SPORT BUSINESS

Operational and Theoretical Aspects

....

PETER J. GRAHAM

University of South Carolina

WCB Brown & Benchmark

PUBLISHERS

Madison, Wisconsin • Dubuque, Iowa

Book Team

Executive Editor *Ed Bartell*
Editor *Chris Rogers*
Project Editor *Scott Spoolman*
Production Editor *Karen A. Pluemer*
Visuals/Design Developmental Consultant *Marilyn A. Phelps*
Visuals/Design Freelance Specialist *Mary L. Christianson*
Marketing Manager *Pamela S. Cooper*
Advertising Manager *Jodi Rymer*

 **Brown &
Benchmark**

A Division of Wm. C. Brown Communications, Inc.

Executive Vice President/General Manager *Thomas E. Doran*
Vice President/Editor in Chief *Edgar J. Laube*
Vice President/Sales and Marketing *Eric Ziegler*
Director of Production *Vickie Putman Caughron*
Director of Custom and Electronic Publishing *Chris Rogers*

 Wm. C. Brown Communications, Inc.

President and Chief Executive Officer *G. Franklin Lewis*
Corporate Senior Vice President and Chief Financial Officer *Robert Chesterman*
Corporate Senior Vice President and President of Manufacturing *Roger Meyer*

Cover and interior designs by Fulton Design

Copyedited by Carol Kozlik

Library of Congress Catalog Card Number: 93–70168

ISBN 0–697–16648–1

Printed in the United States of America by Wm. C. Brown Communications, Inc.,
2460 Kerper Boulevard, Dubuque, IA 52001

10 9 8 7 6 5 4 3 2 1

CONTENTS

Preface   vi

PART 1   SPORT AND THE MARKETPLACE

1 Marketing Tools for Sports
Management   2
Ellen M. Moore and Sandra J. Teel

2 The Significance of Sports Marketing
and the Case of the
Olympic Games   14
Vernon R. Stauble

3 Marketing Exercise/Fitness
Programs: An Examination of
Consumer Shopping Styles   22
Rodney B. Warnick

4 Estimating the Market Potential for
Golf and Tennis   34
Richard B. Morrison

PART 2   STRATEGIC PLANNING IN SPORT

5 Strategic Planning for Athletic
Departments in Small-to-Moderate-
Sized Two-Year Public Institutions:
Focus on the Future   39
Richard A. Stull and Lou Hammen

6 Strategies for Increasing Participation
in Recreational Sports   47
W. Dennis Berry

7 Strategic Planning for an Olympic
Games: The Complexity of Work and
the Performance of People   54
Vernon R. Stauble

8 Back to the Future: Trends in the
Recreational Sports Market   62
Rodney B. Warnick

PART 3   SPONSORSHIP IN SPORT

9   **Corporate Sponsorship: A Framework for Analysis 82**
John Kuzma and William Shanklin

10   **Two Different Examples for Sponsoring, Advertising, and Financing Sport in the Former West Germany: The Trimm-Campaign and the National Soccer League 88**
Horst Ueberhorst

11   **Possible Effects of Corporate Sponsors on Intercollegiate Athletics 93**
Paul Glenn and Patrick Cobb

12   **The University and City: A Unique Partnership in the Successful Solicitation of Major Sporting Events 111**
Celia Regimbal and Scott Breckner

PART 4   SPORT AND THE LAW

13   **Financial Benefits of Trademark Licensing 115**
Dick Irwin

14   **Our Legal System and the Insurance Industry: The Two Most Effective Facets of Society Affecting Sports in America 121**
Marc A. Rabinoff

15   **Artificial Turf: Injuries, Economics, Emotion, and Ethics 132**
Donald P. Foshee and James H. Conn

PART 5   FINANCE AND SPORT

16   **Using Economic Models to Measure the Impact of Sports on Local Economies 145**
Frank Hefner

17   **Major League Baseball Salaries: The Impacts of Arbitration and Free Agency 159**
Lawrence Hadley and Elizabeth Gustafson

18   **Athletic Cost Containment 175**
William Eng and Susan Larkin

19   **Educational and Financial Considerations in Planning Sport Facilities 179**
Marcia L. Walker

PART 6 — QUALITY MANAGEMENT AND SPORT

20 The Use of Information Technology in Sport Management to Provide the Competitive Edge: An Illustration in a Multipurpose Sport and Health Facility 187
Brian McNamara and Bernard Mullin

21 An Analysis of Golf Management Programs 199
William L. Shelburn

22 Beyond Winning: An Expanded Model for Evaluating Athletic Program Quality 204
Scott E. Branvold

PART 7 — HUMAN RESOURCE MANAGEMENT IN SPORT

23 A Double-Edge Sword: Drugs in Sport 212
Joanna Davenport

24 Marketplace Value and Gender Representation of Successful Coaches in Women's Intercollegiate Athletics 223
Connee Zotos

25 Returning to the "Real World": Athletes Adjusting to Life After Sports 231
Leonard Lipton

26 Unity of Force and Diversity of Caring: A Systematic Approach for Enhancing Athletic Performance 234
Nena R. Hawkes, John F. Seggar, and Betty J. Vickers

PART 8 — AWARENESS EXPANSION: SOME AREAS OF INTEREST

27 The Business of Sportscasting 251
Linda K. Fuller

28 How Big Is the West German Sports Market? 262
Arnd Krüger

29 Bridging the Gap Between Research and Practice 276
William J. Rudman and Alar Lipping

Index 283

PREFACE

Interest in the business of sport has expanded at an exponential rate within recent years. Sport business represents a 70 billion dollar per year industry, ranking twenty-third in contribution to the gross national product of the United States.

This volume targets three distinct audiences: sport administration students at both the undergraduate and graduate levels, sport administration faculty, and the vast array of professionals engaged in the day-to-day business operations of sport. Each audience has particular informational needs that this has been developed to address.

The range of topics examined is reflective of the sport industry's multifaceted profile. Each essay is written in a straightforward manner and was selected on the basis of the valuable information it presents and insights it offers. Students, professors, and practitioners will benefit from reading these essays and deliberating on the points discussed.

This volume is unique to the sport business field because its contents are restricted neither to the thoughts of a single author nor to the viewpoints of a small number of contributors who share a similar perspective. Quite the contrary. Thirty-nine authors from North America and Europe—each actively involved in the business of sport as a practitioner, researcher, educator, or a combination thereof—have produced the twenty-nine essays that appear in the following pages. Their individual and collective contributions have been grouped into eight sections, each representing a particular segment of the sports business enterprise.

Marketing is a prime area of concern for many sport business professionals. Part One, Sport and the Marketplace, contains four essays that focus on a variety of marketing issues. Ellen M. Moore and Sandra J. Teel, both members of the College of Business Administration at the University of South Carolina, describe the various tools associated with the marketing of sport. Vernon R. Stauble, an Olympian and member of the Marketing Management Department at California State Polytechnic University, reports on the value of marketing strategy to the growth and success of the Olympic Games. One of the fastest growing industry segments over the past two decades has been exercise/fitness programs. In the third essay, Rodney B. Warnick, member of the Leisure Studies and Resources Program at the University of Massachusetts–Amherst, discusses how consumer shopping styles can be used to help market these programs. Richard B. Morrison, director of the Sport and Fitness Graduate Program at Northeastern University in Boston, concludes the section by presenting a methodology for estimating the market potential for sport activities.

Effective planning concepts are presented in Part Two—Strategic Planning in Sport. Richard Stull, a member of the Physical Education faculty at Humboldt State University and Lou Hammen, director of Development for Dundalk Community College in Baltimore, discuss how the athletic departments at two-year colleges of small and moderate size can effectively apply strategic planning concepts. Recreational sports are extremely popular with college students. W. Dennis Berry, director of Recreational Sports at Washington College in Maryland, presents strategies that have been effective in increasing student participation in campus recreational sports. In his second essay, and using the Olympic Games as an example, Vernon R. Stauble reviews the strategic planning process necessary to successfully stage a major sport event. Rodney B. Warnick contributes his second essay to complete the section, proposing the need to understand past trends in order to successfully plan for the future.

Part Three is titled Sponsorship in Sport. Sponsorship is an aspect of sport business that has enjoyed significant popularity and growth while producing increasing concern for its possible consequences. Business School professors John Kuzma of Mankato State University and William Shanklin of Kent State University explain the concept of corporate sponsorship and its potential role in sport, and identify some measurement techniques for assessing its effectiveness. Horst Ueberhorst, former director of the Sport Management Program at Ruhr Universitat in Bochum, Germany, discusses two ways in which sport is sponsored, advertised, and financed in Germany. Georgia Southern University Sport Science and Physical Education Department members Paul Glenn and Patrick Cobb present potential positive and negative effects of allowing corporations to sponsor intercollegiate sport programs and events. In increasing numbers, institutions of higher learning and local governments have launched cooperative efforts designed to attract major sport events. Celia Regimbal, a member of the Health Promotion and Human Performance faculty at the University of Toledo, and Scott Breckner, director of Michigan State's Breslin Events Center, explain how educational institutions and governmental bodies can effectively join forces to bring major sporting events to their campuses and communities.

Part Four, Sport and the Law, opens with an essay discussing financial protection through trademark licensing, written by Dick Irwin, a member of the Sport Administration Graduate Program at Kent State University. Next, Marc A. Rabinoff, of the Physical Education, Recreation, and Health Department at Metropolitan State College of Denver, contends that our legal system and insurance industry are the two culprits most responsible for forcing a reduction in American sport programs. Finally, issues surrounding the use of artificial playing surfaces are reviewed in an essay by Donald P. Foshee, a member of the Psychology Department at Valdosta State College, and James H. Conn, representing the Physical Education Department at Central Missouri State University.

Frank Hefner, an economist with the University of South Carolina's College of Business Administration, leads off Part Five—Finance and Sport. Hefner presents a model that measures the economic impact of sports on local economies. Lawrence Hadley and Elizabeth Gustafson, both with the Department of Economics and Finance at the University of Dayton, then discuss the impact of arbitration and free agency on major league baseball salaries and demonstrate the effectiveness of their model for predicting the real salary value of professional baseball players. William Eng and Susan Larkin, athletic directors at Baruch College and John Jay College of Criminal Justice, respectively, review the dramatic increase in the cost of maintaining athletic programs. In their essay, they discuss some of the reasons for the escalating costs and offer suggestions for cost containment. Considerable resources are expended on the planning and construction of sport facilities at institutions of higher learning. Marcia L. Walker, a member of the College of Health and Human Sciences at the University of Northern Colorado, concludes the section by presenting a case for basing sport facilities planning on known educational requirements, user needs, and the financial ability to maintain and operate the facility.

Product and service quality has become a critical issue throughout the world of business. Part Six, Quality Management and Sport, includes three essays that focus on the quality issue. Brian McNamara, a member of the School of Business and Public Administration at California State University at Bakersfield, and Bernard Mullin, vice president of business operations for the Colorado Rockies Major League Baseball Club, explain how to gain a competitive advantage in providing quality service through the use of information technology. Four higher-education programs in the United States are designed specifically to prepare students for entry into the field of professional golf management. William L. Shelburn, a member of the College of Business Administration at the University of South Carolina at Aiken, reviews these programs in terms of their history, curriculum, and quality. Winning tends to be the primary criterion for assessing athletic programs. However, Scott E. Branvold of the University of Oklahoma's Health, Physical Education, and Recreation faculty, believes that a winning program is not automatically a quality program. Branvold presents the elements that he contends should be included in the quality assessment process.

Athletes and coaches play a major role in the sport business. Research covering all segments of the business world has demonstrated that effective personnel management is critical to the success of the enterprise. Part Seven, Human Resource Management in Sport, is made up of four essays related to personnel management issues. Joanna Davenport, a member of the Health and Human Performance Department at Auburn University, examines the problem of athletes using drugs. She reviews the history of the use of anabolic steroids, discusses the reasons why some athletes continue to use performance enhancement drugs even when they are aware of the potential physical, moral, and legal dangers, and presents possible solutions for stemming usage. From another perspective, Connee Zotos, athletic director at William Smith College in Geneva, New York, reviews the marketplace value and gender representation of successful coaches in women's intercollegiate athletics. Her findings are based on a comparison of data she collected from identical studies conducted in 1983–1984 and 1988–1989. For many athletes, the toughest challenge they face is not the athletic competition but rather the difficulty of making the transition from the sport world into the "real world" when playing days are over. This challenge becomes increasingly difficult for athletes forced into sport retirement without sufficient notice and preparation. Leonard Lipton, a free-lance writer from Santa Monica, California, explores the problem of adjusting to life after sport and offers some suggestions sport administrators might adopt to help players make this transition. The final essay in this section is written by three professors from Brigham Young University. Physical educators Nena R. Hawkes and Betty J. Vickers, together with John F. Seggar of the Sociology Department, present an argument for enhancing athletic performance through a systematic approach consisting of unity of force and diversity of caring.

Part Eight, titled Awareness Expansion: Some Areas of Interest, concludes the volume. It is imperative that sport business personnel continually expand their knowledge of sport. However, this is often easier said than done given the vast breadth and depth of the sport business world. The last three essays cover topics of which most sport business personnel have little understanding. Virtually everyone can name their favorite sportscaster. But how many individuals understand the business of sportscasting? Linda K. Fuller, a faculty member in the Media Department at Worcester State College in Massachusetts, provides an in-depth review of sportscasting from the perspectives of history, economics, and sociology. She concludes by presenting some concerns and considerations related to the future of sportscasting. The second-largest producer of sporting goods in the world is Germany. The unification of East and West Germany has only served to strengthen this position. Arnd Krüger, director of the Sport Studies Department at Georg-August Universitat, Gottingen, Germany, reports on the depth and scope of the German sport market and its effects on sport participation and spectator opportunities throughout the nation. Far too often, information uncovered through research fails to reach the application stage simply because researchers and practitioners fail to communicate with one another. William J. Rudman, a member of the University of Pittsburgh Health Care Management and Supervision Department, and Alar Lipping, representing the

Health and Physical Education Department at Northern Kentucky University, discuss how the research process contributes to this problem. The authors use the example of corporate fitness to illustrate ways in which the gap between research knowledge and practical application can be bridged.

Peter J. Graham
Columbia, South Carolina

ACKNOWLEDGMENTS

A note of appreciation must be extended to the many individuals who assisted with the creation of this volume. I am grateful to each of the contributing authors, to Carol Kozlik for her outstanding editing skills, and to Chris Rogers, senior editor at Brown & Benchmark Publishers, for his insight into the rapidly changing world of sport business and for his desire to publish this book.

A word of thanks is extended to Dean Harry E. Varney for his support of the Sport Administration Department at the University of South Carolina and to the following people who reviewed this book and offered many helpful suggestions: Herb Appenzeller, Guilford College; James G. Mason, University of Texas–El Paso; and Carl Schraibman, Kent State University.

And last but not least, a very special thanks goes to my wife Barbara who, throughout the many hours this project has required, has provided me with unwavering support and encouragement. It is to her that I dedicate this volume.

SPORT AND THE MARKETPLACE

Marketing Tools for Sports Management

Ellen M. Moore and Sandra J. Teel

INTRODUCTION

The purpose of this essay is to examine marketing tools with specific attention to their use in sport administration. A major concern is the sports consumer, namely, the spectator.

Sports inc. and Wharton Econometrics Forecasting Associates have quantified the sports economy following the standards set by the U.S. Commerce Department for computing the nation's gross national product (GNP). The survey revealed that the gross national sports product (GNSP) was $47.2 billion in 1986. And the sports industry is listed as number 23 in the top U.S. industries by GNP (Sandomir 1987). Sports is indeed big business.

As the sports economy has continued to grow, sports marketing has become increasingly important. At the outset, it should be noted that the term ''sports marketing'' does not have a single, consistent definition. It may be defined

Ellen M. Moore and Sandra J. Teel are with the College of Business Administration, University of South Carolina, Columbia, South Carolina.

as (a) the use of sports entities (defined as athletes, events, and/or programs) in a firm's marketing plan, such as corporate sponsorship; (b) the generation of revenues for sports entities, such as athlete and team endorsements; and (c) the development of a marketing plan to achieve the greatest benefit for the sports entity.

Many companies have been built upon a good idea that occurred at the right time and in the right place. Yet, as is too often seen, a good idea may sustain the life of a firm for only a limited time period. In some ways, sports events are like companies which have survived on the strength of a good idea—but the good idea is no longer new, and attention to marketing tools is long overdue. Strong emphasis on consumer/customer satisfaction is the key to survival for any business. Sports events are no exception. Further, proper manipulation of marketing variables is a constantly changing, evolving task; tactics chosen during the growth stage of a product life cycle are different from tactics chosen during its mature stage.

Since the 1980s corporate sponsorship of sports entities and athlete endorsements of products have grown to become the two most popular marketing tools. Both tactics offer many advantages and enormous potential for gain (Cook, Melcher, and Welling 1987; McGeehan 1987; Steinberg 1987; Walley 1987; Tractenberg 1989). Within the last few years, however, corporate sponsors have shown signs of concern about the net payoffs of continued sponsorship (*Marketing News* 1987; Moran 1987; McGeehan 1987). These concerns have prompted a few authors to write ''How to's'' for achieving the most cost-beneficial match between sponsor and sports entity (Frankel 1986; Pearsall 1987; Lapin 1987; Wilber 1988).

Yet, the focus of these efforts appears to exclude other marketing tools which might also be used, perhaps to greater advantage. The objective of this essay is to critically examine alternatives to the marketing tools currently used in sports marketing. A major concern is the sports consumer—the spectator. Thus, this essay approaches sports marketing as defined in the third of the three definitions given above—the development of a marketing plan to achieve the greatest benefit for the sports entity.

MARKETING VARIABLES

The marketing environment for any organization is dynamic in nature. As with all organizations, the sports firm must adapt quickly to changes. Rigid firms may incur a rapid life cycle transition through the stages of introduction, growth, maturity, and decline. An adaptive organization uses marketing inputs for strategic planning to be ready to restructure and align itself with opportunities. Primary concerns are identifying target markets (and segments), developing tactics to compete with similar firms, and designing an effective marketing mix to reach and serve the targeted consumer. These elements will dictate the specific combination of the product, its price, the place or point of distribution, and the promotion that the firm will use to reach and serve its target market efficiently and effectively. The relationships among these ''four P's'' (a term coined by McCarthy in 1960 to refer to product, price, promotion, and place) of the marketing mix and the target market are shown in Figure 1.1.

Sports entities serve many publics (e.g., sponsors, fans, media). One public, audiences of sporting events, must be segmented by markets and profiled to serve as the target of all marketing efforts. For example, the spectator market may be segmented into nonattenders, media spectators, and attending spectators. The latter may be subclassified into casual attenders and frequent season attenders. Each sports audience may be further segmented by demographic, geographic, and psychographic variables. Major segmenting variables for consumer markets are shown in Figure 1.2.

The target market and consumer analysis will be sport specific and will vary with the complexity, costliness, and riskiness of the purchase of the sports product or service. Thus, an optimal sports marketing mix of service, price, place, and promotion will vary with the type of buyer. Understanding the target market's needs, wants, and buying behavior is at the heart of marketing analysis and an essential task of management. The sports consumer, like other consumers, is influenced also by cultural, social, personal, and psychological factors (see Fig. 1.3). Crucial to the development of a sports marketing program are elements such as who buys tickets (businesses, individuals, families), how (cash, credit card), when (preseason, day of game), where (ticket outlets, telephone, mail, at the gate), and why (personal, family, business). Of equal importance in developing a marketing strategy is understanding the purchase decision. An example of the purchase decision related to sports is shown in Figure 1.4.

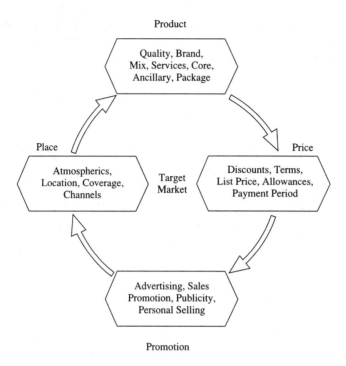

Product

Quality, Brand,
Mix, Services, Core,
Ancillary, Package

Place

Atmospherics,
Location, Coverage,
Channels

Target
Market

Price

Discounts, Terms,
List Price, Allowances,
Payment Period

Advertising, Sales
Promotion, Publicity,
Personal Selling

Promotion

FIGURE 1.1 Marketing Mix Variables

In summary, the specific combination of marketing variables used by a firm is dictated by the target market the firm wishes to attract, to attend, or to view or listen to the sporting event. The consumer demand for a sporting event is ultimately generated by the potential spectator. Thorough knowledge of the characteristics of the spectator market is the essential first step in the development of the four P's. What are the four P's for sport? In what way do the four P's fit into the development of the sports marketing plan?

PRODUCT

A product is anything that can be offered to a market for attention, acquisition, use, or consumption that might satisfy a want or need (Kotler and Armstrong 1987). The term "product" may refer to a service, idea, organization, person, place, or activity. In essence, the product of the sports organization is a service—entertainment. A service is any activity, benefit, or satisfaction that one party can offer to another; it is essentially intangible and does not result in the ownership of anything. A service cannot be seen before it is purchased or separated from the provider and cannot be stored for later use.

Services can vary in quality. McDonald's is renowned for standardizing quality for a service. Variability in sports events, however, is a major attraction for the audience. For example, University of Virginia football fans eagerly await the half-time performance of the "we can march if we want to" band, which strolls onto the field, without benefit of uniforms, and

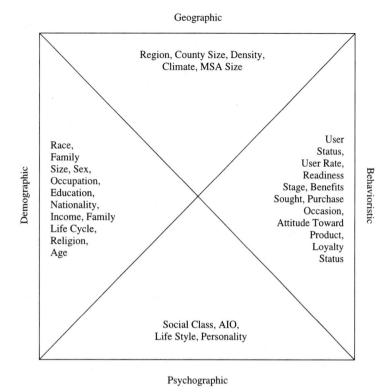

Geographic

Region, County Size, Density,
Climate, MSA Size

Demographic

Race,
Family
Size, Sex,
Occupation,
Education,
Nationality,
Income, Family
Life Cycle,
Religion,
Age

User
Status,
User Rate,
Readiness
Stage, Benefits
Sought, Purchase
Occasion,
Attitude Toward
Product,
Loyalty
Status

Behavioristic

Social Class, AIO,
Life Style, Personality

Psychographic

FIGURE 1.2 Market Segmentation Variables

performs nontraditional music in a nontraditional way. Another type of variation is the disadvantage that any coach knows will result from a losing streak.

Kotler (1982) proposes that an organization must make several basic decisions to determine the product area that may be applied to the service sector: product mix decisions, product line decisions, product item decisions, and product life cycle decisions.

The product mix of any organization may be discussed in terms of its length, width, and depth. Figure 1.5 illustrates the product mix of a hypothetical university sports program, which includes three principal product lines—team, paired, and individual sports. Within each product line are revenue- and nonrevenue-generating sports. Depth of product line would include, for example, football and men's basketball under revenue-generating team sports or, if describing Old Dominion University, women's basketball.

In this example, the department could expand its product mix in three ways: (1) by broadening its product mix (adding intramural sports); (2) by extending the width of its product line (adding an individual sports line under revenue-generating sports); or (3) by lengthening the product mix (adding volleyball under nonrevenue-generating team sports). Conversely, the department may consider decreasing its product mix, product lines, or product items to become more specialized and cost efficient. A major

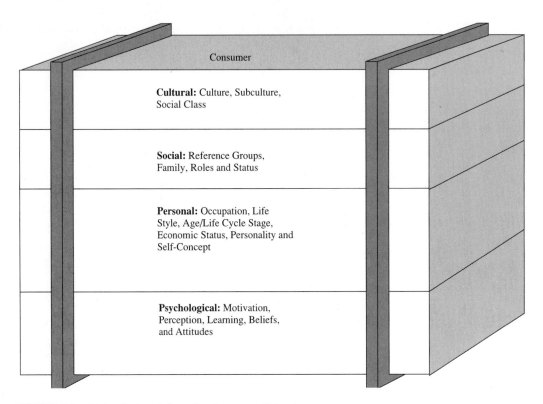

FIGURE 1.3 Major Factors Influencing Consumer Behavior

consideration is what constitutes the organization's core and ancillary products. As in this example, revenue-generating sports are the core or primary product of a university sports program, and nonrevenue-generating sports are an ancillary or secondary product. The product mix is also the source of the program's costs. The nonrevenue-generating sports product line may generate good will and create alumni and community support, yet be costly to the program as a whole. The firm must be attuned to the cost vs. benefit of each product line.

Central to the decision-making process is the question: What need is being met by the product or service? While the primary service is entertainment, the tangible product is the form in which the product may be seen (spectator games) or touched by the consumer. Additional services (accessible concessions) and benefits (half-time entertainment) augment the product offer and become increasingly important as competition increases over time. Each stage of a product life cycle will present new marketing challenges and require adjustments in the target market and marketing mix.

The product life cycle may be shortened or lengthened by economic, cultural, and technological changes in the environment. More specific changes may occur among competitors, suppliers, or purchasers of the product or services. For the typical product or service, the introduction stage is the period of entry into the market and is characterized by slow sales growth and negative profits. During the

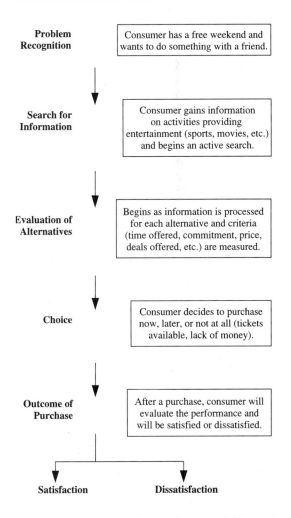

FIGURE 1.4   High-Involvement Decision Making

tant point is that the marketing manager is challenged in each stage to develop effective marketing strategies to prolong the product's life cycle.

PRICE

Pricing objectives, such as survival, market-share leadership, and product quality leadership, are critical to the task of setting price. The more clearly defined the objective, the easier it becomes to set a price. Kotler and Armstrong (1987) suggests several factors, both within and outside the firm, to consider when setting price objectives. Ticket pricing for sporting events is based on the demand, competition, and cost considerations for the single ticket purchase. Price adjustments are made from the base price of a single ticket. Season subscribers may be offered a subscription series price, similar to a quantity discount, which represents some savings over single ticket prices.

Some sports providers will adjust basic prices by offering different prices to different customers. For example, students, senior citizens, and veterans are often charged a lower ticket price. Basic seat prices are also adjusted by offering different prices for different locations within the arena. Promotional pricing may be used by sports organizations as a temporary pricing technique to increase audience size. Several forms are available to the sports firm.

Special Events Pricing

In this situation, ticket prices may be increased or decreased based on the event and the projected demand for tickets (e.g., a well-known sports figure(s) performing at half time; a drawing for big-ticket prizes to raise money for a charitable organization).

maturity stage, the market fully accepts the product or service, the competition is entrenched, and sales and profits stabilize. In the decline period, sales drop off markedly and profits deteriorate. Not all products or services will have the same life cycle pattern. For example, the life cycle of a university sports team is different from that of an NFL team. And, remember the USFL? All products or services go through a life cycle. The impor-

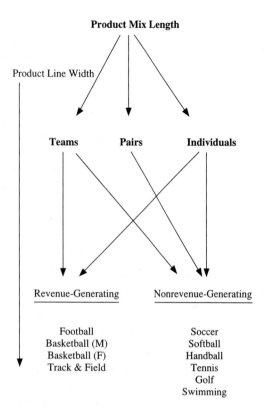

FIGURE 1.5   Length, Width, and Depth of a University Athletic Program

Special Product Discounts

The ticket price may reflect special offers on other products at the event. A food or beverage may be offered at two for the price of one; discounts may be available on promotional products such as banners, hats, or T-shirts; coupons may be given out for products inside or outside the arena; or cents-off coupons on the next admission may be offered.

Pricing is only one of the tools of marketing and must be coordinated with the other mix decisions when designing a marketing strategy. In the long run, the consumer determines if the value and price are right by comparing the value of the product to its price as well as to the price of the competitor's product. A price change decision by a firm is subject to the customer's and competitor's reactions. In addition, suppliers, middlepersons, and the government may react to price changes.

PLACING PRODUCTS

Making products available and accessible to the target market is another major marketing decision. Sports organizations are concerned with locating a set of facilities to serve a widespread population. The level and quality of service has to be determined first. Maximum customer convenience may be ideal (e.g., air-conditioned viewing rooms with free food and beverages), but costs of distribution must also be considered. Clearly, a football stadium cannot move to better serve its market, but Kotler's (1982) four decision areas for designing a service facility, adapted to the sports situation, provide suggestions for creating facilities that serve the needs of the customer.

- What should the facility look like on the outside? The grounds outside a facility, (e.g., a ball field or golf course) are part of the facility itself. Grounds and buildings can look awe-inspiring or ordinary. Decisions about this aspect of the facility will be influenced by the type of sport and the general message management wants to convey about the sport.

- What should be the functional and flow characteristics of the facility? The grounds and buildings must be designed to handle capacity crowds, avoid long lines, and minimize congestion moving into and out of parking, concession, and restroom areas. Will the facility be leased or rented when not in use for the sports event to provide additional income?
- What should the facility feel like on the inside? And, on the outside? Every building (and playing ground) conveys a feeling, whether intended or unplanned. Does it feel awesome, exciting, somber, bright, modern, warm?
- What materials would best support the desired feeling of the facility? The feeling of a facility is conveyed by visual cues (color, brightness, size, shapes), aural cues (volume, pitch), olfactory cues (scent, freshness), and tactile cues (softness, smoothness, temperature). Even the choice of building materials can create or reinforce the desired feeling.

These decision areas describe the "atmospherics" within and outside sports facilities. (Atmospherics describes the conscious designing of space to create or reinforce specific effects on buyers, such as the feeling of well-being, safety, intimacy, or awe [Kotler 1984].) Contrast the Augusta National Masters complex with many competing golf courses. Sports marketers can and should use atmospherics creatively to convey the degree to which the sports organization has adopted the marketing concept.

PROMOTION

In general, all organizations communicate with their markets. A firm must manage all of the promotional tools in a complex system to communicate well. Each communication involves the pertinent elements shown in Figure 1.6. Two parties, a sender and a receiver, send and receive messages through media, engaging in the major communication functions of encoding, decoding, response, and feedback. The noise in the communication process is the unplanned, extraneous factors that can distort the message the receiver gets from the one that was sent. The sender and receiver must share similar knowledge and understanding, called fields of experience, to communicate effectively (Berkowitz, Kerin, Rudelius 1986).

The fourth P, promotion, is a catch-all term defined as the development of persuasive communication. The promotional tools consist of personal selling, publicity, advertising, and sales promotion. Each tool has a subset of tools by which it operates. Listed below are the promotional tools, defined by the American Marketing Association (1961), as they relate to the sports situation:

- **Personal selling: oral presentation in a conversation with one or more prospective purchasers for the purpose of making sales.** The job of service personnel is to provide service in a warm and friendly manner to increase customer satisfaction and loyalty. The costs per contact associated with personal selling are high, but face-to-face communication can be most effective in achieving a firm's marketing objectives. A friendly, personable ticket sales agent, ticket taker, or concessions person can build good will or perhaps make a long wait in line less irritating.
- **Publicity: nonpersonal stimulation of demand for a product, service, or business unit by placing commercially significant news about it in a published medium or by obtaining favorable presentation of it on radio, television,**

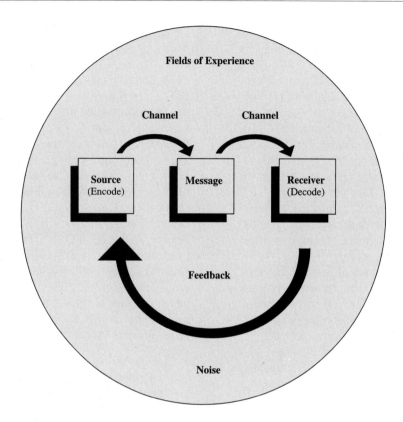

FIGURE 1.6   The Communication Process

or stage that is not paid for by the sponsor. Publicity has high credibility because of its ''nonpaid or indirect payment'' aspect. When one reads a favorable story or hears Tom Brokaw report it, there is a predisposition to believe it because the firm cannot pay to have the story printed or reported. Publicity may be in the form of an editorial or announcement, or a news story on the radio or television or in a publication or speech. Positive publicity has played a major role in generating a sizable audience for the Charlotte Hornets, for example. Articles about the Hornet fans have appeared in almost

every major newspaper and sports magazine and news stories have been broadcast on all major networks, serving to stimulate an already enthusiastic audience.

Unfortunately, not all publicity is positive. Negative publicity appears harder to overcome and longer-lived than positive publicity. Consider the Pete Rose gambling infractions that dominated the sports news for months or the publicity about steroid use and abuse by athletes. Publics want to be informed about the negative—about harmful products, destruction to the environment, or drug abuse. Acting as good citizens, the public's concern can help invoke social consciousness and good will among firms. A good public relations staff is on guard to respond to any negative publicity that may occur. Publicity is difficult to control and, fortunately, is only one element in the promotional mix.

- **Advertising: any paid form of nonpersonal presentation and promotion of goods, services, or ideas by an identified sponsor.** The paid, nonpersonal elements of this promotional tool are important because a firm can control what is said and to whom the message is sent when the firm decides to send it. The costs to produce and place an advertisement are usually quite high, and the feedback is not immediate. The media are varied, and the purposes are diverse. A marketing manager must focus on the four W's in the development of an advertising program (Berkowitz, Kerin, Rudelius 1986):

1. *Who* is the target audience? Are they people from New England, aged 20–34, with 2.5 children, earning over $30,000, with some college education, and who are compulsive, gregarious, seek quality products, drink light beer, and take vacations to play sports?
2. *What* are the advertising objectives? Increased attendance? Overcome negative publicity? What is the budget for the program? Is it sufficient to allow the use of any advertising medium or to respond to negative publicity? What kinds of copy should be used?
3. *When* should the advertisements run? Pre-season? In season? Prime time? Late night? During sitcom or sports-specific programs?
4. *Where* should the advertisements be placed? Radio? TV? Billboards? Magazines?

    An important final step in the effective use of advertising is to evaluate the program once the advertising program has been produced and delivered to the target audience. Post-testing can determine if the objectives were met and what changes are needed for future advertising.

- **Sales promotion: short-term incentives to encourage purchase or sales of a product or service.** A number of short-term incentives are frequently used to increase the market's response to a firm's goods and services. Sales promotion tools may be classified as: (a) consumer promotion (e.g., T-shirts, coupons, hats); (b) dealer or trade-oriented promotion (e.g., free beverage supplies with beverage concession); and (c) sales force promotion (bonus for achieving quotas of box seat sales).

Since the mid-1970s, sales promotion budgets have grown annually at a rate of twelve percent, compared with a nine percent growth rate for advertising budgets; more money has been spent in sales promotion than in advertising (Yovovich 1983). Sales promotions can encourage new product trial (Teel, Williams, and Bearden 1980), increase repeat purchases by customers (Seipel 1971), reduce price cutting, obtain broader distribution, maintain or increase market share, reduce inventories, or meet the competition (Neilsen 1965; Schwartz 1966), and build customer good will (King and Summers 1970).

The purpose of persuasive communication is to influence the target market to engage in a desired behavior. The sports firm must understand how communication works to determine what message will be most effective in producing the desired response. Each promotional tool may be needed to effectively communicate with the target market. Using promotional tools in combination may achieve the desired response and meet the communication goals and objectives of the sports firm. However, and most importantly, the target market and its characteristics need to be identified before determining the promotion campaign (including the media selection).

CONCLUSIONS

This essay has critically examined sports marketing tools and the way they may be used in sports management to meet and serve the needs of the audiences of sports events. Analysis of the target market is at the heart of the marketing task and is essential to the development of a sports marketing program and the marketing tools it uses. The product is not the game, per se, but the entertainment it provides. The sports firm must understand the ticket purchase or viewing decision process. Pricing objectives must be clearly defined and based on knowledge of the target market. The sports event should be made both available and accessible to satisfy the needs and wants of the consumer. A persuasive communication package may then be used to influence behavior in the target market.

Thus, we have come full circle—the core of the sports marketing mix is the target market. The four P's must be viewed from the target's perspective. So, while sports marketers view the product as entertainment, a segment of the target market may define the product more narrowly—''a way to fill a Sunday afternoon when the NFL is not being broadcast on ABC.''

As competition for the consumer's leisure time becomes more intense, a greater understanding of the target's needs and responses to the marketing mix is critical to the success of a sports program. The path for sports marketers and sports marketing educators is clear—more research is needed to better define target markets, identify segments of target markets, and measure and evaluate the target's response to manipulations of the marketing mix variables.

REFERENCES

American Marketing Association. 1961. Report of the Definitions Committee of the American Marketing Association. Chicago: American Marketing Association.

Berkowitz, E., R. Kerin, and W. Rudelius. 1986. *Marketing.* St. Louis: Times Mirror/ Mosby.

Cook, D., R. A. Melcher, and B. Welling. 1987. Nothing sells like sports. *Business Week* 31 August: 48–53.

Frankel, B. 1986. Sports marketing program wins big if it's done right. *Marketing News 7 November: 5.*

King, C. W., and J. O. Summers. 1970. Overlap of opinion leadership across consumer product categories. *Journal of Marketing Research* 7 (February): 43–50.

Kotler, P. 1984. *Marketing management: Analysis, planning, and control.* 5th ed. Englewood Cliffs, N.J.: Prentice-Hall.

Kotler, P. 1982. *Marketing for nonprofit organizations.* 2d ed. Englewood Cliffs, N.J.: Prentice-Hall.

Kotler, P., and G. Armstrong. 1987. *Marketing: An introduction.* Englewood Cliffs, N.J.: Prentice-Hall.

Lapin, J. 1987. Workshop: How to win with sports. *Public Relations Journal,* February, 1987: 31–32, 34.

Marketing News. 1987. USA Today now pitching all-star baseball balloting. 19 June: 3.

McCarthy, E. J. 1960. *Basic marketing: A managerial approach.* Homewood, Ill.: Richard D. Irwin.

McGeehan, P. 1987. Signing 3M—An Olympian effort. *Advertising Age 9 November: S11–S12.*

McGeehan, P. 1987. There's more to marketing than sports. *Advertising Age* 13 July: S4, S6–S7.

Moran, B. 1987. Sponsors, packages key to cautious nets. *Advertising Age 13 July: S18, S20.*

Nielsen, A. C. 1965. The impact of retail coupons. *Journal of Marketing* 29 (October): 11–15.

Pearsall, J. 1987. Four point research plan improves sports marketing. *Marketing New 2 January.*

Sandomir, R. 1987. GNSP: The gross national sports product. *Sports inc.,* 16 November: 14–18.

Schwartz, A. 1966. The influence of media characteristics on coupon redemption. *Journal of Marketing 30 (January): 41–46.*

Seipel, C. M. 1971. Premiums—Forgotten by theory. *Journal of Marketing 35 (April): 26–34.*

Steinberg, J. 1987. Grand prix gets jump on affluent fans. *Advertising Age* 9 November: S10.

Teel, J. E., R. H. Williams, and W. O. Bearden. 1980. Correlates of consumer susceptibility to coupons in new grocery product introductions. *Journal of Advertising* 9(3): 31–46.

Trachtenberg, J. A. 1989. Does sports marketing make sense? *The Wall Street Journal 19 April: B1.*

Walley, W. 1987. Companies learn to play the game. *Advertising Age* 9 November: S1–S2, S4, S6.

Wilber, D. 1988. Linking sports and sponsors. *The Journal of Business Strategy,* July/August: 8–10.

Yovovich, B. G. 1983. Stepping into a new era. *Advertising Age* 22 August: M30.

The Significance of Sports Marketing and the Case of the Olympic Games

Vernon B. Stauble

INTRODUCTION

This essay examines the basic function of marketing in an attempt to describe the significance of the role marketing plays in meeting the biggest challenge facing an Olympic Organization—the challenge of producing results. Discussion will focus on the importance of marketing applications in supporting and enhancing the Olympic Games.

Marketing, as a basic function and central dimension of the Olympic enterprise, requires specific planning and the performance of distinct activities. This essay focuses on several of these areas of planning and activity:

1. Recognition of the potential contribution of marketing.

Vernon R. Stauble was a competitor in the 1968 and 1972 Olympic Games in the sport of cycling. A member of the U.S. College Hall of Fame, he is currently a professor of marketing management at California State Polytechnic University, Pomona, California, and adjunct professor at the University of Redlands, Redlands, California.

2. Identification of a major marketing task of resource attraction (obtaining money). It has long been a stated intention to provide Olympic Games that generate enough direct revenue to pay for themselves.
3. Creation and maintenance of demand.
4. Specific questions for effective marketing planning.
5. Some approaches to financing.
6. Methods and programs of stimulation.

THE SIGNIFICANCE OF MARKETING

Marketing is seen as an important function within the total business system and is particularly central to the operation of the Olympic Organization. Marketing is a major means of support for the activities aimed at producing positive business results.

The basic reason for the marketing function is to enable the organization to achieve its objectives in an effective manner. Marketing provides a foundation upon which objectives are set. The particular objectives of the organization

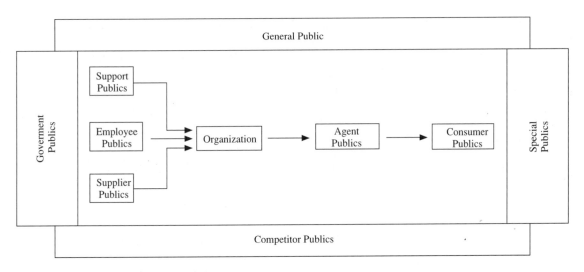

FIGURE 2.1   An Organization's Publics

will have an impact on the appropriate marketing strategy or strategies. Such strategies could involve:

1. Maximizing profit during Game time
2. Maximizing profit in the long run
3. Establishing a reputation for outstanding performance and high quality

An approach to profit maximization suggests the development of a high-quality offering to attract target market(s) that can afford and are willing to pay higher prices to achieve their objectives. For example, a firm like Exxon might respond favorably to a request for funds and be willing to contribute a major portion of the money needed to build an Olympic facility if they could gain publicity for as long as the facility was in use.

An exchange is definitely needed to accomplish objectives. A major responsibility of the Organizing Committee is to identify and concentrate on tasks that facilitate a direct two-way exchange among publics (a public is any group with potential interest in and impact on an organization). Proper incentives have to exist in order to create or stimulate these exchanges.

The Olympic Organization is dependent upon this exchange relation to attract resources. Resources must be attracted and customers found. According to marketing consultant Benson Shapiro, resource attraction (obtaining revenue) is a highly sophisticated marketing task that includes the basic elements of business-oriented marketing. The first assignment is a dual one: first, to segment the donor "market" into homogeneous groups; then to determine which appeal or "product" position will be most effective for that segment. Different segments are amenable to different approaches. An important aspect of resource attraction is determining the amount to be raised from fees for goods and services.

The Olympic Organization, viewed as a resource conversion machine, takes the resources of various publics (supporters, employees, and suppliers) and converts these into products or services that go directly to consumers (Fig. 2.1). The focus is toward providing the supporter or contributor with positive reasons for giving. Of course, the self-interest aspect of the exchange is always considered in providing a basis for marketing thought and action. Consequently, programs are designed to bring about the desired exchanges with target audiences for the purpose of mutual gain.

In addition, the popular image of marketing is that it deals primarily with the problems of creating and maintaining a demand for something—making sure that there is a demand for the organization's products or services in terms of its objectives. And, what about the conversion of the latent demand into effective demand? Marketing cannot, by itself, create purchasing power, but it *can* uncover and channel the purchasing power that exists. It can, therefore, create rapidly the conditions of a much higher level of economic activity than existed before and can create opportunities for the entrepreneur.

As in the case with a proportion of the organization's main publics, it would be fair to say that there is a need to develop a plan involving this latent demand situation. Latent demand is a definite marketing problem because the demand must be recognized, the right product or service developed, the right price chosen, the channels of distribution put together, and adequate and convincing product information disseminated. These elements are combined in order to create customers and keep them satisfied.

QUESTIONS FOR EFFECTIVE PLANNING

Specific questions can be broadly identified as follows:

1. What is being sold?
2. Who are the targets?
3. What is the purpose or benefit of buying?
4. What are the most profitable means to sell the products?
5. What is the appropriate timing of sales?
6. What are the sales areas?

Information needs to be designed to answer questions about the what's and who's so that further action can be taken. The answers to these questions, in terms of the Olympic Movement, are essential to the formulation of effective plans for stimulating demand.

What Is Being Sold?

What desire is being satisfied? For example, does an Olympic Games satisfy the same need as a ball game? What real satisfaction does this product offer the customer? Is its international flavor the key to customer satisfaction? Research will be required to find precise answers to these questions, best accomplished by identifying the final (or end product) desire. The most important reason for conducting marketing research is to discover the needs and wants of the publics and their attitudes towards the organization's services or products. Once aware of these needs and desires the organization can better attempt to deliver satisfaction to its target publics.

Who Are the Targets?

In identifying its targets the Olympic Committee ought to look not only at the sector they are trying to reach and sell to or the person who buys, but the person who makes the buying decision. Those who make buying decisions influence many other factors, including product/service design, sales approach, advertising appeal, and media selection.

The best way to approach this question is to proceed from the general to the particular. First, identify the total market, then the segment or segments of direct concern, and finally who makes the buying decision.

This is an area in great need of research. Once it is known who makes the buying decision, it is essential to learn as much as possible about the person or persons in order to decide the most appropriate marketing mix for the desired results. How many individuals are involved? Where are they? What are their socioeconomic characteristics? Are they male or female? How many are married or have families? What do they read? Do they listen to the radio or watch television? How often?

What Is the Purpose or Benefits of Buying?

Obviously, return-on-investment and profit from a business point of view are primary purposes and benefits of buying. On the other hand, why do people want to buy such things as souvenir items, for example? Is their value real or psychological? Certainly, coin and stamp purchases are recognized as investments, which is why emphasis might be placed on the sale of these items.

What Are the Most Profitable Means to Sell the Products?

Different ways for distribution could be utilized through agents, wholesalers, retailers, or a combination of these channels. What are the trading terms, discounts, overriding payments? What kind of retailers, in numbers and proportions, could and would handle the products?

What Is the Appropriate Timing of Sales?

Focus should not just be directed towards seasonality but the most opportune time for maximum benefit. Carefully timed advertising, promotional, and sales efforts should be seriously considered.

"When" and "why" questions are often closely related. It may be appropriate to start sales as much as two years before the Game time. As in the case of admission tickets to the various events, sales could be in the form of vouchers until a short period before the start of the Games (for example, six weeks), after which the vouchers could be exchanged against actual tickets. Why time ticket sales in such a way? To maintain better control and prevent tickets from being counterfeited. (Canada '76 printed tickets on paper with a watermark especially made for this purpose.)

What Is the Sales Area?

Identifying the sales area is a matter of analyzing area, or customer, strengths and weaknesses to determine the answer to the question: Does the potential of the region justify the investment?

As in the case of limited-supply items, such as admission tickets, a quota system could be adopted for adequate distribution to ensure a fair and reasonable allocation to all countries. Montreal's criteria were:

a. Population of the country
b. Per capita income
c. Distance from host city
d. Number of tourists who visit the host city
e. Number of athletes from the country
f. Accommodation facilities

In theory, all the admission tickets to the Games can be sold to the host country. However, this would be contrary to the international spirit of the Olympics and also would hurt tourism, which is a major profitability concern and interest in staging the Games.

SOME APPROACHES TO FINANCING

The revenue-sharing controversy began soon after the 1956 Games. Growing operating costs for the international federations, resulting from increases in the number of members, necessitated alternate forms of raising capital; the proscription method was no longer adequate. The federations felt that since they had loaned their world championships to the Olympic Games, they had a right to share in the revenues (Epsy 1979).

One report during the XVII Olympiad (Rome) indicated that the international federations had demanded one-third of the television revenues. This demand was carried over into the XVIII Olympiad (Tokyo). The International Olympic Committee (IOC) position remained the same. It had obligations to four revenue recipients—itself, the federations, the organizing committee, and the national committees. In 1966, the IOC came up with a comprehensive method of distribution in which the first million would be divided between the federations, the national committee, and the IOC. Of the second million, one-third would go to the organizing committee, and two-ninths each to the federations, the national committees, and the IOC. Of each successive million, the organizing committee would receive two-thirds, with each of the other three receiving one-ninth, respectively (Kotler 1966).

Television

The Organizing Committee sells television rights according to IOC Rule 48. Radio broadcast rights and written press rights to the Games are free.

Receipts from any television network are for the Olympic rights and for the provision of services and facilities. The payments for each are determined by negotiations; the art of negotiating for rights is an Olympic feat in itself.

The procedure for making arrangements and negotiations are stated in the Olympic guidelines:

> The Organizing Committee first approaches the national broadcasting organizations of the host country. The selected host broadcasting organization will then be responsible for making detailed arrangements with visiting broadcasting companies or groups.

The contract negotiation is the responsibility of the host broadcasting organization in conjunction with the Olympic Organizing Committee and the International Olympic Committee. After the world broadcasting rights have been negotiated, the host broadcasting organization then sublets to regional broadcasting groups for use by their members.

Reviewing the balance sheet for the 1976 Games in Montreal, the Canadian Organizing Committee concluded a $25 million contract with ABC and a $10 million contract with the European Broadcasting Union. These contracts, added to the $4–5 million received from the sale of special services to the broadcasters brought total receipts of $40 million to Montreal.

The Moscow Organizing Committee for the 1980 Olympics sold the American television rights to NBC for $85 million. For the 1984 Los Angeles Games, Olympic coverage and television services were negotiated with the ABC network for $225 million. South Korea needed to sell a total of $1 billion of commercials to break even on their network investments.

Stamps and Coins

The basic idea in the coin program is to earn seigniorage—the difference between the legally designated face vale of a coin and its cost of production. The coins are legal tender.

Admission Tickets

Ticket decisions are made on the basis of two principles:

1. The percentage of tickets to be made available for sale abroad and to the host country
2. The national allocation of tickets for all sports to each country competing in the Games

Criteria for setting prices of admission tickets for the various competitions are as follows:

a. Popularity of the sport in that part of the world
b. Category of the event
c. Location of the seat
d. Time of day the contest is scheduled
e. Current prices in that part of the world for similar competitions
f. Per capita income within the host country
g. Prices charged at the most recent Games
h. Inflation rate since previous Games

Corporate Support

Corporate support programs are pursued whereby large local and international firms are solicited to supply goods and services to the Olympic Organization at no cost or at a substantial reduction in the wholesale prices.

The aim of support programs is very specific, and thus provides the opportunity for manufacturers to participate in the Games as an official sponsor or supplier. The official supplier is one who is willing to provide the Olympic Committee with such items as technical equipment, services for the Olympic Village, and sports equipment. The sponsor, on the other hand, is a firm not involved in the sale of a product. Rather, in exchange for the rights to use the of-ficial emblem of the Games, the sponsor provides assistance in the recruiting of specialized personnel and certain services. Financial institutions and airlines commonly provide Olympic sponsorship.

Corporate support may also take these forms:

1. Supply of cars for the transportation of officials and athletes
2. Supply of official boats for competition
3. Supply of fuel and lubricants for both cars and boats
4. Supply of food and beverages for the athletes and officials
5. Hotel accommodations for delegation authorities and dignitaries
6. Donation of timing equipment
7. Donation of services (including professional)
8. Donation of sporting equipment
9. Loans of reproduction equipment

Montreal's receipts in this category were $20 million. According to David Green, marketing director of the Canadian Organizing Committee, this figure would have more than doubled if only the Canadian Organization had recognized the need and importance of the marketing function sooner than one and one-half years prior to the starting date of the Games.

Montreal's policy as part of the sponsorship program was as follows:

- Donations of $150,000 or more to be considered an official sponsor
- Donations of $51,000–$149,000 to be considered a supporter
- Donations up to $50,000 to be considered a promoter

For the 1980 Moscow Games, the *Moscow News* noted that Western business firms were sought out to donate equipment and to pay for the rights as "official suppliers." Such firms included IBM, Kodak, Omega, and Longines.

Finally, contributions to the Olympic effort can be of great value to a firm in the form of favorable publicity for both the company and its products and services.

Marketing of Rights— Merchandising and Licensing

The rights to market saleable items bearing symbols, emblems, trademarks, and logos in connection with the Olympic event are offered, and royalities are paid to the Organizing Committee. The Olympic Organizing Committee receives a percentage of the income from the sales of those products bearing the emblem, with souvenirs being a major contributing source.

PROMOTIONAL METHODS AND PROGRAMS

In promoting an Olympic event, various promotional methods and programs have been utilized including personal selling, advertising, sales promotion, and publicity.

Each of these promotional tools involves complex issues in strategy and tactics. To promote through advertising, the marketer has to determine the size of the total marketing budget, the choice of appeals, the development of attention-getting copy, the selection of effective and efficient media, the scheduling of the advertising inputs, and the measurement of the overall and segment-level results.

When using personal selling, the marketer must determine the size of the total salesforce, the development of sales territory boundaries and assignments, the development of personal presentation strategies, the degree and type of salesforce motivation and the level of supervision, and the evaluation of salesforce effectiveness.

Publicity requires that arrangements be made for significant news about the product to appear in various media. Sales promotion includes the development of special displays, contests, and games that might be useful in stimulating interest or action.

The purpose of any promotional effort is to get the attention of the consuming public, arouse their interest and desire, and motivate them to take action with respect to the product or service offered. Serious campaigns should focus on personal selling and providing supplemental information to businesses. Publicity for the Olympic Games, in particular, can be enhanced by the regular issue of information on Olympic progress to the local and international press.

Marketing is certainly an important role, first, in creating favorable publicity towards the people of the host city and country. It is also a major means of support in the direction of reducing operating expenses. As favorable publicity increases from the initial communication program, offers of assistance and gifts from the large firms and organizations encouraged to participate will also increase, thereby expanding contributions toward the financing of the Games.

In summary, the first major task of the marketing department is to determine the current status of the intended markets and customers by obtaining answers to the following questions:

1. Markets
   a. Who are the organization's major markets and publics?
   b. What are the major segments in each market?
   c. What is the present size and expected future size of each market and market segment, and what are their distinguishing characteristics?

2. Customers
  a. How do the customers and publics feel toward and perceive the organization?
  b. How do customers make their purchases or adoption decisions?
  c. What is the present level of customer satisfaction and what are likely to be their future needs?

One conclusion to be drawn from this essay is that support programs have enormous potential to positively affect the Olympic effort, as evidenced by companies' demonstrated eagerness to underwrite sporting events. The profit motives of both the organizers of the Olympic Games and of those organizations providing support for the Games can be fulfilled through cooperative efforts.

REFERENCES

Epsy, Richard. 1979. *The politics of the Olympic Games.* Berkeley: University of California Press.

Kotler, Philip. 1972. A generic concept of marketing. *Journal of Marketing* 36 (April).

———. 1966. Minutes of the meeting of the Executive Board of the IOC with delegates of the IFs, 23 April, Brundage Papers, Box 93.

3

Marketing Exercise/Fitness Programs: An Examination of Consumer Shopping Styles

Rodney B. Warnick

INTRODUCTION

The fitness industry has been one of the fastest growing components of the recreation and leisure field over the past two decades. During the growth phase of the fitness industry, few methods were applied to understanding the movement from a marketing point of view. Efforts instead seemed to be focused on meeting both current demand and anticipated industry expansion (Managed Recreation Research Report 1988). However, in the early 1980s signs appeared that seemed to indicate that this fragmented industry was becoming more competitive and mature (Managed Recreation Research Report 1988; DeMarcus 1986; Huntley 1983; Lynch 1983). The Managed Recreation Research Report of 1987 stated that the fitness craze finally appeared to have leveled off, likely due to significant decreases in construction, more conservative budgetary approaches, and fierce competition for membership recruitment.

Rodney B. Warnick is with the Leisure Studies and Resources Program, University of Massachusetts—Amherst.

As the fitness craze cools, as fitness interests change and mature, and as the competition increases, fitness agencies will begin to pay more attention to market strategies and techniques. According to Kotler (1982), responsive agencies, who have a strong interest in how their markets see them and their programs, will examine the consumer behavior of various target markets and develop proactive market strategies.

As fitness agencies develop proactive marketing strategies, more attention will need to be given to the buying or shopping styles of various target markets. Essentially, these agencies will need to identify the shopping orientations of their consumers and determine how they "shop" for programs and memberships. Understanding consumer behavior, in general, and buying and shopping behavior, specifically, will help agencies to improve the effectiveness of their marketing strategies.

RELATED LITERATURE

The study of how consumers select or purchase products and services has been recognized as a critical area of marketing research (Engel, Kil-lat, and Blackwell 1973). One group of methods employed to understand how people choose among products is to identify different types of consumers or target markets. This research involves the development of improved market segmentation approaches. Segmentation approaches, although successful in dividing markets into different types of consumers, have for the most part failed to improve the understanding of consumer choice or purchasing behavior (June and Smith 1987). The shortcomings of market segmentation has produced the development and testing of new models and theories that more adequately explain consumer behavior. These have stemmed largely from the field of social psychology.

The second group of methods generally reflects the traditional thinking in social psychology that attitudes lead to behavior. Understanding attitudes can lead to greater insight into consumer choice and purchasing behavior.

Finally, a third set of methods involves the discrepancies between "buying" behavior and "shopping" preferences and is categorized under patronage behavior theory (Sheth 1983). Patronage behavior theory is a radical departure from attitude research and suggests that "shopping" preference and actual "buying" behavior are two different processes, and that they cannot be combined into a single conceptual framework with a common set of constructs.

The "shopping" preference refers to the customer-specific factors that influence a customer's general shopping motives with respect to a variety of different products or services and may be manifested in a shopping "orientation" or "style." For example, brand-loyal shoppers who go shopping for an automobile may consider only one brand of automobile as they shop. The preferences and intentions of the shopper do not always result in a "buying episode."

Actual "buying behavior" is the activity and decision process of gaining ownership of the product or service in exchange for money or something of value. Taking the automobile example a step further, the brand-loyal person may be mostly oriented to one name brand of automobile. He or she holds a preference toward the brand name car; however, constant advertising from another automobile company and a significant rebate program, which has reduced the price of the second car, results in the shopper's purchase even though it is not the preferred name brand.

The theory of patronage behavior consists of two distinct and separate subtheories, one called a shopping preference and the second where the focus is on the actual buying behavior (Sheth 1983). Shopping preference subtheory consists of shopping predisposition, choice rules, shopping motives, and shopping options. Influencing shopping preference are various determinants: market determinants (location, retail structure, and positioning); company determinants (merchandise, service, promotional efforts); personal determinants (personal, social, epistemic); and product determinants (product type, usage type, and brand loyalty) (Sheth 1983).

Shopping preference, as a subsystem of patronage behavior theory is specifically concerned with the area of personal determinants. Personal determinants affect the individual's shopping style by influencing a customer's general shopping motives. They may be thought of as personal values—the individual's own beliefs about what to look for when shopping; social values—the values imposed by others, such as family and friends, reference groups, or society at large; or epistemic values—those factors which prompt curiosity, exploration, and the search for new knowledge.

The research on shopping orientations has spanned nearly three decades and has identified a variety of different types of shopping orientations among many different products. Some of these orientations are specific to product classes such as food, clothing, and automobiles. Others have identified shopping orientations that cut across a number of product categories. Shopping styles are usually classified into type categories. Stone (1954), in his seminal and classic research on shopping styles, identified four major types among grocery shoppers: the economical shopper, the personalizing shopper, the ethical shopper, and the apathetic shopper. Stone's typology of shoppers was supported in Darden and Reynolds' (1971) research of these four types of shoppers. Consumers of food products have also been identified as convenience shoppers, bargain shoppers, compulsive shoppers, and store-loyal shoppers (Stephenson and Willett 1969). Moschis (1976) further refined the list of shopping orientations by identifying additional lifestyle categories such as the psycho-socializing shopper and the name-conscious shopper.

Bellenger, Robertson, and Greenberg (1977) and Bellenger and Korgaonker (1980) expanded the typology system of shopping orientations or styles by identifying a classification system of economic versus recreational shoppers. They defined recreational shoppers as those who seek a recreational experience that provides satisfaction beyond the actual purchase of goods or services. Economic shoppers, on the other hand, were defined as those who seek convenience as well as lower prices. Shopping styles were then linked within one of these two major types, recreational or economical.

Shopping orientations have also been examined in other product-specific and situational cases. Automobile buyers have been classified as having four major shopping profiles: (1) constructive shoppers, who work hard at gathering and using information, (2) surrogate shoppers, who spend time in shopping but who rely heavily on others in the family, (3) preparatory shoppers, who spend more time talking to friends and who are less influenced by in-store promotional efforts, and (4) routinized shoppers, who exhibit considerable loyalty* to the same brand and provider because of past satisfaction (Furse, Punj, and Stewart 1982). Recent studies have linked shopping style orientations to non-store retailing (Korgaonker 1984), segmentation of elderly consumers (Lumpkin 1985), convenience consumption (Bellizzi and Hite 1986), and typologies of shopping browsers (Jarboe and McDaniel 1987). While these studies have produced insights into shopping orientations specific to products and situations, some private market research firms have collected shopping style orientation information on an annual basis.

Simmons Market Research Bureau (1987b) has annually collected shopping profile information over the past decade, but has not yet linked the profiles to the shopping orientations toward recreation products, programs, or services. To date, only one other study has linked shopping styles to fitness or recreation products (Warnick 1986). He found the five most frequently stated shopping styles of fitness participants were economy minded, style/trend conscious, cautious, conformists, and impulsive. In order to benefit recreation and fitness managers, it seems important to further develop and link the various shopping orientations to the marketplace behavior of recreation and fitness patrons.

Numerous questions still need to be addressed. Is convenience a factor in shopping behavior for fitness programs? Do fitness consumers exhibit completely different and specific shopping styles, or do shopping orientations cluster together? Do shopping orientations appear to cut across different product categories? Do shopping styles vary by sex and participation levels? Lack of answers for such questions indicates a need for more comprehensive research on the marketplace behavior of consumers of recreation and fitness programs and services in order to further refine market strategies. The absence of research may be attributed to the rapid growth of the fitness industry and lack of concern regarding consumer behavior. It may also be a result of the product or sales orientation of many agencies. June and Smith (1987) indicated that the lack of attention to consumer behavior in recreation and tourism is due to a presumption that these purchases are modest and unimportant categories within personal expenditures. However, the value and costs of many fitness and recreational program purchases indicate that these items are salient and significant purchases in the minds of most consumers.

JUSTIFICATION AND PURPOSE OF THE STUDY

Fitness clubs and recreation businesses may benefit in several ways from an improved knowledge of consumer shopping styles. First, an understanding of the predominant shopping styles among fitness participants should facilitate creation of improved media messages in marketing communications. Second, differentiation of consumer shopping style behaviors may improve target market strategies and the positioning of fitness products and programs. An identification of the predominant shopping styles may assist in building an understanding of why consumers select a specific program from among various alternatives. Eventually, the study of shopping styles when linked with product attributes should provide evidence of the influence of shopping orientation to actual buying behavior.

The purposes of the exploratory research described in this essay were: (1) to identify the predominant shopping styles of consumers of exercise/fitness programs through a survey instrument of eleven shopping style statements;

(2) to determine if shopping styles vary by selected demographic or involvement characteristics; and (3) to explore the existence of various shopping style factors.

METHODS

To examine the shopping styles of the exercise/fitness market, data were compiled from a structured questionnaire. Rather than focusing on a wide range of consumers, one specific consumer group was selected—the college student market. This consumer group, primarily made up of 18- to 24-year-olds, was selected because it constitutes the second highest penetration (19.9 percent) of total participation across all age categories and accounts for about one-fifth (20.7 percent) of all adults 18 years and older who participate in physical fitness/exercise programs (Simmons Market Research Bureau 1987a).

Trained interviewers collected information from 250 college students residing in a regional area of two major towns with five colleges located either within or bordering these towns. Total student population of the area was approximately 40,000. Of the 250 interviews conducted, information from 229 was considered complete and eligible for analysis. Only those individuals who were interested or who had participated in an exercise/fitness program were considered eligible in the interview process.

For the purposes of this research, shopping styles were examined by descriptive statistics (percentages), chi-square analysis, and factor analysis. A .05 level of significance was used; however, relationships at the .10 level were also reported. The method of examining shopping styles was developed by Simmons Market Research Bureau (1987b) and has been consistently tested and verified over the past twelve years by the firm.

To examine the shopping styles of the college student exercise fitness market, subjects were asked to respond to ten shopping style statements on a four-point Likert-type rating scale of "strongly agree" to "strongly disagree." Simmons Market Research Bureau (1987b) verified the first ten shopping style statements; however, pretests conducted in this study indicated that a significant number of participants may be convenience oriented. Therefore, an additional statement about convenience was included with the ten statements developed by Simmons, for a total of eleven statements.

Eleven shopping style categories were used for purposes of data analysis (Simmons Market Research Bureau 1987b): brand loyal; cautious; conformists; ecologists; economy minded; experimenters; impulsive; persuadable; planners; style/trend conscious; and convenience oriented. The subjects were not aware of these labels and responded only to the shopping orientation statements. Each individual was then also asked to indicate which shopping style statement best describes his or her shopping orientation for exercise/fitness programs.

Factor analysis of the eleven shopping style statements was conducted according to guidelines set forth by Kass and Tinsley (1979). Kass and Tinsley (1979) recommended Barlett's test, a chi-square test of the significance of the correlation matrix, to determine if factor analysis is appropriate. Principal components with Kaiser normalization was the factor analysis method selected because the goal of the research was to explore data related to shopping styles and because the data collected was descriptive. The internal consistency of the factors was examined by randomly assigning the data to two groups and factor analyzing the eleven statements again within each data set. Statements were loaded in a similar fashion for each of the split half samples; however, the low number of cases did not substantiate a reportable statistic. The factor structure was considered representative, although no measure of stability was derived. Factors with eigenvalues greater than one were determined to be one factor set. Even when the order of entry into the factor loading was randomized, the statements continued to aggregate in a similar factor structure. Statistical analysis was conducted using SPSS (Nie et al. 1975).

RESULTS

The convenience sample of 229 college-aged students was primarily composed of undergraduates (91 percent), 57.9 percent female and 42.1 percent male. The average length of residency in the market area was approximately three school years; and the average age was 21.9 years. The sample indicated that, on average, the maximum amount of time they would travel one-way to participate in an exercise/fitness program was 20 minutes.

The shopping style analysis revealed some useful insights into the shopping behavior for fitness programs of the college-aged target market. When each of the individual shopping style statements was examined, the target market most strongly agreed with the following descriptive statement types: (1) convenience oriented (93.4 percent agreed or strongly agreed); (2) style/trend conscious (73.4 percent agreed or strongly agreed); (3) economy minded (63.6 percent agreed or strongly agreed); (4) ecologist (63 percent agreed or strongly agreed); (5) conformists (61.4 percent agreed or strongly agreed); and (6) planners (53.4 percent agreed or strongly agreed). The respondents tended overall to disagree more with the other descriptive shopping style statements. The results of the sample's responses to each of the eleven shopping style statements are listed in Table 3.1.

Each subject was also asked to select from the eleven statements the one that best describes

TABLE 3.1 Description of Shopping Style Statements for Exercise/Fitness Programs

Shopping Style Statement[a]	Mean	Percent Agree or Strongly Agree
Convenience oriented "Enroll in programs that are conveniently located and scheduled"	1.59	93.4
Style/trend conscious "Keep abreast of changes in programs and techniques"	2.21	73.4
Economy minded "Shop around to take advantage of specials or bargains"	2.28	63.6
Ecologists "Activities and products that are unhealthy should be banned"	2.24	63.0
Conformists "Enroll in programs that my friends/family would approve of"	2.35	61.4
Planners "Generally plan far ahead to enroll in expensive programs"	2.42	53.5
Brand loyal "Always look for the name of the sponsor. . . ."	2.69	47.6
Cautious "Do not 'buy' unknown brands/programs to save money"	2.48	47.1
Impulsive "Enroll on the spur of the moment"	2.68	36.4
Persuadable "Advertising presents a true picture of programs or services"	2.75	34.9
Experimenters "Change sponsoring agencies often for the sake of variety or novelty"	2.81	22.2

[a] Statements adapted from Simmons Market Research Bureau's "Study of Media and Markets," abbreviated here. Mean calculated by average score to scale of strongly agree (1); agree (2); disagree (3); and strongly disagree (4).

his or her shopping style for exercise/fitness programs. The six most frequently selected shopping orientation descriptors were: (1) convenience oriented (33.7 percent); (2) economy minded (13.7 percent); (3) style/trend conscious (13.2 percent); (4) impulsive (9.8 percent); (5) brand loyal (8.8 percent); and conformists (8.3 percent). The frequencies of the other "best" descriptors of shopping styles were considerably lower—all less than 4 percent (Table 3.2).

When each of the shopping style statements was examined by sex and involvement levels, only five of the twenty-two chi-square analysis statements were significant. The chi-square statistics are listed in Table 3.3. For males and females, differences were found in experimental, impulsive, and style/trend conscious shopping

styles. Males were more likely than their female counterparts to disagree that they change sponsoring agencies more often for the sake of variety or novelty. Females were more likely than males to agree that they like to keep abreast of the latest programs and techniques. For involvement level, fitness participants were asked to rate their intensity of involvement or participation on a one-to-ten scale (1 = low intensity involvement and 10 = high intensity involvement). Based on the ratings, three types of involvement were created: low (below four rating), moderate (four to six rating), and high (seven and above rating). Significant differences were found between these involvement types of participants and impulsive and experimental shopping styles. Low-involvement participants

TABLE 3.2 Best Descriptor of Shopping Style Statements for Fitness Programs

Statement	Times Selected	Percent
Convenience oriented	69	33.7
Economy minded	28	13.7
Style/trend conscious	27	13.2
Impulsive	20	9.8
Cautious	18	8.8
Conformists	17	8.3
Ecologists	8	3.9
Brand loyal	6	2.9
Experimenters	4	2.0
Persuadable	4	2.0
Planners	4	2.0

were more likely than high-involvement participants to agree with the statement that they are impulsive. On the other hand, high-involvement participants were more likely than their counterparts to agree that they would change agencies for the sake of variety or novelty. They were more likely to experiment.

A factor analysis of the eleven shopping style statements revealed four composite shopping style dimensions. Bartlett's chi-square test to determine if factor analysis would be appropriate was found to be significant at the .001 level. The results of the principal components factor analysis with a varimax rotation and Kaiser normalization are presented in Table 3.4. In interpreting the meanings of the factors, statements with loadings of .50 or above were considered.

Four principal factors were derived from the data analysis. The first factor represents a "conformist–economy-minded–ecologist–experimeters group." They are shoppers who look to friends and associates for information, who seek out bargains or high value, who value healthy products and environments, and who will change for the sake of variety or novelty in a new program or a new environment. This factor group

was labeled "external cues." They appeared to be driven by external social values. The second factor represents the group of planners and style/trend conscious shoppers. Individuals in this group plan ahead for purchases but also seek out programs which offer the latest in fitness techniques. This group was labeled "innovators." The next factor represents a group of participants who are impulsive and persuadable in their shopping style. This group was labeled "impulsive." The final factor represents a group composed of cautious, brand-loyal shoppers, but who are not driven by a convenience orientation. This group was labeled "loyal."

DISCUSSION

First, a discussion of the purely descriptive aspects and implications of the study is presented. When the individual shopping style statements alone were examined, it was evident that the findings should have direct implications for fitness center managers as they develop and refine their promotional strategies aimed at this particular target market. When the shopping styles of the college-aged target market were examined as a whole, a significant portion of the market indicated they were convenience minded, style/trend conscious, and economy minded. In other words, they appear to desire less expensive programs that offer the latest fitness trends and/or techniques located at convenient locations and during convenient times. This may be a difficult task for many agencies because it means they must keep costs low, but be innovative and willing to change and adapt to new fitness techniques. Furthermore, if fitness agencies want to locate in areas convenient to the college student market, they will probably need to compete directly with other convenience oriented establishments. Other important shopping styles that agencies should consider in the

TABLE 3.3 Chi-Square Analysis of Demographic, Involvement, and Shopping Style Statements

Variable[a]	Chi-Square	df	Significance Level[b]	Contingency
Sex with . . .				
Experimenters	13.46	3	.004	.25
Impulse	12.99	3	.005	.24
Style/trend conscious	7.65	3	.053	.19
Involvement with . . .				
Impulse	12.11	6	.059	.24
Experimenters	18.25	6	.006	.28

[a] Variables examined included sex (male or female) and intensity of involvement level (low, moderate, high) with the responses to each of the eleven shopping style statements.

[b] Significance level = .05; however, those relationships significant at .10 level also reported.

TABLE 3.4 Factor Loadings on Shopping Style Statements

Statement	Factor 1	Factor 2	Factor 3	Factor 4
Brand loyal	.48	.33	−.05	.50
Cautious	−.02	.13	.02	.78
Conformists	.57	.13	−.001	.10
Convenience oriented	.05	.37	.03	−.67
Ecologists	.60	−.44	−.22	.03
Economy minded	.68	.15	−.008	.14
Experimenters	.71	.08	.43	−.05
Impulsive	.07	−.30	.71	−.25
Persuadable	.02	.12	.76	.14
Planners	.16	.78	.04	.02
Style/trend conscious	.20	.62	−.42	−.03
Eigenvalues	2.22	1.73	1.38	1.15
Percent of variance explained	20.20	15.80	12.60	10.50

The underlined factor loadings are the most salient on each factor; a cutoff value of .50 was used for item selection. Varimax rotation matrix after rotation with Kaiser normalization is presented above.

Factor 1 = Conformist – Economy-minded – Ecologist – Experimenters **(External Cues)**

Factor 2 = Planners – Style/trend Conscious **(Innovators)**

Factor 3 = Impulsive – Persuadable **(Impulsive)**

Factor 4 = Cautious – Brand Loyal – Non-convenience-oriented **(Loyal)**

college-aged or young adult market are the "brand loyal," "conformists," and "impulsive" styles.

A direct implication for fitness center management is the adaptation of advertising messages and promotional techniques that communicate to these shopping styles. For example, advertisements geared toward the majority of this target market should include such items as convenience, latest fitness trends, and cost of programs or memberships. For agencies seeking to attract "impulsive" shopping style individuals, the agency must advertise heavily and selectively to keep their name in the minds of the college-aged fitness shoppers. Based on this analysis, an agency that strives to attract fitness participants through an impulse-buy approach may be wasting a great deal of money. Less than 10 percent of all potential fitness participants indicated that they buy fitness programs on an impulse. However, much more can be gained from this analysis than just looking at the purely descriptive statements of the respondents.

Although a simple descriptive approach does shed some light on the shopping orientations of fitness program participants, a more meaningful explanation of shopping styles was gained when the factor analysis was conducted. It was felt that most consumers do not respond to a product category with one specific type of shopping predisposition but carry with them a collection or bundle of shopping characteristics or orientations which may have been learned over a lifetime. The typical consumer, for example, may talk to friends, consider price or shop for the best bargain, and/or plan ahead for membership purchases. The findings of this study suggest that four groups of shopping orientations exist among the college student or young adult market: "external cues," "innovators," "impulsive," and "loyal." The factor with the most loadings and explaining the most variance was "external cues." Although this particular factor was not particularly neat in its descriptive powers, it seemed to be best characterized by those external situations or social values which describe an individual's shopping orientation. One might also see this group as influenced by word-of-mouth. Because of the number of items which loaded on this factor, the external cue group should be considered to be important, and it further suggests the salience of the word-of-mouth impact on consumer behavior.

The "innovator" shopper seems to be similar in some ways to the "early adapters" of the diffusion of innovation theory. Rogers (1962) stated that "early adapters" seek out new innovation and techniques, try new programs early in their life cycles, and then may move on to new products or programs and innovative approaches to program delivery. The "innovator" described in this study appears to have some similar characteristics. They plan ahead for purchases that may give some insights into their search behavior about new programs, and they try to keep up with the latest trends and techniques in fitness programming. An "impulsive" shopper does exist. Surprisingly, a large amount of fitness club and program membership advertising appears to assume that all shoppers are impulsive. While this research documented their existence, they are not the dominant type.

On the other hand, there does appear to be a shopper who exhibits signs of loyalty. The "loyal" shopper is the one who is cautious and who looks for brand-name programs. Their loyalty is such that they would forego convenience. This shopping orientation of fitness participants appears to reinforce a portion of the work of Selin and his colleagues (1988) who found that most participants of recreation programs were only spuriously loyal to agency programs and who suggested that loyalty may be more a factor of habit or convenience. In this study, the shopping orientation of the "loyal" customer appears to suggest that a portion of participants do carry loyal tendencies; however, the negative orientation to convenience suggests that convenience is not part of the loyal customers' predisposition to the program as suggested in the Selin (1988) study. Whether their loyalty is a matter of choice or repeat behavior, it is not possible to tell from these findings. Obviously, much more work on the development of loyal tendencies is needed.

The convenience dimension was probably the most difficult of all the orientations to understand. It did not load positively on any of the other orientation statements with the exception of the negative loading on the "loyal" factor. It appears that convenience is a totally separate issue considered when shopping for fitness programs. Shoppers may carry one of the four predisposed shopping styles with them, but consider convenience as a totally separate issue. Convenience may override or enhance any of the other shopping orientations. The high percentage of individuals (over 90 percent) who indicated agreement with the convenience statement is an indication of the importance of this variable. It may influence shopping behavior, but appears not to be linked to any shopping orientation except that is negatively related to the loyalty orientation.

Although this study did not examine the evolution of shopping orientations, it appears likely that shopping styles evolve over time. For example, it is unlikely that one initially exhibits loyal shopping tendencies. Shopping orientations probably evolve as a result of behavior and experience. Shopping orientations also need to be examined by usage rates and repeat purchase behavior.

Finally, it should be noted that shopping orientations are descriptions of shopping predispositions, and these styles of shopping do not automatically result in behavior. Many other systematic and sometimes managerially planned promotions, events, and efforts intervene between preferences and behavior and result in what Sheth (1983) terms preference–behavior discrepancy. This study of shopping orientations is only a small part of the broader examination of patronage predisposition and behavior needed in the development of consumer behavior research theory for the recreation and leisure marketplace. This research has indicated that shopping styles do exist and differences within some styles are significant by certain demographic and participation involvement variables, but more research is needed. Research should continue to examine shopping orientations of other market groups within other recreation programs and product categories so that more refined marketing and program strategies may be matched to consumer needs.

REFERENCES

Bellenger, Danny N., and Pradeep K. Korgaonker. 1980. Profiling the recreational shopper. *Journal of Retailing* 56 (Fall):77–82.

Bellenger, Danny N., Dan H. Robertson, and Barnett A. Greenberg. 1977. Shopping center patronage motives. *Journal of Retailing* 53 (Summer):29–38.

Bellizzi, Joseph A., and Robert E. Hite. 1986. Convenience consumption and role overload convenience. *Journal of the Academy of Marketing Science* 14(4):1–9.

Darden, William R., and Fred D. Reynolds. 1971. Shopping orientations and product usage rates. *Journal of Marketing* 8 (November):505–508.

DeMarcus, Rachel. 1986. Non-profit commercialism: A growing problem. *Club Business* 6(10):57–58.

Engel, James F., David Killat, and Roger D. Blackwell. 1973. *Consumer behavior.* New York: Holt, Rinehart & Winston.

Furse, David H., Girish N. Punj, and David W. Stewart. 1982. Individual search strategies in new automobile purchases. In *Advances in consumer research,* edited by A. Mitchell, 379–384. Ann Arbor, Mich.: Association for Consumer Research.

Huntley, Steve. 1983. The not-so-healthy health spa industry. *U.S. News and World Report,* 7 November, 60–61.

Jarboe, Glen R., and Carl D. McDaniel. 1987. A profile of browsers in regional shopping malls. *Journal of the Academy of Marketing Science* 15(1):46–53.

June, Leslie, and Stephen L. J. Smith. 1987. Service attributes and situational effects on customer preferences for restaurant dining. *Journal of Travel Research* 26(2):20–28.

Kass, Richard A., and Howard E. A. Tinsley. 1979. Factor analysis. *Journal of Leisure Research* 11(2):120–138.

Korgaonkar, Pradeep K. 1984. Consumer shopping orientations, non-retailers, and consumers' patronage intentions: A multivariate investigation. *Journal of the Academy of Marketing Science* 12(1):11–22.

Kotler, Philip. 1982. *Marketing for nonprofit organizations.* 2d ed. Englewood Cliffs, N.J.:Prentice Hall.

Lumpkin, James R. 1985. Shopping orientation segmentation of the elderly consumer. *Journal of the Academy of Marketing Science* 13(2):271–289.

Lynch, R. B. 1983. The new wave in health clubs. *New York Times,* 13 November, 21.

Managed Recreation Research Report. 1988. The recreation, fitness and leisure industry in 1988. *Recreation, Sports and Leisure* 8(6):5–13.

Managed Recreation Research Report. 1987. The recreation, fitness and leisure industry in 1987. *Recreation, Sports and Leisure* 7(6):7–10.

Moschis, George P. 1976. Shopping orientations and consumer use of information. *Journal of Retailing* 56(4):5–22.

Nie, Norman K., C. Hadlai Hull, Jean G. Jenkins, Karin Steinbrenner, and Dale H. Bent. 1975. *Statistical package for the social sciences.* 2d ed. New York: McGraw-Hill, 1975.

Rogers, E.M. 1962. *Diffusion of innovation.* New York: Free Press.

Selin, Steven W., Dennis R. Howard, Edward Udd, and Ted T. Cable. 1988. An analysis of consumer loyalty to municipal programs. *Leisure Sciences* 10(3):217–223.

Sheth, Jagdish N. 1983. An integrative theory of patronage preference and behavior. In *Patronage behavior and retail management,* edited by W. R. Darden and R. F. Lusch, 9–28. New York: North-Holland.

Simmons Market Research Bureau. 1987a. *The 1987 study of media and markets: Sports and leisure,* vol. P-10. New York.

Simmons Market Research Bureau. 1987b. *Technical guide to study of media and markets,* vol. P-10. New York.

Stephenson, R. Ronald, and Ronald P. Willett. 1969. Analysis of consumer retail patronage strategies. In *Marketing involvement in society and the economy,* edited by P. R. McDonald, 316–322. Chicago: American Marketing Association.

Stone, Gregory P. 1954. City shoppers and urban identification: Observations on the social psychology of city life. *American Journal of Sociology* 60:36–45.

Warnick, Rodney B. 1986. Marketing exercise and fitness programs: An examination of image analysis and consumer buying style. Leisure Research Symposium. Anaheim, Calif.: National Recreation and Park Association.

Warnick, Rodney B., and Dennis R. Howard.
1985. Marketing fitness: It's about time.
Leisure Information Quarterly 6(4):2–5.

Warnick, Rodney B., and Dennis R. Howard.
1985. Market share analysis of selected
leisure services from 1979 to 1982. *Journal
of Park and Recreation Administration*
3(2):64–76.

4

Estimating the Market Potential for Golf and Tennis

Richard B. Morrison

Estimates of market potential are essential in determining how well an organization performs within its market and against its competitors. Such estimates underlie market share and trend analyses and provide a basis for improved strategic planning for a business. In this essay, the factors affecting market potential and a method for estimating market potential are outlined. The participant sports of golf and tennis are used to provide illustrations.

MARKET SEGMENTATION

In contrast to mass marketing, market segmentation is the process of partitioning the total market for a product or service into segments of potential customers with similar characteristics. Customers in a segment have similar buying patterns, and marketing efforts can be targeted to that segment. A market is typically segmented along the following dimensions:

Geographic   What are the primary and secondary trade areas for the product or service? This is often measured in travel time from home or work to the point of purchase or consumption. Does consumption of the product or service vary by geographic area?

Demographic   To what extent do age, gender, education, income, and other socioeconomic characteristics describe the most likely purchasers of a product or service? (See *American Demographics,* February 1987, p. 45 for an example applied to TV sports.)

Psychographic   To what extent do a person's values and lifestyle influence buying behavior? (See *American Demographics,* July 1989, p. 25 for a discussion of the VALS approach to market segmentation.)

Buyer Behavior   Heavy users of a product or service are typically a small percent of all users, but they usually account for a big percent of all sales. For example, in a

Richard B. Morrison directs the Sport and Fitness Graduate Program, Northeastern University, Boston, Massachusetts.

recent survey on product usage in the beer and wine industries, 18 percent of beer drinkers consumed 63 percent of the beer, and 21 percent of the wine drinkers consumed 74 percent of the wine.

In determining which combination of characteristics to use as a basis for segmenting a market, each potential market segment must be evaluated on four dimensions, referred to as the four R's:

1. Can it be *rated* relative to other markets? Is information available on the size, location, media habits, and buying power of the segment?
2. Is it *realistic* in size? Is there enough buying power in the segment to make it worthwhile to try to gain market share?
3. Can customers be easily *reached?* What access do you have to the segment through electronic or print media, or otherwise? Can you target your marketing messages to the segment?
4. Will customers *respond* to marketing efforts? What evidence do you have that this segment is likely to yield improved sales? Are there indicators that such improvements will yield an adequate return on investment?

FACTORS AFFECTING MARKET POTENTIAL

Geographic Factors

How far will most people travel to play golf or tennis? The answer to this question helps define the target market area, the area from which most participants will be drawn. Answering the question is not as simple as it may appear; it depends on one's assumptions.

What is meant by "most people"? Half of them? Seventy-five percent? Ninety percent? What is meant by the term "people"? Occasional golfers or tennis players? People who play very often? What do the terms "golf" or "tennis" mean? A nine-hole course that is crowded and poorly maintained? A championship course that is not crowded and in superb condition? Clay courts in good condition? Composition courts indoors?

It is clear that how far people will travel to play golf or tennis greatly depends on the assumptions one makes about these factors. How does one know which assumptions are most reasonable? Answers will be seen further into this essay!

Demographic Factors

To what extent do factors such as age, gender, and income affect participation in golf or tennis? Does everyone participate at about the same rate? Or, more likely, are some demographic subsets of the population playing golf or tennis at a much higher rate than average? If so, one can use this information to help estimate the potential number of golfers or tennis players in a given region. More about this later in the essay.

Which age groups should one use when collecting information from participants or potential participants? Always ask the person's age in years, and never ask "How old are you?" because it carries an **"OLD"** connotation and may encourage a nonresponse. Also, never use age groups in the questionnaire—always ask for age in years. You can then tailor make your own age groups once the data have been computerized. If questionnaire responses are restricted to specific age groups, then your data are forever limited to those groups. Experience has shown that over 90 percent of persons in telephone surveys will give their age in years.

One is unlikely, however, to get such a high response rate if a person is asked to report his or her income in dollars. Here, unlike age, grouping is best, but the income groups depend on the persons being surveyed. Income can also refer to individual or household income; these are often very different figures. In the most recent sports marketing research completed by this author, the lowest individual income group was under $25,000; the highest of the five groups was over $100,000. By contrast, a recent alumni survey from one of this author's academic institutions used ''under $100,000'' as the lowest income group. Know your market!

Buyer Behavior Factors

Consumers, in this case participants, can be roughly classified into two groups: regulars and dabblers; heavy users and light users; frequent participants and occasional participants. A measure can be taken by asking how many times within a given period a person participated in golf or tennis. The question could ask about the number of occasions, or number of holes of golf, or number of hours of tennis. Experience has shown that persons can readily approximate the number of days on which they participated in golf or tennis, hence this measurement technique is recommended.

In addition to determining the basic unit by which to measure golf or tennis participation, one needs to determine an appropriate time frame. If, in January, a sample of residents in the northeast part of the United States were asked how many times they played golf within the last month, precious few would have played. The same question asked at the same time of residents in the southeast would elicit many golfers. The key point is that where seasonal variation is likely to affect participation rates, a time period that covers the entire seasonal variation, typically one year, should be used in the data collection.

ESTIMATING MARKET POTENTIAL

In the example that follows, geographic, demographic and buyer behavior variables will be used to estimate the market potential for golf and tennis. Here's the basic formula.

$$\text{Days of Market} =$$
$$\text{Potential Participation Rate} \times$$
$$\text{Population} \times$$
$$\text{Participation Days}$$

This formula can be applied to different market segments, using geographic, demographic, and buyer behavior variables to identify segments. Here's an example of how it is done, including the key assumptions made about the market segments.

Assumptions

Assumptions are based on market research which has determined the following:

1. The frequent golfer represents 7 percent of the general population, travels about 45 minutes to play golf, and plays golf about 30 days annually.
2. The occasional golfer represents 4 percent of the general population, travels about 30 minutes to play golf, and plays golf about 4 days annually.
3. The market area has a population of 200,000 within 45 minutes of the golf course and a population of 100,000 within 30 minutes of the course.

Note that more specific statements about smaller market segments, such as by age group, by gender, or by income could be made using the same assumptions. For simplicity of explanation, the more general example will be used. Following, the appropriate values have been substituted in the formula and the calculations performed to provide an estimate of the market potential, measured in annual days of golf.

$$\text{Annual Days of Golf} =$$
$$(.07 \times 200,000 \times 30) + (.04 \times 100,000 \times 4)$$
$$= (14,000 \times 30) + (4,000 \times 4)$$
$$= 420,000 + 16,000$$
$$= 436,000$$

This is an estimate of market potential for golf for the entire market area noted. Once the size of the potential market is known, then one can measure one's own performance in terms of market share. What percent (share) of those 436,000 annual days of golf are accounted for by your golf course?

The same methodology can be readily applied to tennis, but most likely with a different set of assumptions. Tennis players will travel fewer minutes to play tennis, about 10–15 in the northeast. They will also play more times per year, whether they are frequent or occasional players.

Start simple, using a formula such as the one described above. Then modify your assumptions and make your formula sufficiently detailed to account for the smallest important market segments for your business. Get better and better information each year and keep refining your method for estimating demand, saving your information from year to year. This *is* important information, and it *can* help assure business survival as market conditions change. Chart your annual progress and you'll have clear feedback on how well you are performing.

STRATEGIC PLANNING IN SPORT

5

Strategic Planning for Athletic Departments in Small-to-Moderate-Sized Two-Year Public Institutions: Focus on the Future

Richard A. Stull and Louis Hammen

INTRODUCTION

The challenge for the athletic department at the two-year public institution is to develop, maintain, and enhance the athletic program in an era of limited resources to meet the demands of an ever changing student body and community of constituents. How does the athletic director strategically position the athletic program for the future, maintain program viability, and continue to promote the institutional mission?

The purpose of this essay is to develop an awareness of the strategic planning process in order to help effect a symbiotic relationship between the mission of the athletic department and the mission of the college. The focus is on three general institutional objectives that would enhance the mission of all small- to moderate-sized institutions; student enrollment, public image, and revenue development.

Organizations, like individuals, pass through several stages during their life cycle. In its infancy (entrepreneurial stage) an organization generates energy to meet its goals and objectives. Peter Drucker (1977, 153) describes the innovative organization as one that "organizes itself to think through rapidly even the wildest and apparently silliest idea for something new to the point where it feasibly can be appraised."

After appraisal and implementation, the organization moves into a maintenance stage but must make changes to meet new challenges or markets. The successful organization then enters a creative stage in which specific strategies change and create a new list of priorities. When entering periods of decline, those organizations

Richard A. Stull is with the Department of Health and Physical Education, Humboldt State University, Arcata, California, and Louis Hammen is Director of Development for Dundalk Community College, Baltimore, Maryland.

that are able to assess or recognize the symptoms will be the ones that may sustain or even expand their respective missions. Such organizations usually commit to a process of strategic planning in which they review their current functions and services, assess their existing constituencies (those to whom they provide services), and create a new set of priorities to meet the current and future variables of the environment (market place).

In their book, *A Passion for Excellence*, Peters and Austin (1985, 62) indicate the single most important variable in developing a marketing strategy is "relative perceived product quality." For a college athletic/recreation program, the products of high quality facilities and services will produce a positive relationship with the community they serve. The strategic planning process should be used to identify and create this type of perception for the college athletic department's offerings.

We recognize that the athletic department in the small- to moderate-sized institution is beset by a number of limitations. Often the athletic director has a myriad of responsibilities, including teaching classes, coaching sports, and administering budgets. In addition, time for recruitment is often minimal and there is often inadequate money for scholarships.

It is believed, however, that the acceptance and application of the following three important concepts will enable the athletic director to position his or her program for the future:

1. The planning process is no longer exclusively a private sector mechanism used by large corporations or educational institutions to anticipate changes in their market, but is appropriate for small public institutions as well (Miller and Miller 1988, 32).
2. One approach to success entails embracing the concept of the athletic department as a "small sports industry." By implementing creative, entrepreneurial, and ultimately auxiliary enterprises as a result of the strategic planning process, the athletic director will be able to achieve program viability and enhance the institutional mission by advancing the objectives of student enrollment, public image, and revenue development.
3. The successful implementation of the strategic planning model and its results will enable the athletic department to sell itself up to the administration and ensure that the planning process is in concert with the institutional objectives and mission of the college.

Definitions and Terms

Strategic planning has been defined by Peat Marwick's Resource Development System, copyrighted and marketed by Peat Marwick Main and Company (1988, 5) as "the blueprint for the organization which integrates the work of internal functions to achieve stated goals and objectives and to deliver identified results to your constituencies."

The strategic planning process is the mechanism by which the athletic department connects to the institutional mission and its institutional objectives of student enrollment, public image, and revenue generation. But, what is strategic planning and why should anyone spend time and energy with the process? Most experts in the area of organizational leadership and management view planning as essential to effective management. Procaccini (1986, 71) asserts, "To the extent that you plan you will reduce the number of surprises and increase the likelihood of goal attainment."

There are two types of planning: strategic and operational. The strategic process involves looking at the big picture and setting long-range goals (2–3 years) for the organization. The operating plan defines the day-to-day tasks and responsibilities necessary to ensure the organization serves its clients and market. The clients of an athletic department are students and community members, and their markets are those segments of the population in the local community that use their athletic/recreational services.

Methodology

This essay focuses specifically on the activities and actions that support the organization's overall mission. Utilizing Peat Marwick's (1988) Resource Development System as the methodological framework, the strategic plan will employ four tactical approaches, each of which will serve as a specific blueprint for action for the athletic director at the two-year, small- to medium-sized public institution. The following tactics should be exercised:

- Develop a clear plan for targeting constituents (constituency development)
- Communicate with identified constituencies (communications) and market services to identified constituencies (marketing). Identify services for resource development activities or projects (resource development).

With these elements of the strategic plan in place, the athletic director will be able to think of the athletic department and its facilities, course offerings, and other services as a small sports industry or business. As the entrepreneur (or leader) of this small sports industry, the athletic director will have a proposal and operational plan to present to his or her supervisors and college administration.

The elements of the tactical plan build upon each other in enabling the athletic director to select specific activities that meet the general institutional objectives of enrollment development, public image, and revenue generation. Included in these criteria are the following assumptions:

1. Small institution with a small staff
2. Recruitment activities hampered by limited or no operational funds
3. Resource development activities must support academic and institutional missions.
4. Self-sufficiency, program expansion, and institutional image enhancement are desired outcomes derived from the successful implementation of the strategic plan.

Data compiled by the Office of Institutional Research and Grants at Dundalk Community College (1989, 2) indicate that "seventy-five percent of revenues for all public institutions are dependent on enrollments and hence are vulnerable to enrollment decline." It is clear that alternatives must be found so as to not be solely at the mercy of enrollment-driven funding.

CONSTITUENCY DEVELOPMENT

The initial step in preparing a strategic plan for the small sports industry must be to make an assessment of the community it currently serves (constituency). For general purposes, constituency development is defined as "those programs and activities an organization implements to identify, reach, and retain a constituency." (Peat Marwick 1988, 6)

The constituency development phase of the plan seeks three outcomes:

1. To identify constituents (who are presently served, who were previously

served, who might be interested in being served).

2. To maintain interest of identified constituents through involvement and understanding (better defined services offered through increased communication and evaluation of services by constituents).

3. To enhance constituent participation by encouraging increased levels of interaction (improve and increase services to each constituents group).

The identification of a constituent comes from an assessment of current services and current participants. Following identification, each constituent group must be further defined by some criteria to categorize them for subsequent phases of the plan. It is suggested that each group utilizing current services be defined by (1) demographics (age, sex, community), (2) motivation for using services, and (3) appeal for new/enhanced services.

At Dundalk Community College, the athletic/recreational facilities were opened to the entire community. As demand for facility usage time increased, the schedule of use was developed to meet the times of day a particular constituency was present in the facility.

With demand increasing, it became apparent that facility usage was a marketable commodity and that, if properly priced and marketed, sufficient revenue could be generated to increase and enhance services. The following constituency groups were observed and identified:

- Full and part-time students
- Senior citizens
- Business and industry groups
- Alumni
- Community members
- Special groups (police, National Guard, etc.)

Each group was then assessed for current interests and what services they felt should be offered.

COMMUNICATIONS

"Communication is the mix of messages an organization aims at targeted constituencies." (Peat Marwick, 1988, p. 6) Communication within the strategic model is not simply the transmitting of information, however. As stated by Bennis and Nanus (1985), communication is the "management of meaning." (p. 111) Communication strategies in this case should be designed for those external constituencies that are predisposed to support the organization's mission. The purpose of such strategies include the following:

1. Generating awareness
2. Maintaining existing constituents
3. Attracting new constituents

It is recommended that the athletic director spend some time alone and with colleagues to assess the future mission of athletics. How does this mission reflect and advance the mission of the institution?

The Commission on Higher Education, Middle States Association of Colleges and Schools (1987) states that sports and athletics of all kinds—intercollegiate, intramural, and recreational—are deeply rooted in American society and are often major components of student affairs. Their bearing on the quality and integrity of an institution requires that they be conducted in a manner consistent with its educational mission and goals and with the fundamental purposes of higher education.

This is a highly recommended exercise which, apart from the practical value of helping determine future directions, gives pause for reflection on the nature of athletics and its role in communities for the future.

Having clarified the mission, the next step is to list the general messages to be communicated, always remembering to link these messages back to the mission of athletics and of the institution. This cannot be taken for granted. By linking the mission of athletics with the institutional mission, the college administration will be more inclined to view the athletic program as a positive and powerful ally in effecting the three institutional objectives of public image, student enrollment, and revenue development. For example, athletics has long been extolled as a training ground for developing leadership, competitiveness, cooperation, physical well-being, management skills, socialization, and personal growth. Additionally, athletics can provide access to higher education for minority populations and serve as a door to a greater opportunity for those individuals who might not otherwise have considered college.

After completing the preceding exercises, the athletic director must assess which communications vehicles are available. They might include but are not by any means limited to the following media:

1. Television
2. Radio
3. Newspapers
4. Magazines
5. Flyers, posters
6. Billboards
7. Personal appearances
8. Community activities

Cable television, for example, can be an extremely effective vehicle for getting specific messages to targeted constituencies. Many community colleges have facilities on site or have local public access channels. The Health/Life Fitness Division of Dundalk Community College implemented a "Focus on Health and Fit-

ness Show" highlighting topics on community health concerns, showcasing instructors, and covering events within the division. An athletic director could conceptualize similar activities showcasing coaches and athletes in season, announcing fundraising events, and presenting a variety of other features. This could be done ideally on a regular monthly basis in order to institutionalize the show and the message for its external constituents. Activities can be publicized generally or specifically through any or all of the communication vehicles listed above.

Having gained a grasp of the messages to be used, the athletic director should ask the following questions:

1. Which specific constituencies deserve the most attention?
2. Which messages are most appropriate and appealing?
3. Which vehicles best serve my purposes for reaching these specific constituencies?

Finally, having targeted a message to a selected constituency via a specific vehicle, ask whether all three of the following questions can be answered in the affirmative.

1. Is the message timely?
2. Is the message meaningful?
3. Is the message motivational?

This systematic process will help to clarify the communications component of the strategic plan. The communications component cannot be overlooked as it is the critical unifying factor in linking your institution, the athletic department, and your constituents.

MARKETING

According to Peat Marwick (1988, 6), marketing is the "utilization of the organization's products, program and services to build a constituency.'' There are two purposes of marketing in the strategic planning system. The first is to strengthen and expand programs while building constituencies. The second purpose is to maximize existing resources within your organization.

Marketing is believed to be the key to strategic positioning for small athletic departments in the future. Miller and Miller (1988, 10) state that ''considerable progress has been made in identifying strategic objectives, perhaps an unintended consequence of the strong push in the 1970s on marketing, which was a reaction to diminished enrollments and funding, particularly in the private sector.''

Marketing wedded to the effective use of communications can be galvanized by the creative athletic director, using the small sports industry concept as the pragmatic engine. The careful development of entrepreneurial programs with auxiliary accounts can not only greatly augment traditional funding sources, but will enable certain enterprises to become self-sustaining and profitable so that monies can be reinvested for continued growth.

The first step in marketing is to do a program assessment, namely, listing all the programs you are currently using to market athletics. Programs that indirectly market athletics should be included in this list as well. For example, recreation memberships for use of the college weight room does not raise money directly for athletics, yet student and athletic memberships or privileges can be marketed as an inducement for prospective athletes. A sample list of programs in an assessment might include:

1. Facility rentals
2. Recreation memberships
3. Weight room memberships
4. Sale of advertising
5. Donations and gifts
6. Workshops and camps
7. Venture capital
8. Video seminars
9. Equipment rental

The Health/Life Fitness Division at Dundalk Community College has three accounts with revenue earning potential. Revenue from memberships is generated through student, faculty, alumni, and community constituents for the use of the weight room and various cardiovascular exercise machines. A wellness laboratory account derives income through body composition analysis, work tolerance testing, nutritional analysis capabilities, and counseling. The wellness laboratory, in addition to its primary instructional value, serves a variety of constituents and the needs of athletics through the measurement and screening of athletes. Finally, income is derived from the rental of a large tent owned by the college and contracted out to community groups for outdoor functions such as picnics, sales, fairs, or special events.

Another creative use of existing resources might be video seminars presented in conjunction with coaching clinics at camps. There are numerous options and possibilities. The athletic director in concert with the department chair and the college administration needs to determine what is best for meeting the needs of the department, institution, and community.

In many instances, institutional resources are quite limited. Nonetheless, numerous combinations and permutations of activity exist for raising money creatively using the available resources. It is critical, however, to specifically outline to the college administration how an investment will advance the institutional objectives of increased revenue, student enrollment, and public image. The following is a sample list of questions the athletic director must ask in developing a marketing plan, as well as answer for the college administration:

1. What is your product or service?
2. What market(s) are you serving and who are your competitors?
3. Do you have data indicating the way in which your product or service will meet a specific need in your market(s)?
4. What are your marketing strategies and what will they cost?
5. How will you fund your marketing plan?
6. How will you implement your marketing plan?
7. Have you compared and contrasted the short-term versus the long-term potential for your product or service?

RESOURCE DEVELOPMENT

The fuel to sustain the sports industry concept will be the revenue generated from the use of services, programs, and products. The administration will take notice of a proposal that enhances program offerings, satisfies constituent requests, and generates revenue to supplement the operating budget. As with any business, the development of a price structure is dependent on demographics and market share. Demand can be influenced by effective marketing and communication strategies. Information and analysis of the research assists in formulating accurate price and cost projections for your operation.

Peat Marwick (1988, 6) defines revenue generation as ''the implementation of strategies that encourage a constituency to support your organization financially.'' This definition expands the process of revenue generation beyond earned income or value exchange to include revenue produced from donations, gifts, or investment in your operation.

In an educational institution, revenue can be generated from any or all of the following resource development activities:

- Solicitation for donations
- Gifts from alumni
- Corporate gifts
- Grant and foundation proposals
- Contracts for services and programs

By separating each of these activities into a specific project, a strong link can be established to particular programs of interest. Dundalk Community College uses all of these activities in some form to generate revenue, adding to that generated from contracts for services and programs using the small sports industry concept. The small sports industry concept at Dundalk Community College allows participants to enter or join programs and services as students, members (senior citizens, students, alumni, community), special groups, and community groups.

Each constituent group is charged a specific rate for credit/noncredit courses, recreational memberships, and facility usage. Member rates include the use of these facilities:

- Fitness testing labs
- Wellness center
- Circuit center
- Gymnasium, pool and racquetball courts
- Outdoor facilities

Since the initial charge for services was instituted, nearly $25,000 annually has been generated and used to enhance and improve program offerings and recreational/fitness services. The athletic program contributions came from special events and tournaments that generated community interest and revenue from sponsors and ticket sales.

Employing communication and effective marketing strategies, these facilities have and will continue to serve a diverse population of community constituents while generating additional revenue.

CONCLUSION

Strategic planning need not be a time-consuming theoretical exercise used only by large businesses or educational institutions. On the contrary, an awareness of the strategic planning process can help the athletic director in the small- to moderate-sized institution to focus on objectives that are in concert with the institutional objectives of student enrollment, enhanced public image, and revenue generation. By placing the small sports industry concept within the strategic plan, the athletic director can take a systematic approach to the use of specific tactics such as constituency development, communications, marketing, and resource development to enhance the athletic mission. In an era of limited resources and rapid change in the nature of the student body and community constituents, the athletic director can develop a strategic plan to position the athletic program for the future while maintaining program viability and continuing to promote the institutional mission.

REFERENCES

Bennis, Warren, and Bert Nanus. 1985. *Leaders.* New York: Harper & Row.

Commission on Higher Education, Middle States Association of Colleges and Schools. 1987.

Drucker, Peter. 1988. The coming of the new organization. *Harvard Business Review* 50:41.

Drucker, Peter. 1977. *People and performance: The best of Peter Drucker on management.* New York: Harper & Row.

Miller, R. I., and P. Miller. 1988. Promises and perils of planning. *CUPA Journal* (Winter):32.

Office of Institutional Research and Grants. 1989. Background information for strategic planning activities. Dundalk Community College, Baltimore.

Peat Marwick Main and Company. 1988. *Resource development system,* 6–9. New York: Peat Marwick Main and Company.

Peters, Tom & Nancy Austin. 1985. *A passion for excellence.* New York: Warner Books.

Procaccini, Joseph. 1986. *Mid-level management: Leadership as a performing art.* Lanham, MD: University Press of America.

6

Strategies for Increasing Participation in Recreational Sports

W. Dennis Berry

INTRODUCTION

As part of Washington College's self-study, a campuswide survey was conducted to identify student needs and interests in the general area of recreation activities and in the particular area of intramural sports. In response to student replies, the Department of Physical Education and Athletics developed the Recreational (REC) Sports program. In the pages that follow, the strategies employed in marketing this program to the various campus populations are reviewed.

THE PROBLEM

A small liberal arts institution, Washington College is located one mile from the Chester River on the eastern shore of Maryland. The student body of the college is 850 undergraduates. Sport facilities are shared between the physical education, recreation, and athletic programs. Among the existing facilities are a gymnasium (which includes a fitness center and small dance studio), the Casey Swim Center, a boathouse on the Chester River, six outdoor tennis courts, and approximately 9.5 acres of athletic fields. The college offers fourteen varsity sports—seven for men and seven for women. Approximately 29 percent of the student body participates in one or more segments of the intercollegiate athletic program.

Student interest in the intramural sports program had experienced a decline over a five-year period, and a concise strategy for recapturing student participation was planned as a result. Included in the strategic plan were a needs assessment, program redesign, target groups, and a marketing campaign to regenerate interest in intramural sports, and thereby establish it once again as a solid component of the Physical Education and Athletic Department.

W. Dennis Berry is Director of Recreational Sports at Washington College, Chestertown, Maryland.

ASSESSMENT OF STUDENT LEISURE AND RECREATIONAL NEEDS

To assess the leisure and recreational needs of the student body, a questionnaire was designed to identify perceived needs and interests in the area of general recreation and intramural sports. Specific areas of focus were recreational facility usage, selection of intramural activities, factors that encouraged or hindered participation, and desire to enroll in noncredit leisure-oriented courses.

Survey Analysis

Thirteen percent of the student body completed and returned the questionnaire. The distribution of male and female respondents was even. Twenty-three percent of the respondents had participated in intercollegiate athletics—a figure that corresponded with the Athletic Department records identifying 24 percent of the total student body as having participated on intercollegiate athletic teams. This statistic validated data obtained from a random sampling of the general student body.

Facility Usage

Many of the questions answered provided insight into facility usage and students' level of awareness relative to the availability of specific activities and facilities. Interestingly, responses related to the dance studio indicated that 91 percent of the student body never utilized the facility. Yet when comparing responses to activity preferences, aerobic dance, and jazzercise were identified as desired activities by 64 percent of the female respondents. Such data serve to identify problems with student awareness versus facility and activity availability. Respondents also incorrectly perceived that intercollegiate athletic teams were granted priority, if not sole, access to facilities. These data further revealed that an aggressive marketing campaign would be needed to rectify false perceptions and attract students to these recreational sites.

PROGRAMMING

The most revealing statistic gained from the survey related to the low participation rate of female students. While 42 percent of the men indicated they had participated in intramural activities, only 6 percent of the women responded to this question in the affirmative.

Responses to the preferred types of recreational activities made it apparent that gender plays a significant role in activity preferences. Males did not demonstrate a strong preference between organized games (44 percent) and unstructured free activity (37 percent), whereas females preferred unstructured recreational activity (60 percent) over organized games (26 percent). Men identified team sports as their most desired form of activity (86 percent). Their top choices were competitive tournaments (72 percent) and league play (51 percent). Women (57 percent) identified self-structured leisure activities (i.e., one-day special events, trips, and overnight events) as their most preferred activity form. However, a marked difference was observed (on the basis of gender) in particular intramural activity interests. Following are the top three intramural team activities identified by males and females:

Men		Women	
1. Football	58%	1. Volleyball	42%
2. Basketball	56%	2. Softball	34%
3. Volleyball	53%	3. Racquetball	28%

Students also expressed an interest in taking noncredit leisure-oriented courses as an extension of the recreational offerings. Overall, 59 percent of the respondents indicated they would be interested in noncredit courses. This option was preferred by 62 percent of the female respondents. Following are the five most desired noncredit leisure-oriented courses identified by males and females:

Men		**Women**	
1. Racquetball	53%	1. Water skiing	70%
2. Scuba diving	47%	2. Aerobic Dance	64%
Canoeing	47%	3. Scuba diving	58%
3. Water skiing	44%	4. Sailboating	45%
Sailing	44%	5. Tennis	42%

The survey data revealed the presence of several important issues in regard to recreation, intramurals, and possibly physical education participation. Fewer women participated in the intramural program due to the activities available for them. Since intramural activities in previous years had been limited to traditional team sports (either all male or co-ed teams), the data helped to explain why such a low percentage of women (6 percent) elected to become involved in the program. Women identified both poor selection of activities and a resultant lack of interest as factors which precipitated their lack of participation. The analyzed data made it quite clear that the recreational and intramural activities offered needed to be redesigned in order to comply with the leisure time activities desired by the female students. Overall, there was strong student interest in unstructured recreational activities and in noncredit leisure-oriented courses. The survey response may indicate a shift in student preferences away from just those activities that generate academic credit.

The results of this study provided the impetus to create a recreational sports program focusing on the traditional intramural competition and leisure activities designed to promote individual fitness, concepts of lifetime wellness, and an enhanced quality of campus life.

DESIGNING PROGRAMS TO MEET IDENTIFIED NEEDS

Implementation of the REC Sports program required the creation of a positive, new image with a commitment by the Department of Physical Education and Athletics to support this effort on the campus. Specific program components needed to address student needs and preferences as suggested in the recreational activity study. The term "REC Sports" was coined to represent a three-tiered approach to leisure activities encompassing self-structured *R*ecreation, *E*ducational leisure activities, and traditional intramural *C*ompetition. Program development and activity selection reflected the needs and preferences identified in the activity study.

Targeting Special Groups

The key to the success of the REC Sports program required direct involvement with a diverse group of students. The first of two student participation target groups were the Greek organizations on campus. Targeting fraternities and sororities created a direct line to a segment of students who were already organized, competitive by nature, and in search of challenging group activities. Women were the second targeted group for the first year of operation. Although co-ed (co-rec) activities might be considered more contemporary, it was felt that competition specifically designed to accommodate women was important to reestablish. Faculty and staff participants looking for a wellness-oriented program to improve their quality of life constituted a third target group.

Marketing the Program

Once activities were selected for the specially targeted participants, the final step involved

REC Sports

FIGURE 6.1 REC Sports Logo

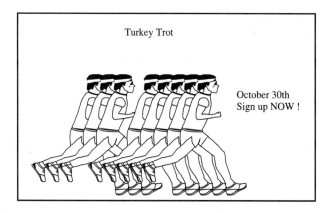

FIGURE 6.2
No Traveling Logo

FIGURE 6.3 Turkey Trot Publicity Graphic

"selling the concept" of a new service to the campus. This required a creative approach to marketing that ultimately called for designing a program logo and implementing a multifaceted "media blitz."

It was felt that the program's image would be visualized most effectively through iconic association. With the assistance of the College's Department of Publications, a text logo was created to establish the implied action of REC Sports (Fig. 6.1).

A second logo was created which, in addition to making a statement, was eye catching. The "no suitcase college" logo (Fig. 6.2) was used on shirts to send a message to students that REC Sports was an alternate to leaving campus on weekends, a concern that the administration hoped the program would be able to address.

With the assistance of a Macintosh SE computer, REC Sports developed from an activity idea into a mechanism for determining facility availability, identifying scheduling conflicts, and creating and producing graphic publicity within a relatively short time span. In fact, the entire REC Sport program, from activity selection and scheduling to brochure development and distribution occurred within a fifteen-day period prior to the return of students to campus. By utilizing the Macintosh and its graphic applications, traditional activities were publicized in a new and visually creative way (Fig. 6.3).

Another effort to reach students involved a campuswide computer network link using the

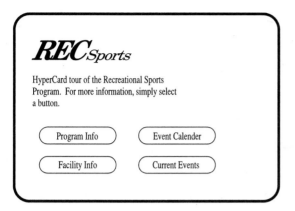

FIGURE 6.4 REC Sports Menu

HyperCard application. This application allowed several campus departments to provide updated information on services and programs which was accessed by students in the library, in the computing center, and in the dorms using the Apple Share Network. By creating an informational stack on upcoming REC Sport activities and intramural competition results, students were provided a "nontraditional" avenue for sending and receiving program information (Fig. 6.4).

In scheduling activities, aside from traditional intramural events, the main thrust of the REC Sports program during the first year was special events and instructional-based leisure action minicourses. This provided for expanded aquatic offerings at the Casey Swim Center and Waterfront where recreational preferences were specifically identified by students. It also provided activities aimed at weekend participa-tion in an effort to provide an alternative to alcohol-related parties which had created a growing problem on campus.

FIRST-YEAR PROGRAMMING

At the conclusion of the first year under the new programming format, the following analy-sis of campus recreational participation was compiled.

Participants	Number	Percent
Men Students	646	58
Men Faculty/Staff	60	5
Women Students	373	33
Women Faculty/Staff	42	4

When analyzing names contained on team rosters against actual enrollment figures (Hegis Report published by the Washington College Office of the Registrar), 53 percent of the total student body were identified as having partici-pated in the REC Sports program. Seventy-nine percent of the men on campus had participated in at least one intramural activity. And, 29 per-cent of the women on campus had participated in at least one intramural activity compared to only 6 percent the previous year.

Programming

To assess interest in activities offered through-out the academic year by the recreational sports program, three broad activity categories were created. The analysis produced the following data:

Activity Type	Number Offered	Number of Participants		Participation Percentage
Competitive	21	609 men	215 women	74%
Education	7	16 men	35 women	5%
Recreation	8	82 men	164 women	21%

Most Successful Programs

Men's

Football	69 participants (10 teams)
Basketball	106 participants (12 teams)

Women's

Basketball	23 participants (4 teams)
Flag football	30 participants (3 teams)
Aerobics	25 participants (2 sessions)
Indoor soccer	32 participants (4 teams)

Co-Ed

Turkey trot	33 participants
REC Sport weekend	55 participants
Spring softball tourney	148 participants

These data provided a good indication of student interest in different categories of activities offered. Although 74 percent of the students participated in traditional intramural competition, 26 percent participated in the structured drop-in recreation activities and the noncredit courses offered. These two new areas appear to have met a student need not previously identified.

The intramural survey indicated that 62 percent of the women were interested in noncredit/ nongraded activity classes such as aerobic dance, scuba diving, and sailing. When these three courses were offered, women comprised 70 percent of the enrollments. Men had indicated a preference for team sports and competition rather than self-structured recreation. Participant records showed that men comprised 74 percent of the intramural/team sport competitions.

Several other interesting observations included:

1. Women preferred to participate in co-ed special events such as recreational volleyball, aerobic dance, the REC Sports All Activity Weekend, and the turkey trot.

2. During the survey year, the thirty-six program offerings surpassed the number available in the two previous years combined.

3. A review of the event entry forms resulted in a conservative estimate that 53 percent of the student body participated in structured competitions. It was also projected that over 70 percent of the student body used the college's facilities/programs for recreation purposes during the academic year.

4. Participation in the recreational sports program by students increased by over 300 percent from the previous year. And, women comprised 38 percent of the total number of program participants.

5. Programs designed with a noncredit/nongraded format were very popular, especially with women. The 9 percent participation rate by faculty and staff members indicates the program offerings were providing the first stage in a total fitness/wellness service for employees.

The main goals of student involvement and creation of an image that would attract students to the program appear to have taken hold. The increase in activity offerings and subsequent increase in student participation is a promising start, but the program will require constant monitoring and student input to establish the stable base needed for continued growth. The support of the college administration and Department of Physical Education and Athletics plays a large part in the increased student interest in recreational activity. A REC Sports brochure was completed with the assistance of the College Relations Department and was distributed to students during the spring semester. A redesigned brochure was mailed to incoming freshmen.

REC Sports was an idea created out of a need to improve the quality of student life. The program was developed less than fifteen days prior to the return of students to campus, and it quickly provided a service to which students responded. By meeting with student leaders throughout the year and conducting another recreational activity survey, Washington College has developed a structure for addressing the recreational needs of its students. The key to the program's success will be its responsiveness to changing student needs and its accessibility to students for activity ideas. REC Sports has established itself as a fine example of a program focused on student service. The sense of excitement and involvement on campus has allowed for levels of growth and visibility within the college community that have far exceeded initial hopes for the program.

REFERENCES

Amezaga, M., S. Cole, and F. Dudenhoeffer. 1987. Student governments can be actively involved with organizing and supporting an intramural program. In *Cultivation of recreational sports programs.* Proceedings from the 38th Annual NIRSA Conference, New Orleans.

Bialeschki, M. Deborah. 1988. Why don't students play intramurals? *NIRSA Journal* 12 (Spring):46–51.

Chestnut, J.T., N. Kovac, and W. Taylor. 1986. An examination of evaluation procedures utilized by recreational sport programs. In *Growth & development in recreational sports.* Proceedings from the 37th Annual NIRSA Conference, Las Vegas.

Fink, Ira, and David Body. 1985. Developing a sports and recreation master plan. *NIRSA Journal* 10 (Fall):25–36.

Haderlie, Brian M. 1987. Influences of campus recreation programs and facilities on student recruitment and retention. *NIRSA Journal* 11 (Winter):24–27.

Oatey, Jennifer Sue. 1987. Strategic planning: A look to the future. *NIRSA Journal* 12 (Fall):21–23.

Rokosz, Francis M. 1987. A rating system for evaluating an intramural program. *NIRSA Journal* 12 (Fall):47–50.

7

Strategic Planning for an Olympic Games: The Complexity of Work and the Performance of People

Vernon R. Stauble

INTRODUCTION

This essay reports on the planning and intricate coordination of resources in line with the recent trends of the Olympic Games. The trend toward decentralization of Olympic effort and impact was particularly beneficial to the 1976 Games held in Canada, where large distances between major points are commonplace. Observed with interest was the practice of scheduling certain sports in centers other than the host city.

The Olympic Games is the largest sports program in the world today and is acclaimed the world's greatest spectacle. The task of organizing this event is not confined to the activities of two short weeks of elite athletic competition; the Games are the climax to years of preparation, recruiting and training of staff, and plain hard work.

Dr. Vernon R. Stauble was a competitor in the 1968 and 1972 Olympic Games in the sport of cycling. A member of the U.S. College Hall of Fame, he is currently a professor of marketing management at California State Polytechnic University, Pomona, California, and adjunct professor at the University of Redlands, Redlands, California.

The complexity of the work is summarized in the objectives which guide the host city:

1. To accommodate the requirements of the individual sports federations and the International Olympic Committee (IOC) with regard to the competitions.
2. Through construction of new facilities and modification of existing ones, to accommodate the needs of the twenty-one sports on the program, including maintenance services and the provision of modern equipment.
3. To accommodate the needs of athletes, spectators, journalists, broadcast commentators and technicians, film camerapeople, and still photographers.
4. To ensure maximum utilization of Olympic facilities both during the Games and after.

Although a general pattern of work does exist, variations inevitably take place from one Olympiad to the next. Adaptations have to be made to meet particular circumstances. Consequently, the Organizing Committee finds itself at the head of an immense enterprise made up of many parts calling for planning that is both far reaching and minutely detailed, and intricate coordination of resources in order to meet diverse requirements.

The basic purpose of this essay is to examine the systematic planning and project control techniques used to enhance the coordination of diverse projects and large amounts of work to be done. Included will be major phases of activity developed by the Canadian Organizing Committee for the 1976 Olympic Games.

In essence, the real challenge is not whether the city can stage the Games or not but how effectively the Games are staged. The Games activity is not limited to the sixteen days that are called Game Time but is inherent in every decision and action of the Organizing Committee leading to and including those days on which the actual events take place.

In light of the scope and complexity of the work involved and the uncertainties that assail the Organizing Committees at each stage, the study of the magnitude and requirements of the Olympic Games organization and planning is the focus of this essay.

ORGANIZATIONAL AND ADMINISTRATIVE STRUCTURE OF AN OLYMPIC GAMES

The Organizing Committee of the 1976 Games in Montreal, Canada, was established on principles of line and staff functions. Everyone had a defined task with enough authority to execute their responsibilities and everyone had a superior. At the top of the line-staff pyramid was a board of directors whose members represent the sports, government, and financial points of view vital to the success of the Games.

A subset of the board of directors was the Executive Committee made up of the president, the executive vice president, and four other members of the board. In order to achieve the objectives defined by the board of directors, the work was divided into approximately 130 units referred to as subprojects. Each subproject was the responsibility of a project leader, and the subprojects were logically grouped into departments. The activities of these departments interfaced through a network plan computed by a staff planning unit in consultation with all project leaders. The work of all departments was coordinated by a management committee chaired by the executive vice president and made up of all the department heads.

Figure 7.1 depicts the actual organizational structure of the Organizing Committee of the 1976 Games as compared to the organization scheme (Fig. 7.2) proposed by the International Olympic Committee (IOC). This is indeed a demonstration of the need for organizational structure to be flexible to growth and change.

PROJECT CONTROL PLANNING

The 1976 Games Organization applied systematic planning and project control techniques especially suited to coordinating large mixtures of projects and making complex things happen on time.

Beginning with the end project and working backward, each of the different stages and work activities that must come together in time were identified to provide a skeleton for the detailed planning and scheduling of work. According to Paul Howell, vice president of Planning/Canadian Organizing Committee, use of this technique helped to build the Organizing Committee with the right people at the right time. Furthermore, it formulated their plan in a detailed, systematic way, thus showing the impact of each activity on other activities and the coming together of completed work at the desired time.

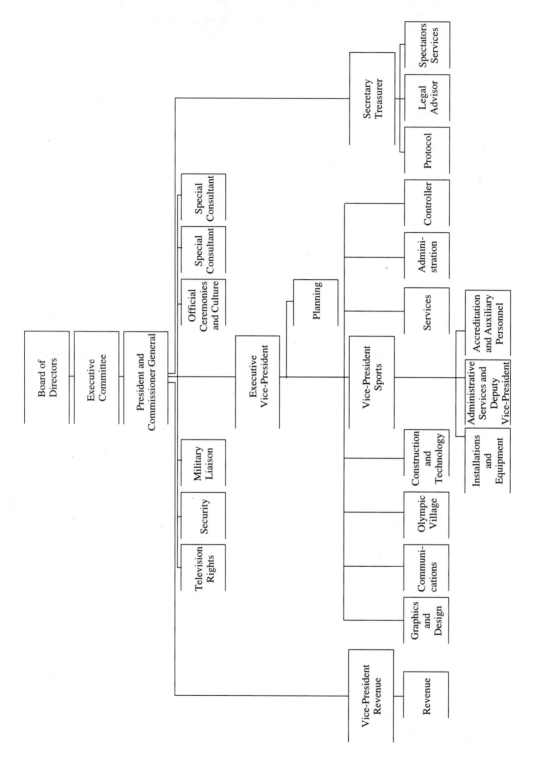

FIGURE 7.1 Organizational Structure of the 1976 Olympic Games

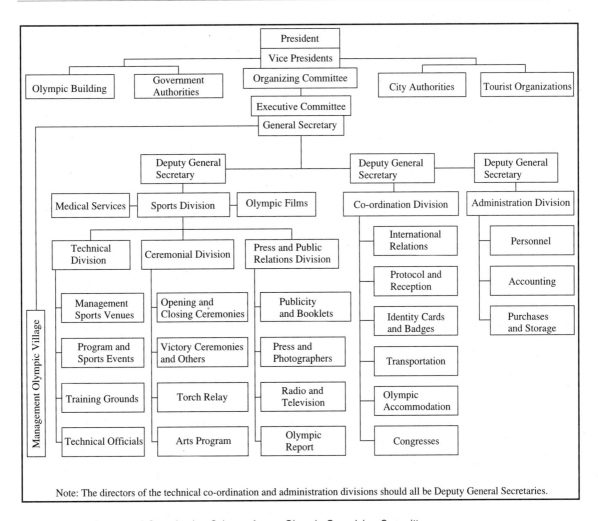

FIGURE 7.2   Suggested Organization Scheme for an Olympic Organizing Committee

MATRIX ORGANIZATION

Staging the Olympic Games probably means doing two different things. First, the facilities, systems, and services used in staging the Games must be developed or built. When this has been done, all are subject to modular tests in the "on-stream" phase. Second, actually staging the Olympic Games for sixteen days is another matter. This is done in the operations phase by the same individuals who developed or built the systems, facilities and services in the "on-stream" phase, but takes place in a different organizational context.

To stage the Games, the Canadian Organization reorganized by operational units. One unit was assigned to operate the facilities, systems, and services in each venue, and a matrix organization was applied (Fig. 7.3). According to management consultant Peter Drucker, a matrix

Functional Subprojects
in Planning and "On-
Stream" Phases

Work Locations, Particularly
Venues during Competition

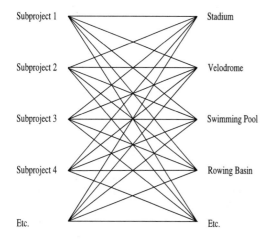

Subproject 1   Stadium

Subproject 2   Velodrome

Subproject 3   Swimming Pool

Subproject 4   Rowing Basin

Etc.   Etc.

FIGURE 7.3   Matrix Organization: Montreal 1976

organization is a mode of organizing, especially of large technological projects, that includes persons having both task and function assignments and, as a consequence, being attached to two units of the organization at one time. The "matrix" is suggested by a diagram that has functional units across the top and task units down the side with entries indicating persons from various functions assigned to a given task.

The critical point in organizing the Games is switching from the functional organization which built the necessary facilities, systems, and procedures to the operational organization which actually makes those facilities, systems, and procedures work in remote locations. The Canadian Organizing Committee reorganized for this purpose and established the operational units in early 1976 to prepare for the Games in July of that year.

MAJOR PHASES OF ACTIVITY

The three major phases of activity are: (1) the planning phase, (2) the "on-stream" phase, and (3) the operational phase. Figure 7.4 includes the Canadian Olympic Games Organization's activities and time periods for Montreal 1976.

Planning Phase

In this phase, the Organization was preoccupied with planning and finding money. Planning included:

1. Financial planning (revenue).
2. Identifying objectives (i.e., answering the question: What does the staging of the Olympic Games mean?).
3. Planning the organization to stage the Games: this included the development of the work breakdown structure, subproject definitions, task descriptions, work scheduling, designing the chart of accounts for budgeting, designing the purchasing procedure, designing the personnel procedure, designing the project approval procedure, developing the operational unit concept, and launching the Management Committee.

The next section will discuss the development of the operational unit and project approval procedure as a fundamental decision-making process.

Project Approval Procedure. In the case of the 1976 Games Organization, the Planning Department proposed the project approval procedure (PAP) to the Executive Committee on July 17, 1973. In December 1973, formal preparation, review, and approval of procedures started after the computerized network plan was completed.

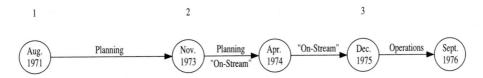

FIGURE 7.4   The Three Major Phases of Canadian Olympic Games Organization Activity

The use of this system required organization by subprojects involving the grouping of related subprojects in one department. In Montreal '76, there was one subproject for each sport, plus one for International Federation relations and a consolidated one for sports equipment—all in the Sports Department. All technological activities, including closed-circuit TV and sound, printing, scoreboards, Swiss Timing, computerized results, and telecommunications were grouped together in the Technology Department. The Planning Department then gave each project leader a task description, a description of the subproject, and a work schedule.

According to Paul Howell, the system works best if one qualified specialist is appointed project leader for each subproject; it is easier to teach such specialists how to plan than to teach planners all about the specialities required in delivering the Olympic Games.

Preparation of the project approval procedure was the responsibility of the project leader. This PAP is a document containing the following:

1. Statement of objectives: a statement of the problem and a brief description of what is to be accomplished in the subproject.
2. Raison d'etre: the project leader's explanation of why the Olympic Organizing Committee should execute this particular subproject. For example, it is easy to see that a facility is required for the cycling subproject, but if a project leader wants to publish a particularly expensive brochure,

justification might be required. This section of the PAP helps top management determine the project leader's level of capability.
3. Method of operation: how the problem described in the statement of objectives will be solved.
4. Subproject organization chart: a visual representation of the subproject structure with the project leader as director of activities, and the personnel resources and particular functions that the subproject requires.
5. Manloading schedule: the start date, end date, descriptive title, and salary of each person working on the subproject.
6. Work schedule: a milestone schedule of approximately fifteen important dates per year to catch schedule slippage; working closely with the Planning Department to prepare an accurate and realistic work schedule.
7. Budget: The Canadian Organizing Committee used a modified PERT-COST system which showed budget costs by nature of cost by month for each subproject; working closely with the chief accountant to prepare an accurate and realistic budget.

From the above, it seems that the PAP has the following advantages:

1. It shows simply and briefly, yet with detail, exactly how every Organizing Committee's responsibility is to be carried out.

2. It motivates the project leaders by implicating them in both the plan and the budget; in essence, it becomes a "contract" between the Organizing Committee and the project leader.

3. It makes it easy to centralize and control personnel; in fact, the Personnel Department itself is a subproject the purpose of which is to consolidate and satisfy personnel requirements in all other subprojects.

4. It makes it easy to centralize and control purchases; in fact, the Purchasing Department itself is a subproject the purpose of which is to consolidate and satisfy purchasing requirements in all other subprojects.

5. It makes it easy to centralize and control costs.

6. It makes it easy to centralize and control schedules.

7. It makes it easy to ensure that no two people are doing the same thing and that no Organizing Committee's responsibility has been overlooked.

8. It makes it easy to identify problems early so that top management can solve the problems by making the correct adjustment to the proper part of the organization.

Finally, completed project approval procedures were turned over to the department head who, in turn, presented it to the Management Committee for level 2 approval. Upon approval of the Management Committee, it can then be included in the plan and budget for level 1 approval.

"On-Stream" Phase

Activity in this phase is preparatory and centralized. The following are developed to be used in staging the Olympic Games themselves:

1. Facilities: building or renovating venues.
2. Systems: building the computerized results system.
3. Services: determining who will be transported where, how, and when during the Games.

In this phase, testing of these facilities, systems, and services was carried out one at a time, and all work was done in the form of "executing approved PAP plans within approved PAP budgets" under the control of the Executive Committee. This control was maintained through the use of monthly progress reports and the monthly cost summaries prepared by the Planning Department with the close cooperation of all the project leaders and the comptroller.

Operational Phase

Operations refers to staging the competitions and executing other activities identified in the Organization's plan. More specifically, operations means implementing the plan on time, within budget, and in a style appropriate to the Olympic Games.

In this phase, concern is no longer with developing systems, facilities, and services, but with operating them. In the case of Montreal 1976, this phase involved a switch from the functional organization (concerned with development) to a decentralized organization (concerned with operation of facilities, systems, and services in the competition venues, training venues, airports, hotels, warehouses, and so forth). This decentralized organization featured operational units, a new structure for operations, and consolidated operations plans.

Operational units were designed to guarantee that these transitions were smooth and that execution was controlled and consistent with approved PAP plans. The mandate of each operations unit is presented in the official reports on the Games of the XXI Olympiad: to organize and integrate the human and physical resources placed in projects by the various departments so that all necessary tasks at each competition and/or training site are accomplished with a view to satisfying the requirements of the International Olympic Committee and the Organizing Committee.

Consolidated Operations Plans

The first responsibility of the operational units was to develop venue operating plans in a prescribed format based on approved PAP plans. While consolidated PAP plans in the "on-stream" phase comprised about 4,000 entries, consolidated venue operating plans contained about 15,000 entries. These venue plans showed what was to be done each hour and who was responsible for doing it. The entire plan was stored on a computer file in the Operations Center—the "war room." Monitors and analysts in the Operations Center periodically checked by telephone throughout the day to ensure that planned activities were carried out. As stated by Paul Howell, problems during operations usually occurred where a necessary activity had been left out of the plan, not with the planned activities.

CONCLUSION

One conclusion that emerged from this study is that the organizational momentum and the quality of the coordination are important factors leading to overall efficiency. The aim was to develop an awareness of the range of issues and main areas of concern pertaining to management in order to optimize business effectiveness.

In regard to general coordination, according to Jean-Yves Perron, director-general of Operations/Canadian Organizing Committee, "It would have been preferable to have a center linked to the executive from the beginning. The staff of such a center would, therefore, have always been kept up-to-date with the projects and sites, and would have had a hand in developing policies. Thus, being involved every step of the way, it would have been able at all times to orient more quickly the ever increasing number of newcomers into an ever more complex organization."

Furthermore, regarding the general organization, members of the Organizing Committee often asked this question: Was it better to plan first and organize later, or vice-versa? Designing an organizational structure is not the first step, but the last. The first step is to identify and organize the building blocks of organization, to ensure that key tasks are encompassed in the final structure.

8

Back to the Future: Trends in the Recreational Sports Market

Rodney B. Warnick

INTRODUCTION

Research has indicated that a number of recreational sport pursuits have increased in popularity over the decades of the 1970s and 1980s. However, much of this research has been conducted sporadically with no real indication of what changes or trends the activity represents. The interest in recreational sport activities has prompted growth in sport businesses, fostered tourism by attracting people to special events throughout various regions, spurred private investment, and even contributed to the quality of life of individuals who seek to live in areas where participation in these activities may occur and are abundant. This study examines the markets represented by people who participated in a variety of selected recreational sports from the period of 1979 through 1987. This, in a sense, is a "look back to the future."

With the exception of the National Sporting Goods Association (NSGA) survey (Feld 1988),

no major public recreational sports trends have been documented on an annual basis. Although a number of private market research studies have been conducted over the years, consistency in data collection and methods and in-depth analyses have been lacking. The need for reliable recreational sport trend data is imperative from both management and planning perspectives. The NSGA survey (Feld 1988) is a step toward the creation of a national data base; however, it was only started in 1984 and does not provide the long-term trend data that is needed. With the rapid changes in many activities and participant interests, there is indeed a need for a yearly national recreational sport trend data base. *Within the last decade,* Simmons Market Research Bureau of New York began to collect and release findings of their annual study of the media and markets. These data give us an opportunity to monitor trends over the long term. The fact that these were collected with consistency is but one of the advantages to the study process they used. Furthermore, Simmons provides a wider cross-section of recreational sport activities and more in-depth analyses than the NSGA survey.

Rodney B. Warnick is with the Leisure Studies and Resources Program, University of Massachusetts–Amherst.

Data, when examined over a longer period such as this eight-year span from 1979 to 1987, provide an opportunity to monitor longitudinal recreational sport trends. These data also help address a number of important marketing questions. For example, to what extent has the public's total demand for recreational sport activities grown? What market trends are visible and what might we expect in the future? What changes, if any, have occurred with respect to the types of participants within selected recreational sport activities? Has the size and composition of light and heavy participant segments changed significantly over time? These questions, among others, serve as the focus of this study.

The purposes of this research are two-fold: (1) to examine market analysis participation trend data and market size as applied to a variety of recreational sport groupings (outdoor resource-based, indoor-based, water-based, and winter-based activities) from 1979 to 1987 within the U.S. and its respective regions; and (2) to examine selected market segment trends of four selected recreational sport activities (power boating, downhill skiing, racquetball, and golf).

METHOD

To analyze the trends, data were compiled from the annual surveys presented in the *Study of Media and Markets* (Simmons Market Research Bureau 1979–1987). This research firm annually measures respondents' participation rates, demographic characteristics, and media use for a wide variety of leisure, sport, and outdoor recreation activities. Data were obtained from household interviews collected on a national stratified random probability sample for each year from 1979 through 1987. (Note that 1981 data were not available.) The data collection process included self-administered question-

naires and telephone interviews. The sample sizes ranged from approximately 15,000 individuals to as high as 20,000 adults. Results were then projected to the adult population, aged 18 years and over, living in the contiguous 48 states of the United States. Respondents were asked to indicate the recreational activities each played, or participated in, during the previous 12 months.

The four groupings of recreation activities examined here included outdoor resource-based, indoor-based, water-based, and winter-based activities. Outdoor resource-based activities included tennis, golf, bicycling, and distance running. Indoor-based activities included racquetball, bowling, basketball and volleyball. Basketball and volleyball are team games which Simmons began monitoring in 1983. Water-based activities included swimming, sailing, power boating, and water skiing. Winter-based activities included downhill skiing, cross-country skiing, snowmobiling, and ice skating. The market size for one activity from each grouping was then examined by the participants' demographic characteristics—age, sex, educational status, and income. The outdoor resource-based activity examined was golf, the indoor-based activity was racquetball, the water-based activity was power boating, and the winter-based activity was downhill skiing.

Participation rate is defined as the percent of the total U.S. adult population who participate in the selected recreational sport activity. Market size is a weighted estimate of the total number of participants engaged in the activity on a yearly basis. Market volume or participation volume is derived from multiplying the market size of each participation level category (defined as participation days using categories of 1–4 days, 5–9 days, 10–14 days, 15–19 days, etc., through 60 days or more) by the median number of days for each category. Participation volume is presented in three segments: light

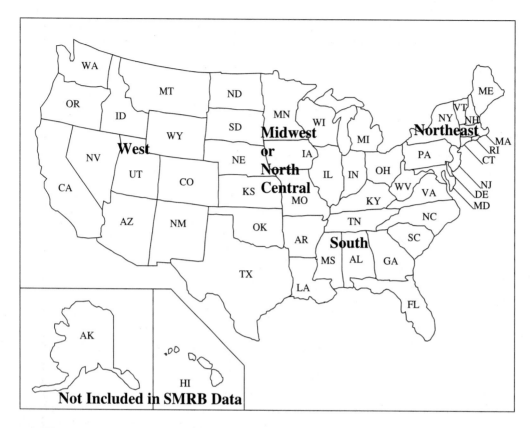

FIGURE 8.1 Simmons Market Research (1987) Regions of the U.S.
SOURCE: Simmons Market Research Bureau. 1979 to 1987. Study of Media and Markets. Volume
P–10. Sports and Leisure. New York, New York.

(1–4 participation days); moderate (5–19 participation days); and heavy (20 or more participation days). The total number of days the activity is played is presented for each of these volume categories and is called market volume. The total number of participants in each category is also presented. Market size and market volume changes are presented for three periods: 1979 through 1983, 1983 through 1987, and 1979 through 1987. Periods were modified where data were not available. The regions examined in this study included the Northeast, the South, the Midwest or North Central, and the West. The states within each of these regions are defined in Figure 8.1. Alaska and Hawaii were not included within the regional configuration.

SELECTED FINDINGS

National Participation Rates

Participation patterns by activity participation rate for the U.S. over the nine-year period revealed some dramatic changes in the resource-based and winter-based activities. However, the participation rates for the water-based and indoor-based activities remained relatively stable with a few exceptions (Figure 8.2).

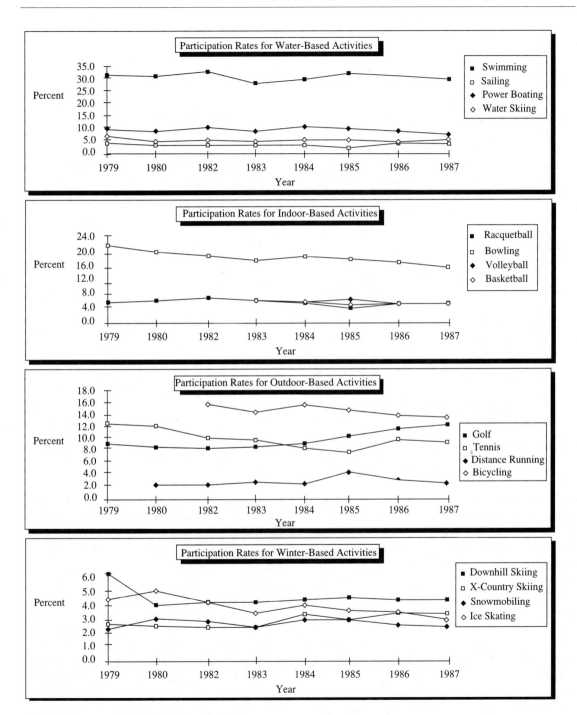

FIGURE 8.2 Participation Rates by Activity Group.
SOURCE: Simmons Market Research Bureau. 1979 to 1987. Study of Media and Markets. Volume P–10. Sports and Leisure. New York, New York.

Outdoor resource-based activities. Participation in golf grew steadily. The participation rate in 1982 was approximately 8 percent, and by 1987 it had increased to 11 percent. Tennis experienced a continuous downward spiral of participation from 1979 through 1985. A substantial increase took place in 1986, but the rate dropped off again in 1987.

The participation rate for distance running peaked in 1985 at nearly 4 percent. Bicycling has continued to decline in participation rate since 1982. However, Simmons began to define bicycling as both an indoor (stationary bicycling) and an outdoor activity in 1985. Prior to 1985, the activity was not differentiated. It is likely that further segmentation of the activity will occur in the future and separate statistics for such segments as bicycle touring will be presented.

Indoor-based activities. Participation in most of the indoor activities examined has remained relatively stable over the past decade. Bowling is the exception. Participation rates have declined since 1979 for this activity. Participation rates for volleyball and basketball have remained roughly between 4 and 5 percent since data were first collected in 1983. Racquetball's participation rate peaked in 1982.

Water-based activities. Participation rates for sailing, power boating, and water skiing remained relatively stable over the period examined. Swimming participation rates fluctuated through 1985; however, since 1985 participation rates have dropped nearly 3 percent and the national participation rate dropped below 30 percent in 1987.

Winter-based activities. The most dramatic finding within the winter-based activities was the sustained drop in participation rates for ice skating. Those rates dropped steadily from 1980 through 1987 with the exception of 1984 which saw an increase in the participation rate. Participation rates for downhill skiing grew slightly from 1980 through 1985, then began to decline. Rates for cross-country skiing increased from 1982 through 1987. Snowmobiling participation rates fluctuated during this period, but showed a steady decline from 1985 through 1987.

Participation rates alone do not indicate the total story of market changes by activity. Next, the changes in market size (number of actual participants) by region are examined.

Market Size Change by Region

Participation does vary by region of the country. The market size, in terms of numbers or participants, is important for making market decisions. In some cases, recreational participation rates may be declining slightly, even while the overall market size by number of participants is actually increasing. This is partly due to population growth and demographic changes over time. Therefore, careful review of market size data is essential in monitoring recreational sports trends. While statistics are not presented here, it would be informative to examine the population and demographic changes within specific regions to more fully understand how these changes relate to participation. In this section, changes in market size for each recreation activity group are presented relative to three time periods (1979 through 1983, 1983 through 1987, and 1979 through 1987). The comparisons over these time periods provide both long-term and short-term trends. For additional insights, compare the rates of changes by region with overall U.S. changes. See Tables 8.1–8.4 for market sizes and changes by U.S. region.

Regional statistics do reveal variations across the country; however, over-time participation also varies by demographic characteristics. Next, the national demographic changes, which affect outdoor recreation participation, are presented for selected recreation activities.

Demographic Characteristics of Participants for Selected Activities

For this section, four recreational sport activities were examined: golf, power boating, downhill skiing, and racquetball. Each of the demographic characteristics (age, sex, educational status, and income level) was measured by market size (number of participants within the category). (Note that these statistics are national, and not by region.) See Tables 8.5–8.8 for market sizes by demographic characteristics and their percentage changes across time periods.

More people of nearly all ages and backgrounds are playing golf than ever before. Golf, an activity formerly associated primarily with older adults, is today being played by an increasing number of adults under the age of 44. Substantial growth in market size among women has also been noted. The adult female golf market size has increased by 62 percent from 1979 through 1987. More college-educated individuals are also playing golf. Although statistics specific to income levels were only partially presented (Simmons redefined household income levels over this period), it is clear that the market size among upper-income households is growing.

For downhill skiing, the age segment with the biggest participation increase was the 35-44-year-old group. The number of skiers in this age segment grew by 102 percent from 1979 through 1987. The market of downhill skiers with high incomes ($36,000 per year or more) has continued to grow since 1982.

There appear to be two different growth markets for power boating: older adults (age 55 and above) and college-educated adults. The market of adult power boaters with high incomes ($35,000 per year or more) has increased in size since 1982.

Although participation in racquetball has declined since 1982, the 35- to 44-year-old age segment has increased in market size by 50 percent. The college-educated market has also increased in size as have the upper-income level markets. Finally, the changes in volume generated by three user segments for each of these four activities are presented.

Participation Volume for Selected Recreation Activities

Each of these selected recreational sport activities was examined by the number of participants within each use segment and the number of activity days generated within each of the three segments: light (1–4 days); moderate (5–10 days); and heavy (20 or more days). See Table 8.9 for information on number of participants and participation volume.

While the amount of golf played increased in all use segments, the percentage change in number of golfers and the number of golf days played was the highest among the light and moderate participation segments for the nine-year period of 1979 through 1987. Overall, the number of golfing days is up by 24 percent and the number of golfers is up 42 percent. The number of light and moderate participation players has increased the most.

The number of days of downhill skiing participation declined by approximately 4 percent from 1979 through 1987. Nevertheless, over that period and within the heavy use segment, there was a 22 percent increase in the number of days skied and a 26 percent increase in the number of skiers. This growth slowed in the more recent years of 1983 through 1987. During that same period there was also an increase of 10 to 12 percent in the number of skier days and the number of skiers among the light and moderate use groups.

TABLE 8.1 Market Size of Outdoor Resource-Based Activities by U.S. Region (in thousands)

Tennis

Region	1979	1980	1982	1983	1984	1985	1986	1987	'80–'83 Change	'83–'87 Change	'80–'87 Change
Northeast	NA	4,377	3,331	3,967	3,143	2,554	3,313	2,294	−9.4%	−42.2%	−47.6%
Midwest	NA	4,526	3,938	3,250	3,357	2,946	3,495	3,417	−28.2%	5.1%	−24.5%
South	NA	4,909	4,827	4,465	3,892	3,524	4,770	4,837	−9.0%	8.3%	−1.5%
West	NA	4,322	2,648	2,857	3,098	2,818	3,386	3,218	−33.9%	12.6%	−25.5%
U.S. Total	19,735	18,133	14,744	14,539	13,490	11,841	14,964	13,767	−19.8%	−5.3%	−24.1%

Bicycling

Region	1979	1980	1982	1983	1984	1985	1986	1987	'82–'83 Change	'83–'87 Change	'82–'87 Change
Northeast	NA	NA	5,218	5,686	5,374	5,081	3,830	3,645	9.0%	−35.9%	−30.1%
Midwest	NA	NA	9,039	7,791	8,226	7,631	8,335	7,472	−13.8%	−4.1%	−17.3%
South	NA	NA	6,012	5,993	6,340	6,319	6,264	5,226	−0.3%	−12.8%	−13.1%
West	NA	NA	5,830	5,264	5,803	5,676	4,918	4,777	−9.7%	−9.3%	−18.1%
U.S. Total	NA	NA	26,098	24,734	25,743	24,708	23,346	21,120	−5.2%	−14.6%	−19.1%

D. Running

Region	1979	1980	1982	1983	1984	1985	1986	1987	'80–'83 Change	'83–'87 Change	'80–'87 Change
Northeast	NA	434	504	736	796	1,141	955	606	69.6%	−17.7%	39.6%
Midwest	NA	380	779	701	840	1,468	1,288	1,052	84.5%	50.1%	176.8%
South	NA	866	672	805	904	1,761	1,767	1,376	−7.0%	70.9%	58.9%
West	NA	850	594	939	712	1,549	1,375	885	10.5%	−5.8%	4.1%
U.S. Total	NA	2,530	2,549	3,181	3,252	5,919	5,385	3,919	25.7%	23.2%	54.9%

Golf

Region	1979	1980	1982	1983	1984	1985	1986	1987	'79–'83 Change	'83–'87 Change	'79–'87 Change
Northeast	2,645	2,439	2,665	3,261	3,264	3,046	3,885	3,360	23.3%	3.0%	27.0%
Midwest	4,412	4,799	4,655	4,660	5,084	5,348	6,565	6,611	5.6%	41.9%	49.8%
South	3,613	2,941	3,012	2,999	3,407	3,304	5,156	4,830	−17.0%	61.1%	33.7%
West	2,639	2,916	2,687	2,813	3,132	3,402	4,107	4,102	6.6%	45.8%	55.4%
U.S. Total	13,309	13,095	13,019	13,733	14,888	15,110	19,713	18,903	3.2%	37.6%	42.0%

SOURCE: Simmons Market Research Bureau. 1979 to 1987. Study of Media and Markets. Volume P–10. Sports and Leisure. New York, New York.

TABLE 8.2 Market Size of Indoor-Based Activities by U.S. Region (in thousands)

Activity				Year					Market Size Change (%)		
Region				Market Size (Number of Participants)							
Racquetball	1979	1980	1982	1983	1984	1985	1986	1987	'80–'83 Change	'83–'87 Change	'80–'87 Change
Northeast	NA	1,544	2,238	2,289	2,223	1,726	1,866	1,567	48.3%	−31.5%	1.5%
Midwest	NA	3,118	3,071	2,327	2,521	2,231	2,049	2,618	−25.4%	12.5%	−16.0%
South	NA	1,777	2,250	1,881	1,562	1,813	2,883	2,483	5.9%	32.0%	39.7%
West	NA	3,087	3,035	2,519	2,582	2,761	2,871	2,499	−18.4%	−0.8%	−19.0%
U.S. Total	7,858	9,525	10,595	9,016	8,888	8,531	9,669	9,165	−5.3%	1.7%	−3.8%
Bowling	1979	1980	1982	1983	1984	1985	1986	1987	'80–'83 Change	'83–'87 Change	'80–'87 Change
Northeast	NA	7,524	7,277	7,051	7,502	7,335	6,469	5,834	−6.3%	−17.3%	−22.5%
Midwest	NA	10,474	10,937	9,451	9,962	9,395	9,909	9,761	−9.8%	3.3%	−6.8%
South	NA	7,578	7,069	6,969	7,588	7,888	7,805	6,828	−8.0%	−2.0%	−9.9%
West	NA	6,399	5,254	4,976	5,685	5,855	5,485	5,505	−22.2%	10.6%	−14.0%
U.S. Total	NA	31,974	30,536	28,448	30,737	30,474	29,667	27,907	−11.0%	−1.9%	−12.7%
Basketball	1979	1980	1982	1983	1984	1985	1986	1987	'79–'83 Change	'83–'87 Change	'79–'87 Change
Northeast	NA	NA	NA	2,031	2,022	1,828	1,584	1,248	NA	−38.6%	NA
Midwest	NA	NA	NA	2,461	2,556	2,422	2,305	2,234	NA	−9.2%	NA
South	NA	NA	NA	2,944	2,889	3,523	3,727	3,715	NA	26.2%	NA
West	NA	NA	NA	1,483	1,936	1,625	1,730	1,803	NA	21.6%	NA
U.S. Total	NA	NA	NA	8,919	9,403	9,398	9,346	9,000	NA	0.9%	NA
Volleyball	1979	1980	1982	1983	1984	1985	1986	1987	'79–'83 Change	'83–'87 Change	'79–'87 Change
Northeast	NA	NA	NA	1,971	2,281	2,201	1,764	1,424	NA	−27.8%	NA
Midwest	NA	NA	NA	2,798	3,282	3,105	3,135	3,235	NA	15.6%	NA
South	NA	NA	NA	2,321	2,395	2,686	2,970	2,720	NA	17.2%	NA
West	NA	NA	NA	1,340	1,884	2,450	2,017	1,711	NA	27.7%	NA
U.S. Total	NA	NA	NA	8,429	9,842	10,443	9,886	9,090	NA	7.8%	NA

SOURCE: Simmons Market Research Bureau. 1979 to 1987. Study of Media and Markets. Volume P–10. Sports and Leisure. New York, New York.

TABLE 8.3 Market Size of Water-Based Activities by U.S. Region (in thousands)

Activity	Year								Market Size Change (%)		
Region	Market Size (Number of Participants)								'79–'83 Change	'83–'87 Change	'79–'87 Change
Swimming	1979	1980	1982	1983	1984	1985	1986	1987			
Northeast	12,129	12,070	11,870	12,150	12,985	12,870	11,668	10,039	0.2%	-17.4%	-17.2%
Midwest	12,554	11,589	14,066	11,704	14,308	14,348	12,910	13,628	-6.8%	16.4%	8.6%
South	13,190	13,454	14,867	13,166	14,022	14,866	14,428	12,947	-0.2%	-1.7%	-1.8%
West	11,217	11,068	10,249	9,392	10,923	11,583	9,118	9,979	-16.3%	6.3%	-11.0%
U.S. Total	49,090	48,181	51,052	46,412	52,238	53,667	48,124	46,593	-5.5%	0.4%	-5.1%
Sailing	1979	1980	1982	1983	1984	1985	1986	1987	'79–'83 Change	'83–'87 Change	'79–'87 Change
Northeast	1,348	1,523	1,419	1,646	1,530	1,508	1,513	1,175	22.1%	-28.6%	-12.8%
Midwest	1,470	1,240	1,279	1,053	1,139	965	1,460	1,259	-28.4%	19.6%	-14.4%
South	1,368	1,056	1,325	1,264	1,525	1,054	1,897	1,596	-7.6%	26.3%	16.7%
West	1,676	1,426	1,282	1,256	1,748	1,388	1,158	1,310	-25.1%	4.3%	-21.8%
U.S. Total	5,862	5,245	5,305	5,219	5,942	4,915	6,028	5,340	-11.0%	2.3%	-8.9%
Water Skiing	1979	1980	1982	1983	1984	1985	1986	1987	'79–'83 Change	'83–'87 Change	'79–'87 Change
Northeast	1,299	972	1,044	1,149	1,193	1,141	1,045	830	-11.5%	-27.8%	-36.1%
Midwest	2,243	2,262	2,611	2,064	2,549	2,239	2,007	2,696	-8.0%	30.6%	20.2%
South	2,856	2,044	2,579	2,421	2,252	2,436	1,992	2,162	-15.2%	-10.7%	-24.3%
West	2,331	1,891	1,717	1,542	2,239	2,249	2,024	1,972	-33.8%	27.9%	-15.4%
U.S. Total	8,729	7,169	7,951	7,176	8,233	8,065	7,068	7,660	-17.8%	6.7%	-12.2%
Power Boating	1979	1980	1982	1983	1984	1985	1986	1987	'79–'83 Change	'83–'87 Change	'79–'87 Change
Northeast	2,401	1,818	1,992	1,843	2,305	2,097	2,043	1,496	-23.2%	-18.8%	-37.7%
Midwest	3,487	3,497	4,374	3,174	3,405	3,765	3,517	3,878	-17.5%	22.2%	0.8%
South	4,002	2,871	3,067	2,965	3,404	3,115	2,993	2,881	-25.9%	-2.8%	-28.0%
West	2,341	2,336	2,217	2,196	2,425	2,420	2,169	1,955	-6.2%	-11.0%	-16.5%
U.S. Total	12,591	10,522	11,650	10,178	11,539	11,397	10,722	10,210	-19.2%	0.3%	-18.9%

SOURCE: Simmons Market Research Bureau. 1979 to 1987. Study of Media and Markets. Volume P-10. Sports and Leisure. New York. New York.

TABLE 8.4 Market Size of Winter-Based Activities by U.S. Region (in thousands)

Activity Region	Year								Market Size Change (%)		
	1979	1980	1982	1983	1984	1985	1986	1987	'79–'83 Change	'83–'87 Change	'79–'87 Change
Snowmobiling				*Market Size (Number of Participants)*							
Northeast	761	1,047	917	902	1,149	1,080	687	958	18.5%	6.2%	25.9%
Midwest	2,614	2,015	2,439	1,861	1,917	2,344	1,934	1,574	−28.8%	−15.4%	−39.8%
South	132	324	220	176	250	353	358	349	33.3%	98.3%	164.4%
West	267	880	498	482	415	394	705	563	80.5%	16.8%	110.9%
U.S. Total	3,774	4,266	4,074	3,421	3,731	4,171	3,684	3,444	−9.4%	0.7%	−8.7%
X-Country Ski									'79–'83 Change	'83–'87 Change	'79–'87 Change
Northeast	982	924	957	1,076	1,387	1,188	1,034	1,065	9.6%	−1.0%	8.5%
Midwest	1,565	1,538	1,578	1,348	1,557	1,604	1,968	2,196	−13.9%	62.9%	40.3%
South	233	393	187	148	178	387	468	523	−36.5%	253.4%	124.5%
West	1,304	1,002	730	910	910	1,078	1,321	989	−30.2%	8.7%	−24.2%
U.S. Total	4,084	3,857	3,452	3,482	4,032	4,257	4,791	4,773	−14.7%	37.1%	16.9%
Downhill Ski									'79–'83 Change	'83–'87 Change	'79–'87 Change
Northeast	1,986	1,427	1,622	2,396	1,685	1,808	1,874	1,459	20.6%	−39.1%	−26.5%
Midwest	1,420	1,358	2,009	1,333	1,550	1,778	1,382	1,743	−6.1%	30.8%	22.7%
South	1,187	952	996	874	951	1,013	1,049	1,195	−26.4%	36.7%	0.7%
West	3,254	2,207	2,108	2,208	3,051	3,040	2,876	2,885	−32.1%	30.7%	−11.3%
U.S. Total	7,847	5,944	6,735	6,811	7,237	7,639	7,181	7,282	−13.2%	6.9%	−7.2%
Ice Skating									'79–'83 Change	'83–'87 Change	'79–'87 Change
Northeast	2,739	3,292	2,379	2,078	2,398	2,056	1,594	1,279	−24.1%	−38.5%	−53.3%
Midwest	1,893	2,233	2,140	1,928	2,075	1,702	1,677	1,471	1.8%	−23.7%	−22.3%
South	1,051	1,152	1,401	756	1,056	989	1,047	733	−28.1%	−3.0%	−30.3%
West	1,141	1,312	931	778	1,121	690	717	790	−31.8%	1.5%	−30.8%
U.S. Total	6,824	7,989	6,851	5,540	6,650	5,437	5,035	4,273	−18.8%	−22.9%	−37.4%

SOURCE: Simmons Market Research Bureau. 1979 to 1987. Study of Media and Markets. Volume P–10. Sports and Leisure. New York, New York.

TABLE 8.5 Demographic Profiles for Golf (market size by demographic descriptor, '000)

	Year								Market Size Changes (%)		
	1979	1980	1982	1983	1984	1985	1986	1987	'79–'83 Change	'83–'87 Change	'79–'87 Change
				Number of Participants							
Age:											
18–24	2,242	2,359	2,334	2,401	3,009	2,950	3,806	3,067	7.1%	27.7%	36.8%
25–34	3,266	3,465	3,458	3,546	4,167	4,175	5,078	5,743	8.6%	62.0%	75.8%
35–44	2,458	2,630	1,782	2,571	2,969	2,863	4,300	3,996	4.6%	55.4%	62.6%
45–54	2,362	1,932	2,132	2,279	2,058	1,899	2,408	2,410	-3.5%	5.7%	2.0%
55–64	1,965	1,765	1,852	1,705	1,624	1,940	2,317	2,028	-13.2%	18.9%	3.2%
65 & Over	1,017	943	1,361	1,231	1,062	1,284	1,806	1,659	21.0%	34.8%	63.1%
Sex:											
Male	9,831	9,468	8,974	9,764	10,789	10,855	13,206	13,231	-0.7%	35.5%	34.6%
Female	3,478	3,626	4,045	3,968	4,099	4,255	6,508	5,672	14.1%	42.9%	63.1%
Education:											
Grad. College	3,977	3,698	3,495	4,497	4,675	4,712	6,054	5,891	13.1%	31.0%	48.1%
Attend. College	3,465	3,359	3,330	3,109	3,730	3,911	4,648	5,337	-10.3%	71.7%	54.0%
Grad. H.S.	4,342	4,568	4,678	4,709	5,178	5,211	6,864	5,985	8.5%	27.1%	37.8%
No Grad. H.S.	1,525	1,469	1,517	1,418	1,305	1,277	2,148	1,691	-7.0%	19.3%	10.9%
Household Income:											
$60,000 plus	NA	NA	NA	NA	NA	NA	2,957	3,168	NA	NA	NA
$50,000 plus	NA	NA	NA	NA	2,879	3,506	4,683	4,902	NA	NA	NA
$40,000 plus	NA	NA	3,485	4,639	5,046	5,928	7,927	1,940	NA	-58.2%	NA
$35,000 plus	NA	3,686	NA	NA	NA	NA	NA	NA	NA	NA	NA
$30,000 plus	NA	NA	6,211	NA	8,346	9,223	11,841	12,086	NA	NA	NA
$25,000+/30–39,999	NA	6,973	8,425	NA	10,303	10,924	3,914	4,146	NA	NA	NA
$20–24,999/29,999	5,589	1,757	1,322	3,154	1,445	1,298	3,937	3,604	-43.6%	NA	NA
$10–19,999	3,515	3,521	2,422	2,156	2,365	2,172	2,839	2,210	-38.7%	2.5%	-37.1%
$10,000 under	660	842	851	838	775	717	1,097	1,003	27.0%	19.7%	52.0%

Note: Income categories changed in 1986 from $20–$24,999 to $20–29,999 and from $25,000 plus to $30–39,999.
SOURCE: Simmons Market Research Bureau. 1979 to 1987. Study of Media and Markets. Volume P-10. Sports and Leisure. New York, New York.

TABLE 8.6 Demographic Profiles for Racquetball (market size by demographic descriptor, '000)

	Year								Market Size Changes (%)		
	1979	1980	1982	1983	1984	1985	1986	1987	'80–'83 Change	'83–'87 Change	'80–'87 Change
Age:											
18–24	NA	3,621	3,724	3,097	3,240	2,688	2,884	2,497	−14.5%	−19.4%	−31.0%
25–34	NA	3,328	3,793	3,369	3,261	3,001	3,415	3,333	1.2%	−1.1%	0.2%
35–44	NA	1,314	1,604	1,602	1,374	1,576	1,843	1,974	21.9%	23.2%	50.2%
45–54	NA	676	631	622	617	805	627	736	−8.0%	18.3%	8.9%
55–64	NA	385	320	223	223	315	536	366	−42.1%	64.1%	−4.9%
65 & Over	NA	202	221	105	173	146	365	259	−48.0%	146.7%	28.2%
Sex:											
Male	NA	5,844	6,337	5,625	5,996	5,720	6,360	5,767	−3.7%	2.5%	−1.3%
Female	NA	3,682	4,258	3,391	2,891	2,811	3,309	3,398	−7.9%	0.2%	−7.7%
Education:											
Grad. College	NA	2,734	3,497	3,262	2,812	2,835	2,819	3,042	19.3%	−6.7%	11.3%
Attend. College	NA	2,739	2,928	2,545	2,540	2,213	2,630	2,830	−7.1%	11.2%	3.3%
Grad. H.S.	NA	3,066	3,101	2,536	2,547	2,749	2,909	2,390	−17.3%	−5.8%	−22.0%
No Grad H.S.	NA	986	1,068	673	989	734	1,311	904	−31.7%	34.3%	−8.3%
Household Income:											
$60,000 plus	NA	NA	NA	NA	NA	NA	1,496	1,635	NA	NA	NA
$50,000 plus	NA	NA	NA	NA	1,537	1,942	2,124	2,466	NA	NA	NA
$40,000 plus	NA	NA	2,800	3,042	2,853	3,319	3,578	4,036	NA	32.7%	NA
$35,000 plus	NA	2,354	NA	NA	NA	NA	NA	NA	NA	NA	NA
$30,000 plus	NA	NA	4,938	4,813	4,742	4,943	5,300	5,962	NA	23.9%	NA
$25,000+/$30–39,999	NA	4,527	6,540	5,900	5,861	5,801	1,721	1,927	NA	NA	NA
$20–24,999/$29,999	NA	1,331	1,039	934	871	929	1,891	1,742	NA	NA	NA
$10–19,999	NA	2,945	2,046	1,452	1,302	1,288	1,559	868	−50.7%	−40.2%	−70.5%
$10,000 under	NA	732	969	730	854	513	919	588	−0.3%	−19.5%	−19.7%

Note: Income categories changed in 1986 from $20–$24,999 to $20–29,999 and from $25,000 plus to $30–39,999.
SOURCE: Simmons Market Research Bureau. 1979 to 1987. Study of Media and Markets. Volume P–10. Sports and Leisure. New York, New York.

TABLE 8.7 Demographic Profiles for Power Boating (market size by demographic descriptor, '000)

| | Year | | | | | | | | Market Size Changes (%) | | |
	1979	1980	1982	1983	1984	1985	1986	1987	'79-'83 Change	'83-'87 Change	'79-'87 Change
				Number of Participants							
Age:											
18–24	3,845	2,779	3,027	2,009	2,320	2,473	2,254	2,317	-47.8%	15.3%	-39.7%
25–34	3,381	3,140	3,857	3,504	3,358	3,496	3,209	3,163	3.6%	-9.7%	-6.4%
35–44	2,472	1,809	2,028	1,978	2,558	2,641	2,169	2,138	-20.0%	8.1%	-13.5%
45–54	1,438	1,553	1,492	1,412	1,677	1,293	1,432	1,093	-1.8%	-22.6%	-24.0%
55–64	1,029	720	808	833	1,056	915	1,072	937	-19.0%	12.5%	-8.9%
65 & Over	427	521	440	444	570	580	587	563	4.0%	26.8%	31.9%
Sex:											
Male	8,044	5,842	6,173	5,870	6,398	6,601	5,636	5,942	-27.0%	1.2%	-26.1%
Female	4,548	4,681	5,478	4,310	5,141	4,796	5,086	4,268	-5.2%	-1.0%	-6.2%
Education:											
Grad. College	2,471	1,945	2,212	2,239	2,730	2,623	2,654	2,776	-9.4%	24.0%	12.3%
Attend. College	3,075	2,576	3,223	2,265	2,813	2,958	2,602	2,696	-26.3%	19.0%	-12.3%
Grad. H.S.	5,047	4,851	4,835	4,313	4,551	4,598	4,363	3,744	-14.5%	-13.2%	-25.8%
No Grad H.S.	1,997	1,151	1,381	1,362	1,445	1,217	1,103	995	-31.8%	-26.9%	-50.2%
Household Income:											
$60,000 plus	NA	NA	NA	NA	NA	NA	1,452	1,757	NA	NA	NA
$50,000 plus	NA	NA	NA	NA	NA	NA	2,308	2,887	NA	NA	NA
$40,000 plus	NA	NA	2,634	2,793	1,947	2,477	NA	NA	NA	NA	NA
$35,000 plus	2,317	2,059	4,955	4,643	NA	NA	NA	NA	NA	NA	NA
$30,000 plus	NA	NA	NA	NA	NA	NA	NA	NA	NA	NA	NA
$25,000+/30–39,999	5,161	4,485	6,607	6,124	7,452	7,996	NA	NA	18.7%	NA	NA
$20–24,999/29,999	2,205	1,889	1,359	1,183	1,182	1,067	NA	NA	-46.3%	NA	NA
$10–19,999	4,254	3,503	2,715	2,080	2,022	1,855	1,410	1,147	-51.1%	-44.9%	-73.0%
$10,000 under	723	493	969	791	910	479	482	568	9.4%	-28.2%	-21.4%

Note: Income categories changed in 1986 from $20–$24,999 to $20–29,999 and from $25,000 plus to $30–39,999
SOURCE: Simmons Market Research Bureau. 1979 to 1987. Study of Media and Markets. Volume P–10. Sports and Leisure. New York, New York.

TABLE 8.8 Demographic Profiles for Downhill Skiing (market size by demographic descriptor, '000)

	Year								Market Size Changes (%)		
	1979	1980	1982	1983	1984	1985	1986	1987	'79–'83 Change	'83–'87 Change	'79–'87 Change
				Number of Participants							
Age:											
18–24	3,463	2,084	2,762	2,518	2,319	1,935	2,427	2,153	−27.3%	−14.5%	−37.8%
25–34	2,536	1,901	2,023	2,271	2,458	2,860	2,248	2,513	−10.4%	10.7%	−0.9%
35–44	763	1,028	1,036	1,094	1,675	1,560	1,463	1,544	43.4%	41.1%	102.4%
45–54	649	606	391	594	409	848	583	709	−8.5%	19.4%	9.2%
55–64	295	254	426	221	271	300	380	220	−25.1%	−0.5%	−25.4%
65 & Over	142	72	97	113	105	135	81	143	−20.4%	26.5%	0.7%
Sex:											
Male	4,718	3,352	3,831	3,758	3,985	4,256	4,100	4,426	−20.3%	17.8%	−6.2%
Female	3,129	2,592	2,904	3,053	3,252	3,382	3,081	2,856	−2.4%	−6.5%	−8.7%
Education:											
Grad. College	2,494	2,144	1,900	2,522	2,564	2,758	2,423	2,610	1.1%	3.5%	4.7%
Attend. College	2,178	1,509	2,160	1,870	2,089	2,363	2,199	2,127	−14.1%	13.7%	−2.3%
Grad. H.S.	2,587	1,908	2,140	1,950	2,046	2,006	2,038	2,079	−24.6%	6.6%	−19.6%
No Grad H.S.	588	382	535	469	538	512	522	465	−20.2%	−0.9%	−20.9%
Household Income:											
$60,000 plus	NA	NA	NA	NA	NA	NA	1,299	1,600	NA	NA	NA
$50,000 plus	NA	NA	NA	NA	1,481	1,892	1,842	2,356	NA	NA	NA
$40,000 plus	NA	NA	2,209	2,592	NA	NA	NA	NA	NA	NA	NA
$35,000 plus	2,067	1,621	NA	NA	NA	NA	NA	NA	NA	NA	NA
$30,000 plus	NA	NA	3,677	4,002	NA	NA	NA	NA	NA	NA	NA
$25,000+/30–39,999	3,942	3,231	4,405	4,836	5,238	5,647	NA	NA	22.7%	NA	NA
$20–24,999/29,999	924	764	569	585	612	615	NA	NA	−36.7%	NA	NA
$10–19,999	2,271	1,535	1,272	940	854	854	711	652	−58.6%	−30.6%	−71.3%
$10,000 under	496	251	490	451	522	522	482	339	−9.1%	−24.8%	−31.7%

Note: Income categories changed in 1986 from $20–$24,999 to $20–29,999 and from $25,000 plus to $30–39,999

SOURCE: Simmons Market Research Bureau. 1979 to 1987. Study of Media and Markets. Volume P-10. Sports and Leisure. New York, New York.

TABLE 8.9 Participation Volume of Recreational Sport Activities by Size and Volume

Activity Market Size	Year Number of Participants ('000)			Trend Size Change (%)		
Racquetball	**1979**	**1983**	**1987**	**'79–'83**	**'83–'87**	**'79–'87**
Light Participants	2,645	2,937	3,241	11.0%	10.4%	22.5%
Moderate Participants	3,261	3,485	3,758	6.9%	7.8%	15.2%
Heavy Participants	1,952	2,594	2,166	32.9%	−16.5%	11.0%
Total Participants	7,858	9,016	9,165	14.7%	1.7%	16.6%

Market Volume	Number of Participation Days ('000)			Volume Change (%)		
Racquetball	**1979**	**1983**	**1987**	**'79–'83**	**'83–'87**	**'79–'87**
Light (1–4 days)	6,613	7,343	8,103	11.0%	10.3%	22.5%
Moderate (5–19 days)	34,652	35,120	38,971	1.4%	11.0%	12.5%
Heavy (20 days or more)	70,843	104,362	89,148	47.3%	−14.6%	25.8%
Total Participation Days	112,108	146,824	136,222	31.0%	−7.2%	21.5%

Market Size	Number of Participants ('000)			Size Change (%)		
Downhill Skiing	**1979**	**1983**	**1987**	**'79–'83**	**'83–'87**	**'79–'87**
Light Participants	3,955	3,396	3,815	−14.1%	12.3%	−3.5%
Moderate Participants	3,459	2,654	2,924	−23.3%	10.2%	−15.5%
Heavy Participants	433	762	543	76.0%	−28.7%	25.4%
Total Participants	7,847	6,812	7,282	−13.2%	6.9%	−7.2%

Market Volume	Number of Participation Days ('000)			Volume Change (%)		
Downhill Skiing	**1979**	**1983**	**1987**	**'79–'83**	**'83–'87**	**'79–'87**
Light (1–4 days)	7,910	6,792	7,630	−14.1%	12.3%	−3.5%
Moderate (5–19 days)	34,868	27,348	30,188	−21.6%	10.4%	−13.4%
Heavy (20 days or more)	13,280	21,978	16,238	65.5%	−26.1%	22.3%
Total Participation Days	56,058	56,118	54,056	0.1%	−3.7%	−3.6%

Market Size	Number of Participants ('000)			Size Change (%)		
Golf	**1979**	**1983**	**1987**	**'79–'83**	**'83–'87**	**'79–'87**
Light Participants	4,560	4,874	6,696	6.9%	37.4%	46.8%
Moderate Participants	4,532	4,988	6,911	10.1%	38.6%	52.5%
Heavy Participants	4,217	3,871	5,297	−8.2%	36.8%	25.6%
Total Participants	13,309	13,733	18,904	3.2%	37.7%	42.0%

Market Volume	Number of Participation Days ('000)			Volume Change (%)		
Golf	**1979**	**1983**	**1987**	**'79–'83**	**'83–'87**	**'79–'87**
Light (1–4 days)	9,120	9,748	13,392	6.9%	37.4%	46.8%
Moderate (5–19 days)	48,269	54,916	72,312	13.8%	31.7%	49.8%
Heavy (20 days or more)	180,395	157,350	209,179	−12.8%	32.9%	16.0%
Total Participation Days	237,784	222,014	294,883	−6.6%	32.8%	24.0%

TABLE 8.9—*Continued*

Market Size	Number of Participants ('000)			Size Change (%)		
Power Boating	**1979**	**1983**	**1987**	**'79–'83**	**'83–'87**	**'79–'87**
Light Participants	4,498	4,173	3,853	–7.2%	–7.7%	–14.3%
Moderate Participants	4,899	3,937	4,221	–19.6%	7.2%	–13.8%
Heavy Participants	3,196	2,069	2,137	–35.3%	3.3%	–33.1%
Total Participants	12,593	10,179	10,211	–19.2%	0.3%	–18.9%

Market Volume	Number of Participation Days ('000)			Volume Change (%)		
Power Boating	**1979**	**1983**	**1987**	**'79–'83**	**'83–'87**	**'79–'87**
Light (1–4 days)	8,996	8,346	7,706	–7.2%	–7.7%	–14.3%
Moderate (5–19 days)	50,813	41,759	49,477	–17.8%	18.5%	–2.6%
Heavy (20 days or more)	118,007	73,700	79,258	–37.5%	7.5%	–32.8%
Total Participation Days	177,816	123,805	136,441	–30.4%	10.2%	–23.3%

SOURCE: Simmons Market Research Bureau. 1979 to 1987. Study of Media and Markets. Volume P–10. Sports and Leisure. New York, New York.

Over the long-term period from 1979 through 1987, the use levels in power boating appeared to decline. Interestingly, however, if only the years from 1983 to 1987 are considered, there was growth in both the number of boaters and the number of boating days for the moderate and heavy use groups. The growth in power boating is most noticeable in the moderate use group. The size of this segment increased by approximately 7 percent and the volume by nearly 19 percent from 1983 to 1987.

Although participation rates peaked in 1982 for racquetball, the market size and volume actually increased from 1979 to 1987. Participation among heavy players declined over the most recent years of the period, from 1983 through 1987. The market size declined by nearly 17 percent and market volume declined by nearly 15 percent.

DISCUSSION

An examination of market recreational sport activity trends on a year-to-year basis for the period of 1979 through 1987 reveals specific patterns and changes in the various participant markets. While not all-inclusive, some discussion points are raised here.

Participation Rates and Regional Differences

It is again evident from this data that the vast majority of American adults do *not* participate in many of the most common recreational sport activities as suggested by Robinson (1987) and Warnick and Howard (1985). While overall participation rates are low, market size in some cases is actually growing or at least has remained relatively stable. On the other hand, the data presents striking regional differences within recreation activities. For example, power boating grew in market size (number of adult boaters) more within the Midwest for the period of 1983 through 1987 than in any other region. While it would be logical to assume that boating would be more popular in the coastal states, evidence indicates that the largest shares of boat registrations per state are held by Michigan (highest with 746,979 registrations) and Minnesota (third highest with 673,503) (Boat Owners Association of the United States, *USA Today*, 1989).

Regional differences within recreational sport activities do exist and do vary greatly. For example, the Northeast appears to vary dramatically from other parts of the United States. Over the period of 1983 through 1987 the Northeast demonstrated (1) much slower market size growth in golf compared with that of other regions; (2) a declining market size for sailing while all other regions indicated growth; and (3) a declining market size for downhill skiing while all other regions indicated growth. It may be that the supply of facilities for some of these activities may present more of a problem in the Northeast than in other regions. The high cost of real estate can certainly limit the number of new golf courses that can be built, and there appears to be a real shortage of boat slips and moorings within the region. Consequently, regional supply factors do need to be monitored and appear to limit and slow growth if they are not sufficient to keep up with demand. Poor weather conditions for downhill skiing may have also impacted participation in this region.

Demographic Impacts on Outdoor Recreation Participation

Over a relatively short period of time (less than ten years), demographic changes have had substantial impact on market sizes and market shifts within recreational sport activities. For example, the effect of baby boomers on participation in downhill skiing and racquetball is clearly evident. The market segment with the largest growth in both of these activities is the 35- to 44-year-old segment. For golf, the biggest growth segments are the younger adult and the female markets. Agencies which carefully monitor demographic changes may be able to create market niches or anticipate changes more quickly over the next decade.

The Golf Boom

Of all the recreational sport activities examined over this period of time, golf is clearly the one with the longest period of sustained growth in market size, participation rate, and participation volume. Market size showed growth in nearly all demographic, use, and regional variables examined here. However, it is unlikely that growth will continue at such a pace without significant changes in the supply and without innovations in the game. First, the rate of building new golf courses has slowed. In 1988, approximately 200 new golf courses were built as compared to the building rate average of 500 per year between 1959 and 1971 (Shuster 1989). The shortage of golf courses and the slower building rate may well restrict the expansion or market growth of the game. Furthermore, waiting times and crowded courses may lead to dissatisfaction among a significant number of golfers. Innovations to speed up the game may help alleviate some of the problems. Shorter or down-sized courses, specially designed practice facilities, golf simulators, and other innovations will help. However, the provision of new facilities and the careful management of player conflicts are necessary to ensure sustained growth in this activity.

Evidence of Environmental Problems

Swimming is one of the country's most popular activities. Various studies have indicated relatively high and stable participation rates. However, this review suggests the presence of some problem within the activity. From 1985 through 1987, the participation rate and market size of participants declined, perhaps due to environmental problems associated with unsafe beaches, rivers, and lakes. On the other hand, the demand for the construction of private swimming pools is high. One would think that "at-home" swimming would offset the decline or at least result in a more stable market condition. But because Simmons does not differentiate between swimming at public, private, or residential facilities, it is difficult to arrive at a firm conclusion. Nevertheless, safety is a problem at public open-water facilities and appears to have had some impact on swimming participation. The extent of its relationship to declining participation rate cannot yet be established.

Impact of Special Events

There appears to be some indication that special events do have real impact upon participation in some activities. For example, a special event such as the Olympics appears to have had impact upon ice skating and distance running participation. The participation rate and overall market size for ice skating has declined every year with the exception of the Winter Olympic years of 1980 and 1984. There were rate "spikes" in each of these years. Distance running participation increased substantially in 1985, the year after the Summer Olympics. Agencies should anticipate the impact of such events within their programming and marketing and should probably work to build interest prior to the event and to sustain interest in the activity after the event.

Use Segment Size and Volume

Warnick and Howard (1985) suggest that in addition to assessing overall participation patterns within recreational activities, managers should also strive to understand the importance of carefully analyzing the distribution of existing users along a continuum from light to heavy users. Managers within particular leisure service industries should seek to analyze the mix of light, moderate, and heavy users and the volume created by each segment. Indeed, analysis by participant use segments has revealed some interesting findings. For example, even though the overall participation rate of an activity may be declining, there may also be a pronounced growth rate within one of the activity's participant use segments. This was evident in downhill skiing. The analysis of this type of information, if incorporated into a marketing information system, may provide keys to maintaining and building market shares, constituencies or loyal customers, and public support or repeat business. This analysis of selected activities has indicated that use segments within an activity are distributed differently and have dissimilar growth and decline rates.

Two-Tier Society

Although income levels and participation rates were not extensively examined within this study, the data on income levels by activity market size appear to indicate that participation in recreational sport activities reflects conditions within society. There is evidence that the United States is becoming a two-tier society: one tier of rather wealthy individuals and another tier of relatively poor individuals, and a rapidly declining middle class overall. Within nearly all of the activities examined here, participation rates and market sizes are increasing within the wealthier market segments and declining drastically among the lower-income market segments. This may also reflect that many recreation sport activities are now more expensive than in past decades. It appears that a "recreation ethic" needs to be developed which strives to provide increased enjoyment among all Americans in recreational activities and not just among those who can afford it.

CONCLUSION

The findings produced by these data do present definite recreational sport participation patterns and provide useful insight when monitored on an annual basis. There is also indication that monitoring trends in this fashion may help to anticipate changes in participation patterns. Even within declining markets, growth segments may be found. Those agencies which incorporate some type of yearly monitoring process into their market information systems should more readily be able to develop sound marketing and planning strategies for the years ahead. A look back may very well help us to plan for the future.

REFERENCES

Clawson, Marion. 1985. "Trends in the use of public recreation areas." In *Proceedings of the 1985 national outdoor recreation trends symposium II.* Clemson, S.C.: Department of Parks, Recreation and Tourism Management.

Feld, Jon. 1988. NSGA sports survey. *Club Industry* 4(12):20–26.

Harris Poll. 1985. Leisure time survey. (Chicago) Cited in *Boston Globe,* 26 December, 5.

Hartmann, Lawrence A., H. Ken Cordell, and Helen R. Freilich. 1988. The changing future of outdoor recreation. *Trends* 25(4):19–23.

Kelly, John R. 1988. *Recreation trends: Toward the year 2000.* Champaign, Ill.: Management Learning Laboratories.

Manuel, Bruce. 1988. New poll shows leisure time shrinking. *Christian Science Monitor,* 27 March, 27.

O'Leary, Joseph T., F. Dominic Dottavio, and Francis McGuire. 1988. Participation shifts in outdoor recreation activities. *Trends* 25(4):14–18.

Parker, Susan. 1989. Boating states. *USA Today,* 26–29 May 1.

Richard, Jerome. 1988. Out of time. *New York Times,* 28 November, Sec A, p. 25.

Robinson, John P. 1987. Where's the boom? *American Demographics* 9(4):34–37, 56.

Shuster, Rachel. 1989. Golf's big boom: Waiting now a big part of the game. *USA Today,* 26–29 May 2.

Simmons Market Research Bureau. 1979–1987. *Study of media and markets: Sports and leisure,* vol. P–10. New York.

Simmons Market Research Bureau. 1987. *Technical guide to study of media and markets.* New York.

U.S. Department of the Interior, National Park Service. 1983. *National outdoor recreation survey.* Washington, D.C.

U.S. President's Commission on Americans Outdoors, A Literature Review. 1986. Washington, D.C.: Government Printing Office.

Warnick, Rodney B. 1988. Outdoor recreation trends in the northeast. In *Northeast recreation research proceedings.* Burlington, VT: U.S. Forest Service.

Warnick, Rodney B. and Dennis R. Howard. 1985. Market share analysis of selected leisure services from 1979 to 1982. *Journal of Park and Recreation Administration* 3(4):64–76.

SPONSORSHIP IN SPORT

Corporate Sponsorship: A Framework for Analysis

John Kuzma and William Shanklin

INTRODUCTION

Corporate sponsorship, also known as events marketing, has been recognized as a potential means of achieving promotion strategies. This essay discusses the potential role that sponsorship can play in helping a company achieve its promotion objectives. The literature is reviewed with regard to the impact of promotion strategies using corporate sponsorship versus the other elements of advertising, personal selling, publicity, and sales promotion. Other areas of the reviewed literature include alternative promotion objectives addressed by corporate sponsorship and potential methods of measuring sponsorship effectiveness. Finally this essay discusses the areas that need to be addressed by empirical research.

John Kuzma is with the School of Business, Mankato State University, Mankato, Minnesota, and William Shanklin is with the School of Business, Kent State University, Kent, Ohio.

DEFINING CORPORATE SPONSORSHIP

As we go about living our daily lives, we are continually exposed to evidences of corporate sponsorship activity. In fact, it is difficult to read a newspaper, watch television, or attend any type of public function without encountering some form of information about corporate sponsorship activity. When one listens to the sports announcer laud the winner of the Manufacturers Hanover New York City Marathon, watches the Sunkist Fiesta Bowl on television, or attends a concert of the Merrill–Lynch Great Performers series they are being exposed to corporate sponsorship. Companies have made concerted efforts to have their names prominently displayed to the viewing public. But what is corporate sponsorship?

Corporate sponsorship has had its foundation in the philanthropic giving by companies who recognize both their community responsibility and the fact that their own economic vitality is linked to the vitality of the community. The reduction of governmental funding of nonprofit organizations (Kovach 1984, 29) and an increased emphasis on corporate promotions (Bernstein 1988) have created greater demands for corporate dollars. As a result, companies are taking a more goal-oriented approach to their philanthropic contributions. Companies are becoming more selective and are attempting to realize tangible returns from their contributions (Mescon and Tilson 1987, 49).

Corporate sponsorship has been defined as the support that is provided to various events by corporations with the intent of achieving specific objectives (Shuman 1986; Gross, Traylor, and Shuman 1987; Gardner and Shuman 1987, 1988). The terms corporate sponsorship and events marketing can be and have been used interchangeably. The specific objectives underlying the sponsorship may be to create, maintain, or reposition the corporate image, to generate sales revenue, to provide community support, or to recognize corporate social responsibility. The events that receive this sponsorship support may include such activities as sports activities, concerts, festivals, dance programs, theater performances, museum programs (Shanklin 1988), charitable events, public television programs, and community events (Gardner and Shuman 1988). The spectrum of activities, objectives, and sponsorship roles are, seemingly, limited only by the imagination of the event or the sponsor.

Companies enjoy opportunities for great promotion flexibility through corporate sponsorship. Opportunity is presented for addressing different promotion objectives or different target audiences either by using different events or by using events that offer multiple levels of sponsorship and financial commitment (Lapin 1987; Ukman 1984, 1986). The various levels of sponsorship participation may be represented by such terms as title sponsor, sole sponsor, cosponsor, presenting sponsor, official supplier, participating sponsor, or licensee (Ukman 1984; Lapin 1987; Jaffe 1986; Taylor and Silverman

1984). Companies should be constantly searching for those combinations of events and sponsorship commitments that will provide the maximum benefits toward achieving their objectives. The company's objectives, financial constraints, need for flexibility, and competitive environment may help to determine the role of corporate sponsorship among the promotion alternatives.

CORPORATE SPONSORSHIP'S ROLE IN PROMOTION

The popularity of corporate sponsorship in the promotion mix and promotion strategies increased throughout the 1980s (Mescon and Tilson 1987; Gardner and Shuman 1987; Bernstein 1988). The commonly recognized elements of the promotion mix are advertising, publicity, personal selling, and sales promotion. Ukman (1984, 21) states that "event marketing will soon join advertising and public relations as an element of the overall marketing mix." Companies have classified corporate sponsorship in a variety of ways—as a function of public relations, advertising, sales promotion, and personal selling, as well as a hybrid form of communication (Mescon and Tilson 1987, 49–51). However, the flexibility provided by corporate sponsorship indicates that it deserves consideration as an independent element of the promotion mix. Some companies have already begun to recognize events marketing as an independent component by establishing separate events marketing departments. The number of U.S. companies with separate corporate sponsorship departments grew from approximately 10 companies in 1982 to more than 400 by 1987 (*Business Week* 1987, 48). Corporate sponsorship can provide many of the same benefits that are provided by other promotion alternatives.

Contrasting the attributes of corporate sponsorship with the other elements of the promotion mix yields an interesting comparison. Advertising and corporate sponsorship both offer geographic, target market, and cost flexibility. Flexibility in advertising is provided through the use of different types of media and different sizes of ads, while corporate sponsorship provides flexibility through different types of events (Gardner and Shuman 1988; Shanklin 1988) and different levels of sponsorship participation (Gross, Traylor, and Shuman 1987; Lapin 1987; Jaffe 1986). A shift toward promotions has taken place because of the perceived decline in advertising's effectiveness (Bernstein 1988) and the clutter associated with the number of advertisements aired during commercial breaks (Walley 1987, S–4).

Many similarities exist between corporate sponsorship and publicity. Both offer the opportunity for companies to receive free media coverage (Ukman 1984), to generate higher levels of credibility than the same level of media advertising (Ukman 1984, 23), and to reach prospects not accessible through normal sales and advertising efforts. Corporate sponsorship and publicity are both used to improve the company image (Kovach 1984, 32) and generate higher levels of awareness (Taylor and Silverman 1984, 28). However, with corporate sponsorship, the sponsor may accrue benefits from the credibility associated with a particular event (Ukman 1984, 24; Ukman 1986, 9). Though many of the benefits that result from corporate sponsorship can be attributed to publicity, it must be remembered that the publicity would not be available without the sponsored event or program.

Corporate sponsorship helps to make personal selling more effective by increasing the awareness of a company's products and services (Ukman 1984). Since the awareness is generated in the consumer's leisure environment, corporate sponsorship helps to reduce the natural adversarial barriers that may exist in a buyer-seller relationship.

Corporate sponsorships have often been classified as forms of sales promotion (Mescon and Tilson 1987, 56). Both corporate sponsorship and sales promotion offer opportunities for companies to address various short-term objectives, provide product sampling, and develop point-of-sale merchandising. Regardless of the fact that a sponsorship or a promotion may be short-term, residual longer-term effects may be accrued through the continued use of memorabilia or premiums (Gadsden 1985, 33). One major advantage of using corporate sponsorship rather than sales promotion is that continued use of a sales promotion tends to diminish a company's or product's image, while the extended use of a corporate sponsorship appears to enhance a company's or product's image (Mihalik 1984, 25).

The substitutability of corporate sponsorship for other elements of the promotion mix should be determined by measuring the effectiveness of corporate sponsorship. Measurements performed in a manner consistent with the procedures used to measure other promotion alternatives, provide a basis for comparison of these elements.

MEASURING CORPORATE SPONSORSHIP EFFECTIVENESS

In order for a company to determine if a corporate sponsorship effort has been worthwhile, some attempt at measuring the level of effectiveness is necessary. The literature indicates that many companies either do not measure or have not found a useful method for measuring sponsorship effectiveness. Although a few exceptions exist, Gross, Traylor, and Shuman (1987, 544) note that measurement has generally been ''haphazard and anecdotal.''

Many forms of measurement could be used in determining the contribution of sponsorship to achieving a company's marketing and promotion objectives. Some of the measurement methods referred to in the literature include: awareness and attitude surveys (Gross, Traylor, and Shuman 1987); measurement against objectives and monitoring market share (Gadsden 1985); frequency counts of name/logo exposure, sales volume increases, and the extent of media coverage (Mihalik 1984); and the pre- and post-buying habit measurement of event attendees (Ukman 1984). The appropriate choice of a measurement method depends on the data available and the information required by the company.

Burson-Marsteller, the public relations unit of Young and Rubicam, has developed several tools to select and track their clients' events. One tool called Relative Value Assessment evaluates an event against the objectives and strategy associated with a product. Another tool, the Sports Compatibility Profile, matches the customer profile of clients against the demographic appeal of forty-five amateur and professional sports (Lafayette 1989).

As companies start paying more attention to evaluating the results of corporate sponsorship, the value and effectiveness of using sponsorships in the promotion mix will become more apparent (Shanklin 1988; Mescon and Tilson 1987).

FUTURE RESEARCH

Since the recognition of corporate sponsorship as a potential element of the promotion mix is in its relative infancy, a number of areas require research consideration. Areas of needed research indicated by the literature include identifying measurement methodologies capable of providing useful data for determining sponsorship ef-

fectiveness, identifying target markets or the company or product characteristics that are conducive to successful sponsorships, and identifying corporate sponsorship's role and position within the promotion mix. Other research might include answering questions such as why companies use corporate sponsorship, what are the objectives companies are trying to achieve through sponsorships, and who makes the corporate decision to participate in sponsorships.

The result of such research would be useful both to companies deciding whether or not to participate in sponsorships and to events and nonprofit organizations seeking funding. Companies trying to make sponsorship decisions might be able to identify conditions that would improve the likelihood of success. Events and nonprofit organizations might be able to identify selling points that could be used when approaching corporations for funding.

SUMMARY

This essay has presented a brief overview of corporate sponsorship and its growing importance to both companies and nonprofit organizations. The obvious conclusion that can be drawn from the discussion is that much more information needs to be gathered if companies are going to make intelligent decisions with regard to using corporate sponsorship in their promotion strategies. The need for information also applies to the nonprofit organizations who must direct their funding efforts toward the proper sources. The allocation of corporate sponsorship to promotion or philanthropy will be determined by time.

REFERENCES

Athletic Business. 1986. Sports in the boardroom: The politics of sponsorship, December.

Bernstein, Sid. 1988. War of words: 'Ad' vs. 'promo'. *Advertising Age,* 9 May.

Brock, Fran. 1987. Special events: A sponsor away? *Adweek,* 6 April, 29–31.

Business Week, 1987. 31 August, 50.

Caesar, Patricia. 1986. Cause-related marketing: The new face of corporate philanthropy. *Business and Society Review* 59(Fall):15–19.

Ensor, Richard J. 1987. The corporate view of sports sponsorship. *Athletic Business,* September.

Feuer, Jack, 1987. Making the most of arts sponsorships. *Adweek,* 17 November.

Freeman, Laurie, and Wayne Walley. 1988. Marketing with a cause takes hold. *Advertising Age,* 16 May.

Gadsden, Shelia E. 1985. Sports events score many goals in one package. *Advertising Age,* 31 October.

Gardner, Meryl P., and Philip J. Shuman. 1988. Sponsorships and small businesses: Conceptual, strategic, and tactical issues. *Journal of Small Business Management* 26 (October).

————. 1987. Sponsorship: An important component of the promotions mix. *Journal of Advertising* 16(1):11–17.

Goldin, Greg. 1987. Cause-related marketing grows up. *Adweek,* 17 November.

Gross, A. C., M. B. Traylor, and P. J. Shuman. 1987. Corporate sponsorship of art and sports events in North America. Paper presented at the 40th Esomar Marketing Research Congress, September, at Montreux, Switzerland.

Hamaker, Ralph M. 1984. Live from the Met. *Public Relations Journal* (June):26–27.

Jaffe, Andrew. 1986. Welcome to Margaritaville. *Adweek,* 17 June.

Kovach, Jeffrey L. 1984. Charitable investments: Is this growing practice true philanthropy? *Industry Week,* 1 October.

Lafayette, Jon. 1989. Y&R steps up event marketing. *Advertising Age,* 9 October, 53.

Lapin, Jackie. 1987. How to win with sports. *Public Relations Journal* 43(2):30–32, 34.

Madlin, Nancy. 1986. Finding the hot sports for sponsorship. *Adweek,* 17 June.

Maher, Philip. 1984. Sports: The Medium of '84. *Business Marketing,* January.

Mescon, Timothy S., and Donn J. Tilson. 1987. Corporate philanthropy: A strategic approach to the bottom-line. *California Management Review* 29(2):49–61.

Mihalik, Brian J. 1984. Sponsored recreation: A look at sponsor's program objectives and tactics, and guidelines for administration. *Public Relations Journal* (June):22–25.

Murphy, Liz. 1986. The controversy behind event marketing. *Sales and Marketing Management* (October):54–56.

Robins, J. Max. 1986. The liberty hoopla: Who really benefits? *Adweek,* 17 June.

————. 1987. Choosing the right event. *Adweek,* 17 November.

Shanklin, William L. 1988. The promise of events marketing to thoroughbred horse racing. *Thoroughbred Times,* 4 March.

Shuman, P. J. 1986. *The power of perceptual marketing: An analysis of sponsorships.* New York: Burson-Marsteller.

Stevent, Art. 1984. What's ahead for special events. *Public Relations Journal* (June):30–32.

Taylor, Alan, and Ira Silverman. 1984. Sports sponsorships. *Public Relations Journal* (June):28–29.

Ukman, Lesa. 1988. The special event: Finding its niche. *Public Relations Journal* (June):21.

————. 1986. What works and what doesn't. *Adweek,* 17 June.

————. 1984. Sports is it. *Marketing Communications* (November):23–32.

Walley, Wayne. 1987. Companies learn to play the game. *Advertising Age,* 9 November.

Yovovich, B. G. 1987. Special event promoters are taking stock—before and after. *Adweek,* 13 April, 12.

Zaharadnik, Rich. 1987. Big companies, small events. *Adweek,* 17 November.

10

Two Different Examples for Sponsoring, Advertising, and Financing Sport in the Former West Germany: The Trimm-Campaign and the National Soccer League

Horst Ueberhorst

INTRODUCTION

This essay examines the relationship between sports and the economy in the former West Germany using the examples of the Trimm-Campaign and the National Soccer League. Some understanding of the historical context is important—of the development of sport in the former West Germany, in general, and of the efforts made to popularize sports through advertising, marketing and new project development, in particular.

The sport clubs and federations in what was the Federal Republic began to act as autonomous units when the German Sports Federation (DSB) was founded on December 10, 1950. The DSB was the umbrella organization for the German gymnastics and sports movements comprising fifty-two national sport federations, including soccer, track and field, skiing, handball, basketball, and volleyball—to name only a few. Each was responsible for the rules and regulations of their discipline. From 1960 to 1990 the membership in these federations increased at the rate of about 8 percent annually. In 1990, the German Sports Federation had 20 million members, an inordinate number of the most recent of which were women and older men. One apparent reason for the shift in membership was the attraction of jogging and other physical fitness programs offered by the "Sport for All" program.

SPORT FOR ALL—FROM THE BEGINNING TO 1990

The success of Trimm-Campaign of the DSB from 1970 to 1990 can be attributed to cover the span between recreational and elite sport. The target group of Sport for All included the

Horst Ueberhorst is a former Director of the Sport Management Program, Department of Sportwissenschaft, Ruhr Universitat, Bochum, Germany.

entire range of the population. In 1990, however, school-aged children and senior citizens represented 60 percent of the program's participants—double the percentage when the campaign commenced in 1970. Throughout that period the DSB recognized the enormous potential of the Trimm-Campaign to improve the living conditions of the whole society. The main goals and purpose of Sport for All were to provide a balance against the one-sidedness found in civilized societies; to create better opportunities for personal creativity and individual development; and to further communication and social participation.

To bring these ideas to reality, following the examples of Norway, Netherlands, and Sweden, it was necessary to wage the Federal Republic of Germany's first social marketing campaign. Through the use of an advertising agency, the cooperation of the media, and by securing sponsors the Trimm-Campaign succeeded in reinforcing the importance of sport for all of society and improving the position of mass sport compared to elite sport. To create this new popular image of sport, millions of brochures and posters were distributed as well as advertisements placed in newspapers and magazines and television. In the first part of the campaign, organizers focused on improving the stamina of the population by promoting aerobic sports in the attempt to fight the major coronary diseases from which more than half a million of the nation's people suffered. This could be done easily and economically by offering organized programs of jogging, cycling, swimming, dancing, and aerobic gymnastics. The so-called Trimm-Trot, was an effective but not too strenuous running program offering advantages similar to jogging: physical self-experience, social contacts with running mates, experience of success, and emotional effects and sensual awareness of nature. The Trimm-Trot was advertised in the

late seventies using posters, T-shirts, TV commercials, and cartoon figures.

Later, the Trimm-Campaign discovered a new deficit in leisure sports and so turned its focus to families by emphasizing the aspect of play. "Come play with us—where there is play, there is life" became an effective slogan. The Play-Campaign promoted community rather than competitive playing and was not limited to children but extended to all age groups. To improve the social and recreational chances of acceptance, lawns and parks were opened to public play and a special advertising agency was founded. The symbol became a red ball inscribed with "come and play with me." Numerous brochures were printed. Three thousand copies of "Great Games Book" were published; posters designed by cartoonists were distributed by post-offices, banks, and schools; and, the campaign was advertised on television. The campaign was financed by sponsors and the broadcasting of television commercials was free of charge. The peak of the campaign was a Games Festival demonstrating about a hundred different activities. The whole Trimm-Campaign was financed by 30 million DM contributed by businesspeople and industry. The financial capacity was further improved after 1980, when Sport-Billy-Productions began to work on a contract basis to offer royalties to business and industry. So sponsors and licensees paid royalties to finance printed materials and other projects. Companies were attracted to participate who were primarily producers of goods related to the health, sport, and leisure industries and who enjoyed a strong reputation throughout the country. The advertising value of the campaign grew from 6 million DM in 1970 to 30 million DM by 1990.

To increase the visibility of the Trimm-Campaign famous politicians including the chancellor and the president of the Federal Republic, participated actively. So did Emil

Zatopek, the well-known gold medalist of the 1952 Helsinki Olympics, who started a running program supported by his personal philosophy of staying active, lifelong. His words: "A bird flies, a fish swims, and a man runs."

Other examples of Trimm program sponsorship included a jogging and walking event, whose participants ranged from 6 to 80 years of age, and which was sponsored by a large health insurance institution. A Family-Sport-Award was also sponsored by the German Sporting Goods Manufacturers Association and presented to families in which at least three members had participated together in at least two programs. Games-Festivals were sponsored by the Community Banks and Building Saving Banks who provided advertising materials and the necessary goods and game equipment. Eight million German marks were contributed by newspapers and magazines to promote "Trimming 130," a mild but effective form of physical exercise, in the effort to publicize the research findings that aerobic activity can improve the cardiovascular system of a trained adult person and helps to slow down the aging process. The reference to "130" means that the heart beats around 130 times a minute for a period of at least ten minutes during aerobic activities such as running, swimming, cycling, and dancing.

The "active together" campaign was established in 1987. The stability of physical exercise habits through the course of a lifetime depends strongly on social conditions. Research shows that the probability of staying active is much higher if participation takes place in a group rather than alone. The slogan was: "In the club, sport is at its best." In 1990, forty-five different sport federations sponsored this campaign. Partners gave support to the campaign act for different reasons. Health insurance companies were confident that the sport campaign had tremendously sharpened the consciousness of the population. The Federal Chamber of Physicians

stated, "There is no medicine or treatment which has an effect comparable to physical training." The local sport governing bodies declared, "The states are interested in reducing the financial costs that arise through a wrong way of life and are interested in making more people experience sport and its positive effects on health, personality, and society."

How is such rational language translated into the language of advertising? An appropriate slogan might be "Movement is the best medicine." Slogans for Trimming 130 could include these: "It is so easy to feel well"; "Good for your figure, good for looking well"; "Take more out of life with Trimming"; or, "Get your pulse up to 130—when cycling." Eighteen months after the campaign's start an opinion poll confirmed that the effects of Trimming 130 were extremely positive. More than half of the population declared they were physically active and had changed their lifestyle in a major way, not only through exercise but also in the areas of nutrition and general body care. Based on other research data, personal sport activity helps to make people more aware of their physical being. Swimming (67 percent), cycling (64 percent), jogging (44 percent), hiking (43 percent), and gymnastic (40 percent) were the participation sports most frequently cited. It would not be an exaggeration to conclude that the Trimm-Campaign provided a strong contribution toward the adoption of a popular, economical, and practical health policy.

THE NATIONAL SOCCER LEAGUE: HOW TO GET LICENSED AND FINANCE THE BIG GAMES

As a result of a federal decision in 1962 the First National Soccer League was founded; ten years later, in 1972, a resolution was passed to establish a Second National Soccer League. In both cases, permission was given after having established and checked all technical, economic, and sporting criteria for qualification. The essential difference between amateur and professional soccer clubs is mirrored in legal status. Amateurs are club members; professionals, or licensed players, are bound by special contract. Licensed clubs are seen as business enterprises and therefore must pay taxes, while amateur clubs are viewed as nonprofit institutions and so are tax exempt. The German Soccer Federation (DFB) kept a transfer list for licensed players: Players not on this list were not allowed to take part in a professional league soccer game. The real purpose of the transfer list was to regulate the exchange of players from one club to another and thereby eliminate ''transparency'' in the player market. Furthermore, the list provided a guarantee to clubs interested in special players that these players had fulfilled their obligations to their present club and were free to participate in a transfer. When a player moved from one club to another, a compensation had to be paid for the transfer. Both clubs were free to negotiate their pay. For an amateur player to secure a contract with a licensed club, required a basic transfer compensation of a total of 22,500 DM to be paid to the First National Soccer League and 18,000 DM to the Second National League. Points of controversy were settled by the control committee of the DFB.

The introduction of a Second National League with licensed clubs achieved one main goal: Moves from the First League to the Second League and vice versa could not affect the legal contract of clubs or players. The employed player was still obliged to give his full strength and physical power to the club, to participate in all games, courses of instruction, and training, to respect sport medical and therapeutic measures, and to support the club by public presentations via television, radio, and the press. The player was obliged to wear the club's sport dress and emblem on these occasions; was restricted from advertising for rival businesses; and was not allowed to make any public statements without the club's permission. Profits made from advertising and public relations activities (i.e., player pictures and autographs) reverted back to the club. Players were prohibited from using drugs in any form.

How did the clubs finance the big games? Besides tickets, advertising, and contracts with firms, big games were financed mainly through television. For example, in 1980 a private TV company (RTL) paid 50 million DM for the exclusive rights to televise the big games of the First National League over the span of three years. Prior to that the public television stations ZDF (Second German TV Company) and ARD (General Broadcasting Company) had each paid only 5 million DM per year for the broadcast rights.

Interestingly, the number of stadium spectators decreased significantly. Why? One reason was the advent of a variety of new spectator sports, especially tennis, which attracted the masses and ranked second in televised sport. In addition, people's weekend interests had changed. Until this point many families went to the soccer stadium and their weekends were focused on soccer games. But their customs and habits changed to the point where women and children refused to watch soccer all the time.

Furthermore, stadiums were too ''prosaic.'' There were no areas where kids could play, no nearby shopping and amusement centers, no entertainment zones, and no creature comforts. The stadiums, mostly located on the outskirts of towns, had a stereotyped construction based on the concept of combining track and field events and with soccer games. Aside from the long distances that had to be traveled to get to the stadium, another problem was the disparity between the incomes of the players and that of the ticket-buying fans. Escalating ticket prices reduced the number of families who could afford cost of admission. Finally, some clubs tried to reduce their financial risks by selling season tickets. The famous soccer club ''Borussia Dortmund,'' near Bochum, sold more than 10,000 tickets at the beginning of the season, a truly unique event. But this kind of marketing includes both advantages and risks. The club gets a lot of advance money, but prices cannot be increased during the season, even for the top games.

Another opportunity for First or Second League soccer clubs to secure additional money is through the transfer of players to foreign clubs as long as no continuous contract exists. The UEFA (European Soccer Association) typically exercises a fixed fee of 2.5 million DM per player transfer. Finally, endowments paid by big firms for advertising (soccer players wear emblems of firms on their T-shirts) represented a viable source of additional financial support. The Opel automobile factory in Bochum paid the local soccer team, a member of the First National League, 500,000 DM per year for advertising. The Bayern Munchen team has received 3 million DM annually. Why? Because Bayern has led the First National League for the past five years.

Nonetheless, membership in juvenile clubs is declining, an indication that identification with soccer lacks the strength it has had in the past. There is greater opportunity to participate in a wide variety of sports.

CONCLUSION

Sport has severed purposes in the former Federal Republic of Germany that range from professional sport, to commercially run sport institutions, to the utilization of sport as a means of advertising. The commercialization of top sport has represented a special sales market with a significant potential for profit. In general, sport as an economic factor has long been an important element of German society. Its business volume in the advertising industry as well as in professional sports (due to its considerable contribution to mass entertainment market) has reached billions. The question is: Is this an inevitable development, a national consequence of societies within a market economy, or is it a dangerous threat leading to the loss of autonomy of sport organizations to business enterprises?

11

Possible Effects of Corporate Sponsors on Intercollegiate Athletics

Paul Glenn and Patrick Cobb

The past decade has witnessed intercollegiate athletics come under fire for unethical conduct time after time. Issues such as drug abuse, steroids, invalid entrance examinations, Title IX, Propositions 42 and 48, pay for play, graduation rates, lawlessness, and athlete privileges appear in the headlines daily, causing severe damage to the reputations of our academic institutions. Many colleges and universities have separated their athletic association operations from that of the rest of the financial structure. As a result, athletic programs currently tend to operate in insulated climates.

Collegiate athletics are in an unenviable situation because they are required to operate at a profit despite rising operating costs and higher expectations for academic quality. This pressure to operate in the black and remain self-supporting has created a difficult environment for athletic programs. Consequently, intercollegiate athletic programs are at the forefront in the use of cor-

Paul Glenn and Patrick Cobb are both with the Department of Sport Science and Physical Education, Georgia Southern University, Statesboro, Georgia.

porate sponsorships as a marketing tool. Corporate sponsorships could become a key ingredient in the marketing mix of collegiate athletics, primarily due to their cost effectiveness and suitability as a supplement income.

Without dwelling upon the unethical behavior that has plagued the reputation of collegiate athletics in the past, it does point to the need for examining corporate sponsorship as it relates to possible opportunities for escalating ethics violations. By analyzing current issues, potential users can evaluate the readiness of their programs for introducing corporate sponsorship. The concerns include the who, what, when, and why of usage; professionalism and commercialism; management and NCAA regulations; state versus private funding and revenue; the prostitution of athletics for the sake of money; and the compromise of academic integrity and the institution's image. Examination of these concerns may serve as a gateway on the road to greater awareness of the complexity and possible complications of building an association between a corporation and a university. Collegiate athletic programs must be aware of the potential consequences before actively pursuing corporate sponsors.

What is meant by corporate sponsorship? One definition identifies corporate sponsorship as a corporation's use of its product, image, and financial backing to fund an event or program to allow a diversion of costs, to increase public awareness and patronage, and to ensure a revenue status for the event or program. To a certain extent, corporate sponsorships already have widespread involvement in college sports. College bowl games have used corporate sponsorships to increase monetary rewards, thereby attracting higher quality competition. Basketball shoe contracts, golf and tennis equipment free lists, and scoreboard advertisements have transitional connections with business. Where corporate sponsorship needs further examination is in regard to the actual subsidization of college athletics. This refers not only to event sponsorship such as football games, but the subsidizing of an entire sports program.

The stage was set for corporate sponsorship of college athletics when a group of major universities began to negotiate television contracts for their major sports events. For corporations, the increasing costs of television advertising, its cost effectiveness, and the desire to associate with sports have made college athletics an integral part of their marketing plan. The trend in sponsorships seems to have flourished particularly since the 1984 Los Angeles Summer Olympiad. Many sponsoring corporations made little, if any, profit, but gained significant media exposure and enhanced the image of the firm.

Naturally, big business seeks opportunities to associate itself or its product with collegiate sporting events because of the immense viewership and image of amateur athletics. Collegiate sports remain one of the last vessels of sponsorship left for corporations. The question is: Is it prudent to assume that our college and university athletic programs are ready for this form of marketing? Pertinent concerns should be examined for their possible effects on institutions of higher learning and their athletic programs.

WHO, WHAT, WHEN, AND WHY OF USAGE

Who?

Who examines the level of collegiate sport best suited for corporate sponsorship? Obviously, the additional funds and revenues that accompany sponsorships could benefit programs experiencing financial difficulties. A southern university with a nationally recognized academic reputation has become one of the first institutions to actively pursue corporate sponsors for its home football games. Low attendance as a result of a series of mediocre seasons was part of this university's rationale in seeking sponsorship. Despite a strong academic tradition and thousands of wealthy alumni, this university is not immune to the financial strain of having a revenue-producing sport in the red. Nevertheless, the question must be posed: Should an institution with this prestigious academic reputation use a corporate-based form of revenue production?

On the other hand, several Division I powerhouses throughout the United States have fallen under extreme criticism for various academic infractions. Many of these visible and successful programs would be viewed as quite a prize to corporate sponsors. These so-called superconference schools, in most cases, have proven revenue-producing capabilities, which raises questions of the need for using corporate sponsorship. In addition, would the increased revenue only further corrupt an academically perplexed institution? Each institution's situation will carry with it a different set of concerns about introducing a sponsorship program.

A third level available to corporate sponsorship includes smaller Division I and I-AA programs. Typically, these are regionally popular, but less visible programs. Sometimes they rely on guaranteed money games against larger Division I competition as a means of supplementing the budgets of their entire athletic program.

Division I-AA programs, like Arkansas-Little Rock, have had to cut sports due to financial strain. A corporate sponsorship could help the situation these schools face, but at what price to the institution's pride and reputation? Also, because of the limited television coverage of smaller schools, corporate sponsors might be hesitant to negotiate with institutions located outside a major market area. The decision on who should use corporate sponsorship is complex because of the variables that exist in our academic institutions.

What?

What sport should be sponsored and what is the level of return that corporations are looking to receive from their investment? The sport and corporation of choice should go hand-in-hand depending on the image and patron. The largest sponsors of the collegiate revenue-producing athletic events generally include major U.S. breweries. (Wilber 1988, 25) The representation of a program within an institution of higher learning by a beer company seems a questionable practice. Any benefit to a large program could potentially be offset by damage to the image of the program and the school. On the other hand, minor college sports like golf and tennis are developing strong ties to corporations already established as leaders in their area of sport. Up-and-coming sports like volleyball, gymnastics, and track and field are increasingly popular during years of Olympic, Pan American, and World Games. Corporations continuously aim to tie themselves or their products to the image of these amateur events. Collegiate

sport administrators may look more strongly toward corporate subsidization of nonrevenue sports in order to reduce pressure on a revenue sport. In any case, the university or college seeking sponsorship must determine whether the image of the business seeking entrance into the market is compatible with the desired image of the university as well as the athletic program itself.

When?

In answering the question of when to establish a corporate sponsorship factors like revenue needs and justifying the basis of the decision must be addressed. As indicated earlier, cost containment in college athletics is a different proposition. If there is reliance on a single revenue-producing sport, as is often the case, the budgeting process can leave otherwise fine-caliber programs in shaky positions. The tragic irony of the situation is that corporations, in general, are interested primarily in sponsoring successful programs, not mediocre ones. Use of corporate backing by sponsoring unrelated sport and social events aimed at potential boosters is a use of corporate backing that could combat this situation. A golf tournament or dinner with a business backing could garnish positive exposure for the corporation and create a climate of positive giving for the institution.

The decision to introduce any form of sponsorship must consider the proper entry point. A program that initiates corporate sponsorship during a crisis period places obvious obstacles in the path of acquiring and retaining a sponsor. On the other hand, a tradition-laden and successful program is likely to be able to pick and choose sponsors with ease. However, many intercollegiate athletic administrators feel that establishing a corporate sponsorship is not necessary for programs that are already successful. Establishing the proper entry point is a key criterion for understanding when this form of marketing should be used.

Why?

Why establish a corporate sponsorship? The answer to this question will help administrators understand the benefits to a corporation of investing money in sponsorship and why an institution of higher learning might consider this type of marketing tool. There are two reasons that contribute to why a corporation would sponsor a sports event (Gardner 1987, 12). First, sponsorship is a means for corporations to invest in events that support corporate objectives or enhance the corporate image. Secondly, corporations are looking to sponsor events that maintain marketing objectives or increase product awareness. Big business knows that sponsorships are a cost effective way of using groups to establish or clarify perceptions of the corporations and the products they offer. Because of skyrocketing costs in advertising, big business is interested in sponsoring areas of sport that can help provide mass exposure and promote the image they desire.

The reasons why a university may consider using promotional tools like sponsorships are rooted in government and NCAA guidelines. Title IX has created a double whammy for many programs (Skousen 1988, 43). An increasing number of athletic programs are being required to beef up traditionally nonrevenue women's sports, a tedious task for programs desiring to move up to the Division I level. An attempt to meet Division I requirements without proper financing can be treacherous because of the enormous cost of adding new sports (Oberlander 1988b, A37). A corporate sponsorship could seemingly benefit a university or college wishing to beef up its athletic program; however, this does not always prove true.

Why might a financially solvent athletic program desire to experiment with corporate sponsorship? As indicated earlier, sponsorship is a wide open field and can be used in innovative ways. One argument in favor of corporate contributions is that they can provide more opportunities for academic endowment. A problem, however, is that many universities experience adverse relationships between the athletic and academic communities. The increasing academic tribulations of athletic programs portrayed by the media could be changed with a combined corporate and athletic department effort toward improving the image of the institution's athletic and academic endeavors. A possible application would be to permit institutions suffering from academic woes to develop sponsorship revenue that would be used for making academic improvements from within the athletic program. Most flagship universities do not need additional revenue to support their athletic programs. Yet, a corporate-sponsored academic program could greatly benefit a tarnished academic image and present a positive and uplifting image for a sponsor. This could also benefit the recruitment of athletes under the controversial Propositions 42 and 48.

Summary

The first section of this essay has attempted to demonstrate the relationship between the who, what, when, and why of introducing a corporate sponsorship to the intercollegiate environment. The considerations must be inspected and weighed against the goals and objectives of the athletic and academic communities. Some of the complexities associated with the merger of two forms of big business has been presented. Now, the drawbacks and limitations of using this form of marketing will be discussed. A major concern in using corporate sponsorship is how it can be used to advance athletics, and at the same time restore and maintain amateur athletics and academic integrity.

PROFESSIONALISM AND COMMERCIALISM

A discussion of college athletics must, at some point, address the concerns of professionalism and commercialism. But first, the reader should gain an appreciation of attributes new to sport. A primary concern is the current trend of requiring intercollegiate athletics to operate on a for-profit basis. This is a tedious task because of the wide variety of regulations and limitations placed on athletics by the NCAA. Another concern is that sport is no longer self-promoting. Marketing is as essential to a successful program in collegiate athletics as it is in business. And finally, sport is a product whose consumers exhibit a strong emotional attachment and therefore requires a harder sell than other commodities. Demographics have demonstrated that almost all Americans come into contact with sports on a daily basis. Consequently, our academic institutions, public or private, and their athletic program performances are constantly under media and consumer scrutiny.

Webster's II Riverside Dictionary describes commercialism as a distinctive use of a system designed for profit and supported by advertisement. Does this sound vaguely familiar? The point is that athletic programs in our cherished universities and colleges are vehicles of commercial entertainment and enterprise (Chu, Seagrave, and Becker 1985). A question worthy of reflection is whether the consumer and/or alumni might actually prefer less commercialism. Or does the hype and glamor of big-time programs satisfy a public desire for attention? Tulane University disbanded its basketball program because of game-fixing allegations and connections with professional gambling. They

vowed not to restore the program unless three conditions were met: the end of commercialization of college sports; the elimination of the culture to win at all costs; and the removal of the economic incentives in intercollegiate athletics (Cramer 1986, K2).

From what we understand about commercialism and its often negative connotation, is the addition of corporate sponsorship likely to perpetuate such an image? As was previously highlighted, indirect corporate endorsements in shoe, equipment, and scoreboard contracts have high visibility and are forms of commercialism accepted as part of the game. According to Fred A. Miller, athletic director at San Diego State University, 80 percent of all college sports have some sort of corporate sponsorship (Lederman 1988, A37). San Diego State has used this form of marketing to reduce a $1 million deficit. The choice was economic—engage in sponsorship or reduce the athletic program. But is there time after program revitalization to end this form of revenue production? In effect, an athletic association may become addicted to corporate dollars.

Commercialism in smaller programs can make or break the entire department. Big-time programs grow faster with less effort. Some universities look for event sponsors for their home football games asking between $75,000 to $300,000 per game. Smaller programs may also use corporate-sponsored events to supplement special occasion days designed to increase attendance. For example, a Hardees Hall of Fame Day or Holiday Inn Alumni Day could be promoted as special occasion events. More radical types of promotion could be used during capital campaigns. A small but dynamic program may have problems generating donations for a new facility. Picture General Motors Stadium or McDonalds Field at your favorite institution. Although it seems extreme and unbelievable, once open to invitation the results could be surprising.

Professionalism, as defined by *Webster's II Riverside Dictionary,* is the participation in a profession, like organized athletics, for pay. This includes professional standing, techniques, attributes, or ethics. With little question, college athletics supports the second part of the definition. Some students participate in college athletics with a single-minded determination to make it to the professional ranks. Even though the odds of achieving this goal are astronomically stacked against these visionaries, thousands continue to pursue this dream, reluctant to acknowledge that their probability of succeeding is limited. Bona fide student-athletes do exist in the minor and revenue sports in college athletics. These individuals participate in sport as an avocation but do not make participation the focal point of their lives. Obviously, this is a preferred situation to that where the winning-at-all-costs attitude prevails.

What effect would corporate sponsorships have on professionalism in college athletics? Should we set higher standards for our intercollegiate athletes, or should we adopt policies similar to those of the Olympics and allow athletes to retain their amateur status while endorsing or wearing a sponsor's product? The purpose is not to debate the amateur status of student-athletes, but to consider the question of professionalism with regard to intercollegiate athletic programs in their entirety. Would the sponsorship of an entire program or event be considered a breach of amateur athletics under the interpretation of NCAA rules? The NCAA disallows the payment of individual athletes, but permits big dollar payoffs from corporate-sponsored games. Why couldn't corporations or individuals sponsor players, positions, or entire teams? To a certain extent, this is already being done in the form of endowment, where individuals do not receive pay directly, but scholarships for sponsored positions are guaranteed. Presently, this form of sponsorship is providing valuable resources for teams needing scholarship stability. Unfortunately, it also creates the potential for corruption, win-at-all-cost attitudes, and misappropriation of funds.

Needless to say, commercialism and professionalism in intercollegiate athletics exists, if only in attitude, techniques, and ethics. Considerations of corporate sponsorship in college programs must be accompanied by effort to prevent its misuse. Used appropriately for containing the costs of single events, corporate sponsorships could be developed into a successful and ethical tool of college sport marketers.

MANAGEMENT AND NCAA REGULATIONS

Minimally speaking, the administration of college athletics is a precarious profession. Athletic administrators encounter external pressure from academicians, boosters, conference and association forces, and media; and they regularly face internal pressure from coaches and players. Balancing the interests of all parties and managing all the hands that touch athletics is, at best, an ulcer-producing responsibility. Traditionally, successful coaches of multimillion dollar programs have also performed the critical role of athletic director. While many coaches offer outstanding abilities in scheduling and motivating, they often lack the skills needed to properly conduct and oversee the business and booster functions. Additionally, conflicts of interest often exist among the sports in such a program. Athletic departments run by improperly trained administrators are often those programs in which rule improprieties are discovered. Eventually, these programs become the subject of NCAA investigations and are penalized for violation of the rules. A prime media target for 1989 was a coach/athletic director at a major southern university. In another program, a regional university recently suspended its basketball program for a year and fired its first-year athletic director because of a $80,000 debt incurred in the attempt to restore the football program (Oberlander 1988a, A37). Poor management can inhibit or destroy institutional growth, with or without corporate sponsorship. Corporate sponsorship added to an already mismanaged program can be a death threat to our athletic and academic communities.

Just as a president or chancellor is the chief executive officer of an institution, an athletic director is the CEO of the athletic department. Little doubt exists as to whether college athletics is big business. The issue in question is the readiness of some administrators to properly plan, direct, organize, and control big-time athletic programs. Some educators see college athletics as out of control (Ivey & Recio 1986, 136). Presently, the marriage of high-powered athletics and corporations is made in corporate board rooms and television negotiation sessions (*NCAA News,* 13). Corporations and broadcasting companies already have the power to persuade colleges and the NCAA to make schedule changes. The seemingly inevitable use of corporate sponsorship can become a vehicle for increased corporate influence on college athletic activities. Will we see corporate executives included in booster and athletic executive committees?

The term "out of control" is not as much a threat as a reality in college athletics. The deemphasis of faculty-controlled athletics is said by some to be a factor that encourages booster and athletic department improprieties. The damages include the demise of professional reputations and the degradation of academics (Oberlander 1988a, A38). An athletic program that is sincerely interested in restoring its academic standards should see to it that institutional control can be exercised through its faculty. Argu-

ments for and against a return to this procedure could be presented. Whatever the path taken, an authentic effort to reestablish a fundamental system of control should begin with a cooperative effort between the academic and athletic communities of an institution.

Any issue of control in athletics must include an understanding of the National Collegiate Athletic Association. The constitution of the governing body of intercollegiate athletics clearly states its purposes and fundamental policy for guiding member institutions. Article Two, Section One of the NCAA Constitution has nine indicated purposes, which include improving programs for student-athletes and promoting and developing educational leadership (Tow 1988, 7). In Article Two, Section Two, the Constitution of the NCAA (in Tow 1988, 7–8) states its fundamental policy:

> A basic purpose of this Association is to maintain intercollegiate athletics as an integral part of the educational program and the athlete as an integral part of the student body and, by doing so, retain a clear line of demarcation between college athletics and professional sports.

Impressive on paper, but in reality the only difference between college and professional sports is that college athletes can not legally receive payment for playing the game. The recent exposure of illegal athlete privileges at many institutions also raises questions of whether student-athletes are an integral part of the student body. The NCAA remains, in most cases, helpless in enforcing the true purposes and policies in its constitution. The NCAA enforcement efforts are to be commended, but reform can only be managed from within the athletic and academic communities of individual institutions.

If the NCAA regulations are examined closely loose references to corporate sponsorship can be found in the Executive Regulations on Championship Meets and Tournaments. The NCAA is a competent administrator of these events and has established policies excluding advertisements that are not in the best interest of higher education (Exec. Reg. 1–19, A). The statement most closely related to corporate sponsorship is in Executive Regulation 1–19, C on advertising. The regulation states, "No commercial advertisement may relate, directly or indirectly, the advertising company or the advertised product to the particular institutions or their athletes, or the association itself, unless prior written approval has been granted by the NCAA executive director." (Tow 1988, 221). Some would suggest that corporate sponsorship is a form of promotion, so the restrictions indicated in the regulations do not apply. Others would say that corporations are still relating themselves to an institution and its athletes indirectly in sponsorship.

Two problems arise from managing the marriage of corporations and college athletics: the potential for new avenues for cheating to open up and the increased likelihood that attitudes of winning at all costs will be perpetuated. Article Three, Section One of the NCAA Constitution follows through the Principles of Amateurism and Student Participation (Tow 1988, 9). A student-athlete can be declared ineligible if he or she commercially endorses a product while still under the umbrella of the institution. Yet, an institution will accept a corporation as a sponsor, use its products, and thereby help the corporation to improve its image, gain exposure, and enrich its financial position. Operating in this manner, a corporation may use the institution and its athletes as indirect endorsers of itself and its products. The NCAA clearly defines its legislation in order to prevent the exploitation of student-athletes, but should regulations be proposed to guard the university or college? The rules applying to individual athletes endorsing products is under constant criticism. To revoke

the regulation would create an obvious situation of professionalism, and would undoubtedly place even more pressure on student-athletes and their time than that which already exists. Relaxing the existing regulations could totally undermine the purpose of education.

Regulations with regard to athletic equipment permit manufacturers to publicize a school's use of their product provided they do not name or picture individual athletes. Equipment advertising through an already attached and standard logo on the athletic uniform is allowed. In a sponsorship plan, a manufacturer could contract for exclusive product usage in exchange for advertising privileges. There are those who say this already exists, but at what point does good business turn dirty as sponsors compete for contracts? Unfortunately, even though corporate sponsorships would cut costs, the drawback is that it compounds the growing commercialism of college athletics.

One goal of the NCAA is to protect the status of amateur athletics. The task of member institutions is to assist the NCAA in the supervision process. The political and emotional climate that accompanies athletic programs has accelerated tendencies toward commercialism and professionalism. A win-at-all-cost attitude, sometimes combined with poor management, has given rise to the deterioration of the ethics of athletics and of the image of educational institutions.

STATE VERSUS PRIVATE FUNDING AND REVENUE

It is important to the total picture of a college athletic program to establish a clear understanding of the rationale underlying athletic funding and its support base. The source of funding, although not tied directly to ethics in athletics, often gives rise to philosophical differences within an institution's athletic program. Two basic concepts are examined: (1) the influence gained by the funding agent and (2) where education and athletics stand in relationship to funding provided. Influence refers to the power that sources may exercise as a result of funding, either directly or indirectly, to sway or affect a program's direction or decision making. Few would dispute that athletic departments choose to remain autonomous, whether or not state legislatures permit the use of state money to fund athletics. Some schools have chosen to cut back programs rather than accept state funding (Lederman 1988b, A34). The administrators point out that the taxpayer's money was designed for academic purposes only; however, there are those who believe that broader uses of the money are also appropriate.

Institutions facing budget deficits are wary of losing program autonomy and falling prey to the influence of state legislators. Let us say, that an institution decides to subsidize its program by using business or corporate funding. Would this create the same probability of influence? Either method could be used as a cost containment measure and could serve as a vehicle for sponsoring nonrevenue sports. State-supported schools will typically pay coaches' salaries, give tuition waivers, and assist in facility renovation and maintenance (Lederman 1988a, A25). Likewise, referendums for additional sales taxes on cigarettes or beer have been proposed to support nonrevenue sports. Contrast this with the addition of corporate dollars and the adoption of a corporate name. This choice of funding may allow the department to maintain autonomy from the state, but can possibly result in image damage or influence peddling. Dangers in many forms are created when an athletic program operates under financial strain. The question to be addressed is which influence is worse.

A second aspect of funding strikes at the heart of the issue, namely, the university's over-

all funding policies as they relate to the funding of an athletic association. A major concern eventually arises relating to just how important athletics are to the state. Does college athletics hold a position of importance over other state programs such as health care, prison overcrowding, and elementary and secondary education? Or should the state give athletics increased support when academic salaries remain substandard to national averages? These are emotional questions for educators and political land mines for legislators. The complexity of this issue may explain why Americans hesitate to support programs for athletics with state taxpayers' money and serves as a major reason why funding by the state has such limited place in collegiate athletic programs. Even so, limited state funding could still serve a purpose in association with collegiate sports. Improved student development programs with strict accounting systems could help fill the gap between education and athletics.

The future success of many programs depends upon meeting the expected profits from revenue sports. This brings about a situation in which a program must be successful in order to turn the profit necessary for maintaining the projected yearly budget. Is it morally or ethically proper to force the athletic program for an entire college to survive off the revenue of a single sport? Is corporate funding a feasible alternative for increasing revenue?

As pointed out earlier, many states do not permit state funding of college athletics. This is probably good in that these states, as well as their governing agencies, may show considerable capital funding favoritism to the larger, more politically prudent, institutions. The ancestral support of the football programs at flagship institutions insures growth and revenue. The additional monies available from bowl games and television appearances enhance an already exorbitant income. In contrast, a smaller institution with dwindling attendance figures is forced to solicit sponsorship to offset a loss in income after a decade of losing seasons. Hundreds of smaller schools are surviving on bare bones budgets. Even successful Division I-AA football programs need the big money payoff from games against Division I competition to adequately budget nonrevenue sports.

Revenue and funding, no matter at what level, are of incredible importance to program survival. Consequently, improprieties often arise and win-at-all-cost attitudes develop in pursuit of this success. If tradition is failing and losing is prevalent, additional income sources are necessary to sustain an active program. This places enormous pressure on administrators, coaches, and athletes. The donations to successful programs rise as teams succeed or as aggressive booster campaigns are waged. A successful revenue sport like football can eliminate debts almost overnight. Vehement arguments occur over how much winning increases attendance. Regardless, we do know that a combination of success and good promotion can certainly affect attendance and alumni giving, thus increase the revenue of an athletic program.

PROSTITUTION OF COLLEGE ATHLETICS FOR THE SAKE OF MONEY

Prostitution means ''to devote to an unworthy or debasing cause.'' These are strong words that represent an issue of critical concern to athletic departments looking to begin corporate sponsorship drives. Two primary considerations are (1) the corporate influence on and sponsorship preferences for institutions and (2) the less than expedient handling of money in college athletics. A background discussion of business growth and prostitution of college athletics is presented first.

In the book *The Political Economy of College Sports* the term ''corporate athleticism'' is used to describe the influence of the business ethic on the new sports system (Hart-Nibbrig and Cottingham 1986). In the business world, the rate of failure is astronomical. A case in point is the savings and loan industry. Once numerous and thriving, the forces of inflation, decreasing trends in saving, and the move toward total banking have caused the savings and loan industry to crumble. Consequently, today it is survival of the fitness among saving and loan enterprises. Correspondingly, college athletic programs that, in the past, were not forced to work at generating profits, are now under pressure to perform or face the elimination and extinction of certain sports. Inflated costs in housing, tuition, feeding, travel, equipment, and maintenance have provoked many into cutting back on the number of athletic teams sponsored. Intercollegiate athletics has reached a point, like any good business, where crucial evaluation of its entire program must be done to maintain financial stability.

Another concern is the potential price athletics may pay by losing its character as a form of amateur athletics. The NCAA has an entire manual set out to protect the amateur status of the athlete. Conversely, intercollegiate athletics is a business and is certainly a commercial enterprise. Hart-Nibbrig and Cottingham (1986) were quite accurate in their assessment of corporate athleticism. The incredible obsession with winning and making money has seen college athletic programs fall prey to the principles and ethics of business. The result is the prostitution of a program, designed for amateur athletics, for the sake of money.

To this point, considerable attention has been placed on a corporation's institution of preference. Corporations will attempt to use the largest and most visible institutions to project the corporate product or image. The unification of corporations with intercollegiate sports could enhance an already questionable business philosophy in college athletics. The dilemma is, at what point or level does a program need corporate subsidy, and when is a sponsor likely to exert pressure on a university's product or operation. The prevailing belief is that with increasing participation and funding, a corporation will desire greater influence over the decisions surrounding the event or program being sponsored. As this occurs, the door is left open to the unethical business practices that are becoming increasingly evident in college athletics.

America loves a winner and exalts the programs and athletes that have proven themselves to be winners. To the vast majority of coaches, players, and administrators, success on the field is of utmost priority, no matter the cost. Imagine the attraction of the options available to a highly successful athletic program as the result of added revenue from corporate sponsorship. Now, picture a struggling athletic program using the revenue to finance the rebirth of its revenue-producing sports. Finally, envision the cost savings represented by having nonrevenue sport participants outfitted exclusively with a corporate product in exchange for advertising rights. The level of influence that corporations could establish within our athletic programs is alarming.

The influx of corporate dollars into a department could compromise the independence that athletic departments cherish. In return for their investment, business leaders may demand to be a part of the decisions made on sport policy. An athletic department with designs on using a corporate sponsor must evaluate the potential damage to their autonomy and image. A college sport marketer must critically appraise all aspects of usage in order to safely receive the best results. Once penetrated by business, what is next for college athletics? The selling of common stock in athletic programs and establishing

a board of directors? Let's hope that common sense prevails.

Another potential problem is the unwise allocation of money in college athletics. The addition of corporate sponsorships to a mismanaged program will undoubtedly accelerate any existing irregularities. A business that has a stake in an athletic program's success may use its influence to recruit athletes. On the other hand, the increased revenue may bloat already exorbitant budgets in many Division I schools while leaving needed academic programs untouched. A smaller school could use the increased revenue to legitimately boost its athletic budget, but at what cost?

The inherent danger in using corporate sponsorships is having good intentions turn sour. The casual use of one-time events sponsorship could bring about a situation where an institution becomes addicted to the monies that accompany corporate sponsorships. Like any form of dependence, a point is foreseeable when an institution becomes subservient to its addiction. The greatest fear is that an athletic department becomes self-absorbed in turning a profit and loses sight of the aims of the educational institution and of amateur athletics. This is no more than the selling out of our universities through an overemphasis and prostitution of its sport entities.

A false perception prevails about the use of corporate sponsorship. Popular belief is that use of marketing promotion methods like sponsorships will help improve program deficits. The reality is that it is just another form of marketing subject to widespread exploitation without proper management. Benefits do exist from using an arrangement such as corporate sponsorship, but administrators must recognize that it may increase the commercialization of college sport and deface the integrity of an institution. The following discussion attempts to clarify this concept by investigating the relationship of academics and athletics.

ACADEMIC INTEGRITY AND INSTITUTIONAL IMAGE

The precedent-setting actions of a few college athletic programs that are actively searching out corporate sponsors may further damage a wounded prey. The prey refers to the state of academics and the diminishing respect of institutions as a whole. The picture materializes as a no-win scenario. Athletic departments face increased pressure to produce profits and winning teams. The academic community faces charges of catering to athletes and giving them special privileges. Athletics faces negative media exposure resulting from low graduation rates and the individual athlete's attitude on class attendance (Gup 1989, 55). Include in this the pressure of Propositions 42 and 48 and the press coverage of academic irregularities regarding athletes.

The media's focus on the negatives of the relationship between athletics and education has smudged the dignity and images of many of our prominent institutions of higher learning. The issues of academic integrity and an institution's image will be discussed separately to assist in differentiating the potential problems that corporate sponsorships can bring to these facets of higher education.

Academic Integrity

Corporate sponsorship is not the Darth Vader of the business empire that has come to destroy the academic system. However, an incompetent approach to handling corporate sponsorships could prove devastating to an institution's academic integrity. College athletics, and sports, in general, have long been labeled as a form of commercial entertainment that leads to a displacement of academic concerns. Some suggest that it is the student's obligation to pursue their educational opportunities as well as meet their curriculum requirements. Unfortunately, the attitude and maturity level of some student-athletes yields a single-minded determination to make the starting lineup or to attract the attention of professional scouts. Legitimate student-athletes desire, but seldom receive, legal tutoring in academics and, subsequently, they drop out of school short of a degree when their eligibility expires (Gup 1989, 58). This condition is the result of a decreased emphasis on academic quality while in pursuit of athletic excellence.

What effect could corporate sponsorship have on academic integrity? The first, and most obvious, theory says sponsorship could further entrench academics in a pit of disrepute. A more positive approach envisions the relationship as offering aid to the recovery of academic quality. Some speculation suggests that the increased revenue and athletic income sponsorship could provide would actually increase the opportunity for upgrading academic endeavors. For example, a major southern university's athletic association recently gave $2 million in surplus income to academics. It probably would have been very easy for this university to form a capital project, purchase essential equipment, or initiate some other project to reinvest that surplus into athletics. On the other hand, this money could have been used toward improving the educational success of academically deficient student-athletes. Revenue produced from corporate sources could also help toward providing better tutoring, student development, and career counseling.

The major concern associated with any increased revenue is tied to the question of who is the supervising agent of the athletic program. The philosophy of faculty-controlled athletics may be present in principle, but is often an illusion worthy of Harry Houdini in practice. Faculty control of athletics means that committee members should regulate the activities of that department. The faculty athletic committee may have the power to approve policies and procedures, but is sometimes clueless about the way athletics operates (Oberlander 1988a, A37). The use of corporate sponsorship could further undermine the efforts of educators and signal an increased deemphasis on academics. Although only a speculation, consider the harsh reality of the commercial power that sponsoring corporations hold. The influence brought forward by groups could accelerate revenue, but at a tremendous cost to education.

Institutional Image

The image and integrity of an institution stands to sustain the most serious damage as a result of mishandling their major college sports. Presently, the image of successful basketball programs at some universities are quite different than those of other, more academically oriented universities. The trend seems to be that successful athletic programs are experiencing image problems. Trend busters include outstanding athletic and academic programs like Stanford, Notre Dame, Duke, and the University of North Carolina at Chapel Hill. Additionally, the Ivy League schools are striving to remain the last bastion of amateur athletics by holding to the purpose of intercollegiate athletics as it was originally conceived.

Traditional "football schools" are relentlessly chastised for poor academic standards and lack of educational commitment. These programs present such a powerful image from their "on the field" success that the academic inequalities are often overlooked or ignored. The increased attention given to Propositions 42 and 48 have unearthed buried statistics on low graduation rates and other educational improprieties by athletes and administrators. Schools suspected of preferential academic treatment are receiving counterproductive publicity of these standards for athletes. Without question, this can significantly effect the image of any institution established for purposes of higher learning. Will an intense marketing program be necessary to improve the image and integrity of a university's academic and athletic programs? If so, where would a corporate sponsor fit into the scheme?

The suspicion is that the reputation of a college could be blemished by associating itself too closely with a business or its executives. It is entirely possible that the influence of corporate sponsorship may one day reach into the academic realm. Although it sounds a little far-fetched, the time could come when a struggling academic department will search for a corporate sponsor to provide resources for its program. Picture your favorite institution with the IBM Management Information Systems Computer Resources Center, the Ralston-Purina School of Veterinary Medicine, the Georgia Pacific School of Agriculture, or the CBS School of Communications and Broadcasting. As ridiculous as that sounds, how much different are these notions from an Anhauser-Busch Stadium or a General Motors Stadium? The distinctions are slight when discussing the commercialization of our educational institutions.

This is conjecture about the possible ways in which the fragile reputation of an institution can be damaged by its athletic program. A good public image can positively affect how legislators, as well as boosters, perceive an institution. State-supported schools maintain a delicate balance between governing boards and state legislators. A school that accepts corporate sponsorship for anything more than a single athletic event may jeopardize its reputation as an institution of higher learning. A perception of overemphasis on commercial exploitation of college sports programs could jeopardize the future of intercollegiate athletics.

EVALUATION

The material presented thus far is a critique of foreseeable outcomes stemming from the use of corporate sponsorships. While some appear unlikely, the consequences are conceivable and therefore should be addressed. Corporate sponsorship is a marketing tool that should not be seriously considered without giving equal thought to the possible repercussions. Sport resides in a place of such importance in the American lifestyle that it affords business the opportunity to use athletics and individual athletes as a means of reaching their target markets. The intercollegiate athlete is protected at least partially by the NCAA; however, those who support paying for play think the NCAA should abandon regulations against compensation. All of these problems are surfacing at colleges and universities at a time when corporate America is drawing criticism for misleading advertising and unethical management practices. The merger of two powerful and visible entities like collegiate athletics and corporate business may remove any remaining vestige of amateur athletics.

Six concerns were raised to provide insight into the nature of college athletics and its unstable relationship with the media and consumer. The use of a corporate sponsor may be a good choice if it can be channeled toward curtailing increasing costs and supporting nonrevenue sports. Understandably, unwise use could establish the sponsor as the key element in the program's success. Collegiate athletic administrators must be prepared to use corporate sponsorships positively and ethically.

The quest for a corporate sponsor should be planned from the beginning to provide benefits to the university or college as a whole. Too many collegiate athletic teams carry the entrenched attitude that "winning is everything," which has stemmed from decades of coaching to that single-minded philosophy and from administrators who have placed academics on the back burner. Similarly, the increased commercialism, glamor, and money associated with professional sports have inspired schoolboy athletes to concentrate solely on their athletic mission. Athletic administrators have allowed the recruitment and management of athletes to go unchecked for too long. The addition of corporate sponsorships could pose yet another roadblock toward restoring the integrity of a college education.

Tables 11.1 and 11.2 list some of the circumstances that would favor or should discourage the development of a corporate sponsorship. These lists are not all-inclusive depictions of when corporate sponsorship are appropriate or inappropriate. The number of possibilities and variability of climates make it impossible to establish hard-and-fast rules in this regard. Instead, these lists may serve as a starting point for athletic departments when discussions of corporate sponsorship are begun.

A program looking toward gaining exposure for the university as a whole, as well as its athletic program, has good cause for using a corporate sponsor. The one-time establishment cost to move up to the Division I level is phenomenal. Increased exposure will help the academic program by increasing enrollments and expanding the number of available course offerings. As indicated earlier, the less visible Division I-AA and II programs can barely afford to finance the required sports in their programs. Division I-AA teams that reach the football playoffs sometimes lose money by the time all expenses are paid.

Division I programs looking to improve their academic reputation could benefit by using a corporate sponsor as a promotional tool. Image-enhancing efforts may include tutoring, student development, and career counseling. Schools looking to reestablish revenue-producing sports are facing large start-up costs. A successful

TABLE 11.1 Circumstances Favorable for Corporate Sponsorship

1. A new or small Division I program that needs to gain exposure and increase cash flow to meet the budget demands of its sports.
2. A Division I-AA or Division II program, successful or not, that is having difficulty financing nonrevenue sports and needs greater visibility.
3. Division I or Division I-AA programs that desires to use increased revenue to improve the educational opportunities for athletes.
4. Any level program under a firmly educational-minded administration that desires to upgrade a revenue-producing sport or reduce a deficit, and then return to a self-supporting status.
5. Any level program that desires to use corporate funds as an endowment to improve the stability and number of available scholarships.
6. Any level program that desires to subsidize and promote single events or occasions.

TABLE 11.2 Circumstances Not Favorable for Corporate Sponsorship

1. Established Division I football or basketball programs with already exuberant revenue and budgets.
2. Any level program that desires to subsidize an entire athletic department.
3. Any level program subject to NCAA investigations for recruiting violations or that is looking to increase revenue through indirect income.
4. Any level program willing to use sponsors to promote products not viewed as positive to higher education.
5. Any level program cited for operation mismanagement, unethical behavior, or preferential treatment of athletes.
6. Any level program suspected of using corporate influence to foster win-at-all-costs attitudes or to promote avenues for cheating.

one-time promotion could pave the road to a self-supporting status. Following the successful lead of the University of Southern California, corporate-backed endowments for scholarships could assist struggling programs. This is of greatest concern to Division I and I-AA programs that cannot afford to give all the scholarships allowable by the NCAA. Special events can be profitable for schools using corporate sponsors for general fundraising and charitable functions.

Earnings figures on the 1989 NCAA Championship Basketball Tournaments indicated that the top ten conferences in the country earned nearly $25 million. Sports like big-time college basketball or football do not need any added commercial support. Television contracts and postseason tournaments are already subject to hefty payoffs. Unfortunately, these are the programs lusted after by corporate sponsors because of the exposure they receive. The second point follows from a total aberration of the purpose of intercollegiate athletics and the image of the educational institution. Corporate sponsors should be used to subsidize the costs of nonrevenue sports, but allowing them to subsidize an entire athletic program is selling out at its worst.

Schools whose athletic boosters are notorious for recruiting improprieties should be discouraged from using corporate sponsors. Third, boosters banned from recruiting involvement could discover new and unique approaches by using their business resources to influence a recruit or his parents. The fourth point is straightforward and includes enterprises whose interests to higher education are questionable.

Fifth, athletic programs run by athletic directors not schooled properly in business or marketing typically demonstrate little concern for education. Corporate sponsorship should be avoided at all costs where this condition exists. Coaches as athletic directors represent a conflict of interest and offer the greatest opportunity for schools to be exploited by corporate marketers.

RECOMMENDATION

Finally, an attempt will be made to recommend positive applications for corporate sponsorship programs (Table 11.3). This is a brief and concise list of issues relating to corporate sponsorship in college athletics. Polarities of thought will always be present: one will focus on athletic administrators as genuinely concerned about educational problems among student-athletes; the other will emphasize the danger that tradition and academic integrity will be traded for financial stability and one more win. For athletic administrators and educators, the key to total program success is careful and active control of the available resources through public opinion surveys and internal monitoring of student and faculty opinions. Each of the tables of recommendations has been presented to permit potential initiates to evaluate their environment and judge the merit of corporate sponsorships for themselves.

Article Three, Section One (H,I,V) of the NCAA Constitution states that institutions may provide student-athletes with tutoring, student development, and career counseling services, and may cover the expenses of those services even if they are provided by sources outside of the institution (Tow 1988, 9). An intensive development and counseling program that includes time management could help to turn athletes back into student-athletes. Numerous articles have highlighted the lack of availability of these resources to student-athletes. The positive image and results that could be gained by corporations and institutions are numerous.

Scholarships and grants-in-aid could be administered through the athletic budget and the institution's financial aid department. Although

TABLE 11.3 Recommendations on Corporate Sponsorships

1. Corporate sponsorships used to develop academic programs for student-athletes including special tutoring, student development, and career counseling programs.
2. Corporate sponsors used to fund the grant-in-aid process and help to extend scholarships beyond athletic eligibility years to assist former student-athletes in completing their graduation requirements.
3. Corporate sponsorships used through special events to attract noncorporate sources of funding.
4. Corporate sponsorships in nonrevenue sports whose traditional participants are bona fide student-athletes.
5. Corporate sponsorships used as endowment funds for improving scholarships and academic capabilities.
6. Corporate sponsorships used to fund a one-time or annual event held for purposes of improving exposure, fostering enthusiasm, or promoting self-supporting methods of program operation.

a somewhat radical concept, the benefit to the institutions and athletes as well as the corporation's image would be invaluable. This is especially plausible because the average student, without the load of athletics, generally takes more than four years to graduate. This program, resembling a pension fund, would allow qualified, nonredshirted student-athletes to receive a full or partial endowment and/or possible job placement assistance while finishing their education.

Public events like golf tournaments, arts festivals, and $100-a-plate dinners could be enhanced by corporate backing to foster booster pledges and funding. Special events like these can provide excellent results in combination with charity or youth functions in the community. The baseball program at the University of

Miami is well known for the use of special-event booster campaigns. Today's Hurricane baseball program consistently plays to packed crowds. Campaigns similar to this would make athletic departments less dependent on corporate priorities and preferences.

Minor sport and women's athletic programs are usually the hardest hit during budget cuts. The increased popularity of Olympic and women's professional sports has given rise to new avenues of corporate sponsorship. Corporate sponsors of professional tours would jump at the opportunity to further their image and exposure at the collegiate level. Equipment contracts and academic grants could be negotiated in this process. The only drawback is the likely increase in charges of commercialism and professionalism. Yet, most minor sports like golf and tennis have sponsors at the professional level that consumers recognize as associated with those sports. Adding corporate sponsorship at the collegiate level could benefit the total program.

The University of Southern California has used endowments as safeguards of the future of its scholarships. An individual or business could put down a one-time amount for a position in any program, and the interest from the investment could be used by the school to annually fund that scholarship. This type of arrangement is an excellent way for smaller schools to establish scholarships for an entire program. Smaller schools make good targets because it would open up the budget for smaller sports. Sponsors could gain a lifetime of recognition by sponsoring entire sports through one-time gifts.

Finally, new or smaller Division I and Division I-AA programs could use event sponsorship as a vehicle to solidify budgets. This is the traditional public view of corporate sponsorship. It is also very difficult to obtain because of a corporation's desire to boost its image through a winning program. The drawback of event sponsorship is that it may encourage influence peddling by corporate personnel; however, one-time usage can sometimes bring about enough enthusiasm to return the program to a self-supporting status.

CONCLUSION

The combination of corporations and collegiate athletics is still a relatively new and unpredictable proposition. It is dangerous and should be approached with great caution. If an athletic program is looking to increase its revenue, big business can certainly provide it, especially if the trend of sponsorship saturation in professional events is any indication. What price is intercollegiate athletics willing to pay to maintain autonomy? Corporate sponsorship in college sports is a concept whose time is coming. It is foreseeable that a large number of institutions will put themselves on the auction block. Is it an ethical dilemma or just a false alarm? Only tomorrow will tell.

REFERENCES

Chu, D., J. O. Seagrave, and B. J. Becker, eds. 1985. *Sports and higher education.* Champaign, Ill.: Human Kinetics Publishers.

Cramer, J. 1986. Winning or learning? Athletics and academics in America. *Phi Delta Kappan* 67(May):K1–K8.

Gardner, M., and P. Shuman, 1987. Sponsorship: An important component of the promotions mix. *Journal of Advertising* 6:11–17.

Gup, T. 1989. "Foul!" *Time,* 3 April, 54–60.

Hart-Nibbrig, N. E., and C. Cottingham. 1986. *The Political Economy of College Sports.* Lexington, Mass.: Lexington Books.

Ivey, M., and M. Recio. 1986. How educators are fighting big-money madness in athletics. *Business Week,* 27 October, 136–140.

———. 1989a. I-A consortium out to attract new sponsors. *The NCAA News,* 14 June, 13.

———. 1989b. 60 colleges that play big-time sports debate forming a consortium to use corporate sponsors. *The Chronicle of Higher Education,* 22 February, A37.

Lederman, D. 1988a. Oregonians debate whether to use tax funds to bolster the state universities' flaggering sports programs. *The Chronicle of Higher Education,* 8 June, A24–A28.

———. 1988b. U of Arkansas' Little Rock campus cuts back sports rather than use state funds to make up deficit. *The Chronicle of Higher Education,* 13 July, A34–A35.

Oberlander, S. 1988a. Big-time college sports: The seductions and frustrations of NCAA Division I. *The Chronicle of Higher Education,* 11 May, A37.

———. 1988b. Chapel Hill professors fear that abuse in big-time sports upset university's traditional athletics-academics balance. *The Chronicle of Higher Education,* 9 March, A37–A38.

Skousen, C. R., and F. A. Condie. 1988. Goal posts or test tubes? *Management Accounting* (November):43–49.

Tow, T. C. 1988. *NCAA manual.* Mission, Kans.: National Collegiate Athletic Association.

Wilber, D. 1988. Linking sports and sponsors. *The Journal of Business Strategy* (July/August):20–25.

12

The University and City: A Unique Partnership in the Successful Solicitation of Major Sporting Events

Celia Regimbal and Scott Breckner

Centers for higher education evaluate performance in three areas: education, research, and service. The University of Toledo is no exception to this evaluation model. What does differentiate this university from others is the sometimes "unusual" way in which it becomes involved with the city of Toledo in the performance of the service component. The city and university combine resources to recruit activities for the benefit of both organizations. The University of Toledo and the city of Toledo have realized the benefits of a strong cooperative relationship and have been successful in attracting national sporting events. This can be attributed to aggressive marketing of both the university and the city to sports organizations that have activities that occur regionally and nationally. It can also be credited to exceptionally well-developed bid plans that have responded to every aspect of the request for bids. This essay focuses on the

interface between the university and the city and the resources each can contribute in attracting major sporting events.

Sporting events offer a variety of options for spectators and participants, and "by attracting sporting events, business leaders across the country have realized, they also attract dollars and, perhaps, new business and industry" (Wendel 1988, 14). Facilities are not the only key in attracting major sporting events. Meeting planners are also interested in housing, transportation, staff support, recreational opportunities, and ancillary activities, just to mention a few concerns (Welch 1989).

Members of the University of Toledo work closely with the members of the Greater Toledo Office of Tourism and Conventions (GTOTC) in planning a bid, promotion of an event, and arranging for local and university services and meeting assistance. The executive director of the Office of Tourism and Conventions has developed good working relationships with most of the business and political entities in the community and is able to persuade all the constituents to work together. Nichols' (1987) description of

Celia Regimbal is with the Health Promotion and Human Performance Department, University of Toledo, Ohio, and Scott Breckner is Director of the Berslin Events Center, Michigan State University, East Lansing, Michigan.

convention and visitors bureaus as ''a group of allies eager to make the job easier and quicker'' is a fitting description of the GTOTC.

In preparation for the bid it is necessary to research the particular event, remembering that there is never ''too much'' information to be gained. Each sport has its own national governing body (NGB) which conducts the bidding process for a national event. The process differs depending on the NGB, and it is important to know exactly what the board members are looking for (Welch 1989). Information can be gained from the board itself, past directors of the event, participants in the event, and people in the communities that were affected by the event.

Most national level sporting events have specific requirements for facilities and equipment. Depending on the event, these requirements could include metric court or field measurements, minimum ceiling height, number of courts or fields available in one area, number of locker rooms per facility, meeting rooms for officials, and special athletic equipment that may include particular brand names, electric score boards, public address systems, and training facilities. The bid should include information on all the sites that would be used and how they meet the necessary requirements. Other information may also be helpful in the bidding process such as: unique features of a facility, ability to accommodate the various media, seating capacity, accessibility, and parking accommodations. The research of athletic facilities should include all possible locations in the city and surrounding area so that alternatives can be provided if an emergency change in plans should happen to occur. This information should also include the names of contact persons and their phone numbers. Educational institutions usually provide excellent settings for large sporting events because of the numerous educational, recreational, and athletic facilities in close proximity.

Prior to bidding it is also necessary to take an inventory of hotels and restaurants in the area. It is important to most NGB to know how many beds are available in a city and the price range, since most participants in their events list cost as a major factor when considering whether or not to participate. Not only is cost important when it comes to food and beverage, but in some cases, the ease with which an establishment can handle a large group of people in a short period of time is a factor. Again, the college campus could be a viable as well as affordable resource. With dorms, cafeterias, and staffs capable of handling large groups the NGB might look favorably on the use of these facilities as an option.

Also important in preparing to bid for an event is a plan for funding the various activities that will take place. ''Funding for the running of an event is a major concern that requires thorough evaluation'' (Welch 1989, 51). In order to develop the funding plan it is necessary to develop a detailed budget, one that sets out everything you are going to need before, during, and after the event. This endeavor will alert you to many aspects of the project you are considering. It might even help lower cost by making apparent the areas in which donations of time, services, or materials might be possible. It is also appropriate at this time to develop a staffing plan. Most sporting events take more staff to run them than the NGB provides and in most cases volunteers are a must. The community can be invaluable in providing the necessary manpower and should be involved as much as possible so that the members feel ownership in the event. This involvement carries many benefits including the increased cooperation of the city and the feeling among the participants that the city regards the event as important. Participants are likely to feel more welcome and enjoy the city more, no matter how they fare in the event itself.

As the budget and staffing plans are developed it is also critical to identify local organizations that might enhance the site's chances of qualifying for the event. Regional companies that are involved in the support of the organization on the local or national level, local clubs that are affiliated with the national organization, sports medicine facilities, and sporting facilities which might be nationally recognized are all important in the development of the bid and possibly in the bid process itself. There may also be nationally known celebrities or Hall of Fame members in the community who actively promote sport and would be both willing and able to help bring the event to the city.

As with most convention and visitors bureaus, the GTOTC is invaluable in helping to market the university and the city to the NGBs. The office compiles publicity materials, including videotape, promoting the city as a destination. Very often the videotape is prepared expressly for the group to whom the bid is being made. Also included in the materials are packages offered by hotels that desire consideration as the conference hotel, visitor guides and other informational brochures about the city, maps of the city and surrounding area, airlines and ground transportation information, and any other information deemed important to familiarize the NGB with the city and the university.

The university considers its involvement in soliciting major sporting events to be a significant part of its role as the institution within the city, especially with regard to its commitment to service. The university is able to provide facilities for activities at little or no cost, and members of the university community are able to provide professional service by staffing positions of leadership and skilled labor. In fact, having a person identified as the general chair of an event that can be contacted at any time by the board of directors of the NGB gives credibility to a bid and is advantageous to the bidding process. At the time of the bid presentation, the NGB should be able to meet the general chair, be given an organizational chart with key people identified, know what commitments have been made by the university and the city, and have received a firm commitment for facilities and hotel packages.

Because organizations are judged by the impressions they make on those around them, it is imperative to develop and maintain a high positive profile. Universities that strive to become involved in community affairs and in events that promise to have a positive impact on the community and the participants, convey an image of responsiveness to the needs of both the community and the consumer. If, in fact, $47 billion was spent on sports in 1986 (Wendel 1988, 14), then it is clear that sporting events can have a very positive influence on the economics of the community. Welch (1989) agrees that money, exposure, and prestige all result from hosting a major sporting event. This essay supports that perspective and further contends that any major event that brings hundreds of people into the community and onto the college campus can only be beneficial. This aggressive posture can provide a definite return on effort which will accrue to the institution, as well as the city in which it resides.

REFERENCES

Nichols, D. 1987. CVBs: Allies in your corner. *Corporate Meetings & Incentives,* October, 77–81.

Welch, A. 1989. Competing in the big leagues. *Sports Travel,* August, 49–52.

Wendel, T. 1988. Civic pride gets aggressive. *Sports Inc.,* 19 September, 14–21.

SPORT AND THE LAW

13

Financial Benefits of Trademark Licensing

Dick Irwin

Corporate trademark licensing, a $60 billion a year industry, has been tabbed as the fastest growing corporate marketing strategy (Gareau 1988). Sport managers have also found the licensing of team logos, symbols, and designs equally beneficial, especially as a supplemental revenue source. It has been estimated that by 1995 the annual sales of officially licensed sport merchandise will exceed $4 billion (Sport licensing 1990).

In 1963, the National Football League pioneered the concept of a sport organization granting a second party a license to produce and distribute merchandise bearing logos of franchise teams (Rosenblatt 1988). In the following years, other sport organizations such as Major League Baseball (1967), the National Collegiate Athletic Association (1976), National Hockey League (1979), the National Basketball Association (1981), and the United States Olympic Committee (1985) adopted similar programs. In

Dick Irwin is with the Sport Administration Graduate Program, Department of Physical Education, Kent State University, Kent, Ohio.

1973, the University of California at Los Angeles (UCLA) became the first college to adopt a licensing program (Revoyr 1984), a practice soon to be followed by over 200 universities worldwide. One of the major benefits of licensing is that it has enabled sport organizations to enter the market with little or no capital outlay and minimal risk (Battersby and Grimes 1986).

The consumer demand for "officially licensed" sports merchandise has skyrocketed within the last few years. The sales of NFL licensed merchandise was anticipated to exceed $700 million in 1990 (Vandewater 1990) while NBA merchandise sales soared from $50 million to $350 million during the 1980s (Macnow 1988). Moreover, the growth experienced by Major League Baseball paraphernalia alone quadrupled from $250 million to approximately $1 billion in annual sales during the last decade (Sandomir 1988) primarily as a result of the demand for baseball trading cards and the development of Baseball Clubhouse stores carrying the Authentic Diamondwear collection (McLaughlin 1988). At the same time, expanded media markets have increased the consumer's affiliation with sports teams and thus has increased their demand for their favorite team's merchandise.

From this consumer hysteria for sport licensed merchandise, retailers have significantly benefited. Licensing has been an effective tool in expanding the market for sport merchandise. No longer must a consumer visit the campus bookstore to purchase an alma mater's sweatshirt, nor must they attend a major sporting event to buy a T-shirt; these items are available at the local mall. Merle Harmon, a sports commentator, first coined the concept of "officially licensed outlets" when he founded the Fan Fair retail chain in 1977, and now these types of outlets tally more than $600 million in annual sales (McLaughlin 1988). Furthermore, the manufacturers of the licensed products have benefited from basic supply and demand principles. The unmarked product has little or no market value until the sport logo is applied. Many licensees have been able to capitalize on the recognition and demand associated with being an "official licensee of . . ." some sport organization. However, it is the benefits realized by the licensors that are of significant interest.

In return for granting the right to a manufacturer to produce products bearing their logos, each league, organization, or college (licensor) receives a royalty, generally 6 to 10 percent of the manufacturer's (licensee) wholesale price (Revoyr 1984). The royalties of the NFL, MLB, NBA, NHL, NCAA, and USOC have collectively grown 458 percent since 1985 while the royalties from collegiate licensing have risen 443 percent within the same time frame.

More specifically, the NCAA has seen licensing royalties for the Final Four and other championship events grow from $50,000 to $3.2 million during the 1980s (Krupa 1988) while the USOC, through the Amateur Sports Act of 1978, has exclusive use in the United States of all symbols associated with Olympics (including the word "Olympic") generated $70 million in royalties for the last quadrennium (Rosner 1988). Additionally, each NFL, MLB, and NHL franchise has realized at least $1 million in licensing royalties (Fichtenbaum 1988; Rosenblatt 1988; Sandomir 1988). Several college programs have approached the million dollar royalty figure, and Notre Dame has already surpassed it (Grassmuck 1990).

In addition to simply issuing license agreements to manufacturers, the sport licensing administrator can also implement a number of operational strategies to assist in maximizing royalty revenues. A number of other activities, suggested from the results of a recent study of the operational practise of the NFL, MLB, NHL, NBA, NCAA, USOC, and over 100 colleges nationwide, address the fundamental benefits of trademark licensing—protection of unauthorized logo usage and promotion of the licensing organization.

INVEST IN THE LICENSING PROGRAM

In order for the licensing program to be effective, appropriate resources should be allocated for a general operating budget: legal consultation, including trademark registration; licensing program literature; program promotional mediums; and staffing. It was found that for every dollar "invested" in the licensing program, three were returned in royalties. While financial data were not made available from several of the professional sport organizations, the average collegiate licensing operating budget was $34,000 with several programs reporting expenditures in excess of $250,000.

A full-time licensing directorship with part-time support staff, as is the norm among the sport licensing programs, is fundamental to the program effectiveness at the league or governing body level. Factors examined in determining the appropriate staff size for franchises, universities, or special events include market size, the number of products licensed, and the number of licensees.

IDENTIFY ALL LICENSABLE PROPERTY

The sport licensing administrator should take stock of all logos, designs, symbols, names, and slogans that may have commercial appeal. This may even include facility names where events are held.

LICENSE APPLICATION FEES

Parties interested in obtaining a license should be required to make a formal application, for which a fee can be charged. An application for license, required of all sport licensing programs and a majority of collegiate programs, should request information from the prospective licensee regarding financial reliability, production capacity, marketing and distribution channels, logo usage intent, and past licensing references. Common among several sport and collegiate licensors is to charge the applicant an application fee of $25.

LICENSE AGREEMENT VARIABILITY

The sport licensing administrator has several possible ways to execute licensing agreements. These include the basic agreement to license which may be executed on an exclusive or nonexclusive basis, joint-use or multiple licensor agreements, and promotional licensing agreements. Each method provides the sport licensing administrator with revenue production opportunities.

Exclusive versus Nonexclusive License

Licenses may be executed by sport organizations on either an exclusive or nonexclusive basis. The exclusivity may be based per product category, where the nonexclusive agreement enables numerous manufacturers to produce merchandise in the same product category while the exclusive agreement limits the number of manufacturers for each product category to one. Or, exclusivity may be geographically based, where licensees are designated for local, regional, national, or international distribution. The nonexclusive licensing agreement, favored among collegiate licensing programs, inherently promotes competition among similar product manufacturers in a manner that has been beneficial to the industry. The exclusive agreement, preferred by sport organizations, provides the licensor with greater leverage in negotiating licensing fees, expedites communication and production, and more efficiently combats unauthorized use of logos.

Joint-Use License

Joint-use agreements are utilized by a majority of sport organizations, and they promote cooperative effort between two or more parties who split royalties proportionally. Joint-use agreements have been executed by the NCAA with member institutions participating in national championships (Krupa 1988); by the University of Calgary with the International Olympic Committee for the 1988 Olympic Games, a venture that netted the university $75,000 in royalties (Sykes 1989); and by various sport and collegiate licensors with prominent cartoon figures the likes of Disney characters, Garfield, The Simpsons, and Peanuts. Each of these programs has enabled the licensors to tap into new consumer markets and generate additional royalty revenues.

Promotional License

A sport licensing administrator may wish to grant a license for logo usage in conjunction with a corporate promotion campaign. For instance, a local fast-food restaurant may be interested in using the franchise logo in a premium giveaway promotion. The fee structure for a promotional license used by a number of the sport and collegiate programs surveyed may be equivalent to regular royalty rates or a flat rate.

ADVANCE ROYALTIES

A common practice among sport and collegiate licensing administrators is to request a royalty advance from licensed manufacturers. Similar to earnest money, the royalty advance is nonrefundable and is applied toward royalties accrued during the term of the agreement. While all professional sport organizations negotiate royalty advances with licensees, collegiate licensing advances were reported to range from $25 to $2,000, often on a per product category basis.

ROYALTY PRODUCTION GUARANTEE

It is not uncommon for sport licensing programs to establish royalty production standards for licensees. For instance, the NCAA requires each licensee to generate a minimum of $10,000 annually, and the NBA commands annual royalty payments of $185,000 from national retail distributors. Failure to meet the production guarantee within the term of the agreement is frequently a basis for nonrenewal of the license agreement.

ROYALTY EXEMPTION LIMITATIONS

At the discretion of the licensing administrator, royalty exemptions may be granted to certain manufacturers, retailers, or organizations. For university licensing programs, items purchased for internal consumption (e.g., athletic and school supplies) are frequently granted exemptions as are items supplied to team members or franchises among the sport organizations. Licensing revenue maximization and operational consistency are more easily achieved through a compulsory compliance, nonexempt policy.

CONDUCTING LICENSEE COMPLIANCE REVIEWS

Compliance reviews, which include the inspection of licensee's accounting records, reveal underpayment of royalties due approximately 50 percent of the time, and in amounts of as much as $100,000 (Harrison 1985). While these underpayments frequently result from honest accounting errors it is imperative that a review system be established to validate the accuracy of royalty payments. Compliance reviews, conducted on a regularly scheduled basis by all sport organizations, should be initiated within the first twelve months after the agreement is executed and repeated as necessary.

MARKET SURVEILLANCE

A program should be implemented for detecting, reporting, and reducing unauthorized use of licensed marks. Program activities should include active "policing" of the marketplace (e.g., retail outlets, gameday vendors) by licensing staff. There should also be personal contact with manufacturers and retailers of unlicensed merchandise and their products confiscated. Cease and desist orders should be issued and, if necessary, litigation started. All of the sport organizations and a number of the colleges analyzed used a type of special identification (e.g., hangtag) to make the licensed merchandise more recognizable. Without a system of licensing program enforcement, sales of unlicensed merchandise will undermine the operational integrity of the program and directly effect royalty revenues and return on the licensing program "investment."

LICENSING PROGRAM PROMOTIONS

Promoting the availability of the licensed products as well as the organization's intent to prosecute against unauthorized usage should have a direct impact on royalties generated. Low-cost, accessible promotional mediums available to the sport licensing administrator include sporting event program ads, event public address announcements, publicity in the local media, and advertising space negotiated to be included in radio and television packages. The NCAA has relied extensively on publicity at Final Four locations to inform the public about the availability of licensed products as well as their intent to confiscate unlicensed merchandise (Krupa 1988; Souvenirs must be licensed 1990). Several of the sport licensing programs and collegiate licensors include an adverting requirement in their licensing agreements thereby passing promotional responsibility on to the licensee.

To complete the licensed merchandise promotional mix, the inclusion of paid media advertising, trade journal publicity, and a direct mail campaign of a licensed merchandise brochure or catalog is suggested. The costs of the catalog production and mailing have been underwritten for numerous licensors by a licensee whose merchandise is prominently displayed. Donations of licensed products for usage in tele-

vision shows, movies, and auctions have also stimulated demand for several sport licensing programs and may serve as an effective means of overcoming advertising restraints. A fully attired fan, otherwise known as a "walking billboard," may make a stronger impression than expensive advertising.

The administrator of the sport licensing program should also design promotional information to generate interest among new licensees. For the administrator utilizing nonexclusive agreements, more licensees in each product category will stimulate competition among manufacturers, which can mean higher royalty revenues. Furthermore, the licensing administrator should actively pursue licensees that can provide an opportunity to extend into diverse product categories or geographical markets.

PROFESSIONAL LICENSING AGENCY CONSULTATION

An alternative to independent licensing program administration is to employ the services of a professional licensing agency. At one time all of the sport organizations and almost 90 percent of the collegiate licensing programs held agreements with licensing agencies. However, today only one sport organization and 60 percent of the colleges retain those services.

Contracting with a licensing agency sensitive to the practice of the industry can insulate the sport licensing administrator from many time-consuming responsibilities. Qualified licensing agencies provide services for legal consultation, compliance reviews, and promotional assistance, as well as an existing bank of licensees. A licensing agency's fee is generally based on a percentage of royalties generated, typically 30 percent. While this fee structure can severely cut into the sport organization's licensing revenues, it can also serve as motivation for the agency to maximize royalties.

As can be seen, there is little question that licensing can provide the sport administrator with added means of producing revenue. Not only is the domestic consumer demand for licensed merchandise projected to grow, but the international market will continue to expand as well due to the "export" of American sports through the media. Therefore, all sport organizations, including newly established major and minor professional leagues, national governing bodies, colleges, and high schools, are encouraged to investigate opportunities for establishing a licensing program. Licensing is an excellent method for organizations to use in controlling their valuable property in, as well as financially benefiting from, a merchandising society. However, if protecting the integrity of the sport logos or the promotional opportunities gives rise to too much emphasis on the profitability available through licensing, problems are sure to arise. A proper balance can be achieved by developing operational strategies for the sport licensing administrator to use in building a solid foundation for royalty revenue maximization.

REFERENCES

Battersby, G., & C. Grimes. 1986. Merchandising revisited. *The Trademark Reporter* 16:271–307.

Fichtenbaum, P. 1988. Hockey comes out of the ice age. *Sports Inc.,* 5 December, 26.

Gareau, R. N. 1988. Corporate licensing—the world's fastest growing marketing discipline. *Trademark World* 14:22–26.

Grassmuck, K. 1990. Colleges fight bootleggers as sales boom for goods that bear logos and emblems. *The Chronicle of Higher Education,* 21 February, A32–33, 36.

Harrison, T. 1985. Solutions to recurring errors in reporting royalty payments. *The Licensing Book* 2(7):10–12.

Krupa, G. 1988. Big bucks on campus. *Sports Inc.,* 5 December, 24–25.

Macnow, G. 1988. Takin' it to the bank. *Sports Inc.,* 5 December, 22–23.

McLaughlin K. 1988. Licensed pro sportswear, it's a hit. *Entrepreneur,* August, 48–54.

Revoyr, J. D. 1984. Licensing: Historical perspective. *The College Store Journal* 51(5):1–3.

Rosenblatt, R. 1988. The profit motive. *Sport Inc.,* 5 December, 18–21.

Rosner, D. 1988. K-Mart, USOC settle counterfeit suit. *Sports Inc.,* 5 February, 16.

Sandomir, R. 1988. "Baseball comes from behind." *Sports Inc.,* 5 December, 16–17.

Souvenirs must be licensed. 1990. *Rocky Mountains News,* 28 March, 19.

Sport licensing. 1990. *The Licensing Book* 7(10):16–17.

Sykes, W. 1989. Collegiate licensing in Canada—a market profile. *Trademark World* 18:46–51.

Vandewater, J. 1990. Walking ads. *St. Louis Post Dispatch,* 30 January, 10.

14 Our Legal System and the Insurance Industry: The Two Most Effective Facets of Society Affecting Sports in America

Marc A. Rabinoff

Professionals in the business of sports and fitness in America have witnessed major growth changes in their field. Major changes have included higher salaries for professional athletes, drug abuse by athletes at all levels, more reports of corruption, and ethics violations by coaches, administrators, boosters, parents, and athletes themselves. We have also seen greater athletic performances—triumphs never thought possible, increasing numbers of adults becoming physically active and living longer, and children gaining greater exposure to recreational sport facilities in schools and in the private sector. A common element links all aspects of the sports, recreation, and fitness business—the good as well as the bad; that element is the influence of the legal and insurance systems on the sports industry.

There are no simple solutions to the problems facing sports in America. This is apparent when the effects of the American legal and insurance systems on the sports industry are examined. An in-depth review of related literature written between the years 1979 and 1989 is presented in the following pages. This review is derived from the study of nineteen journals, ranging from *Glamour* to *Athletic Business;* twenty newspapers, from Denver's local *Up the Creek* to the *Wall Street Journal;* speeches by consumer groups advocating tort reform; and presentations delivered by respected experts including Betty van der Smissen, an attorney and university professor. A bibliography of articles published by *Athletic Business* magazine during the ten-year period of 1977 to 1987 is also provided.

While reviewing this diverse body of literature, issues were categorized in such a way that both professionals and consumers would be able to relate to the picture they provide. Following is a list of those topics:

1. An overview of the impact of the legal and insurance industries on sports in America

Marc A. Rabinoff is with the Human Performance, Sport and Leisure Studies Department, Metropolitan State College of Denver, Colorado.

2. Examples of highly unusual as well as extremely important legal cases
3. Opinions pertaining to tort reform research and product liability
4. The best and the worst of our legal system
5. Schools as victims of the liability crisis
6. Tort reform legislation and malpractice issues
7. The insurance crisis and insurance plans for schools, colleges, and professionals
8. Youth sports, recreational and fitness activities, and the insurance crisis
9. Risk management
10. Update on the insurance industry and sports in America, 1989–1991

These references, as a group, clearly demonstrate that no matter who you are, no matter where you go, you can be sued. There are no waivers or excuses for poor teaching, coaching, or administration, especially when it results in injury or other damages to people or property. The legal system has our number. We are fertile ground for litigation, and the American public is responding as such. Courts and juries are receptive to bringing large awards to plaintiffs seriously injured by incompetent coaches, teachers, or administrators. Yet, they still remain sensitive to professionals who did nothing wrong, even though injury and damage occurred on playing fields, in fitness centers, or in other recreational settings.

We are all part of the problem, as the overview articles illustrate, so we must all be part of the solution. Because of the many strange lawsuits filed, we get a feeling that anyone can sue anybody at anytime, anywhere, for anything, and we are right. However, there are no guarantees the plaintiff will win. As professionals, we all must realize that stupid people can sue just as intelligent individuals can. Age, race, relig-

ion, sex, or intelligence have absolutely no bearing on who sues or who ultimately prevails in these litigations. Sports professionals are well advised to continuously review and reflect on these issues, the results of lawsuits, the awards granted, and the way in which the insurance industry is responding to these litigations.

The research dealing with tort reform and the concepts of liability reveals that this area represents a multifaceted problem that involves a multifaceted solution. Presentations by Richard Feldman, executive director, Product Liability Sports, and Howard Bruns, Product Liability Sports president, delve into the issues concerning the demise of sports and put a lot of the blame on plaintiff attorneys. In Howard Bruns' presentation of March 30, 1987 in Washington, D.C., he states that the "plaintiff bar has been maligned (deservedly) as the *Judas of our society* for its opportunist attack on the weak flank of a judicial system gone awry." Richard Feldman goes on in his presentation to talk about the survival of schools, mainly public schools, in the litigious-natured society into which we have evolved. Feldman says, "We are all in this battle together. It's the sports community versus The American Trial Lawyers Association and they've been winning in the courts up until now. It's high time we fight back and we can kick some political and legislative field goals." The Product Liability Sports organization, now called CAPS (Concerned Americans for Protection of Sports) and located in North Palm Beach, Florida, has been leading the way for tort reform and for changes in our American system to ensure that sports remain part of our system.

The comments of Bruns and Feldman point to the need for assessing the legal system and the functional relationship between the insurance industry and that system—how they work together, where their differences and similarities lie, and how the sports, fitness, and recreation industries can best survive. The majority of people do not understand concepts such as the "anatomy of a lawsuit" which examines how a lawsuit evolves, and the process and procedures lawyers and their clients must go through from the beginning to the end of a lawsuit. This topic has been covered in various journals, texts, law schools, and physical education, sport medicine, and human performance departments throughout the United States. A number of the articles reviewed help to clarify the concept of settling out-of-court, the outcome of 80 to 90 percent of tort cases. Cutting back on jury verdicts, attempting to eliminate the lawsuit in the first place, and greater use of referee systems—all will contribute to slowing the legal system and limiting the legal process to only those cases that truly warrant a jury trial. When these lawsuits ultimately reach the courtroom and juries are asked to render verdicts, it becomes interesting to attempt to understand just how the juries arrive at their decisions. Do they make them based on the evidence, or do other criteria contribute to the judgment? The research clearly shows that juries make decisions for a multitude of reasons, some of which may not include the actual truth or the evidence presented.

Schools can be seen as victims of this liability crisis, and much has been written about the potential for the fear of lawsuits to cripple schools. With serious injuries on the increase, as budget cuts force schools to look for ways to save money, and with a lack of understanding from parents about the value of athletics in the schools, we find schoolboards making decisions to ban or eliminate sports for the wrong reasons. Sport and fitness professionals recognize that accidents will happen, injuries will take place, even death may occur in sport because that is the nature of things. The incident may or may not be the fault of the athlete, the fault of the student, or the fault of the parent. At times, the fault may be poor coaching, lack of supervision, or failure to warn, and when serious accidents take place as a result, multimillion dollar lawsuits can follow. To truly separate out legitimate from frivolous litigations, tort reform is required. Tort reform is the movement at the grass roots level of local, state, and national government to look seriously at who is liable and who should pay for damages rendered. The tort reform issue and liability crisis threatens everyone in sports, and is everyone's problem, including manufacturers who supply the materials and tools of the game. Their obligation is to make sure that this equipment meets the standards as determined by the professionals in the field and that it can be used for its intended purpose without adding greater danger or risk to the fitness, wellness, or recreational activity.

Tort reform legislation started making gains in 1987 as many states began to look for ways of changing the laws to better render liability to the defendants who are most liable, not just to those with the deepest pockets, or the greatest ability to pay the damages. Court reform has made major inroads in Colorado where the state legislature recently enacted the Ski Industry Bill preventing a ski resort from being sued for any inherent risks involved in the sport of skiing. Colorado has given the same protection to equestrian centers. Although some experts believe this will make it very difficult for a plaintiff to sue even if there is negligence on the part of the professional, it nevertheless is a step toward the objective consideration of who is liable and who is not, and who should pay and who should not pay for damages caused in sporting, fitness, wellness, and recreational activities. These debates will continue for many years to come at both the state and national levels, especially as the cost of insurance skyrockets. States such as Florida are approving legislation to relieve the rising cost of medical malpractice and to limit awards and liability for emergency room care for physicians. This may lower insurance premiums for physicians in the future, but care must be taken to avoid protecting incompetent physicians as well as incompetent coaches behind legislation that could unfairly prevent plaintiffs from seeking restitution for damages that a jury may have found were due. Today we find more insurance companies, due to this type of legislation, looking toward the area of risk management. The issue is clear here for insurance companies: exercise risk management before insurance coverage is awarded to a client. The risk management should include a complete analysis of the facility, personnel, staffing, equipment, policies, and facility operations. This study should be conducted by experts in the field who can clearly let the insurance carrier know where the exposure and potential risk is and what is recommended to minimize it. In the short and long run, injuries will be kept to minimum, damages will be kept to a minimum, and lawsuits will be kept to a minimum. This should make everyone happy.

This insurance crisis has certainly had its effect on businesses related to sport, and the literature bears this out. Lawyers have urged federal insurance regulations, since the insurance companies basically have federal control over what it is they do and how they do it. Small companies are being affected by insurance premium increases, with the result that fewer and fewer people are able to remain in business because of the cost of their premiums. For the last few years, the insurance industry has been in a soft market, but developments in 1991 and 1992 indicate a return to a hard market. This would result in fewer insurance companies offering insurance coverage to the sports, fitness, wellness, and recreation industries. Consequently, insurance companies will be looking to risk management as a means of keeping costs down, in turn making it easier for businesses to purchase the insurance necessary for their financial security.

As the market changes through cycles, new concepts for insuring high school athletics, college athletics, and even professors and coaches are developed. The NCAA now has a checklist for its members' insurance coverages. In 1986 and 1987, the NCAA budgeted $947,000 for catastrophic insurance as compared to $0 in 1986. General liability rose to 24 percent during the same period. Along with these increases, we find many colleges and universities forming self-insurance pools. School districts and municipalities have also decided to form self-insurance pools as the cost of insurance continues to escalate. The concept of self-insurance is a good idea, but only if risk management programs are in place to ensure that an injured athlete will be covered. Additionally, the welfare of the athlete will be given greater priority than ever before through the consideration of the facility, the coaching, and all the other elements that can affect the safety and effectiveness of the environment in which the athlete performs. Many studies have examined the principles of no-fault insurance and the reduction of injuries due to the addition of certified high school trainers. These studies clearly show that as more professionals are hired, the rate and severity of injuries continues to decline. The immediate question is whether school districts, boards of trustees, and governmental agencies can afford to pay for these professional employees. The answer is that they must. If they fail to do so, the cost of insurance will continue to skyrocket, as will injuries.

Faculty members and administrators are now beginning to obtain their own professional liability insurance. The coverage is geared toward, but not limited to, legal action that may come from dismissals, suspensions, disciplinary sanctions, layoffs, salary disputes, or nonreappointment of probationary personnel. Professional organizations such as the American Alliance for Health, Physical Education, Recreation and Dance, the American College of Sports Medicine, and the American Council of Exercise have established insurance programs for professionals who are licensed, certified and/or degreed. The future will see increasingly creative plans for insurance coverage offered by carriers who are taking a look at their industry in a new light and with a new vision.

Youth sports and recreational activities are not immune from the insurance crisis. One area that has been greatly affected has been team travel, especially out-of-state. We see that coverage for transportation is limited and has caused school districts significant increases in premiums. In Colorado, the premium for one school district in 1989 went from $5,541 to $18,741. Similar increases have seriously jeopardized varsity team travel for many school districts throughout the country. We find many recreational districts and municipalities closing their doors to taxpayers and consumers due to their inability to obtain insurance coverage. This reduction in opportunities for youth will certainly affect the ability to train and condition future athletes. The research presented is not biased. It presents arguments representing all sides of the controversy.

Ultimately, one must look at solutions to these problems, one of which is risk management. Risk management is a systematic analysis and the review of potential risks in the settings in which the sports, fitness, wellness, and recreation industries operate. Plaintiff attorneys, defense attorneys, and the insurance industry share the responsibility for setting up the potential demise of sport in America. The injured party sometimes recovers financially, the contested sport is often dropped or significantly modified, and the public becomes frustrated by news accounts of the various litigations. Meanwhile, the attorneys, both plaintiff and defense, go away well paid and move on to their next case. When awards are directed to the plaintiff,

the insurance companies either raise premiums substantially or simply drop coverage altogether. The sports professionals remain to battle, to explain, and to regroup, seeking only to survive until the next insurance battle arises. This cycle must be broken. How can it be accomplished?

For starters, sport professionals need to be better educated in the operation of the legal system and the way the insurance industry conducts business. This may be accomplished by attending seminars or workshops. More articles on these issues must be written, and we must begin to talk with attorneys, not avoid them. Information in the form of statistics must be gathered, and insurance companies must be compelled to provide evidence of number of claims, awards paid out, premium incomes, and net profits. Only then can the questioned existence of an insurance crisis be firmly established.

The second step is to become actively involved as a professional and to keep updated on the latest techniques related to coaching, teaching, or administration. The basic guidelines: Never violate people's rights, abuse the system in which you operate, or let your operating standards fall below those established by professional societies or existing legal statutes.

The third step is risk management. This is a method of systematically analyzing facilities, programs, staffing, policies, procedures of operation, and even philosophy and goals as they relate to the safe, effective, and efficient delivery of services to clients. Clients can be students, athletes, adults, or children, in team or individual settings, competitive or just recreational. Risk management provides a sense of where we are and how we can get better in providing these services. The articles presented here offer a clear sense of the purpose of risk management, its value, and the way such programs can be implemented in a variety of settings.

Risk management continues to be the only solution to keeping injuries and lawsuits to a minimum. A complete risk management program requires a basic understanding of liability and legal terms, of the responsibilities of the participant as well as those of management and operations, and of the activities it involves and how they are to be carried out. One way we can understand these issues is to learn from the mistakes of others and review the related literature.

The list of references provided here together establish the depth and breadth of necessary understanding. The use of checklists, safety lists, facility analysis reports, and the employment of outside consultants experienced in the area of risk management for sports, fitness, wellness, and recreation are critical to the success of a complete risk management program.

A new company named Fitness Risk Management Incorporated was established in Denver, Colorado in 1989. Its mission is to work with insurance carriers, providing expert assistance in analyzing facilities, staffing, personnel, and equipment used in the fitness, recreation, wellness, and sports industries. The evidence provided by this company clearly shows that more and more insurance carriers in the 1990s will be seeking this kind of expertise to help them determine who is meeting the standards of care and who is not. This information will influence the issuance and rates of insurance policies. The hope of Fitness Risk Management, and that of the insurance companies, is to make facilities increasingly safer for the consumer. In the 1990s, many insurance companies will offer insurance premiums at a discount to those facilities that have risk management programs. The American Alliance for Health, Physical Education, Recreation and Dance, in updating their facility management text, has for the first time included a chapter dealing with risk management. The material is especially geared to those who are renovating or establishing new facilities.

A November 1991 editorial in the *Journal of Fitness Risk Management* (vol. 1, no. 8), quoted an author in the September 23, 1991 issue of the *Crittenden Excess Surplus and Insider* who wrote, "Claims are increasing faster than premium income as the property/casualty insurance industry creeps along on its painful journey towards a tighter but more lucrative market." The editor goes on to say, "This translates into higher premiums and more difficulty for health, fitness, sport, recreation, and athletic facility owners in obtaining insurance." The point this editor was making was that because the industry is seeking to cut insurance costs, potential risks are going uncovered. Even though this decreased demand prevents premiums from skyrocketing, the exposed risks may very well lead to increased claims and thus increased premiums. Therefore, the editor states, "These companies which implement comprehensive risk management programs may be those least affected by this transition into the hard market. A good risk management program allows health, fitness, sports, recreation, and athletic facilities to enjoy lower premiums even in the face of a hardening market. Insurance carriers and facilities must cooperate to ensure that all appropriate actions are taken to minimize risks in any particular environment."

In conclusion, we are all responsible for the survival of sport, fitness, and recreation in America. No single person or industry is responsible for existing problems, but cooperative effort can help ensure that sports, fitness, and recreation, ingrained and valued as they are in our culture, are given the opportunity to grow and survive rather than disappear.

REFERENCES

I. Overview Articles on the Demise of Sport Due to the Lawsuit and Insurance Crisis in America

Insurance, liability, and the American way of sport. *The Physician and Sportsmedicine,* September 1987.

Sorry, America, your insurance has been cancelled. *Time,* 24 March 1986.

Sport liability insurance. *Athletic Business,* May 1986.

II. Actual Law Suits: What Some People Sue For and Win!

Accused drunken driver blames seeing-light dog. *Rocky Mountain News,* 3 July 1986.

Aurora woman sues over softball injury. *Rocky Mountain News,* 8 April 1989.

Climber's lawsuit a bad precedent. *Rocky Mountain News,* 8 April 1988.

Colorado high court rules W. of Denver is not liable for student's injury. *The Chronicle of Higher Education,* 2 December 1987.

Court orders damages for injured cheerleader. *The Chronicle of Higher Education,* 9 December 1987.

Ex-Denver teacher sues over firing. *Rocky Mountain News,* 3 January 1987.

Father sues school. *Denver Post,* 24 March 1985.

$5 million judgment chills ski industry. *Denver Post,* 8 November 1987.

Golfer's errant shot costs him $22,800. *Denver Post,* 6 December 1987.

GW boy's parent sues to get her son a chance to try out for girls team. *Rocky Mountain News,* 5 September 1987.

Jealous husband gets revenge. *Foreign,* 27 June 1986.

Jeffco schools ruled fair game for lawsuit by injured student. *Denver Post,* 9 September 1987.

Jury awards ex-CU star $250,000 for off-field injury. *Rocky Mountain News,* 31 October 1987.

Jury awards man $1.45 million for wasp sting. *Rocky Mountain News,* March 1988.

Platte diving victim loses damage claim. *Denver Post,* 21 October 1979.

Player's father banned from arena. *NCAA News,* 4 March 1987.

Python's bite prompts $1 million suit. *Rocky Mountain News,* 21 May 1986.

Town to appeal award for frisbee injury. *Denver Post,* 16 April 1988.

Turning paddle on principal draws jail. *Denver Post,* 13 November 1987.

Wife sues over spouse's injury in softball game. *Detroit Free Press,* 8 April 1988.

III. Rabinoff on Sports Liability, Tort Reform, and Product Liability Sports

Braum, Karl. Metro prof lobbies for sports. *The Metropolitan,* 16 October 1987.

Bruns, Howard J. Product liability—sports. Presentation at meeting with members of the U.S. Congress, Washington, D.C., 30 March 1987.

Feldman, Richard J. The extinction of American sports—where have all the Mary Lou Retton's gone? Position paper of

National Sporting Goods Manufacturers Association, North Palm Beach, Florida.

Kenney, Jerry. Lawyers gunning for sports. *Manhattan Daily News,* 22 September 1987.

Mellman, Gerald. Dr. Marc Rabinoff takes the forefront to assure recognition of higher standards in sports industry. *Intermountain Jewish News,* 18 March 1988.

Otterson, Chuck. Mobilizing against insurance dilemma. *The Palm Beach Post,* 10 April 1988.

Rabinoff, Marc A. Who can stop the high cost of insurance? *Looking Fit,* March 1987.

Silva, Lisa Jean. PE professor pushes sports safety. *Metropolitan,* 7 March 1984.

IV. Our Legal System: The Best and the Worst

Barry, Dave. Sue the tar out of everybody. *Miami Herald.*

Big law firms reported getting bigger. *Rocky Mountain News,* 7 July 1987.

Court to study punitive damage awards. *Rocky Mountain News,* 6 December 1988.

Courtroom victors net 71 cents on the dollar from awards. *Denver Post,* 9 July 1987.

Goldie, Diane. Courts are becoming hot-tempered arenas. *Rocky Mountain News,* 20 February 1989.

Goldie, Diane. Court committee works to keep lawyers honest. *Rocky Mountain News,* 6 August 1989.

I'm dumb; therefore I sue. *Denver Post,* 12 January 1986.

Lane, George, and Pat McGraw. Jump in lawsuits worries officials. *Denver Post,* 6 July 1986.

Pankratz, Howard. Case overload jams state's appeals court. *Denver Post,* 31 August 1986.

Quinn, Jane Bryant. Cutting back verdicts. *Newsweek,* 7 July 1986.

Scher, Zeke. Lawyer grievances often without merit. *Denver Post,* 15 April 1984.

Scher, Zeke, and Karen Odom. The megabuck lawsuits: Legal lottery, or reality? *Denver Post,* 3 February 1985.

Shuiruff, Lawrence. Flood of lawsuits inundates courts. *Denver Post,* 28 July 1985.

Simon, Roger. About lawsuits and lawn mowers. *Denver Post,* 3 August 1986.

Taylor, Gary. See you in court. *Spirit,* July 1988.

True, Bob. Settling out of fear—out of court. *Creek,* 4 April 1986.

Welles, Glaris. Lawyers on retainer: Not just for the rich. *USA Weekend,* 20–22 March 1987.

Wishman, Seymour. Guilty or innocent? *Glamour,* September 1986.

The verdict: Litigation is paralyzing America. *Rocky Mountain News,* 15 November 1988.

Vinson, Donald E. What makes jurors tick? *Trial,* June 1988.

V. Tort Reform and Schools as Victims of the Liability Crisis

A window of opportunity for liability tort reform. *Athletic Business,* June 1987.

Eskey, Kenneth. Fear of suits cripples schools. *Rocky Mountain News,* 30 August 1989.

Fairness the real issue in tort reform. *Athletic Business,* November 1987.

The fight for reform. *Athletic Business,* June 1985.

Howe, Jonathan. School sports: A victim of the liability crisis. *School Board News,* 8 July 1987.

Liability crisis threatens everyone in sports. *Athletic Business,* July 1987.

Liability tort reform: Why should you be involved? *Athletic Business,* June 1987.

More states expected to consider tort reform. *Athletic Business,* April 1988.

Product liability reform. *Athletic Business,* January 1987.

Tort system adds 'safety tax' to everyday life. *Athletic Business,* June 1987.

Triathlons' growth brings liability costs. *Athletic Business,* June 1988.

VI. Tort Reform Legislation and Malpractice Issues

Blake, Peter. Senate OKs revising tort reform. *Rocky Mountain News,* 21 January 1989.

Doctors need protection from suit-happy patients. *Rocky Mountain News,* 18 April 1988.

Florida malpractice bill goes to the governor. *USA Today,* 5 February 1988.

Malpractice reform too new to be judged either way. *Rocky Mountain News,* 18 October 1988.

MD's won't deliver for lawyers who sue. *Denver Post,* 14 May 1986.

Sanko, John. Debate over liability to dominate session. *Rocky Mountain News,* 6 January 1986.

Tort reform bill passes first test. *Athletic Business,* September 1988.

Tort reform is working in Colorado. *Denver Post,* 12 October 1986.

Tort reform legislation gains in 1986. *Athletic Business,* September 1987.

Tougher liability laws lauded. *Rocky Mountain News,* 19 September 1987.

Westergard, Neil. Insurance disaster hits Colorado, everyone hurt. *Denver Post,* 22 December 1985.

Westergard, Neil. Tort reform addresses one side of insurance crisis. *Denver Post,* 18 May 1986.

VII. Insurance Crisis: Its Effects on Business and Sports

Aetna hides behind red herring of 'lawsuit abuse.' *Rocky Mountain News,* 23 October 1988.

Best, Allen. Insurance firms catch blame for cost jumps. *The Denver Post,* 24 August 1986.

Carhahan, Ann. Lawyer, Aetna clash over liability awards. *Rocky Mountain News,* 1 December 1988.

Fleming, Robert. Rink takes spill over liability. *Daily News,* 6 May 1986.

Insurance cost rated as top concern. *Athletic Business,* August 1987.

Is there a liability insurance crisis? *Phi Delta Kappan,* September 1989.

Lawrence, John F. Liability: Top worry for business. *Business Outlook,* 23 December 1985.

Lawyers urge federal insurance regulation. *Albuquerque Journal,* 28 December 1988.

Liability's broad impact. *Nation's Business,* June 1986.

Munhall, Kate. Shopping around: The insurance marketplace. *Looking Fit,* March 1988.

Newcomer, Kris. Ski industry told to expect lower rates of liability. *Rocky Mountain News,* 20 June 1986.

Olsen, William. Insurance firms created crisis, Woodard charges. *Rocky Mountain News,* 23 March 1988.

Size of damage awards growing, but slower. *Athletic Business,* March 1989.

Waldman, Peter, and Beatrice E. Garcia. Four big insurers charged with scheme to limit commercial liability coverage. *The Wall Street Journal,* 23 March 1988.

VIII. Insurance Plans for High School Athletes, College Athletes, and Professors

ACSM offers liability insurance. *The Physician and Sportsmedicine,* January 1984.

Berg, Rick. Catastrophic injury insurance: An end to costly litigation? *Athletic Business,* November 1984.

Evangelauf, Jean. Liability insurance for colleges: Costs up and coverage down. *The Chronicle of Higher Education,* 5 February 1986.

Fuchsberg, Gilbert. Colleges forming liability-insurance companies to guarantee coverage, keep premiums down. *The Chronicle of Higher Education,* 16 November 1988.

Heller, Scott. Faculty members, administrators obtaining their own professional liability insurance. *The Chronicle of Higher Education,* 28 March 1984.

Insurance-plan growth continues. *NCAA News,* 9 November 1987.

Insurance plan to aid injured athletes under investigation by Iowa officials. *The Chronicle of Higher Education,* 13 December 1983.

Lederman, Douglas. Colleges and officials face huge costs when injured athletes sue for negligence. *The Chronicle of Higher Education,* 27 July 1988.

NCAA budgeted spending, 1986 and 1987. *The Chronicle of Higher Education,* 30 September 1987.

NCAA to offer insurance against injuries to athletes. *The Chronicle of Higher Education,* 14 September 1983.

No-fault insurance tested in Washington. *The Physician and Sportsmedicine,* November 1983.

Participation in NCAA insurance programs is growing. *The NCAA News,* 20 October 1986.

Sidelines. *The Chronicle of Higher Education,* 26 March 1986.

25 colleges and common fund form company to provide liability insurance coverage. *The Chronicle of Higher Education,* 3 December 1986.

Wong, Glenn M. Athletes, injuries and worker's comp. *Athletic Business,* November 1985.

IX. Youth Sports and Recreational Activities and the Insurance Crisis

Bonacci, Bob. Insurance fees threaten parks. *Lakewood Sentinel,* September 1985.

Canceling the quality of life. *Athletic Business,* June 1986.

The crisis in athletics. *Parents,* May 1987.

Duncan, Pat. Liability forces changes in sports, equipment. *Argus Leader* (Sioux Falls, S.D.), 27 September 1987.

Enough is enough. *Athletic Business,* October 1987.

Lijewski, Paul. Cost of liability insurance may hurt athletics. *The Des Moines Register,* 21 August 1987.

Smith, Bob. Insurance jeopardizes prep trips. *The Denver Post,* 11 May 1986.

X. Risk Management

A payoff for prevention? *Athletic Business,* March 1987.

Aquatic maintenance: Don't confuse the urgent with the important. *Athletic Business,* December 1984.

Baron, Ron. How to limit high school liability. *Sports Inc.,* 16 November 1987.

Carpenter, Linda Jean. Negligence: Who pays? *Strategies,* January 1989.

Dougherty, Neil J. Learning from the mistakes of others. *Athletic Business,* August 1988.

Graham, Laurence. Avoiding the "sue syndrome". *The Physician and Sportsmedicine,* February 1986.

Insurance premiums up despite safety record. *Athletic Business,* December 1987.

Negligence can be avoided, but not escaped. *Athletic Business,* January 1989.

The problem: Legal liability of athletic trainers. *The Physician and Sportsmedicine,* November 1983.

Program links risk management with insurance discounts. *Athletic Business,* July 1989.

Risk management—an ounce of prevention . . . *American Coach,* November/December 1987.

Risk management may encourage insurance discounts. *Athletic Business,* March 1987.

van der Smissen, Betty. Legal liability & risk management. *Physical Education and Sport,* March 1984.

15

Artificial Turf: Injuries, Economics, Emotion, and Ethics

Donald P. Foshee and James H. Conn

The question of which playing surface, artificial or natural turf, poses the greatest threat of injury to athletes has been the subject of considerable research and debate among independent researchers (Barnett and Tancred 1990), turf manufacturers (*Technical Topics* 1981), athletic administrators (Ingram 1990), coaches (Fry 1989), players (*Valdosta Times,* 26 November 1989, 8–C), physicians (Adkison, Requa, and Garrick 1974), and others. Presently, a significant difference in opinion pervades the athletic community of players, turf manufacturers, researchers, athletic coaches and directors, sports writers, and sportscasters. The media have sustained high levels of interest in the issue of playing surfaces for sport participation through coverage of events and through debates, discussions, and television documentaries. The question becomes even more complicated when the

Donald P. Foshee is with the Department of Psychology, Valdosta State College, Valdosta, Georgia, and James H. Conn is with the Department of Physical Education, Central Missouri State University, Warrensburg, Missouri. Originally published in the *Journal of Legal Aspects of Sport,* Vol. 1, No. 1, (Fall 1991). Original title is "Artificial Turf: Injuries, Economics, and Ethics."

appropriate surfaces for all-purpose recreational arenas are considered. The purposes of this essay are to (1) synthesize the findings of empirical studies on artificial and natural turf injuries; (2) examine the effects the turf issue has had on emotion and litigation; and (3) present the comments of prominent individuals in the sport community. The summary comments review the current status and probable future course of a complex and irreconcilable conflict.

INJURIES—SYNTHESIS OF EMPIRICAL STUDIES

Injuries are an inherent part of sport regardless of the type of surface on which the participants are playing. The purpose of this review is to provide a brief overview of previous turf investigations including (1) a description of the subjects, (2) a report of the findings, and, (3) comments on the procedures and design. The studies presented are illustrative and do not serve as an exhaustive review of the research. Subjects have been included from a variety of interscholastic, intercollegiate, and professional sports as well as recreational programs. Interscholastic subjects are primarily high school football players (Adkison, Requa, and Garrick 1974; Olson 1979; Culpepper and Morrison 1987). Intercollegiate subjects include football (Clanton, Butler and Eggert 1986; Kerin et al. 1980; Keene et al. 1977; Keene et al. 1980; Walsh and Petr 1987; Clarke and Miller 1977; Clarke and Miller 1978), baseball (Rapoport 1984; Stevenson 1973), and soccer players (Robichon 1973; Kerin et al. 1980; Clarke and Miller 1977). Professional subjects are football (Powell 1987; Nicholas, Rosenthal, and Gleim 1988) and soccer (Janoff 1980) players. Recreational subjects are collegiate intramural football players (Stevenson and Anderson 1981).

Procedures and Designs

Procedures and designs for collecting information and analyzing data are varied and are not without criticism. The earliest turf studies were conducted in the 1970s (Morehouse and Morrison 1975) to ascertain the type of turf on which most injuries occur. However, many of those studies and subsequent investigations suffered from procedural and design problems which posed questions of internal and external validity. The major independent variables investigated were the types of playing surfaces, and the primary dependent variables were the categories of injuries sustained. The designs of these studies and the particular statistical tools that were used failed to control for contamination effects such as the type of artificial and/or natural surfaces; the type of surface underneath the artificial surface; the description of footwear; condition of the playing surface; fatigue and previous condition of the injured athlete; weight of the individuals; strength and skill differential of opponents; proper mechanics; levels of arousal; game or practice conditions; violation of rules; and a myriad of other variables,

each of which contributes to the injury potential. The authors are inclined to agree with John Powell (1989a) who stated, "Using univariate statistics to analyze existing data is inappropriate."

Findings

The review of the literature was guided by the following question: Are there significant differences in the number of athletic injuries that athletes sustain while participating on artificial turf as compared to those received when playing on natural turf? The findings are divided into two sections. The first section of findings purport that fewer injuries occur on synthetic surfaces. In contrast, findings displayed in the second section suggest that fewer injuries occur on natural turf.

Section One

In 1974 Adkison, Requa, and Garrick (1974) reported the overall injury rate for high school football players on artificial turf (Tartan Turf) to be significantly lower than injuries which occurred on natural turf (natural grass). Furthermore, a significantly lower number of major ligament injuries were recorded on this artificial turf than on natural grass (Keene et al. 1980). The National Athletic Injury/Illness Reporting System (NAIRS) found no difference in injury rates on the two types of surfaces (Clarke and Miller 1978, 1977). Ursula Walsh, NCAA director of research and data processing inferred from an NCAA study of fifteen Division 1–A football teams during the 1987 regular season that there was no significant difference in injury rates between natural and artificial surfaces in Division I–A football (*The NCAA News,* 3 Feb. 1988, 1). However, Walsh and Petr (1987) reported that the number of serious knee injuries on natural turf was significantly greater than on artificial turf. Clear conclusions could not be drawn from a NATA study of 21,233 high school football players during the school years of 1986 to 1988 with regard to natural grass versus artificial turf since the use of artificial surfaces in high school sports was minimal. But for the record, 96 percent of the injuries occurred on natural grass (Powell 1989b).

Section Two

In 1973, the Stanford Research Institute (SRI) reported that more major ligament injuries occurred on artificial turf (Tartan Turf) than on grass among National Football League (NFL) players during the 1969 to 1972 seasons (Grippo 1973). A 1978 follow-up study found that 83 percent of the players responding to the questionnaire preferred playing on grass (Macnow 1988). The rate of injury while playing on the artificial Astro Turf was significantly higher than the number recorded on natural grass or artificial Tartan Turf (Adkison, Requa, and Garrick 1974). As cited in Morehouse and Morrison (1975), injuries to high school football players were 50 percent more prevalent on artificial Astro Turf than on natural grass (Bramwell, Requa, and Garrick, cited in Morehouse and Morrison 1975). A synthesis of the NFL weekly status reports from 1971 to 1980 suggested that more knee, head, and shoulder injuries are expected because more fields are covered with artificial turf (Atkinson, cited in Moore 1982). Data gathered for the years 1980 to 1985 demonstrated a higher rate of injury to players on all types of artificial surface (Astro Turf, Tartan Turf, and Super Turf) when compared with natural turf (Powell 1987). A twenty-six-year analysis of football injuries occurring to the New York Jets suggests there were no significant differences between injuries sustained on artificial turf and natural turf (Nicholas, Rosenthal, and Gleim 1988).

Stevenson and Anderson (1981) found that 69 of 107 injuries to intramural touch football players occurred on artificial surfaces, while the remaining 38 injuries were sustained on natural grass—a statistically significant difference. Nearly half of the 80 NFL players from the New York Giants and San Francisco 49'ers suffered from turf toe and 83 percent of this group indicated they were initially injured while playing on artificial turf (O'Brien et al., cited in Lieber 1988). Injuries to the metatarsophalangeal joints of 63 athletes (primarily football players) from 1971 to 1985, were attributed to artificial Astro Turf and a hyperflexible shoe (Clanton, Butler and Eggert 1986). Another survey of 465 NFL players conducted in 1985 found that 82 percent of the players favored playing on grass fields rather than on synthetic turf (Duda 1986).

Conclusion

These findings suggest that the question of which surface propagates the most athletic injuries lacks overwhelming support for either position. Is there a need for additional studies? Dr. James G. Garrick (Duda 1986) takes a very dim posture. Prior to 1985, Garrick, director of the Center for Sports Medicine at St. Francis Memorial Hospital in San Francisco and former medical adviser for the NFL Management Council and the NFLPA Joint Safety Committee, made a very strong statement when he said, "I'm not sure additional (general) studies are necessary. Virtually all studies indicate that artificial turf is more hazardous, although not all have been statistically significant." Three years later he was quoted as saying, "The continued use of turf cannot be justified" (cited in Macnow 1988).

Barnett and Tancred (1990) claim to have found the answers to the following questions: (1) What way can the disparity which exists between comparative safety of artificial turf and natural turf be measured effectively?, and

(2) Why has there been no definitive test method constructed to deal with the problem once and for all? Barnett and Tancred (1990) completed an extensive desk study which secured information and articles from all over the world (e.g., New Zealand, Australia, Saudi Arabia, and Israel). They concluded that there was no definitive method for selecting a "safe" surface and to attempt to state which surface is better than another is both fruitless and dangerous as it can only be achieved by a total rejection of the interrelating variables. Those variables include the age of the two types of turf, the weather conditions under which both were tested, the individual ability of the athletes tested, the sport being played, and even the number of time the surfaces were being compared. The consideration of the number of possible contaminating variables and athletic surfaces across the country raises many questions with regard to the validity and reliability of these findings.

ECONOMICS

The debate over artificial turf versus natural turf has frequently been reported in the tabloids as an economic issue. The following treatise of economics was solicited from college and university athletic personnel whose programs have recently undergone a change in turf. Bill Davis (1990), assistant athletic trainer at Ohio State University, recently stated that costs for natural turf are higher than for synthetic turf. The installation of natural turf required the employment of a full-time turf management person. In addition, the athletic department was forced to build additional locker facilities, separate from the football stadium, because the natural turf did not allow an equal range or number of activities as could be performed on synthetic turf (e.g., band, soccer). Another conversation with Hooti

Ingram (1990), University of Alabama athletic director, produced his comment that converting from artificial turf to natural turf would reduce costs. Ingram reported the cost for initial installation at Florida State University was approximately $400,000 but was expected to slightly exceed $500,000 at Alabama. Ingram noted the additional costs for fertilizer and the purchase of a $25,000 mower would offset the costs of replacing artificial turf at a cost of $875,000 every seven to eight years.

Economics can also be viewed from the amount of use a playing surface can support. The amount of wear and tear a surface can take without replacement must be considered as part of the economic equation. Leonard (1988) writes that artificial turf is valuable to owners because it can be kept esthetically pleasing. Arnold and colleagues (1979) added that artificial surfaces not only offer economic advantages but practical advantages as well. Reportedly, a number of public playgrounds have installed artificial surfaces. Edward M. Milner, president of Astro Turf Industries, suggests the value of Astro Turf is its durability. In addition, a number of metropolitan stadiums (Legion Field in Birmingham, Alabama; Memorial Stadium in Seattle, Washington; Joe Albi Stadium in Spokane, Washington) have made the change to artificial surfaces. These particular facilities accommodate as many as five or six football games each weekend.

EMOTIONS—SYNTHESIS OF COMMENTS

Participating in sporting activities on artificial surfaces has generated controversy among members of the sporting community. Commentaries have appeared in the media reflecting the emotional feelings of sportscasters, sports announcers, medical personnel, participants, and others. The following emotional responses are a representative sample of comments. Frank De-Ford, former editor of *The National,* remarked on NBC's NFL Today show in 1988 that the NFL should realign the divisions. On a more humorous note, he suggested one of the divisions be referred to as the Synthetic Division because they play their games on artificial turf. These are the players who do not have any knees left when they finish playing. Joe Theisman, a color analyst for ESPN and former NFL player, has stated on numerous occasions that "artificial turf is lousy for a football player." A more critical assessment of playing football on artificial turf was raised in *Sports Illustrated* by Underwood (1985):

> There are reasons why football is played on grass instead of on terrazzo floor or on I-95 and most of them are good ones. They are pretty much the same reasons football should not be played on artificial surfaces; those scouring pads over asphalt whose plastic hides are now spread across more than 200 of the football fields of America.

Gene Upshaw, executive director of the NFLPA has reported that it is not uncommon for an all-pro team to be out for much of the season because of artificial turf injuries. The players prefer not to play on it, and although they put up with the hazards, they remain unconvinced that grass cannot be grown inside a dome.

Larry Csonka, a former Miami Dolphin, is convinced that he would never have had a knee injury had it not been for playing on artificial turf. "My worse enemy was the damned turf." "I hate the stuff," says new Redskin linebacker Matt Millen. NFL pro-bowler Art Still, recently retired from the Buffalo Bills, has tendinitis in both knees and says, "[The turf] just eats 'em up." Albert Lewis, a Kansas City Chiefs cornerback, expressed concern for playing on artificial turf from a different prospective. He was concerned with the potential for self-destruction because of the greater force generated by players colliding with one another while participating on artificial turf. An additional concern was alluded to by Roy Green, wide receiver for the Phoenix Cardinals when he indicated that having to practice the entire week on artificial turf made him too tired to perform to his potential on artificial turf on game day (Herberg 1988).

Intercollegiate performers have also expressed reservations about participating on artificial surfaces. Mike Gundy, varsity football player for Oklahoma State University was quoted in *The Dallas Morning News* as saying, "I'll tell you, the (artificial) turf is really bad. As soon as we go back on turf (from a natural-grass practice field) when the season starts, after a week, I will get tendinitis and my knee will start cracking when I walk just from the pounding I will take. I think that in 10 years, turf will be gone. I think the NCAA or someone will force it out." Football players at the University of Florida enjoyed the 1990 spring practice more than in past years. "I think almost everybody likes it more than before," free safety Andy Newman said. "It's so much better on your knees, ankles, on all your joints. The old field, with the [artificial] turf, had an asphalt base, and it was real hard on you." "I like grass a lot better," defensive tackle Philip Johnson said, "except when it rains. The artificial turf is a lot better than grass when it is wet. But that is the only time" (*The Florida Times-Union,* 7 April 1990, D–1; D–4).

Major league baseball players have expressed similar concerns about having to participate on artificial surfaces. George Brett, first baseman for the Kansas City Royals, after catching his spikes in the artificial turf as he released the ball and reinjured his knee, expressed his feelings in the following manner: "I remember the first words I said to them [Royals officials] were 'You can take this turf and shove it.' . . . I'd never play on this Astro Turf the rest of my life . . . Everyone says 'You've got to get off the turf, because the turf's killing you . . . I don't think I've ever been real adamant about not playing on turf, but I've never liked playing on it . . . but what can you do? It's where I play, and that's the type of surface they want, so you've got to go out and play'' (*The Sporting News,* 22 May 1989). Padres third baseman Jim Presley is quoted as saying, prior to being traded by the Mariners, ''If I am traded, I hope it's to a team that plays on grass. I like playing outside and on real grass. I know it would help me physically. My back and legs have taken a beating from the hard Kingdome surface. At the time, I had to wear a back brace.'' (*The Sporting News,* 3 October 1988, 27) Richie Allen, a former major league player and owner of racing horses, said: ''If a horse won't eat it, I don't want to play on it'' (cited in Macnow 1988). Although the nature of baseball injuries is similar to those found in football, and although baseball presents less complex situations for undertaking a comparison of surfaces, data are not available from which to draw definite conclusions.

The impressions of collegiate sport management personnel are mixed. Bill Cousins, sports information director for Rice University, comments on artificial turf: ''There is a limited amount of maintenance and it provides a nice, even, smooth, all-weather workout area . . . When high school players first run on artificial turf in college, it makes them feel as if they're flying and gives them great self-confidence. They think it's the greatest thing since sliced bread'' (cited in Keever 1988). However, coaches for the most part do not favor participating on artificial turf. Larry Smith, now head football coach at the University of Southern California, said that after his third year at Tulane they changed to regular grass for practice and cut their injuries by 60 percent. In 1988, Hayden Fry reported the University of

Iowa would return to natural turf because too many injuries were occurring on artificial turf. During the Iowa-Michigan football game the following year, Fry commented: ''Last year we had eight major injuries on artificial turf and an assortment of abrasions and this year we have none on natural turf. Gene Stallings, University of Alabama head football coach stated, ''As soon as the game [with L.S.U.] is over, we'll be taking out the artificial turf . . . I am 100 percent in favor of that'' (*Valdosta Daily Times,* 9 November 1990, 2B). ''I just believe grass is a far safer playing surface,'' said Steve Spurrier, coach of the Duke University football team. ''We play on natural turf at Duke and have had very few injuries'' (*The Florida Times-Union,* 1 January 1990, 1).

In summary, these comments from individuals who either have participated on or are currently playing on artificial surfaces are not supportive of synthetic surfaces. Admittedly, these remarks do not represent everyone who has an opinion on the subject, but this review did not uncover any written statement in support of artificial turf. The point is not to sensationalize the issue but rather to emphasize that these comments are falling on the deaf ears of those who are in the position to make decisions about the type of surface on which the athletes will participate.

ETHICS—EXPOSURE TO LITIGATION

Management has reportedly made decisions to install artificial turf because of its aesthetic value and low cost of maintenance. On occasion management groups have listened to the views of players and coaches who have expressed their strong dislike for playing on artificial turf. Where this has taken place litigation may result.

During the 1970s and 1980s, increasing numbers of representatives of the sport community appeared in the courts for rulings on questions of negligence. When a serious injury occurs requiring extensive medical assistance and postinjury care and after the insurance assistance is depleted, the claimant (injured party) will, generally, look toward others (via the lawsuit) for financial relief. It is not uncommon today to find lawsuits in which players are suing other players (*Nabozny v. Barnhill* 1975), coaches other coaches (*Gasper v. Freidel* 1990), administrators other administrators (*Vargo v. Svitchan* 1980), and product manufacturers other manufacturers (*Rawlings Sporting Goods v. Daniels* 1981) in an effort to gain compensation for injuries sustained. The individuals responsible for control of the environment are at risk. The facility owner(s) or those in ''control'' of the facility owe a duty of care to facility users. The question of negligence is decided on the basis of whether (1) the owner of the facility owed a duty; (2) the owner of the facility breached that duty; and (3) the breach of duty was the proximate cause of the injury.

Today's athlete, unlike those of the past, are not willing to accept the risk of injury resulting from faulty equipment or unsafe environments, especially when such conditions can be proven as the proximate cause of injury. The athlete as a participant and consumer of sporting activities has grown to *expect* the equipment they are using and the facility in or on which they are participating to be reasonably safe. Judges and juries will be confronted with having to weigh the claim of injury caused by artificial turf with empirical research findings which do not support the claim. Furthermore, previous court action has clearly implied that sports managers (boards of education) are responsible for providing safe equipment and a well-maintained facility for athletes (*Berman v. Philadelphia Board of Education* 1983; *Prest v. Sparta Community School District No. 140* 1987; *Gerrity v. Beatty* 1978), spectators (*Board of Education of Richmond County v. Fredericks* 1966; *Gravely v. Lewisville Independent School District* 1986; *Lepkowski v. Eagan* 1990), and custodial workers (*Woodring v. Board of Education of Manhasset Union Free School District* 1981). In sum, coaches and athletic administrators must consider the actions of previous court rulings and inspect the conditions of facilities and equipment. Since the playing surface can be considered a piece of equipment or part of the facility, then sport managers need to consider the condition of the playing surfaces as a major part of safety.

As previously mentioned, defective equipment and unsafe facilities have resulted in a large majority of negligence cases involving athletics. Indeed, individuals unknowingly using faulty equipment or facilities (e.g., defective helmets, slippery floors) often enjoy a false sense of security (*Gerrity v. Beatty* 1978).

High school, collegiate, and professional athletes may have a false sense of security when participating on artificial turf. Historically, the equipment manufacturer (*Filler v. Rayex Corporation* 1970), the coach/teacher (*Montague v. School Board of Thornton Fractional Township North High School District 215* 1978), school administrators (*Vargo v. Svitchan* 1980; *Cook v. Bennett* 1980), school districts (*Rutter v. Northeastern Beaver County School District* 1981; *Thompson v. Seattle School District* 1982), and colleges and universities (*Lowe v. Texas Tech University* 1976; *Eddy v. Syracuse* 1980) have been named as defendants. When it is proven (as in the cases named) that those in control of the facility and equipment had prior knowledge of a hazardous condition and did nothing to solve the problem, court action typically is taken in favor of the injured athlete. However, attempting to persuade a judge and jury that artificial turf was the proximate cause of injury is difficult due to conflicting research findings.

Litigation

Kent Waldrep was a victim of a paralyzing injury sustained on artificial turf. The former Texas Christian University football player suffered an injury to the cervical area of his spine while playing at the University of Alabama in 1974. Waldrep sued the American Biltrite Company, the manufacturer of Poly-Turf, and the contractors who installed the turf. Underwood (1985) reported that the action was settled out of court in 1984. In another case, Gil Byrd, a defensive back with the San Diego Chargers, sought compensation for an injury attributed to artificial turf. However, in both cases, the proceedings were sealed by the court.

In a nonfootball related injury, a cheerleader at Washington State University won a judgment of $350,000 when she fell onto the Astro Turf and landed on her elbow, resulting in permanent damage. In this particular case, it was noted that the supervisor was aware that the Astro Turf was harder and caused more injuries than the natural turf on which the cheerleaders were accustomed to practicing (*Kirk v. Washington State University* 1987).

The case of *Thomas v. Chicago Board of Education* (1979) attempted, in part, to address the basic issue of synthetic turf and the cause of injuries. On October 4, 1974, Kyle Thomas, a Lakeview High School varsity football member sustained injuries during a varsity football game. The plaintiff alleged the facility was owned and operated by the school board. One of the charges against the plaintiff was their requirement that teams or individuals play on a synthetic turf which, the plaintiff claimed, was improperly constructed, installed, and maintained. However, the court ruled the complaint failed to state a cause of action based on negligence in supervisory capacities for requiring students to play on synthetic turf field. However, dissenting Justice Simon believed the defendants failed to provide safe playing conditions, and that a party should be held responsible when the defect that gives rise to injury results from their failure to inspect and test the playing surface. Playing fields are just as much a part of the equipment used by a football team as are helmets, in both the potential for causing injury and the constant need for proper inspection (*Thomas v. Chicago Board of Education* 377 N.E. 2d p.60). The major point of *Thomas* is that the turf itself was not claimed as the proximate cause of the injury. The claim was the failure of the district to properly maintain the turf.

Other claimants have sought compensation for injuries but reportedly have agreed to settle out of court. A conversation with Ehrlich (1988), a practicing Philadelphia attorney, produced the following statement in response to this question: Why is there a lack of artificial turf cases reported?

> Claimants have filed a number of suits against manufacturers of synthetic turf claiming disabling injuries. However, all have been settled out of court and sealed by court order. Consequently, the settlement information is not accessible to the public. Additionally, the parties are at risk of losing their settlements if they make settlement terms public. The rationale for settling artificial turf litigation out of court is clear. It prevents the establishment of a legal precedent, thus negating future legal action based on a previous court ruling. In addition, a financial settlement between the defendant(s) and plaintiff(s) is generally more cost effective for the insurance companies.

Finally, Congressman John Dingel of Michigan may have summed up the issue best when he said at a Sporting Goods Manufacturing Association conference in Washington D.C. that it costs $3 to deliver $1 of restitution (Bruns 1988).

SUMMARY

Recent reports contend there are no significant differences between injuries sustained on artificial turf and those that take place on natural turf. Unfortunately, a rational and logical preference for a particular playing surface can neither be supported by technical data nor research data. Further studies are extremely unlikely to provide additional support for either position. Even if the assumption is made that the artificial turf is a proximate cause, the inherent contaminating variables (type of shoe, base surface, condition of the turf, and lack of comparability among studies) will make it impossible to gain definitive results. Based on this review of the literature, the detrimental effects of playing on artificial turf have not been sufficiently demonstrated to allow generalization to all situations.

It is virtually impossible to compare the costs associated with natural versus artificial turf because they differ greatly in their levels of potential use. Quite probably, the trend will continue in major football programs to switch back to natural grass. However, those institutions or organizations unable to afford a dedicated football field will continue to use artificial turf. The tendency to settle related cases out of court has helped to prevent any precedent from being established. Therefore, questions that remain for the courts to decide include: Who is at risk for athletic injuries sustained on artificial surfaces? What are sport managers doing to reduce their risks of litigation as a result of artificial turf injuries? What is the sport manager's legal duty when they allow players to participate on artificial surfaces? It is unlikely that any court will provide definitive answers to these questions.

Future problems are likely to focus on the conditions of the playing surface and type of shoe being used (substantial evidence has been offered to suggest that enhancing the quality of traction increases the chances of serious injury).

Opinions of athletic community members about competing on artificial turf are markedly divided. Management has taken a posture in support of artificial surfaces. Players and coaches prefer natural turf. A standard of care can be reached through consensus among professionals, acting in good faith and under reasonable circumstances. The questions and controversy are much more likely to be resolved in this context than in the courts.

REFERENCES

Adkison, J. W., R. K. Requa, and J. G. Garrick. 1974. Injury rates in high school football. *Clinical Orthopedics:* 99, 131–136.

Arnold, J. A., C. A. Morehouse, J. Linville, E. M. Milner, M. A. Ritter, and H. A. Kretzler. 1979. Artificial vs. natural turf. *Physician and Sportsmedicine* 7:41–53.

Barnett, E., and B. Tancred. 1990. Natural or artificial turf. Project funded by the Health Promotion Research Trust, University of Sheffield, Sheffield, England.

Berman v. Philadelphia Board of Education. 1983. 456 A. 2d 545 (Pa. Super.).

Board of Education of Richmond County v. Fredericks. 1966. 113 Ga. App. 199, 147 S.E. 2d 789.

Bruns, H. 1988. Time to deal with tort reform. *Sports Inc.,* 26 March, 56.

Clanton, T. O., J. E. Butler, and A. Eggert. 1986. Injuries to the metatarsophalangeal joints in athletes. *Foot & Ankle* 7(3):162–176.

Clarke, K. S., and S. J. Miller. 1978. An epidemiological examination of the association of selected products with related injuries in football 1975–77. U.S. Consumer Product Safety Commission, contract no. CPSC–77–0039. Washington, D.C. U.S. Government Printing Office.

Clarke, K. S., and S. J. Miller. 1977. Turf-related injuries in college football and soccer: A preliminary report. *Athletic Training* 12(1):28–32.

Cook v. Bennett. 1980. 288 N.W. 2d 609 (Mich. App.).

Culpepper, M. I., and T. Morrison. 1987. High school football game injuries from four Birmingham municipal fields. *The Alabama Journal of Medical Sciences* 24(4):378–381.

Davis, B. 1990. Telephone interview, 4 December.

DeFord, F. 1988. Comments on NBC Sports ''NFL Live,'' 11 December.

Duda, M. 1986. NFL players survey shows safety concerns. *The Physician and Sportsmedicine,* December, 34–43.

Eddy v. Syracuse. 1980. 433 N.Y.S. 2d 923.

Ehrlich, N. 1988. Telephone interview, 12 December.

Filler v. Rayex Corp. 1970. 435 F. 2d 336 (7th Cir.).

Fry, H. 1989. Comment made on television during the Iowa–Michigan football game, 21 October.

Gasper v. Freidel. 1990. 450 N.W. 2d 226 (S.D.).

Gerrity v. Beatty. 1978. 71 Ill. 2d 47, 15 Ill. Dec. 639.

Gravely v. Lewisville Independent School District. 1986. 701 S.W. 2d 956 (Tex. App.).

Grippo, J. 1973. NFL injury study 1969–1972. Final project report (SRI–MSD 1961).

Stanford Research Institute, Menlo Park, California.

Herberg, L. 1988. Green finds God's sod refreshing. *The Sporting News,* 12 December, 36.

Ingram, H. 1990. Telephone interview, 27 November.

Janoff, B. 1980. Scorecard on artificial turf. When all the votes were counted, the professional players unanimously chose natural grass over artificial surfaces which are covering most U.S. stadium grounds. *Soccer World* 7(1):42–45.

Keene, J. S., W. G. Clancy, R. G. Narechania, and K. M. Sachtjen. 1977. Football injuries occurring on natural grass and Tartan Turf. A comparison study covering 17 years at the University of Wisconsin, ED184995. Arlington, Va: ERIC.

Keene, J. S., R .G. Narechania, K. M. Sachtjen, and W. G. Clancy. 1980. Tartan Turf on trial. A comparison of intercollegiate football injuries occurring on natural grass and Tartan Turf. *American Journal of Sports Medicine* 8(1):43–47.

Keever, J. 1988. Sherrill prefers grass field, but gets little support in SWC. *The NCAA News,* 27 April, 25.

Kerin, T., E. Milner, S. Plagenhoef, E. Lane, and R. D. Wilson. 1980. How to live with synthetic turf. *Athletic Training* 15(3):150–158.

Kirk v. Washington State University. 1987. 109 Wash. 2d 448, 746 P. 2d 285.

Leonard, M. 1988. *A sociological perspective of sport.* 3d ed. New York:Macmillan.

Lepkowski v. Eagan. 1990. Supreme Court Docket No. 13202–89 (NY: June).

Lieber, J. 1988. Turf: The NFL's most pesky agony of DA feet. *Sports Illustrated,* 12 December, 8–9.

Lowe v. Texas Tech University. 1976. 540 S.W. 2d 297 (Sup. Ct. Tex.).

Macnow, G. 1988. Artificial surfaces feel the heat. *Sports Inc.,* 18 July, 14–21.

Montague v. School Board of Thornton Fractional Township North High School District 215. 1978. 57 Ill. App. 3d 828.

Moore, M. 1982. NFL players hear injuries quantified and analyzed. *Physician and Sportsmedicine* 10(6):199–203.

Morehouse, C. A., and W. E. Morrison. 1975. *Artificial turf story: A research review.* University Park, Pa: Penn State University.

Nabozny v. Barnhill. 1975. 334 N.E. 2d 258 (Ill. App.).

The NCAA News. Opinions, 14 November 1988, 4.

NFL players survey shows safety concerns. *The Physician and Sportsmedicine* 14(12):34–43.

Nicholas, J. A., P. P. Rosenthal, and G. W. Gleim. 1988. A historical perspective of injuries in professional football: Twenty-six years of game-related events. *JAMA* 260(7):939–944.

Olson, C. O. 1979. The Spokane study: High school football injuries. *Physician and Sportsmedicine* 7(12):75–82.

Powell, J. T. 1989a. Telephone conversation, 16 October.

Powell, J. T. 1989b. 3-year study finds 'major injuries' up 20% in high school football. *Injury Report: High School Sports.* Greenville, N.C.: National Athletic Trainers Association.

Powell, J. T. 1987. Incidence of injury associated with playing surfaces in the National Football League 1980–85. *Athletic Training* 22(3):202–206.

Prest v. Sparta Community School District No. 140. 1987. 157 Ill. App. 3d 569, 109 Ill. Dec. 727, 510 N.E. 2d 595.

Rapoport, R. 1984. Artificial turf: Is the grass greener? In *Newton at the bat: The science in sports,* edited by Schrier, E. W. and W. F. Allman, New York: Scribner.

Rawlings Sporting Goods v. Daniels. 1981. 619 S.W. 2D 435 (Tex. Civ. App.).

Robichon, J. G. 1973. Round table discussion: Knee injury, knee treatment. Conference proceedings at the International Symposium on the Medical Aspects of Soccer (Football), Oct. 19–21. Toronto.

Rutter v. Northeastern Beaver County School District. 1981. 437 A. 2d 1198 (Pa.).

Stevenson, M. J. 1973. Effects of artificial and natural turf on injuries, and selected player, team and game variables in college intramural touch football. Ph.D. diss., University of Minnesota. Ann Arbor: University Microfilms.

Stevenson, M. J., and B. D. Anderson. 1981. Effects of playing surfaces on injuries in college intramural touch football. *Journal of the National Intramural Recreational Sports Association* 5(3):59–64.

Technical topics. 1981. Monsanto Company: St. Louis, Mo.

Theisman, J. Comment during the Los Angeles Raiders–San Diego Chargers NFL game, 12 November, 1989.

Theisman, J. Comment during the New York Jets–Indianapolis Colts NFL game, 19 November, 1989.

Thomas v. Chicago Board of Education. 1979. 60 Ill. App. 3d 729, 17 Ill. Dec. 865, 377 N.E. 2d 55.

Thompson v. Seattle School District. 1982. Case No. 851225 (King County, Wash.).

Underwood, J. 1985. Turf: Just an awful toll. *Sports Illustrated,* 12 August, 48–50, 53–54, 56–59, 61–62.

Vargo v. Svitchan. 1980. 100 Mich. App., 809, 301 N.W. 2d 1.

Walsh, U. R., and T. A. Petr. 1987. Division I-A football injuries on natural and artificial turf. Study conducted for the NCAA.

Woodring v. Board of Education of Manhasset Union Free School District. 1981. 79 A.D. 2d 1022, 435 N.Y. 2d 52 (1981), appeal denied, 53 N.Y. 2d 603, 439 N.Y.S. 2d 1027, 421 N.E. 2d 854.

FINANCE AND SPORT

16 Using Economic Models to Measure the Impact of Sports on Local Economies

Frank Hefner

INTRODUCTION

Economic impact studies have been applied to a wide range of sporting and recreational events, ranging from a study of the 1987 Florida Citrus Bowl to the effect of the 1987 football strike on the Chicago area economy and from the total effect of the Atlanta Falcons on the Atlanta economy to the Newport Tall Ships Celebration (1976). Whether the researcher is trying to measure the impact of sports, aviation, a military base, or business expansion, the same methodology is applied. The importance of measuring economic impact correctly cannot be overemphasized.

Often, the net revenues from a sporting facility are not the only justification for its construction. For example, in a study of the economic impact of the municipal auditorium in Mobile, Alabama, Chang (1981) claimed that "the true

value of the Mobile Municipal Auditorium should thus be judged not by whether its present operation is running at a deficit or a surplus but by the amount of revenue and economic activity the auditorium brings into Alabama from outside." (p. 12) He recognized that there may be ripple effects benefiting the local economy which are not directly observable, but which justify the construction of the auditorium in this case.

This example is an illustration of the value of economic impact studies. The auditorium may not be able to balance its budget, but the total value added to the local economy may generate enough tax dollars to justify the public expenditure to maintain the auditorium. The increased nonobservable benefits are measured by a "multiplier." The multiplier, in effect, determines the multiplication factor that must be applied to each dollar spent to arrive at the total economic impact.

There has been much discussion of the validity of using a multiplier. Davidson and Schaffer (1984), in justifying the use of a multiplier in their analysis of the impact of a sports festival, state that "to successfully argue that a multiplier does not apply—that is, that the multiplier

Frank Hefner is with the Division of Economic Research, College of Business Administration, University of South Carolina, Columbia, South Carolina. Note: A revised version of this essay has been published in the *Journal of Sport and Social Issues,* Vol. 14, No. 1 (Spring 1990).

is 1.0—one of the following observations must be true: either all direct income due to the festival accrues immediately to nonresidents or the propensity to consume locally must be zero, with all purchases from direct incomes being from out-of-area suppliers.'' In other words, either all of the income "leaks" out of the local economy immediately or all the income earned by local residents is spent immediately outside the local economy. The probability of both conditions being fully met is rather remote, so one may assume that a multiplier of some number larger than one is appropriate. In any case, the size of the multiplier is subject to empirical measurement.

The multiplier concept is used frequently, and its correct application is very important in determining the economic impact of a sports event or facility. Policymakers need to know the total impact in order to measure the resulting tax revenues. This is especially the case when tax dollars are used to subsidize the facility or event. Sports stadiums are a prime example. Brade and Dye (1988) have pointed out that, by conventional accounting measures, no sports stadium constructed since the 1960s has been profitable. Many of these projects have been publicly financed. The issue, then, is whether the use of tax dollars to build the stadium are justified by the benefits.

The ability of a city and its citizens to shoulder the additional tax burden to publicly finance the stadium depends on what the stadium can contribute to the city's tax base. The economic rationale for a sports stadium that cannot be expected to generate an operating profit depends on the size of the multiplier. It should be noted that there may be other reasons for constructing a sports stadium. For example, Moon Landrieu, as mayor of New Orleans, stated: "The Superdome is an exercise of optimism. A statement of faith. It is the very building of it that is important, not how much it is used or its economics.''

Schaffer and Davidson (1985) have commented on the intangible benefits of the Atlanta Falcons. Since these intangible benefits are not measurable, the remainder of this essay will concentrate on the economic and measurable aspects. Brade and Dye (1988) have noted four values that may be analyzed in determining the benefit of a sports facility:

1. Direct revenue projections
2. Indirect multiplier benefits
3. Booster benefits (the stadium may act as a magnet, drawing people to the area and boosting economic activity)
4. Intangible benefits

Brade and Dye found no statistically supported evidence for the existence of the booster benefit and the intangible benefits, by definition, are unmeasurable. This essay will focus on those benefits which are measurable, namely, direct revenue projections and indirect multiplier benefits.

A technically correct example of an impact study is found in Davidson and Schaffer's (1984) study of the economic impact of the Atlanta Falcons. In their study, they found that

> while total expenditures by all fans amounted to almost $12 million, $5.5 million can be attributed to outsiders. When this is combined with the expenditures by the Falcons of almost $21 million and then modified to eliminate double counting and expenditures outside the local economy, the Falcons are responsible for a healthy injection of $17.3 million into the Atlanta economy. These additional dollars mean new business activity of $37.1 million as this money circulates among local businesses and citizens, eventually resulting in additions to household incomes of $16.0 million and in new revenues for local government of $1.1 million. (p. 5)

The objective information provided by the Davidson and Schaffer study is useful to policymakers and local governments. Using measurable data on spending, employment, and taxes assists the local government with planning. The correct measurement of an economic impact can aid in determining not only the added tax base for the local economy, but also the demand on public services.

All too often the multiplier and the total impact are presented as if they were generated by a "black box," with no attempt to clarify the theoretical basis from which these numbers were derived. The two basic models used to determine multipliers are the economic base model and the input-output model. An explanation of the method for deriving these multipliers should dispel some of the mystery of their creation. The section on economic base multipliers will be followed by a presentation of a simple input-output model. Each theoretical approach will be reviewed in terms of its application to sports.

ECONOMIC BASE MULTIPLIERS

A local economy in equilibrium exhibits a pattern of expenditures rotating within the economy. In order for growth to occur, injections of funds into the local economy are necessary. These injections occur because goods and services are "exported" from the local economy. Regional economists consider the tourist trade, for example, as an export activity since it causes funds to be injected into the local economy. These funds are then spent again according to observable patterns. For example, assume that consumers spend half of their income and save the other half. The half that is spent is called the marginal propensity to consume (i.e., the fraction of additional income spent). The difference between what is earned and what is spent is saved, ignoring taxes for the moment. A consumer who earns a dollar as a result of the expenditure of a tourist visiting a local sporting event will spend fifty cents of that dollar. If the entire fifty cents is spent locally, it becomes local income.

Adding up this chain of spending, the total economic activity generated by this one additional dollar of tourist trade is $2.00. Thus, if the one dollar initially spent has a total impact of two dollars, the multiplier is 2. This can be derived from the following expression:

$$M = 1 / (1 - c)$$

where M = the multiplier, and c = the marginal propensity to consume.

Taxes and other factors which would reduce the amount available for the consumer to spend are called *leakages* since the original concept for a circularly flowing economy was modeled on a water system. Anything which does not continue to move within the cycle is a leakage. If taxes are taken into account, the formula for the multiplier becomes

$$M = 1 / (1 - c (1 - t))$$

where t = the effective tax rate.

The fact that some of the money that consumers spend is not spent locally has an effect on the size of the multiplier. There are a number of ways to take this into account. Smith and Wheeler (1986), in forecasting the impact of new business in Michigan, calculated a local marginal propensity to consume (i.e., they determined the proportion of additional income spent locally). They also calculated the effective local tax rate. They determined that the local marginal propensity to consume was 0.674 and the local effective tax rate was 0.234. It follows that the Michigan multiplier is

$$1 / ((1 - 0.674) (1 - 0.234)) = 2.06$$

An equivalent approach to handling the problem of imports, which constitute a leakage to the local economy, is found in Archer and Owen (1972) in their discussion of methods for calculating a regional tourist multiplier. They use the formula

$$M = A / (1 - (B \times C))$$

where

M = the multiplier
A = the percentage of money initially spent and remaining in the region, including the amount of money spent in the region
B = the proportion of income local people spend on local goods and services, including imports which only use the amount spent locally
C = the proportion of expenditures of local people that accrues as local income

This approach is equivalent to that of Smith and Wheeler who determined the proportion of expenditure that remained in the region and applied a regional marginal propensity to consume. Some researchers state the formula with a consumption proportion and modify the multiplier with an import coefficient. In other words, the marginal propensity to consume indicates the amount that is spent on consumption, while the import coefficient indicates the amount of consumption expenditure that is imported and thus does not have an impact on the local economy. Davidson and Schaffer (1984) used this method as seen in the formula

$$M = 1 / (1 - (C - M)(1 - T))$$

where

C = the marginal propensity to consume
M = the marginal propensity to import
T = the effective tax rate

Although the formulas are different, if proper attention is given to imports and taxes, the results from using either formula should be the same.

A number of data problems need to be addressed concerning the use of this multiplier. The marginal propensity to consume is usually found in published sources documenting consumer spending patterns; likewise, the effective tax rate may be determined from published sources. The determination of the import coefficient is not so easily determined. Most local and state economies do not have import coefficients calculated for them and the cost of performing an original survey to determine the import coefficient would be prohibitive for the researcher interested in the impact of sporting events on a local economy. The researcher already has the difficult task of tracking the initial spending that occurs due to the sports event or facility. The raw data used for determining total spending and the distribution of this spending are the same for both the economic base multiplier and for the input-output model.

THE INPUT–OUTPUT MODEL

To measure the total impact of new spending on an economy, all changes in demand must be determined. The initial construction of a $10 million sports facility provides an initial impact of $10 million on the local economy. This is called the *direct impact*. Clearly, the construction of the facility will require concrete, steel, construction workers, and so forth. The money spent on these materials and services comprises indirect expenditure, or the *indirect impact*. The mechanism used to measure total indirect expenditures is the input-output (I-O) table. The I-O table makes two statements about an economy. First, it is an accounting scheme that accounts for the flows from one industry to another in the production of goods and services. Secondly, it is a model of the production technology of the economy. These models are often termed *fixed coefficient models*.

	Construction	Manufacturing	Final	Final Output
Construction	200	100	700	1000
Manufacturing	400	500	1100	2000
Construction	Z_{11}	Z_{12}	F_1	X_1
Manufacturing	Z_{21}	Z_{22}	F_2	X_2

where Z_{ij} = inter-industry flow from sector i to sector j

F_i = final demand of industry i

X_i = total output of industry i

FIGURE 16.1   Hypothetical Input-Output Table

As an example, consider the following simplified economy with two sectors: construction and manufacturing. An I-O table using hypothetical data is presented in Figure 16.1. In this example, the manufacturing sector delivers $1,100 worth of goods to final demand. Final demand is the finished product that is used by a consumer. From the column of manufacturing data, it is apparent that to produce the $1,100 of final goods, the manufacturing sector used $500 worth of its own output and $100 of output from the construction sector. These demands for goods to be used in the production of goods delivered to final demand are termed *intermediate demands*.

Often the I-O table is called an *interindustry flow matrix* because it accounts for the production of one industry that is used in the production of another industry. The total output of manufacturing is the sum of all the intermediate demand and the final demand. Manufacturing produces $400 worth of goods that are used in the construction sector in its production of construction. The total output for manufacturing is the row total, or $2,000.

In Figure 16.1, the same scheme is used to obtain a general notation. The total output from each sector is the sum of the intermediate demands and the final demands, or

$$X1 = Z11 + Z12 + F1$$
$$X2 = Z21 + Z22 + F2$$

which can be put into a matrix form

$$\begin{matrix} X1 \\ \\ X2 \end{matrix} = \begin{matrix} Z11 & Z12 \\ \\ Z21 & Z22 \end{matrix} + \begin{matrix} F1 \\ \\ F2 \end{matrix}$$

and finally

$$X = Z + F$$

Dividing the interindustry flows by the total output produces the technical coefficients matrix, as seen in Figure 16.2. An illustrative interpretation of these technical coefficients shows that it takes $.20 worth of construction output and $.40 worth of manufacturing output to produce $1.00 worth of construction output.

$$
\begin{array}{cc}
& \text{Construction} \quad \text{Manufacturing} \\
\begin{array}{c} \text{Construction} \\ \\ \\ \\ \text{Manufacturing} \end{array}
&
\begin{pmatrix}
\dfrac{200}{1000} & \dfrac{100}{2000} \\ \\
\dfrac{400}{1000} & \dfrac{500}{2000}
\end{pmatrix}
\end{array}
=
\begin{array}{cc}
& \text{Construction} \quad \text{Manufacturing} \\
\begin{array}{c} \text{Construction} \\ \\ \\ \\ \text{Manufacturing} \end{array}
&
\begin{pmatrix}
.2 & .05 \\ \\
.4 & .25
\end{pmatrix}
\end{array}
=
\begin{pmatrix}
a_{11} & a_{12} \\ \\
a_{21} & a_{22}
\end{pmatrix}
$$

FIGURE 16.2   Direct Coefficient Table

Since total output equals the sum of the interindustry flows and the final demand, one can derive the following equations:

$$X = Z + F$$

and

$$Z = AX$$
$$X = AX + F$$

by substitution,

$$X - AX = F$$

by subtraction,

$$X(I - A) = F$$

by factoring, and finally

$$X = (I - A)^{-1}F.$$

The term $(I-A)^{-1}$ is called the *Leontief inverse* and provides a powerful tool in I-O analysis. The numerical result of $(I-A)^{-1}$ in our example is found in Figure 16.3. To understand what these numbers mean, consider what will happen to this economy should the demand for construction increase by $100 to $800, while that of manufacturing remains the same. Obviously, to meet this demand, the construction sector will have to produce an extra $100 of output. Additionally, the I-O table shows that construction uses construction services in its

own production process. In fact, matrix A shows that to produce $1.00 worth of output, it takes $.20 worth of construction production as an input. Thus, $20 worth of construction will be needed as an input to increase output by $100; and, to produce that $20-worth, construction will use $.2 \times \$20$ as an input.

This round-by-round process continues, and the impact caused by this change on the manufacturing sector has yet to be calculated. The Leontief inverse is an effective tool for performing this task. The following substitutions are made in the basic equation to demonstrate this method for finding the total effect of a change in demand:

$$X = (I{-}A)^{-1}F$$

$$
\begin{pmatrix} X_1 \\ \\ X_2 \end{pmatrix}
=
\begin{pmatrix} 1.2931 & 0.0862 \\ \\ .6897 & 1.3793 \end{pmatrix}
\begin{pmatrix} 800 \\ \\ 1100 \end{pmatrix}
=
\begin{pmatrix} 1129.3 \\ \\ 2069 \end{pmatrix}
$$

Therefore, a $100 increase in the demand for construction output requires a total increase of about $129 in construction output and an increase of $69 in manufacturing output. The $(I{-}A)^{-1}$ matrix contains all of the direct and indirect effects of a change in final demand. Thus, the entries in the Leontief inverse provide a tool for analyzing the complete "multiplier" effects of a change in final demand.

$$I-A)^{-1} = \begin{pmatrix} 1.2931 & 0.0862 \\ & \\ & \\ 0.6897 & 1.3793 \end{pmatrix}$$

FIGURE 16.3   Leontief Inverse

In our example, the first entry in the $(I-A)^{-1}$ is approximately $1.29, which means that for a $1 change in final demand for construction, $1.29 worth of construction output will have to be produced. Due to the interrelationships of the sectors of the economy, it also takes $0.69 worth of manufacturing production to meet this $1.00 change in construction demand; that is, the $1.00 gets multiplied by 1.98.

The multiplier derived from this example incorporates both the direct and indirect impacts in demonstrating the I-O model. By adding a row for payments to labor by the firm (wages) and a column of expenditure patterns (the marginal propensity to consume each type of product), the multipliers derived from the Leontief inverse will incorporate the direct, indirect, and induced impacts. The induced impacts are additional expenditures resulting from increased earnings by local residents as a result of the increase in final demand.

The U.S. Department of Commerce maintains RIMS II, an I-O model for each state in the nation which easily yields regional multipliers. Table 16.1 is a reproduction of the RIMS data for South Carolina. For example, the multiplier for new construction in South Carolina, according to RIMS II, is 2.2228. Thus, a new sports facility costing $10 million will generate a total economic impact in the state of about $22 million. Included in this $22 million are the direct impacts, the resulting indirect demands by the firms involved in constructing the facility (or the indirect impacts), the additional wages paid to workers, and the impact of their spending within the state. Using statistical techniques, RIMS II takes into account all the leakages that may occur, and the effect of taxes, imports, and savings, to make the multiplier truly regional. The RIMS II model also provides separate multipliers for the impact on earnings, which is useful for tax determination, and for employment, which is useful for handling economic development issues. The construction of the new facility will generate $7.249 million in earnings and 484 new jobs. These numbers are calculated as $10 million times the earning multiplier of 0.7249 and 10 times the jobs multiplier of 48.4.

Precautions should be taken to avoid the misapplication of the RIMS model because of double-counting. The output multiplier already includes wages and a consumption multiplier. To correctly apply the RIMS model, the investigator must find the appropriate industry for the category of spending being considered. Sporting events are included under the industry label "hotels and lodging places and amusements." For every dollar spent on sporting events, $1.92 is generated as a total impact on the state. If the researcher has also determined that the sporting event attracts consumers to restaurants and hotels they would not have visited otherwise, the expenditures at these establishments may also be included in the total impact.

The figures in Table 16.1 provide a multiplier that can be used easily and quickly. Furthermore, these results are published. For an additional fee, RIMS II will further localize the multipliers to a county or region. In some cases, major universities have ongoing I-O modeling projects or have acquired the RIMS II model for their own internal research. These research institutes are often available by contract to perform detailed impact studies.

TABLE 16.1 RIMS II Multipliers
South Carolina
Total Multipliers, by Industry Aggregation, for Output, Earnings, and Employment

	Output/1/ (dollars)	Earnings/2/ (dollars)	Employment/3/ (number of jobs)
Agriculture, forestry, and fisheries:			
Agricultural products and agricultural, forestry, and fishery services....................	1.8934	0.5412	74.3
Forestry and fishery products	1.6651	.3121	36.2
Mining:			
Coal mining	1.6558	.5014	47.3
Crude petroleum and natural gas	1.4646	.2273	15.1
Miscellaneous mining	1.7991	.5165	31.4
Construction:			
New construction	2.2228	.7249	48.4
Maintenance and repair construction	2.1619	.8150	53.9
Manufacturing:			
Food and kindred products and tobacco	2.1428	.4401	39.9
Textile mill products	2.7121	.6382	43.5
Apparel	2.6766	.7092	57.0
Paper and allied products	2.1521	.5223	27.9
Printing and publishing	1.9635	.6180	41.4
Chemicals and petroleum refining	2.0123	.4696	23.9
Rubber and leather products	2.0094	.5225	28.5
Lumber and wood products and furniture	2.3169	.5778	43.0
Stone, clay, and glass products...................	2.0217	.6021	34.1
Primary metal industries	1.7852	.4031	20.8
Fabricated metal products	1.8268	.5004	28.9
Machinery, except electrical	1.8913	.5649	31.8
Electrical and electronic equipment	1.9682	.5953	36.2
Motor vehicles and equipment	1.8136	.4997	27.2
Transportation equipment, except motor vehicles	1.9979	.6936	37.8
Instruments and related products	1.9722	.6064	36.7
Miscellaneous manufacturing industries.............	2.0675	.5759	41.8
Transportation, communication, and utilities:*			
Transportation	2.0039	.7837	44.2
Communication	1.5086	.4213	21.1
Electric, gas, water, and sanitary services	1.3956	.2403	12.4

TABLE 16.1—*Continued*

Wholesale and retail trade:

Wholesale trade	1.7920	.6396	40.1
Retail trade	1.8501	.7472	64.5

Finance, insurance, and real estate:

Finance	1.7317	.5321	34.2
Insurance	1.9845	.6833	38.9
Real Estate	1.3720	.1445	12.0

Services:

Hotels and lodging places and amusements	1.9155	.6109	66.9
Personal services	1.8857	.7161	81.3
Business services	1.8367	.7779	63.2
Eating and drinking places	1.9505	.5735	70.1
Health services	2.0048	.8776	50.1
Miscellaneous services	1.9516	.6992	49.0
Households	1.0431	.3191	26.1

*Includes government enterprises.

1. Each entry in column 1 represents the total dollar change in output that occurs in all row industries for each additional dollar of output delivered to final demand by the industry corresponding to the entry.

2. Each entry in column 2 represents the total dollar change in earnings of households employed by all row industries for each additional dollar of output delivered to final demand by the industry corresponding to the entry.

3. Each entry in column 3 represents the total change in number of jobs in all row industries for each additional 1 million dollars of output delivered to final demand by the industry corresponding to the entry.

SOURCE: Regional Input-Output Modeling system (RIMS II), Regional Economic Analysis Division, Bureau of Economic Analysis. Previously published in the *Journal of Sport and Social Issues,* 1990, 14 (1), pp. 1–13, by Frank L. Hefner, Asst. Professor of Economics, University of South Carolina.

DATA

In order to use the I-O model, the amount of the increase in final demand must be determined. Often, the raw data that needs to be entered into the I-O model to determine the economic impact of a sports event is acquired through surveys. This part of the analysis is labor intensive, and a more budget-conscious study may use other methods.

Two basic types of surveys are being used. In the consumer or participant type, questionnaires are used to discover the spending in the region directly related to the event. The purpose of the survey is to determine the amount spent and the consumption patterns of the visitors and local residents that are attributable to the sports event. By directly asking these groups how much they have spent, one can obtain an estimate of the direct economic impact of the event. The second type, the business sector survey, focuses directly on the firm and how much sales rose due to the event. Problems associated with all surveys certainly apply to these, although they are not unique to sports-related survey. Davidson and Schaffer point out some of the drawbacks:

- People attending the events are rarely eager to provide accurate responses.

- It is difficult to determine whether the consumer came specifically for the event or for other reasons.
- Sales of the firm may have increased because of seasonal variation rather than the event.
- Merchants may not be willing to release sales data.

Since most studies adopt some kind of survey, the following issues must be addressed:

- What is the appropriate region for the analysis?
- How is a visitor to the events defined and should visitor expenditures be isolated from local expenditures?
- What are the appropriate spending categories?
- What is the correct spending unit?

An example of the first issue is given by Davidson and Schaffer (1984) who report that, in the Tall Ships Festival in Newport, Rhode Island, the researchers only had the multiplier for the state available to them. The application of the state multiplier may not have been appropriate in this case since the festival was located in a subregion.

The importance of isolating visitor expenditures is evident because most of the spending by locals would have occurred anyway. Furthermore, an operational definition of a visitor must be determined. Some people interviewed may have been in the area for other reasons and their participation may not be attributable to the event.

Not only must the amount spent be determined, but the total must be allocated across various commodities and attributed to the various sectors of the input-output table. In the construction of a new facility, it is clear that the $10 million should be allocated to that RIMS category. However, the allocation of the purchase of souvenirs is not so clear. In one case, Chang (1981), an industrial multiplier was used in determining the impact of a municipal auditorium. This is clearly not the most satisfactory way to resolve the problem.

People may attend sporting events alone, in large groups, with families, with friends, and with family and friends. Since it is individuals who are being interviewed, it is important to determine the appropriate spending unit. Miller and Jackson (1984), for example, determined the number of ticket holders to the event and multiplied by the average expenditure per ticket holder to determine the total direct spending attributable to the football games.

In some cases, previous research may provide adequate data for the measurement of direct impacts. For example, the American Hotel and Motel Association has developed a formula for the Memphis area that determines the direct economic impact of hotel visits on a community. Using the estimated number of people attending the 1988 Liberty Bowl, this formula was employed to determine the Bowl's economic impact on the Memphis area.

Table 16.2 presents the type of data used as input for the study of the impact of the football strike on the Chicago area. Once these data are acquired, they must be sorted into appropriate categories to be applied to the I-O model. Table 16.3 presents the effect on the different industrial sectors and the total effect of the strike. Miller and Jackson were able to utilize an I-O model developed at Northern Illinois University for their multipliers.

CONCLUSION

Input-output modeling is the accepted method of measuring the economic impact of sports on a local economy. The main outcome of this type of analysis is the multiplier effect. Proper use of

TABLE 16.2 Input Data Summary

In-Facility Expenditures	
Tickets	$ 959,068.70
Concessions	167,903.44
Total	$1,126,972.14

Out-of-Facility Expenditures	
Food/Entertainment	$669,488.40
Lodging	265,670.00
Shopping	98,297.90
Parking	
($51,933.81 × .539466)	33,411.18
Public Transit	25,813.20
Player's Salaries	
(after tax and consumption)	$507,704.50

SOURCE: Miller and Jackson (1988). Previously published in the *Journal of Sport and Social Issues,* 1990, 14 (1), pp. 1–13, by Frank L. Hefner, Asst. Professor of Economics, University of South Carolina.

TABLE 16.3 Total Effect of the 1987 Football Strike on Chicago BEA ($ millions)

	Output	**Wages**	**Value Added**
Agriculture	0.009	0.002	0.004
Agriculture Service, Forestry, and Fish	0.009	0.004	0.004
Mining	0.002	0.000	0.001
Construction	0.063	0.041	0.049
Manufacturing	0.171	0.027	0.050
Transportation and Public Utilities	0.228	0.046	0.114
Wholesale	0.113	0.047	0.080
Retail Trade	0.656	0.235	0.374
Finance, Insurance, and Real Estate	0.361	0.070	0.260
Services	1.277	0.562	0.755
Government	0.023	0.006	0.011
Total	2.911	1.041	1.701
Multipliers	1.735	1.563	1.762

Previously published in the *Journal of Sport and Social Issues,* 1990, 14 (1), pp. 1–13, by Frank L. Hefner, Asst. Professor of Economics, University of South Carolina.

the methodology cannot be overemphasized, as the value of impact studies hinges on correct application of the model and appropriate interpretation of the data. As a cautionary word, one must guard against the use of overinflated multipliers.

As in most empirical economic studies, problems with data exist, such as determining local expenditure patterns. Furthermore, since economic impact studies often rely on survey data, these problems are compounded by the statistical problems inherent in survey data analysis. Data problems notwithstanding, the measurement of the economic impact of sporting events and facilities provides valuable information for policymakers.

Often, these studies are criticized because of the data problems, but this criticism is shallow since all studies face similar problems. To criticize the methodology of the model shows a lack of understanding of the alternatives. A correctly applied input-output analysis, even with its weaknesses, offers relevant and useful information about the impact of sports on a local economy.

REFERENCES

Archer, Brian, and Christine Owen. 1972. Towards a tourist regional multiplier. *Journal of Travel Research* 11(2):9–13.

Blin, J. M., and F. Murphy. 1974. On measuring economic interrelatedness. *Review of Economic Studies* 41:437–440.

Brade, Robert, and Richard Dye. 1988. An analysis of the economic rationale for public subsidization of sports stadiums. *The Annals of Regional Science* 22(2):37–42.

Chang, Semour. 1981. Measuring economic impact of the Mobile Municipal Auditorium upon Alabama. *Journal of Travel Research* (Spring):12–15.

Davidson, Lawrence, and William Schaffer. 1984. A discussion of methods employed in analyzing the impact of short-term entertainment events. *Journal of Travel Research* (Winter):12–16.

Meltone, Harvey, and Randall Jackson. 1988. The Impact of the professional football strike on the Chicagoland area. *Illinois Business Review* 45(3):3–7.

Miller, Harvey, and Randall Jackson. 1984. The impact of the professional football strike on the Chicagoland area. *Illinois Business Review* 45(3):3–7.

Schaffer, William, and Lawrence Davidson. 1985. Economic impact of the Falcons on Atlanta: 1984. Atlanta: The Atlanta Falcons.

Smith, Dean, and John Wheeler. 1986. How to determine the impact of new business on a local economy. *The Journal of Business Forecasting* (Spring):20–21.

The State. 1988. Game to add $11 million to Memphis' economy. December 12.

APPENDIX

Atlanta Falcons' Economic Impact Survey

QUESTIONS FOR EVERYONE

1. With whom did you come to the game:
   1–family only   3–friends and family   5–alone
   2–friends only   4–organization (_____)

2. How many are in your party (including yourself)? _____

3. How did you get to the Stadium:
   1–car, parked in Stadium lot   5–MARTA system only
   2–parked in Stadium area   6–taxi
   3–car to town, shuttle bus   7–walked
   4–charter bus   8–other (_____)

4. Are you a season-ticket holder?   1–yes   2–no

4–a. IF YES: Do you plan to buy season tickets again next year?
   1–yes   2–no   3–not sure

4–b. IF NO: Do you plan to buy season tickets next year?
   1–yes   2–no   3–not sure

4–c. IF NO: Is your ticket for today:
   1–your purchase   3–gift from friend
   2–purchased by your firm 4–business gift

4–d. IF NO: Why did you decide to come today?
   1–curiosity   3–saw an ad in the paper
   2–invitation   4–other (_____)

5. How do you get the most information about the Falcons?
   1–radio   3–television
   2–newspaper   4–discussion with friends

5–a. Was this source of information important in your deciding to come today?
   1–yes   2–no

6. Where do you live?
   1–City proper   6–DeKalb   11–S. Fulton   16–Rockdale
   2–Butts   7–Douglas   12–Gwinnett   17–Walton
   3–Cherokee   8–Fayette   13–Henry   18–Other Ga. County
   4–Clayton   9–Forsyth   14–Paulding   (_____)
   5–Cobb   10–N. Fulton 15–Newton   19–Other State
                                                    (_____)

6–a. Zip Code? _____

QUESTIONS FOR AREA RESIDENTS
(Area is 1–17 in question 6)

7. How far do you live from the Stadium? _____

8. If you live in the city, in which quadrant?   1–NE   2–NW   3–SE   4–SW

9. Do you expect to dine out before or after the game?
   1–yes, before   3–yes, both
   2–yes, after   4–no

10. IF YES: How much do you expect to spend on food outside the stadium (even dollars)?
   _____

11. IF YES: Would you be dining out anyway if there were no game today?   1–yes   2–no

----

QUESTIONS FOR VISITORS FROM OUTSIDE THE AREA

12. What is the principal reason for your trip to Atlanta?
   1–to see the Falcons play   3–vacation   5–convention
   2–visiting friends or relatives   4–business   6–other (_____)

13. How far do you live from Atlanta (approximate miles)? _____

14. How did you travel to Atlanta?
   1–car   3–bus   5–other
   2–plane   4–train   (_____)

15. How many nights will you be here? _____

16. If overnight, are you staying
   1–in hotel or motel   3–other
   2–with friends or relatives   (_____)

17. Please estimate (in even dollars) how much your party will spend (for your entire stay) for
   FOOD (OUTSIDE STADIUM) $ _____   GASOLINE $ _____
   OTHER ENTERTAINMENT $ _____   LODGING $ _____
   SHOPPING $ _____

THANK YOU VERY MUCH. HOPE YOU ENJOY THE GAME.

SOURCE: Schaffer and Davidson (1984). Previously published in the *Journal of Sport and Social Issues*, 1990, 14 (1), pp. 1–13, by Frank L. Hefner, Asst. Professor of Economics, University of South Carolina.

17

Major League Baseball Salaries: The Impacts of Arbitration and Free Agency

Lawrence Hadley and Elizabeth Gustafson

Earnings are estimated for major league baseball hitters and pitchers using salary data for the 1989 season. The results indicate that final-offer salary arbitration and long-term contracts have a large positive impact on salaries. The impact of free-agency eligibility is also positive, but smaller than arbitration eligibility. This implies that some players have used the arbitration process to extract above-market salaries. Therefore it is concluded that it would be in the interest of the owners to replace arbitration with earlier eligibility for free agency.

Labor relations between players and owners in major league baseball have been in a constant state of turmoil since Curt Flood's lawsuit attempted to overturn the reserve clause in 1972. To date, the major changes in the collective bargaining agreement include formal procedures for final-offer salary arbitration and free agency. Final-offer arbitration of salary disputes was voluntarily adopted by players and owners while renegotiating the basic collective bargaining agreement in 1973. It has become one of the most disputed issues, as indicated by the renegotiation of the basic agreement in 1990. The owners attempted to scuttle arbitration entirely while the players steadfastly held out for arbitration eligibility after two years of major league service instead of three years.

The traditional reserve clause that tied a player to one team for his entire major league career was overturned via grievance arbitration in the Andy Messersmith/Dave McNally case on 23 December 1975. Since that time the owners and players have voluntarily agreed to a revised reserve clause that ties a player to one team for the first six years of his major league career. After that period, players are eligible to declare as free agents and contract with any major team.

Because of its unusual structure, the labor market for major league baseball players has frequently been the subject of economic research. The seminal theoretical contribution was made by Simon Rottenberg (1956) and the seminal empirical contribution by Gerald Scully

Lawrence Hadley and Elizabeth Gustafson are with the Department of Economics and Finance, University of Dayton, Dayton, Ohio. Previously published in the *Journal of Sport Management,* Vol. 5, No. 2, pp. 111–127. Copyright © 1991 by Human Kinetics Publishers. Reprinted by permission.

(1974). Scully's econometric model for analyzing players' actual earnings versus their expected earnings in perfectly competitive markets has been respecified, or at least reestimated, by several economists (Bruggink and Rose 1990; Cassing and Douglas 1980; Medhoff 1976; Raimondo 1983; Sommers and Quinton 1982).

On the surface, arbitration and free agency have greatly favored the players, as indicated by the explosion of salaries beginning in the mid-1970s. Sommers and Quinton (1982), Raimondo (1983), and MacDonald and Reynolds (1989) provide some empirical evidence that this is indeed the case. But it is not easy to know exactly how much either area of change has added to the players' salaries. Other factors may also have been at work to cause salaries to rise over the past fifteen years. The separate impacts of arbitration and free agency on players' salaries can be isolated by estimating regression equations for the 1988 salaries of hitters and pitchers (Hadley and Gustafson 1989). In this essay, 1989 salary data is used to update and improve an analysis of the effects of arbitration and free agency on players' salaries. It also examines some interesting performance-related issues believed to be relevant to the use of major league baseball salary predictions in studying the business of baseball.

A SINGLE-EQUATION MODEL OF BASEBALL SALARY

Regression analysis is the most commonly used statistical technique for isolating the effect of a specific variable on another variable while controlling for possible interdependent effects with related variables. This essay estimates separate salary regression equations for hitters and for pitchers where major league salaries are determined by an appropriate set of explanatory variables.

The form of both salary equations is semilogarithmic as follows:

$$\log(\text{Salary}) = B_o + B_1X_1 + B_2X_2 + \ldots + B_nX_n + E.$$

Log(Salary) is the dependent variable determined by the equation. It can easily be converted to a predicted value for the variable Salary. The X variables (independent variables) are the ones thought to determine a player's salary. The B coefficients of the X variables measure the independent impacts of each variable on log(Salary). An increase of 1 in X_i leads to a B_i (100 percent) increase in salary when all other Xs are held constant. The E is a random disturbance term.

Complete listings of the independent variables (X variables) used in our hitter's and pitcher's salary equations are presented in Table 17.1. The variables can be categorized as player performance variables, player characteristic variables, and team characteristic variables. Player performance variables are unique to each of the two equations while player and team characteristic variables are common to both equations. Variables 2 through 9 in the table of nomenclature are the player characteristic variables; variables 10 through 13 are the team characteristic variables. Variables 14 through 22 and 23 through 31 are the player performance variables in the hitter's and pitcher's equations, respectively.

The player performance variables are self-explanatory. Our empirical analysis indicates that a wide range of these variables produces a much better explanation of salary than do summary performance variables such as the slugging percentage of hitters or the strikeouts/bases-on-balls ratio for pitchers. Performance variables are measured for the players' careers through 1988. Most of the hitters' performance variables

TABLE 17.1 Nomenclature for Variables in Earnings Equations

Player and Team Characteristic Variables

1. Salary = a player's 1989 salary
2. Serve = a player's years of major league service
3. Servesq = $(Serve)^2$
4. Arbit = a binary variable equal to 1 for players who have been eligible for arbitration in 1989 or earlier
5. Free = a binary variable equal to 1 for players who have been eligible to declare free agency in 1989 or earlier
6. Cont90 and Cont91 = two binary variables equal to 1 for players whose contracts expire at the end of the 1990 and 1991 seasons, respectively
7. Star = a binary variable equal to 1 for players with exceptional career performance statistics
8. Black = a binary variable equal to 1 for Black players
9. Hispanic = a binary variable equal to 1 for Hispanic players
10. Attend = the player's team's average home attendance in 1988
11. Teampct = the player's team's winning percentage in 1988
12. SMSA = the population of the metropolitan area of the team
13. NL = a binary variable equal to 1 for National League players

Player Performance Variables in the Hitter's Equation

14. AB = career at-bats divided by years of major league service
15. Hits = career hits divided by career at-bats (career batting average)
16. HR = career home runs divided by career at-bats
17. RBI = career RBIs divided by career at-bats
18. Runs = career runs scored divided by career at-bats
19. SB = career stolen bases divided by career at-bats
20. SO = career strikeouts divided by career at-bats
21. BB = career bases-on-balls divided by career at-bats
22. C, B1, B2, B3, SS, and DH = six binary variables equal to 1 for players whose primary fielding positions are catcher, first base, second base, third base, shortstop, and designated hitter, respectively

Player Performance Variables in the Pitcher's Equation

23. IP = career innings pitched divided by years of service
24. Wins = career wins divided by career innings pitched
25. Loss = career losses divided by career innings pitched
26. Save = career saves divided by career innings pitched
27. ERA = career earned run average
28. SO = career strikeouts divided by career innings pitched
29. BB = career bases-on-balls divided by career innings pitched
30. CG = career completed games divided by career innings pitched
31. Starter = a binary variable equal to 1 for starting pitchers

SOURCE: From "Major League Baseball Salaries: The Impacts of Arbitration and Free Agency" by L. Hadley and E. Gustafson, 1991, *Journal of Sport Management*, Vol. 5, No. 2, pp. 111–127. Copyright © 1991 by Human Kinetics Publishers. Reprinted by permission.

are measured relative to career at-bats; most of the pitchers' performance variables are measured relative to career innings pitched.

The team characteristic variables are included in the equation to control for the possibility that successful teams are in a position to pay higher salaries, other things being equal. Three variables are included to proxy the financial success of the team: the team's winning percentage for the previous season, home attendance for the previous season, and size of the metropolitan area in which the team is based. The league in which the team competes is also included as a variable (the NL binary variable). This controls for the fact that there is one variance in the rules between the two leagues (the American League uses a designated hitter) and that the perceived style of play of the two leagues may differ. These differences may systematically affect the financial success of teams in the two leagues and, therefore, affect the salaries they pay their players.

The player characteristic variables include years of major league service, the square of the number of years of service, four variables that describe a player's employment situation, two binary variables (Black and Hispanic) to identify the player's race, and a binary variable (Star) to identify exceptional players. The employment situation of all players is defined by the collective bargaining agreement between the Players' Association and the team owners. In 1989, players with fewer than three years of service were bound by the reserve clause, which ties players to one team; the only restriction on a player's salary is the 1989 minimum figure of $68,000 (raised to $100,000 in the 1990 contract).

Players with three to six years of major league service are also bound to one team by the reserve clause, but they are eligible to have their salary determined by final-offer arbitration. By the terms of the bargaining agreement, one arbitrator must select either the salary requested by the player or the salary offered by the player's team. The player and his team may agree on a compromise salary prior to the arbitration hearing, but the arbitrator is limited to one of the two salaries. The equation identifies players who have been eligible for salary arbitration at least once during their career by defining a binary variable (Arbit) equal to 1 for all players with three or more years of major league service.

Players with six or more years of major league service are not bound by the reserve clause. Rather, they are eligible for free agency, which gives them the right to negotiate a contract with any major league team. Our equation identifies players who have been eligible for free agency at least once during their career by defining a binary variable (Free) equal to 1 for all players with six or more years of major league service.

Players and teams are free at any time to negotiate a long-term contract. This practice is most common among players who are approaching eligibility for free agency. A player is not likely to sign a long-term contract unless he receives a salary similar to the one he expects via free agency. Most free agents also sign long-term contracts, so there is no incentive for a player approaching eligibility for free agency to sign for a salary below his market value. We identify players on long-term contracts with two binary variables (Cont90 and Cont91). Cont90 identifies players who had two years remaining on their contract at the start of the 1989 season; Cont91 identifies players with three or more years remaining on their contract.

The Star variable is included in our expanded equations because earlier earning equations seemed to consistently underestimate the salaries of the top hitters and pitchers. This problem has been discussed by Rosen (1981) and MacDonald (1988), whose "superstars" model predicts disproportionately high compensation for the star players compared to the average players. The Star variable is included in this equation to control for such an effect.

For hitters, the Star variable is defined as players who have at least 1,500 career at-bats and who have a career batting average of at least .300, or career home runs per at-bat of at least .15. Of the 349 hitters in this sample, 53 are ''stars.'' For starting pitchers, the Star variable is defined as players who have pitched at least 500 career innings and who have won at least .067 career games per inning pitched, or have a career ERA below 3.40, or have at least .8 career strikeouts per inning pitched. The same criteria are used for relief pitchers except that the boundary for career ERA is set at 3.15. There are 42 ''stars'' in this sample of 247 pitchers. The criteria for star hitters and pitchers were chosen with the intent of approximately identifying the top 15 percent of players on the basis of their performance.

The analysis is based on salary data released by the Associated Press Wire Service in April 1989. The bulk of the baseball data are obtained from *The 1989 Baseball Encyclopedia Update, The 1989 American League Red Book,* and *The 1989 National League Green Book.* The hitter's equation is based on data for 349 players for whom salaries were released by the AP and who had 100 or more career major league at-bats through the 1988 season. The pitcher's equation is based on data for 247 pitchers for whom salaries were released and who had 50 or more major league innings pitched through the 1988 season.

REGRESSION RESULTS

The regression coefficients (the B_x) for both salary equations are estimated by ordinary least squares. The results for both hitters and pitchers

are presented in Table 17.2. Overall, these results make it clear that a systematic process determines the salaries of major league hitters and pitchers. The main indication of this is the R^2 values for these equations. R^2 measures what percent of the variation among salaries is explained by the independent variables in the equation. For hitters, R^2 indicates that 88.7 percent of the variation of log(Salary) is explained by the equation variables. For pitchers, 84.9 percent of the variation is explained.

Generally the most important variables that determine salaries are years of major league service and its square, the market structure variables (Arbit, Free, Cont90, and Cont91), and the baseball performance variables. The impact of specific variables on log(Salary) and their levels of significance are indicated in Table 17.2.

A cross-sectional analysis of earnings may become dated for purposes of prediction if the process that determines salaries is unstable over time. Previously estimated regression coefficients for 1988 salaries are available (Hadley and Gustafson 1989), making it possible to test the structural stability of these salary equations over a two-year period. The appropriate statistical test for the stability of a regression equation over time is the Chow test (for a technical discussion of this statistical test, see Maddala 1988, 130–137). This test applied to our 1988 and 1989 regression results, indicates that the equations are indeed stable for both hitters and pitchers at the .05 level of significance. Conceptually, this means that the structures of both salary equations have not changed over this one-year period. In other words, the systematic process that relates these explanatory variables to players' salaries is similar for the two years.

TABLE 17.2 Regression Equations for Hitters and Pitchers

Hitters' variables	Mean	SD	Regression coeff.	SD of regression coefficient	Pitchers' variables	Mean	SD	Regression coeff.	SD of regression coefficient
Serve	5.710	4.186	.253***	.036	Serve	5.395	4.202	.241***	.038
Servesq	50.073	67.721	-.0118***	.00168	Servesq	46.69	75.42	-.0094****	.0015
Arbit	.696	.461	.607***	.084	Arbit	.636	.482	.707***	.098
Free	.398	.490	-.173**	.083	Free	.352	.479	-.355***	.113
Cont90	.106	.308	.296***	.066	Cont90	.121	.327	.192***	.089
Cont91	.092	.289	.304***	.071	Cont91	.101	.302	.514***	.096
Star	.152	.359	.311***	.067	Star	.170	.376	.110	.081
Black	.264	.441	-.0059	.050	Black	.045	.207	-.155	.126
Hispanic	.155	.362	.013	.057	Hispanic	.081	.273	-.043	.096
Attend	26,090.0	7508.0	.0000058	.0000037	Attend	25,645.0	7664.0	-.0000033	.0000053
Teampct	504.1	71.5	.000847**	.000353	Teampct	500.7	73.27	.00118**	.000507
SMSA	3833.0	2079.0	.0000086	.0000105	SMSA	3839.0	2036.0	-.0000054	.0000015
NL	.467	.500	-.0354	.0393	NL	.482	.501	-.073	.054
AB	374.8	135.2	.00216***	.00019	IP	140.78	49.42	.0049***	.0011
Hits	.260	.026	3.886***	1.235	Wins	.058	.014	3.542*	2.008
HR	.024	.016	1.793	2.802	Loss	.056	.015	.544	2.186
RBI	.116	.033	3.062**	1.313	Save	.036	.067	1.990***	.606
Runs	.129	.028	1.149	1.276	ERA	3.77	.689	-.148***	.0557
SB	.027	.029	1.705	1.056	CG	.015	.014	-.152	3.220
SO	.163	.058	-.039	.506	SO	.659	.180	.523***	.169
BB	.091	.035	.187	.673	BB	.372	.094	.335	.334
C	.169	.375	.213***	.069	Starter	.510	.501	.140*	.081
B1	.092	.289	.098	.076					
B2	.123	.329	.0089	.070					
B3	.112	.316	.022	.068					
SS	.100	.301	.304***	.077					
DH	.049	.216	-.161	.099					
Constant			8.506		Constant			10.132	
R^2			.887					.849	
F statistic			93.0					57.2	
Sample size			349.0					247	

*,**,*** indicate statistical significance at the .10, .05, and .01 levels, respectively.

SOURCE: From "Major League Baseball Salaries: The Impacts of Arbitration and Free Agency" by L. Hadley and E. Gustafson, 1991, *Journal of Sport Management*, Vol. 5, No. 2, pp. 111–127. Copyright © 1991 by Human Kinetics Publishers. Reprinted by permission.

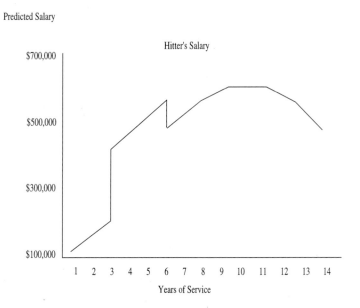

FIGURE 17.1   Earning Profiles for Hitters

SOURCE: From "Major League Baseball Salaries: The Impacts of Arbitration and Free Agency" by L. Hadley and E. Gustafson, 1991, *Journal of Sport Management*, Vol. 5, No. 2, pp. 111–127. Copyright © 1991 by Human Kinetics Publishers. Reprinted by permission.

COMPENSATION ISSUES

The mean salary for hitters in 1989 was $581,135, and for pitchers it was $563,083. Career earnings profiles are shown in Figures 17.1 and 17.2 for average hitters and average pitchers, respectively. These profiles document the impact of major league service, eligibility for arbitration, and eligibility for free agency on the earnings of the average hitter and pitcher. The profile peaks at 10.7 years for hitters (Salary = $673,413) and at 12.8 years for pitchers (Salary = $759,575). The profiles decline over the later years of an average player's career because of the significant negative B coefficient of Service^2. This is a common pattern for earnings in all occupations, and it is attributable to the decline in skills that typically occurs with age. Although our equation controls for a player's historical performance, expectations regarding future performance are related to years of service.

The most surprising result is the statistically significant negative sign for B_{Free} = −.173. The average pitcher has the same experience, with a 70.7 percent increase after three years and an offsetting 35.5 percent decline after six years.

This result should not be misunderstood. Free agency does have a significantly positive impact on salaries. The average salary of a free-agent pitcher is 43.4 percent higher than one who is ineligible for either free agency or arbitration. This number represents the difference between the arbitration and free-agency coefficients in our equation (.607 − .173 = .434). Likewise, the average salary increase of a free agent pitcher over one who is ineligible for both free agency and arbitration is 35.2 percent (.707 − .355 = .352). Similar results were obtained in the 1988 analysis of salaries.

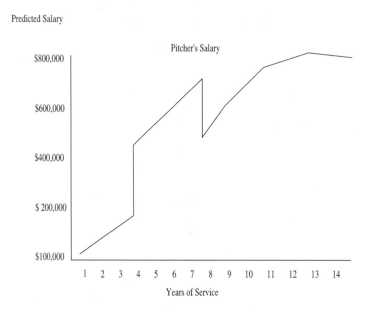

Predicted Salary

FIGURE 17.2 Earning Profiles for Pitchers

SOURCE: From "Major League Baseball Salaries: The Impacts of Arbitration and Free Agency" by L. Hadley and E. Gustafson, 1991, *Journal of Sport Management,* Vol. 5, No. 2, pp. 111–127. Copyright © 1991 by Human Kinetics Publishers. Reprinted by permission.

One possible problem with these results is that the particular players who are actually eligible for free agency during a given contract season are unidentified. Instead, the free agent variable definition includes all of the players who could have been eligible for free agency at some time during their career.

Clearly, all major league players who survive six years of service have the contractual right to declare as a free agent. Some sell their free-agent right in the form of a long-term contract prior to actual eligibility. Others may simply choose not to exercise this right for reasons particular to their situation. However, the right to declare as a free agent should increase salaries even for those who choose not to exercise that right because they would not willingly give it up without compensation. In other words, the players who do not exercise the free agent right can still use the threat effects of this right to

their advantage. Therefore we believe that our definition of the free agency variable is the most accurate for purposes of measuring the impact of free agency on salaries.

Nonetheless, in anticipation of possible criticism of the definition of our Free and Arbit variables, we have reestimated our equations with alternative definitions for these variables. In these reestimated equations, Free is set equal to 1 only for those players who were actually eligible to declare as free agents in November 1988. (The list includes ninety-two players and was compiled by the baseball owners' Player Relations Committee.) We also have redefined Arbit to equal 1 only for those 177 players eligible to submit for salary arbitration in January 1989. In the reestimated hitter's equation, the B_{Arbit} is +.288 and B_{Free} is −.124. For pitchers, the reestimated coefficients are +.487 for B_{Arbit} and −.234 for B_{Free}. All these coefficients are statistically significant. Although the magnitudes of the coefficients are not as large in these equations, the qualitative result regarding the impact of free agency on salaries is substantiated. The conclusion, that arbitration has a significantly larger impact on salaries than free agency, is inescapable.

We believe this result can only be understood in the context of the historical development of owner–player relations over the past fifteen years. Scully (1974) has documented that before 1975 all players were paid salaries well below those that would be obtained in a competitive labor market, and Sommers and Quinton (1982) were among the first to document the large positive impact that free agency has on salaries. The large salaries currently earned by players eligible for arbitration are the result of arbitrators' partially basing their awards on the salaries of comparable free-agent players. Dworkin's (1986) summary of the salary arbitration process describes the institutional mechanism by which this occurs. Therefore, the salary explosion in major league baseball began as the direct result of the free-agent revolution and the partial demise of the reserve clause that it entailed.

The free-agent revolution was temporarily derailed by owner collusion from 1985 to 1987. Owners were found guilty of agreeing among themselves not to bid on each other's eligible free agents. By the 1989 season, however, free-agent bidding appeared to have fully recovered.

This issue is important to the interpretation of the regression results in Table 17.2 because the discussion is based on the assumption that the players eligible for free agency earned salaries equal to their value in a competitive market by the 1989 season. It is a controversial assumption, in part because of the years of known owner collusion against a competitive market. However, the fact that competitive bidding for free agents revived prior to the 1988 season and continued into the 1989 salary season lends sup-

port for this assumption. More specifically, the average annual 1989 salary for the twenty-eight frontline players eligible for free agency in November 1988 increased 43.75 percent over their 1988 salaries. Excluded from this group were any who retired before the end of the 1989 season as well as any marginal players who were released or signed minor league contracts.

The assumption is controversial in another way because economists debate the competitiveness of labor markets in general. Our analysis follows the conventional neoclassical position by assuming that the free agents' salaries in 1989 were free to adjust upward in response to market conditions. Other economists see market failure as the norm. Readers interested in this debate can find nontechnical discussions in Solow (1980, 1990) and an excellent review of the professional literature in Kniesner and Goldsmith (1987).

Arbitration would not have the large effects on salaries in the current labor market were it not for the free-agent revolution of the late 1970s. But the free-agent revolution of the seventies cannot explain the finding that, in 1989, the salary increments from arbitration greatly exceeded those from free agency. If arbitrators had awarded salaries that were consistent with market conditions as indicated by the free agents' salaries, then the entire adjustment to market salaries would occur when players became eligible for arbitration after three years, and no further adjustment would occur when the players became eligible for free agency. This implies that the expected value of the coefficient of Arbit is positive, while that of Free is zero. However, our econometric results indicate a downward adjustment in salaries associated with free agency, implying that the arbitration adjustment was too large.

Our explanation is that arbitrators have consistently overshot competitive market salaries in making their salary awards. This may be due to some bias, inherent in the arbitration process, in favor of the players. Perhaps the arbitrators sympathize with the players because of the way the reserve clause has exploited players for decades; perhaps their awareness of the collusion of the mid-1980s has generated sympathy for the players. Whatever the reasons, these results indicate that arbitration awards have favored the players.

This arbitration result is an unfair outcome for the owners. Owners should pay salaries as determined by a competitive labor market, but they should not pay salaries that are above competitive market levels just because arbitrators consistently overshoot the salaries that prevail in a competitive market.

The remedy appears rather simple. Arbitration should be eliminated and all players with three years of service should be eligible for free agency. For the stability of the game, this right should be qualified by offering the player's current team the right of last refusal, giving a free agent's current team the option to match the terms of any preferred contract and thus retain his service. This is a very weak form of the reserve clause that in no way prevents a player from being paid a competitive market salary. However, it would enable owners to achieve greater stability in player personnel than the current system of free agency allows. Such stability may be an important ingredient in fan loyalty, which is the real basis of high salaries. This proposed modification of free agency may prevent players from playing for the team of their choice, but would seem to establish a reasonable market restriction in the interest of the players.

BASEBALL PERFORMANCE ISSUES

The regression equations in Table 17.2 can be used to generate a predicted salary for any major league player, real or hypothetical. This predicted salary is the amount that compensates the player for his years of service and his performance on the field at the same rate as the average major league player. Tables 17.3 and 17.4 compile 1989 predicted salaries for some well-known players. These predicted salaries are compared with the players' actual 1989 salaries by computing the gaps between the actual and predicted salaries. Players with positive gaps have actual salaries greater than their predicted salaries. This means they are being rewarded for their service and performance at a higher rate than the average player. The reverse is true for players with negative gaps.

On an individual player basis, it is interesting to speculate on the possible reasons, or lack thereof, for the direction and magnitude of each gap. But this exercise involves subjective judgment and is therefore left to the reader.

Two players deserve mention here. According to Table 17.4, Nolan Ryan is the most overpaid pitcher, by $900,225. This anomaly is due to the fact that he has 21.6 years of major league service. Most players have retired long before this point in their career, but Ryan continues to be one of the premier pitchers in the game. The career earnings profile for pitchers indicates that the average pitcher experiences declining earnings after 12.8 years of service due to the negative effect of Serve[2], the factor that causes Ryan's predicted salary to be low relative to his actual salary. This illustrates that the application of our equation to an individual player must be tempered with use of good judgment in recognizing exceptional circumstances.

Ozzie Smith also deserves mention. Our analysis of 1988 salaries indicated that he was the most overpaid player, by about $1.4 million. This analysis indicates that he was still overpaid in 1989, in the amount of $958,197. Critics have pointed out that Smith is the premier fielder at one of the game's most difficult positions. In response, it should be noted that our earnings equation for hitters includes variables

TABLE 17.3 Predicted 1989 Salaries for Selected Hitters

Player	Actual 1989 Salary	Predicted 1989 Salary	Gap
Baines, Harold	$1,189,751	$1,342,709	$-152,958
Bell, George	1,900,000	1,681,674	218,326
Brett, George	1,803,979	1,929,362	-125,383
Boggs, Wade	1,700,000	1,525,500	174,500
Canseco, José	1,600,000	1,328,685	271,315
Carter, Gary	2,160,714	1,444,249	716,465
Carter, Joe	1,630,000	1,102,179	527,821
Clark, Jack	2,000,000	1,242,828	757,172
Coleman, Vince	775,000	994,007	-219,007
Davis, Alvin	1,250,000	1,517,386	-267,386
Davis, Eric	1,350,000	1,074,966	275,034
Davis, Glenn	1,085,000	1,022,540	62,460
Dawson, Andre	2,100,000	1,918,204	181,796
Deer, Rob	760,000	921,815	-161,815
Dunston, Shawon	550,000	551,502	-1,502
Esasky, Nick	570,000	845,176	-275,176
Evans, Dwight	1,100,000	1,256,323	-156,323
Fernandez, Tony	1,400,000	1,472,099	-72,099
Fisk, Carlton	1,200,000	680,307	519,693
Franco, Julio	1,225,000	1,019,681	205,319
Gaetti, Gary	1,466,667	1,749,254	-282,587
Gibson, Kirk	1,833,333	1,647,715	185,618
Guerrero, Pedro	1,833,333	1,829,586	3,747
Gwynn, Tony	1,190,000	1,539,857	-349,857
Hayes, Von	1,300,000	756,759	543,241
Henderson, Rickey	2,120,000	1,625,783	494,217
Hernandez, Keith	2,000,000	1,112,033	887,967
Hrbek, Kent	1,560,000	1,620,589	-60,589
Lansford, Carney	1,275,000	1,437,908	-162,908
Larkin, Barry	292,500	323,191	-30,691
Leonard, Jeffrey	800,000	818,477	-18,477
Mattingly, Don	2,200,000	2,654,322	-454,322
Murphy, Dale	2,000,000	1,573,165	426,835
Murray, Eddie	2,244,462	2,710,653	-466,191
Palmeiro, Rafael	212,000	190,384	21,616
Parker, Dave	875,000	1,017,643	-142,643
Puckett, Kirby	2,000,000	1,759,429	240,571
Raines, Tim	2,100,000	1,784,234	315,766
Sandberg, Ryne	890,000	1,203,687	-313,687
Santiago, Benito	310,000	269,655	40,345
Sierra, Ruben	350,000	426,386	-76,386
Smith, Ozzie	2,340,000	1,381,803	958,197
Strawberry, Darryl	1,420,000	2,071,741	-651,741
Trammell, Alan	1,100,000	1,699,764	-599,764

SOURCE: From ''Major League Baseball Salaries: The Impacts of Arbitration and Free Agency'' by L. Hadley and E. Gustafson, 1991, *Journal of Sport Management*, Vol. 5, No. 2, pp. 111–127. Copyright © 1991 by Human Kinetics Publishers. Reprinted by permission.

TABLE 17.4 Predicted 1989 Salaries for Selected Pitchers

Player	Actual 1989 Salary	Predicted 1989 Salary	Gap
Andersen, Larry	$425,000	$354,336	$70,664
Anderson, Alan	200,000	229,143	−29,143
Bedrosian, Steve	1,450,000	1,081,760	368,240
Belcher, Tim	225,000	218,753	6,247
Blyleven, Bert	1,225,000	1,141,210	83,790
Browning, Tom	1,025,000	733,146	291,854
Candiotti, Tom	505,000	609,564	−104,564
Clemens, Roger	2,300,000	2,047,029	252,971
Darling, Ron	1,566,667	1,862,816	−296,149
Davis, Mark	600,000	489,578	110,422
Davis, Storm	587,500	672,865	−85,365
DeLeon, José	662,500	792,066	−129,566
Eckersley, Dennis	812,500	1,171,974	−359,474
Flanagan, Mike	887,500	1,050,524	−163,024
Franco, John	1,067,500	880,636	186,864
Gooden, Dwight	2,416,667	2,014,537	402,130
Gubicza, Mark	1,375,000	879,316	495,684
Hershiser, Orel	2,766,667	1,996,687	769,980
Higuera, Ted	1,525,000	1,063,738	461,262
Honeycutt, Rick	650,000	820,033	−170,033
Howell, Ken	225,000	338,439	−113,439
LaCoss, Mike	500,000	568,980	−68,980
Landrum, Bill	75,000	73,910	1,090
Langston, Mark	1,300,000	1,076,688	223,312
Magrane, Joe	150,000	175,817	−25,817
Martinez, Dennis	735,000	1,236,135	−501,135
Montgomery, Jeff	95,000	112,028	−17,028
Moore, Mike	1,191,667	1,256,700	−65,033
Morris, Jack	1,989,000	1,343,246	645,754
Reardon, Jeff	1,150,000	1,121,301	28,699
Reuschel, Rick	800,000	1,125,682	−325,682
Reuss, Jerry	325,000	604,466	−279,466
Righetti, Dave	1,450,000	1,094,491	355,509
Robinson, Don	900,000	1,012,062	−112,062
Ryan, Nolan	1,800,000	899,775	900,225
Saberhagen, Bret	1,300,000	1,013,885	286,115
Scott, Mike	1,300,000	1,267,681	32,319
Smith, Bryn	550,000	641,587	−91,587
Stewart, Dave	950,000	832,426	117,574
Stieb, Dave	1,500,000	1,999,285	−499,285
Tanana, Frank	925,000	1,026,946	−101,946
Viola, Frank	1,550,000	1,403,809	146,191
Welch, Bob	1,133,333	1,586,118	−452,785
Williams, Mitch	365,000	468,223	−103,223
Worrell, Todd	875,000	751,180	123,820

SOURCE: From ''Major League Baseball Salaries: The Impacts of Arbitration and Free Agency'' by L. Hadley and E. Gustafson, 1991, *Journal of Sport Management*, Vol. 5, No. 2, pp. 111–127. Copyright © 1991 by Human Kinetics Publishers. Reprinted by permission.

TABLE 17.5   Predicted Salaries for Model Players

Hitters									
Model*	AB	Hits	HR	RBI	Runs	SB	SO	BB	Predicted salary
Power hitter	550	150	40	100	75	10	125	75	$1,835,486
Batting champ	600	200	5	75	100	10	50	50	$1,992,043
Balanced hitter	550	175	25	100	75	10	60	75	$2,095,192
Leadoff/ speed	600	175	5	60	110	60	60	60	$1,848,599
Pitchers									
Model*	IP	W	L	SO	BB	ERA	CG	SV	Predicted salary
20-game winner	225	20	6	150	100	3.00	15	0	$1,845,181
Power pitcher	225	15	10	250	100	3.00	10	0	$2,180,394
Control pitcher	225	15	10	125	50	3.00	10	0	$1,513,350
Middle relief	90	7	5	60	30	2.75	0	10	$1,022,612
Bullpen closer	75	7	5	50	25	2.50	0	35	$2,127,557

*Defined as excellent seasonal performance for hypothetical players. Predicted salaries based on assumptions that players have seven years of major league service, are playing on a three-year contract, and play in the American League on a team with a .500 record. Hitters assumed to be outfielders. First three pitching models assumed to be starters.

SOURCE: From ''Major League Baseball Salaries: The Impacts of Arbitration and Free Agency'' by L. Hadley and E. Gustafson, 1991, *Journal of Sport Management*, Vol. 5, No. 2, pp. 111–127. Copyright © 1991 by Human Kinetics Publishers. Reprinted by permission.

that measure a player's primary fielding position. The average shortstop receives a statistically significant 30.4 percent salary premium over the average player. The result in Table 17.3 indicates that he is paid almost another million dollars on top of the 30.4 percent, since that premium is built into Smith's predicted salary. Our own judgment is that the few spectacular plays that Smith makes every season cannot be worth the amount by which he is overpaid; however, the additional numbers of fans who attend games just to see Smith play shortstop may very well make up the difference.

The salaries of various hypothetical players are presented in Table 17.5, the purpose being to compare the predicted salaries of ideal player models. Four ideal models are defined for hitters: the power hitter, the batting champ, the hitter who balances power with the ability to make contact at the plate, and the hitter who combines speed with the ability to get on base. Players who personify these models well are José Canseco or Darryl Strawberry for the power hitter, Wade Boggs or Tony Gwynn for the batting champ, George Brett or Don Mattingly for the balanced hitter, and Rickey Henderson for the speed player.

All nonperformance variables are held constant in calculating the predicted salaries for these model players. The values of the baseball performance variables are defined to represent an outstanding season for each model player, and these values are presented in Table 17.5 along with the predicted salaries. The results indicate little difference among the four model types in terms of the money they receive. Of the four, however, the power hitter is the lowest paid.

The same method has been used to generate predicted salaries for five ideal pitchers. These include the twenty-game winner, the power pitcher, the control pitcher, the middle relief pitcher, and the bullpen closer. Players who may best personify these five models are Brett Saberhagen or Dave Stewart for the twenty-game winner, Nolan Ryan for the power pitcher, Rick Reuschel or Bryn Smith for the control pitcher, Larry Anderson for the middle reliever, and Mark Davis or Dennis Eckersley for the closers.

It is important to remember that a player's salary is a business decision. Even when an arbitrator decides a player's salary, the owner must implicitly ratify that salary by keeping the player on the team. If the salary demand set by an arbitrator is too high, the owner can trade the player or release him. If an owner chooses to keep a player, it indicates that his salary is within the acceptable range. Ultimately, this range is determined by the owner's subjective view of the player's ability to contribute to the team in terms of winning baseball games and generating revenue.

CONCLUSION

Our statistical results confirm that baseball salaries are the outcome of a systematic process. This process is greatly influenced by the collective bargaining agreement and the role it defines for the reserve clause, arbitration, and free agency. Our analysis indicates that eligibility for arbitration has a significantly larger impact on player salaries than eligibility for free agency. This represents a deviation from the expected outcome of a competitive market.

These results are noteworthy for the professional sports industry. Player personnel costs typically represent over a third of the total expenses of a major league baseball team in the free-agent era (Scully 1989), so there is obvious sensitivity to the issue of players' salaries. Team owners' attempts to monopolize the players' labor market via reserve clauses, player drafts, roster restrictions, and so forth, is characteristic of the labor market in most professional team sports.

To understand the significance of our empirical results from the viewpoint of the team, it is necessary to recognize the owners' skepticism toward free and competitive labor markets in the professional sports industry. We believe this skepticism is an outgrowth of the industry's success in monopolizing labor markets during the 1950s and 1960s. The exploitation of baseball players by paying salaries well below the competitive market level has been documented by Scully (1974). The success of the owners led to player attempts to undermine the owners' advantage by manipulating the labor market to their own advantage. Generally players gained this level of control in the 1970s through use of collective bargaining.

The evidence provided here indicates that the players have managed to reverse the earlier advantage of the owners to the point that some players now extract above-market salaries through arbitration. Given this reversal, it would seem to be in the interest of the owners to allow the free market to play a greater role in the salary process. Our proposal for extending free agency to players with three years of service, combined with the right of last refusal, is one method of increasing the role of the free market. The owners may be slow to accept such ideas, but their bargaining tactics in 1990 would indicate they do recognize their current disadvantage in the labor market. Finally, it should be pointed out that there is extensive literature in economics which concludes that competitive market salaries are fair to buyers and sellers alike.

We believe these findings are also significant from the viewpoint of the individual player. The figures generated by earnings equations analytically summarize the entire salary process. We believe that the variables in our salary equations capture most of the important aspects of that process, as indicated by the high R^2 values.

These R^2 values are excellent results by statistical and econometric standards, but a small portion of the process remains unexplained by the equations. Therefore, it is not surprising that some players are paid salaries that differ from their predicted salaries. On the other hand, if a player's salary deviates greatly from his predicted salary, the owner and/or an arbitrator should carefully examine the reasons for the deviation. In other words, predicted salary is a potentially useful tool for helping to guide the salary process.

It is noteworthy that the baseball owners proposed a formula-determined salary process during the 1990 renegotiation of the basic agreement. They used the phrase "pay for performance" to describe the proposal, and its main purpose was to eliminate arbitration from the salary process. Nevertheless, their proposal serves as an illustration of the potential usefulness of statistical analysis as a guideline in the salary process. If the Arbit and Free variables are dropped from our equation, then the predicted salaries derived from these equations would essentially be based on player and team performance. Still, we remain convinced of the inherent superiority of a free market salary process over any administered salary process (arbitration or statistically generated salaries) in professional sports. We also believe our proposal for extending free agency to players with three or more years of service, combined with the right of last refusal to owners, would greatly improve the labor market in major league baseball.

REFERENCES

Bruggink, T., and D. Rose. 1990. Financial restraints in the free agency labor market for major league baseball: Players look at strike three. *Southern Economic Journal* 56(4):1029–1043.

Cassing, J., and R. Douglas. 1980. Implications of the auction mechanism in baseball's free agent draft. *Southern Economic Journal* 47(1):110–121.

Dworkin, J. B. 1986. Salary arbitration in baseball: An impartial assessment after ten years. *Arbitration Journal* 41(1):63–69.

Hadley, L. H., and E. F. Gustafson. 1989. Earnings in a three-tier market: The case of major league baseball. Working Paper 89–26. Center for Business and Economic Research: University of Dayton.

Kniesner, T. J., and A. H. Goldsmith. 1987. A survey of alternative models of the aggregate U.S. labor market. *Journal of Economic Literature* 25(3):1241–1280.

MacDonald, G. 1988. The economics of rising stars. *American Economic Review* 78(1):155–166.

MacDonald, D. N., and M. O. Reynolds. 1989. Are baseball players paid their marginal revenue products? Unpublished manuscript. University of North Texas and Texas A&M University.

Maddala, G. S. 1988. *Introduction to econometrics.* New York: Macmillan.

Medhoff, M. H. 1976. On monopsonistic exploitation in professional baseball. *Quarterly Review of Economics and Business 16*:113–121.

The 1989 American League Red Book. 1989. New York: American League of Professional Baseball Clubs.

The 1989 Baseball Encyclopedia Update. 1989. New York: Macmillan.

The 1989 National League Green Book. 1989. New York: National League of Professional Baseball Clubs.

Raimondo, H. J. 1983. Free agent's impact on the labor market for baseball players. *Journal of Labor Research 4*:183–193.

Rosen, S. 1981. The economics of superstars. *American Economic Review 71*(5):845–858.

Rottenberg, S. 1956. The baseball players labor market. *Journal of Political Economy 64*:242–258.

Scully, G. W. 1974. Pay and performance in major league baseball. *American Economic Review 64*(6):915–930.

Scully, G. W. 1989. *The business of major league baseball.* Chicago: University of Chicago Press.

Solow, R. M. 1980. On theories of unemployment. *American Economic Review, 70*(1):1–11.

Solow, R. M. 1990. *The labor market as a social institution.* Cambridge, MA: Basil Blackwell.

Sommers, P. M., and N. Quinton. 1982. Pay and performance in major league baseball: The case of the first family for free agents. *Journal of Human Resources 17*(3): 426–436.

18

Athletic Cost Containment

William Eng and Susan Larkin

As pressures increase on athletic directors to reduce the rate of operating costs, the need to examine management philosophies and practices becomes an absolute necessity. Old cost-reimbursement orientations must be replaced with a focus on, and daily attention to, cost containment, productivity monitoring, and sound business planning. Although some athletic directors have found that cost containment has actually resulted in lower operating margins, it is only a matter of time until their department will have to be managed like any other business operating in a competitive environment. The athletic department must become a financially sound "enterprise," rather than just a funded operation.

Many reasons have been identified for the rapidly increasing athletic costs in the United States. New technology continues to appear at a fantastic rate. It usually requires the expenditure of capital and the commitment of higher levels of operating expenses for space and labor. The aspect of equity in women's athletics is placing a greater and greater load on schools and colleges. Finally, the general rate of inflation in the United States continues to raise the price of labor and equipment, the two largest cost items in an athletic department budget. Some colleges experiencing excessive costs have found it fairly easy to reduce the rate of inflation by eliminating nonessential expenditures. Other colleges, not as effectively managed and more "obese," have found it extremely difficult to reduce the rate of inflation in their operating costs. These colleges have been forced to reduce or delay expansion of the number of teams in their programs. Some colleges have placed severe expenditure restraints on athletic business managers and forced them to live within restricted budgets. Still other colleges have instituted extensive management and cost containment programs aimed at improving productivity and the way in which athletic contests are handled.

William Eng is the Director of Athletics for Baruch College, City University of New York, and Susan Larkin is the Director of Athletics for the John Jay College of Criminal Justice, City University of New York.

Since labor costs constitute nearly 60 percent of the typical short-term operating budget for an athletic department, the effective utilization of this expensive resource is extremely important. Many factors affect the productivity of the athletic department's labor resources. Controlling and managing these factors to improve labor utilization is the focus of this article.

It is difficult to discuss athletic cost containment apart from operations. Athletic operations change continuously. New technology, new rules, new procedures, changing populations, and increasing shortages of skilled personnel make athletic operation planning and management a complex task. A rapidly increasing component of the athletic department's operation involves purchased goods. The control of material (equipment) costs involves not only the proper organization and management of material-related labor resources, the institution of material control, material handling, and material selection procedures, but also appropriate purchasing and inventory control mechanisms.

It is clear from the experience of a large number of colleges and universities that no one athletic department can hope to successfully implement all available management methods of improving productivity. Many situations place constraints on the maximization of productivity. Indeed, maximizing productivity is not the intent. Productivity levels must be balanced with the quality of the services provided, the morale of the staff, the particular physical characteristics of the facility, the level of management talent within the department and, in many cases, the financial restrictions that have been placed on capital expenditures. Whether an athletic department is half as productive, or twice as productive, as another is irrelevant. The major concern is to improve upon a particular athletic department's existing productivity.

THE PRODUCTIVITY AUDIT

Before effective productivity improvement techniques can be applied, problem areas must be identified. It costs money to manage and change operations. Thus, problem areas should be addressed first, in order to maximize the return of each dollar invested in productivity improvement. To identify problem areas, several techniques are described which, collectively, can be termed a "productivity audit."

Not all of these techniques need to be applied in every case. Many athletic directors know where major operating or productivity problems exist. Over the long term, however, good athletic administration will apply these productivity audit techniques the same way they utilize annual financial audits—as a gauge of management effectiveness.

Let's start by asking ourselves a simple question: What is an audit? Webster says that to audit is "to examine, adjust, and certify." Thus, to perform the athletic audit involves examining present operation, organization, staffing, resource utilization, and costs. The athletic productivity audit should be designed to identify areas in which the use of resources may be improved. For example, many athletic departments are faced with building a new gymnasium or stadium because the present facility is old or outdated. Some serious questions present themselves in this situation.

1. Where should the new gymnasium (stadium) be located?
2. How many seats should be installed?
3. What type of design should be used?
4. What type of equipment should be purchased?
5. How much will the new gymnasium and equipment cost?

These questions and many others must be answered before a new facility can be built. As these questions are examined and alternatives are suggested, the staff is essentially conducting a productivity audit related to this new building project.

Because of the problems involved in building a new gymnasium or in changing the systems, operations, and procedures of an existing athletic department, an outside objective analyst who has knowledge of new systems and successful operating approaches utilized by other institutions can be a valuable asset. These individuals offer greater opportunities for selecting the best and most profitable alternative from the many that are discussed and analyzed.

It should not be assumed that the audit scope is confined to buildings, equipment, and staff. Many improvements can be made in the internal operating systems of an athletic department. Specific questions regarding operating systems can be included as part of the audit process: How can better communication be accomplished between athletes, coaches, trainers, information directors, and administrators? How can the organizational structure be improved? How can staff be better utilized? What improvements can be achieved? The athletic department audit may bring to light one or more alternatives to improve upon the current system.

ORGANIZATION

The goal of creating a more functional organizational structure is to develop a proper balance between what the athletic director does and what he/she delegates. The administrator who knows precisely the functions of his/her job and knows what functions should be delegated will achieve high marks in performance.

Athletic administration can be viewed from many different angles, but an athletic department audit should include these basic tasks:

1. Enumerate the activities involved.
2. Determine the functions under which these activities can be performed effectively.
3. Develop the titles of positions under which the various functions are performed.
4. Train the particular individuals who occupy titular positions.
5. Link the activities leading toward a common goal.
6. Guide personnel performances so that the common goal can be achieved.
7. Locate the various departments in the organization so that effective coordination can be implemented.

In some athletic departments confusion exists not only with general titles, but also with the functions performed under the titles. For example, what functions should be performed by the athletic director, the associate or assistant director, or the administrative assistant to the athletic director? These positions must be structurally and functionally defined in precise terms so that little or no overlap occurs and so that the activities to be performed by each position are clearly presented and understood.

Athletic departments should demonstrate certain principles of organization.

1. All job functions should be carefully defined.
2. Functions should be assigned to particular job titles.
3. A sufficient number of functions should be assigned to each job title.

4. Each "boss" should have the necessary authority and responsibility to manage the employees under his or her jurisdiction.
5. Job functions should be assigned within the scope of the employees' ability to perform them effectively.
6. Organizational structure should promote cooperation between people, departments, and administrators.

SUMMARY

To summarize, an athletic department should be managed to achieve these fundamental objectives:

1. To render invested capital and staff effort productive
2. To establish major policies
3. To set up rules and regulations
4. To enumerate activities, functions, and duties of departments
5. To develop an effective organization to carry out the activities, functions, and duties
6. To operate the athletic department through the organization

The approach recommended here is to examine all factors that affect productivity and to explore the use of techniques to positively affect those factors and their impact on productivity.

19

Educational and Financial Considerations in Planning Sport Facilities

Marcia L. Walker

From the beginning of organized sports activities, it has been important to develop and design facilities that serve the needs and purposes of the people. In 329 B.C. the first great Roman amphitheater, the Circus Maximus, was built to quench the thirst of the great crowds demanding to see professional contests. Then, in the first century A.D., the Roman Coliseum was built to provide an arena for spectators to watch the sports of the day (Lee 1983).

Facilities play a major role in the success of sports programs. The type of programs being offered should determine the type of facilities which should be developed. It is difficult to establish and conduct a superior program with less than adequate facilities. It is also necessary to update and renovate the facilities which house sports activities and programs.

Facilities require a great amount of planning prior to their construction. Carefully designed plans are critical to the development of func-

tional and adequate facilities. This has been even more critical on the level of the small institution where flexibility is a necessity. Many organizations have developed versatile sports complexes which are cost effective and serve a variety of functions. Mable Center for Physical Education at William Jewell College, with an enrollment of 1400 undergraduate students, is such a complex. "At any one time, the floor can handle three basketball games, five tennis matches, or three volleyball games" (*Athletic Purchasing* 1981).

It has become more critical for institutions to be accountable for the resources they have and for the money they spend. Because of the vast expenditure of funds for sports facilities, it is imperative that these facilities meet the needs and fulfill the purposes for which they have been designed. Administrators are increasingly aware of the scarcity of funds as well as the growing demand for new programs and facilities.

In developing facilities for sports programs, administrators and planners need to know what space standards and guidelines will best suit the

Marcia L. Walker is with the College of Health and Human Sciences, University of Northern Colorado, Greeley, Colorado.

needs identified in the plan for the facility. An important point to remember is that once a structure is complete the planners are stuck with what has been built, and that includes the mistakes.

The trend in sports programs today is diversification. Examples of special programs in sport science, human performance, wellness, and exercise technology are adapted. Particularly at small institutions, the facilities must be flexible enough to provide space for many different types of programs in a limited area.

Many educational institutions and sports organizations have been caught in the battle between too few recreational sports facilities and little money with which to build. This is a dilemma which has seemingly existed since such facilities were first built.

A thorough investigation, which must include a needs assessment, should be undertaken before the determination is made whether or not to build or to renovate. Investigations sometimes generate interest and financing where none was available previously.

Some organizations have generated funding through innovative means such as self-assessed student fees (University of Southern Mississippi), brochure fund-raising (University of Michigan), twenty-five-year master plans to spread out spending (Ohio State University), and multipurpose sharing with other associations or institutions (Coe College shares such a facility with the community).

Many factors should be taken into account when planning to build a sports facility. Following are some of the considerations:

1. Purpose of the facility. Who uses the facility? Is it multipurpose? Is there a broad base of participation?

2. Needs of the community for which the facility is designed. What are the desired activity areas and educational requirements? Philosophy, goals, and programs should be examined.

3. Predesign factors. This includes space programming, scheduling dates (start, completion, phases, etc.) and setting up a cost model (structure, finishes, floors, mechanical costs).

4. Who comprises the planning committee? Include potential users and a representative from each program area.

5. Use of consultants. Should an experienced consultant be hired? An experienced planner will save time, money, and effort. Few architects have experience in building sports facilities.

6. Building materials: encapsulated, pre-fab, steel, etc.

7. Site and geological factors. Considers zoning and environmental impact analysis.

8. Legal concerns and risk management. Looks at the proper placement of activity and program areas.

9. Money to build. How much money will the project require? A cost assessment should be completed.

10. Money to finance. How will the necessary funding be obtained? Who is financially responsible for this project? Identify possible sources.

11. Money to maintain. How much money will be needed to operate the facility once it is completed?

12. Architectural firm. Who will it be? Are they reputable? Have they built similar facilities?

13. Future trends. Are there foreseeable changes in programs, enrollments, and demographics?

14. Computerization. Should computerized systems be designed for specific functions such as security, programming, or laboratories?
15. Handicapped access. Is the building totally accessible?
16. Energy-efficient design. Explore possible uses such as solar, south-facing design, skylights, or thermal storage systems.
17. Flexibility of design. Is the building designed for multipurpose use?
18. Building codes. Are there any discrepancies between the planned designed and local building codes?
19. Adequate space. Does the facility fulfill the space requirements according to the established standards?
20. Alternatives. Consider all the possibilities and evaluate the existing facilities. Explore renovation and rental as well as new construction. Perhaps there is available space underground or over traffic areas.
21. Environment and climate. Should attention be paid to the local conditions and development of appropriate facilities? Is there greater need for indoor or outdoor space?
22. Miscellaneous. Don't forget about acoustics, aesthetics, video stations, etc.

This essay will discuss only the issues of space standards in the college and university setting. Space standards are norms that have been established to serve as criteria and provide guidance for developing and evaluating facilities. They act as measures of the quantity, quality, weight, extent, or value of a program (Athletic Institute 1985). Space standards have been developed for numerous types of facilities from the elementary school indoor activity areas to college and university indoor activity areas.

These standards are useful to administrators who are planning to build, since relating standards to predicted enrollment results in assured space for all disciplines involved.

These standards include "A" space—activity space such as gymnasium floors, mat areas, swimming pools, weight training rooms, dance and aerobic rooms, therapeutic exercise rooms, and exercise physiology laboratories. Four types of "A" space have been established: A1 includes large gymnasium areas with relatively high ceilings and should account for approximately 55 percent of all activity space; A2 includes activity areas with relatively low ceilings and should account for approximately 30 percent of all activity space; A3 includes swimming and diving pools and should account for approximately 15 percent of all activity space; and A4 includes handball, racquetball, and squash courts and should amount to one court per every 800 students (Athletic Institute 1985).

To help in understanding the standards for college and university indoor sports activity areas, one should be aware of the enrollment relationships. The applied student population (ASP) of an institution is the total undergraduate enrollment plus 30 percent of the graduate enrollment (Athletic Institute 1985).

Also, it is important to understand that a minimum requirement states that any college or university having fewer than 3,000 undergraduate students enrolled should meet the minimum space standard of 3,000 students. Institutions with more than 3,000 students should calculate the necessary square footage by the standard of 12 square feet per student (Athletic Institute 1985).

Standards also have been established for ancillary space. This includes areas such as faculty and staff offices, conference rooms, seminar rooms, classrooms, locker rooms, dressing and shower rooms, laundry rooms, libraries, training rooms, equipment storage areas, supply rooms, and secretarial and reception space.

Seven types of ancillary space have been identified: Type I is locker, shower and dressing areas; Type II is classrooms, seminar rooms, and conference rooms; Type III is faculty, part-time faculty, and graduate assistant offices; Type IV is secretarial and reception space; Type V is storage, supply, equipment, and laundry rooms; Type VI is laboratories, research areas, libraries, and computer rooms; and Type VII is athletic training rooms (Strand 1988).

The recommended standard for ancillary space is 35 percent of the total indoor activity space. For example, 100,000 square feet of activity space would equal 35,000 square feet of ancillary area. The net usable area is considered to be a combination of activity and ancillary areas (i.e., 100,000 plus 35,000 equals 135,000 square feet) (Athletic Institute 1985).

Recent space standard studies have been conducted on both large and small college and university facilities. Such research provides valuable information in determining appropriate and adequate space standards which are extremely helpful to the developers of sports facilities. A brief history of the development of space standards has been included in this essay.

One of the first records identifying the necessary space for sports facilities was recorded in 1864 by Dio Lewis. He stated that the floor of the gymnasium should be marked with lines which "must be fifty-five inches apart, both lengthwise and crosswise of the room." This was to mark the place for students to stand. Therefore, the necessary room size would be based on the number of students in the class (Lockhart and Spears 1972).

In 1879, "the wonder gymnasium of the age" was built at Harvard University. Hemenway Gymnasium cost $100,000 and contained a wooden swimming pool (Lee 1983). Because there were no standards for developing facilities, this became the model to follow.

Between 1879 and 1920 the number of college sports facilities increased to 209 and included gymnasiums, playing fields, swimming pools, running tracks, boathouses, skating rinks, and courts for tennis, handball, and squash. Even with the rapid growth during this period, no concerted effort to standardize facilities took place (Lee 1983).

In 1938, standards for various aspects of college and university buildings were established. Evenden, Strayer, and Englehardt (1938) recommended that 50 square feet per student be the set standard for the size of a corrective exercise gymnasium. This was determined from the number of students who needed treatment and with regard to the number of treatments needed per week. The study emphasized that variations in enrollments and in programs within the health, physical education, and athletic departments would require a wide range of different facilities.

Donovan Smith, a planning analyst for the University of California, recommended space standards for colleges and universities in 1954. Then, in 1959 at the University of Illinois, the College of Physical Education was requested to take part in the development of a master plan for that institution. Without existing space standards to serve as a guide, the department established a standard for the square feet per student needed for physical education, intramural, and athletic facilities for colleges and universities. The work was completed by Sapora and Kenney (1961) and involved visiting each of the Big Ten universities and several institutions of similar enrollment size in the midwestern area of the United States. The result was the formation of a tentative standard and space classification.

In January 1965, the National Facilities Conference adopted the standards from the Sapora-Kenney study. These authorities disagreed on the standards in terms of square feet per student for indoor facilities in colleges and universities. They recommended 8.5 to 9.5 square feet of indoor activity space per student for the total undergraduate enrollment as opposed to 12 square feet suggested by Sapora and Kenney. They also proposed that 1,500 students should represent the minimum space needs of any collegiate institution; Sapora and Kenney had recommended 3,000 students as the minimum space requirement (Athletic Institute 1985).

The 1968 College and University Facilities Guide recommended that ancillary space should be a square footage equaling approximately 35 percent of the "A" space within a facility. Twelve square feet of indoor activity space per student in institutions with an enrollment of 3,000 or above was also recommended. Another division of "A" space was added to the guidelines. This space was called "A4" representing indoor handball and squash courts; the guideline recommended one court per 800 students (Athletic Institute 1968).

A description of ancillary area including percentages was developed by Strand in 1988. Strand did a follow-up study of the Sapora-Kenney study in the Big Ten universities. Walker's study in 1988, the first to deal specifically with space standards in small colleges and universities, found the current standards for activity space in small colleges and universities to be inappropriate. The purposes of this study were (a) to compare, by means of a questionnaire, interview, and square footage measurements, the physical education space guidelines established in 1967 by the National Facilities Conference with the "A" space and ancillary space in schools from the Rocky Mountain Athletic Conference and in the Midwest Collegiate Athletic Conference; (b) to establish ancillary space percentages for the schools in the two conferences within the seven types according to the criteria developed by Strand; and, (c) to determine whether the arbitrary space standard (which was set to represent the minimum physical recreation space needs of any collegiate institution based on 3,000 student enrollment) is a reasonable and adequate figure.

This study followed these procedures: (a) the president and department chair for each institution were contacted, (b) questionnaires were submitted to all institutions, (c) a visitation was made to each institution which included interviews with key personnel, (d) space measurements were acquired, (e) collected data were analyzed, and (f) conclusions and recommendations were stated.

The study included the following institutions:

Rocky Mountain Athletic Conference

Adams State College (Alamosa, Colorado) 2,400 students

Colorado School of Mines (Golden, Colorado) 2,300 students

Fort Lewis College (Durango, Colorado) 3,700 students

Mesa College (Grand Junction, Colorado) 2,800 students

University of Southern Colorado (Pueblo, Colorado) 3,500 students

Western New Mexico University (Silver City, New Mexico) 1,900 students

Western State College (Gunnison, Colorado) 2,700 students

Midwest Collegiate Athletic Conference

Beloit College (Beloit, Wisconsin) 1,000 students

Coe College (Cedar Rapids, Iowa) 1,200 students

Cornell College (Mount Vernon, Iowa)
   1,100 students
Grinnell College (Grinnell, Iowa)
   1,100 students
Illinois College (Jacksonville, Illinois)
   800 students
Knox College (Galesburg, Illinois)
   1,000 students
Lake Forest College (Lake Forest, Illinois)
   1,050 students
Lawrence University (Appleton, Wisconsin)
   1,200 students
Monmouth College (Monmouth, Illinois)
   750 students
Ripon College (Ripon, Wisconsin)
   900 students
St. Norbert College (DePere, Wisconsin)
   1,750 students

This investigation revealed an extreme difference between the recommended standard for indoor activity space and the mean for indoor activity space at the institutions reviewed. This study found 25 square feet per applied student population, which was more than double the recommended guideline of 12 square feet per applied student population. (Applied student population is the total undergraduate enrollment of the institution plus 30 percent of the graduate student enrollment.)

Walker's research also found a statistically significant difference between the types of ancillary space at each institution and the standard established by Strand. The largest differences existed between space provided for classroom, laboratories, and training rooms.

It is important to recognize that the space standards were developed for institutions with very large enrollments and, therefore, adjustments may need to be made for smaller institutions.

So what do space standards have to do with financial concerns? Sports facilities require vast expenditures of funds. It is critical that the planners of these facilities be accountable for those resources. Therefore, it is imperative that those facilities measure up to the needs and fulfill the purposes for which they have been designed.

Space standards and guidelines are available to aid those who are planning and developing sports facilities. To clearly define the amount of space and how that space is to be appropriated is essential to proper planning for building or renovating a facility. It is also of great importance to recognize spatial relationships and the effective and efficient management of those spaces.

Following are some final thoughts on cost saving measures related to space standards:

1. Design with the future in mind. Anticipate growth in enrollment and programs. Consider fads and sports that are being developed (e.g., indoor and outdoor soccer, squash, and team handball).
2. Hire a consultant who is familiar with sports facilities and the space standards associated with those facilities.
3. Select an architectural firm that has had experience designing the type of facility to be constructed.
4. Look at all the alternatives.
5. Visit similar facilities. Talk to staff. Find out features that need to be altered, additions that need to be made, and what mistakes to avoid.
6. Compare renovation costs with new construction costs. Are there areas which could easily be converted for other uses (e.g., indoor tennis courts converted to an indoor soccer area)?

7. Determine the space needs for your program and build the facility with these in mind.
8. Build for dual or multipurpose use when possible.
9. Plan ahead. Last-minute changes are costly.
10. Allow space for future expansion. Build extra seating, counting for ten years ahead.
11. Provide extra storage space for unanticipated needs.

REFERENCES

Athletic Institute and American Association for Health, Physical Education and Recreation. 1968. *College and university facilities guide for health, physical education, recreation and athletics,* Washington, D.C.

Athletic Institute and American Association for Health, Physical Education and Recreation. 1985. *Planning facilities for athletics, physical education and recreation,* Chicago.

Athletic Purchasing and Facilities. 1981. Small college realizes flexibility in its physical education complex. September, 46–47.

Evenden, E.S., G.D. Strayer, and N.L. Englehardt, 1938. *Standards for college buildings.* New York: Teachers College, Columbia University.

Lee, M. 1983. *A history of physical education and sports in the U.S.A.* New York: John Wiley & Sons.

Lockhart, A.S. and B. Spears. 1972. *Chronicle of American physical education.* Dubuque, Iowa: Wm. C. Brown.

Sapora, A., and H. Kenney. 1961. *A study of the present status, future needs and recommended standards regarding space used for health, physical education, physical recreation and athletics.* Champaign, Ill.: Stipes.

Smith, D.E. 1954. College and university space requirements. *The American school and university,* 287–295.

Strand, B.N. 1988. A space analysis of physical education activity areas and ancillary areas in Big Ten universities. Ph.D. diss., University of New Mexico, Albuquerque.

Walker, M.L. 1988. A space analysis of physical education activity areas and ancillary areas in selected small colleges and universities. Ph.D. dissertation, University of New Mexico, Albuquerque.

QUALITY MANAGEMENT AND SPORT

20

The Use of Information Technology in Sport Management to Provide the Competitive Edge: An Illustration in a Multipurpose Sport and Health Facility

Brian McNamara and Bernard Mullin

INTRODUCTION

Recent advances in computer applications have made a new technology readily available to the vast majority of small businesses (Dologite 1981). The increased power of computers, their ease of operation, and the decrease in their size and cost have all helped to make it feasible for many businesses to make computers available to their management and clerical staff. Furthermore, as the management approach to buying moves away from a traditional cost orientation and places more emphasis on revenue generation, greater future use of computers can be expected (Massey 1986).

If managers utilize present modes of computer technology, it is possible to obtain more accurate, comprehensive, and timely informa-

Brian McNamara is with the School of Business and Public Administration, California State University, Bakersfield, California, and Bernard Mullin is Vice President of Business Operations, Colorado Rockies Major League Baseball Club.

tion, which will have a direct impact on the competitive position of any business. Computer technology may have an immediate effect on a small company's competitive edge in two distinct areas: (a) cost reduction and (b) product differentiation (Porter and Millar 1985).

There is no doubt that computer systems can contribute substantially to cost reductions through increased efficiency and productivity in the performance of day-to-day clerical tasks. As confidence in using computers increases and the need for greater accuracy in defining the rules for decision making is realized, at all levels of management, a greater degree of automation of business activities can be expected. These automated activities may contribute to additional cost savings. It has become increasingly evident that the adoption of computer technology is resulting in a more productive work force for organizations with computerized management and operational functions (Issiki 1982).

Every small business has fixed and variable costs associated with various production, marketing, and support activities required to operate the business (Porter and Millar 1985). With the introduction of computer technology many of the cost items can be effectively controlled. Thus, a business can cut costs relative to that of a competitor and, as a result, gain an economic advantage. Computer technology can help a small business define its market segment in more detail. Detailed information can be used to help the organization customize its activities in the way that best serves this defined segment. Ultimately, these activities can improve service to customers and thus make the organization more competitive.

Rather than make generic theoretical claims about the benefits of computer technology for small businesses, this essay focuses on a multi-purpose sport and health facility (MSHF) and demonstrates how computer technology can improve its competitive position.

The MSHF industry is a service industry facing two major problems: (a) how to collect and control accounts receivables, and (b) how to minimize member attrition rates. Many computer information systems have been designed to assist in solving management-oriented problems. Besides serving the basic needs of MSHF managers, the computer information systems also provide information needed to improve management efficiency. This enables the management and support staff to operate more effectively in dealing with their members, proactively providing a better service and giving the organization a competitive edge in this area.

The competitive intelligence information system (CIIS) menu depicts all the primary and support activities necessary to operate a MSHF (Fig. 20.1).

The following sections will discuss each of the options displayed on the menu and demonstrate how each type of information can be used to improve the competitive position of an MSHF.

OPTION 1—MEMBER RECORDS AND LISTINGS/REPORTS

The database containing a member's record (Fig. 20.2) allows management to get a better handle on who belongs to the organization. It provides instantaneous access to information such as current membership counts, customer profiles, or geographic, demographic, psychographic, and behavioristic breakdowns. Information can be added, deleted, changed, retrieved, and printed. Furthermore, the information can be sorted by combinations of characteristics and can be combined to produce customized reports and lists in the format best suited to meet the managers' requirements. Target mailings can be selected from this database, thus improving the marketing efficiency of the organization.

A flexible report generator allows the decision maker to obtain counts of individual characteristics or combinations of characteristics as defined by the user and to produce census reports or other lists of information. For example, information generated can differentiate the types of members using the facility. This gives the management a better knowledge of its customer base, and activities can be planned and scheduled to meet the customer's needs.

OPTION 2—MEMBER BILLING (ACCOUNTS RECEIVABLE)

The various functions available under this option allow the accountant to prepare bills by accessing and retrieving debits and credits in a member's account (Fig. 20.3). In addition, one of the functions automatically posts annual dues and other regularly scheduled charges; charges at different profit centers; and multiple payment plans and partial payments. This is a highly efficient system giving management added control over its accounts receivable.

```
              THE COMPETITIVE INTELLIGENCE INFORMATION SYSTEM


    TYPE  1    MEMBER RECORDS AND LISTINGS/REPORTS

          2    MEMBER BILLING (ACCOUNTS RECEIVABLE)

          3    FINANCIAL MANAGEMENT PROGRAMS

          4    FRONT DESK CONTROL

          5    FITNESS AND WELLNESS PROGRAMS

          6    WORD PROCESSING, FORM LETTERS AND MAILING LABELS

          7    SALES AND PROSPECT MANAGEMENT




    PLEASE TYPE YOUR CHOICE AND TOUCH ENTER,
    OR TYPE 0 (ZERO) AND TOUCH ENTER TO EXIT
    THE PROGRAM:
```

FIGURE 20.1   The Competitive Intelligence Information System Menu

The electronic fund transfer program (EFT) function offers the MSHF a method for quick collection of receivables with an attendant low bad-debt ratio (around 3 percent at the most). Transactions can be transferred electronically by modem, disk, or paper. If the MSHF is fortunate enough to have a bank that offers EFT, accounts receivable is no longer a serious problem. There are no invoices to produce, no postage to pay, and no overlooked bills or late payments. Competition in the financial services industry is intensifying and as it does, EFT will be a service commonly offered to customers. Because these functions are repetitive in nature, computer technology can be used to perform the tasks at cost reductions and cost savings to the user.

Computer technology is responsible for revolutionizing the MSHF industry, changing from a sales-oriented industry (lifetime memberships and high fees paid up front) to a service-oriented industry (flat monthly fees paid over time).

OPTION 3—FINANCIAL PROGRAMS

The financial options allow the MSHF to have maximum control over their financial transactions (Fig. 20.4). The programs provide instantaneous financial reports and reduce dependence on outside services, resulting in savings to the club because cash is instantaneously deposited in the club's bank account. Here again, the

```
MEMBER # 000001      FIRST: Brian    INIT: M     LAST: McNamara

HOME ADDRESS                         LOCATION

STREET: 4321 Sugar Cane Avenue
CITY: Bakersfield                    SOCIAL SECURITY #: 012-68-5124
STATE: CA    ZIP: 93313              MEMBERSHIP STATUS: A


HOME PHONE: (805)397-3564: BUS:PHONE: (805)397-1232: EXT:      :
Gender: M      D.O.B.: 04/23/55   COUNSEL DATE: 09/09/88
LOCKER COMBINATION: 32-29-14

INTERESTS:      K,S               AVAILABLE: DD
ADD INTERESTS: Squash


SPOUSE: Karen


PHYSICIAN: Dr. Wong               PHYS PHONE: (805)354-1459


DIVISION: 124        PAYMENT METHOD: 10        COMPANY CODE: 04


TOTAL ATTENDANCE TO DATE: 10        :LAST DATE OF ATTENDANCE: 11/10/88
COMMENTS: Came third in the Local Mini Marathon
```

FIGURE 20.2   Member Information Screen

repetitive nature of these operations lend themselves to cost reductions provided by computer technology.

OPTION 4—FRONT DESK CONTROL

Steven is a member of a MSHF and he walks into the facility. The desk attendant asks for Steven's membership number and types it into the computer to reveal the screen in Figure 20.5.

What is the most important piece of information on this screen, keeping in mind that the MSHF industry is a service industry? The answer, obviously, is the person's name—Steven. Steven is pleased when the desk clerk addresses him by his name. In addition, the desk clerk may note additional information and congratulate Steven on his birthday and on the birth of his first baby. Not only does the clerk congratulate Steven but may give him two free drink vouchers to celebrate. What is Steven likely to tell his friends about the personal attention he receives at his MSHF?

What if Steven has an outstanding bill at the MSHF? Management's policy will dictate how the front desk clerk will act. The key point is that the information is immediately available and shows that Steven owes money to the club. How the club deals with Steven is another important issue. It is obvious that the MSHF, through computer technology, has an immediate control mechanism to deal with outstanding payments. This should bring to an end the problem facilities have faced where members fail to pay their dues for months but continue to use the club because faces are so familiar to club personnel.

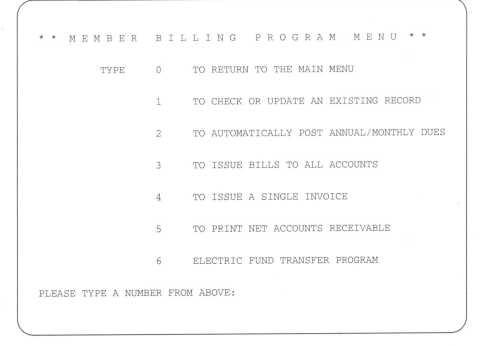

```
* *  M E M B E R    B I L L I N G    P R O G R A M    M E N U  * *

     TYPE     0     TO RETURN TO THE MAIN MENU

              1     TO CHECK OR UPDATE AN EXISTING RECORD

              2     TO AUTOMATICALLY POST ANNUAL/MONTHLY DUES

              3     TO ISSUE BILLS TO ALL ACCOUNTS

              4     TO ISSUE A SINGLE INVOICE

              5     TO PRINT NET ACCOUNTS RECEIVABLE

              6     ELECTRIC FUND TRANSFER PROGRAM

  PLEASE TYPE A NUMBER FROM ABOVE:
```

FIGURE 20.3   Member Billing Program Menu

In addition, the information on the screen includes the telephone number to call in case of an emergency. The type of membership is also displayed, telling the staff member which services are available to that member. The expiration date serves as a reminder to the desk clerk when it is time to issue a renewal notice.

The date, member's number, activity codes, and the time can all be stored in a database. What good is this information? A report can be generated from the data detailing the use of the facility on any given day (see Appendix 20.1). In addition, the data can be manipulated easily to produce weekly, bi-weekly, and monthly breakdowns. The manager can use this information in scheduling staff assignments.

Keeping in mind the MSHF industry is a service organization, the management needs to develop appropriate plans to overcome "bottlenecks" and effectively schedule staff assignments. These actions directly influence customer service in a positive manner—nobody likes to wait to be served. Conversely, management wants to minimize staff salaries when services are not needed.

In addition, the manager can ask for attendance reports at various levels (see Appendix 20.2). This is the most critical part of an "early warning system" designed to reduce member turnover.

```
* * F I N A N C I A L   M A N A G E M E N T   P R O G R A M S   M E N U * *

         TYPE          0      TO RETURN TO THE MAIN MENU

                      11      TO WORK WITH FINANCIAL STATEMENTS

                      12      TO WORK WITH GENERAL LEDGER

                      13      TO WORK WITH ACCOUNTS PAYABLE

                      14      TO WORK WITH INVENTORY

                      15      TO WORK WITH PAYROLL

                      16      TO WORK WITH DAILY TRANSACTIONS FILE

     PLEASE TYPE YOUR CHOICE:
```

FIGURE 20.4 Financial Management Programs Menu

What can management do with this information? A sales force could use the list to call members who have not made recent use of the facility to ask them if there is a problem and what the club can do to get them back.

Management can create lists of members who are heavy users of the club's services and, from these lists, develop demographic and socioeconomic profiles of those members using the club regularly. The information obtained from these interviews can be examined and a better understanding of the club's customers can be established.

These examples demonstrate the importance of computer technology as a tool to be used to provide management with greater internal control over the primary and support activities involved in the daily running of the organization.

Furthermore, close attention to the attendance data can facilitate effective communication between the MSHF and its members, which will have a direct positive influence on marketing efforts.

OPTION 5—FITNESS AND WELLNESS PROGRAMS

Fitness and wellness are the two hot topics of the nineties in MSHF. It is important for a facility to creatively involve its members in the learning process. Adoption of fitness and wellness programs in a MSHF (Fig. 20.6) can generate new profit centers. These sophisticated programs offer an opportunity to provide a new fee-based service which can attract new members and help maintain existing memberships.

```
Steven          Platt

MEMBER NUMBER 44444     MEMBERSHIP EXPIRATION DATE   01/01/94

YEARLY MEMBERS                          HOME PHONE   (805)589-5125
                                        BUS PHONE    (805)397-8645
Wife 1st baby — Cindy




BALANCE                 170.00

OTHER FAMILY MEMBERS — Naomi, Antonia




PLEASE TYPE ACTIVITY CODE:              :
```

FIGURE 20.5   MSHF Member Information Screen

As members have become more sophisticated in their knowledge of exercise and nutrition, personally tailored fitness programs have become the fashion. Such programs provide a competitive edge over less sophisticated competition.

OPTION 6—WORD PROCESSING, FORM LETTERS AND MAILING LABELS

This option serves as a word processor (Fig. 20.7). Form letters and a mailmerge option allow the club to send personalized mail to selected segments of its members. For example, the club might send a letter to every member who has an outstanding balance; the computer can generate a list of the applicable members. Once the standard letter has been written, it is a simple matter to combine the list of members with the letter. The use of personalized direct mailings will help improve communication between the members and the facility and thereby

contribute to the success of marketing efforts. Mailing labels are an obvious saving, particularly if the list to be printed has already been presorted by zip code. Again, the potential for realizing significant cost savings by using word processing with a mailmerge option is excellent.

OPTION 7—SALES AND PROSPECT MANAGEMENT

This application gives a MSHF a superior handle on sales and prospect management, which translates into increased membership sales (Fig. 20.8). Information is stored on all sales prospects and guests and provides complete lead analysis and sales staff performance reports such as closing ratios and average sales dollars. The membership database can be automatically updated when a prospect or guest becomes a member. This action means one point of entry for all data. In addition, a tickler file can help

APPENDIX 20.1
Daily Summary for '11/30/94'

MORNING SESSION
PAGE NO. 00001
12/08/94

TIME	TEN	RACQ	NAUT	SWIM	LIFE	AERO	RUN	OTHER	TOTAL
6:00	1	1	1	1	1	1	1	1	8
7:00	4	3	0	0	0	0	0	0	7
8:00	2	0	3	3	0	1	3	3	15
9:00	1	2	4	2	1	1	1	3	15
10:00	0	1	1	1	1	1	1	0	6
11:00	0	0	0	0	0	0	3	5	8
** TOTAL **									
	8	7	9	7	3	4	9	12	59

AFTERNOON SESSION
PAGE NO. 00001
12/08/94

TIME	TEN	RACQ	NAUT	SWIM	LIFE	AERO	RUN	OTHER	TOTAL
12:00	7	0	0	0	0	0	0	0	7
13:00	0	3	0	4	0	0	0	0	7
14:00	0	0	0	0	3	0	0	0	3
15:00	0	0	0	0	1	3	1	0	5
16:00	0	0	0	0	0	0	1	0	1
17:00	0	0	0	0	0	0	0	6	6
** TOTAL **									
	7	3	0	4	4	3	2	6	29

APPENDIX 20.1—*Continued*

EVENING SESSION
PAGE NO. 00001
12/08/94

TIME	TEN	RACQ	NAUT	SWIM	LIFE	AERO	RUN	OTHER	TOTAL
18:00	0	0	1	3	0	3	0	1	8
19:00	0	0	2	0	0	0	0	0	2
20:00	0	0	1	3	0	0	0	0	4
21:00	0	0	0	3	0	0	0	0	3
22:00	0	0	0	1	0	3	0	0	4
23:00	0	0	0	0	0	3	0	0	3
** TOTAL **									
	0	0	4	10	0	9	0	1	24

ACTIVITY SUMMARY FOR '11/30/94'

TENNIS	15	RACQUETBALL	10	NAUTILUS	13
SWIMMING	21	LIFECYCLE	7	AEROBICS	16
RUNNING	11	OTHER	19		

TOTAL NUMBER OF PERSONS USING THE CLUB =   113

APPENDIX 20.2
****** ATTENDANCE DATA ******

LOWER ATTENDANCE LEVEL =   0
UPPER ATTENDANCE LEVEL =   0

NAME		MEMBER #	HOME PHONE	BUSINESS PHONE	EX
Paul	Calvillo	000020	(805) 231-7575	(805) 323-7585	
Peter	Carr	000021	(805) 343-8687	(805) 345-8474	21
Joseph	Derr	000022	(805) 589-5674	(805) 324-7858	11
Sidney	Halbrook	000023	(805) 589-4356	(805) 434-6474	
Leslie	Haskins	000024	(805) 589-7485	(805) 434-7575	
Francis	Howard	000025	(805) 379-7858	(805) 355-4748	23
Frank	Jones	000026	(805) 357-6475	(805) 343-8585	
Mary	McNabb	000027	(805) 397-3564	(805) 589-5373	12
Jessie	Mills	000028	(805) 589-5125	(805) 647-8484	
Wally	Roberts	000029	(805) 233-8976	(805) 893-8484	14

```
*  *  F I T N E S S   A N D   W E L L N E S S   P R O G R A M S   M E N U   *  *

    TYPE    0     TO RETURN TO THE MAIN MENU

           21     TO WORK WITH FITNESS/WELLNESS EVALUATION FILE

           22     TO WORK WITH EXERCISE ACTIVITY LOG AND CALORIES
                  BURNED/AEROBICS POINTS FILE

           23     TO WORK WITH EXERCISE PRESCRIPTION PROGRAM

           24     TO WORK WITH CORONARY RISK FACTOR ANALYSIS PROGRAM

           25     TO WORK WITH STRESS PERSONALITY PATTERN PROGRAM

           26     TO WORK WITH STRESS FACTOR IDENTIFICATION AND
                  WELLNESS ASSESSMENT

           27     TO WORK WITH LIFE EXPECTANCY ASSESSMENT PROGRAM

           28     TO WORK WITH NUTRITIONAL EVALUATION AND PRESCRIPTIVE
                  DIET PROGRAMS

        PLEASE TYPE YOUR CHOICE — THANK YOU:
```

FIGURE 20.6   Fitness and Wellness Programs Menu

the sales staff in follow-up on potential members. The information gained can be put to good use to define the membership base more accurately. In turn, this information can be used to design training programs for sales personnel, accurately design sales material, and pinpoint a target population for more productive advertising campaigns (Massey 1986).

One cautionary note: It is important to ensure that managers and staff understand what information is available to them and how to apply it. Application training is the most critical piece of the information technology jigsaw puzzle.

Inadequacies in overall performance may stem from the quality of personnel and their inability to make the best use of the information rather than from any deficiencies in the information itself or the computer system that provides it.

CONCLUSION

This essay has provided an overview of a computer information system and how it may be used by MSHF management. There is no doubt that such an information system, when used appropriately, provides solutions to the problems

```
* * F O R M   L E T T E R S   A N D   M A I L M E R G E   M E N U * *


    TYPE   0    TO RETURN TO THE MAIN MENU


           1    TO CREATE FORM LETTER FILE


           2    TO PRINT MAILING LABELS


           3    TO PRINT FORM LETTERS







    PLEASE TYPE A NUMBER AND TOUCH ENTER:
```

FIGURE 20.7   Form Letters and Mailmerge Menu

of the MSHF industry. The system can increase cash flow through faster receivables collection, higher guest and no-show fee receipts, and reductions in the number of delinquent accounts. When exclusive marketing programs are utilized effectively, a higher percentage of prospects can be converted into sales and can significantly reduce member attrition rates. There can be real savings through reduction of salaries and outside service costs for bookkeeping, invoicing, IFT, and payroll. The addition of the fitness and wellness programs can provide new profit centers and be used to gain a competitive advantage by offering personalized fitness programs.

This example shows how the adoption of computers can reduce costs, provide revenue-generating opportunities, and make management and staff more effective, productive, and best of all, proactive. All these benefits directly influence cost reductions and contribute toward providing a MSHF with a competitive advantage.

The cumulative effect of all these benefits allows an organization to have greater internal management control over its primary and support activities. This control, in itself, provides a competitive advantage over rival businesses who do not employ computer technology.

```
* *  S A L E S   A N D   P R O S P E C T   M A N A G E M E N T  * *

  TYPE   0     TO RETURN TO THE MAIN MENU

         1     TO WORK WITH PROSPECT FILE

         2     SALES PERSONNEL ACTIVITY LOG

         3     TO WORK WITH CASH/CREDIT SALES FILE

         4     TO WORK WITH SALES ANALYSIS FILE

         5     TO WORK WITH SALES PERSONNEL PERFORMANCE FILE

         6     TO TRANSFER THE PROSPECT FILE TO THE MEMBER
               RECORD FILE

         7     TO WORK WITH SALES AND MARKETING UTILITY MENU



      PLEASE TYPE A NUMBER:
```

FIGURE 20.8   Sales and Prospect Management Menu

REFERENCES

Dologite, D. G. 1981. Using small computers for more effective business management. *American Journal of Small Business* 5(4): 36–47.

Issiki, K. R. 1982. *Small business computers.* Englewood Cliffs, N.J.: Prentice-Hall.

Massey, T. K. 1986. Computers in small business: A case of under-utilization. *American Journal of Small Business* 11(2): 51–59.

Porter, M. E., and V. E. Millar. 1985. How information gives you the competitive edge. *Harvard Business Review* (July–August): 149–160.

21

An Analysis of Golf Management Programs

William L. Shelburn

INTRODUCTION

The intent of this essay is to examine the development of golf management programs at colleges and universities in the United States. Four programs will be reviewed, their curricula examined, the reasons for their establishment analyzed and compared, and the benefits these programs provide to their respective schools evaluated.

The growth of the golf industry in the United States has been exceptional (Table 21.1). In 1978 there were 14 million golfers in the U.S. By 1988 that figure had risen to 23.4 million, an increase of 67 percent over this ten-year period. The number of rounds played by golfers has also gone up significantly. In 1978, 337 million rounds were played in the United States, and by 1988 that number had increased to 487 million (Benson 1988, 2).

TABLE 21.1 Growth of Golf in the United States

	Golfers (millions)	Rounds Played (millions)
1978	14.0	337
1979	14.6	346
1980	15.1	358
1981	15.6	368
1982	16.0	379
1983	16.5	391
1984	17.0	403
1985	17.5	415
1986	20.2	421
1987	21.7	434
1988	23.4	487

Source: National Golf Foundation, 1992.

The appeal of the game can be explained in part by the comment of one golf enthusiast. "Golf is a lot like sex; you don't have to be good at it to enjoy it." Not only are people enjoying golf, they are spending a great deal of money in the process. The golf industry generates $20 billion annually, a number that analysts expect to double by the year 2000. In addition,

William L. Shelburn is with the College of Business Administration, University of South Carolina–Aiken.

expenditures for golf-related travel and lodging were $7.8 billion and equipment and apparel sales were $2 billion in 1988 (Benson 1988, 2).

The real estate industry is also benefitting from the popularity of golf. Many of the new golf courses being built in the United States are associated with housing developments. Developers realize that the popularity of golf can be used as an inducement to sell homes. Land worth little more than $1,000 an acre suddenly appreciates to $160,000 or more per acre when it is developed around a golf course. Quarter-acre lots on Hilton Head Island, an area once considered to be only marginal farmland, now sell for $75,000 or more if they lay adjacent to one of the island's many golf courses.

With this increase in golf course construction has come a burgeoning demand for golf professionals to manage the pro shops at these courses. These people need to possess increasingly sophisticated marketing and management skills in order to do their job. It is no longer enough for a golf professional to be able to give a lesson, regrip a club, and run a blind bogey tournament. Golf professionals have become retailers and marketers. Most club professionals do not earn their livelihoods simply from giving golf lessons; the sale of merchandise in their shops accounts for an increasing proportion of their incomes. The head professional at a large municipal course or country club needs managerial and motivational skills to supervise employees.

SANCTIONED PROFESSIONAL GOLF MANAGEMENT PROGRAMS

For this reason, as well as a desire to have more golf professionals with a broader background than just the ability to play the game, the Professional Golf Association (PGA) has entered into an agreement with two universities and one college in the United States. These three schools offer golf management programs, providing the student with an opportunity to earn a bachelor's degree in business administration and twenty-four of the thirty-six credits required for Class A PGA professional status.

The Class A status is extremely important for those students who want to work as golf professionals. Virtually all private and municipal courses in the United States and Canada require this status of their head professional.

The first program of this type was established in 1975 at Ferris State College in Big Rapids, Michigan. More recently, Mississippi State University and New Mexico State University have developed golf management majors. These programs consist of 120 hours of academic credit and twenty months of co-op work with Class A professionals at a country club, public course, or golf resort. In addition, four PGA workshops must be completed by the student. These workshops are taught on campus by PGA professionals and cover topics such as the rules of golf, club repair, cart repair, and golf instruction.

The co-op programs provide the students with an opportunity to learn what it would be like to be a municipal course or club professional. In addition, they receive a degree in marketing which they can use to enter the world of business should they decide, after their co-op experience, that being a golf professional is no longer their goal. This is the beauty of co-op work: An individual can experience an occupation but not have to commit to it.

The growth of these programs at Ferris State and Mississippi State have been phenomenal. Ferris State, which is the oldest of the three existing programs, has 300 students enrolled. They graduate 50 students each year and are forced to reject many applicants. The program is so popular that the 100 students they admit for the fall semester are selected by January. Each Ferris

State graduate has been successfully placed in the industry. This outstanding placement rate is testimony to the quality of their program. Almost all of the graduates accept positions as assistant professionals at public or private golf courses.

Mississippi State's program is much newer. Established in 1985, this program graduated its first full class in December 1988. There are presently 120 students enrolled in the curriculum. Students who enroll in the professional golf management program must have a minimum golf handicap of 8 or lower, as certified by a PGA pro or a golf coach. Transfer students must have a 2.5 cumulative grade point average on all college work attempted. The university also requires that the student go through a formal orientation during which he or she receives academic and/or career advice from three different individuals. The advising team consists of a marketing professor, the cooperative education director, and the Mississippi State University Class A PGA director of golf course operations.

This program has benefitted Mississippi State in several ways. First, the program has been an excellent means of attracting out-of-state students. Students from the northeastern region of the United States, in particular, have been attracted by the uniqueness of the program, the warm climate, and the fact that the university has its own golf course. These out-of-state golf management students have convinced some of their nongolfing friends to attend the school.

Second, enrollments in the professional golf management program have justified efforts to make significant improvements in the university golf course. The university now has a par 72 championship layout capable of accommodating major collegiate tournaments. This, of course, has aided Mississippi State University in recruiting young players for its golf team.

The third PGA-sanctioned program in the country is at New Mexico State University. Its program, like the other two, can be completed in four and one-half years and includes twenty months of co-op work with a Class A PGA professional. New Mexico State University's program is the newest of the three. They admitted their first group of students in the fall of 1988.

CURRICULA

The golf management program curriculum at the three schools are quite similar. They are divided into four areas: general education requirements, business foundation courses, marketing concentration, and golf management courses. The general education requirements include English, math, natural science, and social science courses. The business foundation courses include principles of accounting, management, marketing, and finance. In addition, business policy and production management are both required by Mississippi State and New Mexico State. There are some differences in the curricula. Mississippi State requires courses in money and banking, and statistics, while New Mexico State and Ferris State do not. The marketing concentration requirements at the three schools are very similar. Courses in marketing research, consumer behavior, and marketing management are required by all three schools.

The golf management segment, sometimes referred to as the technical courses, is similar among all three schools. Ferris State developed the first courses in this area with the guidance of the PGA. Mississippi State and New Mexico State have simply duplicated Ferris State's offerings. As Dr. Lynn Loudenback, professional golf management program director at New Mexico State stated: "There is no need to reinvent the wheel. The skills required of a Class A PGA professional are thoroughly covered in the courses developed by Ferris State and Mississippi State and we see no need to deviate from their format in offering these courses on our campus.''

The goal of requiring these eighteen or nineteen hours of credit is to provide the student with a general knowledge of course maintenance, swing mechanics, and even food service operations. In addition to these golf management courses, professional golf management majors must complete four separate PGA workshops taught by Class A professionals. The subjects include the rules of golf, club repair, cart repair, and teaching the golf swing.

The programs at these three schools are all sanctioned by the PGA. Presently, the PGA is not providing sanctioning for any additional programs. Henry Thrower, director of golf management programs for the PGA, has stated that their purpose is to avoid saturating the market with professional golf management graduates. The PGA is pleased with the acceptance their graduates have received to this point, and it will be at least two years or more before another program will be started.

NONSANCTIONED PROFESSIONAL GOLF MANAGEMENT PROGRAMS

There is, however, one other professional golf management program in existence in the country and it is located at Methodist College in Fayetteville, North Carolina. A small private college located in the Sandhills region of North Carolina, Methodist decided to start their own major without PGA sanctioning. Their campus is situated in a region famous for its many golf courses and enjoys a climate conducive to year-round play.

A reluctance on the part of the PGA to expand their sanctioned programs, a need to increase enrollment, and a location attractive to young golfers in the East prompted Methodist to offer a professional golf management program. The school has been extremely successful in attracting students from outside the state of North Carolina. Cost and climate are the primary reasons for this. Methodist's annual fees and tuition of over $9,000 are quite high for most students in North Carolina. This figure is reasonable, however, for a student from the Northeast where tuition and fees at many private colleges exceed $18,000 annually. Also, a warm climate and the proximity of so many good golf courses, including the acclaimed Pinehurst courses, are other reasons why the program has grown so rapidly.

Methodist's program is very similar to those at the three sanctioned schools, with a few exceptions. First, the degree Methodist offers is a general business degree without a concentration in marketing. Second, they do not require the courses in food service management and anatomy and kinesiology required by the other programs. Third, and most important, they have a different co-op arrangement. Students co-op during the summer and not during the school year, which is the format at the other three schools. Because of this policy, most of the golf courses where the students are working are in the Northeast. This arrangement allows the student to complete all requirements for the program in four years. It does require, however, a great deal of travel by the professional golf management director, who visits over forty different courses each summer to evaluate student work performance.

The professional golf management program at Methodist College has been quite successful. There are 150 students enrolled out of a student body of approximately 1,000. It has filled a need that existed in this area of the country for a golf management program. The program has attracted more students to Methodist, made their golf team more competitive, and prompted the college to begin construction of an eighteen-hole golf course.

CONCLUSIONS

Professional Golf Management programs are an answer to a growing need for well-trained golf professionals. The skills required of a PGA professional have become more varied and demanding. A knowledge of business concepts, in particular, has become essential. This need has spawned the development of these programs. At the four schools where professional golf management degrees are granted, enrollments have increased, the schools have enhanced their reputations, and their golf facilities have been improved. With the continued growth in the number of golfers and golf facilities, it seems certain that more of these programs will be established.

REFERENCE

Benson, Gordon G. 1988. *Golf projection 2000,* vol. 2 (October). Palm Beach Garden, Fla.: National Golf Foundation.

22

Beyond Winning: An Expanded Model for Evaluating Athletic Program Quality

Scott E. Branvold

Athletic programs within the educational setting are frequently criticized for what is considered to be an overemphasis on winning, yet winning tends to be the primary criterion by which athletic success is measured. This is magnified at the major college level where the financial incentives to win have grown dramatically in recent years. The visible, revenue-producing sports receive most of the attention and support, and they also carry the program's image and provide its financial lifeline. This has created a highly pressurized environment in which winning football and basketball teams have become *the* measures of program quality. This narrow view is one of the major problems with athletics in the educational setting. While appropriate at the professional level, it distorts the purpose of intercollegiate and interscholastic sport. It is

incumbent upon both school and athletic administrators to broaden the focus for evaluating athletics by developing a set of program goals that will address athletics within the educational setting in a realistic way. The model proposed here suggests some basic parameters within which athletic program quality can be assessed. The model for athletic quality (Fig. 22.1) outlines five fundamental considerations that should be assessed and evaluated. While these parameters are not new concerns for the athletic administrator, they may serve to clarify and formalize methods for evaluation.

The first two parameters, winning and financial sufficiency, are standard and interrelated criteria in the assessment of athletic success. Winning will often increase gate receipts and increase media-related revenue in some cases. Some contend that winning will result in more generous alumni, although the research does not support this contention. Sack and Watkins (1985) concluded that football performance has little or no impact on the amount of money alumni contribute each year but cautioned

Scott E. Branvold is with the Department of Health, Physical Education and Recreation, University of Oklahoma, Norman, Oklahoma.

204

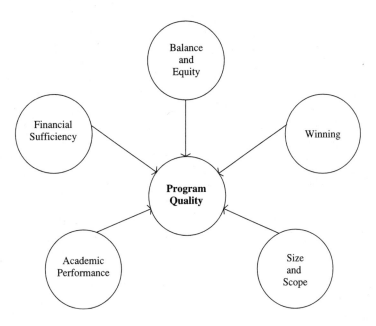

FIGURE 22.1 Model for Athletic Quality

against the idea that athletic programs cannot affect donations in a variety of other ways. Gaski and Etzel (1985) found no apparent connection between donations and football and basketball performance, although they also suggest that a more complex relationship may exist.

The other side of this interrelationship involves the influence money has on the ability to win. Sufficient financial resources will dictate the (a) number of scholarships available, (b) ability to attract and keep quality coaches, (c) quality of facilities, (d) extensiveness of recruiting efforts, and (e) extent of support services available. This cycle in which wins generate revenue, which leads to more wins, exists primarily in the NCAA Division I programs and tends to perpetuate a system in which there is relatively limited access to the elite levels in the major sports of football and basketball.

This is particularly true in football which requires a large number of players. The Division I football powers have changed very little over the past twenty-five years. Only eighteen schools (17.1 percent of Division I institutions) comprised 76 percent of the final top ten ratings positions from 1964 to 1988, and the dominance is even greater if only the top five are considered (Earle 1989). The "haves" willingly subsidize the "have-nots" to maintain the system. Huge guarantees lure weak opponents into the large stadia of the major powers to give one side a big pay day and the other side a victory to impress the pollsters. This relationship and the risks it represents is dramatized by the consequences of the penalties the NCAA imposed on the University of Oklahoma football program. While the bowl and television sanctions and the scholarship and recruiting limitations clearly penalize Oklahoma, other schools in the Big Eight Conference rely on the shared bowl and television money generated by Oklahoma. Oklahoma is far more capable of absorbing the loss of these funds than most of the other schools in the conference so, in some respects, Kansas State or Iowa State may suffer more from Oklahoma's NCAA penalty than Oklahoma will. If winning and financial sufficiency are the sole or primary determinants of program quality, the chances of achieving success are quite limited for many programs.

At other competitive levels (Division II and Division III NAIA), the "wins leads to revenue leads to wins" cycle is not as relevant a consideration because the financial rewards for winning are not as substantial. The athletic programs at these levels are rarely operated at a profit, and the financial objective may simply be to minimize the budget deficit. Winning will likely help in this endeavor, but financial incentive is greatly reduced at this level. The most successful programs tend to be the ones with the most financial support, but the disparity between the "haves" and "have-nots" is not nearly so dramatic or imposing a barrier.

The emphasis (and overemphasis) on winning as the only acceptable result is a sociological issue largely beyond the focus of this essay. Rather than trying to minimize the importance of winning as a reflection of program quality, effort should be made instead to establish a more realistic set of standards for what can be accomplished. Winning, for example, frequently creates a focus on football and basketball, often to the exclusion of other sports. There have been efforts, usually at the conference level, to give "All Sports" awards to recognize success across all conference-sponsored sports. Unfortunately, the attention to such an award is usually minimal, with the announcement buried on the back page of the sports section in the newspaper. This is shabby treatment for what many would consider to be a much better representation of the overall quality of an athletic program than whether the football team was invited to a bowl game. Greater emphasis on such

an award would encourage a more cooperative and supportive program environment and help raise public awareness of other sports and athletes.

Financially, most athletic programs struggle, but the struggle tends to be a relative one. The largest programs seem to operate under the philosophy that everything must be done "first class" in order to be competitive. The assessment may be accurate, but it creates an insatiable appetite for money that manifests itself in the constant search for revenue sources. Cases in point are the recent marketing consortium formed by twenty-two Division I schools under the guidance of Fred Miller at San Diego State and the trend toward corporate sponsorship for individual games (Dunnavant 1989, *The NCAA News* 14 June 1989). Many are critical of this type of commercialization of college athletics, yet often athletic programs are divorced from the institutional funding process and expected to be self sustaining.

The other side of the financial equation, expenses, is a less appealing alternative in balancing the books. Reducing costs often takes the form of dropping nonrevenue sports rather than tightening the expenditures of football or basketball. The NCAA has formed a committee charged with addressing the issue of cost control. Expense areas to receive special attention include recruiting, financial aid, staffing, and competitive policies (*The NCAA News* 7 June 1989). With salaries, scholarships, and travel comprising 60 to 80 percent of the typical athletic budget, these are certainly the areas which require the closest scrutiny (Raiborn 1986).

In smaller programs, the financial struggle tends to be more of a day-to-day effort to minimize the deficit through innovative revenue generation, tightly monitored expenditures, and institutional and student subsidization. In some respects, smaller programs are, by necessity, more fiscally responsible and aware than their larger and more famous cousins, but their stakes are considerably lower. Regardless of size, however, there are means of assessing the financial performance and operations of the program beyond profit and loss.

Any well-run business has certain industry guidelines it can use as a basis for comparison to assess its own status and performance. While such industry standards are not readily available in the athletics literature, the NCAA has commissioned periodic reports that can provide valuable information regarding the financial operations and conditions of athletic programs at various competitive levels. The most recent of these was completed for the years 1981 to 1985 and includes some trend analysis dating back to 1973 (Raiborn 1986). For example, the percentage of the revenue of typical programs from contributions or the average percentage of expenses attributed to recruiting, travel, equipment, and salaries may be used as indicators of operating strengths or weaknesses. Revenue and expense ratios such as these can help administrators compare their programs against norms and against the performance of high-quality programs. In addition to the large-scale data from sources such as the Raiborn analyses, more relevant cohort groups such as conference affiliations may be used to help establish an even more meaningful set of comparative norms. Once norms and standards have been established and realistic goals and objectives have been set, the process of evaluating financial performance becomes a more precise and focused exercise.

The emphasis on winning and financial considerations is difficult to diminish, but looking at program quality requires going beyond these parameters to assess other aspects of the athletic program. One of these factors is program size or scope. Broyles and Hay (1979) suggest that growth is an implicit objective of most athletic organizations, yet many programs have cut

sports in reaction to the financial strains of expanding women's programs or that arise from difficult economic conditions. The number of sports and the number of athletes in the program are both readily available measures of size. There are ways to expand such an evaluation that can be useful in supporting the role and assessing the impact of athletics in the college community. Criteria such as the athlete-to-student ratio, the number of students involved as band members or cheerleaders, and the number of student spectators expands the perspective of program impact. This can be taken even further to include analyses of the economic impact on and recreational value of the program to the community using a model such as those devised by the U.S. Army Corps of Engineers (Allen 1988). Several athletic departments have conducted such impact studies. The Center for Economic and Management Research at the University of Oklahoma estimates nearly $24 million per year comes to the Norman–Oklahoma City area from those attending Oklahoma football games (Terry 1988). Penn State's Center for Regional Business conservatively estimates an impact of over $40 million from Penn State football (*The NCAA News* 8 July 1987). The combination of all these factors provides important information that more completely portrays the scope and impact of the athletic program.

The two other parameters in this expanded model for program evaluation are what Berg (1989) refers to as integrity issues that challenge athletic administrators. One of these parameters, academics, has been an issue of concern for many years. Program equity is a more recent concern the origins of which, in one context at least, are closely tied to the Title IX legislation of the mid-1970s.

The relationship between athletics and academics has been characterized by abuses in many instances. Altering transcripts, awarding grades for little or no work, double standards for athletes, meaningless or directionless coursework, recruiting marginal or incompetent students, hiring test takers are all a part of the litany of academic shenanigans seen in athletics over the years. Many efforts have been made to address and reduce some of the abuses, as evidenced by the voluminous NCAA Manual. Some recent NCAA actions have included rules requiring progress towards a degree and limitations on recruiting marginal students through the controversial Proposition 48 (Bylaw 5–1–j) and the even more controversial Proposition 42. One suggestion that has received some preliminary consideration involves tying scholarship availability to graduation rate (Schultz 1989).

Several factors can be assessed to provide indicators of a program's level of commitment to academics at all stages, from recruitment to graduation. Evaluation should begin with assessment of the academic capabilities of recruited athletes. While this is routinely done by looking at high school GPAs and college board scores, a telling comparison could be any noted differential between athletes and nonathletes. Another possible indicator involves the policy of many institutional entrance standards. The percentage of athletes in this group should be compared with the percentage of athletes in the student body.

Measures of academic commitment during an athlete's career should include the amount of counseling and tutoring assistance available and measured progress toward a degree. Graduation rate is certainly another reflection of academic performance that should be assessed in the context of the institutional graduation rate. Care should be taken to monitor each team's graduation rate rather than merely looking at the overall rate, which can be somewhat misleading. Recent figures indicate the overall graduation rate for athletes and nonathletes is very similar (around 50 percent), but football and men's bas-

ketball graduation rates lag well below the average (41 percent and 33 percent, respectively, in Division I) (Schultz 1989). Dick Schultz, executive director of the NCAA, contends that the athletic rate should be 10 percent higher than for the general student body (Maisel 1988).

While athletic personnel (athletes, coaches, athletic directors) must bear much of the blame for academic abuses, institutional administrators also share in the responsibility. Regardless of public posturing about the importance of academics, the hiring (and firing) of coaches frequently is tied almost exclusively on winning, while concern for academics is ignored. The pressure imposed by alumni and the community to build and maintain winning programs can create some difficult conflicts of interest for administrators. Submitting to such pressures undermines the commitment to academics.

Perhaps the single most important factor in attaining real academic success lies in hiring coaches who are first committed to the educational goals of the organization. Employing coaches with a history of academic unconcern reflects programmatic unconcern as well. Some institutions are now attaching academic performance clauses to their coaching contracts, but it remains to be seen how programs will react to coaches who produce academically but do not win consistently (Copeland 1989).

The other parameter for assessing program quality can be termed equity or balance. There are multiple elements that make up this parameter with the most prominent and publicized concern being that of equity between men's and women's programs. This became a significant issue in athletics with the passage of Title IX in the mid-1970s, and many male administrators continue to grumble about the problems it has created. Establishing standards of equity is the difficult part of assessing this aspect of program quality. The task is complicated even more in circumstances where large football or basketball programs underwrite many or all of the other sports in the program. In reality, however, only about half (48 percent) of the Division I football programs operate at a profit, and even fewer Division I basketball programs are profitable. Outside of Division I, 90 percent or more of the football and basketball programs operate at a loss and provide no subsidy at all for the rest of the sports (Raiborn 1986).

Absolute parity may not be a possible or even advisable goal in some circumstances, but there are many other situations in which the preferential treatment given to the ''major'' men's sports cannot be justified on the basis of their financial support for the rest of the program. Regardless of the philosophical position taken as to what constitutes equity, there are several measures that can be used to assess the fairness of an athletic program. The ratio between scholarships allocated and scholarships allowed is one measure of program emphasis. If the full complement of allowable scholarships is available for men's basketball but not for women's basketball, the equitability of such an arrangement should be questioned. Coaching expertise, travel opportunities and conditions, training and practice facilities, quality of equipment, medical care, academic support, and publicity efforts are all factors that can be assessed rather easily in determining the balance of an athletic program (*The NCAA News* 4 January 1989).

In addition, such assessments should not be based solely on gender differences but should address the ''major sport–minor sport'' dichotomy where these same factors can be applied. The ''minor'' sports participants certainly have a right to expect that their efforts to excel merit equitable treatment despite the limited acclaim they receive. A program of quality will demonstrate a concern that all athletes feel a sense of worth and contribution. As an outstanding golfer stated when asked why he chose a particular university, ''They made me feel like my sport was important.''

The five parameters outlined here can be used as the foundation for program evaluation. Indeed, the NCAA's efforts at program certification may ultimately provide very specific direction in this endeavor (*The NCAA News* 26 April 1989, 16 August 1989). The institutional self-study plan already mandated by the NCAA will serve as the basis for the accreditation process and will include assessment of institutional control, finances, personnel, recruiting, support services, and student-athlete profile (Schultz 1989).

Great diversity and many philosophical differences exist across athletics programs. Without dictating priorities, this model provides the foundations of evaluation and allows individual programs to determine the appropriate emphasis. If clear, concise, and realistic goals and objectives are developed around each of these parameters, measures to assess program quality are readily available. It is important, however, to articulate all program objectives, disseminate and publicize them, and provide recognition and reinforcement for their attainment. Without such efforts, athletic program goals will continue to focus on the ''win-money-win'' cycle to the exclusion of other important aspects of athletics. Such a consequence will merely perpetuate the philosophical lip service that is so prevalent in justifying athletics within the educational system.

REFERENCES

Allen, L. R. 1988. Learn the impact of your recreation & athletic program. Paper presented, December, at the Athletic Business Conference, New Orleans.

Berg, R. 1989. The money game. *Athletic Business,* September, 28–40.

Broyles, J. F., and R. D. Hay. 1979. *Administration of athletic programs.* Englewood Cliffs, N.J.: Prentice-Hall.

Copeland, J. L. 1989. Academics no longer 'silent partner' in membership's athletics programs. *The NCAA News,* 30 August, 1, 3, 18.

Dunnavant, K. 1989. Sponsorship consortium putting accent on numbers. *The Sporting News,* 18 September, 61.

Earle, M. V., ed. 1989. *NCAA football.* Mission, Kans.: National Collegiate Athletic Association.

Gaski, J. F., and M. J. Etzel. 1985. Collegiate athletic success and alumni generosity: Dispelling the myth. In A. Yiannakis, T. D. McIntyre, M. J. Melnick, and D. P. Hart, eds., *Sport sociology.* 3d ed., 166–171. Dubuque, Iowa: Kendall/Hunt.

Maisel, I. 1988. Some doubt utility of linking bonuses to graduation rate. *The NCAA News,* 15 June, 13.

The NCAA News. 4 January 1989. NCAA will provide Title IX compliance guide to members.

The NCAA News. 26 April 1989. Council approves concept of certification program.

The NCAA News. 7 June 1989. Committee on costs maps plan.

The NCAA News. 14 June 1989. I-A consortium out to attract new sponsorship.

The NCAA News. 8 July 1987. Penn State football gives local economy $40 million boost.

The NCAA News. 16 August 1989. Council will proceed with certification program.

Raiborn, M. H. 1986. *Revenues and expenses of intercollegiate athletics programs.* Mission, Kans.: National Collegiate Athletic Association.

Sack, A. L., and C. Watkins. 1985. Winning and giving. In D. Chu, J. O. Segrave, and B. J. Becker, eds., *Sport and higher education,* 299–306. Champaign, Ill.: Human Kinetics.

Schultz, R. D. 1989. Text of Schultz's written testimony in congressional hearing. *The NCAA News,* 24 May, 3, 5, 7, 8, 27.

Terry, J. 1988. Recent study looks at yearly revenues from football games. *The Oklahoma Daily,* 1 July, 15.

HUMAN RESOURCE
MANAGEMENT IN SPORT

23

A Double-Edge Sword: Drugs in Sport

Joanna Davenport

A past feature article in *Sports Illustrated* titled, "Caracas: A Scandal and a Warning" (Neff 1983) described how fifteen athletes were disqualified from the Pan American Games because their urinalysis detected anabolic steroids—one of the substances banned by the International Olympic Committee (IOC). In addition, twelve United States track and field athletes chose to fly home from Caracas before their events, presumably to avoid being tested. As could be expected, there was an avalanche of TV and newspaper coverage of the incident and an immediate demand that more stringent rules be imposed and a cleanup campaign started. As often happens where sensational events are concerned, the media coverage soon died down; articles appeared only infrequently on new rules, with allegations of steroid use, about athletes being caught and punished, and on the enactment of testing procedures by different sport governing organizations.

Joanna Davenport is with the Department of Health and Human Performance, Auburn University, Auburn, Alabama.

Then, at the 1988 Seoul Olympics came the shocking news that Ben Johnson, track and field star and 100-meter gold medal winner, had been disqualified and stripped of his medal because he tested positive for anabolic steroids. This incident focused attention again on the recurring allegations that many athletes are using drugs to enhance performance. This time, media attention did not fade. Almost daily newsclips, articles, books, and documents about the use of drugs by athletes who want a competitive edge are written. The banned drug that appears to be most widely used is anabolic steroids, and is the focus of this essay.

First, what are anabolic steroids and why, since the 1988 Olympics, are we hearing more about them? For a complete understanding, one must go back to 1935 when scientists succeeded in isolating the male hormone, testosterone (Almond, Cart, and Harvey 1984). The original research was done with the purpose of trying to discover why men became less virile with age. Original purpose aside, it was discovered that testosterone was useful for a variety of medical purposes. When administered, it speeded up the process by which protein became muscle. Thus, it began to be used to treat postoperative patients, burn victims, and undernourished prisoners of war from World War II who needed to gain weight.

In 1952, Russia participated in the Olympic Games for the first time and did amazingly well in the weight lifting events, winning a total of three gold, three silver, and one bronze medal. There was suspicion at the time that the Russian weight lifters were being aided somehow and thus, were bigger, stronger, and able to lift heavier weights. Two years later at the World Powerlifting Championships the doctor of the Soviet team told the United States team physician, Dr. John Zeigler, that the Russians were experimenting with the synthetic testosterone. Testosterone was being used to increase the weight lifters size and strength in an attempt to improve performance. Zeigler was no stranger to possible aids for increasing athletic performance as he had engineered many of the prototypes for the early Nautilus exercise machines. Thus, he returned to the United States and worked with CIBA Pharmaceutical Company to further refine testosterone. The result was Dinabol which is believed to be the first synthetic anabolic steroid used by American athletes (Almond, Cart, and Harvey 1984).

When Dinabol became available, Zeigler took it to the York Barbell Club in Pennsylvania where many of the top lifters of the 1950s did their training. There, he hoped to do careful experiments combining isometrics with the new drug. But he soon lost control of the project and isometrics were discarded in favor of these steroids which the athletes, on their own, began to take in increased dosages. Years later, Dr. Zeigler commented that he wished he had never heard of the word ''steroid'' (Almond, Cart, and Harvey 1984).

Before continuing with the historic overview, it is necessary to explain briefly what steroids do. They enable the body to synthesize protein, which is the key to tissue and muscle growth. Athletes believe that the new tissue combined with vigorous training and good nutrition enables better performance, and the results attained by athletes who have used steroids seem to bear this out. But are advantages physical or psychological, and what accounts for the varied explanations that doctors offer? These issues will be examined shortly.

By 1960 and the Rome Olympics many world-class athletes training for events where great bulk was an advantage, such as weight lifting and the field events in track, were using steroids. There were not yet rules against steroid use, and even if there were, no scientific measures were available to test for use of the drug. It did not go unnoticed, however, that athletes in certain events were becoming very large. For example, according to Olympic records, the average weight of shot putters increased by 14 percent between 1956 and 1972 (Donohoe and Johnson 1986, 11). Some researchers have labeled this period the Steroid Era.

Two remarks about that period are worthy of mention. Dr. Ted Thompson, a neurologist and former competitive weight lifter, stated ''. . . as a blanket statement, all of the world-class athletes from the 1960 Rome Olympics on have used them. . . . (the) Steroid Era . . . begins for us in the West with the Rome Games in 1960 and has never let up . . . and which should continue'' (Almond, Cart, and Harvey 1984, 1). Randy Matson, 1968 Olympic shot put champion, revealed, ''The first time I heard about steroids was in California at the 1964 Olympic Trials . . . They were passing them around like candy . . . From 1968 on, I think most weightmen and throwers were taking them'' (Almond, Cart, and Harvey 1984, 2).

It was estimated that, when the United States team trained at Lake Tahoe and before going on to Mexico City, more than one-third of all the field men in track and field were using steroids. In 1972 at the Munich Olympics Jay Silvester, world-record holder in the discus, conducted his own personal survey among the athletes and found these results:

> Two-thirds of the competitors had taken steroids at least sometime during their training period; . . . 61 percent had used them during the 6 months prior to the Games; (and) with the exception of long distance running, their use was prevalent among most track and field events. (Donohoe and Johnson 1986, 12)

About this same time, a test was developed to detect the use of anabolic steroids, and by 1974 the IOC added steroids to the banned drug list. The first testing for these drugs was done in 1976 at the Montreal Olympics. The media exposure was not extensive but seven weight lifters, including two from the United States, and a Polish discus thrower tested positive and were disqualified. It is significant to note that the discus thrower was a woman indicating that female athletes were also using anabolic steroids (Donohoe and Johnson 1986). Even though she was the first woman to be disqualified, evidence was fairly strong that the East German female swimmers were on steroids at the Olympic Games in 1972.

One more item should be mentioned about the 1976 Olympic Games. It was quite likely that the majority of athletes who used steroids were not caught because they knew when they needed to stop use to avoid detection. Dr. Samuel Fox of Georgetown University remarked that the steroid use was rampant and added that "just about all the weightlifters, wrestlers, and participants in . . . events . . . requiring sudden explosive muscle strength [were] using them" (Almond, Cart, and Harvey 1984, 3).

By the 1980 Moscow Olympics, it was speculated that the Russians, who had earlier switched from testosterone to steroid use, had gone full circle and were now back to using testosterone, as they had been before it was added to the banned list. But it was banned for the 1984 Olympic Games and the Los Angeles Olympic Games of 1988. For these Games $2 million was budgeted for drug testing, and it was predicted to be the most sophisticated ever used in the sport world. Was that really true or was the extensive publicity used to scare the athletes? Reliable sources claim the testing was no different than that used at the Olympic Trials or at Caracas (Rosen 1989). Regardless, the publicity worked—no American tested positive and the number of guilty athletes was minimal. However, in order to present the most positive image of the 1984 Olympic Games, media exposure about the drug testing and the athletes who failed the test was kept to a minimum. Mention should be made, though, of one individual whose instant denial was similar to the instant denial made by Ben Johnson. A male runner from Finland won the silver medal in the 10,000 meters but then was disqualified for taking steroids. He vehemently protested his innocence and yet, upon arriving back in Helsinki, said, "I have to carry the burden. My career as a sportsman is apparently over" (Donohoe and Johnson 1986, 16). Sad to say, months later it was revealed that he had tested positive prior to the Games but it had been covered up so he could make the national team. The ensuing negative fallout forced the resignation of the national coach (Donohoe and Johnson 1986).

It is important at this point to examine more closely some of the complex questions that surround the use of testosterone and anabolic steroids. It was mentioned previously that testosterone is the male sex hormone; it takes two types of action—androgenic and anabolic. The androgenic effects are masculinizing, producing the deep voice, affecting the amount and distribution of body hair, and so forth. Anabolic effects are those that stimulate the growth of muscle. Thus, anabolic steroids are synthetic modifications of testosterone designed to enhance anabolic action (muscle growth) and decrease the androgenic effects. It is a drug obtained legally only by a doctor's prescription and as mentioned before, is one of the more than 100 drugs banned by the IOC. It is now believed that those who take steroids are not just weight lifters and field contestants in track and field, but include numerous athletes who want or need additional strength or bulk. This gives rise to many questions: Do they work? Are they safe, and are there long-term effects? If you use them, are you cheating? What percentage of athletes use them? Are there ways to control the use of anabolic steroids?

First, do they work? Any container of anabolic steroids purchased in a pharmacy comes with a label that states: Anabolic Steroids Do Not Enhance Athletic Ability. Sadly, an anonymous spokesperson for the drug company has remarked that the warning is not provided based on the results of any scientific study, but was added to discourage calls from athletes wanting additional information about the drug (Almond, Cart, and Harvey 1984, 5). Because it is a prescription drug, many athletes do not purchase anabolic steroids in a drug store but obtain them illegally "on the street." Dan Duchaine, author of the *Underground Steroid Handbook,* truly believes steroids build strength. He also believes that if medical people were better informed, it would not be necessary for a layman, like himself, to write such a book. To obtain his information, Duchaine conducted interviews in gymnasiums, in doctors' offices, and in warehouses where drugs are sold by mail order. Thus, his book covers such topics as which drugs supposedly pump up a man or woman with the fewest undesirable side effects,

where athletes can obtain drugs legally and illegally, and what strategies may work to obtain drugs from reluctant doctors (Almond, Cart, and Harvey 1984, 13).

So do anabolic steroids work? The athletes believe they do. Some state use of the drug allows them to have three times longer workouts, which means they are working harder, which means they are getting stronger. In addition, some athletes claim that when they are on steroids, the small injuries that are the inevitable result of hard training heal twice as fast. However, all agree steroids are not a crutch, and they have to be used in combination with good training to produce positive effects. But the key question is do they really work or do athletes perform better because they *think* steroids work. The evidence is contradictory and needs elaboration. Furthermore, some evidence is scientific while other claims of results are anecdotal.

Two significant studies were completed by Dr. Gideon Ariel when he was on the faculty at the University of Massachusetts. He studied elite athletes and the psychological effects of steroids. In the first half of the study, all of the athletes were on weights. In the second half, they were told they were getting steroids but were really getting placebos, or sugar pills. Everyone improved on the weights after they started taking the so-called steroids. So, it was obvious that psychological factors had influenced their performance. Ariel was so fascinated by these results that he followed up with a double-blind study using both the drug and placebos. The subjects were placed into two equal groups whereby Group A received steroids for the first four weeks and were given placebos in the last four weeks. Conversely, Group B received placebos for the first four weeks and steroids the last four weeks. All improved but improvement was greater during the drug period (Almond, Cart, and Harvey 1984, 6).

The power of the placebo effect is illustrated in this account by a trainer for the St. Louis Cardinals:

> In 1964 I devised a yellow RBI pill, a red shutout pill, and a potent green hitting pill. Virtually every player on the team took them, and some wouldn't go out on the field until they took my pills. They worked so well that we won the pennant. They worked because I never told them the pills were placebos. (Goldman 1984, 36)

In other words, the assumption is that the placebos give the athletes such a feeling of confidence that they perform better. And according to some doctors and researchers, all anabolic steroids provide is a psychological boost to the confidence of the user. The difficulty is that authentic testing is hard to achieve because the dosages clinically prescribed for scientific study is far different than the dosages athletes use on their own. Of twenty-five scientific studies undertaken to determine whether steroids improve athletic skill, twelve concluded they do and thirteen concluded that they do not, but cause a placebo effect because the athletes believe they work (Almond, Cart, and Harvey 1984, 6).

Another investigation to discover whether anabolic steroids make a difference in athletic performance was conducted by Howard Payne, a British track athlete of the 1960s and a leading crusader against drug use. He theorized that if steroids make the difference in performance then the records set for events after steroids began to be used should be markedly better than records set prior to that time. Examining many events, he calculated the average of the world's ten best results for the years covering the alleged use of anabolic steroids. Quite to his surprise, there seemed to be no sudden improvement in records for the shot put or discus, two "heavy" events almost certain to be affected by anabolic drugs. Furthermore, every event he analyzed showed improvement. Thus, it is hard to conclude whether the gains were due to drug use or better training methods (Donohoe and Johnson 1986, 42), even though most athletes who have admitted using steroids are convinced the drugs helped their performance. The following examples demonstrate both real belief in the positive connection between steroid use and performance and skepticism of the drug's value to performance.

1. A university shot putter and discus thrower was administered steroid injections four times per week using 25 milligrams per injection. Keep in mind the recommended dosage is 25 to 50 milligrams per week. The athlete gained weight and improved performance under this drug regimen (Donohoe and Johnson 1986, 15).

2. A pentathlete used 24 milligrams of steroids per day resulting in an increase in weight and marked improvement in both swimming and running times (Donohoe and Johnson 1986, 15).

3. The last case is represented by the remarks by Harold Connolly, a four-time Olympian, who competed for many years without using drugs and for eight years used anabolic steroids. He began using steroids at the 1960 Olympics because he felt he was putting himself at a decided disadvantage if he didn't (United States Senate 1973, 273).

   Connolly comments: "The dilemma for me is that I have no doubts (steroids) increased my sheer weight and strength . . . The odd thing . . . is that [I] set world records in the hammer throw when [I] was on drugs and when [I] was off them." The difference in the distance of the throws was a little over two feet further when on the steroids, about which Connolly concluded, ''The difference . . . was certainly not significant'' (United States Senate 1973, 273).

Harold Connolly notwithstanding, we all know that in some events the margin of difference is tenths or even hundredths of a second.

With the growing body of scientific research more authorities are realizing what the athletes who have used or are using anabolic steroids already knew—the drug does help performance. Before moving on to the next question, two comments on this issue should be cited. Dr. Charles Yesalis, a well-known researcher on steroid use, recently stated that steroids not only work but ''they work exquisitely well'' (*MacLean's* 13 March 1989, 40). And Dr. Anthony Franks, writing in the *British Medical Journal,* contended that ''the benefit [of anabolic steroids] is simply that you can do things with them that you could not do without them (*MacLean's* 13 March 1989, 40).

Are they safe and are there long-term effects? On one side of the question you have the majority of athletes who state they are safe and do not care even if they are not safe. On the other side of the question, you have the majority of doctors who say they are harmful to a person's health. The researchers and doctors who condone steroid use insist that physicians who profess the dangers of steroids do not have sufficient information to make those dire conclusions. Furthermore, as indicated previously, the research is not only limited but is confusing and often contradictory. Nevertheless, consider the statement by one doctor who refutes proponents of the drug and comments, ''Make no mistake. There is no such thing as drug use, only drug abuse'' (Almond, Cart, and Harvey 1984, 9). The abuse lies in the possible dangerous effects. It is reported that some athletes use

50 to 100 times the recommended dose and according to Dr. Gary Wadler, author of *Drugs and the Athlete,* this will make it almost impossible to ever determine through research exactly what the long-term effects of anabolic steroids are (*JAMA* 16 December 1988, 3398). There is grave concern that heavy users will suffer serious side effects down the road.

What side effects are possible? Some of the manifestations are grounded in scientific evidence and others are more anecdotal. They range in degree of seriousness from acne to liver, kidney, and heart disease. For men, there have been reports of the following: alteration of the reproductive process through atrophy of the testicles and decreased sperm production; thickening of the vocal cords so the voice is lower and deeper; increase in sex drive for some and a decrease for others; and increased amounts of body and facial hair. For women, there is evidence of irregular menstrual flow, increased body and facial hair, and deeper voices. Most of the symptoms for the female disappear with discontinuation, but damage to the vocal cords may be permanent. For both sexes, steroid use may result in acne, baldness, swelling of the nipple area to such a degree that surgery may be necessary, increased susceptibility to tendon pulls and injuries, possible tumors, liver dysfunction, and heart disease.

When an athlete who has used steroids suffers an early death or is incapacitated by health problems, there has been a tendency to attribute the cause of the tragedy or sickness to the use of anabolic steroids. Following are a few examples of such cases:

1. A 26-year-old weightlifter who took anabolic steroids for four years died from cancer of the liver. His doctor remarked that there is no proof that anabolic steroids caused the disease but that ''. . . it's pretty well established

that these drugs are carcinogenic and it certainly has to be suspected'' (Donohoe and Johnson 1986, 56).

2. *Sports Illustrated,* in a feature article titled ''The Death of an Athlete,'' described the steroid use and death of Benji Ramirez, who took the drug ''to get big.'' Although he died of a heart attack, ''it [was] the strong opinion of the coroner . . . that the use of anabolic steroids did in some way contribute to his death . . .'' (Telander and Noden 1989, 70–72). If the coroner's opinion is correct, ''Ramirez is the first United States athlete whose death has been linked officially to the use of steroids . . .'' (Telander and Noden 1989, 71).

3. Steve Courson, a former NFL player, sought a heart transplant and blamed all of his problems on years of using steroids, although his doctor, Richard Rosenbloom, has doubts that drugs are the cause. Dr. Rosenbloom's comments about the case provide yet another illustration of the lack of real knowledge about the effects of anabolic steroids:

I'm more suspicious of a virus as . . . steroid use usually results in a thickening . . . of the heart—the opposite of what has happened to Courson's heart—but we don't know that Steve's condition is not the result of many years of heavy anabolic steroid use. We just don't know. There's not that much research. (*Sports Illustrated* 3 April 1989, 34)

Another effect of steroids is the psychological manifestations that athletes develop while either on the drug or when trying to discontinue use. There are many stories of heightened aggressiveness by athletes when using steroids. One NFL player on steroids admitted, ''[They] made me real moody, violent. I wanted to kill somebody.'' (Voy 1989, 11) A weightlifter who used steroids for five years said that ''[he] felt more aggressive and would fly into uncontrollable rages . . .'' (Voy 1989, 11). Evidence that psychological problems can also arise when an athlete decides to discontinue use of the drug has been presented. Dr. Ritchie Morris, a New York sports psychologist, examined sixteen athletes who used steroids to find that all sixteen suffered severe depression when they discontinued the drug and that three out of sixteen developed psychological dependency on the steroids. Furthermore, each of the individuals displayed less confidence when off the drug then when using steroids (*The First Aider* 1989, 1). Other researchers point out that the data are slim and that much more investigation is needed before it can conclusively be determined that steroids produce psychological problems (*The Physician and Sportsmedicine* 1989, 178).

Dr. Gary Wadler, author of *Drugs and the Athlete* speaks to this question of the effects of using steroids and the lack of scientific data, reminding his readers that steroids are hormones:

. . . hormones are different from drugs like cocaine and marijuana and they have long-acting, down the road effects. I think we should compare it with the . . . DES story. The effects didn't show up in the mothers but in the offspring. The evidence on long-term effects of anabolic steroids taken for nonmedical reasons may be a long time in coming. It certainly isn't now. (*JAMA* 16 December 1988, 3398)

Are you cheating if you use anabolic steroids? By the rules of the IOC, you are. By the rules of the using athletes, you are not. These athletes feel that if it works, use it. Its pervasiveness, even years ago, is exemplified by the statement Frank Shorter made after he did not repeat as a gold medal winner in the 1976 marathon: "I needed a better doctor" (Almond, Cart, and Harvey 1984, 5).

The athletes are faced with a double-edge sword. On one hand they feel pressure to win at all costs, and on the other hand they have been taught the elements of fair play and sportsmanship since they first played games and sports. Proponents for the use of the drug feel it is no less legal than all the other training aids in this day of sophisticated equipment, coaching, and training. These aids are designed to enhance performance and, by their reasoning, anabolic steroids are just another means of assistance. These same people, undoubtedly, would feel that not taking advantage of all resources available is not being smart. Furthermore, the attitude this represents is no different than that which prevails in other domains, whereby if the athlete thinks everyone else is doing it, they have to do it too. Following is the comment of Tom Ecker, the national coach of Sweden:

Today it's a great rarity for someone to achieve athletic success who doesn't take drugs. I normally assume that the winner of a sports contest is one who has a better pharmacist than his opponent. Drug usage has gone to such extremes that you are handicapped in competition if you don't take some. The way drug usage has accelerated, it seems inconceivable that one could hold his own without drugs. (United States Senate 1973, 148)

Or, as one Olympian remarked, "It's kind of like nuclear war. We'll stop when you stop. We don't want to risk our health but it's a competitive sport and you have to be competitive (Almond, Cart, and Harvey 1984, 16) Then you have those who truly believe using anabolic steroids is illegal, harmful, and dishonest. And yet, is it any consolation to those who abide by the rules when they are beaten by those who do not? Many believe it is due to the "winning is everything" attitude that prevails in the world of today.

Consider these remarks by John Thomas, American high jumper, who was predicted to win the gold medal in the 1960 Rome Olympics but instead placed third. He lamented that both sportswriters and fans turned against him:

They only like winners. They don't give credit to a man for trying. I was called a quitter, a man with no heart. American spectators are frustrated athletes. In the champion, they see what they would like to be. In the loser, they see what they actually are, and they treat him with scorn. (Donohoe and Johnson 1986, 129)

Harold Connolly, back in 1973, startled many people when he said: "The overwhelming majority of athletes I know would do anything, and take anything, short of killing themselves to improve athletic performance" (Donohoe and Johnson 1986, 1).

Peter Lawson, secretary of the English Council for Physical Recreation, in 1984 remarked that "unless something is done soon, international sport will be a competition between circus freaks manipulated by international chemists" (Donohoe and Johnson 1986, 124).

Perhaps a fitting ending to the section are these comments by Payne, previously mentioned as a crusader against drug use:

. . . we should emphasize the ethics of the situation, that drug-taking is cheating, right from the start, instead of harping on the harmful side effects. We should have cared about sport as a whole . . . we should have pointed out and tried to educate people that the important thing in sport is to compete honorably, that to win at all costs is a contradiction of the meaning of sport. (Davies and Geoffrey 1982, 109–110)

How many athletes are using anabolic steroids? Since use by elite athletes is prohibited, it is difficult to gather exact figures, and many of the estimates that have been made are pure speculation. The numbers and percentages released after testing are undoubtedly low because many athletes know when to discontinue so that the urinalysis will be negative. For example, National Collegiate Athletic Association (NCAA) policy only mandates testing at championship events or bowl games. In the 1988–89 season, the NCAA tested 3,700 athletes and only 0.8 percent tested positive for drugs. Of that figure, 60 percent tested positive for use of steroids. Dick Schultz, executive director of the NCAA had this to say about the number of athletes who use steroids:

> That eight-tenths of 1 percent sounds exciting, sounds great, like we've done a great job. But, unfortunately, I think we only catch the dumb ones. There is so much sophistication, so many gurus out there that they are trying to stay one step ahead of the testing techniques that if a person wants to take anabolic steroids today, they can cycle those if they know they are going to be tested and probably pass the test. (*Atlanta Constitution* 6 October 1989, 1)

Schultz is hoping that a proposal will be approved whereby NCAA athletes will be subject to year-round random testing.

Estimates of the number of Olympic athletes that used steroids while training for the 1988 Summer Games range from 10 to 90 percent, and many authorities agree the number exceeds 50 percent (Siegal 1989, 6). And yet, the IOC reported that for the past year only 2.45 percent of the athletes tested positive (Woodward 1989, 1C). Again, like Mr. Schultz says, the athletes who were "caught" were just the dumb ones who miscalculated when to stop using before being tested. It is important to remember in this regard that 50 percent of the athletes tested positive for anabolic steroids in 1984 and 1985 when the United States Olympic Committee (USOC) conducted testing with no punitive actions (*NASPE News* 1989, 1). Among the athletes, allegations and finger pointing are frequent, epitomized by the accusations of Darrell Robinson against Florence Joyner-Kersee that she not only used anabolic steroids but that he sold them to her (Rogers 1989, F1, F11).

Returning to the question: How many athletes actually use steroids? The "guestimates" range from 300,000 to 500,000 people. The size of this number clearly suggests that not just elite athletes who wish to gain an edge are using this drug.

A nationwide study on the use of anabolic steroids by male seniors in high school produced some startling results. Over 6 percent of the seniors sampled said they had used steroids by the time they were 16 years old or before. Thirty percent used the drug by injection and 21 percent reported they had been given the steroids by a doctor, pharmacist, or veterinarian. The other 79 percent obtained the drug through friends or on the black market. U.S. federal officials estimate that the black market sale of steroids earn the traffickers $100 million a year (*MacLeans* 13 March 1989, 40). It was also discovered that 35 percent of the users were not involved in sports but used steroids to enhance appearance (*Sports Illustrated* 26 December 1988, 21). Similar to the high school student who died, many steroid users do so "to get big." Ironically, one of the effects of steroids on youth is premature closing of the growth plates in bones. Thus, these youngsters who are rushing "bigness" may not ever be as big and tall as they were meant to be (Sellers 1989, 3).

USA Today estimates that 1 million people in the United States use anabolic steroids. The newspaper's national telephone hotline held for sixteen hours shortly after the Seoul Olympics produced revealing findings similar to those of the high school study and indicate that the U.S. faces a drug problem that extends far beyond the realm of athletics (*United States Sports Academy News* 1989, 12).

1. Fifty percent of the calls were from athletes, but that means 50 percent were from nonathletes. The majority of the callers were users.
2. Some callers were as young as 10 years old.
3. One hundred percent of the users declared they had no difficulty in getting the drug, legally or illegally.

Are there ways to control the use of anabolic steroids? Or in other words, where are we in this perennial struggle of excellence in athletics and the means by which excellence is attained? As mentioned before, most authorities believe athletes will do anything today to enhance performance and to gain an edge. If anabolic steroids provide this edge, athletes will use them or anything else that produces comparable results. The degree of prestige and potential amount of money that accompanies winning is too great to worry about ethical questions or medical consequences. It is estimated that Ben Johnson lost $18 million in endorsements and sponsors by his public fall from grace (*JAMA* 16 December 1988, 3398). The importance of fame and being Number 1 is exemplified in the simple exercise of trying to remember who was Number 2 in many athletic events, especially in the Olympics. How is the problem to be tackled so that athletic competition becomes like competition of years ago where everything was, for the most part, fair, square, and legal?

Many authorities feel education is the answer, and there has been considerable attention to the topic of anabolic steroids in sports in educational materials, conferences, and meetings of sports organizations. A step in the right direction, but will these things alone do the job? The question must be addressed with great care to not lose credibility as happened to the medical profession when it warned of the bad side effects of drug use without the support of scientific evidence.

Testing is another solution, and year-round random testing such as that used by The Athletic Congress (TAC) may be a significant means of deterring drug use. No agreement as to when to test, who to test, and the appropriate punishment for guilty offenders has yet been determined. But many experts feel the clever athletes are one step ahead of the testing procedures. Just as an example, athletes are now using a human growth hormone that appears on the banned list but for which no test to detect it has been developed.

Ethical concerns are compounded by the different values of athletes and coaches. How do you legislate morality? Attempts must be made to change attitudes so that elite athletes, regardless of the rewards, will commit to the ethic that the use of drugs is cheating and against the rules.

Some hold the opinion that the current drug problem in sport and in society is simply a reflection of a changing world with a new set of values and ethical standards. In that context, the promise of solutions seem dim. As Robert Helmick, past president of the USOC, said, "... drugs could destroy the very foundation of amateur sport ... You're not going to get our athletes off of steroids until we can assure them the world is off steroids" (Patrick 1989, 1C). Dr. Robert Voy, the past sports medicine and science director for the USOC states, "I don't see any end to the problem. As long as we have scientists who like to dabble in illegal substances that supposedly improve and enhance performance, we'll continue to have ... problems" (Voy 1986, 51).

It is obvious that, at the moment, there is no single solution to this complex problem of drugs in sports. The suggestions outlined here offer some good beginnings, but it is going to take years to eradicate the use of drugs. More research is needed to establish better understanding, not just of the way in which anabolic steroids work but of their short- and long-term effects. Testing must be expanded and continued in a sophisticated manner, keeping one step ahead of the athlete's knowledge. To quote Sebastian Coe, gold medal-winning runner: ''[Drug use] is the very antithesis of fair play'' (Donohoe and Johnson 1986). Let us hope Mr. Coe's statement is universally heard and that the problem of drug use in sport can be solved.

REFERENCES

Almond, Elliot, Julie Cart, and Randy Harvey. 1984. Olympians finding the drug test a snap. *Los Angeles Times,* 29 January.

Atlanta Constitution. 6 October 1989. NCAA Director Schultz: Drug tests only catching 'dumb ones.'

Davies, Bruce, and Thomas Geoffery, eds. 1982. *Science and sporting performance: Management or manipulation?* Oxford: Clarendon Press.

Donohoe, Tom, and Neil Johnson. 1986. *Foul play.* New York: Basil Blackwell.

The First Aider. 1989 (January–March). Steroid depression.

Goldman, Bob. 1984. *Death in the locker room.* South Bend, Ind.: Icarus Press.

JAMA. 16 December 1988. Accord on drug testing, sanctions sought before 1992 Olympics in Europe.

MacLean's. 13 March 1989. Looking for a chemical edge.

NASPE News. 1989 (Fall). Steroid abuse in secondary schools.

Neff, Craig. 1983. Caracas: A scandal and a warning. *Sports Illustrated,* 5 September.

Patrick, Dick. 1989. NCAA boss wants steroid tests all year. *USA Today,* 6 October.

The Physician and Sportsmedicine. 1989 (February). Does steroid abuse cause—or excuse—violence.

Rogers, Prentis. 1989. Griffith Joyner goes on TV to deny drug use. *Atlanta Constitution,* 22 September.

Rosen, Mel. 1989. Personal interview, 16 October.

Seigal, Arthur J. 1989. The effects of anabolic steroids. *Your Patient and Fitness,* March–April.

Sellers, Tom. 1989. Wild mood swings may be tipoff to steroid use. *The Center Circuit,* Summer.

Sports Illustrated. 3 April 1989. Was the X factor a factor.

Sports Illustrated. 26 December 1988. Steroids and the young.

Telander, Rick, and Merrell Noden. 1989. The death of an athlete. *Sports Illustrated,* 20 February.

United States Senate. 1973. *Proper and improper use of drugs by athletes.* Senate hearings held June 18 and July 12–13. Washington, D.C.: U.S. Government Printing Office.

United States Sports Academy News. 1989 (Spring). Findings of *USA Today* poll on steroid use.

Voy, Robert O. 1986. Drug testing—it's heading to a clear bill of health in sports. *The Olympian,* December.

Voy, Robert O. 1989. Rambo drugs and their psychological impact. *U.S. Olympic Committee Drug Education News,* January.

Woodward, Steve. 1989. Medical official opposes lifetime ban. *USA Today,* 31 August.

24

Marketplace Value and Gender Representation of Successful Coaches in Women's Intercollegiate Athletics

Connee Zotos

For almost two decades, women's athletics has been in a state of constant change. In 1975, the regulations for implementing Title IX of the 1972 Education Amendments Act were promulgated by the Office of Civil Rights of the Department of Health, Education, and Welfare. Over the next five years, opportunities in women's athletics dramatically increased. In the early 1980s, failure to ratify the Equal Rights Amendment, the National Collegiate Athletic Association's (NCAA) takeover of the Association for Intercollegiate Athletics for Women (AIAW), and the Grove City decision of Title IX significantly tempered the women's sport equity movement (Uhlir 1987). Despite this slowdown in the momentum, women's programs have continued to grow in popularity and public interest.

An ever present "growing pain" of women's athletics has been finding the money to support

these programs. Even in the most successful programs, expenses far exceed revenues (Raiborn 1986; Ortiz 1988). Administrators are continually being faced with having to budget funds and prioritize spending in a manner that will improve, or at least not diminish, the participation and quality of women's athletics. A major budgetary consideration is coaches' salaries. One can hardly debate that the success of any athletic program is highly dependent on the abilities of the coaching staff. Administrators must constantly assess the monetary value of coaches by determining the desired success level of their athletic program and investigating the marketplace value of quality coaches who can produce that success.

A second issue surrounding the growth of women's athletics has been the decline in the percentage of females in coaching and administrative positions. According to Acosta and Carpenter (1988), in 1972 the percentage of females coaching women's intercollegiate teams was 90.0 percent. By 1988, that percentage had dropped to 48.3 percent. Similarly, the percentage of females

Connee Zotos is the Director of Athletics at William Smith College, Geneva, New York.

holding the position of head athletic director of women's programs went from more than 90.0 percent in 1972 to 16.0 percent in 1988 (Acosta and Carpenter 1988).

In 1983, Zotos (1984) designed a survey instrument to gather data on collegiate women's athletics budgets from selected Division I institutions for the 1983–84 academic year. Part of the study investigated salaries and gender representation of head coaches among the top-ranked Division I programs in each of seven sports. One of the purposes of the study reported in this essay was to replicate Zotos's earlier (1984) study for the 1988–89 academic year to determine what changes in the financial commitment had taken place with regard to coaches' salaries among the most successful women's athletics programs. In addition, gender representation of coaches in each sport and gender differences in salary were investigated.

Another purpose of this study was to determine how many top-ten women's sport programs reside within combined athletic departments with a male as head athletic director or within separate athletic departments with a female as the director of women's athletics. Once top-ten sport programs are categorized by department structures, what happens to the salary and gender representation data?

Hopefully, the information from this study can be used to aid administrators and coaches in making informed salary decisions based on marketplace data. In addition, the results will indicate whether females are holding their own.

METHOD

The sampling method, survey instrument, and method of data analysis used in this study were identical to those of the Zotos (1984) study so that the two sets of data could be compared.

Data collection pertaining to athletic department structure was done specifically for this study.

Sample

The institutions included in the sample were those Division I schools that had one or more women's sports ranked in the top ten in the sports of basketball, volleyball, softball, track, tennis, golf, and swimming. Top-ten status was determined by finish in NCAA Championships from the two previous academic years and by current national rankings in four sport polls: (1) the Associated Press basketball coaches' poll, (2) the Volvo Tennis collegiate rankings, (3) the preseason *Track and Field News* rankings, and (4) the American Volleyball Coaches Association rankings. Due to variations in rankings and championship finishes, sample sizes for each sport often exceeded ten. A total of fifty institutions were included in the sample. Budget data were requested for eighty-eight top-ten sport programs within the fifty institutions. Budget data were collected on seventy-one of the eighty-eight top-ten sport programs for a return rate of 80.6 percent.

Procedure

Once an institution was targeted as having one or more sports ranked in the top ten, a survey instrument was mailed to the athletic director requesting budget data for the 1988–89 academic year. The survey instrument requested salary information for the head coaches of those sports ranked in the top ten. For example, if a specific university had a top-ten basketball and golf program, salary information for the head basketball and head golf coach was requested. Athletic directors were asked to report salary figures that included the total salary paid by the institution but excluded fringe benefits, retirement packages, summer camp income, and the like. Follow-up phone calls to the athletic directors were conducted to encourage completion of the survey or to get salary information over the phone.

After the budget survey was sent to the athletic director, gender data were recorded. A content analysis was conducted of The 1988–89 National Directory of College Athletics (women's edition) which contains the names of coaches by institution and sport. When gender could not be determined by name, the researcher called the institution's sports information office.

Data were also collected on the structure of each athletic program. Each top-ten sport program was coded into the following three categories: (1) sport program is within a merged athletic department (both men's and women's athletics under a single structure) with a male as head athletic director; (2) sport program is within a merged athletic department with a female as head athletic director; and (3) sport program is within a women's athletics department with a separate administrative structure. These data were easily collected due to the fact that of 294 NCAA Division I member institutions 2 (0.68 percent) fit into category 2 and 9 institutions (3.06 percent) fit into category 3 (Lopiano 1989). All institutions with separate athletic departments had a female as director of women's athletics (Lopiano 1989).

Analysis

Because respondents were assured confidentiality, statistical analysis pertaining to salary figures was limited to mean, median, and range scores. Trends in funding were reflected through calculation of percent increases in salary from 1983 to 1989. In addition, mean and median salary figures were separated by coaches gender. A chi-square analysis was calculated to determine whether a relationship between gender and salary was present.

Percentages of female representation among coaches in the top ten for both academic years (1983–84 and 1988–89) were calculated. These percentages were compared to the data of Acosta and Carpenter (1988) which reflect female representation in the NCAA Division I coaching ranks by sport.

Percentage of top-ten programs within the three different athletic department structures were calculated. Gender representation and salary differences were noted between coaches in top ten programs according to athletic department structure.

RESULTS

In some instances, an extremely high or low salary dramatically affected the mean salary. Therefore, median salary was determined to be the more accurate indicator of average salary for purposes of interpretation. Mean salaries have been included in selected tables, but discussion focuses primarily on the figures representing salary range and median salary.

Head Coach Salaries

A comparison of median head coach salary figures in all seven sports from 1983–84 to 1988–89 indicates that salaries increased anywhere from 17.6 percent to 90.0 percent over that period of time depending on the sport. Median salaries for basketball coaches increased the most while median salaries for tennis coaches increased the least. Reported minimum, maximum, and median salary figures were highest for basketball coaches in both studies. In 1983–84, the median salary ($30,000) for basketball coaches was 0.0 to 20.0 percent higher than the median salary for coaches in five of the other six sports. By 1988–89, the median salary ($57,000) for basketball coaches was at least

TABLE 24.1 Range, Mean, and Median Salaries by Sport and by Year

Sport	1983–84			1988–89		
	Range	Mean	Median	Range	Mean	Median
Basketball	24.3–44.5 (n = 12)	32.3	30.0	45.0–68.1 (n = 9)	56.1	57.0
Volleyball	19.1–38.0 (n = 14)	28.2	30.0	31.5–60.1 (n = 11)	41.5	40.7
Softball	13.0–43.3 (n = 10)	22.5	19.0	21.5–61.0 (n = 11)	40.0	35.7
Track	22.7–39.4 (n = 11)	27.5	26.0	21.0–52.6 (n = 11)	36.8	37.3
Swimming	19.2–37.1 (n = 10)	28.2	28.6	26.0–60.0 (n = 9)	39.0	37.0
Golf	13.2–31.7 (n = 10)	23.9	25.0	17.0–41.5 (n = 12)	35.6	32.0
Tennis	18.8–38.0 (n = 13)	26.4	25.0	16.0–45.1 (n = 9)	30.2	29.4

Note: Salary figures are expressed in thousands of dollars and rounded off to the nearest one hundred dollars.

40.0 percent higher than the median salary for coaches in all of the other sports. Table 24.1 depicts range, mean, and median salaries of head coaches by sport and by year.

In 1983–84, the median salary ($19,000) for softball coaches was the lowest reported among all seven sports. The median salaries in golf ($25,000) and tennis ($25,000) were tied for the second lowest salary reported. From 1983–84 to 1988–89, the median salary for softball coaches increased 87.9 percent. This increase, coupled with low percentage increases in golf (28.0 percent) and tennis (17.6 percent), caused the median salary of softball coaches to move up two positions when comparing all sports.

The range of salaries for softball coaches was larger than salary ranges in all other sports during both years surveyed. When comparing salary ranges in 1983–84 with salary ranges in 1988–89 by each sport, all salary ranges increased somewhere between 14.4 percent (basketball) and 89.9 percent (swimming).

Gender Representation

The percentage of female coaches in top-ten programs for both the 1983–84 and 1988–89 academic years varied dramatically by sport. Top-ten basketball programs had the highest percentage of female coaches during both academic years surveyed, 75.0 percent and 69.2 percent, respectively. Conversely, top-ten swimming programs had the lowest percentage of female coaches during both academic years. In

TABLE 24.2   Percent of Female Coaches by Sport and by Year

Sport	Female Coaches Top Ten (1983–84)	Female Coaches Top Ten (1988–89)	Female Coaches NCAA Div. I (1987–88)*
Basketball	75.0	69.2	57.2
Volleyball	21.4	35.7	61.5
Softball	70.0	61.5	69.5
Track	9.1	27.3	18.3
Swimming	0.0	18.2	16.2
Golf	54.5	69.2	54.9
Tennis	46.2	23.1	47.4

*All data in this column were taken directly from the Acosta and Carpenter study (1988).

1983–84, 18.2 percent of top-ten swimming coaches were female. Combining all seven top-ten sports programs in 1983–84, 39.5 percent (32 of 81) of the coaches were females. That figure rose to 44.3 percent (39 of 88) in 1988–89. Table 24.2 depicts the percentage of females coaching in the top ten by sport for both academic years included in the survey. The table also includes the results of the Acosta and Carpenter (1988) study that investigated the percentage of Division I women coaches by sport.

Results of a chi-square analysis indicated no statistically significant relationship between gender and salaries. In 1988–89, the difference in mean and median salaries, when controlling for gender, indicated that the median salary for all female coaches ($36,300) was less than that of their male counterparts ($39,000). However, the mean salary of female coaches ($39,500) was higher than that of male coaches ($37,800).

Athletic Department Structure

Of the eighty-eight top-ten sports programs included in the sample for the 1988–89 academic year, 81.8 percent of the programs were within merged athletic departments with a male as the head athletic director, while 18.9 percent of the programs were in separate athletic departments with a female as the head athletic director. The percentage of female coaches in separate athletic departments (64.3 percent) was higher than the percentage of female coaches in merged departments (40.5 percent).

When calculating salaries of coaches in merged versus separate departments, 58.3 percent of all coaches in separate departments had salaries higher than the median salary for their sport. In contrast, 43.3 percent of the coaches in merged departments had salaries higher than the median salary for their sport. Salaries for female coaches in separate departments were above the median 62.5 percent of the time while salaries for female coaches in merged departments were above the median 36.4 percent of the time. Salaries for male coaches in both separate and merged departments were above the median 50.0 percent of the time.

DISCUSSION

Head Coaches' Salaries

Salary increases in the sport of basketball were higher than in any other sport. In fact, in 1983–84 the median salary for coaches in five of the six sports were within 20.0 percent of the median salary for basketball coaches. By 1988–89, the median salary for basketball coaches was at least 40.0 percent higher than the median salary for all other coaches. This was an anticipated result because basketball is the most popular and visible women's collegiate sport. Women's basketball has a higher number of participants and higher number of sponsoring institutions than all other sports (*Annual Reports* 1987–1988). Due to its popularity, basketball has also become the number one revenue-producing sport in women's athletics, a factor which impacts on the availability of funds for higher coaching salaries (Ortiz 1988).

The median salary for three sports (volleyball, track, and swimming) were within 15.0 percent of each other in 1983–84. The median salary for softball coaches was at least 32.0 percent lower than any other sport. The median salary for softball coaches increased almost as much as for basketball coaches over the five-year period, making softball salaries competitive with volleyball, track, and swimming salaries. However, it must be remembered that the range of softball coaches salaries is larger than any of the other sports, probably due to the fact that almost half of the top-ten softball institutions were located in California. The state-mandated pay scale for California institutions of higher education is one of the highest in the country.

Median salaries for golf and tennis coaches did not seem to keep pace with the other sports. The median salary increases for golf and tennis coaches over the five-year period were 17.6 percent and 28.0 percent, respectively. More than one-third of the institutions with top-ten tennis and golf programs were private. Many private institutions pay lower salaries than public institutions, which may have contributed to this result. In addition, golf and tennis, relative to the other sports included in the sample, typically have fewer players on the roster, shorter seasons, and fewer scholarship athletes on their teams. Salary decisions may be partially based on these factors.

Gender Representation

As anticipated, the data showed that more males than females coach top-ten women's athletic teams. However, there were large variations of gender representation by sport. More females than males were coaching top-ten basketball, golf, and softball teams, and fewer females were coaching the other four sports. The percentage of women coaching top-ten teams in basketball, softball, track, swimming and golf were comparable to the percentages in the Acosta and Carpenter (1988) study of women coaching NCAA Division I teams in those sports. It is interesting to note that the overall percentage of females coaching top-ten teams (44.3 percent) was slightly higher than the percentage of women coaching at all Division I institutions (43.8 percent) as identified by Acosta and Carpenter (1988).

According to Barrett (1988), Census Bureau figures in the mid 1980s indicated that women's salaries were 60.0 to 74.0 percent of their male counterparts. This was not found to be the case in this study. There was no significant difference in salary between males and females coaching women's teams. The median salary for females was 7.4 percent lower than the men's median salary, but the mean salary for women was 4.5 percent higher than their male counterparts. This equal pay result may be different than the wage gap found in other professions because men have stepped into coaching positions traditionally held by women, rather than vice versa.

Athletic Department Structure

Results pertaining to the number of top-ten sports programs within separate versus merged athletic departments and the relationship of department structure and gender representation were very interesting. Only 3.1 percent of all

NCAA Division I programs have separate athletic departments for men and women, yet 18.9 percent of the top ten teams in the seven sports were produced by departments where women's athletics was separate from men's. The result being that women's sport programs located in separate departments attained top-ten status at a rate six times higher than what would be proportionally expected. In addition, more than 60.0 percent of the coaches of top-ten teams in separate athletic departments were females in contrast to 40.0 percent in merged departments.

Despite the fact that there were no significant coaching salary differences between males and females, some interesting findings resulted from comparing salary figures for coaches in separate departments and merged departments. A higher percentage of those who coached in separate departments received salaries in the upper half of the pay scale. When separating out the two groups by gender, more than 60.0 percent of the females coaching in separate departments were paid in the upper half of the pay scale. Fifty percent of the males, regardless of the department structure, were paid in the upper half of the pay scale, while only 36.4 percent of the females coaching in merged departments were paid in the upper half of the pay scale.

CONCLUSIONS

The following conclusions were drawn from the results of this study:

1. Funding patterns pertaining to coaches' salaries in women's intercollegiate athletics seem to be approaching a major-minor sport model. More money, in terms of higher salaries, was allocated to the sport that produced the highest amount of revenue.
2. Despite the fact that all sport programs in the sample were ranked in the top

ten, coaches salary ranges within each sport were quite large. There were several possible explanations for this result. First, despite the growth in women's athletic programs, funding commitment is still in the infant stage. Some athletic administrators believe that increasing funding for women's athletic programs will result in the demise of men's athletic programs, even though participation data indicate that more men are participating in intercollegiate athletics than before implementation of Title IX (Lopiano 1989). Secondly, large ranges of salaries could easily be a reflection of demographics. State-mandated pay scales vary considerably. The type of institutions included in the sample may have been another factor affecting salary ranges; some private institutions pay less than public institutions. In addition, some institutions with a history of successful men's intercollegiate athletic programs and that pay high salaries to the coaches of men's teams may be increasing the salaries they pay to coaches of women's teams in an attempt to narrow the wage gap that has been documented by Uhlir (1987) and Lopiano (1989).

3. Despite the fact that there were more males coaching women's top-ten teams, the percentage of female coaches in the sample was equivalent to the percentage of females coaching in the NCAA Division I institutions. In addition, by 1988–89, the percentage of females coaching top-ten teams in four of the seven sports was higher than the percentage of females coaching those sports in NCAA Division I institutions. Therefore, females appear to be

"holding their own" among the ranks of the most successful coaches in the country.

4. Separate athletic departments were proportionally more successful than merged departments in producing top-ten teams. In addition, there was a higher percentage of females coaching top-ten teams in separate departments than in merged departments. Coaches in separate departments had a better chance of being paid in the top half of the salary scale within their sport than coaches in merged departments. This was particularly true and not surprisingly for female coaches. Women's athletics within merged departments are often categorized as minor sports; therefore, funding may be lower and may result in lower salaries and a lower recruiting budget, which could affect overall success. It is also logical to assume that a female administrator directing a women's athletics program may be more sensitive to hiring women and closing the wage gap between coaches of women's athletic teams and coaches of men's athletic teams.

REFERENCES

Acosta, V., and L. Carpenter, 1988. Women in intercollegiate sport: A longitudinal study—eleven year update: 1977–1988. Bi-annual report to athletic administrators, Brooklyn College.

Annual reports of the National Collegiate Athletic Association, 1987–88. Mission, Kans.: National Collegiate Athletic Association.

Barrett, N. 1988. Women and the economy. 1988. Edited by S. Rix. *The American woman: 1987–88,* New York: W. W. Norton.

Lopiano, D. 1989. The facts on race and gender discrimination. Statement before the Subcommittee on Postsecondary Education of the Committee on Education and Labor, U.S. House of Representatives, May.

The 1988–89 national directory of college athletics (women's edition). Amarillo, Tex.: Ray Franks.

Ortiz, C. 1988. 1987–88 budget analysis of women's intercollegiate athletics. Master's project, The University of Texas at Austin.

Raiborn, M. H. 1986. *Revenues and expenses on intercollegiate athletic programs: Analysis of financial trends and relationships, 1981–1985.* Mission, KS: National Collegiate Athletic Association.

Uhlir, G. G. 1987. Athletics and the university: The post-women's era. *Academe* 73(4): 25–29.

Zotos, C. 1984. What's the price of success in women's intercollegiate athletic programs? *Athletic Business* 8(6):20–26.

25

Returning to the "Real World": Athletes Adjusting to Life After Sports

Leonard Lipton

The toughest challenge most athletes have to face usually does not take place during "the big game" played in front of thousands of cheering fans. Instead, the toughest challenge most athletes experience usually occurs after the cheering stops and their playing days are over.

Pro basketball Hall-of-Famer and former Los Angeles Laker Jerry West says, "the worst time of all for an athlete is when he has to retire" (pers. int. 11 September 1987). Baseball Hall-of-Famer and former San Francisco Giant pitcher Juan Marichal says, "Probably the most difficult phase of the transition to my life after baseball was the time immediately following my retirement. It was difficult for me to stay in San Francisco as a retired person at the age of 36. I didn't know what I wanted to do with my life" (pers. int. 18 August 1987).

Boxing Hall-of-Famer and former world heavyweight champion Floyd Patterson says,

"The worst thing about being a professional boxer is stepping down . . . After devoting 23 years of my life to the ring, it was very difficult to say 'goodbye' to my career as a boxer" (pers. int. 12 October 1987).

For the majority of athletes, the hardest hurdle to overcome is the adjustment to life after sports. For most of their lives, athletes train to take on opponents in "must-win" situations. But few athletes are trained for their ultimate "must-win" situation: making the inevitable transition from the sports world to the "real world."

What happens to these athletes after they leave the game? How do they adjust to life after sports? Many tragic stories appear in the media about former athletes who succumb to alcohol and drug addition. Others even committed suicide.

These are examples of what happened to some former professional athletes. What about former athletes who played at the high school and college levels, but never played in the pro ranks? Many of them once envisioned making a living as professional athletes and, when they

Leonard Lipton is a free-lance writer residing in Santa Monica, California.

did not make it, were lost. They did not know what to do. Even worse, they were not prepared to do anything else.

Sadly, many athletes believe their playing careers will go on forever. However, as former major league pitcher Al Downing knowingly observes:

> . . . the reality of pursuing a career as a professional athlete should be put in the proper perspective. If you where to think of your life as if it were a book your career as a professional athlete would be only one chapter in that book. You can utilize your athletic talent for what it's worth, but also you have to understand that you still have a long life to live after your sports career is over. And you had better be prepared to take care of yourself for the rest of that life. (pers. int. 11 March 1987).

It is that preparation, or lack of it, that should be of primary concern to today's leaders of college athletics. For college athletes in the 1990s, it could be said that "it is the worst of times and the best of times."

It is easy to see why these are the worst of times. There has been an avalanche of negative publicity concerning widespread corruption and abuses in college athletics. The charges of recruiting violations, poor graduation rates among athletes, crimes allegedly being committed by college athletes, and the NCAA sanctions against programs in violation of the rules have been well documented in the media.

The titles of separate stories in two different national magazines illustrate the extent of the problem in college athletics today. The following article appears in the 27 February 1989 issue of *Sports Illustrated*:

> ••An American Disgrace: A Violent and Unprecedented Lawlessness Has Arisen Among College Athletes in All Parts of the Country." On 3 April 1989, *Time Magazine* ran the story
> ••FOUL!: How the National Obsession with

> Winning and Moneymaking is Turning Big-Time College Sports Into an Educational Scandal That, for Too Many Players, Leads Down a One-Way Path to Broken Dreams."

Right now, the climate for college athletic administrators is uncomfortable. Federal legislation is being proposed to require universities to make public the graduation rates of their student-athletes. Individuals are threatening to organize college athletes into unions. There is strong sentiment for paying college athletes "over the table" for playing on their college teams.

The pressure on college athletic programs is mounting. On the one hand, universities are expected to recruit quality players and produce quality teams. The alumni apply pressure by demanding winning teams. On the other hand, universities are expected to provide a quality education for their student-athletes and to see to it that they graduate. Educators, legislators, members of the media, and the general public apply pressure by crying out against exploitation of athletes.

As a result of the heated criticism they are receiving, college administrators are on the defensive. Their public image is not what it used to be. Many people believe that college athletic programs have lost their integrity.

According to an Associated Press story by Gary Langer that ran in the 3 April 1989 edition of the Los Angles Times:

> Americans widely doubt the integrity of the nation's major sports colleges, believing they commonly give secret payments and inflated grades to student athletes, a Media General-Associated Press poll has found.
> A majority of respondents in the national survey also suspected athletic booster clubs of making secret payments to players. And two-thirds said the colleges overemphasize sports and neglect academic standards for athletes.

Despite the negative publicity being generated concerning the state of college athletics today, and despite the general public's feeling that college athletic programs lack integrity, the decade of the nineties could also be viewed as "the best of times" for college athletics.

How can this be possible? It can be possible if university presidents, college athletic directors, and academic advisors for athletes recognize that the opportunity for change is knocking right now! If college and university administrators are willing to test their imaginations and take risks, they can turn a negative situation into a positive one.

The following steps need to be taken:

1. College administrators should start taking positive action instead of reacting defensively to the negative publicity about their athletic programs.
2. Colleges and universities should begin to fight back (against negative criticism) on behalf of their athletes.
3. The same effort made to recruit student-athletes should be made to prepare student-athletes for the future when they leave campus.
4. Colleges should better prepare athletes for the "real world" by establishing "Life After Sports" courses for athletes. These courses could help athletes improve their communication skills; explore new career choices outside of sports; and learn from on-the-job training experience through internships in business and industry.
5. College administrators should work more closely with high school administrators to better prepare young athletes for the academic as well as the athletic demands of college.
6. Colleges should communicate more closely with professional sports leagues. Perhaps the leagues could provide scholarships to enable college athletes to complete their education regardless of whether or not they play at the professional level.
7. Colleges should work more closely with corporations to provide internships and computer literacy programs enabling athletes to improve their reading skills.

In order for these steps to be taken and for meaningful change to occur, colleges and universities must take on a leadership role. If university presidents, athletic directors, and academic advisors are willing to make a combined commitment to help their student-athletes adjust successfully to life after sports, then college athletics in the 1990s can experience the best of times!

Working together with parents, coaches, teachers, administrators, guidance counselors, business and community leaders, and the athletes themselves, every college and university can have a winning academic record.

The goal is not to kill "the dream" that millions of young people have of one day becoming professional or Olympic athletes. Instead, the goal is preparing the ones who make their dreams come true—and the ones who don't—to make a successful adjustment to life after sports.

REFERENCES

Downing, Al. 1987. Personal interview, 11 March.

Langer, Gary. 1989. *Los Angles Times,* 3 April.

Marichal, Juan. 1987. Personal interview, 18 August.

Patterson, Floyd. 1987. Personal interview, 12 October.

West, Jerry. 1987. Personal interview, 11 September.

26

Unity of Force and Diversity of Caring: A Systematic Approach for Enhancing Athletic Performance

Nena R. Hawkes, John F. Seggar, and Betty J. Vickers

THE MODEL

Superior athletic performance is rooted in athletic ability; however, many other factors are equally important in influencing performance. As competition becomes more intense, these other factors take on an increasingly prominent role in affecting the athlete's success. To recognize and effectively manage the influence these other factors exert on the athlete, we have developed a model which analyzes complexities of athletic performance. Our model assumes a holistic approach to the preparation of an athlete and includes intellectual, social, and psychological factors in addition to physical skill. Extraneous and environmental factors must also be considered. The following discussion presents the factors included in this holistic approach.

Nena R. Hawkes and Betty J. Vickers are with the Department of Physical Education/Sports, and John F. Seggar is with the Department of Sociology, Brigham Young University, Provo, Utah.

Means of Control

Means of control refers to certain critical elements of a support system (Fig. 26.1) and the means by which these elements can be controlled, monitored, or regulated. Management of these critical areas enable athletes to be fine-tuned and achieve the ultimate in performance.

Conditions

Conditions are the external factors that must be evaluated, such as time cycles, personal equipment, practice and the competitive environment. The existing conditions are observed and evaluated to determine their effect on an athlete's performance.

Performance Preparation

Performance preparation identifies the areas crucial to competitive readiness. Each of these areas can be measured by using a simple checklist or by administering a physical performance

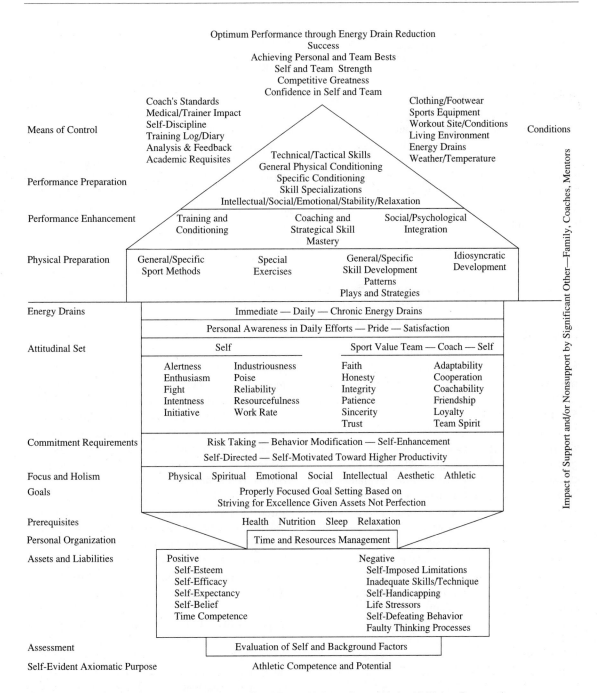

FIGURE 26.1   The Holistic Model © 1988 by The Mentor Makers, Provo, Utah. All Rights Reserved.

test. To compete without adequate preparation in the areas noted might well produce emotional or physical trauma.

Performance Enhancement

Performance enhancement results when reinforcement is received from the three major areas (social, intellectual, and psychological) directly related to physical performance. The refinement of the four crucial developmental processes assures the athlete and the coach of greater competitive readiness.

Physical Preparation

Physical preparation draws attention to the body and is more universally understood than other factors affecting athletic performance. It is important, however, to remember that all aspects of performance, including conditioning, general and specific skill development, and individual physical capabilities must be considered.

Energy Drains

Energy drains may be categorized into the four general areas of social, intellectual, psychological, and physical. These need to be evaluated on a daily basis. Each of these areas can be appraised based upon the data received from the athletes on their preworkout assessment questionnaires. These data will be most helpful when necessary intervention is made prior to a workout or a competition.

Very little affects the performance of a skilled athlete more than extraneous factors which sap energy. Optimum achievement can only be attained when the athlete has managed these inhibitors. Overcoming daily social or emotional problems, fear of failure, and other stressful situations is the key to attaining the maximum level of individual performance.

Attitudinal Set

Attitudinal set is the catalog of specific individual perspectives that tend to limit or facilitate an athlete's willingness to exert effort to achieve personal and team success. The making of a champion is largely determined by the individual's attitudinal set. The true champion is a "winner" even when first place is not attained. Competition must be entered with a predetermined set of individual goals which are realistic and yet constantly challenge the athlete to raise his or her level of expectation.

A coach or team consultant is well equipped to assist the athletes in forming workable attitudinal sets when they are armed with charted results of daily energy drain questionnaires.

Commitment Requirements

Commitment requirements are the characteristics associated with risk taking, behavior modification, self-enhancement, self-direction, and self-motivation considered to be prerequisite to athletic success. Just as skill and performance is assessed and regulated by "stats" taken during events, data gathered on other behavioral factors can be used to assess and regulate behavior during competition.

The "soul" of great athletes is often measured by their commitment. Committed athletes are those who are willing to take the risks of attempting extraordinary feats regardless of the outcome and who continue to strive for seemingly impossible goals. These individuals are always anxious to receive critical analysis, seek new and better ways to improve performance, arrive early and stay late, and give 100 percent in every drill as well as in every contest. The committed athlete is a complete player who takes equal delight in contributing to the success of the team and in making a great individual play.

Focus and Holism

Focus and holism refers to the fact that the whole is greater than the sum of its parts. For example, the sum total of the parts of a dismantled watch is less than a fully functional assembled watch. Likewise, optimum performance is more likely to occur when an athlete is in a balanced state and operating holistically or, as it is sometimes described, is in a state of "flow." Clear intentions help the athlete to focus their energies and become centered. When intentions are clear, centered, and in focus, the athlete's physical, spiritual, emotional, social, and intellectual characteristics are integrated. The balanced interplay of all of the athlete's various needs results in an unrestricted and completely focused athlete capable of achieving consistency and excellence in performance.

John Wooden's "Pyramid of Success" effectively illustrates his concern with developing the complete or whole individual as an athlete. Athletics needs a system of values to have any real focus or purpose.

Goals

Goals are the long-range aspirations and intentions of an athlete. Individual aspirations are often planned in conjunction with the coach and imply reaching for excellence. Goals are not an overnight achievement, but they result from meeting carefully planned objectives step by step. Goals that achieve the purpose of time-honored success measures such as honesty, integrity, dependability, stalwartness, and consistency within sport must be uppermost in the development of a team.

Prerequisites

Prerequisites classify vitality features paramount to an athlete's well-being. Programming for personal excellence is based upon these factors. The athlete must have a sound body, be free from stress, and have total confidence in the purposes and aims of the athletic program.

Personal Organization

Personal organization relates to all the elements an athlete must manage and organize in order to be in a state of readiness to become a more effective athlete. Effective planning and time management are essential in today's competitive environment, where athletes must often compress two-a-day workouts, education, work, and family into a short, twenty-four-hour day.

Assets and Liabilities

Assets and liabilities specify the most relevant positive and negative personal characteristics of the athlete that must be regulated to attain quality performance (refer to Fig. 26.1).

Assessment

Today's dedicated athletes must make choices that have serious potential to affect them socially, physically, spiritually, intellectually, and emotionally. The less-than-committed athlete cannot succeed in the stressful environment of elite competition and the constant evaluation, imposing work demands and unexpected crises that come with it. Assessment of each athlete must be determined by the coach or sports consultant in terms of these factors. Assessing these factors provides the basis upon which the coach or sports consultants can determine and address the needs to be met in order to grow the athlete.

Significant Others

Significant others are those outside the athletic environment that provide a system of support for the athlete. These often include parents, spouses, and friends, but may also be represented by anyone who is willing to support and sustain the athlete, even without an obligation to do so. These supporters accept, sustain, and promote the athletes for themselves rather than support the athlete out of a sense of responsibility or duty.

APPLICATION OF THE MODEL

The model addresses energy management to enhance optimal performance. Optimal performance is not a chance happening but a consequence of several important factors blending in the right configuration. This configuration may vary from one athlete to another, however, and the athlete must fit whatever criteria are defined by a particular sport. There must be a balance between arousal and relaxation, and there must be a high level of motivation, with a minimum energy drain.

Assessing Energy Drains

One of the more critical components of the model, the assessment of daily energy drains, is the major focus of this essay. In this day of rapidly expanding technology, stress has become a regular phenomenon. Some of us cope with stress more effectively because we have learned to manage it better. To be better able to manage stress, we must know why and to what extent stress exists. In the assessment of daily energy drains, collegiate coaches and athletes were asked to identify the kinds of things that distract them from performing at their maximum.

Development of Questionnaire

Coupled with these assessment results and by researching the works of others, including Poole's "Potential Exploration Program (PEP),"

Wooden's "Pyramid of Success," Swartz's "Blueprint for Excellence," and the "Total Training Scheme," cited by McInnis, we designed a questionnaire to identify energy drains in athletes (Fig. 26.2). The resulting questionnaire asked athletes to provide information concerning stress factors related to the following four areas: intellectual, physical, social, and psychological.

Collecting Data

Athletes from women's basketball, gymnastics, tennis, and volleyball were asked to fill out a self-administered questionnaire in the training room each day before practice. This questionnaire took approximately two minutes to complete. A person trained to score the responses, scored and calculated scale scores for each of the four components. Cumulative scores were calculated throughout the playing season on each team member. Collecting the data almost daily allowed us to compose profiles for each athlete (Figs. 26.3, 26.4, 26.5).

Composing Profiles

Since athletes respond to their life situations in unique ways, team homogeneity was not expected. Furthermore, every athlete seemed to develop some specific normative patterns. From the daily summary sheet of each team we were able to determine the self-perceived emotional state of each athlete. It became apparent after several weeks of monitoring, that scores usually fell between 10 and 25 on the scale. When an individual's scores exceeded 30 or established an unusual pattern, intervention was recommended. The coach and the trainer were notified that an athlete's score was higher than usual and counseling was recommended. In some cases, particularly in the physical area, the trainer suggested treatment alternatives to reduce physical pain, stiffness, or overuse.

Energy Drain Factor Scale

Circle the number that most closely represents your perception.

Name or #:_____ Team:_____ Date: _____Day: M   T   W   TH   F   SA

1. Number of exams and papers due today   0   1   2   3   4   5   6   7   8   9

2. Number of exams and papers due rest of this week   0   1   2   3   4   5   6   7   8   9

3.	Feel caught up in classes	Way behind and very stressed 10	Behind and slightly stressed 9 8 7	Behind but not stressed 6 5 4	Slightly behind 3 2 1	Caught up 0
4.	My classes right now are	Overwhelming 10	Considerably difficult 9 8 7	Moderately difficult 6 5 4	Slightly difficult 3 2 1	Easy 0
5.	My teachers are generally	Unsupportive 10	Slightly supportive 9 8 7	Moderately supportive 6 5 4	Considerably supportive 3 2 1	Extremely supportive 0
6.	Feel rested—caught up on sleep	Not at all 10	Slightly 9 8 7	Moderately 6 5 4	Considerably 3 2 1	Extremely 0
7.	Food satisfaction–level of satisfaction with meals in past 24 hours	Not satisfied 10	Slightly 9 8 7	Moderately 6 5 4	Considerably 3 2 1	Extremely 0
8.	Energy and vitality level for today's workout was	Very low 10	Moderately low 9 8 7	Pretty high 6 5 4	Considerably high 3 2 1	Optimum 0
9.	Feeling of health/strength level	Very weak 10	Slightly weak 9 8 7	Moderately strong 6 5 4	Considerably strong 3 2 1	Very strong 0
10.	Wellness level	Extremely sick 10	Considerably sick 9 8 7	Moderately sick 6 5 4	Well 3 2 1	Extremely well 0
11.	Pain level	Unbearable 10	Considerable 9 8 7	Moderate 6 5 4	Slight 3 2 1	No pain 0
12.	Stiffness level	Unbearable 10	Considerable 9 8 7	Moderate 6 5 4	Slight 3 2 1	None 0
13.	Weight level (too fat or too thin)	Unsatisfied 10	Slightly satisfied 9 8 7	Moderately satisfied 6 5 4	Considerably satisfied 3 2 1	Very satisfied 0
14.	Recovering from injury or sickness	Just injured or sick 10	Slightly recovered 9 8 7	Moderately recovered 6 5 4	Considerably recovered 3 2 1	Completely recovered 0
15.	Experiencing now (please circle if applicable)	PMS	Pregnancy (week)	Menstrual cramps	Other pains	
16.	Estimate of my work rate for today's workout	0% 10 10% 9	20% 8 30% 7	40% 6 50% 5 60% 4	70% 3 80% 2 90% 1	100% 0

FIGURE 26.2a Energy Drain Factor Scale

17. Estimate of my satisfaction with workout

Unsatisfied	Slightly satisfied	Moderately satisfied	Considerably satisfied	Extremely satisfied
10	9 8 7	6 5 4	3 2 1	0

18. Burnout factor—combination of intellectual, emotional, and physical fatigue

Extremely	Considerably	Moderately	Slightly	None
10	9 8 7	6 5 4	3 2 1	0

19. Estimate of team's work rate for today's workout

0% 10%	20% 30%	40% 50% 60%	70% 80%	90% 100%
10 9	8 7	6 5 4	3 2	1 0

20. Estimate of team's satisfaction with today's workout

Unsatisfied	Slightly satisfied	Moderately satisfied	Considerably satisfied	Extremely satisfied
10	9 8 7	6 5 4	3 2 1	0

21. Satisfaction with length of workout

10	9 8 7	6 5 4	3 2 1	0

22. Satisfaction with difficulty of workout

10	9 8 7	6 5 4	3 2 1	0

23. Satisfaction with competition schedule

Unsatisfied	Slightly satisfied	Moderately satisfied	Considerably satisfied	Extremely satisfied
10	9 8 7	6 5 4	3 2 1	0

24. Estimate of how I see the coach #1

Rejecting	Resentful	Indifferent	Accepting	Friend/Mentor
10	9 8 7	6 5 4	3 2 1	0
Hostile	Cool	Civil	Warm	Affectionate
10	9 8 7	6 5 4	3 2 1	0
Very critical	Disapproving	Impartial	Approving	Praising
10	9 8 7	6 5 4	3 2 1	0

25. Estimate of how I see the coach #2

Rejecting	Resentful	Indifferent	Accepting	Friend/Mentor
10	9 8 7	6 5 4	3 2 1	0
Hostile	Cool	Civil	Warm	Affectionate
10	9 8 7	6 5 4	3 2 1	0
Very critical	Disapproving	Impartial	Approving	Praising
10	9 8 7	6 5 4	3 2 1	0

26. Estimate of how I see the coach #3

Rejecting	Resentful	Indifferent	Accepting	Friend/Mentor
10	9 8 7	6 5 4	3 2 1	0
Hostile	Cool	Civil	Warm	Affectionate
10	9 8 7	6 5 4	3 2 1	0
Very critical	Disapproving	Impartial	Approving	Praising
10	9 8 7	6 5 4	3 2 1	0

27. How I feel towards my teammates as a group

Rejecting	Resentful	Indifferent	Accepting	Close friendship
10	9 8 7	6 5 4	3 2 1	0
Hostile	Cool	Civil	Warm	Affectionate
10	9 8 7	6 5 4	3 2 1	0
Very critical	Disapproving	Impartial	Approving	Praising
10	9 8 7	6 5 4	3 2 1	0

28. What I feel from the team towards me

Rejection	Resentment	Indifference	Acceptance	Friendliness
10	9 8 7	6 5 4	3 2 1	0
Hostility	Coolness	Civility	Warmth	Affection
10	9 8 7	6 5 4	3 2 1	0
Very critical	Disapproving	Impartial	Approving	Praising
10	9 8 7	6 5 4	3 2 1	0

FIGURE 26.2b

29. Difficulty with significant-other relationships:	Serious difficulty	Considerable			Moderate			Slight			No difficulty
Coach	10	9	8	7	6	5	4	3	2	1	0
Family	10	9	8	7	6	5	4	3	2	1	0
Partner/Fiance/Spouse	10	9	8	7	6	5	4	3	2	1	0
Boyfriend/Girlfriend	10	9	8	7	6	5	4	3	2	1	0
Roommates	10	9	8	7	6	5	4	3	2	1	0

30. Social life satisfaction	Unsatisfied	Slightly satisfied			Moderately satisfied			Considerably satisfied			Extremely satisfied
	10	9	8	7	6	5	4	3	2	1	0

Right now I feel	Extremely	Considerably			Moderately			Slightly			Not at all
31. Depressed	10	9	8	7	6	5	4	3	2	1	0
32. Angry	10	9	8	7	6	5	4	3	2	1	0
33. Troubled	10	9	8	7	6	5	4	3	2	1	0
34. Harried	10	9	8	7	6	5	4	3	2	1	0
35. Tense	10	9	8	7	6	5	4	3	2	1	0
36. Bad tempered	10	9	8	7	6	5	4	3	2	1	0
37. Aggressive	10	9	8	7	6	5	4	3	2	1	0
38. Discouraged	10	9	8	7	6	5	4	3	2	1	0
39. Burned out	10	9	8	7	6	5	4	3	2	1	0
40. Anxious	10	9	8	7	6	5	4	3	2	1	0

41. My feelings about being here now doing what I am doing	Unsatisfied	Slightly satisfied			Moderately satisfied			Considerably satisfied			Extremely satisfied
	10	9	8	7	6	5	4	3	2	1	0

42. Any other problems?		
Housing	Yes	No
Car/Transportation	Yes	No
Financial	Yes	No
Other	Yes	No

Note: PLEASE GO BACK AND MAKE SURE YOU HAVE COMPLETED *EVERY* LINE.

ACADEMIC   PHYSICAL   SOCIAL   EMOTIONAL   TOTAL

FIGURE 26.2c

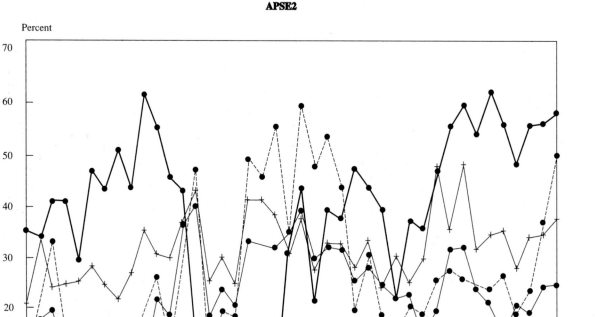

FIGURE 26.3 Individual Athlete Profile—Basketball

Implementing the Questionnaire

Recommendations with regard to the social, intellectual, and psychological areas were made to the coaches as well. Some coaches chose to act upon these recommendations, whereas others did not. As we were dealing with four different head coaches, the protocol was determined by the coach's perception of the program. Frequently, coaches requested direct intervention by the research team, who then worked individually with an athlete. Counseling was done in the training room, office, or other setting that insured privacy. Athletes were then made aware of what specific, elevated stress levels were causing their energy drain and were invited to discuss these problems. Once the nature of the stressor was identified, efforts were made to

APSE 8

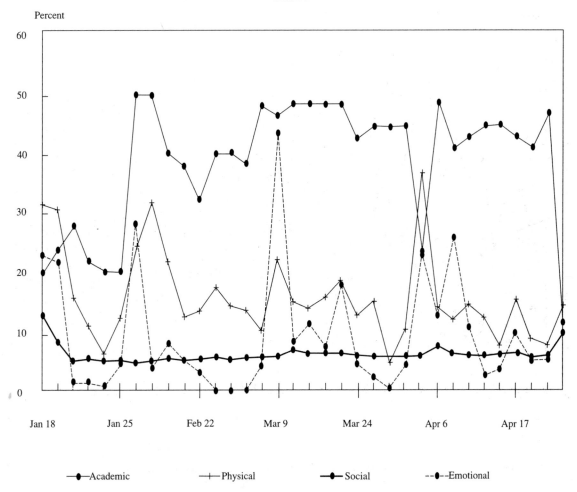

FIGURE 26.4   Individual Athlete Profile—Tennis

determine if there were other, more obscure, factors underlying their stress. The person doing the intervention then explored (with the athlete) ways in which the draining situation could be reduced. Reducing the stress often produced other recommendations which included allowing an athlete to miss practice, permitting special makeup tests, or engaging in relaxation exercises.

Results

Although the data gathered are not conclusive, we have learned many important facts: (a) this method of gathering data gives a viable, daily reading of an athlete's current stress level; (b) we know that changes occur in levels of precipitate dysfunction and emotional disequilibrium; and (c) we can talk with athletes and assist them in

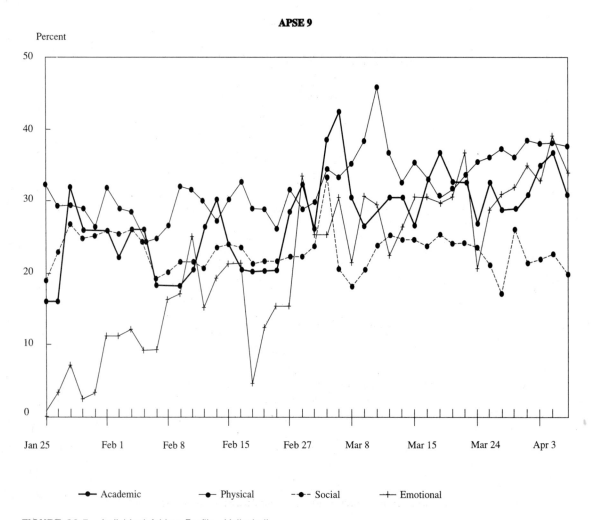

FIGURE 26.5 Individual Athlete Profile—Volleyball

diffusing some stresses that can be distracting, whether they be physical, psychological, social, or intellectual.

Further study was suggested by the data gathered. The success of the stress inventory has been in discovering problematic areas. Each athlete has shown consistency in reporting these problematic areas, and successful intervention was made frequently, which resulted in a relief

of the inhibiting factor. However, further study is needed to address whether or not scores reported in any or all of the four-part form had any relationship to athletic performance.

A correlation analysis was done to give a preliminary idea as to whether items within the subscales actually clustered. This essay will only discuss the factor analysis results for the physical subscale. Figures 26.6–26.9 show that the physical

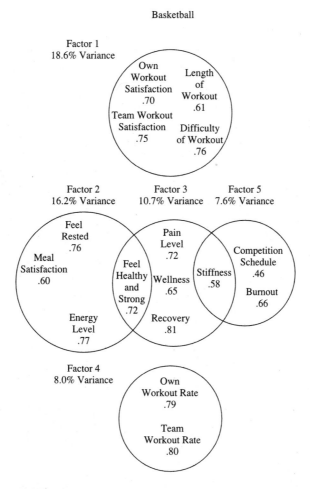

FIGURE 26.6   Physical Stress Factor Analysis—Basketball

stress items cluster in different configurations for the four different teams. Possible explanations for these differences include (a) the physical, psychological, intellectual, or social demands made by each particular sport, or (b) modalities of response that have tendencies to be sports-specific (i.e., a tennis team schedule that requires matches to be played against three nationally ranked universities in one weekend or during midterm examinations as compared with a home gymnastics meet against a local, mediocre team).

Ineffective performance caused by stress drains energy from the store of energy required for an athlete's optimal performance. This state of stress, perceived by and subjective to each athlete, may be independent of real environmental conditions. But the fact that the athlete *thinks* that things are not in a state of equilibrium may be sufficiently disruptive to siphon energy from the task at hand.

Some examples of this state of disequilibrium or ineffectiveness may be illustrated, at least at

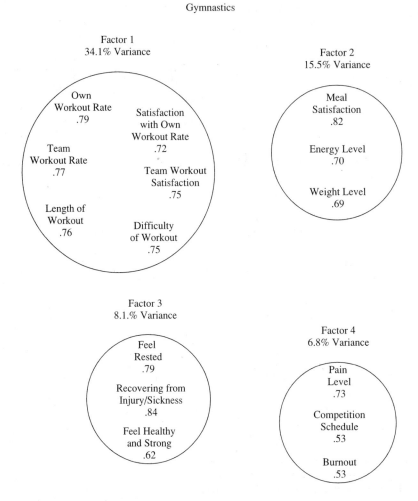

FIGURE 26.7   Physical Stress Factor Analysis—Gymnastics

the qualitative level, by such statements as "I do [or I don't] feel upset." It is also believed that persons are capable of differentiating between a bipolar perception such as, "I felt lousy yesterday, but I feel great today."

The fact that the measuring or numbering system is not exact or precise may be irrelevant. What is relevant is that the athletes are discerning their own inner experiences and that they recognize that their social, intellectual, and psychological structure is resulting in ineffective performance. They are able to share with another person that they are sufficiently disturbed that changes are needed to make the conditions right again. Since these stressors can be described on at least four levels, the athlete can probably identify causality even though it may not be based on external factors. The disparity

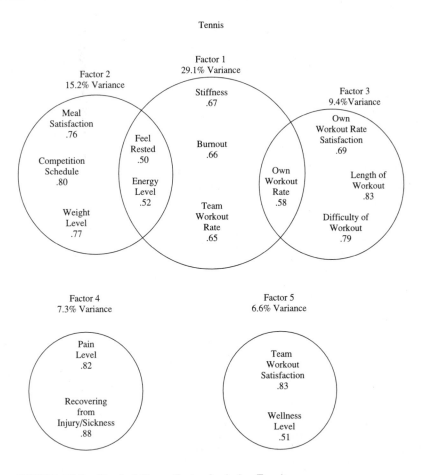

FIGURE 26.8   Physical Stress Factor Analysis—Tennis

between a desired state of equilibrium and the perceived state of equilibrium varies with individual experiences and the magnitude of the resulting effect on performance.

The ability of an athlete to cope has no relationship to their skill, but it requires an ability to muster the energy to focus attention, to relax, or to continue striving for a desired goal. Athletes who do not cope well have greater difficulty handling real or perceived disequilibrium, while athletes who do cope well can often proceed with reckless abandon. Elite ath-

letes, however, must consider long-term goals when forced to cope with an immediate problem. Handling disequilibrium must be planned as efficiently in an athlete's training program as are their physical skills and mental strategies.

APPLICATION OF THE STUDY TO SUPPORT BUSINESS

The model and questionnaire provide invaluable information for coaches, athletes, and sports consultants involved in competitive experience.

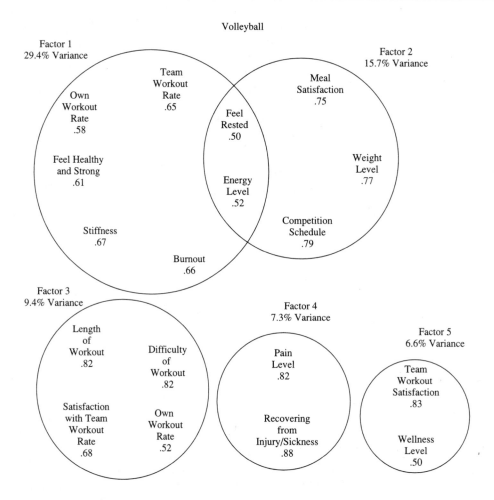

FIGURE 26.9 *Physical Stress Factor Analysis—Volleyball*

The model provides for a mentoring process to occur between willing athletes and willing coaches by enhancing awareness, caring, and shared knowledge and skills, and by building positive interpersonal relationships. It also helps identify areas that may need intervention, such as what is needed to prevent or solve problems. Because teams are made up of individuals, we find that the configurations for stress factors vary from team to team. The emerging pattern is a result of what is going on in the daily lives of individual athletes. How they handle their experiences greatly affects the team's performance.

Professional Sports

Although this program was designed to evaluate the stressors or energy drains that affect collegiate athletes, it can be easily adapted to the professional sports scene. Questionnaires were developed which measure daily stresses that occur in any or all of the four general areas of social, psychological, intellectual, or physical factors.

Ideally, professional sport would apply the model in the following way: (a) Team members would fill out their questionnaires in the training room. (b) Results of the questionnaires would be faxed to the sports consultant's office where the staff would score them and identify individual problems. (c) The consultant would then either fax or call the appropriate member of the coaching staff with suggestions for intervention. (Intervention could be handled on site if the team has a sports psychologist.) A season inventory should be developed from a composite of the team stress profiles. This information could provide data for planning future coaching schemes.

Fitness Program

The model and questionnaire data can also be incorporated or applied to the expanding world of corporate fitness, racquet clubs, health spas, and wellness clinics. Using the questionnaire to understand the daily condition of club members or employees may provide opportunity for improving the daily workout routine or for reducing stress levels and energy drains over time.

In conclusion, one of the positive outcomes of this type of holistic approach is that the athlete, club member, or employee feels like they are being dealt with as a complete human being. Secondly, a positive, caring rapport is developed between coaches or leaders with team members, club members, or employees.

One of the major findings of this research is that individuals change from day to day and yet they are generally resilient if they have emotional support. People with support systems appear able to accomplish things more quickly and

more effectively. Knowing the stress factors that are present and being able to manage those energy drains are keys to creating an atmosphere for success.

REFERENCES

Dunphy, M. 1981. *John Robert Wooden: The coaching process.* Ph.D. diss., Brigham Young University, Provo, Utah.

Gill, D. 1986. *Psychological dynamics and sport.* Champaign, Ill.: Human Kinetics.

Hendricks, G., and J. Carlson. 1982. *The centered athlete.* Englewood Cliffs, N.J.: Prentice-Hall.

Jones, B., J. Wells, R. Peters, and D. Johnson. 1982. *Guide to effective coaching: Principles and practice.* Boston: Allyn and Bacon.

Landers, D. 1982. *Social problems in athletics.* Urbana, Ill.: University of Illinois Press.

Martens, R. 1982. *Coaches guide to sport psychology.* Champaign, Ill.: Human Kinetics.

Nideffer, R. 1978. The relationship of attention and anxiety to performance. In *Sport psychology: An analysis of athletic behavior,* edited by W. F. Straub. Longmeadow, Mass.: Movement Publications.

Pate, R. 1984. *Scientific foundations of coaching.* Philadelphia: Saunders.

Straub, W. 1978. *Sport psychology: An analysis of athletic behavior.* Longmeadow, Mass.: Movement Publications.

Wooden, J. 1972. *They call me coach.* Waco, Tex.: Word Books.

AWARENESS EXPANSION:
SOME AREAS OF INTEREST

27

The Business of Sportscasting

Linda K. Fuller

INTRODUCTION

This essay could arguably have been titled ''Sportscasting as Business'' because it discusses the evolution of sportscasting from information to entertainment in terms of its profitability. Part of a wider research project,[1] it is approached from a number of perspectives—historical, economic, in terms of the audience, as part of the media, and from the sociological point of view. It aims to tackle some sticky issues and begin dialogue on many more.

BACKGROUND

A would-be sports announcer would do well to learn everything possible about the different sports that are broadcast. The rules and requirements of the games must be thoroughly absorbed. The phraseology distinctive of the game or sport should be studied and used in broadcasts only if it is generally understood by sport fans and by the average listener. The sport pages of newspapers written by experts will be a learning tool, providing a dictation that is picturesque and a style that is speedy. The history of the sport and of those who have participated and gained renown are important resources. The signs or gestures used by the officials are part of what must be learned. But most of all, the broadcaster must never forget that the event is not watched for personal amusement, but is reported to an audience who is listening closely to that description.

The development of sportscasting, for quite logical reasons, evolved with that of radio. Arguments abound as to when the very first sportscast was actually made, but the year was 1921. With Johnny Ray and Johnny Dundee as contending parties in a boxing event on April 11 at Motor Square Garden in Pittsburgh, a blow-by-blow description went out over local crystal sets. In August of that same year, KDKA reported both the Davis Cup tennis matches and a National League baseball game. Grantland Rice broadcast the 1921 World Series.

Linda K. Fuller is with the Department of Media, Worcester State College, Worcester, Massachusetts.

And on November 5, Harold Arlin, of KDKA, broadcast the first college football game—Pittsburgh versus West Virginia; the word is that he yelled so excitedly on one touchdown that he knocked the station off the air.

Radio station WJY of Jersey City was later created by David Sarnoff, general manager of RCA, for the occasion of broadcasting a world heavyweight championship prize fight between Jack Dempsey ("The Manassa Mauler") and Georges Carpentier of France, "with an antenna strung between a steel tower and the clock tower of the Lackawanna railroad terminal" (Archer 1971, 213). The first live sporting event broadcast on television was the second game of a baseball double-header between Columbia and Princeton, covered by Bill Stern out of New York's Baker Field 17 May 1939 (Warburton 1987, 16).

Rather than reviewing the entire history of sportscasting here, the important point to underscore is the fact that oftentimes sportscasters themselves have become more the focus of audience concern and comment than the sporting event itself.

Technically, production improvements aided by such technological capabilities as instant replay facilities, multiple cameras, computer graphics, and statistical data processors have further changed the role of the sportscaster from that of simple blow-by-blow announcer to that of complex analyst and showperson.

Bruce Garrison of the University of Miami in Coral Gables (1987) summarizes a report on the evolution of professionalism in sports by pointing out these basic characteristics:

1. Movement toward more process-oriented reporting rather than exclusively event-oriented reporting.
2. Increased use of innovative reporting methods, including use of new technology for investigative and public opinion reporting.
3. Sports story topics of a wider range—such as courtroom litigation, high finance, and international politics.
4. Participation in sports reporting by women, both in print and on the air.
5. Increase in sports newsmaking by women.
6. Reduction of "cheerleading" of local teams and reporting of both the positive and negative activities of teams.
7. Sensitivity about professional behavior standards through creation and enforcement of codes of ethics by groups such as APSE.
8. Concern for reporting credibility.
9. Reaction by print sports media to the impact of the instantaneous coverage by electronic media.
10. Adoption of new computer-based technologies for faster and more accurate coverage of sports in print and on the air.
11. Spot and feature photography of sports action at a higher level of quality through better talent and better technology.
12. Better use of available print space and air time for sports reporting.
13. Large news holes for sports in newspapers and, probably, for television networks and local stations.
14. Reduction of bias against coverage of women's sports, primarily at amateur levels.
15. More common use of features about sports people and their activities.
16. Concern for credibility, ethics, and professionalism in the behavior of sports reporters.
17. Pulitzer Prize Committee recognition in 1985 and 1986 for excellence in sports reporting.

"In many instances," David A. Klatell and Norman Marcus of Boston University's Institute in Broadcast Sports remind us, "the broadcast booth, rather than the action on the field, has become the center of the telecast, with multiple on-air personnel orchestrating a combination of entertainment, network promotion, and commentary for the benefit of non-sports fans and their impact on ratings" (1988, 16).

ECONOMICS OF SPORTSCASTING

Economics is what sportscasting is all about. As the electronic media become evermore our preferred source of sports information (so much so, in fact, that radios and televisions are becoming continually more noticeable at actual sporting events), the multimillion dollar sportscasting business must be factored in.

Advertisers are clearly aware of the importance of who will be anchoring the shows where their products are being pushed. The name of the game is, after all, ratings. Toward that end, television executives and advertisers are interested primarily in sportscasters who can draw and sustain audiences. Their concern, for example, is not with the sportscaster's level of expertise in sport or television, but how many ratings points the individual can garner for a particular program. Neither are advertisers concerned whether the audience likes or dislikes the sportscaster, as long as that audience tunes in— a classic case of "Cosell-itis," when large numbers of people admit to tuning in to the man they love to hate.

The symbiotic relationship of the sports-media complex has been well documented. A number of books have been written about the interdependence between television and sport,[2] about sportswriters and sportscasters,[3] and by sportswriters and sportscasters.[4]

A number of sportscasters have become sponsors in their own right. Some examples that come to mind are Mel Allen for White Owl cigars; Pat Summerall for True Value; Merlin Olsen for FTD; Bob Uecker for Miller Lite; Howard Cosell for Fruit of the Loom; Phil Rizzuto for The Money Store; and Jim Palmer for Jockey shorts. No doubt you can think of many more.

THE AUDIENCE(S) FOR SPORTSCASTING

As mass entertainment, intensively commercialized spectator sports play a larger role in American culture than in any other society, past or present. In no other country today do the amounts of money spent, tickets bought, games played, livelihoods involved, words printed, hours televised, or spinoff industries concerning sports match American totals, either by absolute or proportional measures.

Sports audiences in the United States are the target market for the greedy programmers who hope to sell them to greedy advertisers. Allen Guttmann (1988), professor of English and American Studies at Amherst College, sees the American fascination with sport as a reflection of our culture due to the fact that sports are "secular, bureaucratic, and specialized," and theoretically democratic in terms of equality among competitors. According to Benjamin G. Rader (1983), we are living in the Age of Spectators, and television keeps adding more "trash-sports."

While the Super Bowl attracts more than 100 million viewers from its massive hyping on television, studies have shown that nearly one-third of Americans follow television sports daily and another 50 percent listen to them on the radio (Morse 1984, 45).

International audiences for events such as the Olympic Games and the World Soccer Championship exceed 80 million people, with those numbers increasing exponentially with the advent of satellite communications. And we must not forget the 8,250 accredited media representatives for the 1988 Summer Olympics in Los Angeles outnumbered the 7,800 competing athletes.

Special sporting events in the United States such as the Indianapolis 500, Super Bowl, Masters, U.S. Open, NBA finals, World Series, and Kentucky Derby make particularly interesting case studies in terms of sportscasting and its audiences. Regularly scheduled programs such as ABC's Wide World of Sports, Monday Night Football, and/or Canada's Hockey Night will be future subjects of similar study.

MEDIA INTERDEPENDENCE

Although the topic of this essay is sports reporting via telecommunications, it must include both print and electronic media. "Like it or not," writes Kramer (1987, S9), "sportswriting is no longer the art of writing about athletes as though they sprang from Zeus's head and live on Mount Olympus." The rules of the golden age of sportswriting have been rewritten by the double whammy of electronic media and tabloid journalism.

Instead, we have the age of realism or what one observer calls "the age of the human side of the athlete combined with the 'if I don't write it someone else will' school of journalism." Sports coverage in the print media has been revolutionized with the advent of *USA Today,* whose pages of graphics, statistics, and wide-ranging sports coverage have spurred nearly all other newspapers to improve sports coverage. *Sports Illustrated* has long dominated the magazine field, but more specialized sports-related tabloids frequently appear on the stands.

As mentioned, sports-related books on the market include Jim Spence's *Up Close & Personal: The Inside Story of Network Television Sports,* Bill Carter's *Monday Night Football,* and an analysis of network sports divisions by Terry O'Neill, a former television executive at both ABC and CBS.

The role of radio in sportscasting remains a strong one, but television's influence has come to reign supreme. Much has been written about the power of television to frame interpretation, and how it has affected rules and rulings, statistics and salaries, sweeps and scheduling, and, most of all, our perceptions of sports. The question posed here is of the role sportscasters play in that interdependence between sports and television. Bemoaning a decline in the art of sportswriting, Andrews (1987, 8) comments: "Television sports coverage seems perpetually at odds with itself. It spends a small fortune to bring you the game and then devotes much of its vast technical resources to distracting your attention from the game. When there is action on the field you are frequently getting instant replay of what is already past."

Traditionally, the three commercial networks have held the monopoly on the audience for sports and sportscasting. Many people would agree that "ABC has traditionally been the master of milking sports coverage." (Robins 1988, 74). Under the tutelage of Roone Arledge and his introduction of "Wide World of Sports," ABC became the undisputed network leader, with NBC anxiously hoping to gain a share of the sports ratings. Yet, Stephen Singer (1987, 5), a former editor for *Sports Magazine,* rated CBS the best all-around network for sportscasters, especially citing Brent Musburger and John Madden. And not to be discounted, the success of twenty-four-hour sports programming on ESPN since 1979 has made major inroads into garnering the sports audience, introducing lesser-known sports and making networks evermore edgy about losing audiences to cable and other competition.

More than a decade ago, Roone Arledge was quoted as saying, ''You must use the camera—and the microphone—to broadcast an image that approximates what the brain perceives, not merely what the eye sees. Only then can you create the illusion of reality.'' (Talen 1986, 50) The pictures in our heads of sports on television are a topic unto themselves.

THE "JOCKOCRACY" ISSUE[5]

Robert Lipsyte's term ''jockocracy'' refers to television's hiring of former athletes as broadcasters. In reference to that practice, Howard Cosell (1985, 134) first makes a broad disclaimer that there have been some exceptions, then states:

> But, generally speaking, these alleged analysts and colormen serve a limited role—and they rarely proved themselves capable of bridging the gap between entertainment and journalism. The bottom line: they are not communicators.
>
> Put an ex-jock in the booth, and their cliche-ridden presentation of a game is the least of their sins. As a result of their lack of training, most of them are blessedly lost when trying to establish a story line for a telecast—i.e., detecting trends, keying on the personality and experiences of a player as they relate to his performance on the field, knowing his strengths and weaknesses, recalling the flow of events from earlier in the game as a series of plays rather than as a contest, and often they are ignorant of the human perspective.

The issue is not a new one. Even prior to television, Abbot (1941, 62) discussed it: ''Undoubtedly a good background knowledge of sports is essential; but the knowledge of how to dramatize the voice, to pick vivid, descriptive words quickly, to keep on giving information in the midst of excitement, and to inject the thrill

of the game without hesitation into the microphone are more essential than previous participation in the sport.''

This point is illustrated by Ken Coleman (1973) in ''Well-Known Announcers and How They Got That Way.'' He indicates that many of the greats may have played a sport but that most possess a journalistic background. He cites those that fit such a description: Curt Gowdy, Chris Schenkel, Vin Scully, Jim Simpson, Lindsey Nelson, Ray Scott, Don Dunphy, Jack Brickhouse, Marv Albert, Dan Kelly, Ernie Harwell, Chuck Thompson, Bob Prince, Merle Harmon, Harry Kalas, Al Michaels, Danny Gallivan, Jim Woods, Harry Jones, Howard Cosell, Dick Enberg and Don Wells. One of the first athletes to become a broadcaster was Marty Glickman, a member of the U.S. track team at the 1936 Olympics in Berlin; he was joined some time later by other athletes who ''made the transition from the playing fields to the broadcast booth'': Frank Gifford, Joe Gargiola, Tom Harmon, Bud Palmer, and Bill White. Cosell would add the names of Paul Christman (''the first ex-jock to take to the air with literacy and a willingness to criticize''), Pat Summerall, and Bob Uecker, adding that ''newcomer Ahmad Rashad has potential.''

Emmy Award-winning CBS sports broadcaster Warner Wolf (1983, 5) gives his opinion: ''I've got nothing against ex-athletes being on the air—some are great as analysts and some as play-by-play men because they have been down on the field. But you don't see many ex-athletes become sportscasters on the 6 P.M. and 11 P.M. news. The reason is they haven't learned the business. Synder and Spreitzer (1983) suggest that some observers consider former athletes as having a special advantage as sportscasters in the sense of ''having been there'' and being able ''to tell it like it is,'' giving the impression of offering the fan an inside view of strategies, respective team strengths and weaknesses, and locker room scuttlebutt. Many of television's color commentators are ex-jocks who, according to Klatell and Marcus (1988, 17), "have taught us several valuable lessons: it isn't nearly as easy as it looks; being good at an activity like sports is not the same as being good at understanding or explaining it; mediocrity is so commonplace anyone with a little spark or originality will shine through."

SOCIOLOGICAL PERSPECTIVE

The sheer pervasiveness and salience of sports must be noted here, both in terms of their use of our time and of our money. From a wider perspective, our bent toward Western enthnocentrism must also be considered—it colors not only how sportscasters present the games but the way in which the audience-receiver perceives them.

In light of such current scandals as the Len Bias and Ben Johnson drug cases, SMUs football probation, Pete Rose's gambling, or the positive role Magic Johnson has chosen as a spokesperson for "safe sex" after discovering that he has tested positive for the AIDS virus, the issue of our athletes as role models and heroes becomes a topic of great concern to sportscasters.[6]

Race and gender issues also abound. Regarding the former, evidence runs the gamut from what was not said forty years ago when Jackie Robinson entered baseball's major league to what Isaiah Thomas said about basketball's white Larry Bird or what Jimmy "The Greek" Synder's said "in jest" about blacks being better athletes due to selective breeding. Women sportscasters, a rare breed, typically emerge via the former-athlete route, with exceptions being Phyllis George, Becky Dixon, and Gayle Gardner.[7]

Then too comes the issue of the sportscaster as newscaster, a role in which Jim McKay found himself during the Olympic Games in Munich and Al Michaels took on during the San Francisco earthquake. More and more, our sportscasters are required to be able to ad-lib about more than just the sporting event at hand.

And what about the politics of sportscasting? Should audiences be able to expect the nonbiased, objective description and interpretation, or should they be subjected to team-preferred sportscasters? In the one camp is Bob Prince of KDKA, the Pirates broadcaster known as the Prince of Homers, who states: "We are not journalists as such. We are part-reporter and part-entertainer. We are there to make our rooters happy—and the other teams' rooter mad." (Durslag 1975, 2). Surely Johnny Most made no pretense of being an objective Celtics reporter. Jim McKay (1973, 212) feels very strongly about objectivity: "Reporting, I think, is simply the communication to someone not on the scene of a given event, a happening. The reporter's job is to tell as clearly and accurately as he can the facts of the situation and, in the case of television, to explain the meaning of the visual image on the screen. More subtly, I think the reporter must communicate the mood of the moment. What is the inner emotional reaction to the scene, in the words of one who is there?" John Madden (1984) has been quoted as joking that he knows he has done a good job on a game when each team complains about his favoring the other. And then, too, it can backfire, as with Patriot audiences' dislike of Bob Griese as their sportscaster because of his longtime association with the Dolphins.

Synder and Spreitzer (1983, 218) remind us that, "the sports announcer has three constituencies to please in addition to the listener or viewer—the owner of the sports franchise, the corporate sponsors who buy the advertising time, and the owner of the television or radio station."

SPORTSCASTERS AS CELEBRITIES

The question here is, Did Howard Cosell create Muhammad Ali, or vice versa? Whatever the case, the phenomenon of the sportscaster as celebrity is upon us. Klatell and Marcus (1988, 15–16) comment:

> The •star' announcers and commentators—the Maddens, Giffords, Musburgers, Michaels, and Cosells of the industry—are so removed in salary, visibility, and status from the humble local announcers or nightly sportscasters that they hardly seem employed in the same business. In fact, a case can be made that they are not employed in the same business. The million-dollar salaries and incessant promotional campaigns mounted by their employers place them at a level equal to or higher than that of the athletes they are covering. In some cases, the television announcers, their associated personnel and vans full of high-tech equipment, have overwhelmed the event and its erstwhile participants.

SPORTSCASTERS—SOME PROFILES

From his half-century of broadcasting, sportscaster great Red Barber (1970, 225) shares the fact that for many years he has kept this stanza from Rudyard Kipling's "The Elephant Child" on his desk:

I keep six honest serving men

(They taught me all I knew):

Their names are What and Why and When

And How and Where and Who.

He adds: "These six are, of course, the essentials of reporting. For the sports announcer they are so basic as almost to be taken for granted. Without trying to top Kipling, let's name an additional six serving-men for the radio-television sports broadcaster to call upon in his play-by-play profession. They are preparation, evaluation, concentration, curiosity, impartiality, and, if such can be achieved, imperturbability.''

In 1979, the National Sportscasters and Sportswriters Association decided to elect people for an annual Sportscaster of the Year award. Named for Ford C. Frick, a sportswriter who later became commissioner of baseball, the names of the award winners are located on a plaque in the Baseball Hall of Fame at Cooperstown, New York. The winners have been:[8]

1978—Mel Allen and Red Barber

1979—Bob Elson

1980—Russ Hodges

1981—Ernie Harwell

1982—Vin Scully

1983—Jack Brickhouse

1984—Curt Gowdy

1985—Buck Canel

1986—Bob Prince

1987—Jack Buck

1988—Lindsey Nelson

1989—Harry Caray

A list is being compiled of sportscasters who should be profiled for their contributions to both sports and the media. The list that follows is preliminary and will grow as time moves on and additional names emerge: Mel Allen, Red Barber, Len Berman, Jack Brickhouse, Jack Buck, Buck Canel, Harry Caray, Don Cherry, Ken Coleman, Bud Collins, Howard Cosell, Bob Costas, Dizzy Dean, Don Dunphy, Bob Elson, Dick Enberg, Julius Erving, Joe Garagiola, Frank Gifford, Marty Glickman, Curt Gowdy, Bryant Gumbel, Ernie Harwell, Chick Hearn, Tom Heinsohn, Russ Hodges, John Madden, Bill McAtee, Tim McCarver, Al McGuire, Jim McKay, Al Michaels, Johnny Most, Brent Musburger, Lindsey Nelson, Merlin Olsen, Tony Kubek, Bob Prince, Ahmad Rashad, Bill Russell, Chris Schenkel, Vin Scully, Bill Stockton, and Pat Summerall.

FUTURE CONCERNS AND CONSIDERATIONS OF SPORTSCASTING

"The work of a television sportscaster is an odd job," wrote William O. Johnson, Jr. in 1971. "It is neither art nor science, neither common labor nor honored profession. To criticize its practice, or its practitioners, is difficult and perhaps even unfair, since it really has no strict standards or firm procedures by which one can make documentable judgments. Beyond bad grammar, mispronounced names, or perhaps a cheap haircut, one may have trouble finding either a norm or a mean for complaint. The sportscaster is easier to define by what he is not than by what he is. He is not quite a journalist, not quite a carnival barker, not quite an orator or an interlocutor or master of ceremonies or trained seal. Yet he is a little of all of them" (p. 192).

Thus, one may ask, Are sportscasters a cultural reflection of television's dominance? Are they an elite, speaking "boothtalk" (Jackson 1986, 45) to inform audiences, or to entertain them? Is sportscasting a "profession," as such? What rules and roles do women and minorities adopt in breaking into the field? What is the relationship between sportscasting and celebrity-hood? Between sportscasting and sponsors? But most of all, what role do sportscasters play for their audiences, for sports fans? As the role of sportscaster continues to be explored and discussed, the answers to these questions will evolve.

NOTES

1. Linda K. Fuller, *Sportscasters/Sportscasting,* book in progress.
2. Allen Guttman, *A Whole New Ball Game* (U. of North Carolina Press, 1988); Dale Hoffmann and Martin J. Greenberg, *Sport$biz* (Leisure Press, 1989); David A. Klatell and Norman Marcus, *Sports For Sale* (Oxford University Press, 1988); Leonard Koppett, *Sports Illusion, Sports Reality* (Houghton Mifflin, 1981); Richard Lipsky, *How We Play the Game* (Beacon, 1981); Douglas A. Noverr, *The Games They Played* (Nelson-Hall, 1983); Ron Powers, *Super Tube* (Coward-McCann, 1984); Benjamin G. Rader, *In Its Own Image: How Television Has Transformed Sports* (Macmillan, 1984); and Michael Real, *Super Media* (Sage, 1989).
3. Ira Berkow, *Red* (Smith) (Times, 1986); Frank Graham, *A Farewell to Heroes* (Viking, 1987); Jerome Holtzman, *No Cheering in the Press Box* (Holt, Rinehart, Winston, 1974); Curt Smith, *Voices of the Game* (Diamond, 1987); Bert Randolph Sugar, *The Thrill of Victory* (ABC) (Hawthorn, 1978); and George Vecsey, *A Year in the Sun* (Times, 1989).
4. Red Barber, *The Broadcasters* (Dial, 1979); Heywood Hale Broun, *Tumultuous Merriment* (Richard Marek, 1979); James J. Cannon, *Nobody Asked me, but . . .* (Holt, Rinehart, 1978); Ken Coleman, *So You Want to Be a Sportscaster* (Hawthorn, 1973); Howard Cosell, *Like it is* (Playboy Press, 1974), with Mickey Herskowitz, *Cosell* (Playboy Press, 1974), and with Peter Bonaventre, *I Never Played the Game* (William Morrow, 1985); Frank Deford, *The World's Tallest Midget* (Little, Brown, 1987); James F. Fixx, *Jackpot!* (Random House, 1981); Frank Gifford, *Gifford on Courage* (Evans, 1976); Ralph Hubbell, *Come Walk with Me* (Prentice-Hall, 1975); Mike Lupica, *Shooting from the Lip* (Bonus, 1988); John Madden, with Dave Anderson,

Hey, Wait a Minute, I Wrote a Book! (Villard, 1984) and *One Size Doesn't Fit All* (Villard, 1988); Tim McCarver, with Ray Robinson, *Oh, Baby, I Love It*! (Villard, 1987); Jim McKay, *My Wide World* (Macmillan, 1973); Lindsey Nelson, *Hello Everybody, I'm Lindsey Nelson* (Beech Tree, 1985); Blackie Sherrod, *The Blackie Sherrod Collection* (Taylor, 1988); Hank Stram, with Lou Sahadi, *They're Playing My Game* (William Morrow, 1986); Dick Vitale, with Curry Kirkpatrick, *Vitale* (Simon and Schuster, 1988); and Warner Wolf, with William Taaffe, *Gimme A Break*! (McGraw-Hill, 1983).

5. This section is excerpted from my conference paper ''Olympics Access for Women: Athletes, Organizers, and Sportsjournalists,'' presented 1987 at the International Congress on The Olympic Movement and the Mass Media, in Calgary, Canada.

6. My interest in this particular topic was generated from my study of ''The Baseball Movie Genre: At Bat, or Struck Out?,'' which I first presented at the Popular Culture Association conference in St. Louis in April 1989, and which will soon be published in *Play & Culture*. It has spurred me on to further research that appears as ''Triumph of the Underdog in Baseball Films'' in volume two of a series on American popular film I am coediting with Paul Loukides. The series is called *Beyond the Stars* and is published by Popular Press. See also Frank Graham's *A Farewell to Heroes* (Viking, 1987).

7. Marilyn Hoffman's article titled ''Women Sports Stars Tackle Broadcast Journalism'' in the *Christian Science Monitor* (2 August 1984, 27) is what initiated my interest in researching sportscasting and sportscasters.

8. I am grateful to William J. Guilfoile, director of public relations for the National Baseball Hall of Fame and Museum, for this information.

REFERENCES

Abbot, Waldo. 1941. *Handbook of broadcasting*. New York: McGraw-Hill.

Andrews, Peter. 1987. The art of sportswriting. *Columbia Journalism Review* (May/June): 25–30.

Archer, Gleason L. 1971. *History of radio to 1926*. New York: Arno Press/New York Times.

Barber, Red. 1970. *The broadcasters*. New York: Dial Press.

Berkow, Ira. 1986. *Red: A biography of Red Smith*. New York: Times Books.

Broun, Heywood Hale. 1979. *Tumultuous merriment*. New York: Richard Marek.

Cannon, James J. 1978. *Nobody asked me, but . . . The world of Jimmy Cannon*. New York: Holt, Rinehart.

Coleman, Ken. 1973. *So you want to be a sportscaster: The techniques and skills of sports announcing by one of the country's most experienced broadcasters*. New York: Hawthorn Books.

Cosell, Howard. 1974. *Like it is*. Chicago, Ill.: Playboy Press.

Cosell, Howard, with Mickey Herskowitz. 1973. *Cosell*. Chicago, Ill.: Playboy Press.

Cosell, Howard, with Peter Bonaventre. 1985. *I never played the game*. New York: William Morrow.

Deford, Frank. 1987. *The world's tallest midget: The best of Frank Deford.* Boston: Little, Brown & Company.

Dunphy, Don. 1988. *Don Dunphy at ringside.* New York: Henry Holt & Company.

Durslag, Melvin. 1975. I don't care who wins, as long as *we* do!: An unblushing defense of announcers who root for the home team. *TV Guide,* 17 May.

Fixx, James F. 1981. *Jackpot!* New York: Random House.

Fuller, Linda K. 1987. Olympics access for women: Athletes, organizers, and sports journalists. In *The Olympic movement and the mass media: Past, present and future issues.* International conference proceedings, The University of Calgary, February 15–19. Calgary, Alberta: Hurford Enterprise.

Garrison, Bruce. 1987. The evolution of professionalism in sports reporting. In *The Olympic movement and the mass media: Past, present, and future issues.* International conference proceedings, The University of Calgary, February 15–19. Calgary, Alberta: Hurford Enterprises.

Garrison, Bruce, with Mark Sabljak. 1985. *Sports reporting.* Ames, Iowa: Iowa State University Press.

Gifford, Frank. 1976. *Gifford on courage.* New York: Evans.

Graham, Frank. 1987. *A farewell to heroes.* New York: Viking Press.

Guttman, Allen. 1986. *Sports spectators.* New York: Columbia University Press.

———. 1988. *A whole new ball game: An interpretation of American sports.* Chapel Hill, N.C.: University of North Carolina Press.

Hofmann, Dale, and Martin J. Greenberg. 1989. *Sport$box: An irreverent look at big business in pro sports.* Champaign, Ill.: Leisure Press.

Hoffman, Marilyn. 1984. Women sports stars tackle broadcast journalism. *Christian Science Monitor,* 2 August, 27.

Holtzman, Jerome, ed. and rec. 1974. *No cheering in the press box.* New York: Holt, Rinehart & Winston.

Horowitz, Ira. 1974. Sports broadcasting. In *Government and the sports business,* edited by R. C. Noll. Washington, D.C.: Brookings Institution.

Hubbell, Ralph. 1975. *Come walk with me.* Englewood Cliffs, N.J.: Prentice-Hall.

Jackson, Herb. 1986. Watch 'em single coverage the wide receivers and collision the quarterback! *TV Guide,* 8 March, 45–46.

Johnson, William O., Jr. 1971. *Super spectator and the electric lilliputians.* Boston: Little, Brown.

Klatell, David A., and Norman Marcus. 1988. *Sports for sale: Television, money, and the fans.* New York: Oxford University Press.

Koppett, Leonard. 1981. *Sports illusion, sports reality: A reporter's view of sports, journalism and society.* Boston: Houghton Mifflin.

Kramer, Staci D. 1987. The rewritten rules of sports journalism. *New York Times,* 2 August, S9.

Lipsky, Richard. 1981. *How we play the game: Why sports dominate American life.* Boston: Beacon Press.

Lupica, Mike. 1988. *Shooting from the lip: Essays, columns, quips, and gripes in the grand tradition of dyspeptic sports writing.* Chicago: Bonus Books.

———. 1988. *One size doesn't fit all.* New York: Villard Books.

Madden, John, with Dave Anderson. 1984. *Hey, wait a minute, I wrote a book!* New York: Villard Books.

McCarver, Tim, with Ray Robinson. 1987. *Oh, baby, I love it!* New York: Villard Books.

McKay, Jim. *My wide world.* 1973. New York: Macmillan.

Morse, Margaret. 1984. Sport on television: Replay and display. In *Regarding television: Critical approaches—an anthology,* edited by E. Ann Kaplan, 44–46. University Publications of America.

Nelson, Lindsey. 1985. *Hello everybody, I'm Lindsey Nelson.* New York: Beech Tree Books.

Noverr, Douglas A. 1983. *The games they played: Sports in American history, 1865–1980.* Chicago: Nelson-Hall.

Powers, Ron. 1984. *Super tube.* New York: Coward-McCann.

———. 1984. *In its own image: How television has transformed sports.* New York: Macmillan.

Rader, Benjamin G. 1983. *American sports: From the age of folk games to the age of spectators.* Englewood Cliffs, N.J.: Prentice-Hall.

Rashad, Ahmad, with Peter Bodo. 1988. *Rashad: Vikes, mikes, and something on the backside.* New York: Penguin.

Real, Michael. 1989. *Super media: A cultural studies approach.* Newbury Park, Calif.: Sage Publications.

Rice, Grantland. 1954. *The tumult and the shouting: My life in sport.* New York: Barnes.

Robins, J. Max. 1988. NBC's year to be a big sport. *Channels of Communication,* June, 74–75.

Sherrod, Blackie. 1988. *The Blackie Sherrod collection.* Dallas: Taylor Publishing.

Singer, Stephen. 1987. The best sportscasters on television. *TV Guide,* 21 November, 5–6.

Smith, Curt. 1987. *Voices of the game: The first full-scale overview of baseball broadcasting, 1921 to the present.* South Bend, Ind.: Diamond Communications.

Snyder, Eldon E., and Elmer A. Spreitzer. 1983. *Social aspects of sports.* 2d ed. Englewood Cliffs, N.J.: Prentice-Hall.

Stram, Hank, with Lou Sahadi. 1986. *They're playing my game.* New York: William Morrow.

Sugar, Bert Randolph. 1978. *The thrill of victory: The inside story of ABC sports.* New York: Hawthorn Books.

Talen, Julie. 1986. How the camera changes the game. *Channels of Communication,* April, 50–55.

Underwood, John. 1984. *Spoiled sport: A fan's notes on the troubles of spectator sports.* Boston: Little, Brown.

Vecsey, George. 1989. *A year in the sun: The games, the players, the pleasure of sports.* New York: Times Books.

Vitale, Dick, with Curry Kirkpatrick. 1988. *Vitale: Just your average bald, one-eyed basketball wacko who beat the ziggy and became a PTP'er.* New York: Simon and Schuster.

Warburton, Terrence L. 1987. Sports and the media: The evolution of sportscasting. Paper presented, March, to the Popular Culture Association, Montreal.

Wolf, Warner, with William Taaffe. 1983. *Gimme a break!* New York: McGraw-Hill.

28

How Big Is the West German Sports Market?*

Arnd Krüger

Germany has a long sporting tradition, successful international teams, a high percentage rate of memberships in sports clubs, and a successful sporting goods industry with such companies as Adidas and Puma. However, in West Germany there is very little solid information about what is actually going on in sports on a business level. Neither leisure nor sports is a separate entry in the *German Statistical Year Book*. The German Sports Federation Deutscher Sportbund (DSB) has no exact data on its 21 million members, and many of the other important facts can only be acquired by indirect means.

What can be learned of the past and present of the sports market shows that it is tied into general social, political, and economic developments. Therefore, it can be safely assumed that

Arnd Krüger is with the Department of Sport Studies, Georg-August Universitat, Gottingen, Germany.

*Note: The essay was written before the German reunification.

future trends in this part of the leisure industry will follow the more general trends of society (DSB 1988b; Krüger 1989). Sports are part of the service sector, and West Germany lags far behind comparable countries in this field. Only 12 percent of the work force is actively employed in health, education, and social services as compared to 15 percent in Great Britain, 18 percent in the United States, and 25 percent in Sweden (Krupp and Wagner 1988).

THE SPORTING TRADITION

The German sports tradition is distinct from that of other countries. The German Revolution of 1848 was fought among other issues about the right to freely form associations. This affected not just political parties and trade unions, but gymnastic and sport organizations. For example, the Turners, had more than 2 million members by World War I and were larger than the AAU or any other sports organization in the world. The right to form a nonprofit organization with

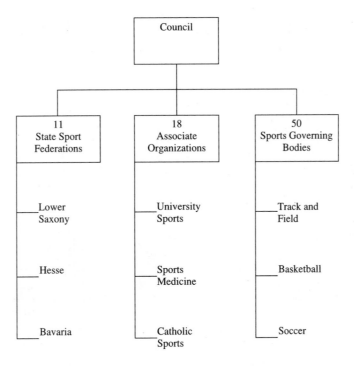

FIGURE 28.1   Structure of DSB

a minimum of seven members has been the core of the German sports movement ever since. This concept survived two world wars and the Nazi era and was the basis of the sports movement in West Germany. Prior to 1933 sports clubs were members of many rival national sports federations. The Nazi government then forced the coordination of all voluntary organizations (Gleichschaltung) and made sure that all sports clubs were organized under a single national sport governing body. At each administrative level of government representatives of the sport organization also formed an association with bargaining power toward the state authority.

After the World Wars practically all nonprofit sports clubs were members of at least two organizations—their local multisports federation and their local single-sport association—which in turn are members of their state multisports federations and state single-sport associations. There was also a national sports federation (DSB) in which the eleven state sport federations and fifty national sports governing bodies spoke with one voice, lobbied together, and formed a single pressure group (Fig. 28.1). What started as sports organizations' lopsided bargaining position under Nazi totalitarian conditions soon became a standing of tremendous power.

The smallest clubs had seven members and the largest, which was Bayern Munich, claimed more than 14,500 members. Their structures were extremely different: There were clubs with just one sport and other clubs with many, which in turn belonged to many sport governing bodies. Some clubs charged low membership fees, and some were considerably higher; some were managed by amateurs and others by professional athletes and coaches. Even the large,

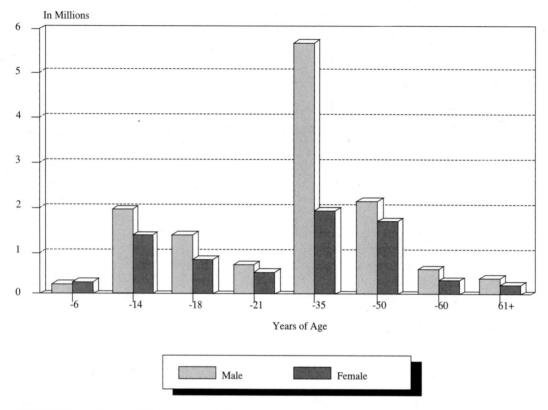

FIGURE 28.2 Membership Structure of DSB (1988)

internationally successful and profitable soccer clubs were run as a nonprofit organization with highly paid employees. In 1988 there were about 66,000 clubs with some 21,000,000 members (i.e., one-third of the West German population). The age and sex distributions are shown in Figure 28.2. Low fees allowed many persons to hold membership in more than one club. In reality, about 25 percent of the German population were members of one or more sports clubs (Fig. 28.3).

The distribution of the various sized clubs is shown in Figure 28.4 (DSB 1988a). Fifty percent were single-sport clubs, whereas the other 50 percent offered multiple sports. The trend was clearly moving to the multiple-sports club.

In 1982 the distribution was 57 percent single sport and 43 percent multiple sports.

The DSB was a federation of federations rather than of clubs, and did not have much information about the basic membership. The autonomy lay with the individual club, but through laws and subsidies, the state and the DSB exerted some influence on structure and content of the sports activities. From a financial standpoint, an investment into any nonprofit sports club could be deducted from the income tax as a donation—even if the purpose of the involvement was purely avocational. To demonstrate the point of the tax law: If you bought a yacht with your friends you were certainly engaging in your private lifestyle. If you formed

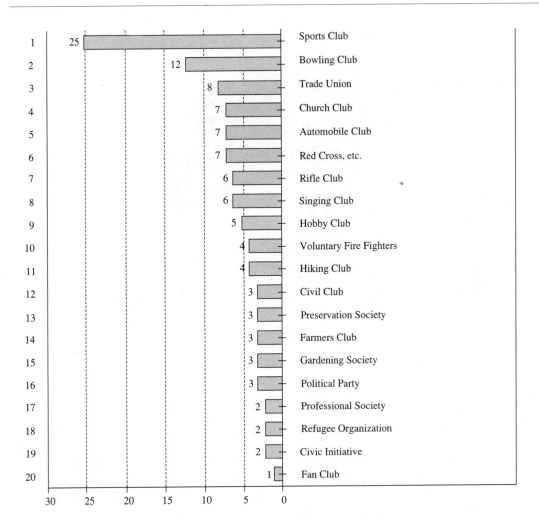

1	25	Sports Club
2	12	Bowling Club
3	8	Trade Union
4	7	Church Club
5	7	Automobile Club
6	7	Red Cross, etc.
7	6	Rifle Club
8	6	Singing Club
9	5	Hobby Club
10	4	Voluntary Fire Fighters
11	4	Hiking Club
12	3	Civil Club
13	3	Preservation Society
14	3	Farmers Club
15	3	Gardening Society
16	3	Political Party
17	2	Professional Society
18	2	Refugee Organization
19	2	Civic Initiative
20	1	Fan Club

FIGURE 28.3 Members of Organizations in Germany (a representative sample of 1000)

a club with at least six of your friends and donated the money to the club to buy the yacht, you could deduct the yacht from your income tax (Isensee 1989) and sail with it just as before.

The sports federations were subsidized by local, county, state, and federal governments from the nineteenth century onward. Exact amounts are difficult to estimate as there were many indirect subsidies such as the granting of school physical education facilities to the clubs free of charge. In general, however, around 2 billion West German Deutschmark (DM) ($1.1 billion) per year were provided in addition to the tax benefits. Only the support of international athletes was directly financed by the federal government in the name of national representation, a practice that had its beginnings in 1914 (Krüger 1981).

West Germany maintained a web of sporting facilities throughout the country. Under the

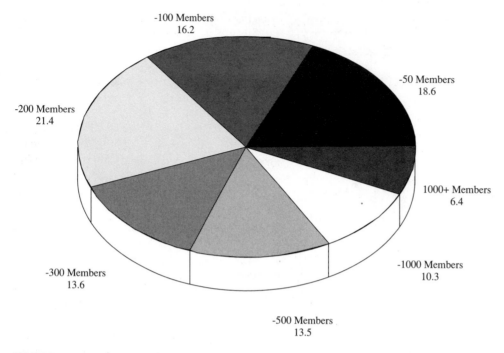

FIGURE 28.4   Size of Sports Clubs (in percent)

so-called Golden Plan, the local authorities, with the help of the state and the federal governments, provided financial help to sport facilities at a cost of more than $15 billion. The necessary land was also provided at no cost from 1960 onward. Since 1988 the annual expense has been almost 400 million U.S. dollars per year plus land for new constructions and more than 1 billion U.S. dollars in maintenance per year from the communities.

Keep in mind that West Germany, although it had a population of about 62 million in 1988, is not much larger in size than North and South Carolina combined, or about two-thirds the size of California. The first figure developed in 1965 identified almost 70,000 public sport facilities. That number more than doubled to over 150,000 over the next twenty years (Schmickler 1988). There were as many

sporting facilities in West Germany as there were pubs and restaurants (DGF 1989).

The Golden Plan required a community of less than 5,000 inhabitants to provide 6.5 square meters (65 square feet) of sport field per citizen, and in the larger communities 4 square meters (40 square feet). In addition, there was to be .3 square meters (3 square feet) of gymnastic halls or other covered sports grounds in the smaller and .2 square meters (2 square feet) in the larger communities. These values were adapted every ten years to the changing attitudes of the population. As the trend toward more indoor activities and a stagnation in outdoor games (with the exception of golf) developed, an additional 6000 gymnastic halls or 2.7 million square meters was needed to provide the 100 percent coverage called for in the current Golden Plan. Specific figures for indoor and outdoor swimming pools and for special sport facilities like ice stadia were established. Golf courses were not included because they use a disproportionate amount of space.

The purpose of the Golden Plan was to provide similar living conditions throughout the country. It should be pointed out that these were public facilities which, in most cases, were attached to a school, which used it in the morning and early afternoon. The clubs used the facilities free of charge in the afternoons and evenings. Where there were no schools, sporting facilities were constructed and provided free of charge under similar conditions. With the inexpensive availability of sports facilities, it was often not financially desirable for a club to own its sports ground because public ones were so much cheaper.

The authorities provided these services in most cases without any firm legal basis. The bargaining power of the sports organizations was strong enough that the contributions of the authorities came voluntarily. Only three of the eleven states had sport laws regulating what sports organizations could legally ask from the government—there was no explicit federal sports law (Krüger 1981). In the small communities, the pressure group power of the sports clubs was most easily achieved. The smaller the community, the larger the percentage of residents who were members of the local sports club because there was most likely only one club available. In such instances, it was not unusual for 50 percent of the community residents to be enrolled members. Thus, the club's board was often well represented on the town council. The larger the city, the less people tended to belong to a club simply to be part of it and the more they sought membership for the specificity and adequacy of the services it could provide. The common denominator of the sports clubs, in all their competition for members and particularly gifted athletes, was the free facilities and

financial subsidies for coaches, youth leaders, and members. A voluntary coach could earn 200 DM ($110) per month tax free in addition to their normal taxed income. If the club paid more, the voluntary coach would often donate the excess amount back to the club and thus receive an additional tax benefit.

In 1987 there were 167,000 registered voluntary and only about 6,000 full-time coaches within the club structure (DSB 1988a). With such a system, a club could be run for relatively little money. Consequently, the monthly membership fee in U.S. dollars for most sports clubs was around $5.00 for adults. But, in small communities the price was closer to $3.00 and in larger communities it could be as much as $12.00. Generally the fee for children, youth, university students, soldiers, senior citizens, and the unemployed was half the amount adults were charged. Those clubs that provided more extensive facilities, like golf or tennis, naturally charged higher costs. The national average fee for all members was about $2.75 per month (DSB 1988a), which accounted for less than 40 percent of the club's income. The distribution of the various incomes is shown in Figure 28.5 while the various expenditures appear in Figure 28.6.

The top level elite sports became better managed and somewhat professionalized from the 1970s onward (Heinemann 1987). This was, however, only for the benefit of relatively few athletes. No more than 3,500 were nationally selected to be subsidized. In all fifty sports combined, no more than 15,000 people were part of the elite system. But, due to media coverage and the constant search for young talent, this became the most visible segment of sport. The professionalization process took place at different speeds within the various sports. Soccer and tennis were the ones with the highest degree of professional management and the highest visibility. This did, however, change somewhat

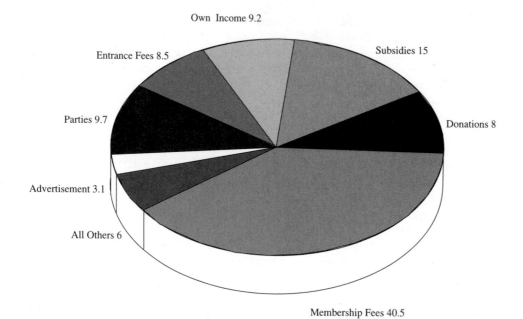

FIGURE 28.5 Income of Sports Clubs (in percent)

over time, depending on the international success of German athletes in the various sports (Fischer 1986).

The DSB sports advertising programs were very successful. Mass participation based on the long Turner and sport tradition produced a counter movement looking for social exclusiveness and high quality professional services.

COMMERCIAL SPORT FACILITIES

There have always been commercial sports organizations alongside the nonprofit enterprises. The first Turner teachers from the 1820s onward tried to have classes of students who paid them directly. There were the Zander studios of mechanotherapy at the turn of the century which provided what we would now call body building facilities. Dancing schools also thrived. East Asiatic sports such as judo and karate were generally taught in commercial studios—which had a club attached so that the competitions could be performed under the auspices of the sport governing body. There were private gymnastic and ballet studios from the 1920s onward which generally had a strong female clientele. These boomed when the aerobic wave passed through West Germany just as it did in the United States.

Commercial body building studios then became the new wave. In 1988 there were about 4,500 studios and that number was growing at an annual rate of about 15 percent. They employed 40,000 full-time and part-time persons, many of whom were certified by the sport government bodies. Also included in this employment group were physical education teachers unable to gain appointments in the school system. Body building combined with commercial tennis, badminton, and squash centers and the

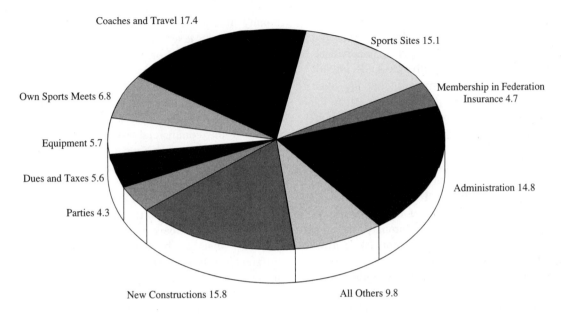

Coaches and Travel 17.4

Sports Sites 15.1

Membership in Federation
Insurance 4.7

Own Sports Meets 6.8

Equipment 5.7

Dues and Taxes 5.6

Parties 4.3

Administration 14.8

New Constructions 15.8

All Others 9.8

FIGURE 28.6   Expenditure of Sports Clubs (in percent)

judo and ballet schools, attracted about 6 million clients annually who paid approximately 1.2 billion West German DM (or $660 million) (Kappler 1988). The 21 million members of the DSB paid about the same amount annually.

Why do people join commercial clubs when similar programs are available through community clubs for a quarter or a fifth of the expense? The cleaner, more friendly atmosphere and the freedom to use the club when desired rather than only when certain activities are offered were among the reasons most frequently given (Krüger and Dreyer 1988). There also seemed to be a generational problem. The clients of the commercial institutions were generally between 20 and 40 years of age. They did not like to be involved in the activities of large clubs, but preferred to be active with their friends. They were not necessarily a part of the yuppy culture, but did strive to yuppy ideals. Both the older and younger members were

happy with sports clubs. Many members in this age group were also sport club members (Fig. 28.2). Ironically, the clubs tended to be competition-oriented for this age group while most of the participants were not (Schinkel 1987). It was quite common for this age group to take the services where they were provided, to join a club without participating in any of the social activities other than the sport itself, and to avoid any long-term personal commitments. This was quite dangerous for the long-term development of the nonprofit club structure, as it was based on the voluntary help of its members (Winkler 1988). It is obvious that the younger generation lacked a firm commitment to the club ideal and used the club simply to receive subsidized athletic services. All clubs of the sports federation combined are estimated to have received 185 million hours of unpaid voluntary work per year (i.e., 15.4 hours per month by almost 1 million male and almost 400,000 female volunteers).

Parents and other helpers also drove, free of charge, 240 million miles annually using their private vehicles to transport teams and individuals participating in other club activities (DSB 1988b).

It should be noted, however, that the older age group was not fully reached by either the commercial fitness clubs or the traditional nonprofit sports clubs. It is very difficult to find the right health arguments. "I am not that old yet" and "I don't want to hear about all those diseases" are constant arguments against the health appeal (Kuhr et al. 1988). The traditional sports clubs, with the help of health insurance, offered special groups for coronary patients. Health insurance paid the clubs for the certified personnel rather than offering the courses themselves or having the commercial studios offer them. The commercial studios were not available in small towns with fewer than 5,000 inhabitants and they were more expensive. The clubs accepted this new charge because it provided them with more income, more members, and additional time to spend on the club's many administrative duties.

Positive fitness and health attitudes are far easier to market than negative ones. On the whole it can be argued, however, that the leisure industry has just started to realize the tremendous sales potential of the senior citizen market (Pöggeler 1989). It was first the tourist trade which provided long-term winter vacations in the Mediterranean for this age-group market. Very slowly the sports industry is catching on. The mean age of the average German citizen is constantly growing. In the long run, both the commercial studios and the nonprofit sports clubs will have to adapt to meet this new situation (Fig. 28.7).

The commercial sport establishments faced two major disadvantages when they were forced to compete against the nonprofit sports clubs. They had to provide their own sports facilities instead of receiving them from the local community free of charge, and they had to pay taxes: property taxes on their facility, a 14 percent value-added tax on their fees, and as much as 53 percent income tax on their profit. It is surprising that, in spite of this unfair disadvantage, the commercial sport establishments grew at a even faster rate than the nonprofit ones. Some of the commercial establishments, however, attempted to combine the benefits of the nonprofit sports club with their own profit. Many clubs of the German Body Building Federation were offsprings of commercial studios and many nonprofit sports clubs started studios for their own members on the basis of an extra fee. So, what can be seen as two completely different sports organization set ups have complemented each other in this process.

THE SPORTS INDUSTRY

The sporting goods industry has been a very spoiled market. For more than a decade it saw such an increase in annual sales that many of the large companies became rather complacent in their marketing efforts. This attitude changed, however. The two largest German sporting good companies, Adidas and Puma are cases in point. When the last chairman from the controlling and founding Adolf Dassler family died, Puma started to concentrate on profit rather than expansion. The constant expansion had strained the resources of Puma to such an extent that it went public to maintain its high profile. Neither company really needed to advertise their name anymore. Their companies were household names; they could concentrate on their products. The actual size of the sporting goods market is difficult to delineate. The sporting good shops also sell leisure clothes, and sports clubs buy clothing and shoes for their members wholesale and often import directly. It has been estimated that sporting goods is a 10 billion West German

Age Grouping in Intervals of Five Years

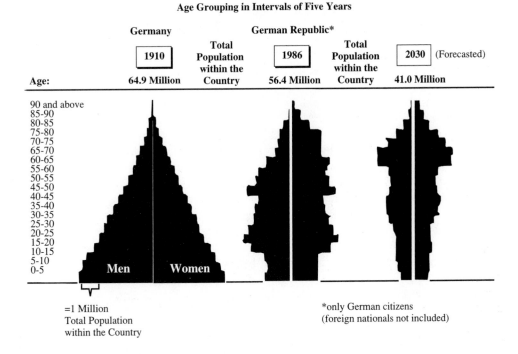

FIGURE 28.7 The Changing German Population
SOURCE: Copyright © 1993 by Arnd Krüger.

DM ($5.5 billion) industry (Krupp and Wagner 1988). Included in this figure is about $1 billion worth of equipment sales. Another estimate of more than $6 billion included bicycling and leisure boating (DGF 1989). This figure was derived from the sales of 5,400 sporting goods shops, 2,800 play shops, 67,500 clothing stores, and 13,500 shoe shops (DGF 1988).

Most of these products came from within the European Community. All American sport shoe companies are represented on the German market, but as far as clothing and equipment are concerned there is a clear dominance by German-based companies. Figure 28.8 shows the potential of the German sporting goods market.

Because goods are sold in supermarkets, department stores, and, of course, special sporting goods shops it is difficult to estimate the exact

number of people employed by this industry. However, Krupp and Wagner (1988) estimate about 250,000 are employed in the sales sector alone.

Due to the nonprofit nature of most sports clubs it has taken a relatively long period to develop effective marketing tools for amateur sports (Gieseler 1988). It is estimated that the annual amount expended on sports marketing surpassed the 1 billion West German DM mark for the first time in 1989. In 1984 this figure was just one-tenth of what it was only a few years later (Kappler 1988). In 1989, sports marketing expenditures represent about 5.5 percent of the total advertising budgets spent in West Germany overall. Per capita, West German companies spend on advertising only 43.2 percent of the amount of expended in West Germany by

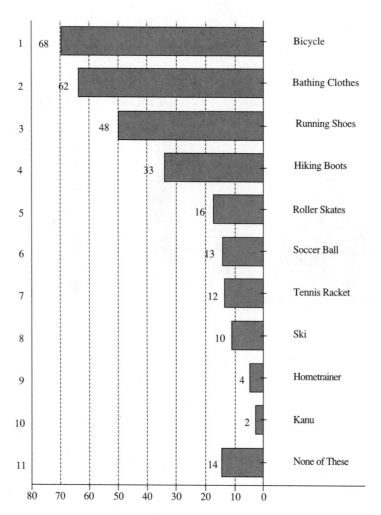

FIGURE 28.8 Germans Own the Following Sporting Goods
(a representative sample of 1000)
SOURCE: Copyright © 1993 by Arnd Krüger.

American companies. And most of that money is directed toward motor sports (Fig. 28.9).

A comparative study by ISL-Marketing of the public acceptance of sports marketing in West Germany, the United States, Singapore, and Portugal showed that the highest level was recorded in Singapore (91 percent), followed by the U.S. (81 percent), and West Germany and Portugal (69 percent each). Only 22 percent of the West German population (as compared to 28 percent in Singapore, 29 percent in the United States, and 47 percent in Portugal) admitted that sport advertising influenced their purchasing decisions (ISL 1988).

Contrasted to the United States, West Germany took much longer to accept commercial

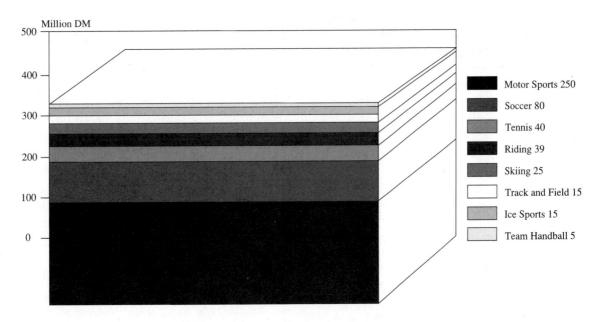

FIGURE 28.9 Sponsorship Income (1987) for Eight Major Sports

television (Dahms 1988). With the clear dominance of paid public television, the fees for television coverage are relatively low. In spite of the relatively new opportunities to advertise extensively in some new television and radio stations, the advertising budgets of the print media did not suffer (Steinbach 1988). As the amount of money needed to run a sport increased, the clubs began to search for forms of revenue other than the traditional subsidies by the government.

Dreyer (1986) has analyzed the image of the various sports for advertising purposes. He shows a very differentiated picture which indicates that even a sport considered to be a minor one has a particular appeal—if it is successful enough. Herrmanns (1988) shows that the whole trend will increase the role of sport-sponsoring for the sport itself as well as for the various businesses.

One of the most frequently employed advertising vehicles has been the athlete's jersey.

However, the rules for this type of advertising vary considerably from sport to sport (Furhmann 1989). Some of the clubs sold their names to corporate sponsors. While the former form of sponsorship is generally accepted, with certain limitations on size and placement, some federations stopped corporate sponsorship because it was felt to project an unfavorable image of sport (Ryssel 1989). Thus, for a long time public relations activities dominated over clear-cut sponsoring in sports (Krüger 1988). Title sponsoring of events developed slowly, with tennis and golf in the forefront. National sports federations were reluctant to have advertisement on the jerseys of national teams. But the winter sports federations paved the way and allowed advertising on the athlete's equipment in much the same manner as found in motor sports. Sometimes a conflict of interest arises when an athlete is under contract with one company and then competes for the national team which is under contract to another. This was a problem for the national soccer team which, for a long time, used Adidas equipment. Players with their own private Puma contracts or who had contracts with other manufacturers were required to wear Adidas while playing or not play on the national team at all (Netzle 1988).

CONCLUSIONS

To an investor, the West German sports market was of considerable interest. It was not rewarding to invest in the service industry due to the largely subsidized, nonprofit nature of the sport and its wide distribution. On the other hand, this wide basis of sport activism of all classes and ages created a solid and growing market for equipment and sporting goods. Directly related forms of sports advertising were made possible and more widely accepted. The educational system rapidly accepted the challenge of the new nature of sport, and colleges and universities began to prepare graduates with a sports management and business administration background. Increasing numbers of students began to graduate with degrees in sports administration and sports economics.

It was speculated that the traditional nature of sport on the basis of nonprofit organizations would have to change. Krupp and Wagner (1988) contended that this would occur because the state would need revenue from the service sector of employment. Pressure was exerted by unemployed physical education teachers to be hired by the clubs. The clubs, on the other hand, needed more full-time professional personnel to cope with increasing memberships and the decreasing willingness of members to devote time to the club on a constant, volunteer basis. When a club sport can no longer be offered at inexpensive rates, attitudes toward the sport tend to change. While sport is among the cheapest forms of leisure (although considerable sums are expended on sport during winter and/or summer vacations) the trend shows that the readiness to spend money on sport is constantly rising. These current changes make the West German sports market not only an interesting field of research for the social scientist but also a profitable area for the investor.

REFERENCES

Bundesinstitut für Sportwissenschaft, ed. 1989. Neue Medien und Sport. Ergebnisse einer Studie. *Sportsponsor* 2: 1, 27–29.

Bundes minister des Innern, ed. 1987. 6. *Sportbericht der Bundesregierung*. Bonn: BMI.

Dahms, H. 1988. Sport im Fernsehen. Eine Analyse von Angebot und Nutzung. *Sportsponsor* 1: 2, 30–34.

Deutsche Gesellschaft für Freizeit, ed. 1988. *Deutscher Freizeit Kongress 1987*. Erkrath: DGF.

Deutsche Gesellschaft für Freizeit, ed. 1989. *Freizeit-Daten*. Erkrath: DGF.

Deutscher Sportbund, ed. 1988a. *Aus der Finanz- und Struktur-analyse 1986*. Paper presented at the Sport und Wirtschaft. 27. Magglinger Symposium.

Deutscher Sportbund, ed. 1988b. *Menschen im Sport 2000*. Schorndorf: Hofmann.

Dreyer, A. 1986. *Werbung im und mit Sport*. Göttingern: Cognos.

Fischer, H. 1986. *Sport und Geschäft*. Berlin: Bartels & Wernitz.

Furhmann, H. 1989. Trikotwerbung und Trikotnummern. Werbevorschriften der nationalen Sportverbände. *Sportsponsor* 2: 1, 57.

Gieseler, H. H. 1988. Die Wirtschaft liebt den Glanz des Sports. *Sportsponsor* 1:2, 43–44.

Heinemann, K., ed. 1987. *Betriebswirtschaftliche Grundlagen des Sportvereins.* Schorndorf: Hofmann.

Herrmanns, A. 1988. *Formen der Vermarktung.* Paper presented at the Sport und Wirtschaft. 27. Magglinger Symposium.

Isensee, J. 1989. Skatverein mit Adelsprädikat. Gemeinnützigkeit zwischen Selbstlosingkeit und Selbstverwirklichung. *Frankfurter Allgemeine Zeitung* 251:15.

ISL, ed. 1988. Sport-Sponsoring im Länder-Vergleich. *Sportsponsor* 1:1, 26.

Kappler, E. 1988. *Ressourcenstruktur der Sportorganisationen.* Paper presented at the Sport und Wirtschaft. 27. Magglinger Symposium.

Krüger, A. 1989. Das Jahrhundert des Sports naht. In *Vision 2000. Hoffnungen—Ängste—Chance,* edited by H. A. Piper, 107–122. München: Orta.

Krüger, A. 1988. PR Aktivitäten im Sportberich. *Sportsponsor* 1:1, 10–14.

Krüger, A. 1982. Sport—State—and the Olympic Games. In *5th Canadian symposium on the history of sport and physical education,* edited by B. Kidd, 369–379. Toronto: University of Toronto.

Krüger, A. 1981. *Sport und Gesellschaft.* Berlin: Tischler.

Krüger, A. 1975. *Sport und Politik. Vom Turnvater Jahn zum Staatsamateur.* Hannover: Fackelträger.

Krüger, A. & A. Dreyer. 1988. *Die kommerziellen Sportanbieter in Göttinger.*

Eine Betreiber- und Verbraucheranalyse. Unpublished manuscript, Göttingen.

Krupp, H. J., & G. Wagner. 1988. *Die Wirtschafliche Bedeutung des Sports.* Paper presented at the Sport und Wirtschaft. 27. Magglinger Symposium.

Kuhr, J., R. Lanker, H. Oberste-Lehn, et al. 1988. *Alter und Freizeit. Zur Grundlegung einer Freizeitgerontologie.* Erkrath: DGF.

Netzle, S. 1988. *Sponsoring von Sportverbänden.* Zürich: Schulthess.

N. N. 1989. Plädoyer für eine größere Trikotwerbung beim Fußball. *Sportsponsor* 2:1, 56–57.

N. N. 1988. Einschaltquoten und Reichweiten von Sportsendungen. *Sportsponsor* 2:1, 68.

Pöggeler, F., ed. 1989. *Freizeit-Alter-Lebenszeit.* Erkrath: DGF.

Ryssel, C. 1989. Das Image des Sportlers als Kriterium für den Sponsor. *Sportsponsor* 2: 1, 32–36.

Schinkel, J., ed. 1987. *Situationsanalyse im Hochschulsport.* Ahrensburg: Czwalina.

Schmickler, E. D. 1988. Die Bundesrepublik is unangefochten Weltmeister im Sportstättenbau. *Frankfurter Allgemeine Zeitung* 235: 26.

Steinbach, J. 1988. Der Werbemarkt 1987. Die Entwicklung der Werbemedien. *Sportsponsor* 1:2, 61–66.

Wehr, W., ed. 1987. *Freizeit-Sport-Bewegung. Stand und Tendenzen in der Bundesrepublik Deutschland.* Erkrath: Medienpoon.

Winkler, J. 1988. Das Ehrenamt. Zur soziologie ehrenamtlicher. *Tätigkeit dargestellt am Beispiel der deutschen Sportverbände.* Schorndorf: Hofmann.

29

Bridging the Gap Between Research and Practice

William J. Rudman and Alar Lipping

This essay examines the practical application of scientific research and theory in the field of corporate fitness. The purpose is to show how research and theory may be used to (a) increase involvement in corporate fitness programs; (b) better understand the role of health and fitness at the workplace; and (c) help define the social and psychological effects of implementing a health and fitness program on work culture. Unlike most research reports that concentrate on the results of the data analysis, the focus of this essay is on the research process. As such, the discussion details where errors of analysis and interpretation were made and where consultation with fitness practitioners helped to correct these mistakes and provide a better understanding of the data.

William J. Rudman is with the University of Pittsburgh Health Care Management and Supervision Department, Pittsburgh, Pennsylvania. Alar Lipping is with the Health and Physical Education Department, Northern Kentucky University, Highland Heights, Kentucky.

THEORETICAL PERSPECTIVE

The interpretation of findings is based on an organizational culture theoretical perspective (Schein 1984; VanMaanen and Barley 1984; Van Maanen and Schein 1981; Schein 1986). According to this perspective, whether or not a corporate fitness program is started and maintained is directly dependent on the perceived success of the program (e.g., cost effectiveness, reduction in absenteeism, improved work conditions). If a corporate fitness center is to be successful it is necessary for the staff to understand (a) the various dimensions that stratify an organization, and (b) how health and fitness programming is perceived in the work culture. According to the literature in this area, work organizations are stratified along three basic dimensions or boundaries: (1) hierarchical, (2) functional, and (3) inclusionary. These three boundary demarcations determine and define the role of exercise and fitness in the workplace. For example, hierarchical boundaries might focus on how health and fitness programs are supported by upper management. Does support come in the form of written messages and memos? through active participation in the program? or by changing the organizational structure and goals to accommodate the fitness program (e.g., flextime)?

Understanding the functional boundaries might help the practitioner to better promote and market the program in keeping with the expected goals and required image of the corporation. Whether the director takes an aggressive or passive approach in promoting the program depends on the ideology of the corporation. For example, certain corporations are aggressive in trying to capture the consumer market with a particular product. Other corporations have a set portion of the market share and are content to take a passive approach in advertising and promotion. If the director of a fitness program deviates from the corporate norm, the program is likely to fail. Finally, understanding the inclusionary boundaries helps the fitness practitioner develop both informal and formal networks of support for the program. This understanding helps in answering a number of questions: Are the fitness programs incorporated into the lifestyles of the employees? Are the fitness programs seen by employees as another means of management control over workers?

In the particular corporation under study, the fitness program can be easily identified in terms of each of the three boundaries. First, support primarily comes in the form of memos and written materials. While a majority of the upper management personnel are involved, their involvement is not high profile (i.e., participation is at low usage time periods). Most of the upper management personnel work out at times of the day when there is little if any interaction with other employees. Moreover, upper-level management did not participate in company sponsored social activities (e.g., softball games, races). In order to promote the program, the di-

rector had to take a passive approach in terms of marketing strategies. The corporation has maintained a solid share of the market with little fluctuation over the past decade. Consequently, marketing of the corporate product is conservative and passive. If the fitness director had used an aggressive approach, given the conservative nature of the company, the program most likely would have failed. Finally, most workers viewed the program as a positive gesture on behalf of management. Very few, only 10 percent, thought the program was designed to infringe on the rights of employees.

DATA

Data for this study were collected from a major oil-producing company in southwest Texas. Only full-time employees from the corporate world headquarters participated in the study. Two data sets are used in the analysis. The first data set consists of 968 survey questionnaires (48 percent return rate). The second data set consists of 110 personal interviews. As might be expected, given that the analysis was conducted at a world headquarters, respondents were either lower white collar (clerical), secretarial, middle- and upper-level management, or professionals (e.g., lawyers, geographers, etc).

The results are presented in three sections. The first section focuses on the perceived outcomes and barriers to involvement in physical activity. This section deals with ways a corporation might change promotional strategies to improve involvement in the program. The second section deals with the impact on the work culture of implementing a fitness program. Here, a variety of ways are offered in which the practitioner may use the data to demonstrate the impact of the program on the work environment. The third section provides the fitness director a new method of understanding attendance patterns.

It is hoped that, by differentiating between active and nonactive members, better promotional strategies may be developed.

Perceived Outcomes and Barriers to Involvement in Physical Activity

Regardless of the quality of the facility or equipment, if participation rates are low the program is not a success. As prior research has shown, very few workers engage in exercise programs at levels sufficient to maintain a healthy lifestyle (identified in the American College of Sports Medicine guidelines as three times per week, for 20 minutes). Indeed, only 10 to 15 percent of Americans exercise at these intensity levels. In this study, 17 percent of those interviewed met ACSM standards for exercise.

Regression analysis is used to examine which employees are currently using either the corporate or a private fitness club and to determine what factors either restrict or facilitate involvement in these programs. Findings from the regression analysis show that those most likely to use the corporate facility are (a) between the ages of 19 and 34; (b) in lower-management positions (in the fast track lines); and (c) participate in order to reduce workplace stress. The primary reasons for involvement in the corporate program are related to work pressure (e.g., relieve work anxiety, stress, or tension), for general health (e.g., improve health, stay in shape, reduce weight). The most important factors restricting involvement are related to time (e.g., too busy, not enough time). The least important factors restricting involvement are related to access (e.g., too inconvenient, hours open).

While these findings provide a basis from which to start, they do not provide the practitioner with information that can be applied or with the complete picture of corporate fitness behavior. As prior research suggests, in order to understand involvement in physical activity it is important to understand how age interacts with patterns of participation (McPherson 1984; Rudman 1986). There is a need to know how both involvement and the factors that influence involvement change throughout the life cycle. Age-specific factor analysis and regression analysis was conducted on three specific age groups: 19 to 34, 35 to 49, and 50 and above. Age categories were based on prior research which found that passages through family and work rituals were the primary determinants of involvement in sport activities (Rudman 1984, 1986).

Age-specific regression analyses were conducted on both involvement and adherence in the corporate program and involvement in private clubs. As expected from prior research, reasons for involvement in corporate versus private club membership changed across the life cycle based on ideology and philosophy. It is important for the practitioner to understand why an individual would pay $1,500 per year to join a private club when membership in a corporate program of equal quality is free. As will be discussed later, this finding points to the way in which the philosophical and ideological base of involvement, in conjunction with work and family responsibilities, determine the type and place for physical activity.

For those 34 and younger, the psychological benefits (e.g., release of tension and stress) were the most consistent factors influencing involvement and adherence in the corporate program. Members of the corporate program were not likely to use excuses (e.g., inconvenient, lack of facility) as reasons for noninvolvement. In contrast, members of private clubs were not likely to perceive the psychological benefits as a reason to join. Similarly, outside members were also less likely to use motivation (e.g., too tired, bored) or time as a barrier to involvement. This would seem to indicate that those who are in outside clubs are more dedicated to the idea of exercise. They were more willing to travel and pay, and were less likely to use motivational excuses as barriers to involvement.

In the 35 to 49 age group, ideological reasons for involvement in fitness programs began to impact the decision of where to participate in fitness activities. While psychological factors influence both members and nonmembers, the desire to compete in sport activities became increasingly important. The desire to become involved in competitive activities is the most important predictor of involvement in private clubs. This competitive philosophy contrasts sharply with the noncompetitive philosophy of the corporate program.

In the 50 and over age group, the competitive dimension coupled with the desire to "play" with friends and family was the most important reason for joining an outside program. This is in contrast to the corporate policy of excluding family. Perhaps more importantly for the fitness practitioner, those joining outside programs were senior-level upper management. This is important when we consider the hierarchical boundaries which in essence provide support for the program.

These findings have two important (and immediate) implications for the practitioner: the need to consider upper-level management's desire for social competition; and the need to stratify promotional efforts in order to meet the needs of all age groups. The current strategy employed by the fitness staff was focused exclusively on younger employees without taking the needs of older workers into consideration.

At first glance it would seem that a general restructuring of the program needs to occur in order to increase involvement, in general, and among upper-level management, specifically. After further consultation with the director and staff it was found that over 70 percent of the top-level management is currently involved in the corporate program. The analysis went astray because of the complicating occurrence that 90 percent of the senior upper management belonged to both the corporate and a private club. Furthermore, all of those involved in the corporate fitness program were also members in outside clubs. Membership in a private club is seen as a sign of power and status within the corporation. Moreover, involvement in the private club is purely for pleasure. What the directors need to do is to encourage upper management to participate in the social functions sponsored by the fitness center. Increasing visibility and interaction with other employees would provide the impression of stronger management support for the program.

The second consideration, targeting promotional efforts by age, does have some important programmatic and policy implications. The data clearly identify ideological differences that impact participation. The program is attracting younger participants simply because the marketing and promotional strategies are designed for younger adults. In order to attract middle- and older-aged adults, social and family activities must be included. Moreover, the family must be allowed to participate in the fitness center programs. This will be perceived as a symbolic gesture of care and concern about the whole individual (e.g., the family) on behalf of management. This finding is consistent with prior research (Rudman 1984, 1986) and with the personal interviews that suggest a "pure fitness emphasis" is "intimidating" to older adults. This position suggests that those intimately involved in exercise or fitness programming often fail to recognize the complete picture of the fitness movement.

Due to a lack of training or a deeply ingrained belief system, practitioners seem to concentrate on the physical aspects of fitness, while ignoring the social and psychological dimensions. "Getting into shape" and "being physically healthy'' are seen as the only reasons for involvement. As a result, fitness programs themselves become a source of tension and stress. Including the family or scheduling intramural competition in social situations would be a way to reduce this stress and anxiety. Although this would seem like a logical solution, it is interesting to note the resistance encountered from the practitioners. This finding lends even more importance to the need for practitioners to carefully monitor their programs.

Fitness and Work Culture

This section examines how employees perceive the effect of the health and fitness program on work environment, and focuses on beliefs concerning the benefit of involvement in physical activity. Both members and nonmembers believe the corporate fitness program has a positive effect on the work environment. Of those interviewed, 76 percent believe the program had a positive effect, 24 percent believe the program had no effect, and 0 percent believe the program had a negative effect. Statements by both members and nonmembers strongly support the value of the health and fitness program. For example, a member commented that ''the fitness center has had a positive effect on company employees . . . the attitude is better around here.'' A nonmember noted, ''not for me personally [physically] . . . for those who are involved it seems to make a difference [physically] . . . [however] it makes us all think more highly of the company.''

In terms of directly increasing personal productivity, 73 percent believed their involvement in the program would help them to be more productive at work. Involvement in exercise and fitness programs were seen as helping employees relate better to each other and to become more productive. Over 80 percent believed their involvement would reduce work related stress and anxiety.

At this point in the research process there was excitement about demonstrating the universal impact of having a fitness center at the work site. The next step was to regress our proxy measures of satisfaction and productivity on measures of involvement and adherence controlling for certain demographic and economic factors. Specifically, job satisfaction, work satisfaction, importance of having a job, importance of producing quality work, job autonomy, and company loyalty are used to measure employee attitudes and work culture. All measures were scales with alpha loadings above 0.69.

Results from the regression analysis were both surprising and disappointing. Membership in the fitness program did not have an effect on any of our measures concerning work or company culture. This was surprising given the earlier findings, which were overwhelmingly positive. At this point, it was necessary to retrace the thought processes and to discuss the findings with the fitness staff. It was strongly believed, given the positive oral responses received, that eventually the underlying forces that statistically attenuated the initial response effects in the regression analysis would be uncovered.

To better understand the results and to provide more applicable information, a three-step process was employed: (1) employee attitudes toward the company and their jobs in general were examined; (2) these findings were then compared with similar research in the area of organizational culture; and (3) theory and research in the sport and organizational literature was used to help interpret and redesign the next step in the analysis.

In general, employees had very favorable opinions and attitudes toward the company and their work, and had a strong commitment to producing quality work. For example, 75 percent noted that they were satisfied with their current job, 68 percent found "real" enjoyment in their work; 80 percent felt loyalty toward the company; and over 98 percent felt committed to producing quality work.

Compared with the results of similar studies in the organizational literature, respondents in this study, on the average, had higher levels of job and company satisfaction and higher levels of commitment to producing quality work. For example, in the more than twenty studies examined (see Cook, Flepworth, Wall, and Warr 1981; Price and Mueller 1986) the average range of scores for work satisfaction ranged from X of 3.30 to 3.55, as compared to our study with an X of 3.81. Similarly, on measures of work commitment the average scores ranged from an X of 3.6 to 4.2, as compared to our study with an X of 4.6.

These findings, in conjunction with earlier findings, provide reasonable support for a belief in the overall impact of the fitness programs on work culture. To help understand the lack of effect in the regression equations, sport and organizational culture theories are used. According to these two bodies of literature, there should be a contrasting effect of these two forces on attitudes that would indeed attenuate the effects in the regression analysis. Literature in the area of sport studies suggests as age increases involvement in physical activity decreases. Literature from the organizational culture literature suggests as age increases work and company satisfaction increase. Both of these findings were substantiated in the analysis. The age-specific regression revealed significant effects of involvement and adherence on the measures of work/job satisfaction and productivity.

These findings are important for the practitioner in documenting the effectiveness of the program and in providing a better understanding of how fitness is viewed within the various economic status strata at the workplace. These findings are encouraging in that they suggest

that future support of the fitness center is likely. Those who are now involved in the fitness program are in the "fast track" occupational strata within the company. As they are promoted to positions of power, support of the facility and programs should be forthcoming.

INTERPRETING THE NUMBERS

The final section focuses on a variety of ways the fitness practitioner may interpret attendance patterns. The intent will be to identify core and peripheral users. This will help by allowing the practitioner to directly target efforts to those individuals who are interested but not yet committed.

The two most common measures of attendance look at the percent of employees who are members and at the times and days the facility is used. In this program, over a four-year period of time, between 63 and 66 percent of the employees were members. Monday and Wednesday mornings (6–7:30 A.M.) and immediately after work (4–6 P.M.) were the highest-use time periods.

While these data provide valuable information for the practitioner, they do not adequately explain participation. For example, finding that 63 percent of the employees are members may be misleading when trying to establish a core participant base or design programs that will be effective in increasing program adherence. One method not commonly used in defining core participants and facility usage has been termed the Bradford-Zipf distribution. The Bradford-Zipf measurement allows both the researcher and the practitioner to identify core and peripheral members as well as to establish usage indicators for the facility.

Data from a Bradford-Zipf table show that 4,947 visits were made to the facility during a one-month period. Of the members, 1.7 percent account for 10 percent of the facility use. The core group is represented by 5.3 percent of the members and accounts for 27 percent of the facility use. Finally, only 53 percent of the members used the facility during the course of the month under observation.

This information is most useful in identifying the moderate user (6–12 times per month). Regardless of how the program is marketed, it is highly unlikely that the 5 percent core or the 47 percent nonactive member will be affected. The initial push, therefore, should be directed toward the 48 percent moderate-to-low users. These individuals have already shown interest, but may need an extra incentive to develop a commitment. Here special efforts need to be made, most likely in personalizing service for members of this group in order to increase the likelihood of their involvement.

DISCUSSION

The most important result from this study concerns the need for the researcher and practitioner to work together in developing an integrative approach to understanding fitness in the workplace. Problems encountered in the interpretation of contrasting results were greatly aided by the help of the fitness staff. Without the firsthand knowledge and experience of the fitness practitioner, several mistakes in the interpretation of the data and suggestions for programmatic changes might have been made. The data also strongly suggest the need for practitioners to seek out and utilize research to improve their individual fitness programs. Information generated in this study should provide a solid base for future efforts to improve both new and existing programs and to help the practitioner better understand the role of fitness in the workplace.

REFERENCES

Bailyn, L. 1982. Resolving contradictions in technical careers. *Technology Review* (November/December): 40–47.

Cook, J. D., S. J. Flepworth, T. D. Wall, and P. B. Warr. 1981. *The experience of work.* London: Academic Press.

McPherson, B. D. 1984. Sport participation across the lifecycle: A review of literature and suggestions for future research. *Sociology of Sport Journal* 1(3): 213–230.

Price, J., and C. Mueller. 1986. *Handbook of organizational measurement.* Mansfield, Mass.: Pitman Publishing.

Rudman, W. J. 1984. Lifecourse socio-economic transitions and sport involvement: A theory of restricted opportunity. In *Sport and Aging,* edited by B. McPherson, 25–36. Champaign, Ill.: Human Kinetics Press.

Rudman, W. J. 1986. Sport as a part of successful aging. *American Behavioral Scientist* 29(4): 453–470.

Schein, E. H. 1984. Coming to a new awareness of organizational culture. *Sloan Management Review,* vol. 25(2) (Winter): 261–295.

Schein, E. H. 1986. *Organizational culture and human performance.* San Francisco: Jersey-Bass.

VanMaanen, J., and S. R. Barley. 1984. Occupational communities: Culture and control in organizations. *Research in Organizational Behavior,* November, 287–365.

VanMaanen, J., and E. H. Schein. 1981. Toward a theory of organizational socialization. *Research in Organizational Behavior,* vol. 1, 209–264.

INDEX

a

Abbot, W., 255, 259
academic integrity, 104
accounting, 201
accounts receivable, 188
Acosta, V., 223–25, 227–28, 230
activity
  co-ed, 49
  community, 43
  "on-stream" phase, 58, 60
  operational phase, 58, 60
  phases, 58
  planning phase, 58
Adams State College, 183
Adidas, 270, 274
Adkinson, J. W., 132–33, 134, 140
advertisers, 253
advertising, 83, 88–89, 271, 273
  campaigns, 196
  what, 11
  when, 11
  where, 11
  who, 11
aerobics, 268
  dance, 49, 52
  gymnastics, 89
Albert, M., 255
alcohol addiction, 231
Ali, M., 257
Allen, L. R., 207, 210
Allen, M., 253, 257
Allen, R., 137
Almond, E., 212–13, 215–17, 219, 222
Amateur Athletic Union (AAU), 262

American Alliance for Health,
  Physical Education, Recreation
  and Dance (AAHPERD), 124,
  126
American Broadcasting Company
  (ABC), 12, 18
American College of Sports Medicine,
  125, 278
American Council of Exercise, 125
American Marketing Association, 9
American Motel and Hotel
  Association, 154
American Volleyball Coaches
  Association, 224
Amezaga, M., 53
Amherst College, 253
ancillary products, 6
Anderson, B. D., 133–34, 142
Anderson, D., 258, 261
Andrews, P., 254, 259
Apple Share Network, 50
arbitration, 159–60, 162, 167–68,
  172–73
Archer, B., 147, 156
Archer, G. L., 252, 259
Ariel, G., 215
Arledge, R., 254–55
Arlin, H., 251
Arnold, J. A., 135, 140
artificial turf, 132, 134–36, 138–40
assessment, 47
Association for Intercollegiate
  Athletics for Women (AIAW),
  223
Astro Turf, 134–36, 139
Astro Turf Industries, 135

athletic
  business manager, 175
  department, 177–78
  director, 40, 41–44, 46, 175, 208,
    224, 227, 233
  operations, 176
  performance, 234
  profile, 242–44
  programs, 204
  quality, 204–5
Atkinson, G., 134
Atlanta Falcons, 145
atmospherics, 9
attitudinal set, 236
attrition rates, 188, 197
Augusta National Masters, 9
Austin, A., 40, 46

b

badminton, 268
Bailyn, L., 282
ballet, 268, 269
Barber, R., 257–59
Barley, S. R., 276, 282
Barnett, E., 132, 134–35, 140
Barrett, N., 228, 230
Barry, D., 128
baseball, 159–60, 167, 252
basketball, 52, 69, 88, 204–6, 208–9,
  224, 226–27, 228, 238, 242, 245
Basketball Hall of Fame, 257
Battersby, G., 115, 120
Bayern Munchen (Munich) Soccer
  Club, 92, 263

Bearden, W. O., 11, 13
Becker, B. J., 109, 210
Bellenger, D. N., 24, 31
Bellizzi, J. A., 24, 31
Beloit College, 183
Bennis, W., 42, 46
Benson, G. G., 199, 203
Bent, D. H., 32
Berg, R., 130, 207, 210
Berkow, I., 258–59
Berkowitz, E., 9, 11–12
Berman, L., 257
Bernstein, S., 83–84, 86
Best, A., 129
Bialeschki, M. D., 53
Bias, L., 256
bicycling, 68
Big Ten Conference, 182
billboards, 43
Bird, L., 256
Blackwell, R. D., 23, 31
Blake, P., 129
Boat Owners Association of the
    United States, 78
Body, D., 53
body building, 268
Boggs, W., 171
Bonacci, B., 130
Bonaventure, P., 258–59
booster benefits, 146
Borussia Dortmund Soccer Club, 92
Boston University, 253
boundaries
    functional, 276–77
    hierarchical, 276, 279
    inclusionary, 276–77
bowling, 69
Brade, R., 146, 156
Bramwell, J., 134
Branvold, S. E., 204
Braum, K., 127
Breckner, S., 111
Brett, G., 136
Brewtt, G., 171
Brickhouse, J., 255, 257
broadcaster, 251
Brock, F., 86
Brokaw, T., 10
Broun, H. H., 258–59
Broyles, J. F., 207, 210
Bruggink, T., 160, 173

Bruns, H., 139–40
Buck, J., 257
budget deficit, 101, 206
budget survey, 225
Buffalo Bills, 136
Burson-Marsteller, 85
business administration, 274
business policy, 201
Butler, J. E., 133–34, 140
buyer behavior, 23, 25, 36
buying decisions, 16–17
Byrd, G., 139

Cable, T. T., 32
Canadian Organizing Committee, 18,
    19, 55, 57–58
Canel, B., 257
Cannon, J. J., 258–59
canoeing, 49
Canseco, J., 171
Caray, H., 257
Carhahan, A., 129
Carlson, J., 249
Carpenter, L. J., 131, 223–24, 225,
    227–28, 230
Carpentier, G., 252
Cart, J., 212–13, 215–17, 219, 222
Carter, B., 254
Cassing, J., 160, 173
Ceasar, P., 86
Chang, S., 145, 154, 156
Charlotte Hornets, 10
Cherry, D., 257
Chestnut, J. T., 53
Christman, P., 255
Chu, D., 97, 109, 210
CIBA Pharmaceutical Company, 213
Circus Maximus, 179
Clancy, W. G., 141
Clanton, T. O., 133–34, 140
Clarke, K. S., 133, 140
Clawson, M., 80
coaching clinics, 44
Cobb, P., 93
Coe, S., 222
Coe College, 180, 183
Coins, 18
Cole, S., 53

Coleman, K., 255, 257–59
collective bargaining, 159
Collins, D., 257
Colorado School of Mines, 183
Columbia University, 252
commercialism, 97–98
commercial sport, 270
Commission on Higher Education,
    42, 46
communications, 9, 41–42, 117
    decoding, 9–10
    encoding, 9–10
    face-to-face, 9
    feedback, 9–10
    message, 10
    persuasive, 11–12
    receivers, 9–10
    response, 9
    senders, 9
    source, 10
competition, 236
competitive tournaments, 48, 52
computer, 187, 197, 252
    applications, 187
    technology, 187–89, 197
Concerned Americans for Protection
    of Sport, 122
Condie, F. A., 110
Conn, J. H., 132
Connolly, H., 216–17, 219
constituency development, 41
consumer, 23
    analysis, 3
    behavior, 22, 25
    choice, 23
    shopping styles, 22
consuming public, 20
Cook, D., 3, 13
Cook, J. D., 281–82
Copeland, J. L., 208, 210
Cordell, H. K., 80
core products, 6
Cornell College, 184
corporate
    fitness, 276
    promotion campaign, 118
    sponsors, 93–100, 102, 107, 109
    sponsorship, 2, 82–85
    support, 19
Cosell, H., 253, 255, 257–59

cost
  containment, 175
  fixed, 187
  flexibility, 84
  variable, 187
Costas, B., 257
Cottingham, C., 102, 109
country club, 200
Courson, S., 218
Cousins, B., 137
Cramer, J., 97, 109
cross country skiing, 71
Csonka, L., 136
Culpepper, M. I., 133, 141
customers, 21
cycling, 89–90

d

Dahms, H., 273–74
dance studio, 48
dancing, 89, 268
Darden, W. R., 24, 31–32
Dassler, A., 270
database, 188
Dattavio, F. D., 80
Davenport, J., 212
Davidson, L., 145–46, 148, 153–54, 156
Davies, B., 219, 222
Davis, B., 135, 141
Davis, M., 172
Davis Cup, 251
Dean, D., 257
decision making, high-involvement, 7
Deford, F., 136, 141, 258, 260
DeMarcus, R., 22, 31
Dempsey, J., 252
Dingel, J., 139
direct revenue projections, 146
Disney, 117
distribution channels, 117
Dixon, B., 256
Dologite, D. G., 187, 198
Donohoe, T., 213–14, 216, 218–19, 222
Dougherty, N., 131
Douglas, R., 160, 173
downhill skiing, 63, 67, 71, 76, 88
  demographic characteristics, 67, 75

market volume, 76
participation volume, 76
Downing, S., 232–33
Dreyer, A., 269, 273–75
Drucker, P., 39, 46, 57
drugs, 212, 216, 221–22
  abuse, 10, 93
  addiction, 231
  effects of, 217
Duchaine, D., 215
Duda, M., 134, 141
Dudenhoeffer, F., 53
Duke University, 137
Duncan, P., 130
Dundee, J., 251
Dunnavant, K., 206, 210
Dunphy, D., 249, 255, 260
Durslag, M., 256, 260
Dworkin, J. B., 167, 173
Dye, R., 146, 156

e

Earle, M. V., 205, 210
Eastern Broadcasting Union, 18
Ecker, T., 219
Eckersley, D., 172
econometric model, 160
economics, 132, 135, 253
  development, 262
  impact, 145–47, 153–54, 156
  models, 145, 147
  multipliers, 145–47, 150–51, 154
Eggert, A., 133–34, 140
Ehrlich, N., 139, 141
electronic fund transfer, 189
Elson, B., 257
emblems, 20
emotions, 135
Enberg, D., 255, 257
energy drains, 236, 238–39, 242
Eng, W., 175
Engle, J. F., 22, 31
Englehardt, N. L., 182, 185
Ensor, R., 86
environmental problems, 78
epistemic values, 23
Equal Rights Amendment, 223
equipment advertising, 100
Erving, J., 257

ESPN, 136
Espy, R., 18, 21
estimating market potential, 34, 36
ethics, 132, 137
Etzel, M. J., 205, 210
European Soccer Association (UEFA), 92
Evangelauf, J., 130
Eveden, E. S., 182, 185
events marketing, 83
exercise
  market, 25
  programs, 22, 25
external cues, 30
Exxon, 15

f

facilities, 179–81
facility usage, 48
Family Sports Award, 90
fan fair, 116
Feld, J., 62, 80
Feldman, R. J., 122, 127
Ferris State College, 200–202
Fever, J., 86
Fichtenbaum, P., 116, 120
finance, 91, 201
financial programs, 189
financial reliability, 117
Fink, I., 53
First National Soccer League, 90–92
Fischer, H., 268, 274
fitness, 49, 276–77, 279–80, 282
  clubs, 25
  consumers, 24
  market, 25
  programs, 22, 192, 197
Fitness Risk Management, Inc., 126
Fixx, J. F., 258, 260
Fleming, R., 129
Flepworth, S. J., 281–82
Flood, C., 159
Florida Citrus Bowl, 145
Florida State University, 135
flyers, 43
football, 52, 102, 204–6, 208–9
  flag, 52
  touch, 134
form letters, 193

Fort Lewis College, 183
Foshee, D. P., 132
Four P's, 3–4, 12
Fox, S., 214
Frankel, B., 3, 12
Franks, A., 217
free agency, 159–60, 162, 166–68, 172
Freeman, L., 86
Freiolich, H. R., 80
Frick, F. C., 257
front desk control, 190
Fry, H., 132, 137, 141
Fuchsberg, G., 130
Fuller, L. K., 251, 258, 260
Furhmann, H., 274
Furse, D. H., 24, 31

Gadsden, S. E., 84–86
Gallivan, D., 255
Garcia, B. E., 130
Gardner, G., 256
Gardner, M. P., 83–84, 86, 96, 109
Gareau, R. N., 115, 120
Garfield, 117
Garagiola, J., 255, 257
Garrick, J. G., 132–34, 140
Garrison, B., 252, 260
Gaski, J. F., 205, 210
gender, 209, 223–25, 228, 256
Geoffrey, T., 219, 222
George, P., 256
German Body Building Association, 270
German Soccer Federation (DFB), 91
German Sporting Goods Manufacturers Association, 90
German Sports Federation (DSB), 88–89, 262–63, 267–68, 270
Germany, 262
Gieseler, H. H., 271, 275
Gifford, F., 255, 257–58
Gill, D., 249
Gleim, G. W., 133, 142
Glenn, P., 93
Glickman, M., 255, 257
goals, 237
Golden Plan, 266
Goldie, D., 128

Goldin, G., 86
Goldman, B., 216, 222
Goldsmith, A. H., 167, 173
golf, 34–37, 63, 67–68, 76, 95, 109, 224, 226–28, 266–67
    demographic characteristics, 67, 72
    industry, 199
    management, 199–200
    management programs, 199–203
    market volume, 76
    participation volume, 76
    professionals, 200
Gowdey, C., 255, 257
graduation rate, 93, 208, 232
Graham, F., 258–60
Graham, L., 131
Grassmuck, K., 116, 120
Greater Toledo Office of Tourism and Conventions, 111, 113
Green, D., 19
Green, R., 136
Greenberg, B. A., 24, 31
Greenberg, M. J., 258, 260
Griese, B., 256
Grimes, C., 115, 120
Grinnell College, 184
Grippo, J., 134, 141
Gross, A. C., 83–86
Guilfoile, W. J., 259
Gumbel, B., 257
Gundy, M., 136
Gup, T., 104, 109
Gustafson, E., 159–60, 163–66, 169–71, 173
Guttmann, A., 253, 258, 260
Gwynn, T., 171
gymnastics, 88–89, 95, 238, 246, 266, 268

Haderlie, B. M., 53
Hadley, L., 159–60, 163–66, 169–71, 173
Hamaker, R. M., 86
Hammen, L., 39
handball, 88
Harmon, M., 116, 255
Herskowitz, M., 258
hiking, 90

Hilton Head Island, 200
Hite, R. E., 24, 31
Hodges, R., 257
Hoffman, D., 258, 260
Hoffman, M., 259, 260
holistic approach, 234
holistic model, 235
Holtzman, J., 258, 260
Horowitz, I., 260
Howard, D. R., 32–33, 77, 79–80
Howe, J., 129
Howell, P., 59, 61
Hubbell, R., 258, 260
Hull, C. H., 32
Huntley, S., 22, 31
Hypercard, 50

IBM, 19
ice skating, 71
Illinois College, 184
impact
    direct, 148, 151, 154
    indirect, 148, 151
Indianapolis 500, 254
indirect multiplier benefits, 146
indoor soccer, 52
information technology, 187, 196
Ingram, H., 132, 135, 141
injuries, 132
innovators, 30
Input-Output model, 147–51, 153–54, 156
institutional image, 104–5
insurance, 121, 123–25
    health, 270
    no-fault, 124
    professional, 124
    self-insurance, 124
intangible benefits, 146
intercollegiate athletics, 47–48, 93, 103, 223
intercollegiate sports 132, 204
interindustry flow matrix, 149–50
intermediate demands, 149
International Olympic Committee (IOC), 18, 54, 117, 212, 214–15
interscholastic sports, 132, 204

intramural
    activities, 48–49
    program, 49
    sports, 47
Iowa State University, 206
Irwin, D., 115
Isensee, J., 265, 275
Issiki, K. R., 187, 198
Ivey, M., 99, 110

Jackson, H., 258, 260
Jackson, R., 154, 156
Jafee, A., 83–84, 86
Janoff, B., 133, 141
Jarobe, G. R., 24, 32
jazzercise, 48
Jenkins, J. G., 32
jogging, 89–90
Johnson, B., 212, 214, 249, 256
Johnson, D., 249
Johnson, M., 256
Johnson, N., 213–14, 216, 218–19, 222
Johnson, P., 136
Johnson, W. O., 258, 260
Jones, H., 255
Joyner-Kersee, F., 220
judo, 268, 269
June, J. L., 25, 32

Kalas, H., 255
Kansas City Chiefs, 136
Kansas City Royals, 136
Kansas State University, 206
Kappler, E., 269, 271, 275
karate, 268
Kass, R. A., 26, 32
Keene, J. S., 133, 141
Keever, 137, 141
Kelly, D., 255
Kelly, J. R., 80
Kenney, J., 128
Kentucky Derby, 254
Kerin, R., 9, 11, 12
Kerin, T. E., 133, 141
Killat, D., 23, 31

King, C. W., 11–12
Kipling, R., 257
Kirkpatrick, C., 259, 261
Klatell, D., 253, 256–58, 260
Kniesner, T. J., 167, 173
Knox College, 184
Kodak, 19
Koppett, L., 258, 260
Korgaonker, P. K., 24, 31
Kotler, P., 4, 5, 7, 9, 12, 18, 21–22, 32
Kovac, N., 53
Kovach, J. L., 82, 84, 86
Kramer, S. D., 254, 260
Kretzler, H. A., 140
Kruger, A., 262, 267, 269, 273, 275
Krupa, G., 116–17, 119–20
Krupp, H. J., 262, 272, 274–75
Kubek, T., 257
Kuhr, J., 270, 275

labor
    costs, 175–76
    relations, 159
Lafayette, J., 85–86
Lake Forest College, 184
Landers, D., 249
Landrieu, M., 146
Lane, E., 141
Lanker, R., 275
Lapin, J., 3, 12, 83–84, 86
Larkin, S., 175
latent demand, 16
Lawrence, J. F., 129
Lawrence University, 184
Lawson, P., 219
league play, 48
leakages, 151
Lederman, D., 97, 101, 110, 130
Lee, M., 179, 182, 185
legal system, 121
leisure industry, 262, 270
Leonard, M., 135, 141
Leontief inverse, 150–51
Lewis, A., 136
Lewis, D., 182
liability, 123
Liberty Bowl, 154

license
    compliance, 118
    exclusive, 117
    joint-use, 117
    nonexclusive, 117
    promotional, 118
licensee, 83
licensing, 20
    administrator, 117–19
    agency, 119
    program enforcement, 119
Lieber, J., 134, 142
Lijewski, P., 131
Likert-type rating scale, 26
Linville, J., 140
Lipping, A., 276
Lipsky, R., 258, 260
Lipsyte, R., 255
Lipton, L., 231
Lockhart, A. S., 182, 185
logo, 20, 49, 85, 100, 115–18, 120
Longines, 19
Lopiano, D., 225, 229–30
Loudenback, L., 201
Louisiana State University, 137
Lumpkin, J. R., 24, 31
Lupica, M., 258, 260
Lusch, R. F., 32
Lynch, R. B., 22, 32

MacDonald, G., 160, 173
Macintosh computer, 50
Macnow, G., 115, 120, 134, 137, 142
Madden, J., 254, 256–58, 261
Madison Square Garden, 251
Madlin, N., 86
magazines, 43
Maher, P., 86
mailing labels, 193
mailmerge, 193
Maisel, I., 208, 210
Major League Baseball (MLB), 115
Managed Recreation Research Report, 22
management, 40, 201
    committee, 60
Manddala, G. S., 163, 174
Manuel, B., 80

Manufacturers Hanover New York
    City Marathon, 82
Marcus, N., 253, 256–58, 260
Marek, R., 258
Marichal, J., 231, 233
market
    determinants, 23
    potential, 34
    segment, 78–79
    segmentation, 23
    segmentation variables, 5
    share, 34, 277
    size, 63–64, 66, 76–78, 117
    strategies, 22
    surveillance, 118
    trends, 63
    volume, 63–64, 76–77
marketing, 14–16, 20, 22, 41, 43–44,
    47, 88, 97, 103, 117, 201
    campaign, 47–48
    communications, 25
    environment, 3
    mix, 3
    mix variables, 4, 12
    plan, 2
    research, 16, 23
    rights, 20
    strategy, 3, 277
    tools, 2, 93
    variables, 3
marketplace behavior, 24
markets, 20
Martens, R., 249
Massey, T. K., 187, 196, 198
Masters Golf Tournament, 254
matrix organization, 57
Matson, R., 213
Mattingly, D., 171
McAtee, B., 257
McCarthy, E. J., 3
McCarver, T., 257, 259, 261
McDaniel, C. D., 24, 32
McDonald's, 4
McGeehan, P., 3, 13
McGraw, P., 128
McGuire, A., 257
McGuire, F., 80
McIntyre, T. D., 210
McKay, J., 256–57, 259, 261
McLaughlin, K., 115–16, 120
McNamara, B., 187

McPherson, B. D., 278, 282
Medhoff, M. H., 160, 172
media, 251, 253, 257
media coverage, 85
media messages, 25
Melcher, R. A., 3, 12
Mellman, G., 128
Melnick, M. J., 210
Meltone, H., 156
member
    billing, 188
    records, 188
mentoring, 248
merchandising, 20
Merrill-Lynch Great Performers, 82
Mesa College, 183
Mescon, T. S., 83–86
Messersmith, A., 159
Methodist College, 202
Miami Dolphins, 136
Michaels, A., 255–57
Midwest Collegiate Athletic
    Conference, 183
Mihalik, B. J., 84–86
Millar, V. E., 187–88, 198
Millen, M., 136
Miller, F., 206
Miller, F. A., 97
Miller, H., 154, 156
Miller, P., 40, 44, 46
Miller, R. I., 40, 44, 46
Miller, S. J., 133, 140
Milner, E. M., 135, 140–41
Mississippi State University, 200–202
Mitchell, A., 31
Mochis, G. P., 24, 32
Monmouth College, 184
Moore, E. M., 2
Moore, M., 134, 142
Moran, B., 3, 13
Morehouse, C. A., 133–34, 142
Morris, R., 218
Morrison, R. B., 34
Morrison, T., 133, 141
Morrison, W. E., 133–34, 142
Morrow, W., 259
Morse, M., 253, 261
Most, J., 256–57
Mueller, C., 281–82
Mullin, B., 187

multiplier
    consumption, 151
    economic base, 147
    output, 151
    tourist, 148
Munhall, K., 129
municipal golf courses, 200
Murphy, L., 86
Musburger, B., 254, 257

Nanus, B., 42, 46
Narechania, R. G., 141
National Athletic Injury/Illness
    Reporting System (NAIRS), 133
National Athletic Trainers Association
    (NATA), 133
National Broadcasting Company
    (NBC), 18, 136
National Collegiate Athletic
    Association (NCAA), 93,
    96–100, 102, 106–8, 115-19,
    124, 136, 205–9, 220, 223–24,
    228–29, 232
National Facilities Conference, 183
National Football League (NFL), 12,
    115, 134, 136, 218
National Football League Players
    Association (NFLPA), 134, 136
National Governing Body (NGB),
    112–13
National Hockey League (NHL),
    115–16
National League Baseball, 251
National Park Service, 80
National Soccer League, 88
National Sporting Goods Association,
    62
natural turf, 133–35, 137, 139–40
Neff, C., 212–22
Neilsen, A. C., 11, 13
Nelson, L., 255, 257, 259, 261
Netherlands, 89
Netzle, S., 274–75
Newcomer, K., 130
Newman, A. 136
New Mexico State University, 200–201
Newport Tall Ships Celebration, 145,
    154

newspapers, 43
New York Giants, 134
NFL Management Council, 134
Nicholas, J. A., 133, 142
Nichols, D., 111, 113
Nideffer, R., 249
Nie, N. K., 26, 32
Noden, M., 218, 222
Noll, R. C., 260
non-credit leisure oriented courses, 48–49
nonrevenue-generating sports, 6
Northern Illinois University, 154
Norway, 89
Notre Dame University, 105
Noverr, D. A., 258, 261

Oatey, J. S., 53
Oberlander, R. S., 96, 99, 105, 110
Oberste-Lehn, H., 275
O'Brien, K., 134
Odom, K., 128
official supplier, 83
Ohio State University, 135, 180
Oklahoma State University, 136
Old Dominion University, 5
O'Leary, J. T., 80
Olsen, M., 253, 257
Olsen, W., 130
Olson, C. O., 133, 142
Olympic
  Committee, 15, 16, 19, 54–55, 59–61
  Games, 14, 16–18, 20–21, 54–57, 60, 95, 212–13, 254, 256
    Los Angeles, 18
    Montreal, 18, 55
    Moscow, 19
    Rome, 18
    Toyko, 18
  Movement, 16
  Organization, 14–15, 19
  Organizing Committee, 18, 20
  Village, 19
Omega, 19
O'Neill, T., 254
Opel, 92
operational planning, 41

organization, 177
  leadership, 40
  personal, 237
organization life cycle, 39
  appraisal stage, 39
  creative stage, 39
  entrepreneurial stage, 39
  implementation stage, 39
  maintenance stage, 39
organized games, 48
Ortiz, C., 223, 228, 230
Otterson, C., 128
Owen, C., 147, 156

P

Palmer, B., 255
Palmer, J., 253
Pan American Games, 95
Pankratz, H., 128
Parker, S., 80
participating sponsor, 83
participation
  rate, 63–64
  volume, 63, 67
Pate, R., 249
Patrick, D., 221–22
patronage behavior theory, 23
Patterson, F., 231, 233
pay-for-play, 93
Payne, H., 216
Peanuts, 117
Pearsall, J., 3, 13
Peat Marwick Main and Company, 40, 42–43, 46
Peat Marwick's Resource Development System, 40–41
Pennsylvania State University, 207
performance
  enhancement, 236
  preparation, 234
  reports, 193
Perron, J. Y., 61
personal
  appearance, 43
  determinants, 23
  presentation strategies, 20
  selling, 9, 20, 83, 84
PERT-COST System, 59
Peters, R., 249

Peters, T., 40, 46
Petr, T. A., 133, 143
philanthropic contributions, 82–83, 85
Phoenix Cardinals, 136
physical fitness programs, 25
placing products, 8
Plagenhoef, S., 141
planning, 40, 237
  effective, 16
  process, 40
Play Campaign, 89
player
  characteristic variables, 160–62
  performance variables, 160–61
Poggeler, F., 270, 275
political development, 262
Poly Turf, 139
Porter, M. E., 187–88, 198
post-buying habits, 85
posters, 43
Powell, J. T., 133, 142
power boating, 63, 67, 70, 77
  demographic characteristics, 67, 74
  market volume, 77
  participation volume, 77
Powers, R., 258, 261
pre-buying habits, 85
Presley, J., 137
Price, J., 281–82
pricing, 7–8
  objectives, 7, 12
  special events, 7
primary products, 6
Prince, B., 255–57
Princeton University, 252
Procaccini, J., 40, 46
product, 4
  determinants, 23
  distribution, 17
  life cycle, 2–3, 6–7
  mix, 5, 8
production
  capacity, 117
  management, 201
productivity
  levels, 176
  monitoring, 175
Professional Golf Association (PGA), 200–203
professional sports, 132
profit maximization, 15

program assessment, 44
Project Approval Procedure (PAP),
    58–61
promotion, 9, 279
    mix, 83, 85, 119
    strategies, 82–83, 85
promotional
    opportunities, 120
    pricing, 7
    strategies, 277
    tools, 9, 12
Proposition 42, 93, 96, 105, 208
Proposition 48, 93, 96, 106, 208
publicity, 9–10, 20, 83–84
    negative, 10–11
Puma, 270, 274
Punj, G. N., 24, 31
purchasing
    behavior, 23
    power, 16

q

questionnaire, 25, 35, 48, 63, 277
Quinn, J. B., 128
Quinton, N., 160, 167, 174

r

Rabinoff, M. A., 121, 128
race, 256
racquetball, 49, 63, 67, 69, 76
    demographic characteristics, 67, 73
    market volume, 76
    participation volume, 76
Radar, B. G., 253, 258, 261
radio, 43
Raiborn, M. H., 206–7, 209–10, 223,
    230
Raimondo, H. J., 160, 174
Ramirez, B., 218
Randolph, B., 258
Rapoport, R., 133, 142
Raschad, A., 255, 257, 261
Ray, J., 251
Real, M., 258, 261
real estate industry, 200
Recio, M., 110

recreation
    activities, 48–49
    businesses, 25
    ethic, 79
    needs, 47
    programs, 24
recreational sport
    activities, 62–63
        indoor-based, 63, 65–66
        outdoor resource-based, 63, 65–66
        water-based, 63, 65–66
        winter-based, 63, 65–66
    facilities, 180
    market, 62
REC Sports Program, 47, 49, 50–53
Redelius, W., 9, 11–12
Regimbal, C., 111
Relative Value Assessment, 85
Requa, R. K., 132–34, 140
research process, 276
reserve clause, 159, 162, 172
resource development, 41
return-on-investment, 17
Reuschel, R., 172
revenue-generating sports, 6
revenue-sharing, 18
Revoyer, J. D., 115–16, 120
Reynolds, F. D., 24, 31
Reynolds, M. O., 174
Rice, G., 251, 261
Rice University, 137
Richard, J., 80
RIMS II, 151–52, 154
Ripon College, 184
risk management, 124–26
Ritter, M. A., 140
Rizzuto, P., 253
Robertson, D. H., 24, 31
Robichon, J. G., 133, 142
Robins, J. M., 86, 254, 261
Robinson, D., 220
Robinson, J., 77, 80, 256
Robinson, R., 259, 261
Rocky Mountain Athletic Conference,
    183
Rogers, E. M., 30, 32
Rogers, P., 220, 222
Rokosz, F. M., 53
Rose, D., 160, 173
Rose, P., 256
Rosen, M., 214, 222

Rosen, S., 162, 174
Rosenblatt, R., 115–16, 120
Rosenbloom, R., 218
Rosenthal, P. P., 133, 142
Rosner, D., 116, 120
Rottenberg, S., 159, 174
royalties, 20, 116, 120
    advance, 118
    exemption, 118
    revenues, 117
Rudman, W. J., 276, 278–79, 282
running, 68
Russell, B., 257
Ryan, N., 168, 172

s

Saberhagen, B., 172
Sachtjen, K. M., 141
Sack, A. L., 204, 210
Sahadi, L., 259, 261
sailing, 49, 70
St. Norbert College, 184
salaries, 223, 225–29
sales
    area, 17
    force evaluation, 20
    force motivation, 20
    promotion, 11, 20, 83–84
    promotion budget, 11
    territory, 20
    volume, 85
San Diego Chargers, 139
San Diego Padres, 137
San Diego State University, 97
Sandomir, R., 2, 13, 115–16, 120
San Francisco 49ers, 134
Sanko, J., 129
Sapora, A., 182–83, 185
Sarnoff, D., 252
Schaffer, W., 145–46, 148, 153–54,
    156
Schein, E. H., 276, 282
Schenkel, C., 257, 269, 275
Scher, Z., 128
Schmickler, E. D., 266, 275
Schwartz, A., 11, 13
Scott, R., 255
scuba diving, 49
Scully, G., 159, 167, 172, 174

Scully, V., 255, 257
Seagrave, J. O., 109, 210
Seattle Mariners, 137
secondary products, 6
Second National Soccer League, 90–92
Seggar, J., 234
segmentation
    buyer behavior, 34
    demographic, 34–35
    geographic, 34–35
    market, 34
    pyschographic, 34
Seipel, C. M., 11, 13
self-structured leisure activities, 48, 52
Selin, S. W., 30, 32
Sellers, T., 220, 222
service, 4
Shanklin, W. L., 83–86
Shapiro, B., 15
Shelburn, W. L., 199
Shenkel, C., 255
Sherrod, B., 259, 261
Sheth, J. N., 23, 31–32
shopper
    apathetic, 24
    bargain, 24
    brand-loyal, 23, 26–31
    cautious, 26–28
    compulsive, 24
    conformist, 26–29
    constructive, 24
    convenience, 24–28
    ecologist, 26–28
    economical, 24–28
    ethical, 24
    experimenter, 26–28
    impulsive, 26–30
    name-conscious, 24
    personalizing, 24
    persuadable, 26–28
    planner, 26–28
    preparatory, 24
    psycho-socializing, 24
    recreational, 24
    routinized, 24
    store-loyal, 24
    style/trend conscious, 26–28
    surrogate, 24
shopping
    behavior, 22
    orientation, 22, 24–25

preferences, 23
    styles, 24–25, 28
Shorter, F., 218
short-term incentives, 11
Shuiruff, L., 128
Shultz, R. D., 208–10, 220
Shuman, P. J., 83–86, 109
Shuster, R., 80
Siegel, A., 220, 222
Silva, L. J., 128
Silverman, I., 83–84, 87
Silvestern, J., 214
Simmons Market Research Bureau,
    24–26, 62–63, 66, 79
Simon, R., 128
Simpson, J., 255
Singer, S., 254, 261
Ski Industry Bill, 123
skills
    managerial, 200
    promotional, 200
Skousen, C. R., 96, 110
Smith, B., 131, 172
Smith, C., 258, 261
Smith, D., 147–48, 156, 182, 185
Smith, L., 137
Smith, O., 168, 171
Smith, S. L. J., 25, 32
snowmobiling, 71
Snyder, E. E., 255–56, 261
Snyder, J., 256
soccer, 88
social development, 262
softball, 52, 224, 226–28, 277
sole sponsor, 83
Solow, R. M., 167, 174
Sommers, P. M., 160, 167, 174
Southern Methodist University, 256
South Korea, 18
space standards, 181–84
    activity, 181, 183–84
    ancillary, 181–84
Spears, B., 185
sponsors, 253
sponsorship program, 19
sport
    business, 62
    clubs, 263, 267, 270, 274
    consumers, 3
    economics, 274
    entities, 3

events, 111–12
    facility, 180, 182, 184, 187
    management, 187, 274
    market, 262, 274
    marketer, 9, 12
    marketing, 2, 14, 271, 272
    marketing educators, 12
    marketing mix, 12
    marketing research, 36
    nonprofit clubs, 270
    pages, 251
sport announcers, 251
sportscasters, 252–58
sporting goods industry, 270
Sporting Goods Manufacturers
    Association, 139
sportscasting, 251–52
Sports Compatibility Profile, 85
sports federations, 263
Sports for All, 88–89
Sports inc., 2
sportswriters, 253
Spreitzer, E. A., 255–56, 261
Spurrier, S., 137
squash, 268
Stallings, G., 137
stamps, 18
Stanford Research Institute (SRI), 134
Stanford University, 105
Statistical Package for the Social
    Sciences (SPSS), 26
statistics
    Barlett's chi square test, 26, 28
    Bradford-Zipf distribution, 281
    chi-square analysis, 25, 27–29, 225,
        227
    Chow test, 163
    correlation analysis, 244
    descriptive, 25
    factor analysis, 25, 28, 30
    fixed coefficient model, 148
    Kaiser normalization, 28–29
    regression analysis, 160, 278, 280
    regression equation, 163, 168
    salary equation, 160
Stauble, V. R., 14, 54
Steinbach, J., 273, 275
Steinberg, J., 3, 13
Steinbrenner, K., 32
Stephenson, R. R., 24, 32

steroids, 10, 93, 212–18, 220–21
  anabolic, 212, 214–17, 219–22
  Dianabol, 213
Stern, B., 252
Stevenson, M. J., 133–34, 142
Stevent, A., 87
Stewart, D. W., 24, 31, 172
Still, A., 136
Stockton, B., 257
Stone, G., 24, 32
Stram, H., 259, 261
Strand, B. N., 183–85
strategic planning, 3, 34, 39–41, 46, 54
strategic planning system, 44
Straub, W. F., 249
Strawberry, D., 171
Strayer, G. D., 182, 185
stress, 238, 242, 245–49, 278
Stull, R. A., 39
Sugar, B. R., 261
Summerall, P., 253, 257
Summers, J. O., 11–12
Sunkist Fiesta Bowl, 82
Super Bowl, 253
Super Turf, 134
supervising
  sales force, 20
Sweden, 89
swimming, 70, 89–90, 224, 226–28,
  266
Sykes, W., 117, 120
symbols, 20, 115, 117

Taaffe, W., 259, 261
Talen, J., 255, 261
Tancred, B., 132, 134–35, 140
tangible product, 6
target
  audience, 11, 16
  groups, 49
  market, 3, 11–12, 22–23, 84
  market strategies, 25
Tartan Turf, 133–34
Taylor, A., 83, 87
Taylor, G., 128
Taylor, W., 53

team
  characteristic variables, 160–62
  endorsements, 2
  sports, 48, 52
Teel, J. E., 11, 13
Teel, S. J., 2
Telander, R., 218, 222
telephone interviews, 63
television, 43, 91
  cable, 43
tennis, 34–35, 37, 49, 68, 95, 109,
  224, 226–28, 238, 243, 247
Terry, J., 207, 210
Texas Christian University, 139
The Athletic Congress, 221
The Simpsons, 117
Theisman, J., 136, 142
Thomas, I., 256
Thomas, J., 219
Thomas, K., 139
Thompson, C., 255
Thompson, T., 213
Thrower, H., 202
ticker file, 193
tickets, admission, 19
Tilson, D. J., 83–86
time management, 237
Tinsley, H. E. A., 26, 32
Title IX, 93, 96, 207–8, 223, 229
title sponsor, 83
Toledo, 111
tort reform, 122–23
tourism, 25, 62
Tow, T. C., 100, 108, 110
track, 88, 95, 224–28
Tractenberg, J. A., 3, 13
trademarks, 20
  licensing, 115–16
  registration, 116
Traylor, M. B., 83–86
trend analysis, 34
Trimm-Campaign, 88–89
Trimming, 90, 130
Trimm-Trot, 89
True, B., 128
Tulane University, 97, 137
turf studies, 133
turkey trot, 52
Turners, 268

U.S. Commerce Department, 2, 151
U.S. Open Golf Tournament, 254
Udd, E., 32
Ueberhorst, H., 88
Uecker, B., 253, 255
Uhlir, G. G., 223, 229–30
Ukman, L., 83–84, 87
Underwood, J., 136, 139, 143, 261
United States Olympic Committee
  (USOC), 115–16, 220–21
University of
  Alabama, 135, 137, 139
  Calgary, 117
  California, 182
  California at Los Angeles, 115–16
  Florida, 136
  Illinois, 182
  Iowa, 137
  Massachusetts, 215
  Miami, 109, 252
  Michigan, 137, 180
  North Carolina, 105
  Oklahoma, 205–7
  Pittsburgh, 252
  Southern California, 107, 109, 137
  Southern Colorado, 183
  Southern Mississippi, 180
  Toledo, 111
  Virginia, 4
Unstructured free activity, 48–49
Upshaw, G., 136

van der Smissen, B., 121, 131
Vanderwater, J., 115, 120
Van Maaney, J., 276, 282
Vatele, D., 259, 261
Vecsey, G., 258, 261
Vickers, B. J., 234
video seminars, 44
Vinson, D. E., 128
volleyball, 69, 88, 95, 224, 226–28,
  238, 244, 248
Volvo Tennis, 224
Voy, R. O., 218, 222

Wadler, G., 217–18
Wagner, G., 262, 271, 274–75
Waldman, P., 130
Waldrep, K., 139
Walker, M. L., 179, 183–85
Wall, T. D., 281–82
Walley, W., 3, 13, 84, 86–87
Walsh, U. R., 133, 143
Warburton, T. L., 252, 260–61
Warnick, R. B., 22, 24, 32–33, 62, 77, 79–80
Washington College, 47
Washington Redskins, 136
Washington State University, 139
water skiing, 49, 70
Watkins, C., 204, 210
Wehr, W., 275
Welch, A., 111–13
Welles, G., 128
Welling, B., 3, 12

wellness, 49
  laboratory, 44
  programs, 192, 197
Wells, D., 255
Wells, J., 249
Wendel, T., 111, 113
West, J., 231, 233
Westergard, N., 129
Western New Mexico University, 183
Western State College, 183
West Germany, 88, 262
West Virginia University, 252
Wharton Econometrics Forcasting
  Associates, 2
Wheeler, J., 147–48, 156
White, B., 255
Wilber, D., 3, 13, 95, 110
Willett, R. P., 24, 32
William Jewell College, 179
Williams, R. H., 11, 13
Wilson, R. D., 141
Winkler, J., 269, 275
Wishman, S., 128
Wolf, W., 255, 259, 261
women's programs, 207
Wong, G. M., 130

Wooden, J., 237–38, 249
Woods, J., 255
Woodward, S., 220, 222
word processing, 193
World Games, 95
World Series, 254
World Soccer Championships, 254

Yesalis, C., 217
Yiannakis, A., 210
Young and Rubicam, 85
Yovovich, B. G., 11, 13, 87

Zaharadnik, R., 87
Zatopek, E., 89
Zeigler, J., 213
Zotos, C., 223–24, 230

Analyzing Public Policy

Analyzing Public Policy

Concepts, Tools, and Techniques

SECOND EDITION

Dipak K. Gupta
San Diego State University

CQ PRESS

A Division of SAGE
Washington, D.C.

CQ Press
2300 N Street, NW, Suite 800
Washington, DC 20037

Phone: 202-729-1900; toll-free, 1-866-4CQ-PRESS (1-866-427-7737)

Web: www.cqpress.com

Cover design: www.designfarm.com
Composition: C&M Digitals (P) Ltd.

⊗ The paper used in this publication exceeds the requirements of the American
National Standard for Information Sciences—Permanence of Paper for Printed Library
Materials, ANSI Z39.48-1992.

Printed and bound in the United States of America

14   13   12   11   10   1   2   3   4   5

Library of Congress Cataloging-in-Publication Data
Gupta, Dipak K.
Analyzing public policy : concepts, tools, and techniques / Dipak K. Gupta. — 2nd ed.
    p.   cm.
  Includes bibliographical references and index.
  ISBN 978-1-60426-570-5 (alk. paper)
1. Policy sciences—Statistical methods. 2. Policy sciences—Mathematical models.
I. Title.

H97.G868 2010
320.6072′7—dc21

2009051866

To Chitra and Samar Das

Contents

Tables, Figures, and "A Case in Point"   xv

Preface   xxi

CHAPTER 1   REASON, RATIONALITY, AND PUBLIC POLICY:
**   THE PUZZLE OF HUMAN BEHAVIOR**   **1**

Government in Our Lives   1
Politics and Rationality   2
The World of the "Rational Fool"   5
    The Illogic of a "Rational Being"   6
    The Un-rational Being and Political Behavior   9
Government's Goals and Their Impact on Public Policy   15
    Efficiency   16
    Equity   18
    The Equity-Efficiency Trade-off   19
    Liberty   20
    Security   21
    The Liberty-Security Trade-off   22
Key Words   23
Exercises   24
Notes   24

CHAPTER 2   THE ANALYSTS: THEIR ROLE AND THEIR TOOLS   **27**

The Prince and the Pundits: Analysts, Academics, and Advocates   28
    The Politicos and In-house Policy Analysts: An Uneasy Cohabitation   30
    Exit, Voice, and Loyalty: What's an Analyst to Do?   32
The Use of Quantitative Techniques in Public Policy Analysis   35
Structure above a Swamp: Public Policy Analysis and Professional Ethics   40
Key Words   43
Exercises   43
Notes   44

CHAPTER 3   GOVERNMENT AND THE MARKET   **47**

The Fundamental Contributions of Economic Analyses   49
    Marginal Analysis   49
    Opportunity Costs   52
Market Failure: Why Government Interferes in a Free Market   52
    Lack of Competition   53
    Barriers to Entry and Exit   55
    Restricted or Asymmetrical Flow of Information   57
    Externalities and Social Costs   59
    Rising Service Costs: The Appearance of Market Failure   61
Government Failure   62
    Inability to Define Social Welfare   63
    The Limits of Democracy and the Paradox of Voting   63
    Inability to Define the Marginal Benefits and Costs of Public Goods   64
    Political Constraints   65
    Cultural Constraints   65
    Institutional Constraints   65
    Legal Constraints   66
    Knowledge Constraints   66
    Analytical Constraints   66
    The Timing of Policies   67
Limiting Government Intervention: Joint Partnership in a Mixed Economy   67
    Stimulating the Market   68
    Simulating the Market   69
Key Words   72
Exercises   72
Notes   73

CHAPTER 4   THE POLICY PROCESS   **75**

Agenda Setting   76
    The Pluralist Model   77
    The Elitist Model   81
    Impact of Sensational Events   83
    Evaluating Costs and Benefits   86
Policy Formulation   87
    Explaining Behavior   88
    Forecasting Effects   88
    Conflict, Inaction, and Nondecision   89
Policy Adoption   91
Policy Implementation   92
Policy Evaluation   93

Policy Change 94
Policy Termination 96
Key Words 97
Exercises 97
Notes 98

CHAPTER 5   CRITICAL THINKING AND RESEARCH DESIGN   **101**

Five Steps of Objective Analysis 102
Setting Goals 104
    Utilitarians and the Pareto Principle 106
    The Kaldor-Hicks Compensation Principle 107
    The Rawlsian Challenge 108
    Setting Public Policy Goals 109
Choosing a Method of Analysis 109
    Experimental Design 110
    Quasi-experimental Design 112
Choosing the Right Model 115
Forecasting Outcomes and Unintended Consequences 116
Designing Policy Research 117
    Limiting the Number of Alternatives 117
    Accepting or Rejecting a Project 119
    Ensuring the Process Is Fair 121
Challenges to Critical Thinking: Biases in Reasoning 122
    Representativeness 122
    Availability of Information 125
    Adjustment and Anchoring 127
A Few Parting Suggestions 127
Key Words 128
Exercises 128
Notes 128

CHAPTER 6   BASIC STATISTICS   **131**

Numbers as Storytellers 131
Methods of Descriptive Statistics 131
    Measures of Central Tendency 132
    Measures of Dispersion 137
    Which Measure of Central Tendency to Use 144
    A Quick Glance at the Distribution: The Stem-Leaf Method 144
    Correlation Coefficient: Pearson's r 145
Key Words 147

Exercises   148

Notes   148

CHAPTER 7   PROBABILITY AND HYPOTHESIS TESTING   **149**

Objective Probability   149

  Probability Distribution   151

  Hypothesis Testing and Confidence Intervals   157

  The Chi-Square Test   165

Subjective Probability   169

Key Words   171

Exercises   171

Notes   176

CHAPTER 8   SOURCES OF DATA   **177**

What Are We Measuring?   177

  Types of Measurement   177

  Accuracy of the Measuring Scales   178

Primary Data: Conducting a Survey   179

  Designing a Survey   180

  Systematic Errors in Sampling   180

  Random Sampling Errors   184

  Choosing the Sample Population   185

  Choosing the Size of the Sample   186

  Choosing Effective Survey Instruments   187

  Choosing Polling Methods   189

Quantification of Survey Data   189

Reporting Survey Results   190

Conducting Focus Groups   190

Secondary Data   192

  Searching for Information   193

  Online Searches   193

  Searching the Old-fashioned Way   200

  When Data Are Not Available   200

Key Words   201

Exercises   201

Notes   202

CHAPTER 9   MAKING SENSE OF NUMBERS   **203**

A Picture's Worth: Graphical Methods of Analysis   203

  Current versus Constant Dollars   204

Percentage Change	208
Creating an Index	209
Choosing the Type of Graph to Use	210
Graphical Methods in Decision Making	211
To Tell the Truth and Nothing but the Truth	213
Interpretation and Deception	214
Tabular Presentation of Data	221
Those Not-so-Innocent Numbers	222
Key Words	223
Exercises	223
Notes	224

**CHAPTER 10   PROJECTION TECHNIQUES: WHEN HISTORY IS
                    INADEQUATE   225**

Projection versus Causal Prediction	225
Inadequacy of History	227
Single-Factor Projection	227
Fiscal Impact Analysis	229
Problems of Single-Factor Analysis	230
Judgmental Methods of Projection	232
The Delphi Technique	232
The Feasibility Assessment Technique	238
The Expected Utility Model	242
Origin of the Numbers	244
Shortcomings of the Judgmental Methods	245
Key Words	246
Exercises	246
Notes	247

**CHAPTER 11   PROJECTION TECHNIQUES: ANALYSIS OF
                    HISTORICAL DATA   249**

The Components of a Data Series	249
The Patterns of Time Trends	253
Adjustment Methods	256
Seasonal Adjustment	258
Trend Adjustment	259
Smoothing Out the Fluctuations	260
Projecting the Immediate Past: Naive Projection	261
Projecting by the Mean	263
Moving Average	263
Choice of Projection Technique	265

The Politics of Forecasting   265

Key Words   266

Exercises   267

Notes   269

**CHAPTER 12   PROJECTION TECHNIQUES: THE METHODS OF
             SIMPLE AND MULTIPLE LEAST SQUARES   271**

The Logic of the Least Squares Method   272

Linear Time Trend: Simple Regression Model   275

  Accuracy of the Results   278

  High R^2   280

  Relevance of the Estimated Coefficients   280

  The Significance of Individual Coefficients   283

  Presentation of Estimation Results   286

  The Number of Observations   286

Trend Changes: Building Multiple Regression Models   287

  Abrupt Changes in Trend   288

  Abrupt Changes in Slope   292

Gradual Changes in Trend: Estimation of Nonlinear Trends   296

  Polynomial Forms   296

  Higher Order Polynomials   299

  Log-transformed Forms   301

  Inverse Forms   302

  The Problem of Irrelevant Independent Variables: Adjusted R^2 303

  The Significance of Coefficients Taken Together   304

  Choosing the Correct Functional Form   305

Forecasting and Its Problems   305

  Point Forecasts   306

  Interval Forecasts   307

Explaining the Present with the Past: Lagged Dependent Variables   311

Key Words   313

Exercises   314

Notes   317

**CHAPTER 13   THE ELEMENTS OF STRATEGIC THINKING: DECISION
             TREE AND GAME THEORY   319**

Getting a Grip on Uncertainty   320

Decision Making and Expected Payoff   321

The Decision Tree   322

  Structuring a Decision Tree   324

  Evaluating Flood Damage Reduction   325

  Risk Tolerance and Expected Payoff   330

Two Active Players: Game Theory 332
    Game Theory in Local Government Decision Making 337
    The Golden Rules of Decision Making under Uncertainty 338
Strategies to Overcome the Prisoner's Dilemma 339
Other Strategies: Trust and Bargaining 341
Key Words 341
Exercises 341
Notes 343

CHAPTER 14   CHOOSING THE BEST ALTERNATIVE:
                 COST-BENEFIT ANALYSIS   **345**

Social versus Private Cost-Benefit Analysis 346
Defining Goals 347
Identifying Alternatives 347
Listing the Costs and Benefits of the Alternatives 347
Estimation and Valuation of Benefits and Costs 350
    Can We Put a Price Tag on the Intangibles of Life? 351
    How Can We Measure Future Loss or Gain? 353
Introduction of Time: Present Value Analysis 355
    Choice of Time Horizon 359
    Choice of Discount Rate 360
    The Internal Rate of Return 362
Choosing the Best Alternative 364
    Sensitivity Analysis 364
    Cost-Benefit Ratio 364
    The Limits of Cost-Benefit Analysis: Redistribution of Income 366
    Cost-Effectiveness Analysis 366
Key Words 369
Exercises 369
Notes 370

CHAPTER 15   SO YOU WANT TO BE AN ANALYST?
                 SOME PRACTICAL SUGGESTIONS   **373**

Before You Start 374
    "Know Thyself" and Your Organization 374
    Be Aware of Biases 375
    Be Aware of External Constraints 376
Begin Your Analysis 377
    Organize Your Thoughts: A Quick Analysis 377
    Conducting a More Elaborate Analysis 378
Tell a Good Story: Effective Presentation 382
    Know Your Audience 383

Know What You Don't Know 383
Say It with Numbers 384
Tell a Compelling Story 385
Whose Ball Is It Anyway? Zen and the Art of Public Policy Analysis 387
Exercises 387
Notes 387

Appendix A Example of a Policy Analysis Report 389
Appendix B Models of Causal Prediction: Multiple Regression 412
Appendix C Areas of the Standard Normal Distribution (the *Z* table) 447
Appendix D Critical Values of the *t* Distribution 448
Appendix E Critical Values of the *F* Statistic: 5 Percent Level of Significance 449
Appendix F Critical Values of the *F* Statistic: 1 Percent Level of Significance 450
Appendix G The Chi-square Distribution 451
Index 453

Tables, Figures, and "A Case in Point"

TABLES

1.1	Ranking of Nations Based on Academic Performance of 15-Year-Olds	4
1.2	Classification of Goods	6
3.1	Voters' Preferences on the Decision to Purchase Fire Engines	64
3.2	Voters' Preferences on the Decision to Purchase Fire Engines: Strategy Change by Group A	65
4.1	Comparison of Pluralist and Elitist Models of Agenda Setting	83
4.2	Outcomes for Diffuse and Specific Costs and Benefits	86
5.1	Multiple Goals: Building a New Stadium	105
5.2	Correlation Analysis: Marital Status versus Student Achievement	114
6.1	Distribution of Housing Prices	133
6.2	Weighted Observations	136
6.3	Grouped Data	137
6.4	Relative Distribution of Housing Prices between Two Neighborhoods	138
6.5	Relative Distribution of Housing Prices: Deviation from the Mean	139
6.6	Calculation of Variance	140
6.7	Comparing the Dispersion of Two Distributions	141
6.8	Data Showing a Symmetric Distribution	142
6.9	Examples of Symmetric and Asymmetric Distributions	143
6.10	Mean, Median, and Mode in Symmetric and Asymmetric Series	144
6.11	Stem-Leaf Analysis: Drug Arrests, $N = 16$	145
6.12	Crime Rate and City Size	147
7.1	Probability and Cumulative Probability Distribution of Caseloads for a Social Worker on a Given Day	153
7.2	Comparison of Means	164
7.3	Example of a Contingency Table	166

7.4	Errors of Hypothesis Testing	168
7.5	Risk Assigned to Parolees	170
7.6	Quadratic Score Matrix for Parolees	170
9.1	State and Federal Grants to Masters, Pennsylvania, in Current Dollars, 2000–2009	204
9.2	State and Federal Grants to Masters, Pennsylvania, in Current and Constant Dollars, 2000–2009	204
9.3	Consumer Price Index (CPI): All Urban Consumers, 1990–2008	206
9.4	State and Federal Grants to Masters, Pennsylvania, as a Percentage of Revenue, 2000–2009	208
9.5	Yearly Percentage Change in State and Federal Grants to Masters, Pennsylvania, in Constant Dollars, 2000–2009	208
9.6	Index of State and Federal Grants to Masters, Pennsylvania, 2000–2009	210
9.7	Spending by Function and Level of Government, 1995	222
10.1	Projected Demographic Profile of New Community	229
10.2	Relative Issue Positions	238
10.3	Availability of Resources	239
10.4	Potential for Policy Influence	240
10.5	Ranking of Resources	240
10.6	Calculated Policy Influence	241
11.1	Tourist Population of Masters, Pennsylvania	257
11.2	Calculation of Quarterly Adjustment Factors	258
11.3	Seasonally Adjusted Quarterly Tourist Population	258
11.4	Calculation of Yearly Adjustment Factors	260
11.5	Trend-adjusted Quarterly Tourist Population	260
11.6	Quarterly Series on the Number of Tourists Visiting Masters, Pennsylvania	262
12.1	Population over Time	277
12.2	Calculations for a Straight-line Regression Equation	278
12.3	Calculation of R^2	280
12.4	Calculations for Tests of Significance	286
12.5	Per Capita Federal Grant Expenditures	288
12.6	Setting Up an Intercept Dummy Variable	290
12.7	Expenditures on Drug Rehabilitation Programs	292
12.8	Setting Up Slope Dummy Variables	294
12.9	Comparison of Estimated Data	296
12.10	Budget Deficit as a Percentage of GDP (five-year average)	297
12.11	Transformation of Data for the Estimation of a Quadratic Equation Form	298
12.12	Yearly Crime Statistics	312
13.1	Hypothetical Expected Payoff Matrix for President Ford's Response to Possible Swine Flu Epidemic	323
13.2	Estimated Flood Damage with and without Flood Wall	325

13.3	Estimated Flood Damage with Flood Wall and Levee	327
13.4	Total Estimated Cost of Flood Wall and Levee	330
13.5	Payoff Matrix for Mayor and Garbage Collectors' Union	334
13.6	Possible Days of Allied Bombing	336
13.7	The Prisoner's Dilemma	338
14.1	Benefits and Costs of Convention Center	349
14.2	Comparison of Costs and Benefits for Projects A and B	357
14.3	Contradictory Decision Based on Net Difference and Benefit-Cost Ratio	364
14.4	Costs and Benefits of Library Facilities	365
14.5	Costs and Benefits of Library Facilities, Ranked According to Benefit-Cost Ratio	365
15.1	Steps in Conducting an Effective Analysis	374

FIGURES

1.1	Goals and Their Trade-offs	15
1.2	World Military Spending	22
2.1	Four Models of Policymaking	31
2.2	Alternative Responses to Value Conflict	34
3.1	The Foundation of Economic Reasoning: Market Equilibrium	48
3.2	Marginal Utility and Consumer Surplus	50
3.3	Rent Seeking	57
4.1	The Policy Cycle	76
4.2	The Pluralist Model of Agenda Setting	77
4.3	The Elitist Model of Agenda Setting	81
4.4	The Subgovernmental Model of Agenda Setting	82
4.5	Decision and Nondecision in Policy Formulation	90
4.6	Impact of External Shocks on Policy Coalitions	93
5.1	The Pareto Principle	107
5.2	Methodology for Policy Analysis	110
5.3	Solomon Four-Group Experimental Design	111
5.4	Post-test-only Control Group Design	112
6.1	Class Divisions in Presidential Voting, 1952–2004	132
6.2	A Symmetric Distribution	134
6.3	Distribution with an Extreme Value	135
6.4	Distribution with the Modal Value	136
6.5	The Effects of Different Dispersions	138
6.6	The Range, the Midspread, and Hinges	139
6.7	Example of a Symmetric Distribution	142
6.8	Comparison of Symmetric and Asymmetric Series	143
6.9	Stem-Leaf Method and Histogram	145

6.10	The Extent of Correlation between Two Variables	146
6.11	The Nature of Correlation	146
7.1	Probability and the Number of Tries	151
7.2	Plot of Probability Distribution	154
7.3	Normal Distributions with Different Means	154
7.4	Normal Distributions with Various Levels of Dispersion	155
7.5	Standard Normal Distribution	155
7.6	One-tailed Test	159
7.7	Two-tailed Test and Confidence Interval	161
8.1	Measuring the English Shoreline	179
8.2	Errors in Sampling	181
8.3	Random Sampling Errors	185
8.4	Searching with the Computer	194
9.1	State and Federal Grants to Masters, Pennsylvania, in Current Dollars, 2000–2009	205
9.2	State and Federal Grants to Masters, Pennsylvania, in Current and Constant Dollars, 2000–2009	207
9.3	State and Federal Grants to Masters, Pennsylvania, as a Percentage of Local Government Tax Revenue, 2000–2009	209
9.4	Yearly Percentage Change in State and Federal Grants to Masters, Pennsylvania, in Constant Dollars, 2000–2009	210
9.5	Yearly Percentage Change in State and Federal Grants to Masters, Pennsylvania, by Indexing, 2000–2009	211
9.6	Expenditures on a Drug Prevention Program in Masters, Pennsylvania	212
9.7	Ratio of Nonwhite to White Unemployment Rate	218
9.8	Ratio of Nonwhite to White Unemployment Rate (stretched graph)	219
9.9	Ratio of Nonwhite to White Unemployment Rate (elongated vertical axis)	219
9.10	Ratio of Nonwhite to White Unemployment Rate (1960, 1970, and 1980)	220
9.11	Ratio of Nonwhite to White Unemployment Rate (1960, 1970, and 1980; shortened vertical axis)	220
9.12	African Elephant Population, 1980–1990	221
10.1	Trend Projection versus Causal Prediction	226
10.2	Problems of Single-Factor Projection	231
10.3	Relative Issue Positions on Public Funding of AIDS Information	239
10.4	Expected Payoff of the Government and Its Opposition	243
10.5	Dynamics of the Policy Outcome	244
11.1	Number of Tourists in Masters, Pennsylvania	250
11.2	Linear Trend Patterns	251
11.3	Horizontal, or No-Trend, Pattern	251
11.4	Seasonal Trend Pattern	252

11.5	Effects of Economic Cycles	252
11.6	Discerning Trend Patterns in the Tourist Data from Masters, Pennsylvania	253
11.7	Quadratic Trends	254
11.8	Exponential Trends	255
11.9	Logistic Trend	255
11.10	Catastrophic Trend	256
11.11	Plot of Number of Tourists per Quarter	257
11.12	Plot of Seasonally Adjusted Quarterly Data	259
11.13	Plot of Trend-adjusted Tourist Data	261
11.14	Adjusted and Unadjusted Data on Tourists Visiting Masters, Pennsylvania	264
12.1	U.S. Gross Domestic Product per Capita (in 1972 constant dollars)	272
12.2	Time-series Model	273
12.3	Errors of Estimation	274
12.4	The Problems of Summing the Errors	275
12.5	Explanation of a Straight-line Equation	276
12.6	Population Trend	279
12.7	Curve of Normal Distribution	281
12.8	Increasing Accuracy of Estimated Coefficients	287
12.9	Abrupt Shift in a Series	289
12.10	Shift in Expenditure Pattern	290
12.11	Plot of Trend in Government Expenditures for Drug Rehabilitation	293
12.12	Comparison of Estimated Trend Lines	295
12.13	Publicly Held Federal Debt as a Percentage of GDP: Linear Estimation	298
12.14	Publicly Held Federal Debt as a Percentage of GDP: Quadratic Estimation	299
12.15	Prediction with a Third-degree Polynomial	300
12.16	Symmetry Forced by a Quadratic Form	300
12.17	Double-Log Functional Forms	302
12.18	The Inverse Form	303
12.19	Errors of Prediction	310
13.1	Hypothetical Decision Tree for Swine Flu Threat	323
13.2	Decision Tree for Swine Flu	324
13.3	Probability of Flood Damage	326
13.4	Decision Tree for Flood Control	326
13.5	Expanded Decision Tree for Flood Control with Levee Option	328
13.6	Decision Tree for Flood Control with Total Expected Costs	329
13.7	Risk and Payoff in a Television Game Show	331
13.8	Strategies in the Battle of the Bismarck Sea	335
13.9	Decision Tree for Allied Strategy in the Battle of the Bismarck Sea	336
14.1	Classification of Costs and Benefits	348
14.2	Consumer Surplus and Social Benefits	350
14.3	Time Preference and Discount Rate	357

14.4   Plot of Present Values as a Function of Discount Rates   359
14.5   The Effects of Choosing a Time Horizon   360
14.6   The Internal Rate of Return   363

"A CASE IN POINT"

Moral Hazard and the Banking Crisis   10
What Do You Mean by Government Efficiency, Equity, and Liberty?   17
The Numb and Number: The Exploding Domain of Public Policy Analysts   29
Ignored Advice and the Global War on Terror   33
The Saboteur, the Whistleblower, and the Loyal Protester   36
Poverty in America: Contrasting Perspectives   40
Too Big to Fail: How Monopolies Can Hold the Government Hostage   54
Drug Policy: Our Addiction to Failure?   58
College Affordability: Should Government Intervene?   60
Trading Pollution: Simulating the Market   71
What's in a Name? The Case of the Mexican Swine Flu Pandemic   78
The Power of a Focus Event: Making Schools Safe   84
Halliburton and Government Patronage: Rent Seeking during the War   118
Do You Give a Dam? The Fate of the Snail Darter   121
Probability in Baseball: Revenge of the Nerds   152
Errors of Observation: The Hawthorne Experiment   183
Focus Group for Growth Management Policies   191
Politics and Government Statistics   197
The Politics of Data Collection: The Case of Terrorism Research   198
Racial Profiling   212
Digging Deep into the Numbers: A Stolen Election?   216
Single-Factor Analysis: The Fiscal Impact of Illegal Immigration in
        San Diego County   231
The Use of the Delphi Technique in Devising a Public Policy Curriculum   236
Fighting over a Fiction? The Budget Surplus in the Presidential Debate   266
Campaign Contributions and Judicial Impartiality: How Regression
        Analysis Can Help   282
Who Wins Olympic Medals? Beijing 2008   308
Risky Business: Orange County Bankruptcy   332
Fitting Seat Belts in Texas School Buses   367

Preface

I began writing the first edition of this book in early 2000. Since then, the world of public policy has felt the shock of several catastrophic national and international events. At the start of the decade, anxiety surrounded the turn of the new millenium (dubbed Y2K), and the stress of a contested presidential election followed shortly. The devastating attacks of 9/11 shocked the world in 2001 and led the United States to protracted wars in Afghanistan and Iraq. Nature demonstrated its fury with a tsunami in Asia in 2004 that killed more than 200,000 people, and with Hurricane Katrina in 2005, whose aftermath exposed grave social problems in the United States. There were concerns about global warming heating up not only the world but also the political climate in America. Finally, in the waning days of the decade, the world experienced the worst economic decline since the Great Depression. No wonder the December 7, 2009 issue of *Time* carried the cover story "The Decade from Hell."[1] These momentous events have led to policy conundrums, exposing the vulnerability of our most strongly held beliefs about what the government should do.

The cover of a July 2009 issue of the *Economist* featured a picture of a melting textbook on "modern economic theory," evoking Salvador Dali's surreal melting clocks, with the caption "Where it went wrong—and how the crisis is changing it."[2] It is hard to believe that about a year earlier, newly minted economists fresh out of universities were being hired by hedge funds with unlimited money and matching ambition to develop complex models of market behavior based on the traditional assumptions of human behavior. We believed that we had tamed the monster called the "market" by reducing it to a finite number of stylized, interconnected components. Yet, as demonstrated by the economic crisis, the rough edges of reality can cut deeply into our ability to manage the vast outside world.

Meanwhile, however, there was a sea change of ideas taking place. As one part of the academic and policy world remained rooted in tradition, another was changing rapidly. Several disciplines—from behavioral economics and decision sciences to social psychology and cognitive sciences—were shedding new light on the complexities of the human mind. With these advances in knowledge, along with the exposure of the vulnerability of traditional positivism, which sees human beings as "rational" actors, a number of related disciplines have been paving a new way of looking at the policy world. This second edition attempts to sort out this confusion and the complexities of finding the right policy prescription. It emphasizes that policy analysis is less a slavish creed than a prism through which to understand the world. This world is devoid of a single optimal solution and the corresponding ability to engineer all its sides; it is a world in which there is perhaps no right answer, only compromises among conflicting goals, aspirations, interests, and ideologies.

To this end, I have completely revised the first chapter to more fully explore the complex relationship of human behavior to public policy, as well as the social goals that government must balance in its crafting of policy. Additionally, chapter 2 has undergone a thorough revision; the political and ethical forces in policy analysis receive special consideration as I discuss the tools and structure of the field. I also have added a final chapter that offers some straightforward, practical suggestions for aspiring (and established) policy analysts. Finally, readers will note the inclusion of an excerpt from a Government Accountability Office report on poverty in Appendix A, as well as several end-of-chapter exercises that refer to it. This report serves as a valuable starting point for a real-world policy analysis, and I encourage readers to reflect on the issues I bring up throughout the book as they peruse the report.

In addition to updating and streamlining the content of all chapters, I have added many new "Case in Point" features. In choosing these cases, drawn from all areas of public policy, I have used the dual criteria of relevance and student interest. I have made sure that the cases show the practicality of the topics under discussion, and I have made every attempt to make the narratives of interest to students. Books don't dream, but their authors do: I fervently hope that these cases generate discussion and debate not only within the structured classroom, but also outside in the hallways, in the parking lots, and in front of the elevators. After teaching for more than three decades, I strongly believe that students excel only when they take an active interest, which is generated when they discover the real-life relevance of what they are learning in classrooms.

Since the aim of this book is to present a comprehensive picture of policy analysis, I had to be mindful of its size and coverage. As a result, I decided to move the old chapter 12, "Models of Causal Prediction: Multiple Regression," to Appendix B. Multiple regression and causal prediction are introduced in chapter 12 of this edition, but instructors who would like to draw upon the more extensive discussion of these topics from the previous edition will find it in the appendix.

While I have made some serious changes in preparing this second edition, I have not altered the fundamental orientation of the original volume. In the vast marketplace of public policy texts, nearly all of which are written from a particular perspective, this book stands virtually alone in its pursuit of a comprehensive outlook. By looking at numerous syllabi collected from many institutions of higher learning, I have made the prosaic discovery that almost nobody uses a single textbook when teaching public policy; some emphasize the ethical considerations and some the economic principles, some concentrate on the policy process, some stress the methodology of analysis, some focus on statistical tools, and others teach public policy courses as case studies of actual policies. It is my hope that when instructors use this text, they will be able to expand it to their desired ends by incorporating other great books available in the market.

In the construction of my ideas I have benefited a great deal from many of my friends and colleagues and, thanks to the modern technology of the Internet, students from many parts of the world. Among the former group, my intellectual debt to C. Richard Hofstetter, Madhavi McCall, and Ron King runs deep. Among the latter, I have received many constructive comments from students, including one from New Zealand who complained that in the previous edition I did not draw the map of Papua New Guinea accurately. In this current edition, an accurate map of the island has replaced the "glob." I also benefited from the candid feedback of several reviewers commissioned by CQ Press: Matthew Cahn, California State University, Northridge; Amy Dreussi, University of Akron; Kurt Gaubatz, Old Dominion University; Mark

Imperial, University of North Carolina Wilmington; Robert Stoker, George Washington University; and Jill Tao, University of Hawaii. I am also thankful to James Kelly for an extremely professional editing job.

Finally, I must acknowledge my good luck. A decade ago, my good karma brought an energetic and highly competent editor (any author's dream), Charisse Kiino, to my office for an unscheduled appointment, which resulted in the writing of the book. For this revised edition, my good karma still held; I was ably aided by Allison McKay. Without her active help and support, this version of the book might not have been completed.

Notes

1. Andy Serwer, "The Decade from Hell—and Why the Next One Will Be Better," *Time*, December 7, 2009.
2. "What Went Wrong with Economics," *The Economist*, July 18–24, 2009, www.economist.com/printedition/displayStory.cfm?Story_ID=14031376.

1 Reason, Rationality, and Public Policy: The Puzzle of Human Behavior

GOVERNMENT IN OUR LIVES

In "Tradition," the opening number of the hit Broadway musical turned movie *Fiddler on the Roof*, Tevye the milkman introduces the rabbi as the most important person in the tiny Jewish village of Anatevka: "[The rabbi] tells us what to eat, when to eat, how to dress, when to pray." The audience wonders about this distant land and its alien customs. Life in this nineteenth-century village seems so different from modern life in our own country; here, no one tells us how to live. Or do they? Upon reflection, we realize that an outside force shapes practically every aspect of our lives. In the modern world the government regulates almost everything we breathe, touch, use, ride, inject, and ingest, from our birth to our death. The government sets air and water quality standards and criteria for serving food and administering drugs. It levies taxes, circulates currency, makes education policy, and resolves questions of our personal welfare. The government tries to protect us by keeping law and order. It maintains a military to keep us safe from attack. It even passes laws affecting the most personal aspects of our lives, including laws regulating sexual behavior. State governments determine the age of consent, prohibit or permit same-sex marriages, and define acceptable sexual practices. It would be difficult, if not impossible, to list all the government regulations and standards to which we must adhere in our daily lives.

Consider, for example, the birth of a baby. The hospital must follow strict rules and regulations governing medical equipment, medicines, and medical personnel. The parents must register the child's birth. When they leave the hospital and get into the family car, they cannot simply place the newborn on the mother's lap. In many states, the infant must be strapped into an approved car seat. Similarly, when we die, many government regulations tell us how our family may dispose of our remains. Imagine how long the list would be if you wrote down all the ways government policies have touched your life since you got out of bed this morning.

The government does not make public policies in a vacuum. Its control over its citizens depends on several factors that determine what are and what are not acceptable domains of public policy. These factors include the nation's norms, values, culture, history, traditions, constitution, and technological sophistication. Together, these factors form the environment in which public policies are made. In the United States and other Western nations, the rights of the individual reign supreme; citizens challenge immediately any policy that impinges on these rights. Therefore, policymakers seek to uphold individual rights. In contrast, in collective societies ruled by national religions or communism, lawmakers value the needs of the group more highly than the rights of individuals. In making public policy, such societies seek to uphold not the rights but the duties of citizens. Some countries arrest those who do not pray during specified times of public prayer, or impose fines for violating the Sabbath. Other countries severely curtail the right of political expression. Although most Western countries consider property rights sacred, other nations balance these rights against competing national goals, such as eliminating poverty or meeting society's general needs, as defined by the political elite.

The extent to which government intrudes in the lives of its citizens is partly determined by technology. As technology advances, so does society's need for regulations. A simple agrarian society requires minimal government intervention. However, today's complex world, characterized by rapid changes in technology—from the Internet to genetically altered food, from the possibility of cloning animals and humans to the specter of global warming caused by unrestrained human activities—demands regulations with increasing urgency.

In the wide-open field of public policy analysis, the analyst performs a high-stakes balancing act. Like the fiddler perched precariously on a slippery roof, playing his fiddle, public policy analysts ply their trade by balancing a number of competing demands, confusing perceptions, and other pitfalls of scientific reasoning.

POLITICS AND RATIONALITY

Politics is sometimes defined as deciding "who gets what, when, and how." In a democratic free market system, government allocates scarce resources among competing demands. In giving someone or some group something, government often has to take it from someone else. As a result, society is always rife with conflict. The study of politics allows us to understand the process by which actors receive government-allocated public goods, while the study of *public policy* lets us understand the rationale for the allocation. In other words, it adds to the four questions—*who, what, when,* and *how*—the fifth important question of *why*. Policy analysts provide the rationale and draw up the roadmap for the allocation of goods, advising the decision makers—elected public officials—regarding the proper course of action. In order to understand the rationale of allocation, however, we must begin with an understanding of **rationality**.

Do you consider yourself to be a rational individual? Of course you do. Few of us would admit to being otherwise. Although we take it for granted and use it in our everyday parlance, what does the term *rational* really mean? To most of us, being "rational" means analyzing a situation based on logic, without any interference from emotion or instincts. Separation of emotion from reason has been the cornerstone of Western philosophy. Plato, René Descartes, and Immanuel Kant all proclaimed that what separates humanity from all other species on Earth is our ability to overcome natural instincts and emotion. Following this tradition, Adam Smith, the father of modern economics, in his 1776 book *The Wealth of Nations*, assumed that everyone is a "rational" actor. His assumption was based on three principles: (1) each of us is aware of what is best for us; (2) our behavior is dictated by the simple principle that we act when the benefit of an action is greater than the corresponding cost; and (3) among various alternatives, we choose the one that gives us the most benefit compared with the cost. Smith argued, "It always is and must be the interest of the great body of the people to buy whatever they want of those who sell it cheapest. The proposition is so very manifest, that it seems ridiculous to take any pain to prove it."[1]

Thus, Smith rhetorically asked, if you are in a shop to buy a piece of cloth and one is more expensive than the other, will you spend more money to get an identical product? Obviously not. If you are a seller and you ask for more money for your product than your competitors, nobody will buy from you. On the other hand, if you are offering a price that is less than market value, the demand for your product will be so overwhelming that you will be forced to raise your prices. (For a fuller explanation of this supply-and-demand process, see chapter 3.) In a free market, therefore, nobody can get more than what the market will bear. To Adam Smith, the market process was not only inherently the most efficient but also the fairest: nobody will be able to get more or less than what he or she deserves. This market process is rational, since you don't make your market decisions according to emotions; rather, you buy or sell according to the market price. You may cooperate with another person, but only on the basis of your self-interest. When we all behave in our best individual interest, the market achieves its greatest point of efficiency and reaches the pinnacle of distributive justice. Adam Smith called this process the **invisible hand**, which solves all market-related problems through the working of an unseen force, greater than the wisdom of any one individual or group. This force is always impersonal, totally impartial, often cruel, but, in the end, always fair. Therefore, the best course of action for the government is to interfere as little as possible in the natural course of the market, only providing internal security through maintaining the rule of law and protecting the nation from external threats.

Unfortunately, however, as we will see in the following chapters, the market does not always behave "efficiently." The shortcomings of the market were clearly exposed during the Great Depression of the 1930s. Economists, starting with John Maynard Keynes, pointed out that at certain times the market fails to correct itself, and the government must step in to remedy market inefficiency through regulation, restriction, or direct infusion of money. Keynes's economic theories shaped our economic policies during the Great Depression and laid the foundation for the Obama administration's efforts to stimulate the lagging economy in 2009.

In the policy world, the identification of a social need, caused by market inefficiency, usually starts in the political arena. Let us take a hypothetical example to illustrate this process of rational decision making, which is also often called the **policy cycle**. We will have an opportunity to examine this policy cycle in greater detail in chapter 4.

TABLE 1.1	Ranking of Nations Based on Academic Performance of 15-Year-Olds

Math (2006)	Reading (2003)
1. Finland	1. Finland
2. South Korea	2. South Korea
3. The Netherlands	3. Canada
4. Switzerland	4. Australia
5. Canada	5. New Zealand
6. Japan	6. Ireland
7. New Zealand	7. Sweden
8. Belgium	8. The Netherlands
9. Australia	9. Belgium
10. Denmark	10. Norway
11. Czech Republic	11. Switzerland
12. Iceland	12. Japan
13. Austria	13. Poland
14. Germany	14. France
15. Sweden	**15. United States**
16. Ireland	16. Denmark
17. France	17. Iceland
18. United Kingdom	18. Germany
19. Poland	19. Austria
20. Slovak Republic	20. Czech Republic
21. Hungary	21. Hungary
22. Luxembourg	22. Spain
23. Norway	23. Luxembourg
24. Spain	24. Portugal
25. United States	25. Italy

Source: National Governors Association, Council of Chief State School Officers, and Achieve, Inc., "Benchmarking for Success: Ensuring U.S. Students Receive a World-class Education," 2008, www.nga.org/Files/pdf/0812BENCHMARKING.PDF. © National Governors Association. Reproduced by permission of the National Governors Association. Further reproduction prohibited.

It is an easily demonstrable fact that education is the key to economic success. Yet as Table 1.1 shows, the standardized test scores of high school students in the United States are among the lowest compared with other developed countries. Since the academic preparation of our youth determines the future prosperity of the country, let us suppose that this has prompted the president of the United States to ask the Department of Education (ED) to develop appropriate policies to increase the scores by a certain percentage within a specific time frame. The policy analysts in the ED accept the task and proceed to formulate appropriate policy prescriptions.

Policy analysts begin work by observing the real world and collecting relevant data to measure where we are at this particular point in time and where we need to be at the end of the policy period. Therefore, the policy formulation process begins by collecting data on current student performance. Once armed with those data, the analysts will consider alternative plans to bridge this performance gap, since there is no single "correct" method for achieving the policy goal. These **alternatives** might include strategies such as providing additional funds for hiring qualified teachers, appointing educators to improve the curriculum, increasing the time students spend in school, emphasizing charter schools, starting after-school tutoring programs, working with parents to instill the value of education in their children, or even providing greater assistance to school lunch programs so that poor children are not distracted by hunger.[2]

The next step toward a scientific analysis is to develop a **model**. A model is a scaled version of complex reality that allows us to test our hypotheses regarding cause and effect. The ED analysts will take each alternative and project how it will improve test scores—we will discuss these methods of projection at length in later chapters. The foundation of scientific reasoning lies in our ability to test the validity of hypotheses with empirical evidence. The eminent philosopher of science Karl Popper called this **falsifiability**. For example, the hypothesis that hiring better prepared teachers is the most cost-effective way of improving students' performance is falsifiable—it can be proven false with contrary evidence. In contrast, questions regarding the existence of God, the soul, or spirits, which cannot be observed, measured, or tested, are essentially beyond the scope of scientific inquiry.

Based on the projected costs and benefits produced by the models, the ED analysts will make their recommendations to the president, who will propose a course of action. Once legislators are able to pass a bill on the action, and the president signs it into law, money starts flowing from the treasury to fund the new policy. This is the beginning of the implementation stage of the policy cycle. After the policy is formulated, legislated, adopted, and implemented, the analysts evaluate the results against evidence from the real world. Did the policy achieve its goals? What did we learn from our experience? In policy analysis, this step is known as evaluation research.

This process sounds simple and makes sense. If we were all "rational" beings, in the strict economic sense of the term, social concerns would be readily validated by data, models would produce irrefutable projections of costs and benefits, and the most efficient policy would be adopted and implemented without any dissent. In short, we would achieve our policy goals. Unfortunately, as we will see, at each stage of the process our lives become complicated as the precepts of "rationality" are violated. Let us now see why this eminently "reasonable" description of policy analysis becomes convoluted in actual life.

THE WORLD OF THE "RATIONAL FOOL"

Adam Smith took it for granted that we are all eminently rational.[3] And why not? Individuals are selfish—they are motivated by self-interest. This assumption of human nature permeates political discourse and is enshrined in our Constitution. It is so commonplace that we are barely conscious of this underlying assumption of human nature while discussing public policies.[4] Yet how valid is such an assumption? Political scientist George Lakoff points out, "Most of us have inherited a theory of mind dating back at least to the Enlightenment, namely, that reason is conscious, literal, logical, unemotional, disembodied, universal, and functions to serve our interests. This theory of human reason has been shown to be false in every particular, but it persists."[5] Since public policies aim at altering individual behavior, their formulation requires us to understand the roots of motivation; we need to know what incentive will nudge people to act in a certain way. Thus, the Nobel laureate economist Amartya K. Sen, in his influential essay "Rational Fools," points out that "universal selfishness as *actuality* may be false, but universal selfishness as a requirement of *rationality* is patently absurd."[6]

Over the past few decades, research from fields as diverse as biology, cognitive science, primate behavior, social psychology, and even experimental economics has painted a much more complex picture of this intensely social being. In this chapter, I will argue that the two interrelated obstacles to the rational model of policy analysis arise out of our own nature and the society we have created as a consequence. Specifically, I will show that

- the assumption of a self-utility-maximizing being leads us to a logical contradiction, particularly when it comes to the provision of public goods, the core of public policy analysis;
- as social and emotional beings, we often understand the world in profoundly different ways; and
- group identities are extremely important in the understanding of the public policy process.

The Illogic of a "Rational Being"

The concept of a perennially self-utility-maximizing human being, the fundamental building block of economics, presents a strong logical contradiction when it comes to the provision of public goods, the core subject matter of this book. Before I present my arguments, let me first define the term **public good**.

We can classify all goods with the help of two characteristics, **excludability** and **exhaustibility**, which is also called the **rivalrous** quality of a good (see Table 1.2). If your friend asks to borrow this book from you, you can say no, since this is your own copy and you have every right to deny access to it (although you may not have a friend much longer). In contrast, if the book belongs to the library, after your time is up, your friend has an equal right to borrow it. The difference between these two cases lies in the book's excludability; a user can exclude others from using certain types of goods. Exhaustibility, on the other hand, depends on whether the utility of a good to its user goes down when an additional user joins in. In other words, is there any rivalry in the good's use? For example, if you are driving down the highway, your ability to use the highway does not go down simply because one more car is on the road (the way it does when another person wants to read your book at the same time); thus, the utility of the highway is nonexhaustible. I have provided a matrix in Table 1.2 to classify four types of goods that we enjoy in life.

Let us go back to the example of the book you are reading. If you own it, it is purely a **private good**. You can limit access to it, since sharing it with someone else will decrease its utility to you. You may also decide to buy the book jointly with a few other friends.

TABLE 1.2	**Classification of Goods**	
	Exhaustible (rivalrous)	Nonexhaustible (nonrivalrous)
Excludable	Private goods	Toll goods
Nonexcludable	Club goods (common pooled resources)	Pure public goods

In that case, although it is essentially a private good within your friend circle, you decide to use it as a public good. Everyone within this small group has an equal right to it. In economics, this is known as a **club good** (or, alternatively, a **common pooled resource**), because the benefits of owning it remain within the group, or the "club." On the other hand, there are some goods that are actually meant to be shared, such as a bridge, a road, public transportation, or a national park. Yet because of the possibility of overuse when they are provided free of charge, or because they need to be financed, a toll may be required in order to use them. The fee on a **toll good** restricts its use only to those who are willing to pay and excludes those who are unable or unwilling to do so. Finally, we are left with the category of **pure public goods**. These are goods that must be shared with everyone, even those who cannot or will not pay for their use. Suppose you live in Miami Beach, Florida, a town known for its beautiful beaches. It costs the city (and the local taxpayers) money to provide lifeguards at the public beaches. If I am visiting Miami Beach and, therefore, do not pay city taxes, I am still fully eligible to swim in the ocean under the watchful eyes of the lifeguards, and should I need their services, they will be provided to me equally as to any other local taxpaying citizen.

Among these four types of goods, the question of the allocation of pure public goods is most problematic. For the other three types of goods, there is a strong link between benefits and costs. When you pay for a private good, club good, or toll good, you know what you are getting in return for your money. As a result, consumers are able to adjust their demand according to price. However, when it comes to public goods, the link between benefits received and the price paid is obscure. For example, we pay for clean air, a public good, through our tax dollars that are spent on monitoring the levels of pollutants in the air. We also pay for it through higher prices when, say, a tax is imposed on gasoline, or the government directs oil companies to use less polluting but more expensive additives or forces car manufacturers to install hybrid engines. As we pay directly or indirectly for the quality of the air, we have no control over "how much" clean air we "purchase." Some of us might want cleaner air and be willing to pay a higher price for it, but others would rather keep their costs down. Yet when the government sets air pollution standards, one size must fit all. On top of these variations, there are many poor people or visitors from other nations who also enjoy a clean environment without paying anything at all for it. In other words, the adjusting market mechanism of costs and benefits, which functions for the other three types of goods, does not operate for public goods. As a result, there are constant debates on the best use of government money and the allocation of these public goods.

The aftermath of World War II and the onset of the Cold War era represented a "feel good" time in public policy literature. The contrast between a free market democracy and communism was stark. An overarching sense of triumph was pervasive as American scholars of public policy often predicted the eventual victory of democratic values over the twin evils of dictatorship and communism. It was assumed that a free society, in which every person was dictated to by nothing other than his or her self-interest, would find ways of allocating government-provided goods efficiently and ethically. For example, if there was a need or inefficiency, the citizens would band together, lobby the government, and correct the inefficiency. Suppose the folks in your community noticed that a busy street intersection needed a traffic light. They would immediately form a neighborhood committee, work through the democratic processes, and get the local government to install a traffic light. If the authorities were unresponsive to the popular demand, they would risk getting booted out of office in the next election. How different, people wondered, were lives in a communist or a nondemocratic country, where common people were deprived of their ability to mobilize for collective action.

However, in the late 1960s influential scholar Mancur Olson created a stir by showing that when it comes to the allocation of public goods through individual effort, the assumption of the self-utility-maximizing economic being, or *homo economicus*, runs us into a logical quagmire. Simply put, the problem for Olson was that since the benefits of a public good are not dependent on an individual's effort, why should a rational person—figuring out that she can get something for nothing—contribute toward its procurement? As I drive to school, I listen to National Public Radio (NPR) without paying anything, just as I can to any other station. NPR differs from other radio stations, however, in that a large part of its funding comes from its listeners' contributions. As I contemplate contributing money, I realize that even if I don't contribute a single penny, others will, and I will continue to get something for nothing. Second, I also know that my contribution of "a dollar a day," which is a significant amount in my own finances, will make only a marginal difference in the survival of my favorite station. Taken together, does it make any *economic sense* for me to send in my pledge? Absolutely not. If we all act rationally, no one will choose to contribute to NPR. And as a result, no public good—from a neighborhood streetlight to measures against global warming—would ever be produced. Olson called this dilemma the **free-rider problem**, and in political science, it is also known as the **collective action problem**.[7]

Mancur Olson's work paved the path for brand new ways of looking at society, especially for those who want to know how to make the government more efficient. Among many interrelated issues, we can talk about a few. First, let us consider **moral hazard**.[8] Suppose you know that your insurance policy covers car theft. In that case, what is your incentive to take the extra step to make sure to lock your car doors? To extend this example, when Congress bails out yet another very large bank or an automobile manufacturer, what is the incentive for those receiving bailout money to run an efficient shop if they know that their own risks for bad decisions are close to zero (see "A Case in Point")? What is the guarantee that in a large workplace, some workers will not be tempted to **shirk** their responsibilities, knowing that nobody would find out that they are not pulling their weight?[9] These questions illustrate the problem of moral hazard.

Consider another class of problems. If I make a commitment to you, and there is no oversight and I face no cost for going back on my word, what is my incentive to keep my word when it does not suit my purpose to do so? In other words, if my commitment is not credible, why should anyone trust me? In the literature, this is known as the **credible commitment problem**.[10] For instance, the United States is extremely concerned that Iran might build its own atomic weapon, which might destabilize the entire region. Therefore, in order to dissuade Iran from becoming a nuclear power, the United States threatens "severe consequences" whenever Iran makes a move that indicates its progress toward manufacturing nuclear weapons. Yet in the international arena, particularly facing opposition from Russia and China, the hands of U.S. foreign policymakers are tied. Therefore, without a credible commitment, Iran may soon develop the dreaded weapons.

Finally, the free-rider problem can lead to the **tragedy of the commons**.[11] Imagine a town in which large plots of public land are set aside for grazing cattle. If everybody in the village lets their cattle feed on the grass for a set amount of time, the grass has time to regenerate, and everyone benefits from the continuing use of the land. However, if I keep my cattle on the land a bit longer, then my better fed cattle are fatter, and they fetch a higher price in the market. But if everybody lets their cattle feed for longer hours (since we are all self-utility-maximizing *homo economicus*), we will soon see an environmental catastrophe in which the grass dies out and everybody suffers. Viewed from a different angle, what is my incentive to abide by the rule? If I limit the time my cows are grazing on the public land, but if I am the only one doing so, my noble self-restraint does little to improve the overall condition of the grazing land. Such a situation can be extremely real and pose huge policy problems.

In his book *Collapse*, biologist Jared Diamond shows how the unrestrained pursuit of self-interest brought about an environmental collapse on Easter Island in the Pacific Ocean. When tribes started competing with each other for natural resources on the isolated island, they irrevocably damaged the fragile environment, which did not have the opportunity to regenerate, causing mass starvation, wars, and the death of most Easter Islanders. We can also see the same scenario being played out in our world as unchecked commercial fishing depletes stocks all over the ocean; homeowners do not conserve groundwater and overwater their lawns, which lowers the groundwater to a level where it is nearly impossible to access; or the industries that belch pollutants from their smokestacks help create acid rain that kills many living things in the vicinity. In short, the free-rider problem points to our irresponsible behavior in pursuit of short-term, selfish utility, as well as the need for suitable regulatory action by authorities who are mindful of the welfare of the entire community (a public good).

The "Un-rational Being" and Political Behavior

Insightful as Mancur Olson's arguments are, the timing of his book's publication, in 1965, was a bit ironic. Just as Olson was pointing out why "rational actors" would not participate in a collective action, tumultuous mass movements were occurring in the United States. The 1960s saw the development of the civil rights movement, joined by people of every color who were inspired by Dr. Martin Luther King Jr. and prodded by the sight of racial intolerance in the South. There were also violent movements, such as the Weather Underground organization, an anarchist group that wanted to bring down organized society and its manifest inequalities, and the Black Panthers and the Symbionese Liberation Army, both of which wanted to end segregation through violent means. The members of these groups did not think that their individual actions would bring about social change, and they knew very well that they were risking pain, prison sentences, or even death. Regardless of the validity of their vision, each member set aside his or her personal welfare in order to seek a certain public good, to change the nation in their way. Olson was not oblivious to these developments and thought that many human actions were not based on "rational" calculations. He pointed out, "It is not clear that this is the best way of theorizing about either utopian or religious groups. . . . Where nonrational or irrational behavior is the basis for a lobby, it would perhaps be better to turn to psychology or social psychology than to economics for a

A CASE IN POINT

Moral Hazard and the Banking Crisis

In our economic system commercial banks play a central role by lending money to consumers to buy homes, cars, and other consumer goods, and to businesses for their expansion. If this money spigot is turned off, the entire economic system comes to a grinding halt, yet the banks cannot print money. They depend on us to open accounts and deposit money. Suppose I deposit $100 in a checking account at my neighborhood bank. The bank knows that I will not come back tomorrow and withdraw all my money, so it keeps, say, 10 percent in reserve and lends out $90 to someone who needs to borrow it. When the loan is approved, the bank manager does not come back with a satchel full of money but instead opens a checking account, showing a deposit of $90. The process starts once again, when the bank keeps $9 and lends out $81. If you continue this calculation, you will see that at the end, the bank has created a total of nearly $900 from my $100 deposit. In effect, this is similar to a Ponzi scheme of borrowing from Peter to pay Paul. The banks make money when they lend money and the borrowers pay interest. However, if a significant number of borrowers fail to repay, the bank can fail. Therefore, banks have to be extraordinarily careful and resist the temptation to make risky loans.

The Great Depression began with the failure of a number of banks. As the news spread, people scrambled to get their money. The ensuing panic nearly brought down the entire monetary system. In order to prevent such a catastrophe, the Roosevelt administration created the Federal Deposit Insurance Corporation, which, by taking a small fee from all bank deposits, guaranteed that no individual depositor would lose money up to $100,000 per account. (In 2009, the Obama administration increased this limit to $250,000.) This move calmed the market but created a moral hazard for the banks. Since banks and bank executives make money when they lend, if

relevant theory. The beginning of such a theory may already exist in the concept of "'mass movement'." [12]

Professor Olson was correct. Economists' method of analysis, as their critics point out, assumes that people are rational, predictable, and pretty much the same, regardless of culture, religion, or upbringing. In the four decades since the publication of Olson's book, research in diverse fields has shed new light on the mind of what I call the *un-rational* being. The flip side of the term *rational* is *irrational*, which implies a complete absence of reason or even insanity. We clearly are not so; we are simply not "rational" in the sense that the term is defined in traditional economics. It is important to note that this assumption about human nature plays a significant part in how we devise policies to deal with less desirable behavior. [13] If the assumption regarding a person's motivations is not correct, it may also reflect in the policy that we prescribe to address a pressing social need. *New York Times* columnist David Brooks saw that a faulty assumption about human nature lay at the roots of the policy failure that led to the economic disaster of 2008 and 2009. [14] He points out, "The nation essentially bet its future on economic models with primitive views of human behavior." To Brooks, there is no risk (and cost) to their bad decisions, what is the guarantee that they will not become too greedy and engage in overtly risky business practices?

In order to prevent this, Congress enacted the Glass-Steagall Act of 1933, which created a barrier between commercial and investment banks. The commercial banks were not allowed to invest in the stock and real estate markets, and the investment banks were barred from normal banking operations. The bank executives' excesses created such a public outrage that, a year later, Congress was able to create another important agency to oversee the powerful financial executives—the Securities and Exchange Commission. These measures worked well, but the banks chafed under the regulatory firewall and myriad rules governing their conduct.

The election of conservative president Ronald Reagan (who famously declared that government is not the solution but the problem) in 1980 opened the door for weakening the government's financial regulations. Over time, with the inclusion of banking industry insiders as heads of the agencies, the distinction between regulation and advocacy became blurred. Finally, in 1999, Congress passed and President Clinton signed into law the repeal of the Glass-Steagall Act, thus allowing commercial lenders to trade risky securities. Although there is no unanimity, there is a growing consensus among economists that the roots of the banking crisis of 2008 can be traced to the condition of moral hazard created by weak government oversight and a system that rewarded the banks for taking risks without much thought for the consequences of their actions.

Discussion Points

1. How is the notion of risk involved in the condition of moral hazard?
2. How does government temper the act of regulation in a free market system?
3. Does government intervention in the market amount to socialism?

the blame for the policy failure should be placed on the "policymakers and experts who based estimates of human psychology on mathematical equations." The complexity of the human mind stands in the way of objective scientific inquiry, particularly in the area of public policy. This complexity results from two interconnected concepts: the way social beings understand the world, and the way society influences policy research.

In the Western tradition, it is assumed that rational people keep their emotions separate from the cold calculations of benefits and costs. Cognitive scientist Antonio Damasio would beg to differ.[15] Damasio cites the case of a man he calls Elliott, a successful business executive and a caring family man. After Elliott had a benign tumor removed from the frontal lobe of his brain, he successfully regained all his faculties, awareness, and speech, but he was a completely changed person in a profound way—he was unable to make a decision. Damasio discovered that the surgery had damaged a part of his brain tissue and permanently separated the emotional part of his brain from the analytical part. As a result, Elliott could perfectly analyze a complex situation, but he did not have the emotional backing to make the final decision.

While Damasio examined individual decision-making processes, Drew Westen, another prominent neuroscientist, studied how people make political decisions. During the heated presidential election between George W. Bush and John Kerry in 2004, Westen and his colleagues recruited fifteen diehard Democrats and fifteen diehard Republicans and scanned their brains in order to study how extreme partisans reason when they come face to face with information that directly challenges their strongly held beliefs—in other words, a contradiction between data (facts) and desire (political ideology).[16] The scientists showed participants two slides: The first contained a statement that Bush or Kerry supposedly made (some were true, and others were fabricated), and the second showed another statement that to any reasonable person would seem contradictory. When the partisans saw the obvious contradictions, they reacted very similarly; the part of the brain that controls negative emotions fired up when Republicans saw contradictory statements made by Kerry, and Democrats' brains did the same when Bush's contradictory statements were shown. However, when it came time for their own candidates, a funny thing happened in the brains of both groups. At first a network of neurons that produces distress became active, indicating that the subjects were keenly aware of the contradiction and were distressed by it. However, the brain quickly "registers the conflict between data and desire and begins to turn off the spigot of unpleasant emotion. We know that the brain largely succeeded in this effort, as partisans mostly denied that they had perceived any conflict between their candidate's word and deeds."[17] Even more amazingly, Westen found that "once partisans had found a way to reason to false conclusions, not only did neural circuits involved in negative emotions turn off, but circuits involved in positive emotions turned *on*."[18] In other words, when it comes to politics and public policy, we most often make our decisions using our gut and political instincts, which may or may not involve questions of rationality or self-interest. Thus, emotion is not only legitimate but is also central to political persuasion.

As Westen's experiment demonstrates, people tend to seek affirmation of their core beliefs—especially through news sources that best fit their worldview—and this has resulted in polarization and a deepening of partisanship in the United States.[19] A 2009 Pew Research Center poll shows that the gap in the public's perception of how the president is performing is getting wider with time. Traditionally, a newly elected president enjoys a "honeymoon" period, when Republicans and Democrats set aside their differences and give the incoming administration the benefit of the doubt. For example, a majority of Republicans actually approved of Jimmy Carter's job performance early in his term, and a majority of Democrats backed Richard Nixon at a similar point in his administration. A gap began to emerge when Reagan was elected, after he ran a highly ideological campaign. However, Barack Obama has the biggest partisan gap in his early job approval rating of any president in the past 40 years. The Pew poll shows that 88 percent of Democrats approve of the president, but only 27 percent of Republicans think he's doing a good job—a stunning 61-point gap that demonstrates the polarization between the collective identities of the two parties.[20]

An examination of the "partisan brain" leads us to a discussion of the importance of group formation in our reasoning process. Our brains have evolved to gear us toward forming groups.[21] For instance, social psychologist Henri Tajfel's experiments showed the universal human need to belong to a group and to strive for the group's welfare, even when the act comes at the expense of one's own personal interest. Do you root for a professional sports team? If you do, does your mood depend on how "your team" performs on a specific day? If our teams do badly, some of us get mildly annoyed, some get angry, and some may even become violent, as English soccer fans in the 1980s and 1990s demonstrated.[22] If you think about it, why should anyone be so emotionally wrapped up in what a group of millionaire athletes do on the field playing for their wealthy owners? In many instances, neither the players nor the owners have any permanent loyalty to any city; they often readily change teams or leave town when offered more money or better prospects. Yet so many of us remain loyal fans. Through our identification with a team (as opposed to a single player, such as Tiger Woods or Serena Williams), we exhibit our deep-rooted desire to belong to a group.

This need to have a group identity takes many different forms. Sociologist Benedict Anderson, for instance, points out that many of our cherished feelings, such as patriotism, are based on the creation of an "imagined community."[23] This preference for our groups or communities allows us to overcome the natural inertia of free riding; for example, young men and women—often spurred by patriotism or a sense of civic duty—join the armed services in times of war, knowing full well the risk of being sent to the front lines. We abide by the rules—both official and unofficial—of the "group" of society. Following our group norm, we dutifully lock our car doors even when we know that we are fully insured, we tip a certain percentage of the total bill, and we put in an honest day's work even when there are ample opportunities for shirking. Contrary to the rationality of *homo economicus*, we often behave altruistically toward others.[24] Most of these actions reflect our group behavior.

The formation of group identity is not accidental or random; it is often shaped by the deliberate acts of political leaders. In the political science literature, these leaders are referred to as **political entrepreneurs**, and they range from good to evil, from Gandhi, Lincoln, and Martin Luther King Jr. to Hitler, Stalin, and Osama bin Laden.[25] These political entrepreneurs often mobilize people by **framing** an issue. In psychological terms, a "framer" can change another person's perception of an issue by putting it in a certain context.[26] Take for instance the case of the federal inheritance tax. This tax was set for those who would inherit very large amounts of wealth and is known as the "estate tax." But in the 1990s, conservatives started calling it the "death tax." This new term was designed by a marketing expert to tap into the resentment that many feel toward government in general and taxes in particular. By changing its name, the Republican Party was able to mobilize public opinion, especially among the working class, against the tax.

Our group memberships lead to the formation of what social psychologists call collective identity—in other words, an "us" versus "them" mentality. When we separate ourselves into the categories of allies (the "in group") and enemies (the "out group"), we view the world through partisan glasses, allowing our group affiliations to dominate our rationale. Often this may prompt us to go against our self-interest. For instance, during his presidential campaign, Barack Obama advocated increasing taxes for those making over $250,000 a year. Yet many affluent supporters of Mr. Obama rallied behind him and his economic agenda, even though his tax plan would disadvantage them personally. The fact of the matter is, when we view the world through the prisms of our group affiliations, we often violate the first principle of scientific inquiry: It is not that we observe the world and understand; we often "understand" the world and then observe. If it were otherwise, by the fundamental precept of rationality, we would all come to the same conclusion when presented with the same set of facts. Even when there is no controversy over a fact, we tend to interpret it according to our political affiliations and ideological orientations (as Westen's experiment demonstrated).[27]

In the realm of public policy, group psychology explains consumer behavior during periods of inflation and recession. Take for instance the recent economic downturn, much of which was caused by troubles in the housing sector. The prosperity of the global economy fueled an increased demand for homes. As prices increased and stories of people making huge profits by buying homes and then selling them quickly began to circulate, everyone wanted to get in on the game. Fearing that they would be pushed out of the market, people lined up to buy homes in any way they could, often taking out loans (many of which seemed favorable in the short run, but became very expensive after the periods of "teaser rates" expired). With interest rates on mortgages at an all-time low, the risks of borrowing reduced, and an overabundance of available homes, many people threw caution to the wind—builders built too many houses, banks lent too much money, and homeowners bought too many properties. In short, the herd mentality took root. As the housing market took a sudden downward turn (or if homeowners lost their jobs), many homeowners suddenly faced bankruptcy and financial ruin, and it was inevitable that a large number of them would default on their loans. Indeed, Federal Reserve chair Ben Bernanke has singled out the herd mentality as an element that brought about the catastrophic swings in the market in 2008.[28]

Finally, no discussion of public policy can be complete without noting that the fear factor dominates public discourse on policy changes. Every new policy introduces the prospect of change, and the uncertainty involved in change elicits fear and strong reactions, because of the human tendency to remember impending threats.[29] Fear is most often the primary motivator for collective action that produces the NIMBY (not in my backyard) factor, demonstrated most recently by the highly emotional debates surrounding comprehensive health care reform in the United States. Evolutionary biologists bolster the findings of **prospect theory** offered by Kahneman and Tversky,[30] which simply states that in the process of evaluating the benefits and costs of an action, human beings often place a far greater weight on the fear of a loss than the prospect of a gain. Jonathan Haidt points out, "If you were designing a fish, would you have it respond as strongly to opportunities as to threats? No way. The cost of missing the sign of a nearby predator, however, can be catastrophic. Game over, end of the line of those genes."[31] Any species that is fearless and does not take into account the prospect of a loss is destined to be extinct. Therefore, we must understand the essence of our primordial nature; in most policy debates, fear moves us in a profound way.

In sum, it is interesting to note that while most of us think of ourselves as "freethinking" individuals, our perceptions on issues become colored by many factors, including the groups in which we claim membership and the leaders and opinion makers to whom we listen.[32] We also are guided by inherent moral and ethical concerns. If you recall my example of contributing to NPR, you should note that while there is no "rational" reason for me to contribute money, in reality I do, because I feel that contributing to the broadcast is the "right thing to do." This simple appeal to our internal ethical code propels us to overcome our natural inertia to free ride.

GOVERNMENT'S GOALS AND THEIR IMPACT ON PUBLIC POLICY

If we draw out the concept of Adam Smith's "invisible hand," whereby competition in the free market process makes the government largely unwanted, we reach the ideal world of the libertarian philosophy. However, as we will see in chapter 3, the market process is not without its own shortcomings. Therefore, government intervenes in the market process to provide us with four desired goals: **efficiency, equity, liberty,** and **security.** Yet, as discussed above, these four cherished goals of public policy often imply different things to different people, since our perceptions are colored by our varying ideologies, group affiliations, and economic interests. Plus, as you can see in Figure 1.1, these goals often conflict with one another. The most hotly debated trade-offs are the ones between equity and efficiency and between liberty and security.

However, before discussing the concepts of efficiency, equity, liberty, and security, we should also be mindful of the influence of another extremely important influencing factor: time. Time is important, since everything in life must be evaluated within a certain time period. For example, if I put some money away for my children's college education, I would seek investments where my benefits would peak around the time my children would be graduating from high school. In contrast, if I wanted short-term gains, I would use a different set of investment strategies. Similarly, the same person looking at a public investment at two different points in time may come to two radically different conclusions about its desirability. For instance, when the United States purchased Alaska from Russia for $7.2 million in 1867, the move had severe critics, who saw Alaska as nothing more than a polar bear infested frozen wasteland. However, oil was soon discovered there, and during the Cold War period, Alaska's location was vital to U.S. efforts to monitor and check Soviet power; thus, the

---

FIGURE 1.1   **Goals and Their Trade-offs**

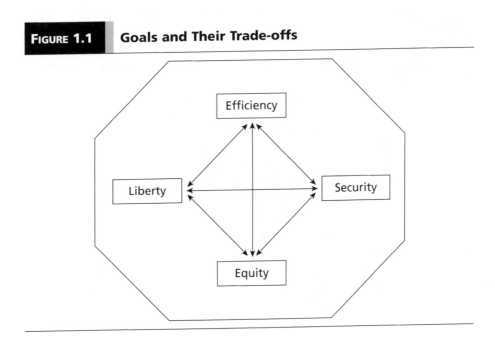

purchase of Alaska became accepted as a prudent use of public money.[33] In contrast, in 2003, when President George W. Bush announced the invasion of Iraq, some polls indicated that his decision was supported by an unprecedented nearly 90 percent of Americans. As U.S. forces became bogged down in a protracted war at a huge cost—both in lives and in money—public support evaporated quickly. With these caveats, let us briefly look at how our individual perceptions as well as group affiliation can color the way we look at public policies.

Efficiency

Of all the good things to which we aspire in public policy, efficiency seems to be the easiest to understand, as well as one of the most important. Efficiency is defined as the ratio between output and input—in other words, "are we getting our money's worth?" This question of efficiency can be measured in two different ways. One way of determining efficiency is by an **absolute measure**: are we getting our money's worth from a specific government expenditure? We can also ask if an expenditure is the most efficient use of money given all other needs. This is referred to as the **relative measure**, or the **opportunity cost**. Take for instance the example of the U.S. government's decision to bail out the failing auto industry in Detroit. As Uncle Sam uses taxpayers' money to shore up General Motors and Chrysler, many people ask whether these are wasted efforts, since much of their problem stems from the fact that U.S. consumers are increasingly purchasing foreign cars. This argument uses the absolute measure of efficiency. If we evaluate the efficiency of the bailout using a relative measure, we would examine the other ways in which the bailout money could be used; for example, that money could have been used to help out the states (which are in dire straits as a result of huge budget deficits), improve education initiatives, or repair crumbling infrastructure. The notion of opportunity cost in public policy debate is perhaps most pronounced in the allocation of money for NASA and the National Endowment for the Arts. Critics point out that while there are so many worthy causes and policy problems on Earth, it would be inefficient to spend money on exploration of the universe or promotion of the arts. These criticisms stem from the agencies' inability to place monetary value on or produce physical evidence of their outputs; thus, it makes it difficult to weigh these outputs against expenditures.

The concept of efficiency is deeply ingrained in our everyday thinking. Yet when we look at it closely, we realize how it can look different from different perspectives, particularly when it comes to what we do in the name of the general public. Some of us assume that government is by nature inefficient, while others see it as a necessary instrument to correct the shortcomings of the market. The chasm between these two camps defines the difference in core beliefs between conservatives and liberals, Republicans and Democrats in the United States. As a result, we engage in endless debates about issues such as "pork barrel spending" (wasteful government spending to satisfy the special interests of politicians) and government efforts to help those who are poor and powerless (or even to act quickly to address a pressing need).[34] Given the sheer number of alternatives and divisions within the nation along the ideological divide, politicians communicate with their respective political bases with "glaring examples" of government waste of public money.

A CASE IN POINT

What Do You Mean by Government Efficiency, Equity, and Liberty?

In 2002 I was lecturing at prestigious Peking University to a group of students and government bureaucrats on the issue of efficiency in public policy. Before I started talking, I asked the audience to raise their hands if they thought the U.S. government was very efficient in implementing the goals of approved public projects. Most hands went up. I told them that in my hometown of San Diego, there is a significant traffic bottleneck. The two major highways run north and south, and there was a critical need to build a connecting road. The road, I told the audience, was placed in the regional master plan in 1958, when in China Mao Zedong's disastrous plan of social engineering, the Great Leap Forward, was beginning to take shape. Yet nearly forty-five years later, the road had not been constructed.[35] A stretch of about six miles had been built, but a series of lawsuits by environmental groups had stopped the construction of a one-mile section in the middle. In the meantime, the city and its population had expanded rapidly, and not only was the connecting road needed for ease of transportation, its absence also posed a serious security threat to citizens in one of the most fire- and earthquake-prone regions of the country. Without the connecting road, any quick evacuation plan would have been in serious jeopardy.

This example was particularly puzzling to the Chinese, who were looking to me, the U.S. expert, to tell them how to increase government efficiency. In a nondemocratic nation, government projects, from highway construction to building colossal dams for hydroelectric projects, are implemented immediately. Visitors to China are amazed at the breakneck speed with which buildings go up in its glittering, modern cities. And thanks to persistent double-digit income growth, the massive country, to its credit, has been able to cut its poverty rate in half over the past three decades. To many, therefore, China epitomizes government efficiency. Others, however, complain that there are hidden human costs in terms of lost liberty. Its critics argue that China's economic progress is possible because the Communist Party attempts to remain in power by silencing all opposition.[36]

Discussion Points

1. Given this contrast, how do you define government efficiency? Do you think the Chinese government is more efficient than the U.S. government?
2. How does government strike a balance between efficiency and equity?

For instance, President Reagan, a conservative, evoked the image of a "welfare queen" in order to rally support during his 1976 campaign. According to Reagan, the welfare queen "has 80 names, 30 addresses, 12 Social Security cards and is collecting veterans benefits on four nonexisting deceased husbands. And she's collecting Social Security on her cards. She's got Medicaid, getting food stamps and she is collecting welfare under each of her names."[37] In contrast, during the presidency of George W. Bush, nothing rallied his opponents like the picture of oil executives or the no-bid contracts granted to Vice President Dick Cheney's former associates at Halliburton to support the war effort in Iraq. These examples, to the minds of the faithful, served as perfect examples of government waste and inefficiency.[38] As you also can tell from these examples, the question of "objectivity" is a slippery concept.[39] Apart from outright corruption and mismanagement, the perception of efficiency often arises out of a group's ideological position.

Another important aspect of government inefficiency, and one that is often overlooked in the literature, is the ability of a democratic government to move quickly. This has been a source of heated debate among those who study the process of economic development and democratization in the countries of the developing world. As we contemplate the question posed in my example of highway construction in the United States (see "A Case in Point"), it shows that democracies are, by their very design, inefficient. This "planned inefficiency" is also known as the system of "checks and balances." Because no one has the supreme authority to push a nation to accept any single vision, democracies are often seen as vacillating, chaotic, inefficient, and mired in bureaucratic red tape. This debate has taken on a much bigger global context and rests at the core of a comparison between the processes of development in authoritarian China and democratic India.[40]

Equity

There are few, if any, on Earth who oppose equity as a policy goal. The equity of every human is enshrined as a "self-evident truth" in the U.S. Declaration of Independence. But what did equity really mean to the Founders? In their nascent nation, women, slaves, and white men who did not own property were not allowed to vote. Although significant progress has been made in gender and racial equity, the meaning of equity remains vague today.

Suppose you are engaged in developing admissions standards for a very competitive state university. Since this is a state university and the bulk of its funding comes from the taxpayers of the state, should you make an immediate distinction between in-state and out-of-state students? This is a matter of equity based on *membership*. If I am a citizen of the state, whether I pay taxes or not—even if I am too poor to pay taxes—you may think that my candidacy to attend the school should be judged by different admissions and tuition standards.

The question of equity is also closely intertwined with the notion of *eligibility:* who is eligible to receive public goods? You could base eligibility on merit using a certain academic standard, which may include high school grade point average, the quality of a written essay, or standardized test scores. So, have you defined equity through defining merit? Not quite. In your effort to make admissions standards equitable, you will have to determine the relative weights you will place on the three areas of consideration. If you place too much emphasis on grade point average, you will be reminded that not all high schools have similar standards of grading and competition. A very high grade from a school with a poor performance record may not measure up against those from high-performing schools. Should you therefore take into account the relative standing of the schools? What about the essay? While we might think it surely reflects a student's ability to think critically and articulate properly, unfortunately some students get help from their parents, friends, or even paid "essay consultants." So, perhaps we should place the most weight on SAT scores? Alas, even setting aside lingering doubts about the ability of SAT scores to predict a student's performance in college, standardized tests contain a number of systematic biases. Race, gender, ethnicity, religious affiliation, first-generation language skills, as well as parents' educational levels all play a role in determining the average test score of a candidate. You may take into account not only the current disadvantages, but also the lingering effects of past discrimination.

Finally, in your admission criteria you may consider applicants whose parents or siblings have attended or are currently attending the school. These "legacy" applicants receive special consideration, even when they don't meet the strict measures of merit. Since most of these students come from particularly successful parents who may have given a lot of money to the university, it may be considered not only a good business practice but also fair to admit them, even if their academic achievement doesn't measure up to that of other incoming students.

As you can see, each of these special considerations is bound to raise strong opinions on all sides. As a result, even a seemingly straightforward application of "equity" runs into all sorts of controversies.

The Equity-Efficiency Trade-off

During his campaign for president, Barack Obama vowed that he would give a tax break to 95 percent of American wage earners but would increase taxes on the top 5 percent, who earn more than $250,000. The Republicans saw elements of "class warfare" in his position and bitterly complained that such a move amounted to a tax on "success." Their debate rests at the core of the trade-off between efficiency and equity.

Those on the right point out that the capitalist system is based on individual initiative and entrepreneurship in a free market. If I know that I am going to have to share my profits with the government, where is my incentive to take risks, work hard, and do better than everybody else? If we stifle such initiatives don't we strike at the heart of efficiency? If, by trying to redistribute income, we slow the pace of economic growth, then the equity in the distribution of income comes at the expense of market efficiency.

The left responds by saying that over the past twenty-five years, the income distribution in the United States has become exceedingly skewed in favor of the rich. Such a concentration of income not only gives economic power to a small group of oligarchs, it also gives them an undue share of political power. Furthermore, they argue that the money people can keep after taxes is not their only source of motivation. Our work is often the source of our satisfaction. We also have other needs, including the need to belong and to have a secure future not only for ourselves but also for our children. Thus when people work hard, they also seek these other nonmonetary ends, which may not hamper their desire to work hard even if they face higher taxes.

In contrast to those who see an inevitable trade-off between equity and efficiency, others have argued that when we look at economic growth over the long term, the apparent zero-sum game between equity and efficiency seems to disappear. Nations with a large middle class are inherently more stable than those with extremes of income.[41] They further point out that Japan as well as many European countries enjoy high rates of economic growth despite having much higher tax rates (and more social programs) than the United States.

Liberty

"Give me liberty or give me death." In the face of an impending attack by British forces in 1775, Patrick Henry made this impassioned declaration and secured his firm place as one of the original American patriots. *Freedom* is one of the most overused terms in American political rhetoric, and the Statue of Liberty stands as the most recognized symbol of the entire nation. Yet our liberty is not absolute. Although we have the right to free speech, we cannot yell "Fire!" in a movie theater or smoke in many public places. The nineteenth-century English philosopher John Stuart Mill argued in his famous essay "On Liberty" that a man should be allowed to do whatever he wants to do—unless it harms others in the process. That is, the state must intervene and our liberty must be curtailed if in our pursuit of happiness we imperil others' well-being.

On the face of it, the notion of preventing someone from doing harm to others as a rationale for state interference seems fairly obvious. However, this harm is not confined to the physical integrity of a person or property. Think about the case of same-sex marriage or polygamy. Several states have passed referenda declaring marriage as a union solely between a single woman and a single man. These results are likely to work through the court system for several years as arguments are made for their unconstitutionality. If such a prohibition on same-sex marriage is upheld by the Supreme Court, it will in effect state that marriage as an institution will be harmed if we allow homosexuals to get married. Although there is no move to legalize multiple marriages—as are allowed in a number of Muslim countries—their prohibition makes the same statement about their harm.

How about harm to one's own self? It is a crime to try to commit suicide, since it is declared that the state has an abiding interest in our being, and thus taking one's own life would also harm the state's interest. What about doctor-assisted suicide in the case of terminally ill patients? Once again, you can see that no easy answer is available to address these tortuous questions.

Let us take another example. Should we legalize marijuana? *Time* magazine columnist Joe Klein has argued, in a somewhat lighthearted way, that with plenty of legal and illegal mind-altering drugs around, we should seriously consider legalizing marijuana.[42] He points out that any harm to individuals may be overcome by the economic benefits of commercializing the drug, since it is estimated to be the largest cash crop in California, with an annual commercial value of $14 billion. A 10 percent tax on marijuana could bring $1.4 billion to the cash-strapped state. It also could create a large number of legal (and that means taxpaying) jobs in the agricultural and manufacturing sectors. And, more important, it could save the expenses of prosecuting and imprisoning a large number of drug offenders. On the other hand, the liberty of legally smoking marijuana and generating tax revenue must be weighed against a number of outcomes that can adversely affect society's welfare. For instance, the legalization and commercialization of marijuana would surely increase the number of users and enhance the legally produced drug's potency; neither of these consequences would be beneficial for society's health. Especially considering the global effort to reduce cigarette smoking, the introduction of another smoking agent makes little sense.

When discussing liberty and state sanction, we cannot overlook another extremely difficult question: if the authorities overstep their bounds and curtail our liberty, do we have a moral obligation to oppose tyranny? Mill was very aware of this issue and wrote about *social tyranny* and the *tyranny of the majority*. Social tyranny takes place when the ruler(s) of a nation becomes despotic and makes decisions that harm the people, who have no way of escaping the harm. Mill also acknowledged that sometimes the majority of the people make decisions that are harmful to a small minority. In this "tyranny of the majority" scenario, the citizens have the right and even a moral obligation to oppose these policies. For instance, the Jim Crow legislation in the South, which discriminated against and oppressed African Americans, was based on consent of the majority of those whites who were living in southern states. Thus, although the laws might have had legal justification, based on every accepted standard of human rights, the laws' utter injustice cried out for opposition.

In sum, although Mill put his arguments in philosophical terms, in the real world, we can translate his theory into practice by emphasizing that, as in medicine, the first principle of public policy is to do no harm. We will have a chance to discuss this at length later in the book.

Security

Ever since humans began forming organized societies, kings sought to protect their subjects from external and internal threats. Security remains an important goal for governments. Even in the most libertarian interpretation of Adam Smith's "invisible hand" and the primacy of market forces, the role of government in providing a secure environment is universally recognized. To do otherwise is to invite anarchy.

Security, however, is a very broad notion, encompassing physical security (which justifies military and police actions), as well as protection from natural disasters or ecological collapse. In recent years two images have clearly marked our collective memory with a strong sense of insecurity: the two hijacked planes that crashed through the twin towers of New York's World Trade Center and the sight of New Orleans residents stranded on housetops and victims' bodies floating in flooded streets after Hurricane Katrina. As a result, there are endless debates regarding how to allocate resources for the military and police. In 2008, the Stockholm International Peace Research Institute, a respected think tank, estimated that the total global military expenditure amounted to $1.339 trillion, which is about 2.5 percent of the world's gross domestic product, or $202 for each person in the world.[43] The top fifteen countries with the highest spending account for 83 percent of the total expenditure, and the United States is responsible for 45 percent of the world total, distantly followed by the United Kingdom, China, France, and Japan, each with 4 to 5 percent of the world share (see Figure 1.2). Therefore, there is an ever-present debate in the United States about whether the government spends too much of its resources on the military. Those who stress security needs point out the necessity of maintaining a strong defense in an increasingly volatile world. In contrast, others point to the alternative uses of this vast sum of money—from the alleviation of poverty to education and health care.

External threats, particularly those posed by terrorism, traditionally have been the domain of the federal government. However, after the 9/11 attacks, the city of New York took a different tack and established its own intelligence unit.[44] Established by Raymond Kelly, the pragmatic commissioner of the New York Police Department (NYPD), and David Cohen, a former analyst at the Central Intelligence Agency, the NYPD's counterterrorism division, which stations more than 600 police officers and operatives stateside and around the world, is credited by some as the most effective force in the nation.

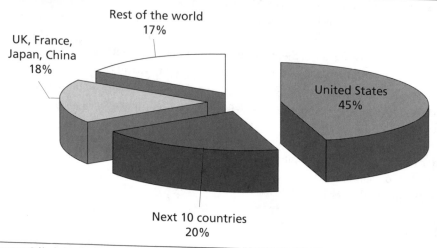

FIGURE 1.2   **World Military Spending**

Rest of the world
17%

UK, France,
Japan, China
18%

United States
45%

Next 10 countries
20%

Source: Stålenheim, Perdomo, and Sköns, "Chapter 5. Military Expenditure," *SIPRI Yearbook 2008.*

The demands of internal security in the United States also are overwhelming. By compiling data from the U.S. Department of Justice, the Pew Center on the States estimates that the total U.S. correctional population—those in jail, in prison, on probation, or on parole—stood at 7.3 million in 2007, or one in every thirty-one adults. Astoundingly, the United States has 5 percent of the world's population, but 25 percent of the world's prison inmates. This huge correctional population is also highly skewed in its composition; black adults are 4 times as likely as whites and nearly 2.5 times as likely as Hispanics to be in the prison system. Also, while the number of female offenders continues to grow, the number of imprisoned men (of all races) is 5 times that of women. This enormous prison population has created overcrowded facilities that have put many states' budgets in dire straits. This is particularly true in California, where the effects of "three strikes and you're out" legislation, in which three felony convictions result in exceedingly long mandatory prison sentences, have contributed greatly to the problem. Some have argued that overcrowding leads to inhumane treatment of prisoners, which ultimately contributes to their radicalization and thus increases threats to safety and even national security.[45]

The Liberty-Security Trade-off

First and foremost, we desire security from our governments; this desire comes under sharper focus in times of crisis. After the 9/11 attacks, the federal government was forced into action, and many of the actions the George W. Bush administration took placed extraordinary power in the hands of the president and the executive branch. President Bush obtained the power to declare U.S. citizens "enemy combatants" and hold them indefinitely without trial, and the Department of Justice and the attorney general argued for the abrogation of the Geneva Convention, which protected detainees at Guantanamo Bay against torture.[46] Wiretaps were also authorized without any judicial oversight. These extraordinary steps were justified in the name of providing security to the

American people against future attacks. When the nation felt insecure, the general public accepted these assaults against individual liberties as necessary steps. As the threat of a further attack seemed to fade and the wars in Iraq and Afghanistan turned into quagmires, however, resistance to these security measures built up among the public.

When we define security in the traditional sense of managing internal and external threats, we can clearly see a trade-off with liberty. Recently, however, a group of notable scholars have been promoting the concept of **human security**. In 1994, Pakistani economist Mahbub ul Haq crystallized the concept of human security in a United Nations Development Programme report, defining the term according to seven factors:

1. *Economic security*—A minimum income through meaningful employment or from government assistance.
2. *Food security*—The assurance of enough food for everyone.
3. *Health security*—Protection from diseases and unhealthy living conditions, including access to clean drinking water.
4. *Environmental security*—Protection from natural or manmade disasters.
5. *Personal security*—Protection to individuals who are threatened by violence from ethnic and religious conflicts or criminal groups.
6. *Community security*—Protection to groups that are threatened by ethnic, religious, cultural, or political conflicts.
7. *Political security*—The ability to express political beliefs without fear of repression from governments or other groups.

In a 2003 United Nations Commission on Human Security report, the economist Amartya Sen argued that the concept of security is meaningless without freedom and people's ability to have economic security, health security, and freedom.[47] To Sen, security, economic development, and freedom constitute parts of a larger whole.[48] In this broader definition of security, it is not a zero-sum game; there is indeed no trade-off between security and liberty.

As we have seen throughout this chapter, public policy analysis involves intricate balancing on multiple levels. Governments, for one, must balance notions of liberty and security, efficiency and equity, in order to maintain a functioning society. As political beings, all of us also perform a balancing act, weighing the self-interested impulses of our inner *homo economicus* against our subjective and collective perceptions. Within this complex puzzle of rationality, human behavior, and government action, public policy analysts work to sort out the pieces and find the best ways in which they fit together.

KEY WORDS

Absolute measure (p. 16)
Alternatives (p. 4)
Club good (or common pooled resource) (p. 7)
Collective action problem (p. 8)
Credible commitment problem (p. 8)
Efficiency (p. 15)
Equity (p. 15)
Excludability (p. 6)

Exhaustibility (p. 6)
Falsifiability (p. 5)
Framing (p. 13)
Free-rider problem (p. 8)
Human security (p. 23)
Invisible hand (p. 3)
Liberty (p. 15)
Model (p. 5)

Moral hazard (p. 8)
Opportunity cost (p. 16)
Policy cycle (p. 3)
Political entrepreneurs (p. 13)
Politics (p. 2)
Private good (p. 6)
Prospect theory (p. 14)
Public good (p. 6)

Pure public goods (p. 7)
Rationality (p. 2)
Relative measure (p. 16)
Rivalrous (p. 6)
Security (p. 15)
Shirk (p. 8)
Toll good (p. 7)
Tragedy of the commons (p. 9)

EXERCISES

1. Why is it difficult to define human rationality? Why is understanding rationality important for the discussion of public policy?
2. What are the major ethical trade-offs in the realm of public policy? Consider government responses to recent catastrophic events, such as the 9/11 attacks, Hurricane Katrina, or the economic meltdown of 2008. At times of stress, how do we, as a society, deal with the contradictions between equity and efficiency or liberty and security?
3. What is human security? How is it defined, and how does its acceptance reduce conflict with equity and efficiency?
4. A report on poverty in the United States prepared by the U.S. Government Accountability Office (GAO) appears in Appendix A. The report explains how poverty creates its own vicious cycle. Read the report and discuss in a group what the role of government in ending this cycle of poverty should be. Explain how individuals with different political ideologies might interpret the results differently.
5. How does the concept of human security relate to the GAO's report on poverty?

Notes

1. Adam Smith, *An Inquiry into the Nature and the Causes of the Wealth of Nations* (New York: Modern Library, Random House, 1937), 461. (Originally published in 1776.)
2. Walter Isaacson, "How to Raise the Standard in America's Schools," *Time*, April 27, 2009.
3. It is interesting to note that while Adam Smith's assumption of self-utility-maximizing human being, proposed in *The Wealth of Nations*, gained widespread acceptance and became the foundation of modern economics, he had argued for a much more nuanced view of human nature in his lesser known earlier work *The Theory of Moral Sentiments*.
4. French philosopher Michel Foucault calls the assumption of me-centric individualism "positive consciousness of knowledge," which he defines as "a level that eludes the consciousness of the scientists yet is a part of scientific discourse." Michel Foucault, *The Order of Things: An Archeology of the Human Sciences* (New York: Pantheon Books, 1970), xi.
5. George Lakoff, *The Political Mind: Why You Can't Understand 21st-Century American Politics with an 18th-Century Brain* (New York: Viking, 2008), 3.
6. Amartya K. Sen, "Rational Fools: A Critique of the Behavioral Foundation of Economic Theory," *Philosophy and Public Affairs* 6 (1977): 317–344 (italics in the original).
7. See Elinor Ostrom, "A Behavioral Approach to the Rational Choice Theory of Collective Action: Presidential Address, American Political Science Association, 1997," *American Political Science Review* 92 (March 1998): 1–22.

8. Bengt Holmstrom, "Moral Hazard in Teams," *The Bell Journal of Economics* 13 (Autumn 1982): 324–340.

9. Armen Alchain and Harold Demsetz, "Production, Information Costs and Economic Organizations," *American Economic Review* 62 (1972): 777–792.

10. Gary Miller, "Credible Commitment and Efficiency in the Design of Public Agencies," *Journal of Public Administration Research and Theory* 10 (2000): 289–328.

11. Garrett Hardin, "The Tragedy of Commons," *Science* 162 (December 1968): 1243–1248.

12. Mancur Olson, *The Logic of Collective Action: Public Goods and the Theory of Groups* (Cambridge, Mass.: Harvard University Press, 1965), 161–162.

13. For an alternative formulation of human nature in social sciences, see Dipak K. Gupta, *Understanding Terrorism and Political Violence: The Life Cycle of Birth, Growth, Transformation, and Demise* (London: Routledge, 2008). Also see Dipak K. Gupta, *Path to Collective Madness: A Study in Social Order and Political Pathology* (New York: Praeger, 2001).

14. David Brooks, "Peering into Our Economic Future," *New York Times*, February 13, 2009.

15. Antonio R. Damasio, *Descartes' Error: Emotion, Reason, and the Human Brain* (New York: Avon, 1994). Also see Daniel Goleman, *Emotional Intelligence* (New York: Bantam, 2006).

16. Drew Westen, *The Political Brain: The Role of Emotion in Deciding the Fate of the Nation* (New York: Public Affairs, 2007), x–xv.

17. Ibid., xiii–xv.

18. Ibid., xiv (italics in the original).

19. It may interest you to note that some cognitive psychologists argue that we are predisposed to our ideologies. One study concludes that your answers to two completely unrelated questions can predict your ideological orientation. The first question is, How willing would you be to slap your father (with his permission) as a part a comedy skit? The second is, How disgusted would you be to touch a faucet in a public restroom? The study's authors argue that your answers to similar questions can place you on a scale between extreme conservatism and extreme liberalism. They contend that the fundamental difference between the two rests on one's willingness to accept authority and the feeling of disgust one feels in various life situations. Conservatives have greater respect for authority and feel greater disgust than liberals. Visit www.yourmorals.org to take the test and find out your own value position.

20. Pew Research Center for the People & the Press, "Partisan Gap in Obama Job Approval Widest in Modern Era," April 2, 2009, http://pewresearch.org/pubs/1178/polarized-partisan-gap-in-obama-approval-historic.

21. See Robin Dunbar, Louise Barrett, and John Lycett, *Evolutionary Psychology* (Oxford, United Kingdom: Oneworld, 2005).

22. For an amusing yet frightening discussion of English soccer fans, see Bill Buford, *Among the Thugs* (New York: Norton, 1992).

23. Benedict Anderson, *Imagined Communities: Reflections on the Origin and Spread of Nationalism* (New York: Verso, 2003).

24. For an explanation of our altruistic behavior, see Kristen Renwick Monroe, *The Heart of Altruism: Perceptions of a Common Humanity* (Princeton, N.J.: Princeton University Press, 1996).

25. By expanding Joseph Schumpeter's concept of an economic entrepreneur from *The Theory of Economic Development*, the noted economist William J. Baumol made a useful distinction between "constructive" and "destructive" entrepreneurs, whose behaviors are guided by the reward system within a society. See William J. Baumol, "Entrepreneurship: Productive, Unproductive, and Destructive," *Journal of Political Economy* 98 (October 1990): 893–921.

26. For one of the best explanations of "irrationality" due to framing, see James N. Druckman, "The Implications of Framing Effects for Citizen Competence," *Political Behavior* 23 (September 2001): 225–256. Also see James N. Druckman, "Political Preference Formation:

Competition, Deliberation, and the (Ir)relevance of Framing Effects," *American Political Science Review* 98 (2004): 671–686.

27. See Samuel Kernell and Gary C. Jacobson, *The Logic of American Politics* (Washington, D.C.: CQ Press, 2000).

28. See David Ignatius, "Bernanke, or New Tiger atop the Fed?" *Washington Post*, May 28, 2009.

29. See Rose McDermott, James H. Fowler, and Oleg Smirnov, "On the Evolutionary Origin of Prospect Theory Preferences," *Journal of Politics* 70 (2008): 335–350.

30. Daniel Kahneman and Amos Tversky, "Choice, Values, and Frames," *American Psychologist* 39 (1984): 341–350.

31. Jonathan Haidt, *The Happiness Hypothesis: Finding Modern Truth in Ancient Wisdom* (New York: Basic Books, 2006), 29.

32. For a delightful discussion of our lemming-like behavior, see Robert B. Cialdini, *Influence: How and Why People Agree to Things* (New York: Morrow, 1984).

33. Ronald J. Jensen, *The Alaska Purchase and Russian-American Relations* (Seattle: University of Washington Press, 1975).

34. For an interesting discussion of legislators' motivations behind "bringing home the bacon" ("pork barrel" to others), see Philip Keefer and Stuti Khemani, "When Do Legislators Pass on Pork? The Role of Political Parties in Determining Legislator Effort," *American Political Science Review* 103 (2009): 99–112.

35. For a history of Highway 56 in San Diego, see "Highway 56 History: 1958–Present," July 18, 2004, www.gbcnet.com/roads/hwy_56/56_history.html.

36. See, for example, Elizabeth C. Economy and Adam Segal, "China's Olympic Nightmare: What the Games Mean for Beijing's Future," *Foreign Affairs*, July/August 2008.

37. "'Welfare Queen' Becomes Issue in Reagan Campaign," *New York Times*, February 15, 1976. For a contrary view, see Susan J. Douglas and Meredith W. Michaels, *The Mommy Myth: The Idealization of Motherhood and How It Has Undermined All Women* (New York: Free Press, 2005).

38. Despite widespread press, there were many who saw the case against Halliburton differently. See, for instance, Byron York, "Halliburton: The Bush/Iraq Scandal That Wasn't," *National Review*, July 14, 2003.

39. For an excellent discussion of the subjective nature of government's participation in the market, see Deborah Stone, *Policy Paradox: The Art of Political Decision Making* (New York: W. W. Norton, 2002).

40. See, for example, Daniel Deudney and G. John Ikenberry, "The Myth of the Autocratic Revival: Why Liberal Democracy Will Prevail," *Foreign Affairs*, January/February 2009.

41. See Dipak K. Gupta, *The Economics of Political Violence: The Effect of Political Instability on Economic Growth* (New York: Praeger, 1990).

42. Joe Klein, "It's High Time: Why Legalizing Marijuana Makes Sense," *Time*, April 13, 2009.

43. Petter Stålenheim, Catalina Perdomo, and Elisabeth Sköns, "Chapter 5. Military Expenditure," *SIPRI Yearbook 2008*, http://yearbook2008.sipri.org/05.

44. Christopher Dickey, *Securing the City: Inside America's Best Counterterror Force—The NYPD* (New York: Simon & Schuster, 2009).

45. See Mark S. Hamm, *Terrorism as Crime: From Oklahoma City to Al-Qaeda and Beyond* (New York: New York University Press, 2007).

46. For an excellent discussion, see Jane Mayer, *The Dark Side: The Inside Story of How the War on Terror Turned into a War on American Ideals* (New York: Doubleday, 2008).

47. Commission on Human Security, *Human Security Now*, 2003, http://www.humansecurity-chs.org/finalreport/English/FinalReport.pdf.

48. See Amartya Sen, *Development as Freedom* (New York: Knopf, 2009).

2 The Analysts: Their Role and Their Tools

The field of public policy is so vast that those who study it may be compared to a group of blind people who have been asked to describe an elephant: some people describe it by its trunk, some by its tusks, some by its large belly, some by its large, floppy ears or by its thin tail. According to the University of California's electronic library catalog, Melvyl, no fewer than 4,586 books with the words *public policy* in their titles have been published during the past ten years. This enormous number of publications clearly indicates that there are many ways of studying public policy.

While some students of public policy focus on the political, cultural, and judicial contexts in which policies are made, others study how policies are adopted. Economists concern themselves primarily with the effects of policies, while operations researchers and those who use quantitative techniques examine the management policies that promote efficiency in public organizations' delivery of services. Philosophers worry about the ethical aspects of government involvement in our everyday lives. Students of public administration examine the role of bureaucracy in the allocation of public goods. Political scientists, in contrast, typically are most interested in the role of interest groups in public policy.

If you define the study of public policy as advising those who govern, the field has a long history.[1] If, on the other hand, you define it as a systematic, objective, and institutionalized approach to improving the art of government, then policy science has a short past. Let us keep in mind both definitions as we discuss the evolution of the profession and the tools developed by policy analysts.

THE PRINCE AND THE PUNDITS: ANALYSTS, ACADEMICS, AND ADVOCATES

Throughout history, kings and princes depended on counsel from their ministers. These ministers were the first policy analysts, since they were the advisers to the ultimate authorities (and the actual decision makers) in the land. Today, in a large democracy, the role of policy analysts is much more diffuse. Although it is not always clear whom we should call a "policy analyst," this large group may be divided into *staff analysts*, *academics*, and *advocates*.

Policy analysts are typically employed by governments to help executive decision makers at all levels of government—federal, state, and local—on issues ranging from budgeting to law enforcement to health and human services (see "A Case in Point"). They also may be employed by the legislative and the judiciary branches of the government or by multinational agencies, such as the World Bank, the International Monetary Fund, the United Nations Children's Fund, the World Meteorological Organization, and the International Labour Organization.[2] Policy analysts are experts in their fields, and often become repositories of information. They collect reports written by other agencies, articles in professional journals, and scholarly books in their areas of expertise, and become the "go-to persons" for the decision makers in all branches of the government.

Apart from those who are directly employed by governments, many analysts work as hired consultants. They can be academics or employees of private consulting firms or nonprofit organizations. These experts are typically hired to work on specific projects for which government agencies do not have "in-house" capability. For instance, suppose your city's administration has noted that fatal car accidents along a certain corridor have increased significantly, and they need a plan to reduce this number. If there is no one in the transportation department to conduct the study, the department may issue a request for proposal and hire an individual contractor or a firm to do the job. Applicants for the job might include experts in the field, former transportation officials, consulting firms, private think tanks, or professors teaching transportation planning or traffic engineering at your university. Government-funded institutes (as opposed to those directly run by the government), such as the National Science Foundation, the National Institutes of Health (NIH), and the United States Institute of Peace, may also hire policy analysts to evaluate specific programs. For example, the NIH may fund a program to evaluate the relative success of various antismoking campaigns among teens.

Finally, the world of policy analysts is also composed of nongovernmental organizations that approach policy problems from a strict advocacy position. As opposed to the analysts working for government agencies or institutes, advocacy analysts are part of a large network of interest groups. Their clients are specific interest or ideological groups, and their effort is ultimately directed toward the benefit of their clients. For instance, the Tobacco Institute, which was founded by the powerful tobacco industry in 1958, for decades produced or funded studies that fraudulently disclaimed any link between smoking (and exposure to secondhand smoke) and lung cancer, hypertension, and other forms of cardiovascular disease.[3] Similarly, in the political arena, some research institutes have clear ideological orientations. For example, the Cato Institute, the American Enterprise Institute, and even the Stanford University–affiliated Hoover Institution are seen as "right wing," while the Brookings Institution is regarded as "liberal." As a result, analyses conducted by these think tanks often carry signs of an ideological slant.

A CASE IN POINT

The Numb and Number: The Exploding Domain of Public Policy Analysts

Since the government allocates money, which is spent—at least partially—according to what policy specialists recommend, the domain of policy analysts is enlarging both in relative and in absolute terms. The amount of government spending is so huge that the numbers can truly numb our minds. As I write this book in 2009, the United States is in the grips of a deep recession. As the number of foreclosed homes rises and many people find themselves out of work, newly elected president Barack Obama has attempted to jump-start the economy with a direct infusion of public money. The question, however, is how much money?

We all know that a million dollars is a lot of money. Each year *Forbes* magazine lists the wealthiest people in the world, and their worth is now counted in billions. However, when it comes to the federal government, the operative word is *trillion*. Facing the daunting task of restarting the economic engine, President Obama proposed a budget of $3.6 trillion. At this moment, the total federal debt—the amount Uncle Sam owes to those who have lent him the money—stands at an astounding $10 trillion.

How large is the number 1 trillion? If I were to ask you what you were doing a million seconds ago, would you be able to remember? You should, because a million seconds equals approximately 11.5 days. Now, let me ask you what you were doing a trillion seconds ago. Well, if you cannot recall, there is a good reason for it. Since a trillion is a million millions, a trillion seconds translates into 11.5 million days—or about 32,000 years.

These trillions of dollars in government expenditures, however, do not fall from the sky. Like any borrower, the government must repay its debts. Every time the government undertakes a new program, it creates "winners" and "losers": those who benefit from it and those who pay for it. Given the enormous size of the government's expenditures, the question therefore is how to make sure the money is spent efficiently and with due consideration to justice and equity. These questions constitute the domain of the public policy analyst. As the size of the government increases, so do the responsibilities of those who must make sure that its funds are being spent wisely.

Discussion Points

1. What do you think is the appropriate role of government in a free market society?
2. Does the overwhelming amount of public spending make the job of policy analysts more important? Explain.

The ranks of policy analysts also include journalists and columnists, who often take the side of a particular political party or a specific ideology. You could take some of the best-known columnists and, based on their articles or media appearances, place them along the ideological spectrum.

Policy analysts generally serve specific client groups. The idea of a completely impartial, rational, scientific analysis is often a figment of the imagination in an otherwise subjective world. Therefore, it is hardly surprising that within the democratic system, the role of unelected bureaucrats in general, and staff policy analysts in particular, will be of great interest. Some have accused these bureaucrats of having too much influence, while others have placed greater faith in these trained professionals than in the elected "political animals." Let us therefore further examine the complicated role of policy analysts in a democratic system.

The Politicos and In-house Policy Analysts: An Uneasy Cohabitation

The Framers of the Constitution minimized the role of the government, particularly at the federal level. However, as the new nation took on greater responsibilities on an ever-larger scale, government officials recognized the need for true professionals to run the government and make its policies. In the early years, the administration and politics were inseparable, and elected politicians hired their own supporters to fill administrative positions. However, as the government grew more complex, untrained administrators drew criticism for mismanagement and corruption, which prompted a public call for change.

The first serious study of public administration and the role of the bureaucracy began three years after the passage of the Pendleton Act (1883), which sought to reform the civil service by instituting merit-based selection procedures. The author of the study, a young political scientist named Woodrow Wilson, stressed the importance of a strict separation between elected officials and nonelected bureaucrats.[4] His model advocated a perfect dichotomy between the two groups: elected officials defined policy objectives while public agencies and administrators performed purely technical and professional functions. Policymakers did not interfere in administration, and administrators did not get involved in policymaking. The horizontal line bisecting the sphere in Figure 2.1 (a) shows this strict hierarchy: elected officials make public policies, and administrators remain fully accountable to their political bosses while translating adopted policies into action. This **policy-administration dichotomy model** primarily emphasizes democratic control over a burgeoning bureaucracy. Insulated from the corrupting influences of the political spoils system, in which elected officials ignore the merits of job applicants and offer administrative posts to their loyal supporters, administrators work toward achieving greater degrees of neutrality, professionalism, and efficiency. Introduced in the 1930s, this model withstood strong attacks from various academic quarters to become, until the mid–1960s, the dominant model in the field.

In 1968, during a tumultuous period in American history, a group of young academics founded the "new public administration," a school of policy analysis. Like most young men and women of that time, they were deeply affected by the riots, the assassinations of prominent political leaders, and the ongoing war in Vietnam, which fostered in them a strong distrust of elected officials. These scholars distanced themselves from the policy-administration dichotomy model, which seemed to them to prescribe a machinelike devotion by administrators to the policies of elected officials.[5] They also questioned the loyalty of administrators to their political bosses.[6] They

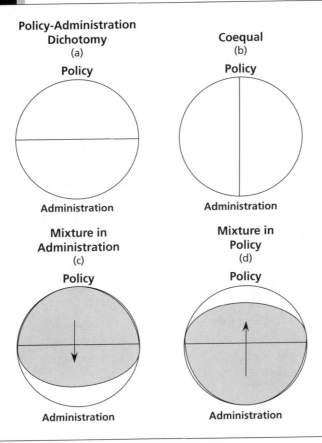

FIGURE 2.1   **Four Models of Policymaking**

Policy-Administration
Dichotomy
(a)

Policy

Administration

Coequal
(b)

Policy

Administration

Mixture in
Administration
(c)

Policy

Administration

Mixture in
Policy
(d)

Policy

Administration

Source: Based on James H. Svara, "Dichotomy and Duality: Reconceptualizing the Relationship between Policy and Administration in Council-Manager Cities," in *Ideal and Practice in Council-Manager Government*, ed. H. George Fredrickson (Washington, D.C.: International City-County Management Association, 1995), 3–19.

advocated a nonhierarchical, coequal arrangement in which administrators were loyal not to the hierarchy but to their ethical principles—their belief in the equality of policymakers and administrators and their commitment to protecting the rights of the powerless.[7] Radical in their approach, they urged administrators to become activists by developing a direct link with the people. The young academics admitted that such direct contact might sometimes conflict with the policies of elected representatives. Figure 2.1 (b) illustrates the **coequal model**: a vertical line divides the policy-administration sphere into two equal domains.

Another group of scholars went in the opposite direction in the 1960s. They developed models in which elected officials questioned the role of administrators in policymaking. The **mixture-in-administration model** (see Figure 2.1 (c)) observes that elected officials prevent nonelected administrators from gaining too much authority in a democracy by encroaching on the domains of administrators. At the national level, elected officials encroach on administrative domains when different parties control the White House and the legislative branch. For example, the Democratic-controlled 110th Congress that came to power in 2006 called Bush administration officials to testify about their operations. As U.S. forces became bogged down in Iraq and the need to take quick and decisive action against terrorism was replaced with calmer reflections, the Bush administration was forced to defend its actions at home and abroad. The use of the USA PATRIOT Act of 2001 (Uniting and Strengthening America by Providing Appropriate Tools Required to Intercept and Obstruct Terrorism) and allegations of torture at the Guantanamo Bay detention camp became the preoccupation of numerous congressional oversight committees.

In contrast to the mixture-in-administration model, the **mixture-in-policy model** (see Figure 2.1 (d)) describes the increasing role of bureaucracy in public policy making.[8] Three developments fostered this rapid encroachment by nonelected policy analysts and executives with specific expertise, particularly in local governments. First, as the nation grew more populous and urban, the demand for public services increased more than proportionately. New demands for public policies on crime control, education, health care, infrastructure, drug abuse, poverty, and environmental protection particularly challenged city governments, which typically were ill equipped to deal with such a wide variety of issues. Second, at the federal level, the Great Depression and Keynesian economics, which prescribed an involved government, changed people's attitudes. People started expecting the government to act on such issues as raising children's test scores in public schools and reducing gun violence. As a result, public administrators and elected officials faced new rules of engagement. Finally, rapid advances in technology—from stem cell research to invasive security procedures at airports, from genetically modified food to climate change and global warming—required that government regulate and promote activities that the Founders never could have imagined.

Exit, Voice, and Loyalty: What's an Analyst to Do?

From the earliest days of recorded antiquity, the relationship between princes and high priests has been like a marriage, with alternating periods of gleeful bliss and contentious acrimony. Although the princes have depended on the pundits to chalk out the proper course of action, history is clear about the fate of those counselors who gave their masters advice they did not want to hear. King Henry VIII, although respectful of his advisers Cardinal Thomas Wolsey[9] and Sir Thomas More,[10] did not let his admiration of these men stand in the way of virtually imprisoning Wolsey and beheading More. Policy analysts do not suffer the same fates in today's world, yet at times they may experience a deep ambivalence working within an organization (see "A Case in Point").

When conflicts based on value and ethical considerations become deep, analysts face three broad choices. They can voice dissenting opinions, quit their organizations, or become disloyal to them. Based on the seminal work of Albert Hirschman,[11] Weimer and Vining[12] presented these three choices with three intersecting circles that illustrate seven different courses of action (other than simply being quiet and going along with one's supervisor) (see Figure 2.2). When facing a conflict with your organization, your first option is to voice dissent and *protest*. In this option you voice your opinion

A CASE IN POINT

Ignored Advice and the Global War on Terror

As a seasoned veteran of the intelligence community who had advised three presidents, Richard Clarke had spent years following the activities of a Saudi millionaire named Osama bin Laden and the radical Islamic fundamentalist group that he established, al-Qaida. Clarke linked the group to multiple attacks against the United States, including the 1998 bombing of the U.S. embassies in the East African cities of Dar es Salaam, Tanzania, and Nairobi, Kenya. He was convinced that the same group was responsible for the attack on the warship U.S.S. *Cole* off the coast of Yemen in 2000. And by 2000, he strongly suspected that al-Qaida was about to launch a devastating attack on U.S. soil. In fact, he had persuaded the Clinton administration to carry out missile attacks on bin Laden's alleged hideout in Afghanistan and a suspected bomb factory in Sudan. Clarke maintains that President Clinton was aware of the gravity of the situation and became increasingly obsessed with stopping al-Qaida. With Clarke, the Clinton administration had developed workable plans to neutralize bin Laden and his group but was thwarted by political infighting and the sex scandal that led to Clinton's impeachment by the House.

When the Bush administration took charge, they were skeptical of Clarke's claim that a ragtag group was targeting the United States. Some of the new politicos in town, known as the neoconservatives, or neocons, came in with the notion that it was the Iraqi dictator Saddam Hussein who should be the primary target of U.S. counterterrorism policy, and they aimed to change the political landscape of the Middle East by tumbling Hussein's regime. As Clarke tried in vain to convince Vice President Dick Cheney, Defense Secretary Donald Rumsfeld, and others in the administration of the ominous threat, he was told to concentrate on Saddam Hussein rather than wasting his time on bin Laden.

After al-Qaida's devastating attacks on the United States on September 11, 2001, the political powers in Washington kicked into full gear their plans to invade Iraq and take out Saddam Hussein. President Bush and Vice President Cheney disregarded the adversarial relationship between bin Laden and Hussein and made every effort to lump the two enemies together. As a frustrated Clarke watched, the United States was soon embroiled in a two-front war in Afghanistan and Iraq.

Discussion Points

1. When a politician ignores an analyst's recommendation, who is responsible for the consequences?
2. What would you have done if you were in Richard Clarke's position?

---

internally and do nothing to undermine the organization by going public with your grievances. If you feel that your position is being sufficiently undermined, you may be ready to exit and submit an *ultimatum;* unless the organization alters its position, you will leave. If you don't want to jeopardize your position within the organization, you

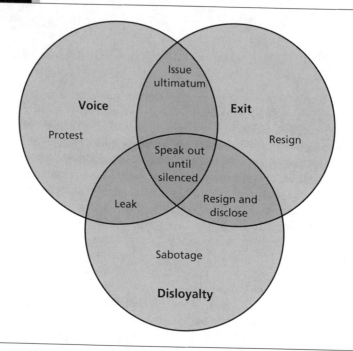

FIGURE 2.2 | **Alternative Responses to Value Conflict**

Source: From David L. Weimer and Aidan R. Vining, *Policy Analysis: Concepts and Practice*, 3rd edition. Upper Saddle River, N. J.: Prentice-Hall, 1999. © 1999 by Prentice Hall Inc. Reprinted by permission by Pearson Education Inc.

may secretly *leak* information to outsiders. The risk, of course, is that your involvement may be discovered, and punitive actions may be taken against you. You may not want to remain loyal to the organization and thus may talk to the media or other outside departments. If you do, this would be regarded as a case of disloyalty. If you choose to be disloyal, perhaps the most honorable course of action is to *speak out* until you are silenced. People who do this are often called **whistleblowers**. A number of state and federal laws have been enacted to protect whistleblowers. If you are not willing to become a whistleblower, you may *resign* from your position and, once out of the organization, *disclose* its inner workings by writing a "tell-all" book. This has been the time-honored path of many in positions of power in Washington and elsewhere. Facing a moral dilemma, they carefully accumulate evidence, keep secret memos, and, after resigning as loyal followers, decide to publish memoirs for considerable sums of money. Finally, you may decide to *sabotage*. This typically happens when a disgruntled worker, finding no other option to stop an organization from moving forward in a way that the worker finds abhorrent, decides to work secretly against the organization's goals. Most often these acts are hidden from the outside, since the organization and its supporters are too strong, or the laws do not protect those who might otherwise have come out in the open and opposed its policies. These saboteurs, when caught, can be severely reprimanded, and their stories often are fodder for Hollywood dramas (see "A Case in Point" for examples of these courses of action).

THE USE OF QUANTITATIVE TECHNIQUES IN PUBLIC POLICY ANALYSIS

In the un-rational world separated by group identities and ideological divisions, the search for scientific objectivity in public policy analysis has been a matter akin to finding the Holy Grail. From the beginning, the founders of policy analysis as a distinct field of inquiry—defined by Robert Lynd in the 1930s and 1940s and by Harold Lasswell in the 1940s and 1950s—sought to improve government efficiency by making better use of knowledge from the social sciences.[13] Over the next half century, numerous scholars established the academic credentials of policy analysis, and today nearly all major universities either offer stand-alone academic degrees in public policy or offer the subject as an emphasis within an established program.[14] As governmental organizations have striven to become more efficient by using mathematical models and quantitative techniques, the new fields of decision sciences and operations research have emerged.[15] Together, they have come to be known as the **rational model** of decision making.

One of the primary drawbacks of mathematical reasoning is that it often gives the impression of objectivity and, as a result, raises expectations far beyond what it can possibly deliver. For example, on August 12, 1965, President Lyndon Johnson issued an executive order requiring every agency to institute what he called a "revolutionary" new system based on a systems approach—the Planning-Programming-Budgeting System (PPBS).[16] Before the PPBS was implemented, the traditional federal budgeting process was incremental: each department's budget request was considered individually in light of its allocation from the previous year. For example, if the Department of Defense submitted a budget request under the incremental system, policymakers focused on how much the department had received the previous year and asked whether the department could keep up with inflation and other relevant demands. Then, after complex political bargaining, legislators allocated the money. What was lost in this process, however, was the question of whether any of the programs were worth continuing. In contrast, the PPBS used a series of rigorous steps—such as defining the overall goal, finding alternative plans for achieving the goal, developing productivity indicators, and using a decision model such as cost-benefit analysis—to determine department budgets, ignoring how much funding an office had received in previous years. In this way, its proponents claimed that the PPBS eliminated "politics" from the budget process and allocated more resources to the most productive programs while curtailing or even eliminating those that were inefficient. In his statement introducing the PPBS, President Johnson promised that it would "improve our ability to control our programs and our budgets rather than having them control us." This new system, bristling with the tools of the objective decision sciences, came to be known as the rational model of decision making. Pinning the term *rational* on one method made all other tools seem, at least implicitly, "irrational." Two decades later, President Ronald Reagan issued an executive order directing that lawmakers analyze the costs and benefits of every federal regulation before recommending it for adoption.[17]

Despite the enthusiasm of President Johnson and many others in the policy field, the PPBS failed to meet expectations. Decision makers, doubting their ability to control the programs and budgets, instead were controlled by something they did not fully understand. As political scientist Aaron Wildavsky emphatically stated, "No one knows how to do program budgeting (PPBS)."[18] Moreover, Wildavsky claimed that a "rational"

A CASE IN POINT

The Saboteur, The Whistleblower, and the Loyal Protester

They were some of the darkest days of American history, in early 1973, when a paranoid president used his power to subvert the democratic processes of the nation. As President Nixon faced widespread criticism for his increasingly futile war efforts in Vietnam, he and his advisers resorted to all sorts of illegal means—from unauthorized wiretapping and espionage to breaking into the Democratic Party's Washington office—to silence their opposition. Two young *Washington Post* reporters, Bob Woodward and Carl Bernstein, began investigating the administration's scandalous actions, and they were aided by a political informant whom they dubbed Deep Throat. Hiding beneath a broad-brimmed hat and behind the upturned collar of his trench coat, Deep Throat would meet the reporters in an empty parking garage or other secret locations and provide them with tantalizing clues to push their investigation along. Even after the reporters' published their exposé and Nixon resigned, the journalists kept Deep Throat's identity a mystery. Finally, on April 30, 2005, the *Washington Post* revealed Deep Throat's name: he was Mark Felt, the number two man in the Federal Bureau of Investigation at that time. According to Figure 2.2, Felt acted as a disloyal "leaker." Shortly after the disclosure of Felt's identity, which was done with his consent, he passed away. During his eulogies, he was hailed as a true American patriot.[13]

In the late 1990s, Enron was the envy of Wall Street. It began as a natural gas pipeline company and quickly got involved in the trading of energy-related products in Texas. With its success came access to power. Enron's chair and CEO, Kenneth Lay, was a personal friend of President George H. W. Bush, his chief of staff James Baker, and President George W. Bush. As the company became involved in trading instead of producing, it began to gamble on an unprecedented scale. However, some of its financing was fraudulent, and shady bookkeeping allowed it to hide its true nature from the outside world—that is, until it imploded from within, spurring a congressional investigation into its failure. The congressional hearings revealed that a little-known analyst named Sherron Watkins had written several memos to Kenneth Lay voicing her deep concern over

method of budgeting is unknowable and warned that we should not even try to implement such a system. In sum, he argued that "rational" models deny a fundamental principle of democratic government: the political rationality by which elected representatives balance the numerous and often contradictory concerns of their various constituents. In a democracy, politics is not about efficiency; rather, it is about bargains and compromises among competing interests. Wildavsky dismissed the PPBS because of its single-minded pursuit of economic efficiency—measured in terms of maximum output (benefits) relative to input (costs). Running the government with the efficiency of a private business, he said, was "downright undemocratic and un-American."

While Wildavsky questioned the criteria by which government programs should be evaluated, scholars such as Charles Lindblom and David Cohen pushed to the extreme the argument denouncing quantitative techniques and scoffed at the idea of the way the company was operating. Her protests were completely ignored. Ms. Watkins quickly came forward and began testifying against her own company and her supervisors, becoming one of the nation's most famous whistleblowers in the process.[20]

In another dark chapter in American political history, this time in 2004, news began to break that American soldiers were abusing Iraqi detainees in the notorious Abu Ghraib prison. Soon, pictures taken by military police personnel of humiliated, tortured, and abused Iraqi men began to circulate. Freedom from torture is a part of the Universal Declaration of Human Rights and is considered to be the hallmark of any civilized nation. Yet a secret memo, written primarily by then White House lawyer John Yoo, opined that torturing prisoners held in secret U.S. prisons outside its territories was permissible.[21] He also argued that the Fourth Amendment to the Constitution did not apply to domestic military operations as a part of the larger global war on terror. Such techniques had strong support from most high-level Bush administration officials, including Vice President Dick Cheney and Defense Secretary Donald Rumsfeld.[22] Yet none understood the risk of torturing prisoners and abrogating the Geneva Convention better than the Secretary of State Colin Powell. Apart from moral questions surrounding the torture techniques, Powell's military experience allowed him to see the danger that every future American prisoner would face in wars yet to be fought as a result of the practices. He tried to protest forcefully, but lost his own battle within the administration. However, perhaps his military training prevented him from resigning, or he might have reasoned that his presence was an asset as a moderating force. In any case, he remained, continuing to voice his protests behind closed doors.[23]

Discussion Points

1. Why do values sometimes conflict within organizations?
2. Compare and contrast how Mark Felt, Sherron Watkins, and Colin Powell dealt with the moral dilemmas they faced.
3. If you were in their place, would you have taken a different action?

using statistics to conduct "professional social inquiry." Instead of quantitative methods, Lindblom and Cohen urged policymakers to use "ordinary knowledge" when making decisions.[24] Lindblom declared forcefully, "For all the effort and for all its presumed usefulness, I cannot identify a single social science finding or idea that is undeniably indispensable in any social task or effort. Not even one."[25]

Lindblom overstates his case and too quickly throws out the proverbial baby with the bathwater by dismissing all quantitative techniques. Peter deLeon notes that policy analysis has made significant contributions to many government programs, such as those created by the 1988 Family Support Act and the 1990 Clean Air Act.[26] Besides these highly publicized cases, it is obvious that policymakers—from the chair of the Federal Reserve to the directors of financial management divisions in state and local governments—are influenced by economic analyses conducted in-house or outside their agencies. They use analytical techniques when projecting revenues and costs, when evaluating the overall desirability of a project, and when submitting an environmental impact statement, which is required for all public projects. They may not always use the most sophisticated techniques of analysis, but they do use systematic, logical thinking, which takes them far beyond the reaches of "ordinary knowledge," far beyond the realm of unstructured, subjective assessment.

However, we should note that quantitative techniques, by themselves, cannot solve all of our problems. The wise people of antiquity told us that although it is important to know what we do know, it is even more important to know what we do not know. Before we discuss the techniques of analysis, we must first describe their limits. These limits arise because

1. we cannot prove or disprove our hypotheses with the precision of laboratory experiments;
2. we cannot eliminate uncertainty;
3. our techniques may offer a limited view of reality;
4. our predilections, prejudices, and biases often cloud our judgment; and
5. we cannot define social welfare.

First, for the most part, hypotheses posed in the natural sciences can be proved or disproved by controlled experiments. If I hypothesize that two hydrogen atoms combined with a single oxygen atom produce water, I can prove my assumption conclusively in a controlled laboratory experiment. This result can then be replicated. However, if a president up for reelection claims that his economic policies caused national prosperity, we have no way of proving the claim (see chapter 5). As a result, eighty years later, liberals credit President Roosevelt's policies for ending the Great Depression, while conservatives remain unconvinced.

Second, in an uncertain world, we make our predictions based on mathematical models. Mathematician John Casti reminds us that regardless of how accurate our measurements and our analytical techniques are, we are never able to completely penetrate the core of uncertainty.[27] As you will see in later chapters, there are several techniques designed to aid our decision making in an uncertain situation, but they cannot reach certainty. At the end of one highly mathematical textbook on macroeconomics, a discipline that is useful in analyzing public policy, the author concludes the chapter "Policy Making under Uncertainty" with this startling admission:

> Economic analysis has a long way to go until we can specify models with as little residual uncertainty as the ones posited in this chapter, and unfortunately economic analysis has little to say about the appropriate conduct of policy when there is uncertainty as to the correct model of the economy. Therefore, the actual practical usefulness of the analyses of this chapter may be quite limited.[28]

Third, when we make models of human behavior, we must make assumptions regarding its essence. Since all public policies aim to alter existing patterns of behavior through incentives (tax breaks, monetary rewards, etc.) and disincentives (taxes, fines, quotas, etc.), we must make assumptions regarding human nature. As we have seen in the first chapter, the concept of economic rationality has gathered a lot of scorn from many quarters. Thus, Alice Rivlin, former president of the American Economic Association and former director of the Office of Management and Budget, took her colleagues to task in the early 1990s for relying too heavily on models: "Economists . . . in their usual fashion, have been short on realism and long on theory and prescription."[29] Journalist Anatole Kaletsky even places the blame for the current economic crisis squarely on economists: "The economics profession must bear a lot of the blame for the current crisis. If it is to become useful again it must undergo an intellectual revolution—becoming both broader and more modest."[30] Yet the assumption of the "rational" *homo economicus* remains prevalent. Political scientist Elinor Ostrom takes a kinder view of economists and their assumptions about human nature; in a 1997 address to the American Political Science Association, she stated, "While incorrectly confused with a general theory of human behavior, complete rationality models will continue to be used productively by social scientists, including the author."[31] Echoing Ostrom's sentiment, another political economist asserted that models based on economic rationality are "neither always true nor always good, merely almost always useful."[32] Because quantitative techniques are based on a fragmented model of reality, they will always be open to criticism from those who do not agree with the models we have selected. Furthermore, the conclusions we reach using one technique may contradict the results we get using another, or they may vary when we rearrange the data (see chapter 7).

Fourth, as we discussed in the previous chapter, our biases affect our judgments. When we observe, we receive information through filters of culture, religion, and personal life experience. In the social sciences our observations (and the data we gather) admit biases of many kinds. If our data are biased, we do not get an objective result that is accepted by everyone, regardless of how sophisticated our analytical techniques may be (see chapter 6 and the discussion of imperfect data in chapter 9).

Finally, analytical techniques fail us because we cannot define social welfare. Although we are quick to call for the "common good," in reality, it is almost impossible to agree on what is best for society, and the public policies that will achieve it. Every policy creates winners and losers. When we build a new airport, the region as a whole may win through increased trade, commerce, and ease of transportation, but those with buildings near the flight paths lose property value. Spending on education helps the young but takes money from elderly people and those who do not have school-age children. As we will see in chapter 4, developing a satisfactory framework in which to "size up" the winners' wins and the losers' losses may exceed our powers of analysis.

Taking a comfortable middle road, however, will not end the debate over the usefulness of quantitative techniques in public policy analysis. Without a controlled experiment, we cannot prove the effectiveness of our analytical techniques. Even with only "ordinary knowledge," without the aid of "scientific models," we can safely forecast that we will continue to debate this issue—and fill the pages of professional journals—for the foreseeable future. In the meantime, we will use quantitative techniques to analyze public policy. However, we must do so with full knowledge of their strengths and weaknesses. I argue that scientific methods and their claims to objectivity apply only to the relatively narrow process that begins once we have defined the problems, identified the alternatives, and specified the techniques of analysis. *We must make matters of subjective judgment clear at every step of the way, and understand how decisions reflect the goals and principles of public policy analysts and their political bosses.* From observation to analysis,

A CASE IN POINT

Poverty in America: Contrasting Perspectives

After reading the Government Accountability Office report on poverty in Appendix A, you might be persuaded as to the plight of poor people in America, the land of plenty. However, like beauty, nearly every aspect of public policy is based on perception. For instance, the conservative Heritage Foundation published a report on what it means to be poor in America, arguing that most of those whom we call poor are, in fact, not destitute.[33] As evidence, Robert Rector points out the following statistics:

- Forty-three percent of all households identified as poor by the Census Bureau actually own their own homes, which typically have three bedrooms, one and a half bathrooms, a garage, and a porch or patio.
- Eighty percent of these homes have air conditioning.
- About 6 percent of the homes are "overcrowded," and more than two-thirds have more than two rooms per person.
- Compared with the average (middle-class) European living in Paris, London, Vienna, Athens, and other cities, poor people in America enjoy larger accommodations.
- Almost 93 percent of poor Americans own cars, with 31 percent owning two cars.
- Over 97 percent of poor households in American have color televisions, with half having two.
- Similarly, most of these "poor" households have microwave ovens, stereos, automatic dishwashers, DVD players, and cable or satellite television.

Rector concludes, "The living conditions of persons defined as poor by the government bear little resemblance to notions of 'poverty' promoted by politicians and political activists." For him,

the most wonderfully complex computers in the world guide us: our brains. The quality of our analysis will be judged in the end not by the sophistication of our technique but by the wisdom of our judgment.

STRUCTURE ABOVE A SWAMP: PUBLIC POLICY ANALYSIS AND PROFESSIONAL ETHICS

Now you may be confused. If everything about public policy is so vague and subjective, what is the use of learning methods of objective research? On one hand, I emphasize the relative nature of truth, and on the other, I advocate objective analysis. A quotation from Karl Popper, the eminent philosopher of science, may resolve this contradiction:

> The empirical basis of objective science has thus nothing "absolute" about it. Science does not rest upon rock-bottom. The bold structure of its theories rises, as it were, above a swamp. It is like a building erected on piles. The piles are driven down from above into the swamp, but not down to any natural or "given" base; and when we cease our attempts to

poverty, when it does exist, is caused by the fact that "the typical poor family with children is supported by only 800 hours of work during a year: That amounts to 16 hours of work per week." He identifies children born out of wedlock as another major contributing factor. Therefore, Rector recommends that any antipoverty measure must include incentives for mothers to work longer hours as a condition for receiving aid and that welfare and tax laws should be amended to promote marriage.

Ron Haskins and Isabel Sawhill of the liberal Brookings Institution, using the same set of information, come to a radically different conclusion, and consequently, their policy prescriptions are different from those of Rector. They see inequality in the United States as growing rapidly and recommend the following[34]:

- Strengthen work requirements in government assistance programs.
- Increase the minimum wage.
- Expand the earned-income tax credit.
- Subsidize child care for low-wage workers.
- Promote marriage as the best environment for rearing children.
- Fund effective teen pregnancy prevention efforts, premarital education, and family planning.
- Invest in high-quality early childhood education.

Discussion Points

1. How do differences in values affect an analyst's judgment?
2. Discuss how the two perspectives on poverty stem from the respective ideological stances of the two reports' authors.
3. If you were working as a policy analyst, what would you do to avoid an ideological bias?

---

drive our piles into a deeper layer, it is not because we have reached firm ground. We simply stop when we are satisfied that they are firm enough to carry the structure, at least for the time being.[35]

Therefore, although we can empirically test "scientific laws" regarding society, we cannot know their truth. The ability to test hypotheses has lent social sciences and policy science a considerable degree of credibility. Hence, on this shifting ground of "truth," we want to achieve objective analyses by being systematic in our definitions of goals, consistent about our methods of analysis, and forthright about our implicit assumptions.

In building castles over shifting sand, we must rely not only on the appropriateness of the tools but also on the integrity of those who must use them. The ethics of public policy is an important area of consideration. In this discussion, I can point to two broad areas of bias: personal honesty and the recognition of ideological biases.

At the personal level, analysts must overcome a number of ways in which their positions of power and knowledge can make them vulnerable to corruption. Analysts may often face a **conflict of interest**. One of the most difficult conflict-of-interest situations to grapple with—since it may happen under the radar and go unnoticed—is **honest graft**. Suppose I am employed by the city planning department and am working on a proposal for the expansion of mass transit to an area that is currently known for urban blight. I know that when the project is implemented and the new rapid transit system is introduced, the land value will increase substantially. Armed with this privileged knowledge, I choose to invest in the area that will benefit the most from the ensuing economic boom. If I do that while I am preparing the report, my analyses and my recommendations may be influenced my own selfish interest. I may want to emphasize the benefits and downplay the costs.

To take another example, say that during your work as a policy analyst, you have developed specialized knowledge that may be of interest to a private corporation. You believe that the corporation may be willing to offer you a high-paying job. If you are writing a report that has a significant impact on the company, you may be tempted to alter your report to make your policy recommendations favor your future employer. If you want to be totally impartial, in such a situation you must make full financial disclosure and, under certain circumstances, may recuse yourself from the project.

Your professional integrity may also be compromised if you orient your report to fit with the ideological or political agenda of your superiors. In most federal agencies, the party in power appoints the top management. Therefore, for career advancement, you may be tempted to slant your analysis to support your ideologically driven boss.

Finally, you may be driven by your own ideological position. In that case, you may deliberately ignore evidence that is contrary to your value position and cherry-pick information in a way that supports your view. Once again, it is exceedingly difficult to completely eliminate the biases arising out of your own ethical norms, since you may not even recognize it as an **ideological bias**.

In an otherwise subjective world, riven by prejudiced assessment, skewed perception, and the influence of personal interest, how do we maintain objectivity? I argue that these corrupting influences can be addressed only when analysts take pride in their profession. Their professional integrity is the guiding light that, at the end of the day, must ensure that their analyses are protected from systematic biases. In this context, perhaps, the work of prominent philosophers can provide an answer. We may recall John Stuart Mill's admonition of doing no harm as a moral compass. To this we may add John Rawls's (see chapter 5) assertion that a society should be judged by the welfare of those who are at the bottom. Thus, in evaluating public policies we must make sure that the burden of cost does not fall primarily on those who can least afford it.

In this book we will learn a number of different statistical techniques that are used for policy analyses. These tools carry with them an aura of objectivity, which can be extremely misleading. In their scientific garb, these "objective" analyses can hide strong ideological biases. In psychology it is often held that the strength of one's character can also be the source of one's weakness. Similarly, the appeal of objective methods of policy analysis is the ability to present complex phenomena with simple, easy-to-understand numbers and figures. At the same time, the unquestioned acceptance of these statistical approaches can lead to serious flaws. Therefore, we should know how to use with skill the extremely useful and powerful tool called statistics. This skill is honed with practice and by knowledge of the methods of manipulation. As we embark upon learning the tools of the trade for policy analysis, we may begin where John Maynard Keynes ended his seminal 1936 book, *The General Theory of Employment, Interest and Money.* He correctly warned,

> The ideas of economists and political philosophers, both when they are right and when they are wrong, are more powerful than is commonly believed. Indeed, the world is ruled by little else. Practical men, who believe themselves to be quite exempt from any intellectual influences, are usually the slaves of some defunct economist. Madmen in authority, who hear voices in the air, are distilling their frenzy from some academic scribbler of a few years back. I am sure that the power of vested interests is vastly exaggerated compared with the gradual encroachment of ideas. Soon or late, it is ideas, not vested interests, which are dangerous for good or evil.[36]

As the profile of policy analysis has risen in recent years, so has the volume of literature covering the hard issues of professional ethics. Echoing their colleague Mark Lilla,[37] social scientists David Weimer and Aidan Vining suggest that the profession of policy analysis should work toward a new standard of conduct that "explicitly recognize[s] our obligations to protect the basic rights of others, to support our democratic processes as expressed in our constitutions, and to promote analytical and personal integrity."[38] As an analyst attempting a high-wire act, balancing conflicting values, interests, and concerns, you can do no better than observe this standard.

KEY WORDS

Coequal model (p. 31)

Conflict of interest (p. 42)

Honest graft (p. 42)

Ideological bias (p. 42)

Mixture-in-administration model (p. 31)

Mixture-in-policy model (p. 32)

Policy-administration dichotomy model (p. 30)

Rational model (p. 35)

Whistleblowers (p. 34)

EXERCISES

1. Write an essay on the role of a policy analyst in a public agency. Discuss the various balancing acts this analyst must perform.
2. There is a continuing debate on the use of statistical and operations research techniques in the public policy making process. What are the strengths and weaknesses of these techniques?
3. Should policy analysts be dispassionate scientists, or should they express their deeply held values? Consider an important public policy issue that your community is currently debating. How would you analyze the issue? Do you think your analysis would be influenced by your values, your ideology, or the organization you work for? If so, should your analysis be considered "objective"?

Notes

1. For a delightful discussion, see Peter deLeon, "Reinventing the Policy Sciences: Three Steps Back to the Future," *Policy Sciences* 27 (March 1994): 77–95. Also see Herbert Goldhamer, *The Adviser* (New York: Elsevier, 1978), and Arnold J. Meltsner, *Rules for Rulers: The Politics of Advice* (Philadelphia: Temple University Press, 1990).

2. Although it is a bit dated, for an excellent discussion, see Arnold J. Meltsner, *Policy Analysts in the Bureaucracy* (Berkeley: University of California Press, 1976). Also see Robert Formaini, *The Myth of Scientific Public Policy* (New Brunswick, N.J.: Transaction, 1990), and Robert A. Heineman, *The World of the Policy Analyst: Rationality, Values, and Politics*, 2nd ed. (Chatham, N.J.: Chatham House, 1997).

3. See Allan M. Brandt, *The Cigarette Century: The Rise, Fall, and Deadly Persistence of the Product That Defined America* (New York: Basic Books, 2007).

4. Woodrow Wilson, "The Study of Administration," *Political Science Quarterly* 2 (1887): 197–222.

5. The articles by the "rebel academics" were published in *Toward a New Public Administration: The Minnowbrook Perspective*, ed. Frank Marini (San Francisco: Chandler, 1971).

6. Frederick C. Thayer, *An End to Hierarchy! An End to Competition! Organizing the Politics and Economics of Survival* (New York: New Viewpoints, 1973); later republished as *An End to Hierarchy and Competition: Administration in the Post-affluent world* (New York: New Viewpoints, 1981).

7. Lewis C. Mainzer, *Political Bureaucracy* (Glenview, Ill.: Scott, Foresman, 1973).

8. Svara, "Dichotomy and Duality."

9. In 1514, Henry requested that Pope Leo X perform the highly unusual but not entirely unprecedented action of making Wolsey (then a bishop) a "Cardinal Sole." In his letter to the Pope on August 12, Henry claimed that he "esteemed Wolsey above his dearest friends and could do nothing of importance without him." Jasper Ridley, *Statesman and Saint: Cardinal Wolsey, Sir Thomas More, and the Politics of Henry VIII* (New York: Viking, 1982), 48.

10. Henry showed deep personal respect and friendship for More and often stated that he "valued no one's approval more than his." See Carolly Erickson, *Great Harry: The Extravagant Life of Henry VIII* (New York: Summit, 1980), 120.

11. Albert O. Hirschman, *Exit, Voice, and Loyalty: Responses to Decline in Firms, Organizations, and States* (Cambridge, Mass.: Harvard University Press, 1970).

12. David L. Weimer and Aidan R. Vining, *Policy Analysis: Concepts and Practice*, 3rd ed. (Upper Saddle River, N.J.: Prentice-Hall, 1999).

13. See, for example, Robert S. Lynd, *Knowledge for What? The Place of Social Science in the American Culture* (Princeton, N.J.: Princeton University Press, 1939); Harold Lasswell, *Power and Personality* (New York: Norton, 1949); and Daniel Lerner and Harold Lasswell, eds., *The Policy Sciences* (Palo Alto, Calif.: Stanford University Press, 1951).

14. Frank Fischer, *Evaluating Public Policy* (Chicago: Nelson-Hall, 1995), chap. 1.

15. For a comprehensive look at the field of operations research and quantitative methods of decision making in the area of public policy analysis, see Göktuğ Morçöl, ed., *Handbook of Decision Making* (Boca Raton, Fla.: CRC, 2007).

16. See, for example, Virginia Held, "PPBS Comes to Washington," in *Planning-Programming-Budgeting: A Systems Approach to Management*, ed. Freemont J. Lyden and Ernest G. Miller (Chicago: Markham, 1968), 11–26. For one of the earliest explanations of "systems theory" in politics, see David Easton, "An Approach to the Analysis of Political Systems," *World Politics* 9 (1957): 383–400.

17. For a discussion of President Reagan's executive order and the use of quantitative techniques, see William Ascher, "The Evolution of Policy Sciences," *Journal of Policy Analysis and*

Management 5 (1986): 365–389; and Peter deLeon, *Advise and Consent: The Development of the Policy Sciences* (New York: Russell Sage Foundation, 1988). Also see Douglas Torgerson, "Between Knowledge and Politics: Three Faces of Policy Analysis," *Policy Sciences* 19 (1986): 33–60.

18. Aaron Wildavsky, *The Politics of the Budgetary Process*, 3rd ed. (Boston: Little, Brown, 1979), 197.

19. David von Drehle, "FBI's No. 2 Was 'Deep Throat': Mark Felt Ends 30-year Mystery of *The Post*'s Watergate Source," *Washington Post*, June 1, 2005.

20. For an excellent discussion, see Bethany McLean and Peter Elkind, *The Smartest Guys in the Room: The Amazing Rise and Scandalous Fall of Enron* (New York: Portfolio Trade, 2004).

21. For an excellent discussion of moral debate on the issue, see Karen J. Greenberg, ed., *The Torture Debate in America* (Cambridge, Mass.: Harvard University Press, 2006).

22. For a real-life experience of an interrogator on the effectiveness of torture as a tool for extracting information from accused terrorists, see Matthew Alexander (with John R. Bruning), *How to Break a Terrorist: The U.S. Interrogators Who Used Brains, Not Brutality, to Take Down the Deadliest Man in Iraq* (New York: Free Press, 2008).

23. Jane Mayer, *The Dark Side: The Inside Story of How the War on Terror Turned into a War on America's Ideals* (New York: Doubleday, 2008), 292.

24. Charles E. Lindblom and David K. Cohen, *Usable Knowledge: Social Science and Social Problem Solving* (New Haven, Conn.: Yale University Press, 1979).

25. Charles Lindblom, *Inquiry and Change: The Troubled Attempt to Understand and Shape Society* (New Haven, Conn.: Yale University Press, 1990), 131.

26. deLeon, "Reinventing the Policy Sciences," 78.

27. John L. Casti, *Searching for Certainty: What Scientists Can Know about the Future* (New York: Morrow, 1990).

28. Stephen McCafferty, *Macroeconomic Theory* (New York: Harper & Row, 1990), 360–361.

29. Alice M. Rivlin, "A New Vision of American Federalism," *Public Administration Review* 52 (1992): 315–320.

30. Anatole Kaletsky, "Goodbye, Homo Economicus," *Prospect*, April 26, 2009.

31. Elinor Ostrom, "A Behavioral Approach to the Rational Choice Theory of Collective Action: Presidential Address, American Political Science Association, 1997," *American Political Science Review* 92 (March 1998): 1–22.

32. Mark I. Lichbach, *The Rebel's Dilemma* (Ann Arbor: University of Michigan Press, 1995), 344.

33. See Robert E. Rector, "How Poor Are America's Poor? Examining the 'Plague' of Poverty in America," The Heritage Foundation, August 27, 2007, www.heritage.org/research/welfare/bg 2064.cfm.

34. Ron Haskins and Isabel V. Sawhill, "Attacking Poverty and Inequality: Reinvigorate the Fight for Greater Opportunity," Brookings Instition, 2008, www.brookings.edu/papers/2007/~/media/Files/Projects/Opportunity08/PB_Poverty_Haskins_Sawhill2.pdf.

35. Karl Popper, *The Logic of Scientific Discovery* (New York: Harper & Row, 1959), 65.

36. John Maynard Keynes, *The General Theory of Employment, Interest and Money* (New York: Harcourt, Brace, 1936).

37. Mark T. Lilla, "Ethos, 'Ethics,' and Public Policy," *Public Interest* 63 (1981): 3–17.

38. Weimer and Vining, *Policy Analysis*, 57.

3 Government and the Market

The city of Boston and its surrounding region faced a housing crisis in the 1990s.[1] As the region experienced a nearly decade-long economic boom, jobs were created and new housing developments sprang up everywhere. However, housing was priced far beyond the reach of low-income residents. According to a government study, only eleven communities in the greater Boston area set aside more than 8 percent of their housing for low-income families. Ninety-three communities failed to do even that much. After months of pressuring reluctant suburban politicians, Mayor Thomas Menino submitted legislation to the city council to penalize neighboring cities if they did not set aside at least a tenth of their housing in the affordable price range. If they did not meet this goal, and made no effort to meet it, the legislation recommended that the state would withhold housing funds. Today, many cities across the land, particularly those with very high housing costs, have passed similar ordinances. This example may cause you to wonder why government interferes in a free market system. If some of its citizens cannot afford to live in a particular city, is it the proper role of the government to force the city to create housing for them? If so, on what basis should it intervene?

History tells us that governments have always strongly influenced the lives of citizens. In fact, until recently, the grip of the king and the church was quite strong. Protests against such domination started in Europe. In 1776, as the first shots of rebellion were being heard in the colonial states, a revolution of a different sort was taking place on the Atlantic's other shore. Adam Smith, an ex–customs official and a tutor to an aristocratic child, published *An Inquiry into the Nature and the Causes of the Wealth of Nations.*[2] As noted in chapter 1, Smith wrote his book to repudiate the then popular theory of **mercantilism**, which argued that a nation becomes prosperous when it maintains a trade surplus by maximizing exports and minimizing imports. To limit imports, mercantilism erected trade barriers. In contrast, Smith argued that the wealth of a nation increases when all restrictions to the free functioning of the market are removed. He reasoned that individuals, when free of outside restrictions, pursue their self-interest, allowing the nation to prosper.

Adam Smith's arguments regarding the efficient working of a market are shown in Figure 3.1.[3] The curve DD depicts the demand for a certain commodity, while the SS curve traces its supply. The point of **equilibrium** is reached where the curves intersect. This point is called *equilibrium* (a term borrowed from mechanics) for two reasons:

1. When the market rests at that point, no internal force will cause it to move away from equilibrium.
2. If the market departs from this point, the push and pull of demand and supply will bring it back to equilibrium (point E).

If a producer asks for a price higher than is warranted by the market (P_o), the demand for the product will dwindle, and ultimately the seller will have to lower the price. Similarly, if one producer makes an abnormally high profit by selling a new product, soon other suppliers will flood the market with copycat products. A situation of oversupply will occur, pushing the price down from P_o to P_e. The opposite scenario will take place if the market price is below the equilibrium point. Consumers will attempt to purchase more goods while suppliers cut down on production. This situation of excess demand drives the market price from P_u to P_e.

FIGURE 3.1	**The Foundation of Economic Reasoning: Market Equilibrium**

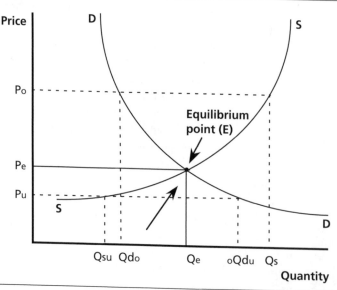

Note: The demand curve, DD, is downward sloping because as the price of a commodity goes down, its demand increases. In contrast, the supply curve, SS, slopes upward. When prices go up, supply increases in response to a greater expectation of profit. The point of intersection of the two curves is called the equilibrium point.

This diagram—perhaps the most well-known illustration in the social sciences—forms the foundation of the entire field of economics. As you can see, if there is any outside intervention, the market is corrupted; it becomes inefficient because it cannot reach the point of equilibrium. When supply is arbitrarily restricted, buyers pay a higher price than they should be paying. This situation leads to unemployment and other market inefficiencies. On the other hand, when supply is increased beyond the point of equilibrium, buyers consume more than they should, leading to overuse and waste.

You may note the normative implications of this discussion, which are apparent from our use of the imperative *should*. The government *should* stay away from the marketplace so that prices reflect the "true" forces of demand and supply. When the government does not interfere, the invisible hand of market forces clears the market and allocates resources among the four factors of production—land, labor, capital, and organization—in the fairest way. Landowners get the rent they deserve, and laborers get the wages they merit. Moreover, market forces allocate the most appropriate amount of interest to the owners of capital and the right level of profits to the entrepreneurs. When anyone is paid more than he or she deserves, the market wipes out the excess profit through free competition.

THE FUNDAMENTAL CONTRIBUTIONS OF ECONOMIC ANALYSES

The success of an academic discipline can ultimately be gauged by the extent to which its core doctrines permeate our daily lives, social values, and accepted norms. By that measure, the intellectual revolution sparked by the bored Scottish tutor of a nobleman's son is unparalleled in social science. In his analysis of a nation's prosperity, Smith placed the individual at the forefront of the economic system. Over the 200 years following the publication of *Wealth of Nations*, economics has grown in many diverse directions. If we were to point out the most fundamental contributions of economics as an analytical tool, we might mention the related concepts of **marginal analysis** and **opportunity costs**. These concepts are so integral to systematic analysis that it is virtually impossible to engage in a meaningful academic discourse about public policy without taking them into account.

Marginal Analysis

In the economic literature the term *marginal* means "additional." Although the word is used in classrooms as well as boardrooms, policymakers often make serious mistakes when they confuse *marginal* with *average*. Let me explain marginal utility by giving you an example. Suppose you are thirsty and you come upon a stand selling cold drinks. You are so thirsty that you are willing to pay $2 for the first drink. However, the drink is too small to quench your thirst, so you want a second one. Because you are already somewhat satisfied, you are willing to spend up to $1.75 for it. After quaffing the second drink, you are still thirsty. You are willing to pay $1 for a third and $0.50 for a fourth. We plot your willingness to pay in Figure 3.2. Remember, these numbers reflect only

FIGURE 3.2   **Marginal Utility and Consumer Surplus**

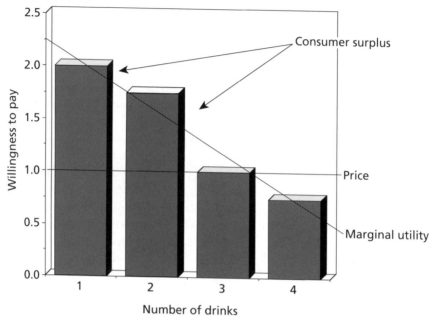

your psychological willingness to pay, not the actual prices for the marginal, or additional, drinks. They represent the marginal utility you receive from the drinks.

The important question becomes, at what point would you stop buying drinks? Let us say the price of a drink is $1. You will stop after you have consumed three drinks. You will not stop before then, because you are getting a bargain with each drink, and each provides you with more utility than it costs you. However, the price of the fourth drink is below your marginal utility. The first rule of **consumption efficiency** is to *stop consuming at the point where the marginal utility of the good is exactly equal to its **marginal cost**.* Your marginal cost (the cost of an additional drink) is fixed at $1. In a perfectly competitive market, you are a **price taker**. That is, because the market is too large for you to manipulate, you cannot influence the market price with your purchase. The additional utility you derive from three drinks, the amount above your market price ($1), is your **consumer surplus**. It is the difference between the market price and the total utility. For the first drink, the consumer surplus is $1 ($2 – $1); for the second drink, it is $0.75 ($1.75 – $1); and for the third drink, there is no consumer surplus ($1 – $1). The full implications of this concept are discussed in chapter 14.

So as a consumer, you know when to stop buying. What about the producer? A producer produces to the point where his or her **marginal revenue** equals the price. Suppose I am the owner of that drink stand and I am deciding how many gallons of drinks to produce. As I sell each drink, I make a certain amount of revenue. I keep buying the ingredients until I reach the point where the marginal cost (of buying, transporting, storing, and serving) is equal to the marginal revenue from the product. Because I am a small producer and cannot influence prices in the market, I am—like the customer—a price taker. Therefore, *I will stop producing when my marginal revenue is equal to the marginal cost.* Together, the two dictums about consumption and production constitute the iron laws of microeconomics. They give us both the point at which a consumer would stop buying and the one at which a producer would set limits for production.

Marginal Versus Average: Cause for Policy Confusion. Although marginal costs and benefits are basic concepts of microeconomics, they are often misunderstood. Two examples, one drawn from the private sector and the other from a public policy debate, can help us understand the confusion.

The next time you board an airplane, look around the aircraft. Although each passenger will travel the same distance, the fares they pay will vary widely. Some passengers have paid full fare for, say, buying the ticket after the minimum number of stipulated days or for not spending a Saturday night at their destinations. There are those who bought tickets at a discount due to their age (senior citizens or children), special promotional deals, or special arrangements with travel agencies. Besides these passengers, there may be students on board with cut-rate standby fares or those who are flying free of charge on a "frequent flyer" arrangement. Does this wide variation surprise you? Does the airline lose money for selling certain tickets at a discount, since each discounted ticket brings down the average price per ticket?

The surprising answer is that the airline makes money even when it sells tickets at a significant discount (awarding free tickets to frequent flyers may fall under the separate category of giving incentives or promoting passenger loyalty). This is because most of the costs of flying an airplane are fixed. The salaries of the crews and the ground staff must be paid regardless of the number of passengers on board. The port authorities must be paid for landing rights at the airport. The costs of maintenance will not vary significantly with the *additional* number of passengers. Therefore, the marginal cost of carrying an additional passenger is negligible. After those paying full price have covered maintenance costs, any revenue received from a senior citizen or a standby passenger will result in positive marginal revenue for the airline. If decision makers look only at the average fare—which goes down with every discounted ticket—they will surely miss the opportunity to increase the company's profit by carefully instituting discounted prices.

When it comes to the public sector, the confusion about average and marginal costs can lead to serious policy mistakes. Take, for example, the controversy over the cost of illegal immigration in California. During the mid–1990s, the state was caught up in a divisive debate over the cost of educating the children of illegal immigrants. A referendum was passed barring these children from public education. During the debate the proponents of the ban estimated the costs by taking the *average cost* per child (the entire state education budget divided by the number of students) and multiplying it by the number of children of illegal immigrants enrolled in California's public schools. In contrast, those who opposed the measure pointed out that much of the education budget is fixed. They argued that if we want to calculate the true cost of educating these children, we must look at the *marginal cost*. It is interesting to note that the two sides were arguing past one another without realizing the sources of the two widely varying figures.

Opportunity Costs

To understand opportunity costs, let us go back to the case of affordable housing in the Boston area. The state of Massachusetts set aside $400 million in housing aid as an incentive for cities to supply affordable housing to low-income families.[4] The mayor's plan also called for using some of the state's surplus funds to supplement this housing trust fund. Of course, it is a noble idea to encourage cities to build houses for low-income people. But the money spent on affordable housing projects could have been put to other uses, such as making the streets safer, providing children with a better education, or assisting elderly people and those who are homeless. This argument is normal in public debate; when we spend money for a project, other deserving projects remain unfunded or underfunded. When considering a project, it is common to take into account the costs of alternative projects. In other words, *what must you give up to get the project you are buying*? The answer to this question allows you to determine the opportunity cost of an activity.

Let us take a look at the cost of higher education. How much are you paying for your college education? If you are a full-time student, you would calculate your expenses for tuition, room and board, supplies, transportation, and so on. In addition, you must factor in another cost. You gave up a job you otherwise would have had, had you not attended college. We must add the monetary costs and the estimated forgone income. It is impossible to overlook opportunity cost in public policy decisions, because no resource is infinitely abundant and without alternative uses. Space, clean air, and ocean water all have alternative uses and opportunity costs associated with their exploitation. Harvesting an old-growth forest in the Pacific Northwest clashes with saving the endangered spotted owls. The sudden popularity of fishing for orange roughy off the Australian coast has deprived giant squid of their primary food source. A proposed ballpark vies for public money with other city needs, such as library facilities, garbage collection services, and programs to care for the downtown homeless population. When it comes to public policy analysis, economics—as a powerful analytical tool—teaches us to look beyond the market value of a resource to its opportunity cost.

MARKET FAILURE: WHY GOVERNMENT INTERFERES IN A FREE MARKET

Adam Smith saw the market as inherently self-correcting. If only we let the market run its course, he said, most of our miseries would be solved—if not immediately, certainly in the long run. Yet his critics pointed out that not all markets are self-correcting. The problems of market failure became painfully clear in 1929, when, following the stock market crash, the Great Depression set in. John Maynard Keynes argued that the free market, if left on its own, would not be able to extricate itself from the quagmire of high unemployment (recession or depression) or high prices (inflation). For the economy to reach full employment with stable prices, it would require active government intervention. Furthermore, Keynes famously commented that the market may indeed correct itself in the long run—a favorite term of conservative economists—but "in the long run we are all dead."

Under the guidance of Keynes, the role of the government in the domestic and international economies became firmly rooted. Building on his work, Keynes's intellectual descendants determined that the government has four major roles: *allocation, distribution, stabilization,* and *growth.* First, because the market cannot allocate public goods (see chapter 1), the government must step in. For example, the government builds infrastructure, mandates clean air, and provides public education and military protection because the market fails to supply them. Second, because the market inherently favors rich and powerful people, the government must help those who are caught in an endless cycle of poverty. In this way it plays a redistributive role, whereby through taxation, similar to the mythical Robin Hood, it takes money away from the wealthy and spends it on the poor. Third, with active government intervention through stabilization policies, the market is protected from wild swings of inflation and recession and safeguarded against the extremes of business cycles. Finally, because the market is a poor allocator of resources between current consumption and future investment, an activist government—through its policies that support research and development in science, technology, and education—can ensure future prosperity for the nation.

A society based on free market principles and requiring no government intervention—except to maintain external and internal security and a fair judicial system—sounds good in theory. Upon close scrutiny, however, the society that self-corrects and attains equilibrium loses some of its appeal. When we realize that a perfectly competitive market depends on some of the most restrictive assumptions and truncated views of reality, it is apparent that the market will not always self-correct. A free market is based on four drastic assumptions:

1. There are numerous buyers and sellers.
2. There is perfect exit from and entry into the market.
3. There is a perfect flow of information.
4. There is no **externality**, or no one is affected by the activities of any other person.

A perfectly competitive market is shattered when any of these four conditions is violated. Let us examine these conditions in more detail.

Lack of Competition

The competitive market that emerged from Adam Smith's analyses was rooted in the early days of the industrial revolution, when there were no significant monopoly forces in the market. When there are numerous buyers and sellers, no individual or firm can single-handedly influence the outcome of the market. Each participant in the market is a price taker, as opposed to being a monopolistic **price maker**. Every buyer and seller must adjust his or her respective demand and supply in view of prevailing market prices. Landowners, laborers, moneylenders, and business entrepreneurs earn according to their respective merit. If anyone makes more than that, the excess profit will bring in other competitors, thereby eliminating any profit over what is warranted by merit.

Market conditions have changed significantly since the eighteenth century. Today the market is often plagued by monopoly power. The federal government's antitrust case against Microsoft is an example. The government argued that by bundling its Internet Explorer Web browser with its Windows operating system, Microsoft made it hard for consumers to use another browser, such as Netscape. In its price-making capacity, a monopolist sets a price that guarantees a profit over what it would have earned if there

A CASE IN POINT

Too Big to Fail: How Monopolies Can Hold the Government Hostage

I have explained the theory behind the hypothesis that a monopoly is inherently less efficient than a perfectly competitive market. However, with its economic power a monopoly also acquires political power and positions of special privilege, which can be squarely in conflict with the national well-being. The abuse of power from corporate monopoly became apparent as the nation and the entire world were industrializing. And the most essential ingredient in the process was oil. Sensing an opportunity, the Standard Oil Company brought it under the control of a single entity. Through a series of innovative and stealthy business practices in the 1870s, the legendary John D. Rockefeller, his brother William, and a handful of other men created a huge monopoly by forcing out the competition. They created a "trust," which was a conglomeration of a number of powerful companies. This type of economic giant quickly became known for its predatory practices, leading Congress to pass sweeping antitrust legislation, including the Sherman Act of 1890 and the Clayton Act of 1914.[5] While they were minimally able to curb the power of the monopolies in the area of oil production and distribution, monopoly thrived in other areas.

Of course, monopoly is not restricted to industry; it involves labor unions as well. As the monopoly power of the United Auto Workers increased, it forced car manufacturers (particularly General Motors and Chrysler) to grant its workers salaries and benefits that were unsustainable in the face of international competition. The rapidly increasing gas prices and environmental concerns associated with large trucks and SUVs, however, soon caught up with GM; it saw its sales plummet and faced the ominous prospect of bankruptcy when the recession of 2008 took hold. Yet GM's going out of business was unthinkable for the policymakers in Washington, leading them to pass a $14 billion bailout for the automaker. Not only did the automakers employ a

were competition. In 1999, the court decided that in a competitive market, Microsoft would have charged $29 for Windows 98, but because it was a monopolist, it could charge $49, nearly double the competitive amount.[9]

A market can sustain a higher price only when the supply is restricted; to hold a high price, a monopolist must reduce the total supply in the market. In a monopolistic market, society loses because of the restricted supply. In addition, a monopolist can choke off innovations because it has little financial incentive to make improvements for a captive group of buyers.

A monopolist does more than simply restrict its output to raise the prices of its products. Some economists have argued that because a monopolist has little incentive to lower costs to achieve maximum efficiency, it often operates at a less than optimal level of efficiency. Harvey Leibenstein coined the term *x-inefficiency* to describe such a situation.[10] In the late 1980s the Defense Department found itself in a public relations controversy when someone pointed out that it was purchasing items such as toilet seats and screwdrivers at exorbitant prices from its monopolistic suppliers. In summer 2000 huge number of people in the nation, they were highly concentrated in certain areas, such as Michigan, where their collapse would have led to an unmitigated disaster.[6]

The American International Group is the largest insurance company on the planet, the eighteenth largest company of any kind in the world. It commanded $1 trillion in reported assets, roughly equal to the gross domestic income of India,[7] and it is a component of the Dow Jones Industrial Average. AIG began to experience problems, however, when one of its subsidiaries wrote insurance protection against losses on debts and loans of borrowers to the tune of $447 billion, spurring a chain of disastrous events. When the housing market was hit by a flood of mortgage defaults and debt piled up in 2008, AIG was hit hard and was left with a very low level of capital reserves. The government stepped in to prevent its total collapse, bailing it out for an eye-popping $173.3 billion. In return, taxpayers received an 80 percent stake in AIG.

How did these corporations get to be too big to fail? Republicans and Democrats alike had paid scant attention to the problems that monopoly creates for the market. President George W. Bush's Justice Department did not file a single case against a dominant firm for violating the antimonopoly laws.[8] At the time of this writing, the Obama administration's new policy more closely aligns the American antitrust policy on monopolies and predatory practices with the views of antitrust regulators at the European Commission. If history is any predictor, however, as soon as the economy turns around and public attention shifts, the economic power of the corporate giants will ensure that the concentration of economic power will continue to grow unabated.

Discussion Points

1. Should we be concerned about monopoly power in the current economic market? Why or why not?
2. How can we ensure that the government enforces antitrust laws when public focus on the ills of concentration of economic power shifts?

the oligopolistic oil industry was accused of price gouging. In response, President Bill Clinton, as a stopgap measure, decided to release some of the strategic oil reserves held by the government for such an emergencies.[11] (See "A Case in Point" for a more in-depth discussion of monopolies and government actions.)

Barriers to Entry and Exit

The concept of ease of entry into the market has three aspects. The first is **factor mobility**. Take, for example, unemployment. In a perfectly competitive market, it does not exist. This is because an unemployed person is one who is able and willing to accept a job at the going wage.[12] If I want to become a guard in the National Basketball Association but lack the necessary talent and physical skills, I cannot be classified as unemployed, because I am willing to play the position. Similarly, if I decline to take a job at the going rate because it is far below what I expect to earn, I am not considered unemployed, because I can always take this job. If wages are too high, the demand for labor goes down and exerts a downward pressure on the wage rate. In contrast, if wages are too low, firms hire more people until the market wage rate becomes equal to the market-clearing equilibrium rate. This typically has been the conservative argument in the United States against minimum wage restrictions; if there is unemployment it is because the government has set a minimum wage rate, which is a barrier to hiring.

The second aspect of ease of entry relates to what is known as **indivisibility**. For some industries, the biggest impediment to entry is the size of the required investment. For instance, in the early part of the twentieth century, a profusion of car manufacturers opened for business. Because the technology was not that complex, many prospective producers entered the market. However, as technology advanced, and as Henry Ford radically altered manufacturing through his innovation of assembly line production, it became increasingly difficult for new manufacturers to spring up with new automobile designs; a huge investment was required to compete with the established car manufacturers. This impediment to market entry created an **oligopoly** (dominance by a few large sellers) in the automobile industry.

The outcome of the barriers to entry is known as **rent seeking**. When the market is restricted, any source of unusual profit attracts those who can exploit product scarcity and make a quick buck. Restrictions can creep in from a variety of sources, both public and private. In the public sector, restrictions on factor mobility result from government regulations. When there is a huge demand for a particular good but the government imposes a limit on its availability, the resulting excess demand causes its price to increase and revenues to climb. This increased revenue becomes excess profit for some. For those regulating the supply of the product, it can take the form of a bribe.

For those in the private sector, it provides a select group of business owners with the opportunity to make a monopoly profit. In the 1990s, California's milk producers successfully lobbied state politicians to set wholesale milk prices at an artificially high level and to impose restrictions on imports from neighboring states. In October 1999, the California Department of Food and Agriculture increased the wholesale price by 33 percent, one of the biggest increases in state history. The hike allowed California dairy farmers to earn an extra forty-two cents for every gallon of milk they sold to processors. As a result Californians spent about $650 million more a year for milk than they would have in a free marketplace.[13] In Figure 3.3, the shaded area represents this $650 million rent.

Consider another example, drug trafficking in the United States. Without any government restrictions, the market price of an illicit substance would find its equilibrium, at which point the supply would satisfy all those who are willing to consume it at the going rate. However, when the government imposes sanctions, the supply is immediately restricted. This restriction increases its price and acts as a windfall to the drug smugglers—or as a bribe to corrupt law enforcement agents. In many developing countries, government corruption can be traced to officials' penchant for imposing too many restrictions on the economy (see "A Case in Point").

Rent seeking, therefore, leads to market inefficiency and can take many forms. Suppose your state awards a contract to a firm to build highways, at a profit deemed higher than normal by the firm's competitors. Say the normal profit for a similar project is $10 million, but firm A will receive $15 million. This situation may prompt firm A's competitor, firm B, to allocate up to $5 million to fight the decision in court. If the decision is reversed in favor of firm B, and the firm spends only $3 million in legal costs, then it makes a windfall

| FIGURE 3.3 | Rent Seeking |

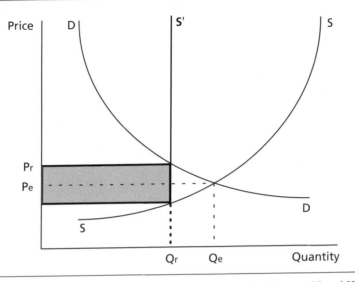

Note: The diagram shows the effects of an artificial restriction on supply. The curves DD and SS show the demand and supply of a commodity that, without any restriction, would reach its point of market-clearing equilibrium at price P_e and quantity Q_e. However, because the government has restricted the supply to SS, this action creates an artificial quantity decrease to Q_r and a price increase to P_r. The shaded area shows the possibility for rent seeking or corruption.

of $2 million over what it would have earned in a competitive market. In the meantime, the project is delayed, and waste and inefficiency are introduced into the market.

Restricted or Asymmetrical Flow of Information

We are told that the secret formula for Coca-Cola is kept in a vault in Atlanta. In a perfectly competitive market, it would be anathema to have such a secret. However, contrary to the ideal constructs of a perfectly competitive market, a producer can often benefit from secrets. If the recipe for the fizzy drink had not been a secret and had been as available as the formula for hot dogs, another company might have posed stiff competition when the drink was introduced. But the secret kept competition at bay. In its early days, as the drink became wildly popular, other firms could not break into its newly created niche market. Later, with clever advertising and controlled distribution, the company established its influence over the soft drink industry.

Theories of perfect competition assume that information is free-flowing between buyers and sellers, so if you are in the market for a certain product, you can determine its true value to you. Yet in actuality, information is neither readily available nor free. In the case of some products, you can easily evaluate whether they are worth their prices. For instance, if you are considering buying a painting, you can look at it and determine if you like it or not. This type of good is called a **search good**—its quality is readily apparent. However, if the seller claims that it is an authentic painting by a reputed artist, and if you are not an art expert yourself, you may want to go to a certified appraiser and get it authenticated. To do so will cost you money—this is the cost of information. In the

A CASE IN POINT

Drug Policy: Our Addiction to Failure?

Since President Richard Nixon declared war on drug abuse in 1971, the nation has been spending nearly $10 billion a year to combat the movement of illicit drugs from Latin America to the United States. The war on drugs has not only cost money and lives in the United States, it has also destabilized a large part of Latin America. The insatiable demand for drugs created the twin-headed monster of money and guns, which has devoured many to the south of us and is ultimately threatening U.S. national security. Money has corrupted the political systems of many Latin American countries, and lax gun laws in the United States have led to a steady stream of the most sophisticated guns flowing into Latin America, overwhelming the firepower of traditional police forces.[14] At the time of writing, law and order are deteriorating rapidly in Mexico. Pictures of gruesome murders, including beheadings, committed by warring factions are becoming commonplace. In 2009 the U.S. State Department issued an advisory for Americans visiting Mexico, and many U.S. colleges discouraged students from crossing the border for traditional spring break revelry.

The profits from the drug trade have been the lifeblood of many violent organizations, such as the Revolutionary Armed Forces of Colombia (FARC), the Shining Path in Peru, and even the Taliban in Afghanistan, which directly threaten the United States. Although Colombia has seen a recent decline in violence and a weakening of FARC, and the Shining Path has been defeated in Peru, there is more cultivation of coca in Latin America and opium in Afghanistan.

In 2009, the Latin American Commission on Drugs and Democracy declared that despite trillions of dollars in spending, thousands of deaths, and hundreds of thousands of imprisonments, the war on drugs was "lost."[15] It plainly pointed out that "prohibitionist policies based on eradication, interdiction and criminalization of consumption simply have not worked."[16] In light of this failure, the commission proposes a paradigm shift based on three strategies:

1. Drug abusers should be treated as patients in need of public health services, rather than as criminals who need to be locked away.
2. The demand for drugs should be reduced by spending more on educating the public on the harmful effects of drug abuse.
3. The drug distribution network, run by organized crime, should be targeted more aggressively through police and intelligence work.

Discussion Points

1. What kinds of policies should we consider to combat illegal drug use? Public education about harmful effects of drugs? Amending gun laws to prevent guns from crossing borders and landing in drug traffickers' hands? Legalizing certain types of drugs?
2. What kind of metrics should we use to determine the success or failure of our policies?
3. What are the political, cultural, and historical impediments to a radical change in our drug policies?

eighteenth-century world of Adam Smith, such considerations were not as important as they are today. Therefore, in today's highly litigious society, the traditional warning of "buyer beware" is not sufficient, as it can lead to severe market inefficiencies.

In contrast to search goods, there are certain products you need to experience (or consume) before you can know their characteristics. By the time you have consumed a product and realized that it was not up to its billing and that the seller had withheld information about its limitations, it may be too late for you to receive compensation for your loss. These are called **experience goods**. We often hear about pharmaceutical companies being sued for selling drugs with unacceptable side effects that were not known to their users. Any drug will have some undesirable side effects. However, if a company knowingly engages in false advertising, which a consumer cannot be expected to verify, the government must step in and try to eliminate the market inefficiency.

Government attempts to correct these inefficiencies by passing proper disclosure laws, which can cover many aspects of trade, large and small. For instance, in several states, such as California, New York, and Missouri, a seller of real property must disclose any known occurrences of paranormal activities to a potential buyer. If you purchase a house that you believe is "haunted" and the seller was aware of this reputation at the time of sale, you can sue the seller for not disclosing the unwanted resident of your house.[17] In another example, in 2009, the Food and Drug Administration (FDA) demanded that General Mills cease making its highly exaggerated claims of the cholesterol-reducing properties of its Cheerios cereal. The company claimed that its product could reduce "bad" cholesterol levels by 4 percent in just six weeks and ward off heart disease and cancers of the colon and stomach. These extraordinary claims were printed boldly on Cheerios packages, featured on the General Mills Web site and in television commercials, and even announced over loudspeakers in supermarkets as part of the company's promotional efforts. The FDA finally took the necessary step to stop the food giant from deceiving the consumers with its false claims.[18]

Externalities and Social Costs

Markets are efficient at producing goods that consumers want at prices they are willing to pay. This efficient process of allocating resources works well as long as an exchange between a buyer and a seller affects only those two parties. Unfortunately, their transaction often affects other parties. When it does, it creates an externality. The costs or benefits of individual externalities add up to what are known as **social costs** or **social benefits**. Externalities occur when the decisions of an economic actor (an individual, a firm, or a government unit) have an impact on another actor's well-being without the affected party's consent or compensation. If the impact is favorable, it is called a **positive externality**. If it is adverse, it is called a **negative externality**.

Suppose your town wants to attract a large retail outlet. The outlet is interested but would like a significant tax break. How can you justify using public money to help a privately owned company? Supporters of the proposal will point out the positive externalities: the creation of new jobs, the ability to attract other small businesses, and the influx of additional customers for bars and restaurants. These businesses will need employees, so even more jobs will be created. All of these activities will generate tax revenues for your town. They are examples of social benefits. Opponents of the project, on the other hand, will note the negative externalities, such as traffic congestion, an increase

A CASE IN POINT

College Affordability: Should Government Intervene?

The cost of higher education in the United States is rising much faster than the rate of inflation and parents' ability to pay for it, according to a report from the National Center for Public Policy and Higher Education.[19] The report found that college tuition and fees increased 439 percent from 1982 to 2007, while the median family income rose 147 percent. As a result, college loans have more than doubled in the past decade. Compounding the problem, students from lower income families, on average, are getting smaller grants from the colleges they attend than students from more affluent families. While in many parts of the world, a child's future is tied to his or her parents' socioeconomic status, this country was founded on the principle of providing everyone the opportunity to prosper. Yet the rapid increases in college costs are threatening this "American dream" and some of our most cherished national goals.

We know that the completion of each successive level of education makes it possible for students to earn more money. In 2009, the U.S. Department of Education reported that while the average yearly income of a four-year college graduate was $65,000, those with two-year college educations could expect to earn substantially less, $38,000. This average goes down even further, as those with only high school diplomas earn, on average, $26,000, and those without diplomas must get by on a meager $18,000 a year.[20] It is no wonder that young men and women have looked at higher education as the key to success. This becomes particularly true during periods of economic downturn, when those who get thrown out of work attempt to increase their future earning capabilities by enrolling in institutions of higher learning, particularly state colleges and universities. Ironically, times of huge budget shortfalls cause state governments to cut back their support for higher education. In the spring of 2009, in the midst of the deepest recession since the days of the Great Depression, the University of California system announced a 9.6 percent tuition increase, while the California State University system also announced a 10 percent increase. Florida was talking about a 15 percent increase, while Washington State considered a

in crime, and the possible degradation of both the environment and the overall quality of life. These are the social costs of the retail outlet locating in your town.

The actor who generates positive externalities cannot redeem any of them. Similarly, those hit by negative externalities cannot recoup their losses through the market process. The private, or market, cost reflects the price of a good, the price we pay in stores. However, another cost may be associated with the consumption of this good. When I buy a pack of cigarettes, I pay the private, or market cost. However, cigarette smoking is associated with a host of ailments that cost states huge amounts of money to care for patients suffering from these illnesses. When society (or the government, as the agent of society) pays for their care, that cost should be added to the product's market price. When it is not, the cost of the negative externality of smoking causes the social price to exceed the market price. That is, if you are a smoker, the price you are paying for the cigarettes is lower than what you should be paying when you take into account all the costs that you are imposing on the others. Since the market is unable to take corrective action on its whopping 20 percent jump. The National Center for Public Policy and Higher Education reported that in 2007, the net cost of a year at a four-year public university amounted to 28 percent of the median family income, while a four-year private university cost 76 percent of the median family income. The situation is particularly daunting for those families with incomes in the lowest 20 percent; for them, the net cost of a year at a public university was 55 percent of the median income, up from 39 percent in 1999–2000. At community colleges, long seen as a safety net, that cost was 49 percent of the poorest families' median income in 2007–2008, up from 40 percent in 1999–2000. It is no wonder that in 2008 the cohort of twenty-five to thirty-four-year-olds was less educated than that of older workers.

According to a survey conducted by the Chronicle of Higher Education in 2008, 42 percent of Americans think that controlling college costs is "extremely important" and needs to be addressed by the federal government. Support for federal intervention in the rise of college tuition was strongest among parents (55 percent) and those with incomes under $35,000 (65 percent).[21] While lawmakers continue to debate intervention measures, such as creating a public watch list of universities whose tuition increases outpace inflation, the middle class has begun to assume higher debts for education costs, and many low-income students are left unable to afford college. As you can see, this phenomenal cost increase can tear apart some of the basic expectations of the people and create a permanent underclass, which, by any measure, is a harbinger of conflict and social discord.

Discussion Points

1. Why are college costs, particularly at public universities, rising so rapidly? Are these examples of market or government failure?
2. Should the government be involved in the education business? What should state governments do during the times of economic recession?

own, the government steps in with a tax to set the market price equal to the social cost. In the same way, when the government imposes taxes on a polluting firm, it bridges the gap between the market price and the social cost of the firm's product. In either case, the tax may be shifted to customers. The tax will reduce the demand for the good, thereby lowering the cost of consuming a socially harmful product.

Rising Service Costs: The Appearance of Market Failure

Another curious matter makes the functioning of the free market somewhat complicated. The cost of providing services—from education to health care, from personal services, such as plumbing, to car repair—is increasing much faster than are general commodity prices in the economy.[22] This phenomenon, although not directly related to market failure, calls for government intervention. As a society, we are bewildered by rising health care costs and appalled at the cost of higher education—especially at public universities (see "A Case in Point"). We wonder why the costs of government service delivery, at all levels of government, keep increasing, far outstripping the inflation rate. Moreover, as prices rise, the quality of many of these services seems to fall.

Although market failure and government intervention are responsible for some price increases, the major causes of such increases are rooted in simple economics, not "price gouging," moral hazard (see chapter 1), or other kinds of market failure. Price increases also have very little to do with inefficiency in the government sector, though comparisons of government with the private manufacturing sector may suggest otherwise. For example, due to dizzying advances in computer technology, the cost of information processing is falling at an exponential rate. Technology is moving so fast that by the time this book is published, my one-year-old computer will have become obsolete. As we take advantage of computer-assisted design and manufacturing, worker productivity continues to shoot up at an astronomical rate. However, most service delivery by the government and public health providers remains impervious to technological advances. Even in our technology-saturated society, a postal worker still must deliver mail one house at a time, garbage must be picked up at the curb in front of each house, doctors must spend time with individual patients, and teachers must observe class-size restrictions. As a result, cost escalation is typical of many labor-intensive services, such as restaurant businesses, retail stores, and automobile repair shops.

GOVERNMENT FAILURE

In many ways the 1960s were magical, particularly for the United States. An awestruck nation watched astronaut Neil Armstrong take a "giant leap for mankind" to become the first person to step on the moon. The space race was over, and the United States had beaten the Soviet Union to the moon. The United States was indisputably on top in terms of military might and advancement in science and technology. However, in the midst of this exuberance, the nation faced widespread, endemic problems, from poverty and racism to political assassinations and street riots. A bewildered nation asked, if we can send men to the moon, why can't we solve our earthly problems? President Lyndon Johnson unveiled his Great Society program as a way to solve some of these vexing social problems. In the area of public budgeting, Johnson introduced the Planning-Programming-Budgeting System (PPBS), a process of allocating money through analytical means (see chapter 2). In the area of planning, physical planning based on technology was in vogue. In the realm of public policy, "systems analysis" was used to dissect every social problem into neat analytical components.

Unfortunately, the government failed to deliver. The Great Society program did not eliminate poverty,[23] the PPBS was a dismal failure, physical planning that emphasized building new public housing and freeways was unable to cure urban blight, and systems analysis grappled unsuccessfully with social problems. It was indeed easier to remove technological hurdles to landing on the moon than to find solutions to the age-old problems of human society. If in an imperfect world the market often fails to deliver, so does the government. There are ten reasons for this failure, each of which we will discuss briefly:

1. Inability to define social welfare
2. The limits of democracy and the paradox of voting

3. Inability to define the marginal benefits and costs of public goods
4. Political constraints
5. Cultural constraints
6. Institutional constraints
7. Legal constraints
8. Knowledge constraints
9. Analytical constraints
10. The timing of policies

Inability to Define Social Welfare

Recall the lofty list of inalienable rights in the Declaration of Independence. The sentence beginning "We hold these truths to be self-evident" boldly assumed that "we" included everybody in the new nation. Yet history has shown repeatedly that not everybody in the nation has held the fundamental rights guaranteed by the Declaration, rights deemed universal regardless of race, religion, sex, or national origin.

Similarly, we frequently hear phrases such as "the welfare of society" or "the good of the people" in political rhetoric or social discourse. Yet in a secular, pluralistic political culture, a thoughtful reader of public policy analysis recognizes the fragility of such confident phrases. We can think of no policy that is a boon to every individual in society. Instead, we are apt to find cases in which there are winners and losers, victors and vanquished, benefits and costs (see chapter 14).

The Limits of Democracy and the Paradox of Voting

If we cannot define "social welfare," then we can assume that people will articulate their wishes through the electoral process. Let us say that a rural county has recently experienced a spate of devastating forest fires. It is now trying to decide how many fire engines to buy—one, two, or three. The county population is divided over the issue. Three public opinion groups have emerged: those in a small minority who are most threatened by the possibility of another fire next summer (group A), those who are more concerned about the solvency of the county than about the prospect of another fire (group B), and those who are taking a centrist position (group C).

As you can see in Table 3.1, if a referendum were held and each group were allowed to vote for its first choice, we would observe no conclusive outcome. Although the moderate group is numerically the strongest, it does not command the majority of the votes. However, if each group were to vote on two alternatives, we would discern a conclusive majority preference. When the choice is between two fire engines or three, the two-engine option receives 80 percent of the votes (groups B and C prefer two to three). When groups must decide between one engine or two, two still wins (garnering 65 percent of the votes), because those who are most concerned about another forest fire would rather have two engines than one. In this case, a social consensus will be reached, and the outcome will reflect the will of the majority.

However, the situation gets more complicated if group A changes its preference ranking. Suppose group members are so frightened by the prospect of living without

Group	Strength (percentage of votes)	Number of fire engines First choice	Second choice	Third choice
Those most threatened by the prospect of fire (A)	20	3	2	1
Fiscal conservatives (B)	35	1	2	3
Moderates (C)	45	2	3	1

adequate fire protection that they vote for only one fire engine if they cannot have three. Perhaps in protest they move to another county.

Suppose that group A, the smallest and most intense, finds the compromise position of two fire engines just as unacceptable as that of only one (see Table 3.2). In that case, group members have made the strategic decision to rearrange their preference pattern. Now they do not prefer two to one, even though two is closer to their desired position of three. You can see that there will be no unique outcome of this election. The outcome will depend on who controls the agenda:

Choice between 1 and 2	1 wins with	55 percent of the votes
Choice between 3 and 1	3 wins with	65 percent of the votes
Outcome	3 wins	

Choice between 3 and 2	2 wins with	80 percent of the votes
Choice between 1 and 2	1 wins with	55 percent of the votes
Outcome	1 wins	

As a result of this new strategic position, group A has effectively eliminated the middle position. If it can control the agenda, it can win the election with only 20 percent of the vote! This is the paradox of voting. Its broad implications are obvious: *even with the fairest voting rules, the outcome of an election may not reflect the true preferences of the community.*

Inability to Define the Marginal Benefits and Costs of Public Goods

If we are at a loss defining "social welfare," we are similarly confounded defining the marginal utility from an additional dose of public expenditure. When President Ronald Reagan took office, during the height of the Cold War with the Soviet Union, he declared that he wanted a 700-ship navy. Nearly a decade later, Bill Clinton, presiding over the lone superpower, opted for a navy of fewer than 400 ships, nearly half the number requested by Reagan. Why those numbers? Why not 701 ships or 420 ships? Would you, as a voter, sleep more soundly if you knew that one more navy destroyer than before

		Number of fire engines		
Group	Strength (percentage of votes)	First choice	Second choice	Third choice
Those most threatened by the prospect of fire (A)	20	3	1	2
Fiscal conservatives (B)	35	1	2	3
Moderates (C)	45	2	3	1

TABLE 3.2 Voters' Preferences on the Decision to Purchase Fire Engines: Strategy Change by Group A

were guarding your shores? These questions reveal the difficulty of calculating the marginal utility of a government purchase.

Political Constraints

In his first meeting with President Franklin D. Roosevelt, Keynes did not seem practical to the savvy politician. In Keynes's mind the policy implications of his economic strategy—expand government spending, even beyond revenues, during times of recession and reduce expenditures and government size during periods of inflation—did not affect the soundness of his theory. But as Keynes, Roosevelt, and the rest of the nation soon learned, it is much easier to raise the levels of expenditure than to reduce them. Every time policymakers create a government program, the program creates its own constituents. As a result, even when its utility is in question, closing it down often becomes nearly impossible.

Cultural Constraints

Like political constraints, the cultural context influences the public policy process. To be adopted and successfully implemented, public policies must conform to the cultural norms of the community. This cultural context perplexes us when we travel across the nation or to another country. A visitor to India might wonder why cows are allowed to roam freely through the already overcrowded city streets. In the same way, outsiders in America might ask about the cultural attachment of ordinary Americans to guns in the face of gun-related violence. They might also question those who oppose international abortion and birth control initiatives, even as United Nations population control programs in poor, lesser developed countries buckle under unsustainable population growth. Without cultural acceptance, even a perfectly reasoned public policy may not be considered appropriate for a community.

Institutional Constraints

Any public policy must depend on bureaucratic institutions for its formulation and implementation. An organization, like any other entity—collective or individual—develops its own cultural ethos, goals, and mythology. As a result, policies promoted by the social services division of a city can come into direct conflict with the mandates of its law enforcement branch. These conflicts, often seen as "turf battles," can render a policy ineffective. The Commerce Department promotes international trade. Therefore, it seeks to maximize the export of American goods. Yet its goals may collide with those of the State Department, which manages the country's foreign policy. For political reasons the State Department may bar U.S. companies from selling their wares, such as weapons and high-speed computers, to other countries.

Legal Constraints

Public policies must be formulated and implemented within a nation's legal framework. Generally speaking, laws from six sources govern our daily lives in the United States: constitutional laws, laws made by legislatures, executive orders, interpretations of laws by the judicial branch, agency rules, and public referenda. In our democratic system of checks and balances, laws passed by legislatures, executive orders, referenda, and agency rules can all be declared null and void by the courts. In certain cases the legislative branch fights the executive branch for control of the national agenda. Although Congress passed the War Powers Resolution of 1973 to curtail the president's ability to send U.S. troops into combat in other countries, it failed to enforce its own laws when President George W. Bush sent U.S. forces to fight in Iraq and Afghanistan.

Knowledge Constraints

Any public policy is constrained ultimately by our present knowledge. As we learn more about the world around us, we realize the failings of our past policies. Take the problems of malaria abatement in many countries around the world. Malaria was once the top killer in the world's tropical regions. As scientists learned that the disease spread through mosquitoes, they sparked a huge international effort to kill the pesky insects in their places of breeding—swampy areas with stagnant water. Thanks to the massive spraying of the insecticide DDT, many lesser developed countries declared victory over malaria's scourge. Yet within a decade people started noticing the chemical's devastating effects on the fragile ecology of marshland, which is essential to the survival of many species of flora and fauna. Again, policies had to be developed to eradicate not the disease but the effects of past policy. As these devastated habitats were restored, the disease came back, often with a vengeance.

Analytical Constraints

Analytical techniques tapped for public policy analysis, either at the formulation stage or the implementation stage, use numbers. Numbers have a magical quality. They give the impression of being totally objective. As we will see, however, there are many opportunities for subjectivity to creep into our analysis. When we learn statistical methods or the various techniques of operations research, they exude the impartiality of scientific reasoning. Yet when we dig deeper, we discover that *objectivity relates solely to deriving the conclusion once the problem has been formed*. In each stage of formulating the problem, we may confront not just confusion but also pressure to make quick decisions, which are often rendered for the convenience of the analyst or to suit the particular quantitative technique chosen for the analysis. These analytical constraints may creep into the analysis from a number of sources discussed throughout this book.

The Timing of Policies

Biases or inefficiencies may arise due to the timing of policy measures. Consider a business cycle that moves the economy through a series of booms and busts. Critics of government's anticyclical policies point out that several steps must be taken before a policy is implemented and its effects felt. If the government decides to enact countermeasures to keep the economy on an even keel, it must first recognize that the economy is going into a recession. As we note in chapter 4, though, forecasting is sometimes like looking in the rearview mirror while driving a car. We consult past data to gauge where we should be going. But the data have been collected from the quarter before. We encounter a **recognition gap**, which requires that we study trends to understand its causes. Because it takes time to analyze a trend, unless we are studying a rapidly escalating situation, policies can become delayed. A time gap often occurs as analysts come up with appropriate policies. This gap is called a **prescription lag**. After a policy has been recommended, the appropriate legal body must consider it for adoption, causing an **adoption lag**. Finally, an **implementation lag** results when adopted policies are translated into action. In the meantime, if the economy has made a turn on its own, the "lagged" policies may backfire and choke off a natural recovery. This policy failure then creates a new set of problems.

The timing of an anticipated change in government can also lead to market inefficiency. Thus, if I expect the market price of an item to go up, I may run to the store and stockpile, buying in quantities that I may not need for some time. Furthermore, if this fear is widespread, the surge in market demand can create shortages and an artificial increase in prices. For instance, immediately after the election of Barack Obama, many gun enthusiasts feared a looming restriction on gun and ammunition sales. This caused a frenzy in sales of guns and even created a shortage of ammunition for public safety officials. As a result, many even jokingly called Obama the "Gun Salesman of the Year."[24]

LIMITING GOVERNMENT INTERVENTION: JOINT PARTNERSHIP IN A MIXED ECONOMY

The standard theory of economics tells us that the market achieves its highest level of efficiency when government resists the temptation to interfere in it. Yet this theory yields many questions. Why does the market go through cycles of boom and bust? Why does unemployment exist even when there is no minimum wage to discourage firms from hiring workers? Why does an unchecked market produce extremes of wealth and poverty? Rather than attributing these problems to government interference, Keynes thought they were caused by humans' tendency to respond "irrationally" to a number of cues. He called this the **animal spirit**. Building on this, the Nobel Prize–winning economist George Akerlof and the Yale economist Robert Shiller argue that if the market is to avoid the disruptive influences of the animal spirit, it must understand human nature in its fuller context and not be tied to its restrictive assumption of self-utility maximizing *homo economicus*.[25]

However, government interference in the market is a double-edged sword, and sometimes governments do fail. When this happens, because of government inefficiency or corruption, the market forces of unencumbered demand and supply must be brought in to remedy the situation. The reintroduction of market forces can either stimulate or simulate the market. **Market stimulation** takes place when the barriers of entry into the market are removed, whereas **market simulation** requires the government to provide public goods through exclusionary pricing. Akerlof and Shiller insist that the ill effects of the animal spirit can be brought under control only through a properly balanced partnership between the market and the government.

Stimulating the Market

Market stimulation is achieved when the government *deregulates, legalizes, privatizes,* or *infuses money.* As we have seen, government intervenes in the market through regulations when it deems such actions to be beneficial to society. One of the most regulated sectors in U.S. economic history is the banking industry. Through their lending, commercial banks create an economy's money supply. As the backbone of the monetary structure, banks can function only when people trust the system and deposit money. When we open a checking account, the Federal Deposit Insurance Corporation requires the bank to pay a small premium to buy insurance against a possible bank failure. If the bank fails, each of the checking accounts, up to a maximum of $250,000, will be fully insured. When bank insurance was originally proposed during the Great Depression, President Roosevelt was deeply suspicious of it. He feared that because customers could not lose a penny, bankers would be irresponsible with deposited money. In the 1980s, the so-called supply-side economists successfully advocated **deregulation** of the market, which erased many of the restrictions that had prevented banks from engaging in highly speculative activities, such as selling risky commercial stocks or investing in commercial real estate. A decade after deregulation, the savings and loan crisis engulfed the nation. Many critics blamed the freewheeling practices of unregulated banks and sought to reregulate the sector.[26] As we have seen in the previous discussion of the failure of the insurance giant AIG (see "A Case in Point" earlier in this chapter), many of these same mistakes have been repeated in recent years.

Another area that is heavily regulated by the government is electricity. Regulations have caused inefficiency, prompting the U.S. government to deregulate the industry. Although advocates of deregulation often tout its virtues, evidence indicates that it has had mixed results. In North Carolina, the deregulation of electricity did not reduce consumers' rates.[27] In fact, in the late 1990s, largely because of deregulation, electricity rates in fifty-one cities jumped by 25 to 30 percent. In winter 2001 the deregulation of electricity brought California perilously close to an economic disaster. Not surprisingly, one study found that deregulation of the airline industry failed to increase efficiency as had been predicted.[28] It is extremely difficult to establish unequivocally a causal relationship between deregulation and market failure, so the debate on deregulation's merits is likely to go on.

Legalization brings a previously illegal act into the realm of taxable, legal activities. The Supreme Court's judgment in *Roe v. Wade* legalized abortion for American women within a certain period of pregnancy. This action drastically reduced the number of unsafe abortions. However, as the opposition to the Court's opinion in *Roe v. Wade* demonstrated, the acceptance of a public policy may not always be based strictly on economic grounds or the health considerations of a pregnant woman but can come from a host of moral and religious perspectives. Similarly, in certain European nations, as well as some counties in Nevada, laws permit prostitution. This generates tax revenues for these governments (as the sex workers work within the legal system), lowers the risk for spreading sexually transmittable diseases, and may restrict the power of pimps and organized crime. Yet many in the society recoil at the idea on moral, ethical, and religious grounds.

Privatization turns previously government-operated services over to the private sector. The conservatism prevailing in the nation following the election of President Reagan spurred a huge demand for the privatization of government services. Although the initial enthusiasm waned with time, privatization continued to advance at all levels of government.[29] Despite the common assumption that privatization is a quick way out for cash-strapped governments, it also has been used by solvent governments to acquire superior management talent and specialized expertise. However, despite the growing interest in privatization, fierce political opposition, particularly from labor unions, continues to make outsourcing a hard sell. Proponents of privatization say that competition from private firms can often raise productivity in government-provided service areas. In the municipal waste disposal industry, evidence suggests that parallel providers have helped both private and public sector firms become "better, faster, smarter, and more cost-effective." Residents of cities and counties across the United States have been the primary beneficiaries of this competition.[30]

Government also tries to stimulate the market through the **direct infusion of money**. In times of recession the aggregate demand for goods and services goes down. As a result, market prices fall, and industries start laying off workers. As these unemployed workers lose their purchasing power, prices go down even more, prompting another round of layoffs. This process continues, sending the entire economy into a downward spiral. Keynes pointed out that, unlike the situation shown in Figure 3.1, there is no market mechanism that can bring the economy out of this whirlpool of an economic abyss. The only way the economy can be saved is by the government's borrowing huge sums of money and injecting them into the economy. As the government funds projects, which employ the previously jobless, the reverse process takes hold: workers spend their money and boost aggregate demand, which increases prices and profits businesses. The Obama administration's decision to pass an enormous stimulus package is rooted in Keynesian theory. On the other hand, those who believe in the market argue that government intervention only brings about inefficiency, corruption, and public debt, which binds future generations to a higher level of taxes.

Simulating the Market

When it is not possible to stimulate a market, federal, state, and local governments reduce the inefficiencies of government control by simulating the market—that is, by charging prices for the products and services once offered free of charge (see "A Case in Point"). Charging fees for government services has become critical for cash-starved cities in many parts of the country. This has been particularly true in California, where in

1978 voters organized a "tax revolt" and passed a sweeping referendum, known as Proposition 13, that reduced their property taxes. This proposition also significantly reduced the government's ability to impose new taxes. Because the voters said no to the government's request for finances but did not at the same time curtail their demand for services, the only answer to the problem was to charge user fees. More recently, some cities, such as Coon Rapids, Minnesota, have considered charging their citizens when they use emergency services like fire extinguishing or cleanup after car accidents.[31] With government as the service provider, users pay for the services they demand, simulating the market process.

Apart from allowing financially strapped cities to provide the services their citizens demand, simulating the market through user fees offers several other advantages. First, prices act as a signal for demand. Because it is impossible to quantify the demand for public goods, if a local government charges a fee for its services, each consumer can bring his or her demand for public goods in line with their cost. Returning to our example of voting for fire engines, we may satisfy all three groups by charging them different rates for different levels of fire protection. The group that wants the most fire protection can pay for extra fire engines dedicated to their community, while the rest are charged the regular rate. This situation is known as **consumption efficiency,** in which an economic actor's marginal utility matches the marginal cost. Because nothing dispels enthusiasm more than a small entry fee, user fees often can curb the abuse of a publicly provided service.[32]

Along with consumption efficiency, the simulation of the market may also introduce **production efficiency** by forcing government units to bring their marginal revenues in line with marginal costs. In fact, sending price signals through user fees may help even the private market correct itself. In the market the social cost of a product often becomes significantly higher than its market cost. Suppose the authorities of the indoor sports arena in your town want to host a pop music festival lasting several days. Although it may be profitable, this concert may impose extra costs on the surrounding areas in terms of higher street-cleaning expenses and more traffic, pollution, and crime. Each business may have to hire extra help to clean up or protect its property during the festival. In addition, the city may have to pay police officers overtime to direct traffic and keep the festival orderly. As you might expect, festival organizers pass on their costs to the rest of the community. Therefore, if the city charges the organizers a fee for the privilege of holding such an event, an amount that compensates the affected parties, no one will be economically harmed, yet many (promoters, stadium authorities, musicians, and fans) will benefit from the festival. This strategy is effective for many nonprofit organizations, such as charitable, religious, and educational institutions, which are exempt from property taxes. By imposing user fees, they can bring their private costs in line with those of society.

The decision to charge for publicly provided services must be considered very carefully. Some services provide benefits not only to those who use them but also to the rest of the community. As a society we have decided that when children in grades kindergarten to 12 are educated, the benefits are not restricted to them but spill over to the rest of society. Therefore, it is not always prudent to emulate the market and charge tuition fees. Charging a fee may have an adverse effect on poor people. If a city wants to impose a fee for using public facilities such as basketball courts and baseball fields, the fee may

A CASE IN POINT

Trading Pollution: Simulating the Market

Ronald Coase of the University of Chicago, who won the Nobel Prize in economics in 1991, had a novel idea. He argued that if people were allowed to market their property rights, many problems resulting from negative externalities could be solved.[33] Take the case of environmental pollution.[34] Factories emit pollutants—sources of negative externalities—as by-products of their operations. However, some factories are more efficient than others and produce fewer pollutants. Regulating environmental pollution has a high opportunity cost because it causes production shutdowns, loss of income, and unemployment. If there are too many restrictions, the government imposes undue burdens on society, but if the laws are too lax, the social costs of the products far outweigh their market costs.

Guided by Coase's arguments, government experts determine the amount of pollution that can safely be tolerated, then give each polluting plant a permit to pollute up to its quota. If some plants pollute below their quota, they can sell their "rights to pollute" to plants that cannot meet the regulatory standard. Through trading pollution rights, the social costs can be brought in line with the market costs. Thus, the Clean Air Act of 1990 introduced what is now known as emissions trading, by which the government sets pollution quotas and efficient firms sell their unused pollution rights to inefficient ones.

In response to pressure to reduce the emission of greenhouse gases, BP-Amoco's Western Gas business unit installed thousands of new valves that shunt fluids from the firm's network of wells. The old valves emitted whiffs of methane, a potent greenhouse gas; the new valves do not. Today, Western Gas sells its unused pollution rights to other subsidiaries of Amoco at a profit.[35] This sort of emissions trading has been steadily increasing every year. In 2005, 374 million metric tons of carbon dioxide equivalent were exchanged, a 240 percent increase over the 2004 level.[36] Although by many measures this injection of market forces into the allocation of public goods has been a success, critics have argued that the overall cap on total emissions is too high. As a result, some firms have found new ways of making money by spreading pollution in previously unpolluted parts of the world.

Discussion Points

1. How can we bring social costs close to market costs through government action?
2. Do you think trading emissions offers a viable solution to the problem of global warming?
3. Can you think of other negative externalities that could be treated with Coase's prescription?

---

have an adverse effect on the children of a poor neighborhood. In contrast, if the city wants to raise the fee for using public golf courses, such effects may not be felt.

Even in the face of overuse or high social cost, charging a fee may not be technically feasible, or the cost of collection may be too high. Suppose your city's traffic department wants to reduce congestion during peak traffic hours. It may make sense to charge motorists a fee for using the highways during those hours.[37] However, it may not be possible to collect those fees without creating an even bigger traffic jam. In such cases, simulating the market is not a viable option.

Besides being technically unworkable, imposing fees for services that previously were provided free of charge may not be politically feasible. If services are free, consumers view them as having no cost. Toward the end of the nineteenth century, San Diego faced a small tax revolt of its own. The city, like most other cities in the nation, was collecting fees for picking up garbage. When it became known that the city was selling this garbage to nearby hog farms, irate citizens passed a referendum to eliminate garbage collection fees. More than 100 years later, the city has grown substantially and the pig farms have long since left the vicinity. Yet it remains politically infeasible to reinstate a collection charge, one of the most common municipal fees in the United States.

KEY WORDS

Adoption lag (p. 67)
Animal spirit (p. 67)
Consumer surplus (p. 50)
Consumption efficiency (p. 70)
Deregulation (p. 68)
Direct infusion of money (p. 69)
Equilibrium (p. 48)
Experience goods (p. 59)
Externality (p. 53)
Factor mobility (p. 55)
Implementation lag (p. 67)
Indivisibility (p. 56)
Legalization (p. 68)
Marginal analysis (p. 49)
Marginal cost (p. 50)
Marginal revenue (p. 50)
Market simulation (p. 68)

Market stimulation (p. 68)
Mercantilism (p. 47)
Negative externality (p. 59)
Oligopoly (p. 56)
Opportunity costs (p. 49)
Positive externality (p. 59)
Prescription lag (p. 67)
Price maker (p. 53)
Price taker (p. 50)
Privatization (p. 69)
Production efficiency (p. 70)
Recognition gap (p. 67)
Rent seeking (p. 56)
Search goods (p. 59)
Social benefits (p. 59)
Social costs (p. 59)
X-inefficiency (p. 54)

EXERCISES

1. Your city wants to contract out fire prevention and firefighting services to a private firm. Argue for and against such a move.
2. Write an essay on the uses and limits of economic analysis, incorporating an appropriate example from your local or state government.
3. Write an essay on the deregulation of utility prices. When do you think deregulation works, and when does it not?

Notes

1. Stephanie Ebbert, "Menino Bill Would Boost Low-income Housing," *Boston Globe*, November 30, 2000.
2. The instant success of the book—it went through five editions during Smith's lifetime—made the author famous, but his work failed to have a significant influence on British public policy of the time. For a discussion of Adam Smith's contribution to modern economics, see David D. Raphael, *Adam Smith* (Oxford, United Kingdom: Oxford University Press, 1985).
3. Smith did not draw the famous demand and supply curves. Developing the geometry of his theory took about 100 more years and a combined effort on both sides of the English Channel. For a detailed discussion, see Mark Blaug, *Economic Theory in Retrospect* (Homewood, Ill.: Richard D. Irwin, 1968), 38–67.
4. Ebbert, "Menino Bill."
5. Daniel Yergin, *The Prize: The Epic Quest for Oil, Money, and Power* (New York: Simon & Schuster, 1991).
6. See Liam Pleven, "AIG Sees Long Road Back from the Brink," *Wall Street Journal*, May 11, 2009.
7. See the World Bank's "Key Development Data & Statistics" page at www.worldbank.org/data/ (select "Data" from the menu at the left side of the page).
8. Stephen Labaton, "Administration Plans to Strengthen Antitrust Rules," *New York Times*, May 11, 2009.
9. Joel Brinkley, "The Verdict: Microsoft Is a Monopoly," *New York Times*, November 7, 1999.
10. Harvey Leibenstein, *Beyond Economic Man: A New Foundation for Microeconomics* (Cambridge, Mass.: Harvard University Press, 1976). See also Roger S. Franz, *X-Efficiency: Theory, Evidence and Applications* (Boston: Kluwer Academic, 1988).
11. Kate Gillespie and Clement Moore Henry, eds., *Oil in the New World Order* (Gainesville: University Press of Florida, 1995).
12. There is no single, worldwide definition of unemployment. The official U.S. definition carries many restrictions, and the definitions of other nations vary significantly.
13. The Department of Food and Agriculture defended its action by arguing that it was only trying to ensure the survival of California's dairy farmers. Although this rhetoric evokes the image of small family farmers getting up with the sunrise every morning to milk their herds, in fact, dairy farming is a huge, $3.6 billion industry. The average farmer is a corporation with 602 cows and annual sales of $1.6 million.
14. See Brian Loveman, ed., *Addicted to Failure: U.S. Security Policy in Latin America and the Andean Region* (Lanham, Mass.: Rowman & Littlefield, 2006). Also see David R. Mares, *Drug Wars and Coffeehouses: The Political Economy of the International Drug Trade* (Washington, D.C.: CQ Press, 2005).
15. Drug Policy Alliance Network, "The Latin-American Commission on Drugs and Democracy (Co-chaired by former presidents Fernando Henrique Cardoso [Brazil], César Gaviria [Colombia], and Ernesto Zedillo [Mexico]) Releases Groundbreaking Report," February 11, 2009, www.drugpolicy.org/news/pressroom/pressrelease/pr021109lar.cfm. For an interesting demonstration of the costs of the drug war, see Drug Sense, "Drug War Clock," www.drugsense .org/wodclock.htm.
16. Fernando Henrique Cardoso, César Gaviria, and Ernesto Zedillo, "The War on Drugs Is a Failure," *Wall Street Journal*, February 23, 2009.
17. In a famous case, often called the *Ghostbusters* case, a seller in New York was held liable for withholding information about the existence of poltergeists from the buyer (*Stambovsky v. Ackley*, 169 A.D.2d 254, N.Y. App. Div. 1991). This case has become a textbook example in contract and property law cases. There have since been other cases of similar litigation.
18. A large literature on information asymmetry and the cost of information began with the publication of George Akerlof's "The Market for 'Lemons': Quality Uncertainty and the Market Mechanism," *Quarterly Journal of Economics* 84 (1970): 488–500.

19. John Immerwahr and Jean Johnson (with Paul Gasbarra, Amber Ott, and Jonathan Rochkind), "Squeeze Play 2009: The Public's Views on College Costs Today," Public Agenda and the National Center for Public Policy and Higher Education, 2009, www.highereducation.org/reports/squeeze_play_09/index.shtml.

20. U.S. Department of Education, www.ed.gov/index.jhtml.

21. Jeffrey Selingo, "Americans Split on Government Control of Tuition," *Chronicle of Higher Education*, April 4, 2008.

22. This concept of productivity lag was first presented by William J. Baumol, "Macroeconomics of Unbalanced Growth: The Anatomy of Urban Crisis," *American Economic Review* (June 1967): 415–426.

23. Although the poverty rate did decline during periods of economic expansion, poverty was merely cut in half between 1959 and 1972.

24. Judson Berger, "Obama Driving Surge in Gun Sales, Firearms Groups Say," FoxNews.com, January 16, 2009, www.foxnews.com/politics/2009/01/16/firearms-associations-claim-obama-drove-surge-gun-sales.

25. George A. Akerlof and Robert J. Shiller, *Animal Spirits: How Human Psychology Drives the Economy, and Why It Matters for Global Capitalism* (Princeton, N.J.: Princeton University Press, 2008).

26. See, for example, Alan Gart, *Regulation, Deregulation, Regulation: The Future of the Banking, Insurance, and Securities Industries* (New York: Wiley, 1994).

27. Buster Kantrow, "Electricity Deregulation Runs into Static in N.C.," *Wall Street Journal*, July 26, 2000.

28. Zinan Liu and E. L. Lynk, "Evidence on Market Structure of the Deregulated US Airline Industry," *Applied Economics* 31 (1999): 1083–1092.

29. "Privatization on the Rise Despite Surpluses," *USA Today*, August 1, 1999.

30. Christi Clark, "How Privatization Helped Raise the Bar in the Solid Waste Field," *American City and County* 113 (February 1998): 52–60.

31. Maria Elena Baca, "Cities May Charge Fees on Emergency Services," *Minneapolis Star-Tribune*, May 2, 2009.

32. Although this statement is made somewhat in jest, there is strong evidence that people are willing to pay for a public resource if doing so improves service. Kelly McCollum found in a survey of 3,000 students in the California State University system that about 65 percent of the students would be willing to pay higher than usual student fees for better on-campus computing resources. Of those students who were willing to pay, more than 71 percent stated that they would spend an extra $10 per month for better on-campus computing, while 15 percent were ready to pay more than $20 per month. See Kelly McCollum, "65% of California State U. Students Back a Technology Fee, Survey Finds," *Chronicle of Higher Education*, September 17, 1999.

33. For an excellent discussion of the theoretical issues, see Neil Bruce, *Public Finance and the American Economy*, 2nd ed. (Boston: Addison-Wesley, 2001), 99–115.

34. A. Denny Ellerman, Paul L. Joskow, Richard Schmalensee, Juan-Pablo Montero, and Elizabeth M. Bailey, *Markets for Clean Air: The U.S. Acid Rain Program* (Cambridge, United Kingdom: Cambridge University Press, 2000).

35. John Carey, "A Free-Market Cure for Global Warming," *Business Week*, May 15, 2000.

36. See the World Bank's Carbon Finance Unit (www.carbonfinance.org) for the latest data and information.

37. In some parts of the country transportation departments have experimented with issuing permits for single motorists to use carpool or high-occupancy vehicle (HOV) lanes. These permits are often expensive because they must pay for highway patrol officers to enforce HOV restrictions.

4 The Policy Process

Something interesting is happening on the street corners of my city, though I did not notice it at first while driving through my neighborhood. I approached a yellow light, and instead of coming to a stop at the signal, I made a quick turn a split second after the light had turned red. Three weeks later, I received an envelope from the Department of Motor Vehicles. Inside were a picture of my license plate and a clear shot of this author looking intense while making an illegal turn in a hurry. The pictures came with a hefty fine and an invitation to spend a weekend at traffic school. On my next trip to that same intersection, I noticed the little birdhouse-type structure at the corner, its shiny camera lens sticking out, busily snapping away at delinquents. Within a few months I observed that most of the city's intersections, and many in neighboring towns, had been outfitted with these Orwellian devices. In June 2000 the cameras operated in forty-one U.S. cities; today, nearly all major U.S. cities use them.[1]

These devices clearly were installed as a result of deliberate public policies. Students of policy analysis might ask, who placed the cameras on the policy agenda? How did policymakers decide to install them? How are city officials implementing the policies? How effective are the devices at preventing traffic violations? As the cameras become part of our daily lives, we may ask whether they raise constitutional issues. If so, how might this concern change future policies for catching red light runners? Finally, if policymakers find the cameras ineffective, how do they go about eliminating them? We may answer all of these questions by examining the **policy cycle**, or **policy formation**, the process through which policy is formed (see Figure 4.1).[2]

Before examining each stage of the cycle, we must remember an important caveat: the process is not as neatly segmented as the figure suggests. Rather, it is much more complex, resembling a seamless quilt in which all phases of the cycle are woven together.

FIGURE 4.1   The Policy Cycle

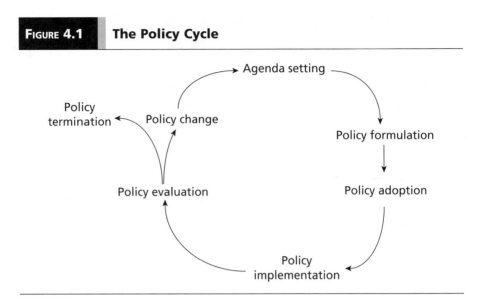

AGENDA SETTING

The policy cycle starts when the government pays serious attention to an issue. If you look around, you notice that thousands of areas cry out for corrective action. However, not everything that needs the government's attention gets it. You may notice a particularly dangerous intersection in your neighborhood. When you turn into the intersection, your view is blocked by a large tree. You are concerned, and so are some of your neighbors. Yet years go by and no one takes action. Or you may worry about the so-called greenhouse gases that reportedly cause global warming. You may wonder why political leaders do not pay more attention to a problem with such enormous consequences for our future.[3] You may also ask why some issues suddenly crop up, dominate the agenda, and surprise everyone, including those who study such matters for a living.[4]

Policy scientists identify two kinds of agendas: those that government institutions act on, known as institutional, or governmental, agendas, and those on which they delay action, called systemic, or noninstitutional, agendas.[5] **Systemic agendas** "percolate" in society, waiting to be elevated to the active agenda. A systemic agenda "consists of all issues that are commonly perceived by members of the political community as meriting public attention and involving matters within the legitimate jurisdiction of existing governmental authorities."[6] In contrast, an **institutional agenda** consists of those problems on which "legislators or public officials feel obliged to take appropriate measures."[7] Sometimes an issue remains the focus of intense public debate but still never makes it onto the institutional agenda. At other times an issue surprisingly and suddenly moves to the active list. Take, for example, the issue of teen smoking. Despite the fact that for years many prominent health care professionals had documented tobacco's ill effects and highly addictive qualities, the issue failed to reach the institutional agenda until the late 1990s, when some states sued tobacco companies, the Food and Drug Administration issued stronger tobacco regulations, and the media covered the issue more widely—Congress responded by passing measures that sought to reduce underage tobacco use by prohibiting certain types of cigarette advertisements and reforming retail distribution practices.

The White House and Congress initiate official or institutional agendas at the federal level. The courts also set institutional agendas through their decisions and legal opinions. Because of the system of checks and balances, all three branches of government must cooperate to adopt an institutional agenda. All legislation must be passed by both houses of Congress. If a bill conflicts with the Constitution, the judiciary must step in. Just as government actors often pull institutional agendas from the vast pool of systemic agendas, they may at any time toss back an institutional agenda into the pool.

How does an issue reach the active agenda, and who ushers the issue through the policy cycle? Those who hold demand-side theories of agenda setting believe that policymakers determine institutional agendas in response to widespread popular demand. This view is known as the **pluralist model**. In contrast, those who support the **elitist model**, a supply-side view, believe that the power to set the agenda resides at the top of the political and economic hierarchies.

The Pluralist Model

The pluralist model is based on theories of American democracy developed in the 1950s and 1960s.[8] In this somewhat romanticized view of the American power structure, power rests with citizen activist groups. The model makes no permanent distinction between the elite and the masses, though a hierarchy may exist in which the elite control some institutional agendas. Any issue can reach the institutional agenda, and its success in doing so depends on the abilities of citizen activist groups (see Figure 4.2).

In the early 1970s Roger Cobb and his associates explained how an inactive agenda becomes active in the pluralist model.[9] To attain institutional status, an issue must possess the following characteristics: specificity, social significance, temporal relevance, simplicity, and categorical precedence. Cobb's argument can be best understood with the help of

FIGURE 4.2   **The Pluralist Model of Agenda Setting**

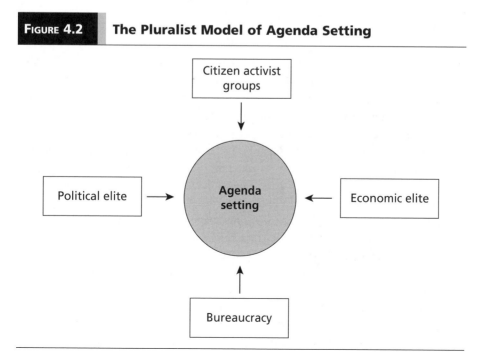

A CASE IN POINT

What's in a Name? The Case of the Mexican Swine Flu Pandemic

Shakespeare's Juliet famously asked, "What's in a name? That which we call a rose by any other name would smell as sweet." True, but in the world of thirty-second sound bites and coded political communication, names can have devastating consequences.

In the late spring of 2009, the news of a pandemic popularly referred to as "swine flu" swept the world. As the disease spread from country to country, the World Health Organization elevated the risk to level 4 on a five-point scale for a global pandemic, and panic set in. Although the virus turned out to be much less virulent than the seasonal flu virus that afflicts the world every year, it created problems on several fronts.[10]

First, the name "swine flu" created problems for the $15 billion U.S. pork industry.[11] Although the genetic makeup of the offending virus contains parts of human as well as avian flu, fearful consumers began avoiding pork products despite assurance from the U.S. Centers for Disease Control and Prevention that any properly cooked pork product was perfectly safe. In the wholesale market, pork prices instantly dropped from $70 to $59 per 100 pounds of hog. Some small operations in agricultural states like Iowa faced economic ruin. China, Russia, and the Ukraine—some of the largest consumers of pork products—canceled imports from Mexico and parts of the United States. In Egypt, Muslim crowds attacked pig farms operated by Coptic Christians. The Christians claimed that the fear of the pandemic gave the perfect cover for the attack. In Israel, an ultra-Orthodox deputy health minister declared that his country would call it "Mexican flu" in order to prevent Jews from having to say the word "swine."

the story of Elián González, a castaway boy from Cuba. In November 1999, the six-year-old, his mother, her boyfriend, and eleven others fled the Communist-controlled island for a better life in the United States. In the middle of the ocean, their boat sank, and little Elián was the only survivor. After a fishing boat plucked him from the ocean, he was turned over to the U.S. Coast Guard, and a custody battle began to brew between Elián's father in Cuba and the fiercely anti-Castro exile community in Miami. Elián's father was his legal guardian and had full rights to take him back to Cuba, but the battle instantly became a political issue, a rallying point against the Communist regime. After the 11th Circuit Court of Appeals ordered the boy returned to his legal guardian and the U.S. Supreme Court refused hear his case, the Clinton administration (in particular Al Gore, who was preparing to run as the Democratic candidate for the presidency) was caught in the middle. The executive branch was obliged to follow the law, but politics dictated that they support the Cuban community in Florida. This political dimension was complicated by the fact that the Cuban American community has traditionally supported the Republican Party. The complex battle spurred a media spectacle that gripped the nation, but Attorney General Janet Reno ended it when she ordered that federal agents whisk the terrified child away in the middle of the night and return him to Cuba.

Mexico suffered the most serious damages from being associated with the flu. Although names are given to the area where the virus is first detected—such as the Spanish flu of 1918 or the Hong Kong flu of 1967—that does not mean that the virus originated from that exact location. Most medical historians believe that nearly all flu viruses originate in southeastern China, where animals and people live in close proximity in densely populated areas. Nevertheless, the term "Mexican flu" caused China to quarantine Mexican nationals for a prolonged period, spurring diplomatic tension between the two nations. Mexico finally sent a chartered plane to China to pick up some of its stranded citizens.

Fear can bring out the worst in us. In the United States, the "Mexican flu" gave a boost to those who were out to make political capital by spreading xenophobia against illegal immigrants from our neighbor to the south. A number of politicians and political commentators began conflating the two unrelated issues of illegal immigration and the pandemic, elevating xenophobia to a new height.

Finally, the term pandemic conjures up images of the black death of medieval times or the flu epidemic of 1918 that killed millions of people and depopulated parts of the world. Yet the definition of pandemic is simply the spread of an infectious disease within a significant proportion of the population in several countries. While the swine flu killed fewer than 100 people worldwide in a matter of a couple of months, we should keep in mind that every single day nearly 100 people die from influenza, most of whom are elderly or have immune deficiencies. The combination of the three terms Mexican, swine, and pandemic created havoc by shaping the definition of the problem and how the public viewed it. In the end, many agencies started referring to the virus by its neutral technical name, H1N1.

Discussion Points

1. Why are names important in the process of public policy making?
2. What do the problems caused by naming the flu virus say about human nature?

Although Elián's eight-month turn in the media spotlight is now a minor footnote in history, in retrospect it might have changed the history of the world. Al Gore was defeated in Florida in 2000 by a handful of votes. If the Gonzalez saga had not pitted the Cuban American community against the Democratic administration, Al Gore might have secured a few more votes in Florida and George W. Bush might not have won the electoral vote. Let us now examine the pluralist model in light of the Elián González saga.

Specificity. This characteristic describes how broadly an issue has been defined. When advocates of an issue define it in a way that attracts wide public support, it is more likely to be picked up by the political elite. When Elián González requested asylum from the United States, his Republican supporters portrayed his cause as a fight between freedom and communism. From a different angle, it could have been seen as a simple case of a custody battle over an unfortunate little boy. However, the issue was framed in political terms, which helped inflame passion and translated into a political agenda. There are numerous examples of systemic agendas being translated into political action due to their framing (see "A Case in Point"). For instance, pro–tobacco forces depicted the debate over underage tobacco use as a battle for an individual's right to choose, while those in opposition framed the issue in terms of public health and, perhaps more important for some voters, in terms of money spent on combating the consequent illnesses. In both cases, by using terms that raise emotion, activists on both sides improved the chances that their issues would reach the institutional agenda. By framing them in a wide context, they attracted far greater public support than they would have if they had construed the issues narrowly—as one child's request for asylum or as a single industry's campaign to advertise its products as it wishes.

Social Significance. When advocates frame a complex issue in a way that makes sense to constituents, the issue attains a level of social significance. This simplification makes it easier for a political leader to champion the cause and for others to lend support. Similarly, when setting an agenda for the courts, especially the Supreme Court, advocates give their issue social clout by defining its broad constitutional implications. The question of whether grandparents should retain visitation rights when their sons or daughters get divorced might be resolved by a family court, unless advocates couch their argument in terms of the parents' right to make decisions for their children. Such an argument could elevate the issue to the high court. In the case of Elián González, the social significance of opposing the repressive regime was readily understood by the Cuban American community and, in fact, the rest of the nation.

Temporal Relevance. This term refers to whether an agenda has only short-term relevance or deep and enduring implications. Supporters of Elián González claimed that they fought not only for Elián but also for Cuba's future generations, to liberate them from dictator Fidel Castro. Proponents of a ban on teen smoking asserted their intention to save today's children from future addiction, illness, and death.

Simplicity. An issue improves its chance of being embraced by the political elite if it can be easily understood. Supporters of Elián González asked this simple question: should Elián be reunited with his father, or should he settle in America to fulfill his mother's last wish? When advocates frame issues in a straightforward manner, they can communicate them easily to the general public. In contrast, when they convey complex scientific information—about global warming, for example—their arguments are likely to languish in the arena of public debate unless they can be summarized in terms of costs and benefits.

Categorical Precedence. Finally, lawmakers are more likely to champion an issue that is a matter of routine legislative action—or has categorical precedence—than one that is unique and far from routine. Issues such as environmental protection and global warming tend to face greater resistance in Congress than, say, a specific military procurement measure. In the case of Elián, the fight against the Castro regime was part and parcel of the politics of the Cuban American community. Therefore, it was easy for politicians to pick up the issue and to force it through the political processes.

    In his later work Cobb extended the pluralist model of agenda setting. In his original model, he had noted that agendas reach the institutional level when driven by public demand, as voiced through community leaders or the media. In his revised model Cobb observed that agendas also flow to institutions when initiated by political leaders, who rally widespread public support. Moreover, some agenda setting goes on out of public view, in the corridors of the legislative and executive branches.[12]

The Elitist Model

While some scholars ask *how* policy concerns reach the agenda, others ask *who* sets the agenda. Proponents of the hierarchical, or elitist, theory of agenda setting focus on the structure of decision making. They note that power is concentrated in the hands of a few. Political elites wield authority over a multitude lacking ready access to the corridors of power. The power structure resembles a pyramid, with power flowing from top to bottom (see Figure 4.3).[13]

Scholars favoring the elitist, pyramidal model adopt one of two views of agenda setting. The first view, described by decision scientists James March and Johan Olsen, points out that elites focus on issues in three ways.[14] First, they select issues randomly from a wide universe of possibilities. If you are a freshman representative in the House, you can focus on an infinite number of issues. You can pick up issues here or there—perhaps military appropriations now, the environment next, and possibly welfare down the road. Second, elites choose issues in which they specialize. If you are on the Defense Appropriations Subcommittee, you tend to pay attention to the issues in your area of expertise. You focus on defense spending while ignoring or setting aside other issues. Third, when selecting issues, elites observe hierarchies. A hierarchy governs the work of the Appropriations Committee. When the committee considers an issue, your staff reviews it first. As the member of Congress, you deal only with those issues that your staff has already vetted. If you are a junior member, your area of attention differs from that of the chair of the subcommittee. Within an organization, participants focus their attention in a hierarchical way. Therefore, the process of agenda setting is inevitably hierarchical.

The second view of elitist agenda setting, advanced by political scientists Thomas Dye and Harmon Ziegler, argues somewhat cynically that society's elites select issues that serve their own interests.[15] Separated from the masses, who are by and large apathetic, elites such as lawmakers, corporate representatives, and other interest groups

FIGURE 4.3   The Elitist Model of Agenda Setting

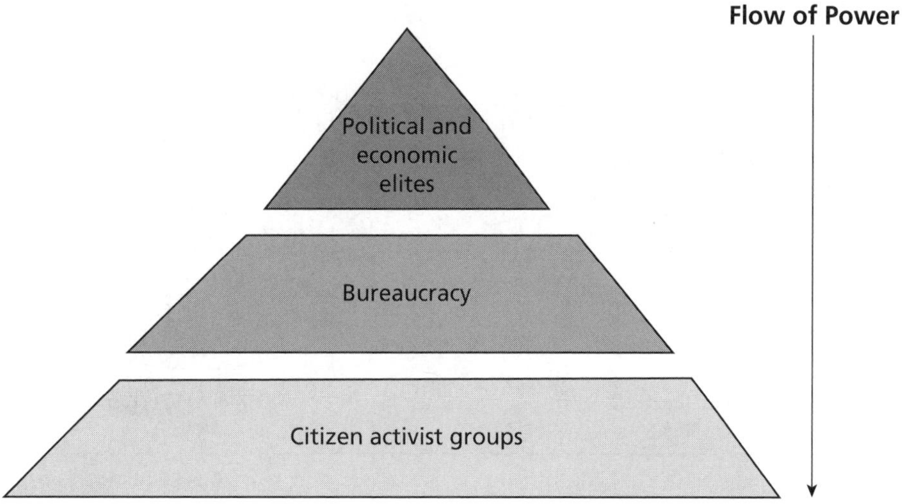

exercise overarching influence on the institutional agenda.[16] Only when issues become important to elected officials or bureaucrats are they placed on the government agenda. Political and bureaucratic elites give priority not to the most salient issues but to those that best serve their own interests.[17] For example, critics of President George W. Bush's energy and environmental policies argued that they protected the corporate interests, especially those of the oil, natural gas, and manufacturing industries.

Another model of agenda setting, one closely linked to the elitist model, is the **subgovernmental model** (see Figure 4.4).[18] The model describes an **iron triangle**, with political elites (Congress) at the apex and, at the base, those who dominate agenda setting—administrative elites (the bureaucracy) and special interests, along with their staffs and other experts. This rigid model assumes a stable coalition of players in the policy-making process. Some scholars have proposed a model slightly different from this one, in which the coalitions are flexible and open to outsiders. Outside players such as think tanks, academics, and journalists often make significant contributions to policy processes.[19] By publishing an insightful book or article, or by broadcasting a penetrating investigative report, these players can join a loose, informal coalition with policy advocates and community activists.[20]

John Kingdon presents another model of agenda setting, one that combines features of the pluralist, elitist, and subgovernmental models.[21] According to the **garbage can**

FIGURE 4.4　　**The Subgovernmental Model of Agenda Setting**

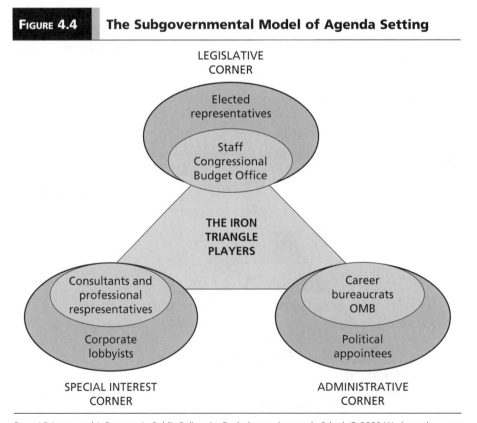

From J.P. Lester and J. Stewart, Jr. *Public Policy: An Evolutionary Approach,* 2d ed. © 2000 Wadsworth, a part of Cengage Learning, Inc. Reproduced by permission. www.cengage.com/permissions.

Note: OMB is the Office of Management and Budget.

TABLE 4.1	Comparison of Pluralist and Elitist Models of Agenda Setting	
	Pluralist model	**Elitist model**
Power	Based on size of group and its access to resources	Concentrated in the hands of a few
Centers of power	Multiple	Few
Values	Shared by masses and elites	Basic consensus among elites; values of elites differ from those of masses
Social mobility	High; elites permit input from masses and confer when making a decision	Low; masses exert minimal influence over elites
Influence	Individuals can influence elites	Individuals cannot sway elites; elites are highly insulated from apathetic masses
Outcome	Depends on many compromises among competing groups	Depends on elites' directing policy from top to bottom, serving their own interests

model, when making decisions we act like a magician reaching inside a black hat and pulling out a rabbit. That is, we make choices in seemingly chaotic fashion, in a policy-making environment of "organized anarchy." We do not seek the absolute best decision. If we were to do so, we might spend our entire lives looking for it. Even if we did find the absolute best choice, the cost of the search might outweigh the benefits. Instead of searching, we choose the option that **satisfices**—that is, the one that is satisfactory and sufficiently good.[22] According to Kingdon, we make decisions using "imperfect rationality" (satisficing behavior), incomplete preferences (preferences that cannot be placed in strict order), and fluid participation (participation without structure or hierarchy). We make decisions in a mixed environment—one characterized both by the structure of the cozy iron triangle and by the randomness of the pluralistic model, in which we participate in give-and-take based on the mobilization of groups. Recent studies present evidence of this garbage can, or semichaotic, model of agenda setting but give greater weight than does Kingdon to the model's elitist, top-down features.

The distinguishing characteristics of the pluralist and elitist models, which present contrasting views of American politics, are listed in Table 4.1.

Impact of Sensational Events

Our discussion of how an agenda attains institutional status would not be complete if we did not mention the effects of sensational events on policymaking. In his exhaustive work, Thomas Birkland analyzed the impact of hurricanes, earthquakes, and oil spills on agenda setting.[23] He found that we are easily moved by pictures of human suffering; incensed, we sometimes demand immediate action. The devastation wreaked by Hurricane Katrina in New Orleans in 2005 provides a perfect example to support Birkland's thesis: reports and images of the horrific conditions endured by residents of the predominantly poor Lower Ninth Ward served to thrust several issues, such as poverty and emergency preparedness, to the forefront of the national agenda. However, the most clear-cut case of a sensational event causing rapid political action is, of course, the 9/11 attacks. The sights

A CASE IN POINT

The Power of a Focus Event: Making Schools Safe

The worst nightmare of every parent came true in April 1999, when TV news programs showed terrified students streaming out of the Columbine High School campus in Littleton, Colorado. Responding to the bloodshed caused by two troubled teenagers, Eric Harris and Dylan Klebold, the federal Bureau of Alcohol, Tobacco, and Firearms (ATF), along with school boards all over the country, moved aggressively to combat school violence and prevent another tragedy. Although policymakers had debated school safety for years, the incident at Columbine brought the issue to the institutional level, and the American public demanded action.

While many schools responded by installing expensive metal detectors at school entrances, the ATF worked with a threat assessment company to help school administrators identify troubled students who might be on the verge of committing violent acts. The controversial program, known as Mosaic 2000, tested students in twenty schools—primarily high schools—as part of a national pilot study.[24] Mosaic identified potentially violent students at Reynoldsburg High School, in a suburb of Columbus, Ohio, by asking students 150 questions crafted by experts in law enforcement and psychiatry. Administrators also asked parents, friends, and school counselors to evaluate students. The students were then rated on a scale of one to ten.

Needless to say, the Mosaic study provoked controversy. At Reynoldsburg High, school administrators, parents, and the school board favored the program, as did Ohio's attorney general. However, the Ohio chapter of the American Civil Liberties Union expressed concern that the program breached students' civil rights, including their right of confidentiality. The group called Mosaic a "technological Band-Aid" that fed on parents' fear. Critics also questioned the program's effectiveness in identifying potentially violent students. At Columbine, the perpetrators were good, though troubled, students with access to guns, students who unexpectedly snapped because they felt victimized by bullies and the school system. In a recent book, journalist Dave Cullen pointed out that although Harris probably was a sadistic psychopath and Klebold was clinically depressed, there was no specific characteristic that would have identified the two young men before the incident took place.[25] When such students are involved, is Mosaic just as helpless as school administrators in identifying the potential assailants?

Similar to many other sensational events, the Columbine massacre created its own copycats. As shown in the graph below, incidents of school (and college) shootings took more lives in subsequent years. In addition to a rising trend in the United States, other nations, such as Germany and Finland, have also seen senseless killings by young people.

of the collapsing twin towers and hapless people jumping to their deaths have been seared in our collective memory ever since. Terrorist organizations know the importance of sensational events in shaping a nation's agenda; as a result, Alex Schmid and Janny de Graaf have argued that these acts are forms of political communication.[26] For the past forty years, international terrorist acts have killed about 370 people per year—while this is a deplorable amount, it is still slightly fewer than those who drown in bathtubs in the United States every year.[27] Because terrorist attacks generate such a spectacle, though, they force governments to overreact. Thus, President Bush felt the need to respond to the

School Shootings in the United States

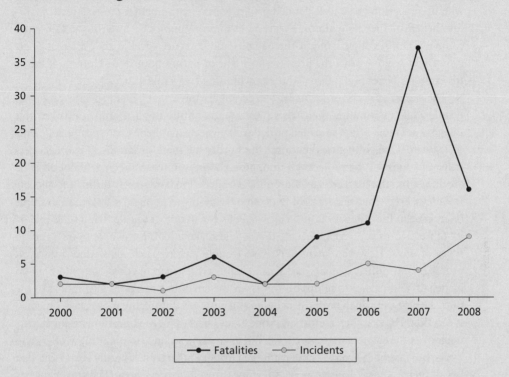

Discussion Points

1. How did school safety reach the institutional agenda?
2. How did the Reynoldsburg school board respond to public concern? Do you think their response was effective?

9/11 attacks in a dramatic manner, quickly declaring a global war on terror and launching a two-front war in Afghanistan and Iraq.[28]

However, sometimes it takes more than shocking pictures of disaster to force an issue from the systemic to the institutional agenda. Birkland argues that an agenda can be activated by a **focus event** that spurs a community to organize and demand legislation (see "A Case in Point"). The most effective community is a coherent group of professionals, experts, and activists—policy entrepreneurs—who mobilize and initiate a plan of action.

Evaluating Costs and Benefits

Although the process by which policymakers give a systemic agenda official status is complex, we can develop a simple model that explains which agendas are likely to make the official list. We begin by evaluating systemic agendas in terms of their relative costs and benefits. If the benefits and costs are diffuse, they fall on a large number of people who do not belong to a well-defined group. Most environmental projects provide diffuse benefits—they help almost everyone in the community by fostering a clean environment. On the other hand, if the benefits and costs are specific, they affect a single group, which alone bears the project's favorable or harmful outcome. Hunting licenses, for example, benefit only those who enjoy hunting (see Table 4.2).

The easiest projects for lawmakers to accept are those that benefit specific groups of people while distributing their costs over a large, diffuse population. Included in this category are most of the so-called pork barrel projects that help a few specific segments of legislators' constituencies. Because the burden of these programs falls on faceless taxpayers, most of the projects go unopposed. However, when the benefits of an issue are diffuse but the costs are specific, political leaders find it extremely difficult to allocate resources, even when encouraged to do so by widespread popular support. An example of an issue in this category is gun control. Polls consistently indicate that a solid majority of Americans support a measure that would make it hard for people to own certain types of guns. However, lawmakers have trouble passing such legislation because it promises only diffuse benefits, lacks a single powerful group of constituents to fight on its behalf, and faces strong opposition from the small but powerful gun lobby. In the third category, in which both the benefits and costs are diffuse, the most likely outcome is inaction. For example, almost everyone agrees that we need educational reform, particularly at the elementary school level. But lawmakers struggle to pinpoint winners and losers, because both groups come from the citizenry at large. It is hardly surprising that for all their rhetoric, legislators pass few measures in this category. The final category comprises measures with clear winners and losers. These bills address the most controversial redistribution issues. Examples of such measures include bills that support or oppose a new airport, pit environmentalists against the timber industry in the Pacific Northwest, or redress past injustice through programs such as affirmative action.

Having explored agenda setting in terms of benefits and costs, we are prepared to briefly discuss the two ways people commonly assess the benefits and costs of a policy. Those who favor a narrow view hold that when considering costs and benefits, people strive only to maximize their own short-term self-interest. If the potential benefits for a

TABLE 4.2	**Outcomes for Diffuse and Specific Costs and Benefits**	
	Benefits (winners)	
Costs (losers)	*Diffuse*	*Specific*
Diffuse	Inaction	Likely acceptance
Specific	Likely rejection	Conflict

group are diffuse, the group is likely to lose, because no one in the group will be willing to bear the cost of a policy that will benefit the entire group, whether or not the other members share the costs. Mancur Olson called this situation the free-rider problem, asserting that "rational" people do not want to participate in a collective action when they can get something for nothing (see chapter 1). Olson pointed out that as group size increases, the problem becomes more pronounced.[29] In contrast, those who advocate the broad view contend that people are motivated not just by short-term self-interest but also by commitment,[30] group utility,[31] and ideology.[32] Supporters of this theory assert that if people defined benefits and costs as narrowly as the self-interest camp says they do, they would never embrace the most challenging causes—from improving the environment to supporting national liberation movements. Because environmental policies benefit so many of us, we find it almost impossible to answer the question, why should I give my time to support these issues? Indeed, we cannot answer this important question if we assume that people follow only their narrowly defined self-interest. However, if we accept the premise that people often look beyond their own selfish needs and are inspired to contribute benefits to a larger community, we can explain a wide variety of altruistic behavior. When group members define an issue's benefits and costs as "specific" to them, they may fight to keep it in front of the political elite and get it onto the institutional agenda. By taking this approach, volunteers for Mothers Against Drunk Driving spurred the passage of many local laws that got tough on drunk driving.

POLICY FORMULATION

Once an agenda attains institutional status, specific policies must be formulated. Legislators outline the course of action that the policy will follow. This plan can then be enacted into law. To determine the plan, lawmakers specify objectives, identify policy alternatives, and adopt the one alternative that gives the best results. Although analysts may participate in each stage of the policy cycle, their involvement is most critical in the phases of policy formulation, implementation, and evaluation.

Suppose we want to achieve a completely drug-free society—a desirable objective, though highly improbable. If we set an impossible goal, our policies, no matter how effective, will fail. Therefore, we start with the goal of reducing illegal drug use by, say, 10 percent in the next five years. How do we achieve this policy goal? We attack the problem by trying to curtail either the demand for drugs or their supply. We may choose to adopt one or more of the policy solutions outlined below. These policies may be enacted through legislation, executive orders, ordinances, or judicial decisions.[33]

Policies tend to provide either positive or negative incentives. Many drug users want to quit but cannot do so because of the high cost of treatment. To provide a positive incentive for quitting, the government may open rehabilitation centers for treating users free of charge. As a further inducement, the government may protect the privacy of those receiving treatment. On the flip side, negative inducements include stiffer penalties for drug possession and mandatory sentencing guidelines for repeat offenders. The government also may empower law enforcement agents to confiscate property gained through drug trafficking.

Another option available to us is to modify behavior by changing the rules. We might pass laws to make detection easier or to authorize locker searches. Students' fear of getting caught would raise the cost of using illicit drugs and might discourage them from bringing drugs to school. Moreover, we might decide to alter behavior with educational campaigns. We could distribute factual information on the physiological and psychological impacts of drug abuse. Such information might take the form of advertisements, leaflets, or curricula on drug abuse, such as the Drug Abuse Resistance Education (D.A.R.E.) program for children.[34] We could also pass laws to give people rights that protect them from injuries or injustice related to drug enforcement and sentencing. Finally, we might accomplish the aims of our institutional agenda by shifting power over the agenda to a specific agency. In one of the most controversial anti-drug proposals, the federal government considered engaging the air force to intercept low-flying airplanes crossing the U.S.-Mexican border. It also authorized the navy and the Coast Guard to seize high-speed boats and ships dropping off drugs.

Explaining Behavior

Before we formulate policy and do everything necessary to achieve our policy goals—offer incentives, change the rules, distribute factual information, give people rights, or transfer power—we first must determine if our proposed solution will be effective. To make this determination, we develop a behavioral model, making certain assumptions about human nature.

If we educate potential users about the ill effects of drug use on their bodies and minds, will we significantly affect their behavior? If so, why? The answer to this question will help us develop a fuller understanding of why people become addicted in the first place, and this information will shape the policies we propose. We might want to know where our target population is most likely to get its information. That way, if we conduct an advertising campaign, we will know from our behavioral model what the ads should say and what kind of ads to run.

To check our behavioral model we can use statistical techniques, testing our hypotheses with existing, **secondary data** or with data collected by the researcher, known as **primary data** (see the discussion of statistical techniques in chapters 7 and 9; see also information on data gathering in chapter 8).

Forecasting Effects

We can use our behavioral model to make a forecast. Scientific forecasting is not fortune-telling. The primary distinction between the two is that although fortune-telling makes a prediction about a single unique event, answering a question with a definitive yes or no, scientific forecasting takes place in the context of probability. When a scientist forecasts a 99 percent probability and the event does not take place, the forecast may still be valid. Embedded in the forecast is a small but definite 1 percent chance of the event's not taking place. What the scientist intends to say with the forecast is that if the same conditions prevail over many tries, the event will occur 99 percent of the time. In forecasting we can never develop a model that fully eliminates uncertainty.[35]

Scientists base their forecasts on explicit or implicit assumptions about people's behavior, assumptions that they test by using control variables. Similarly, policymakers manipulate control variables to achieve their stated goals. If we assume that a rational human being is more inclined to abstain from drugs if given enough information about their harmful effects, such information becomes our control variable, or the factor designed to induce certain behavior. Forecasting is often like looking in the rearview mirror while driving a car. If we want to understand the future, we must study the past. We make most forecasts using past data. If the road behind is the same as the one ahead, we are in a good position to forecast our future. However, when the road changes, curving and zigzagging, our forecasts lose their accuracy (see the discussion of forecasting techniques in chapters 10–12).

After setting goals and identifying alternatives, we pick the best possible option. We make our choice using cost-benefit or cost-effectiveness analysis (see chapter 14).

Conflict, Inaction, and Nondecision

We define public policy as what the government decides to do and not to do. The government can make as loud a statement by refusing to get involved as by taking action. Many agendas, from poverty to nuclear weapons, swirl around in society and are debated on college campuses, discussed in community halls, and written about on editorial pages. However, the vast majority of them do not make it to the institutional agenda. The government and the power elite may actively prevent some of the agendas from ever reaching the institutional stage, either by force or through deliberate neglect. Government officials in the South did not make a concerted effort to address black poverty and discrimination until civil rights legislation compelled them to take action. Authorities frequently used brute force to block attempts to discuss the relevant issues.[36]

The government, however, does not need brute force to keep certain agendas from reaching institutional status. Most often, it blocks consideration of agendas unpopular with the elite simply through benign neglect. Why does it prevent some agendas from achieving institutional status? Evidence suggests two reasons for such failures (see Table 4.2). First, some issues provoke huge conflicts in society, especially when these issues identify specific winners and losers. If passions run high on both sides, political leaders often try to sidestep the issues. The primary goal of politics is managing conflict. No organized society can survive without suppressing certain disagreements that can develop into huge conflicts. Take, for instance, the issue of gun control. Suppose the governor of your state fervently believes that banning weapons is the only way of reducing violence. If the governor's party controls the legislature, the governor may feel free to take a radical stance on the issue. However, if others in the state passionately defend their right to own guns, the clash between the two viewpoints may lead to open conflict. Facing this ominous prospect, the political elites of both parties may refrain from pushing the agenda forward.[37]

In addition, if both the winners and the losers are diffuse, policymakers have no incentive to elevate an agenda from the nebulous systemic zone to the institutional stage. Many issues with merit never achieve institutional status. Thus, despite their scientific relevance, numerous environmental issues of global proportion remain unaddressed.

On the other hand, sometimes an issue that has been neglected for years suddenly commands the attention of the general public and the power elite. Adapting the arguments of social scientist Anthony Downs, we can show how an issue goes through an

| FIGURE 4.5 | Decision and Nondecision in Policy Formulation |

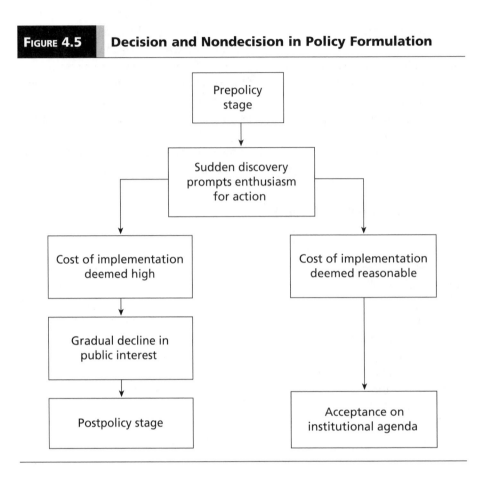

"attention cycle." As it proceeds through the cycle, it either fades from the public agenda or pushes toward institutional acceptance (see Figure 4.5).[38] At the systemic, prepolicy level, an agenda remains dormant. If a sudden discovery—such as news about the spread of the AIDS virus, the existence of an ozone hole over the Antarctic, or the alleged security leaks at Los Alamos National Laboratory—mobilizes influential members of the policy community, they may issue an enthusiastic call for action. However, if they perceive an unacceptably high cost, the agenda may lose public interest and drop into "a twilight calm of lesser attention and spasmodic recurrences of interest." Downs suggests that such agendas have three things in common: they affect numerical minorities (for example, poor people, homeless people), they advocate social arrangements providing benefits (such as high-speed rail transport or new subway systems) to a majority or a powerful minority, and they no longer captivate the public with exciting ideas (for example, the space program's lunar landing missions—routine flights to the moon did not sustain initial public fascination).

If influential policymakers find the costs to be reasonable, a sudden discovery may motivate them to transform a long-standing agenda into an accepted public policy. In the late 1990s, advances in DNA analysis brought capital punishment to the forefront of public awareness. A shocked public learned that new methods allowing researchers to read an individual's genetic code had proven the innocence of a number of inmates slated to face capital punishment. In 1999 Illinois governor George Ryan, a Republican, suspended executions until he could be sure that only the guilty would be put to death.[39] In the Senate, Patrick Leahy, D-Vt., and Gordon Smith, R-Ore., jointly proposed that defendants be guaranteed competent lawyers and provided with DNA testing that might prove their innocence. Some states, including California, made similar proposals. Several religious leaders and anti–capital punishment advocates called for a moratorium on capital punishment. Once nearly forgotten, the movement questioning the appropriateness of capital punishment quickly returned to the public consciousness. Foes of capital punishment drew strength from a steadily declining crime rate during the past decade, which enhanced the public's willingness to accept shorter sentences. Because policymakers saw as reasonable the cost of making DNA testing mandatory and abandoning capital punishment, the policies quickly gained the government's attention.

POLICY ADOPTION

Policy adoption comes at the end of the formulation process. Once policy analyses are complete, they are sent to the official decision-making bodies, which enact legislation or issue executive orders. In the long cycle of policy formation, the adoption stage is for the most part well-defined—if not at the beginning, then certainly at the end of the stage, when the legislature takes a vote or the chief executive issues a formal executive order. Typically the analyst's job ends with policy formulation, when decision makers review the alternatives and analyses of their respective impacts.

In a policy analyst's ideal world, his or her recommendations will be seriously discussed, and policymakers will pick from the alternatives he or she has identified. However, in the real world, lawmakers and the chief executive may be guided by a welter of conflicting concerns, of which the analyst's recommendation is but one. As the formal decision stage approaches, the outcome may reflect a long history of bargaining and deal making based on the decision makers' values, their constituents' concerns, their party affiliations, public opinion, and pressure from special interest groups.[40]

When we look at how decision-making bodies work, we may become cynical about the motives of elected officials. In opinion polls the American public repeatedly expresses its skepticism about Congress's ability to lead the country.[41] The question is, when deciding policy issues, do elected representatives vote only their self-interest (defined as the interest of their constituents and their political action committees), or are they also guided by "ideology"? In an interesting study, researchers Joseph Kalt and Mark Zupan followed legislation through the adoption stage of the policy cycle.[42] They evaluated the voting records of U.S. legislators debating the Surface Mining Control and Reclamation Act (SMCRA), which resulted from a protracted political struggle. Congress passed two versions of the act, in 1974 and 1975. President Gerald Ford vetoed them on both occasions. President Jimmy Carter finally signed the SMCRA into law in 1977. The act required that strip-mined land be restored to its pre-mining state. It also established the Abandoned Mine Reclamation Fund and clarified previously undefined rights to water and land in strip-mined areas.

The self-interest theory says that lawmakers vote only the economic interests of their constituents, with a view toward winning reelection. However, the survey indicated that self-interest, as measured by the importance of mining in a lawmaker's state or district, does a poor job on its own of explaining voting records. The theory was a better predictor of voting behavior when researchers considered not only self-interest but also ideology, as measured by the League of Conservation Voters, an ideological watchdog. The survey indicated that when voting on legislation, U.S. senators and representatives are guided by both self-interest and ideology. Several other studies found similar results.[43]

POLICY IMPLEMENTATION

After a public policy has been adopted, it must be implemented. Adopted policies, particularly legislative acts, almost never specify exactly what is to be done. If a city council passes an ordinance prohibiting skateboarding on public sidewalks, it rarely tells administrators how to implement the measure. Administrators have numerous options. To understand the complexity of their choices, consider the following facts. Because it is impossible to patrol every street corner at all times, the city police department must decide where and when to enforce the new law. Police must decide whether to monitor only those streets with a high volume of pedestrian traffic or to patrol both these areas and those where young people are active, such as parks, schools, and beaches. They also must decide whether to patrol on foot, on bicycles, or in cruisers, which are fast but inefficient in crowded streets. Even after making these decisions, administrators must figure out what fraction of the police department's resources should be devoted to enforcing this new law. In some areas, the new mandate might come with a specific allocation of money, but that is not always the case. Because the police department might prompt legal challenges when enforcing the new law, officers must try to strike a balance between the rights of individuals and the demands of cities.

During the past fifty years, scholars have devoted a great deal of energy to understanding the major players and coalitions in agenda setting and policy formulation. But what happens after the laws have been passed? Do the formal and informal coalitions developed in the previous stages of the policy cycle disappear in the implementation stage? Or does the power coalition that brought about policy change remain active in overseeing implementation? If the power coalition continues to shape implementation, does the structure of the original coalition remain the same, or does it change?

In a series of studies conducted primarily in the 1990s, policy analysts made a number of useful observations about the implementation stage.[44] Figure 4.6 illustrates their findings. As shown in the figure, institutional agendas are set and policies formulated by a loose coalition that may include several formal as well as informal players, who cluster around a set of "core values." According to Paul Sabatier and Hank Jenkins-Smith, these core values are the glue that holds together a disparate coalition.[45] This belief system is highly resilient and often resists changes, particularly by members of the advocacy groups in the broad coalition. Without any strong external shocks, these coalitions tend to remain stable throughout the implementation process. However, when economic conditions change, new information comes to light, or unexpected events occur—such as legal challenges or technical glitches—the

FIGURE 4.6   Impact of External Shocks on Policy Coalitions

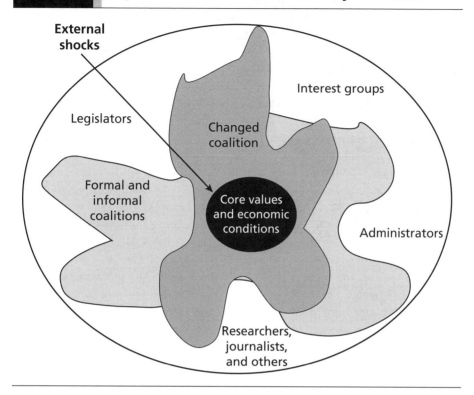

composition of these coalitions may alter significantly. For example, Brian Ellison studied the Animas–La Plata River project in Colorado, near the New Mexico border.[46] Originally seen as a water project, it enjoyed the support of a pro–water development coalition. However, when a government study questioned the financial feasibility of the project and noted that it could jeopardize the river's endangered squawfish population, these external shocks changed the configuration of the coalition of Indian tribes, environmentalists, and probusiness groups, thereby altering the project several times during implementation.

POLICY EVALUATION

If there is one area over which policy analysts exercise primary responsibility in the policy cycle, it is the evaluation phase. Analysts inquire about the possible impact of an adopted policy. Does the policy meet the greater needs of society, and is it achieving its goals? The first question is broader than the second. We hope that the goals of society and those of the policy are compatible, but they sometimes conflict with each other. Suppose your state government has initiated a new education policy to boost school performance. It has allocated funds to prepare students for national standardized achievement tests. If at the end of a certain period the average test score has improved, we may conclude that the program has achieved its goals and that the money has been well spent. However, a broader question arises if we look at the total impact of the program, particularly on children from traditionally disadvantaged and non-English-speaking families. Suppose that while average test scores have improved, the program's curricular changes have devastated less prepared students, increasing dropout rates. In addition, suppose that legislators funded this program at the expense of another project, a state-funded special initiative for children with learning disabilities. We might find that the opportunity cost of such a program exceeds the benefits. When we evaluate the policy on its stated goals, we get a much more positive picture than when we analyze its overall impact on society.

We may evaluate the impact of a policy on several levels. For example, we may examine **policy output**.[47] Returning to our example of traffic cameras on street corners, we note that in June 2000, traffic officials in San Diego cited 4,000 drivers per month for violations, fining them $271 per ticket.[48] Lockheed Martin IMS, the local manufacturer of the cameras, received $70 from each ticket. Therefore, we estimate that the policy output equals the city's net revenue per ticket ($271 − $70 = $201). At this rate, the city expects to make annual collections of about $9.65 million (4,000 × $201 × 12).[49]

We also measure the effect of public policy by conducting a **performance evaluation**—that is, by gauging the policy's impact on target groups. Our target group includes drivers who typically run red lights, causing accidents. However, performance evaluation does more than measure how many people in the target group are affected by a program; it also evaluates the program's total effectiveness. Analysts measure the performance of the cameras by looking at accident data and conducting research to see if the devices reduced the total number of accidents.

In addition, policy analysts may want to evaluate the impact of a policy from an even broader perspective than the one afforded by performance evaluation. In that case, they look at **policy outcomes**. The effects of a policy may not be confined to the target group or even to the immediate program objectives. Instead, they may spill over into other areas of social behavior and social conditions. Because of the traffic devices, motorists may drive carefully not only where cameras are located but also everywhere else they drive, making areas beyond the monitored intersections safer for both pedestrians and drivers.

Finally, analysts measure policy impacts by evaluating feedback. A number of motorists complained that the cameras were unsafe. The drivers argued that if they were to stop suddenly to avoid hefty fines, they might cause accidents. They also argued that at night the blinding flashes from the cameras caused confusion, which led to accidents.[50] This kind of feedback helps analysts change policies to better fit objectives.

POLICY CHANGE

As alluded to above, policies evolve and go through numerous changes until some of them finally are terminated. If we follow the life of any single public policy, we find that it is constantly shaped and reshaped by at least seven factors:

1. Incremental changes in the dynamics of society smooth out the rough edges of implementation.
2. New statutes contradict or invalidate parts of the existing policy.

3. Lawsuits or questions of constitutionality challenge the policy in court.
4. New technology alters the feasibility of the policy.
5. New discoveries or revelations change public support for a program.
6. Political and economic circumstances change, imposing different conditions on an existing policy.
7. Elections cause a major ideological shift that changes the policy.

In other words, as the world around us changes, so do all major policies.

If we look at capital punishment, we see how society's attitudes have changed over the years. A strict "eye for an eye" attitude of swift justice has given way to a more reasoned approach, one that considers carefully the social effects of such a policy. The history of capital punishment goes back to the earliest period of recorded penal codes. The Code of Hammurabi (1790–1750 BCE) recommended capital punishment for twenty-five different crimes.[51] In the seventh century BCE, Draco, the Athenian lawgiver, from whom we get the term *draconian*, prescribed death for every kind of offense. It is interesting to note that Sir Thomas More explained in *Utopia* that in his imaginary land, where pure reason guided all public policy, capital punishment for most offenses, such as stealing, was prohibited. This is because if thieves knew their punishment, they would have every incentive to kill anyone wanting to turn them in. In contrast, capital punishment was prescribed for anyone discussing politics outside the Senate.[52] Brought to the new world by European colonists, capital punishment was liberally administered for high crimes against the state as well as for petty theft. Soon, though, a movement to abolish capital punishment gained ground in the United States. As governor of Virginia, Thomas Jefferson recommended capital punishment only for treason and murder, but after a stormy debate, the legislature defeated the bill by one vote. In 1972, the Supreme Court, reviewing three separate cases, struck down capital punishment in several states and set the standard for capital punishment. Under this guideline, the Court would consider capital punishment "cruel and unusual" if it (a) was too severe for the crime, (b) was arbitrary (that is, not uniform—applied to some but not to others in similar situations), (c) offended society's sense of justice, or (d) was less effective than another punishment.[53] However, during the next seventeen years, the pendulum of the Court's position on the issue swung back hard and fast. In a series of challenges, the Court upheld capital punishment in a number of state cases.[54] When opening old cases in the 1990s, several state courts started admitting DNA evidence. Capital punishment remains an important issue today, as demonstrated by the repeal of capital punishment in New Jersey and New Mexico in 2007 and 2009, respectively.[55]

Policy scientists note four patterns of policy change:

1. **Linear**, when one policy is replaced by another.
2. **Consolidated**, when programs with similar goals are combined.
3. **Split**, when an agency enforcing a certain policy grows too large to administer the policy effectively. The agency is broken into smaller components, and each of them receives part of the original policy.
4. **Nonlinear**, when social conditions change or technological advances generate new information, prompting drastic or major policy changes.

POLICY TERMINATION

As the government accumulates trillions of dollars of public debt more than sixty years after John Maynard Keynes recommended to President Franklin Roosevelt that the government increase spending during recessions and reduce spending during periods of inflation, some policy scientists charge that Keynes ignored political realities. They note that government spending has been elastic in only one direction: upward. Government officials have found it easier to increase spending or propose a new public policy than to terminate one after it has been implemented. As Garry Brewer and Peter deLeon point out, the cavalry did not gallop into the sunset with the introduction of mechanized regiments; the March of Dimes did not stop marching after the invention of the polio vaccine.[56]

Scholars define policy termination as "the deliberate conclusion or cessation of specific public sector functions, programs, policies, or organizations."[57] They have identified four types of termination: functional, organizational, policy, and program.[58]

- **Functional termination** is sweeping. If the government decided to abandon its educational responsibilities, that decision would fall in this category. This termination would cause the complete privatization of education, with the private sector managing the entire field.
- When the government does not want to end its involvement in a field but does wish to withdraw support for an agency, it engages in **organizational termination**. Although nobody expects the government to drop its educational duties entirely, many conservatives in U.S. politics have urged the federal government to end its involvement in the field by eliminating the Department of Education.
- **Policy termination** takes place when lawmakers abandon a specific policy to address changing social needs. In the American South legislators discarded discriminatory Jim Crow laws to respond to changes in the post–civil rights era.
- **Program termination** occurs when the government ends a specific program. For example, in 2006 the Bush administration ended the State Planning Grant Program, which provided funds for states to collect data and develop strategies for dealing with people without health insurance, because it was found to be ineffective and duplicative of other programs.

Why is policy termination a problem for government? Lawmakers adopt a specific public policy to address a specific human problem. They rarely solve a problem completely. Therefore, the policy lingers. It goes through many changes, but the essential goals of the policy remain intact. When legislators terminate a program, they must contend with the losers. Lawmakers' failure to distribute the losses effectively causes many of these programs to continue. This is particularly true when the costs of termination fall on a small, specific group (employees working at a military base, for example, and those who depend on the business generated by the base). It is equally true when the benefits remain diffuse (savings for U.S. taxpayers). A cynical observer would argue that every government program creates its own constituencies. These entrenched interests prevent political leaders from taking the hard step of terminating a policy, program, or agency. Many military bases were established in the United States to fight Native Americans during the early days of the nation's settlement. Yet most of those bases remain in use even a century after their original purpose was fulfilled. Anytime lawmakers try to close a military base, the agencies near the base lobby Congress to keep it open.[59] This pattern repeats itself when political leaders debate whether to end other government programs. As a result, few programs are ever completely terminated.

KEY WORDS

Consolidated policy change (p. 95)

Elitist model (p. 77)

Focus event (p. 85)

Functional termination (p. 96)

Garbage can model (p. 82)

Institutional, or governmental, agenda (p. 76)

Iron triangle (p. 82)

Linear policy change (p. 95)

Nonlinear policy change (p. 95)

Organizational termination (p. 96)

Performance evaluation (p. 94)

Pluralist model (p. 77)

Policy cycle (p. 75)

Policy formation (p. 75)

Policy outcomes (p. 94)

Policy output (p. 94)

Policy termination (p. 96)

Primary data (p. 88)

Program termination (p. 96)

Satisfices (p. 83)

Secondary data (p. 88)

Split policy change (p. 95)

Subgovernmental model (p. 82)

Systemic, or noninstitutional, agenda (p. 76)

EXERCISES

1. Every newly elected president goes to the White House promising to alleviate poverty and economic inequality. Yet in the end, many research and policy debates produce only marginal changes in this area. After reading through the Government Accountability Office report on poverty in the United States in Appendix A, write an essay explaining why it is difficult to make radical changes in public policies. Specifically, why is it challenging to devise a comprehensive program to deal with poverty?

2. Despite recognition of the fact that we should try to substantially reduce poverty in America, the issue remains confined within the broader systemic agenda. How do you explain this in view of our discussion of agenda setting? Is there anything that can be done to bring the issue of poverty to the forefront of political debate?

3. What is the importance of interest group coalitions in public policy formation? Take an important policy that has recently been adopted and determine whether the coalition supporting it has been stable or whether it has changed over time.

4. Write an essay on the role of quantitative analysis—and those who use it—in public policy formation. Given the political nature of the process, should we look to economic analyses and statistical techniques for answers?

Notes

1. Jennifer Hanrahan, "Motorists Taking San Diego's Red-light Cameras to Court," *San Diego Union Tribune*, May 7, 2000.

2. James E. Anderson, *Public Policymaking: An Introduction*, 3rd ed. (Boston: Houghton Mifflin, 1990), 78.

3. See, for example, Nick Mabey, Stephen Hall, Clare Smith, and Sujata Gupta, *Argument in the Greenhouse: The International Economics of Controlling Global Warming* (New York: Routledge, 1997).

4. James P. Lester and Joseph Stewart Jr., *Public Policy: An Evolutionary Approach*, 2nd ed. (Belmont, Calif.: Wadsworth, 2000), 65–86.

5. Roger W. Cobb and Charles D. Elder, *Participation in American Politics: The Dynamics of Agenda-Building*, 2nd ed. (Baltimore: Johns Hopkins University Press, 1983).

6. Ibid., 85.

7. Anderson, *Public Policymaking*, 3rd ed., 83.

8. David B. Truman, *The Governmental Process: Political Interests and Public Opinion* (New York: Knopf, 1951). See also Robert A. Dahl, *Who Governs? Democracy and Power in an American City* (New Haven, Conn.: Yale University Press, 1961).

9. Roger W. Cobb and Charles D. Elder, "The Politics of Agenda Building," *Journal of Politics* 33 (1971): 892–915; Cobb and Elder, *Participation in American Politics*; Roger W. Cobb, Jennie-Keith Ross, and Marc H. Ross, "Agenda Building as a Comparative Political Process," *American Political Science Review* 70 (1976): 126–138.

10. Keith Bradsher, "The Naming of Swine Flu, a Curious Matter," *New York Times*, April 29, 2009.

11. Mike Baker and Michael J. Crumb, "Name Given to Virus Pains Pork Industry," Associated Press, May 1, 2009.

12. Cobb, Ross, and Ross, "Agenda Building."

13. Thomas R. Dye and L. Harmon Ziegler, *The Irony of Democracy: An Uncommon Introduction to American Politics*, 5th ed. (Monterey, Calif.: Duxbury, 1981). See also Thomas R. Dye, *Understanding Public Policy*, 9th ed. (Upper Saddle River, N.J.: Prentice Hall, 1998).

14. James G. March and Johan P. Olsen, *Ambiguity and Choice in Organizations* (Bergen, Norway: Universitetsforlaget, 1976).

15. Dye and Ziegler, *The Irony of Democracy*.

16. James E. Anderson, *Public Policymaking* (New York: Praeger, 1975).

17. Barbara J. Nelson, *Making an Issue of Child Abuse: Political Agenda Setting for Social Problems* (Chicago: University of Chicago Press, 1984).

18. Douglas Carter, *Power in Washington* (New York: Random House, 1965). See also J. L. Freeman, *The Political Process: Executive Bureau-Legislative Committee Relations*, rev. ed. (New York: Random House, 1965).

19. For an excellent, detailed discussion of how conservative think tanks have shaped public policy, see Trudy Lieberman, *Slanting the Story: The Forces That Shape the News* (New York: New Press, 2000).

20. See, for example, Hugh Heclo, "Issue Networks and the Executive Establishment," in *The New American Political System*, ed. Anthony King (Washington, D.C.: American Enterprise Institute, 1978), 87–124. See also Paul A. Sabatier and Hank C. Jenkins-Smith, eds., *Policy Change and Learning: An Advocacy Coalition Approach* (Boulder, Colo.: Westview, 1993), 105–128.

21. John W. Kingdon, *Agendas, Alternatives, and Public Policies* (Boston: Little, Brown, 1984).

22. The term *satisficing* was coined by Herbert Simon. See, for example, Herbert Simon, *Administrative Behavior: A Study of Decision-Making Processes in Administrative Organization* (New York: Free Press, 1945).

23. Thomas A. Birkland, *After Disaster: Agenda Setting, Public Policy, and Focusing Events* (Washington, D.C.: Georgetown University Press, 1997).

24. See Alex P. Schmid and Janny de Graaf, *Violence as Communication: Insurgent Terrorism and the Western News Media* (Beverly Hills, Calif.: Sage, 1982).

25. See John Mueller, *Overblown: How Politicians and the Terrorism Industry Inflate National Security Threats, and Why We Believe Them* (New York: Free Press, 2006).

26. The Nobel laureate economist Joseph Stiglitz and Linda Blimes estimate the cost of the war in Iraq to be more than $3 trillion. See Joseph E. Stiglitz and Linda J. Blimes, *The Three Trillion Dollar War: The True Cost of the Iraq Conflict* (New York: W. W. Norton, 2006).

27. Francis X. Clines, "Schools Await High-tech Help for Evaluating Who's a Threat," *New York Times*, October 24, 1999.

28. Dave Cullen, *Columbine* (New York: Twelve, 2009).

29. Mancur Olson, *The Logic of Collective Action: Public Goods and the Theory of Groups* (Cambridge, Mass.: Harvard University Press, 1965).

30. Amartya K. Sen, "Rational Fools: A Critique of the Behavioral Foundation of Economic Theory," *Philosophy and Public Affairs* 6 (1977): 317–344.

31. Howard Margolis, *Selfishness, Altruism, and Rationality: A Theory of Social Choice* (Cambridge, United Kingdom: Cambridge University Press, 1982).

32. Dipak K. Gupta, *Path to Collective Madness: A Study in Social Order and Political Pathology* (New York: Praeger, 2001).

33. Deborah A. Stone, *Policy Paradox and Political Reason* (Glenview, Ill.: Scott, Foresman, 1988).

34. For an example of factual information designed to change behavior, see D.A.R.E.'s Web site at www.dare.com.

35. For an exciting discussion on forecasting, see John L. Casti, *Searching for Certainty: What Scientists Can Know about the Future* (New York: Morrow, 1990).

36. See, for example, Peter Bachrach and Morton S. Baratz, *Power and Poverty: Theory and Practice* (New York: Oxford University Press, 1970).

37. E. E. Schattschneider, *The Semisovereign People: A Realist's View of Democracy in America* (New York: Oxford University Press, 1960).

38. Anthony Downs, "Up and Down with Ecology: The Issue-Attention Cycle," *Public Interest* 32 (Summer 1972): 38–50.

39. Richard Cohen, "We Can Never Be Really Certain of Eliminating Mistakes in Capital Cases," *Washington Post*, April 20, 2000.

40. For an excellent discussion, see Anderson, *Public Policymaking*, 3d ed.

41. In a continuing national survey, the Gallup organization found in May 2009 that 37 percent of the public approved and 57 percent disapproved of the job Congress was doing. See Gallup, "Congress and the Public," 2009, www.gallup.com/poll/1600/Congress-Public.aspx.

42. Joseph P. Kalt and Mark A. Zupan, "Capture and Ideology in the Economic Theory of Politics," *American Economic Review* 74 (1984): 279–300.

43. Edward J. Mitchell, "The Basis of Congressional Energy Policy," *Texas Law Review* 57 (1979): 591–630; James B. Kau and Paul H. Rubin, "Self-Interest, Ideology, and Logrolling in Congressional Voting," *Journal of Law and Economics* 22 (1979): 365–384; Joseph P. Kalt, *The Economics and Politics of Oil Price Regulation: Federal Policy in the Post Embargo Era* (Cambridge, United Kingdom: Cambridge University Press, 1981).

44. Daniel A. Mazmanian and Paul A. Sabatier, *Implementation and Public Policy* (Lanham, Md.: University Press of America, 1989); Sabatier and Jenkins-Smith, *Policy Change and Learning*, 105–128; Hank C. Jenkins-Smith and Paul A. Sabatier, "Evaluating the Advocacy Coalition Framework," *Journal of Public Policy* 14 (1994): 175–203; Hank C. Jenkins-Smith, Gilbert K. St. Clair, and Brian Woods, "Explaining Change in Policy Subsystems: Analysis of Coalition Stability and Defection over Time," *American Journal of Political Science* 35 (1991): 851–880.

45. Paul A. Sabatier and Hank C. Jenkins-Smith, "The Advocacy Coalition Framework: An Assessment" (paper presented to the Department of Political Science, University of Amsterdam, February 1997), 7–8.

46. Brian A. Ellison, "The Advocacy Coalition Framework and Implementation of the Endangered Species Act: A Case Study in Western Water Politics," *Policy Studies Journal* 26 (1998): 11–29.

47. Melvin J. Dubnick and Barbara A. Bardes, *Thinking about Public Policy: A Problem-solving Approach* (New York: Wiley, 1983), 203.

48. In this example I measure output in dollars. However, we need not gauge public policy outputs in monetary terms. For example, we can measure the output of a drug education policy by the size of the target audience reached.

49. Hanrahan, "Motorists Taking San Diego's Red-light Cameras to Court."

50. Ibid.

51. Michael H. Reggio, "History of the Death Penalty," in *Society's Final Solution: A History and Discussion of the Death Penalty*, ed. Laura E. Randa (Lanham, Md.: University Press of America, 1997), 1–11.

52. See Jasper Ridley, *Statesman and Saint: Cardinal Wolsey, Sir Thomas More, and the Politics of Henry VIII* (New York: Viking, 1982), 66–67.

53. Reggio, "History of the Death Penalty," 10.

54. *Gregg v. Georgia*, 428 U.S. 153 (1976); *Thompson v. Oklahoma*, 487 U.S. 815 (1988); *Penry v. Lynaugh*, 492 U.S. 302 (1989).

55. William Glaberson, "Fierce Campaigns Signal a New Era for State Courts," *New York Times*, June 5, 2000.

56. Garry D. Brewer and Peter deLeon, *The Foundations of Policy Analysis* (Homewood, Ill.: Dorsey, 1983), 386.

57. Ibid., 385.

58. Lester and Stewart, *Public Policy*, 2nd ed., 156–157.

59. Louis Jacobson, "City, State Lobbyists Work to Head Off Base Closings," *Planning* 65 (August 26–27, 1999): 26.

5 Critical Thinking and Research Design

Within a mere six-month span in 2009, four professional sports teams in New York—the Mets, Yankees, Giants, and Jets—opened the doors to brand new stadiums. By 2011, several other professional New York–area teams (including the Rangers, Liberty, Knicks, Nets, Devils, Islanders, and Red Bulls) plan to be playing in new or renovated stadiums, hoping to lure fans, corporate sponsors, and free-agent athletes.[1] These cushy, high-tech stadiums come with huge price tags. The costs of these projects often exceed $500 million, and the cost of the legendarily spendthrift Yankees' new stadium is well over $1 billion. Therefore, team owners nearly always ask for public financing of their extravagant sports facilities.[2]

Professional sports have come a long way since May 15, 1862, when William Cammeyer enclosed the ballpark on Union Grounds in Brooklyn, New York, to keep out nonpaying spectators. Today, professional sports teams—participants in a multibillion dollar enterprise—seek partnerships with cities all over the country.[3] Suppose the professional sports team in your city requests public financing of a new facility. You have been hired by the city to conduct an analysis. How do you proceed?

In the course of a day, decision makers in public organizations are bombarded with questions: What are the present and future needs of our clients? Should we invest in that project? Of three possible projects, which one is best? When can we expect to finish this project? How much, how many, when, which one? As the questions pile up, decision makers can make up their minds by drawing on personal experiences or by acting on hunches. If they are really desperate, they may call on their policy analysts or go outside their organizations and hire consultants to provide them with the answers. If these individuals want to make sense of a jumble of seemingly meaningless numbers—or if they want to use reports submitted by consultants or in-house analysts—they will need a deep appreciation for the abilities and limits of the various tools of statistics and operations research.

FIVE STEPS OF OBJECTIVE ANALYSIS

The strength of modern social science is its ability to translate vague philosophical discourse into rigorous objective analysis. The *New Webster's Dictionary of the English Language* defines objectivism as a "doctrine which postulates that reality exists independent of mind," an outlook free of prejudice, feeling, or subjectivity.[4] This outlook, also known as objective professionalism, has shaped the twentieth-century development of Western social science in general and that of policy analysis in particular. **Objective professionalism** is rooted in inductive logic—the practice of inferring a general conclusion from premises that can be verified empirically, through observation or experience. In contrast, medieval reasoning depended to a large extent on deductive logic, in which conclusions were drawn from premises whose validity was never questioned. Despite empirical evidence supporting Galileo's discovery that the earth revolved around the sun, the scientific authorities of his day could not accept his conclusion. They rejected his finding because it contradicted the established, church-sanctioned view, which was based purely on faith.

With the birth of scientific reasoning, the authorities gradually accepted empirical verification as the best way to conduct scientific inquiry. In fact, today, empirical verification is the hallmark of objective, scientific reasoning.[5] However, this principle runs counter to human nature, for we humans think subjectively, unscientifically. To gather information, we observe the world through filters of culture, upbringing, knowledge, values, ideologies, tastes, and personal interests. Despite our subjective perceptions, however, our reasoning is shaped by our communal existence in a scientific society, which has developed a framework of objective analysis. Our paradigm of scientific reasoning has helped us identify the following five-step process for analyzing a complex problem:

1. Define the fundamental issue and lay out the goals of the analysis.
2. Identify the alternative courses of action.
3. Forecast the consequences of the alternatives.
4. Compare and evaluate systematically all possible outcomes.
5. Choose the most preferred alternative.

We must begin our objective analysis by clearly defining our investigation's content and goals. In other words, we must make sure that we know what the fundamental issue is and what we want to establish by this analysis. In the case of stadium financing, we might ask ourselves, for whom are we building the stadium, and what needs will it serve? We also must define the goal of our study. In other words, for whom are we conducting the analysis? Although the proposed ballpark may benefit the city and downtown businesses (including the team owners), it may harm some of the other neighborhoods in the city, or it may draw resources from regional or other local governments, such as the county or a neighboring city. The project may be good for the city's sports fans but bad for those who had hoped for a new library. It may favor one professional sports team (say, football) at the expense of another (say, baseball). Before starting our analysis, we must determine the purpose of our study.

Having defined our objective, we move to the second step of problem analysis, identifying the alternative courses of action. Our choice of alternatives will be guided by two factors: consistency and feasibility. Our alternatives should be consistent with our goal. While considering the proposed new stadium, we will want to identify the alternatives. Our first choice may be between doing the project and doing nothing. Next, we might consider building in several locations, ever mindful that we can choose not to do the project if none of the other alternatives meets our goals.

We then proceed to the third step in objective public policy analysis, forecasting the consequences of the alternatives. During public debates, the supporters of a new stadium will note the benefits of sports to the community—from creating jobs to reducing youth crime—in the loftiest terms. As an analyst, you must make an exhaustive list of these possible benefits.[6] You may note the following reasons for providing subsidies to a private enterprise, such as a professional sports team:

- *Increase in tax revenue.* Cities prosper when more people and businesses move in. As more people work, live, and spend their income in a city, they generate revenues for the city in the form of income taxes, sales taxes, license fees, other fees, and even fines. Building a new stadium may mean that more people will work for the club, more fans will flock to the games, and more businesses will flourish because of the increased economic activity.

- *Positive externalities.* Many local governments value major league sports teams because they elevate their cities to the "major leagues." "If the Jacksonville Jaguars aren't well known in other parts of the country, they will be—soon," announced the lead story in a Jacksonville newspaper on the eve of an American Football Conference (AFC) championship game against the Tennessee Titans in 2000.[7] "Basically, this game will be a three-hour commercial for the city and the team," said Mike May, director of communications for the Sporting Goods Manufacturers Association. Suddenly a second-tier city in Florida was talking about worldwide exposure. Some stadium proponents even suggested that the civic pride generated by a better sports facility would reduce crime among area youth.[8] The project's supporters also predicted increased business for the local service sector. Between the AFC championship game and the Jaguars' matchup against the Miami Dolphins the previous week, city officials estimated that more than 50,000 visitors had traveled to Jacksonville and spent $1 million in the city, with $800,000 going to local hotels.

In addition to considering these benefits of the stadium project, you must evaluate the stadium's costs. Publicly financing a privately owned sports club could have the following negative effects:

- *"Blackmail" potential.* A professional team creates a strong constituency of fans. As a result, teams demand new stadiums or expensive repairs to existing facilities. If their demands are not met, they threaten to leave their cities. In December 1982, after a highly public five-month battle leading to an agreement between the Raiders, a National Football League franchise, and the city of Los Angeles, the city controller announced that the Los Angeles Coliseum was on the verge of bankruptcy. The controller estimated that because of the deal extracted from the city, the Coliseum would run a deficit of $4 million in the third year of its lease.[9] Two years after the Raiders' agreement with the city, at least thirteen of the forty-two cities with professional sports franchises were asked to provide their teams with tax incentives or to improve their sports facilities, or risk losing their teams.[10]

- *Wealth transfer.* When a city provides a team with subsidies, it transfers wealth from city taxpayers to wealthy athletes and multimillionaire club owners. Because the tax burden falls only on city residents, out-of-town fans receive, in effect, subsidized tickets.

- *Negative externalities.* Building a new stadium, or renovating an existing one, often displaces residents or small businesses from surrounding areas. For many of them, the cost of relocating far exceeds what the city is willing to give as compensation.

In the fourth step of objective policy analysis, we conduct a systematic *valuation of all possible outcomes*. At this stage, we place monetary values not only on the outcomes that are readily measurable in monetary terms but also on the intangible aspects of positive and negative externalities. Unfortunately, such valuations often lead to heated controversies.[11] In 1998, when San Diego was debating the merits of Proposition C, which would have authorized public funding of the Padres' new baseball park, city hall projected that it would need an investment of $275 million. However, the city's consultant, Deloitte & Touche, sidestepping the fact that the project could not sustain itself from its own revenues, estimated that the project would generate $1.8 million annually in net revenues.[12]

Finally, after conducting a thorough analysis, we *choose the most preferred alternative*, in light of the goal of the project and on the basis of some *decision criteria*. These decision criteria can take several forms. When the costs of the alternatives are the same, the criterion should be to maximize the total benefits. On the other hand, when the benefits are the same, we should choose the alternative that costs the least. When both costs and benefits vary, we try to maximize the net benefit (the difference between benefits and costs).

In real life, our criteria for thinking critically about a project can become complex, particularly when we include uncertainty in our thinking. When faced with uncertainty, decision makers may not choose the alternative with the highest expected net benefit. If you are an extra-cautious person (in technical terms, a **risk averter**), you may choose the certainty of low earnings over the lure of more attractive but uncertain returns. On the other hand, if you are a **risk taker**, you may aggressively pursue high returns, regardless of the risk. Your ability or willingness to take a risk plays a significant role in the real world—especially in a democratic, pluralistic society—because you will find that many of the steps in policy analysis do not provide certain, definitive answers. To deal with uncertain outcomes, we must follow a number of specific strategies (see chapter 13).

SETTING GOALS

Defining the goals of a project may be the most difficult step in policy analysis, because they are set not by analysts but by elected officials or higher level government officials.

TABLE 5.1	Multiple Goals: Building a New Stadium	
Project goals	Expected benefits	Expected costs
Enhance the city's image	National and international exposure from having a major league sports franchise	Excessive traffic on already heavily used highways—city could be labeled overcrowded
Foster urban renewal	Extensive construction of new hotels, restaurants, and other business facilities	• Uprooting of existing businesses • Loss of identity of established communities • Relocation of low-income residents in other poor and already congested areas of the city
Generate tax revenue for the city	Increased city revenues through licenses; fees; and property, sales, and income taxes	• Tax subsidies for the sports franchise • Increased financial liabilities for the city, particularly if the team does not live up to expectations

Quite often public policy goals are not well formed, even in the minds of those who make the ultimate decisions. In inviting a professional team to a city, the mayor and other elected officials may be thinking only about the immediate benefit of creating a better image of the city. An analyst, then, should point out the other goals the city ought to consider.

The project might have multiple goals, some of which may be vague or ill defined, while others may be contradictory. A city may build a stadium to attract a new sports franchise, which will enhance the image of the city.[13] If the city builds in a blighted area, the project may have an urban renewal objective. At times these goals may be complementary, while at others they may be contradictory. A stadium may help rebuild the neighborhood around it, but if it creates congestion and traffic problems by clogging up the surrounding highways, it may ultimately harm the city's image. In any case, when you set multiple goals, you should conduct your analysis with respect to each of them. You may present your finding in a table (see Table 5.1), so that decision makers can honestly debate the project's merits.

The primary goal of any public policy is maximizing social welfare, but we have yet to find a way to define "social welfare" to everyone's satisfaction. Terms like *the people* and *the nation* are staples of political rhetoric. Politicians of all shades, from democrats to demagogues, take liberty with these terms. The president sets a national agenda and boldly declares what the nation needs. The opposing party claims to know what "the people" really want. The question of who is "the nation" or who are "the people" has occupied some of the best minds in our intellectual history. French philosopher Jean-Jacques Rousseau, the most celebrated proponent of "general will," assumed its existence as a self-evident truth. As political theorist George Sabine points out,

> The general will . . . presented a unique fact about a community, namely, that it has a collective good which is not the same thing as the private interests of its members. In some

sense it lives its own life, fulfills its own destiny, and suffers its own fate. In accordance with the analogy of an organism, which Rousseau had developed at some length in the article on political economy, it may be said to have a will of its own, the "general will (volonté générale)."[14]

The problem with accepting the existence of an overarching **social objective** is that it often conflicts with individual freedom and individual rights. If you assume the existence of a collective will or, in economic terms, a social objective, you implicitly assume its predominance over individual aspirations. If you believe that for the world's collective good, the hunting of whales must stop, the interests of the whaling industry and the people dependent on it must be sacrificed for the greater good of the community. Similarly, public officials fund antipoverty programs by taxing the upper and middle classes. Building a freeway helps some groups (communities near the freeway, the trucking industry, motorists, the suburbs) while hurting others (communities bypassed by the freeway, the railroad industry, people and businesses displaced by the highway, the city center). Because very few public policies let everyone win and no one lose, to make wise policy choices, we must find a way of comparing the winners' gains with the losers' losses.

Utilitarians and the Pareto Principle

Toward the end of the eighteenth century, a group of British social thinkers called the **utilitarians** tried to define "social welfare." Jeremy Bentham, the best known member of this group, argued for the maximization of total utility in society. The utilitarians, in effect, argued that the marginal utility of a dollar diminishes with a person's level of income. A wealthy person, they asserted, would probably pay less attention to the loss of a dollar than would a poor person. Extending this logic, you could argue that by taking, say, $1,000 from the wealthiest individual on Earth and giving it to a starving person, you would reduce the rich person's marginal utility to an extent less than the increase to the poor person's. As a result, the redistribution of income would increase the total utility of society. By following this formula, we could keep taxing rich people to fund social programs for poor people until the two groups' marginal utilities (one negative and one positive) were equal. The problem with such a plan is that interpersonal utilities are not measurable. We cannot quantify personal feelings about utility. If we take from a miserly rich person and give to a happy-go-lucky poor person, the redistribution of income may not affect the total utility of society at all.

Following this logic—that calculations of interpersonal utilities cannot be made—Italian economist and sociologist Vilfredo Pareto argued that a society's welfare cannot be improved by a redistribution of income from rich to poor individuals. The only way society can be considered better off is if one member gets more income (by stumbling on an oil well, for example) without taking anything away from the other members. This theory is known as the **Pareto principle** (see Figure 5.1).

Suppose our society is composed of two individuals, A and B. A commands twice as many resources as B. If as a result of a new public project A makes an extra $10 and B makes nothing, we move along the vertical axis from the point of initial distribution between the two members. If the reverse takes place and B makes money while A makes nothing, we proceed along the horizontal axis from the initial position. Extending rules to mark A's and B's respective positions in the two scenarios, we call the shaded space

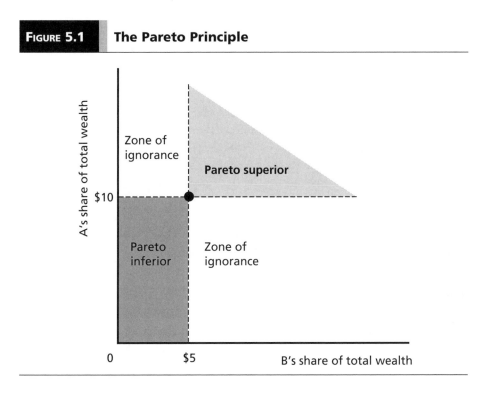

FIGURE 5.1   **The Pareto Principle**

bounded by these lines **Pareto superior**, the region where either A or B or both gain and neither loses. If a project places us in this zone, we should immediately recognize it as desirable. In contrast, if a project causes either individual to lose with no one gaining, we should readily discard the project, because it will take us to the **Pareto inferior** position. Public projects that benefit one group at the expense of another fall in the **zone of ignorance** and cannot be justified in the name of aggregate social welfare. The implications of the Pareto principle are extremely conservative. First, it passes no judgment on the initial distribution of wealth, regardless of how unfair that distribution may be. Second, because it is almost inconceivable that a public policy would have no redistributive component, the Pareto principle is incompatible with any sort of government activism. According to Pareto, we would quickly reject any spending on public goods— national defense, health care, access to free education, or environmental protection— because they would have to be financed by tax revenue, the burden of which would fall mostly on the upper and middle classes.

The Kaldor-Hicks Compensation Principle

Two British economists, Nicholas Kaldor and John Hicks, developed a theory of policy analysis that sought to balance the needs of society and those of individuals. Kaldor and Hicks separately argued that society was better off when pursuing projects that generated sufficiently large gains for the winners, gains great enough so that the winners could compensate the losers for their losses and still remain better off.[15] Suppose a project causes A to gain $10 while costing B $7. A can pay B $7 as compensation, which leaves A with $3 of net gain. This arrangement does not violate the Pareto principle, because one person's gain has taken nothing away from someone else. The question remains: how do we compensate the losers? In all democratic nations, if the losers can be clearly identified (as is the case when the government declares eminent domain to acquire land for building roads), the laws require that the losers be paid adequate compensation. Yet in many cases the losses are spread over a large part of society, the losers cannot be identified, or their losses cannot be adequately measured. In such cases, Kaldor and Hicks argue that we should not worry about paying compensation. As long as we can demonstrate that the benefits outweigh the costs, we can proceed with the project with a clear conscience. Such a position ultimately rejects the Pareto principle in favor of a greater "social good" but fails to help those who have no recourse when denied adequate compensation for their losses. We can cite many examples of the most well-meaning public policies' creating misery for small groups of individuals. Examples include much-needed highways that cut through the heart of a community, and dams that, while producing electricity and irrigation, flood valuable land and ruin it for inhabitants.

The Rawlsian Challenge

In contrast to the Kaldor-Hicks principle, the theory of philosopher John Rawls offers different criteria for judging social welfare.[16] To deduce the fairest rule of distribution, Rawls proposes a method illustrated in the following scenario. Suppose I have a delicious pie that I plan to distribute to your class. I can cut the pie in unequal portions (with one person getting the largest share, while others literally get the crumbs), or I can divide the pie equally among the students. These portions will be distributed by a random drawing over which the students have no control. The question is, before the pie is cut, if you were given a chance to decide, how would you like it to be cut? Remember, if I cut the pie unequally, if you are lucky, you might get the biggest piece; otherwise you will surely go hungry. Rawls calls this random drawing "the veil of ignorance." According to the principles of game theory (discussed in chapter 13), when we face uncertain outcomes, the most rational course of action is to choose a strategy that minimizes our potential loss. Therefore, Rawls argues that if the students follow the precept of rationality, they should opt for an equal distribution, since that would minimize their chances of the maximum loss (known as the *minimax* strategy) of getting only a few crumbs. Extending this logic, Rawls draws a radical conclusion regarding the distribution of wealth in a society. He argues that because of the veil ignorance (since we cannot choose our parents), if we could make a conscious decision *before we are born*, we would surely choose an equal distribution of wealth. In other words, Rawls imagined that if he could put the question to babies before they knew whether they would be born into privileged, wealthy families or to impoverished parents, they would surely choose an equal distribution. Therefore, according to the **Rawlsian criterion**, the fairness of a distribution of income should be judged by the absolute level of well-being of the community's least fortunate ones.

Suppose there are two communities, A and B, with the following sets of income distributions:

$$A = [\$10, \$25, \$8]$$

$$B = [\$200, \$150, \$5]$$

The figures in brackets show the wealth of the six members of the two communities. According to the Rawlsian criterion, you should prefer the distribution in A because the poorest member of A is better off than the poorest member of B. A drawback of the Rawlsian principle is that it throws its entire weight behind the well-being of the least advantaged members of society and disregards the welfare of others. We all know our relative positions in society, and if we are privileged members of community B, we are not likely to move to community A without serious prodding, a medicine that can be far worse than the ailment and, more important, nearly unattainable in a democratic system. However, as a standard for an ethical norm, the Rawlsian principle provides us with an extremely important method of setting public policy goals.

Setting Public Policy Goals

I may sum up our discussion as follows: When using the quantitative techniques discussed in this book, we must define a goal to be maximized. However, despite centuries of intensive searching, we have not yet found an adequate definition of social welfare. Even if we settle on one definition that benefits poor people, those who are disadvantaged, and even the largest segment of society, the goals of socialism inevitably clash with individual aspirations. And, more important, since these collective goals are articulated by a small group of powerful elite, as we have seen in communist regimes, they lead to stifled creativity, economic progress, and significant curtailment of individual rights. On the other hand, if we concern ourselves only with individual goals, we are left with extreme concentrations of income, which often ushers in political instability and social conflict. Our philosophical inadequacy and our inability to define social welfare leave a gaping hole in our understanding of project evaluation. We will return to this important problem several times in the course of this book.

CHOOSING A METHOD OF ANALYSIS

Public policy analysts strive to link project goals (output) to investment (input). The purpose of policy analysis is threefold: to choose the methods or analytical processes that will identify a **causal link** between the dependent and independent variables, to **generalize** the results, and to establish the **control**, or the policy direction. We may illustrate this complex process by drawing an analogy from the game of pool. Suppose the object of our game is to send the eight ball to a pocket by striking the white cue ball with a cue (see Figure 5.2). Our **policy objective** is to shoot the eight ball (the **dependent variable**) into the pocket by hitting it with the cue ball (the **independent variable**). The cue ball is driven by the cue, which represents the **control variable**, or the strength of our action. To properly execute our shot, we must exert correct pressure in the right direction. If the eight ball goes in the pocket, we can claim to have a successful policy. If it does not, the policy will be considered a failure. If the eight ball hits other balls on the way and makes our position on the table extremely difficult, we call this position an **unintended consequence** of the policy. Let us assume that our goal in constructing a new stadium is to increase tax revenues for the city. Our policy objective is positive net tax revenue. The dependent variable is the revenue, which is influenced by the independent variable, the new stadium. The amount of investment toward the construction is the control variable. If the new stadium causes traffic gridlock and

FIGURE 5.2 Methodology for Policy Analysis

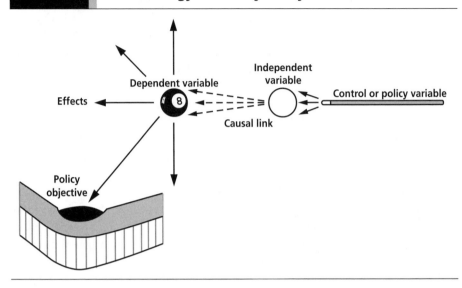

harms local businesses, we will regard these problems as the unintended consequences of the project.

Suppose we are concerned about the rising number of teen pregnancies in our state. We decide that our policy goal is to reduce the number by 15 percent in the next three years. If our analysis demonstrates a causal link between preventing pregnancy (the dependent variable) and disseminating information on reproduction through television advertising (the independent variable), we can estimate the amount of money (the policy, or control variable) we will need to accomplish our goal. In this process, then, our first task is to establish the causal relationship between the dependent and independent variables through proper **research design**.

Research design, or the plan of inquiry, links the dependent variable with a set of independent variables. It can take a number of forms that vary in scientific rigor. Broadly speaking, we classify research designs under the headings **experimental** and **quasi-experimental**. With experimental designs, we randomly assign the subjects of inquiry across experimental groups and control stimuli, and we manipulate the independent variable as we like. Using a controlled experiment, we make inferences from the results about the strength of the causal link. We then generalize our inferences to design an appropriate policy to achieve a certain goal. In contrast, with quasi-experimental research designs, we do not use these criteria. The following examples will help explain these terms.

Experimental Design

We find the classic experimental design in controlled group experiments, conducted primarily in the fields of medicine, the natural sciences, and experimental psychology. The most rigorous of all designs is the so-called **Solomon four-group design** (see Figure 5.3).[17] If we want to prove the effectiveness of a new drug, we randomly assign our

Solomon Four-Group Experimental Design

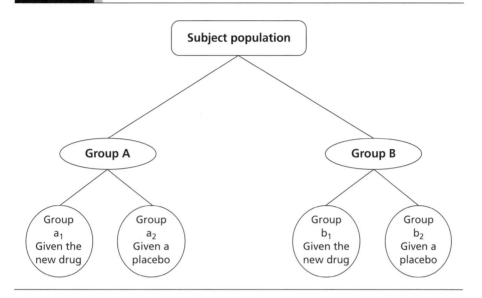

subjects to two groups, A and B. We further divide each group into two more groups. We give the new drug to one subject from group A and one from group B, while others receive a placebo. After administering the new drug, we monitor our patients' progress. If we find that the differences between the control groups $(a_1 - b_2)$ and $(b_1 - a_2)$ are significant, we can experimentally establish a causal link between the new drug and the disease.

In medical or biological experiments, researchers often exert such control over the subject population, drawing inferences and proving them with repeated experiments. New drugs come on the market, evidence mounts about various carcinogens, and clinical tests establish human behavioral patterns.

Although Solomon four-group tests are the strongest in establishing a causal link between dependent and independent variables, conducting these elaborate tests can be extremely expensive, time-consuming, and, in many cases, particularly in the area of social sciences, virtually impossible. Therefore, we must frequently be satisfied with **post-test-only control group experimental designs**, in which we simply observe the effects of experimental drugs on those who were exposed to them and on those who were not (see Figure 5.4).

In this less restricted research design, we randomly assign subjects to two, rather than four, groups: one exposed to the stimulus and one not. If we find the difference between the two groups to be statistically significant, we can establish the string of causality. Important to this research design is the random assignment of the subjects for the experiment. If we do not assign them in random order, we may allow systematic biases to creep into the experiment and contaminate the results. If we separate the groups by sex, for example, our results may be invalid if the division along gender lines introduces another independent variable along with the independent stimulus variable (in our

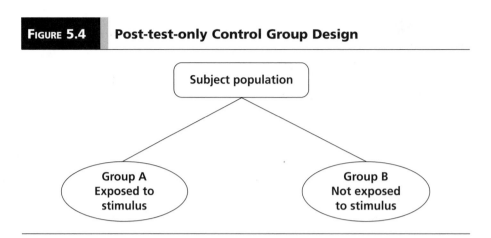

FIGURE 5.4 **Post-test-only Control Group Design**

example, the new drug). Unfortunately, however, even this less restricted research design is generally impossible to implement in the social sciences, because it requires a laboratory setup, in which subjects are randomly selected into two groups.

Quasi-experimental Design

The problem with conducting research in the social sciences is that we cannot control the real world in a manner comparable to that of a researcher working in a lab. Experimental research designs require us to distribute subjects randomly, separate them into distinct groups, guard against time lapses that dilute the effect of the stimulus, and eliminate the influence of past government policies. Therefore, in public policy research we must adopt quasi-experimental designs, in which we relax the rigors of experimental designs to meet the challenges of open society. These compromises create a number of problems for researchers.

If we want to use a strict scientific research design to test the hypothesis that the strength of family ties bears directly on a student's educational performance, we must be able to assign family stability to the subject group in a random fashion. But this clearly is not possible. Similarly, when the control variable is not amenable to change, we may have to make do with a comparison between groups that are not strictly similar. While trying to establish the relationship between family stability and educational achievement, we might find two groups, one with stability—perhaps measured by whether the parents are divorced or separated—and one without. Clearly, however, the marital status of the parents will not be the only difference between the two groups. The experiment will be affected by a variety of other intervening variables, such as the strength of the extended family, the status of religious and social community ties, and other factors.

A second problem with quasi-experimental research designs is that, in contrast to researchers in medicine, the natural sciences, and experimental psychology, those in the social sciences seldom seek to discern a stimulus-response reaction in the subject population. Instead, social scientists want primarily to understand the causal link between preexisting social or economic characteristics and revealed preferences, attitudes, values, and orientations. Suppose we try to examine the impact of a school voucher system on a group of minority pupils. We give parents at a low-performing school the opportunity to send their children to the private school of their choice. After a year, we compare the test scores of those who went to the private schools with those who remained in the public school. If we see a significant difference between the average test scores of the two groups of children, can we positively attribute the change to the voucher system? Not necessarily—at least not according to the strictest of the scientific criteria of experimental research design. We can argue that those parents who chose to send their children to private schools may have introduced some self-selection bias into the experiment. That is, they may be more concerned about their children's education, and more involved in it, than those who did not take advantage of the voucher system. Unlike medical research, social science experiments do not permit us to randomly assign students to private schools. As a result, we cannot completely rid ourselves of the effects of self-selection and other such biases.

Another important source of bias is the passage of time. The experimental design assumes an instantaneous response to a stimulus, a response that is free of time's influence. Suppose you are conducting research in microbiology and are interested in the impact of a certain chemical compound on the growth of a particular bacterium. If after applying the compound to the bacteria-coated dish you receive instantaneous feedback, you can clearly see the test results. If, on the other hand, you must observe the gradual growth of the culture over time, you will take precautions to protect the dish from exposure to the outside environment, because you do not want the results to be contaminated by an external agent. However, in society no such protection from outside elements can be provided. This situation creates a number of intriguing problems. To continue our discussion of the voucher system, let us say that we decide to test the impact of the system on minority students by tracking those children who left the public school. If we can get data on their progress before and after the transfers, we can build a strong case for testing our hypothesis. Even under these circumstances, though, we may doubt the reliability of our data because of the possible contaminating effect of the passage of time. As children grow older, they go through many developmental stages. Critics of our experimental design may ask how much of our result may be attributed to the two school systems and how much to child development.

Take another example, national crime rates. A weary nation, jaded by sensational news stories, watched in disbelief as the crime rate declined steadily during the 1990s. President Bill Clinton claimed credit for the decrease by linking it to his recruitment of 100,000 new police officers. Matching his zeal, Republicans declared that their get-tough policies caused this welcome trend. In fact, in every city or town where the rate declined, police chiefs and city fathers claimed victory for their own programs. Can we end the debate and prove through research what reduced the crime rate? Unfortunately we cannot. To be sure, some public policies were responsible, but so were a number of broad social trends that had little or nothing to do with anticrime policies adopted at any level of government. This period saw unprecedented growth in the economy, with the lowest recorded level of unemployment in history. With more people working, fewer idle wrongdoers lived on the street. The nation was going through a major demographic shift. The children of baby boomers were passing through a crime-prone age group (between sixteen and twenty-five), but boomers had fewer children than their predecessors, causing the crime rate to decline nationwide.

You can see how difficult it is to establish a causal relationship in an open society. It is therefore not surprising that social scientists seldom resolve theoretical controversies, even when such disputes are part of accepted academic orthodoxy. So how do we discern a causal relationship between dependent and independent variables? First, we look at the strength of the correlation between the variables and, with the help of statistical tests, try to minimize the possibility of accepting a false hypothesis as true. Second, if external variables threaten to sway the results, we design the research plan carefully to remove their contaminating influence. The analyst addresses these two concerns by selecting the appropriate experimental design.

Quasi-experimental designs can take several forms: **one-shot case studies**, **correlation analyses**, **cross-sectional analyses**, or time-series analyses. Analysts typically conduct one-shot case studies on unique events of history. Consider a state road made obsolete by recent highway construction. A close-knit small town that depended on the state route is economically devastated. If you want to study the town's plight, you may need to conduct a one-shot study. The problem with one-shot case studies is that they do not give us the advantage of a valid comparison, without which we often are unable to test our hypotheses. In these studies, the best we can do is to make sure that our arguments are logically consistent and supported by valid observations. Although one-shot studies may lack scientific rigor, they can shed important light on the problem in question.

Correlation analyses consider the degree of association between two variables. If we see that an increase or decrease in one variable is associated with an increase or decrease in another, we can hypothesize a correlation between the variables. As you can see in Table 5.2, this hypothetical data set indicates that a correlation may exist between parents' marital status and children's academic achievement. We will discuss correlation analysis and hypothesis testing in chapter 7. Because researchers conduct correlation analyses by collecting comparable data for a number of cases, these analyses, unlike one-shot case studies, are amenable to statistical testing.

Analysts make cross-sectional analyses to compare the outcomes in a number of cases at a single point in time. We can compare the crime rates of similarly sized cities and ask why variations occur from city to city. The strength of cross-sectional studies is that the data are not contaminated by the passage of time. Their primary weakness concerns our ability to select cases that are directly comparable with one another. If we compare the crime rate of Billings, Montana, with that of Atlanta, Georgia, the validity of our results might be questioned because the two cities are quite different from each other. To avoid the proverbial comparison of apples and oranges, we must take special care to eliminate the effects of external variables.

TABLE 5.2   **Correlation Analysis: Marital Status versus Student Achievement**

	Student achievement	
Marital status	*Percentage low*	*Percentage high*
Parents divorced or separated	60	40
Parents together	30	70

Trend analyses study a single case over time. We may conduct research on the respective crime rates of Billings and Atlanta during a certain period. Much of econometric analysis involves trend, or time-series, analysis. We will discuss time-series analysis at length in chapters 11 and 12. Its strength is that it permits us to study the same case over a long period of time. The problem with time-series analysis is that time itself has an important impact on the case we are studying. If we are studying Atlanta's crime rate over the past twenty years, we may ask whether the city has changed culturally, demographically, or economically during that period. If these variables have changed over time, they may have altered Atlanta in a significant way.

CHOOSING THE RIGHT MODEL

Because we as social scientists are restricted to the quasi-experimental design to conduct our research, we must choose a model. But what model should we use? Our fundamental problem is that we are trying to match two dissimilar worlds. We superimpose the world of quantitative techniques, based on objective, structured, scientific reasoning, on a largely unstructured, subjective world of public policy analysis. This incongruity raises two important issues: (1) A model is by definition a truncated version of reality. Can we trust it to shed light on real-world problems? (2) Models that seek to maximize social welfare assume agreement on the goal of society. How relevant are such models in a pluralistic, democratic society, in which there are multiple and diverse policy goals?

Analysts use abstract quantitative models to represent a complex reality. A model, by definition, always deviates from reality, and this deviation makes it suspect. As a model truncates reality by making assumptions, questions about its relevance become paramount. Because they use models extensively, often to reduce reality to unrecognizable forms, economists have been the objects of derision—and awe.[18] We should not reject a model just because it makes simple assumptions about the real world. Because of the world's complexity, we frequently need these restrictive assumptions to separate fundamental, global patterns from local, particular, or ephemeral effects. Assumptions help us define the domain where results are expected to hold. We can then expand the boundaries of this narrow domain by systematically removing some of the assumptions to make the results resemble reality more closely. Another important reason for building models is that they help us examine the internal consistency of our reasoning. If we build a model on the premise that education discourages illegal drug abuse, we can conduct statistical tests on the basis of empirical evidence. Moreover, if we see that other variables are important in determining an individual's tendency toward drug abuse, we can take them into consideration. We can also drop a variable (for example, race or gender) if we see that it is not very useful to the explanation. Using this structured logic, models frequently explain behavior and reveal unsuspected relationships. They also eliminate the need for ad hoc reasoning and help us understand our mistakes when our predictions go awry.

Let us say that you want to forecast the number of students who might be using illegal drugs on a college campus.[19] You base your forecast on a survey that shows how many freshman students used drugs last year and are continuing to do so. The survey also tells you how many nonusers have begun to use drugs since starting college. Guided by these findings, you assume that the ratios will persist throughout the college careers of the entering freshman class. You also suppose that no external factors will have a significant effect on the trend suggested by the ratios.

We easily find reasons to question the validity of these bold assumptions. For one thing, the study does not include entering transfer students, who may behave differently than the students surveyed. In addition, the forecast does not consider the effect of education or the psychological maturity of the student population. Including these factors could alter your projections in important ways. In support of your forecasting model, you may argue that given your assumptions, you have identified the most likely trend. If you find reasons to believe that students' levels of addiction go down as they mature and become better educated, you can modify the model to allow for this change of relationship. Furthermore, if you find at the end of four years that your projections were seriously flawed, you can go back to your original set of assumptions and try to correct the mistakes. The assumptions and structure of your model allow you to process feedback in a way that would have been impossible had you made your projections based solely on "gut feelings," intuition, or ad hoc reasoning.

While it is difficult to accurately forecast the outcome of each alternative, it is even more problematic to understand and forecast the unintended consequences of government policies. These unforeseen consequences of public policies can happen because of many factors, such as a lack of scientific knowledge at the time of the adoption of the policies, an inability to fully understand complex social relationships, moral hazard, overregulation, rent seeking, and the inability to properly time a government program (see chapter 3).

FORECASTING OUTCOMES AND UNINTENDED CONSEQUENCES

The government makes decisions within the bounds of existing scientific knowledge. As science develops, it finds the follies of our previous actions. For example, in the late 1940s an agricultural research station in Mexico created a hybrid variety of rice and wheat, which was quickly described as "miraculous." It substantially increased the production of those crops and allowed many poor nations, including the perennially famine-prone India, to sustain their own food supplies. The program was so successful that it was called the "green revolution." Unfortunately, few people could have anticipated the social and political upheavals it created in India. The introduction of these new varieties of crops, which substantially increased total production, required more intensive cultivation, more irrigated water, and more fertilizer, which only the wealthier farmers could afford. The wealthier farmers also started using more mechanical devices instead of hiring day laborers.[20] As a result, income inequality in rural India increased, which ultimately led to social unrest; quickly, the so-called green revolution turned bloody red.[21]

Another source of unintended consequences of public policies is moral hazard (see chapter 1). It results from insulating people from the adverse consequences of their actions. For instance, terrorism expert Marc Sageman has argued that in France, extended unemployment benefits and other social safety net programs, coupled with overt and covert racism and discrimination, have made idle urban youth of North African origin into the main source of Islamic radicalism.[22]

Government restrictions can create different types of unintended market distortions. For instance, in 1973, the United States learned a painful lesson about its dependence on imported oil when, as a result of U.S. support for Israel during the Yom Kippur War, the oil-producing Arab nations imposed an embargo on oil exports to the United States. Looking for alternative sources of energy at home, the nation turned toward nuclear power. However, on March 28, 1979, a valve in the Three Mile Island nuclear power generator near Harrisburg, Pennsylvania, malfunctioned and released a large quantity of radioactive coolant into the atmosphere. While the accident itself would have been a cause for concern, public anxiety was further heightened when the popular movie *The China Syndrome* depicted the nightmarish effects of a nuclear power plant accident. Suddenly, opinion swung drastically against nuclear power. Its fate was permanently sealed after the 1986 Chernobyl disaster in the Ukraine. As the government slapped stringent safety regulations on nuclear power, plant building projects were halted. As a result, the energy-hungry nation turned to the other readily available source of energy—coal. Unfortunately, coal is the worst producer of greenhouse gases, which many suspect contribute to global warming. In any case, sensing the public mood, the government's restriction of the nuclear industry gives us a clear example of market distortion from government overreaction.

Government involvement in the market can also produce the unintended consequence of creating artificial entry into the market. This results in rent-seeking behavior (see chapter 3). Firms that benefit from the restrictions suddenly capitalize on excess demand over its supply; these firms reap the benefits in terms of windfall profits (see "A Case in Point").

DESIGNING POLICY RESEARCH

Our discussion confirms that there is no easy and elegant escape from the theoretical quagmire in which we find ourselves when we try to define social welfare. As professors Edith Stokey and Richard Zeckhauser eloquently put it,

> Philosophers and economists have tried for two centuries to devise unambiguous procedures for measuring and combining welfare of two or more individuals to provide a measure of total social welfare. Their quest has been as successful as the alchemists' attempt to transmute lead into gold. The occasional flickers of hope have all been extinguished; not only have no feasible procedures been developed, none are on the horizon.[23]

Confronted with limited insight into the question of how to define social welfare, Stokey and Zeckhauser offer pragmatic advice. They suggest that an analyst take a limited and practical view, seeking the best solution within a narrowly defined boundary instead of the one that optimizes outcomes globally, across boundaries.

Limiting the Number of Alternatives

In our stadium financing example, our alternatives were to build the arena or not build it. Our decision to build may be complicated by the issue of location. For a project like this one, a number of sites are possible. Some may be attractive but also prohibitively expensive because of the land value. Others may offer all the desirable characteristics (adequate lot size, traffic flow, parking, and so on) but may be in environmentally

A CASE IN POINT

Halliburton and Government Patronage: Rent Seeking during the War

Stories of war profiteering have been told for as long as large armies have marched across the land. The demand for logistical supplies along with the risk of being on the front line of an active hostility creates the perfect opportunity for many to make huge profits. The case of Halliburton during the Iraq war energized the critics of President George W. Bush's policies like few others. Competitive bids for government contracts are the essence of efficient practices. They allow market forces to determine the best supplier at the least possible cost for government projects. However, war has its own logic of expediency, which often trumps concerns for efficiency. As the U.S. military invaded Iraq, the need to supply food and fuel became paramount. Since quick actions were needed, Halliburton and its subsidiary, Kellogg Brown & Root (KBR), were awarded a series of "no-bid" contracts—without having to compete with other firms. This abandonment of the normal bidding process elicited charges of foul play and corruption from many quarters. Furthermore, in the view of economists, the problem became one of rent seeking. That is, if Halliburton did not have to submit a bid to receive a contract, the government was putting up barriers to all other companies to compete with it. Therefore, Halliburton could potentially charge more than it should have by taking advantage of this barrier.[24]

Erle Halliburton, who was born in poverty and worked in the dusty oilfields of Oklahoma and West Texas, started an oil company in the early 1920s. Today, the company is a huge conglomerate, with its declared revenues surpassing $18 billion in 2008. Since Vice President Dick Cheney,

sensitive areas. If you want to evaluate each possible location, you may find that the cost and time required for the study are excessive. In this case, you should eliminate those alternatives that clearly are inferior to the more feasible ones and those that obviously are not workable because of cost or other factors.

Consider Only Changes in Social Welfare. Suppose you are analyzing a program to provide inner-city youths with summer jobs. Rather than getting hopelessly entangled by the question of how to stop inner-city poverty and by the larger problem of how to eliminate social injustice, you decide to evaluate the program incrementally, asking how much this program will change the youths' economic condition. In doing so, you limit the evaluation to a manageable framework by concentrating only on the marginal instead of the total change in social welfare.

Use Income as a Proxy for Welfare. "Money cannot buy happiness" goes the proverb, implying that the relationship between wealth and happiness (or utility) may not be a direct one. Yet in practice, we have no choice but to accept money as the measure of individual utility. In a situation in which one gains at the expense of another, we must be able to compare the gains and the losses in monetary terms. When we accept this proposition, we escape from the theoretical quicksand of utility measurement, only to seen as a chief architect of the unpopular invasion of Iraq, had served as the chief operating officer of Halliburton, it quickly became the poster child of Bush administration's cronyism; Cheney, fairly or unfairly, became the face of public corruption. Although the company agreed to pay $579 million in fines resulting from an allegation of bribing foreign government officials (not in Iraq), the largest ever imposed on a U.S. company,[25] Halliburton vigorously denied allegations of corruption, overcharging, and war profiteering. It argued that in supporting U.S. war efforts from military bases in Iraq and in Afghanistan, and from facilities at Guantanamo Bay, the company and its operators have taken an undue amount of risk. The substantial payment for its services by the U.S. government, Halliburton claimed, reflected that risk.

Although Cheney was most closely associated with influence peddling by Halliburton, its association with power in Washington predates the former vice president. In fact, the company developed its political ties by teaming up with a young and ambitious Democratic member of the U.S. House of Representative from Texas, Lyndon B. Johnson, over fifty years ago.[26] There is no doubt that Halliburton, like other companies large and small, has cultivated its political patrons. Its practices are rooted in the time-honored nexus of public need, private profit, and war making.

Discussion Points

1. How do governments create conditions for rent seeking?
2. Would you have conducted the government's operations any differently than the Bush administration, considering that the circumstances called for quick action?

land in another sort of trap—the confusion of imputing monetary values to gains and losses. Be assured, though, that our new trap is a practical problem with practical solutions rather than a theoretical problem with no solution at all.

Accepting or Rejecting a Project

To summarize, the utilitarian position does not provide us with workable criteria for analyzing public policy, because we have no way of measuring interpersonal utility. The Pareto principle turns out to be equally unhelpful, because it builds barriers against government intervention. The Kaldor-Hicks compensation principle does not address the concerns of those who might lose as a result of a public project, while the Rawlsian criterion focuses too narrowly on the welfare of the poorest members of a community. Setting aside these unworkable theories, you should make your recommendations on the basis of the following criteria.

You should accept the project if the following are true:

1. The gains are much larger than the losses, the winners and losers are roughly equal in social stature, and the losses pose only a minor problem for the losing group. Suppose you are evaluating a project to build an access road linking two major

thoroughfares. The majority of inhabitants will benefit from the road; however, a small group of people living near the project are complaining about increased traffic, with all its accompanying problems. The commissioned environmental impact report detects no significant loss to the environment or to the community. In such a case, you may recommend the project over the objections of the adversely affected group on the basis of this first criterion.

2. The benefits to society greatly exceed the cost to a specific group, or the cost of inaction is enormous. The government's power of eminent domain entitles it to purchase, confiscate, or expropriate private properties for the greater public good as long as it provides property owners with adequate compensation. In the United States we usually associate eminent domain with the government's takeover of private lands to build highways. Other countries use similar powers to confiscate property or nationalize businesses. In any case, countries justify such actions by citing the overwhelming needs of society as compared with the costs to a specific person or a small group.[27]

3. The benefits of a proposed policy to the winners are greater than the costs to the losers, and the gains equalize some losses resulting from past discriminatory policies. Many affirmative action plans and other projects to remedy racial inequality, such as forced school desegregation and busing, would fall in this category. In addition, if a group, community, or state has received special benefits in the past, as did California during the 1980s, when the state profited from increased defense expenditures, we may make a case for bypassing it when the time comes to allocate a second round of benefits. We also may argue for equalizing the beneficial effects of public investment and diverting the second-round benefits to communities that did not receive money the first time.

In contrast, a proposed project should be rejected if the following are true:

1. The net benefit is positive, but the cost imposed on a specific group is significant. Many of our laws enforcing the Endangered Species Act of 1973 (ESA) are based squarely on this principle. Although a project may produce great benefits for the community, if it also may cause irreparable damage to a threatened species, the project will be rejected (see "A Case in Point").

2. The effect of redistribution is highly desirable, but the project does not pass the test of positive net social benefit. We frequently encounter cases in which the cause is noble but the costs do not justify action. It is desirable to provide the most comprehensive health care to everybody in the country regardless of income, age, or level of care needed. Yet not only are the costs of doing so extremely high, but any attempt to provide comprehensive government-funded health care is deemed by many as against the principles of free market capitalism. Because of their opposition, the United States, unlike most European nations and Canada, has been unable to meet the health care needs of the poorest of its citizens, although President Barack Obama has advocated passing more comprehensive health care legislation.

These criteria are by no means perfect. However, given the practical needs of public agencies, the guidelines are probably the best we can come up with. When we support our analysis with generally accepted guidelines of fairness, we make our analysis more efficient and more acceptable to the vast majority of people.

A CASE IN POINT

Do You Give a Dam? The Fate of the Snail Darter

One of the most celebrated controversies in the battle to protect endangered species involved the snail darter, a three-inch-long member of the perch family. The rare fish's habitat was threatened in the mid-1970s by the construction of Tellico Dam on the Little Tennessee River.[28] After four years of construction, local landowners filed a lawsuit charging that the dam violated the Endangered Species Act (ESA), bringing the $100 million project to a halt.

This event divided the country. The United States was in a recession caused largely by a nagging energy crisis, and most studies showed that the benefits of the project exceeded the costs. The Tennessee Valley Authority (TVA) estimated the net benefits from the project to be about $11.51 million (approximately $33.5 million in 2000 constant dollars). Although the estimated net benefits later were revised to $3.66 million (about $10.65 million in 2000 dollars), the project's support among southern legislators was overwhelming.[29] Responding to their demands, Congress tried to bypass the ESA by exempting the Tellico project from the law. A highly reluctant President Jimmy Carter, aspiring to leave a legacy as an environmentalist, signed the exemption measure in 1979. The day after the president's action, the TVA's bulldozers started rolling. The project was quickly completed, destroying the snail darter's habitat.

Nearly a decade later, long after the dust had settled on the banks of the Little Tennessee River, policy analysts proved that the controversy had revolved around a dam that should not have been built and a species that did not require protection. They found the projected benefits to be even smaller than TVA's revised estimates. The project continued to run at a loss even before environmental impacts were factored into the calculation.[30] The fish thrived in the undammed parts of the river. On August 6, 1984, the U.S. Fish and Wildlife Service downgraded the status of the snail darter from "endangered" to "threatened."

Discussion Points

1. How was the Tellico Dam project stopped and how was it revived? What criteria did policymakers on both sides of the argument use to evaluate the dam?
2. What lessons can we draw from this case study about the problems of critical thinking?

Ensuring the Process Is Fair

We will now explore issues of justice and fair play from the standpoint of procedural justice. The goal of **procedural justice** is not to alter the final outcome to achieve fairness but to ensure that the process by which resources are allocated is fair. We can promote the notion of fairness by using quantitative techniques to expose hidden assumptions and values.[31]

Lotteries are unfair because one ticketholder wins most of the money, while small amounts go to other winners. For the majority of players, the lottery yields nothing. Why do we not complain about the gross inequality? We do not protest because we know that the process of choosing the winner is fair. That is, we accept the final outcome because we believe that each person buying a ticket has an equal shot at winning the prize money. We know the process by which a winner is determined (because the drawings are often televised), and when purchasing a ticket, we agree to play by the rules of the lottery. If these conditions were violated, we would be extremely dissatisfied with the outcome. When people go over the speed limit and get a ticket, they seldom complain about the ticket itself, focusing instead on the amount of the fine or the way they were treated by the police or the court system.

Political scientist Robert Lane points out that procedural justice has four important components. It must include dignity, relief from procedural pain, a uniform standard of justice, and justice itself.[32] The process must recognize, protect, and preserve the self-esteem of every individual. If you are stripped of your dignity, even the most equal distribution of wealth will seem oppressive, arbitrary, and capricious. Every individual should be assured of the swift disbursement of justice. If the process is cumbersome and time-consuming, justice cannot be served. The process also must guarantee resonance between the standards of justice followed by the judge and those recognized by the judged. If you are judged by a standard that is completely alien to you, you cannot accept the verdict as just. Finally, procedural justice must include some minimum guarantee of economic well-being.

CHALLENGES TO CRITICAL THINKING: BIASES IN REASONING

Critical thinking requires that we conduct dispassionate, objective analyses of real-life problems with uncertain outcomes. Yet our biases and preconceived notions prevent us from being completely objective in our analysis. To help us guard against biased results, we must know the most common pitfalls of critical thinking. Research in social psychology has shown that people rely on a few principles to simplify the complex task of assigning probability. Although these principles are useful in appraising an uncertain situation, they sometimes lead to systematic biases that cause severe errors in judgment.

These principles, which Amos Tversky and Daniel Kahneman call **heuristics**—the way we see and understand the world—permit us to predict the probability of rain by looking at the sky or to judge distance by looking at the size of an object (although our judgments may be flawed or inaccurate).[33] Tversky and Kahneman reduced these heuristic principles for analytical thinking into three broad categories: **representativeness**, **availability**, and **adjustment and anchoring**. When asked to make a judgment about an object or event, we make decisions on the basis of representativeness, or how closely the object or event resembles others in our experience. We also make subjective judgments on the basis of the availability of information. Finally, when our predictions differ from reality, we use new information to adjust and anchor our appraisal of the future.

Representativeness

At the root of all scientific discovery is association. If we draw a connection between the coat of a woolly caterpillar and the coming winter, or between a groundhog's shadow and the imminence of spring, we have in effect predicted the arrival of the seasons. Such associations have led scientists to make discoveries by causally linking events. At the same time, reasoning by association also has produced old folk tales and prejudices. When we cringe at the sight of rowdy youths in a subway but look favorably on individuals wearing business suits, we are making a judgment on the basis of representativeness. Because we often base our associations on long-term observations, our predictions often turn out to be correct. However, unless we are careful, blind adherence to association can lead us to biased policy decisions.

Guard Against Biases of Irrelevant Information. Biases may result from our insensitivity to the probability of outcomes. In a psychological experiment, subjects were told that a group contained 70 percent farmers and 30 percent lawyers.[34] If we choose an individual at random from this group, the probability that we will select a farmer is 0.7. The subjects in this experiment used this prior probability to compute the odds of getting a farmer or a lawyer in a random pick. Subjects were given worthless information on a person from the group, such as

> Dick is a thirty-year-old man. He is married with no children. A man of high ability and high motivation, he promises to be quite successful in his field. He is well liked by his colleagues.

After reading this passage, subjects were asked to estimate the probability that Dick was a farmer. Because the passage contains no information about Dick's profession, subjects should have stuck to the overall probability of 70 percent, the proportion of farmers in the group. Yet they ignored the prior probability and assigned a 50 percent likelihood of Dick's being from either group. In life we often are misled when confronted with useless information, which can trigger judgments on the basis of representativeness. Despite conflicting prior information, we decide to ignore it.

Pay Attention to the Sample Size. The second set of problems may arise from our insensitivity to sample size. Suppose I ask you the following question:

> In your city, you can have your baby delivered at one of two hospitals, one large and one small. The probability that you will have a boy is 50 percent, and the chance that you will have a girl is also 50 percent. If each hospital records the days in a year when the percentage of boys exceeds 60 percent of its births, which hospital can expect to have counted more such days at the end of the year?

You would be incorrect to choose the large hospital or to assume that both hospitals would have an equal number of days with 60 percent or more boys. This is because, as we will see later in the book, as the number of tries increases, the samples become less likely to stray from the average probability figure. Therefore, large hospitals, with more births, are less likely than small hospitals to record days with more than 60 percent male births. If you made the wrong choice, take heart in the fact that many people make decisions on the basis of faulty statistical reasoning—including the people whose profession is to teach statistics.

Remember that Chances Do Not Self-Correct—They Merely Dilute. Suppose you are losing a game of cards. Do you tell yourself that because you have had a string of bad luck, your luck is due for a change? If so, you are making an erroneous inference about an independent probability distribution. As you may recall from our discussion of the independence of probability, if you receive four heads in a row in a coin toss, your chances of getting tails do not go up on the fifth try. Thinking that chances self-correct is a common mistake. But the anomalies of chances are not corrected over many tries; they are merely diluted. This idea is especially true for small samples. Remember that the smaller the sample, the less representative it will be of the larger population. Therefore, we place less faith in results based on small samples than in those drawn from large ones.

If You Do Not Have the Relevant Information, Do Not Predict. Suppose your department wants to complete a project in a tight time frame. You have been asked to recommend one out of numerous applications from a group of vendors. Because the vendors are not aware of the time constraint when they apply for the contract, their applications do not mention their ability to deliver on time. Instead, the applications contain the usual information: lists of projects the vendors have been involved in, the qualifications of the project team, and, of course, budget estimates.

What would you do in this situation? You might look into vendors' relative experience and qualifications and predict their ability to meet the accelerated deadline. If you did, you would be committing the error of judgment that Kahneman and Tversky[35] call the error of insensitivity to predictability. Because the available information tells you practically nothing about the vendors' ability to complete the job in a hurry, and because this ability depends on their present workload and capacity to devote key personnel to the project, you would need more information to make your selection. Without this information, you would be better off making no prediction at all.

Beware of Picking the "Right" Evidence. The heuristics of representativeness require that we match an unfamiliar, observed event with a familiar one whose outcomes are known to us. Because an event has a number of characteristics, you must choose the most significant ones in determining this representativeness. Chances are good that you will choose evidence to suit your preconceived biases. This likelihood raises tough issues, especially if it involves your deeply held values and biases.[36]

Do Not Ignore the Regression Toward the Mean. Suppose you are an avid but average golfer, and you know your handicap. This morning you drive the ball well from the tee, and you nearly get a hole in one. However, you bogey the next hole, failing to put the ball in the cup from a close distance. You are disappointed, and you have every reason to be. But statistically speaking, you should not despair, because your performance shows simply that you cannot beat the mean. In other words, you are merely playing your average game. If you make one exceptional shot after another, then you are playing at a level much higher than your natural average. English scientist Sir Francis Galton noted more than 100 years ago that outcomes tend to gravitate to the mean. He called this tendency the regression toward the mean.

Ignoring the regression toward the mean is another important source of error in subjective judgment. If you can find a long history of past performance, you will be much better off basing your prediction on the mean of that performance than on an optimistic or pessimistic extreme that reflects minor variations in external conditions.

Consider the Allais Paradox. The precepts of objective reasoning state that when faced with an uncertain outcome, you should choose the option that maximizes your expected returns. We define expected return as the probability of winning multiplied by its reward. If I offer you $10 for calling a coin toss correctly, your expected return is 0.5 × $10 = $5. When facing two options, either the possibility of winning $10 in a coin toss or that of gaining $25 by rolling a die, you should stick with the coin, because the expected return of tossing the coin ($5) is greater than that of rolling the die (1/6 × $25 = $4.17). Unless you are a real gambler (a risk lover), the laws of probability dictate that despite the chance of a larger reward with the die, you should choose the coin. In real life most of us fail to follow this principle, which is known as the **Allais paradox**, named after French mathematical economist Maurice Allais.[37]

Suppose you have been offered two options. The first option gives you a 100 percent chance (certainty) of winning $1 million; the second option gives you a 50 percent chance of winning $5 million. In experiments most people choose the first option in violation of the rules of expected returns (1.0 × $1 million = $1 million, which is less than 0.5 × $5 million = $2.5 million). Why do people ignore the laws of probability? When we expect an outcome to occur with certainty or near certainty, we tend to focus less on the probability factor than we do when anticipating an uncertain result.

Consider two other options. In the first option you have a 1 in 10,000 chance of winning $1 million, and in the second, your chance of winning $20 million is 1 in 1 million. Which option do you choose? Most people choose the chance to win $20 million, despite the fact that expected returns are higher for the $1 million option. Again, contrary to the principles of statistical reasoning, when probabilities are small (1 in 10,000 vs. 1 in 1 million), people tend to focus more on the reward than on the odds of winning. Allais unearthed some important biases in human reasoning that often prove critical in the decision making of a public organization.

Availability of Information

We often estimate the probability of an event by observing the frequency of similar events. If your city is considering whether to build its own garbage recycling plant, you can appraise the probability that the plant will succeed by examining the available information on similar ventures. Tversky and Kahneman call this decision-making device *availability*. They assert that information on similar events yields valuable clues about future possibility. This information points toward a more certain outcome when similar examples are numerous than when they are scarce. As we gather information, the following biases may cloud our judgment: **relative retrievability**, the **effectiveness of a search**, **biases of imaginability**, and **illusory correlation**.

Biases of Relative Retrievability. Our memory works like a filing cabinet. If we know where to search, we can retrieve a stored item quickly. However, if we file it in the wrong place, we cannot retrieve it easily, even information that is quite important. One way to keep track of information is to associate an event with some recognizable pattern or some other event. We then retrieve the information we need by recalling this other pattern or event. For example, most people remember the day of the 9/11 attacks vividly. We may not recall something important that happened in the past three weeks, but we remember many details about an important national event that took place years ago. When we recall memorable events or those associated with other facts that made a strong impression on us, we are susceptible to biases in judgment. These biases may lead to biases of availability, causing us to give relatively unimportant factors more weight than they deserve. Our awareness of life-threatening diseases may be only cursory until we hear that a celebrity has a particular malady, or until we learn about the illness of a friend or relative. Then our awareness of that disease goes up, prompting fear and, often, hysteria. We may focus on the probability of getting that particular disease more than is warranted by our personal habits, lifestyle, or genetic history. We also may disregard another source of illness, one more plausible than that suggested by the condition of the celebrity or friend.

The Effectiveness of Search. Have you ever conducted a computer search for information through a library information retrieval system? Suppose you are looking for information on a certain subject (say, drug abuse in North Carolina). If you define your key words properly for this search, you will be rewarded with information on a number of highly relevant publications. However, if your choice of key words is too wide (simply *drugs*), you will be inundated with irrelevant information. On the other hand, if you define your key words too narrowly, you may miss a large number of important works on the subject. In our minds we use key words to retrieve information effectively. Our effectiveness depends very much on our ability to define the parameters of our search.

Biases of Imaginability. If you are considering a risky venture, you would start your assessment by first listing both the difficulties and the advantages of the project. You would consider a full slate of possibilities before taking any action. Your options are limited only by your imagination. If you have difficulty estimating the relative risks and payoffs of a project, you may leave yourself open to biases. These sorts of biases seem to be most prevalent when a decision must be made about extraordinary events (such as when a disaster-preparedness program must respond to catastrophic and unpredictable events like floods, tornadoes, earthquakes, or large-scale riots).

Illusory Correlation and Organizational Myths. People often make decisions on the basis of long-held beliefs born out of illusory, or faulty, correlation. For example, do you believe that you have a "lucky" article of clothing that helps you during an uncertain situation? If so, you may be guilty of illusory correlation, which is described by the Latin phrase "post hoc, ergo propter hoc," or "after this, therefore because of this." In other words, you are taking past co-occurrences as signs of correlation. If you conclude that your decisive victory in a tennis match was due to the shirt you were wearing, you are guilty of finding a causal link between the two events (wearing the shirt and winning the match) when, in fact, there is no connection.

The errors in judgment caused by illusory correlation are often deep-rooted and cannot be easily corrected. We create myths on the basis of such errors, myths that affect not only our individual decisions but also the decisions we make at the organizational level. We find in some of the taped conversations between President Richard Nixon and his aides during the Watergate crisis classic examples of organizational decisions made on the basis of a paranoid worldview. Time and again, Nixon and his staff made decisions rooted in a fortress mentality, ultimately contributing to the demise of his administration. In any organization the vision of a decision maker can be clouded by myths of illusory correlation created by a single key staff member or by collective myths produced by a number of people in an organization.

Adjustment and Anchoring

In estimating the uncertain outcome of a project, we are frequently influenced by the first estimate. In social psychology this tendency is known as anchoring. You can witness anchoring on a popular television game show, when a group of contestants is asked to judge the price of an item. You will notice that the first contestant's answer seems to have a great deal of influence on the answers of the rest of the contestants. Contestants appear to be calibrating their own answers by the previous answers. In real life we often arrive at a quantitative judgment by working from an initial number. This tendency can cause serious errors in assessing an event's probability.

In this section I have tried to show some of the major sources of cognitive bias that can produce errors in critical thinking. The list of sources is long but by no means exhaustive. Thanks to the prolific work of social psychologists, we are learning more about these natural biases. The most important conclusion we can draw from this discussion is that these distortions of judgment are not necessarily caused by self-serving motivations such as wishful thinking, desire for reward, or fear of punishment. Instead, they are rooted in our thinking and the ways we process information. Proper knowledge of our cognitive biases may alert us to the pitfalls of objective analyses.

A FEW PARTING SUGGESTIONS

Quantitative models and numerical analyses are simply tools, aids to your natural analytical capabilities. Like all other tools, by themselves they are neither good nor bad—their ultimate value to you, your organization, and society at large depends on the way you use them. Along with knowing what you know, it is imperative to know what you do not know. Analysts should identify their zones of ignorance. By using an objective analysis, you can proceed up to a certain point, beyond which you must make judgments using personal, political, or social values. Quantitative techniques will take you to this point. To go further, you must seek help beyond the scope of these techniques. You must enter the arena of the decision makers and goal setters.

Another important contribution of quantitative techniques is that they force us to disclose our biases, hidden values, prejudices, and presuppositions. The light of quantification significantly illuminates the dark, hidden crevasses of subjective analysis. When we fully specify a problem in numerical terms, we can agree or disagree about the nature of the problem on level ground, without hyperbolic rhetoric masking our value judgments. When a policy based on an objective analysis fails, we can learn from its failure and recalibrate the policy by listening and responding to feedback.

As we have seen, the usefulness of objective techniques goes far beyond their substantive contributions to policy analysis. They also affect procedural justice in a public policy debate. Objective analysis not only provides policymakers with clearly defined evidence and a set of corresponding arguments but also gives them an intellectual framework for open discussion. Even when we find its conclusions unacceptable or infeasible, objective analysis shapes the structure, language, and issues of a policy debate.[38] The debate, focused on the ways of reaching the conclusion rather than on the conclusion itself, sets the stage for a broader understanding and an acceptance of the policy process. Once a policy has been adopted, its success depends on its economic viability, administrative feasibility, and, above all, political acceptability, as filtered through the legitimacy of the policymakers.

KEY WORDS

Adjustment and anchoring (p. 122)

Allais paradox (p. 125)

Availability (p. 122)

Biases of imaginability (p. 125)

Causal link (p. 109)

Control (p. 109)

Control variable (p. 109)

Correlation analyses (p. 114)

Cross-sectional analyses (p. 114)

Dependent variable (p. 109)

Effectiveness of a search (p. 125)

Experimental research designs (p. 110)

Generalize (p. 109)

Heuristics (p. 122)

Illusory correlation (p. 125)

Independent variable (p. 109)

Objective professionalism (p. 102)

One-shot case studies (p. 114)

Pareto inferior (p. 107)

Pareto principle (p. 106)

Pareto superior (p. 107)

Policy objective (p. 109)

Post-test-only control group experimental
   designs (p. 111)

Procedural justice (p. 121)

Quasi-experimental research designs (p. 110)

Rawlsian criterion (p. 108)

Relative retrievability (p. 125)

Representativeness (p. 122)

Research design (p. 110)

Risk averter (p. 104)

Risk taker (p. 104)

Social objective (p. 106)

Solomon four-group design (p. 110)

Trend analyses (p. 115)

Unintended consequence (p. 109)

Utilitarians (p. 106)

Zone of ignorance (p. 107)

EXERCISES

1. Your city is considering upgrading its sewage treatment plant, and you have been hired to make a recommendation. Think critically and discuss how you would approach the problem.

2. Write an essay on the pitfalls of objective analysis. How can you reduce their effect on your reasoning?

3. Suppose your local government is proposing the construction of a halfway house for nonviolent juvenile offenders in a city neighborhood. You have been hired to evaluate the project. Explain how you would begin your job and what problems you would face in arriving at an objective conclusion.

4. Explain the Rawlsian theory of distributive justice. After reading the Government Accountability Office report on poverty in America in Appendix A, do you think the Rawlsian theory is a politically and economically viable principle to guide our national public policy?

Notes

1. Richard Sandomir, "Tickets for New Stadiums: Prices, and Outrage, Escalate," *New York Times*, August 25, 2008.

2. Mandy Rafool, *Playing the Stadium Game: Financing Professional Sports Facilities in the '90s* (Denver, Colo.: National Conference of State Legislatures, 1997).

3. Dean V. Baim, *The Sports Stadium as a Municipal Investment* (Westport, Conn.: Greenwood, 1994). See also Neil deMause and Joanna Cagan, *Field of Schemes: How the Great Stadium Swindle Turns Public Money into Private Profit* (Monroe, Maine: Common Courage, 1998).

4. Sidney R. Bergquist, ed., *New Webster's Dictionary of the English Language* (Melrose Park, Ill.: Delair, 1981), 653.

5. Karl R. Popper, *The Poverty of Historicism* (Boston: Beacon, 1960).

6. See, for example, Robert A. Baade and Richard F. Dye, "An Analysis of the Economic Rationale for Public Subsidization of Sports Stadiums," *Annals of Regional Science* 22 (July 1988): 37–47.

7. Mya M. Borger, "Having a Ball: Sunday's AFC Championship Game a Financial Jag-ernaut for Team, City," *The Business Journal* (Jacksonville, Fla.), January 24, 2000.

8. Baim, *The Sports Stadium*, 5.

9. "Danger of Coliseum Going Broke Seen," *Los Angeles Times*, December 17, 1982.

10. Arthur Johnson, "Municipal Administration and the Sports Franchise Relocation Issue," *Public Administration Review* 6 (November/December 1983): 519–529.

11. We will discuss the problems of valuation later in the book. At this point, we will keep in mind that we are always assigning monetary values to intangible items, such as a human life, a person's reputation, and the pain and suffering claimed by a plaintiff in legal proceedings.

12. Philip J. LaVelle, "Proposition C Is about a lot More Than a Ballpark," *San Diego Union-Tribune*, October 20, 1998. Needless to say, this figure of $1.8 million in net benefits was used liberally by supporters of the project. The proposition passed by a wide margin, and by September 2000 the half-completed project had already run into financial problems.

13. In 1957 C. Norris Poulson, the mayor of Los Angeles, chided the opponents of his plan to bring baseball's Brooklyn Dodgers to the city. He charged that they wanted to keep the city in the "bush league." See "LA Council Votes Dodgers Deal, 11-3," *Los Angeles Times*, September 17, 1957 (quoted in Baim, *The Sports Stadium*, 5).

14. George H. Sabine, *A History of Political Theory*, 3rd ed. (New York: Holt, Rinehart & Winston, 1961), 588–589.

15. Nicholas Kaldor, "Welfare Propositions of Economics and Interpersonal Comparison of Utility," *Economic Journal* 39 (September 1939): 549–552. See also John R. Hicks, "The Foundations of Welfare Economics," *Economic Journal* 49 (December 1939): 696–712.

16. John Rawls, *A Theory of Justice* (Cambridge, Mass.: Belknap, 1971).

17. For a detailed discussion of research design, see David Nachmias and Chava Nachmias, *Research Methods in the Social Sciences* (New York: St. Martin's, 1976). See also Carl V. Patton and David S. Sawicki, *Basic Methods of Policy Analysis and Planning* (Englewood Cliffs, N.J.: Prentice Hall, 1986).

18. You may have heard the story of an economist who is stranded with a group on a desolate island, with only a can of beans. The economist suggests, "Let us assume a can opener."

19. For information on how to use quantitative methods for this kind of forecasting, see the discussion of Markov's chain in chapter 12.

20. For a more complete picture, see, Stanley A. Freed, *Green Revolution: Agricultural and Social Change in a North Indian Village* (New York: American Museum of Natural History, 2002).

21. See, for example, Bernhard Glaeser, *The Green Revolution Revisited: Critique and Alternatives* (London: Allen & Unwin, 1987).

22. Marc Sageman, *Leaderless Jihad: Terror Networks in the Twenty-first Century* (Philadelphia: University of Pennsylvania Press, 2008).

23. Edith Stokey and Richard Zeckhauser, *A Primer for Policy Analysis* (New York: W.W. Norton, 1978), 276.

24. See Pratap Chatterjee, *Halliburton's Army: How a Well-Connected Texas Oil Company Revolutionized the Way America Makes War* (New York: Nation Books, 2009).

25. Zachary A. Goldfarb, "Halliburton, KBR Settle Bribery Allegations," *Washington Post,* February 12, 2009.

26. Dan Birody, *The Halliburton Agenda: The Politics of Oil and Money* (New York: Wiley, 2005).

27. For a discussion of eminent domain, see Ralph C. Chandler and Jack C. Plano, *The Public Administration Dictionary,* 2nd ed. (Santa Barbara, Calif.: ABC-CLIO, 1988), 62–63.

28. Mark Van Putten and R. J. Smith, "At Issue: Has the Endangered Species Act Been a Success?" *CQ Researcher,* September 15, 2000.

29. Robert K. Davis, "Lessons in Politics and Economics from the Snail Darter," in *Environmental Resources and Applied Welfare Economics: Essays in Honor of John V. Krutilla,* ed. V. Kerry Smith (Washington, D.C.: Resources for the Future, 1988), 211–236.

30. John V. Krutilla and Anthony C. Fisher, *The Economics of Natural Environments: Studies in the Valuation of Commodity and Amenity Resources,* rev. ed. (Washington, D.C.: Resources for the Future, 1985).

31. For a classic exposition of essentially the same arguments, see Allen Schick, "System Politics and Systems Budgeting," *Public Administration Review* 29 (March–April 1969): 139–150. The flip side of these views is that an agency might use quantitative techniques either to rationalize its preordained decisions or to conduct a public relations campaign to placate critics and ward off outside interference. A later study by Harvey Sapolsky claimed that, contrary to the highly touted success stories, Program Evaluation and Review Technique network analysis had nothing to do with the progress and problems of the navy's Polaris project. See Harvey M. Sapolsky, *The Polaris System Development: Bureaucratic and Programmatic Success in Government* (Cambridge, Mass.: Harvard University Press, 1972).

32. Ibid.

33. Amos Tversky and Daniel Kahneman, "Judgment under Uncertainty: Heuristics and Biases," *Science* 185 (September 1974): 1124–1131. Derived from the Greek word *heuriskein* (to find out), "heuristics" is defined by the *New Webster's Dictionary of the English Language* as "teaching principles which allow students to make their own discoveries."

34. Ibid.

35. Ibid.

36. I will illustrate my point about self-selection bias by telling a story about two friends. One friend held an unshakable faith in astrology, while the other did not. All their lives they argued about the validity of astrology. One day, the believer in astrology learned that he would have to make a long trip across the state by car. Having consulted all the relevant astrological signs, he chose the most auspicious day to start his journey, only to have a serious accident within half a mile of his home. The poor man was taken to a nearby hospital, where his nonbelieving friend went to greet him with his best-rehearsed arguments against putting faith in such superstitious nonsense. Before the visitor could say anything, the injured man looked up from his hospital bed and asked, "You believe in astrology now, don't you? Can anybody survive such an accident without guidance from the stars? I am lucky to have consulted my chart before I started my trip. What do you think of astrology now?"

37. Maurice Allais, "Fondoments d'une théorie de choix comportant un risqueet critique des pustulates et axiomes de l'eloce Americane" ("The Foundations of a Positive Theory of Choice Involving Risk and a Criticism of the Postulates and the Axioms of the American School"), in *Expected Utility Hypothesis and the Allais Paradox: Contemporary Discussions of Decisions under Uncertainty with Allais' Rejoinder,* ed. Maurice Allais and Ole Hagen (Dordrecht, the Netherlands: D. Reidel, 1952).

38. Giandomenico Majone, *Evidence, Argument, and Persuasion in the Policy Process* (New Haven, Conn.: Yale University Press, 1989). See also E. S. Quade, *Analysis for Public Decisions,* 3rd ed. (New York: North-Holland, 1989).

6 Basic Statistics

NUMBERS AS STORYTELLERS

The footprints of history are preserved in recorded information. Properly collected and analyzed numbers can shed a great deal of light on the past. We know that we can numerically extend information collected from autopsies of Egyptian mummies to the general population of the time. But numbers can even reveal seemingly nonnumerical aspects of human lives, such as feelings. For example, some political scientists claim that income class has increasingly polarized American politics.[1] The data that I have plotted in Figure 6.1 support this claim by showing the rise in differences in presidential voting choices between the classes. Now, on the basis of this scenario, you can develop many different stories about current political conditions in the United States and draw conclusions about its future. This is the task of quantitative analysis: to make sense of the story behind the numbers. Facing a torrent of information, an analyst or researcher discards the unnecessary information and arranges and rearranges the rest to create something new—a logically coherent set of arguments.

METHODS OF DESCRIPTIVE STATISTICS

There are many ways of looking at the world of information. We may look at the world **ex post facto** and **ex ante facto**—that is, what has already taken place (ex post) and what will take place (ex ante). The basic tools for analyzing ex post data are the measures of **central tendency** and **dispersion**, and the tool for analyzing ex ante data is probability theory. Certainty is what has already taken place; uncertainty is what may follow.

Analysis of data expressed in numbers starts with the measures of central tendency and dispersion. Together these two are called descriptive statistics. The term *descriptive* obviously implies description—yet from description, one starts analysis; from the understanding of the

| **FIGURE 6.1** | **Class Divisions in Presidential Voting, 1952–2004** |

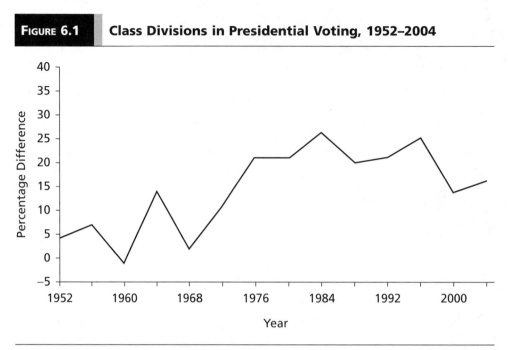

Source: American National Election Studies, "ANES Cumulative Data File" (October 31, 2005 version, 1948–2004), www.electionstudies.org/studypages/download/datacenter_all.htm.

past, one looks for clues to forecast the future. Therefore, in this chapter we will start with the methods of descriptive statistics and correlation, and in the following chapter we will introduce the theories of probability.

Measures of Central Tendency

The aim of descriptive statistics is to describe a situation or assess the prevailing condition with numbers. In our daily communications we can describe a situation verbally without the use of numbers. Anthropologists tell of primitive tribes whose abilities to express quantities with numbers are limited.[2] However, the power of description increases with the proper quantification of the situation. Thus, one may describe the day's temperature as "unusually hot," or one can express the temperature as a measure of degrees Fahrenheit or Celsius. The use of a recognizable index for measuring temperature immediately facilitates its understanding at the absolute level ("it is really hot today"), as well as its comparative evaluation ("the highest recorded temperature in twenty years" or "it was hotter here today than it was in Phoenix").

A series of numbers do not readily convey a coherent picture. The purpose of descriptive statistics is to look for the number around which a series has a tendency to cluster, so that it can be seen as the representative of that series. The tendency of a numerical series to cluster around a number is called the *central tendency*. By this measure, we offer the number that best represents the series. For example, consider Table 6.1, which presents the prices of five houses in a neighborhood. To convey a quick impression about this neighborhood, we can reproduce the entire table, which is rather cumbersome, or we may try to describe it using a single number. Of the many measures of central tendency, three are most commonly used in the area of social sciences: the mean, median, and mode. The **mean** is the arithmetic average of a series, expressed as

$$\mu = \frac{\sum_{i=1}^{n}(x_i)}{n} \tag{6.1}$$

where x is a variable with n number of observations, and μ is the mean.

This is the formula for the arithmetic average. Those of you who don't often look at mathematical expressions may recall that the Greek capital letter sigma (Σ) is used as a sign for summation. The term x with subscript i is a **variable** (in Table 6.1, it is the prices of the houses, which vary with each house). The subscript i refers to the specific observation, or in this case an individual house. If $i = 2$, then x_2 refers to the second observation in the series, which in this case is the price of the second house, $65,000. The term n is a **constant** and measures the number of observations, which in this case is 5. The subscript below and superscript above the summation sign Σ are read as "the sum of variable x, with observations (i) varying from 1 through 5." Therefore, in this case, we add up the values of our five observations to arrive at $900,000. Dividing by 5, we get the average value of a neighborhood house: $180,000.

You may notice that I have expressed the mean with the Greek letter μ (pronounced "meu"). However, sometimes you will find the mean written as $\bar{X}$ (said as "X bar"). It is important to note that it is a common tradition in statistics to denote the mean of a **population** (the entire group in question) as μ and the mean of a **sample** (a small fraction of the population chosen by a researcher to observe) as $\bar{X}$. Unless I note otherwise, I am speaking of a population.

The arithmetic mean is the most commonly used measure of central tendency. You may notice that most quantitative techniques (many of which are discussed in this book) are built around the analytical anchor provided by the mean. This is because the implication of the mean is rather intuitive. Also, in mathematical statistics, the mean as the measure of central tendency has the highly desirable property of **asymptotic convergence**. Suppose I have an unbiased coin, which I flip, and every time I flip heads, I note it. If the coin is not flawed, as I repeat my experiment a number of times, the ratio of the number of heads to the total number of tosses will come closer and closer to .5 as the number of tosses increases. This number (.5) is the same as the theoretically derived ratio of **relative frequency**—the number of desired alternatives divided by the total number of alternatives. In this case we have just one desired alternative, heads, and two possible alternatives, heads and tails. Using this rule we can calculate that the odds of flipping heads are 1:2 = .5. Because a die has six sides, the possibility of getting either a

TABLE 6.1	Distribution of Housing Prices
House	**Price**
I	$65,000
II	$65,000
III	$150,000
IV	$230,000
V	$390,000

1 or a 6 with a throw of the die is 2:6 = .333. This neat mathematical property allows the mean to be used in statistical theorems.

However, extreme values in a series influence the mean, especially when the sample size is small. In our example of the unequal prices of a small number of houses in a neighborhood, the mean price of housing is $180,000, which is higher than two-thirds of the houses in our sample. The house priced at $390,000 has influenced the mean.

The **median** is the middle number in a series. In our example, the median price of a house in the neighborhood is $150,000. Because it is the middle number, it is impervious to the extremes in the series. However, determining the median requires the physical inspection of the series, and thus it cannot be calculated as easily as the mean. Also, it does not have the asymptotic property of unbiasedness that makes the mean such an attractive measure of central tendency in statistics and mathematics.

Finally, the **mode** is the most frequent number in a series. In this simple example, it happens to be $65,000.

Since the mean price of housing is $180,000, the median is $150,000, and the mode is $65,000, which of these three considerably different numbers should represent the average price of a house in the neighborhood? Let us elaborate.

Consider, for example, Figure 6.2. The distribution is clearly symmetric. The choice of a measure of central tendency is not going to be controversial because, for this distribution, the mean, median, and mode will coincide. Controversy will soon ensue if the distribution is not symmetric. In Figure 6.3, for example, all the numbers cluster close to one another, except for one, which is an extreme value. This unusually large number will unduly influence the mean. In this situation either the median or the mode can be used to represent the series. In Figure 6.4, one observation with a particular value predominates. Therefore, the modal value will best represent the series. The extreme value makes the mean an inappropriate measure. Similarly, because of the prevalence of one value, even the use of the median may be considered less than appropriate.

FIGURE 6.2   A Symmetric Distribution

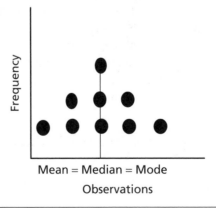

Mean = Median = Mode

Observations

Note: The distribution of observations shows a clear tendency to cluster around the middle number. Therefore, since this series of numbers is evenly distributed, we may accept any of the three measures of central tendency as appropriate. Still, one should always calculate the mean when reporting the central tendency, unless there is a special reason not to do so.

FIGURE 6.3   Distribution with an Extreme Value

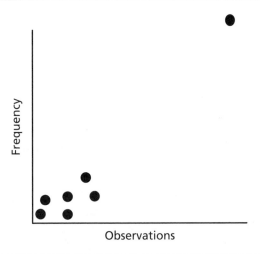

Note: When there is an extreme value, the total picture of a distribution becomes complex. In these cases, the use of any one measure of central tendency would be controversial, since one can always question the "representativeness" of the number.

At the outset, presenting the day's temperature in your city on a local television station's weather map looks like a simple enough task. However, controversy would arise if the city recorded a high temperature at noon and the temperature then fell precipitously as a cold weather front moved in. The question would be to decide which measure to choose as representative of the day's temperature. Varied geographical areas with several small climate zones within the city would further complicate the problem. In this case, a weather station located in a coastal area may record a significantly different temperature from one located inland.

The fundamental question is, Why do such problems arise? We encounter these kinds of controversies any time we try to describe a complex, multidimensional phenomenon with a one-dimensional measure. The more complex the situation, the more problematic its representation with just one set of numbers. The alternative is to describe a multidimensional phenomenon with several different sets of numbers. However, more than one number tends to numb one's senses. Representing a complex situation with just one number may have its disadvantages, but the alternative does not seem all that attractive either. The choice of the best measure of central tendency often calls for subjective judgment.

Weighted Estimates. If I ask you, "How long would it take you to go to the airport?" you might say, "If the traffic is *exceptionally* heavy, it can take fifty-five minutes; if it is *unusually* light, fifteen minutes; but *in general,* it takes me about twenty minutes." Not knowing the traffic conditions, we may estimate the travel time to the airport by averaging the three numbers. If we do that, we come up with an estimate of thirty minutes. Notice that this time is far too pessimistic, because it is one and a half times the time it usually takes to drive to the airport. This average reflects the extreme nature of the most pessimistic assessment of the situation. In such cases, when you do not want to be influenced by the presence of extreme values, yet you do not want to disregard them, you

FIGURE 6.4   **Distribution with the Modal Value**

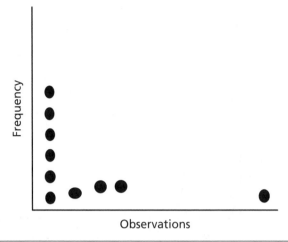

Note: This figure shows a hypothetical situation in which the use of the mode would be appropriate. Since there is an extreme value, the mean would be unduly influenced by it.

may derive your estimate by giving **weights** to the observation. That is, you may give a weight of 4 to the average time. We can write the series as shown in Table 6.2.

From these data, we can calculate the weighted average as $[(15 \times 1) + (20 \times 4) + (55 \times 1)]/6 = 25$. Notice that now we are not dividing the sum by the number of observations; instead, we are dividing the sum by the total of the weights. Also notice that this number (25) is a lot closer to the "most likely" number (20) than the unweighted average (30). By attributing weights, we have made the estimate a lot more realistic. In mathematical symbols, the calculation of weighted average is written as

$$\mu = \frac{\sum(f_i \times x_i)}{\sum f_i} \tag{6.1a}$$

where f_i represents the respective weights for the observations.

"Grouped" Data. Similar logic is applicable when data are available in **groups**. The range of a group is called the **interval**. The data on housing prices for a neighborhood may be available only in groups. I have written the housing price data given in Table 6.1 in group form in Table 6.3.

TABLE 6.2   **Weighted Observations**

Assessment	Time (in minutes)	Weight
Optimistic	15	1
Most likely	20	4
Pessimistic	55	1

TABLE 6.3	Grouped Data		
Price range	Number of houses (f_i)	Midpoint of intervals (x_i)	Midpoint × number of houses (f_i × x_i)
$0–$99,999	5	$50,000	250,000
$100,000–$199,999	17	$150,000	2,550,000
$200,000–$400,000	3	$300,000	900,000
	$\Sigma f_i = 25$		$\Sigma f_i x_i = 3,700,000$

Using the formula given by equation 6.1a, we can calculate the weighted mean as $3,700,000/25 = \$148,000$.

The median for interval data is calculated somewhat differently. To calculate the median, first inspect the data to locate the middle observation. As you can see from Table 6.3, there are twenty-five houses in the sample. Therefore, the midpoint is located at the thirteenth house. However, we don't know the exact price of the thirteenth house in the sample series. Hence, we assume that all the observations are evenly spaced within the range, which in this case is equal to $99,999. We can estimate the spacing of the prices by dividing the length of the range by the number of units within it. In other words, we assume that the difference between two successive houses is $99,999/17 = $5,882.30.

If we assume that within the range $100,000 to $199,999, the seventeen houses are evenly spaced in price, the thirteenth house (the sixth one within the price range) will be priced at $100,000 + ($5,882.30 × 6) = $135,293.80.

Therefore, *weighted averages are only approximations of the actual ungrouped data. So, whenever possible, use ungrouped data for the calculation of central tendency.*

Measures of Dispersion

A series is characterized not only by its central tendency but also by how strong this central tendency is. That is, how closely does the series cluster around the measure of central tendency? In Figure 6.5, both series have the same mean, but obviously the first series (Figure 6.5 (a)) is more bunched together than the second (Figure 6.5 (b)).

The closer this clustering is, the more confident we can be of the representativeness of our measure of central tendency. To understand the measures of dispersion, let us compare our first neighborhood with a second neighborhood. We can measure the relative dispersion, or the "scatteredness," of a series by using range, mean absolute deviation, variance, or standard deviation (see Table 6.4).

The **range** simply measures the difference between the highest and the lowest values in a series. In Table 6.4, the houses located in neighborhood A have a range of $325,000, while the range for neighborhood B is $50,000. The concept of range is also associated with what are known as the hinge and the midspread. One-quarter of the observations in the series lie below the **lower hinge**, and one-quarter lie above the **upper hinge**. The distance between the two hinges, containing half the observations around the median, is called the **midspread**. For example, the series of numbers 3, 17, 69, 85, 97, 117, 198, 211, 217, 300, and 301 does not tell us very much about the nature of its distribution,

FIGURE 6.5	The Effects of Different Dispersions

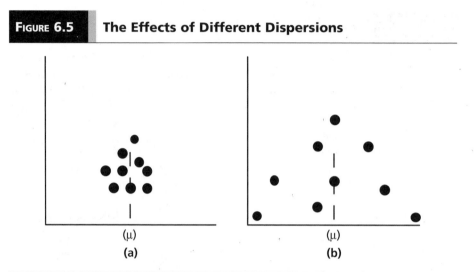

(μ) (μ)
(a) (b)

Note: If the observations are closely bunched together, the distribution has a smaller level of dispersion (a) compared with the one in which the observations are widely scattered (b).

but we may express it with the help of the range, the median, and hinges, as shown in Figure 6.6. This depiction sheds more light on the characteristic of the series. As you can see, in this series, 117 is the median value of the series of eleven numbers, the third and the ninth observations are the two hinges, and the difference between them is the midspread.

To measure how scattered or dispersed a distribution is, we need to find out the deviation from the mean, or the average distance between an individual observation within the series and the mean. However, if we add up the different distances from the mean, the positive numbers cancel out the negative numbers. Thus, we get the results shown in Table 6.5 if we subtract the mean value of the series ($180,000) from the various values of the housing prices of the two neighborhoods. From this table, it should be apparent that if we try to compare the deviation from the mean for the two series, the sum of column 3 $(x_i - \mu)$ will give us 0, as will the sum of column 6 $(x_j - \mu)$. Therefore, it is important to note that *the sum of deviations from the mean is always equal to 0.*

We can avoid the problem of measuring dispersion from the mean by either disregarding the signs of the deviations or by squaring them (since the square of a negative

TABLE 6.4	Relative Distribution of Housing Prices between Two Neighborhoods

House	Neighborhood A	Neighborhood B
I	$65,000	$150,000
II	$65,000	$180,000
III	$150,000	$180,000
IV	$230,000	$190,000
V	$390,000	$200,000

FIGURE 6.6   The Range, the Midspread, and Hinges

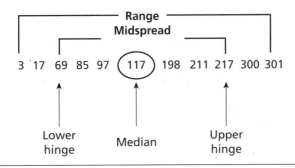

number is positive). The first method of calculating the average dispersion of a series is called the **mean absolute deviation**, written as

$$\text{Mean absolute deviation} = \frac{\sum_{i=1}^{n} |x_i - \mu|}{n} \tag{6.2}$$

Using this formula, we can see in Table 6.5 that the mean absolute deviation for the first neighborhood is $104,000 = ($520,000/5), and for the second, $12,000 = ($60,000/5). According to the mean absolute deviation measure, the second neighborhood is nearly 8.7 times more homogeneous (less dispersed) in its distribution of housing prices than the first neighborhood.

However, the mean absolute deviation poses two problems. First, computationally it is cumbersome; second, it does not possess some of the most desirable mathematical properties. Therefore, we may try another way to eliminate the negative signs in the deviation from the mean—that is, by squaring the deviations. This process can be written as

$$\sigma^2 = \frac{\sum_{i=1}^{n} (x_i - \mu)^2}{n} \tag{6.3}$$

This is the measure of **variance**, expressed as σ^2. To calculate the variance of the two neighborhoods, we need to square the deviations from the mean (the third and sixth

TABLE 6.5   Relative Distribution of Housing Prices: Deviation from the Mean (in dollars)

House	Neighborhood A			Neighborhood B		
	(x_i)	$x_i - \mu$	$|x_i - \mu|$	(x_j)	$x_j - \mu$	$|x_j - \mu|$
I	65,000	−115,000	115,000	150,000	−30,000	30,000
II	65,000	−115,000	115,000	180,000	0	0
III	150,000	−30,000	30,000	180,000	0	0
IV	230,000	50,000	50,000	190,000	10,000	10,000
V	390,000	210,000	210,000	200,000	20,000	20,000
Total		0	520,000		0	60,000

| | Neighborhood A (squared deviation | Neighborhood B (squared deviation |
House	from the mean) $(x_i - \mu)^2$	from the mean) $(x_i - \mu)^2$
I	13,225,000,000	900,000,000
II	13,225,000,000	0
III	900,000,000	0
IV	2,500,000,000	100,000,000
V	44,100,000,000	200,000,000
Total	73,950,000,000	1,200,000,000

TABLE 6.6   Calculation of Variance

columns in Table 6.5), add them up, and divide by 5. The problem with variance is that the numbers are often extremely large (see Table 6.6). In this case the calculated variances for the two neighborhoods are 14,790,000,000 (73,950,000,000/5) and 240,000,000 (1,200,000,000/5). We can reduce the size of the variance by taking its square root. The resulting number is called the **standard deviation** of the series. Because of its several highly desirable mathematical properties, the standard deviation (expressed as σ) is by far the most frequently used measure of dispersion. The standard deviation of a series is calculated using the following formula:

$$\sigma = \sqrt{\frac{\sum_{i=1}^{n}(x_i - \mu)^2}{n}} \tag{6.4}$$

By taking the square roots of the variances of the two series, we calculate the standard deviations, which turn out to be $121,614.14 and $15,491.93. Obviously, these numbers are much more manageable than the variances. From these measures, we can see that the dispersion for the first neighborhood is more than seven times the dispersion for the second neighborhood.

When we are speaking in terms of population variance and standard deviation, we use the Greek alphabet: σ^2 and σ. When we consider sample variance and standard deviation, we use the Roman (English) alphabet: s^2 and s. This is a rather important convention in statistical terminology: *When denoting population mean, variance, and standard deviation, we use the Greek alphabet: μ, σ^2, and σ. However, sample mean, variance, and standard deviation are written $\bar{X}$, s^2, and s.*

At this point, you should note another significant difference between the formula for calculating the population standard deviation σ and sample standard deviation s. The sample standard deviation, which is only an estimate of the population standard deviation, must be corrected for bias by dividing the sum of squares by $n - 1$, instead of n. This implies that as the size of the sample (n) increases, the subtraction of 1 will have less and less impact on the calculated value of the standard deviation. I discuss the rationale for subtracting 1 from the number of observations, known as the **degrees of freedom**, in the next chapter. The formula for calculating the **sample standard deviation** is given by

$$s = \sqrt{\frac{\sum_{i=1}^{n}(x_i - \bar{X})^2}{n - 1}} \tag{6.4a}$$

TABLE 6.7	Comparing the Dispersion of Two Distributions	
	Series I	Series II
	0	0
	1	5
	2	10
	3	15
	4	20

Dispersion of Distributions. Suppose we want to know which of two distributions has more variations within it. Unfortunately, unlike the mean, we cannot readily use standard deviations to compare the relative dispersion of distributions. The problem with the standard deviation is that it is an absolute measure. That is, it is influenced by the unit of measurement. Consider two sample distributions, I and II. You will notice that series II is series I × 5 (see Table 6.7).

The sample standard deviation (*s*) is calculated to be 1.58 for series I and 7.91 for II. Because series II is five times the value of series I, so is the value of the respective standard deviation. This can sometimes pose a practical problem. Suppose we want to compare the dispersion of housing prices in two diverse cities, Tijuana, Mexico, and San Diego, California. These two cities probably offer the greatest contrast in relative prosperity among neighboring cities around the world. When we try to compare the two, we face a problem: Because housing prices in San Diego are much higher than those in Tijuana, the dispersion in the San Diego real estate price will be magnified by the absolute difference in the price level. However, it is entirely possible that the disparity in housing prices is greater in Tijuana than in San Diego. To compare the relative dispersion between the two cities, we must divide the standard deviation by the mean. This measure, known as the **coefficient of variation**, is written as

$$\text{Coefficient of variation} = \frac{\sigma}{\mu} \tag{6.5}$$

Looking at the two neighborhoods in Table 6.4, we can calculate the coefficient of variation for them as

$$\text{Neighborhood A} = \frac{135,968.70}{180,000} = 0.755; \text{Neighborhood B} = \frac{18,708.30}{180,000} = 0.104$$

The calculated coefficients of variation show that the variance for the first neighborhood is more than 7 times (7.26, to be precise) that of the second one. Incidentally, you may also notice that by using this measure, we conclude that despite the difference in scale, the distributions of values for series I and II have the same relative dispersion.

Skewness and Symmetry of Distribution. A question often asked about a series of numbers is, Where are the mean, median, and mode of the distribution? The positions of these three measures of central tendency can give decision makers extremely valuable clues about the distribution of the series. Take, for example, the series of numbers shown in Table 6.8.

The data from Table 6.8 are plotted in Figure 6.7. The perfect bell-shaped distribution shown in this figure is called symmetric. For distributions like these, all three

TABLE 6.8	Data Showing a Symmetric Distribution

Observation	Frequency
1	5
2	8
3	12
4	15
5	21
6	35
7	21
8	15
9	12
10	8
11	5

measures of central tendency—the mean, median, and mode—fall on the same point. If you calculate the mean for the distribution shown in Table 6.8, you can see that it is approximately (with the appropriate rounding off for the decimal point) equal to 6. Also, since there are five numbers above and five numbers below, the median for the distribution is also 6. Finally, because the observation 6 has the highest frequency, it is also the modal point for the distribution.

However, this happy situation changes if the distribution is tilted to the right or to the left of the perfect bell shape. A tilted distribution is called a **skewed distribution**. A distribution tilted to the right is called a **positively skewed distribution**; one that tilts to the left is called a **negatively skewed distribution** (see Figure 6.8). Consider, for example, two new series along with the one given in Table 6.8. Data for three different series are presented in Table 6.9. The symmetric series is called frequency A, and the two subsequent series are labeled frequencies B and C. If you plot these three series, you will see the curves shown in Figure 6.8.

Notice that the median for the three distributions remains the same. Because we have eleven observations, the sixth observation is the middle point for each of these

FIGURE 6.7	Example of a Symmetric Distribution

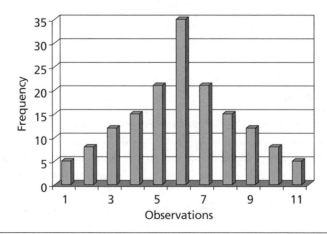

FIGURE 6.8   Comparison of Symmetric and Asymmetric Series

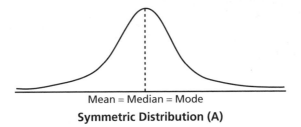

Mean = Median = Mode
Symmetric Distribution (A)

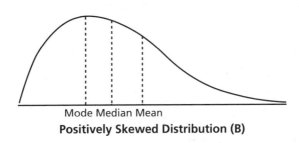

Mode Median Mean
Positively Skewed Distribution (B)

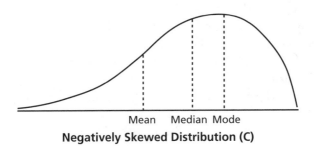

Mean   Median Mode
Negatively Skewed Distribution (C)

TABLE 6.9   Examples of Symmetric and Asymmetric Distributions

Observation	Frequency A	Frequency B	Frequency C
1	5	25	5
2	8	35	6
3	12	20	7
4	15	18	8
5	21	15	10
6	35	12	12
7	21	10	15
8	15	8	18
9	12	7	20
10	8	6	35
11	5	5	20

TABLE 6.10	Mean, Median, and Mode in Symmetric and Asymmetric Series		
	Mean	**Median**	**Mode**
Symmetric distribution (A)	6.0	6.0	6.0
Negatively skewed distribution (B)	4.3	6.0	2
Positively skewed distribution (C)	7.6	6.0	10

distributions. The means for series B and C are 4.3 and 7.6, respectively. The mode for series B is 2, and for series C it is 10. Table 6.10 summarizes this information.

For a policymaker who needs to make a quick judgment about a data series, it is extremely important to remember that *for a negatively skewed distribution, the mean is less than the median, and for a positively skewed distribution, the mean is greater than the median.* These two figures can give a rough picture of the distribution. In fact, you may notice that the greater the difference between the two, the greater the extent of skewness of the distribution.

Which Measure of Central Tendency to Use

Previously I argued that the choice of a measure of central tendency depends on the subjective assessment of the person making a statement. However, there are a few rules of thumb:

1. In a symmetric distribution, all three measures are the same. Therefore, one could choose any one of the three.
2. In a highly skewed distribution, the median may be the most useful measure of central tendency.
3. An overwhelming preponderance of one number may indicate the use of the mode.
4. The arithmetic mean should be used to calculate the average, unless there is a special need to do otherwise.
5. If for any reason the median or mode is used, this should be made clear to the reader.

A Quick Glance at the Distribution: The Stem-Leaf Method

A series of numbers often does not convey a coherent picture. For example, assume that over a fifteen-week period, local police officers arrested varying numbers of individuals on drug-related charges: 15, 23, 8, 31, 9, 45, 41, 18, 11, 3, 13, 25, 33, 40, 10, 102. Clearly, one cannot draw many conclusions from these numbers. Nevertheless, a policy analyst must frequently draw quick conclusions about a distribution, such as housing prices in a neighborhood, the ages of children in a detention center, or the time taken by various employees to complete a task. In such cases, the **stem-leaf method** offers a helping hand.

The stem-leaf method arranges a series of numbers by *stems* and *leaves*. For example, in the preceding series of numbers, the first digit of a number is the stem, and the second digit is the leaf. For the number 15, 1 is the stem and 5 is the leaf. For a single-digit number, such as 3, the stem is 0 and the leaf is 3. You may notice that you can produce a histogram or a bar chart simply by rotating the stem-leaf diagram (see Figure 6.9).

FIGURE 6.9   Stem-Leaf Method and Histogram

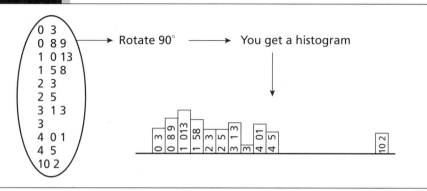

The advantage of the stem-leaf method is that it presents a lot more information regarding the distribution. For instance, we can tell from Table 6.11 that although the data vary a good deal, the median value, 25, is much closer to the minimum, 3, than to the maximum, 102. Therefore, it is clearly a negatively skewed distribution. The output also indicates that the maximum value is an outlier, or a real exception to the rest of the values in the series. In many decision-making instances, this method can provide some rather important insights.

Correlation Coefficient: Pearson's *r*

You may often wonder if two sets of data are correlated. Throughout the ages, patient observers have gained scientific knowledge by discovering close associations between two phenomena. Ancient astronomers noted that the tides change with changes in the lunar cycle. In social science research, the extent and nature of the association between two variables are often the subject of inquiry.

We may want to know if being a victim of child abuse is correlated with later criminal behavior. The nature of the correlation between two variables is described as positive or negative. In Figure 6.10 two variables, Yellow and Blue, are shown with Venn diagrams. If the two overlap, there is a correlation. As the two move toward each other, the

TABLE 6.11   Stem-Leaf Analysis: Drug Arrests, *N* = 16

0 3	
0 89	
1 013	Lower Hinge
1 58	
2 3	
2 5	Median Value
3 13	
3	Upper Hinge
4 01	
4 5	
Outside value	
10 2	

Note: Minimum = 3.000; lower hinge = 10.500; median = 25.000; upper hinge = 36.500; maximum = 102.000.

FIGURE 6.10   **The Extent of Correlation between Two Variables**

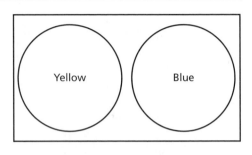

Extent of Correlation   No Correlation

---

extent of correlation increases. The two circles correlate perfectly when they completely overlap and thus become indistinguishable from each other. If they do not correlate at all, they do not intersect.

If an increase in one variable corresponds to an increase in the other, there is a **positive correlation**. If the presence of childhood abuse is linked with higher levels of criminal behavior, we call it a positive correlation. In contrast, the presence of an abusive relationship linked to a child's lowered academic achievement is an example of a **negative correlation**. I have shown this in Figure 6.11.

We can numerically measure the extent and strength of correlation with the help of Pearson's r, or simply the **correlation coefficient**. Suppose we have two sets of variables, X and Y. The correlation coefficient between them is measured by the formula

$$\text{Correlation coefficient} = \frac{\sum(X_i - \bar{X})(Y_i - \bar{Y})}{\sqrt{\sum(X_i - \bar{X})^2 \sum(Y_i - \bar{Y})^2}}$$

(6.6)

FIGURE 6.11   **The Nature of Correlation**

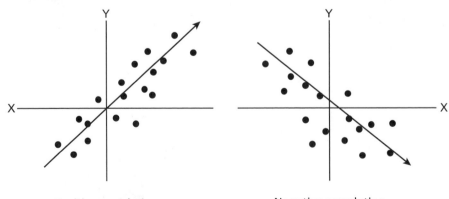

Positive correlation   Negative correlation

TABLE 6.12	Crime Rate and City Size	
City	Population (×1,000)	Crime rate (per 1,000 inhabitants)
A	50	1.5
B	57	1.7
C	65	1.6
D	68	2.9
E	88	2.0
F	92	3.1
G	96	2.5
H	100	3.5
I	120	3.8
J	125	3.7

The size of the coefficient indicates the extent of correlation. If it is equal to 1, there is a perfect correlation (or a complete overlap) between the two variables, and if it is equal to 0, the two variables are independent of each other (there is no overlap). The sign of the correlation coefficient shows the nature of their relationship. If the sign is positive, the relationship is positive, and vice versa. Therefore, the correlation coefficient equals 1 when there is a perfect positive correlation, it equals −1 when there is a perfect negative correlation, and it equals 0 when there is no correlation at all.

Let us suppose the crime rate in your city has gone up in recent years. Of late, a few local newspaper articles have condemned this trend. Your police chief, however, contends that because the city is growing rapidly in size, the crime rate can be expected to rise as well. You want to know if there is a correlation between the crime rate and the population size. You have collected the data series shown in Table 6.12. Using the formula in equation 6.6, you can calculate the correlation coefficient, which turns out to be .8655. The positive number corroborates your police chief's assertion regarding a strong correlation between the crime rate and the population size of a city.

KEY WORDS

Asymptotic convergence (p. 133)

Central tendency (p. 131)

Coefficient of variation (p. 141)

Constant (p. 133)

Correlation coefficient (Pearson's *r*) (p. 146)

Degrees of freedom (p. 140)

Dispersion (p. 131)

Ex ante facto (p. 131)

Ex post facto (p. 131)

Grouped data (p. 136)

Interval (p. 136)

Lower hinge (p. 137)

Mean (p. 133)

Mean absolute deviation (p. 139)

Median (p. 134)

Midspread (p. 137)

Mode (p. 134)

Negative correlation (p. 146)

Negative skew (p. 142)

Population (p. 133)

Positive correlation (p. 146)

Positive skew (p. 142)

Range (p. 137)

Relative frequency (p. 133)

Sample (p. 133)
Sample standard deviation (p. 140)
Skewed distribution (p. 142)
Standard deviation (p. 140)
Stem-leaf method (p. 144)

Upper hinge (p. 137)
Variable (p. 133)
Variance (p. 139)
Weight (p. 136)

EXERCISES

1. What is the implication of the name *descriptive statistics*? What are the measures of central tendency and dispersion? Explain the term *central tendency*. Why do we face controversies regarding the appropriate choice of a measure of central tendency?
2. Consider the following series and choose the most appropriate measure of central tendency for each series. Explain your choices.

Series A	Series B	Series C	Series D
10	5	3	5
11	8	7	7
9	11	9	9
27	13	25	11
16	16	7	9
15	18	7	7
17	21	7	5

Suggestion: You may want to plot the data to determine the patterns.

3. What do we measure by the coefficient of variation? Give an example of its possible use in public sector decision making. Using this method, comment on the relative dispersions of the four series of data presented in the preceding table.
4. Which one of the measures of central tendency is most commonly used in mathematics and statistics? Why?
5. How is the correlation coefficient useful? Give an example of its possible use and abuse.
6. We often hear the argument that increased size of the government retards economic growth. The Central Intelligence Agency collects the most reliable cross-national data in its *World Factbook*. Go to its Web site at https://www.cia.gov/library/publications/the-world-factbook/index.html and collect data on the size of government (budget revenue/gross domestic product) for Japan, Australia, and New Zealand, and for Western Europe and North America. Also gather data on rates of growth with regard to per capita income. Prepare a table, calculate the correlation coefficient between the two variables, and explain your finding.

Notes

1. Jeffrey M. Stonecash and Mack D. Mariani, "Republican Gains in the House in the 1994 Elections: Class Polarization in American Politics," *Political Science Quarterly* 115 (Spring 2000): 93–113.
2. The people of the Nambiquara tribe of the Mato Grosso forest in Brazil, for example, lack any system of numbers. The closest they come to expressing equality between two sets of items is by using a verb that means "they are alike." *The Guinness Book of Records 1992* (New York: Facts on File, 1991), 269.

7 Probability and Hypothesis Testing

As the old adage goes, the only certainties in life are death and taxes. Even then, we cannot predict the time of our demise or foretell changes in the tax law. Therefore, we must venture into the world of uncertainty. The presence of uncertainty in public policy analysis means that decisions must be made *before* we know which one of many conceivable and perhaps even inconceivable outcomes will come to pass. While deciding on a possible outcome, we assign probability values, as we do when we assess the odds of winning the lottery, the chances of a rainstorm, or the behavior of the stock market. The sources of probability measures are either objective (based on actual facts) or subjective (based on personal judgment). Let us discuss these two sources of probability.

OBJECTIVE PROBABILITY

The **objective** measure defines probability as the ratio of the occurrence of a given event from a finite number of possible outcomes. Therefore, objective probability is also known as **relative frequency**. Say that 245 students with a certain range of grade point averages and SAT scores applied for admission to a public university and that 35 of them were selected. We can calculate the probability of a student's being admitted as

$$p = \frac{35}{245} = .143$$

In other words, the probability (p) of a student in that particular academic achievement category gaining admission is 14.3 percent. The formula for calculating objective probability by the measure of relative frequency can be written as

$$p = \frac{\text{Observed frequency}}{\text{Total frequency}} \tag{7.1a}$$

However, defining probability by observed frequency alone is problematic. If I ask you, for example, what the probability is of flipping heads in a coin toss, you will notice that it is impossible to use the above definition of probability, because we cannot observe all the coin tosses and record their outcomes. In that case, we may define objective probability as

$$p = \frac{\text{Target outcome}}{\text{Total number of possible outcomes}} \qquad (7.1b)$$

Suppose we toss a coin looking for one specific outcome, heads, out of two possible outcomes. Using formula 7.1b, we can calculate that the probability of flipping heads is $1/2 = .5$. Similarly, the probability of getting a 5 in the roll of a die is $1/6 = .17$.

We cannot keep on tossing the coin an infinite number of times to prove that the probability of flipping heads is 1/2. Thus you must recognize that calculated probability in actual practice is only an approximation of the "true" probability. As the number of experiments becomes larger and larger, approximation poses less of a problem (see "A Case in Point"). Let us take a moment to explain this extremely important concept properly.

It is obvious that a weather forecast of a 50 percent chance of rain does not imply that it would rain half the day or that it would rain every half hour. In fact, it will either rain or it will not (even drizzle should count as rain). Interpreting such a forecast is the same as interpreting the outcome of a coin toss. Since by tossing a coin you will either win or lose, you should interpret the probability measure as if you were to toss the coin an unlimited number of times. You will see that as the number of tosses increases, the ratio of heads to the total number of attempts approaches .5 (see Figure 7.1). Suppose we are tossing a coin in groups of four tosses. After each set of tosses, we record the number and average it over the previous ones. Suppose that on the first try, we flip heads one time and tails three times. This gives us a ratio of 1:3. Suppose that on the next try, we flip heads twice and tails twice. Averaging the total number of tosses, the ratio of heads to tails is 3:4. If we continue to do this, we will see a curve similar to the one presented in Figure 7.1. In the beginning, the fluctuations may be wide, but as the number of tries increases, the average approaches the "true" probability figure of .5.

This is the basis of objective probability. Embedded in this simple example of a coin toss are some of the most important assumptions and axioms that form the basic building blocks of statistical reasoning. A proper understanding must begin with an examination of these properties of objective probability. First, the events in a probability experiment (in this case, each toss) must be **independent**. Perhaps the most common cause of misinterpreting probability is the question of independence. Suppose you have placed a bet on a coin toss. You are calling heads, and you have called it correctly four times. On the fifth try, should you call heads again, or should you try to be smart by calling tails? Because the tosses are independent, what happened last time or any time before has no bearing whatsoever on what may happen this time.

The second assumption of objective probability is that the events are **mutually exclusive**, meaning that they cannot take place simultaneously. For example, we cannot get both heads and tails on a single try. But it is entirely possible to have both rain and sunshine within a single day. Therefore, whereas the outcomes of a coin toss and the roll

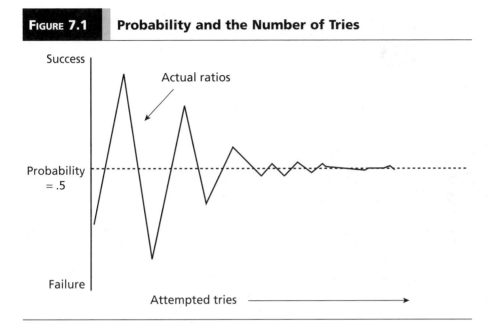

FIGURE 7.1   **Probability and the Number of Tries**

Success

Actual ratios

Probability
= .5

Failure

Attempted tries

of a die are mutually exclusive, rain and sunshine are not, unless we define the outcome as "having rain any time during the day."

Finally, the probability measures are **asymptotic**. That is, the probability of flipping heads with an unbiased coin is .5. However, that does not imply that we will get exactly two heads and two tails in four tries. It simply means that if we repeat the experiment many times, as the number of tosses increases, the ratio will approach .5. Similarly, going back to our previous example, we must interpret the meteorological prediction as follows: if the weather conditions (temperature, barometric pressure, wind condition, humidity, and so forth) become the same as the condition we are having at this time, over a long period of time, this combination of conditions will produce rain half of the time.

Probability Distribution

When we assign probability to a series of independent and mutually exclusive events, we get a **probability distribution**. Suppose we want to find the probability of the size of a social worker's caseload on a given day. We record the number of cases each day—say, for 100 days. Then, by dividing each day's frequency by the total number of arrivals, we can construct the probability column of the arrival of the cases. These hypothetical data are presented in Table 7.1 and Figure 7.2. By looking at the table, you can tell that the probability that the social worker would handle just one case is 5 percent, two cases is 10 percent, and so on. The third column of the table shows the cumulative probability totals. Called a **cumulative probability distribution**, the numbers are the probability of having a value less than or equal to a specific value of x. The cumulative probability distribution data reveal that the probability of the social worker's having four or fewer cases on a given day is 47 percent.

A CASE IN POINT

Probability in Baseball: Revenge of the Nerds

At first glance, it is hard to believe that Bill James (b. 1949) is responsible for winning so many baseball games; he is pudgy, middle aged, and in sum the antithesis of an athlete. His secret: a deep understanding of probability theory and the statistics that explain the outcome of the game. Every sport is ultimately about probability. Even if all the "best" players are on a team, they are not assured victory every time.

Among all the professional sports, baseball is perhaps the best suited for statistical testing, because of the huge number of chances players get during the season. The regular season of major league baseball consists of 162 games, each with at least nine innings. Assuming each player gets 3 shots at the plate per game, a starter can appear at the plate 486 times in a season. Therefore, keeping statistics has been a preoccupation of baseball fans ever since 1845, when Henry Chadwick invented the box score (a brief numerical summary of the outcome of a baseball game that lists each player's contributions—times at bat, hits, runs batted in, and so on—and describes how runs were scored over the course of the game).

Bill James, however, took this score keeping to a new level.[1] By looking at the detailed statistics, he would calculate the probability of success and test his hypotheses with the actual outcomes of ball games. Over the years, James dispelled many bits of conventional wisdom about the game, but perhaps his most important contribution was related to walks (in which a batter proceeds to first base after four pitches are thrown outside the strike zone, referred to as balls). Old-fashioned coaches and managers never kept count of the number of walks batters had; instead they were fixated on the number of hits. However, Bill James asked the most basic

Knowledge of the mean and standard deviation of a probability distribution provides us with a good deal of information about the nature of the distribution. Most important, this information gives us some of the most powerful analytical tools in the field of applied statistics. Probability distributions can take on an infinite number of shapes. However, for analytical purposes, a perfectly symmetric distribution, known as the **normal distribution** (or, in common parlance, the bell curve), serves as the fundamental building block. Again, a symmetric distribution can also take on various shapes. In Figure 7.3, I have drawn three normal distributions with different means.

Symmetric distributions can also have the same mean and yet be different. In Figure 7.4, the three distributions, despite having the same mean, have their relative levels of dispersion, measured in terms of standard deviation, σ. Clearly, of the three normal distributions, the tall and skinny one has the lowest standard deviation, whereas the short and fat one has the largest dispersion. Because of these variations, a **standard normal distribution** is defined as the one whose mean is equal to 0 and standard deviation is equal to 1. This standard normal distribution serves as the "ideal type," or the benchmark against which the probabilities of an uncertain world are measured.

question: what is the purpose of batting? To him, the entire purpose of batting was to score runs. When he analyzed the records, he came up with the following formula:

$$\text{Probability of runs created} = \frac{\text{Total bases} \times (\text{Hits} + \text{Walks})}{\text{Plate appearances}}.$$

When he plugged in the variables, he was spot on in explaining the total number of runs made. As you can see from his formula, a batter's ability to stay on the field and avoid getting out is just as important as getting hits.

James also dispelled many other old ideas about the game. For instance, he showed that sending in "clutch hitters" in pressure situations made no difference in the outcome of the game. James also paid special attention to the men on the field; he noted that although the number of catches can indicate a fielder's capabilities, a wider measure of the number of assists to get the other side out also had to be taken into account. James called this the "range factor."

On the basis of his findings, teams started keeping records that were more detailed than standard box scores. Since major league baseball is really a business, many other decisions—such as the position of the outfield wall, the percentage of left-handed versus right-handed batters, and the value of a player on the basis of his age—have been guided by James's calculations.

Discussion Points

1. What does Bill James's story tell us about the use of numbers in decision making?
2. Can you think of areas in the sphere of public policy in which gathering more information can help us achieve greater efficiency?

TABLE 7.1	Probability and Cumulative Probability Distribution of Caseloads for a Social Worker on a Given Day		
Number of cases (x)	Observed frequency	Cumulative probability distribution	Probability distribution
1	5	.05	.05
2	10	.10	.15
3	15	.15	.30
4	17	.17	.47
5	20	.20	.67
6	15	.15	.82
7	8	.08	.90
8	7	.07	.97
9	3	.03	1.00
Total	100	—	—

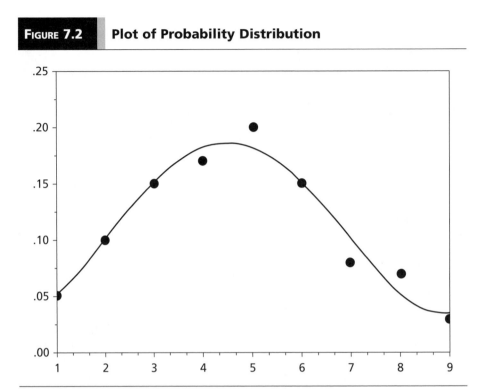

FIGURE 7.2   **Plot of Probability Distribution**

The beauty of a standard normal distribution is that the distribution is standardized, as the name suggests. That is, we are able to measure any segment of it with the utmost precision. Because for a standard normal distribution the standard deviation is 1, any distance from the mean can therefore be measured in terms of the standard deviation. For example, from Figure 7.5, you can see that 68.26 percent of all the observations in the distribution will fall within $+1\sigma$ distance from the mean. Similarly, the area within the boundaries of $+2\sigma$ will capture 95.46 percent of the observations; 99.74 percent of the observations fall within $+3\sigma$, and nearly 100 percent are captured within the bounds of $+4\sigma$. The formula of the normal distribution enables statisticians to calculate any defined area under the curve.

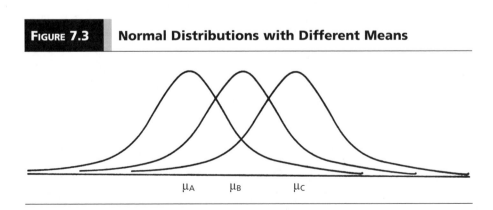

FIGURE 7.3   **Normal Distributions with Different Means**

FIGURE 7.4   **Normal Distributions with Various Levels of Dispersion**

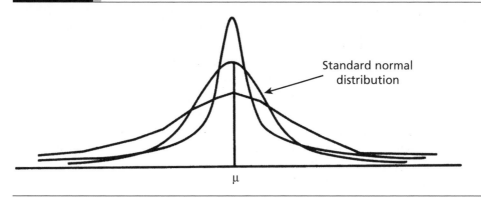

Standard normal
distribution

μ

The standard normal distribution is, of course, a theoretical concept. The **central limit theorem**, perhaps the most remarkable theorem in the field of mathematics and statistics, bridges the gap between the theory and its practical use.[2] This theorem is also often referred to as the **law of large numbers**. An example will help you understand the compelling nature of this theorem. We know that human beings come in all shapes and sizes. Therefore, if we plot the percentages of males in the United States falling in various

FIGURE 7.5   **Standard Normal Distribution**

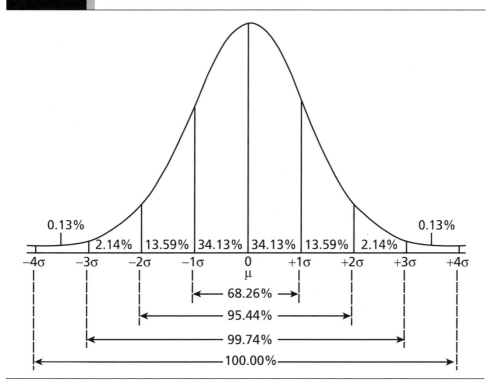

groups of heights, we will see a distribution with a strong central tendency and relatively few observations at the extreme ends of the spectrum (extremely tall and extremely short). This plot will not show a perfectly symmetric distribution, but we can get a standard normal distribution if we follow a simple procedure. Suppose we already know the mean (μ) and the standard deviation (σ) for the height of the U.S. male population. We collect ten males at random, note their average (mean) height, and let them go. We then collect another group of men, note their average height, and let them go. If we perform this operation many times, we will get a series of numbers showing sample means, which we may call $\overline{X}_i$. The reason for the subscript i is that we are referring to a series of means, not just one single value of a mean.

The central limit theorem tells us that if we subtract the sample means from the population mean and then divide by the standard deviation, as we repeat the experiment we will obtain a standard normal distribution, regardless of the shape of the original distribution. Suppose we know that the average height of an adult American male is 68 inches and the standard deviation is 2.0. Now we collect the averages of three groups of ten men and see that their average heights are 72, 73, and 65 inches. We then perform the following operations:

$$\frac{72 - 68}{2} = 2.0; \quad \frac{73 - 68}{2} = 2.5; \quad \frac{65 - 68}{2} = -1.5$$

As the number of samples increases, the series will have a mean of 0 and a standard deviation of 1. We can write this with the help of mathematical symbols as follows:

$$\frac{\overline{X}_i - \mu}{\sigma} \approx (0, 1) \text{ as } i \to \infty \tag{7.2}$$

We read expression 7.2 as follows: the series derived by subtracting the population mean from sample means, and divided by the population standard deviation, will be distributed with a mean of 0 and a standard deviation of 1.[3] Another example will clarify the enormous practical implication of this property.

Several years ago, two neighboring countries in a bitter border dispute claimed the skeletal remains of some prehistoric settlers that had been found in the area. The discovery caused excitement because the racial identity of the ancient inhabitants could decide the current dispute. Thus, researchers took the average cranial measurement of the newly discovered skeletons. Thanks to previous anthropological studies, the average cranial measurement and the standard deviation of the present stock of occupiers of the land were known. It was decided to test the hypothesis that the people whose skeletons were discovered came from the same group of people as today's inhabitants.

However, in mathematics it is often impossible to prove the *existence* of a relationship. If we state that all A's are B, it would be impossible to check every A to prove the relationship. Instead, it is often simpler to nullify an opposite hypothesis in its negative form, such as "there are some A's that are not B." If we do not find any example of an A not being a B in our sample, then as the size of the sample increases we become more and more confident in our assertion that there is no A that is not B. In statistical terminology, this alternate hypothesis is called a **null hypothesis**. We call it "null" (defined by one dictionary as "none," "invalid," or "void") because while testing, the analyst is usually interested in the hypothesis being false.

Figure 7.5 can help explain the idea behind this test. If the cranial average of the skeletal remains is very close to that of the present group, we can assume that they both belong to the same racial stock. However, if the average falls outside the 2σ measurement from the mean, the probability distribution tells us that there is only about a 4 percent chance that these people belonged to the same racial group, because nearly 96 percent of all the observations (in this case, people of this particular race) will fall within this range. The process we just described is known as **hypothesis testing**, part of the fundamental construct of analytical reasoning.

Hypothesis Testing and Confidence Intervals

The theoretical framework derived by the central limit theorem can be used to test the probability of a hypothesis or to estimate a band within which we can reasonably expect to find the "true" value. Suppose the average drop-out rate in a school district is 15.5 percent, with a standard deviation of 1.05. Within the district, one particular school is being touted as exceptional in its achievement of a lower drop-out rate. Last year, this school showed only a 15.3 percent drop-out rate in a graduating class of 100. Is this truly exceptional or merely a result of chance factors? The basis of this question forms the core of hypothesis testing.

Hypothesis testing starts with a question. In the preceding example, the question is whether the drop-out rate of the school in question is significantly smaller than the average for the district. The second step in hypothesis testing is the formulation of a specific null hypothesis. Statistical convention generally expresses the research hypothesis as H_1 and the null hypothesis as H_0.

These two hypotheses can then be written as follows:

H_1: *The school's average is significantly lower than the district average.*

H_0: *The school is not exceptional, and the difference between its mean and the average of the school district can be explained by chance.*

Since it is extremely important to construct a null hypothesis correctly, I offer another example of setting up a research question and a null hypothesis. What to do with juvenile delinquents deeply concerns society. These youngsters should be punished for their offenses, yet sending them to prison might transform them into hardened criminals. Suppose we are attempting to find out if setting up military-style boot camps for first-time juvenile offenders has any bearing on their future criminal activities. We have collected data by tracking two groups of recently paroled offenders: those who were sent to the boot camps and those who were sent through the usual criminal justice system. We can form the two hypotheses as follows:

H_1: *Boot camps do reduce the probability of a juvenile's future conviction rate.*

H_0: *An individual's enrollment in a boot camp has no bearing on his or her future conviction rate.*

In the third step, we must determine the **level of significance** for rejecting the null hypothesis. That is, by using the standard normal distribution, we must determine the level of certainty we must seek for its rejection. This level can be set at 90 percent, 95 percent, or even 99 percent. The level of significance in statistical jargon is often denoted as α (alpha). Suppose, for testing our hypothesis, we have set the α level at 90 percent. If we want to include 90 percent of the observations in a symmetric distribution, the remaining 10 percent must be divided equally between the two tails of the distribution. Therefore, in this case, when we want to know if the sample mean (the average for the particular school) is significantly *less* than the population average (the district average), we set the α value at half of .10, or .05. This is called a **one-tailed test**, shown in Figure 7.6. The probability value corresponding to the predetermined level of α is also called the **critical value**, since it determines the threshold for rejecting the null hypothesis. If we set the critical value at the 95 percent level of probability, we want to be 95 percent certain that what we see in our sample result has only a 5 percent chance of being caused by chance alone. If the sample value falls below the critical value, we will not be able to reject the null hypothesis.

Z test. Let us go back to our example of the school district. We know the mean and standard deviation for the district, so it is a simple matter to calculate how far the individual school's record is from the district average, measured by units of the district's standard deviation. We can then compare this number with a theoretical distribution for rejecting or not rejecting a null hypothesis. If the number of samples is large and we know the population mean and standard deviation, we can derive the value for a **Z distribution**, given by the formula

$$Z = \frac{\overline{X} - \mu}{\sigma / \sqrt{n}}$$

(7.3)

where n is the number of observations in the sample, which in this case is 100 (the number of graduating seniors).

$$Z = \frac{15.2 - 15.5}{1.05 / \sqrt{100}}$$
$$= \frac{-0.3}{0.105}$$
$$= -2.86$$

Our calculated **Z score** is –2.86, which means that the sample mean (the mean of the school in question) is 2.86 times the standard deviation away from the population mean. The corresponding critical value of the Z distribution is given in Appendix C. The table in Appendix C gives the area under the right-hand side of the standard normal distribution, corresponding to the various calculated Z values. To determine the area of the normal distribution below our calculated Z value of 2.86, go down the first column and find 2.8. Then move to the right across the row to locate the number corresponding to column .06. The number corresponding to the row 2.8 and the column .06 is .4979, which is the area under the normal distribution below $Z = 2.86$.

Notice that this number relates only to the right-hand side of the distribution. Since it is a symmetric distribution, the other half contains 50 percent of the distribution. Therefore, by adding .5 to .4979, we get .9979, the cumulative value of the total area

FIGURE 7.6	**One-tailed Test**

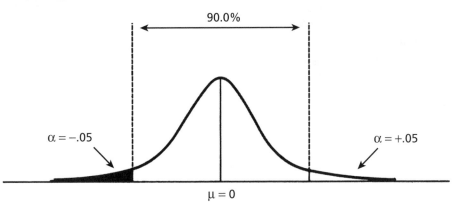

below the area of the *Z* value of 2.86. This implies that we can be 99.79 percent certain that the difference between the average district drop-out rate and the experience of the model school is not due to chance; this school is justified in its claim to have significantly reduced the drop-out rate.

Our calculated *Z* value has a negative sign. Because the *Z* distribution is symmetric, this sign is of no consequence. It simply points to the direction of the difference from the mean. After calculating the *Z* score, you can find the corresponding probability value. If it is greater than the standard level of significance that you have set (usually .05), you can reject the null hypothesis. If it is less, you cannot reject it. You may also set the critical level of the *Z* score value without setting the probability standard. If you set your critical value at .05, you can go down the *Z*-score table to find the approximate point at which the area under the curve covers 95 percent of the distribution ($Z = 1.64$). If your calculated *Z* score is greater than 1.64, you can reject the null hypothesis.

Confidence Interval. The results of the *Z* tables can also be used to develop what is commonly known as the **confidence interval**. Clearly, the "true" values of a population distribution are unknowable. For instance, if we want to know the average height of American females, we have to measure every female in the United States, which is an impossible task. Therefore, we will have to infer the average height from sample results. Sample results converge with the actual value when the sample size becomes extremely large. Unless we want to continue taking larger and larger samples, it would be safer to express the population value with a band or an interval. Without saying that the average is 5 feet 6 inches, we will say that the average will lie between, say, 5 feet 3 inches and 5 feet 8 inches. If we express this band as a probability (for example, "We are 95 percent certain that the average height falls within this range"), then we call it a confidence interval.

A confidence interval tells us the range within which we can expect the population mean to fall with a certain level of confidence or probability. When radio or television newscasters tell us poll results, they almost always include corresponding confidence intervals. We are told that "67 percent of people support the proposed legislation, which has an error margin of plus or minus 3 percentage points." In other words, we are being asked to hold with a high degree of confidence (usually at a 95 or 99 percent level) that the actual percentage of people in the general population who support this legislation falls between 70 and 64 percent. To derive a confidence interval, we need to use a **two-tailed test**, because we are not sure of the direction of deviation from the sample value. Therefore, consider the logic of a critical value for rejecting the null hypothesis on the basis of the Z score once again: reject the null hypothesis if

$$Z = \frac{\overline{X} - \mu}{\sigma/\sqrt{n}} > Z_{.05}$$

or

$$Z = \frac{\overline{X} - \mu}{\sigma/\sqrt{n}} < -Z_{.05}$$

These two expressions tell us to reject the null hypothesis if the Z scores are greater than the stipulated value. Diagrammatically this means that if the Z scores fall outside the shaded area in Figure 7.7, reject the null hypothesis.

The two algebraic forms can be rewritten as follows: reject the null hypothesis if

$$-Z_{.05} > \frac{\overline{X} - \mu}{\sigma/\sqrt{n}} > Z_{.05} \tag{7.4}$$

When we want to construct a confidence interval, we choose not to know a specific estimate for the population value μ. Instead, by manipulating equation 7.4, we can write

$$-Z_{.05} \times \frac{\sigma}{\sqrt{n}} > \overline{X} - \mu > +Z_{.05} \times \frac{\sigma}{\sqrt{n}} \tag{7.5}$$

which is again rewritten as

$$\mu - Z_{.05} \times \frac{\sigma}{\sqrt{n}} > \overline{X} > \mu + Z_{.05} \times \frac{\sigma}{\sqrt{n}} \tag{7.6}$$

Equation 7.6 gives us the confidence interval for our population (μ). In this equation, we set the value for the desired level of confidence, which in this case is 10 percent, or 5 percent on either side of the curve. By looking at the Z table, we can see that the value of $Z_{.05}$ is approximately 1.65. We know that the population standard deviation (σ) equals 1.05, n equals 100, and the population mean (μ) equals 15.5. Therefore, the confidence interval for our population mean is calculated by inserting these numbers in equation 7.6:

$$15.5 - 1.65 \times \frac{1.05}{\sqrt{100}} > \overline{X} > 15.5 + 1.66 \times \frac{1.05}{\sqrt{100}}$$

or

$$15.33 > \mu > 15.67$$

FIGURE 7.7   Two-tailed Test and Confidence Interval

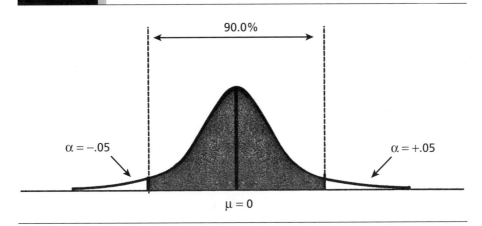

$\alpha = -.05$

$\alpha = +.05$

90.0%

$\mu = 0$

In plain English, the results mean that we can expect 90 percent of all the schools in the district to exhibit drop-out patterns that will vary between 15.33 and 15.67 percent. This information can be of great help to administrators in evaluating the performance of individual schools in the district. Those that exceed a drop-out rate of 15.67 percent are doing significantly poorly. Those that have drop-out rates less than 15.33 percent are doing significantly better than the district at large.

t test. The Z test assumes that we know the population standard deviation and that the number of observations in the sample is large (usually more than 30). However, both of these assumptions are frequently violated in hypothesis testing. In such a case, the Z table becomes inappropriate. W. S. Gossett, writing under the pseudonym Student, devised another test for these kinds of problems, which has since been called the **t distribution**. The results of this distribution are presented in a *t* table (Appendix D). The formula for the use of *t* statistics is similar to that of Z, and with a large enough sample, the two will coincide. The formula for the *t* distribution is given as

$$t = \frac{\overline{X} - \mu}{s / \sqrt{n - 1}}$$

(7.7)

Notice that this new statistic (*t*) differs from Z in that its denominator contains the sample standard deviation (*s*) instead of the population standard deviation (σ), and we take the square root of the number of observations in the sample ($n - 1$). The subtraction of 1 from *n* gives us the **degrees of freedom** (*df*). One can easily explain the concept of degrees of freedom, but its use in statistics is not exactly intuitive. The term *degrees of freedom* refers to the number of free choices one can make in estimating a number. For example, say that the sum of two numbers, X and Y, is equal to 10. There are, of course, infinite counts of two numbers that add up to 10. However, if I choose the value of one number (say, 27), there is only one number (–17) that will result in a sum of 10. Therefore, in estimating the sum of two numbers, we have the free choice of only one number (2 – 1). We call it the degree of freedom, in this case, 1. By extending this logic, we can see that if twenty numbers add up to 10, we will have 19 degrees of freedom; after we have chosen nineteen numbers, the twentieth number is automatically determined. Since we are attempting to estimate the population value with samples, we use $n - 1$ degrees of freedom. Therefore, it is important to remember to subtract 1 from the number of observations for each set of samples. So to calculate the t value, which is done on one set of samples, we use $n - 1$ degrees of freedom. In the following section, we will compare two sets of samples. For that problem, we will subtract 1 for each of the two sets of samples, n_1 and n_2. Thus, the degrees of freedom for the t distribution will be equal to $(n_1 + n_2) - 2.$[4]

Let us go back to the example of the discovered remains of inhabitants of the disputed land. Suppose we found the skulls of seventeen adults, with an average circumference of 21.5 inches and a sample standard deviation of 1.4. The average for the present-day population is 23 inches. To test the null hypothesis that these ancient people belonged to the same race, we set up the t score as

$$t = \frac{21.5 - 23.0}{1.4/\sqrt{17 - 1}}$$
$$= \frac{1.5}{1.4/\sqrt{16}}$$
$$= 4.29$$

Suppose that we want to evaluate the null hypothesis at the .01 level (alternatively, the 99th percentile level), which as a one-tailed test is $\alpha = .005$. Now we can look up the t table (see Appendix D). By going across the columns, pick out the .005 level. Then come down along the rows until this level is matched with 16 degrees of freedom (17 observations minus 1). This will give you the critical t value of 2.921. Our calculated t value is larger than the critical value, so we can reject the null hypothesis and conclude that it is highly unlikely that they belong to the same race of people. *It is important to note that in the empirical sciences, regardless of how large the Z or the t value is, we never establish the absolute "truth"; instead, we maintain that we can reject the null hypothesis.*

Comparison of Two Different Series of Numbers. In the previous examples, we tested the hypothesis that *a particular sample was different from the population*. However, we may frequently need to test whether two samples are *significantly different from each other*. In the previous example, we discussed whether the remains of the ancient settlers belonged to the racial stock of the present population. In contrast, suppose we have found two sets of remains from two different time periods. We want to know whether these two groups of people came from the same stock. In such a case, we will test the null hypothesis that

$$\overline{X}_1 = \overline{X}_2$$

Since we are not making any assumption regarding the relative size of the difference between the two means (that is, if $\overline{X}_1 > \overline{X}_2$ or $\overline{X}_1 < \overline{X}_2$), we must use a two-tailed test. If the number of samples (n_1 and n_2) is more than 30 for each series, we can use a Z statistic; otherwise we need to use a t statistic. To test the null hypothesis that the two means are equal, the difference between the two means is converted to a standard score by dividing it by the standard deviation. That is,

$$t = \frac{\overline{X}_1 - \overline{X}_2}{\sigma_{x_1 x_2}} \tag{7.8}$$

where $\overline{X}_1 - \overline{X}_2$ is the difference between the two means, and $\sigma_{x_1 x_2}$ is the standard deviation of the sampling distribution of the difference between two means.

If the t statistic is applicable, its degree of freedom is given by $(n_1 + n_2 - 2)$, where n_1 is the number of sample observations in series 1 and n_2 is the number of sample observations in series 2. Since we have the observations of the two series, we know their means. However, the question arises, What is the standard deviation of the distribution of the means? If there are reasons to believe that the standard deviations of the two sample series are in fact equal, the standard deviation of the combined series is calculated as

$$\sigma_{x_1 x_2} = \sqrt{\frac{n_1 s_1^2 + n_2 s_2^2}{n_1 + n_2 - 2}} \sqrt{\frac{n_1 + n_2}{n_1 n_2}} \tag{7.9}$$

If, however, there is no reason to believe that the two standard deviations are the same, then we should use the following formula:

$$\sigma_{x_1 x_x} = \sqrt{\frac{s_1^2}{n_1 - 1} + \frac{s_2^2}{n_2 - 1}} \tag{7.10}$$

Of course, the question arises, When should we assume that the standard deviations are the same, and when should we not? The answer to this question may depend on your subjective assessment. However, the rule of thumb is that if the two means are coming from a similar population group, you may assume that the standard deviations are the same. For example, if you are comparing the average number of children per household in two suburbs of the same city that have similar socioeconomic and demographic characteristics, you may safely assume that their standard deviations are the same. However, if you are comparing the mean of an affluent suburb with that of a poor center city area, you may have to assume that the standard deviations are different.

Let us consider a numerical example. Suppose we have data on drug abuse per 1,000 high school students in two school districts, A and B, with the characteristics shown in Table 7.2.

If we believe that the two standard deviations are equal, then using equation 7.10, we can estimate the pooled standard deviation as

$$\sigma_{x_1 x_2} = \sqrt{\frac{28(5.75)^2 + 16(6.05)^2}{28 + 16 - 2}} \sqrt{\frac{28 + 16}{28 \times 16}} = 0.589$$

By substituting this estimated number in equation 7.8, we get

$$t = \frac{25.0 - 20.6}{0.589} = \frac{4.4}{0.589} = -7.47$$

TABLE 7.2	**Comparison of Means**	
	District A	**District B**
Mean	25.0 ($\bar{X}_1$)	20.6 ($\bar{X}_2$)
Standard deviation	5.75 (s_1)	6.05 (s_2)
Number of schools in the district	28 (n_1)	16 (n_2)

Since t has 42 degrees of freedom $(28 + 16 - 2)$, the corresponding probability value for $\alpha = .025$ is approximately equal to 2.02. Because our calculated t score, -7.47, falls outside the critical region of 2.02, we can reject the null hypothesis that the two means are equal. That is, drug abuse in district A is significantly lower than in district B.

If there is no reason to believe that the two standard deviations are the same, using equation 7.8, we estimate the pooled standard deviation to be

$$\sigma_{x_1 x_2} = \sqrt{\frac{5.75^2}{(28 - 1)} + \frac{6.05^2}{(16 - 1)}} = 1.91$$

By plugging the value 1.91 into equation 7.8, we get $t = 4.4/1.91 = 2.30$. Again, this number is greater than 2.02, so we can reject the null hypothesis.

Although in this case both calculations gave us similar answers, it should not be assumed that the standard deviations in two series are equal.

Difference of Proportions Test. While doing a survey, you may face a situation in which you need to compare the proportions and percentages of the two sample populations. For instance, suppose you are conducting a survey to find out the attitude of citizens toward the police. Your survey indicates that 33 percent of the 320 whites polled agreed with the statement that "they do not have a great deal of trust" for the local police department, whereas 45 percent of the 267 minority respondents agreed with that assessment. To determine a policy of community relations for the police department, you want to know if the difference between the two communities is statistically significant. For this, you will have to use the following formula:

$$Z = \frac{\bar{p}_1 - \bar{p}_2}{\sqrt{\left(\dfrac{n_1 \bar{p}_1 + n_2 \bar{p}_2}{n_1 + n_2}\right)\left(1 - \dfrac{n_1 \bar{p}_1 + n_2 \bar{p}_2}{n_1 + n_2}\right)\left(\dfrac{n_1 + n_2}{n_1 \times n_2}\right)}} \tag{7.11}$$

where

$\bar{p}_1$ = proportion of first subgroup,

$\bar{p}_2$ = proportion of second subgroup,

n_1 = sample population of first subgroup, and

n_2 = sample population of second subgroup.

For this example the values are as follows:

$$\bar{p}_1 = 0.38$$

$$\bar{p}_2 = 0.45$$

$$n_1 = 320 \text{ and}$$

$$n_2 = 267$$

When we substitute these numbers in equation 7.11, we get $Z = 1.71$.

The Z table tells us that the critical value of the one-tailed test is 1.645. Our Z value exceeds the critical value, and thus we can conclude that the minority groups have less trust in the police department. Hence, any public policy for community involvement must take into account this difference in perception.

The Chi-Square Test

The preceding examples show that if we are confronted with a problem such as determining whether a subgroup is significantly different from the larger population, we can use the Z test (provided, of course, that we know the population mean and the standard deviation). If we do not know the population values but want to know if two different groups are "truly" different from each other, we can use Student's t test. In contrast to these two common forms of hypothesis testing, we frequently encounter a situation in which we may be interested in finding out whether an observed phenomenon is significantly distinct from its expected behavior.

Suppose the Metropolitan Transit Authority (MTA), which employs 300 bus drivers, has the task of training new recruits and periodically retraining older operators. The MTA used to operate an in-house driver training school; however, in a cost-cutting mood, it is experimenting with replacing trainers with a newly developed computer-based training method. By this method, trainees will sit in front of a computer terminal, go through each lesson, and at the end answer multiple-choice questions. If they pass, they will move on to the next section and will ultimately pass the entire theoretical portion of their training program. Management finds this computer-based program attractive: it offers cost savings on salaries and benefits, and the training school can remain open twenty-four hours a day, thereby allowing the drivers to come at their own convenience and train themselves. As a consultant, your task is to determine whether the system is acceptable to the drivers of the MTA. You conduct a survey that asks the drivers whether they are

1. enthusiastic about computer-assisted training
2. indifferent between the computer and the training school, or
3. upset about the change and would prefer the old training school.

Since fear of computers may be related to an individual's gender, I decided to classify the trainees according to their sex and then look at the survey responses. I have presented the data in the form of a matrix, which is known as a **contingency table** (see Table 7.3). In this table, the numbers next to the word *observed* represent the actual numbers of responses corresponding to the attitudes toward computer-assisted training, classified by the gender of the respondents.

TABLE 7.3	Example of a Contingency Table			
Sex of the trainees	Like computers	Indifferent	Do not like computers	Total
Female	Observed: 15 Expected: 25	Observed: 10 Expected: 13	Observed: 30 Expected: 17	55
Male	Observed: 120 Expected: 110	Observed: 60 Expected: 57	Observed: 65 Expected: 78	245
Total	Observed: 135	Observed: 70	Observed: 95	300

Below each observed frequency of responses is an entry for the expected response. This expected response is based on the hypothesis that there is no age bias in the acceptance of computer-assisted training. Thus, the two figures are exactly the same proportion as the two classifying variables (sex and attitude toward computers). This expected number is derived by multiplying the column total (known as the *marginal*) by the row total for each sex and dividing by the total number of trainees (300). The expected value for the female trainees who like computers is calculated as

$$\text{Expected value} = \frac{\text{Column marginal} \times \text{Row marginal}}{\text{Total frequency}} = \frac{135 \times 55}{300} = 24.75$$

The logic for this operation is that if preference for computers does not depend on the gender of the respondent, the women will prefer it in exactly the same proportion as all those who prefer the computers.

After we have determined the expected value for each cell, we can look into the difference between the actual and the expected values. Similar to the other probability distributions, the sum of the squared differences between actual and expected values is also distributed along a theoretical probability distribution, called χ^2, or **chi squared**. This is written as

$$\chi^2 = \sum \frac{(f_o^i - f_e^i)^2}{f_e^i} \tag{7.12}$$

where f_o^i is the observed frequency of cell i, and f_e^i is its expected value.

Thus, we can write the formula as

$$\chi^2 = \frac{(\text{Observed frequencies} - \text{Expected frequencies})^2}{\text{Expected frequencies}}$$
$$= \frac{(15 - 24.75)^2}{24.75} + \frac{(10 - 12.83)^2}{12.83} + \frac{(30 - 17.41)^2}{17.41}$$
$$+ \frac{(120 - 110.25)^2}{110.25} + \frac{(60 - 57.17)^2}{57.17} + \frac{(65 - 77.58)^2}{77.58}$$
$$= 16.60$$

Like the t distribution, the χ^2 distribution varies with the degrees of freedom. For the χ^2 distribution, the degrees of freedom are calculated as (number of columns − 1) ×

(number of rows – 1). Thus, the degrees of freedom for our example are $df =$ (columns – 1) × (rows – 1) = (3 – 1) × (2 – 1) = 2 × 1 = 2.

Now we can look up the χ^2 distribution given in Appendix G. As you can see, for 2 degrees of freedom, the critical value at the .05 level is 5.99. Since our calculated χ^2 value, 16.60, is greater than this number, we can safely conclude that the results show a definite sex bias in the acceptance of computer-based training for the MTA bus drivers. You may notice that in this case, we did not need to know anything at all about the mean and the standard deviation of either the sample or the general population. This is the strength of this test and why it belongs to a class called **nonparametric tests**. Also, you should note that whereas t and Z distributions compare the difference between only two values, the χ^2 distribution measures the significance of all the cells jointly. Therefore, it is called a **joint probability distribution**.

Testing for Correlation: Pearson's r. In chapter 6 we discussed Pearson's r, or the correlation coefficient. As you know, the relation between two variables in the real world is seldom perfect. Therefore, in observing a less than perfect correlation, you may wonder if the calculated coefficient is statistically significant. One of the advantages of the correlation coefficient is that it can be used to test the hypothesis that two variables are correlated. To test this hypothesis, r must be converted into a t statistic using the following formula:

$$t = \frac{r\sqrt{n-2}}{\sqrt{1-r^2}} \tag{7.13}$$

where n is the size of the sample.

For example, suppose the correlation between X and Y has been found to be .65, with a sample of 26 observations. The correlation is less than perfect, so you can formulate the null hypothesis that there is no correlation between the two variables.

By using the preceding formula, you can calculate t as

$$t = \frac{.65\sqrt{26-2}}{\sqrt{1-.4225}} = 4.18$$

Since there are 26 observations, the degrees of freedom for the t test are 26 – 1 = 25. The critical value for t at a 5 percent level of confidence for 15 degrees of freedom is 2.060. Since our calculated t statistic is greater than this critical value, we can reject the null hypothesis.

The Risks in Hypothesis Testing. In testing hypotheses under uncertain conditions, we run the risk of (1) rejecting the null hypothesis when it is in fact true or (2) accepting a false hypothesis. A true hypothesis rejected as false incurs a **type I error**, whereas a false hypothesis accepted as true creates a **type II error**. The matrix shown in Table 7.4 best explains this dilemma.

Many public sector decisions affecting the health and welfare of citizens are based on the statistical reasoning of hypothesis testing. Therefore, the cost of an erroneous decision can be enormous. Suppose we are considering school funding on the basis of the

TABLE 7.4	**Errors of Hypothesis Testing**	
Decision	Hypothesis is true	Hypothesis is false
Reject hypothesis	**Type I error**	Correct decision
Accept hypothesis	Correct decision	**Type II error**

attendance records of pupils. A particular school shows a higher than average absentee rate, which puts it at risk for losing part of its revenue from the government. If we reject the hypothesis that the school is failing to provide a rewarding education system to keep students in class, and the hypothesis is indeed true, we will be wasting public funds on an inefficient (at least by this particular measure) institution. In contrast, if we accept the null hypothesis and find the school negligent of its duties, when in fact its attendance record is not worse than those of the other schools in the district, we will be inflicting undue pain on a school.

Therefore, we try to minimize these two errors in determining the decision rules. Unfortunately, these two errors are inversely related. That is, when we want to reduce type I error, we create more type II error. If we want to give the benefit of the doubt to the individual schools, we stand to encourage poor schools by failing to take punitive measures. In contrast, if we become extremely strict about attendance records in determining school funding, we inflict unnecessary punishment on some otherwise deserving schools.

In statistics, the type I error is the chosen level of significance, or the α level. Therefore, when we choose an α level of .05, we make sure that we will falsely reject a true hypothesis only 5 percent of the time. If we lower the significance level to .01, we reduce the chance of accepting a false hypothesis but increase the probability that we will inadvertently reject a true one.

The choice of a significance level depends on the type of problem under consideration and the consequences of rejecting a true hypothesis. The criterion for accepting a hypothesis is rather conservative, and given a choice, we would rather err on the side of the status quo than make a false move. An example may clarify the dilemma. In the early 1990s the U.S. Food and Drug Administration (FDA) came under fire from two different groups for two diametrically opposite reasons. On one hand, the FDA was accused of taking too long to test and approve for sale experimental drugs for AIDS. On the other hand, the FDA was heavily criticized for approving silicone gels for breast implants too quickly, without proper testing. If we are dealing with a problem that requires the utmost safety, we would be better off setting the level of significance as small as possible (say, at .001). However, it is a matter of common practice to set the confidence level at 95 percent ($\alpha = .05$) for most research and policy analysis.

Steps in Hypothesis Testing

1. Check theories relating to the comparability of the variables for testing.
2. State the null hypothesis clearly, making sure of the opposite hypothesis.
3. Specify the significance level of α.
4. Specify whether to use a Z or a t test.

5. Compute the value of the test statistic.

6. Draw your conclusion regarding the rejection or nonrejection of the null hypothesis.

SUBJECTIVE PROBABILITY

Ron and Chris are members of the parole board. They are participating in a parole board hearing of Rob. The board must decide whether Rob is a safe enough risk to grant him parole. Ron and Chris have different views. Ron sees Rob as a "high risk" for committing a serious crime, whereas Chris judges him to be a "low risk." Both Ron and Chris are assessing the probability that this convicted felon will be in trouble with the law in the near future. However, in this case, they cannot use measures of objective probability, because each individual parole applicant poses a unique case. The decisions of Ron and Chris are prime examples of rendering judgment on the basis of **subjective** assessments of probability.

In our everyday lives, we all make subjective judgments about uncertain situations. We appraise the future by assigning chance factors or odds. Although in life it is often sufficient to state that "it is likely that the task will be completed within the next week" or that "there is a good possibility that the shipment will not arrive on time," in professional work, these vague chance factors must often be expressed in numerical terms. It is more useful to know that an expert assigns a 30 percent chance of a certain legislation's passing congressional scrutiny, or an 80 percent probability of a survey's results being completed by next Thursday, than simply knowing the odds in qualitative terms ("a small chance" or "highly probable"). This assignment of numerical value gives more precision to the statement and as such can be compared with the assessment of some other expert.

Long neglected by serious researchers, the issue of subjective probability is increasingly becoming a topic of serious scientific inquiry. To Frank Lad, "The logic of probability merely formalizes the coherent implication of specified beliefs about events when beliefs are expressed in a graded scale from 0 (complete denial) to 1 (complete affirmation). . . . The 'scientific method' empowers the scientists with precisely the same inferential principles that it empowers the person on the street in the conduct of daily affairs, no more no less."[5] In fact, many studies in economics have found that subjective assessments of probability by experts can often rival the accuracy of those derived from sophisticated econometric models.[6]

Still, we may need to take a number of steps to ensure the accuracy of a subjective assessment. Returning to our example of the parole board, we may ask the following question: is there a measure of overall accuracy so that we can compare the subjective assessment of one board member with that of another, or the judgment of one parole board with that of another? Statisticians offer a number of different measures of accuracy, but let us discuss the most commonly used measure, the **quadratic score**.[7] The quadratic score (Q) is given by the formula $Q = 1 - (p - A)^2$, where Q is the quadratic score of probability assessment, p is the assessed probability, and A is the actual outcome.

As you can see from this formula, if I assign 0 probability to an applicant and he stays out of trouble ($A = 0$), I have a perfect score of 1. However, if the parolee goes back to prison, my score becomes equal to 0.

TABLE 7.5	Risk Assigned to Parolees		
	Parolee		
Parole board member	Rob	Joe	Phil
Ron	High	High	Low
Chris	Medium	Low	Low

Let us explain the method with the example of our parole board members, Ron and Chris. They had categorized three successful parole applicants, Rob, Joe, and Phil, as high risk ($p = .8$), medium risk ($p = .5$), and low risk ($p = .2$). After a year, Rob and Phil had stayed out of prison ($A = 0$), whereas Joe had committed a serious crime ($A = 1$). On the basis of this information, we can construct the matrix shown in Table 7.5.

On the basis of our method, we can calculate the accuracy score for the two board members with regard to Rob as follows:

Ron's score on Rob: $Q = 1 - (.8 - 0)^2 = .36$

Chris's score on Rob: $Q = 1 - (.5 - 1)^2 = .75$

This measure magnifies the error in judgment by squaring the difference between actual and predicted values. By following this method, we can score the board members on each of their judgments and average the score. From Table 7.6, we can see that Chris has been more accurate than Ron. You may notice that although in this case, we can claim that Chris has been a better forecaster than Ron, you may not say for sure if that is purely by chance. It is of course possible to establish the statistical significance of the differences in performance; for that, however, we need many more observations. If we have a large enough sample size, we can use the techniques of hypothesis testing to find out the statistical significance.

Finally, we should mention the shortcomings of subjective probability. The attribution of probability scores by individual observers will always be open to question. We all assign probability values to uncertain events in our everyday lives. These attempted peeks into the future are based on our individual experiences and expertise, and thus personal biases of judgment influence our assessments of probability. To understand subjective probability, we must know the sources of biases that may obscure our judgments. I have discussed the psychological obstacles to critical thinking in chapter 5. They are equally applicable to the assessment of subjective probability.

TABLE 7.6	Quadratic Score Matrix for Parolees			
	Parolee			
Parole board member	Rob	Joe	Phil	Average score
Ron	.36	.36	.96	.56
Chris	.75	.96	.96	.89

KEY WORDS

Asymptotic probability (p. 151)

Central limit theorem (p. 155)

Chi-squared (p. 166)

Confidence interval (p. 159)

Contingency table (p. 165)

Critical value (p. 158)

Cumulative probability distribution (p. 151)

Degrees of freedom (p. 161)

Hypothesis testing (p. 157)

Independent probability (p. 150)

Joint probability distribution (p. 167)

Law of large numbers (p. 155)

Level of significance (p. 157)

Mutually exclusive probability (p. 150)

Nonparametric tests (p. 167)

Normal distribution (p. 152)

Null hypothesis (p. 156)

Objective probability (p. 149)

One-tailed test (p. 158)

Probability distribution (p. 151)

Quadratic score (p. 169)

Relative frequency (p. 149)

Standard normal distribution (p. 152)

Subjective probability (p. 169)

t distribution (p. 161)

t test (p. 161)

Two-tailed test (p. 160)

Types I and II errors (p. 167)

Z distribution (p. 158)

Z score (p. 158)

Z test (p. 158)

EXERCISES

1. What is an objective probability? What are the sources of bias in how we understand objective probability?

2. What is a subjective probability? What are the main sources of bias an individual faces in assessing subjective probability?

3. With an appropriate example, discuss the use of the central limit theorem as the foundation of statistical reasoning. Explain how it helps build a model of hypothesis testing.

4. The average SAT score for your state is 850, with a standard deviation of 65. The high school in your area has an average score of 980. Is this school an exception? Justify your answer.

5. From the information given in exercise 4, provide a confidence interval to develop a criterion for identifying schools with exceptionally good and unusually poor records.

6. Property tax is levied on the appraised market value of a property. However, it is often alleged that although the appraised values of lower priced houses are quite close to their market values (revealed when the properties are actually sold), the appraised values of higher priced houses are significantly lower than their market values. To investigate this allegation, the city of Masters conducted a study that found that for the forty lower priced houses, the ratio of assessed value to market value (A/M) was 0.89, with a standard deviation of 0.09. For a sample of forty higher priced homes, this ratio was 0.65, with a standard deviation of 0.15. Do you agree that the lower income homeowners in the city are carrying an unfair property tax burden?

7. The financial manager for the city of Masters is considering a switch from the existing money market fund to a new one. On the basis of the presented data series, do

you believe that the difference between the two is significant enough to warrant a change?

Year	Existing	New
1	7.5	6.7
2	8.0	9.3
3	7.9	5.5
4	8.5	10.9
5	7.0	5.3
6	9.2	12.6
7	8.2	6.7
8	7.4	4.3
9	8.8	10.7
10	8.0	12.9

8. The city of Masters has been conducting a survey of police responses to emergency calls. A similar city has been chosen for comparison purposes. The following table shows the distribution of response times during a typical week. Is there any reason to believe that there is any significant difference in the records of the two cities?

Distribution of Police Response Time

Response time (minutes)	Masters	Other city
1–3	23	45
3–5	62	72
5–8	41	59
8–10	38	43
10–15	16	32
15–25	3	21
25–35	0	13
35–60	0	7

9. Let us continue with the example of the MTA's new computer-assisted driver training program. Having examined the possible sex bias in the acceptance of the program, suppose you are trying to discover any possible age bias. Your survey results in the following table. Using a χ^2 distribution, determine whether age imposes an additional barrier to the use of computers in the MTA.

Age of the trainee	Like computers	Indifferent	Do not like computers	Total
18–25	30	25	10	65
26–45	65	30	60	155
46 and older	15	10	55	80
Total	110	65	125	300

10. Suppose we have observed ten individuals to establish the hypothesis that education has a strong correlation with income. Consider the following data, and test the hypothesis:

Education (years of schooling)	12	18	6	17	19	12	16	16	20	8
Income ($\times$ $1,000)	25	35	22	56	85	20	45	48	65	20

11. The crime rate in your state is 4,455 per 100,000 population, with a standard deviation of 289. The city in which you live has a crime rate of 3,990 per 100,000 population. Your police chief is claiming credit for a low crime rate. Is your city an exception? Assume that the city and the state have the same standard deviation.

12. Your state is considering a program for reducing recidivism among its convicted felons. Another state instituted a similar program ten years ago. The following table provides us with information on the two states. On the basis of these data, what advice can you give to the policymakers?

Recidivism per 1,000 Convictions

Year	Your state	State with a running rehabilitation program
1	155	134
2	160	183
3	153	110
4	172	193
5	140	145
6	188	252
7	166	132
8	151	86
9	214	116
10	260	98

13. Your city has been conducting a survey of incidents of lead poisoning among children in the city's school districts. For the purpose of comparison, you have chosen your neighboring city. The following table shows the distribution of toxic incidents among various age groups of school-age children during a six-month period. Is there any reason to believe that there is any significant difference in the records of the two cities?

Distribution of Lead Poisoning Incidents

Age of children	Your city	Neighboring city
5–6	54	53
7–8	51	43
9–10	44	38
11–12	24	29
13–14	10	9
15–16	5	1
17–18	0	1

14. The public health officials in your city are considering using a new type of flu vaccine that is being touted as a better preventive measure. However, the new vaccine costs three times as much per inoculation. On the basis of the following information, would you recommend the use of the new vaccine?

Comparison of Inoculation Using Two Types of Vaccines

Year	Number of flu incidents in your city per 1,000 inoculated (with the old vaccine)	Number of flu incidents in a neighboring city per 1,000 inoculated (with the new vaccine)
1	150	142
2	155	164
3	142	110
4	157	112
5	120	128
6	174	210
7	157	142
8	133	99
9	135	143
10	156	155

15. Write an essay on subjective probability. Suppose you are attempting to determine the odds that your favorite football team will win the Super Bowl. What kinds of biases might cloud your judgment?

16. In 2001 a school district was experimenting with a new policy to reduce absenteeism in its schools. The following table presents the data from the ten schools for two years. The 2000 data do not include the new policy. Using the methods of hypothesis testing, determine whether the district has been successful. Justify your methodology.

Comparison of Absenteeism

School	Rate of absenteeism in 2000	Regional average in 2001
1	4	9
2	3	5
3	4	6
4	5	4
5	3	9
6	9	9
7	2	7
	3	3

17. You are in charge of assessing the effectiveness of four parole board members. They assigned levels of high (H), medium (M), and low (L) risk for recidivism among parolees with corresponding subjective probabilities of .8, .5, and .2. You want to determine if their judgments were borne out by evidence after the parolees had been out of prison for one year. The number in parentheses, 1 or 0, after the name of each parolee indicates whether the parolee was back in prison within a year: the number 1 indicates that the individual went back to prison, and 0 indicates that he did not.

Parolee	Parole board member			
	Chris	Ron	Meg	Bob
A (0)	H	L	L	M
B (1)	H	M	L	M
C (0)	M	L	L	L
D (0)	H	L	L	M
E (1)	H	M	M	H
F (0)	H	H	L	M
G (1)	H	L	M	M
H (0)	M	L	L	L
I (0)	L	L	L	L
J (1)	H	H	L	L
K (0)	M	L	L	M
L (0)	H	M	L	L
M (0)	M	M	M	L
N (0)	H	H	L	L
O (1)	H	M	M	L
P (1)	H	L	L	M
Q (0)	M	M	L	L
R (0)	H	L	L	M
S (1)	H	M	M	M
T (0)	L	L	L	M
U (0)	M	H	L	H
V (1)	H	L	M	M
W (0)	M	M	L	L
X (1)	H	M	M	L
Y (0)	H	M	L	L
Z (0)	M	L	L	M

Notes

1. There are now many books in the market on Bill James and how he revolutionized baseball. Among them, I would recommend Michael Lewis, *Moneyball: The Art of Winning an Unfair Game* (New York: W.W. Norton, 2003); Scott Gray, *The Mind of Bill James: How a Complete Outsider Changed Baseball* (New York: Doubleday, 2006); and Gregory F. Augustine Pierce, ed., *How Bill James Changed Our View of Baseball* (Skokie, Ill.: ACTA Sports, 2007).

2. For an excellent discussion of the central limit theorem and its implication in the field of statistics, see John L. Casti, *Five Golden Rules: Great Theories of 20th-century Mathematics—and Why They Matter* (New York: John Wiley, 1996).

3. The fact that the mean of a normal distribution will be 0 can be easily shown. Since the sample average $\overline{X}$ becomes equal to its true population value μ, with infinite sampling the sum of $(\overline{X} - \mu)$ becomes equal to 0.

4. For the mathematical explanation of degrees of freedom, see Robert S. Pindyck and Daniel L. Rubinfeld, *Econometric Models and Economic Forecasts*, 2nd ed. (New York: McGraw-Hill, 1981), 42–43.

5. Frank Lad, *Operational Subjective Statistical Methods: A Mathematical, Philosophical, and Historical Introduction* (New York: John Wiley, 1996), 13. Lad offers a comprehensive but demanding explanation of subjective probability.

6. See Harinder Singh, "Relative Evaluation of Subjective and Objective Measures of Expectations Formation," *Quarterly Review of Economics and Business* 30 (1990): 64–74; and Roger Frantz, *Two Minds: Intuition and Analysis in the History of Economic Thought* (New York: Springer, 2005).

7. J. Frank Yates, "Subjective Probability Accuracy Analysis," in *Subjective Probability*, ed. George Wright and Peter Ayton (New York: John Wiley, 1994), 381–410.

8 Sources of Data

The first question facing an empirical researcher is, Where do I get the necessary information to prove my hypothesis or to answer my question? Just as the first step of objective analysis is to define a project's goals or objectives, before you look for data, you must define precisely the problem you want to investigate. If your task is to get information on the effectiveness of a particular public policy, you need to plan precisely how you are going to go about your task. Then you must collect the information, which may or may not be readily available. Information available in published form is called **secondary data** (that is, data collected by someone other than the researcher). Data that you must collect on your own are **primary data**. In this chapter we will cover issues of measurement and then discuss primary and secondary sources of data.

WHAT ARE WE MEASURING?

We all like to quantify. We express the amount of rainfall, the speed of automobiles, even intelligence, in numbers. We collect statistical information on income, unemployment, crime, political violence, the extent of democratic values, and the level of authoritarian personality. As analysts, we aim to assign numbers to properties or attributes according to specific rules or measurements. However, controversies arise with regard to the accuracy of those measurements. Therefore, let us first discuss the various types of measurements and then concentrate on their relative merits as measuring units.

Types of Measurement

Phenomena to be measured can be assigned values according to nominal, ordinal, interval, or ratio scales. Of these measurements, the weakest form of assigning numerical value is the **nominal scale**. For example, while filling out the census form or application forms, we are often asked to identify our ethnic background. Each ethnic group is assigned a number (1 through 5, say), a Roman numeral (I through V), or an alphabetic classification (A through E). Because these numbers and letters are not amenable to mathematical treatment, they do not give us any insight into their relative comparability, such as whether group B is closer to group A in any attribute or physical quality than is group E. For nominal scales, assigning numbers is devoid of any intrinsic meaning.

Some phenomena are comparable, so we can arrange them according to some quality but cannot tell precisely the distances among them. We may rank presidential candidates according to their political philosophies, but we may not be able to tell that candidate A is 2.35 times more conservative than candidate B. This process of ranking is called an **ordinal scale**. It is important to note that because numbers for ordinal rankings do not carry any specific meaning, the direction of their assigned values does not make a difference. Thus, among five candidates, the most conservative candidate may be assigned the value 1 or 5 without any consequence, as long as the ordering is in sequence. As you can see, ordinal rankings are stronger than nominal ones, since we can compare the relative position of the case in question (the "conservatism" of the presidential candidates in this example).

Arrangement using an **interval scale** offers us a greater amount of flexibility in comparing cases, both according to the arrangement of rankings and the actual distance between any two cases. If the candidates are assigned numbers on an interval scale, we can compare them by saying not only that A is more conservative than B but also that A is 2.35 times more conservative than B. Because of this desirable quality, the temptation to express orderings according to interval scales is strong. As a consequence, a great deal of effort has been directed toward constructing interval scale measures for various kinds of social, political, and economic phenomena. Various conservative and liberal congressional watchdogs assign numbers to individual members of Congress according to their voting patterns. In other studies, countries have been given numerical values for their development potential, degrees of democratization, and levels of political violence.[1]

An interval scale, however, may not have a fixed and well-defined zero point, at which the quality we are measuring does not exist. In the progressive assignment of points (the higher the number, the higher the level of liberalism) to members of Congress, a senator with a score of zero must show no traces of liberal values whatsoever, an attribute rarely seen in human beings. In contrast, we may order various school districts by the percentage of minority enrollment, or airlines according to the ratio of delayed to total flight arrivals, and in each of these cases, the value of zero will have a specific meaning (a school district with no minority students or an airline that is always on time). This is called a **ratio scale**.

Accuracy of the Measuring Scales

When we try to quantify something, we need to know the accuracy of our measurements. If we want to measure a phenomenon that has a physical manifestation and only one dimension, our efforts are largely free of controversy. Measuring an individual's height or weight is done without any trouble, as long as we are measuring either height or weight. However, we are likely to run into a bit more trouble if we attempt to quantify the "largeness" of a person, a measure that must encompass both height and weight. Therefore, if we want to express a phenomenon that has no obvious physical manifestation, such as an

FIGURE 8.1	**Measuring the English Shoreline**

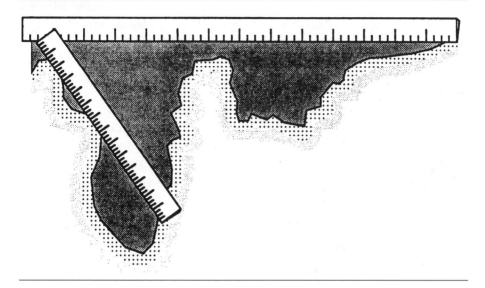

individual's intelligence, attitude, or quality of life, or the regional inflation rate, national growth potential, or international political instability, we are treading in dangerous waters. Even measuring strictly physical, single-attribute phenomena can sometimes be controversial. James Gleick gives an interesting example in a popular book on the mathematical theory of chaos.[2] In encyclopedias and other reference books, one frequently encounters various measures of national geography, such as the total square miles of land area or the length of shoreline. Gleick points out that the measurement of a jagged shoreline must vary with the size of the yardstick. When cartographers measure shorelines, they use approximations. Consider Figure 8.1. When I use a large yardstick, I miss all the little edges. However, by using a smaller stick, I can try to be more precise. In so doing, the measurement of the shoreline will register an increase, as this more precise instrument will include areas that were not measured before. Unfortunately, this smaller stick would not produce a perfect measurement, as it would miss areas smaller than itself. Clearly, as we keep reducing the size of the yardstick, we also increase the measurement of the total shoreline. In the end, when the yardstick becomes infinitesimally small, the measurement of the shoreline would be recorded as infinitely long.

We live in an imperfect world. Therefore, along with everything else, we must live with the shortcomings of our indicators. The only recourse we have is to be aware of their inherent biases and problems and to interpret them with extreme care. With these words of caution, we may examine the types of data and their sources.

PRIMARY DATA: CONDUCTING A SURVEY

Often, the kind of information you need is not available in archival records. In that case, you may need to collect information on your own. You can collect primary information through direct observation or through surveys. Traffic engineers routinely observe traffic patterns for more efficient and safer road design. They can send actual observers or use counters that automatically record the number of vehicles and their speed. Public health officials develop regional statistics by compiling data from local hospitals, and water management departments collect information through laboratory testing of water samples from local rivers, streams, and other sources of drinking water.

Public policy researchers, however, most frequently use surveys to collect primary data. For example, local governments often rely on opinion polls for needs assessments, prioritization of issues, or to shape service delivery systems. If county authorities want to improve health care delivery to a community's elderly residents, they can commission a survey that assesses residents' needs through a series of specific or open-ended questions. A municipal service agency such as a rapid transit authority can design a survey for developing a more efficient mass transit system. A municipal government may also be interested in learning its constituents' views on a specific issue, such as a proposed ban on smoking in public places or the location of a proposed city library. The challenge for these and other surveys is how to collect unbiased information in a systematic way. Because it is often impossible to ask every member of a large group, we have to depend on surveys based on sampling theory. Sampling theory helps us determine the most cost-efficient way to derive unbiased information; more simply, it helps us design a survey.

Designing a Survey

The starting point of any **survey design** is the question of **population**. The term *population* is defined as the entire target group from which the necessary information is to be extracted. Let us suppose that we want to determine whether the residents of a small town are willing to accept a proposed prison facility located on the outskirts of town. In such a case, we may define the population as all the city's adult residents. If we are trying to figure out the effects of a price hike on city buses, then bus riders will form the survey's population.

In a perfect world, with no constraints on time and money, it is desirable to have a complete enumeration, or a survey of each member of the population. However, in reality, we must confine our inquiry to a small group of representatives of the population, called the **sample population**. The single most important quality of the sample population is its representativeness. That is, how closely does this sample group represent the entire population? If it does not represent the population well, the sample population will give us biased (and therefore erroneous) information, as shown in Figure 8.2.

These **sampling biases** are characterized as either systematic or random. Through proper understanding of sampling theory, one can minimize systematic sampling errors, which result from inappropriate survey design. Random variations in the data are what cause random sampling errors, however. Such variations cannot be completely eliminated but can be managed through proper survey design. Let us discuss these in detail.

Systematic Errors in Sampling

Systematic errors result from biased sampling of a population. These biases have many sources. Some of the most common sources of systematic sampling biases are identified below.

FIGURE 8.2   Errors in Sampling

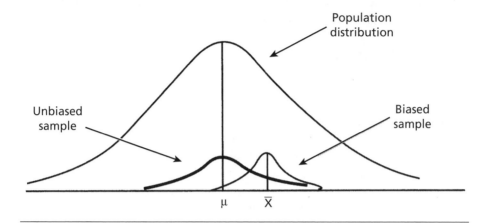

Population distribution

Unbiased sample

Biased sample

μ   X̄

Nonrepresentative Sample. A nonrepresentative sample group produces biased infer- ences about a population. During the 1936 presidential campaign, the now defunct *Literary Digest* conducted a telephone survey. On the basis of its sample of New York residents, the magazine predicted a comfortable margin of victory for Alf Landon against Franklin D. Roosevelt. However, when the actual poll results came out, FDR had won a decisive victory. Why was the survey wrong? The prediction was incorrect because it was based on a sample that did not properly represent the population. Telephones were still a novelty in 1936, restricted to the relatively affluent. The telephone was not the tool of universal communication that it is today. Therefore, a sample of telephone owners was an inappropriate representative for the rest of the population.

The designer of a survey should always guard against this kind of systematic bias. For example, if you pick names of individuals from the property tax roll for a survey to determine the mass transit needs of a low-income neighborhood, your sample may diverge from your intended group—the neighborhood residents. Because most resi- dents rent, rather than own, their homes in a low-income neighborhood, the exclusion of the renter population will cause the poll results to deviate significantly from those of the target population. To avoid this error one must have an intimate knowledge of the population and the existence of biased "cells" or subgroups within it.

Self-Selection Bias Within the Sample. Unfortunately, even correctly specifying the sample group will not always eliminate the problem of getting unbiased information. For example, suppose you carefully identified your sample group and administered a detailed questionnaire. When the results come in, you find out that they are still biased. This may happen because of self-selection within the sample group, when those who choose to respond to a survey turn out to be different from the rest of the population. Thus, going back to my example of mass transit needs in a low-income neighborhood, I may find that the respondents are disproportionately drawn from the English-speak- ing, better educated, older, and nonminority population. In such a case, their opinions will obviously not reflect the entire neighborhood. This self-selection bias may not be restricted to individual respondents. The International City/County Management Association (ICMA) collects data on municipalities. However, its data sets are based on information voluntarily submitted by the municipalities. Such self-reporting can create a bias, because those local governments that are less affluent or are experiencing hard economic times may not have the personnel or the inclination to fill out a detailed questionnaire. Thus, the data sets presented in the ICMA yearbooks carry an appropriate warning.

When People Lie. If you ask a sensitive question, people often do not tell the truth. People may lie about their beliefs regarding race relations, gender equality, homosexuality, or other matters of private attitude because they are afraid to be politically incorrect or are mindful of social sanctions for unpopular opinions. This is a particular problem for AIDS researchers. To make a proper assessment of a community's needs, they must ask extremely sensitive questions regarding people's sexual habits. Unless they do so with the utmost care, their survey may produce inaccurate and biased results.

People are also typically reluctant to reveal their deeply held racial prejudices. As a result, time and again, forecasting the results of certain elections turns out to be incorrect. When Barack Obama became the first African American candidate for president in 2008, many pundits warned of the "Bradley effect," which posits that white voters hide their reluctance to support a black candidate from pollsters. Some saw Obama's defeat in the New Hampshire primary, in which he held a 10-point advantage in the polls leading up to the contest, as evidence of the Bradley effect, but his victory in the general election dissolved much of the buzz around this theory.

Collection Bias. Natural obstacles to reporting may create biases. In several border states the issue of illegal immigration has been rather controversial. Because immigration has a tremendous impact on a region's economy, the U.S. Census Bureau would like a more accurate enumeration of the illegal immigrants in the area and more detailed knowledge of their socioeconomic characteristics. However, for understandable reasons, illegal immigrants have been underreported.

Biases also result from the mode of collection. The *World Handbook of Political and Social Indicators* (1983), by Charles Taylor and Michael Jodice, makes a significant contribution to scholarly research by compiling international social and political data. Yet, as the authors readily admit, much of the political data are collected from the *New York Times* and a few other published reports. These newspapers are more likely to report on events that take place in Western nations than in some obscure country in Asia or Africa, so the data will contain systematic biases.

Errors Due to Observation. In the early 1920s, the physicist Werner Heisenberg performed a series of famous experiments in an attempt to observe the positions of subatomic particles. To ascertain the positions of these particles, they had to be charged with photon particles. But the very act of charging them caused them to change their original positions in a random fashion, thereby making it impossible to know where they were before. These experiments gave birth to what is known as the Heisenberg Uncertainty Principle, which simply states that for certain cases, no experimental design is available that would not create errors caused by the process of observation.

A CASE IN POINT

Errors of Observation: The Hawthorne Experiment

The fact that observation often alters the behavior of those being observed can significantly reduce the validity of research findings. The most celebrated example of this is the so-called Hawthorne experiment. In 1932 a group of researchers reported the results of an experiment they had been conducting for the past five years at the Hawthorne Works, a Western Electric Company manufacturing plant near Chicago. They discovered, by accident, that people generally seem to work better and are more productive when their performance on the job receives the flattering attention of a group of university researchers.

The researchers, headed by Elton Mayo and F. J. Roelithsberger, were originally trying to determine at what level the garment factory's illumination needed to be set to maximize production.[3] They started with a very high degree of light and slowly reduced its intensity to see if it would influence productivity. The workers became aware of the fact that they were being observed. As the light got dimmer and dimmer, they took it as a matter of group pride to work even harder. Needless to say, their sensitivity to being observed spoiled the original intent of the research. However, the results of this experiment made scholars of organizational behavior aware of the strength of group identity as a motivating force in the workplace and started the so-called humanistic school of organizational behavior.

Discussion Points

1. Why should we be extra careful in designing our research, particularly when it comes to observing human behavior?
2. How can you maintain objectivity in observing human behavior or derive truthful answers through survey questions?

In an analogous way, social scientists often alter the behavior of the people they are observing. In other words, if we are told that we are being observed, our behavior may differ from that in our day-to-day lives. In a famous experiment conducted in the early 1970s, the psychologist Stanley Milgram demonstrated the power of authority figures in influencing individual behavior.[4] His subjects were told that they were taking part in a test to determine the effect of punishment on memory. They were asked to give electrical jolts to another "subject," a man in another room, whenever he made a mistake. In fact, the voice from the other room was that of an actor and was taped for the experiment. They were also told to increase the voltage each additional time the "subject" made a mistake. To the amazement of the experimenters, the subjects continued to increase the voltage despite desperate pleas from the unseen voice, simply because they were told to do so by the laboratory psychologist. Nearly 60 percent of the subjects increased the voltage to the fatal level. Although the findings of this sensational experiment paint an unflattering picture of human nature, it is extremely difficult to say whether such blind obedience could be replicated on all of us in an open society.[5]

One of the ways to avoid the errors resulting from observation is to collect data on what is known as **revealed preference**. That is, although people's actual preferences are not apparent to an outside observer, they are revealed through their past choices. If you ask people if they will go to the polls in an upcoming election, those who may not vote may attempt to hide their actual intent because of a reluctance to admit their failure to carry out their civic duty.

Bias in the Survey Instrument. Survey results can be biased if the instruments (the questions) are loaded with hidden values that elicit certain reactions from the respondents. During the early days of the Soviet Union's dissolution, the government of President Mikhail Gorbachev objected to a referendum in a breakaway republic that asked, "Would you like to be free, or are you willing to be dominated by the forces of communist Russia?" Naturally, the election results were never in doubt. In public policy analysis, a faulty survey instrument can often distort the results. For example, when asked in a general context, most people are likely to show their preference for such public goods as a clean environment, abundant wildlife, or a safer and well-maintained infrastructure. However, these answers may not truly reflect public opinion, because people are just as likely to change their minds when these same questions are asked with reference to how much the programs may cost them personally.

Furthermore, calls for subjective judgment can create biases. Asking people to categorize something as "high," "low," "large," "small," and so forth, elicits the subjective nature of people's judgment, which may stand in the way of determining the "true" opinion of the public.

Random Sampling Errors

Random sampling errors occur because of unexplained variations around "true" population values. Because these variations are random (or are caused by factors that cannot be determined), they can fall in any direction around the true values. For example, if you throw stones at the middle of a target, some will hit the bull's-eye and some will not. The stones will have a strong central tendency because you have aimed at the bull's-eye. Therefore, however poor a marksman you are, the stones will form a more or less normal distribution (unless, of course, your arm gets tired and creates a bias as a result), which will look like a Mexican sombrero. Similarly, if the errors are randomly distributed around the mean in a three-dimensional situation, they will form normal distributions in any direction around the mean (μ). I have attempted to depict this in Figure 8.3. As you can see, the true population value (of, say, the proportion of the population favoring handgun control) is μ. However, because of the presence of random variations, the sample value may turn out to be different from this true value.

Because these variations are random, we cannot completely eliminate them. Instead, we try to increase the precision of the sample results by reducing the random error factor. How can we do this? Recalling the discussion of the law of large numbers in chapter 7, we know that as the size of the sample increases, the domain of the error term shrinks. So when the number of samples approaches infinity or the sample size becomes the same as the entire population (in which case it is no longer a sample but a complete enumeration), the sample value becomes equal to the true population value. As already mentioned, however, costs often preclude a complete enumeration. Hence, we need to design a survey that is within our financial means yet provides us

FIGURE 8.3   Random Sampling Errors

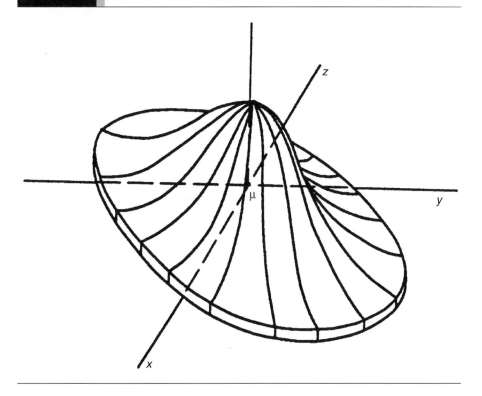

with a tolerably precise result—that is, one with a reasonably low error level. We will discuss this more at length when we tackle the question of sample size later in this chapter.

Armed with the knowledge of possible pitfalls, we may now discuss the process of designing a survey. This process essentially centers on four questions: (1) Who is chosen? (2) How many are chosen? (3) Which questions should be asked? and (4) What is the mode of polling?

Choosing the Sample Population

There are numerous methods of choosing a group of subjects, some of which are called **objective sampling** or **probability-based sampling**, in which the sample subjects are drawn according to a set of rules meant to maximize the probability of achieving an accurate account of the population. In contrast, one may use the **judgmental method of sampling**, in which one uses specialized knowledge about the population to get to the correct information.

The following are methods of objective sampling.

- **Random sampling.** When we conduct random sampling, each element in the population has an equal chance of being picked. There are many ways of ensuring that the samples are drawn in a truly random fashion. For example, you may use computer-generated random numbers to pick the subjects. Or, in a large metropolitan city, you may go by the listings in the telephone book (say, by choosing the tenth person on each page). This method is most likely to give us the desired results when the population is relatively homogeneous. If we are interested in gathering information on social norms and mores, a random sample may be the most appropriate design, because each member of the society has an equal voice when determining individual attitudes.

• *Stratified sampling.* In contrast, when a population is divided into distinct subgroups, or *strata*, it may be better to identify each stratum of society and poll it separately. An example may clarify the situation. Suppose a school district is considering switching from the traditional academic calendar to year-round schooling. To assess the reaction to this proposed change, the school district wants to poll the residents of the district. Because the population is fragmented along the lines of income and race—and because the district authorities want to be sensitive to the special needs of single parents—it is advantageous to poll each subgroup separately.

• *Cluster sampling.* When an extremely large population must be polled, a pollster may find it difficult (or too expensive) to include each member on the list of potential subjects from which the sample is to be drawn. Instead, the pollster may concentrate on a microcosm of the larger population. Let us suppose that we need to examine an aspect of urban America, and we find it impossible to reach every city. We may argue, then, that a particular city (say, Buffalo, New York) can serve as the "typical city." Hence, we can poll the residents of Buffalo and draw conclusions about the rest of the urban areas of the United States. As you can see, the accuracy of this procedure depends on how representative of the population the cluster is.

Choosing the Size of the Sample

The development of theoretical statistics has given us some of the most powerful tools of quantitative decision making. One of these tools helps us determine sample size by linking the concepts of confidence interval and sample error. As discussed in chapter 7, the confidence interval is calculated using the following formula:

$$-Z_\alpha \times \frac{\sigma}{\sqrt{n}} > \overline{X} - \mu > +Z_\alpha \times \frac{\sigma}{\sqrt{n}} \qquad (8.1)$$

where Z_α is the value from the Z-score table (Appendix C) at the desired level of confidence, α; σ is the population standard deviation; n is the population size; $\overline{X}$ is the sample mean; and μ is the population mean.

This formula tells us that we can be confident at any desired level of α that the difference between the sample mean and the population mean will fall within a particular band. We can rewrite this formula as

$$(\overline{X} - \mu) \pm Z_\alpha \times \frac{\sigma}{\sqrt{n}} \qquad (8.1a)$$

or

$$\mu = \overline{X} \pm \left(Z_\alpha \times \frac{\sigma}{\sqrt{n}} \right) \qquad (8.1b)$$

The problem with using this formula is that it uses the population standard deviation, which is unobservable. We can estimate the population standard deviation from the sample standard deviation by correcting the formula with the degrees of freedom:

$$\mu = \overline{X} \pm Z_\alpha \times \frac{s}{\sqrt{n-1}} \qquad (8.1c)$$

where s is the sample standard deviation and n is the size of the sample population.

Let us take an example. Suppose that from a sample of 100 residents of a city, we learn that 67 percent support a proposed referendum. We also know that the survey has a standard deviation of 0.15. To be safe, we want 95 percent accuracy. Therefore, we can consult the Z table for the value of $Z_{.05}$, which turns out to be approximately 1.96. Using these numbers in equation 8.1, we can be 95 percent certain that the population mean, which we cannot observe, will fall within the range

$$\mu = \pm 1.96 \times \frac{0.15}{\sqrt{100-1}} = 0.67 \pm 0.0295$$

That is, we can be 95 percent sure that the opinion of the population will vary within the range of approximately 70 percent and 64 percent. In other words, the sample result contains a sample error of ±3 percent (by rounding off 0.0295).

As you can see, there is clearly a trade-off between the need for accuracy and its cost. If you want a very low sample error, you will have to interview a lot more people, which increases the cost of the survey. For example, you need a high degree of accuracy to predict the outcome of a close election, but you might not demand such a high standard for other policy-related polls.

Choosing Effective Survey Instruments

Although choosing the size of the sample is mechanical, the real art (derived from experience and creativity) of conducting a survey lies in designing the questionnaire. Many concerns arise when developing a questionnaire; we may classify them in five broad categories:

- *Be on a level with the respondents.* Questionnaires must be developed with the respondents in mind. If you are developing a questionnaire for middle school children, would you ask questions with words that are beyond their vocabulary? Certainly not. And since you are asking youngsters, you would be careful about the way you phrase your questions. The same caution applies to questions put to adults. The question "Do you belong to the poor, middle, or wealthy class?" would draw a mixed reaction, because definitions of these class boundaries vary considerably. Instead, you can get a much more specific answer by asking, "Which of the following income groups do you belong to—less than $10,000; between $10,001 and $20,000; . . . ?"

- *Choose the right format for answers.* Questions in a survey can be either open-ended or fixed. With an open-ended question, answers can be long and descriptive. To determine positions on handgun registration, questions may be phrased as, "What is your position on handgun control?" Alternatively, questions may be put within a fixed format, such as

"I believe all handguns within the state should be registered."

_____ Strongly Agree

_____ Agree

_____ Neither Agree nor Disagree

_____ Disagree

_____ Strongly Disagree

_____ No Opinion

Both types of questions have advantages and drawbacks. Open-ended questions draw out a full spectrum of responses without restricting respondents. However, the answers to these questions, by virtue of being unstructured, cannot be easily fitted into a specific coding system for quantitative analysis. A highly structured question, however, may miss an answer that many respondents might have chosen.

- *Avoid words that provoke emotion.* If your goal is to develop an objective set of questions, you should avoid terms that evoke strong emotional reactions. For example, you are trying to determine public support for the U.S. government's food aid to drought-stricken parts of Africa. Consider three questions:

  1. "Do you support U.S. aid to drought-stricken parts of Africa?"
  2. "Do you support U.S. aid to the starving people of Africa?"
  3. "In view of all the problems facing this country, do you support U.S. aid to Africa?"

Although in general, few people are against food aid to a starving group of people, it is fairly obvious that the answers to these similar questions are likely to be quite different. However, to an unsuspecting audience, you can report the results of this survey as "people's opinion on U.S. aid to Africa" by picking the one that suits your purpose the best.

- *Choose the proper sequence of questions.* The sequence in which questions are put to respondents can be crucial. The questions can be asked in a random sequence, or they can be asked in a funnel or an inverted funnel sequence. If respondents are likely to be familiar with the broad issues, it is better to use a funnel-like sequence, starting with the most general question and then narrowing down to a more specific one. Suppose a school district is debating the distribution of literature on birth control devices to its high school students. Because most people hold some kind of opinion on the state of family values, you can start by asking respondents to assess the state of family values and then, within that context, ask their opinion about birth control. In contrast, most people are not well informed about the problem of the external trade deficit and may require some help in framing the issue. Therefore, in such a survey, you may do well by starting out with a set of specific questions, which can help them focus on the broader issue.

- *Choose the appropriate length of questionnaire.* Because conducting a survey is expensive and time-consuming, there is a tendency to load questionnaires with as many questions as possible. This tendency is to be resisted, as most people lose interest in answering questions if they are too long or there are too many. This is particularly true for mail or telephone surveys. Greater latitude is often possible when interviewing face to face.

Choosing Polling Methods

Surveys are about asking questions. Determining the mode of questioning is an extremely important aspect of survey design. Much thought must be given to choosing an appropriate medium. Generally speaking, there are three methods of interviewing:

- *Face-to-face interviews.* The personal, face-to-face interview is the most expensive, although probably the most accurate, method of gathering information about a population. Face-to-face interviews are particularly appropriate when a questionnaire has many open-ended questions or is lengthy. Frequently this form of personal interview can put subjects at ease with the interviewer. Yet this personal contact may have its drawbacks, as the interviewer and the interviewee may find each other less than acceptable, and as a result, the survey results may be skewed.

- *Telephone interviews.* Telephone surveys may be the least expensive type of survey to administer and are not likely to create systematic biases. They are most effective in conducting quick, rather than in-depth, surveys. However, people are often squeamish about opening up to a faceless voice over the telephone and tend to be guarded in their responses.

- *Mailed questionnaires.* Relatively inexpensive and free of the influences of individual interviewers, mailed questionnaires allow subjects to think over their responses and can also be used to elicit long answers to open-ended questions. Also, once the questionnaires are returned, they can be processed and data can be recorded, tabulated, tested, and reported with relative ease. In many cases these surveys are recorded on paper and scanned by a computer, creating files for subsequent testing. However, mailed questionnaires often suffer from extremely low response rates. While for personal interviews response rates are typically about 95 percent, for mail surveys these numbers have been observed to be between 2 percent and 40 percent. A low response rate should warn us that unless we are careful, the results can exhibit a self-selection bias. In other words, as discussed earlier, if the rate of returns is extremely low, those who have taken the initiative to fill out the questionnaires and mail them may represent a special subset of the population.

QUANTIFICATION OF SURVEY DATA

Survey results are typically expressed in absolute numbers or in percentages and ratios. We are also told survey results in terms of means. Because it is difficult to report the results of open-ended questions in numbers, most surveys use fixed-format answers. As noted at the beginning of the chapter, certain questions are answered in numbers (income, age, years of education, and so on), others in nominal scales (sex, race, religion, and the like). Finally, data that relate to matters of attitudes and values cannot be readily translated into numbers. To express these variables in numbers, we use predetermined scales.

In the social sciences, **Likert scales** are the most commonly used. With a Likert scale, respondents are asked to express their feelings on a continuum varying from highly positive to highly negative. On a five-point scale, the respondents will be asked whether they "strongly agree," "agree," are "undecided," "disagree," or "strongly disagree" with a particular statement. These answers can then be assigned weights either in ascending (1, 2, 3, 4, 5) or descending (5, 4, 3, 2, 1) order. On the basis of their answers, respondents will be given points, which will indicate their individual stances on particular issues, or the average of the responses can be calculated for determining the "average" attitude or feeling.

REPORTING SURVEY RESULTS

Surveys are conducted to gather information and to test a specific set of hypotheses. It is very important, then, to report the results of a survey properly. Most are reported with tables, graphs, and charts. I will discuss these techniques in chapter 9. However, because survey data can be misused and misinterpreted, you must spell out in detail the assumptions, sampling method, sample error, level of confidence, and often the questions themselves. In a typical example, the *Los Angeles Times,* when reporting the results of a nationwide opinion survey, informs readers how the poll was taken:

> The *Times* poll interviewed 1,146 registered voters nationwide, by telephone, from August 12 to 14. Telephone numbers were chosen from a list of all exchanges in the country. Random-digit dialing techniques were used to ensure that both listed and nonlisted numbers had an opportunity to be surveyed. Results were weighted slightly to conform with census figures for sex, race, age, education, and household size. The margin of sampling error for the total sample is plus or minus three percentage points. For certain subgroups, the error margin is slightly higher. Poll results can also be affected by other factors, such as question wording and the order in which questions are presented.[6]

CONDUCTING FOCUS GROUPS

Focus groups are becoming increasingly popular as a tool for gauging public opinion regarding policy issues at all levels of government. For a focus group, a small representative group of the target population, usually numbering between eight and twelve, is assembled for in-depth discussions on a certain topic. Under the guidance of a trained interviewer, the group discusses structured questions relating to the central topic. Focus groups can shed light on complex areas of public policies and other important issues that may be missed by a survey, which can be too structured (see "A Case in Point").

In conducting focus groups, which can be powerful tools of policy formulation, you must address a number of methodological and procedural questions. Unlike a survey, there is no set methodology for focus groups. Since they are small and the questions open-ended, strict statistical techniques cannot be used for their verification. A great

A CASE IN POINT

Focus Group for Growth Management Policies

The problem of managing economic growth confronts many regions of the nation. Palm Beach County is one of the largest counties in Florida, comprising 2,223 square miles and thirty-nine municipalities. In the 1990s, the county experienced some of the fastest economic growth in the United States. Located between the ecologically sensitive Everglades, Lake Okeechobee, and the Atlantic Ocean, the county's population grew by an incredible 20 percent per year. In 1998 the Sierra Club ranked Palm Beach County as one of the most sprawling medium-sized metropolitan areas in the nation. Therefore, the problem of managing runaway growth is paramount to the region's planners. However, this issue is quite complex, since it aims to reconcile often contradictory interests of the citizens.

In 1997 the county introduced its Managed Growth Tier System, which divided it into five distinct regions: urban-suburban, exurban, rural, agricultural reserve, and the glade. Palm Beach County's plans were tested by more than twenty-two focus groups for a year-and-a-half. These groups, representing various interest groups in the region, discussed the plans to fine-tune various proposals. At the end, when the growth management plan was approved, it received the American Planning Association's award for 2000.[7]

Discussion Points

1. When is it appropriate to use focus groups in public policy analysis?
2. Why was Palm Beach County successful in using focus group findings?
3. Consider a particular issue in your community. Do you think you can recommend the use of focus groups to determine citizens' positions on the issue? Why or why not?

---

deal of advanced thinking and planning must compensate for methods that are less than rigorous. I can make a few suggestions for developing successful focus groups:

1. *Determine a clear-cut set of goals.* For example, in Palm Beach County, it was decided to concentrate only on respondents' views on the proposed public policy of dividing the region into five distinct zones of growth.
2. *Identify the critical characteristics of potential participants.* In the Palm Beach County case, do the focus groups include "constituents," meaning a group drawn from the resident population, or is the purpose to understand the views of key interest groups (for example, the Chamber of Commerce, small business groups, commuters, builders and developers, agricultural workers, environmentalists, and so forth)?
3. *Recruit skillful group leaders.* You should note that it is extremely important to use skillful discussion leaders who can keep the focus of the group tightly on the

issues at hand. Discussion leaders must balance the need for the participants to freely express their opinions on controversial issues with that of avoiding futile arguments.

4. *Analyze the discussion for summary and conclusion.* There is no set procedure for analyzing focus group discussions. They can sometimes be taped with the permission of the participants, or the discussion leader may take copious notes for analysis. The summary and conclusion must be presented in a clear and concise manner so they answer the decision makers' pertinent questions.

5. *Determine the number of focus groups.* Because focus groups are typically composed of eight to twelve people, you need to have a number of such groups to get a feel for the community's diverse views on public policy questions.

SECONDARY DATA

Opinion polls and focus groups are excellent tools for needs assessment or for prioritizing needs for a local government. However, most public policy research involves the use of secondary information, collected by someone other than the researcher. When you are confronted with an unfamiliar topic, you may be at a loss as to where to begin. Chances are there is a vast amount of information, but you must be able to conduct an effective search so that you can find the information you need.

Let us take an example. Suppose you are a junior analyst, working for your city, which wants to address a great deal of abandoned or dilapidated housing in the downtown area. The city wants to provide an incentive to homeowners to make substantial improvements through a proposed property tax rebate program. Under this program, homeowners in the designated area will qualify for a property tax rebate for three years if they improve their properties. Your job is to research the project's effectiveness.

To fully understand the issues relating to your project, you must first find out what work has already been done on such issues. Your literature review will help you

- gain a fuller view of what other researchers have discovered through their investigations, as well as point to areas that still need to be addressed;
- identify causal linkages that may help explain your hypothesis;
- conceptualize and measure key concepts; and
- identify data sources.

Thus, a literature review will quickly tell you about the experiences of other cities that have experimented with similar programs. These published books and articles will help you develop your own hypotheses and methods of formulating the analysis. On the basis of the literature, you may decide to try to find out if a tax rebate does in fact spur investment in housing renovation.

However, the decision to improve one's property is complex and depends on factors other than property taxes. It involves the calculation of, for example, the condition of the neighborhood (neighborhoods with higher property values would provide investors with higher returns), levels of property tax rates, and current economic conditions. A review of the relevant literature will help you identify the factors that are important to a potential investor in property improvements.

Once you know these causal linkages, you can start thinking about how to define and operationalize (numerically measure) these variables. You can operationalize the economic condition of a neighborhood either by its average household income or by the median property value. Although these two figures are closely linked, they do not convey an identical measure of the neighborhood's relative prosperity. A quick reading of the literature will provide you with a good idea of which measures other researchers have used and why.

After you have decided how to operationalize the relevant variables, you need to find data containing such information. For example, if you know that fifty cities have attempted tax rebate programs in the past, you may start searching for comparable data on those cities. Many sources can provide you with the information you seek (see this and following pages). Once you have gathered the relevant data, you may proceed with your analysis.

Searching for Information

Thanks to advances in technology, sources of secondary information are unlimited, and most college and university libraries offer their students online services. However, before you start searching—and perhaps get frustrated—you must develop a strategy. Not all the searches you attempt will deliver the right information. I have classified information sources into three broad categories (see Figure 8.4). You can conduct an internal search within a library for books and scholarly journals. During such a search, you can explore by using an author's name, a title, a subject, or words in the title. If you know the names of prominent authors in the field, or you know exact titles, you can easily find out if the library has sources you would find useful. If you do not have a good idea about the topic, it is always smart to start with a recognized textbook, because it provides you with a well-rounded introduction to the subject matter. You can also search by key words. For example, for our inquiry, I typed in "property tax" and found a number of useful books. Once you come across a relevant book or article, look at the list of references. These citations can lead you to other relevant works. This process of building a bibliography is called **pyramiding citations**, because you can develop a substantial list from a small number of initial sources. In a library search, you will have to evaluate books and journal articles to see which of these will be useful to you.

Online Searches

An Internet search, in contrast, offers a great deal of information without your having to leave your desk. In an online search, you quickly discover that a world of information awaits you. The problem, however, is how to focus your search to find pertinent information, and once you find that information, how to determine its reliability. In this intimately interconnected information network, the first problem is to find a proper starting point.

Today, most people are familiar with general search engines or portals, such as Google and Yahoo. These search engines are excellent tools for locating institutions, government agencies, particular newspapers, and people. If you Google "property tax," you will receive a large number of hits, which include, among others, tax consultants, the Internal Revenue Service, individuals trying to sell books on how to lower your

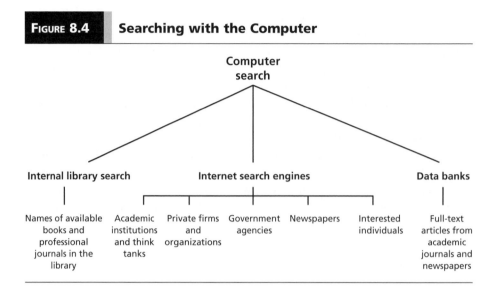

FIGURE 8.4   **Searching with the Computer**

property tax bill, lists of unclaimed properties, and state property tax forms. Conducting an internal search on an institution's Web site also can be useful. For example, on the Web site of the Brooking Institution, a leading think tank, a search for "property tax" generates a list of the institution's publications on the subject. Another strategy is to search in the online archives of a news source.

All search engines depend on key word searches for accessing the right information. As stated above, this type of search (often called a Boolean search) allows you to specify a word or phrase that best represents your area of inquiry. Some engines allow you to use the operators AND, OR, and NOT to create either a very broad or a very narrow search. Say you are interested in looking for articles on school district consolidation. You began the search with the broad key word "school financing." Because this is too broad a search, you get a large number of hits, most of which are of little or no interest to you. In that case, you can narrow the search by adding another key word following the operator AND, which combines search terms so that each result must contain both terms, such as "school AND consolidation." If you are interested in further narrowing the search, you could add another word (say, "Midwest" or "Kansas") along with the two, separated by another AND operator. If you want to broaden your search, use the operator OR. The OR operator combines search terms so that each result contains at least one of the terms. For example, "school OR consolidation" will give you results that contain either term. Some advanced searches also allow you to use the operator NOT. This operator excludes the results that contain the term that follows NOT. For example, if you are interested in the consolidation of individual schools, not school districts, you may restrict your search to find results that contain the term "school" but not the term "district."

The results from a search often hide the information you need within a heap of unrelated, inaccurate, or incomplete materials and links. It is up to you, then, to determine whether a site is to be trusted, if the information is accurate, or if a more advanced search would produce better results. A search for the name Einstein gives me information on the life and work of the famous physicist, but it also produces sites for a garage, a laboratory auction house, and a chain of bagel stores. It is therefore important to remember that anyone can put up a Web site. It is also important to remember that unlike a published book, postings on the Internet have no physical existence. Therefore, a site that looks interesting and useful to you now may not be there tomorrow, or it may change significantly. This lack of permanence can cause problems when you include references to Web sites in your report. There is no better example of this problem than Wikipedia, the online encyclopedia that anyone can edit. The open-source nature of Wikipedia makes it a very up-to-date resource, but it also creates a problem: there is no certainty of the accuracy of its information. Therefore, one must be extremely careful in using Wikipedia and should crosscheck all information from other, more reliable sources. Furthermore, Wikipedia tends to be more accurate in reporting specific facts rather than providing information on issues that can evoke emotion or subjective judgment. You are more likely to find reliable information on the date of birth of Napoleon Bonaparte than on the death penalty, abortion, or gun control.

So exactly how do you judge the reliability of a Web site's information? The answer to this question is less complicated than it may at first appear. Because of the wide variation in the reliability of printed sources as well, you should not accept any kind of information without a critical review. You should always test the information's validity, accuracy, and authority. When getting information from the Web, see if the information follows a valid sequence of reasoning. Analysis based on critical reasoning differs from propaganda based on rhetoric only. However, even if a piece appears to be based on sound reasoning backed by empirical observations, you may question the validity of the data. If the data are not widely available, you may have to establish their accuracy through cross-referencing. That is, you may want to know if the data have been used in published work in a reputable scholarly journal, magazine, or newspaper. You are much safer in accepting the validity of the information if the source is a reputable organization, such as a university, a well-known independent research outfit, a well-regarded publishing house, or an official government entity. But even then you should be aware of the possible shortcomings of the information. The data may contain deliberate biases stemming from ideological positions or from vested interests. If I am looking for information on the effects of environmental pollution, I may have reason to be skeptical of data provided either by an environmental activist group such as the Sierra Club or by an industry with a stake in the outcome of the public debate. In such a situation, you should look for corroboration by other independent sources.

If you are interested in articles published in scholarly journals, magazines, or newspapers, you can go to specialized databases. Databases are different from general search engines in that they cover only a specific pool of information. Some may cover a set number of professional journals. You can log on to such a database and look for articles published in these journals. Most of these databases allow users to download entire articles without having to go to a library. Searching for "property tax" and "abatement" in the ProQuest database, I found some excellent articles detailing the experiences of Syracuse, New York, and Dayton, Ohio, with regard to tax rebates for property improvements.[8] If you are interested in publications from the top social science journals, you should search JSTOR. You may also find many other excellent articles in the area of your interest in various other databases. I discuss a few of these later in these pages. However,

I should mention that accessing these databases can be an expensive proposition, since the information is proprietary. However, if your university has paid the required fees, you may be able to access these datebases as a student.

For public policy analysts, perhaps the best sources of secondary data are U.S. government publications (see "A Case in Point"). Appendix A includes an example of one of these publications—a report conducted by the U.S. Government Accountability Office (GAO) on the state of poverty in America. Government agencies in the United States are inveterate collectors of statistical information. Furthermore, most government organizations are part of this enormous information-sharing network. Although a multitude of extensive databases are available and new ones are being created, I mention a few important ones at this point:

- CIAO (Columbia International Affairs Online) (www.ciaonet.org) is an excellent source of policy-related papers. In addition to a number of scholarly journals, it provides policy briefs and working papers from a large number of think tanks and research institutes.
- EBSCOhost Academic Search Elite (www.ebscohost.com) provides access to a large number of journal articles from various academic disciplines. It covers more than 1,200 periodicals starting around 1990.
- LexisNexis Academic (www.lexisnexis.com/us/lnacademic/) allows you to retrieve full-text versions of national and international news articles. Its coverage generally starts from the late 1980s.
- ProQuest Research Library (www.proquest.com/en-US/catalogs/databases/detail/pq_research_library.shtml) is one of the most comprehensive sources of scholarly articles. Its core research module covers traditional academic journals and is supplemented by subject-specific modules, such as Arts, Education, Humanities, and International and Multicultural Studies. Coverage begins in 1986.
- PAIS International (Public Affairs Information Service) (www.csa.com/factsheets/pais-set-c.php) is also one of the most comprehensive data sources, containing an index to journal articles. This database is particularly important to us because of its primary focus on public policy. Its coverage starts in 1972.
- JSTOR (www.jstor.org) provides access to full-text scholarly journals in the humanities, sciences, and social sciences and some in the natural sciences and population studies. This database provides full texts of published articles in the most prestigious scholarly journals in the fields of social science, demography, environmental sciences, and statistics.

Having gone through the relevant literature, you are now ready to collect numerical data on your topic. You should start with the annual *Statistical Abstract of the United States*, the annual *Economic Report of the President*, the *Handbook of Labor Statistics*, and the *U.S. Census Bureau Catalog and Guide*. Several excellent publications provide state and local government data; the *Census of Governments*, the *County and City Data Book*, the *County Yearbook*, and the *Municipal Yearbook* are a few of them. There are also excellent sources for international data. However, international data are often not comparable, as different governments use different criteria for classifying information, which makes cross-national comparisons problematic. Nevertheless, a number of large international agencies compile information cross-nationally. For example, if you are interested in basic economic, political, and demographic information, you may start

A CASE IN POINT

Politics and Government Statistics

When we use data from U.S. government publications, from census figures to the rate of inflation, we tend to take their objectivity for granted. Yet, like many activities of government, its data collection is not completely free of political considerations. William Alonso and Paul Starr point out that "official statistics do not merely hold a mirror to reality. They reflect presuppositions and theories about the nature of society. . . . Political judgments are implicit in the choice of what to measure, how to measure it, and how to present and interpret the results."[9] This political intrusion can cause serious public policy implications in the collection and interpretation of the data.

Stephen Feingold provides a vivid example of how politics affected the effort of the Centers for Disease Control and Prevention (CDC) to collect data on AIDS.[10] The problem of defining the disease with precision complicated the collection of data. A relatively large number of people carry the human retrovirus known as HIV. Of those who do carry it, only a small portion actually develops AIDS-related complex, and a much smaller proportion of this group actually develops full-blown AIDS. The population groups with the highest incidence of AIDS are homosexual men, intravenous drug users (and their children), and hemophiliacs.

In the 1980s, data on the spread of AIDS were based on an antiquated system of counting that used a much more stringent definition of the disease. Because of its political position that the spread of AIDS was not a serious matter for most Americans, the administration of Ronald Reagan was reluctant to allocate money for a more complete survey.[11] Further complicating the matter was the conflict between the measurement issue and both the government's "war on drugs" and a general prejudice against homosexuals. When the CDC proposed an intensive national survey for an accurate count, Senator Jesse Helms, R-N.C., argued that it was not intended to stop the spread of AIDS but to provide evidence that homosexuality was "just another normal lifestyle." In the end, the survey was conducted in 1992, funded by private donations. When the results came out, much to the surprise of the scientific community, the threat of a rapid spread of the dreaded disease was found to be a lot less than expected.

Discussion Points

1. Discuss how politics can influence data gathering by even the most trusted government agencies.
2. As a policy analyst, how can you guard against biases in the information used in your analysis?

with the Central Intelligence Agency's *World Factbook* (https://www.cia.gov/library/publications/the-world-factbook/). You may also consult the World Bank (www.worldbank.org), the *United Nations Statistical Yearbook* (http://unstats.un.org/unsd/syb/), the *International Trade Statistics Yearbook* (http://unstats.un.org/unsd/trade/default.htm), and the United Nations National Accounts Statistics (http://unstats.un.org/unsd/snaama/Introduction.asp).

A CASE IN POINT

The Politics of Data Collection: The Case of Terrorism Research

In the ideal policy world, hypotheses are tested with empirical evidence. By analyzing data, we either accept or reject hypotheses and project the future outcomes of various alternatives. For instance, when Congress proposes a new tax, it can ask the Congressional Budget Office (CBO) to project the impact of the tax on the economy. The CBO uses readily available, detailed macro-economic data in its statistical models to get the required answers. However, in many other areas of policy analysis, our research agendas can be significantly hamstrung by the paucity of empirical information. As a result, policymakers may be forced to make decisions on the basis of educated guesses, conjectures, or simply conventional wisdom. Because of the "tyranny of data," the availability of statistical information can influence the research agenda.

At the height of the Cold War, when the United States was worried about the causes of open hostilities between nations—notably, between the two superpowers—funding started to flow to research projects on wars. University of Michigan political scientist David Singer and historian Melvin Small began collecting data on wars under the title Correlates of War.[12] The emphasis shifted in the late 1960s, when the United States and Western Europe were rocked by acts of political violence by disgruntled youth. This new reality forced the government to sponsor data collection on a different kind of social conflict. Many of these data sets were published, but they were collected at the national level, so they did not offer researchers a finer grain to analyze violence at regional levels or by groups.[13] However, as the riots, assassinations, and coups d'état that rocked the world in the 1960s and early 1970s subsided, the funding for these data collection efforts quickly dried up.

The availability of data was altered once again after a huge truck bomb devastated the Alfred P. Murrah Federal Building in Oklahoma City in 1995, taking 168 lives in the process. The bomber turned out to be homegrown: a decorated former U.S. army soldier, Timothy McVeigh. In response, a nonprofit organization, the Memorial Institute for the Prevention of Terrorism (MIPT), was established (it later received help from the U.S. Department of Homeland Security) and began collecting and posting terrorism data on its Web site. The MIPT's data sets were managed by the RAND Corporation, but after several years, its funding became depleted, and the RAND Corporation took them off the Web.

In addition to these vast amounts of economic, political, and social information, a huge array of data on attitudes and opinions are available. The Institute for Social Research at the University of Michigan collects and compiles data on many aspects of social, political, and psychological attitudes.

Finally, if your research project involves a particular government agency, the agency's annual budget reports can supply a great deal of information. The agency may collect for its own internal use a good deal of information that may not be available in a ready-to-use form. However, you may be able to make effective use of these pieces of

Horrific attacks by the members of a small group who plotted from the dusty caves of Afghanistan shocked the United States on a September morning in 2001. Stunned, politicians, pundits, and the general public started groping for answers about why it happened and how to prevent future attacks. Those who endeavored to find answers, however, found themselves in a quandary caused by the lack of reliable data on the subject. As a result, everyone came up with his or her own theory. President George W. Bush proclaimed that "they hate us for our freedom." Others, notably in the liberal camp, assumed that poverty caused these men to hate Americans more than they loved their own lives. As a startled nation woke up to the freshly realized threat, there were calls for better collection of data.

This call spurred a debate over who should collect data on terrorism. Terrorism data are collected by governmental agencies such as the U.S. State Department, intelligence agencies, for-profit groups, think tanks, and university-affiliated entities. But because *terrorism* is an intensely political term and defies a single definition, any agency that collects data will be suspected of injecting its own ideological orientation into it.[14] The State Department, for instance, was roundly criticized for politicizing the data that it started to report soon after the 9/11 attacks.[15] As a result, it stopped publishing data. The intelligence agencies in every country collect data, but they are classified and therefore not open to scrutiny by the scholarly community. For-profit organizations, such as ITERATE (International Terrorism: Attributes of Terrorist Events), offer information—sometimes at a stiff price—to private firms, academic institutions, and individual researchers.[16] Since terrorism is a social phenomenon, its wide analysis and understanding is crucial for constructive policy debates. Therefore, the Department of Homeland Security established the National Consortium for the Study of Terrorism and Responses to Terror (START), located at the University of Maryland. Funded by the U.S. government and supervised by independent scholars, START offers the best source of information on global terrorism. Yet in recalling the history of government funding, it is conceivable that if there are no sensational terrorist attacks directed at the United States, this worthwhile effort may also be abandoned as public attention shifts elsewhere.

Discussion Points

1. Why is it important to know who should collect data on terrorism?
2. How can we ensure objectivity in data collection?
3. How do sensational events affect how data are collected?

information by arranging them in a proper way. Most of these sources are open to public use and are available on the agnecies' Web sites. If you are looking for national-level or local-level data, you may consult the following resources:

- The *Statistical Abstract of the United States* (www.census.gov/compendia/statab) provides a large number of national census data sets. It also contains most comprehensive data sets on state and local governments. For more detailed sets, you may have to purchase the CD-ROM.

- If you are interested in data on the Consumer Price Index and information related to labor, visit the Web site of the U.S. Bureau of Labor Statistics (www .bls.gov).
- If your library subscribes, you may also access the online data bank of STAT-USA. This data bank allows you to access daily economic news, frequently requested statistical releases, the National Trade Data Bank, the Economic Bulletin Board, and the U.S. Bureau of Economic Analysis.

Searching the Old-fashioned Way

If your library does not allow you to search electronically, the traditional, time-honored places to start are the published versions of the *PAIS Bulletin*, the *Social Sciences Citation Index*, or the *ABC Index of Political Science and Government*. If you are specifically interested in urban issues, there are selective publications, such as the *Index to Current Urban Documents*. Many specialized indexes for various areas of the social sciences, public policy, and planning are available, as are subject-specific abstracts of important articles in the fields of business, economics, education, law, political science, public administration, public policy, sociology, urban and regional planning, and so on.

Finally, for a thorough literature survey, you may also build on other students' accepted work. This is an often overlooked area of a literature search. Although most Ph.D. dissertations and master's theses are not formally published, upon their acceptance for degrees, they become public documents. Because the students who wrote them have already spent a great deal of time developing bibliographies, access to relevant theses or dissertations can be extremely useful to you as a researcher, especially if you are not familiar with the topic. Accepted dissertations and theses are available online from *Dissertation Abstracts/Digital Dissertations*, a proprietary database to which many libraries across the nation subscribe.

When Data Are Not Available

Having gone through numerous data sources, you might feel frustrated. The specific information you are looking for does not seem to exist anywhere. It may be that your topic is too specific. Or it may be that for political or cultural reasons, such data have not been collected (see "A Case in Point"). You may not find time-series data on the homeless population in your city because the subject is too specific and no agency is currently collecting the information. In some cases, the data for a few crucial years may be missing from an otherwise complete series. Or, suppose you are interested in estimating the possible effect of a new convention center on your city's economy. You will not find much information, because the convention center has not yet been built. Suppose you are looking for data on smoking-related deaths on a cross-national basis. It may be that because of a lack of awareness, such data have not been collected for many countries around the world.

In such cases, your job becomes tenuous. You may consider inferring the data. That is, if you can find a comparable city with a similar demographic, cultural, and economic background, you may draw a parallel. These kinds of inferences are often permissible when no data are available. However, if you must have a series prepared through inference or interpolation, you must make absolutely clear to the reader the nature of your data and the procedure by which they were obtained.

KEY WORDS

Cluster sampling (p. 186)
Focus groups (p. 190)
Interval scale (p. 178)
Judgmental method of sampling (p. 185)
Likert scales (p. 190)
Nominal scale (p. 177)
Objective sampling (p. 185)
Ordinal scale (p. 178)
Population (p. 180)
Primary data (p. 177)

Probability-based sampling (p. 185)
Pyramiding citations (p. 193)
Random sampling (p. 185)
Ratio scale (p. 178)
Revealed preference (p. 184)
Sample population (p. 180)
Survey design (p. 180)
Sampling biases (p. 180)
Secondary data (p. 177)
Stratified sampling (p. 186)

EXERCISES

1. There are many different ways to collect data on and measure poverty. The GAO report on poverty in America in Appendix A provides some examples of different measures. Why do you think the GAO analysts chose to use these measures? How did they go about collecting data? Why is it difficult to devise a universally acceptable measure for poverty?

2. What are primary and secondary data? Discuss the various scales of data. What are their relative strengths and weaknesses? What are their respective uses?

3. The city of Masters (population 150,000) wants to enlarge its airport to accommodate a growing need for a small commuter airline landing. The city wants to conduct a survey to assess public opinion on possible locations for the landing. Specifically, the city wants to know who would support and who would oppose such an expansion effort in certain already identified sites. The survey must be completed within three months. Design a survey, specifying the sampling method (random, stratified, and so forth), the number of people to be surveyed, questions to be asked, and the mode of interview.

4. Write a short essay on the biases of sampling. Collect information from the real world to elaborate on your points.

5. Consider the following three scenarios and give your recommendation regarding which type of sampling method (random, stratified, or cluster) or focus group to use.
   a. The mass transit department in your city is considering a rate hike. Before it makes the final decision, it wants to learn more about the possible effects of such a hike on its customers.
   b. The professional football team in your city is threatening to move to a different city unless yours is willing to spend many millions of dollars to expand and renovate the existing stadium. The city council wants to know the opinion of its citizens.
   c. Your town is concerned about the scarcity of low-income housing. It is considering a new subsidy program that has been found to be effective in a different town of similar size. Your job is to design a survey to determine the effectiveness of the proposed program.

6. Suppose your town has received federal funding for educating the target population about sexually transmitted diseases. Your department has decided to conduct a survey. In an essay, discuss the problems you might face in obtaining a correct picture of the problem.

7. What are the advantages and disadvantages of conducting focus group research over a traditional survey design? Provide specific examples in which a survey would be more appropriate than a focus group and vice versa.

8. Consider an important issue facing your community. If you were to conduct a focus group, what steps would you take and what sorts of questions would you ask? Where would you meet?

9. Write a short essay on information gathering from the Internet. How would you ensure the credibility of the information?

10. Think of an appropriate focus group or survey design for your community. How would you estimate its cost?

11. Consider an important public policy issue. Prepare a bibliography and gather data through a Web search. If it is a controversial issue, such as gun control or abortion rights, rank the sites mentioned in your paper according to their reliability.

Notes

1. Professor Ted Gurr (Polity II database, Inter-University Consortium for Political and Social Research) quantified the degree of "democratization" of countries. Among several others, I have developed indexes of political instability. See Dipak K. Gupta, *The Economics of Political Violence: The Effect of Political Instability on Economic Growth* (New York: Praeger, 1990).

2. James Gleick, *Chaos: Making a New Science* (New York: Viking, 1987).

3. For a review of the implications of the Hawthorne experiment, see J. H. Smith, "The Enduring Legacy of Elton Mayo," *Human Relations* 51 (1998): 221–250.

4. Stanley Milgram, *Obedience to Authority: An Experimental View* (New York: Harper & Row, 1974).

5. For a detailed discussion of the human proclivity towards obedience to authority figures, see Dipak K. Gupta, *Path to Collective Madness: A Study in Social Order and Political Pathology* (New York: Greenwood, 2001).

6. *Los Angeles Times*, August 16, 1992, A6.

7. Stuart Meck, "Growing Smart: Initiatives and Applications—Palm Beach County Managed Growth Program," *Planning*, April 2000, 3–5.

8. On Syracuse, see William P. Barrett, "Willis Carrier's Ghost," *Forbes*, May 29, 2000; on Dayton, see Clifford A. Pearson, "Dayton Tackles Brownfields to Create Houses and Offices," *Architectural Record* 188 (June 2000).

9. William Alonso and Paul Starr, eds., *The Politics of Numbers* (New York: Russell Sage Foundation, 1987), 2.

10. Stephen E. Feingold, "Ethics, Objectivity, and Politics: Statistics in a Public Policy Perspective," in *Statistics and Public Policy*, ed. Bruce D. Spencer (Oxford, U.K.: Clarendon, 1997), 62–83.

11. Ibid., 76.

12. For a description, history, bibliography on related projects, and data, see the Web site of the Correlates of War Project at www.correlatesofwar.org/cowhistory.htm.

13. See Arthur S. Banks, *Cross-Polity Time-Series Data* (Cambridge, Mass.: MIT Press, 1971); Charles Lewis Taylor and Michael C. Hudson, *World Handbook of Political and Social Indicators*, 2d ed. (New Haven, Conn.: Yale University Press, 1972); and Charles Lewis Taylor and David A. Jodice, *Annual Events Data* (Ann Arbor, Mich.: University of Michigan, Interuniversity Consortium, 1982).

14. See Bruce Hoffman, *Inside Terrorism* (New York: Columbia University Press, 2006).

15. See Alan B. Krueger, "To Improve Terrorism Data, the U.S. Should Follow the Lead of Economic Statistics," *New York Times*, July 22, 2004; and Alan B. Kruger and David D. Laitin, "'Misunderestimating' Terrorism," *Foreign Affairs* 83 (September/October 2004): 5–8.

16. Duke University Libraries, "ITERATE—International Terrorism: Attributes of Terrorist Events," June 4, 2009, http://library.duke.edu/data/collections/iterate.html.

9 Making Sense of Numbers

Much of a busy executive's workday involves making decisions. These days executives find themselves increasingly surrounded by information, often expressed in numbers. The spectacular advances in technology have made collecting and storing information inexpensive and data retrieval and the display of their analyses quite simple. A large series of numbers, however, tends to numb our senses and push us beyond our cognitive capabilities. Therefore, decision makers prefer seeing large sets of numbers in an understandable form.

The purpose of this chapter is to provide students and practicing analysts with a guide for rendering social, political, or economic phenomena in graphs or tables. It is important to be creative without being misleading or deceptive. I will take you through some familiar terrain and expose you to the advantages and pitfalls of the most commonly used and abused methods of presenting numerical arguments to decision makers.

Descriptive statistics and graphical techniques are useful in assessing social conditions, such as per capita income, the rate of population growth, and crime rates. These techniques are often neglected in more sophisticated statistics and operations research textbooks because they seem too simplistic. However, an overwhelming number of decisions in both public and private organizations are made on the basis of simple decision rules: a brief assessment of relative desirability based on quick impressions rather than thorough research.

A PICTURE'S WORTH: GRAPHICAL METHODS OF ANALYSIS

Let us consider a hypothetical situation. Suppose the city manager of a medium-sized city, Masters, Pennsylvania, would like to know how much the city depends on state and federal grants. The financial management division of the city gives the city manager breakdowns of the city's state and federal grants for 2000 through 2009 (see Table 9.1).

TABLE 9.1	State and Federal Grants to Masters, Pennsylvania, in Current Dollars, 2000–2009

Year	State and federal grants in current $
2000	71,000
2001	75,000
2002	85,000
2003	89,000
2004	91,000
2005	91,500
2006	93,000
2007	95,000
2008	98,000
2009	102,000

Current versus Constant Dollars

The numbers in Table 9.1 indicate that state and federal funding for the city is growing every year. A better appreciation of the historical trend can be obtained by plotting the data. However, as you will soon discover, there is more than one way of drawing a picture.

Of course, the plotted information shown in Figure 9.1 is a great improvement over the table. The diagram clearly shows the generosity of the state and federal governments to the city. The dollar amounts of the grants have increased steadily over the years, with the greatest increases coming during the early 2000s. However, the city manager is skeptical; this diagram does not take into account the rate of inflation for the period. Therefore, the price deflator (the Consumer Price Index for the United States) was obtained for the period, and the yearly numbers were converted to constant dollars (see Table 9.2).

Time-series data require the conversion of current dollars into constant dollars because the value of money does not remain the same over time. The books that you purchased last year probably cost more today. Such increases make the value of money

TABLE 9.2	State and Federal Grants to Masters, Pennsylvania, in Current and Constant Dollars, 2000–2009

Year	State and federal grants in current $	Consumer Price Index[a]	State and federal grants in constant $
2000	71,000	100	71,000
2001	75,000	110	68,182
2002	85,000	117	72,650
2003	89,000	122	72,951
2004	91,000	127	71,654
2005	91,500	129	70,930
2006	93,000	137	67,883
2007	95,000	139	68,345
2008	98,000	143	68,531
2009	102,000	147	69,388

[a] The Consumer Price Index data are hypothetical.

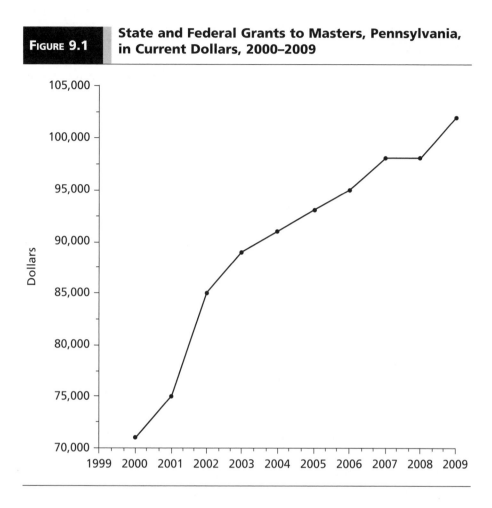

FIGURE 9.1 State and Federal Grants to Masters, Pennsylvania, in Current Dollars, 2000–2009

decrease with the passage of time. Therefore, in using the actual dollars received by Masters from the state and federal governments, we paint a deceptive picture. The rate at which the dollar loses its value is measured by a value known as a price index. In the United States, the Bureau of Labor Statistics (BLS) collects data on price changes and other employment-related information.[1] Price changes are measured in terms of a base year, which is expressed as a value of 100. For example, most of the current series in price indexes measured by the BLS hold the period from 1982 to 1984 as 100.

A price index is calculated on the basis of what is known as **variable weight** or **fixed weight**. The variable-weight price index states price change as a ratio of a set of goods and services in the current period and their costs in the base year. More precisely, it is written as

$$\text{Variable}-\text{weight price index} = \frac{\text{Value of goods at current}-\text{year prices}}{\text{Value of those goods at base}-\text{year prices}}$$

The effects of price changes are, of course, not universal. If you do not like turnips, you are not affected if their prices go through the roof. However, if you practically live on turnips, your well-being will be affected. If you are making the same amount of money

TABLE 9.3	Consumer Price Index (CPI): All Urban Consumers, 1990–2008			
Year	CPI (1982–1984 = 100)	CPI (1990 as the base year)	Annual rate of inflation	Cumulative inflation rate since 1990
1990	130.7	100.0	—	—
1991	136.2	104.2	4.2	4.2
1992	140.3	107.3	3.1	7.3
1993	144.5	110.6	3.3	10.6
1994	148.4	113.4	2.8	13.4
1995	152.4	116.6	3.2	16.6
1996	156.9	120.1	3.5	20.1
1997	160.5	122.8	2.7	22.8
1998	163.0	124.7	1.9	24.7
1999	166.6	127.5	2.8	27.5
2000	172.2	131.8	4.3	31.8
2001	177.1	135.5	3.7	35.5
2002	179.9	137.6	2.1	37.6
2003	184.0	140.8	3.2	40.8
2004	188.9	144.5	3.7	44.5
2005	195.3	149.4	4.9	49.4
2006	201.6	154.3	4.9	54.3
2007	207.3	158.6	4.3	58.6
2008	215.3	164.7	6.1	64.7

as last year, you are poorer this year than you were before. Your income in current dollars is called your **nominal income**, and the true value of your reduced income is called your **real income** (meaning that it is adjusted for price change). You may note that the variable-weight price index takes an overall picture and does not consider whether the price changes will affect any single segment of the population. As a result, the most commonly used variable-weight price index is called the **GDP deflator**, which is used to compare the gross domestic product (GDP) of the past year with that of the current year.

In contrast, the fixed-weight price index considers a typical basket of goods that a consumer would consume and tracks its prices over the years. The fixed-weight price index is used to measure the **Consumer Price Index**, or the changes in prices that will affect a typical consumer. The BLS produces data series on the Consumer Price Index for various regional centers (urban, rural, a specific city, and so forth) as well as GDP deflators. For example, suppose you have job offers from two different cities. By comparing the price levels of the two, you can decide which one is offering you a higher salary in "real" dollars. In Table 9.3, I show the change in prices facing all urban consumers. From this table you can see that between 1990 and 2008, a dollar lost 64.7 percent of its value. That is, a dollar in 2008 was worth about 35 cents in 1990.

You can also calculate the amount of inflation by changing the base. For example, if you want to use 1990 as the base year, you can recalculate the series using the following formula:

$$\pi_{t+1} = \frac{P_{t+1} - P_t}{P_t} \times 100$$

$$(9.1)$$

| FIGURE 9.2 | State and Federal Grants to Masters, Pennsylvania, in Current and Constant Dollars, 2000–2009 |

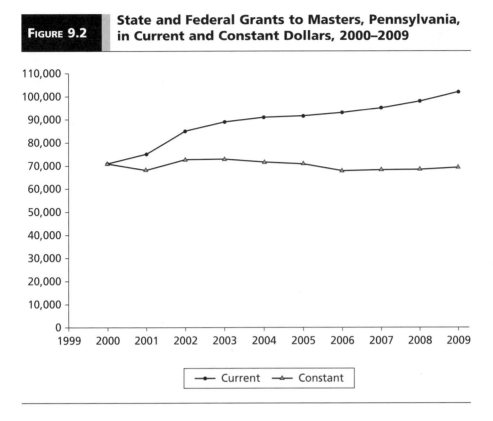

where π_{t+1} is the index of price change for year $t+1$, P_t is the Consumer Price Index for year t, and P_{t+1} is the Consumer Price Index for year $t+1$. The results are shown in Table 9.3 under the heading "Annual rate of inflation."

Looking again at the case of Masters, it is obvious from the calculation of constant dollar figures that the city is not doing as well with state and federal grants as was assumed. In fact, the inflationary forces in the early 2000s eroded so much of the purchasing power that they caused an actual decline in the grant money in **real terms** (see Figure 9.2).

As you can clearly see, we can get radically different conclusions each time we transform the data. You can further transform the data by comparing them with other variables, such as population or the size of the city budget; the data may also be compared with national or regional averages, or the series can be looked at by its rate of increase. In each case, the data will tell us a different story. In a sense, the data are like a kaleidoscope, in which you can see a completely different picture by slightly changing the angle of the device. Let us consider some other ways of looking at the same information.

We can expand the data presented in Table 9.2 to include information on total city revenue during the period of study. If we express the dollar amounts of grants received by the city as percentages of its total revenue, we will be comforted by the fact that we have done well over the years (see Table 9.4). We can be further comforted if we look at the national trend of the ratio of state and federal government assistance to cities as percentages of their total revenue. While external assistance to cities across the nation

TABLE 9.4	State and Federal Grants to Masters, Pennsylvania, as a Percentage of Revenue, 2000–2009			
Year	State and federal grants in current $	Total government revenue in current $	State and federal grants as a ratio of total government revenue	National average of grants as a percentage of local government revenue
2000	71,000	360,000	19.7	35.5
2001	75,000	369,000	20.3	32.3
2002	85,000	382,000	22.3	30.2
2003	89,000	385,000	23.1	26.8
2004	91,000	398,000	22.9	22.8
2005	91,500	410,000	22.3	21.5
2006	93,000	419,000	22.2	20.2
2007	95,000	425,000	22.4	20.3
2008	98,000	432,000	22.7	19.8
2009	102,000	444,000	23.0	19.5

was going down in the 2000s, our city held its ground and was doing better than the national average during the latter part of the decade (see Figure 9.3).

Each of these transformations tells a slightly different story. Through them we get glimpses of different facets of the situation. Therefore, the question is not which one is telling the "true" story but which one contains the most important message from the perspective of the inquirer.

Percentage Change

You may want to look at the information in yet another way. You may calculate the yearly percentage change in constant dollar grants to Masters. This information, presented in Table 9.5 and plotted in Figure 9.4, can be quite useful in discerning year-to-year changes in state and federal assistance to the city.

TABLE 9.5	Yearly Percentage Change in State and Federal Grants to Masters, Pennsylvania, in Constant Dollars, 2000–2009	
Year	State and federal grants in constant $	Yearly percentage change
2000	71,000	—
2001	68,182	−3.97
2002	72,650	6.55
2003	72,951	0.41
2004	71,654	−1.78
2005	70,930	−1.01
2006	67,883	−4.30
2007	68,345	0.68
2008	68,531	0.27
2009	69,388	1.25

FIGURE 9.3	State and Federal Grants to Masters, Pennsylvania, as a Percentage of Local Government Tax Revenue, 2000–2009

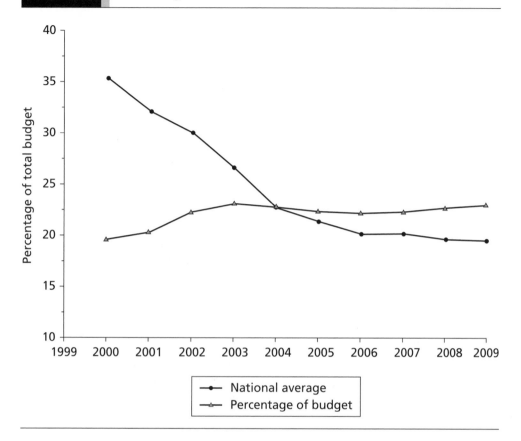

Creating an Index

Finally, it may be useful to look at the data with the help of an index. As noted earlier, an index is created when we take a particular figure as the **base** and then express the series in relation to this particular number. For example, if we take the grants figure for 1990 as the base (expressed as 100), we can calculate the index by dividing each year's data by this number and then multiplying it by 100. That is,

$$\text{Index for } 1991 = \frac{1991}{1990} \times 100$$

or

$$\frac{68,182}{71,000} \times 100 = 96.03$$

The data presented in Table 9.6 are plotted in Figure 9.5. As you can see, each presentation of the same information tells a slightly different story. Therefore, how you present your case will depend on your need.

FIGURE 9.4

Yearly Percentage Change in State and Federal Grants to Masters, Pennsylvania, in Constant Dollars, 2000–2009

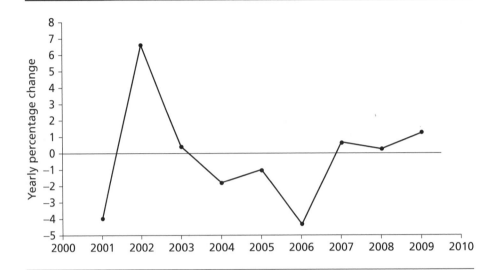

Choosing the Type of Graph to Use

In the previous examples we used only line graphs. Today's managers use a variety of graphs, such as **scatter plots**, **bar graphs**, and **pie charts**. Each kind of graph presents information in its own unique way. You should be familiar with each kind of graph and determine which kind of pictorial rendition gets your intended message across in the most effective way (see "A Case in Point").

TABLE 9.6

Index of State and Federal Grants to Masters, Pennsylvania, 2000–2009

Year	State and federal grants in constant $	Index (1990 = 100)
2000	71,000	100.00
2001	68,182	96.03
2002	72,650	102.32
2003	72,951	102.75
2004	71,654	100.92
2005	70,930	99.90
2006	67,883	95.61
2007	68,345	96.26
2008	68,531	96.52
2009	69,388	97.73

FIGURE 9.5

Yearly Percentage Change in State and Federal Grants to Masters, Pennsylvania, by Indexing, 2000–2009

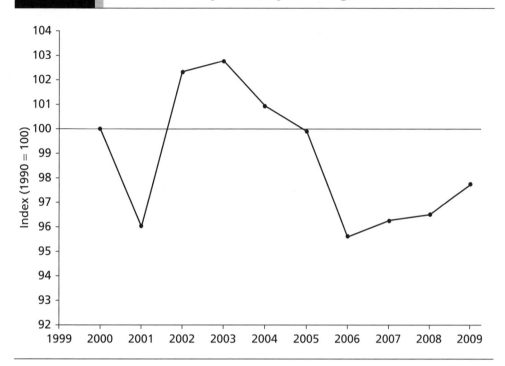

Specifically,

- Line graphs are used for time-series data.
- If you have cross-sectional data, you should use a bar diagram or a scatter plot.
- If the data are in fractions of a total (or in percentages), use a pie chart.

Graphical Methods in Decision Making

Graphical presentations describe a situation by visual means. However, they should not be considered passive tools of description; they can also be used as extremely powerful decision tools. Consider the following situation. The police department in Masters is trying to reach as many youngsters as possible to educate them about the perils of drug use. Last year the department expended considerable effort in arranging school appearances by officers and experts. It also advertised on local radio and television. Suppose that last year, the city spent $7,500 on school lectures, $13,000 on radio advertisements, and $20,000 on local television ads. A recent survey by the city showed that of the children who are aware of the city's drug prevention effort, 35 percent became aware of the issue through face-to-face contact with officers, 15 percent through radio ads, and the remaining 50 percent through watching television. In the two pie charts in Figure 9.6, I show the expenditure for each method of contact.

The side-by-side placement of these two diagrams visually demonstrates that face-to-face contacts are the most cost effective way to disseminate drug prevention

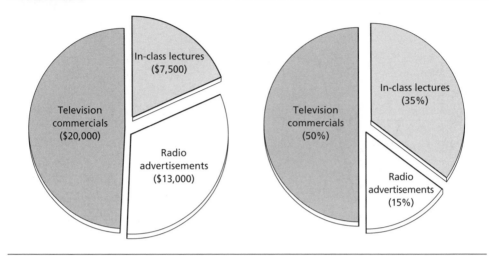

FIGURE 9.6 **Expenditures on a Drug Prevention Program in Masters, Pennsylvania**

information to school-age children. The same information could have been presented as simple percentages in a table. However, as is often the case, a picture is worth a thousand words. For another example of how diagrams may enhance presentation of data, see "A Case in Point."

A CASE IN POINT

Racial Profiling

Many minority drivers have protested racial profiling, a practice in which police stop nonwhite motorists and search their vehicles at a disproportionate rate. Mounting concerns about the practice from San Diego's minority population prompted the city's police department to conduct a study. The study covered more than 90,000 instances of police officers' stopping drivers between January and June 2000. The *San Diego Union-Tribune* published the data as pie charts (see charts below).[2]

The publication of these data created a big stir, particularly when they were presented visually in pie charts similar to the ones here. "We have known this for a long time," said an African American community leader regarding racial profiling. However, in support of police practices, San Diego police chief David Bejarano pointed out that although Latinos made up only about 20 percent of the city's drivers, because San Diego is a border town, a large number of motorists come from Mexico. Furthermore, he pointed out, the figures might be misleading, because police are often deployed in areas close to the border and other high-crime areas. Therefore, considering the entire city population does not allow for a valid comparison. A more detailed study would be required to control for the influence of these two external factors.

TO TELL THE TRUTH AND NOTHING BUT THE TRUTH

Over the years, statistics have been characterized in less than flattering ways. One of British prime minister Benjamin Disraeli's famous quips was "There are three kinds of lies: lies, damned lies, and statistics." We have come to accept expressions such as "statistical artifacts" and "cooked-up statistics." We must recognize that deception, misunderstood implication, or the existence of a bias in the process of collecting information can cause problems.

The deceptive use of numbers must be defined with respect to the intent of the user. Thus, an individual or organization that puts out information knowing full well that the data have no real-life validity is defrauding or deceiving the user. During times of national emergencies or war, government agencies routinely use data for propaganda purposes. A nation at war may exaggerate or downplay claims about its military or industrial strength, or its war casualties, depending on its strategy. China, in the course of suppressing the prodemocracy movement, underreported the number of student casualties and released figures that were widely disputed by such knowledgeable people and agencies as Chinese student groups in the United States and Amnesty International. Similarly, the figures for North Vietnamese war casualties were routinely inflated by Pentagon officials during the Vietnam War.

Another source of contention frequently centers on the "true" implication of a statistic. We often use per capita GDP as a measure of the relative economic development of nations. However, it is obvious that the word *development* used in a national context should imply more than a measure of a country's per capita GDP, because *development* implies a certain degree of progress and maturity in social, political, and economic

Comparison of Police Stopping, by Race

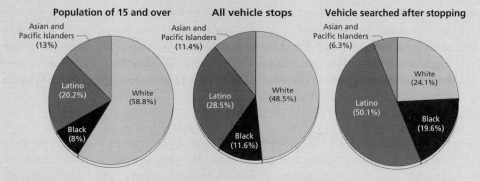

Discussion Points

1. How effective was the presentation of the data?
2. Can you think of a better way to present the information?
3. What are the points raised by Chief Bejarano? How would you respond to these points?

institutions. Tiny oil-rich nations may have the highest per capita GDPs, but one would be hard-pressed to characterize those countries as the most developed in the world.

Biases resulting from other factors may also cause a statistic to be misinterpreted. Valid questions have been raised about whether IQ tests measure relative levels of intelligence in children. For years, entrance to the U.S. Civil Service was based on one's score on a multiple-choice examination. However, it was eventually determined that such an examination was biased in favor of white, middle-class men. Therefore, the test score could not be accepted as the best measure of a candidate's suitability for a position.

Then there are data that, by their very nature, call for subjective judgment in how they are defined and compiled. A good example is the Consumer Price Index, discussed earlier in this chapter. As mentioned earlier, a "typical" basket of goods and services that an "average" American consumes yearly is used to measure the rate of inflation. However, we know that each of us has a unique consumption pattern, based not only on our individual tastes but also on various factors, such as age, income, race, and geographical location. If the price of skateboards goes up, senior citizens are less likely to be affected than are young people. Similarly, an increase in the cost of health care may not affect single young adults as much as the increase in the index would suggest. Whoever compiles this basket of goods thus faces two problems in making the index relevant to the majority of Americans. First, the compiler must discern what is "typical," in terms of what kinds of goods and services and at what levels of consumption. Errors that severely distort the data creep in during the collection of information in many ways; not recognizing this means that the results of analyses may be meaningless, misleading, or even damaging.

You must be extremely wary of accepting data for analysis, and you cannot be too careful in looking at possible sources of bias and errors. At the same time, remember that it is impossible to find a perfect set of data in an otherwise imperfect world. Like the proverbial fastidious eater who dies of starvation, a researcher who is too cautious will know all the flaws of the data and its analyses without being able to draw any useful conclusions from them.

The rule of thumb, then, is to evaluate carefully the sources of bias in the data and be aware of the cost of doing an incorrect analysis. If you are conducting medical research for a new type of vaccine as an antidote for a disease, or calculating trajectories for the reentry of a space shuttle into the earth's atmosphere, the margin of acceptable error is rather low. However, mercifully, in the areas of social science and public policy research, the demand for numerical accuracy may not be that extreme. It is most important to be aware of and open about the shortcomings of the data and the possible sources of bias in their analysis and interpretation.

Interpretation and Deception

The last source of skepticism to keep in mind is that to most people, numbers portray a rigid, self-evident truth. In a cocktail party discussion, a friend claimed that homosexuality was purely biological, since homosexuals seem to constitute 10 percent of every society's population. It is fairly obvious that this statement is the kind designed to end all discussions, as it purports to present a totally scientific, incontrovertible fact of life. To some people, numbers pose a threat because they have the appearance of "scientific" objectivity. However, closer scrutiny will reveal problems resulting from the various biases we have described, and a significant source of disagreement may be that any information (numerical or otherwise) about a complex social situation is bound to be open to interpretation.

In 1954 Darrell Huff wrote an extremely interesting, humorous book, *How to Lie with Statistics,* in which he systematically demonstrated many ways to distort information to suit the purposes of an investigator. In his tongue-in-cheek introduction he states,

> This book is a sort of primer in ways to use statistics to deceive. It may seem altogether too much like a manual for swindlers. Perhaps I can justify it in the manner of the retired burglar whose published reminiscences amounted to a graduate course in how to pick a lock and muffle a footfall: The crooks already know these tricks; honest men must learn them in self-defense.[3]

Huff's highly acclaimed book advanced understanding of the various ways one can use descriptive statistics among generations of undergraduate students. However, in all honesty, we may pose the question differently. If the manipulation of data is always suspected of "distorting" the picture, then there must be a truly undistorted version of real life. In other words, are we to assume the universality of truth? Does it always require a statistician to obfuscate an otherwise obvious situation? A famous early twentieth-century Japanese play *Rashomon,* by Ryunosuke Akutagawa, brings home the point of the relativity of perception. In the play a bandit rapes a young woman traveling with her samurai husband. A number of different individuals witness this terrible act of violence. When they are brought to the trial (including her deceased husband, who speaks through a medium), the incident is found to have variations of interpretation. As the play shows, there may be honest differences of opinion in the way one looks at a situation, even when expressed in "cold, hard, objective numbers." We live in a complex world in which "truth" may have more dimensions than can be effectively captured by any one-dimensional measure. However, if we use multiple indexes to characterize a situation, our cognitive limitations stand in the way of formulating any definitive picture. Like everything else in life, the quantification of social phenomena requires a trade-off between the confusion of a total picture and the clarity a limited view offers.

For example, consider our hypothetical city of Masters, Pennsylvania. The demographic composition of Masters is typical of the region, with a large number of working-class people, along with pockets of urban blight, characterized by persistent levels of high unemployment. However, a few areas of the city house extremely wealthy families. Let us focus on three individuals plying their trades in Masters: a real estate broker, a college professor, and a city planner. All three of these individuals want to present the "true" economic picture of this city with a single number: the average income of the city's people. However, these three have different objectives. The real estate broker wants to portray the city as a nice place to live and raise a family. Therefore, in talking to clients he mentions as "average" the mean income of the residents of the town. However, although small in number, the extremely wealthy households influence the mean. The prospective buyer gets a much rosier picture of the average affluence of the city than that espoused by the professor. The professor is conducting research in urban economics, for which he is using the figure of median income. The median, the middle income across the range from highest to lowest, presents a less attractive picture of the economic well-being of the city because it is not affected by the presence of the wealthy sector of the community. However, even this number is far superior to the one used by the city planner. The city planner of Masters wants to respond to a request for a grant proposal from

A CASE IN POINT

Digging Deep into the Numbers: A Stolen Election?

The 2000 presidential election looms large in the annals of modern American history. Many accused the Republican candidate, George W. Bush, of stealing the election from the Democrat, Al Gore. Others saw the results differently.

As the votes were tallied, in a neck-and-neck contest, Florida took on added prominence because the state's twenty-five electoral votes would determine the outcome of the election. Within the state of Florida, the voting of Palm Beach County residents generated an unexpected twist. In the 1992 presidential election, Ross Perot, the candidate of the newly founded Reform Party, drew a respectable number of votes, which many thought gave the presidency to Bill Clinton. In 2000 the Reform Party candidate was Patrick Buchanan. In Palm Beach County, the election commission approved a "butterfly" ballot, a double-faced ballot on which the names of the candidates appeared side by side. The name Al Gore was opposite that of Pat Buchanan, creating confusion among many Democratic voters. Many Gore supporters mistakenly voted for Buchanan instead. When the votes were tabulated, Buchanan had received about 3,400 votes.

Numbers of Votes Cast for Patrick Buchanan in the Florida Counties

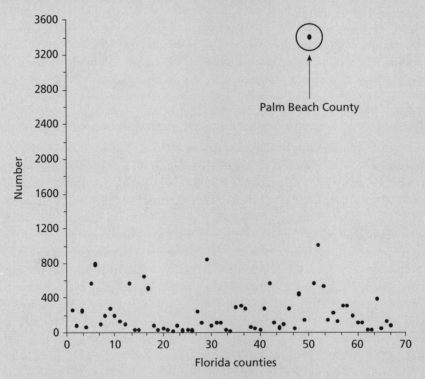

The graph above shows the number of votes garnered by Buchanan in Florida's sixty-seven counties, before they were hand counted, as a scatter diagram. As you can see, the numbers clearly show an unmistakable spike for Mr. Buchanan. The scatter plot clearly identifies those Palm

Beach Buchanan votes as an obvious outlier. However, in the social sciences, for every obvious solution, there is always a different angle. When we calculate the number of votes as a percentage of the total votes in each county, Palm Beach County's record does not appear so strange, as the figure below demonstrates. In fact, in terms of percentages, at least six small counties (Baker, Charlotte, Indian River, Liberty, Suwannee, and Washington) polled higher than did Palm Beach.

Percentages of Votes Cast for Patrick Buchanan in the Florida Counties

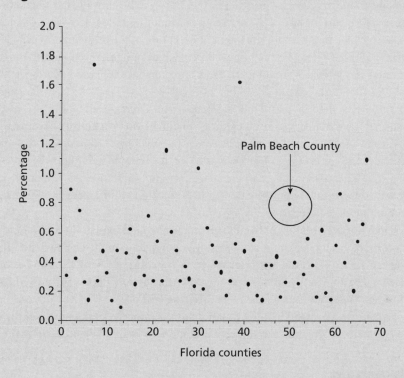

Discussion Points

1. The importance of the U.S. election cannot be overemphasized in terms of its impact on the world stage. In 2009, U.S. Secretary of State Hillary Rodham Clinton went to Pakistan and held a town hall–style meetings with university students. When Clinton pointed out the importance of having legitimate, democratically elected governments in Islamabad and Kabul, some students pointed to the controversial Florida election results as an example of imperfect democracy in the United States. Although there are many aspects to the truth, after reading this case, what conclusion can you derive about the legitimacy of the election in Florida?

2. What lesson can we derive from looking at the two scatter plots about having a healthy skepticism about any data set?

the state government to bring in money earmarked for the economically depressed areas. For this proposal, she uses the modal income of the town, which is the most frequently found income of its inhabitants.

Is it possible to pick out which of the three individuals, who use three different measures of average income because of their different objectives, is engaged in an act of deception? I would argue that none of them can be accused of such an act unless some other kind of deception is present. When it comes to the definition of "average," most people intuitively use the arithmetic mean, median, and mode, in that order. Therefore, by convention, if one uses the term *average* for the mean, one can feel justified. The use of the median may require justification, and the use of the modal income would certainly require its mention in the report, to be ethically fair and aboveboard. However, the use of any of these measures cannot be called deception. Therefore, we must conclude that without the intent of deception, none of the figures can be characterized as a lie. There can be honest difference of opinion, even among those whose business it is to deal with numbers, as to which one of these three represents the most valid picture of the city.

Another source of bias, Huff claimed, comes from the deceptive use of pictorial information—graphs. Because a picture is said to be worth a thousand words, the desire to convey information by graphical means is rather strong. But in the process one might take advantage of a certain trickery. Consider the example in Figure 9.7, which depicts nonwhite unemployment as a percentage ratio of white unemployment. In 1955 the unemployment rate within the nonwhite population was 62 percent higher than that within the white population.

Does this presentation of the information suit your needs, or do you want to portray more dramatically the plight of the minority population in the United States? If you do, you can s-t-r-e-t-c-h the graph for added visual effect, showing the same information (Figure 9.8). Obviously, in this case the difference between nonwhite and white unemployment is portrayed in a much more striking fashion.

What if you contend that the situation for the minority population is really not that bad, or that the situation has not changed appreciably over the years? In that case, you

---

FIGURE 9.7   **Ratio of Nonwhite to White Unemployment Rate**

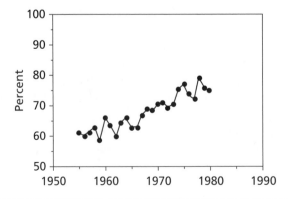

Source: U.S. Bureau of Labor Statistics.

FIGURE 9.8 | **Ratio of Nonwhite to White Unemployment Rate (stretched graph)**

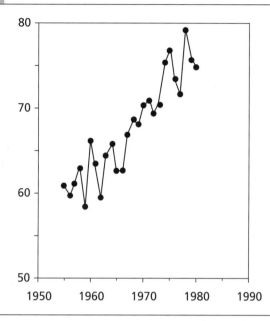

can use another trick. You can increase the range of the vertical axis, which allows you to present the same information in a different light. Against a much wider range of possible ratios of unemployment, the ethnic difference in the relative measure of economic deprivation does indeed look small (Figure 9.9).

Yet another effective way of representing a series is to use selective years for comparison. For example, you may want to present the same information contained in the three graphs, but even more emphatically. You may want to show them in either of the following ways without "lying" with your statistics. The two graphs in Figure 9.10 show only three years: 1960, 1970, and 1980. This restriction removes the distracting effects

FIGURE 9.9 | **Ratio of Nonwhite to White Unemployment Rate (elongated vertical axis)**

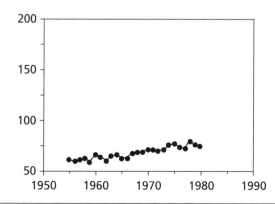

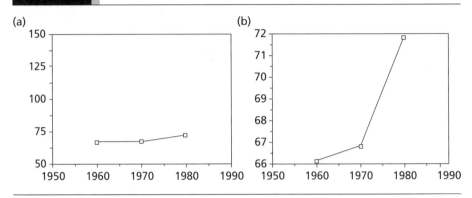

FIGURE **9.10**   **Ratio of Nonwhite to White Unemployment Rate (1960, 1970, and 1980)**

of yearly fluctuations and allows us to present long-term trends. Then, by simply manipulating the vertical axis, we have two radically different visual effects.

Now that I have shown you various ways of presenting the same information, which do you think represents the "true" picture? The answer is simple: we do not know which of these diagrams would be classified as a deceptive representation of the reality. However, Figures 9.9 and 9.10 (a) might be interpreted as edging toward questionable practices, since the vertical axes in those figures have wider ranges than required by the data. But would you call that lying? In real life, truth, like beauty, is in the eye of the beholder.

In the preceding examples, the difference between interpreting and deceiving might have been subtle, but consider the rendition of the same information in Figure 9.11.

FIGURE **9.11**   **Ratio of Nonwhite to White Unemployment Rate (1960, 1970, and 1980; shortened vertical axis)**

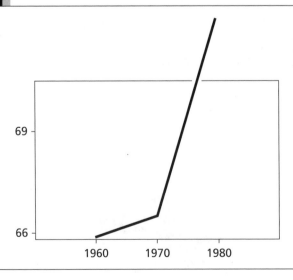

FIGURE 9.12   **African Elephant Population, 1980–1990**

60,000   20,000

| 1980 | 1990 |

In this diagram, you are not only presenting facts but also trying to make a rather loud statement with the obvious analogy of the ratio going through the roof.

Huff pointed out that, intended or unintended, deception may creep in more readily when one uses graphics instead of lines and bars, which are drawn according to scale. Consider a diagram showing the plight of African elephants (Figure 9.12). It is shocking to realize that in ten years the elephant population has diminished to one-third of its 1980 size. Although the numbers themselves speak volumes about the plight of the hapless pachyderms in Africa, the pictures in the figure are not drawn according to scale. We catch the relative size difference in the picture more readily than the difference in magnitude between the numbers, but we may not be able to catch that the 1980 drawing is much more than three times the size of the 1990 drawing. These kinds of disproportionate pictorial renditions are popular with those who present data at legislative hearings and in administrative decision-making sessions because the message is direct and dramatic. With computer graphics so easy to use, the possibility of some creative minds' deceiving the unwary has never been greater.

The power of strong visual presentation is well recognized and well documented. A 1985 *Wall Street Journal* story documents how the use of such a tool helped Caspar Weinberger, then secretary of defense, avert a cut in the Pentagon budget by David Stockman, director of the Office of Management and Budget:

> In staving off Mr. Stockman's assault on the planned buildup, Mr. Weinberger turned to a tactic for which he has since become famous, the chart and easel. The defense secretary's charts, presented in a meeting with President Ronald Reagan, showed large soldiers bearing large weapons, which were labeled "Reagan budget." They towered above small soldiers with small weapons labeled "OMB budget." President Reagan went along with the "Reagan budget."[4]

Tabular Presentation of Data

A long series of numbers pushes us to the limits of our cognitive capacities. For that reason, the value of an effective table as a means of communication cannot be overstated. Presenting data in useful tabular form is an art, which can be perfected only through practice.

TABLE 9.7			Spending by Function and Level of Government, 1995					
	Spending by level of government (in million $)			PS	Percentage of spending by level of government			
Function	Federal	State	Local	(percentage)	Federal	State	Local	Total
Defense	327,231	—	—	9.60	100.00	—	—	100.00
Education	27,270	101,510	276,763	12.10	6.72	25.03	68.25	100.00
Highways	731	48,893	30,216	2.38	0.92	61.24	37.85	100.00
Welfare	57,246	160,421	32,669	7.47	22.87	64.08	13.05	100.00
Police	7,563	5,735	52,329	1.96	11.52	8.74	79.74	100.00
Health	26,517	49,487	56,460	3.95	20.02	37.36	42.62	100.00
Administration	19,416	24,781	35,237	2.37	24.44	31.20	44.36	100.00
Insurance	558,291	93,692	13,648	19.86	83.87	14.08	2.05	100.00
Other	680,857	402,563	262,046	39.93	50.60	29.92	19.48	100.00
Total	1,705,122	887,082	759,368	100.00	50.88	26.47	22.66	100.00

Sources: U.S. Department of Commerce, Census Bureau, and The Tax Foundation (Washington, D.C.).

Notes: PS = percentage of total public spending. Some percentages may not add up to 100 percent because of rounding.

The preparation of an effective table requires considerable thought and time (and therefore money). First, have a clear idea of exactly what you want to communicate to the reader. Second, choose a title that succinctly describes the contents of the table. Third, consider various ways of presenting the raw data so that they make the point you want to make most effectively.

For a table to be useful, its purpose must be absolutely clear from its title. The title should be concise but not so brief that it does not convey the true intent of your presentation. The numbers, taken together, must tell a coherent story. Consider, for example, Table 9.7. You may notice how much information has been packed into a concise table. You can find out from the table how much money the government spent on selected items in 1995. During that fiscal year, education accounted for 12.10 percent of all public spending, and local governments paid the bulk (68.25 percent) of education costs. The table also tells you that the federal government originated half (50.88 percent) of total government spending.

In my discussion of graphical presentation, I have shown you how to look at a data set from different perspectives. Similarly, before preparing a table, you may draw interesting conclusions by using absolute numbers, ratios, percentages, and so on.

THOSE NOT-SO-INNOCENT NUMBERS

It is relatively easy to define outright deception or lying by the measure of intent and the sheer fabrication of data, but the line between deception and differences in interpretation is murky. Often the intentions of presenters are not obvious; nor are we capable of detecting purposeful contamination of data. Because we tend to believe in the objectivity of numerical information more readily than in the subjectivity of qualitative statements, the deceptive use of statistics can bring incredible misery to people.

In 1896 Frederick L. Hoffman, a nationally famous statistician for the Prudential Insurance Company of America, wrote a book titled *Race Traits and Tendencies of the American Negro*. Hoffman's thesis was that since emancipation, African Americans (having left the protective care of their slave owners) had gone back to their "basic racial trait" of "immorality of character." Hoffman based his theory on a number of different statistics he had collected. He noted that in 1890, there were 567 blacks in prison for rape, which constituted 47 percent of the prison population convicted on rape charges. Because this number was significantly greater than the proportion of the African American population (about 10 percent at the time), according to Hoffman, rape and other sexual crimes were reflective of the "Negro racial trait." Hoffman thus concluded that

> all the facts brought together in this work prove that the colored population is gradually parting with the virtues and the moderate degree of economic efficiency developed under the regime of slavery. All the facts prove that a low standard of sexual morality is the main and underlying cause of the low and anti-social condition of the race at the present time.[5]

Hoffman then connected the "Negro racial trait of immorality" to the high mortality rate among the black population. On the basis of this causal linkage, disregarding the fact that the census of 1890 showed a steady increase in the size of the black population, Hoffman predicted that African Americans were doomed to face a "gradual extinction of the race." The name of Hoffman's publisher, the American Economic Association, added a dose of respectability to this statistical study, which was widely used as a weapon in promoting white supremacy for decades to come. However, another important consequence of this and other internal statistical studies was that Prudential judged African Americans to be bad actuarial risks and promptly started to cancel all African American life insurance policies. Within four years, by the end of the century, most insurance companies had gotten out of the business of insuring African Americans.[6] In a similar manner, statistics have been used over the years to perpetrate many kinds of heinous crimes, or their faulty uses have led to extremely inefficient public policies.[7]

Key Words

Bar graphs (p. 210)

Base (p. 209)

Consumer Price Index (p. 206)

Fixed weight (p. 205)

GDP deflator (p. 206)

Nominal income (p. 206)

Pie charts (p. 210)

Real income (p. 206)

Real terms (p. 207)

Scatter plots (p. 210)

Variable weight (p. 205)

Exercises

1. Write an essay on truth and objectivity in quantitative analysis for public policy. Within this context, describe the relative advantages and disadvantages of the various measures of central tendency and dispersion. Provide appropriate examples.

2. After reviewing the U.S. Government Accountability Office report on poverty in Appendix A, consider the yearly poverty rate as measured by the U.S. Census Bureau

from 1959 (see www.census.gov/hhes/www/poverty/histpov/hstpov2.html). Plot the data and examine the trend. Suppose you are an antipoverty advocate; is there any way you can present the information to show that the situation is worsening? On the other hand, suppose you are an ardent proponent of the free market. Can you use the same series and show that the poverty rate is either unchanged or heading downward?

3. Collect data on the growth rate of per capita GDP, the rate of inflation, and unemployment from 1950 (consult the *Economic Report of the President* and the *Statistical Abstract of the United States*). First make the case that the nation has been better served by Republican presidents, and then make the case for the Democrats on the basis of the same set of data.

4. Look at some recent news reports presented with quantitative data. See if you can derive a different conclusion from the same information.

Notes

1. You can access data collected by the BLS at its Web site, http://stats.bls.gov.
2. Mark Arner and Joe Hughes, "Police Stop Blacks, Latinos More Often: Data from Profiling Report Echo Fears of S.D. Minorities," *San Diego Union-Tribune*, September 29, 2000.
3. Darrell Huff, *How to Lie with Statistics* (New York: W. W. Norton, 1954), 9.
4. Tim Corrigan, "Weinberger Finds His Well-worn Strategies Always Succeed in Blunting Defense Budget Axe," *Wall Street Journal*, March 1, 1985.
5. Frederick L. Hoffman, *Race Traits and Tendencies of the American Negro* (New York: Macmillan, 1896), quoted in Joel Williamson, *The Crucible of Race: Black/White Relations in the American South Since Emancipation* (New York: Oxford University Press, 1984), 329.
6. For a detailed discussion, see Williamson, *The Crucible of Race*.
7. For an excellent discussion of measuring people's abilities with numbers, see Stephen Jay Gould, *The Mismeasure of Man* (New York: Norton, 1981).

10 Projection Techniques: When History Is Inadequate

PROJECTION VERSUS CAUSAL PREDICTION

One of the most important of an organization's functions is planning for the future. How would you begin the process? It is not merely a cliché that it is impossible to predict the future without knowledge of the past. In history we look for **trends** and the **causal connections** that offer explanations for the events at hand. We may call the analysis of trends **projection**. In contrast, **prediction** is an inquiry into the causal relationship that binds the variable to be explained (the **dependent variable**) to a set of variables (the **independent variables**) that purport to explain it.

We call trend analysis "projection" because it contains an underlying hypothesis that whatever factor(s) set in motion a past pattern of change will continue to operate in the future, leading to the same rate of growth or the same pattern of behavior. This postulation, called the **assumption of continuity**, is the underlying premise of all forecasting methods. In using projection techniques we aim to find a past trend and project it into the future. Of course, forecasting on the basis of past trends raises the philosophical question of whether history really repeats itself. Without getting embroiled in this age-old controversy, we can safely point out that because progress in the realm of the social sciences is mostly evolutionary and incremental, the study of any long socioeconomic series would point to the existence of some sort of trend pattern.

With causal analysis, in contrast, we hypothesize that the future development of the dependent variable is not related to its past trend (at least not to any significant extent), and therefore, a past pattern cannot solely predict future behavior. Instead, it is determined by a complex causal linkage between the dependent variable and a set of independent variables.

An example may clarify the difference. If we want to know the extent of future health care needs, we can look at past trends and see that health care costs increased by a certain percentage every year and then forecast that in five years, we will need a corresponding amount of money to meet health care needs. Or we may look at various explanatory factors, such as the percentages of children and elderly in the population, expenditures on preventive medicine, trends related to food and nutrition, education levels, or the rate of income growth. Then, by developing a model in which all these factors influence the outcome, we can attempt to forecast future health care costs (see Figure 10.1).

Both projection and prediction methods have their relative advantages and drawbacks. Projection methods often turn out to be easier to use for forecasting—particularly for short-term "policy prescription"—because these models require data points of a single series to calculate the trend. In contrast, causal models require a thorough understanding of the causal linkages between a dependent variable (outcome) and a set of independent variables (causes). These types of models are better suited for policy research and for longer term forecasting. In general, when choosing an appropriate method of forecasting, you should consider the following points. You should choose a trend analysis in preference to a causal model if

- the past trend is stable, which means not much has changed over time, at least in the short run;
- you do not have a good understanding of the causal factors explaining the dependent variable; or
- you do not have a great deal of time and resources to conduct the appropriate research.

FIGURE 10.1   Trend Projection versus Causal Prediction

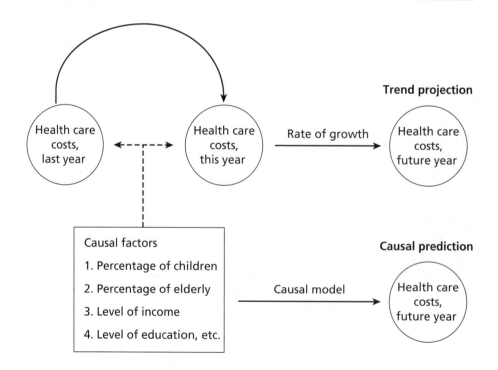

INADEQUACY OF HISTORY

If we want to forecast the future with the help of the past, we need a minimum amount of information from the past to provide us with any kind of meaningful insight into the future. Unfortunately, researchers and policy analysts often face the problem of inadequate past information. This inadequacy may result from (1) a lack of history itself, (2) a past lack of interest in collecting information, or (3) scattered past information whose compilation in a series would require too much time and money.

For example, if you are attempting to forecast population growth for a newly incorporated city, you do not have much of a history to fall back on. Or in an attempt to estimate the influx of tourists in a city, you may find out that such data exist for only the past two years or that no systematic effort to collect them has ever been made. Or you may discover that although various agencies have collected the data over a number of years, each has done so independently, without cooperating much with the others; as a result, the compilation of those data in one continuous series would require a great deal of resources. In such cases, you can still make a projection on the basis of one or two past data points, or none at all. For these kinds of cases, I discuss a number of techniques that can be classified under two broad headings: **single-factor projection** and **judgmental methods of projection**.

Single-Factor Projection

Suppose we are interested in projecting the number of cases of AIDS in our city, which was incorporated a couple of years ago. Our town has data on the number of AIDS victims for only the past two years. Last year, there were 150 reported cases, and the year before, there were 138 cases. Therefore, the rate of AIDS in our area increased by nearly 9 percent last year. On the basis of this information, we may project next year's infection rate by multiplying the number of this year's cases by 1.09. In symbolic terms, this can be written as

$$P_1 = (1 + r) \times P_0 \qquad (10.1)$$

where P_1 is the future year's population, r is the rate of population growth, and P_0 is the present year's population.

Using this formula, we can predict that if the current population of AIDS victims is 150, one year from now, this number will reach 150×1.09, which is equal to about 164. Using the same logic, we can see that the year after, this number will increase by another 9 percent. Thus, if P_2 is the population for the second year, then it can be estimated as

$$P_2 = (1 + r) \times P_1 \qquad (10.1a)$$

Since we know from equation 10.1 that P_1 is equal to $(1 + r) \times P_0$ we can substitute this expression for P_2 to obtain

$$P_2 = (1 + r) \times (1 + r) \times P_0$$

which means

$$P_2 = (1 + r)^2 \times P_0 \qquad (10.2)$$

Therefore, it is obvious that if the population grows at a constant rate, to estimate the second year's population we must multiply the current year's population by a factor of 1 plus the rate of growth to the power of 2. If the population keeps growing at this constant rate, in three years we can expect the number to reach the current year's population multiplied by a factor of 1 plus the rate of growth to the power of 3. Therefore, by generalizing this logic, we can write the formula as

$$P_n = (1 + r)^n \times P_0 \tag{10.3}$$

where n is any year in the future.

Thus, if we want to estimate the number of people who might be infected with the deadly virus ten years from now, we set the number of years equal to ten in the preceding equation ($n = 10$). Thus, we write equation 10.3 as

$$P_{10} = (1 + 0.09)^{10} \times P_0 \tag{10.4}$$

Using this formula, we can estimate that ten years from now, *if the present rate of infection continues*, we can expect to see 355 people infected.[1] This is the formula of geometric growth, which is also used to calculate compound interest rates. The use of this formula can make an analyst's task easy because the size of any future population can be estimated simply by substituting the appropriate numbers in equation 10.3.

For policy analysis, it is often important to know not only the point estimate of the number of cases n years in the future but also the total number of cases for the entire time span. To estimate the total number of people who will develop AIDS during the next ten years, we can estimate the size of the afflicted population for each year using equation 10.5 and then adding these values up. Since this process is cumbersome and time-consuming, we can estimate the sum of any geometric series using the following formula:

$$\sum_{n=1}^{k} P_n = \frac{(1 + r)^{n+1} - 1}{r} \times P_0 \tag{10.5}$$

Using this formula, we can estimate with a hand calculator the total number of patients needing treatment and public assistance to be nearly 2,634.[2] By multiplying this number by the current level of medical costs and public funding per patient, we can provide a rough-and-ready estimate of the total medical costs for these potential patients and the amount of money required in public assistance for the next ten years.

In the preceding example, we projected the future values of a variable on the basis of its past rate of growth. However, we can use many other factors as the basis of projections. For example, suppose a large parcel of vacant land is being considered for rezoning. The new zoning ordinance will allow residential housing, apartments, or commercial buildings. Analysts may use past information on land use patterns and their fiscal impact to project the future needs of the new community. By looking at the prices of the proposed residential units, planners can get a good idea about the economic capabilities of the newcomers. From the data of a larger city or a similar neighborhood, projections can be made for detailed demographic characteristics, such as the number of school-age children and elderly residents, commuting behavior, and recreational needs. If we expect 10,000 people to settle in the new neighborhood, by calculating the percentage for each demographic segment, we can project their numbers. These projections in turn would allow the projection of future resource needs for schools, libraries, recreational facilities, roads, sewer systems, and other necessary infrastructure. These data can also be used for projecting traffic congestion or crime rates.

Fiscal Impact Analysis

Suppose your town is considering a large residential development project. Since the building of new homes will create increased demands for public services and infrastructure, you would like to prepare the town for such a change. The housing development will create demands for new schools, health care facilities, shopping areas, new roads, sewage systems, energy, pollution control, public transportation, and police and fire protection. At the same time, it will create new employment and generate local taxes, such as those on property and sales. To plan for such extensive changes, you must forecast the impact of this new development. **Fiscal impact analysis** is particularly suited for these kinds of predictions.[3]

Let us explain this analysis with an example. A developer is planning to build 500 new single-family housing units, of which 40 percent will have two bedrooms, 35 percent will have three bedrooms, and the remaining 25 percent will have four bedrooms. The houses will sell for $90,000, $110,000, and $150,000, respectively. The demographic profile of your town indicates that on average, each two-bedroom house is expected to accommodate 2.354 occupants with 0.148 children. The figures for three- and four-bedroom units are 2.512 occupants with 0.614 children and 2.689 residents with 1.302 children. From this information, you can find the projected demographic profile for the newly developed community (see Table 10.1).

As you can see, using similar logic we can generate a wide range of forecasts, from employment and income generation to the need for additional police, fire, and city employees. The question then becomes, how do you get the necessary numbers

TABLE 10.1   **Projected Demographic Profile of New Community**

	No. of units	No. of residents	No. of children	Property tax revenue (at 1 percent of sales price)
Two-bedroom units	(500 × 0.40) 200	(200 × 2.354) 471	(200 × 0.148) 30	(200 × $900) $180,000
Three-bedroom units	(500 × 0.35) 175	(175 × 2.512) 440	(175 × 0.614) 107	(175 × $1,100) $192,500
Four-bedroom units	(500 × 0.25) 125	(125 × 2.689) 336	(125 × 1.302) 163	(125 × $1,500) $187,500
Total	500	1,247	300	$560,000

(the "multipliers") to estimate the future demand, revenues, and costs? There are several methods for getting these numbers:

- The **per capita multiplier method** is the most popular among all others for estimating the basis for future projection because it can be done quickly and relatively inexpensively. This method assumes that the resource utilization pattern of tomorrow will not be any different from today's. For example, to estimate the day care needs of a new community, we can look at the citywide estimate of the average number of children of appropriate age per household. Then, by multiplying that number by the number of new homes, we can calculate the expected number of children in the neighborhood. Since only a fraction of these children will require day care facilities, we can consult other sources for information on the average day care requirements of children from similar social and economic backgrounds. Moreover, using this method, we can estimate such diverse aspects as the number of cars, pollutant emissions, and traffic congestion. If the current average occupant of a three-bedroom house owns 1.98 cars, this pattern will remain unchanged in the next two years, when this hypothetical project is scheduled to be completed.

- The **case study method** involves interviewing municipal department heads, school administrators, and other experts in the field. The premise behind such a method is the assumption that these are the individuals who know the conditions best. Therefore, without the analyst's getting data on per capita resource consumption (as in the previous case), we can get the experts' assessments of the relevant multipliers.

- The **comparable city method** looks at an analogous project and can be used profitably as long as the two projects are similar in nature.

Problems of Single-Factor Analysis

The principal advantage of the methods discussed above is that they are relatively inexpensive and provide quick estimates of the future course of events. As a result, these techniques remain the most commonly used in the area of public sector analysis. We frequently come across estimates derived by these methods in policy debates about crime rates, population growth, and the number of drug addicts. The problem with such estimates is the implicit assumption that whatever happened during the previous period will continue unchanged. However, in life, relationships hardly remain unaltered over time. If we project the rate of AIDS growth in the United States on the basis of the past five years, we can see that there is already some empirical evidence to suggest that the disease's rate of growth may have slowed down, at least among some target groups, as a result of greater public awareness through education and media exposure. Therefore, the reality of the future may not turn out to be as dire as predicted by our method.

Figure 10.2 illustrates the predicaments of a single-factor projection. In Figure 10.2 (a) the two black dots represent two known points in history. On the basis of this meager knowledge, we are predicting the linear trend shown by the arrow. However, an infinite number of nonlinear trends can be drawn through two points. In Figure 10.2 (b), I have drawn two such nonlinear trends. If either of these is the actual trend, a projection based on a straight-line trend will cause serious errors. (For an example of how San Diego County used single-factor projection to estimate the cost of illegal immigration, see "A Case in Point.")

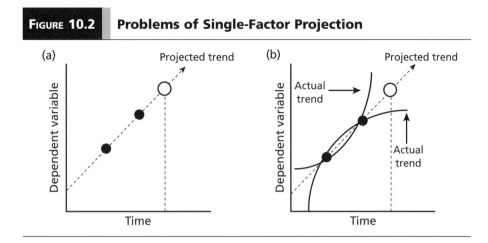

FIGURE 10.2   **Problems of Single-Factor Projection**

A CASE IN POINT

Single-Factor Analysis: The Fiscal Impact of Illegal Immigration in San Diego County

Because of the various problems associated with single-factor projections, they are always highly controversial. Yet when no reliable information is available, they can effectively serve as the starting points of policy debate and eventual policy formation. Since these techniques are extremely common in the public sector decision-making process, let me give you an example.[4]

Located on the border with Mexico, San Diego County faces the problem of large numbers of illegal immigrants, mostly from Mexico and Central American countries. Nearly all of these people are extremely poor, so the county must bear a great deal of the costs of health care, education, and law enforcement. In 1992 the state of California commissioned a study to estimate the number of illegal immigrants in San Diego County. However, the researchers faced the problem that nobody had any information on the number of illegal aliens. Therefore, they used some simple but imaginative methods. They estimated the number of illegal aliens by the following procedure.

During the twelve-month period ending September 30, 1991, the Immigration and Naturalization Service apprehended 540,300 undocumented immigrants in San Diego County. It has been estimated by the San Diego Border Patrol that between one in three and one in five undocumented immigrants are actually apprehended. This implies that 1,080,600 to 2,161,200 undocumented immigrants succeeded in entering San Diego County during the year.[5] The researchers estimated the cost to the state and county governments for the care of the illegal immigrants by calculating their proportion in the total population served by health care services, the education system, social services, and the criminal justice system, and then multiplying that number by the total expenditure. This was claimed to be the total cost to the state and local governments. Following a similar procedure, the researchers estimated the tax revenue contributions by the undocumented alien population of the region. The total net cost to the state and local governments was estimated to be $145,921,845.

Discussion Points

1. Why is the count of illegal immigrants problematic? How did this study use single-factor analysis to estimate the costs of illegal immigration to San Diego County?
2. Discuss the accuracy of the study's methodology. Can you suggest a better one instead?

JUDGMENTAL METHODS OF PROJECTION

Frequently in life we encounter situations in which forecasting cannot be performed in a structured way, either because of a lack of knowledge of the past or because the causal linkages are too complex to be quantified properly. In such cases forecasts must be based on special insights and intuition. Let us consider an example.

The passage of a piece of legislation through the U.S. political process is a highly complex affair. After it works its way through a maze of committees, it must pass both chambers of Congress. After its passage, if the president signs it, it becomes law. Disagreement between the House of Representatives and the Senate or a presidential veto can easily derail this process. However, it may be necessary to predict the future of a particular piece of legislation so that those with a stake in the matter can be prepared for a change in the course of action. Or consider the case of policymakers in the State Department who are waiting for a certain development to take place in a foreign country and want a reliable forecast of the situation. They must depend on forecasts based on the intuition or subjective judgment of experts. Out of this necessity, a good number of techniques have been developed to deal with these unstructured forecasting needs.

In the previous section, we attempted to estimate the spread of AIDS with the help of only two data points. We also saw the problems posed by such simple techniques. For example, one must consider the effects of increased awareness of the disease and the development of curative and prophylactic drugs. With such a complex issue, it is entirely possible that no single individual possesses all the necessary information to draw a realistic conclusion. We must depend on judgmental methods of projection based on the collective wisdom of experts. In the following sections I discuss a few of these methods.

The Delphi Technique

The name **Delphi technique** was coined after the famous oracle in Apollo's temple in the ancient Greek city of Delphi, where the oracle (in fact, the priests hiding behind it) used to forecast the future of the devotees. The Delphi technique is an important subjective predictive tool that was developed in 1948 by researchers at the RAND Corporation and since the mid-1950s has seen wide use in many countries around the world. Like most of the other techniques in the field of operations research, the Delphi technique owes its origins to attempts to solve problems of military strategy systematically.[6]

The Delphi technique brings a systematic, unbiased reasoning process into subjective group forecasting. We may form a panel of experts and let them sit around a table and come to an agreement about what may take place in the future. However, decisions made by a group may suffer from several sources of bias. If there is a well-known authority in the panel, the lesser members may become intimidated. If the rest of the panel is dispassionate about an issue, they may be swayed by one individual with a strong personality who approaches the issue with a particularly strong opinion. Also, research shows that most people are victims of **groupthink**.[7] That is, most of us loathe being the odd person out, with a different point of view from the rest of the group. As a result, more cogent points with differing points of view may never be raised in a group discussion.[8]

One way of solving this problem is to ask the experts to forecast independently. In this case, the problem of succumbing to groupthink will be averted, but if the experts have conflicting conclusions, we will have no way of achieving a consensus. Therefore, the Delphi technique was developed to find a happy medium between preserving the individuality of opinion and a synthesis of ideas. It is based on four principles:

1. *Anonymity.* Individual anonymity is achieved through the strict physical separation of panel members. In some cases, even the names of the members should be kept secret from one another.

2. *Iteration.* The judgments of the panel members are summarized and circulated so that group members can modify their original positions. Each round of individual deliberation initiated by information on others' opinions is called an iteration. During the entire process, there may be two or three such iterations.

3. *Distribution of statistical summary.* The individual responses are tabulated, and the measures of their central tendencies and dispersion are provided to the members. To eliminate the extremes, often the median value is presented for the measure of central tendency. For dispersion, a range of measures is usually provided. The members may also receive detailed graphs and charts specifying the shapes of the distribution of responses.

4. *Group consensus.* Finally, on the basis of this process of iteration and feedback, efforts are made to achieve a group consensus on the issue.

The Delphi technique was created primarily for forecasting technical information from a largely homogeneous group of experts. The overall homogeneity in value creates a strong central tendency for the distribution in the forecast values (like a bell-shaped curve). In such a situation, the mean value is a fair representation of the group's judgment on a particular issue. However, when it comes to forecasting a sociological phenomenon, such unimodality of distribution of opinion may not exist. Let us consider, for example, an emotionally charged issue: the future of race relations in the United States. A group of experts assembled to discuss the matter are likely to reflect diversely held value positions and strongly disagree. The group may not be able to form a consensus. In such cases, a slightly different method, called the **policy Delphi technique**, may be more appropriate. This technique starts with the initial assumption that the experts are not homogeneous in their points of view. In fact, the panel members may not even be experts but instead be individuals who represent various interest groups. Therefore, for the policy Delphi technique, the original steps are modified to reflect the changed reality:

1. *Selective anonymity.* It is recognized that there will be subjectivity in arguments on the basis of interest or value positions. Therefore, the participants are frequently kept anonymous only during the initial stage of discussion. After everybody has a chance to state his or her view, the issue may be debated openly in the subsequent iterations.

2. *Informed multiple advocacy.* Unlike the original Delphi technique, this method directs that the panel members be chosen not for their expertise but for their special

interest in or position of advocacy on the matter. The panel considering policy options on how to contain outbursts of racial or ethnic hostility may include conservative advocates of strict law and order, liberal advocates of social reform, and members of opposing ethnic groups.

3. *Multimodal response.* Since opinions are likely to reflect the multimodal distribution of opinion of such a panel, the statistical summary to be provided to the members for the subsequent iterations may not include an attempt to find the central tendency. Instead, the summary may simply provide, as accurately as possible, a picture of the multipolar distribution of opinion.

4. *Structured conflict.* The original Delphi technique depends on the convergence of views, but the policy Delphi technique is built around conflict. In a contentious world, it is often helpful to be able to define opposing points of view clearly. Therefore, policy Delphi does not always aim at resolution, and sometimes it shows a final unbridgeable gap between parties.

Both Delphi techniques seem deceptively simple. For their successful use, you must follow the same path of structured reasoning as we discussed in chapter 5. The steps are outlined here.

Define the problem. The success of this process depends on the clear definition of an issue. For example, an agency faces a probable cut in funding. Before it assembles a panel, it must decide the perimeter of the issue: should it attempt to forecast the amount of money available for the next fiscal year, or should it tackle the question of specific cuts corresponding to certain levels of funding? An ill-defined issue can easily cause confusion and cost the organization a great deal in wasted effort, time, money, and morale. The proper definition of the issue is even more critical for a policy Delphi analysis, because social issues are likely to be far more complex than a technical problem facing an organization.

Choose the right panel. Choosing the right panel is equally critical for the success of the Delphi technique. Hard thinking must precede the selection of the panel members. Often the individuals designing a Delphi analysis may not have adequate knowledge of the important persons relevant to the issue. William Dunn suggests a practical solution to this problem.[9] Frequently, the planners are at least able to name the most influential figure in the debate. They may ask this individual to identify the person with whom he or she agrees most closely and another with whom he or she disagrees most vehemently. By asking these individuals the same question, the planners are well on the way to selecting an entire panel that shows a full range of opinion.

Develop the first-round questionnaire. The success of Delphi depends on the types of questions that are put before the panel, and you, the analyst, must decide what the questions will be in the first and subsequent iterations. Although there are no hard-and-fast rules about developing a questionnaire, you must develop it for the first round with an eye to the next. Suppose the purpose of the exercise is to obtain a forecast, say, of the number of AIDS victims in the next five years. Some very structured questions regarding the future spread of the disease can start off the discussion. Or the panel can discuss trends in people's attitudes and sexual practices, changing social mores, and the attitude of the administration toward a frank discussion of unsafe sexual and intravenous drug use practices among the target groups and the distribution of prophylactic devices. In this case, the first-round questionnaire can be relatively unstructured and contain a number of open-ended questions. If the questions are not open ended, the answers should be quantified according to some scale.

Analyze first-round results. The results of the first round of questionnaires should be analyzed to determine the position of each panel member. These results should be tabulated, and for each question, the measures of central tendency and dispersion should be calculated. The panel members should have these results available for subsequent rounds. For example, if the question was, "How much do you expect teenage sexual practices to change in view of an increase in awareness campaigns?" and the answers were rated on a five-point scale (5 being significantly changed, 1 being no change at all), the panel members should be given at least the mean, median, standard deviation, and range of distribution of the answers. If you have graphics capability, it may not be a bad idea to show panel members visually the distribution of their answers. This may be a particularly good idea if the members are not expert statisticians.

Develop questionnaires for the subsequent rounds. Comparison of the group results with the individual responses paves the way for further discussion in the Delphi process. If the answers indicate a significant responsiveness of teenage sexual behavior to a concerted ad campaign, a more detailed discussion of this topic can help develop forecasts (and future policies). Also, note that although panel members may not have stated their basic assumptions in the first round, they are allowed to do so in successive rounds. Policy Delphi usually involves three to five rounds, so members have ample opportunity to evaluate one another's arguments in greater detail. These rounds of discussion may cause the members to modify their positions.

Arrange the panel discussion. At the end of the process, a group meeting can allow the panel members to see if a consensus finally emerges through an open, face-to-face discussion. These group discussions can be particularly fruitful, since by now, each member of the panel is thoroughly conversant with the positions, arguments, hypotheses, and logic of others on the panel. Therefore, the group discussion can often take place in an atmosphere of mutual understanding, if not agreement.

Prepare the final report. The last step of a Delphi process is for the analyst to prepare the final report. It should describe the entire process. If an overall agreement appears, the report should mention it, but you should be careful not to ignore minority or extreme positions, if any. If there is no consensus, you must take care to document the diverse points of view and the extent of divergence of opinion. (For a report on how California State University, Long Beach, used the Delphi process to revamp its public affairs program, see "A Case in Point.")

A CASE IN POINT

The Use of the Delphi Technique in Devising a Public Policy Curriculum

I have mentioned the use of the Delphi technique as a forecasting tool. You can extend this and all other techniques of numerical analysis in solving problems far beyond their principal use. For example, the members of the public administration department at California State University, Long Beach, wanted to revise its public policy curriculum, which would fundamentally reorient the direction of the department's program.[10] However, public policy may be taught from many different angles, requiring a wide variety of analytical skills. Since the faculty members could not come to an agreement, they decided to use the Delphi technique to devise the new curriculum. For that, the faculty took the following steps:

1. *Identification of the problem.* The faculty first wanted to know "what practicing public managers, academics, students, and alumni thought MPA [master of public administration] graduates should know and be able to do, and second, to rate or rank the relative importance of those knowledge and skill components." They also wanted to identify "which components should be taught in required courses and which in elective."[11]

2. *Identification of the monitor/team.* Three faculty members with the required skill and knowledge of the Delphi technique were selected to make up the research team.

3. *Identification of the sample.* The team identified the stakeholders (the students, alumni, faculty members, and public managers), from whom they chose more than 100 participants for the first round. The participants were required to have access to e-mail. This requirement was not seen as a bias in the study, since nearly 85 percent of the students worked for public agencies and had e-mail addresses. High percentages of alumni, faculty members, and public managers also had e-mail access.

4. *Round 1.* The participants received two open-ended questions: What should MPA graduates know, and what skills should they have?

5. *Round 2.* The research team tabulated the responses under the headings "knowledge" and "skills" and sent them back to the participants with the request to add, delete, or otherwise modify the lists.

6. *Round 3.* The team compiled complete lists under "knowledge" and "skills" and sent them back to the participants, asking them to award weights from 0 to 10, with 10 being the most important to the MPA students.

7. *Round 4.* The team members tabulated the responses for mean and standard deviation and ranked them according to their relative importance. Finally, they sent the results back to the participants and asked them to assign "core" or "elective" to each of the categories of "knowledge" and "skills."

8. *Sharing of information*. The faculty shared the gathered information and from it devised seven required and five elective courses.

Here is the list of the ten most important topics in the "knowledge" and "skills" categories, ranked from most to least important:

Knowledge	Standard deviation	Mean
1. Economics, politics and markets, microeconomic theory	9.7	0.55
2. Administrative theory, theory of the state	9.5	0.70
3. Research methods	9.5	0.70
4. Policy analysis	9.0	1.40
5. Strategic and comprehensive planning	9.0	1.40
6. Statistics	9.0	1.40
7. Financial management, politics of financial management	9.0	1.40
8. Program evaluation	9.0	1.40
9. Budgeting	8.5	2.10
10. Intergovernmental relations	8.0	1.00

Skills	Standard deviation	Mean
1. Writing skills	9.4	0.55
2. Analytical skills and techniques	9.0	1.00
3. Policy analysis skills	8.6	1.34
4. Leadership skills	8.4	1.14
5. Oral presentation skills	8.4	3.50
6. Finance and budgeting skills	8.2	1.48
7. Political awareness and interaction	8.0	1.58
8. Interpersonal management/behavioral skills	8.0	1.87
9. Cultural competency/diversity management	7.8	1.30
10. Listening skills	7.8	2.95

Discussion Points

1. Discuss the relative importance of the top ten "knowledge" and "skills" requirements, particularly in light of their mean and standard deviation scores.
2. Can you think of other areas in which the Delphi technique can be profitably used?

The Feasibility Assessment Technique

The **feasibility assessment technique** (FAT) is a commonly used judgmental method of projection. This method is particularly useful in forecasting the outcome of a contentious issue, fought by a number of interested parties. Therefore, FAT has found wide application in the forecasting of political, economic, military, and institutional outcomes of a conflict. It is a versatile technique and can be used at any phase of the policy-making process. It can be used for predicting which issues will come to the forefront, what the legislative outcomes will be, or how a policy will be implemented.

For example, suppose we are trying to forecast the outcome of a bill before a state legislature to fund the distribution of AIDS information to high school students. To forecast the outcome of this debate, we need to make a list of the interested parties who play an active role in determining the outcome of the bill. We can make a list of the major players as follows: the governor, the liberal lawmakers, the media, the conservative lawmakers, the public health groups, the conservative Christian church groups, and the gay activist groups. Let us assume that the governor is a moderate conservative who shows mild opposition to the bill. The liberal lawmakers strongly support the measure, and the conservative lawmakers are solidly opposed to it. The public health groups support the issue. Finally, the church groups are vehemently opposed to the public funding of explicit sexual education, and the gay activists are equally visceral in their support for the bill. In FAT terminology, the relative position of the "player" groups (those who exert some power and influence over the policy outcome) is called the "issue position."

An analyst (or a group of analysts) assesses the relative issue position by estimating the probability of support by each player group. This probability measure is assigned to each group, and it varies between +1 and –1. If a group is certain to support the issue, its issue position will have a value of 1. If it is certain to oppose it, its issue position value is assessed as –1. If the group is likely to be indifferent, its value will be 0. It is safe to assume that the gay activist groups should be assigned a value of +1, and the conservative church groups should be given a value of –1. Let us assume that the support of the public health groups is 0.9, the media 0.8, liberal lawmakers 0.6, the governor –0.1, and the conservative lawmakers –0.7. The relative positions are shown in Table 10.2. Note that we are assigning values on the basis of our subjective assessments. In a class exercise, you can simply make your estimations. However, a great deal of serious thinking has gone into "mental modeling," by which an expert in the field can arrive at a subjective

TABLE 10.2 **Relative Issue Positions**

Group	Relative position
Gay activist groups	+1.0
Public health groups	+0.9
Media	+0.8
Liberal lawmakers	+0.6
Governor	–0.1
Conservative lawmakers	–0.7
Conservative church groups	–1.0

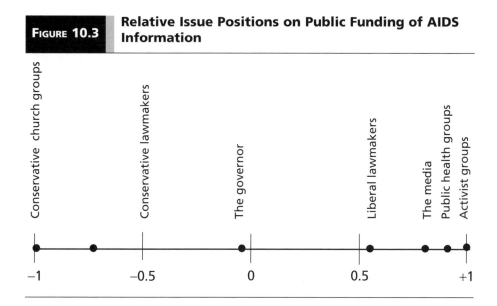

FIGURE 10.3 **Relative Issue Positions on Public Funding of AIDS Information**

assessment. Analysts must conduct these subjective forecasting techniques with the utmost care because of the influence of a great number of possible biases. I have mentioned some of these biases at the end of this chapter.[12]

Looking at Figure 10.3, you might think that because more groups with passion appear to the left of the spectrum (the right-hand side of the diagram), the issue is certain to be decided in favor of funding. Reality, however, is more complicated than that. To begin with, not every player has equal influence over the outcome of the debate. For the next step, we would want to measure the players' available resources on the issue. The resources within the disposal of each group would include prestige, legitimacy, money, time, administrative capabilities, and communication capabilities. The available resources are measured within the range of 1 (having a great deal of resources to bear) and 0 (having no resources whatsoever). We may hypothetically assign values to our lineup as shown in Table 10.3.

TABLE 10.3 **Availability of Resources**

Group	Resource availability
Governor	0.90
Liberal lawmakers	0.40
Conservative lawmakers	0.50
Media	0.80
Conservative church groups	0.30
Gay activist groups	0.10
Public health groups	0.05

| TABLE 10.4 | **Potential for Policy Influence** | | |

Group	Issue position (*a*)	Available resources (*b*)	Potential for policy influence (*a* × *b*)
Governor	−0.10	0.90	−0.09
Liberal lawmakers	0.60	0.40	0.24
Conservative lawmakers	−0.70	0.50	−0.35
Media	0.80	0.80	0.64
Conservative church groups	−1.00	0.30	−0.30
Gay activist groups	1.00	0.10	0.10
Public health groups	0.90	0.05	0.045
Total			+0.285

The potential influence of each player can now be calculated by multiplying the issue position of each group by its total available resources. Thus, we can derive Table 10.4. The total potential of policy influences predicts a positive outcome for the measure. However, the potential does not often foretell the actual outcome. Every player faces a slate of issues it considers to be vital to its mission. The governor has many agendas, of which fighting the funding of the AIDS information project is one. Facing an issue, the players must decide on the relative importance of the issue in relation to their other obligations. In other words, this particular issue, like all others facing each group, must have the group's commitment to invest a percentage of its resources. This commitment is called the "ranking of resources." Let us assume that the players have decided to allocate their total available resources as shown in Table 10.5.

In other words, the liberal lawmakers are willing to commit 15 percent of their resources, and the gay activist groups are estimated to spend 80 percent of their resources, whereas the largely disinterested media are expected to commit no more than 2 percent in promoting this measure. The governor has decided to spend no more than 10 percent of his resources in fighting this measure, but the conservative lawmakers have made this issue a hallmark of their conservative agenda and are expected to spend 30 percent of their available resources. Similarly, the conservative church groups are expected to commit 90 percent of their resources to fight public funding of what they

| TABLE 10.5 | **Ranking of Resources** |

Group	Resource ranking
Governor	0.10
Liberal lawmakers	0.15
Conservative lawmakers	0.30
Media	0.02
Conservative church groups	0.90
Gay activist groups	0.80
Public health groups	0.60

TABLE 10.6	Calculated Policy Influence		
Group	Potential for policy influence (a)	Ranking of resources (b)	Feasibility score (a × b)
Opponents			
Governor	−0.09	0.10	−0.0090
Conservative lawmakers	−0.35	0.30	−0.1050
Conservative church groups	−0.30	0.90	−0.2700
Subtotal			−0.3840
Proponents			
Liberal lawmakers	0.240	0.15	0.0360
Media	0.640	0.02	0.0128
Gay activist groups	1.000	0.80	0.0800
Public health groups	0.045	0.60	0.0270
Subtotal			0.1558
Total			−0.2282

consider to be offensive. This commitment factor multiplied by the total potential determines the outcome. Thus, we may construct Table 10.6.

Table 10.6 gives us the total feasibility score: the opponents of the measure will have more support than will the proponents (−0.3840 as opposed to 0.1558). Therefore, despite popular support (more groups in favor), the measure will be defeated.

You may find the conclusion of this hypothetical study somewhat surprising, especially in view of the initial assessment based on Figure 10.3 and Table 10.4. In fact, the ultimate outcome of any public policy depends on the relative issue position and the fraction of the total resources that the player groups are willing to invest in achieving a favorable outcome. You may notice that although the governor is the most resourceful person in this debate, his reluctance to invest a great deal of resources reduces him to the position of a minor player. In contrast, by combining their total resources and a stronger determination, the coalition between the conservative lawmakers and the church groups becomes a formidable force in stopping public funding. This technique explains very well many different social and political events. Consider, for example, the impact of the so-called Moral Majority, a coalition of right-wing religious groups and conservative politicians put together by the Reverend Jerry Falwell in the late 1970s and early 1980s. Although not supported by the majority of the American public, this group had a profound impact on the course of American politics that went far beyond its numerical strength.

The steps of FAT can be summarized as follows:

1. Identify the issue.
2. Identify the player groups.
3. Estimate the issue positions of the groups.
4. Estimate the available resources for each group.
5. Estimate the resource rank within each group.
6. Calculate the feasibility assessment index.

The Expected Utility Model

Some analysts have found a variation of the feasibility assessment technique to be a useful forecasting tool for predicting the outcomes of an incredible variety of social phenomena, from international relations to banking regulations. Bruce Bueno de Mesquita of the Hoover Institution at Stanford University and his associates are at the forefront of such predictive efforts, which they call the **expected utility model**.[13] Their methodology for forecasting is far too complex to be discussed in this book, but I can give you the basic idea behind these prediction methodologies.

Suppose we are forecasting the probability of a change in a certain government policy. By scanning the political landscape, we can pick out the major players in the game. They may then be classified as proponents of a change or opponents of a change. Let us assume that the government and its allies do not want any change and the opposition groups do. Those groups that are proposing a change are inviting a confrontation with those that prefer the status quo. Each group recognizes that just like investing in a risky project, the investment of resources to fight a rival has its own risks. A loss might cause an embarrassment and expose the group's vulnerability to its foes. In contrast, a win will bring highly desired spoils. Therefore, a group's strategic move in determining whether to confront its opponent and how much to invest in the process will reflect its expectations about the future. The following example can help show the relative positions of the proponents and the opponents of a policy change.

Suppose opposition groups propose a change in government policy (for example, in handgun control, or increased funding for urban renewal, or conservation of open space), whereas the government and its supporters oppose such a change. The expected payoffs of the two groups can be shown with the help of a diagram. In Figure 10.4 the quadrants created by the intersection of the two straight lines have been subdivided into octants. These octants are marked with Roman numerals. The expected payoffs of the two groups are plotted on a Cartesian plane. In the northeastern quadrant, comprising octants I and II, each contestant expects to gain by confronting the other. If both contenders feel that they can win in a confrontation, the chances of open confrontation are extremely high. However, if the government's expectations of the outcome of a confrontation fall in octant I, at point x, then the government expects to gain more than what the opposition parties would gain. Therefore, we can expect the government to take an aggressive posture and start a confrontation. In an authoritarian regime, this confrontation may take the form of cracking down on the opposition. In a democratic system, it may be a presidential veto.

In contrast, if the government's expectations of the outcome of a confrontation fall on a point such as q on octant II, then it would expect to win, but its win would be less than that of its rival. As a result, if mutual expectation patterns fall in this region, we can expect a role reversal, wherein the opposition parties more aggressively seek confrontation with the government. However, since both parties expect to win, the chances of a confrontation are extremely high. In an international context, disputes falling within these two octants have escalated into war about 90 percent of the time.[14]

In the northwestern quadrant (octants III and IV), the opposition expects to win and the government expects to lose. In octant III, although the challenger expects to win, its gains will be smaller than the other's loss. Therefore, seeing the prospect of a relatively small loss, the government will sit down with the opposition and negotiate a compromise that gives the opposition an edge.

FIGURE 10.4   **Expected Payoff of the Government and Its Opposition**

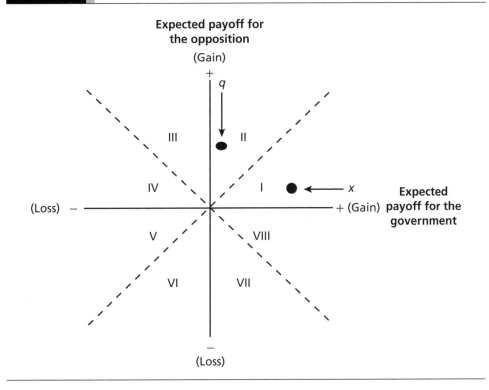

In octant IV, in contrast, the government is expected to suffer a heavier loss than what the opposition would gain. If the government's expectations match this kind of a pattern, we can expect it to accede to the demands of the opposition. In 1990, as part of a wide-ranging budget compromise, President George H.W. Bush decided to go along with the Democrats in increasing taxes. At that time the president decided he had more to lose by opposing a compromise. In view of his earlier unequivocal campaign pledge of not increasing taxes ("Read my lips, no new taxes"), however, his action became a liability and came back to haunt him later.

In the southwestern quadrant, both parties expect to lose. You may note that in octant V, the government's losses are expected to be greater than the losses of the opposition. The situation is reversed in octant VI. Facing the prospect of a lose-lose situation, neither party shows much enthusiasm for a head-on confrontation.

Finally, the southeastern quadrant is the mirror image of the northwestern quadrant. That is, in this case, the government is expected to win in confrontation, and the opposition expects to lose. When the condition of octant VII prevails, the government perceives that it is making a legitimate demand on the opposition, and it has a good deal to gain from its position; but more important, the opposition has a good deal more to lose. Situations such as these prove to turn out peacefully because the opposition is effectively shut off with the prospect of a heavy loss. In the spring of 1984, President Ferdinand Marcos of the Philippines called for elections. President Marcos often used

FIGURE 10.5 | Dynamics of the Policy Outcome

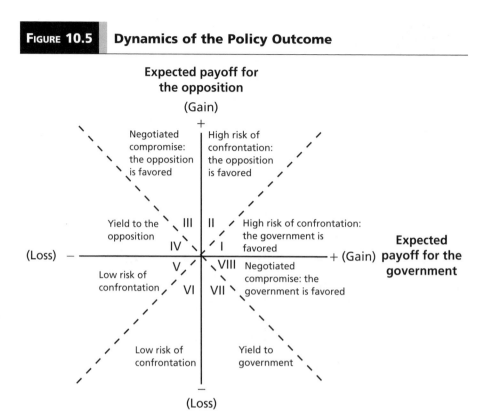

Expected payoff for
the opposition
(Gain)
+

Negotiated compromise: the opposition is favored

High risk of confrontation: the opposition is favored

Yield to the opposition

III

II

High risk of confrontation: the government is favored

IV

I

(Loss) —

+ (Gain)

Expected payoff for the government

V

VIII

Low risk of confrontation

VI

VII

Negotiated compromise: the government is favored

Low risk of confrontation

Yield to government

—
(Loss)

the results of highly corrupt elections to gain political legitimacy for his regime. The widespread disenchantment with his rule prompted many observers to predict organized opposition to Marcos or a call for the boycott of the elections and even violence. However, the leading opposition groups did not expect to defeat Marcos and expected to lose far more than the loss they could inflict on his regime by opposing him in the election. On the basis of their perception, Bueno de Mesquita correctly predicted no serious challenge to Marcos's presidency and a relatively uneventful election. I show the expected outcomes of confrontation in Figure 10.5.

Origin of the Numbers

The numbers in a FAT model or the estimation of the expectations of the two rivals in an expected utility model come from the judgment of those who are experts in the area. The expected utility model requires the identification of the major players and the estimation of their expectations. For these estimations, similar to those in the FAT model, you can use the expertise of those who have direct knowledge of these groups. Having ascertained the groups' positions, you may first plot them in their respective octants to see if a pattern emerges. These results will tell you whether you can expect a confrontation.

Although I have provided examples from international relations, a versatile technique such as the expected utility model can be used to forecast many different outcomes in contentious situations facing all levels of government. Let us suppose that during a police chase in your town, a police cruiser crashed into the car of an innocent citizen, injuring her. The risk management division of your local government is interested in settling the case. However, before offering a settlement amount, the risk manager wants to know if the injured party would want a lengthy and extremely expensive court case. The expected utility model can help you develop a scenario that will justly compensate the victim for her suffering and yet save a good deal of the city's tax dollars.

Shortcomings of the Judgmental Methods

Often in life, issues are so complex that it is extremely difficult to capture all their dimensions within the confines of structured techniques of analysis and forecasting. In addition, in real life you will encounter situations in which there is no history to depend on for predicting the future. In such cases, judgmental methods give us extremely useful alternatives. Time and again, the various subjective methods of prediction have proved their usefulness. However, the very sources of their strength in one situation become their liability in another.

Although the techniques of judgmental methods offer more flexibility than do the other, more rigorous statistical methods (discussed in the following chapters), they still must operate within some structure. In analyses of group interaction (say, between the government and the opposition), we assume that all groups are making their decisions at the same time yet independently. It stands to reason, however, that they are interdependent. Also, group interactions are part of a dynamic process in which groups communicate with one another, compromise, and form or break coalitions. Even the most flexible open-ended forecasting method cannot accommodate many of these complex behaviors.

However, the more serious problem with the judgmental methods is that because there is no systematic way of discussing the assumptions and arguments of the "experts," preconceived ideas, prejudices, unarticulated agendas, self-interest, or other psychological pitfalls and cognitive limitations frequently contaminate their judgments. Few experts (in and out of the government) predicted the first war between the United States and Iraq in 1991. Even at the last minute, most were willing to dismiss the threats and counterthreats (for example, Saddam Hussein's apocalyptic promise that it would be the "mother of all wars") as simple bravado, posturing, or face-saving gestures. When President George H.W. Bush ordered Iraq to get out of Kuwait or face war, he was not bluffing. And when Hussein, facing incredible odds, said that his army would never leave Kuwait of its own accord, he meant it. Yet most experts saw the prospect of this strange war as so far-fetched that they refused to believe the resolve of the two contenders almost until the first bullet was fired. Similarly, because of these psychological impediments, the Central Intelligence Agency was caught off guard by the sudden collapse of the Soviet Union. Having poked and prodded, studied and analyzed the Soviet system for decades, agency experts completely failed to understand the fundamental fragility of the system.

KEY WORDS

Assumption of continuity (p. 225)
Case study method (p. 230)
Causal connections (p. 225)
Comparable city method (p. 230)
Delphi technique (p. 232)
Dependent variables (p. 225)
Expected utility model (p. 242)
Feasibility assessment technique (p. 238)
Fiscal impact analysis (p. 229)

Groupthink (p. 232)
Independent variables (p. 225)
Judgmental methods of projection (p. 227)
Per capita multiplier method (p. 230)
Policy Delphi technique (p. 233)
Prediction (p. 225)
Projection (p. 225)
Single-factor projection (p. 227)
Trends (p. 225)

EXERCISES

1. Consider the following facts in your community and explain how you would go about forecasting them for the next five years:
   a. The number of homeless people
   b. The number of child abuse cases
   c. The number of school-age children
   d. The number of violent crimes
   Explain your data needs, point out the possible sources, and choose a projection model.

2. Suppose the indigent elderly population that depends on public assistance is growing at a rate of 4 percent per year in your county. At present there are 3,500 individuals in this category. How many such people would you expect to see three years from now? Assuming that it costs the county $2,300 per person for health care, estimate the total cost of indigent health care for elderly people in your county.

3. Explain the problems of single-factor projections. Despite these problems, single-factor projection remains one of the most commonly used techniques of projection. Taking a real-life example, account for the widespread use of single-factor projection in public policy analysis.

4. Explain the process of the policy Delphi technique. What are its strengths and shortcomings?

5. The city of Masters, Pennsylvania, faces a controversial issue. The marshland adjacent to a prosperous neighborhood is not being used. A developer has submitted a proposal to make it into a golf course. However, the marshland is the habitat for migratory birds. Hence, the project is opposed by powerful environmental groups. The conservative, probusiness council members support the project. This is a divisive issue, and the mayor has expressed her mild opposition to the project, whereas the liberal members of the city council are in vehement opposition. The table shows the relative positions of the various parties, their available resources, and the ranking of resources. Predict the outcome of the debate.

Group	Issue position	Ranking of resources	Available resources
Mayor	−0.20	0.30	0.80
Developer	11.00	0.90	0.30
Conservative city council members	0.85	0.60	0.40
Liberal city council members	−0.65	0.80	0.50
Environmental groups	−0.90	0.90	0.90
Chamber of commerce	10.50	0.40	0.10

6. Take any current controversial issue facing your community, state, or the nation, such as gun control, abortion, or the amount of national defense funding. Then, working with others in a group project, predict the policy outcome using the feasibility assessment technique. How accurate do you think your predictions are? What are the major weaknesses of your predictions? Would you feel comfortable using these techniques in a real-life situation? Explain. (Suggestion: The size of the group is often crucial to the success of such a project. A group size of about five is best. A larger group can be broken into several groups, each one attempting to forecast the same issue or different ones.)

7. Suppose you are going to forecast the outcome of an upcoming sporting event. As a group, discuss and write down the factors (quality of the players, past performances of the two teams, and so forth) that may help you in your prediction. Then, using the judgmental method, develop a forecast. Compare your forecast with the actual outcome of the game.

Notes

1. Those of you who have hand calculators with a button that says $[y^x]$ can be spared the task of having to multiply 1.09 ten times. The $[y^x]$ key raises a number to the desired exponent. To calculate this number, you need to (1) enter 1.09, (2) hit the $[y^x]$ button followed by (3) the number 10, (4) press the $[=]$ button to obtain the value for the expression $(1 \times 0.09)^{10}$. By multiplying this number by the initial number of cases (P_0), you can estimate the value of P_{10}.

2. To arrive at this number, we write equation 10.5 as follows:

$$\sum_{1}^{10} P_n = \frac{(1 + 0.09)^{10+1} - 1}{0.09} \times 150$$

3. For a detailed discussion of fiscal impact analysis, see Robert W. Burchell and David Listokin, *The Fiscal Impact Handbook: Estimating Local Costs and Revenues of Land Development* (New Brunswick, N.J.: Rutgers University Press, 1978).

4. This study generated a lively controversy on the cost of illegal immigration in the region. Without taking any side in the controversy, I am simply reporting the results as an example of single-factor projection when no other data are available.

5. Auditor General of California, "A Fiscal Impact Analysis of the Undocumented Immigrants Residing in San Diego County," Report C-126, August 1992, 11.

6. For a historical account of the development of the Delphi technique, see Harold Sackman, *Delphi Critique: Expert Opinion, Forecasting, and Group Process* (Lexington, Mass.: Lexington Books, 1975). See also Juri Pill, "The Delphi Method: Substance, Contexts, a Critique, and an Annotated Bibliography," *Socio-Economic Planning Science* 5 (1971): 57–71. However, for an excellent discussion of Delphi and other techniques of subjective decision making, see William N. Dunn, *Public Policy Analysis: An Introduction* (Englewood Cliffs, N.J.: Prentice Hall, 1981).

7. The term *groupthink* was made popular by the psychologist Irving Janis. For a more detailed explanation and many more examples, see Irving Janis, *Groupthink: Psychological Studies of Policy Decisions and Fiascoes* (Boston: Houghton Mifflin, 1982), a revised and enlarged edition of Irving Janis, *Victims of Groupthink: A Psychological Study of Foreign-Policy Decisions and Fiascoes* (Boston: Houghton Mifflin, 1972).

8. People often choose not to express their "true preferences" in public because of peer pressure or the fear of social ostracism. If the need to be "politically correct" overwhelms the need to be truthful, your publicly held views will deviate from what you prefer or believe to be the truth. The price of this distortion of a citizen's preferences may be considerable, as public policies based on misconstrued views can lead to inefficiency or social conflict. For an interesting discussion of the need for anonymous discourse for the articulation of genuine preferences, see Timur Kuran, "Mitigating the Tyranny of Public Opinion: Anonymous Discourse and the Ethic of Sincerity," *Constitutional Political Economy* 4 (1993): 41–78.

9. Dunn, *Public Policy Analysis*, 198.

10. Michelle A. Saint-Germain, John W. Ostrowski, and Martha J. Dede, "Oracle in the Ether: Using an E-mail Delphi to Revise an MPA Curriculum," *Journal of Public Affairs Education* 3 (2000): 161–172.

11. Ibid., 163.

12. See, for example, Herbert Simon and Dorothea Simon, "Individual Differences in Solving Physics Problems," in *Children's Thinking*, ed. Robert S. Siegler (Englewood Cliffs, N.J.: Prentice Hall, 1986). See also David Klahr and Kenneth Kotovsky, eds., *Complex Information Processing: The Impact of Herbert A. Simon* (Hillsdale, N.J.: Lawrence Erlbaum, 1989); Vadim D. Glezer, *Vision and Mind: Modeling Mental Functions* (Hillsdale, N.J.: Lawrence Erlbaum, 1995).

13. See, for example, Bruce Bueno de Mesquita, David Newman, and Alvin Pabushka, *Forecasting Political Events: The Future of Hong Kong* (New Haven, Conn.: Yale University Press, 1985).

14. Douglas Beck and Bruce Bueno de Mesquita, "Forecasting Policy Decisions: An Expected Utility Approach," in *Corporate Crisis Management*, ed. Steven J. Andriole (Princeton, N.J.: Petrocelli, 1984).

11 Projection Techniques: Analysis of Historical Data

Forecasting on the basis of projection techniques requires an understanding of the basic pattern of behavior. Without a pattern, variations are totally erratic or random, in which case future behavior cannot be predicted. In the previous chapter we discussed using forecasting methods when faced with a paucity of past information. In such instances, when making projections, we must rely on one or two data points over time or on expert judgment. To make the most of what little historical data we have, we use projection techniques specially suited to situations of data scarcity, such as single-factor projection and judgmental methods of forecasting. However, we select different techniques when we have a long history of behavior to study. In this chapter we examine those techniques that lend themselves to discerning trends in series of data.

To understand the trend of a series (or the direction in which it is heading), we need to plot the data first. Sometimes, though, a scatter plot does not reveal a strong trend. Consider, for example, a hypothetical series of tourists visiting the Pennsylvania city of Masters, which has a strong tourist industry that attracts vacationers primarily during the skiing and summer seasons. The city's chamber of commerce has collected data on the number of tourists quarterly (in three-month periods) for thirteen years, from 1996 to 2008. These data are plotted in Figure 11.1.

THE COMPONENTS OF A DATA SERIES

You may conclude that the scatter plot of the quarterly tourist population looks quite confusing and that you can determine little from it. Often a series contains elements that obscure our vision. In general, a data series tends to head in a general direction, or contains an element of a trend. A series that grows over time is called a **positive trend**, whereas a series that declines is said to have a **negative trend**. Besides

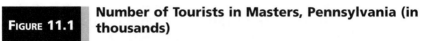

FIGURE 11.1 **Number of Tourists in Masters, Pennsylvania (in thousands)**

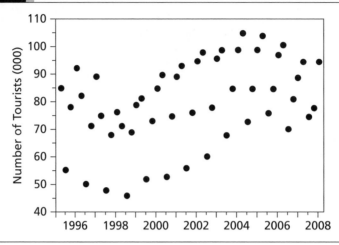

the trend, a data series may also reflect fluctuations resulting from the effects of seasonality. Furthermore, a data series may exhibit the effects of long-term economic cycles. As the economy expands and contracts during the course of a business cycle, it affects many kinds of economic and social activities. Finally, a series contains the effects of purely random fluctuations, which are caused by factors outside our consideration. Natural calamities (floods, earthquakes, devastating tornadoes, and the like), political events (riots, assassinations of important political persons, the election of a new chief executive or political party, and so forth) or institutional factors (such as changes in government regulations) can have an unpredictable effect on a series. The collapse of the Soviet Union had an extraordinarily important but unforeseen effect on the U.S. defense industry. Since these external factors cannot be factored into a model, their effects are called **random errors**. Therefore, time-series data (data recorded over time) may contain the following:[1]

Data = Trend + Seasonality + Cyclical Effect + Random Error

Let us examine these components in greater detail. Figure 11.2 depicts two **linear trend** patterns. Many aggregate social, economic, and demographic data (such as the per capita gross domestic product [GDP] of a country and population growth in the short term) show positive linear growth when plotted over time. However, as shown in Figure 11.2, not all points of observation fall on the trend line. Since these deviations cannot be accounted for within the model, we assume that aberrations reflect the effects of the random error component.

In the case presented in Figure 11.1, the rate of growth does not seem to change over the delineated time period. This trend can be viewed as upward or downward. Despite little peaks and valleys for economic booms and recessions, the GDP per capita, measured in constant dollars, has shown an upward trend over the years in the United States.

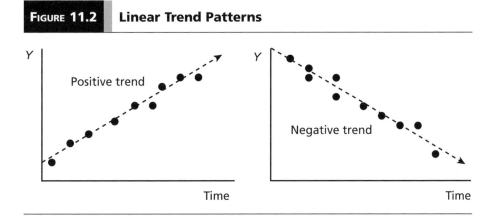

FIGURE 11.2 | **Linear Trend Patterns**

But during the 1980s, federal government assistance to state and local governments demonstrated a steady downward trend.

When data values fluctuate around a constant mean, a **horizontal trend** pattern develops. This is characteristic of a series in which there is no trend and the data seem to fluctuate in a random fashion. In technical terms, such a series is called a **stationary series.** In a stationary series, a trend line will go through the mean ($\overline{Y}$). Since there is no seasonality in the human reproductive process, for example, the daily number of births in New York City hospitals within a year will depict such a series. Figure 11.3 is an illustration of a horizontal pattern of fluctuation.

A **seasonal trend** is shown in Figure 11.4. The quarterly data plotted in the figure depict a trend of regular fluctuations of peaks and valleys during the course of a year. Home construction, unemployment, crime, and highway accidents often tend to show this kind of seasonal variability.

FIGURE 11.3 | **Horizontal, or No-Trend, Pattern**

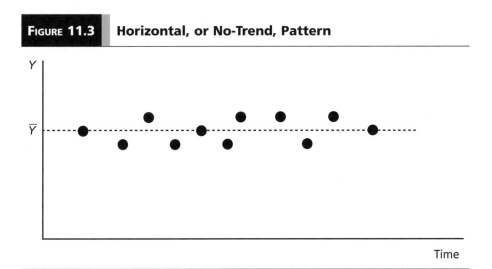

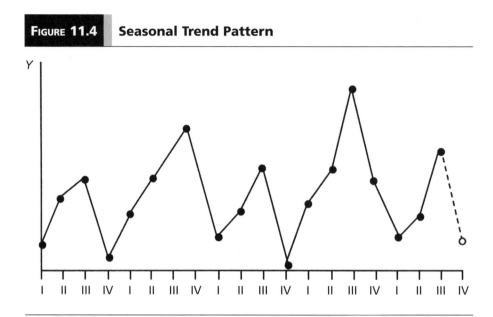

FIGURE 11.4 **Seasonal Trend Pattern**

A **cyclical trend** exists when long-term economic fluctuations associated with the business cycle influence the data. Thus, during a period of slow economic growth, housing construction will decrease. Most economic data tend to be sensitive to the business cycle and fluctuate according to the phase of the cycle. Figure 11.5 reflects the cyclical variability of a series.

Returning to our example of quarterly tourist data, we can plot the data again according to the effects of various elements in a series (see Figure 11.6). Now the patterns are quite clear. The series reflects an overall positive trend over time, although it shows strong seasonal fluctuations, along with effects arising from broader economic

FIGURE 11.5 **Effects of Economic Cycles**

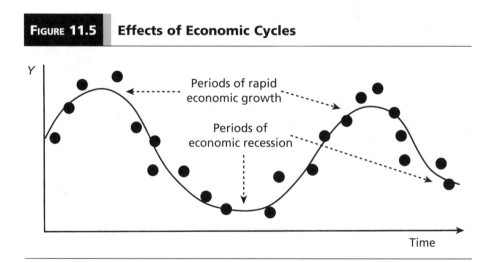

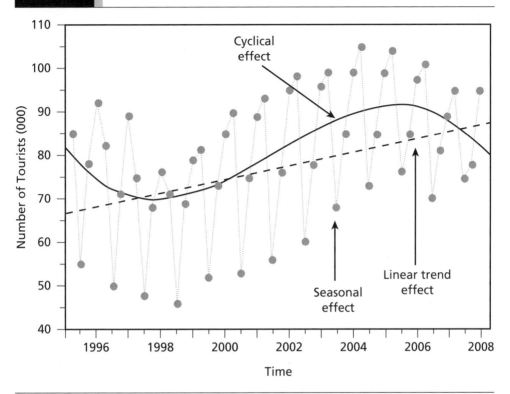

FIGURE 11.6 **Discerning Trend Patterns in the Tourist Data from Masters, Pennsylvania**

trends over the thirteen-year period. Now that we have succeeded in showing definite patterns, our task of forecasting becomes a lot more manageable.

THE PATTERNS OF TIME TRENDS

Seasonal variations, the effects of a business cycle, and other external factors influence a data series. However, data may include a complex relationship with time that can cause a series to change directions in many different ways. Figures 11.7 (a) and 11.7 (b) show patterns of **quadratic trends**. The reverse U-shaped pattern is typical of a situation in which the dependent variable shows a pattern of increase followed by a decline. Data on the percentage of Americans living below the official poverty line demonstrate this kind of quadratic structure during the period from 1950 to 2000. The relation between agricultural production and the application of fertilizer is an example of a causal linkage in a quadratic trend. As one increases the use of fertilizers, the level of production tends to go up. However, after the point of saturation, these chemicals reach a toxic level and, consequently, begin to have a deleterious effect on production.

This U-shaped pattern is also typical of a per unit cost curve in a situation of increasing inefficiency as the scale of operation increases. Consider the operation of a

FIGURE 11.7 **Quadratic Trends**

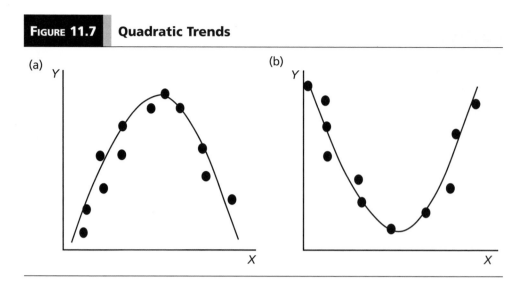

county sheriff's department. If the sheriff's department operates on a very small scale, its cost of operation will be extremely high, because it will have to bear a large fixed cost for administration and other necessary operations. However, as the size of its operation increases (maybe because other small, incorporated cities start contracting their police work out to the sheriff's department), its per unit cost of operation (whichever way it is measured) will go down. But this downward trend cannot continue forever, and at a certain stage the increased size of the department will hamper its efficiency. Beyond this point (which in economics is regarded as the point of maximum efficiency), the unit cost of operation will start to increase. Therefore, by measuring the efficiency of an expanding organization over time, one may discern such a quadratic relationship.

A series may also depict an **exponential trend**, as shown in Figures 11.8 (a) and 11.8 (b). For example, viewed over time, population growth exhibits a negative exponential rate with income. That is, birthrates are highest among the underdeveloped nations in the world. However, these rates drop and then reach a plateau when nations attain high levels of economic prosperity. This pattern is shown in Figure 11.8 (a). In contrast, data on life expectancy show a positive exponential pattern similar to Figure 11.8 (b). Advancements in medical technology have increased people's life expectancy at a fairly rapid rate, but as we approach a biological limit on how long we can survive, the rate of growth slows down considerably.

A series can also depict a rather complex pattern of growth. For example, a series can have a **logistic trend**, or an S-shaped trend, such as the one shown in Figure 11.9. This trend shows a changing pattern of growth. The rate of growth is slow at the beginning of the series but changes during a transition period, at which time the rate of growth becomes quite rapid. After a certain point, this rate slows as the series reaches a steady state or an upper asymptote (a ceiling). This behavior is considered typical of a learning situation. When we try to learn something new (say, a foreign language), at the beginning our progress is painfully slow. After we have mastered the basics, our ability

FIGURE 11.8   **Exponential Trends**

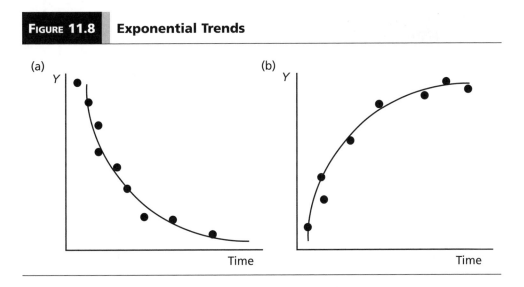

to absorb material accelerates, only to reach a point of saturation when we attain the upper limits of learning.

A series is said to have demonstrated a **catastrophic trend** when there is a sharp discontinuity (see Figure 11.10). This kind of a precipitous rise or fall occurs as a result

FIGURE 11.9   **Logistic Trend**

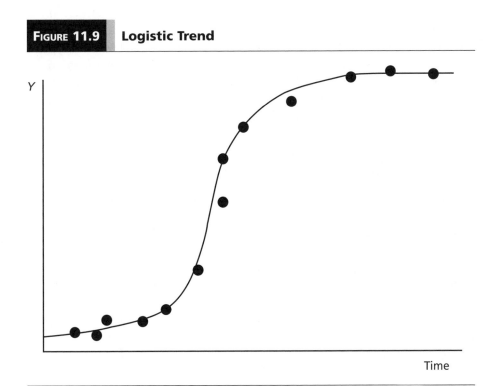

FIGURE 11.10 | **Catastrophic Trend**

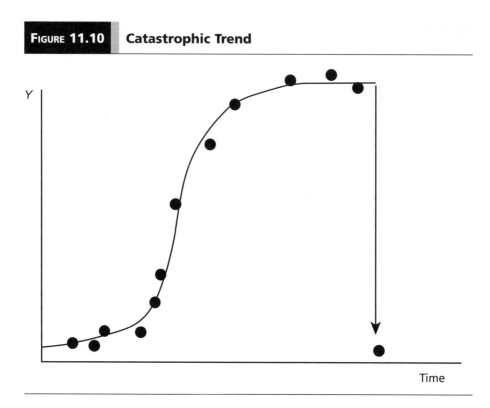

of a war or some other kind of national calamity. If one examines the growth of per capita GDP of the former Soviet republics, the catastrophic impact of the dissolution of the Soviet Union is apparent as their GDPs plunge. The technique of catastrophic **trend analysis** is still in its infancy and therefore is not commonly used in social science research or public policy analysis.

ADJUSTMENT METHODS

Looking again at Figure 11.1, we would probably agree that the true nature of a trend can be lost in the seasonal fluctuations of a series. In such cases, you may want to examine the data by filtering out the effects of these fluctuations. Suppose you want to know if the unemployment rate went up in December. The unemployment data will show the natural effects of a seasonal fluctuation because many types of outdoor work, from construction to agriculture, either stop or slow down during the winter months. To get a proper perspective, you will have to seasonally adjust monthly or quarterly unemployment figures. You may have noticed that the statement "seasonally adjusted" always qualifies quotations of unemployment statistics. Similarly, the presence of a strong trend can muddle the pure effects of seasonal fluctuations. That is, a rapidly growing economy can blunt the seasonal fluctuations in employment statistics. Unless this trend factor is eliminated, the effects of the seasons on the data may

TABLE 11.1	Tourist Population of Masters, Pennsylvania (in thousands)		
Quarter	2006	2007	2008
I	45	46	49
II	35	36	38
III	42	44	45
IV	33	38	42

not be apparent. Perhaps the simplest way of eliminating the effects of seasonal fluctuations and trends is the method of seasonal and trend adjustment.

Let us return to Masters, our Pennsylvania resort town known for its winter and summer recreational facilities. The city's chamber of commerce is trying to understand the nature of tourist demand for its facilities. Consider the records of quarterly figures of tourist populations for the past three years (Table 11.1). The data presented in Table 11.1 do not reveal a great deal of information regarding the nature of the town's tourist industry. Neither does th`eir plot, shown in Figure 11.11. Indeed, we would be hard-pressed to draw too many conclusions from the information we have at hand.

FIGURE 11.11   **Plot of Number of Tourists per Quarter (in thousands)**

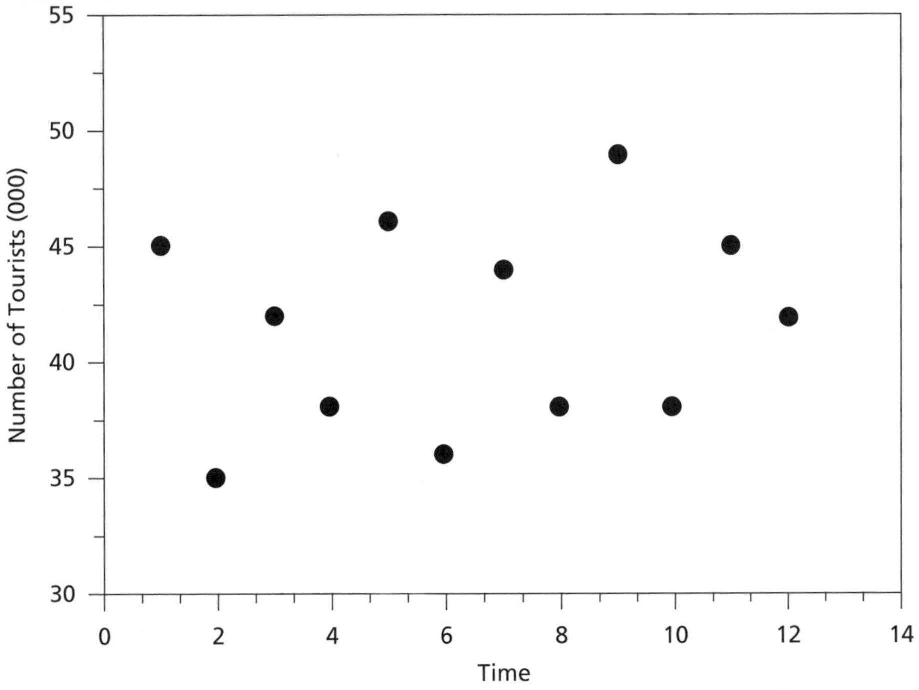

Seasonal Adjustment

The method of seasonal adjustment can lend a helping hand. The reason for this apparent confusion regarding the data is that two factors are at play: the seasonal effect and the trend effect. The presence of these two factors is obfuscating the picture presented by the raw data. Let us begin by suppressing the effects of seasonal variations to accentuate the effects of the trend. If you look at the data carefully, you will see that the first and the third quarters, which cover the peak skiing and summer seasons, tend to bring in more tourists. If there were no seasonal variation whatsoever, the quarterly totals would have been the same. Therefore, we can adjust for this variation by forcing each season to be the same (see Table 11.2).

TABLE 11.2   **Calculation of Quarterly Adjustment Factors (in thousands)**

Quarter	Quarterly total (1998–2000)	Quarterly average	Quarterly adjustment factor (quarterly average minus grand average)
I	140	46.7	+5.6
II	109	36.3	−4.8
III	131	43.7	+2.6
IV	113	37.7	−3.4
Total	493	41.1	

The quarterly totals in the table were calculated by adding the number of tourists for each of the four quarters during the three-year period. During the first quarter, 45,000 tourists visited the town in 2006, 46,000 in 2007, and 49,000 in 2008. Therefore, during the first quarters of these three years, the town had a total of 140,000 visitors. By dividing the quarterly total by three, we calculated the average quarterly figure for the study period. You may notice that during this period there was a total of 493,000 visitors, or about 41,100 tourists per quarter. This is the average number of tourists we could expect if there were no seasonal effect. Therefore, we can calculate the **seasonal adjustment factor** by subtracting the grand average from each quarterly average. This is the adjustment factor, which, subtracted from each individual quarter, will give us a seasonally adjusted figure (see Table 11.3).

TABLE 11.3   **Seasonally Adjusted Quarterly Tourist Population (in thousands)**

Quarter	1998			1999			2000		
	No.	Adjustment factor	Adjusted no.	No.	Adjustment factor	Adjusted no.	No.	Adjustment factor	Adjusted no.
I	45	−5.6	39.4	46	−5.6	40.4	49	−5.6	43.4
II	35	+4.8	39.8	36	+4.8	40.8	38	+4.8	42.8
III	42	−2.6	39.4	44	−2.6	41.4	45	−2.6	42.4
IV	33	+3.4	36.4	38	+3.4	41.4	42	+3.4	45.4

| FIGURE **11.12** | **Plot of Seasonally Adjusted Quarterly Data** |

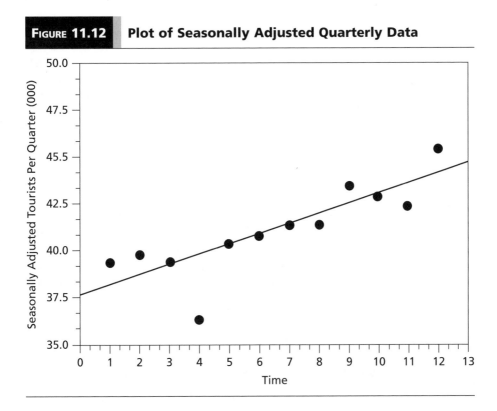

Armed with this new series of numbers, the chamber of commerce can plan more effectively for the future, knowing that at least for the past three years, there has been a definite upward trend in the number of visitors coming to town. By comparing Figure 11.11 with Figure 11.12, you can see how this process of seasonal adjustment has subdued the quarterly variations and emphasized the trend pattern.

Trend Adjustment

The chamber of commerce may also want to understand the patterns of seasonal fluctuations without the distorting effects of a trend. Trends can be eliminated simply by adjusting the data for yearly variations. Again, the logic is the same. If there were no trend pattern, there would be no variation across time. In this situation seasonal factors will be the sole cause of fluctuations. We can calculate the yearly totals for the three years and then subtract each year's total from the yearly average to get the yearly adjustment factors, or the **trend adjustment factors** (see Table 11.4). These yearly adjustment factors show the average change from the mean. By adjusting the data for each quarter by this factor, we will be able to suppress the influence of the trend.

Now, by adjusting the yearly data, we can eliminate the effects of the trend factor and accentuate seasonal variations. This adjustment process can be seen in Table 11.5.

In Figure 11.13 the emphasis is on seasonal changes, and the trend factor has been filtered out. This diagram will help the policymakers in Masters visualize the seasonality of the tourist trend and plan for the future. Although the methods of seasonal and trend adjustment are not methods of forecasting per se, they can shed a good deal of light on

TABLE 11.4	Calculation of Yearly Adjustment Factors (in thousands)		
Year	Yearly total	Yearly average per quarter	Yearly adjustment factor (yearly average minus grand average)
2006	155	38.8	−2.3
2007	164	41.0	−0.1
2008	174	43.5	+2.4
Total	493	41.1	

the behavior of a seemingly chaotic data series. As you can see in Figure 11.13, the trend-adjusted data show that the number of tourists visiting Masters in the first two quarters of the three years remained stable but that the number went up steadily for the fourth quarter. This insight into the data can be a powerful planning and analysis tool for developing appropriate public policies to bring more tourists to the area during the off-season. On the basis of this analysis, the city may hire a public relations firm to publicize the city's attractiveness to potential visitors for the first half of the year.

TABLE 11.5	Trend-adjusted Quarterly Tourist Population (in thousands)								
	2006			2007			2008		
Quarter	No.	Adjustment factor	Adjusted no.	No.	Adjustment factor	Adjusted no.	No.	Adjustment factor	Adjusted no.
I	45	+2.3	47.3	46	+0.1	46.1	49	−2.4	46.6
II	35	+2.3	37.3	36	+0.1	36.1	38	−2.4	35.6
III	42	+2.3	44.3	44	+0.1	44.1	45	−2.4	42.6
IV	33	+2.3	35.3	38	+0.1	38.1	42	−2.4	39.6

SMOOTHING OUT THE FLUCTUATIONS

In the previous section, we discussed ways to smooth out seasonal fluctuations to reveal the underlying trend. However, when we want to consider a time span that is longer (say, a year or six months) or shorter (a week or a month, for example) than a season, or when fluctuations are more random than seasonal effects, we seek the help of a different method of smoothing. In these cases we use such techniques as **naive projection** and **moving average**.[2]

Let us return to the quarterly time-series data on tourists visiting Masters during the thirteen-year period from 1996 to 2008 (see Table 11.6). I plotted this data series in Figure 11.1. As noted earlier in the chapter, the trend line is hidden behind fluctuations caused by seasonal variations and cyclical fluctuation. By examining this figure you can now clearly see a positive trend, the fluctuations caused by the four seasons, as well as the impact of a strong business cycle. Now we want to use this data series to forecast values for the next quarter. If we do not want to be restricted to the four quarterly figures, we will have to use one of the following methods of projection.

FIGURE 11.13	**Plot of Trend-adjusted Tourist Data**

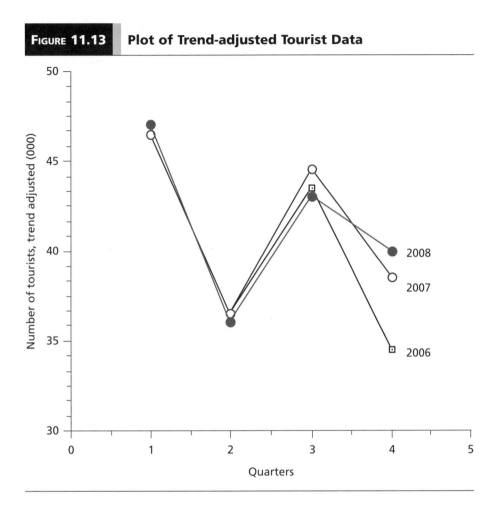

Projecting the Immediate Past: Naive Projection

If I were to ask you to predict your earnings for the coming year, your prediction would probably be based on what you earned this year. Prediction based on the last period's performance is often called the naive method of projection. In Table 11.6, the quarterly data are listed in the first column. In statistics this process is called **lagging**. If we lag a column by one period, we express it in terms of what happened in the immediately preceding period. Similarly, a three-period lag would present the series in terms of what happened three periods ago. When we write in algebraic symbols, we express periods in subscripts. For example, X_t would mean the value of the variable X in period t, which in this case is the current year. Similarly, X_{t-1} would mean last period's value (or the value lagged by one period), and X_{t-10} would be the value lagged by ten periods.

Because an organization's decisions are almost always made on the basis of incremental reasoning (an argument such as, "Last year this program cost \$150,000; therefore, this year we expect it to cost . . ."), forecasting on the basis of what happened last period is probably the most frequently used method. This method produces a reasonably good forecast if there is little trend, positive or negative, and there are few fluctuations. If you have steady salaried employment, your current year's earnings would serve as a good proxy for the next year's prediction. If your income tends to fluctuate, however, this

	Quarterly		Moving	Moving
Year	data	Lag (1 year)	average (2 years)	average (4 years)
1996.1	85	—	—	—
1996.2	55	85	—	—
1996.3	78	55	70.0	—
1996.4	92	78	66.5	—
1997.1	82	92	85.0	77.50
1997.2	50	82	87.0	76.75
1997.3	71	50	66.0	75.50
1997.4	89	71	60.5	73.75
1998.1	75	89	80.0	73.00
1998.2	48	75	82.0	71.25
1998.3	68	48	61.5	70.75
1998.4	76	68	58.0	70.00
1999.1	71	76	72.0	66.75
1999.2	46	71	73.5	65.75
1999.3	69	46	58.5	65.25
1999.4	79	69	57.5	65.50
2000.1	81	79	74.0	66.25
2000.2	52	81	80.0	68.75
2000.3	73	52	66.5	70.25
2000.4	85	73	62.5	71.25
2001.1	90	85	79.0	72.75
2001.2	53	90	87.5	75.00
2001.3	75	53	71.5	75.25
2001.4	89	75	64.0	75.75
2002.1	93	89	82.0	76.75
2002.2	56	93	91.0	77.50
2002.3	76	56	74.5	78.25
2002.4	95	76	66.0	78.50
2003.1	98	95	85.5	80.00
2003.2	60	98	96.5	81.25
2003.3	78	60	79.0	82.25
2003.4	96	78	69.0	82.75
2004.1	99	96	87.0	83.00
2004.2	68	99	97.5	83.25
2004.3	85	68	83.5	85.25
2004.4	99	85	76.5	87.00
2005.1	105	99	92.0	87.75
2005.2	73	105	102.0	89.25
2005.3	85	73	89.0	90.50
2005.4	99	85	79.0	90.50
2006.1	104	99	92.0	90.50
2006.2	76	104	101.5	90.25
2006.3	85	76	90.0	91.00
2006.4	97	85	80.5	91.00
2007.1	101	97	91.0	90.50
2007.2	70	101	99.0	89.75
2007.3	81	70	85.5	88.25
2007.4	89	81	75.5	87.25
2008.1	95	89	85.0	85.25
2008.2	75	95	92.0	83.75
2008.3	78	75	85.0	85.00
2008.4	95	78	76.5	84.25
2009.1 (forecast)	—	95	86.5	85.75

TABLE 11.6 — **Quarterly Series on the Number of Tourists Visiting Masters, Pennsylvania**

method will not give you a very good forecast. For example, because seasonality causes ample variations, the lagged data presented in Table 11.6 act as a poor predictor for the following quarter.

Projecting by the Mean

Another method of projection is calculating the mean. For instance, consider a series:

$$X_1, X_2, X_3, X_4, \ldots X_{t-1}, X_t$$

In this case we can make a prediction for the following period, X_{t+1}, simply by taking the mean of the series—that is, by calculating

$$\overline{X} = \frac{X_1 + X_2 + \cdots X_{t-1} + X_t}{t} = \hat{X}_{t+1} \tag{11.1}$$

where t is the total number of observations and $\hat{X}_{t+1}$ is the projected value for the period $t + 1$.

Therefore, the forecast of X_{t+1} is given by the mean of the series

$$\hat{X}_{t+2} = \frac{X_1 + X_2 + \cdots X_t + X_{t+1}}{t + 1}$$

You might wonder when this simple method is appropriate for forecasting a series. This method is useful only if you have a stationary series with no observable trend (see Figure 11.3). In such cases, the mean of the series would give you the best possible forecast for future behavior. When predicting fluctuations in rainfall, you may do best by taking the yearly average. The same may be true for predicting price movements for a specific period in the stock market.

Moving Average

When there is a clear trend, the variations within a series can be ironed out by what is known as the method of moving average. A moving average is calculated by averaging two or more consecutive values in the series and accepting the computed value to be the forecast for the next period, as shown in Table 11.6. Using this method, we would predict for X_{t+1} as follows:

$$\hat{X}_{t+1} = \frac{X_t + X_{t-1}}{2} \tag{11.2}$$

Lagging the data by one period is called the moving average of order 1, or the first-order moving average. As you can see in Table 11.6, when calculating the moving average of order 2, we lost information on the first two observations because these were used to calculate the forecast for the third period. We can increase the order by taking the average of a larger number of lagged data. If we want to calculate a fourth-order moving average, $\hat{X}_{t+1}$ will be computed as

$$\hat{X}_{t+1} = \frac{X_t + X_{t-1} + X_{t-2} + X_{t-3}}{4} \tag{11.3}$$

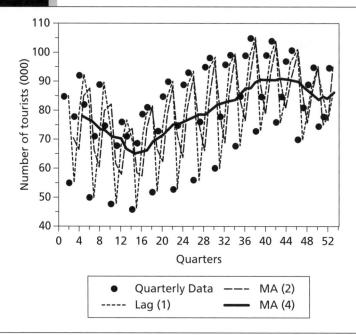

FIGURE 11.14   **Adjusted and Unadjusted Data on Tourists Visiting Masters, Pennsylvania**

Note: MA = moving average.

If you have quarterly data that reflect a strong seasonal effect, a four-period moving average would essentially iron out the seasonal fluctuations. This is shown in Figure 11.14. As the order of moving average increases, the top of the series loses more information, and the series shows a greater degree of smoothing out.

The moving average method requires you to decide on the number of periods to use to smooth the series. You can see from Figure 11.14 that if you want your newly created series to look like the original data, you should choose a smaller lag period. Hence, if a series has a clear trend with a relatively small degree of fluctuation, use a short (perhaps a two-period) lag. However, if the series contains a large degree of seemingly random or seasonal variations, use a larger lag period. Although the choice is highly subjective and dependent on the needs of your client, for the series under discussion, given the high degree of seasonal variation, I would choose a longer lag, perhaps a four-period one.

When you do a trend analysis, it is imperative that you proceed in a systematic way. Here is a quick list of steps you can follow when conducting your analysis:

1. Specify the objective of your study.
2. Plot the data.
3. Look for a trend pattern.
4. If the series is monthly or quarterly, look for seasonal variability.
5. For a long yearly series, look for cyclical effects.
6. Correct for seasonality or trend, depending on the purpose of the study.
7. If there is no trend, use the mean for forecasting.

Choice of Projection Technique

In this chapter we have discussed several different projection techniques. As you can see, each method has its pros and cons. Note that you may obtain a different forecasted value depending on the technique you choose to use. Although there is no definitive roadmap for selecting the "best" method, I suggest following these steps:

1. Define the objective of projection.
2. Plot the data.
3. If there is a great deal of seasonal variability, for comparison purposes, do seasonal and trend adjustments.
4. If there is no trend, use the mean of the series.
5. If there are seasonal fluctuations, use the moving average. Remember, the higher the order of the moving average, the greater the smoothing effect.

THE POLITICS OF FORECASTING

If forecasting on its own merits is a tricky business, forecasting for public policy can be even more problematic. Because a forecast may involve the livelihoods of many individuals and has the potential to cause huge monetary damages, a forecast should be of great concern. Take, for example, the case of Mammoth, a mountain resort town in the picturesque eastern Sierra region in California. Like many other places in the state, this region is susceptible to earthquakes. To complicate the matter, Mammoth Mountain is a dormant volcano. In 1998 the Hollywood movie *Dante's Peak,* set in a mythical resort town meant to mimic Mammoth, showed the plight of the town when the volcano suddenly erupted. This sensational movie, along with some dire predictions from volcanologists, caused the ski town a great deal of anxiety as real estate prices threatened to fall faster than the skiers on its slopes. David Hill, chief scientist with the U.S. Geological Survey and a longtime observer of the region, calmed frayed nerves with his prediction that the odds of a sudden volcanic eruption were grossly overstated.[3]

Although forecasts are supposed to be accurate descriptions of the future, the power they hold in the area of public policy can often make them tools of special interest groups. The current debate on forecasts relating to global warming provides an example of the issues involved. If the cause of global warming could be pinned to the emission of hydrocarbons and other greenhouse gases resulting from human activity, public policies would severely crack down on these polluting agents. Since such agents, in the form of large corporations, are concentrated in the industrial West, such a forecast can be highly significant for its economy.

Forecasts can also be used by scientists and environmentalists for the purpose of raising awareness. In the late 1950s a group of environmentalists became engaged in studying the entire world as one single socioeconomic and environmental system.[4] Their work alerted a generation of young scientists and environmental activists to the dangers of relying on dwindling natural resources. Although the claims of a catastrophe were clearly overblown (and were realized as such at the time of the study), their research was instrumental in educating people about the risks of unrestrained growth. (For a report on how forecasting has affected the debate over the budget surplus, see "A Case in Point.")

A CASE IN POINT

Fighting over a Fiction? The Budget Surplus in the Presidential Debate

During the fierce 2000 presidential campaign, one issue dominated the national debate: how to spend the $4.6 trillion national surplus projected over the next ten years.[5] On the basis of this rosy prediction, Republican George W. Bush wanted to give a third of the surplus back to the taxpayers and use the rest on national defense and education, as well as pay down the national debt. Democrat Al Gore wanted to pay down the national debt, as well as spend on numerous other social and military programs. Gore promised to eliminate the federal debt by 2012; Bush claimed he would do the same by 2016.

While these candidates exchanged barbs and insults and promised the most judicious spending plans, some experts quietly questioned the veracity of the forecasts. Because the budget surplus was based on the performance of a hot economy in 1999, experts feared that if the economy did not keep up with exceptional years of growth, the projected surplus would quickly melt away. In fact, if the economy produced a lower surplus, or no surplus at all, any ambitious spending plan would take the economy back to the days of deficit spending and the consequent burgeoning public debt.

To make the situation worse, the Congressional Budget Office warned that after the next ten years, the government would face a funding crunch from Social Security, Medicare, and Medicaid that could "drive federal debt to unsustainable levels." As the aging baby boomers would demand increasingly more health care and other social service dollars, around 2020 the federal budget

KEY WORDS

Catastrophic trend (p. 255)
Cyclical trend (p. 252)
Exponential trend (p. 254)
Horizontal trend (p. 251)
Lagging (p. 261)
Linear trend (p. 250)
Logistic trend (p. 254)
Moving average (p. 260)
Naive projection (p. 260)
Negative trend (p. 249)

Positive trend (p. 249)
Projecting by the mean (p. 263)
Quadratic trends (p. 253)
Random errors (p. 250)
Seasonal adjustment factor (p. 258)
Seasonal trend (p. 251)
Stationary series (p. 251)
Trend adjustment factors (p. 259)
Trend analysis (p. 256)

would be overwhelmed by these limitless demands. And it could get worse. The projected surplus was divided into two parts: $2.4 trillion in the Social Security program and $2.2 trillion in the rest of the budget. The analysts were comfortable with the projection for Social Security because it was based on relatively stable demographic data. However, it was the surplus in the rest of the federal budget that worried independent observers. On the basis of a different set of assumptions, the Center on Budget and Policy Priorities, a liberal group, estimated that the ten-year surplus outside Social Security would come closer to $700 billion. The Brookings Institution, a somewhat more centrist think tank, estimated that the figure might be as low as $352 billion. If these lower projections came true, the budget surplus would not be much of an issue to fight over.

This "Case in Point" appeared in the first edition of this book, published in 2001. Today, nearly a decade later, the discussion of eliminating the federal public debt by 2012 or even 2016 seems a distant dream from a different land. At the time of writing the present edition, the current year budget deficit—resulting from an economic meltdown, massive bailouts of the banking and automobile industries, and two long wars in Iraq and Afghanistan—is reaching $1 trillion for the first six months of fiscal year 2009, and the total public debt stands at more than $11 trillion and counting.[6]

Discussion Points

1. Why do experts differ on forecasts?
2. What are the political pitfalls of public policy forecasting?
3. Can you ensure an "unbiased" forecast when it comes to public policy?

EXERCISES

1. Write an essay on trend analysis when the past behavior is known. Give examples from real life for the various kinds of trend patterns discussed in this chapter.
2. A typical time series contains wide-ranging fluctuations. Explain, with examples, various sources of fluctuations in a data series. How can you adjust for such fluctuations?
3. After reviewing the U.S. Government Accountability Office report on poverty in America in Appendix A, inspect the U.S. Census Bureau's data on poverty. Using the moving average, can you project the U.S. poverty rate from the Census Bureau's data?
4. In 1987 several states increased the speed limit on their highways in sparsely populated areas. A county analyst is trying to see if the change caused a discernible

increase in the accident fatality rate. She has compiled a table of quarterly fatality data:

Quarter	1985	1986	1987	1988
I	85	76	88	92
II	43	42	52	48
III	51	57	71	78
IV	98	97	110	121

What conclusions can you draw for policy prescription?

5. You are in charge of investing your agency's liquid cash. You are considering investing in a particular security portfolio that has yielded the monthly returns shown below. How would you predict its behavior for the next three months?

Month	Yield
1	7.0
2	3.7
3	1.8
4	0.5
5	9.5
6	0.1
7	2.3
8	6.3
9	3.2
10	0.9
11	4.1
12	9.3
13	7.3
14	7.8
15	6.6

6. The table below shows the number of auto thefts in the city of Masters for the past fifteen years. Use the moving average technique to discern the overall trend and predict the number of auto thefts for the coming year. In this context, explain your choice of lag period.

Year	Auto thefts
1	98
2	87
3	110
4	112
5	108
6	121
7	132
8	125
9	127
10	130
11	145
12	153
13	148
14	151
15	149

7. Collect a series of data on any event of national, state, or local importance. Write a report on its trend pattern and predict its value for the next period.

Notes

1. Also, in reality, a series can assume a much more complex trend pattern. For a more detailed discussion, see Spyros Makridakis, Steven C. Wheelwright, and Victor E. McGee, *Forecasting: Methods and Application*, 2nd ed. (New York: Wiley, 1983).

2. To look at the use of moving average in discerning the underlying trend (and to help you forecast the future trend), log on to the Web page of any Wall Street brokerage firm (for example, Charles Schwab, at www.schwab.com). By choosing the box for a particular company (say, IBM), you can readily see the use of moving average as an aid to the mental forecasting of stock prices.

3. See Robert Lee Holtz, "Southland's Quake Danger Forecast Is Cut," *Los Angeles Times*, March 18, 1998.

4. See Donella Meadows, Dennis L. Meadows, Jorgen Randers, and William W. Behrens III, *The Limits to Growth* (New York: Signet, 1960).

5. Ken Moritsugu and Jackie Koszczuk, "Surplus Could Be a Figment of Faulty Estimates," *San Diego Union-Tribune*, October 7, 2000.

6. Jeff Bater, "U.S. Budget Deficit for 2009 Nears $1 Trillion," *Wall Street Journal*, April 10, 2009, http://blogs.wsj.com/economics/2009/04/10/us-budget-deficit-for-2009-nears-1-trillion.

12 Projection Techniques: The Methods of Simple and Multiple Least Squares

Forecasting is integral to the process of planning. In the previous chapter we discussed the problem of projecting a trend when a long history is unavailable. However, in the current information age, we frequently encounter a long series of past information. When such information is available, forecasting becomes much more systematic, or "scientific" if you will, than forecasting on the basis of a single rate of growth or on subjective judgment.

We do not have to look far to find examples of forecasting in the public sector. State and federal governments routinely forecast revenues from various sources for the preparation of budgets. Local governments, unless they are extremely large, depend primarily on state governments to provide them with such information and do not generally get involved in projecting tax revenues. However, local government agencies frequently engage in forecasting needs for their services. A financial management department may seek permission to raise money from a bond issue for enlarging children's recreation facilities. This may call for a forecast of the number of children in the community for the next five years. In addition to government agencies, branches of the federal reserve banks, research institutes, information consultants, and many other groups get involved in the business of forecasting the future.

We discussed the difference between a trend projection and causal analysis in chapter 10. In this chapter, we will examine one of the most commonly used techniques of trend projection based on a series of data over time (called a time series): the **method of least squares**, or regression models.[1] In a straight or linear trend, we use time as a single independent variable. If you plot the per capita gross domestic product (GDP) of the United States, you will see that the series shows a fairly steady linear trend pattern. I have plotted the data in Figure 12.1. In cases in which there are linear trends, we use **simple regression** models, which have only one independent variable (in our example, time). However, at times a series may exhibit a complex, nonlinear trend pattern. In such a case, you may have to use a nonlinear model with more than one independent variable. These are called **multiple regression** models. The focus of this chapter is on the effects of time. Hence, we will discuss multiple regression within the context of a more complex time pattern in the second half of the chapter. (See Appendix B for a discussion of multiple regression as a part of building causal models.)

THE LOGIC OF THE LEAST SQUARES METHOD

The task of forecasting becomes considerably easier when we have long time-series data that allow us to see if there is a definite trend. When the trend is readily apparent, we can build a model that will help us forecast the future. For example, we can hypothesize from Figure 12.1 that GDP per capita is growing in a linear trend pattern over time. In other words, the elapsed time since the beginning of the study period determines the level of per capita income. The straight line drawn through the yearly data approximates the trend line. By our model we hypothesize that the per capita GDP of the country will continue to grow along this line and, by extending it into the future, we can forecast the future levels of per capita GDP.

In building a model for the projection of a trend, we hypothesize that the fundamental direction in a data series can be explained by the functional relationship proposed by the model. I can best explain the basic idea of a regression model with the help of Figure 12.2. The model in this figure shows the dependent variable (in this case, per capita income) as an input being transformed by the internal logic (or the functional relationship) of the system. An input stimulus (a change in the independent variable—in this case, the passage of time) produces the output (the new level of per

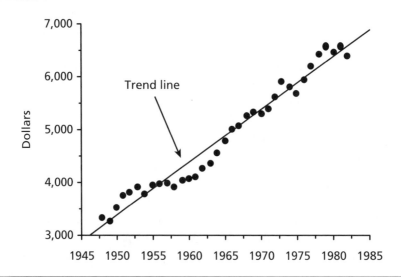

| FIGURE 12.1 | **U.S. Gross Domestic Product per Capita (in 1972 constant dollars)** |

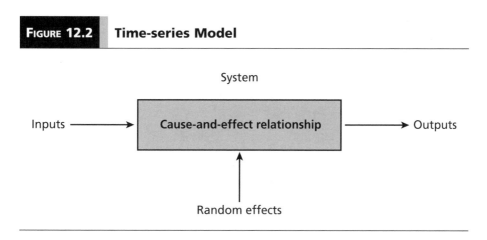

FIGURE 12.2   **Time-series Model**

capita GDP). At this point, it is extremely important to remember that when we are including time as the independent variable, we are in fact claiming to be agnostic regarding the true causal relationship that is propelling the direction of the dependent variable. Thus, multiple factors could affect the growth of the per capita GDP of a nation, including world business cycles, the invention of new technologies, and new areas of trade and commerce (for example, in the case of the United States, trade with a more open China and the former communist nations). War, revolution, or cataclysmic natural disasters, such as earthquakes and hurricanes, are also likely to affect the growth of national domestic products. The basic assumption of a time-series model is that the simple passage of time embodies within it all these complex events, resulting in a steady discernible pattern, which we call a trend.

Despite our hypothesis regarding a simple linear trend, as you can clearly see in Figure 12.1, not all the actual observations fall on the trend line. If they did, we would have a perfect relationship, offering a perfect forecast of the future values. However, one rarely sees a perfect relationship in the realm of the social sciences. When some of the data points do not fall on this line, we claim that the disparity between our forecast and the actual observation is caused by **random errors**. These random events are defined as the effects of those independent variables that we did not include in our model.

Therefore, we assume that the observed system contains two components: the explained and the unexplained. That is,

Data = Trend + Error.

The primary purpose of trend analysis is to uncover the pattern that allows us to project it into the future. In this endeavor, we look for the "best line" that approximates the trend in a data series. In Figure 12.3, for example, we are measuring the values of the dependent variable Y on the vertical axis, while the horizontal axis measures the independent variable X. The plotted observations show a linear trend pattern. By extending the trend (shown by the dashes), we can project the future value of Y on the basis of X. Then the question becomes how to derive the trend line. It should be obvious that to obtain the line that best explains the trend, we must find the one that *lies closest to the*

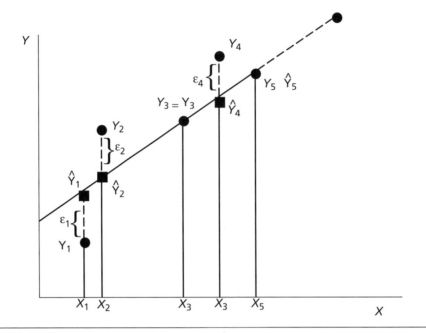

FIGURE 12.3   **Errors of Estimation**

observations, or leaves us with the least amount of unexplained error. Errors are the differences between the projected trend line and the observed data points.

Suppose we have five observations on the dependent variable, Y, the trend of which we are trying to estimate by deriving a line as close as possible to the data points. Suppose we have obtained the trend line for the data series. The points on the trend line are the estimated values. For the first observation, Y_1, we estimate it to be $\hat{Y}_1$ ("Y hat one"). Since our estimate falls short of the actual value, the difference between the actual and the estimated values is the random error, or the error of estimation, which we call ε_1.

It is obvious that drawing the line of estimation by hand (as in Figure 12.3) will not do, because we can never be sure that it is in fact the closest line to the data. However, we can understand intuitively that the best possible line to fit a data set will have to be the least distance from the mean of the series. Consider the following data points:

$$X = 1, 2, 3, 4, 5$$

$$Y = 4, 6, 7, 9, 10$$

If you plot these points on graph paper, you can see that any line that does not go through the point (3, 7.2)—3 being the average of the values of X and 7.2 being the average of the values of Y—cannot be considered closest to the data points.

However, our problem does not go away when we draw a line through the mean values of the two series. Since the deviation from the mean is always the least, the sum total of deviation from the mean is always equal to 0. Therefore, in some cases this rule

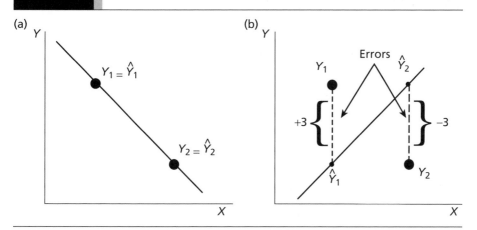

FIGURE 12.4   **The Problems of Summing the Errors**

will not allow us to identify the "best" line. This problem can be shown with the help of Figure 12.4. Suppose I have only two observations, and I want to draw the line to lie closest to these two points of observation. Clearly, as shown in Figure 12.4 (a), the line drawn through the two points will be the best line because for each observation, the error terms are equal to 0. However, suppose I draw this line in the opposite direction, as shown in Figure 12.4 (b). Let us assume that the distances from the trend line to the observed points are 13 and −3, respectively. The problem with simply summing the errors is that the positive errors cancel out the negatives. If we want to choose the best line on the basis of the fewest number of errors, we are at a loss to choose between these two lines, because the sum of errors for both of them is equal to 0. How do we choose between them?

In chapter 6 we discussed the problem of deviations from the mean being equal to 0. Recalling our discussion, we can see that this problem can be avoided if we *square the deviations* from the line. By following this method, the line in Figure 12.4 (a) still gives us an error value of 0, whereas the sum of the squared deviations for the second line is $(+3)^2 + (−3)^2 = 18$. Clearly, we can now choose the first line over the second.

Therefore, we can lay down our criterion for choosing the best line as *the one that gives us the least amount of squared deviation from the observed points.* This is the notion behind the method of least squares.[2] The equation derived through the method of least squares is called the **regression equation.**

LINEAR TIME TREND: SIMPLE REGRESSION MODEL

The regression model for a straight line is given by the following equation:

$$Y = \alpha + \beta X + \varepsilon \tag{12.1}$$

where Y is the **dependent variable** (the one to be explained), α is the **intercept**, β is the **coefficient for trend** (or slope), X is the **independent variable** (the one that explains the

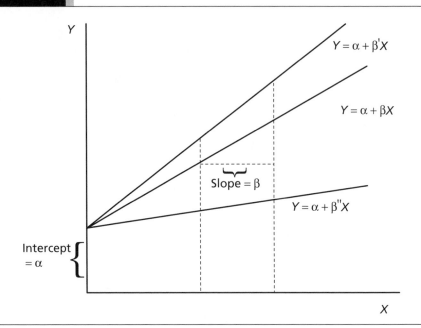

FIGURE 12.5   **Explanation of a Straight-line Equation**

dependent variable), and ε is the **error of estimation** (or the residual difference between actual Y and estimated Y).

Figure 12.5 is an explanation of the meaning of a straight-line equation. The intercept term (α) measures the point at which the trend line meets the vertical axis. Quite often, the intercept term has interesting interpretations. For example, in fitting a Keynesian aggregate consumption function (the relation between consumption and income), the intercept term measures the level of consumption one must have even when income is zero. This is the subsistence level of consumption, which presumably must be met either through government transfer (welfare payment) or private charity.

The trend coefficient β measures the magnitude that a one-unit change in the independent variable causes in the dependent variable. Thus, a higher value of β' would signify a steeper line, implying that a small change in the independent variable would cause a great deal of change in the dependent variable. The reverse would be true for a smaller trend coefficient (β'').[3] A positive trend coefficient implies an upward slope; a negative coefficient a downward slope; and a zero coefficient implies the absence of any relationship between the dependent and independent variable.

An estimated equation for a straight line contains three components: the coefficient (also known as the constant or parameter) for the intercept, the coefficient for the slope, and the error term:

$$\hat{Y}_i = a + b\hat{X}_i \tag{12.1a}$$

where $\hat{Y}_i$ is the estimated value of Y_i, a is the estimated intercept coefficient, and b is the estimated slope coefficient.

It is important to note the difference between the "true" coefficients and their estimated values. The true values are conceptual in nature and, as such, cannot be known. The best we can hope for is to obtain their closest estimated approximation. To help in understanding this important difference, I have denoted the true values with Greek letters and their estimated values with Roman letters.

The **error term** is the difference (the residual) between the *actual* and the *estimated* values of Y: $e_i = Y_i - \hat{Y}_i$ By replacing $\hat{Y}_i$ with $a + bX$ (from equation 12.1a), we get

$$e_i = Y_i - a - bX_i \tag{12.2}$$

As I explained earlier, by the method of least squares we estimate the coefficients of a and b such that we minimize this sum of errors[4]:

$$\text{Minimize} \sum_{i=1}^{n} (e_i)^2 = \sum_{i=1}^{n} (Y_i - a - bX_i)^2 \tag{12.3}$$

From the preceding expression (12.3), we can devise the following formula for the estimated coefficient of b:

$$b = \frac{\sum (Y_i - \overline{Y})(X_i - \overline{X})}{\sum (X_i - \overline{X})^2} \tag{12.4}$$

where $\overline{Y}$ and $\overline{X}$ are the means for the variables Y_i and X_i.

The intercept term is estimated by

$$a = \overline{Y} - b\overline{X} \tag{12.5}$$

Let us consider the following example. Suppose that for the purpose of long-term planning, we would like to estimate the future population of a small town. The population figures for the past five years are shown in Table 12.1. By plotting this series (see Figure 12.6), we can detect the existence of a steady linear trend. We then decide to forecast the future population size using a linear equation form, shown in equation 12.1.

To estimate the coefficients a and b, for a straight-line equation, we need to work out Table 12.2.

TABLE 12.1   **Population over Time (in thousands)**

Population	Year
5	1
8	2
10	3
15	4
17	5

TABLE 12.2	Calculations for a Straight-line Regression Equation				

			Year		
Population (Y_i)	(X_i)	($Y_i - \overline{Y}$)	($X_i - \overline{X}$)	($X_i - \overline{X}$)²	($Y_i - \overline{Y}$)($X_i - \overline{X}$)
5	1	−6	−2	4	12
8	2	−3	−1	1	3
10	3	−1	0	0	0
15	4	4	1	1	4
17	5	6	2	4	12
Total		0	0	10	31

Note: $\overline{Y} = 11.0$ and $\overline{X} = 3.0$.

Recalling the formula for calculating b,

$$b = \frac{\sum (Y_i - \overline{Y})(X_i - \overline{X})}{\sum (X_i - \overline{X})^2}$$

we can calculate the value of b by inserting the numbers from Table 12.2. Thus, we estimate

$$b = \frac{31.00}{10.00} = 3.1$$

Similarly, we can calculate the intercept term a as

$$a = \overline{Y} - (b\overline{X}) = 11 - (3.1 \times 3) = 1.7$$

Therefore, we can write the estimated equation as

$$\text{Population } (\hat{Y}) = 1.7 + 3.1 \text{ Year } (X) \tag{12.6}$$

The plot of the actual data and the trend line are shown in Figure 12.6.

We have plotted the estimated and actual values of population in Figure 12.6. From this derived equation we can project the future population of the city. For example, we can estimate the population for the sixth year (6) as

$$1.7 + (3.1 \times 6) = 20.3$$

Similarly, to obtain the projected figure for the seventh year, we must substitute 7 as the value for the independent variable (X). This arithmetic calculation yields 23.4, the projected population figure for the seventh year.

Accuracy of the Results

Having estimated the trend line, you can legitimately ask, how good are my results? This question has two interrelated parts: First, you may ask whether your model is offering a significant explanation of the variations within the series. Second, you would want to

FIGURE 12.6   **Population Trend**

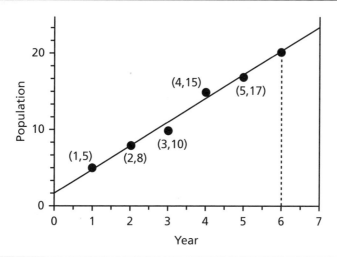

explore how confident you feel about your estimation of the coefficients. That is, are the estimated values reflective of the "true" relationship between the dependent and independent variables, or did you obtain a correlation by chance—a spurious correlation?

Recall Figure 12.3. While estimating the relationship between the dependent and independent variables, we can see that we can explain part of the series through estimation, whereas the remainder (the difference between the observed and the estimated values) is unexplained. A perfect explanation explains all the variations within a series. In contrast, in the absence of any relation between the two variables, none of the variations will be explained. Hence, the measure of goodness of fit is the proportion of explained variance within the total variance. Again, since we want to get rid of the problem of having to add positive deviations with negative deviations, we square the deviations and then sum the results.[5] This ratio is called the **coefficient of determination**, or R^2, and is written as

$$R^2 = \frac{\text{Squared sum of explained variations}}{\text{Squared sum of total variations}} = \frac{\sum(\hat{Y}_i - \overline{Y})^2}{\sum(Y_i - \overline{Y})^2} \qquad (12.7)$$

where Y_i represents the actual values for Y observations, $\overline{Y}$ is the mean of Y, and $\hat{Y}_i$ represents the predicted values of Y_i on the basis of the regression line (calculated using the estimated equation $Y = a + bX_i$).

You may note that when all the Y_i values are correctly predicted, the predicted values are the same as the actual values. In that case, $\hat{Y}_i$ is equal to Y_i, which means that the numerator is equal to the denominator, or the value of R^2 is equal to 1. This is a perfect explanation. When a model cannot explain any variation (or when the variations are completely random), however, the values of $\hat{Y}_i$ form a horizontal line (such as the one shown in the previous chapter in Figure 11.3) that goes through the average value of the distribution. In such a case, $\hat{Y}_i$ is equal to $\overline{Y}$, which makes the numerator equal to 0 and

TABLE 12.3	Calculation of R^2			
Population (Y_i)	Year (X_i)	Projected value ($\hat{Y}_i$)[a]	$(\hat{Y}_i - \overline{Y})^2$	$(Y_i - \overline{Y})^2$
5	1	4.8	38.44	36.0
8	2	7.9	9.61	9.0
10	3	11.0	0.00	1.0
15	4	14.1	9.61	16.0
17	5	17.2	38.44	36.0
Total			96.10	98.0

[a] The projected values are calculated with the help of the estimated equation 12.6.

consequently R^2 equal to 0. Therefore, the value of R^2 will always fall within the limits 0 (no explanation) and 1 (perfect explanation).

Let us calculate R^2 for our example from Table 12.3. We can calculate R^2 using equation 12.7:

$$R^2 = \frac{96.1}{98.0} = 0.981$$

In other words, our model is predicting slightly more than 98 percent of the variations.

High R^2

There is no universally acceptable answer to the question of what a high R^2 is. Generally speaking, if you are dealing with *economic time-series data*, you are likely to find a high degree of correlation, because most economic variables tend to move in the same direction. In times of prosperity, all the good indicators tend to go up (for example, savings, investment, employment, housing construction). The reverse takes place during economic recession. In an interesting study, Edward Ames and Stanley Reiter showed that even when unrelated time-series data were chosen at random and regressed against one another, R^2 values exceeded 0.5.[6] The lesson of their study is that since correlation between two variables only measures co-occurrence and does not necessarily establish a causal linkage, a high value of R^2 should not give cause for celebration, unless such a relationship can be backed up by solid theoretical reasoning.

You should also note that for cross-section data, the R^2 values are typically smaller than those for time-series data. Also, because of greater complexity in their interrelationships, correlation coefficients for sociological or political data are often much smaller than those for economic or financial data.

Relevance of the Estimated Coefficients

Now that we have determined how much of an explanation of the data the model is providing, we may want to know the following: how relevant are the *individual coefficients*, and how relevant are the coefficients *taken as a whole*? To answer these questions, we need to look back at the development of theoretical statistics. One of the most remarkable theorems of the entire field of mathematics and mathematical statistics was derived nearly 200 years ago and provides the basis for hypothesis testing. Suppose you know the average (mean) height of the American male population (μ) and the standard deviation (σ). You are conducting a random survey, whereby you are surveying groups of men and noting their average heights. At every try, you are getting a small sample group together and noting its average height, subtracting it from the **population mean** (μ), and dividing by the **population standard deviation** (σ).[7] You continue with this process, which symbolically can be written as

$$\frac{(\overline{X}_i - \mu)}{\sigma} \tag{12.8}$$

As discussed in chapter 7, if you repeat your experiment, the plotted results will approach a normal distribution. This distribution will have a mean equal to 0 and a standard deviation equal to 1. The remarkable aspect of this theorem is that it does not matter what the distribution of the variable X_i is. Unless there are some systematic biases (such as measuring only basketball players to arrive at the average height of the general public), repeating this procedure will give us the normal distribution as the number of samples increases. This theorem is known as the law of large numbers (see chapter 7). By the property of this standardized distribution, we know how much of the values will fall within what range, which makes the derivation of a normal distribution particularly fortuitous. For example, we know that approximately 95 percent of all values will fall within ±1.96 standard deviations, and nearly 99 percent of all values will fall within ±2.57 standard deviations. Therefore, in our example, suppose we come across a group of Pygmies with an average height that is more than 1.96 standard deviations below the average for men from the United States. We can then state with a 95 percent level of confidence that the members of this particular sample are not Americans. Let me explain this with the help of Figure 12.7.

You may notice, however, that I have emphasized the term *random*. One of the most important assumptions of a regression model is that the model includes all of the

FIGURE 12.7   **Curve of Normal Distribution**

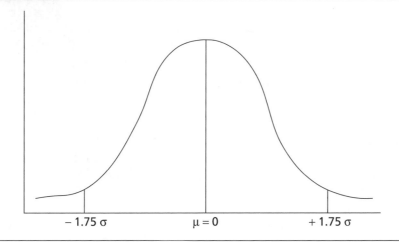

$- 1.75\ \sigma$ $\mu = 0$ $+ 1.75\ \sigma$

A CASE IN POINT

Campaign Contributions and Judicial Impartiality: How Regression Analysis Can Help

Although judges are required to follow the law when deciding cases, there might be enough flexibility in the law to allow for some judicial interpretation. Assuming that a case allows a judge some discretion in decision making, it is generally assumed that judges and justices want to hand down decisions that are consistent with their own personal belief systems. But what if a judge's personal beliefs are inconsistent with the views of a majority of American citizens? Are there any political consequences for rendering unpopular decisions? On the U.S. Supreme Court, to which justices are appointed by the president for life terms, it is unlikely that justices will face any serious ramifications for ruling against the majority. That is not the case, however, on state supreme courts.

Some state high court justices are appointed, but most have set term lengths and keep (or lose) their seats on the bench through popular elections, just like other politicians. And like other politicians, these justices must raise money to fund their campaigns. Most of the money raised by judges comes from special interest groups, many of which have cases before those same judges. If justices' campaign contributors have specific policy objectives and specific rulings they expect justices to deliver, then justices who are reelected may be influenced in their rulings. As such, we can assume that a rational judge has two goals: the judge wants to implement personal policy preferences and wants to get reelected. The question for social scientists is, how do judges balance these two goals?

The question of judicial impartiality came to a head in 2009, when the Supreme Court decided a case that had become a flashpoint in the national debate over potential corruption in state judicial elections caused by big contributors. In a 5-4 decision in the case of *Caperton v. A.T. Massey Coal Company, Inc., et al.*, the Court ruled that "West Virginia Supreme Court Justice Brent Benjamin violated constitutional due process of law when he voted in the dispute after being asked to take himself out because of a conflict of interest."[8] The perception of judicial impartiality is the cornerstone of our political system. Therefore, the question at hand is of great importance to all of us.

The question is, Is there any empirical proof of campaign money influencing judges' decisions? By creatively using regression analysis, in a series of articles Madhavi McCall provided empirical proof for the question of justice for sale.[9] In her model, she presented a list of variables that justices consider when making decisions. This is because before we can truly understand the impact

relevant explanatory variables. Therefore, the variation in the observed data that is not explained is caused by random factors, which are distributed normally around the mean of 0. A variable is considered random if its values are determined by the outcome of a "chance experiment." That is, in our example, if we confined our search to a particular ethnic group, or a group of basketball players, then the outcomes are not being determined by chance. Whether the selection is by design or by some unrecognized bias on the part of the researcher, this theorem of the law of large numbers will not apply; the of campaign contributions on case outcomes, we must control for other factors that might influence judicial choices. For instance, while there may be some flexibility in a justice's ability to interpret the law, the law still matters and is most likely a factor in judicial decisions. Additionally, some judges may choose to follow more closely what campaign contributors want in the months immediately before they face reelection in the hope of generating more contributions, suggesting that the timing of a case during a justice's term also matters. After getting reelected, no longer immediately needing popular votes or campaign contributions, a rational judge may decide that he or she now has an opportunity to decide cases based only on his or her personal view of the law, suggesting that a justice's personal policy preferences are important. Using regression analyses, McCall tested what impact campaign contributions, case timing, the law, and a justice's personal policy preferences have on that justice's eventual vote and determined which factors, when they are all considered together, exert the strongest influence on the justice's rulings.

For instance, when regression was applied to the voting behavior of Texas's elected state supreme court justices, McCall found that the justices' voting decisions appeared to be strongly influenced by campaign contributions and that the Texas justices appeared to be very strategic in their decisions. Immediately before elections, the justices voted with the popular majority so that they could garner sufficient votes to win the elections. However, during the campaign season (several months of fund-raising and campaigning before the actual elections), the justices were more inclined to vote with campaign contributors. This was true even when a campaign contributor held a fundamentally different legal position than the justice typically supported, suggesting that during the campaign season, justices put aside their own personal policy positions and instead favored the positions of campaign contributors. And of course, certain aspects of the law restricted judicial choices. Ultimately, however, the model indicates that during the campaign season, the most significant influence on judicial behavior is the presence or absence of a campaign contribution. The use of regression in this type of study allows for a better understanding of the determinants of judicial behavior.

Discussion Points

1. On the basis of the findings of these studies, what kind of policy would you propose to ensure judicial impartiality? For instance, should judges be appointed for life or, as in some countries, rise through the ranks of civil service?
2. Can you think of and propose testable hypotheses in other areas of policy inquiry?

resulting distribution will not approximate a normal distribution, regardless of the number of experiments. As a result, none of the results described below will hold true.

The Significance of Individual Coefficients

As can be seen in Figure 12.7, a group average sufficiently different from the mean may indicate that the two populations are indeed different. Hence, this theorem serves as the basis for testing the validity of hypotheses. For our purposes, we can use this result to test the null hypothesis that our coefficients are results of chance and, in fact, there is no relationship between the dependent and the independent variables. For example, the level of statistical significance for our estimated trend coefficient (b) can be calculated as

$$\frac{b - \beta}{\sigma} \tag{12.9}$$

where b is the estimated coefficient, β is the true coefficient, and σ is the true standard deviation of the distribution. Since we are testing the null hypothesis that there is no correlation between the dependent and independent variables, we set β equal to 0. Also, since we do not know what the true standard deviation is for population, we approximate it within the estimated standard error of coefficient, which we may call SE_b. Therefore, equation 12.9 can be written as

$$t_b = \frac{b}{SE_b} \tag{12.10}$$

Similarly, to test the statistical significance of the coefficient a, we need to calculate the t ratio given by

$$t_a = \frac{a}{SE_a} \tag{12.11}$$

From equations 12.10 and 12.11, we can see that the larger a coefficient is in relation to its standard error of estimate, the farther out the calculated ratio will be on our normal distribution chart. The farther out it is, the more convinced we will be that the coefficients are not equal to 0. Therefore, the value of this ratio will tell us that the coefficients are **statistically significant**.

Before we get into the process of actually testing the null hypothesis regarding the validity of the coefficients, I would like to repeat a few important properties of hypothesis testing from our discussion in chapter 7. First, as the name suggests, by the law of large numbers, the normal distribution is achieved only when the number of observations becomes extremely large. In such cases one can use the Z table to test hypotheses. However, when the number of observations is relatively small, an approximation of the normal distribution is used to ascertain the critical values. This is called **Student's t distribution**, named after a statistician who wrote under the pseudonym Student.

Since we do not know the true standard deviation of an estimator (an estimated coefficient), we need to approximate it with our sample results. Let us take a concrete example. In our population projection, we estimated two coefficients: $a = 11.0$ and $b = 3.1$. On the basis of that result, we can use the following sample estimate of the true variance σ^2:

$$SE^2 = \frac{\sum e_i^2}{n - 2} = \frac{\sum (Y_i - a - bX_i)^2}{n - 2} \tag{12.12}$$

where SE is the standard error of estimate.

You can see that the numerator of equation 12.12 is the sum of squared errors of estimate. This sum is being divided by $n - 2$ (the number of observations minus 2) to approximate the true variance.[10]

With an estimate of $\sum e_i^2$, we can estimate the variance associated with the estimated coefficients, a and b. The respective standard errors are calculated as

$$SE_a = \sqrt{SE^2 \frac{\sum X_i^2}{n\sum(X_i - \overline{X})^2}} \qquad (12.13)$$

and

$$SE_b = \sqrt{\frac{SE^2}{\sum(X_i - \overline{X})^2}} \qquad (12.14)$$

From the preceding formulas, we can see that to calculate the standard errors of the coefficients, we need to add a column to Table 12.3 (see Table 12.4).

From equation 12.12, the estimate of $SE^2 = 1.9/3 = 0.63$. Substituting the numbers in equations 12.13 and 12.14, we derive the estimated standard error of coefficients a and b as

$$SE_a = \sqrt{0.63\left(\frac{55}{5 \times 10}\right)} = 0.83$$

and

$$SE_b = \sqrt{\frac{0.63}{10}} = 0.25$$

Substituting the respective values in equations 12.10 and 12.11, we get

$$t_a = \frac{1.7}{0.83} = 2.05 \qquad (12.13a)$$

and

$$t_b = \frac{3.1}{0.25} = 12.4 \qquad (12.14a)$$

For an interpretation of these results, we can resort to Figure 12.7. We noted that if the estimated coefficient is located farther away from its critical value, we can be reasonably certain that the estimated value is different from the true value proposed by our null hypothesis.

These values (t_a and t_b) are distributed as t, with $n - 2$ degrees of freedom (see definition in chapter 7). Since we have five observations, our degrees of freedom are $5 - 2 = 3$. By checking a t table for 3 degrees of freedom, we see that for a .05 level of significance (a 95 percent confidence level), the t ratio is equal to 2.353. Therefore, if the ratios are greater than this number, we can state with a great deal of confidence that our estimated coefficients are indeed significantly different from zero. In other words, there is a significant relationship between the dependent and the independent variables.

Because the t value of the intercept term (2.1) is less than the required critical value (2.353), we cannot reject the null hypothesis that the intercept is equal to 0. In contrast, because the t ratio for the slope (b) is greater than this number, we can be sure that this number is statistically significant.

TABLE 12.4	**Calculations for Tests of Significance**				
Population (Y_i)	Year (X_i)	Projected value ($\hat{Y}_i$)	$(Y_i - \hat{Y}_i)^2$	$(X_i - \bar{X}_i)^2$	X_i^2
5	1	4.8	0.04	4	1
8	2	7.9	0.01	1	4
10	3	11.0	1.00	0	9
15	4	14.1	0.81	1	16
17	5	17.2	0.04	4	25
Total			1.90	10	55

Presentation of Estimation Results

Once a regression equation is estimated, the results must be presented to the policy-makers. There are of course many ways of presenting this information. I suggest the following:

$$\text{Population} = 1.7 + 3.1\text{Year}$$
$$t = (2.037)(12.32)^*$$
$$R^2 = 0.98$$
$$\text{Adjusted } R^2 = 0.97 \qquad (12.15)$$
$$n = 5$$
$$F_{(1,3)} = 151.74^*$$

*Significant at the .05 level

The numbers within the parentheses in the estimated equation 12.15 are the respective t values for the individual coefficients. The asterisks point out the significant t values and F value. You may notice that the t value for the slope coefficient and the F statistic are significant, but the t value for the intercept term is not significant at the .05 level. An estimated equation with a high R^2 and significant slope coefficients but an insignificant intercept may seem a bit confusing to you. It may happen for two reasons. First, it may be that the "true" intercept is too close to 0, and thus the regression equation is unable to determine its estimated value. Or it may mean that you have left out some important independent variable in your construction (technically, "specification") of the model.

The Number of Observations

A series with five observations occurs in my example of population growth. You may ask, what is the minimum number of observations I need to establish a proper relationship between the dependent and the independent variables? Remembering the law of large numbers, we can see that as the number of observations increases, so does the accuracy of the estimated coefficients. In Figure 12.8 I have shown how the estimated

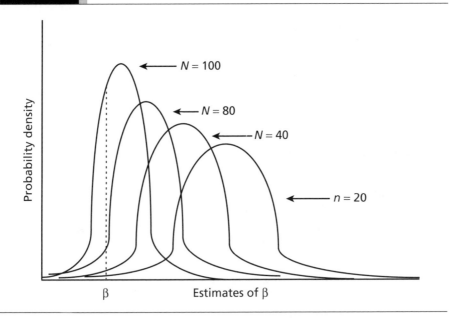

FIGURE 12.8   Increasing Accuracy of Estimated Coefficients

coefficients tend to converge on the "true" coefficients as the number of observations becomes very large (and, consequently, the sample distribution approaches a normal distribution). You may also note that with a larger number of observations, not only do the estimated coefficients come closer to the actual number, but their deviation gets smaller. That is, we are increasingly confident that our estimated **regression coefficients** represent their "true" values. Finally, no number can be considered sufficiently large to estimate the "true" value of the coefficient, so I have drawn the estimated coefficient b, with 100 observations, close to its true value of β, but they are still not equal.

In sum, because there is no definition of a "very large number," as a rule of thumb you should not have fewer than ten observations in a regression model. My examples of the estimated equation have fewer than ten observations solely for the ease of computation.

TREND CHANGES: BUILDING MULTIPLE REGRESSION MODELS

In a straight-line model we hypothesize that the trend has remained unchanged during the period under study. However, it is entirely possible that the data may reflect a changing pattern. This change can be abrupt or can be part of a gradual process. An abrupt change in trend can result from sudden catastrophic events such as war, the changing of a law, a significant invention resulting in a change in technology, or a change in policy resulting from a change in political leadership. These events introduce a **qualitative change** in a series. For example, if we note the trend of per capita GDP in a country such as Iraq, we may notice dramatic downward shifts in trend following Iraq's two devastating wars with Iran and the coalition led by the United States. Similarly, several data series (such as national debt) for the United States will show signs of abrupt changes brought about by significant wars. A study of immigration patterns will clearly show the results of changes in the law. Similarly, the invention of many modern drugs, such as penicillin, caused shifts in the trends of infant mortality in the late 1940s and 1950s.

Abrupt Changes in Trend

Suppose we are studying the trend in per capita expenditure by the local government in a community that incorporated itself as a new city in 1996. The achievement of its city status has enabled it to access more state and federal grants, which has caused a vertical shift in the series. Table 12.5 provides the series of per capita government expenditures.

This abrupt change in trend is shown in Figure 12.9. You may notice that the vertical shift that takes place during the middle of the series (in 1996) does not affect the trend pattern itself.

These sorts of shifts are typical of series in which an extremely important external event has taken place or there is a large gap in the data set. It is clear from this figure that a broken trend line would produce fewer errors of estimation than would an unbroken straight line fitted through the entire series.

For a better visual presentation, I have replotted the data shown in Figure 12.9 (see Figure 12.10). In this figure, we can see the result of a vertical shift. We can account for this vertical shift if we draw a trend line based on our pre-incorporation (before 1996) data and then add a constant to the estimated values for the post-incorporation data (1996 and after). This can be done if we have *two* intercept terms, one for before and one for after the incorporation. We can accomplish this with a trick: we can introduce what is known as an **intercept dummy variable**.

TABLE 12.5	Per Capita Federal Grant Expenditures
Year	Expenditure (constant $)
1991	105.0
1992	110.0
1993	116.0
1994	120.0
1995	125.0
1996	180.0
1997	187.0
1998	193.0
1999	200.0
2000	213.0

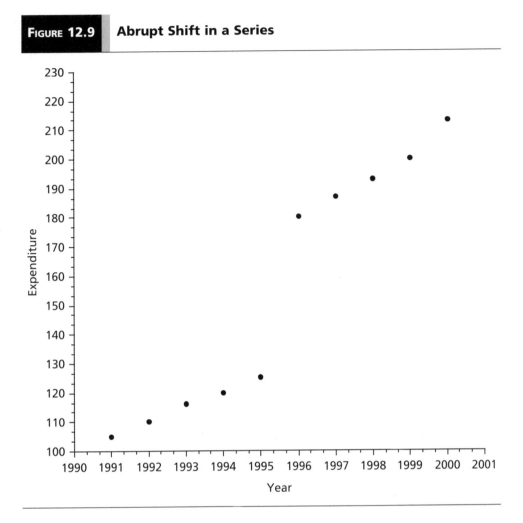

FIGURE 12.9   Abrupt Shift in a Series

An intercept dummy introduces an additional intercept term to account for this kind of a shift. This takes the form of adding an extra independent variable, which has a value of 0 for the observations prior to the time of shift and 1 for periods afterward. Therefore, the equation to be estimated is written as

$$Y_i = a + a' + bX_i + e_i \qquad (12.16)$$

where a' is the dummy variable, which is 0 for years prior to the shift (1991–1996 in our example) and 1 for the years afterward (1996–2000).

Let us proceed with the example of our newly incorporated city. Since we want to introduce an additional independent variable, a', we need to add a new column to Table 12.5, as seen in Table 12.6.

You may realize now that as we introduce an additional independent variable, a', we will be using multiple regression instead of simple regression. The estimation of the coefficients of multiple regression is a bit too complicated to be calculated by hand. Even

FIGURE 12.10 **Shift in Expenditure Pattern**

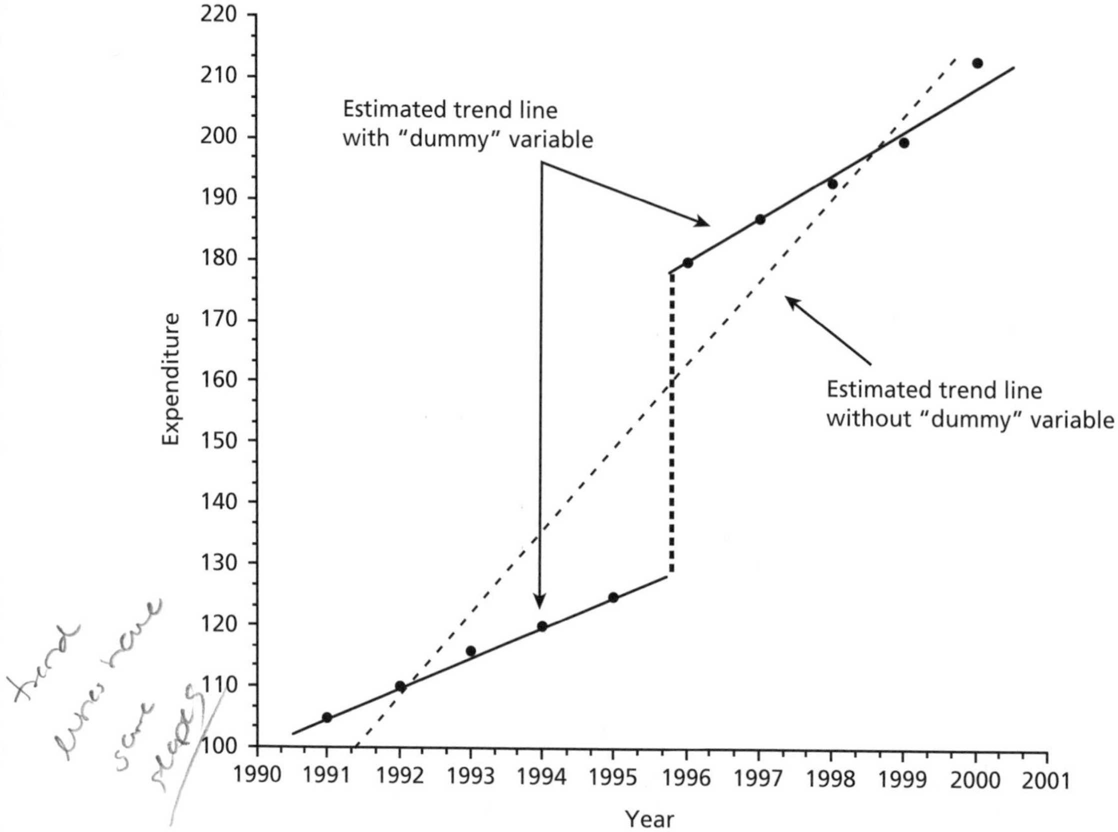
Estimated trend line
with "dummy" variable
Estimated trend line
without "dummy" variable
Expenditure
220
210
200
190
180
170
160
150
140
130
120
110
100
1990
1991
1992
1993
1994
1995
1996
1997
1998
1999
2000
2001
Year
trend
lines have
same
slopes

TABLE 12.6 **Setting Up an Intercept Dummy Variable**

Year	Expenditure (constant $)	Dummy (*a*′)
1991	105.0	0
1992	110.0	0
1993	116.0	0
1994	120.0	0
1995	125.0	0
1996	180.0	1
1997	187.0	1
1998	193.0	1
1999	200.0	1
2000	213.0	1

though generations of students of statistics and econometrics were subjected to this tortuous exercise, the proliferation of computers has made the estimation rather simple. Therefore, you will want to use suitable statistical software to derive the coefficients for this equation.

The use of this dummy variable gives us an excellent predictive model, as shown by the results of the estimated equation[11]:

$$\text{Expenditure} = -12,739.65 + 6.45 \text{ Year} + 47.15 \text{ Dummy}$$
$$t = \quad (-9.768)^* \quad (9.857)^* \quad \quad (12.543)^*$$
$$R^2 = 0.996$$
$$\text{Adjusted } R^2 = 0.995 \quad\quad\quad\quad\quad (12.17)$$
$$n = 10$$
$$F_{(2,7)} = 968.7^*$$

*Significant at the .05 level

where the dummy variable equals 0 for years prior to 1996 and 1 for 1996 and afterward.

I have placed the calculated t ratios under the corresponding regression coefficients. As you can tell from this equation, we are explaining 99.5 percent of the total variance in the series. The dummy variable tells us that as a result of incorporation, an average resident of the city gained $47.15 in government funding. The coefficient for the variable Year tells us that every year, the federal contribution has gone up by $6.45 per city resident. If we want to predict the level of per capita government expenditure for 2001, we will have to write the equation as follows:

$$\text{Projected expenditure } (2001) = -12,739.65 + 6.45 \times 2001$$
$$+ 47.15 \times 1 = 213.95$$

To estimate values for years prior to 1996, we will have to set the dummy variable equal to 0, and therefore the equation will contain only the intercept and slope terms. Thus, we may estimate the value for 1993 as follows:

$$\text{Estimated expenditure } (1993) = -12,739.65 + 6.45 \times 1993$$
$$+ 47.15 \times 0 = 115.2$$

I have plotted the predicted versus the actual values of expenditure in Figure 12.10. The estimated line with the dummy variable has been drawn as a solid line, whereas the straight-line equation has been drawn as a dotted line. You may notice the close approximation of the actual values as a result of the use of the dummy variable. For example, if you estimate the equation without the dummy variable, you get the following result:

$$\text{Expenditure} = -26,971.81 + 13.59 \text{ Year}$$
$$t = \quad (-9.26)^* \quad (9.31)^*$$
$$R^2 = 0.915$$
$$\text{Adjusted } R^2 = 0.905 \quad\quad\quad\quad\quad (12.17a)$$
$$n = 10$$
$$F_{(2,7)} = 86.67^*$$

*Significant at the .05 level

Although this equation looks excellent on its own, the use of the dummy significantly improves the quality of the estimated equation.[12]

Abrupt Changes in Slope

In the previous example, we discussed the situation in which there is a parallel shift in the trend line. In reality there can also be an abrupt change in the slope. This change is more dramatic because this new situation has altered the entire direction of the trend line. There are many examples of this abrupt change in trend. The discovery of gold in California in 1849 caused a huge population influx; the initiation of the Great Society program in the 1960s caused a sudden increase in the trend of social expenditures; the successful launching of the Soviet Union's *Sputnik* satellite caused a big increase in expenditures for NASA for a decade; during the presidency of Ronald Reagan, federal assistance to state and local governments took an abrupt change in the opposite direction. Let us consider a hypothetical example of government expenditures on drug rehabilitation programs for a period of fifteen years. Assume that because of heightened awareness and a change in political leadership during the eighth year of the study, society decided to spend increasing amounts on drug rehabilitation programs (see Table 12.7 and Figure 12.11).

The plot in Figure 12.11 makes it clear that the trend pattern changed after the seventh year. Whereas for the first seven years of the study, government expenditure was increasing at a slow rate, the rate of change accelerated greatly from the eighth year on. This change in trend cannot be accommodated simply by adding an intercept dummy. Therefore, in our projection of trend, we need to account for this change. This abrupt change can be captured adequately by using dummy variables for the two different slopes. Imagine holding a stick at an angle approximating the trend shown at the beginning of a data series. We can visualize the change in trend if we break the stick at the point at which the change took place. To split the series into two distinct trend lines, we introduce two dummy variables, D_1 and D_2, with D_1 having the value 1 for all the points

TABLE 12.7	Expenditures on Drug Rehabilitation Programs
Year	**Expenditure ($\times$$1,000)**
1	76
2	75
3	78
4	76
5	80
6	81
7	80
8	96
9	97
10	102
11	109
12	114
13	116
14	125
15	129

FIGURE 12.11 **Plot of Trend in Government Expenditures for Drug Rehabilitation**

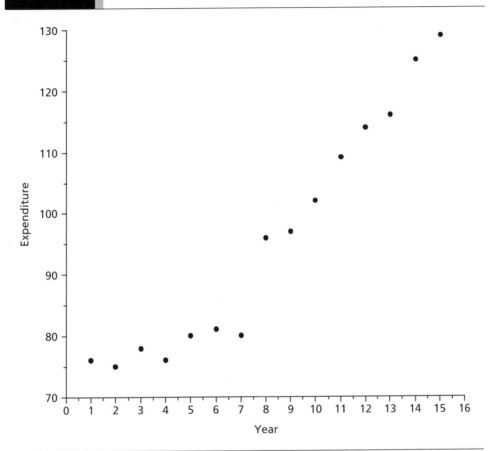

for which the old trend applies and 0 for the rest. D_2 has the values 0 and 1 in the reverse order. Then, by multiplying the independent variable by these two dummy variables, we can create two new sets of independent variables. By running a multiple regression on the dependent variables against these two newly created variables, we can estimate the equation containing two different slopes (Table 12.8).

Using the data shown in Table 12.8, we estimate the trend equation for government expenditure, which yields the following results:

$$\text{Expenditure} = 70.61 + 1.663(D_1 \times \text{Year}) + 3.568(D_2 \times \text{Year})$$
$$t = (27.5)^* \quad (2.8)^* \qquad\qquad (15.0)^*$$
$$R^2 = 0.974$$
$$\text{Adjusted } R_2 = 0.969$$
$$n = 15$$
$$F_{(2,12)} = 222.75^*$$

(12.18)

*Significant at the .05 level

TABLE 12.8	Setting Up Slope Dummy Variables				
Year	Expenditure (×$1,000)	D_1	D_2	$D_1 \times$ Year	$D_2 \times$ Year
1	76	1	0	1	0
2	75	1	0	2	0
3	78	1	0	3	0
4	76	1	0	4	0
5	80	1	0	5	0
6	81	1	0	6	0
7	80	1	0	7	0
8	96	0	1	0	8
9	97	0	1	0	9
10	102	0	1	0	10
11	109	0	1	0	11
12	114	0	1	0	12
13	116	0	1	0	13
14	125	0	1	0	14
15	129	0	1	0	15

From this equation, we can see that the trend coefficient for the second period (3.568) is 2.15 times larger than that for the first period (1.663). This equation can be used to estimate the amount of government expenditure for every year within the study and can be used to predict the values for future time periods.

If you estimate an equation with a **slope dummy**, you may run into a problem when you attempt to forecast. If you estimate an equation with two slope dummies to account for the two phases of a trend, you may have to include an intercept dummy in your model. If you do not include an additional intercept dummy, the model will force each slope to compromise on a common intercept, which will make both the slope lines deviate from their true positions. If, however, you allow for the slope dummies to have their own intercepts, the estimated results will be far superior.

Consider once again the estimated equation (12.18). We can significantly improve the model by including an intercept dummy, D_1. The model is estimated as

$$\text{Expenditure} = 53.77 + 20.51D_1 + 0.929(D_1 \times \text{Year}) + 4.976(D_2 \times \text{Year})$$
$$t = (18.05)^*(6.24)^* \quad (2.98)^* \quad (19.58)^*$$
$$R^2 = 0.994$$
$$\text{Adjusted } R^2 = 0.993 \qquad\qquad (12.19)$$
$$n = 15$$
$$F_{(2,12)} = 630.47^*$$

*Significant at the .05 level

FIGURE 12.12	Comparison of Estimated Trend Lines

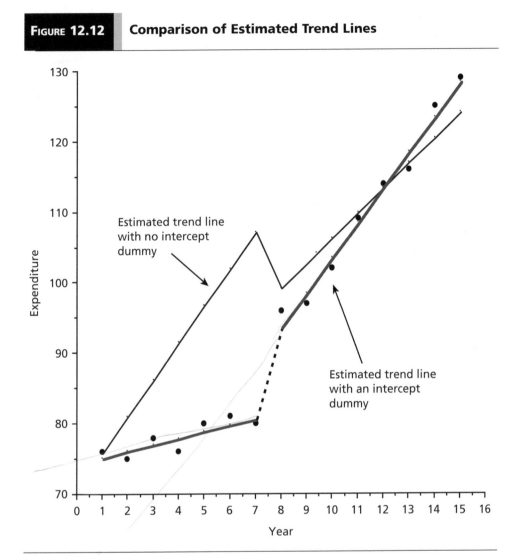

If you compare the estimated results of equation 12.18 with those of equation 12.19, you will notice that all the statistics have improved. However, the real improvement can be seen when the predicted values based on the two equations are plotted side by side against the actual values. In Figure 12.12, I have drawn the predicted values of actual expenditure on the basis of the two models. You can see that the line with a dummy variable is clearly superior (closer) to the actual values. You may also note that the slope of the second phase (4.976) is nearly 5.4 times the slope of the first phase (0.929). I have presented the estimated data in Table 12.9.

TABLE 12.9	Comparison of Estimated Data	
Actual observation	Estimated value (without intercept dummy, equation 12.18)	Estimated value (with intercept dummy, equation 12.19)
76	72.27	75.21
75	73.94	76.14
78	75.60	77.07
76	77.26	78.00
80	78.93	78.93
81	80.59	79.86
80	82.25	80.79
96	99.16	93.58
97	102.72	98.56
102	106.29	103.54
109	109.86	108.51
114	113.43	113.49
116	116.99	118.46
125	120.56	123.44
129	124.13	128.42

GRADUAL CHANGES IN TREND: ESTIMATION OF NONLINEAR TRENDS

Many data series relating to society and the economy can be approximated by a straight line. When a trend is fundamentally nonlinear, however, the use of a straight line will cause severe problems in forecasting. Many nonlinear forms can be captured by regression equations (thanks to advances in computer technology) without a great deal of computational difficulty. Some nonlinear trends can be estimated easily by transforming the data, in which case we do not need to use any special nonlinear estimation techniques (which are beyond the scope of this book). Let us consider a few examples.

Polynomial Forms

A polynomial form expresses a dependent variable as a function of a number of independent variables. Some of these independent variables may be raised to powers greater than 1. The degree of a polynomial is known by the highest power among the independent variables. Thus, a quadratic form, expressed as $Y_i = a + b_1X_i - b_2X_i^2$, is called a second-degree polynomial, the equation $Y_i = a + b_1X_i - b_2X_i^2$ $Y_i = a + b_1X_i - b_2X_i^2 + b_3X^3$ is called a third-degree polynomial, and so on.

It is common to find examples of a quadratic relationship in nature. For example, as we apply fertilizer to plants, they grow at a rapid rate, and we get more flowers, fruits, and vegetables. However, after a certain point, the application of more fertilizer damages their growth. Or, after an initial period of decrease in the cost per flower, we increase our scale of operation. But at a certain point, inefficiency creeps in and unit costs start

TABLE 12.10	Budget Deficit as a Percentage of GDP (five-year average)	
Years	**Percentage of GDP**	**Time**
1970–1974	1.5	1
1975–1979	2.8	2
1980–1984	3.9	3
1985–1989	5.4	4
1990–1994	4.9	5
1995–1999	1.6	6

climbing. As another example, if we start consuming something we highly desire, our satisfaction goes up, but after a point of saturation, we tend to lose interest. These are all examples of quadratic relationships, as discussed in chapter 11. A quadratic form can be U shaped or inverted U shaped.

The quadratic equation is specified as

$$Y_i = a + b_1 X_i - b_2 X_i^2 \tag{12.20}$$

for a U-shaped relationship and

$$Y_i = a - b_1 X_1 + b_2 X_i^2 \tag{12.21}$$

for an inverse U–shaped relationship.[13]

Let us see how these nonlinear forms are estimated. Consider the data series for the federal budget deficit as a percentage of GDP shown in Table 12.10. Note that I have used five-year averages. You may also note that I have replaced the independent variable with a new column, "Time."

During the first twenty years, between 1970 and 1985, the federal budget deficit as a percentage of U.S. GDP showed a trend of steady increase. However, this trend reversed itself in the next decade. Therefore, if we try to fit a straight-line trend, the approximation of the actual data will be rather poor. This is demonstrated when a linear estimation gives us the following result:

$$\text{Percentage deficit} = 2.52 + 0.237 \text{ Time}$$
$$t = (1.52)(0.56) \tag{12.22}$$
$$R^2 = 0.072$$

Since the critical value for t at a .05 level of significance with 5 degrees of freedom is 2.05, we cannot reject the null hypothesis that the coefficients are in fact equal to 0. As you can clearly see in Figure 12.13, the line fitted through the data does not give us a good prediction. The situation changes dramatically, however, when we try a quadratic

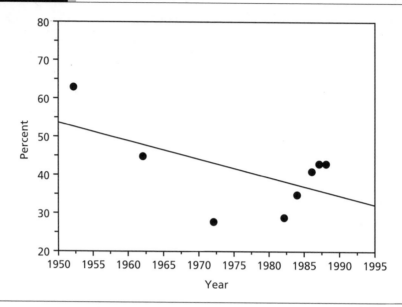

FIGURE **12.13** | **Publicly Held Federal Debt as a Percentage of GDP: Linear Estimation**

Source: *Economic Report of the President* (Washington, D.C.: U.S. Government Printing Office, 1989).

fit. To do that, we need to add one more column of independent variables, "Time²" (see Table 12.11).

Now that we have made the necessary data transformation, we can estimate the desired equation. In the same way we estimated the straight-line equation, we can use our computer software to estimate the three coefficients (a, b, and c). In this case, we will have to indicate that we have two independent variables (Year and Year²) instead of one.

The estimated values of the coefficients are as follows:

$$\text{Percentage deficit} = -2.38 + 3.91 \text{ Time} - 0.525 \text{ Time}^2$$
$$t = (-1.481)(3.72)^* \qquad (-3.57)^* \qquad (12.23)$$
$$R^2 = 0.823$$

*Significant at the .05 level. The critical value for t at a .05 level of significance is 2.0.

TABLE **12.11** | **Transformation of Data for the Estimation of a Quadratic Equation Form**

Year	Percentage of GDP	Time	Time²
1970–1974	1.5	1	1
1975–1979	2.8	2	4
1980–1984	3.9	3	9
1985–1989	5.4	4	16
1990–1994	4.9	5	25
1995–1999	1.6	6	36

FIGURE 12.14	**Publicly Held Federal Debt as a Percentage of GDP: Quadratic Estimation**

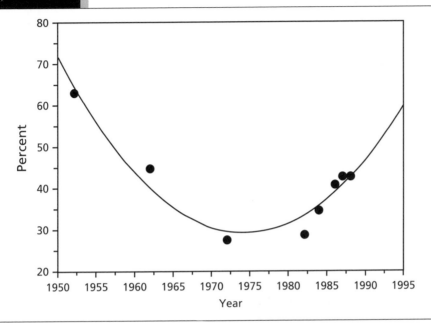

As you can see from Figure 12.14, the estimated quadratic equation (12.23) is clearly superior to the straight-line equation (12.22). From this equation, we can estimate the value for 1982 to be 29.81 percent, much closer to the actual figure.

Higher Order Polynomials

Although the regression results indicate that the quadratic form (equation 12.20) seems to be a definite improvement over the linear form (equation 12.17), can we not improve the results even more by using a third-degree polynomial? If we run a third-degree equation, we get the following result:

$$Y = 17,704,000 + 271,050 \text{ Year} - 13.83 \text{ Year}^2 + 3.0 \text{ Year}^3 \qquad (12.24)$$
$$R^2 = 0.983$$

Indeed, as equation 12.24 and Figure 12.15 indicate, the third-degree polynomial is a better fit than a second-degree polynomial. In fact, if we keep increasing the degree of polynomial, the resulting curve will get closer and closer to the observed points and, when we use $n - 1$ (the number of observations minus 1) degrees, there is no residual. A perfect fit! Unfortunately, such an exercise reduces our result to a mathematical tautology. In fact, it is extremely rare for researchers in the social sciences to use higher than a second-degree polynomial. Apart from the tautological reasoning, the use of a higher degree polynomial imposes undue restrictions on the data. For example, in a third-degree polynomial the predicted values of Y may increase for the initial range of the value of X, then decrease rapidly, and finally increase at a dramatic rate. In the final stage, when the

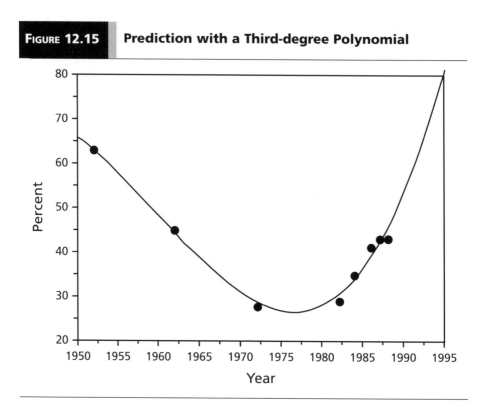

FIGURE 12.15   **Prediction with a Third-degree Polynomial**

coefficient of the extremely large third-degree term becomes dominant, predictions outside the sample range will give a highly inflated figure, as you can see in Figure 12.15.

Even the simpler quadratic form is not free of structural biases. Its strict mathematical structure forces a symmetric specification, which can lead to faulty predictions. The result of this bias is shown in Figure 12.16. If the dependent variable shows a symmetric

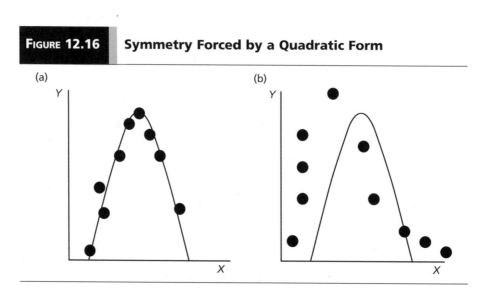

FIGURE 12.16   **Symmetry Forced by a Quadratic Form**

distribution, then you are safe. If the distribution is skewed, however, the predictions will be suspect. Unfortunately, this bias may not be apparent from the regression results, which will show a fairly decent fit. Yet if you plot the actual observations against the predicted values, the quadratic form will reveal its shortcomings.

Log-transformed Forms

In the segment of social science research that uses **regression analysis**, perhaps the most common functional specification after the linear form is the log-log form. To understand log-log functions, you should know what a log, or logarithm, is.

A **log transformation** expresses a number by the exponent of its base. That is, suppose we are using 10 as the base. Since 1,000 is 10^3, we write $\log(1{,}000) = 3$. By following this logic, $\log(100) = 2$, $\log(10) = 1$, and because any number raised to the power of 0 is equal to 1, $\log(1) = 0$. For numbers less than 1, their log values become less than 0, or negative. However, as the logs of numbers come close to 0, they produce large negative numbers and, therefore, the log of 0 is an infinitely large negative number. So *you cannot take the log of 0.* Logs can have any base, but the most commonly used base is 10. Hence, it is called the **common log**. If the base of a log is e (a commonly used number in mathematics, equal to 2.71828), it is called a **natural log**. If you want to get the original values from the log-transformed values, you have to use an **antilog**. Thus, the common log of 10 is 1, and the antilog of 1 is 10. The common log is written as **log**, whereas the natural log is expressed as **ln**. For a better understanding of logarithms, you may try log transforming a few numbers with the help of your hand calculator.

Although you can use either 10 or e as the base, in statistics it is more common to use the e-based natural log. Therefore, in this section, we will use the expression ln for log-transformed variables. By log transforming the dependent and independent variables, a log-log functional form is written as

$$\ln(Y_i) = a + b\ln(X_i) + e_i \qquad (12.25)$$

The log transformation of data offers us a few attractive features. First, a series may exhibit a nonlinear form, such as the ones shown in Figure 12.17 (a). If the coefficient b is greater than 1, the series would grow exponentially. Although it is hard to find examples of series with such explosive growth patterns in the realm of the social sciences, over a short period of time a series may exhibit such a pattern (for example, housing prices in the boom areas of the United States). Many series in the social sciences come close to the lines shown where $0 < b < 1$. For example, cross-national data show that as nations become affluent, their aggregate rates of growth, after periods of rapid expansion, tend to slow. Also, it is relatively easy to find examples where b is negative (<0). For example, we know that as nations become affluent, their population numbers register steady rates of decline. In such cases log-log functions offer a better fit than linear forms. If you plot the data on a log-log form, they will show linear patterns, as in Figure 12.17 (b).

Second, the log transformation of a very large number makes it small; for instance, $\ln(85{,}790) \cong 11.36$. Therefore, the log transformation gives a better fitted equation for data that vary a great deal (which often is the case when the numbers are large). Note,

FIGURE 12.17 **Double-Log Functional Forms**

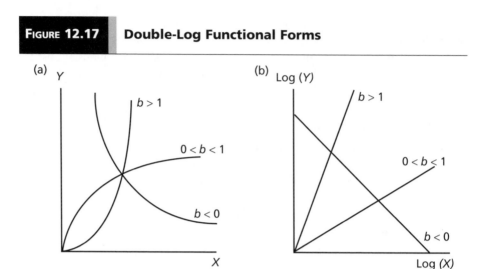

however, that if you estimate a log-log curve, the predicted values will be in log forms. To change to actual numbers, you will have to take their antilogs.

Inverse Forms

The inverse functional form expresses Y as a reciprocal (or inverse) of the independent variable X. An inverse functional form can show a positive or a negative relationship between the dependent and independent variables. You may notice that because it is an inverse relationship, the following expression will give you a negative relationship:

$$Y_i = a + b\frac{1}{X_i} + e_i \tag{12.26}$$

whereas

$$Y_i = a - b\frac{1}{X_i} + e_i \tag{12.27}$$

will show a positive relationship, as shown in Figure 12.18. When using an inverse form, you should remember that since you cannot divide any number by zero, there must be no zeroes in the data series for the independent variable.

You should use the inverse functional form when the value of the dependent variable falls (or rises) sharply and then approaches a certain number without actually ever being equal to it, as the value of the independent variable gets larger. Figure 12.18 illustrates the asymptotic nature of a typical inverse functional form.

FIGURE 12.18   The Inverse Form

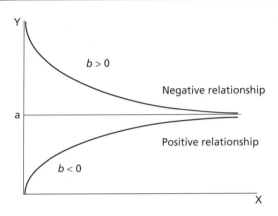

The Problem of Irrelevant Independent Variables: Adjusted R^2

Although R^2 is widely used as a measure of goodness of fit and as a measure for choosing among alternative specifications, it contains some important drawbacks. The most important problem with R^2 is that it measures how much of the total variation is being explained by the model. Therefore, in a multiple regression model, if one keeps adding variables that are only marginally relevant, the total amount of explained variation will go up (or, at the very least, when a variable is absolutely irrelevant, the amount will remain unchanged). Thus, in a model, if we include an independent variable that adds nothing to the explanation of the dependent variable, the R^2 measure *will not go down* to reflect the inclusion of an irrelevant variable. To correct this problem, we use adjusted, or corrected, R^2. The **adjusted R^2** is written as $\overline{R^2}$ ("R bar squared") and can be calculated either independently or from the calculated value of R^2. Because it is easier to calculate it from the calculated value of R^2, I provide the following formula:

$$\overline{R^2} = 1 - (1 - R^2)\frac{n-1}{n-k} \tag{12.28}$$

where n is the number of observations, and k is the number of coefficients in the regression equation.

Note the following features in this formula:

1. There is just one independent variable—that is, where $k = 1$, $\overline{R^2} = \overline{R^2}$. Otherwise, R^2 will always be greater than $\overline{R^2}$ when there is more than one independent variable ($k > 1$). You can have only one independent variable if you run a regression equation without the intercept term—that is, if you are estimating an equation $Y = bX + e$. This is a special form of equation that makes a rather stringent assumption that the intercept

term is equal to zero. Although special reasons to formulate such a model may arise, in general you should not specify a model without the intercept term.

2. If you include an additional independent variable in the model, unlike R^2, $\overline{R^2}$ may go *up* or *down*. If you think about it, this makes sense. Consider once again, for instance, the case of GDP per capita in Figure 12.1. The trend line appears to be linear. However, we want to see if there is a shift in trend. In that case, when we introduce the second independent variable (a dummy variable), the squared value of time, the inclusion will either add significantly to the explanation or be an irrelevant independent variable. If it adds significantly to the explanation, the value of R^2 will increase more than the offsetting effects of an increase in the number of independent variables. As a result, the value of $\overline{R^2}$ will increase from the previous estimation. In contrast, if the improvement in explanation as a result of the inclusion of an additional independent variable is less than the dampening effects of an additional variable, $\overline{R^2}$ will register a decline.

Suppose that five years ago, your city introduced tough youth crime legislation requiring mandatory punishment for gun-related crimes. You have been asked to see if the action has resulted in a change in the city's crime rate. By using a simple time-series regression ($k = 2$) on the data for the past twenty years ($n = 20$), your model explains 60 percent of the total variation ($R^2 = 0.6$), showing a gradual rising trend. From this information you calculate the adjusted R^2 as follows:

$$\overline{R^2} = 1 - (1 - 0.6)\frac{20 - 1}{20 - 2} = 0.58 \tag{12.29}$$

Now you have included a dummy variable starting the year the legislation was passed. By reestimating your equation with two independent variables, you can attempt to provide evidence for the efficacy of the legislation. Let us suppose the new equation shows an R^2 value of 0.62, or a 2 percent improvement in your overall explanation of the city's crime rate. You can now calculate the adjusted R^2 for the new equation:

$$\overline{R^2} = 1 - (1 - 0.62)\frac{20 - 1}{20 - 3} = 0.57 \tag{12.30}$$

As you can see, since the addition of the dummy variable did not improve the overall explanation significantly to offset the dampening effects of fraction ($[n - 1]/[n - k]$), the $\overline{R^2}$ value actually went down, leading you to conclude that there is no significant statistical evidence to suggest that the passage of the legislation has had an effect on the city's crime rate.

The Significance of Coefficients Taken Together

A multiple regression model contains many independent variables, most of which are statistically significant on an individual basis. However, questions may still be raised as to their significance as a set. For this test, we test the null hypothesis that none of the explanatory variables helps explain the variation of the dependent variable around its mean (that is, $b_0 = b_1 = b_2 = \cdots b_n$). In our previous attempt to establish statistical significance of individual coefficients, we used the t distribution. For this test, known as the joint probability test (since we are testing the collective significance of all the independent variables), we use the F distribution. We calculate the F value for the equation as

$$F_{(k-1,n-k)} = \frac{R^2}{1-R^2} \frac{n-k}{k-1} \tag{12.31}$$

The F test is closely linked to R^2 in that while testing the null hypothesis that none of the independent variables is relevant, the F test, in fact, is testing the null hypothesis that $R^2 = 0$. Therefore, for a two-variable linear equation, the null hypothesis is that the slope of the regression line is horizontal (such as in Figure 11.3 in the previous chapter).

From our example, we can calculate the F statistic as follows:

$$F_{(2-1,5-2)} = F_{(1,3)} = \frac{0.9806}{(1-0.9806)} \frac{5-2}{2-1} = 151.64$$

The subscript for F, $(k-1, n-k)$, denotes the degrees of freedom. You will see that the F table (Appendix E) is arranged in a matrix form, where the coordinates are specified by the row and column numbers. For our test, the first number of the subscript $(k-1)$ refers to the numerator (the column), and the second number $(n-k)$ refers to the denominator (the row) of the table. By consulting the table, we can find that the critical value for $F_{(1,3)}$ at a 5 percent level of significance is 10.1. Since our F value, 151.64, is greater than 10.1, we can reject the null hypothesis and conclude that the model is indeed relevant.

Choosing the Correct Functional Form

So far we have discussed quite a few functional forms for regression models. When it comes to choosing the correct functional form, essential for good forecasting, the books on econometric theory are of little use to a researcher. However, I can offer these words of advice: *unless theory, common sense, or your experience tells you otherwise, use a linear form.* Before using any model, read theoretical literature on its behavior, plot the data to see if there is any reason to believe that a form other than a linear one is more appropriate, and draw on your or an expert's experience in choosing the functional form.

Imagine that you have been asked to project the property tax revenue for your county. After plotting the data, you detect a slight upward trend that may tempt you to go for a second-degree polynomial fit. However, you should be careful, because the trend may be the result of a recent economic boom, and its effects may be temporary. Therefore, although the estimated equation with a quadratic form is giving you better R^2 and adjusted R^2 values, your estimations may be too optimistic, particularly when the economy slows down.

FORECASTING AND ITS PROBLEMS

The purpose of estimating a regression equation is to forecast. We depend on forecasting in every facet of modern life. The stock market reacts to the projected future of the economy, revenue and expenditures are forecasted for government budgets, students often choose their careers on the basis of the expected remuneration, orders are placed on the basis of forecasted demand, and investments are made on the basis of expected future trends in the market. Therefore, from private decisions to public policies, forecasting has become an integral part of our lives. However, you often hear such ironic comments as "It's extremely difficult to predict, especially the future." Indeed, there is a great deal of truth to this cynicism. However, since we are in the business of forecasting, let us go about it in a more systematic fashion.

A projected forecast is a quantitative estimate of the likelihood of an event's taking place in the future, on the basis of available historical data. There are two kinds of forecasts. A forecast can be either a point forecast or an interval forecast. A **point forecast** predicts a particular value for our dependent variable, which is likely to take place at a certain future point in time. An **interval forecast**, in contrast, indicates a band within which the future value is likely to lie.

Point Forecasts

We tend to prefer to offer single numbers rather than ranges, so most of our predictions turn out to be point forecasts. Interval forecasts make clear the probability factor associated with the predicted value, but point forecasts do not always do so. However, whether explicit or not, all forecasts contain an element of probability. Thus, when we forecast the government's revenue for next year to be $1.6 trillion or for the population of a city to be 123,758, despite the apparent precision, we are predicting a probable occurrence by extrapolating from a past trend. In a sense, an economic forecaster has a certain handicap compared with a weather forecaster. We associate weather forecasting with a probabilistic outcome, even though the actual outcome is always binary—either it is going to rain or it is not. Thus, when we are told that there is a 40 percent chance of showers, we are not terribly disappointed with the forecaster when it does not rain. Yet the results of forecasts based on a regression model, with its numerical precision and its omission of the probability factor, convey a certain sense of determinism and thus can be extremely deceiving. Therefore, it is important to inquire into the factors that make a forecast good or poor.

The worth of a forecast is in its accuracy. Yet it is possible to have a good predictive model provide an inaccurate prediction, or a prediction based on a poor model turn out to be astonishingly close to reality. However, before we delve deeply into the questions of accuracy and sources of possible error, it is important to clarify certain useful terminology.

Forecasting can be either **ex post** or **ex ante**. Suppose we are predicting on the basis of a series of past data, which ends last year. We know the value of the dependent variable for this year, so we may compare the accuracy of our prediction against this known data. This is called an ex post prediction, in which we know with certainty the values of the dependent and independent variables. It is still a prediction because the model is providing us with values outside of the study period (which had ended the previous year). It is called ex post, or "after the fact," because the event has already taken place. In contrast, an ex ante forecast predicts values that are not yet known.

We can also distinguish between **conditional** and **unconditional** forecasts. An unconditional forecast is made when we know with certainty the values of all the independent variables. If we are predicting on the basis of time alone, measured in years, we know the value of the independent variable in a forecast for the next year. However, if we do not know the values of the independent variables with any certainty, the forecast is called conditional. An ex post forecast is always an unconditional forecast because we know the values of the dependent and independent variables. But an ex ante forecast may be either conditional or unconditional. Clearly, if we do not know for sure the values of the independent variables in the future, this will be an example of both an ex ante and an unconditional forecast. However, like the example of time series for a future year, or when the independent variable is the past year's dependent variable (for example, when we hypothesize that how we will perform next year will depend on how we do this year), then a forecast can be both ex ante and conditional.

Interval Forecasts

An interval forecast is made when a boundary or band is provided, within which the actual value is likely to lie. For this kind of forecast, we need to use the law of large numbers again. We discussed earlier that we can test the validity of our null hypothesis by calculating how many standard deviations away the estimated parameter is from its "true value." Using the same logic, we can predict with a given level of certainty that the actual value of the predicted variable will fall within a particular range. Thus, for example, we are testing at a .05 percent level of confidence the null hypothesis that our estimated parameter b is the same as the "true" parameter β. We write this as

$$-t_{.05} \le \frac{b - \beta}{\sigma} \le t_{.05} \qquad (12.32)$$

where $t_{.05}$ is the value of the t ratio (derived from the t table) at a .05 percent level of confidence, and σ is the standard deviation.

We reject the hypothesis if the calculated value of this ratio is greater than or equal to, or less than or equal to, the critical value of the t ratio. Now it is easy to see that we can use the same logic to state that

$$b - \sigma t_{.05} \le \beta < b + \sigma t_{.05} \qquad (12.33)$$

The preceding equation states that we are 95 percent confident that the actual value of the parameter β will be between $b \pm \sigma t_{.05}$. Therefore, we can use the same technique to derive the band within which we predict with a certain degree of confidence what the future value of our dependent variable will be. This is given by

$$\hat{Y} - \sigma_f t_{.05} \le Y_f \le \hat{Y} + \sigma_f t_{.05} \qquad (12.34)$$

where $\hat{Y}$ is the predicted value of Y, σ_f is the standard deviation associated with forecasting, and Y_f is the future value of Y.

A CASE IN POINT

Who Wins Olympic Medals? Beijing 2008

Problem

Every four years the nations of the world get together and participate in the Summer Olympic Games. As nations compete as teams, a game quickly transforms into a platform for showing patriotic pride. Some countries' governments embrace the games as part of their national policies. At the end of the games, when the medals won by each country are tallied, there is a great disparity; some countries win a lot, while many never win anything. You may wonder why some countries do well in sporting events while others do not. We can explore this question with the help of regression analysis.

Hypotheses

Being engaged in sports requires time and money. If you have visited Olympic training facilities, you understand not just the dedication of the individual athletes but also the investment a society makes in making their young men and women competitive on the world stage. We can hypothesize that as a nation becomes more affluent, it is better able to divert resources into recreational activities. We hypothesize that per capita gross national income (GNI) will have a positive coefficient.

Winning medals depends not only on the amount of money a country can afford to invest, it also depends a great deal on the total number of athletes in the pool. Therefore, it is easy to see that more populous nations, such as China and the United States, will have a decided advantage over tiny nations like Luxembourg and Brunei. We hypothesize that population will have a positive correlation.

Apart from the size of the population and the relative affluence of a country, its probability of winning also depends on its government's active involvement in sport. During the Cold War, the communist bloc countries saw success in sports as the most visible vehicle for demonstrating their competitive edge over their more affluent and technologically advanced adversaries in the West. The tradition has continued even after the fall of the Berlin Wall. Most of the former communist nations pursue sports as a demonstration of national pride and see them as a vehicle for cementing national identity. Therefore, the third variable we can introduce in our model is a dummy variable equal to 1 for a current or former communist country and 0 otherwise. We hypothesize that the coefficient of this variable will show a positive correlation.

In our effort to explain the winning of medals, we can also introduce a fourth variable. If you examine the list of countries that win medals, you will notice the conspicuous absence of certain nations: some of the conservative Islamic nations of the Middle East. This is because their conservative tradition does not allow women to compete in sports; even men wearing immodest athletic outfits are frowned upon. As a result, these nations do not compete very well on the world stage. Once again, to account for this qualitative factor, we must use a dummy variable: these countries will have a value of 1, and all others will have a value of 0. We hypothesize that the coefficient of this variable will show a negative correlation.

Data Collection

One of the best sources of data on cross-national incomes and populations is the World Bank. We will use World Bank data, being mindful of the fact that the data set does not contain information on some countries. For instance, because of the war, it does not post its estimate of 2008 per capita GNI for Iraq. Similarly, it does not show a population figure for Afghanistan. However, the Central Intelligence Agency's *World Factbook* gives an estimate. I have included the CIA's population data for Afghanistan. In the case of other countries for which there were no available data, I eliminated them from the sample, which consists of 136 nations.

Estimation

The hypothesized equation is written as

Number of medals = f (Per capita GNI, Population, Communist, Middle East)

While estimating the equation, I came across two interrelated problems. There are wide variations in the variables of medal count, per capita GNI, and population. Therefore, I decided to log transform these variables. However, since the log of 0 is undefined, I added 1 to the series of medals and then log transformed them. This gave me the log value of 0 for those countries that failed to win a single medal.

Estimation Results

The regression model yielded the following results:

$$\ln(\text{Medals}) = -3.41 + 0.433\ln(\text{GNI}) + 0.334\ln(\text{Population}) + 1.12(\text{Communist}) - 0.675(\text{Middle East})$$
$$t = (-8.9)^* \qquad (6.7)^* \qquad\qquad (10.7)^* \qquad\qquad (7.23)^* \qquad\qquad (-3.18)^*$$
$$\beta = (0.382)(0.597)(0.414)(0.182)$$
$$R^2 = 0.612$$
$$\text{Adjusted } R^2 = 0.600$$
$$F_{(4,128)} = 50.54^*$$

*Significant at the 99% level

Discussion

The estimated equation explains more than 61% of the medal winnings. All the null hypotheses are rejected at the 99% level of confidence. The model clearly indicates the importance of income, population, governments' national sports policies, and culture.

Discussion Points

1. You can find the data used in this equation at www.rohan.sdsu.edu/faculty/dgupta. Calculate the predicted medal winning for each country from this equation.
2. Which countries did better than expected in the 2008 Beijing Olympics, and which did worse? Is there a pattern? Explain.
3. Can you think of other variables that can be used to make this equation even more accurate?

This formula would provide us with the necessary interval for our predicted value if we knew the value of σ_f. Since we do not know this value, we estimate it. To estimate the errors associated with prediction (S_f^2), we need to adjust the standard error of estimation (SE^2) derived in equation 12.34 with the following factor:

$$S_f = \sqrt{S_f^2} = \sqrt{SE^2\left[1 + \frac{1}{n} + \frac{(X_{t+1} - \overline{X})^2}{\sum(X_i - \overline{X})^2}\right]} \qquad (12.35)$$

where X_t is the terminal period of the study. If our study period includes 25 years, then X_t is 25, and when we predict for the next year, X_{t+1} is 26. Therefore, using this measure, we can rewrite equation 12.35 as

$$\hat{Y} - S_f t_{.05} \leq Y_f \leq \hat{Y} + S_f t_{.05} \qquad (12.36)$$

It is interesting to note from the formation of equation 12.35 that because of the expression $(X_{t+1} - \overline{X})^2$, as the prediction moves away from the mean ($\overline{X}$), the error of prediction flares out in an exponential manner. In other words, the further into the future we want to predict, the greater our chance of committing an error and, therefore, the larger the band of prediction interval. This is shown in Figure 12.19.

Looking back at our first example of forecasting population for a small city, we had already calculated the values of S (which is 1.9) and $\sum(X_i - \overline{X})^2$ (which is 10). Hence, for us, the standard error of prediction is

$$S_f = \sqrt{1.9\left[1 + \frac{1}{5} + \frac{(6-3)^2}{10}\right]} = 2.0$$

FIGURE 12.19   **Errors of Prediction**

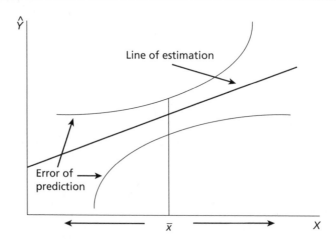

This error of prediction is distributed with $n - 2$ degrees of freedom. Since we had five observations, the relevant t value is 3.182. We can derive the prediction for the sixth year from our estimated equation, which is 20.3. Therefore, the interval of prediction is given by

$$20.3 - 2 \times 3.182 \leq \hat{Y}_f \leq 20.3 + 2 \times 3.182$$

or

$$13.94 \leq \hat{Y} \leq 26.66$$

We are 95 percent confident that the future population for the sixth year will fall between the band 13.94 and 26.66. To check out the flaring effect of the prediction errors, you may calculate it for a few more years in the future.

EXPLAINING THE PRESENT WITH THE PAST: LAGGED DEPENDENT VARIABLES

In the real world, once an incident has taken place, its effects linger for a considerable amount of time. We can argue that the level of crime a city is presently experiencing will be largely dependent on the extent of criminal activities last year. This kind of a lingering relation is particularly true when the relation between the dependent and independent variables is shaped by long-term factors such as culture, poverty, or education. Therefore, it may be true that for a forecast of a city's future crime rate, we need to look at past records of criminal activities. In econometric analysis, this is accomplished by running a regression treating the past year's observation as the independent variable for this year. Thus,

$$Y_t = a + bY_{t-1} + e_t \tag{12.37}$$

In technical terms, this use of the past year's data as the independent variable is called a **lag dependent variable** or an **autoregressive model**. An example may clarify this model for you. Suppose we are trying to forecast the number of violent crimes for future years. We have the data presented in Table 12.12.

In Table 12.12 the yearly crime statistics for the city (Y_t) are presented under the heading "Current year's crime rate." In the column labeled "Previous year's crime rate," the data are lagged by one period (Y_{t-1}). Using this information in equation 12.38, we estimate that the model for the lagged dependent variable will be

$$Y_t = 2.192 + 0.981Y_{t-1}$$
$$t = (1.26) \ (12.53)^*$$
$$R^2 = 0.929$$
$$\text{Adjusted } R^2 = 0.923 \tag{12.38}$$
$$n = 14$$
$$F_{(1,12)} = 156.83^*$$

*Significant at the .05 level

TABLE 12.12	Yearly Crime Statistics	
Year	Current year's crime rate (Y_t)	Previous year's crime rate (Y_{t-1})
1	10	—
2	13	10
3	13	13
4	16	13
5	15	16
6	18	15
7	19	18
8	25	19
9	24	25
10	26	24
11	27	26
12	29	27
13	30	29
14	31	30
15	35	31

You may notice that as a result of lagging, we are missing the first year's data. Hence, the number of observations has become 14 instead of 15. You may also notice that the results of this equation can be used to forecast the future year's crime rate. For instance, for the sixteenth year, we need to plug in the data for the fifteenth year in the equation. That is, the estimated figure for the sixteenth year is

$$\hat{Y}_{t+1(\text{16th year})} = 2.192 + (0.981 \times 35) = 36.52$$

This equation can be used ad infinitum to generate future forecasts. For the seventeenth year, we need to plug in the forecast for the sixteenth year; for the eighteenth year, we need the forecast for the seventeenth year, and so on. As we discussed in the previous section, the further we move into the future years (and therefore away from the mean of the actual series), the progressively larger will be the errors of estimate.

The use of a lagged dependent variable in a regression equation carries some rather important implicit assumptions. Be aware that by accepting the previous year's observation as the independent variable, you are assuming that all the external forces that shaped last year's crime rate will continue to have the same impact in determining future values.

Forecasting by Curve Fitting: A Step-by-Step Approach

- *Review the literature.* Understand the underlying relationship linking the dependent variable with the independent variables. If there is no literature available, prepare the appropriate arguments for your postulated hypothesis.

- *Collect data.* Collect data arranged in a series. Make sure there are no missing or otherwise "contaminated" data.

- *Plot the data.* A scatter plot will show you the nature of the underlying trend.

- *Formulate a projection model.* Decide on the appropriate model of forecasting. When in doubt, use parsimony as the guiding principle. If there is a strong quadratic or exponential trend, use an appropriate nonlinear form. If in doubt, use a linear form. If there are a number of distinct trend patterns or many fluctuations in the series, use the moving average model.

- *Estimate the model.* Use appropriate software to estimate the parameters. Present your findings with all the estimated parameter values and their corresponding t values. Report the R^2 value and the F statistic. Then verbally explain the full implications of the estimated model. If the report is to be read by a nontechnical person, consider placing the results of your estimation in a footnote or an appendix. Make sure that the reader is fully aware of your methodology and assumptions and the data.

When using a trend model, you must remember that the trend method assumes the existence of a continuing trend and therefore cannot predict turning points. If the trend pattern changes or is expected to change, you are better off using a causal model of prediction.

KEY WORDS

Adjusted R^2 (p. 303)
Antilog (p. 301)
Autoregressive model (p. 311)
Coefficient for trend (slope) (p. 275)
Coefficient of determination (R^2) (p. 279)
Common log (p. 301)
Conditional forecasting (p. 306)
Dependent variable (p. 275)
Error of estimation (p. 276)
Error term (p. 277)
Ex ante forecasting (p. 306)
Ex post forecasting (p. 306)
Independent variable (p. 275)
Intercept (p. 275)
Intercept dummy variable (p. 288)
Interval forecast (p. 306)
Lag dependent variable (p. 311)
ln (p. 301)
Log (p. 301)

Log transformation (p. 301)
Method of least squares (p. 271)
Multiple regression (p. 272)
Natural log (p. 301)
Point forecast (p. 306)
Population mean (p. 281)
Population standard deviation (p. 281)
Qualitative change (p. 288)
Random (p. 281)
Random errors (p. 273)
Regression analysis (p. 301)
Regression coefficients (p. 287)
Regression equation (p. 275)
Simple regression (p. 271)
Slope dummy (p. 294)
Statistically significant (p. 284)
Student's t distribution (p. 284)
Unconditional forecasting (p. 306)

EXERCISES

1. The county health authority data show a 3 percent annual increase in the number of indigent emergency care cases. According to a recent survey of area hospitals, there were 3,500 such cases last year. Using a single-factor forecasting model, estimate the number of cases of indigent emergency care in your county for the next five years. If the county is paying $1,500 per case for treatment, estimate the total monetary requirement during this period of time. Having made the estimate, comment on the reliability of your results.

2. A similar method can be used to estimate the number of homeless people, teenage pregnancies, illegal immigrants, and the like. As a part of your project, select a specific issue in your city or state and forecast its course for the next three years.

3. The table below presents three different distributions, all showing a quadratic structure. Explain which one (Y, K, or Z) will be best explained by a quadratic specification.

Dependent variables		Independent variables	
Y	K	Z	Time
2	2	2	1
4	3	10	2
7	5	15	3
10	12	8	4
8	16	4	5
3.5	10	3	6
2	2	2	7

4. Consider the following hypothetical yearly data on garbage collection for the town of Masters, Pennsylvania. Estimate the tonnage of garbage collection for 2009 and 2010. Use various models of forecasting. Which one of these models would you choose and why? Explain your choice of forecasting technique.

Collection of Garbage in Masters, Pennsylvania

Year	Garbage ($\times$ 1,000 tons)
1987	1,325
1988	1,356
1989	1,386
1990	1,402
1991	1,435
1992	1,495
1993	1,550
1994	1,597
1995	1,645
1996	1,701
1997	1,756
1998	1,810
1999	1,899
2000	1,967
2001	1,998
2002	2,030
2003	2,780

2004	3,134
2005	3,753
2006	4,004
2007	4,139
2008	4,356

5. The crime rate in the United States has gone down steadily every year since 1998. The city of Masters is no exception. The following table shows the burglary rate per 1,000 population. Use an inverse functional form to estimate the burglary rates for 2009 and 2010.

Burglary Rate in Masters, Pennsylvania

Year	Burglary rate (per 1,000 population)
1998	2.95
1999	2.65
2000	2.42
2001	1.99
2002	1.90
2003	1.85
2004	1.81
2005	1.78
2006	1.76
2007	1.74
2008	1.74

6. The following table shows per capita chicken consumption (in pounds) for the period 1994 through 2008. On the basis of this information, forecast the per capita demand for 2009, 2010, and 2011. For these years, assume that the actual numbers were 51.6, 53.0, and 53.8. Comment on the accuracy of your model.

Year	Consumption (pounds)
1994	35.6
1995	36.5
1996	36.7
1997	38.4
1998	40.5
1999	40.3
2000	41.8
2001	40.4
2002	40.7
2003	40.1
2004	42.7
2005	44.1
2006	46.7
2007	50.6
2008	50.1

7. Predict the value of Y for X equal to 16, 17, 18, 19, and 20.

X	Y
1	35
2	28
3	25
4	20
5	18
6	16
7	15
8	16
9	21
10	27
11	32
12	35
13	39
14	45
15	53

8. Collect any time-series data (for example, government debt as a percentage of GDP, population, sales tax revenue), and with the help of a regression model, project it for the next five years. Estimate the errors of projection for each year's projection and calculate the confidence intervals.

9. The passage of the Property Tax Limitations Act (Proposition 13) in California in 1978 caused a dramatic shift in local government finances for the state. The following are the property tax rates per $100 of assessed valuation for the city of San Diego. Estimate the tax rate for 1991 and 1992. Also estimate the intervals for those two years.

Year	Tax rate	Year	Tax rate
1971	1.959	1981	0.0860
1972	1,809	1982	0.0195
1973	1.774	1983	0.0170
1974	1.753	1984	0.0160
1975	1.753	1985	0.0147
1976	1,733	1986	0.0130
1977	1,548	1987	0.0117
1978	1.357	1988	0.0112
1979	0.131	1989	0.0103
1980	0.088	1990	0.0099

10. After reviewing the U.S. Government Accountability Office report on poverty in Appendix A, use the U.S. Census Bureau data set on poverty to develop a regression model for projecting the U.S. poverty rate. Explain your choice of dependent variables and fully explain your findings.

Notes

1. Numerous books are available on regression analysis and the method of least squares. For one of the best explanations, see Peter Kennedy, *A Guide to Econometrics*, 2nd ed. (Cambridge, Mass.: MIT Press, 1985).

2. The method of least squares has a long history, with the names of some of the most illustrious mathematicians attached to its development. This method was first proposed in 1806 by Adrien-Marie Legendre. Shortly afterward, Pierre-Simon Laplace and Carl Friedrich Gauss justified its use and demonstrated some of its useful properties. In 1812 Laplace offered proof that every unbiased linear estimator is asymptotically normal when the number of observations tends to infinity. Further, Laplace demonstrated that for the least squares estimators, the asymptotic variance is minimal. In a series of articles (1821–1823) Gauss showed that among all unbiased linear estimates, the least squares estimators minimize the mean square deviations between the true value and the estimated value. Most important, Gauss established that this relationship holds for any distribution of the errors and for any sample size. Later corroboration of his findings came through the work of Andrey Markov (1912). Subsequent developments in the least squares method were the work of mathematicians such as Alexander Aitkens and Ronald Aylmer Fisher from the late 1920s through the 1940s. This method forms the basic building block of the field of econometrics.

3. If you are not well versed in the algebra of a straight-line equation, you may engage in the following exercise. Consider two sets of equations: (a) $Y = 2 + 0.5X$ and (b) $Y = 2 + 2.5X$. By substituting values of 0, 1, and 2 for X, you can see the implications of the intercept and trend coefficient. (Y is equal to 2, 2.5, and 3 for [a] and to 2, 4.5, and 7 for [b]).

4. For those of you who are interested in the logic of derivation of the formulas for a and b, they can be derived using differential calculus. Thus, we are trying to minimize

$$S = \sum_{i=1}^{n} (e_i)^2 = \sum_{i=1}^{n} (Y_i - a - bX_i)^2$$

Therefore, the sum of squares is minimized with respect to the values of a and b. Hence, we have

$$\frac{\delta S}{\delta a} = -2\sum(Y_i - a - bX_i) \tag{12.3a}$$

$$\frac{\delta S}{\delta b} = -2\sum X_i(Y_i - a - bX_i) \tag{12.3b}$$

By setting equations 12.3a and 12.3b equal to 0, we can get two equations that can be solved for two unknowns, a and b. By solving these two equations, we get equations 12.4 and 12.5 for estimating the two parameters.

5. The squared sum of explained variations is also known as the error sum of squares, and the squared sum of total variation is also referred to as the total sum of squares.

6. Edward Ames and Stanley Reiter, "Distributions of Correlation Coefficients in Economic Time Series," *Journal of American Statistical Association* 56 (1961): 637–656.

7. Once again, note that we are using two different sets of symbols for mean and standard deviation. They are μ and $\overline{X}$ for mean and σ and s for standard deviation. This is because we want to distinguish between the population, or the "true," mean and standard deviation and the sample, or "observed," mean and standard deviation. The true values have only conceptual validity, because we can never observe them. Yet in statistical theory, theorems such as the one

shown by equation 12.8 are valid only when we have the true values. Therefore, to get around the problem, we use the estimated or sample values with some necessary modifications.

8. For a history of the case, see William Kistner, "Justice for Sale?" 2009, http://americanradio works.publicradio.org/features/judges/. The entire Supreme Court verdict is available at www .supremecourtus.gov/opinions/08pdf/08-22.pdf.

9. Madhavi McCall, "Buying Justice in Texas: The Influence of Campaign Contributions on the Voting Behavior of Texas Supreme Court Justices," *American Review of Politics* 22 (Fall 2001): 349–373. Also see Madhavi McCall, "Court Decision Making in Police Brutality Cases, 1990-2000," *American Politics Research*, 33 (2005): 56–80; Madhavi McCall, "The Politics of Judicial Elections: The Influence of Campaign Contributions on the Voting Pattern of Texas Supreme Court Justices, 1994-1997," *Politics and Policy* 31 (2003): 314–347.

10. The theoretical justification for dividing the sum of squared errors by $n - 2$ lies in the fact that there are n data points in the estimation process, but the estimation of the intercept and the slope introduces two constraints on the data. This leaves $n - 2$ unconstrained observations with which to estimate the errors of estimate. Hence, the number $n - 2$ is referred to as the number of degrees of freedom.

11. You may notice that here we have estimated the time trend by using the actual values of the years (such as 1991) as the independent variable. For ease of computation, you may also use numbers 1, 2, 3, and so forth for the actual values of the year. This will not change the basic relationship between the dependent and the independent variables; only the values of the estimated coefficients will change. On a computer, try estimating the same equation both ways, and then calculate the predicted or estimated values for the dependent variable. They will not change.

12. Using the two equations, you can compute the values of the dependent variables and examine the relative efficiency of the two models.

13. To see how these equations specify a quadratic relationship, consider the following two equations:

$$\text{(a) } Y = 10.0 - 2.0X + 0.5X^2$$

and

$$\text{(b) } Y = 2.0 + 2.0X - 0.5X^2$$

If you start substituting the values 0, 1, 2, 3, and so on, for X (and squaring them for X^2) and then calculating and plotting the resulting values of Y, you will see the shapes of quadratic curves.

13 The Elements of Strategic Thinking: Decision Tree and Game Theory

In March 1976 President Gerald Ford had a problem. Epidemiologists were concerned about a virulent form of the influenza virus, swine flu, which had broken out at Fort Dix in New Jersey. Experts feared that this new strain would hit the larger population of the United States in the fall, during flu season. Many scientists suggested that the flu was related to a strain that in 1918 and 1919 had caused a worldwide epidemic and taken twenty million lives.

Quickly mutating flu viruses are nightmares for health care professionals. To counter the threat of influenza, manufacturers reproduce strains of the viruses in laboratories, incubate them in eggs, and turn them into vaccines. When injected into humans, these harmless viruses become part of the shield that protects the body from natural viruses. But viruses play hide and seek with researchers by mutating, making them impervious to inoculation. To compound the problem, the protective virus must be reproduced *before* the actual infestation takes place. If people are already infected, there is not much a doctor can do. Therefore, President Ford needed to decide whether to do nothing or to start a massive inoculation program for the entire population, especially people who fell in the high-risk category (for example, older people and those with lung ailments or other chronic health problems). If he chose to do nothing, and the worst fears of the experts were realized, the nation would face a public health catastrophe. But if the experts were wrong, the president would save a great deal of money. Massive inoculation programs carry high price tags, along with the risk that some people may die from complications related to the injection.

On the other hand, if the swine flu virus infiltrated the general population after the president had assumed the associated risks and ordered a nationwide inoculation program, the president would be admired for his prudence by a grateful public, and this gratitude would translate into a considerable amount of political goodwill for the president. However, if the threat failed to materialize, the president's policy would likely be widely ridiculed for wasting valuable public resources. Place yourself in the president's position. What would you have done? At the root of President Ford's problem was uncertainty. He did not know the future course of the virus. It is natural that a decision maker will frequently face uncertainty. So far, our discussion of how quantitative techniques aid the decision process has not addressed the question of uncertainty. Let us now see how introducing this quirk into the process affects our decisions.

GETTING A GRIP ON UNCERTAINTY

Making decisions about an uncertain future is basic to human existence. Without the benefit of hindsight, we cannot expect our decisions to be right on target. In fact, we will never have perfect or complete information about a future event. If we did, every public policy would be a success, and in the end there would be no distinction among the past, present, and future. Since the real world does not operate in this way, we must proceed strategically and establish a logical process for viewing uncertainty from an analytical perspective.

One way of looking at the unpredictable future is to follow the early work of the eminent economist Frank Knight.[1] In his seminal work Knight distinguishes **risk** from **uncertainty**. Risk is present when one can calculate the probability of a future outcome, and uncertainty is present when one cannot. When you buy car insurance, agencies use your age, education, and driving record to estimate the actuarial risk of covering the costs of probable accidents. However, when you encounter a unique event for which there is no probability estimate, you face an uncertain situation.[2] If you are judging the probability of an election result, a legislative outcome in Congress, or a future draft choice by a professional sports franchise in your town, you encounter uncertainty. As suggested by our discussion of probability in chapter 7, I can assert that for a future event, we can use the measures of objective probability to estimate risk, whereas for uncertainty, we must depend on subjective estimates.

You may ask, how does the concept of risk differ from that of uncertainty? The fundamental difference between the two rests on the availability of substantive knowledge. Simply put, risky events are not unique; they take place often enough for a researcher to recognize their pattern. Insurance companies, having covered hundreds of thousands of motorists, can calculate the risk of insuring an individual driver. For example, there is a pattern to how most twenty-one-year-old men drive, and insurers take their past behavior into account when setting rates. In contrast, if you want to know if I will be involved in an accident on my way home, you are dealing with uncertainty. This is because, as you may recall from our earlier discussion of probability (see chapter 7), the outcome of any single event is unpredictable; results are predictable only over a number of tries. That is, you cannot say for sure whether you will flip heads in a single coin toss, but you can predict a 50 percent outcome over a large number of tries.

The literature on uncertainty points out that there are four general sources of uncertainty, which are listed below.[3] You may notice that the first three of these depend on researchers themselves. Luckily, we can use different strategies to reduce their impact. The last source, at the core of uncertainty, is something that we simply cannot avoid and must learn to accept.

The Inadequacy of Knowledge. There are events that are not entirely unknowable but depend on the knowledge and expertise of the inquirer. If I am asked to ascertain the risk for groundwater contamination from a waste treatment plant, without substantive knowledge of the field, I may fail to come up with a reasonable answer. However, if I am a properly trained expert, I am much better equipped to calculate risk levels. To reduce uncertainty, decision makers must look for the proper personnel to evaluate the odds of uncertain outcomes. If the necessary expertise cannot be found in-house, they should look for outside consultants.

Biases of Reasoning. Personal biases can cloud the mental process through which we analyze the future. These biases may crop up from a number of different sources (see chapter 5). A decision maker must be constantly on guard against such biases.

Interdependence of Human Actions. In a society, people work in groups. As a result, the final output depends not on one individual but on a number of actors. Their joint efforts shape the ultimate outcome of a project. Traditional neoclassical economics assumes that people follow their self-interest independent of others. However, research in social psychology and other branches of the social sciences has shown that those around us fundamentally affect our behavior. In dealing with others, we can never be sure of their identities, ideologies, group affiliations, or levels of commitment.[4] Harvey Leibenstein pointed out that any manager who assumes that employees will always work "according to the book" will soon be humbled.[5] Hence, a proper assessment of the future must include a deep understanding of human beings as social animals.

The basic core of uncertainty. The outcome of a future event depends not only on our knowledge and effort but also on factors that are completely beyond our control. Young Back Choi explains this obscured understanding with an old Chinese fable.[6] An old man goes into the field and finds a nice horse. "Lucky me!" he exclaims and gives it to his son. Unfortunately, his son falls off the horse and becomes lame. "This horse has brought me only misfortune," sighs the old man. Soon war breaks out with the dangerous barbarians, and the emperor's army takes away all the young men of the village to fight the enemy. But the army does not take the old man's lame son. The old man is thankful for finding such a lucky horse.

DECISION MAKING AND EXPECTED PAYOFF

The question of how to make the best possible decision under uncertain conditions has come under intense scrutiny. The first analytical breakthrough was derived by John von Neumann and Oskar Morgenstern, two mathematicians from Princeton University, and was developed further over the years by a great number of mathematicians and economists. Let me explain the basic precepts of their analysis. Suppose someone offers you a choice. If you predict correctly, you may win $2 in a coin toss or $5 in a roll of the die. Which option do you choose? Theoretically, you should choose the coin toss because your chances of winning are $1/2 = .5$. On the other hand, with the roll of the die, your chances of calling the right number are $1/6 = .167$. The **expected payoff** in a risky situation is calculated by the following equation:

$$\text{Expected payoff} = \text{Probability of winning} \times \text{Amount of reward}.$$

That is, in our case, the expected payoffs are

$$\text{Expected payoff for coin toss} = .5 \times \$2 = \$1$$

and

$$\text{Expected payoff for roll of the die} = .167 \times \$5 = \$0.83.$$

As you can see, you will be better off betting on the coin toss—that is, unless you are a real gambler or risk taker. In that case, you may prefer the higher reward offered by the die regardless of the chances of winning. For the moment, let us assume that you are neither an excessive risk taker nor an extreme risk averter; instead, you are a risk-neutral decision maker. If you want to maximize your chances of winning in the long run, you will be better off, given uncertainty, following the law of rational decision making and choosing the option with the highest expected payoff. In fact, in every uncertain situation, including those involving gambling or card games, good players will depend primarily on the proper calculation of the odds. At blackjack tables in casinos, the house realizes its profits solely by playing the odds, which are in its favor. Although there are winners among the players, the house always cleans up the table at the end of the day.

THE DECISION TREE

We can use the insights developed by von Neumann and Morgenstern to analyze the optimal course of action. The branch of social science and applied mathematics that is dedicated to the study of decision making under uncertainty is broadly called game theory. However, when a single decision maker evaluates the choice of action, he or she uses a **decision tree**, a diagram showing the sequence of events with their corresponding probability figures.

Let us go back to the uncertain public policy problem of President Ford. Suppose that the experts at the Centers for Disease Control and Prevention estimate the probability of the deadly virus's reaching the United States to be 40 percent. Also suppose that the president's political advisers appraise the benefits of his decision on a scale of +10 through −10, with +10 being the most desirable outcome and −10 being the most undesirable. Because we do not know President Ford's reasoning process, we must hypothesize that if he decides to do nothing and the epidemic becomes real, this outcome will be the least desirable of his options (scored −10). But if he decides to take no action and the epidemic does not materialize, then he has remained calm in the face of an unjustified doomsday prediction and has saved a considerable amount of public money. On his scale this result rates +5.

On the other hand, if he decides to inoculate the population, the most desirable situation arises, from his perspective, if the threat of epidemic turns out to be real. In that case the president will be hailed as a savior—an outcome worth +10 on his rating scale. However, if the epidemic does not show up, the decision to start a mass inoculation program may turn out to be a political liability, which is assessed a −5 rating. Having put numerical values on the probabilities and payoffs, we can calculate the expected payoffs facing the president (see Table 13.1).

TABLE 13.1	Hypothetical Expected Payoff Matrix for President Ford's Response to Possible Swine Flu Epidemic			
Action (1)	Situation (2)	Probability (3)	Payoff (4)	Expected payoff (5) = (3) × (4)
Do nothing (A)	Epidemic occurs	0.4	−10	−4
	Epidemic does not occur	0.6	+5	3
Total		1.0	−5	−1
Start mass inoculation (B)	Epidemic occurs	0.4	+10	4
	Epidemic does not occur	0.6	−5	−3
Total		1.0	5	1

I have drawn the logical structure of President Ford's actions in the form of a decision tree (see Figure 13.1). The branches of a decision tree can be divided into **actions** and **outcomes**. Although actions are deliberate and reflect an individual's conscious decision, outcomes are uncertain. If you inspect Figure 13.1 closely, you will see that it contains four important elements:

1. *Decision nodes:* the points at which a decision maker must choose a possible course of action. In this particular case, President Ford has one decision node that shows two possible actions: do nothing or inoculate. I have represented this node as a square.
2. *Chance nodes:* the points showing the probable outcomes of an action. After the president chooses an action, there are two possible outcomes: the flu breaks out or it does not break out. The chance nodes are indicated with circles.
3. *Probabilities:* estimates of the possible outcomes. Probabilities can be determined either through observation in the case of objective probabilities or through the subjective assessments of experts.
4. *Payoffs:* consequent rewards and losses experienced by the decision makers. Payoffs can be estimated in monetary terms or, as in this case, in terms of some other agreed-upon scale. These payoffs can be actual or perceived profits or losses.

FIGURE 13.1   Hypothetical Decision Tree for Swine Flu Threat

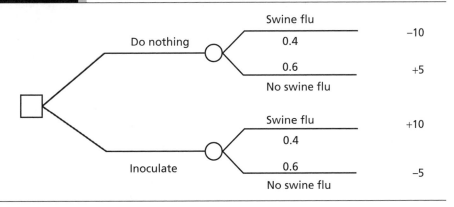

FIGURE 13.2 | **Decision Tree for Swine Flu**

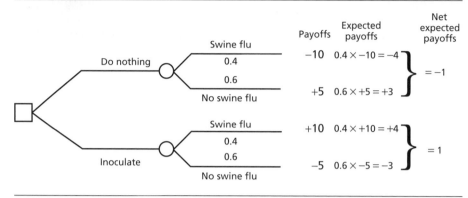

In Figure 13.2 we can see that, facing an uncertain situation, President Ford had a choice between an expected payoff of −1 (for the "do nothing" option) and +1 (for the "inoculate" option). Therefore, given the logical construct, he should have chosen the option to inoculate the entire population against a probable swine flu infestation. As an anecdotal postscript to this analysis, we should note that President Ford did choose to inoculate, and the virus failed to show up in the United States.[7]

Structuring a Decision Tree

From the preceding rendition of a decision tree, you can see that a tree can be a powerful tool of logical reasoning when the outcomes are shrouded in risk. This exercise allows you to see the true nature of a problem more clearly by providing you with a deeper understanding of the role of chance as it relates to the alternative courses of action. Also, the very process of identifying the alternatives, their outcomes, and their sequential interaction with their respective probabilities can reveal more about the core of the problem than you may otherwise have known.

To be an effective tool of analysis, decision trees must be as exhaustive as possible in identifying every conceivable outcome. Thus, in the above example, I have identified two options for President Ford: to do nothing and to inoculate the entire population. If there were other options, such as inoculating only those who were at the highest possible risk, or restricting the inoculations to specific geographic areas, they also should have been fully explored. This process of identifying alternatives, then, should be **collectively exhaustive**. That is, no feasible option should be deliberately left out without an explicit justification for its exclusion.

Furthermore, the options must be **mutually exclusive**. In other words, the options should be defined in ways that do not overlap. Let us say that we have defined the president's three options as (1) do not inoculate, (2) inoculate only the high-risk population, and (3) inoculate everyone. In this case, all options are mutually exclusive, since you cannot meaningfully choose more than one option at one time. If I choose to inoculate only the high-risk segment of the population, that choice would preclude my choosing to inoculate everyone in the nation. However, suppose the president has another option: to immediately launch a research project investigating the causes of the pandemic. The decision tree would have four branches: (1) do not inoculate, (2) inoculate only the high-risk population, (3) inoculate everyone, and (4) start a research project. As you can see, launching a research project does not exclude the other three options, and you can conduct research along with any other action. Therefore, unless your action is predicated on the findings of the research project, you should not include the project in the decision tree.

Evaluating Flood Damage Reduction

Imagine that several neighborhoods in your town have serious problems with seasonal flooding. A recent study commissioned jointly by the Federal Emergency Management Agency and the U.S. Army Corps of Engineers (COE) shows that if your town is hit by a catastrophic hundred-year flood (with a corresponding probability of 1 percent, or .01), the damage may equal $150 million. However, the study also suggests that the construction of a flood wall may significantly reduce the damage from flooding. Table 13.2 presents the estimated damage figures corresponding to the various levels of flooding. The flooding we can expect every other year (with a probability of .5) is not likely to cause much damage. However, a more severe flood that inundates the town every five years (having a probability of .2) may cause up to $25 million of damage. Figure 13.3 plots the data presented in Table 13.2.

As a preventive measure, the town is considering the construction of a flood wall. The COE estimates that the flood wall will cost the town $10 million. The town council is trying to decide whether to finance the structure with a municipal bond issue. I have represented the choices open to the town council in the form of a decision tree (see Figure 13.4). To make the diagram less complicated, I have eliminated the most frequent flooding, which does negligible damage. As you can see, I have numbered the decision nodes and added letters to the chance nodes. The symbol ⊟ indicates the point in the decision process at which a fixed cost has been incurred. This symbol stands for the cost of constructing the flood wall, which we must add to the total expected flood damage.

If you look again at Table 13.2, you may be tempted to conclude that the total savings for the project is $114 million, the total difference in estimated damage, minus

TABLE 13.2	**Estimated Flood Damage with and without Flood Wall**		
	Estimated damage ($\times$ $1 million)		**Difference in estimated damage**
Probability of flood	**Flood wall**	**No flood wall**	**($\times$ $1 million)**
.50	0	0	0
.40	0	18	18
.30	10	20	10
.20	19	25	6
.10	23	40	17
.01	87	150	63
Total	139	253	114

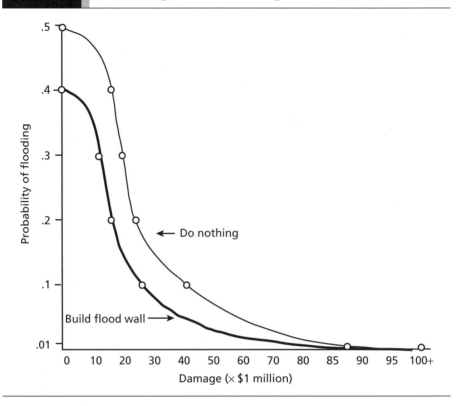

FIGURE **13.3** **Probability of Flood Damage**

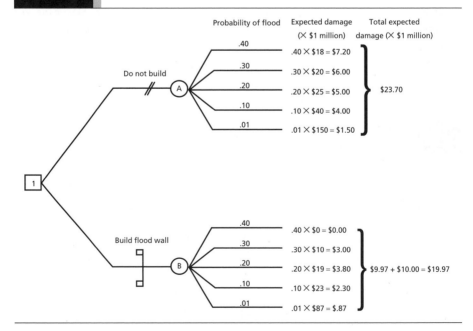

FIGURE **13.4** **Decision Tree for Flood Control**

$10 million, the cost of building the flood wall. However, when you take into account the respective probability measures, you will see that the bulk of the savings comes from limiting the damage of the most devastating flood, which is expected to occur every hundred years. Since the probability of such a monster flood is small (.01), the expected payoff is puny. As you can see from Fig. 13.4, the expected loss without the flood wall is $1.5 million, compared with $0.87 million with the flood wall. The expected savings comes to $630,000. The total benefits of constructing a flood wall are still greater than those of not constructing it. If we go ahead with the construction, our expected damage is $9.97 million plus the cost of construction, $10 million, or a total of $19.97 million. Because this number is smaller than the expected damage of $23.7 million without the flood wall, we should go ahead with the project.

At this point you should note that since we find the "do nothing" option decidedly inferior to the construction of the flood wall, we have crossed it out with an etch mark: //. This mark shows that we have considered this option and rejected it in favor of another.

This example of a decision tree is relatively simple, since it contains only one decision node. However, a decision tree can be much more complex and include many more decision nodes. Let us extend our example to include some additional decision options.

The COE study has come up with another flood control plan. It suggests that the town council consider building, in addition to the flood wall, a small levee of locally available impervious soil. This levee, to be constructed a few miles upstream, may divert enough water to significantly reduce the town's damages, particularly from the more frequent swells. However, there are a couple of caveats. First, the levee may turn out to be ineffective. In that case, the town will incur the same amount of damages as it would have sustained without this new construction. But if the levee is effective, the town will realize significant savings by constructing the flood wall. The COE estimates the construction cost for the levee to be $1 million. The agency further predicts that the probability of the levee's proving effective is 70 percent.

TABLE 13.3	Estimated Flood Damage with Flood Wall and Levee		
	Estimated damage (× $1 million)		
Probability of flood	Flood wall	No flood wall	Effective levee with flood wall	Ineffective levee with flood wall
.50	0.00	0.00	0.00	0.00
.40	0.00	18.00	0.00	0.00
.30	10.00	20.00	0.00	15.00
.20	19.00	25.00	5.00	20.00
.10	23.00	40.00	10.00	40.00
.01	87.00	150.00	180.00	150.00
Total expected flood damage (probability × damage)	9.97	23.70	3.80	14.00

FIGURE **13.5** **Expanded Decision Tree for Flood Control with Levee Option**

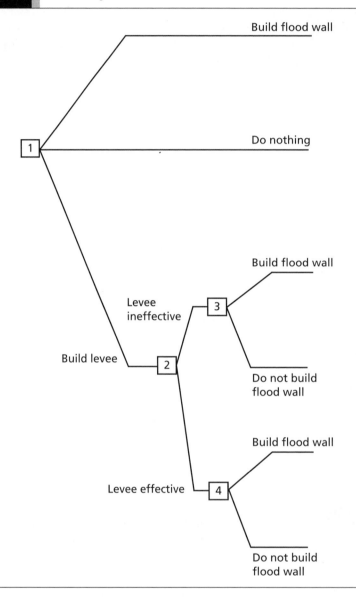

The second caveat is that in the case of a catastrophic flood, the levee is likely to collapse. If it does, the damage from the flood will escalate even more than it would if the levee and flood wall had not been built (see Tab. 13.3). This caveat introduces new options. The town can still decide to do nothing, it can immediately start building a flood wall, or it can wait to see whether the earthen levee is effective. If the levee is ineffective, then it can consider constructing the flood wall. If the levee is successful, it may go ahead and build the flood control device or decide not to build it after all (see Fig. 13.5).

FIGURE 13.6 **Decision Tree for Flood Control with Total Expected Costs**

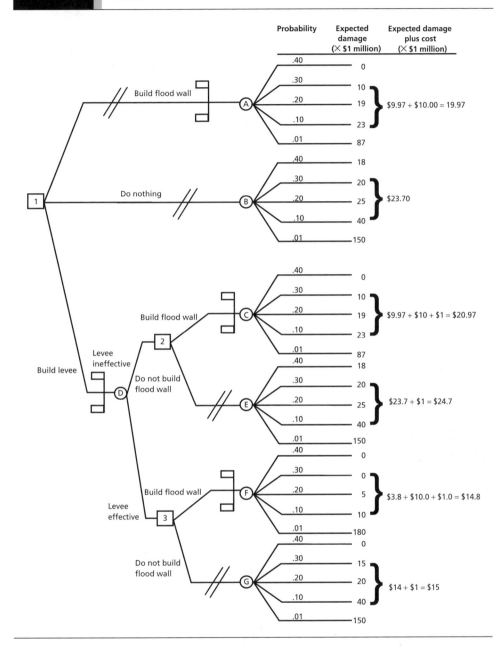

Table 13.3 presents the damage estimates for an effective levee. You may note that I have left out one option: I did not include the damage estimates for when the levee is ineffective. This is because these estimates are the same as those for no levee at all. Combining information from Table 13.2, Table 13.3, and Figure 13.5, we can build the decision tree shown in Figure 13.6.

When there are several decision nodes, the simplest way of working out a decision tree problem is *folding backward*. In this case, the first two options of doing nothing and building the flood wall must be evaluated against the option of constructing the levee first. In evaluating that option, we must consider decision nodes 2 and 3. For decision node 2, if the levee is ineffective, it stands to reason that the flood wall should be built, since the total estimated damage for the option of "do not build" ($23.7 million + $1 million for levee = $24.7 million) is higher than that for the decision to construct the flood wall ($9.97 million + construction cost of $10 million + $1 million = $20.97 million).

If, on the other hand, the levee is found to be effective (at decision node 3), building the flood wall once again seems to be a better option than not building it. That is because the expected damage with an effective levee and a flood wall, $14.8 million ($3.8 million of expected flood damage + $10 million for the flood wall + $1 million for the levee), is lower than the expected cost of not building a flood wall, $15.0 million ($14.0 million + $1 million).

We are now in a position to evaluate the options: do nothing or immediately build the flood wall. As you can see, the estimated damage for the do-nothing option is $23.7 million, while the damage for the immediate construction of the flood wall is expected to be $19.97 million. Since these estimates are higher than those for building the flood wall whether or not the levee is effective, we should recommend that the town council build the levee and the flood wall. I have summarized the findings in Table 13.4.[8]

Risk Tolerance and Expected Payoff

Each of us views risk differently. I was recently watching a game show in which the contestant had two answer choices. If she gave the right answer, she would earn a

TABLE 13.4   Total Estimated Cost of Flood Wall and Levee

| | Estimated damage (× $1 million) | | | | | |
| | | | Ineffective levee | | Effective levee | |
Probability of flood	Flood wall	No flood wall	Flood wall	No flood wall	Flood wall	No flood wall
.50	0.00	0.00	0.00	0.00	0.00	0.00
.40	0.00	18.00	0.00	18.00	0.00	0.00
.30	10.00	20.00	10.00	20.00	0.00	15.00
.20	19.00	25.00	19.00	25.00	5.00	20.00
.10	23.00	40.00	23.00	40.00	10.00	40.00
.01	87.00	150.00	87.00	150.00	180.00	150.00
Total estimated damage	9.97	23.70	9.97	23.70	3.80	14.00
Cost of flood wall	10.00	0.00	10.00	0.00	10.00	0.00
Cost of levee	0.00	0.00	1.00	1.00	1.00	1.00
Total cost	19.97	23.70	20.97	24.70	14.80	15.00

FIGURE 13.7   Risk and Payoff in a Television Game Show

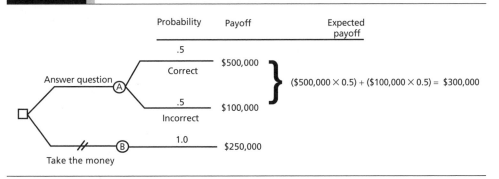

$500,000 prize, doubling her current winnings of $250,000. But if her answer was incorrect, she would receive only $100,000. What would you do if you were in her position? Let us draw her options in the framework of a decision tree (see Figure 13.7).

If her chances of choosing the right answer are 50-50, her expected payoff is greater than that of the sure-bet option (probability = 1.0) of taking the money she has already won. But would you be a cool statistician and risk losing $150,000? If you would, your behavior would be considered **risk neutral**. On the other hand, if you would choose the second, sure-bet option, your action would be regarded as **risk averse**; that is, you would prefer to avoid risk in decision making. In contrast, some people thrive on taking high risks. If you are only 30 percent sure that you know the correct answer, the expected returns for attempting to answer are $220,000, $30,000 less than the returns expected for taking the money. In this case, if you still insist on chasing the high reward of half a million dollars, you will be considered a **risk lover**.

Is it then irrational to be anything but risk neutral? There is a problem with defining human rationality as risk-neutral behavior. As I have shown in chapter 5, the so-called Allais paradox demonstrates that people's preference for risk can vary across the range of probability and reward. From a policy perspective, it may be advisable to take risks as long as you can comfortably bear the consequences of the loss. Consider, for example, our hypothetical example of constructing a levee along with a flood wall. By following the rules of mathematical expectation, we have recommended the construction of both. However, if you examine the payoff matrix carefully, you will see that such a recommendation may be shortsighted. Building both flood control devices significantly lowers the risk of more frequent flooding, but it heightens the risk for damage associated with a cataclysmic flood. A huge increase in the water level may suddenly break the levee, and the breach could exacerbate an already catastrophic incident. The question is, can you afford a small risk that you will incur a devastating loss? After all, the hundred-year flood may not wait another hundred years to show up. If it occurs, the entire town may be wiped out. Given this possibility, can you blame the authorities for taking the less expensive and less risky option of building only the flood wall? For another example of how policymakers weigh risk against expected payoffs, see "A Case in Point."

A CASE IN POINT

Risky Business: Orange County Bankruptcy

On December 6, 1994, officials of Orange County, California, one of the most affluent and fiscally conservative counties in the nation, declared bankruptcy, the result of risky investments made by county treasurer Robert Citron.[9] When the final tallies were made, the county had lost a total of $1.64 billion from its investment pool, which invested money for the county, its thirty-one cities, and more than 150 other, mostly single purpose, government entities.

The primary guiding principles for local government investment pools are safety, liquidity, and yield. That is, when investing public money, pools must safeguard invested money and not take unacceptable risks. Fund managers should also make sure that the municipality has enough liquid cash on hand to meet its obligations. Finally, cash managers seek to maximize return on investment (yield).

Citron was the county treasurer for more than twenty years. He was widely considered a "financial guru," who could consistently earn returns vastly superior to those realized by other municipalities throughout the state and the nation. In fact, Citron had promised that a full 35 percent of the county's 1995 revenue would come from interest income. As it turned out, Citron was paying more attention to the possibility of yield than to the reality, virtually ignoring the safety of his investments by choosing high-risk instruments called "derivatives." The problem with derivatives is that if the market follows your prediction, these securities give you extremely high returns, but if it does not, they can result in enormous losses.[10]

To be sure, Citron did have his critics, who claimed that he was taking unacceptable risks. However, the county, like most other local governments in California, was strapped for tax revenues because Proposition 13 (a sweeping property tax reduction measure) had put the county in a financial straightjacket since its passage in 1978. Because these investments brought in huge sums of money—without requiring that the county impose higher taxes on its highly conservative electorate—such words of caution were ignored by the politicians who supervised Citron.

TWO ACTIVE PLAYERS: GAME THEORY

The decision tree is a schematic representation of decision making under uncertainty. It falls under the more general area of study called **game theory**. Game theory is a mathematical technique to evaluate the strategic interaction between two or more opponents on the basis of expectations about their possible moves. This technique is particularly useful when you are in a situation of active confrontation, must make strategic decisions, and are uncertain about the moves of your opponent(s). The literature on game theory is varied and rich. The beauty of this technique is that it can be used to explain strategies in a variety of scenarios, from chess games to corporate takeovers, from labor union bargaining to the negotiation of international treaties. Also, because it lends itself to mathematical modeling, literature about it varies from simple to extremely complex,

In the end, Robert Citron, the "financial wizard," was convicted of fraud. Most interestingly, during his trial, a neuropsychologist testified in his defense that she found extensive damage in Citron's frontal brain, which "allows you to think, analyze information, and be conscious."[11] Echoing her findings, a clinical psychologist compared him to "an empty bottle put out into the water." The experts claimed that Citron had suffered from brain damage throughout his life.

Derivatives attempt to manipulate the future risks within a complex mathematical model. As a result, many who invest in these products do not fully understand the risks involved and the assumptions that go into the construction of these models. As they pushed Orange County to bankruptcy in 1994, a year later, the British banking giant Barings fell into the same trap when an errant trader in one of its overseas branches gambled on these extremely high risk products. The mounting losses brought down Britain's oldest merchant bank, which had financed the Napoleonic wars, the Louisiana Purchase, and the construction of the Erie Canal. Investment in derivatives, particularly by hedge funds, which often operate outside banking regulations, was also blamed for the financial debacle of 2008. The biggest moral of the saga of the derivatives for the money managers is that they must not invest in anything they do not fully understand. Since the implications of investing in these exceedingly lucrative instruments are extremely dire, and so is the temptation for fund managers to seek them out for quick profits, it appears that the government and regulatory agencies may soon step in order to mitigate their devastating effects in a globalized economy.

Discussion Points

1. Does it always pay to be risk neutral when dealing with an uncertain future? Is it advisable to be a risk lover in certain situations? When?
2. From the standpoint of risk management, why did Orange County face a fiscal disaster?

from eminently practical to highly esoteric.[12] The rules of strategic decision making have been researched by psychologists (to study fallacies about uncertainty), international relations scholars (to predict the strategic moves of nations), and students of corporate strategies (to explore the ways in which corporations interact).[13] Students of negotiating and bargaining have tried to come up with rules for conflict resolution.[14] These diverse inquiries have significantly advanced our knowledge about strategic decision making and sometimes have inflated expectations beyond what these techniques can deliver.[15]

Let us start with a simple game with two players. Although decision trees are shown as diagrams, two-player games are usually written as matrices. Since game theory can explain the outcome of a confrontation between two or more parties, it is useful in analyzing policies of engagement. Let us assume that your city is engaged in a bitter

TABLE 13.5	Payoff Matrix for Mayor and Garbage Collectors' Union	
	Mayor's position	
Union's position	*Accept arbitration*	*Hang tough*
Accept arbitration	3, 2	0, 5
Strike	4, 0	1, 1

labor dispute. The garbage collectors' union is threatening to go on strike during the busy Christmas season. The city has been in negotiation with the union for some time, but the parties remain far apart in their positions. The union believes that the conservative mayor wants to weaken organized labor and has little faith in her commitment to an acceptable negotiated settlement. The mayor, on the other hand, is up for reelection in February. She believes that the actions of organized labor are politically motivated and designed to undermine her candidacy. The state mediators, unable to end the impasse, suggest binding arbitration, in which case an independent board reviews the situation and proposes a compromise binding on both sides. From the perspective of the union, there are two options: to accept arbitration and risk a less than acceptable contract or to go on strike. Similarly, the mayor has two options. She can accept arbitration and run the risk of approving a contract she believes might be fiscally irresponsible for the city, or she can hang tough and not negotiate with the garbage collectors' union. We can analyze the city's dilemma with the help of game theory. Table 13.5 shows the payoff matrix for the two parties.

The table presents the perceived payoffs for the two parties on a scale ranging from 0 (least desirable) to 5 (most desirable). As you can see from this table, the union has two alternatives. It can accept arbitration or go on strike. If it negotiates with the mayor for an arbitration board of its liking, its preference ranking is 3. This, however, is not the best option for the mayor, since she would prefer to take a tough stance against organized labor. In any case, she assigns this option a lukewarm 2.

From the union's perspective, the worst scenario is one in which the mayor refuses to negotiate and the union is forced to accept arbitration. This combination of strategies is valued as 0 by the union and 5 by the mayor.

The union may opt for a work stoppage. If this action brings a reluctant mayor to the negotiating table, it is the most preferred option for the union (4) and least preferred (0) for the mayor. Finally, if the union strikes and the mayor hangs tough in a high-risk game, both parties assign 1 to this option.

The rules of rational choice under uncertain conditions dictate that each player follow a **minimax strategy**, in which each chooses the strategy that minimizes his or her maximum loss or regret. From the perspective of the union, if it chooses to accept arbitration, its maximum loss is to be pinned to the mat by a tough mayor. Thus, for this option, its maximum regret position is 0. However, for the strike option, its worst possible outcome is 1. Hence, from the standpoint of the union, deciding to strike is superior to going for arbitration. Similarly, you can see that the mayor minimizes her maximum loss when she takes a strong position. Therefore, the only possible outcome of this confrontation is a strike by the garbage collectors while the mayor takes an intransigent posture.

This outcome, in the lower right-hand corner of the matrix, is called the solution of **Nash equilibrium**, after noted mathematician John Nash. This solution identifies an outcome from which neither player can gain by unilaterally switching to another strategy.[16] That is, if the mayor chooses to confront the labor union, the union does not gain by unilaterally switching to a compromise option of going for arbitration, since doing so would lower its payoff from 1 to 0. Similarly, if the union chooses to strike, the best option for the mayor is to project a firm position; otherwise, her own payoff would sink from 1 to 0.

The need to devise military strategies in the face of uncertainty has inspired much of the development of game theory. One of the textbook cases of game theory can be found in the Battle of the Bismarck Sea.[17] In early 1943 the allies' counterattack on the Japanese navy was in full swing. By that time U.S. forces had gained a foothold on the island of New Guinea. The northern half of the island was controlled by the Japanese, while the allies controlled the southern part. Intelligence reports produced for Douglas MacArthur, the supreme commander of the allied forces, indicated that the Japanese were sending huge reinforcements for a major counterattack on the allies. General MacArthur ordered General George C. Kenney, commander of the allied air force, to challenge the Japanese convoy and inflict the maximum possible damage. Figure 13.8 presents General Kenney's dilemma.

As you can see, the commander of the Japanese convoy had two options: he could take the northern route or the southern route. Therefore, Kenney also had the corresponding options of sending the bulk of his interceptor forces to the north or directing them to the south. His objective was to deliver the maximum possible

FIGURE 13.8   **Strategies in the Battle of the Bismarck Sea**

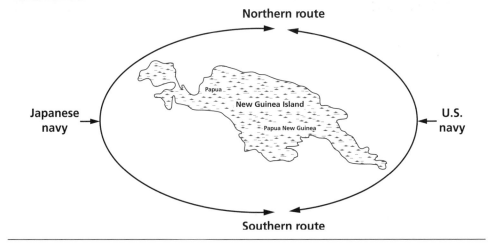

TABLE 13.6	Possible Days of Allied Bombing	
	Japanese strategy	
Allied strategy	*Sail north*	*Sail south*
Search north	2 days of bombing	2 days of bombing
Search south	1 day of bombing	3 days of bombing

damage to the Japanese convoy through relentless bombing. The weather report showed an approaching storm on the north side of the island. The storm would markedly reduce visibility and, consequently, the ability of the allied planes to locate and strafe enemy ships. General Kenney measured his payoff in terms of the expected number of days the allied air force would have to bomb the convoy as the allies headed west. The payoff matrix for the options open to the opposing commanders is shown in Table 13.6.

From General Kenney's standpoint, if he sent his forces up the northern route and the Japanese chose to sail to the north side of the island, since weather was expected to be poor, his pilots would be able to bomb the Japanese for just two days. However, if after flying north in the foul weather the allied bombers discovered that the Japanese had taken the southern route, they would still be able to bomb enemy ships for two days. In contrast, if Kenney sent his forces south, only to find out that the Japanese were on the other side of the island, the allies would have to be content with only one day's bombardment. But if they were lucky and found that the Japanese had taken the calmer waters of the southern route, they would be able to bomb the convoy for three days. We can show the situation facing General Kenney in terms of a decision tree (see Figure 13.9).

FIGURE 13.9	Decision Tree for Allied Strategy in the Battle of the Bismarck Sea

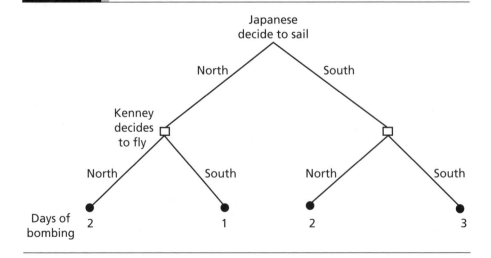

You can see from the decision tree that General Kenney's best option was to follow the northern route. Adopting the minimax strategy (by which you minimize your maximum regret: one day of bombing for the allies and three for the Japanese), Kenney realized that the worst he could do by flying south was to bomb the Japanese convoy for one day. However, if he sent his planes north, the worst outcome for him was to inflict two days of damage. Therefore, his **dominant strategy** was to fly north. That is, that strategy provided him with the highest payoff given what he expected the Japanese to do. Similarly, for the Japanese fleet, its worst fears would have been realized if it had taken the calm waters of the south and had been quickly discovered by the allies for a full three days of attack. Hence, this classic battle situation presented the game theorists with a textbook case of a Nash equilibrium. In reality, the Japanese sent their ships along the northern route. General Kenney also went north, and his planes delivered a devastating blow to Japanese aspirations in the Pacific with two days of incessant bombing.

Game Theory in Local Government Decision Making

The most often cited examples of the use of game theory involve strategic decisions in military operations or international relations. This powerful analytical technique may also be used to aid local government decision makers. We have considered a hypothetical case of a city mayor confronting a labor union. In reality, local governments often face the prospect of strikes resulting from disputes with labor unions. Until about two decades ago, a universal ban prevented strikes by state and local government employees. For example, New York's Taylor law flatly prohibits strikes by public employees and prescribes the forfeiture of tenure and double loss of pay for striking workers.[18] However, in recent years this stance has softened somewhat. By the early 1990s, about ten states permitted certain groups of government workers to strike under specific circumstances.

Needless to say, strikes or work slowdowns by public employees can cost cities millions of dollars. At the same time, a city can get into a financial bind by signing an overly generous pay package with the unions. In fact, many have blamed New York City's brush with bankruptcy in 1975 on politicians too eager to placate the demands of labor unions.[19] Strikes usually do not help workers' unions, either. Unions lose out in terms of public support and may even risk court-imposed sanctions and fines.

If a union and a city administration are not careful, they can get locked into a losing proposition. Such a situation is known as a **prisoner's dilemma**. The name comes from a game in which, because of a lack of mutual trust, understanding, and cooperation, both players must settle for a less than satisfactory resolution. Let us consider the following scenario, portrayed frequently on television in police and courtroom dramas. You and your best friend have committed a crime, but no one saw you do it. The only way the district attorney can get a conviction is if either or both of you confess. Knowing this, the police have kept the two of you in different cells, with no possibility of communication. Your attorney tells you that you have two options: you can either confess or not confess. If you choose to confess, you will face two alternate scenarios. If your unrepentant, bullheaded friend does not confess, you will be rewarded with the witness protection plan while your friend languishes in jail for fifteen years. If, on the other hand, your weak and gutless friend decides to confess as well, both of you will draw five-year prison terms. If you decide not to confess and your friend betrays you, you end up with the fifteen-year prison term. However, if he turns out to be equally trustworthy and

TABLE **13.7**	The Prisoner's Dilemma	
	Your friend's strategy	
Your strategy	*Confess*	*Do not confess*
Confess	5, 5	Witness protection, 15
Do not confess	15, witness protection	0, 0

remains steadfast in not confessing, the prosecution has no case, and both of you are acquitted.

What should you do? Before answering this question, let us consider the payoffs for each strategy (see Table 13.7). You can see in the matrix that *collectively*, both of you will be better off choosing not to confess. However, you will reach this desirable position (from both of your viewpoints) only if you trust each other. Without trust, you will look at only two strategies: confess or do not confess. If you confess, the maximum risk is five years in prison. If you do not confess, the maximum risk is fifteen years in jail. Therefore, following the decision rule of minimizing your maximum loss (the minimax rule), you should choose to confess. Following the same rule, your friend will arrive at the same conclusion, leading to a joint confession and a five-year prison term for both of you. You may notice that in this case, confessing is the dominant strategy for both players.

In our example in Table 13.5, both the mayor and the union could have gone for a negotiated settlement in which both parties would have been better off. The labor union would have improved its position from 1 to 3 and the mayor from 1 to 2.

Game theory, by providing insight into the dynamics of a conflict, can help the involved parties avoid the prisoner's dilemma. The reason parties get locked in a prisoner's dilemma is that they do not trust each other. If the mayor and union had not been as mistrustful of each other, they could have found a mutually acceptable arbitration board. In many areas of decision making under uncertain conditions, an effort to develop trust can save everyone from being locked in an undesirable position.

The Golden Rules of Decision Making under Uncertainty

Identifying the optimal strategic moves in situations of uncertainty has been the subject of a great deal of academic discussion. On the basis of this lengthy discourse, I can offer four rules of advice:

Rule 1: Look ahead and reason back. Successful strategies depend on conscious forward thinking. However, while planning, one must think about the possible reaction of the opponent and the opposing course of action. The old Native American adage of learning to walk a mile in someone else's moccasins has considerable validity. Putting yourself in your opponent's shoes requires you to draw lessons from past experience to anticipate where your moves ultimately will take you.

Rule 2: If you have a dominant strategy, play it. It may not win you many friends, but if you have a dominant strategy, you must play it regardless of the situation. This rule is especially true in **zero-sum games**, in which the players' interests are strictly opposed and one player's gain is the other's loss. If we are playing poker, your win is my loss, and the total amount to be distributed is fixed. The confrontation between the mayor and the union may be construed as a zero-sum game. Everyone must play the dominant strategy and, inevitably, must choose the undesirable outcome—deadlock. However, given the absence of trust, by playing the dominant strategy, each party ensures that it will not be stuck in an even worse position.

Rule 3: Successively eliminate all dominant strategies from consideration. If you have a number of possible alternatives, you should compare the outcomes and eliminate the dominant strategies. We followed this rule during our discussion of the decision tree. You may recall that by the process of elimination, we arrived at the most desirable strategy of building a levee and a flood wall. Proceeding in a similar way in your decision making may bring you to a unique alternative that is better than all others.

Rule 4: In the absence of a unique dominant strategy, look for an equilibrium. In the absence of a dominant strategy, settle for a point that represents the best response under the circumstances, given the players' positions. These circumstances can be quite complicated. Game theorists have pointed out that some situations may have more than one equilibrium position, or none at all. Since the discussion of these complicated scenarios is likely to take us beyond the scope of this book, for the sake of economy I will table these questions for now and simply refer the more curious readers (and certainly the adventuresome) to other books and articles.[20]

STRATEGIES TO OVERCOME THE PRISONER'S DILEMMA

Uncertainty often causes us to take actions that are not in our best interest. This is true for individuals, organizations, and even nations engaged in international strategic moves. Often people get locked into situations that offer poor solutions; however, given the circumstances, there seems to be no other way out.

You can see that following the rules of rational decision making under uncertainty can put you in an undesirable situation. We will discuss some ways of building trust and engineering cooperation in the next section. However, often in life we must proceed without trusting our adversaries. In international relations, nations get into wasteful arms races (even those that can least afford to do so). By engaging in destructive labor disputes, industries around the world have been forced to shut down, causing unemployment for workers and economic hardship and loss of capital for owners and management. Of course, many interpersonal disputes remain unresolved because of lack of trust.

However, trust is not developed in a vacuum. It can evolve only through players' trustworthy actions. If I know an individual to be reliable, I can expect cooperative behavior in response to my cooperative gesture. However, this reciprocity of cooperative behavior can break down because of greed or fear. In our example of the prisoner's dilemma, I can truly win if my friend is made to believe that I will not confess—and then I turn star witness for the prosecution. If I pursue this strategy, I am guilty of greed. If I know that I can win with an unexpected defection, like all other swindlers and con artists, I will slowly develop trust and then defect at the most opportune time. Or I may defect out of fear. I may believe that you are about to break our bond of trust, so I may do it on my own. From violent ethnic strife in Eastern Europe and Africa to broken relationships between friends and relatives, life is full of examples of such defections, which result in suboptimal payoffs for the players.

Greed and fear can be minimized if there is an avenue for punishing defection. The Mafia in southern Italy was able to maintain its iron grip over society by using *omertà*, the universal code of silence. Regardless of the situation, a defector was sure to face the fearsome wrath of the organization. This code kept the system of organized crime going for years. In the United States the court system punishes breach of contract, as defined by clearly understood and vigorously enforced tort laws. If the players are aware of the costs of defection, and the costs are higher than the expected gains, they can be assured of a cooperative game.

However, in many cases, such enforced cooperation is not viable. A great deal of effort has gone into discerning the best strategies under complete uncertainty, when cooperation between two players cannot be guaranteed. In the early 1980s Robert Axelrod, a University of Michigan professor of political science, organized a tournament.[21] Game theorists from around the world submitted computer programs proposing strategies for dealing with uncertainty. These strategies were matched against one another in pairwise competition, in which each computer program was pitted against every other computer program. Each game was repeated 150 times. The strategies varied from nasty (defection on every move) to saintly (cooperation regardless of the opponent's action), from simple techniques to highly complex systems of calculated cooperation and punitive defection. The game that received the highest number of points was one that was submitted by Anatol Rapoport, a professor of mathematics at the University of Toronto. This surprising winner followed a simple strategy: tit for tat. It started out by cooperating (that is, not confessing, in the language of our example). After this it simply repeated the last move of its opponent. In other words, if the opponent cooperated, the tit-for-tat strategy did the same. However, if the opponent defected, the strategy sought immediate retribution and defection. But if the opponent, having defected, went back to cooperation, it was quick to forgive and adopt a cooperative position.

Axelrod attributed the success of the tit-for-tat strategy to four desirable qualities: clarity, "niceness," provocability, and forgiveness. The rules of this strategy are simple and, therefore, *clear*. The strategy is *nice* in the sense that it does not defect unprovoked. Although it is quick to exact retribution for a breach of trust (*provocability*), it is equally quick to *forgive* and go back to the cooperating mode. Axelrod claimed great possibilities for the tit-for-tat strategy and saw through it the evolution of a cooperative system. During the period of the renewed Cold War (after the speech in which President Ronald Reagan referred to the Soviet Union as an "evil empire"), this simple strategy symbolized for many the hope of a new, trusting world order.

However, despite the early hopes for greatness, later scrutiny of the tit-for-tat strategy found damaging flaws in its universality. First, the strategy was the winner only in terms of cumulative score; it could not beat any strategy in a pairwise game. The best it could do was to tie with the cooperative (saintly) games, or the games following strategies close to its own, starting with cooperation. It won overall because, since it echoed the opponent, it always came close, regardless of strategy, a quality that could not be matched by any other strategy.

The tit-for-tat strategy also suffers from some other serious flaws. Avinash Dixit and Barry Nalebuff point out that if two opponents are playing this strategy and one defects by mistake, or the move is seen as a defection, the tit-for-tat strategy will kick in, and the two will not be able to extricate themselves from a never-ending cycle of retribution. Instead of tit for tat, Dixit and Nalebuff suggest a more forgiving strategy.

OTHER STRATEGIES: TRUST AND BARGAINING

It is obvious that no one would want to get mired in a game of "getting even." Mahatma Gandhi often quipped that the strategy of "a tooth for a tooth and an eye for an eye" ultimately leaves contenders toothless and blind. Across the United States a great deal of academic energy is being devoted to finding ways to resolve seemingly intractable disputes. The key to the resolution of conflict lies in developing trust. When trust is lacking, participants need external enforcement of compliance through the imposition of costs for noncompliance, and as always in a conflict situation, they should rely on bargaining. In their widely read book *Getting to Yes*, Roger Fisher and William Ury of the Harvard Negotiation Project spell out a number of strategies to achieve agreement in disputes.[22] Although these strategies make for extremely useful and lively debates—and I strongly recommend that you become familiar with them—their full discussion falls outside the scope of this book.

I leave you with a final word of caution. Because of the very nature of disputes, not all of them have peaceful resolutions. For many different reasons, the contenders may deem open hostility to be more desirable than a negotiated compromise. In such cases, the only outcome is continuing conflict.

KEY WORDS

Actions (p. 323)
Collectively exhaustive (p. 324)
Decision tree (p. 322)
Dominant strategy (p. 337)
Expected payoff (p. 321)
Game theory (p. 332)
Minimax strategy (p. 334)
Mutually exclusive (p. 324)
Nash equilibrium (p. 335)

Outcomes (p. 323)
Prisoner's dilemma (p. 337)
Risk (p. 320)
Risk averse (p. 331)
Risk lover (p. 331)
Risk neutral (p. 331)
Uncertainty (p. 320)
Zero-sum games (p. 338)

EXERCISES

1. What is an expected payoff? How does the concept of expected payoff help analyze a situation of uncertainty? In this context, explain "dominant strategy" and the minimax rule.
2. What is a zero-sum game? With an appropriate example, explain how conflict arises in the area of resource allocation (resulting from a public policy) because of a zero-sum situation.

3. What is the prisoner's dilemma? What are its outcomes for the participants? How can it be prevented in real life?

4. In July the parks and recreation department in your town wants to organize an exhibition of local arts and crafts. The department is considering whether to hold the exhibit inside the downtown sports arena or outside in its open-air parking lot. However, the problem is that while planning the location of the exhibition, the planners face uncertainty about the weather. The weather bureau reports that there is only a 20 percent chance of rain. If the town holds the event inside the sports arena, after paying for the use of the facility, it expects to break even if it rains. If it does not rain, the town will make a profit of $15,000 from the event. On the other hand, if the exhibition is held outdoors, it can be either a great success or a real failure, depending on the weather. If it does not rain, the town will make a tidy profit of $35,000, but if it rains, it stands to lose $10,000. Draw a decision tree and explain the options open to the decision makers. What would be your recommendation?

5. Your town is located on the shores of the Atlantic Ocean, directly in the line of devastating hurricanes. You are evaluating a policy to invest $10 million in emergency preparedness. It is estimated that the chance that a moderate to strong hurricane (categories 2 and 3) will come your way next year is 30 percent. The chance of being hit by a devastating category 4 hurricane is 5 percent. Right now, without this additional preparation, the town can handle small tropical storms without much problem or property loss. If there is a category 2 or 3 hurricane, however, the estimated loss will be about $15 million, and for a fierce category 4 storm, the estimated property loss could rise as high as $50 million.

   The financial administration department estimates that with the $10 million invested, the town will be able to withstand a strong hurricane of category 2 or 3 with a minimum damage of $5 million. Even if there is a giant hurricane of category 4, the damage estimate goes no higher than $20 million. Should the town invest the money in disaster preparedness? Draw the decision tree and write a report explaining your recommendation.

6. Suppose you are an aide to the governor of your state. Because of a much publicized story of a mentally deranged person killing a number of innocent victims in a crowded restaurant with an automatic weapon, the governor is considering a proposal to ban all sales of automatic guns within state borders. This issue is emotionally charged, and the governor is keenly aware of the political cost of an unpopular decision.

   Facing this controversial problem, the governor sees three options: to do nothing, to propose a mild law banning the sale of a few such weapons, or to establish a commission. If the governor does nothing, there would be a political cost, to which the governor's advisers assign a value of −3. If a mild ban is unilaterally imposed, it will cause a net loss of popularity, valued at −2. On the other hand, if an independent commission is set up, the governor may be able to circumvent this lose-lose situation. However, the governor has no control over the recommendations of an independent commission. The commission may come up with a "do nothing" recommendation, which would absolve the governor for not doing anything (value = 0). Another possibility is that the commission will recommend a mild ban, or it could suggest a strict ban on the ownership of automatic weapons. The governor, however, retains the right to go along with the commission or to reject its recommendations. If the commission recommends a mild ban, the governor can accept it for a political payoff of +3, or he may reject it and do nothing for a small loss of –1 (the commission has taken the edge off the governor's inaction).

A real problem may arise if the commission recommends a radical plan of gun control. If the governor accepts it, he will be hit for a loss of –10, but if he rejects the plan, he will incur a loss of –4. The probability that the commission, which will have broad-based support, will recommend doing nothing is .3, the chance that it will suggest a mild ban is .5, and the chance that it will support a strict gun control measure is .2. If you are a political analyst for the governor, what will be your recommendation and why?

7. Many social conflicts arise when rival factions place themselves in a prisoner's dilemma situation. With an appropriate example, discuss the prisoner's dilemma, pointing out the reasons for the intractability of problems and suggesting some possible measures that may help generate cooperation among the parties involved.

Notes

1. Frank Knight, *Risk, Uncertainty, and Profit* (Boston: Houghton Mifflin, 1921).
2. Over the years, authors have altered the definitions of risk and uncertainty proposed by Knight. You may come across a definition of risk that describes it as associated with a project itself, whereas uncertainty is thought to relate to the overall environment. However, in a delightful work on the subject, Young Back Choi argues for the original definitions of these terms. Following Choi, I stick to Knight's definitions of risk and uncertainty. See Choi's *Paradigms and Conventions: Uncertainty, Decision Making, and Entrepreneurship* (Ann Arbor: University of Michigan Press, 1993).
3. Choi, *Paradigms and Conventions*, 13–16.
4. Dipak K. Gupta, "Economics and Collective Identity: Explaining Collective Action," in *The Expansion of Economics and Other Disciplines: Toward an Inclusive Social Science*, ed. Shoshana Grossbard-Shechtman (Armonk, N.Y.: M.E. Sharpe, 2001). A number of eminent economists have broken ranks with the traditional view of utility maximization. See George A. Akerlof and Rachel E. Kranton, "Economics and Identity," *The Quarterly Journal of Economics* 115 (2000): 715–753; Timur Kuran, "Ethnic Norms and Their Transformation through Reputation Cascades," *Journal of Legal Studies* 27, pt. 2 (1998): 623–659; Amartya K. Sen, "Goals, Commitment, and Identity," *Journal of Law, Economics, and Organization* 1 (1985): 341–355; and Howard Margolis, *Selfishness, Altruism, and Rationality: A Theory of Social Choice* (Cambridge, United Kingdom: Cambridge University Press, 1982).
5. Harvey Leibenstein, "The Prisoner's Dilemma in the Invisible Hand: An Analysis of Intrafirm Productivity," *American Economic Review* 72 (1982): 92–97.
6. Choi, *Paradigms and Conventions*, 15–16.
7. Arthur M. Silverstein, *Pure Politics and Impure Science: The Swine Flu Affair* (Baltimore, Md.: Johns Hopkins University Press, 1981). Also see Richard E. Neustadt and Harvey V. Fineberg, *The Swine Flu Affair: Decision-making on a Slippery Disease* (Washington, D.C.: U.S. Department of Health, Education, and Welfare, 1978).
8. For an actual study of the probability of flood damage, see *Flood Proofing: How to Evaluate Your Options: Decision Tree* (Fort Belvoir, Va.: U.S. Army Corps of Engineers, National Flood Proofing Committee, 1995).
9. For a comprehensive review of the problem, see Mark Baldassare, *When Government Fails: The Orange County Bankruptcy* (Berkeley and San Francisco, Calif.: University of California Press and Public Policy Institute of California, 1998). In this section, I concentrate mostly on

risk management. However, a number of studies, in addition to identifying the problem of assuming undue risks, point to fraud and criminal activities in this expensive fiscal fiasco. See, for example, Susan Will, Henry N. Pontell, and Richard Cheung, "Risky Business Revisited: White-Collar Crime and the Orange County Bankruptcy," *Crime & Delinquency* 44 (1998): 367–387.

10. For an excellent discussion of derivatives, see Julian Walmsley, *New Financial Instruments*, 2nd ed. (New York: Wiley, 1998).

11. See Associated Press, "Former Orange County Treasurer Had Brain Damage, Witnesses Say," *San Diego Union-Tribune*, November 19, 1996.

12. For an informative, highly entertaining explanation of game theory, see Avinash K. Dixit and Barry J. Nalebuff, *Thinking Strategically: The Competitive Edge in Business, Politics, and Everyday Life* (New York: W. W. Norton, 1991).

13. David M. Kreps, *Game Theory and Economic Modelling* (Oxford, United Kingdom: Oxford University Press, 1990). Also see Jeremy I. Bulow, John D. Geanakoplos, and Paul D. Kemperer, "Multimarket Oligopoly: Strategic Substitutes and Complements," *Journal of Political Economy* 93 (1985): 488–511.

14. Roger Fisher and William Ury, *Getting to Yes: Negotiating Agreement without Giving In* (New York: Penguin, 1981). Also see Howard Raiffa, *The Art and Science of Negotiation* (Cambridge, Mass.: Belknap, 1982).

15. *Newsweek* magazine, in reviewing Fisher and Ury's *Getting to Yes* (see note 14), called the book "a coherent 'win-win' negotiation which, if it takes hold, may help convert the Age of Me to the Era of We" (quoted on the book's back cover).

16. Bruce Bueno de Mesquita, *Principles of International Politics: People's Power, Preferences, and Perceptions* (Washington, D.C.: CQ Press, 2000), 48.

17. For an excellent discussion of the importance of game theory, see John L. Casti, *Five Golden Rules: Great Theories of 20th-century Mathematics—and Why They Matter* (New York: Wiley, 1996).

18. Robert J. Thornton, "Unions and Collective Bargaining," in *Management Policies in Local Government Finance*, ed. J. Richard Aronson and Eli Schwartz (Washington, D.C.: International City/County Management Association, 1996), 418.

19. "Message to Rudy," *The New Yorker*, May 15, 1995.

20. For a discussion of multiple equilibrium, see John C. Harsanyi, "Advances in Understanding Rational Behavior," in *Foundational Problems in the Special Sciences*, ed. Robert E. Butts and Jaakko Hintikka (Dordrecht, the Netherlands: D. Reidel, 1977). For an example of this kind of situation and its resolution, see Frank C. Zagare, "Rationality and Deterrence," *World Politics* 42 (January 1990): 238–260. Again, for the most readable explanation, see Dixit and Nalebuff, *Thinking Strategically*.

21. For the results of this tournament, see Robert Axelrod, *The Evolution of Cooperation* (New York: Basic Books, 1984).

22. Fisher and Ury, *Getting to Yes.*

14 Choosing the Best Alternative: Cost-Benefit Analysis

Your city is considering acquiring a parcel of vacant land near the center of the city to develop a new convention center with a hotel complex. Your job, as a policy analyst, is to evaluate the proposal and send your recommendation to the city council. The question is, of course, how to go about it.

It is obvious that you will recommend the project if the benefits outweigh the costs. When we make a decision, any decision, we consciously or unconsciously evaluate its potential benefits and costs. In fact, this evaluation process is so fundamental to human cognition that many economists have equated it with the very notion of human rationality.[1] Economists argue that when individuals make decisions, even emotional ones, they have a good sense of the benefits and costs of their actions. How do we choose our mates in marriage? Poets and authors of romantic novels claim that love is blind—anyone can fall in love with anyone else without following any definite pattern of behavior. Yet statistical data show that marriage partners tend to match each other's "endowments" (age, looks, wealth, education, social standing, and so forth). That is, their actual preferences reveal a "rational choice" based loosely on the economic notion of **cost-benefit analysis**.[2] Thus, you will probably not be surprised that this chapter on cost-benefit analysis mirrors chapter 5 on critical thinking. Cost-benefit analysis, which emphasizes monetary evaluation, provides critical thinking with a more formal structure. I mentioned that the techniques of statistics and operations research greatly aid the process of thinking critically. Hence, because cost-benefit analysis draws on all these tools, I am discussing it at the very end of our discussion of analytical techniques.

In sum, the fundamental principles of cost-benefit analysis are the following:

- *When considering a single project, accept it if its benefits are greater than its costs.*
- *When considering alternative projects, choose the one that gives you the highest benefits in relation to the costs.*

In our convention center example, we should go ahead with the project if its benefits are greater than its costs. Similarly, we should evaluate alternative uses for the land (for example, a new public library, a public park, or a shopping mall) with regard to their respective benefits and costs and choose the one that gives us the highest benefit relative to the costs.

If you recommend building a new convention center, how much should the city pay for it? Those who derive their livelihoods from the tourist industry may benefit more than those who do not. Thus, those in the former group may be willing to pay more for it than others. If the total amount the city is willing to pay (reflecting the total utility of the project to its stakeholders) is greater than the cost of the project, it is worth undertaking. This total amount is known in economic terms as the **consumer surplus** (see chapter 3). Therefore, this question goes to the heart of cost-benefit analysis. However, the more we look into the issue, the more complicated it becomes. To fully appreciate the complexity of the problem, we start with the process of conducting a cost-benefit analysis.

Similar to the familiar process of critical thinking, the process of conducting a cost-benefit analysis is as follows:

1. Define the goal(s) of the project.
2. Identify the alternatives.
3. Make an exhaustive list of all benefits and costs, present and future.
4. Estimate and express benefits and costs in monetary terms.
5. Forecast the future streams of benefits and costs, if needed.
6. Choose the alternative with the largest benefit in comparison with the cost.

Let us now discuss in detail each of these six steps. This powerful analytical tool can be used to evaluate almost every social decision. And as you will see from our discussion, its thoroughness (which is directly linked to the cost of the study) must be matched against the importance of the project. If we want to evaluate a proposal for a neighborhood park, we may want to devote a modest amount of time and effort. In contrast, the evaluation for the construction of an atomic power plant, which may affect the health and welfare of hundreds of thousands of residents in the region, would require a much greater degree of precision.

SOCIAL VERSUS PRIVATE COST-BENEFIT ANALYSIS

Before getting to the steps mentioned above, we should briefly discuss the various ramifications for the public versus the private sector. An example may clarify the distinction. An analyst friend, who works for a small neighboring town, called me to say that he was disappointed. The town was negotiating with a national retail chain store to locate within its boundaries. After months of negotiation, the store decided to locate in a more affluent medium-sized city next door. Because my friend's town was coming out of a long fiscal slump and the store would have given it a significant boost, he complained, "Didn't the management of the retail chain know how much social good they could have achieved by choosing to locate here?"

Indeed, if you considered the positive externalities of this relocation decision, you might have agreed with him. However, from the standpoint of the retail chain, the private net benefit was the only calculation that counted. This difference in perception explains the distinction between private and public cost-benefit analysis. Every project, large or small, contains social benefits and costs. Retail stores generate employment, produce sales and income tax, and may even increase property values in the surrounding areas. In contrast, they may also create traffic congestion and pollution. When conducting a cost-benefit analysis for a public project, we must take into account these **positive externalities** and **negative externalities**; because private firms are not rewarded for the positive externalities they generate in the community, nor penalized for negative externalities (unless their actions cause a lawsuit), they do not consider them in their cost-benefit calculations.

DEFINING GOALS

The first task of a cost-benefit analysis is to identify the goals of the project. The clearer the goals are, the easier it will be for an analyst to select the best course of action for achieving them. In chapter 5, I demonstrated the importance of defining the goals of projects. When evaluating the convention center proposal, we must determine whose goals to maximize, the city's, the county's, or the convention center authorities'. We also need to know the goals of the project. We may identify as a goal an increase in tax revenue, urban renewal (as a result of the new convention center), or the enhanced image of the city. Elected representatives may set the goals, or we may determine the wishes of the stakeholders through surveys and focus groups.

IDENTIFYING ALTERNATIVES

The second step in preparing a cost-benefit analysis is to identify the alternatives. Typically, when there are not many identifiable alternatives, we evaluate a project against the option of doing nothing. However, if there are other feasible uses of the site, such as a new public library, a park, or a shopping mall, we should consider them in our analysis.

LISTING THE COSTS AND BENEFITS
OF THE ALTERNATIVES

After selecting the alternatives, one should make as exhaustive a list as possible of the costs and benefits of the various alternatives. It may be useful to use the scheme shown in Figure 14.1 to delineate costs and benefits. They can be broadly classified into two

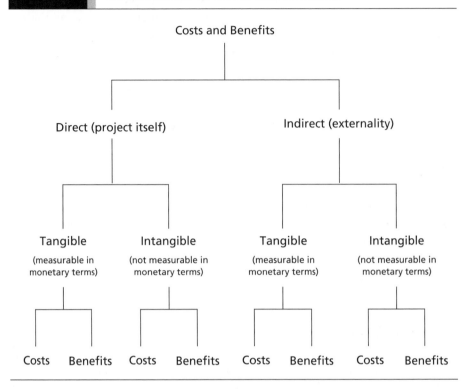

FIGURE 14.1 | Classification of Costs and Benefits

categories: direct and indirect. The **direct costs and benefits** are those that are associated directly with the project itself. The **indirect costs and benefits** are those that affect the surrounding community but do not show up in the ledger of the project.

In our convention center example, the revenues from the new facilities are considered to be the direct benefits, and the construction costs are the direct costs of the project. However, beyond these benefits and costs are the externalities of the proposed project. Thus, the generation of economic activities, such as increased business for the surrounding areas, is to be counted as an indirect benefit. The increased activities, however, may create factors that are detrimental to the city, such as increased traffic, pollution, or crime. These are the social or indirect costs of the project.

Not all costs and benefits are measurable in monetary terms. Many costs and benefits are primarily qualitative in nature and as such cannot be readily expressed in dollars and cents. For example, a beautiful convention center can produce the intangible benefit of newfound pride in the city. Its construction can bring about a change in attitude in the city's citizens. In contrast, such negative conditions as environmental hazards brought about by the construction of the hotel and convention center would constitute part of its social costs. These are the **intangible costs and benefits** of a project. Analysts should be as comprehensive as possible in enumerating the costs and benefits of a public project, both intangible and tangible. I present a list of possible tangible and intangible costs and benefits in Table 14.1.

TABLE 14.1 Benefits and Costs of Convention Center

Benefits				Costs			
Direct		Indirect		Direct		Indirect	
Tangible	Intangible	Tangible	Intangible	Tangible	Intangible	Tangible	Intangible
Revenues from the convention center	Appearance of the new facility	Increased business for the surrounding areas	Increased civic and community pride	Construction expenses and other related costs	Appearance of structure	Increased costs to business as a result of traffic congestion	Increased urban congestion, traffic jams
		Higher property, sales, and transient occupancy taxes for the city		Cost of acquiring land	Reduced property values for some neighborhoods		Increased crime and pollution
		Increased property values for some neighborhoods					Environmental degradation
							Displacement of the poor from the neighborhood

ESTIMATION AND VALUATION OF BENEFITS AND COSTS

One of the most difficult problems of conducting a cost-benefit analysis is that many of the benefits and costs may not be measurable in monetary terms. Another problem is that if they are to be accrued in the future, they must be estimated. It is not enough to state that the construction of a new convention center would increase revenue for the city. We need to come up with a reasonable estimate of how much additional revenue there would be.

A convention center would draw groups of people from outside the region for business meetings. The proposed center would provide large rooms for various gatherings as well as hotel space for convention participants and their guests. Suppose that city hotels can accommodate 300,000 guests per year. The new convention center would increase this capacity to 350,000. The average cost of renting a room in the city is $50, but the increased supply of rooms would reduce this cost to $45 (see Figure 14.2).

You may recall our discussion of consumer surplus from chapter 3. We illustrate this concept in Figure 14.2, in which the demand curve for hotel rooms (D) is shown as a downward-sloping heavy line. Suppose that before construction of the convention center, the supply curve was vertical line S, which gave us an equilibrium occupancy rate of 300,000 rooms at an average room cost per room of $50. At that point, the triangle abc represented the total benefit, or consumer surplus. As a result of the convention center, the supply increased to S′, with an equilibrium room occupancy rate of 350,000 and an average rental rate of $45. As you can see, this increase in supply and reduction in price

FIGURE 14.2   **Consumer Surplus and Social Benefits**

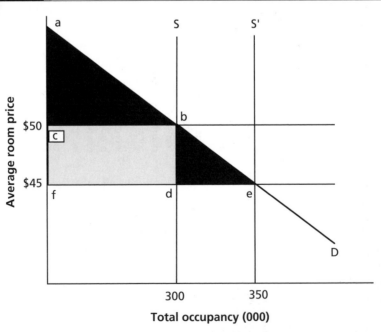

have allowed 50,000 extra guests to visit the city. This new situation has enlarged the area of total consumer surplus to the triangle aef.

Of the total consumer surplus represented by triangle aef, the part described by triangle abc is not new. However, the convention center project has in fact created two new areas of consumer surplus, the rectangle cbdf and the triangle bde. Rectangle cbdf is an added surplus to consumers. That is, as a result of the reduced price of lodging in the city, the gain to consumers is a dollar-for-dollar loss to producers—the hotel and motel owners who had to lower their rates to fill the additional capacity. Rectangle cbdf illustrates what microeconomists call the **pecuniary effect**, which occurs when a change in the welfare of one group of individuals comes at the expense of some other group. Since the gains of the gainers exactly match the losses of the losers, for society as a whole, there is no change in welfare, unless we want to value one group's gain differently from the other group's loss. In that case, society must make a value judgment about the redistribution of income. We will discuss this issue later in the chapter.

Returning to Figure 14.2, we see that the true additional consumer surplus is represented by triangle bde, the area of **net social benefit**. Using the Pythagorean theorem, we can calculate the area of triangle bde as

$$\frac{\text{Height} \times \text{Width}}{2} = \frac{(\$50 - \$45) \times 50,000}{2} = \$125,000$$

Thus, the net gain in consumer surplus to the city is $125,000. Let us suppose that the project has been financed with municipal bonds. The bonds cost city taxpayers $75,000 per year. Therefore, the net gain to the city is $50,000, the difference between the gain in consumer surplus and the cost of servicing the loan ($125,000 – $75,000 = $50,000).

The preceding problem was an easy one to solve. In real life, calculations of costs and benefits are rarely as simple as those in our example. Table 14.1 gives you an idea of the different kinds of costs and benefits that have to be estimated and translated into monetary terms.

One of the most important aspects of conducting a cost-benefit analysis is the valuation of intangibles, which are not bought and sold in the market. Yet for the sake of comparison, an analyst must ascribe monetary values to these items. Let us consider a few examples.

Can We Put a Price Tag on the Intangibles of Life?

How would you value the life of a human being, or the risk of injury that could result in physical disfigurement, or irreparable damage to the environment? Putting a value on such matters evokes controversy, yet it has become a routine matter. For example, when a jury hands down an award for pain and suffering, loss of face, disability, or loss of life, it is imputing a value to the most intangible aspects of life. The case of *State of Alaska v. Exxon Corporation*, resulting from an oil spill in the pristine and ecologically fragile Prince William Sound, is an example of putting a specific monetary value on the loss of habitat. It is indeed legitimate and necessary to consider ways of imputing monetary value to these intangibles when conducting a cost-benefit analysis.

For instance, our large construction project carries the possibility of accidents resulting in severe injuries and even death. In such circumstances, it is essential to include the costs of such accidents. There are several methods for calculating these costs: the **face value of life insurance**, **discounted future earnings**, and **required compensation**. The face value of life insurance measures the monetary worth of one's life by the amount of one's life insurance policy. However, people buy insurance for many different reasons (for example, to some, it is a form of forced saving), and as such, their purchase may have little to do with their perception of the value of their own lives. In the discounted future earnings approach, often used in court cases, a person's life is worth the discounted value of future income. Future earnings are discounted because a dollar in the future is worth less in today's money. But since it evaluates life by one's earning potential, this approach undervalues the lives of those individuals whose talents are not sold in the market or who have stopped earning money. Therefore, it will fail to place much value on homemakers, retirees, and people with disabilities who cannot work.

The market valuation of life does not address the crucial question of the worker's perception of the extent to which the added risk is compensated by the income differential. The answer would imply how much an individual believes his or her life is worth. There are people whose jobs carry almost no risk of death (for example, elementary school teachers, bank clerks), whereas the jobs of others carry an inordinate amount of risk (for example, firefighters, members of a bomb squad). Therefore, if we take an individual's education, age, experience, and other relevant factors of earning determination as constant, we will arrive at a larger payment for the risky jobs to compensate those workers for their added risk. The calculation of this margin of compensation for risk is called the required compensation principle. This is an important issue, and many economists have attempted to estimate the size of this margin. From their studies it seems that this value varies from a lower boundary of $2.5 million to $5 million in 1988 constant dollars. This value turns out to be, on average, five to ten times the value of life calculated under the discounted future earnings principle.[3]

As you can imagine, the imputing of a very high value for human life would make many projects less than economically viable. Therefore, you may think of these numbers as quite excessive, until you realize that an individual who took such a job might not have been totally aware of the risk involved. This is particularly true in the field of high technology; for example, workers whose job was sealing radiation chambers in the construction of atomic power plants complained that they were not adequately apprised of the risk by management. Even individuals who are aware of risk may not have the bargaining power to gain adequate monetary protection against the loss of life. Finally, this measure does not take into account the externalities of such a loss. The death of an individual can destroy a family and cause irreparable damage to the welfare of those who were dependent on this person for financial and emotional security. In light of these kinds of externalities, the U.S. military often exempted only sons from the draft or ensured that two brothers did not serve on the same ship.

As technology improves we come to realize the deleterious effects of substances such as asbestos, whose risks most people were not aware of until many years later. In December 2000 the Environmental Protection Agency (EPA) announced its decision to clean up a dangerous chemical, PCB, from the waters of the upper Hudson River by dredging 2.65 million cubic yards of sediment along a forty-mile stretch. General

Electric had discharged an estimated 1.1 million pounds of PCBs into the river before 1977 from capacitor plants in Fort Edward and Hudson Falls, about forty miles north of Albany. As a result, the EPA claimed that a 200-mile stretch of the river, down to New York City, was contaminated. The project would cost GE an estimated $460 million. However, the effects of PCBs had not been previously known, and therefore they were not banned before 1977.[4]

An example may help you understand the differences among the three methods of valuing a life. Suppose an innocent thirty-five-year-old schoolteacher is killed by the police during a high-speed car chase. Pursuing a suspect, a police cruiser goes through a red light and crashes into the teacher's car. The city is asked to pay compensation for this loss of life. Assume that the young man was earning $35,000 a year and had purchased a life insurance policy worth $150,000. According to the face value of life insurance method, the city will be liable for $150,000. However, if we assume that the young man would have lived for another thirty years and earned his current salary, his lifetime earnings discounted at a 6 percent rate turn out to be $201,022.19 (see the discussion of present value later in this chapter). In contrast, since he was not in a hazardous job, the required compensation method would estimate the value of his life at several million dollars.

Since valuation of most of the intangibles in life is often highly subjective, the numbers can vary, climbing to absurd amounts. In 1991, two years after the Exxon tanker *Valdez* had spilled oil, causing extensive environmental damage in Alaska, Exxon agreed to settle criminal and civil complaints brought by Alaska and the federal government for $1.25 billion. Yet within a relatively short period, a study commissioned by the state and federal governments put the damage to the ecology at $15 billion.[5]

Indeed, as a society we may at times place extremely high prices on projects. If a project threatens a species with extinction or destroys a place of national interest or veneration, then we may assume that the cost of its destruction is too high for any conceivable monetary compensation. To prevent the extinction of spotted owls, the U.S. government declared a moratorium on logging in Oregon in 1991.

How Can We Measure Future Loss or Gain?

The prospect of future loss poses one of the most difficult obstacles to public projects. In popular terminology, this is the dreaded NIMBY (not in my backyard) factor, which community groups can effectively use to stop the construction of projects that have widespread indirect benefits but impose specific costs on a certain community. Thus, while the construction of a new airport may prove to be a boon to a region's economy, the question remains as to which community will have to live with the noise and increased traffic. Although small in proportion to the total gain to the region, the cost of increased noise can have disastrous effects on property values in nearby neighborhoods.

An analyst is often faced with estimating a loss of property value that has not yet occurred. This estimate can typically be carried out using a causal regression model, discussed in Appendix B. We can form a regression model in which the price of property will be a function of changes (D) in

$$\text{Price} = f\Delta \text{ (Noise, Pollution, Travel time, Other factors)} \qquad (14.1)$$

In this case, we hypothesize that the price of property will depend on the altered levels of noise (measured in decibels) and pollution (measured by various standardized emission units), which will have a negative effect on the price. A decrease in travel time (measured in terms of minutes to the airport), in contrast, is likely to increase the price. Other factors include the property's size, location, view, and so forth. For the model we can take these factors as given because the construction of the airport will not change them.

Taking a cross-section of city properties, we can estimate the relevant coefficients for noise, pollution, and travel time. The coefficients for each term measure the impact on the dependent variable of a one-unit change in the independent variable. By multiplying the estimated coefficients with the expected change in that variable as a result of airport construction, we can estimate the total loss to the property. Suppose our regression coefficient for the effect of noise on the price of property turns out to be –$5,000. This would mean that a one-unit increase in decibel level would reduce the price of a piece of property by $5,000. Suppose the environmental impact statement estimates that the new airport would add five decibels to the already existing noise level of a particular neighborhood. We can estimate the loss of property value for that neighborhood to be –$5,000 × 5 = –$25,000. Other coefficients can be used in a similar manner to measure the total impact the new airport would have on property values.

This kind of estimation poses many problems. Property owners are likely to dispute the results, because the estimates certainly will not cover all the costs associated with increased noise and other kinds of pollution (such as the effect on the physical and psychological health of the residents). It is interesting to note that frequently there exists an asymmetry in information between the gainers and losers of large public projects. In some instances a small group of potential losers tends to know and care about its losses a lot more than the larger group of potential gainers. In such cases, well-organized groups are often able to stop a project through political protests or obstructive legal actions. Conversely, in other cases, in which the potential for individual gains is strong, a handful of powerful interest groups are able to get approval for a project that may inflict costs on a wide segment of society.

It should be obvious by now that inferring the value of nonmarketable items is not an easy task and often creates controversy. Yet as an analyst you may have to estimate the value of time saved as a result of a traffic diversion or the emotional cost of destroying a community to build a freeway through it. You have to approach such matters boldly but with caution. For example, a recent report suggested that the construction of high-occupancy vehicle lanes (the highway lanes set aside for vehicles carrying more than a certain number of passengers) on the perennially clogged Atlanta freeways reduced commuting time by fifteen minutes. You may be tempted to put a value on the time saved by multiplying it by the average wages of the commuters multiplied by their number, until you realize that the time saved is not likely to increase the commuters' working hours. Instead the fifteen minutes that would have been spent sitting in a traffic jam will now be spent pursuing enjoyable activities that carry no commercial value. You may instead consider the amount of gasoline saved by having to run the car engine for fifteen minutes and then calculate the money saved by commuters. In addition, you may look for the environmental benefits of reduced auto exhaust emissions.

In the previous pages we discussed the problems of putting monetary values on nonmarketable items. If you find items that are simply not translatable in money, you may do well not to overstretch your imagination. As we have seen, unless you are careful, the valuing of nonmarketable items can quickly veer toward the ridiculous. Therefore, in such cases, an analyst should report accurately the intangible effects of the proposed project so that political decision makers can make informed decisions.

INTRODUCTION OF TIME: PRESENT VALUE ANALYSIS

In the preceding example of the convention center, we have a relatively simple choice to make on the basis of a onetime, lump-sum net benefit. However, the benefits and costs of most projects do not occur at one time. Instead, they come in over a period of time. This inclusion of time adds one more dimension to our problem.

To begin with, a dollar received a number of years down the road may not be worth as much as a dollar already in our pockets. I am always reminded of a local television commercial for an annuity program. The announcer asks viewers to join a "millionaires' club." If a young adult saves a certain amount of money per month, at the end of nearly thirty-five years, this individual will receive $1 million from the annuity. Of course, during the dreamy announcement part of this commercial, the camera lens pans over all the trappings that are commonly associated with the lives of millionaires—a fancy home, a limousine parked in the driveway, and so on. Ask yourself, though, would $1 million thirty-five years from now be worth $1 million in today's money? Obviously, the answer is that the two amounts of money are not equal. But the question of the difference between a dollar in my pocket today and one in the future can be answered only if we understand the process of discounting.

To explain the process of discounting, I must first explain the process of compounding. Suppose I have invested $100 in a certificate of deposit, maturing at the end of the year, at a 10 percent interest rate. At the end of the year, I will receive $110. Thus, $100 invested at 10 percent interest for a year will yield $100 × (1 + 0.1), or $110.

The preceding formulation is perfectly obvious. If I keep this investment one more year at the compounding interest rate of 10 percent, at the end of the second year, I will get back not another $10, but $11, because I will earn interest on the previous year's interest. Therefore, at the end of the second year, I will receive $110 × (1 + 0.1), or $121. By inserting into the preceding equation the formula by which we obtained the result of $110, we get $100 × (1 + 0.1) × (1 + 0.1), or $121, which can be rewritten as $100 × $(1 + 0.1)^2 = \$121$.

If you are observant, you will note that keeping the money for two years requires us to multiply the original amount of money invested by 1 plus the interest rate (10 percent, or 0.1 in this case), the quantity raised to the power of 2. Therefore, if I had kept the money for three years, the exponent of the term within the parentheses would have to be raised to 3. By extending this logic, we can generalize by stating that the original investment of P_0 at a rate of interest of r percent for n years will give us P_n amount of money:

$$P_n = P_0 \times (1 + r)^n \tag{14.2}$$

where P_n is the principal amount at the end of the nth period, P_0 is the original principal amount at period 0, and r is the rate of interest.

Using a calculator, we can determine that $155, invested at a 6.5 percent rate for seventeen years, would yield $155 × $(1.065)^{17}$, or $452.14. This is the formula for the computation of compound interest; it tells you how much a dollar invested today at a certain interest rate would be worth in the future.

In contrast, a dollar in the future may not be worth its full face value in today's currency; the forces of inflation, uncertainty, risk, and the plain fact that you would rather have your money now than at a later date may eat away much of its value. In other words, I may pose the question from the opposite direction: how much would a dollar be worth to you in the nth year in the future? In such a case, without compounding your initial investment, you would have to discount your future income. Let us take a specific example. Suppose I were to receive $100 a year from today. Since I will be getting the money in the future, if I use a **discount rate** (which measures the intensity with which I want my money in the present) of 10 percent, the $100 will be equal to

$$\frac{100}{1.1} = \$90.91$$

As in our previous example, if we are considering n years in the future, our future gain will have to be discounted by 1 plus the rate of discount, raised to the number of years we have to wait for the money. Thus, we can generalize the formula as

$$P_v = \frac{P_n}{(1+r)^n} \tag{14.3}$$

Going back to the example of the millionaires' club, we can see that if the discounting factor is 10 percent, then $1 million received thirty-five years from now will be equal to

$$\frac{\$1,000,000}{(1+0.1)^{35}} = \$35,584.10$$

Alas, in light of this analysis, it appears that the dream of $1 million has to be curtailed; the *present value* of $1 million received thirty-five years in the future is only about $35,000. With this amount, one certainly cannot expect all the trappings required for membership in a millionaires' club. This process is called **present value analysis**, by which we calculate the current or present value of a dollar to be gained in the future. We can use this formula to calculate the present value of a stream of benefits and costs to arrive at the net present value of a project. Notice that the larger the discount rate, the lower the present value of future dollars. If we were to discount $1 million at a 15 percent rate, we would arrive at the paltry sum of $7,508.89 for the same time period.[6] You can see that as we increase the discount rate, the future dollars look smaller and smaller. As a result, gains to be made in the future look increasingly less attractive; similarly, the prospect of losses in the distant future looks less ominous. Therefore, the discount rate captures the strength of the desire to have money now as opposed to sometime in the future. This desire is called **time preference**.

The relationship between time preference and the discounted future value of a dollar is shown in Figure 14.3. In this figure, we have plotted this year's earnings on the

FIGURE **14.3**	**Time Preference and Discount Rate**

horizontal axis and next year's earnings on the vertical axis. If we do not have a time preference, we will be indifferent between $10 today and $10 next year. The line connecting $10 on the two axes shows an **indifference map** (we are indifferent between, or prefer equally, any two points along this line) with no time preference. However, if we discount the future earnings at a 10 percent rate, then to be on the same utility plane, we must earn $11 next year. If we have an even higher time preference, equal to a 15 percent rate of discount, unless we earn $11.50 in the following year, we would prefer to have $10 today.

Let us consider a concrete example. Suppose we are evaluating two projects with the streams of benefits and costs shown in Table 14.2. From this table, it is clear that project A provides us with double the net benefit ($80) provided by project B ($40).

TABLE **14.2**	**Comparison of Costs and Benefits for Projects A and B**

	Project A		Project B	
Year	*Benefits*	*Costs*	*Benefits*	*Costs*
0	0	30	15	5
1	0	15	15	5
2	0	10	15	5
3	10	5	15	10
4	20	5	15	10
5	120	5	15	15
Total	150	70	90	50

Should we automatically choose project A over project B? If we were to jump to this conclusion, we would be remiss, since we would fail to consider that the increased net benefits of project A come at a later stage in the project's life. Our choice between the two projects will depend on the strength of our time preference—the willingness to wait for future returns. Therefore, to compare the two projects on level ground, we must translate these future streams of benefits and costs into their present values. The formula is written as

$$PV = \sum_{t=0}^{n} \frac{(B_t - C_t)}{(1+r)^t}$$

(14.4)

where PV is the present value of the project, B_t is the benefit, and C_t is the cost at time t.

We can expand this expression and write

$$PV = \frac{(B_0 - C_0)}{(1+r)^0} + \frac{(B_1 - C_1)}{(1+r)^1} + \frac{(B_2 - C_2)}{(1+r)^2} + \frac{(B_3 - C_3)}{(1+r)^3} + \cdots + \frac{(B_n - C_n)}{(1+r)^n}$$

Since any number raised to the power 0 is equal to 1, the expression can be written as

$$PV = (B_0 - C_0) + \frac{(B_1 - C_1)}{(1+r)^1} + \frac{(B_2 - C_2)}{(1+r)^2} + \frac{(B_3 - C_3)}{(1+r)^3} + \cdots + \frac{(B_n - C_n)}{(1+r)^n}$$

You may notice that the 0th year's net benefits are not discounted. This makes eminent sense, because the current year's dollar is equal to its face value and hence does not need to be discounted.

If we are willing to wait (that is, it does not matter to us whether we receive our payments today or tomorrow), our time preference is said to be nil. In such a situation, we discount the future stream of net benefits with a zero discount rate and therefore do not discount at all. Thus, if we do not have any time preference, the net benefits for projects A and B are $80 and $40. In contrast, suppose we do have a definite time preference, and we want to evaluate the future stream of net benefits for the two projects at a 10 percent discount rate. In such a case, we can write the present values of project A (PV_A) and project B (PV_B), discounted at 10 percent, as[7]

$$PV_A = (0 - 30) + \frac{0 - 15}{(1 + 0.1)} + \frac{0 - 10}{(1 + 0.1)^2} + \frac{10 - 5}{(1 + 0.1)^3} + \frac{20 - 5}{(1 + 0.1)^4} + \frac{120 - 5}{(1 + 0.1)^5}$$

$$= -30 - 13.64 - 8.26 + 3.76 + 10.25 + 71.41 = 33.52$$

and

$$PV_B = (15 - 5) + \frac{15 - 5}{(1 + 0.1)} + \frac{15 - 5}{(1 + 0.1)^2} + \frac{15 - 10}{(1 + 0.1)^3} + \frac{15 - 10}{(1 + 0.1)^4} + \frac{15 - 15}{(1 + 0.1)^5}$$

$$= 10 + 9.09 + 8.26 + 3.76 + 3.41 + 0 = 34.52$$

From the preceding calculation, we can see that discounted at a 10 percent rate, project A is less preferable than project B because it carries a lower present value.

Plot of Present Values as a Function of Discount Rates

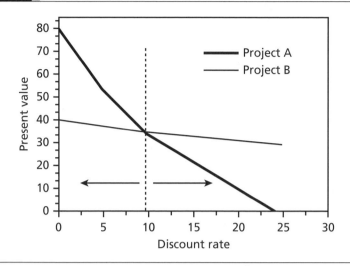

We can also see that the present values of the two projects will depend on the rate of discount, which determines their relative desirability. I have plotted the present values as functions of the rate of discount in Figure 14.4. From this figure, it can be seen that the two projects become equally desirable at a discount rate slightly less than 10 percent. For discount rates below 10 percent, project A is preferable to project B, but the relative desirability changes for discount rates of 10 percent and above. This change reflects how project A's benefits come at the end of its life. In contrast, project B yields positive net benefits from its inception. Therefore, if we can afford to wait (and have a small discount rate), we would prefer project A. However, if we are in a hurry to get back the returns on investment (and therefore have a stronger time preference), we should choose project B.

Finally, if the present value is negative (as project A is for a discount rate close to 24 percent), we should reject the project.

Choice of Time Horizon

The choice of an appropriate **time horizon** is of crucial importance for a cost-benefit analysis. The relative desirability of a project is intrinsically connected to when it ends. The length of a time period affects the desirability of long- and short-term projects. Many projects for drug interdiction are designed for short-term results. In these projects, drug use is considered primarily as a law-and-order problem, and efforts are made to lower the supply of illicit drugs by police action. In contrast, programs treating drug abuse are seen as long-term public health initiatives that require expenditures on education, rehabilitation, and employment opportunities. These demand-side efforts (trying to reduce the drug demand) offer longer term solutions. So unless they are given longer time horizons, their impacts on drug use will not be fully realized. Project desirability dependent on the choice of time horizon is shown in Figure 14.5. You can see that before

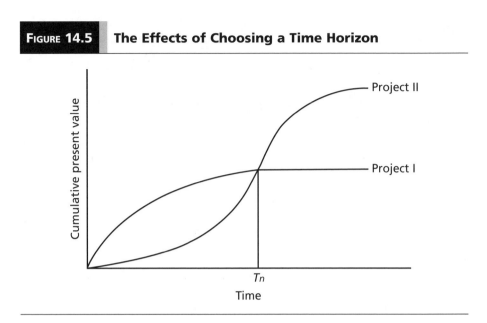

FIGURE **14.5**   **The Effects of Choosing a Time Horizon**

the critical point in time, T_n, the short-term project (Project I) yields higher net present value. However, beyond this point, the long-term project (Project II) becomes more attractive.

Choice of Discount Rate

The results shown in Figure 14.4 demonstrate how sensitive the assessment of a project's desirability can be to a change in the discount rate. Therefore, it is essential that we come up with the "correct" discount rate in evaluating a public project. In fact, the sensitivity of a public investment decision to the choice of discount rate was underscored by a proposed joint water project between Canada and the United States. Whereas the United States analysts, who used a lower discount rate, recommended the project, their Canadian counterparts, who used a higher discount rate, rejected it. There is little mention in the cost-benefit literature of how to choose the "appropriate" discount rate. A simple personal example may explain one of the reasons for this confusion. Suppose I am thinking of investing in a project that yields a certain amount of money over a period of time. In considering the desirability of this investment, I may consider alternative ways to invest the money. I find out that the best return on available investment is 8 percent. In such a case, I would discount the future net benefits of the project at an 8 percent rate. If this discounting provides me with a positive net present value, I should invest; otherwise, I should not. This process of considering alternative uses of money provides the opportunity cost, or the **shadow price**, of money. From the standpoint of a local government, the alternative use of money determines its opportunity cost. That is, if we did not invest in the convention center, we could use the money for some other projects important to the residents. Without full information on the opportunity cost of money, we may not be able to determine the appropriate discount rate.

However, the opportunity cost of money may not be the only guiding principle for investment. I may choose to discount my investment with a rate that reflects my own time preference. People may use many different rates of discount representing different time preferences. Thus, if I want my money right now (or, in other words, I have a strong time preference), I would use a very high discount rate. If, however, I have a long-term perspective, I would be willing to wait for a higher return in the future, in which case the rate of discount would be quite low. In fact, in an extreme case, my time preference could even be less than zero. Imagine that you are the dictator of a small but wealthy country. You have all the money you want for the present. However, what you do not have is security for the future—you may find yourself deposed in a coup or a revolution. In such a case, your discount rate could even be negative, and hence you would be willing to put your money in a Swiss or otherwise secret bank account, whereby the bank would charge you for the safekeeping of your (presumably ill-gotten) assets and would not pay you interest. In other words, depending on my circumstances, it may be perfectly reasonable for me to use a discount rate different from the opportunity cost, in conformity with my personal time preference.

Similarly, in the case of society, economists have argued back and forth regarding the optimum rate of discount on the basis of opportunity cost and **social time preference**. The proponents of opportunity cost for investment argue that government pays for its investments by taking money away from private citizens; thus, unless the returns of these investments are at least equal to those of the private sector, it does not make any economic sense for the government to invest. According to this point of view, when evaluating a public project, an analyst should take into account the opportunity of alternative investment opportunity in the private sector and hence discount the project by a rate equal to the private rate of return. Suppose that NASA is proposing building a new kind of space vehicle, which would be able to deploy satellites with a greater degree of efficiency than do the existing space shuttles. Money for this project must be raised from private taxpayers. If the market is yielding 10 cents on a $1 investment, unless it could be shown that the return from this project would be at least 10 percent (that is, the project carries a positive net present value when discounted at 10 percent), the project should not be undertaken.

This rule of discounting seems reasonable. However, upon further consideration, it turns out to be unsatisfactory. Problems arise because like all other markets, the capital market is characterized by various kinds of imperfections. For example, monopolies can significantly distort security prices.[8] Also, the government may face several political constraints in its investment decisions, which can make any comparison with the private sector invalid. Therefore, by looking at the vast and imperfect capital market, an analyst is likely to be confused about the "appropriate" rate of yield in the private sector.

The comparison of government rate of return with that in the private market is further complicated by the often ill-defined source of government revenue. Thus, if tax money comes out of taxpayers' savings, the consideration of opportunity cost may be valid. However, if it comes from the money that was allocated by taxpayers for consumption, the comparison would not make much sense. In addition, the sources of government revenue are diverse. The government may get its money from taxes, tariffs, licenses and fees, or selling bonds or government property. Not all of these moneys have the same opportunity cost, and it is impossible to pinpoint the exact source of the funding for a project.

Finally, the outputs of government projects may be intangibles and as such cannot be measured in monetary terms. Thus, it would be impossible to convert the benefits of subsidized school lunch programs into strict monetary units. Also, many government programs can generate long-term positive externalities, which are extremely difficult to measure. For example, the development of computer technology, to a large extent, has been a by-product of the space program. Yet at the time of the inception of the program, nobody could have predicted this fortuitous outcome.

The recent literature in economics suggests the use of a discount rate that reflects the subjective time preference of society.[9] Unfortunately, the scholars who have spent a great deal of time contemplating the appropriate discount rate are unable to tell us exactly which number to use.[10] However, the insights derived from these discussions can at least point out the folly of using grossly inappropriate rates. Given the enormous complexity of our world, we may consider that benefit to be a giant step forward. In any case, the confusion about the correct discount rate is reflected in the practices of the highest federal agencies.

At the federal level, the Office of Management and Budget (OMB), the U.S. Government Accountability Office (GAO), and the Congressional Budget Office conduct discounting on a regular basis for capital expenditure programs, lease-purchase decisions, regulatory reviews, and sales of government assets. However, they use different discount rates.[11]

For example, the OMB, which determines rates for all executive agencies, typically uses a 10 percent discount rate, corrected for the rate of inflation, for all tax-financed projects. If an agency wants to use a different rate, it must justify its choice. Since lease-purchase projects are funded by government bond financing, they are evaluated at the Treasury Department borrowing rate with a maturity date corresponding to the project's completion, plus 0.125 percent to cover the Federal Financing Bank's borrowing charge. Thus, a fifteen-year project will be discounted at the fifteen-year Treasury bond rate (say, currently at 4.75 percent) plus 0.125, or at 4.875 percent. In contrast, when a government asset is sold to nongovernmental entities, the OMB uses comparable private sector borrowing rates.

The GAO's use of a discount rate is based on the current yield of Treasury debt between one year and the life of the project. The GAO uses sensitivity analysis through different discount rates (see the discussion of sensitivity analysis later in the chapter).

The Congressional Budget Office, like the OMB, uses an inflation-adjusted Treasury borrowing rate and then looks at the sensitivity of the project by adding or subtracting 2 percent from the chosen discount rate. Also, like the OMB, it uses private sector rates to evaluate asset sales.

Because there is no unanimity at the federal agency level, state budget offices either follow the federal directives or use different rates. Local governments usually follow state guidelines.

The Internal Rate of Return

Since it is so difficult to settle on a universally acceptable discount rate for public projects, a decision maker can often be tempted to use what is known as the **internal rate of return**

FIGURE 14.6   The Internal Rate of Return

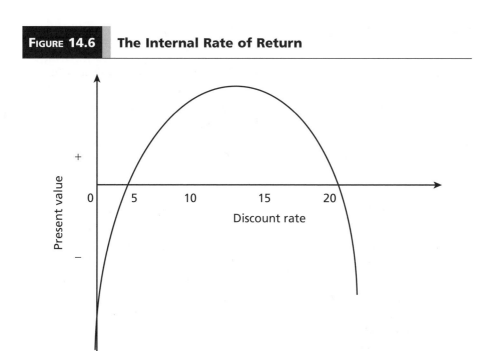

for judging the desirability of a project. The internal rate of return is defined as *the rate of discount at which the present value of a project is equal to zero*. Thus, from Figure 14.4, you can see that the present value for the hypothetical project A approaches zero at about 24 percent, which is its internal rate of return.[12]

The advantage of using an internal rate of return is that it reduces a decision maker's burden of having to make a choice on the basis of a single discount rate. Instead, a project can be accepted if the returns are larger than what can be reasonably obtained in an alternative investment. Going back to our example, if the internal rate of return for a project is 24 percent, it is so much higher than what can be reasonably expected in other possible investments that a decision maker will be hard-pressed to reject it.

However, despite this intuitive appeal, the internal rate of return suffers from some important shortcomings. First, although the internal rate of return is useful in pointing out the desirability of a single project, it is ineffective when choosing between two or more. Second, depending on the configuration of streams of net benefits, projects can often have more than one internal rate of return, as shown in Figure 14.6.

Since there are two rates (5 percent and 20 percent) at which the present value of the project becomes equal to zero, our decision maker is likely to remain confused about the desirability of the project. Edith Stokey and Richard Zeckhauser note that the internal rate of return can point to the correct public policy decisions under some rather unrealistic circumstances, such as when there are no budgetary constraints, there are no comparisons with alternative projects, and the stream of returns is first negative and then positive.[13]

CHOOSING THE BEST ALTERNATIVE
Sensitivity Analysis

After conducting an analysis, you may decide that you do not agree with your finding, or other experts in the field may disagree with you, or you may simply want to know how robust your finding is. In such cases, you may want to conduct a sensitivity analysis. This process allows analysts to change the assumptions underlying their analyses, estimate a different set of numbers, choose an alternative discount rate, and then see if there is a significant change in the outcome. Where there is a nonexistent market, you may impute monetary values on the basis of a different set of criteria. Or you may look into alternative scenarios for estimating future streams of income. For example, you may consider the most plausible case, the most optimistic case, and the most pessimistic case, with their corresponding subjective probabilities. If the probability of a disastrous case scenario poses an unacceptable amount of risk, that risk should be made clear to the decision makers. Finally, the use of different discount rates can also be of tremendous help in understanding the strength of a particular project. In our hypothetical case shown in Figure 14.4, you can demonstrate that project A is preferable up to a 10 percent discount rate, beyond which project B becomes preferable. Such a demonstration of sensitivity strengthens the robustness of your argument more than choosing a single rate and then drawing a conclusion on the basis of it.

Cost-Benefit Ratio

When choosing among alternatives, you may want to consider the ratios between benefits and costs, instead of their difference. In many cases, the use of either of these two criteria will lead to the same conclusion. However, a difference in the scale of operation may bring about a conflict. Consider the problem shown in Table 14.3.

From this table, you can see that the sheer difference in the size of the two projects means that we are really comparing apples and oranges. Therefore, using the ratio method, we are apt to choose project A, whereas using the difference method, we would have chosen project B.

The cost-benefit ratio, however, is often thought of as the efficiency measure. It may be particularly useful when you are evaluating a set of projects with a fixed amount of funds available for them. Let us consider the following hypothetical example. Suppose your city is considering spending $10 million, raised through bond financing, to expand the public library system. Eight facilities are being proposed: one large facility at the center of the city and seven smaller facilities spread through various neighborhoods. Each one has a different cost estimate. The purpose of a public library is making its facilities accessible to the residents of the city, so you have decided to use the projected circulation from each facility as the measure of each facility's benefit. Table 14.4 shows the various benefits and costs.[14]

TABLE 14.3	**Contradictory Decision Based on Net Difference and Benefit-Cost Ratio**			
	Benefit	**Cost**	**Net benefit**	**Benefit-cost ratio**
Project A	10	3	17	3.33
Project B	50	25	125	2.00

TABLE 14.4	Costs and Benefits of Library Facilities		
Location	Benefits (projected circulation per year, ×1 million)	Costs (× $1 million)	Benefit-cost ratio
City center	15.00	7.50	2.000
Neighborhood A	3.00	0.75	4.000
Neighborhood B	1.75	0.50	3.500
Neighborhood C	0.95	0.76	1.250
Neighborhood D	2.10	0.66	3.182
Neighborhood E	6.50	1.78	3.652
Neighborhood F	8.30	5.10	1.627
Neighborhood G	3.90	1.20	3.250

If you add up the costs of all eight facilities, you will quickly find that the project would cost $18.25 million, far beyond the city's allocation of funds. Therefore, you may have to choose among these eight possibilities. In this case (Table 14.5), you may rearrange Table 14.4 according to the relative rates of efficiency, the cost-benefit ratio.

In Table 14.5, the column on cumulative cost tells us how much each facility would add to the total cost. Alas, reality often does not make the life of an analyst easy. In this case, listing the sites on the basis of their efficiency shows that the top five require $4.89 million. Adding the city center facility would mean going over the $10 million budget limit by $2.39 million. Therefore, you may decide to drop this one and include the next efficient site, neighborhood F. In that case, the total expenditure comes to $9.99 million, serving 25.55 million readers.

As you can see, the cost-benefit ratio served as a guide for our choice of the most efficient allocation of public funds. However, efficiency may not be the only consideration. For instance, the mayor may want the grandiose facility at the city's center for political reasons, or a more deprived neighborhood may be more deserving even though it does not score well on the measure of relative efficiency.

TABLE 14.5	Costs and Benefits of Library Facilities, Ranked According to Benefit-Cost Ratio			
Location	Benefits (projected circulation per year, ×1 million)	Costs (×$1 million)	Benefit-cost ratio	Cumulative cost (×$1 million)
Neighborhood A	3.00	0.75	4.000	0.75
Neighborhood E	6.50	1.78	3.652	2.53
Neighborhood B	1.75	0.50	3.500	3.03
Neighborhood G	3.90	1.20	3.250	4.23
Neighborhood D	2.10	0.66	3.182	4.89
City Center	15.00	7.50	2.000	12.39
Neighborhood F	8.30	5.10	1.627	17.49
Neighborhood C	0.95	0.76	1.250	18.25

The Limits of Cost-Benefit Analysis: Redistribution of Income

The preceding discussion of cost-benefit analysis leaves out one important problem: every government project creates winners and losers. How do you balance the gains against the losses? In a zero-sum society one group of individuals almost always comes out ahead of others. It is relatively easy to show the benefits of massive highway construction in the United States. This was especially true during the 1950s, when the increased ease of transportation gave a tremendous boost to trade and commerce. Yet such construction did not come without a long list of those who were adversely affected by this development. Many small towns by the now abandoned but previously well-traversed roads were simply wiped out of existence; many communities lost their identities as the highways caused dislocation, isolation, and a general deterioration of neighborhoods. The trucking industry gained at the expense of a more energy-efficient railroad industry; suburbs gained at the expense of downtown areas.

Yet as a reflection of the state of the art in social sciences and social philosophy, cost-benefit analysis is singularly unable to solve the problem of inevitably having winners and losers. I discussed the problem in chapter 4. Social philosophers have been grappling with the problem of determining distributive justice for centuries, with surprisingly few solutions. Paraphrasing Sir Winston Churchill, rarely in the entire field of social philosophy and social science have so many spent so much effort to produce so few results. The inability to address the question of redistribution not only remains the biggest challenge for cost-benefit analysis but also truly exposes the intellectual poverty of our social philosophy.

Cost-Effectiveness Analysis

The basic principle of cost-benefit analysis is simple enough: choose the alternative that gives you the maximum net benefit. However, in many cases of public expenditure, the benefit schedule is ill defined or impossible to measure: the local fire department wants to buy fire engines that can accomplish more or less the same task as the current trucks; an organization is planning to purchase personal computers of similar capabilities to the ones now in use. In such cases, if it is reasonable to hold that all the alternatives are substitutes, then we can assume that the benefit levels for all of them are equal and, hence, can be regarded as constant. Thus, we can choose the least expensive alternative.

Suppose, however, that money has been allocated to support an outreach program to teach children of homeless families, and proposals are being evaluated for choosing the best alternative. In this case, all the alternatives will spend the full allocation, so the costs are the same. For our comparison we need concern ourselves only with maximizing the benefits. In this circumstance we can use a truncated version of cost-benefit analysis. This is called **cost-effectiveness analysis**. The two simple rules for cost-effectiveness analysis are as follows:

1. If the benefits are the same, choose the alternative with the least cost.
2. If the costs are the same, choose the alternative with the most benefits.

Returning to the fire department example, two different makes of fire engines are under consideration. Both serve the same function, so we can concentrate on various aspects of costs of purchase and operation. Having done so, we can choose the one that is less expensive. Although the process seems simple enough, all the problems of a full-fledged cost-benefit analysis remain just as relevant. For a real-world application of the concepts discussed in this chapter, see "A Case in Point."

A CASE IN POINT

Fitting Seat Belts in Texas School Buses[15]

The problem: In 1985 Texas was confounded by the problem that more adults and children were injured in school bus accidents (a total of 635 in 1985) than in any of the previous eight years. Since Texas did not require school buses to be equipped with seat belts, only a very small fraction of the injured children (1.7 percent) were wearing them.

The goal: Evaluate the potential reduction in serious injury and death to the schoolchildren resulting from the installation of safety belts.

The alternatives: Install seat belts on all the school buses, or do nothing.

Assessment of costs and benefits: The benefit was the avoidance of serious injuries to children, and the cost was the expense involved in refurbishing the existing school buses. Imputing tangible values for intangible benefits was a bit trickier because data on the effectiveness of seat belts in the prevention of serious accidents were not available for school buses. Therefore, it was assumed that seat belt effectiveness in buses was the same as in automobiles, for which data were available. These data were used to calculate the percentage of preventable injuries. The severity of injuries was calculated using the Multiple Abbreviated Injury Scale (MAIS). The results are shown in the table.

Types of Injuries and Preventable Numbers for Texas, 1983–1985

Age and injury category	Number of accidents		Preventable fraction	Number of preventable cases
	Belted	Not belted		
MAIS 0: no injury	4	354		
5–14 years	3	297	0.00	0
15–18 years	1	57	0.00	0
MAIS 1: minor injury	3	253		
5–14 years	2	212	0.00	0
15–18 years	1	41	0.00	0
MAIS 2: moderate injury	1	150		
5–14 years	1	126	0.01	1
15–18 years	0	24	0.23	6
MAIS 3: serious injury	0	91		
5–14 years	0	76	0.07	5
15–18 years	0	15	0.39	6
MAIS 4: severe injury	0	37		
5–14 years	0	31	0.20	6
15–18 years	0	6	0.64	4
MAIS 5: critical injury	0	32		
5–14 years	0	18	0.25	5
15–18 years	0	4	0.71	3
MAIS 6: fatal injury (no fatal injuries were reported)				

Discount rate: A social discount rate of 6 percent was used to calculate the present value of net benefits over time.

Recommendations: The results indicate that the economic benefits from mandatory seat belts would not be cost effective for all the existing buses. However, mandatory seat belts could be cost effective for new buses.

Conclusion: This result is surprising given the widely accepted safety benefits resulting from automobile seat belts. The authors explain this discrepancy by noting that the number of injuries per mile of school bus ride is significantly less than for automobiles. Also, the severity of injuries is much higher in autos. Second, since the injury victims are children, who do not start earning income for years (in contrast to income-earning adults), the use of their discounted earning capability reduces the size of the benefits. Third, the indirect benefit that the habit of wearing seat belts may carry over to private automobiles, as the children learn to use them, was not included in the study. Finally, the study did not consider the cost-effectiveness of requiring seat belts for only the newly acquired buses.

Other considerations: School buses still transport millions of children every year, and every year there are a few accidents that cause death and injury to some children. After each accident, renewed calls are heard for installing seatbelts. However, the National Highway Traffic Safety Administration (NHTSA) claims that current school buses are among the safest forms of transportation. After studying the results of crashes involving school buses, the NHTSA recommended against federally mandated retrofitting of the old buses or installing seat belts on new ones. Since most accidents involving school buses were either frontal or rear collisions rather than side impacts, the NHTSA concluded that because of the length of the buses, the children were amply protected by a safety feature called compartmentalization. This involves seating passengers in rows of padded seats with cushioned backs, so that in the event of a collision, passengers are either pushed back into their seats or thrown forward into the padded backs of the seats ahead.

The NHTSA also believes that belts on school buses may hamper rescue or evacuation efforts, as dazed children, unlike adults, may have difficulty unbuckling themselves. Some mischievous students may also use the heavy buckles as makeshift weapons during fights, creating even more of a safety hazard.

Finally, if seat belt use is made mandatory, there can be the additional problem of compliance. Since bus drivers already have a significant amount of responsibilities, schools might have to hire additional monitors to ride on all the buses. All of these can open up new allegations of negligence and numerous legal actions, which cash-strapped school districts are unable or unwilling to bear.

Discussion Points

1. How was cost-benefit analysis used in determining whether to fit seat belts on existing buses?
2. Do you agree with the study? If you were doing the analysis, would you have altered any of the assumptions? How do you think that might have changed the recommendation?

KEY WORDS

Consumer surplus (p. 346)
Cost-benefit analysis (p. 345)
Cost-effectiveness analysis (p. 366)
Direct costs and benefits (p. 348)
Discount rate (p. 356)
Discounted future earnings (p. 352)
Face value of life insurance (p. 352)
Indifference map (p. 357)
Indirect costs and benefits (p. 348)
Intangible costs and benefits (p. 348)
Internal rate of return (p. 362)

Negative externalities (p. 347)
Net social benefit (p. 351)
Pecuniary effect (p. 351)
Positive externalities (p. 347)
Present value analysis (p. 356)
Required compensation (p. 352)
Shadow price (p. 360)
Social time preference (p. 361)
Time horizon (p. 359)
Time preference (p. 356)

EXERCISES

1. Suppose you are considering buying a new home or renting a bigger apartment. In a report, define your goal, the feasible set of alternatives, and the set of desirable attributes. Then, given your budgetary limitations, write a report describing the process by which you arrived at the optimum choice.

2. Consider a project in your city that proposes to increase the supply of any public good. Indicate the benefits and costs, pointing out the possible area of consumer surplus, the pecuniary effect, and the loss of producer surplus. You many also think of a project that proposes some new government regulation to bring social cost in line with private cost. Point out the area of possible dead-weight loss in consumer surplus, the pecuniary effect, and the gain in producer surplus. Explain your choice of discount rate (you do not need to show any actual calculation of present value).

3. What is a social discount rate? Why is there so much confusion in defining the term *social discount rate*? Why is it important to determine this rate when calculating the relative desirability of a public project?

4. What is a cost-effectiveness study? How does it differ from a full cost-benefit analysis? Give examples of when it is more appropriate to use a cost-effectiveness analysis.

5. Calculate the net social benefit of the two projects in the table by evaluating them at 0, 5, 10, and 20 percent discount rates.

	Project A		Project B	
Year	*Benefits*	*Costs*	*Benefits*	*Costs*
0	10	10	0	55
1	15	10	5	25
2	20	10	15	25
3	30	10	50	15
4	20	10	65	15
5	10	10	95	15

6. Suppose your final answer in a popular game show was correct and you received $1 million. The show offers you two options: you can take your $1 million in a lump sum, or you can receive $145,000 per year for the next twenty-two years. Within the framework of the present value analysis, which option would you choose and why? Explain your choice of discount rate. One more small matter of information: Regardless of when you take your prize money, you are subject to a tax of 40 percent.

7. A recent study has demonstrated the link between death rates and the amount of fine particulates less than ten microns (one-thousandth of a millimeter) across.[16] These particulates come from cars, trucks, power plants, construction, and even agriculture. The study found that for each ten micrograms of particles per cubic meter of air over a twenty-four-hour period, the death rate from all causes rose more than 0.5 percent. That is, in a large city in which 100 people die each day, a rise in the particulate pollution of twenty micrograms per cubic meter can cause an additional death per day. During the study period, New York averaged 190.9 deaths per day. The corresponding figures for Los Angeles and Chicago were 148 and 113.9.

    Suppose you are an EPA analyst in charge of producing a position paper on a new pollution standard reflecting the new findings. How would you develop your study? Specifically, what kinds of information would you seek to demonstrate the desirability of your proposal through a cost-benefit analysis?

Notes

1. This line of reasoning has a long history and a voluminous literature in economics. For a seminal explanation, see Gary S. Becker, *The Economic Approach to Human Behavior* (Chicago: University of Chicago Press, 1976).

2. See Shoshana Grossbard-Shechtman, *On the Economics of Marriage: A Theory of Marriage, Labor, and Divorce* (Boulder, Colo.: Westview, 1993), esp. 5–84.

3. For an excellent discussion of the required compensation principle, see Edward M. Gramlich, *A Guide to Benefit-Cost Analysis*, 2nd ed. (Englewood Cliffs, N.J.: Prentice Hall, 1990), 67–70.

4. Kirk Johnson, "G.E. Facing Order to Remove Poisons from the Hudson," *New York Times*, December 6, 2000.

5. "Secret Studies Put Spill Damage at $15 Billion," *Los Angeles Times*, October 8, 1991.

6. You can calculate the present value by using a simple hand calculator. If you have a y^x button on your calculator, you can make the necessary calculation. To calculate the present value of $1 million thirty-five years from now at a discount rate of, say, 5 percent, punch in the numbers in the following sequence: $1,000,000/(1.05 y^x 35) =. This sequence will give you the answer: $181,290.29.

7. You can calculate the net present value using Microsoft Excel. However, if you do, you should know that Excel assumes that discounting starts at period 0. Therefore, to obtain the results in this book, you should start discounting from the second year on and then add the net present value of the initial year.

8. Recall the security exchange fraud during the late 1980s and early 1990s by the giant trading houses such as Drexel Burnham Lambert and Solomon Brothers, which had a significant impact on the market. Similar irregularities in Japan caused widespread concern over the integrity of Japanese financial institutions.

9. See David F. Bradford, "The Choice of Discount Rate for Government Investments," in *Public Expenditure and Policy Analysis*, 3rd ed., ed. Robert H. Haveman and Julius Margolis (Boston: Houghton Mifflin, 1983), 129–144.

10. Edward Gramlich suggested that the social time preference for the federal government, corrected for inflation, in 1988 was about 4 percent for projects financed by tax revenue and 6 percent for those financed by bonds. See Gramlich, *A Guide to Benefit-Cost Analysis*.

11. John L. Mikesell, *Fiscal Administration: Analysis and Applications for the Public Sector*, 5th ed. (Fort Worth, Tex.: Harcourt Brace, 1999), 253.

12. Using Microsoft Excel, you can calculate the internal rate of return. For the example of project A in Figure 14.4, the internal rate of return is about 23.7 percent.

13. Edith Stokey and Richard Zeckhauser, *A Primer for Policy Analysis* (New York: W. W. Norton, 1978), 167.

14. You may notice here that although I have defined benefits in strict monetary terms, in this case we are using a nonmonetary measure. When a monetary measure is not feasible, and everyone can agree upon a readily available indicator of benefit, there is no harm in using such a nonmonetary index.

15. Adapted from Charles E. Bagley and Andrea K. Biddle, "Cost-Benefit Analysis of Safety Belts in Texas School Buses," *Public Health Reports* 103 (September–October 1988): 479–488.

16. Jonathan N. Samet, Francesca Dominici, Frank C. Curriero, Ivan Coursac, and Scott L. Zeger, "Fine Particulate Air Pollution and Mortality in 20 U.S. Cities, 1987–1994," *New England Journal of Medicine* 343 (December 14, 2000): 1742–1749.

15 So You Want to Be an Analyst? Some Practical Suggestions

In the wide-open field of public policy analysis, the term may conjure up images of a civil servant tucked away in the corner of a sterile office writing long reports on some specific areas of government operation. In today's world, policy analysts come in many different shapes and forms. They may work for the public sector, the private sector, or for-profit or nonprofit organizations. They may work for think tanks or advocacy groups. They may work for politicians or for law firms, for newspapers or radio or television stations, as part of teams or by themselves as private contractors. They may prepare long reports, opinion pieces, position papers, or policy memos. They may contribute to blogs, appear on talk shows, or make slide presentations for their clients. They may look at health policy, foreign policy, or budgetary policy. They also get involved in every level of government: local, state, federal, and international.

In this extremely varied arena, one commonality stands, however: analyzing public policy is more of an art than a science. That is, scientific "objectivity" can get you up to a certain point, but it gives you no guarantee of results. In this book, I have discussed many different tools of scientific research, from simple to relatively sophisticated. Through them we aim to develop "rational" or "scientific" or "objective" analyses. All of these terms imply strict impartiality, adherence to stringent methods of analysis, and an absolute absence of emotion. Yet recent advances in neuropsychology are showing that contrary to the accepted belief, our rationality cannot be separated from our emotions. After all, wisdom is about achieving a proper balance between the emotional and analytical parts of your brain. Unfortunately, nobody really knows where that proper balance might be. Therefore, in a subjective, uncertain, and intensely political world, I can offer you a few guidelines.

Basically, when approaching a problem analytically, we want answers to a stream of related questions: What do we know? What

TABLE 15.1	**Steps in Conducting an Effective Analysis**

Before you start

"Know thyself" and your organization

- Define your role.
- Do you know your client?
- Do you have a basic understanding of the issue?
- Remember that in public policy analysis, "objectivity" simply applies to the process.

Be aware of biases

- Do you think you already know the answer?
- Do you see a value conflict?
- Do you have a conflict of interest?
- Is there institutional pressure?

Be aware of external constraints

- Is there enough information?
- Is there enough staff, money, and time to do the analysis?

Begin your analysis

Organize your thoughts: a quick analysis

- Think, decompose, simplify, specify, rethink.

Conducting a more elaborate analysis

- Define your goal.
- Gather information.
- Measure dependent and independent variables.
- Choose the right tool.
- Project the outcomes and make your recommendation.

Tell a good story: effective presentation

- Know your audience.
- Know what you don't know.
- Tell a compelling story.

don't we know? What do we need to know? What don't we need to know? What do we need to know to know what we do and don't need to know? However, let us go about asking these questions more systematically, in three sections: (1) before you start, (2) begin your analysis, and (3) tell a good story: effective presentation. I have placed the outline of my suggested steps in conducting an effective analysis in Table 15.1.

BEFORE YOU START
"Know Thyself" and Your Organization

To "know thyself" is the first principle of western Hindu philosophy. According to ancient wisdom, it is the most difficult quest in life. Before starting an analysis, it may be worthwhile to look into your own role as an analyst. As part of this query you must address the question, who is your client? For instance, suppose you are working as a staff analyst for one of the U.S. senators from your state, and you have been asked to prepare a position paper on welfare reform. In that case, you have to remember that you are serving a particular elected official from a specific political party. Even within a political party, members are associated with various wings, based on their ideologies. Therefore, unless it goes against your moral compass, one of the goals of your position paper may explicitly or implicitly recognize the senator's ideological orientation or one that the senator may be able to defend politically. When there is a strong moral dilemma, as we have seen in chapter 2, you may need to evaluate your position using a proper mix of exit, voice, and disloyalty within the organization. If, on the other hand, you are working for the neutral Congressional Budget Office, where presumably your client is the entire nation, and you prepare a report on the same topic, your orientation may differ.

When working on a specific issue, you should ask yourself, How much do I know about this? If you work as a staff analyst, you may need to get involved in all sorts of projects. Today, you are preparing a position paper for your senator on welfare reform; tomorrow, you may be asked to write one on a particular matter of military procurement. If you do not have much knowledge of the subject matter at hand, you must develop your own knowledge base through proper research.

In our analyses, we all seek objectivity. Yet as we have seen throughout the book—from the discussion of human nature to political orientation—we must deal with our subjective assessments every step of the way. In this confusion, we would do well to recall that "objectivity" of analysis should involve the process by which we find our solutions, not the solutions themselves.

Be Aware of Biases

Biases, as I have shown, are impossible to avoid. However, what is possible is to know the existence of your presuppositions. For instance, before you start your analysis, ask yourself if you think you already know what your conclusion will be. If you do, and if you are planning to conduct an unbiased analysis, it may be time for you to look at your own motivations. In that case, it will be important for you to get acquainted with opposing points of view. By synthesizing the various perspectives, you may arrive at an impartial assessment.

To be neutral is a worthy goal. However, sometimes it is impossible to avoid such conflicts when it comes to deeply emotional issues relating to religious faith, abortion, or gay rights. In case you do have a very strong view that you know to be immutable, and if your moral, ethical perspective stands against conducting an impartial analysis, you may try to recuse yourself from working on such a project. However, in many organizations, it is impossible to avoid such responsibilities. In such a situation, you may do well to explicitly state—either orally to your supervisor or as part of the written report—your own ideological position on the matter at hand. You should also be clear in your mind about any conflict of interest in the area you have been asked to investigate. Do you or any member of your family or circle of friends stand to gain (or lose) from the project? Sometimes these conflicts can have legal implications; at other times they may pose moral issues. In any case, it should be clear in your mind that there is no conflict of interest.

Finally, you must be aware of any organizational pressure that may be brought upon you to arrive at a certain conclusion. These pressures can be explicit or extremely subtle. Every organization, when examined closely, is built around a central belief structure. For instance, the U.S. Department of Veterans Affairs aims to help retired members of the military, the U.S. Department of Education generally attempts to aid students and schools, and U.S. Customs and Border Protection strives to keep illegal immigrants from coming into the country. Many think tanks promote certain ideologies, while advocacy groups often lean toward cherry-picking evidence to support their client groups or beliefs. In fact, in performing their duties, organizations often embrace a certain philosophical orientation. Therefore, any analysis that is contrary to its central article of faith may be considered heretical and can result in pressure being placed on the messenger. For example, supervisors may try to quash a report and stop its release, prevent a report from going up the chain of command, transfer an offending analyst to a different (often less desirable) position, or even try to fire an analyst. These are matters of explicit reprimand for the dissenting voice. Group pressure can also be subtle, from loss of friendship to being left out of happy hour. Psychologist Irving Janis popularized the concept of groupthink, whereby members of a group, often unconsciously, start thinking along a similar line.[1] Any deviation from this group orientation can result in the ostracism of the offender. Facing such group pressures, you may have to think of your options, among a combination of exit, voice, and disloyalty.

Be Aware of External Constraints

Apart from your own knowledge, experiences, and perceptions, and the organization you work for, there are certain external constraints that can affect your ability to properly analyze a problem. These constraints arise because, after all, life itself is limited. Professor Herbert Simon believed that life was about satisficing—reaching a sufficient result within a set of constraints—not about boundless optimization.

While conducting research on most topics, you may come across information limitations. I call it the tyranny of data.[2] Information is collected by people who may or may not have the same research agenda as you do. Therefore, quite often, what we can prove is dependent on what information is available. For example, if you want to show that students' scores on standardized tests are determined by the stability of their parents' marriages, you may find data on test scores and divorce rates, but the two variables may not correspond. Therefore, unless you want to develop a full-scale survey and collect your own primary data, there is no way for you to test your hypothesis. The problem, however, is that if you want to conduct a survey, it requires money, time, and specific expertise.

This brings us to the next constraints: money and time. The poet Homer famously wrote, "The gods are jealous of men because they die." Analysts, on the other hand, may be jealous of gods because they don't, and have unlimited time. Therefore, in designing your analysis, you must be realistic. You must learn how to cut your proverbial coat according to your cloth. This may seriously affect what you might consider the proper analysis. However, given the realities, you must learn to draw the line somewhere. Furthermore, not every problem merits elaborate analysis. Many are matters of mundane concern. Many require quick decisions. In such cases, you must learn to do a "back of the envelope" analysis on the basis of some accepted "rules of thumb," rather than gathering primary data and using sophisticated statistical analyses. I argue, however, that whether you do a quick "back of the envelope" analysis or design a full-scale research project, the basic steps remain the same. The only difference is in the amounts of time and money that you and your organization commit.

On this point, I will add one more piece of guidance: policy analysts are trained at institutions of higher learning, but the expectations surrounding a policy paper may differ significantly from that of the academic environment where the analysts were educated. Since academics are often not as constrained by time and face a different set of expectations when they publish in scholarly journals, their analyses are often much more extensive. In comparison, a policy analyst's report may appear shallow and superficial. However, we must remember that the two are writing for completely different clients; as a result, an analyst's report rarely would be accepted in an academic journal, and an academic study may be quite inappropriate as a policy report.

BEGIN YOUR ANALYSIS
Organize Your Thoughts: A Quick Analysis

You have just been given the task of analyzing a particular policy issue. Where would you start? Behn and Vaupel have given us some excellent ideas.[3] They propose the following five steps:

1. Think
2. Decompose
3. Simplify
4. Specify
5. Rethink

Think. The process of decision making starts with thinking. The thinking part essentially involves framing the problem. Because no problem in life is one-dimensional, you must look squarely at the heart of a complex, multidimensional problem. This reduction of a large problem into a manageable, bite-sized form often requires the use of simple numbers—numbers that can convey the essence of a problem. The percentage of people living in poverty and the comparative scores of graduating seniors on standardized tests from comparable countries are examples of such core numbers that clearly define a problem.

Decompose. Behn and Vaupel point out that the essence of analysis is decomposition: the ability to see a problem as an amalgam of various elements. Our brains offer us only limited space for processing complex information. Therefore, if we can see a problem in its various parts—some complementary and some contradictory—we have made significant progress in the right direction. Suppose you are writing a term paper on poverty in America. If you are fixated on the entire issue and go to the library and, finding hundreds of books and articles on the topic, get even more frustrated, you will not know how or where to begin. On the other hand, if you quickly choose a working title for your paper, which you can change as you go along, it will help you focus on a specific aspect of a very large problem. The second step for writing a term paper is to develop a table of contents. This is the core of decomposition. Now you are looking at the problem in an organized fashion. Once you have decided on a title and developed a table of contents, you are on your way toward writing a focused paper.

Simplify. If we had unlimited time and money, we could do an exhaustive analysis. However, all of us must work within our means. Therefore, when time is of the essence, we do not have the opportunity to go through all the possible alternatives and outcomes to achieve the best solution. In such cases, we need to simplify the process by drastically eliminating all but the most essential components of the problem. The process of structured simplification is so effective in problem-solving situations because (1) without simplification, a problem can push us beyond our cognitive capabilities; (2) a simplified problem propels it from the realm of intuition or gut reaction to informed judgment; and (3) once a problem has been simplified and broken into essential components, decision makers' intuitions can be used to their fullest advantage. Finally, along this line, I should mention that in life there are people who are obsessed with perfection. There is of course nothing wrong with being a perfectionist, unless it prevents you from making a decision when you absolutely must. The simplification of a complex problem allows you to manage your time effectively. The value of the ability to deliver on time simply cannot be overstated within an organization.

Specify. When faced with a complex problem, after you have decomposed and simplified, try to draw a diagram (such as a decision tree, discussed in chapter 13) that specifies its interrelated components. Make a quick drawing of all the possible alternatives and options, including the option of doing nothing. Doing so will force you to specify the amount of risk and the amount of reward. You may put down your subjective assessment of risk with either probability figures or classifications, such as "highly probable," "probable," or "nearly impossible." Your pictorial rendition of the problem will give you deep insight into its true nature.

Rethink. On the basis of the quick decision rules, you have now arrived at a solution. Should you stick to it? Perhaps not. If there is time, rethink! Since all analysis is ultimately incomplete and is based on aspects of subjective judgment, you should not waste the opportunity to rethink. If there is enough time and you are still uncertain about your decision, start from the beginning once again, and make a second cut. Go on rethinking until you have come to the conclusion that given the constraint of time, you have done your best.

Conducting a More Elaborate Analysis

Define the Problem. Every analysis begins with a problem that needs a solution. It is important to recognize that your client must share the perception of this problem. Sometimes, in our activism, we may lose sight of the fact that our client may not perceive this to be a problem or believe that the solution is politically feasible. If there is a gap in perception, you must begin with identifying reasons it is in the interest of the decision makers to address this particular problem and end with an analysis of the political, economic, and organizational feasibility of the solutions you are proposing. How you define a problem may ultimately determine its fate. This will require many skills far beyond what is needed to conduct a technical analysis. In particular, your definition of the problem must resonate with the organizational needs of your client. For instance, all elected officials see their constituents as their ultimate clients. Therefore, in proposing a project, you may appeal to their ideology or show that it would bring the greatest good to their home districts. Bardach calls this the "issue rhetoric."[4] The art of finding the right rhetoric is something that comes with a deep understanding of your client and the organization for which you are working.

Gather Information. Evidence is key to scientific inquiry. In today's world, the ability to verify hypotheses with facts is as central as breathing oxygen. After you have defined the problem, you must actively engage in gathering facts. In the era of the Internet, a few chosen keywords can bring you a mother lode of information. Unfortunately, it is nearly impossible to have a drink at the mouth of a gusher. With so much information around, you must develop a strategy to gather information before you take a plunge.

Your strategy for gathering information must begin with knowing what you are looking for and what you are not. Your judgment about this must be backed by reason. For instance, suppose you are conducting research on poverty in America. Should you look into cases of comparable countries? At first glance, it may indeed sound like a good idea. However, your decision must be guided by all the external and internal constraints I mentioned above. How much time, money, staff, and expertise you have at your disposal should determine how widely you cast your net.

However, regardless of where you start and how far you want to take your analysis, you must do a quick review of existing books, articles, and reports relating to the problems at hand. In chapter 8, I detailed several sources of secondary information. Many sources and studies will not only provide you with invaluable insight into the causal linkage between your dependent and independent variables but may also offer examples of what happens when a particular policy is implemented. Their experience can allow you to prepare a "best practices" report.

As you look at the prior research and findings, you must be aware of the ideological underpinning of the studies. It will be up to you to determine if these studies' orientations match with that of your own organization. As you go along, you must also consider the veracity of the sources of the information used in the studies.

Finally, in a rapidly changing world, where new technologies are creating brand new issues every single day, you may be hard-pressed to find a comparable case. When that happens, you may look into analogous examples. For instance, there are persistent allegations that photo-enforced intersections have turned into cash machines for local governments and the companies that install these devices. For instance, in 2008, Los Angeles earned more than $3 million from these red-light cameras. As other cities scramble to install the devices, many are questioning the true motives of city officials. For instance in 2009, Kansas City not only began installing red-light cameras but also increased the fine for running a red light to $100, while in other cities, fines are as high $400 per infraction.[5] The introduction of this new technology, much touted for its ability to reduce accidents, has created controversy, as some have suspected that the companies that install the cameras have reduced the time that yellow lights stay lit. While a shorter yellow light catches more offenders, studies of a number of cities (such as Mesa, Arizona, and Fort Collins, Colorado) show that a longer yellow light actually reduces the number of accidents, as drivers don't speed up at the last moment to beat the camera.

A study by the Tennessee Center for Policy Research reports that an increase of 1 second reduced accidents by 73 percent, while a boost to 1.5 seconds reduced the frequency by 94 percent. Yet at the same time, the increase in the time the yellow light remained lit drastically reduced the revenue of the cities and the camera vendors. If you begin to write a report on red-light cameras for your own town, you may not find anything comparable in your area, but you may find plenty of analogous examples from other cities. However, in providing analogies, you must be careful to make sure they actually fit. That is, if you are basing your arguments for New York City on what happened in Mesa or Fort Collins, you must make sure that there are no intervening variables that would make your case null and void.

Measure Dependent and Independent Variables. Once you have reviewed the relevant literature, it is time to set your hypotheses. Calling a statement a "hypothesis" does not necessarily imply a prelude to statistical testing; rather, it simply means that you are making a conjecture that the variable you are targeting to change (the dependent variable) will be affected by altering a set of policy variables (the independent variables). Once you have identified the variables, you can proceed to test their relationships by using statistical tools or simply citing other examples. In the yellow-light example, you can either collect your own data by sending observers or using meters, or you can use the results obtained by other research institutions, academics, or government agencies.

We are inveterate producers of numbers. As I showed in chapter 6, we tend to express in numbers many things we see and even feel. Numbers have a magical quality of appearing precise and objective. However, as we have seen, like all things in life, social data are "contaminated" by subjective judgment. Therefore, once again, I should remind you that before you use any numbers for your dependent and independent variables, you must make sure you are measuring the right thing. For instance, when using data for accidents, you may assume that all data define an "accident" in the same way, but conclusions can be radically different when you look closer into the data and divide them into fender benders, accidents involving injuries, and those that cause fatalities. In each case, the paths of causal links with the independent variables can be significantly different. For example, you may find out that increasing the time of the yellow light reduces fender benders but actually increases the frequency of fatal collisions.

Identify Alternatives. After you have established a causal connection or gained an understanding of what is causing the problem at hand, you can focus your attention on how to achieve your goals of solving, mitigating, or managing it. These are the various policy options the government can use. In the course of conducting an analysis, this is the step that requires the greatest imagination and creativity. There may be many ways to skin a cat, but only a few are acceptable or feasible. While you may cast your net widely and think of many different alternatives, soon you will begin the process of pruning these options, as they are deemed too expensive, too time-consuming, too intrusive, too cumbersome, or politically infeasible. In other words, you will consider only a feasible set of options, given your constraints of time, money, public acceptance, and political feasibility.

However, you must recognize that all of these factors can change. What is considered to be too expensive today may bring money flowing to it under different circumstances.

For instance, after the 9/11 attacks, some raised the specter of terrorists' coming across the border from Mexico. Suddenly, a number of politicians began pushing for an impenetrable wall that would stretch from the Gulf of Mexico to the Pacific Ocean across the entire U.S.-Mexican border. As frenzied speeches raised the temperature and the nation reoriented its priorities, an enormous amount of money was allocated for the border fence. Similarly, as banking regulations weakened with the repeal of the Glass-Steagall Act of 1933 and the Securities and Exchange Commission became less aggressive in developing and enforcing regulations, the nation faced an economic crisis of a magnitude not seen since the Great Depression. The 2008 economic crisis suddenly altered the political climate, allowing both the Bush and Obama administrations to pass sweeping changes as the federal government took over some of the largest financial institutions. Suddenly, these intrusive government actions, which would have been considered infeasible months before the downturn, were accepted. Hence, while judging the feasibility of policy options, we must keep in mind that it is a relative concept that can change dramatically in response to large shifts in economic and political reality.

Identify Criteria. The most commonly used criterion for choosing the best course of action is efficiency, which is defined simply as the "most bang for your buck." However, as I discussed in chapter 1, in reality, monetary efficiency is not the sole criterion for choosing a public project. The drive toward economic efficiency must be weighed against concerns of equity, liberty, and security. Since these concepts are vague, most often the adoption of a criterion depends on how the political elites choose to frame an issue. The idea of global warming, which at one time was considered to be the quaint obsession of a handful of scientists and environmental extremists, has become mainstream over time. As a result, when we evaluate a public project, we not only use the criterion of dollars and cents; along with this, we often look at a project's "greenness." For instance, local government projects, apart from the mandatory completion of environmental impact statements, often tout their beneficial impact on the environment.

Choose the Right Tools. You have learned a good number of quantitative techniques, and you are ready to test your hypotheses or to project the outcomes of a proposed plan of action. Which model should you use? This is a very important question, which I have not addressed in these pages. Sometimes the problem at hand will dictate the type of tool you use. For instance, if there is no past information, you cannot use data-driven techniques such as regression analysis. However, you must keep in mind that every technique has its own limitations. There is nothing you can do about this except be fully aware of these limitations. If you are asked to defend your choice of tool, you should be prepared to do so.

Finally, I should mention that when choosing your tool of analysis, you must not be too enamored of the complexity of the tool itself. Many statistical analyses are extremely complex and fall beyond the scope of this book. Sometimes a researcher may be attracted by the apparent "sophistication" of a technique. You must remember that complexity, by itself, is no virtue. If there is something special in a technique that makes it particularly useful for the problem at hand, you should use it. Otherwise, given a choice, you should always choose the approach that is simpler to understand and to explain.

Project the Outcomes and Make Your Recommendation. Looking into the future is, at best, an inexact science. In this book I have discussed many different methods of prediction, each of which has its own strengths and weaknesses. Although public policy analyses require forecasting, for some outfits, forecasting is their entire business. For instance, the government forecasts future economic growth and inflation, hurricanes and other natural disasters, and the path of the latest epidemic. Therefore, before we get into a discussion of prediction, allow me to remind you of two rules that are worth remembering: (1) it is extremely difficult to forecast, especially the future, and (2) if forecast you must, forecast and forecast often. Although they are said in jest, let me explain why they give us valuable insights.

In forecasting the future, physicist Werner Heisenberg learned that it is of course impossible to fully penetrate the shroud of uncertainty (chapter 8). Therefore, in an open society, public policy forecasts cannot peer into the future without a good deal of uncertainty. Any claim of a guaranteed outcome is bound to be false.

Furthermore, forecasting in the real world must not be confused with oracular pronouncements, made only once and then expected to come true. Rather, similar to weather forecasting, we must continue to update our predictions as the objective conditions change. If we recall these two rules, we may learn to have realistic expectations regarding foretelling what is to come.

Despite these shortcomings, any policy discussion must contain an effort at forecasting. When there are no past data, we must rely on various subjective assessments, from forecasting by analogies to the use of more structured forms, such as the Delphi method. If we have time-series data, we can certainly look for a trend. However, no analysis of trend can predict a turning point. That is, if the economy is on the rise, we can predict where it will be at some point in the future, but if it is currently declining, regression models for projecting the trend may be inadequate to determine where the bottom might be. For those cases, we may use a multiple regression model, looking into the causes of a phenomenon (see Appendix B). Once again, given the fact that these models predict on the basis of an average, our forecasted values may not have a great deal of policy significance, although a causal model may provide us with the knowledge of what is caused by what.

When all manner of "scientific" forecasting fails us, we turn to another method: intuition, or simply a "hunch." Of late, a number of economists have been looking into intuition. Their research has revealed that when an expert is asked to forecast simply on the basis of intuition, the expert often performs better than even the most sophisticated models.[6] After all, the complexity of the human brain is no match for even the most mathematically complicated data-driven statistical analyses. Therefore, while we develop our policies on the basis of forecasting future outcomes, we must learn to live with life's uncertainties. The only danger we need to be concerned about is the presence of systematic biases and wishful thinking (see chapter 10).

TELL A GOOD STORY: EFFECTIVE PRESENTATION

You have done an excellent analysis. Now comes the final hurdle: it is your turn to present it. You can present your findings along with your recommendation in the form of a written report or in front of a group of those whose job it is to make the actual decision.

They can be the president, members of the Congress, other elected officials, or, in the case of private corporations, the directors or your superiors. If you think your findings are the best analysis of the problem, your job now is to convince them of the efficacy of your work. You should know that doing the analysis and making an effective presentation require two different sets of skills. You may do an excellent study but may fail to persuade the decision makers. Therein lies the art of persuasion. Let us discuss some of its essential elements.

Know Your Audience

You must understand your audience. What may be effective in one setting can completely fall flat in front of another group. The groups may differ in their knowledge of the subject matter, their levels of sophistication, and their interest. For instance, in the days after the catastrophic 9/11 attacks, many military planners as well as political leaders in the United States lacked detailed knowledge of the Islamic world; in analyzing the links between various groups, many were unaware of the deep religious divisions that exists between Shi'a and Sunni Muslims. The 9/11 Commission hearings, conducted years later, revealed its members' ignorance of some of the most basic ground realities of the Islamic world. Therefore, if I had given a presentation to these leaders in the aftermath of 9/11 and incorrectly assumed that they understood the links among various militant Islamist groups, I would have completely missed the boat. Similarly, when faced with the exceedingly complicated causes of banking failure, if I write a report and assume that my audience is fully cognizant of the issues, I may fail in my presentation.

On the other hand, I may have an audience that is quite knowledgeable but not technically savvy; they do not have deep knowledge of statistical tools. Suppose that when I present them with my findings I emphasize the mathematics of my analysis; I will quickly lose my audience. Indeed, there is a difference when an expert presents to a conference of other experts as opposed to a congressional panel.

Finally, as I have stressed throughout the book, you must understand the political feasibility of your proposals. In 2009, *New York Times* columnist Thomas Friedman argued that while the Obama administration had been forthright in forcing the failing U.S. automobile giants to produce more gas-efficient vehicles, it had been absolutely "gutless" in giving American consumers incentive to buy these cars. He suggested that there should be a $2 gasoline tax, which he called the "carbon" tax, so that the higher gas prices would induce consumers to go for the pricier fuel-efficient models. Even though Friedman's proposal is backed by impeccable logic, could it ever make much of an impression on lawmakers? No elected official, Republican or Democrat, can be expected to vote for such a measure, because raising taxes on necessity items is deeply unpopular under any circumstances. While the country was in a deep recession, what elected official would even think of proposing a doubling of the tax rate? If you, as an analyst, propose something that will go squarely against the interest of the decision makers, regardless of the cogency of your argument, you will fail to sell the results of your analysis to them.

Know What You Don't Know

The philosopher Socrates said the wise man knows what he does not know. There is nothing that can trip up an effective presentation more profoundly than the revelation of the presenter's ignorance of any key issue. For instance, facing a rapidly escalating banking crisis in 2008, the George W. Bush administration pushed through a $700 billion rescue plan for the failing institutions. As Treasury secretary Henry Paulson appeared before Congress to testify about the Troubled Asset Relief Program, he was asked to show where the vast amount of public money was being spent. Unfortunately, Paulson had to admit that he did not know exactly where the $700 billion went among the banks. This gave the nation the impression that the Treasury was writing blank checks to faltering financial institutions without any accountability. On *The Daily Show*, comedian Jon Stewart mockingly asked if the folks at the Treasury knew how to use Microsoft Excel. Regardless of the cogency of Paulson's banking bailout plan, he had lost his case to the American people.

Say It with Numbers

If you want to persuade an audience with analytical knowledge, a presentation with numbers is often far more effective than one without. Numbers seem to have a magical quality about them for some people; once uttered, they take on an aura of rock-solid objectivity. During a cocktail party discussion of gay rights, someone solemnly declared that 10 percent of American men are homosexual. Immediately the discussion was altered as participants assumed the veracity of this claim. It is interesting to note that this figure came from Alfred Kinsey's pathbreaking study in 1948, when the methodologies of gathering sampling data were less scientific than they are today.[7] Therefore, there could actually be more or fewer homosexual men in the United States, especially because changing social mores have allowed many to come out of the closet and admit their sexual orientations. Yet both sides of the debate tend to cling to the figure as irrefutable truth for political reasons. Numbers have the appearance of being precise, objective, and irrefutable. Therefore, it is no surprise that *Star Trek*'s Mr. Spock, the embodiment of (at least half) human rationality, spouts the odds of survival in a seemingly impossible situation to five-digit precision. Even in our most earthly conversations, if we can phrase our arguments in terms of numbers, our chances of winning increase significantly. A most fascinating demonstration of the power of numbers at the highest level of public policy discussion can be found in the autobiography of George Ball, the undersecretary of state in the Kennedy and Johnson administrations. He writes about his experience in White House cabinet meetings as follows:

> In any group where Robert McNamara (then Secretary of Defense) was present, he soon emerged as a dominant voice. I was impressed by his extraordinary self-confidence—based not on bluster but on detailed knowledge of objective facts. He gave the impression of knowing every detail of the Defense Department's vast operations and had concise and impressive views on any subject that arose, reinforcing his opinion with huge verbal footnotes of statistics. Since I am quite incapable of thinking in quantitative terms, I found McNamara's performance formidable and scintillating. He quoted precise figures, not mere orders of magnitudes. During the Vietnam War, if asked to appraise the chances of success for different optional projects, he would answer with apparent precision: one operation would have a 65 percent chance, another a 30 percent chance. Once I tried to tease him, suggesting that perhaps the chances were 64 percent and 29 percent, but the joke was not well taken.[8]

However impressed he was by the precision of McNamara's numbers, Ball laconically adds,

> [McNamara's] mastery of that capricious behemoth, the defense establishment, was not achieved merely by a virtuosity with statistics: it required force of character. McNamara, moreover is a man of humanity and imagination, capable of strong commitment to cause.[9]

In other words, McNamara was simply "assessing" the probability figures in a most important policymaking body, which were taken as truth because of their seeming numerical precision and the authority and self-confidence with which they were spoken. Despite his apparent confidence, McNamara all but admitted later in his own writings that he had grave doubts about the possibility of winning the war in Vietnam.[10] Therefore, it is important for us to understand the uses and misuses of numbers in policy debates. In chapter 9, I demonstrated how numbers can be manipulated to emphasize a point far beyond what is warranted by reality. Therefore, as policy analysts, we must be fully cognizant of the awful power and responsibility we share in shaping the welfare of a much larger community.

Tell a Compelling Story

The purpose of the last part of your effort is to convince decision makers of the value of your findings and to adopt policies accordingly. As an analyst, there is nothing more satisfying than knowing that your recommendations have formed the basis of an adopted policy. Therefore, your job may not be over until you have had a chance to present your case to your superiors. As you can tell, communication, oral or written, is an art form. However, I can give you some suggestions. In Appendix A of this book, I have presented an actual policy paper from the U.S. Government Accountability Office. You will do well to read my list of suggestions in the light of this excellent report by professional policy analysts.

The information age literally bombards us with innumerable pieces of information every day of our lives. As we see, listen to, and/or read them, very few get through to the realm of our conscious understanding. You may, for example, see a billboard while driving or listen to a lecture, yet a minute later you may recall absolutely nothing about the specific message that was directed at you. On the other hand, you may recall something you heard, saw, or read many years ago. The question is, what causes some messages to stick? Heath and Heath's research in mass communication has shown that a memorable message must be simple, concrete, and credible; have contents that are unexpected; appeal to our emotions; and contain a compelling storyline.[11] Since I am addressing a wide range of professionals who can be called "policy analysts," not all of these factors might be applicable to every situation. You must pick and choose the ones that apply to your own case.

A sticky message depends on simplicity of thought; you will remember a simple message but will soon forget a complex one. Therefore, you must make every effort at reporting your findings in the simplest of terms. In so doing, you must avoid writing in the passive voice. Although it once was fashionable for academics to write in the passive voice, because it allowed them to avoid making categorical statements, many now see the active voice as the core of effective writing. It is also important to maintain simplicity by avoiding archaic words that your audience may not readily understand. Since your job is to make yourself as clear as possible, you should choose simple, everyday words, unless the content dictates that you choose more difficult ones.

Your message must not only be simple, it must be concrete in its conclusion. If you present your report as a list of findings, however strong, it will make little impression on your audience if not backed by a logically derived, well-considered policy recommendation. If you read the opinion pieces in the top newspapers, you will see that the authors not only present their cases effectively but most often propose some concrete steps to achieve what they are advocating.

A message is accepted not only for its contents but also for the credibility of the messenger. Sometimes such credibility comes from your authority or by virtue of the position you have within your organization. For instance, Theodore Roosevelt used to call the presidency the "bully pulpit"; because the president holds the highest office in the country, the country takes notice whenever the president speaks out. However, a president's credibility can be undermined by missteps and poor choices. For instance, in the aftermath of the devastation wrought by Hurricane Katrina, President George W. Bush praised Federal Emergency Management Agency (FEMA) director Michael Brown in front of television cameras, saying, "Brownie, you're doing a heck of a job." As the full extent of the tragedy unfolded and FEMA's ineptitude was revealed, the president lost a good bit of his credibility, and scorn was heaped on the FEMA director when he came before Congress.

The "unexpected" part of a memorable message comes when the analyst "connects the dots" for the listeners and clearly explains the confusing world in which they live. In the context of reporting your findings, empirical evidence showing a strong correspondence between the dependent and independent variables will certainly make a compelling case for you.

As human beings we remember messages that evoke emotions, particularly those that paint the portrait of an impending threat. As I discussed in chapter 1, fear is most often the primary motivator for collective action. Therefore, policy papers that reveal vulnerabilities gather far more attention and receive more urgent action than those that do not. In 1983, at the height of the Cold War, when the United States was particularly concerned about a surprise nuclear missile attack by the Soviet Union, President Ronald Reagan was approached by well-known physicist Edward Teller, who had a plan to build a ground-based laser system that would be able to shoot down incoming missiles.[12] With animation providing vivid conceptual pictures of laser beams zapping enemy ballistic missiles in flight, many were excited about the scheme, which its detractors quickly dubbed the Star Wars program. Despite the infeasibility of building such a system with the existing technology, the fear of missile warfare gripped the nation, and billions of dollars were spent on the powerful laser, which never became a reality.

Finally, memorable messages come with stories. Experimental studies show that when two similar messages are presented to an audience, one supported by statistics and the other by a suitable story, the latter inevitably sticks more than the former. Any good public speaker knows the power of a storyline. Presentations also become effective when they are accompanied by graphs, charts, pictorial renditions, and even pertinent video clips. Recent advances in technology have given us wonderful tools to create these aids.

WHOSE BALL IS IT ANYWAY? ZEN AND THE ART OF PUBLIC POLICY ANALYSIS

My analyst friend looked dejected. Shaking her head, she told me that she had spent a great deal of time preparing an analysis on a particular issue. Her results, based on a sophisticated mathematical model, clearly showed the "correct" course of action. Yet the politicians had rejected her recommendations and made an "obviously wrong decision." As I sympathized with my friend, I wondered if she should feel so dejected. Indeed, if you have spent a large amount of time on a project, it often is impossible to separate your emotions from the project itself. Her problem raises the question of the analyst's role in a public organization.[13]

At the beginning of this book, I invoked the image of the fictional fiddler on the roof, who plays his music on the slippery rooftop, performing an amazing balancing act. As policy analysts, we have more in common with him than with the white-coated scientists sequestered in sterile laboratories conducting dispassionate research. At the end of the day, our job is simply to identify the recommended path to policymakers. As analysts we would do well to remember that although the pundits play the game, within our democratic processes, it is the elected princes who really own the ball.

EXERCISES

1. Take a significant problem facing the world today. Suppose you have been asked to design a policy to deal with it. By making assumptions about your client and your resources (such as time and money), design the steps you will take to complete the task.

2. Examine the question of poverty in America. Write a brief policy paper with recommendations for a national antipoverty initiative.

Notes

1. Irving L. Janis, *Victims of Groupthink: A Psychological Study of Foreign-Policy Decisions and Fiascoes* (Boston: Houghton Mifflin, 1972).

2. Dipak K. Gupta, "Tyranny of Data: Going beyond Theories," in *Tangled Roots: Social and Psychological Factors in the Genesis of Terrorism*, ed. Jeff Victoroff (Amsterdam, the Netherlands: IOS Press, 2006), 37–51.

3. Robert D. Behn and James W. Vaupel, *Quick Analysis for Busy Decision Makers* (New York: Basic Books, 1982).

4. Eugene Bardach, *A Practical Guide for Policy Analysis: The Eightfold Path to More Effective Problem Solving*, 2nd ed. (Washington, D.C.: CQ Press, 2005).

5. E. Thomas McClanahan, "Revenue Quest, Not Safety, Behind Red Light Cameras," *Kansas City Star*, January 3, 2009.

6. See Harinder Singh, "Relative Evaluation of Subjective and Objective Measures of Expectation Formation," *Quarterly Review of Economics and Business* 30 (1990): 64–74; and Roger Frantz, *Two Minds: Intuition and Analysis in the History of Economic Thought* (New York: Springer, 2005).

7. Alfred Kinsey, Wardell B. Pomeroy, and Clyde E. Martin, *Sexual Behavior in the Human Male* (Philadelphia: W. B. Saunders, 1948).

8. George W. Ball, *The Past Has Another Pattern: Memoirs* (New York: W.W. Norton, 1982), 173–174.

9. Ibid, 174.

10. Robert S. McNamara, James Blight, Robert Brigham, Thomas Biersteker, and Herbert Schandler, *Argument without End: In Search of Answers to the Vietnam Tragedy* (New York: Public Affairs, 1999).

11. Chip Heath and Dan Heath, *Made to Stick: Why Some Ideas Survive and Others Die* (New York: Random House, 2007).

12. William J. Broad, *Teller's War: The Top-Secret Story behind the Star Wars Deception* (New York: Simon & Schuster, 1992).

13. For a more detailed discussion of the role of an analyst within an organization, see Martha S. Feldman, *Order without Design: Information Production and Policy Making* (Stanford, Calif.: Stanford University Press, 1989).

Appendix A
Example of a Policy Analysis Report

United States Government Accountability Office

GAO

Report to Congressional Requesters

January 2007

POVERTY IN AMERICA

Economic Research Shows Adverse Impacts on Health Status and Other Social Conditions as well as the Economic Growth Rate

G A O
Accountability * Integrity * Reliability

GAO-07-344

United States Government Accountability Office
Washington, DC 20548

January 24, 2007

The Honorable Charles B. Rangel
Chairman
Committee on Ways and Means
House of Representatives

Dear Mr. Chairman:

According to the Census Bureau, approximately 37 million people in the United States—nearly 13 percent of the total population—lived below the poverty line in 2005.[1] This percentage was significantly larger for particular population groups, specifically children, minorities, and those living in certain geographic areas such as inner cities. The federal government spends billions of dollars on programs to assist low-income individuals and families.[2] These programs included Medicaid, food stamps, Temporary Assistance for Needy Families (TANF), and the Earned Income Tax Credit (EITC), to name some of the largest. While some have taken issue with Census' official poverty measure and proposed alternative measures, it is generally recognized that poverty imposes costs on the nation as a whole, not merely in terms of programmatic outlays but also through lost productivity that can affect the overall economy.

A substantial body of economic research has looked at the effects of poverty and you asked us to discuss (1) what the economic research tells us about the relationship between poverty and adverse social conditions, such as poor health outcomes, crime, and labor force attachment; and (2) what links economic research has found between poverty and economic growth.

To answer these questions, we reviewed the economic literature by academic experts, think tanks, and government agencies, which we collected from searches of various databases, peer-reviewed economic journals, specialty journals, and books. We also provided our draft report

---

[1] In 2005 the poverty threshold for a family of four was $19,971.

[2] Congressional Research Service, *Cash and Noncash Benefits for Persons with Limited Income: Eligibility Rules, Recipient and Expenditure Data, FY2002-FY2004* (Washington, D.C.: Mar. 27, 2006).

to four external reviewers. They are recognized experts who have conducted research and published on the topic of poverty and economic growth and whose work has recommended a variety of approaches and strategies to policymakers. We limited the scope of our work by looking at recent studies published since 1996, excluding anything older, with exceptions made for work that was considered seminal. Thus, our results are not an exhaustive or historical treatment of the topic. Our review was primarily driven by the economic literature focused on the United States either exclusively or including other developed nations; studies from other disciplines were excluded unless they were captured in either the economic study under review or its bibliography. When we refer to poverty in the report, we are using an absolute measure, not a relative one. This means that, for the most part, the studies we reviewed typically used the official poverty line published by the Census Bureau as its benchmark. A few of the studies we reviewed used relative measures such as the poorest 10 percent of the population.

Our work was conducted between October 2006 and January 2007 according to generally accepted government auditing standards. Because we did not evaluate the policies, operations, or programs of any federal agency to develop the information presented in this report, and because we are not making any recommendations, we did not seek agency comments. However, we met with agency officials from the Departments of Commerce, Health and Human Services, Justice, and Labor to obtain information on research they or others had conducted related to our work objectives.

Results in Brief

Economic research suggests that individuals living in poverty face an increased risk of adverse outcomes, such as poor health and criminal activity, both of which may lead to reduced participation in the labor market. While the mechanisms by which poverty affects health are complex, some research suggests that adverse health outcomes are due, in part, to limited access to health care as well as exposure to environmental hazards and engaging in risky behaviors. For example, some research has shown that increased availability of health insurance such as Medicaid for low-income mothers led to a decrease in infant mortality. Likewise, exposure to high levels of air pollution from living in urban areas close to highways can lead to acute health conditions. Data suggest that engaging in risky behaviors, such as tobacco and alcohol use, a comparatively sedentary life-style, and a low consumption of nutritional foods can account for some portion of the health disparities between lower and upper income groups. The economic research we reviewed also points to links between poverty and crime. For example, one study indicated that higher levels of unemployment are associated with higher levels of property crime. The relationship between poverty and adverse outcomes for individuals is complex, in part because most variables, like health status, can be both a cause and a result of poverty. Regardless of whether poverty is a cause or an effect, the conditions associated with poverty can limit the ability of individuals to develop the skills, abilities, knowledge, and habits necessary to fully participate in the labor force.

Research shows that poverty can negatively impact economic growth by affecting the accumulation of human capital and rates of crime and social unrest. Economic theory has long suggested that human capital—that is, the education, work experience, training, and health of the workforce—is considered one of the fundamental drivers of economic growth. The conditions associated with poverty can work against this human capital development by limiting individuals' ability to remain healthy and develop skills, in turn decreasing the potential to contribute talents, ideas, and even labor to the economy. An educated labor force, for example, is better at learning, creating, and implementing new technologies. Economic theory suggests that when poverty affects a significant portion of the population, these effects can extend to the society at large and produce slower rates of growth. Although historically research has focused mainly on the extent to which economic growth alleviates poverty, some recent empirical studies have begun to demonstrate that higher rates of poverty are associated with lower rates of growth in the economy as a whole. For example, areas with higher poverty rates experience, on average, slower per capita income growth rates than low-poverty areas.

Background

Economic growth is one of the indicators by which the well-being of the nation is typically measured, although recent discussions have focused on a broader set of indicators, such as poverty. Poverty in the United States is officially measured by the Census Bureau, which calculates the number of persons or households living below an established level of income deemed minimally adequate to support them. The federal government has a long-standing history of assisting individuals and families living in poverty by providing services and income transfers through numerous and various types of programs.

Measuring the Nation's Well-Being: Economic Growth and Other Indicators

Economic growth is typically defined as the increase in the value of goods and services produced by an economy; traditionally this growth has been measured by the percentage rate of increase in a country's gross domestic product, or GDP. The growth in GDP is a key measure by which policy-makers estimate how well the economy is doing. However, it provides little information about how well individuals and households are faring.

Recently there has been a substantial amount of activity in the United States and elsewhere to develop a comprehensive set of key indicators for communities, states, and the nation that go beyond traditional economic measures.[3] Many believe that such a system would better inform individuals, groups, and institutions on the nation as a whole.[4] Poverty is one of these key indicators. Poverty, both narrowly and more broadly defined, is a characteristic of society that is frequently monitored and defined and measured in a number of ways.[5]

How Is Poverty Defined in the United States.?

The Census Bureau is responsible for establishing a poverty threshold amount each year; persons or families having income below this amount are, for statistical purposes, considered to be living in poverty.[6] The threshold reflects estimates of the amount of money individuals and families of various sizes need to purchase goods and services deemed minimally adequate based on 1960s living standards, and is adjusted each year using the consumer price index. The poverty rate is the percentage of individuals in total or as part of various subgroups in the United States who are living on income below the threshold amounts.

Over the years, experts have debated whether or not the way in which the poverty threshold is calculated should be changed. Currently the calculation only accounts for pretax income and does not include noncash benefits and tax transfers, which, especially in recent years, have comprised larger portions of the assistance package to those who are low-

---

[3] GAO, *Informing Our Nation: Improving How to Understand and Assess the USA's Position and Progress*, GAO-05-1 (Washington, D.C., November 2004), p.4.

[4] GAO-05-01.

[5] GAO-05-01, p.34.

[6] The U.S. Department of Health and Human Services (HHS) establishes poverty guidelines that are similar to the poverty thresholds but are used by HHS and other agencies for administering programs, such as determining program eligibility.

income.[7] For example, food stamps and the Earned Income Tax Credit could provide a combined amount of assistance worth an estimated $5,000 for working adults with children who earn approximately $12,000 a year.[8] If noncash benefits were included in a calculation of the poverty threshold, the number and percentage of individuals at or below the poverty line could change. In 1995, a National Academy of Sciences (NAS) panel recommended that changes be made to the threshold to count noncash benefits, tax credits, and taxes; deduct certain expenses from income such as child care and transportation; and adjust income levels according to an area's cost of living.[9] In response, the Census Bureau published an experimental poverty measure in 1999 using the NAS recommendations in addition to its traditional measure but, to date, Census has not changed the official measure.[10]

U.S. Poverty Rates

In 2005, close to 13 percent of the total U.S. population—about 37 million people—were counted as living below the poverty line, a number that essentially remained unchanged from 2004. Poverty rates differ, however, by age, gender, race, and ethnicity and other factors. For example,

- Children: In 2005, 12.3 million children, or 17.1 percent of children under the age of 18, were counted as living in poverty. Children of color were at least three times more likely to be in poverty than those who were white: 3.7 million, or 34.2 percent of, children who were African-American and 4 million, or 27.7 percent of, children who were Hispanic

---

[7] Congressional Research Service, *Poverty in the United States: 2005* (Washington, D.C.: Aug. 31, 2006).

[8] Danzinger, Sheldon, "Fighting Poverty Revisited: *What Did Researchers Know 40 Years Ago? What Do We know Today?*" Dec. 4, 2006.

[9] For a summary of the NAS panel recommendations see Congressional Research Service Report 95-539, *Redefining Poverty in the United States: National Academy of Science Panel Recommendations*, by Thomas R. Gabe (archived) (Washington, D.C.: 1995).

[10] U.S. Census Bureau, *Poverty among Working Families: Findings from Experimental Poverty Measures* (Washington, D.C.: Sept. 2000).

lived below the poverty line compared to 4 million, or 9.5 percent of, children who were white.[11]

- Racial and ethnic minorities: African-Americans and Hispanics have significantly higher rates of poverty than whites. In 2005, 24.9 percent of African-Americans (9.2 million) and 22 percent of Hispanics (9.4 million) lived in poverty, compared to 8.3 percent for whites (16.2 million).

- Elderly: The elderly have lower rates of poverty than other groups. For example, 10.1 percent of adults (3.6 million) aged 65 or older lived in poverty.

Poverty rates also differ depending on geographical location and for urban and nonurban areas. Poverty rates for urban areas were double those in suburbs, 17 percent compared to 9.3 percent.[12] Poverty rates in the South were the highest at 14 percent; the West had a rate of 12.6 percent, followed by the Midwest with 11.4 percent and the Northeast at 11.3 percent.[13]

The Role of the Federal Government

The U.S. government has a long history of efforts to improve the conditions of those living with severely limited resources and income. Presidents, Congress, and other policymakers have actively sought to help citizens who were poor, beginning as early as the 1850s through the more recent efforts established through welfare reform initiatives enacted in 1996.

Over the years, the policy approaches used to help low-income individuals and families have varied. For example, in the1960s federal programs

---

[11] Beginning in March 2003, the Census Bureau allowed survey respondents to identify themselves as belonging to one or more racial groups. In prior years, respondents could select only one racial category. Consequently, poverty statistics for different racial groups for 2002 and after are not directly comparable to earlier years' data. The term "blacks and whites" refers to persons who identified with only one single racial group. The term "Hispanic" refers to individuals' ethnic, as opposed to racial, identification. Hispanics may be of any race.

[12] Congressional Research Service, *Poverty in the United States: 2005* (Washington, D.C.: Aug. 31, 2006).

[13] Congressional Research Service, *Poverty in the United States: 2005* (Washington, D.C.: Aug. 31, 2006).

focused on increasing the education and training of those living in poverty. In the 1970s, policy reflected a more income-oriented approach with the introduction of several comprehensive federal assistance plans. More recently, welfare reform efforts have emphasized the role of individual responsibility and behaviors in areas such as family formation and work to assist people in becoming self-sufficient. Although alleviating poverty and the conditions associated with it has long been a federal priority, approaches to developing effective interventions have sometimes been controversial, as evidenced by the diversity of federal programs in existence and the ways in which they have evolved over time.

Currently, the federal government, often in partnership with the states, has created an array of programs to assist low-income individuals and families. According to a recent study by the Congressional Research Service (CRS), the federal government spent over $400 billion on 84 programs in 2004 that provided cash and noncash benefits to individuals and families with limited income. These programs cover a broad array of services: Examples include income supports or transfers such as the Earned Income Tax Credit and TANF; work supports such as subsidized child care and job training; health supports and insurance through programs like the State Children's Health Insurance Program (SCHIP) and Medicaid; and other social services such as food, housing, and utility assistance.

Economic Research Links Poverty with Adverse Outcomes for Individuals Such as Poor Health and Crime

Economic research suggests that individuals living in poverty face an increased risk for adverse outcomes, such as poor health, criminal activity, and low participation in the workforce. The adverse outcomes that are associated with poverty tend to limit the development of skills and abilities individuals need to contribute productively to the economy through work, and this in turn, results in low incomes. The relationship between poverty and outcomes for individuals is complex, in part because most variables, like health status, can be both a cause and a result of poverty. The direction of the causality can have important policy implications. To the extent that poor health causes poverty, and not the other way around, then alleviating poverty may not improve health.

Individuals Living in Poverty Experience Higher Rates of Adverse Health Outcomes, in Part because of Limited Access to Health Care, Environmental Hazards, and Risky Behaviors

Health outcomes are worse for individuals with low incomes than for their more affluent counterparts. Lower-income individuals experience higher rates of chronic illness, disease, and disabilities, and also die younger than those who have higher incomes.[14] As reported by the National Center on Health Statistics, individuals living in poverty are more likely than their affluent counterparts to experience fair or poor health, or suffer from conditions that limit their everyday activities (fig.1). They also report higher rates of chronic conditions such as hypertension, high blood pressure, and elevated serum cholesterol, which can be predictors of more acute conditions in the future. Life expectancies for individuals in poor families as compared to nonpoor families also differ significantly. One study showed that individuals with low incomes had life expectancies 25 percent lower than those with higher incomes.[15] Other research suggests that an individual's household wealth predicts the amount of functionality of that individual in retirement.[16]

[14] Centers for Disease Control and Prevention, *Health, United States, 2006; 1998* (Hyattsville, Maryland).

[15] Deaton, Angus, "Policy Implications of the Gradient of Health and Wealth," *Health Affairs*, Vol. 21., No.2, March 2002.

[16] Smith, James, and Raynard Kington, "Demographic and Economic Correlates of Health in Old Age." *Demography*, Vol. 34, No. 1, 1997.

Figure 1: Selected Health Indicators by Poverty Status

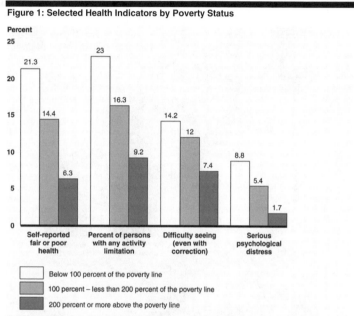

Source: National Center for Health Statistics, *Health, United States, 2006 with Chartbook on Trends in the Health of Americans* (Hyattsville, Maryland: 2006).

Research suggests that part of the reason that those in poverty have poor health outcomes is that they have less access to health insurance and thus less access to health care, particularly preventive care, than others who are nonpoor. Very low-income individuals were three times as likely not to have health insurance than those with higher incomes, which may lead to reduced access to and utilization of health care (fig. 2).

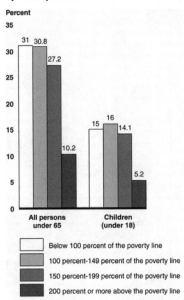

Figure 2: Percentage of Population with No Health Insurance (Private or Medicaid) by Poverty Status

Percent

Data show that those who are poor with no health insurance access the health system less often than those who are either insured or wealthier when measured by one indicator of health care access: visits to the doctor. For example, data from the National Center on Health Statistics show that children in families with income below the poverty line who were continuously without health insurance were three to four times more likely to have not visited a doctor in the last 12 months than children in similar economic circumstances who were insured (fig. 3). Research also suggests that a link between income and health exists independent of health insurance coverage. Figure 3 also shows that while children who are uninsured but in wealthier families visit the doctor fewer times than those who are insured, they still go more often than children who are uninsured but living in poverty.

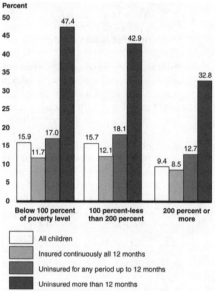

Figure 3: No Visits to Any Health Provider in the Past 12 Months (Children under 18 Years of Age) by Level of Insurance

Percent

- All children
- Insured continuously all 12 months
- Uninsured for any period up to 12 months
- Uninsured more than 12 months

Source: National Center for Health Statistics, *Health, United States, 2006 with Chartbook on Trends in the Health of Americans* (Hyattsville, Maryland: 2006).

Some research examining government health insurance suggests that increased health insurance availability improves health outcomes. Economists have studied the expansion of Medicaid, which provides health insurance to those with low income. They found that Medicaid's expansion of coverage, which occurred between 1979 and 1992, increased the availability of insurance and improved children's health outcomes. For example, one study found that a 30 percentage point increase in eligibility for mothers aged 15-44 translated into a decrease in infant mortality of 8.5 percent.[17] Another study looked at the impact of health insurance coverage through Medicare and its effects on the health of the elderly and also

---

[17] Currie, Janet, and Jonathan Gruber, "Saving Babies: The Efficacy and Cost of Recent Changes in the Medicaid Eligibility of Pregnant Women," *The Journal of Political Economy*, Vol. 104, No. 6, December 1996.

found a statistically significant though modest impact.[18] There is some evidence that variations in health insurance coverage do not explain all the differences in health outcomes. A study done in Canada found improvements in children's health with increases in income, even though Canada offers universal health insurance coverage for hospital services, indicating that health insurance is only part of the story.[19]

Although there is a connection among poverty, having health insurance, and health outcomes, having health insurance is often associated with other attributes of an individual, thus making it difficult to isolate the direct effect of health insurance alone. Most individuals in the United States are either self-insured or insured through their employer. If those who are uninsured have lower levels of education, as do individuals with low income, differences in health between the insured and uninsured might be due to level or quality of education, and not necessarily insurance.[20]

Another reason that individuals living in poverty may have more negative health outcomes is because they live and work in areas that expose them to environmental hazards such as pollution or substandard housing. Some researchers have found that because poorer neighborhoods may be located closer to industrial areas or highways than more affluent neighborhoods, there tend to be higher levels of pollution in lower-income

---

[18] Card, David, et. al., "The Impact of Nearly Universal Insurance Coverage on Health Care Utilization and Health: Evidence from Medicare" National Bureau of Economic Research, Working Paper 10365. NBER, March 2004.

[19] Currie, Janet, and Mark Stabile, "Socioeconomic Status and Child Health: Why Is the Relationship Stronger for Older Children." *American Economic Review*, Vol. 93, No. 5, December 2003.

[20]Additionally, differences in individual health outcomes can sometimes be explained by other factors that may be associated with poverty, but are difficult to detect, such as risk aversion.

neighborhoods.[21] The Institute of Medicine concluded that minority and low-income communities had disproportionately higher exposure to environmental hazards than the general population, and because of their impoverished conditions were less able to effectively change these conditions.[22]

The link between poverty and health outcomes may also be explained by lifestyle issues associated with poverty. Sedentary life-style; the use of alcohol and drugs; as well as lower consumption of fiber, fresh fruits, and vegetables are some of the behaviors that have been associated with lower socioeconomic status.[23] Cigarette smoking is also more common among adults who live below the poverty line than among those above it, about 30 percent compared to 21 percent.[24] Similarly, problems with being overweight and obese are common among those with low family incomes, although most prevalent in women: Women with incomes below 130 percent of the poverty line were 50 percent more likely to be obese than those with incomes above this amount.[25] Figure 4 shows that people living

---

[21] While much of the specific biological mechanism by which air pollution might affect health is still unknown, some recent research by economists has noted a link between pollution and health, especially for infants. Currie and Neidell (2005) find that the decrease in the level of carbon monoxide in California in the 1990s had a significant effect on reducing infant mortality. See Currie, Janet, and Matthew Neidell, "Air Pollution and Infant Health: What Can We Learn From California's Recent Experience?" *Quarterly Journal of Economics*, 120 (3), 2005. Similarly, Chay and Greenstone (2003) find that the reduction in total suspended particulates due to the 1970 Clean Air Act had a significant impact on infant mortality. See Chay, Kenneth, and Michael Greenstone, "Air Quality, Infant Mortality, and the Clean Air Act of 1970." National Bureau of Economic Research, Working Paper No. 10053. NBER, 2003.

[22] Institute of Medicine, Committee on Environmental Justice, "Toward Environmental Justice: Research, Education, and Health Policy Needs", (Washington, D.C.: 1999), p.6.

[23] Adler, Nancy E., and Katherine Newman, "Socioeconomic Disparities in Health: Pathways and Policies." *Health Affairs*, Vol. 21 No. 2, 2002. See also Deaton, Angus. "Policy Implications of the Gradient of Health and Wealth." *Health Affairs*, Vol. 21, No.2: 2002.

[24] Centers for Disease Control and Prevention, *Tobacco Use among Adults–United States, 2005. Morbidity and Mortality Weekly Report* , 2006; 55(42): 1145-1148. Some research suggests that part of the reason why smoking rates are higher may be peer effects, especially among youth smokers. See DeCicca, Phillip, Donald Kenkel, and Alan Mathios, "Racial Difference in the Determinants of Smoking Onset." *Journal of Risk and Uncertainty*. Boston: 2000. Vol. 21, Iss. 2/3; p311. Other studies have shown that educational attainment can affect smoking use as well. See DeCicca, Philip, Donald Kenkel, and Alan Mathios,"Putting Out the Fires: Will Higher Taxes Reduce the Onset of Youth Smoking?" *Journal of Political Economy*. Chicago 2002.Vol.110, Iss.1; p. 144.

[25] U.S. Public Health Service, *Surgeon General's Call To Action to Prevent and Decrease Overweight and Obesity 2001*, Washington, DC, pp. 13-14.

in poverty are less likely to engage in regular, leisure-time physical activity than others and are somewhat more likely to be obese, and children in poverty are somewhat more likely to be overweight than children living above the poverty line. In addition, there is also evidence to suggest a link among poverty, stress, and adverse health outcomes, such as compromised immune systems.[26]

Figure 4: Percentage of Population Who Have a Sedentary Lifestyle, Are Overweight, or Are Obese, by Poverty Status

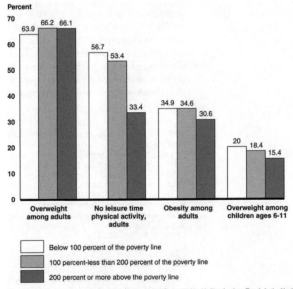

Percent

- ☐ Below 100 percent of the poverty line
- ▨ 100 percent-less than 200 percent of the poverty line
- ■ 200 percent or more above the poverty line

Source: National Center for Health Statistics, *Health, United States, 2006 with Chartbook on Trends in the Health of Americans* (Hyattsville, Maryland: 2006).

---

[26] While access to care, behavior, and environmental factors are some of the most commonly offered reasons for the relationship between poverty and health, recent literature has suggested other alternative theories, of which there is less of a research tradition. These include the effect of short exposures to health shocks as a result of poverty, such as poor nutrition or increased adrenalin due to higher levels of stress, and psycho-social stress that leads to problems with the immune system. See Smith, James P., "Healthy Bodies and Thick Wallets: The Dual Relation between Health and Economic Status." *The Journal of Economic Perspectives*, Vol. 13, No. 2, 1999.

While evidence shows how poverty could result in poor health, the opposite could also be true. For example, a health condition could result, over time, in restricting an individual's employment, resulting in lower income. Additionally, the relationship between poverty and health outcomes could also vary by demographic group.[27] Failing health, for example, can be more directly associated with household income for middle-aged and older individuals than with children, since adults are typically the ones who work.

Economic Research Shows an Association Between Poverty and Crime

Just as research has established a link between poverty and adverse health outcomes, evidence suggests a link between poverty and crime. Economic theory predicts that low wages or unemployment makes crime more attractive, even with the risks of arrest and incarceration, because of lower returns to an individual through legal activities.[28] While more mixed, empirical research provides support for this. For example, one study shows that higher levels of unemployment are associated with higher levels of property crime, but is less conclusive in predicting violent crime.[29] Another study has shown that both wages and unemployment affect crime, but that wages play a larger role.[30]

Research has found that peer influence and neighborhood effects may also lead to increased criminal behavior by residents. Having many peers that engage in negative behavior may reduce social stigma surrounding that behavior.[31] In addition, increased crime in an area may decrease the

---

[27] It is not clear whether these adverse outcomes occur with greater frequency among all individuals living in households below the poverty line or only among those experiencing extreme poverty; those who experience poverty during critical development stages, such as infancy or early childhood; or those who experience long bouts of poverty.

[28] Criminal behavior has been measured by reports to the police in an area, self-reported crime by individuals in surveys or arrests, as well as other measures. See also Freeman, Richard, "Why Do So Many Young American Men Commit Crimes and What Might We Do About It?" *Journal of Economic Perspectives*, Vol. 10, No. 1: Winter 2006.

[29] Raphael, Steven, and Rudolf Winter-Ebner, "Identifying the Effect of Unemployment on Crime." *Journal of Law and Economics*, Vol. XLIV. 2001.

[30] Gould, Eric D., Bruce A. Weinberg, and David B. Mustard, "Crime Rates and Local Labor Market Opportunities in the United States: 1979-1997. *Review of Economics and Statistics*, 84 (1): 2002.

[31] Katz, Lawrence F., Jeffrey R. Kling, and Jeffrey B. Liebman, "Moving to Opportunity in Boston: Early Results of a Randomized Mobility Experiment." *Quarterly Journal of Economics*, May 2001.

chances that any particular criminal activity will result in an arrest. Other research suggests that the neighborhood itself, independent of the characteristics of the individuals who live in it, affects criminal behavior. [32] One study found that arrest rates were lower among young people from low-income families who were given a voucher to live in a low-poverty neighborhood, as opposed to their peers who stayed in high-poverty neighborhoods. The most notable decrease was in arrests for violent crimes; the results for property crimes, however, were mixed, with arrest rates increasing for males and decreasing for females. [33]

Adverse Outcomes, Such as Poor Health and Low Educational Attainment, Lead to Reduced Participation in the Labor Market

Regardless of whether poverty is a cause or an effect, the conditions associated with poverty limit the ability of low-income individuals to develop the skills, abilities, knowledge, and habits necessary to fully participate in the labor force, which in turn leads to lower incomes. According to 2000 Census data, people aged 20-64 with incomes above the poverty line in 1999 were almost twice as likely to be employed as compared to those with incomes below it. [34] Some of the reasons for these outcomes include educational attainment and health status.

---

[32] However, a challenge that researchers face is that, almost by definition, many individuals share the same characteristics in a neighborhood. Therefore, it is difficult to determine whether it is the characteristic of the individual or the neighborhood that is the source of the behavior.

[33] Http://www.huduser.org/publications/fairhsg/MTODemData.html and http://www.hud.gov/prodesc/mto.cfm . Some economists have used data from the Moving-to-Opportunity experiment as a way to attribute causality. Moving-to-Opportunity is a research demonstration in which a number of families, chosen randomly, within five public housing authorities were given housing vouchers to be used in low-poverty neighborhoods. Another group of families acted as the control, and were not given the vouchers. Using these data, some economists have compared the outcomes for children whose families received the vouchers and those that did not. To some extent, the results have confirmed that neighborhood, independent of individual characteristics, affects criminal behavior, but the results have also been mixed. Using data from the randomized housing experiment, Ludwig, Duncan, and Hirschfeld (2001) found that the housing vouchers reduced violent arrests by teens, but may have increased the number of property arrests. Kling, Ludwig, and Katz (2005) also used the Moving-to-Opportunity data, but looked for differential effects by gender. The authors found that for females, there were large reductions in the amount of arrests for both property and violent crime, when compared to those for the control group. For males, there were reductions in violent arrests, but proportionally smaller than the drops for females. In addition, there were significant increases in the rate of property arrests.

[34] U.S. Census Bureau, *Employment Status: 2000, Census 2000 Brief* (Washington, D.C., August 2003), p.4

Poverty is associated with lower educational quality and attainment, both of which can affect labor market outcomes. Research has consistently demonstrated that the quality and level of education attained by lower-income children is substantially below those for children from middle- or upper-income families. Moreover, high school dropout rates in 2004 were four times higher for students from low-income families than those in high-income families.[35] Those with less than a high school degree have unemployment rates almost three times greater than those with a college degree, 7.6 percent compared to 2.6 percent in 2005. And the percentage of low-income students who attend college immediately after high school is significantly lower than for their wealthier counterparts: 49 percent compared to 78 percent.[36]

A significant body of economic research directly links adverse health outcomes, which are also associated with low incomes, with the quality and quantity of labor that the individual is able to offer to the workforce. Many studies that have examined the relationship among individual adult health and wages, labor force participation, and job choice have documented positive empirical relationships among health and wages, earnings, and hours of work.[37] Although there is no consensus about the exact magnitude of the effects, the empirical literature suggests that poor health reduces the capacity to work and has substantive effects on wages, labor force participation, and job choice, meaning that poor health is associated with low income.

---

[35] National Center for Education Statistics, U.S. Department of Education, *Dropout Rates in the United States: 2004* (Washington, D.C. November 2006), p. 4.

[36] Choy, Susan, "College Access and Affordability," *Education Statistics Quarterly*, Vol. 1, Issue 2, Topic: Postsecondary Education.

[37] Several methodological challenges exist in this literature: For example, many of these findings could reflect the effect of income on health rather than vice versa. In addition, results are highly sensitive to the measures of health that are used, with self-reported health status subject to several forms of bias, some of which could overstate the relationship between income and health, and others of which could understate the relationship. For example, individuals who have reduced their hours of work or left the labor force may be more likely to report poor health, in order to justify their reduced labor supply or because government programs provide incentives to report disability; this would lead to an upward bias in the estimated relationship between income and health. On the other hand, it is possible that higher-income individuals, who on average have greater health care utilization, may be more likely to be diagnosed with certain conditions simply because of their greater access to health care. This would lead to a downward bias in the estimated relationship between income and health.

Research also demonstrates that poor childhood health has substantial effects on children's future outcomes as adults. Some research, for example, shows that low birth weight is correlated with a low health status later in life. Research also suggests that poor childhood health is associated with reduced educational attainment and reduced cognitive development. Reduced educational attainment may in turn have a causal effect not only on future wages as discussed above but also on adult health if the more educated are better able to process health information or make more informed choices about their health care or if education makes people more "future oriented" by helping them think about the consequences of their choices. In addition, some research shows that poor childhood health is predictive of poor adult health and poor adult economic status in middle age, even after controlling for educational attainment.

Economic Research Suggests a Negative Association between Poverty and Economic Growth

The economic literature suggests that poverty not only affects individuals but can also create larger challenges for economic growth. Traditionally, research has focused on the importance of economic growth for generating rising living standards and alleviating poverty, but more recently it has examined the reverse, the impact of poverty on economic growth. In the United States, poverty can impact economic growth by affecting the accumulation of human capital and rates of crime and social unrest. While the empirical research is limited, it points to the negative association between poverty and economic growth consistent with the theoretical literature's conclusion that higher rates of poverty can result in lower rates of growth.

Research has shown that accumulation of human capital is one of the fundamental drivers of economic growth.[38] Human capital consists of the

[38]Economic models that consider human capital to be a fundamental driver of economic growth are commonly referred to as endogenous growth models, although the more traditional neoclassical model has also been augmented to include the role of human capital. Endogenous growth theory posits technological growth as occurring through dynamics inside the model. Although there are several competing models, crucial importance in each is given to the production of new technologies and human capital. While the major point these models emphasize is that human capital is the driving force behind growth, the actual modeling of the relationship is still a controversial issue in the economic literature. Some growth models assert that the driving force behind economic growth is the rate of accumulation of human capital, in which the rate of economic growth is proportional to the rate of accumulation of human capital. Another approach considers that high levels of human capital, as embodied in the level of the educational attainment of the workforce, increases the capacity of individuals to innovate (discover new technology) or to adopt new technology.

skills, abilities, talents, and knowledge of individuals as used in employment. The accumulation of human capital is generally held to be a function of the education level, work experience, training, and healthiness of the workforce.[39] Therefore, schooling at the secondary and higher levels is a key component for building an educated labor force that is better at learning, creating, and implementing new technologies. Health is also an important component of human capital, as it can enhance workers' productivity by increasing their physical capacities, such as strength and endurance, as well as mental capacities, such as cognitive functioning and reasoning ability. Improved health increases workforce productivity by reducing incapacity, disability, and the number of days lost to sick leave, and increasing the opportunities to accumulate work experience. Further, good health helps improve education by increasing levels of schooling and scholastic performance.

The accumulation of human capital can be diminished when significant portions of the population have experienced long periods of poverty, or were living in poverty at a critical developmental juncture. For example, recent research has found that the distinct slowdown in some measures of human capital development is most heavily concentrated among youth from impoverished backgrounds. When individuals who have experienced poverty enter the workforce, their contributions may be restricted or minimal, while others may not enter the workforce in a significant way. Not only is the productive capability of some citizens lost, but their purchasing power and savings, which could be channeled into productive investments, is forgone as well.

In addition to the effects of poverty on human capital, some economic literature suggests that poverty can affect economic growth to the extent that it is associated with crime, violence, and social unrest. According to some theories, when citizens engage in unproductive criminal activities they deter others from making productive investments or their actions force others to divert resources toward defensive activities and expenditures. The increased risk due to insecurity can unfavorably affect

---

[39] In general, economists regard expenditures on education, training, medical care, and so on as investments in human capital. Collectively, theoretical growth models suggest economic growth results from improvements in human capital as embodied in the skills and experience of the labor force; from expansion of physical capital in the form of plant and equipment; and from progress in science, engineering, and management that generates technological advance. While many variables have been empirically tested, only a few have been accepted as being statistically significant in explaining growth. The role of human capital is now almost universally regarded as being indispensable in this respect.

investment decisions—and hence economic growth—in areas afflicted by concentrated poverty. Although such theories link poverty to human capital deficiencies and criminal activity, the magnitude of their impact on economic growth for an economy such as the United States is unclear at this time.[40] In addition, people living in impoverished conditions generate budgetary costs for the federal government, which spends billions of dollars on programs to assist low-income individuals and families. Alleviating these conditions would allow the federal government to redirect these resources toward other purposes.

While economic theory provides a guide to understanding how poverty might compromise economic growth, empirical researchers have not as extensively studied poverty as a determinant of growth in the United States. Empirical evidence on the United States and other rich nations is quite limited, but some recent studies support a negative association between poverty and economic growth. For example, some research finds that economic growth is slower in U.S. metropolitan areas characterized by higher rates of poverty than those with lower rates of poverty.[41] Another study, using data from 21 wealthy countries, has found a similar negative relationship between poverty and economic growth.[42]

Concluding Observations

Maintaining and enhancing economic growth is a national priority that touches on all aspects of federal decision making. As the nation moves forward in thinking about how to address the major challenges it will face

---

[40] Human capital deficits experienced by some impoverished individuals cannot always be attributed to experience of poverty. In some cases, low education attainment and poor health, although associated with poverty, may actually be caused by some other factor that is also responsible for poverty. In this case, poverty would be a symptom rather than a cause (i.e., poor health, poor choices, or addiction may erode human capital potential and cause poverty). Similarly, most poor people do not commit crimes, and those that do may be motivated by forces unrelated to their incomes.

[41] The relationship is not always statistically significant in all regions. Statistical insignificance in some cases might be more attributable to data issues such as sample size or multicollinearity rather than an indication of nonrelationship between poverty and income growth in various regions. See S. Dev Bhatta, "Are Inequality and Poverty Harmful for Economic Growth," *Journal of Urban Affairs*, 22 (3-4): 2001. This study provides, arguably, a better comparison group than cross-country studies, since metropolitan statistical areas in the United States are at relatively similar stages of development.

[42] Voitchovsky, S., "Does the Profile of Income Inequality Matter for Economic Growth? Distinguishing between the Effects of Inequality in Different Parts of the Income Distribution." *Journal of Economic Growth*, Vol.10.: 2005.

in the twenty-first century, the impact of specific policies on economic growth will factor into decisions on topics as far ranging as taxes, support for scientific and technical innovation, retirement and disability, health care, education and employment. To the extent that empirical research can shed light on the factors that affect economic growth, this information can guide policymakers in allocating resources, setting priorities, and planning strategically for our nation's future.

Economists have long recognized the strong association between poverty and a range of adverse outcomes for individuals, and empirical research, while limited, has also begun to help us better understand the impact of poverty on a nation's economic growth. The interrelationships between poverty and various adverse social outcomes are complex, and our understanding of these relationships can lead to vastly different conclusions regarding appropriate interventions to address each specific outcome. Furthermore, any such interventions could take years, or even a generation, to yield significant and lasting results, as the greatest impacts are likely to be seen among children. Nevertheless, whatever the underlying causes of poverty may be, economic research suggests that improvements in the health, neighborhoods, education, and skills of those living in poverty could have impacts far beyond individuals and families, potentially improving the economic well-being of the nation as a whole.

Appendix B
Models of Causal Prediction: Multiple Regression

If you are interested in forecasting an event, you may do so by extending the trend or by examining the event's root causes. Forecasting on the basis of trend was covered in chapter 12. This appendix covers causal prediction, the method to be used when models of trend projection may be inappropriate.

As you have learned, trend projection models assume that the present trend will continue, at least for the period of prediction. The problem with an assumption of continuity is that a past trend may not hold true for any length of time. Or the data may not show any obvious trend pattern. In these cases we must think about the causal relations that may link the dependent variable with a set of independent variables.

Causal models based on multiple regression techniques have been used in public policy analyses in many different ways. Many local governments depend on multiple regression models for assessing property taxes.[1] Property tax is assessed on its market value. However, we cannot know the value before a property is sold, so an assessor must estimate, or forecast, the market price.[2] Because a high assessment means a high property tax for the homeowner, property tax assessments have been a source of conflict in many communities across the nation. How do you forecast a property's market price? Let us look at a hypothetical example. Suppose your town's appraiser has assessed the value of a custom-built home at $265,000, which the owner is challenging as far above its market value. Your job is to determine the validity of the owner's claim. You will have to build a causal model for predicting the market value of the property.

BUILDING A CAUSAL MODEL

The first step in building a causal model requires establishing the causal linkage between a dependent variable and a set of independent variables. Once we have inquired into the causes of a specific event (the dependent variable), we begin our analysis by selecting the independent variables. After preparing a list and collecting data, we determine how these independent variables relate to the dependent variable. These two steps constitute the specification of the model. At this stage, the difference between a time-series model and a causal model comes into sharper focus. For building a model in which the only explanatory factor is the trend over time, we do not need to understand the causes of a change. However, in specifying a model for causal analysis, we must develop a deep understanding of the change's causes.

Let us return to our example of predicting the price of a house. As the first step toward specification, we hypothesize that the price of a house depends on the following independent variables: the type of structure and its location. We assume that the type of structure has only one component: the size of the covered area. The location factors include two separate variables: whether the house has a view and whether it is located on a cul-de-sac. You can write your model as

$$\text{Price} = f(\text{Area, View, Cul-de-sac}) \tag{B.1}$$

Expression B.1 is read as "price is a function of (or depends on) area, view, and cul-de-sac." This expression is also known as an implicit function or implicit model. It is called implicit because we are not making any explicit hypotheses regarding the nature of the relationship between the dependent variable and the independent variables. If we express the model by specifying the relationship, the expression is called an explicit function or explicit model. Thus, the implicit function written in equation B.1 can be made explicit by writing

$$\beta_0 + \beta_1\text{Area} + \beta_2\text{View} + \beta_3\text{Cul-de-sac} + \varepsilon \tag{B.2}$$

where β_i are the coefficients for the independent variables, and ε is the error term.

The explicit model (equation B.2) states that we expect the price to go up with the size and relative desirability of the area and location factors. Also, the model states that we are hypothesizing a linear relationship between price and the other independent variables.

CAUSALITY VERSUS CO-OCCURRENCE

One of the most difficult problems of statistical analysis based on regression or a correlation coefficient is that the results can never establish causality; they can only demonstrate co-occurrence. That is, empirical results can establish that the dependent and the independent variables moved in the same direction, but they cannot say whether one caused the other. Actual causality must be established by a theoretical explanation of human behavior. Policy researchers develop their hypotheses by thoroughly reviewing the literature on the theories of human social interactions.

An example may clarify this point. Data show that productivity in the United States, measured in per capita gross domestic product (GDP) and adjusted for inflation (real per capita GDP), is increasing steadily over the years. So is the population of Lima, Peru. If we regress U.S. per capita GDP against the population of Lima, we will find a high degree of statistical significance, leading to the claim that an increase in Lima's population adds to U.S productivity. Yet it is obvious that no such causal connection exists. On the other hand, if you study the literature on economic growth, you find that the accepted theories explain growth in national per capita GDP by pointing to a combination of expenditure on financial capital (total national capital formation) and spending on human capital (for example, education, health care, or research and development).

The issues of causality and correlation are central to our understanding of the methods of scientific research. Hardly a day passes without medical researchers' linking some food or personal habit with some human ailment. Many of these findings, of course, cannot claim causality and instead point out close associations. Sometimes researchers misuse these findings by asserting a causal connection where there is none. In contrast, some people take advantage of the fact that these results do not *prove* causality and deny a significant relationship. Lobbyists for the tobacco industry have tried to dismiss the results linking lung cancer with smoking as a mere co-occurrence. However, in the face of overwhelming evidence, increasing public awareness has prompted public policies that limit tobacco use.

Other than mistaking co-occurrence for causality, we may make significant mistakes by using trivial variables to find a causal linkage. Suppose we want to develop a model for explaining the difference in criminal justice expenditures among cities of similar size. If we include in the model the number of law enforcement officers as an independent variable, we will be engaging in a trivial pursuit, since it is obvious that when we hire more officers, the size of our budget goes up. Instead, we should use variables such as crime rate, population density, and per capita city income. Of course, when trying to exclude trivial independent variables, lines tend to blur. A deep understanding of human behavior, not statistical manipulation, helps you see that link between the dependent and independent variables.

ESTIMATION OF THE MODEL

After specifying a model, we estimate the relevant coefficients. For this step we need to determine how each of the variables is to be quantified or operationalized. Thus, in our example, we can operationalize housing quality as an explanation of price with the help of our independent variables: the size of a house expressed in square feet of covered area, the presence or absence of a view, and the location on or off a cul-de-sac (which is desirable for privacy and the absence of fast-moving traffic). We expressed each location variable (view and cul-de-sac) as an intercept dummy, with a value of 1 if a particular house has a view and 1 if it is located on a cul-de-sac. If, on the other hand, it has no view and is not on a cul-de-sac, each location variable gets a value of 0.

Suppose the assessor's office has provided you with information on thirty houses in the neighborhood sold during the past six months. The information is presented in Table B.1. You can estimate the model with these data.[3]

Using information from Table B.1, you can write the estimated equation as follows:

$$\text{Price} = 6,767.87 + 100.04 \text{ Area} + 40,603.07 \text{ View} + 42,607.31 \text{ Cul-de-sac}$$
$$t = \quad (0.233) \quad\quad (8.18)^* \quad\quad\quad (3.23)^* \quad\quad\quad\quad (3.38)^*$$
$$R^2 = 0.786$$
$$\text{Adjusted } R^2 = 0.761 \tag{B.3}$$
$$F(3,26) = 31.77^*$$
$$n = 30$$

*Significant at the .05 level

TABLE B.1	Housing Prices and Characteristics		
	Price ($)	Area (square feet)	View	Cul-de-sac
1	310,000	2,200	1	1
2	233,000	1,800	0	0
3	400,000	3,500	1	0
4	430,000	3,200	1	1
5	210,000	1,800	0	0
6	240,000	1,700	1	1
7	300,000	2,200	0	1
8	350,000	2,100	1	1
9	385,000	2,600	1	1
10	368,000	3,000	0	0
11	200,000	2,000	0	0
12	298,000	1,750	1	1
13	275,000	1,900	0	1
14	198,000	1,800	0	0
15	253,000	2,200	1	0
16	278,000	2,100	1	1
17	320,000	2,170	1	1
18	178,000	1,200	1	1
19	225,000	2,000	0	0
20	212,000	1,900	0	1
21	288,000	2,800	0	1
22	315,000	2,300	1	1
23	255,000	2,600	0	1
24	284,000	2,700	1	0
25	189,000	1,640	1	0
26	220,000	2,600	0	0
27	248,000	1,900	1	0
28	276,000	2,000	1	1
29	210,000	2,300	0	0
30	205,000	2,200	0	0

The estimated equation (B.3) tells an interesting and convincing story about how home prices are determined. It states that each square foot adds $100.04 to the price of a home. The estimated results also point out that location variables contribute heavily to the determination of price. If the property is located on a piece of land with a view, the price increases by $40,603.07, while sitting on a cul-de-sac boosts the price by another $42,607.31.

The interpretation of the intercept term is often problematic in a regression equation. Equation B.3 indicates that even if there is not a single square foot of covered area, there is still a price. Therefore, the temptation to interpret the intercept term as the price of land is great. Using this logic, we can state that if a parcel of vacant land (square feet = 0) does not have a view (view = 0) and is not located on a cul-de-sac (cul-de-sac = 0), it will still carry a price of $6,767.87. With a view, this price will change to $47,370.94. If the land is located on a cul-de-sac but has no view, it is worth $49,375.18. Finally, when a plot of land in this particular neighborhood has a view and is located on a cul-de-sac, it should command a price of $89,978.25. The danger in such an assertion is that we can interpret the intercept term to be the land price if we accept the model to be perfectly specified. If not, we may have left out one or more significant independent variables, the impact of which will then be captured by the intercept term. For example, we did not use the lot size (or the total land area) for the houses. Since this is a potentially important variable, we cannot readily interpret the intercept term. Therefore, unless the model is fully specified (includes all important variables), any interpretation of the intercept becomes questionable.

The estimated results indicate that the four independent variables explain 78.6 percent of the variations (R^2). Since there are 30 observations, at 29 degrees of freedom, the relevant t value for evaluating the significance of the four estimated coefficients (including the constant) at a 95 percent level of confidence is 1.697. All coefficients except for the constant have t values greater than this number, so all are statistically significant. The critical F value at 3 and 26 degrees of freedom is 2.76. Since the calculated F value is 31.768, we can safely conclude that the equation as a whole is statistically significant.

Now that you are satisfied with the quality of the estimated model, you can predict the price of the house in dispute. The equation states that each square foot of housing area adds $100.04 to the base price of $6,767.87 (value of the intercept). Also, if a house has a view, its price goes up by $40,603.07. Finally, its location on a cul-de-sac increases its value by $42,607.31. This particular house has 2,200 square feet of covered area and, although it does not have a view, it is located on a secluded cul-de-sac. Armed with the information derived from the estimated model, you can forecast the market price as follows:

$$\text{Estimated price} = 6,767.87 + (100.04 \times 2,200) + (40,603.07 \times 0) + (42,607.31 \times 1)$$

Notice that since this house does not have a view, the value of the dummy variable is 0. But because the house is located on a cul-de-sac, the dummy value of this variable is 1. Using this equation, we calculate the estimated price of the property to be approximately $269,463. Therefore, according to your estimation, the owner does not have a strong case. In fact, from the estimated result, we learn that the property has been appraised at a value lower than its estimated market price.

HOW GOOD IS THE MODEL?

Because of its mathematical elegance and ease of explanation, multiple regression is probably the most commonly used technique in statistical research and econometric prediction. Although regression analysis offers a powerful tool for prediction, its quality depends on the model and how close it is to the "true" relationship. Again, as we have mentioned before, we cannot observe the "truth." Therefore, we have no objective way of knowing whether we are sufficiently close to a desired specification. Since the process of specification contains two separate parts, choosing the right set of independent variables and postulating the correct functional form, let us discuss both parts in detail, beginning with the problem of selecting the right set of independent variables.

Choosing Independent Variables

When choosing independent variables, we might omit important variables or include some that are irrelevant. The error of omitted variables occurs because of our lack of understanding of the underlying factors that produce the dependent variable. Such lack of understanding may result from a general dearth of theoretical insight into a particular aspect of social behavior or from a paucity of data. If we want to determine the reasons students engage in random school shootings, we may find out that there is neither a strong theoretical explanation for this puzzling behavior nor a good deal of data on potential offenders to specify a causal model. Therefore, if we attempt to build a model, we are likely to encounter the problem of misspecification and are apt to leave out important explanatory variables or include irrelevant ones. Either error leads to some rather serious problems of estimation. Let me explain. The basic idea of a multiple regression is illustrated in Figure B.1.

As you can see, I have explained the dependent variable, housing price, with the help of two independent variables, view and area. The intersecting parts of the Venn diagram show which aspects of the dependent variable are explained by the two independent variables. The regression model explains the area where the dependent and independent variables overlap. As you can see, the area of overlap is divided into three segments. The area V signifies the price difference among the houses explained by the presence or absence of a view. Segment A is the price that is explained by the size of the structure (area). However, there is also an area of correlation between the size of the house and the view. The correlation may be high, since the lots with prime views

---

FIGURE B.1   **Visual Explanation of Multiple Regression**

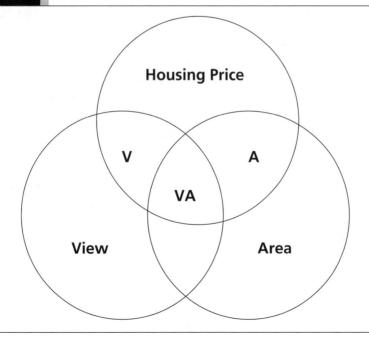

| FIGURE B.2 | **Visual Explanation of Irrelevant Variable** |

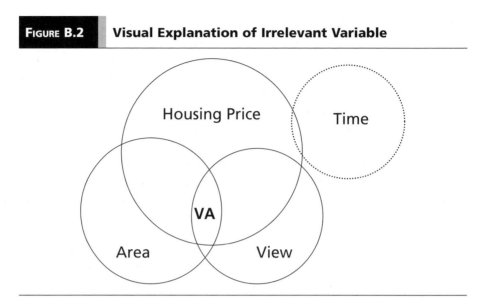

tend to attract larger homes. This area is designated VA. The R^2 value derived from the estimated equation is a ratio of the total area of these three sections to the total area of the dependent variable [(A + V + VA)/housing price]. A high R^2 value would mean that these overlapping areas cover most of the dependent variable, and a low R^2 value would imply a small area of intersection.

We would misspecify a model if we excluded an important variable and/or included an irrelevant one. Thus, in the case of estimating housing prices, if we leave out either the area or the view, we will run into the problem of misspecification. A small R^2 value is the first indication of misspecification (the incorrect construction of a regression model) due to an omitted variable.

On the other hand, if we include irrelevant variables, the overall explanation of the dependent variable will not improve. In Figure B.2, the irrelevant variable (time) is shown with a dotted line. You may notice that compared with the other two independent variables, this one explains very little of the dependent variable (housing price). Therefore, its inclusion has little or no effect on the total explanation (R^2) of the model. Also, when we compare the adjusted R^2 value of the new model with that of the old model (without the variable time), the adjusted R^2 value of the expanded model turns out to be smaller than that of its properly specified predecessor.

Let me now explain the impact of misspecification on t values. Suppose in our housing price example that the true relation is captured by the specification of equation B.2; that is, housing prices depend on these three variables: area, view, and cul-de-sac. In this case the estimated coefficients will reflect their true values. For the purpose of exposition, let us say that we did not include the independent variable area. As a result, equation B.2 is improperly specified and is written as

$$\beta'_0 + \beta'_1 \text{View} + \beta'_2 \text{Cul-de-sac} + \varepsilon \tag{B.4}$$

Since the true relationship includes area (see equation B.3), the effects of the omitted variable will be distributed among the remaining independent variables and error term. This situation will create two problems. First, the estimated coefficients for the independent variables, by illicitly incorporating fractions of another coefficient, will deviate from their true value. Second, the error term will now contain bias due to contamination by the residual factors of the omitted variable, causing the regression to violate the precepts of the classical least squares method. Moreover, the estimated coefficients will not be the best, linear, unbiased estimators. Let us see what happens to our estimated equation as a result of errors of omission. First we will omit an important explanatory variable, and then we will include an irrelevant one. We have reestimated equation B.4 by omitting the variable area from equation B.3, with the following results:

$$
\begin{aligned}
\text{Price} &= 230,560.40 + 43,030.87 \text{ View} + 34,230.87 \text{ Cul-de-sac} \\
t &= \quad (12.72)^* \qquad (1.84)^* \qquad\qquad (1.47) \\
R^2 &= 0.234 \\
\text{Adjusted } R^2 &= 0.177 \\
F(2,27) &= 4.11^* \\
n &= 30
\end{aligned}
\tag{B.5}
$$

*Significant at the .05 level

If you compare the estimated results of equation B.5 with those of equation B.3, you can see the obvious differences. First, both the R^2 and the adjusted R^2 values have dropped significantly, implying that less is explained by the new model. Second, quite significantly, the variable cul-de-sac is no longer statistically significant. To a researcher, these are the telltale signs of a poorly specified model. Therefore, any prediction based on such a model would be erroneous.

Errors of specification, however, are the most difficult to detect. If you have omitted some important explanatory variables, the first indication may be a lower than expected R^2 value. Because R^2 measures the percentage of explained variance, leaving out important explanatory variables will cause it to be low.

As we have seen, the omission of an important variable also causes its effect to be absorbed by the error term. The second probable sign of omission is a high serial correlation, in which the error terms of one period are correlated with those of previous periods. The problem of serial correlation will be discussed later, but it may suffice at this time to point out a few important facts. You may recall that one of the fundamental assumptions of the least squares method is the random distribution of error terms. Now suppose that the properly specified model for determining housing prices consists of the three independent variables, area, view, and cul-de-sac, but that we have failed to include cul-de-sac. In that case, the misspecified model is

$$
\beta''_0 + \beta''_1 \text{Area} + \beta''_2 \text{View} + \varepsilon
\tag{B.6}
$$

Since I have omitted cul-de-sac, its effects are now incorporated in the error term (ε), which, in effect, has become $\varepsilon + \beta''_3$cul-de-sac. As you can imagine, because the variable cul-de-sac is causally linked with price, the effects of its omission will not be random, and its inclusion in the error term will cause a bias. This bias in the error term causes serial correlation. If there is evidence of a high degree of serial correlation, you should look for important explanatory variables that you may have inadvertently left out.

Let me repeat: the error of omitted variables can be corrected not by resorting to any statistical technique but through an understanding of the nature of the dependent variable. This understanding must come from the theoretical literature. If we are trying to build a model to predict the crime rate of a city, we must have a deep understanding of the sociological factors that determine the overall crime rate. In forecasting revenue for the state government, we must look into economic theory and understand the state's fiscal structure.

We noted earlier that the second source of specification error is the inclusion of irrelevant variables in a model. What happens when we include independent variables that do not explain the dependent variable? This error is easier to detect than an error of omission and even simpler to correct (by eliminating irrelevant variables from the model). Let us see what happens when we include irrelevant variables in the model.

Suppose that in estimating housing prices, we decide to include a fourth independent variable, which measures the ease of access from a house. This variable, shown in Table B.2, is measured by the minutes of travel time to reach the nearest highway.

When we include this new variable and reestimate our model, we obtain the following results:

$$
\begin{aligned}
\text{Price} &= 9,291.11 + 99.78 \text{ Area} + 41,496.06 \text{ View} + 43,182.00 \text{ Cul-de-sac} - 180.5 \text{ Time} \\
t &= \quad (0.30) \qquad (8.0)^* \qquad\qquad (3.15)^* \qquad\qquad\quad (3.32)^* \qquad\qquad\qquad (-0.29) \\
R^2 &= 0.786 \\
\text{Adjusted } R^2 &= 0.752 \\
F(4, 25) &= 23.01^* \\
n &= 30
\end{aligned}
$$

(B.7)

*Significant at the .05 level

As you can see from the preceding results, the new variable turns out to be statistically insignificant. This lack of statistical significance may be due to some people preferring easy access to the highway, while others prefer seclusion and distance from it. Therefore, these conflicting preferences do not show up in the determination of demand for housing. Returning to Figure B.2, you can see that when we include an irrelevant variable (time), the area of explanation (where time overlaps housing price) is rather small, and hence its inclusion does not significantly increase the R^2 value.

The inclusion of irrelevant variables poses less of a specification problem than the omission of important variables. Thus, if a new variable is totally random, it will impose no bias on either the estimated coefficients or the error term. However, unless

| TABLE B.2 | Variables for Determining Housing Price | | | |

Price ($)	Area (square feet)	View	Cul-de-sac	Time (minutes)
310,000	2,200	1	1	25
233,000	1,800	0	0	3
400,000	3,500	1	0	17
430,000	3,200	1	1	8
210,000	1,800	0	0	2
240,000	1,700	1	1	35
300,000	2,200	0	1	7
350,000	2,100	1	1	33
385,000	2,600	1	1	35
368,000	3,000	0	0	21
200,000	2,000	0	0	10
298,000	1,750	1	1	1
275,000	1,900	0	1	15
198,000	1,800	0	0	4
253,000	2,200	1	0	15
278,000	2,100	1	1	13
320,000	2,170	1	1	9
178,000	1,200	1	1	32
225,000	2,000	0	0	22
212,000	1,900	0	1	25
288,000	2,800	0	1	1
315,000	2,300	1	1	7
255,000	2,600	0	1	19
284,000	2,700	1	0	20
189,000	1,640	1	0	20
220,000	2,600	0	0	4
248,000	1,900	1	0	3
276,000	2,000	1	1	15
210,000	2,300	0	0	10
205,000	2,200	0	0	25

you are deliberately choosing a random series, few data sets in nature will be randomly distributed with respect to another, especially when a researcher has reason to believe that there is *some* causal link between the dependent and the independent variables. This largely irrelevant variable will impose some biases and can be detected. To locate this variable, look for the following results:

1. If the included variable is not significantly correlated with the dependent variable, this lack of correlation will show up as an insignificant t value for the included variable's estimated coefficient. As can be seen (equation B.7), the variable time has a statistically insignificant t value.
2. Although the R^2 value will remain unchanged or may even go up slightly, the adjusted R^2 value will register a decline. You may recall our discussion of R^2 and adjusted R^2 in chapter 12. R^2 is the measure of total explanation. Therefore, even

if you add an utterly irrelevant variable, the worst it can do is to add nothing to the explanation. In this case R^2 will remain the same (unchanged) when you include such a variable in the original list of independent variables. However, you may recall that the formula for adjusted R^2 is

$$\overline{R^2} = 1 - (1 - R^2)\frac{n-1}{n-k}$$

So unless the new variable adds more to the value of R^2 than does the correction factor, $(n-1)/(n-k)$, made for the inclusion of an additional variable, the value of R^2 will decline. By comparing the estimation results of equation B.3 with those of equation B.7, we can see that the R^2 value has remained unchanged at 0.786 with the inclusion of the irrelevant variable, time. However, since this marginal increase could not compensate for the adjustment factor, the adjusted R^2 value has declined from 0.761 to 0.752.

3. The inclusion of irrelevant variables tends to increase the variance of the estimated coefficients. This increased variance reduces the t values of the coefficients. As you can see, the inclusion of an irrelevant variable has caused a slight reduction in the t values of all three independent variables.

4. An irrelevant variable may mean that the new variable is measuring the same phenomenon as one of the other independent variables. In this case, the analysis suffers from multicollinearity, a problem discussed at greater length later.

Searching for the Proper List of Independent Variables

Among the greatest beneficiaries of computer hardware and software advances have been econometricians. Thanks to the increased computing capabilities of modern computers, the most sophisticated techniques of estimation are available to prospective users at the touch of a button. As a result, the temptation to forgo the thoughtful but time-consuming effort required to build a theoretically sound model and to settle for a model of empirical convenience is strong. Yielding to it can often lead to serious but undetected problems of specification error. To underline the fact that there is no substitute for the deep understanding of the causal interrelationship, I will discuss some of the most commonly misused techniques for solving specification problems.

Suppose I am trying to build a causal model for forecasting a complex sociological phenomenon: drug abuse cases among high school students. An industrious researcher, I have found information on various social and economic characteristics of the general population in the surrounding areas of the school district. However, lacking familiarity with the scholarly literature on the subject, I do not have a clue about which variables are important and which are not. But it is easy to run a regression equation when the data are already in the machine, so there is no stopping me. I proceed to run a large number of equations and then choose the combination that gives me the highest R^2 and best t values. This approach is called a fishing expedition or data mining. The problem is that since the model has been built without a profound comprehension of the causal linkages, what we may be observing is a simple case of co-occurrence. Therefore, this model is likely to give us misleading forecasts, as the future development of these less than relevant independent variables will have little bearing on the course of the dependent variable.

Stepwise regression is a statistical technique that minimizes the tedious job of having to choose manually the best set of independent variables. Given a list of variables, this technique will search for the variable that gives the highest value of R^2. After that, it will pick from the list the second variable that adds the most to this R^2 value, then go to the third, and so on. Many statistical packages come with this stepwise option. The problem with stepwise regression is that it selects independent variables solely on the basis of the strength of association, not on causality.

Predicting on the Basis of the Wrong Functional Specification

Even after we have selected the "correct" set of independent variables, serious errors can arise if we do not choose the right functional form. For example, suppose we have a data set in which the true relationship is a quadratic one. If we assume that the relationship is linear and fits a straight line, we will get a terribly inaccurate predicted value (see Figure B.3). I have discussed this problem in chapter 12.

The only way to avoid the problem of misspecifying the functional form is to graph each independent variable against the dependent variable. Although a linear form is recommended over a more complicated nonlinear one, you cannot always use the linear functional form. If the data are arranged in a way that quickly reveals, say, a quadratic form, you may not have to spend time plotting the data. However, in most cases you cannot be sure until you have plotted them. Consider the two sets of data presented in Table B.3. Series A presents citywide survey results showing support for a public roller-skating

FIGURE B.3	**Errors of Functional Misspecification**

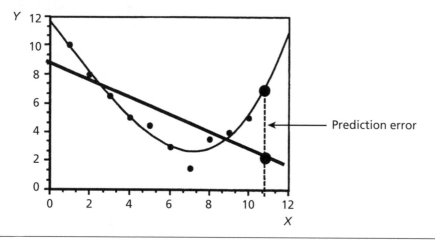

Note: The figure shows a huge error in prediction due to the misspecification of the functional form. Clearly, in this case, the polynomial form is more appropriate. The choice of a straight line causes prediction error.

TABLE B.3	**Detecting the Relationship between Variables in a Series**		

	Community support for roller-skating park		
Series A (1991–2000)		**Series B (2001)**	
Year	Community support (percent)	Household median income (× $1,000)	Community support (percent)
1991	3	60	5
1992	5	19	30
1993	10	25	35
1994	15	30	50
1995	25	52	3
1996	35	36	35
1997	20	17	9
1998	18	58	7
1999	13	28	40
2000	6	45	20

park. The data clearly show that support for the project increased rapidly over the years and then, as the roller-skating fad diminished, support waned. The data are presented in a way (in this case over time) that makes the nature of the relationship between the two variables obvious. However, the results of another series may not be arranged so conveniently for the researcher to discern the shape of the relationship. Take series B, which shows a cross section of support among community residents for the same project in 2001. Since the dependent and independent variables are not arranged in any order, you may not be able to grasp their relationship simply by looking at the data. However, I have plotted the two variables in Figure B.4, which clearly shows a quadratic relationship between them, with support for the park coming solidly from the middle-income neighborhoods. In contrast, poor and wealthy citizens show a distinct lack of interest.

Although Figure B.4 strongly suggests a nonlinear relationship, we have not solved the problem completely. You may still be undecided about the type of polynomial to use. You could try a quadratic or a second-degree polynomial.

The estimation of the second-degree polynomial gives us the following result,

$$P = -24.92 + 3.71\ Y - 0.056\ Y^2$$
$$t = (-0.92)\ \ (2.37)^*\ \ \ (-2.80)^*$$
$$R^2 = 0.69$$
$$\text{Adjusted } R^2 = 0.61 \tag{B.8}$$
$$F(2,7) = 7.91^*$$
$$n = 10$$

*Significant at the .05 level

Community Support for Roller-skating Park, 2001

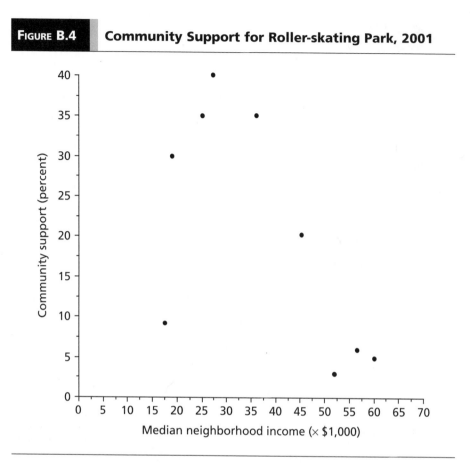

where P is the percentage of support for the project within the community in 2001, and Y is the median income of the community.

The estimated results look fine, with high R^2 and significant t and F values. The estimated curve has been plotted with a heavy line in Figure B.5.

However, we may also be tempted to try a third-degree curve, since the series shows some sign of turning the corner and going up again. In that case, the results are as follows:

$$P = -192.78 + 19.69\ A - 0.515\ Y^2 + 0.004\ Y^3$$
$$t = \quad (4.9)^* \quad (5.45)^* \quad (5.06)^* \quad (4.54)^*$$
$$R^2 = 0.93$$
$$\text{Adjusted } R^2 = 0.90 \qquad\qquad (B.9)$$
$$F(3,6) = 26.88^*$$
$$n = 10$$

*Significant at the .05 level

FIGURE B.5	**Projection and Model Specification**

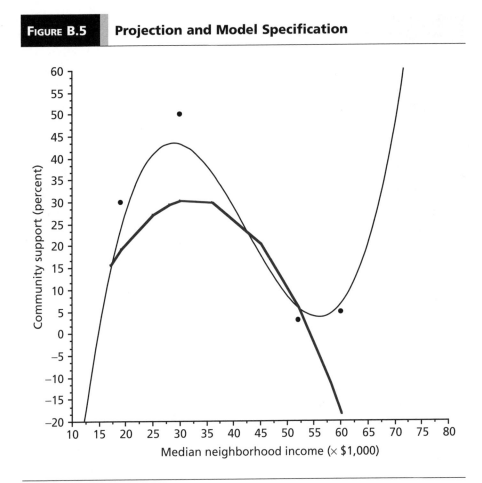

The preceding results indicate that although the second-degree curve gives us a good fit, the third-degree one gives us an even better fit. I have plotted the expected values on the basis of the preceding formulations (equations B.8 and B.9) in Figure B.5. Not only do the two models give us different estimated results for the observations within the sample range, but also the problem of model specification becomes truly critical when we attempt to project outside the sample range. For example, if we want to project for $Y = 75$, the expected value for the quadratic form is -62.42, while for the third-degree polynomial, it is 74.6.[4]

It is important to remember that the functional form you choose may give you forecasts that are significantly different from one another, especially for the independent variables *outside the sample range considered in the model* (the range between the highest and the lowest values of the independent variable). In that case, you may not have any objective way of choosing among the different functional forms.

However, even if a higher order functional form gives you an apparently good fit, there are few, if any, instances in the social sciences that conform to the explosive

FIGURE B.6	Relationship between Housing Prices and Covered Area

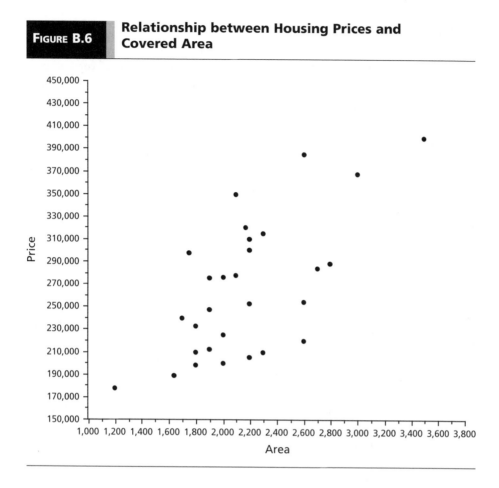

growth of a higher order polynomial. Therefore, to repeat my previous suggestion, always use a linear form when in doubt, and never use a functional form higher than the second order.

Returning to our example of predicting housing prices, to specify the functional form, price is plotted against area in Figure B.6. From the plotted data, we decided that the linear form was the best functional form.

WHEN REGRESSION RESULTS ARE SUSPECT: THE ERRORS OF ESTIMATION

When using regression analyses, a researcher, like the heroes of the Greek epics, can be misled by a number of different errors or may forfeit sound reasoning and be seduced by empirical results that appear to be gorgeous at first glance. However, more careful scrutiny reveals their deceptive nature. Let us discuss the major errors of regression analysis.

Identifying Multicollinearity

One of the premises of the classical least squares method is that the independent variables are not *collinear* (not correlated). In statistical terms this lack of correlation is called *orthogonal*. Take any series of numbers (for example, the square footage measurements of the various houses in our example). If another variable is created by adding, multiplying, dividing, or subtracting a constant, these two variables are perfectly correlated and are called perfectly collinear with each other. Hence, in our housing price equation, if we add another variable that measures the covered area in square meters, we have created a situation of perfect multicollinearity, since this new variable is a multiple of the old variable. The presence of perfect multicollinearity prevents us from deriving any estimate of the slope coefficients.[5] Let me explain why. Suppose we are trying to estimate the following equation

$$Y = a + bX + cZ + \varepsilon \qquad\qquad (B.10)$$

where X and Z are two highly correlated (collinear) independent variables.

You may visualize the effects of multicollinearity with the help of the Venn diagram in Figure B.7.

Let us go back to our example of estimating housing price. Suppose that we have included two independent variables: the square footage of the house (area) and the number of bathrooms (bathrooms). As you can see from this diagram, the two independent variables explain the dependent variable. The parts of housing price that are explained by the two independent variables are the overlapping areas. However, if you compare this figure with Figure B.2, you will see that in this case, the problem is that the two independent variables overlap to a large extent. This result is caused by the simple fact that the larger a house is, the more bathrooms it is likely to have. This is the problem of multicollinearity.

To explain the problem, I have marked the areas of intersection separately. The parts of housing price that are explained exclusively by each of the two independent variables, area and bathrooms, are labeled A and B, respectively. The segment that is jointly explained is marked a + b. Finally, the portion of the figure that is a simple overlap between the two independent variables, without any implication for the explanation of housing price, is labeled A′ + B′. As we have seen before, R^2 is measured by the ratio [A + (a + b) + B]/(total area of housing price).

The problem of multicollinearity shows up in the estimation of the coefficients. If there is a high degree of multicollinearity among the independent variables, we encounter two significant problems. First, we face the problem of estimating the "true" coefficients of the individual independent variables. Thus, in Figure B.7, while calculating the relation between housing price and area, regression analysis concentrates only on segment A. Because it cannot disentangle the area (a + b) jointly explained by the two independent variables, the regression model ignores area (a + b). As a result, *the estimated coefficients turn out to be smaller and more statistically insignificant than they would be if only one of these variables were introduced without the other.*

| **FIGURE B.7** | **Multicollinearity and Its Effects on R^2** |

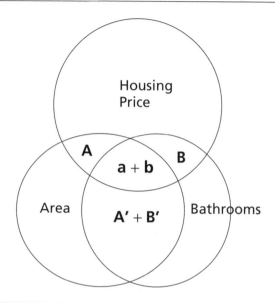

Second, multicollinearity enlarges the standard error of the estimated coefficients. *As a result, the calculated* t *values can become highly questionable* (see Figure B.8).

Computing a multiple regression is extremely time-consuming, so the formulas for calculating regression coefficients for multiple regression models are not included in this book. However, for the purposes of exposition, I would like to point out that when there is more than one independent variable, the estimated standard error of slope coefficients is obtained with the following formula:

$$SE(b) = \sqrt{\frac{\sum_{i=1}^{n} e_i^2 / (n - k)}{\sum_{i=2}^{n} (X_i - \overline{X}_i)(1 - r^2_{XZ})}} \tag{B.11}$$

where e_i^2 is the error sum of squares, n is the number of observations, k is the number of independent variables, and r^2_{XZ} is the square of the correlation coefficient between the two independent variables, X and Z.

From the preceding formula, you can see that when there is no correlation between X and Z (that is, when $r^2_{XZ} = 0$), the term $(1 - r^2_{XZ})$ in the denominator is equal to 1. Therefore, the estimated standard error of the estimated regression coefficient b is at its minimum.

However, as the correlation between X and Z becomes stronger, the correlation coefficient, r^2_{XZ}, approaches 1. If there is a perfect correlation, this term equals 1. In that case, the denominator of the estimated standard error equals 0, which makes

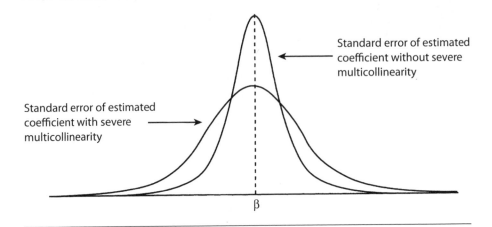

FIGURE B.8   **The Effects of Multicollinearity on the Standard Errors of Estimation**

Standard error of estimated coefficient without severe multicollinearity

Standard error of estimated coefficient with severe multicollinearity

β

the standard error infinite. This result makes the estimation of the standard error of the regression coefficients impossible.

In real life we seldom encounter perfect collinearity between two independent variables unless they are the same variable, simply expressed in two different measurement units. If we accidentally use two perfectly collinear independent variables, our computer software will warn us by posting an error message. What the software cannot tell us, though, is where there is less than perfect correlation. This situation, as we can deduce from the preceding equation, will make our estimated standard error more widely dispersed, as shown in Figure B.8.

What is the immediate effect of this increasing dispersion of the error term of the estimated coefficients? As you may recall, the t values for the estimated coefficients are calculated by dividing the coefficient by its standard error (see equation B.11). Therefore, this increase in the error term will reduce the t value, causing the researcher to reject an otherwise significant independent variable as insignificant.

You may note that despite multicollinearity, the estimated coefficients will remain unbiased, as Figure B.8 indicates. In other words, in our example of housing prices, we estimated the regression coefficients with the help of thirty observations. This calculation gave us an estimate of the true value of b. If we considered another sample group of houses and reestimated the same equation, we would get another estimate of this elusive b. If we continued to repeat this experiment, the distribution of the estimated values of b would have a mean, which would get closer and closer to the true value of b. You may recall that this is the property of unbiasedness in the classical least squares method. The presence of multicollinearity does not make our estimated coefficients biased. Therefore, this property of least squares is not violated.

Since the variance of the distribution of the estimated coefficients goes up with increasing levels of multicollinearity, including a collinear variable will cause the estimates to fluctuate widely. If we include an independent variable that is highly correlated with another independent variable in the model, the variables' estimated coefficients will become extremely sensitive and will change dramatically each time the equation is run with a slightly different set of independent variables. *However, this extreme sensitivity will not affect those independent variables that are not highly correlated with this new variable.*

The presence of multicollinearity does not affect the measures of overall goodness of fit. That is, R^2 and F values in an equation with a high degree of multicollinearity will be unaffected. Consider our example of estimating home prices. Suppose we include two other variables in the model, the number of bathrooms (bathrooms) and the total, as opposed to covered, land area (land). Suppose that these homes are all located in the same tract-home development, and therefore the total land area is highly correlated with the covered area. So is the number of bathrooms. These new variables are presented in Table B.4.

TABLE B.4	Housing Prices and Multicollinearity				
Price ($)	Area (square feet)	Bathrooms	View	Cul-de-sac	Land (square feet)
310,000	2,200	3.5	1	1	4,170
233,000	1,800	2.5	0	0	3,330
400,000	3,500	5.0	1	0	6,175
430,000	3,200	4.0	1	1	6,000
210,000	1,800	2.0	0	0	3,330
240,000	1,700	2.0	1	1	3,045
300,000	2,200	3.0	0	1	4,090
350,000	2,100	3.0	1	1	3,885
385,000	2,600	4.5	1	1	4,810
368,000	3,000	4.5	0	0	5,650
200,000	2,000	2.5	0	0	3,777
298,000	1,750	2.0	1	1	3,237
275,000	1,900	2.5	0	1	3,500
198,000	1,800	1.5	0	0	3,330
253,000	2,200	3.0	1	0	4,100
278,000	2,100	3.0	1	1	3,885
320,000	2,170	3.5	1	1	3,999
178,000	1,200	1.0	1	1	2,220
225,000	2,000	3.0	0	0	3,700
212,000	1,900	2.0	0	1	3,515
288,000	2,800	3.5	0	1	5,280
315,000	2,300	4.0	1	1	4,255
255,000	2,600	3.0	0	1	4,810
284,000	2,700	3.5	1	0	4,995
189,000	1,640	2.0	1	0	3,034
220,000	2,600	3.0	0	0	4,810
248,000	1,900	2.5	1	0	3,515
276,000	2,000	3.5	1	1	3,700
210,000	2,300	3.0	0	0	4,255
205,000	2,200	2.5	0	0	4,070

Let us explore the effects of including these highly correlated independent variables in the model. The results of the newly estimated equation are as follows:

$$\text{Price} = 33,268.056 + 29.92 \text{ Area} + 30,137 \text{ View} + 38,598.56 \text{ Cul-de-sac}$$
$$+ 10.24 \text{ Land} + 31,879.62 \text{ Bathrooms}$$

$$t = \quad (1.10) \quad (0.19) \quad\quad (2.24)^* \quad\quad (3.15)^* \quad (0.12)^* \quad\quad (2.29)$$

$$R^2 = 0.825 \tag{B.12}$$

$$\text{Adjusted } R^2 = 0.788$$

$$F(5,24) = 22.58^*$$

$$n = 30$$

*Significant at the .05 level

By comparing the results of equation B.12 with those of equation B.3, we can see the impact of severe multicollinearity. The most affected variable is area, which is highly correlated with the newly introduced variables, land and bathrooms. Although the estimated coefficients and their respective t values for the other two independent variables (view and cul-de-sac) remained relatively unchanged, the estimated coefficient for area was significantly reduced, and its error term greatly increased, causing a precipitous drop in the t value. You also may notice that the R^2 value was not affected by including the highly correlated independent variables.

Once you understand the problems caused by multicollinearity, the question becomes how to detect it and what to do about it. You should note that multicollinearity should be suspected if you have high R^2 values but low t values.

To detect which independent variables are collinear, you should calculate the correlation matrix among the independent variables. Most software packages can provide you with the matrix of correlation coefficients shown in Table B.5.

Each entry in the table shows the correlation coefficient between the row and column variables. For example, the correlation between bathrooms and area is .867. The diagonal numbers are all 1.000 because, by definition, each variable has a perfect correlation with itself. You can see that three of the independent variables—area, bathrooms, and land—are highly correlated with each other. This would account for the multicollinearity in the estimated equation.[6]

TABLE B.5   **Correlation Matrix**

	Area	Bathrooms	View	Cul-de-sac	Time	Land
Area	1.000					
Bathrooms	.867	1.000				
View	−.003	.208	1.000			
Cul-de-sac	−.078	.060	.330	1.000		
Time	−.079	.035	.289	.237	1.000	
Land	.997	.864	−.022	−.069	−.092	1.000

Resolving Multicollinearity

Multicollinearity poses a dilemma for the analyst. If there is severe multicollinearity between two independent variables, one of the best ways to resolve the problem is to eliminate one of the variables. However, if the eliminated variable happens to be an important variable in explaining the dependent variable, then by eliminating it we will cause specification error with its accompanying problems. Furthermore, as we have noted, multicollinearity among a partial list of independent variables will not affect the other variables, nor will the error term be biased.

Researchers often choose not to do anything about multicollinearity unless the problem is acute. Looking at the correlation coefficients of our previous example, I would be inclined to include the number of bathrooms in the model because it happens to be one of the vital considerations in determining the price of a home. On the other hand, I would reason that with a correlation coefficient of .997, land is not adding much to the explanation of market price beyond that provided by area. I would specify the model by including bathrooms but eliminating land. As you can tell, this decision is purely a line call on the basis of subjective judgment.

Econometricians have tried to walk the tightrope between being comprehensive—including all the important information—and avoiding severe multicollinearity. Although balancing these competing objectives is a matter of subjective judgment and comes through years of practice, you can improve your chances of success immediately by following these practical steps for eliminating multicollinearity among the independent variables:

1. *In certain circumstances the two independent variables can be added together.* This newly created variable will contain information from both variables and may add to the explanation without contributing the problems of multicollinearity. This trick may work provided the two variables do not have opposite expected signs or are not significantly different in magnitude. Suppose we are adding two highly correlated independent variables, X and Z, to form a new variable. If X is positively related to the dependent variable, Y, while Z is negatively related (X and Z are negatively correlated with each other), the newly created variable will have little explanatory capability, because the positive relation will be offset by the negative one. Adding independent variables also will not work if one of the variables has a substantially higher mean than do the others. In this case the smaller variable will be lost in the larger variable, and the linear combination of the two will not provide any more insight into the variation of the dependent variable. Furthermore, the newly created variable may not have any intuitive meaning. For example, for a completely different purpose, economist Arthur Okun created an index by adding the unemployment rate and the rate of inflation, calling the sum the "misery index." This composite measurement has a readily understandable meaning. In contrast, if we add area and land, this composite variable may not convey any definite meaning to policymakers (in this case, the property owners).

2. *For time-series data, the problem of multicollinearity can also be solved if you take the first difference.* That is, you create a new variable by subtracting the preceding time period's data from those of the current period. Suppose we are trying to forecast the sales tax revenue for a state government. We have chosen as independent variables the growth rate of per capita state income and the rate of unemployment. But in formulating our model, we

find that there is a strong negative correlation between these variables (that is, during prosperous times, when the income growth rate is high, unemployment is low, and vice versa). Therefore, we cannot add these two variables together. A way out may be to use the yearly difference in the unemployment rate, which may not have as strong a correlation with the growth rate of per capita income as does the absolute level of unemployment. However, even this method is not a panacea for correcting multicollinearity. Similar to the problem of creating a composite variable, using the yearly difference of a variable may not have the same meaning (or even any meaning) as an independent variable. Even after getting high t and R^2 values, we may be at a loss to explain our results in a meaningful way.

3. *Finally, another (and probably the least controversial) way of dealing with multicollinearity is to increase the sample size.* If doing so is a viable alternative, it is certainly worth pursuing. If the two variables are not simply multiples of each other (perfectly correlated), then as the number of observations increases, the natural variations within the series will sufficiently distinguish themselves and allow the proper estimation of the model. In our example of housing prices, if we can increase the sample size from thirty to, say, 300, the variations within the two series may distinguish themselves enough to allow us to estimate the model properly.

Identifying Serial Correlation

Serial correlation (also known as autocorrelation) means that the order in which the observations are arranged has some effect on the estimation of the regression coefficients. In other words, serial correlation exists if the error of one observation depends on that of the previous one. An example may clarify the point. Many cities across the nation want to reduce lawsuits stemming from work-related injuries. The job of a risk manager is to curtail such lawsuits by offering adequate training to his or her workers. However, the training programs are expensive, so some cities establish benchmarks for the amount of workers' compensation paid out each year. If a city pays more than the specified amount this year, it will invest more money in the training program next year. On the other hand, if the city pays less than this benchmark amount, less money will be allocated for training the following year. Before initiating this benchmark program, the allocation of money followed other guidelines, and the error term from the equation explaining expenditure on training showed a random pattern. I have shown the hypothetical distribution of the error term in Figure B.9, in which the trend line over time is a flat horizontal line.

However, after introducing the benchmark program, the error terms were correlated with the past year's term. That is, if the yearly compensation overshot the target, more money flowed into the training program; if it undershot, money was taken away from the program. Situations such as these, in which the current year's performance is predicated upon that of the previous year, show serial correlation. In contrast to Figure B.9, in which the error terms are randomly distributed, Figure B.10 shows two kinds of serial correlation: positive and negative. If the current period's error term generally shows the same sign as error terms of previous periods, the series is said to have a positive serial correlation. Thus, if a public policy affects the course of the economy for a number of years (as did Proposition 13, the California initiative that cut property taxes and restricted the ability of local governments to raise and spend money), the series shows positive serial correlation.

In contrast, if a series shows alternately positive and negative error terms, it demonstrates negative serial correlation. In this case the error terms oscillate back and forth

FIGURE B.9	**Distribution of Errors Showing No Serial Correlation**

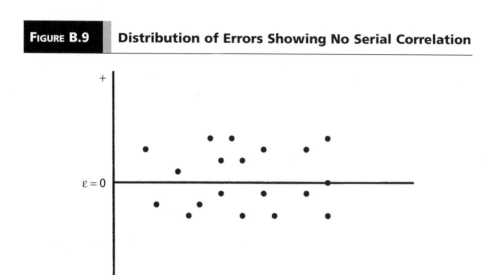

FIGURE B.10	**Serial Correlation**

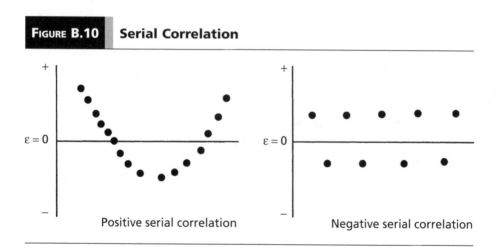

like a pendulum. The equation explaining spending on the benchmark program may exhibit a negative serial correlation.

A correlation between successive error terms violates one of the fundamental principles of the least squares method. The most widely used method for detecting serial correlation is the Durbin-Watson d test.[7] This test applies only in the following cases:

1. The regression model includes an intercept term.
2. The error terms have a first-order correlation, meaning that each year's error is correlated only with that of the preceding year and not with the errors of the previous two or three years. In symbolic terms this can be written as

$$e_t = \rho e_{t-1} + \varepsilon \qquad \text{(B.13)}$$

where e_t is the residual (estimated error term) in year t, e_{t-1} is the residual (estimated error term) in the previous year $(t-1)$, ρ is the correlation coefficient, and ε is the true random error term.

3. The regression model does not include a lagged dependent term.

The Durbin-Watson d statistic is defined as

$$d = \frac{\sum_{t=2}^{n}(e_2 - e_{t-1})^2}{\sum_{t=1}^{n}e_t^2} \tag{B.14}$$

The d statistic varies between 4 and 0. If there is perfect positive serial correlation $(r = 1)$, e_t is the same as e_{t-1}, and the numerator becomes 0. In other words, with a perfect positive correlation, the d statistic equals 0. If, on the other hand, there is perfect negative correlation $(r = -1)$, the numerator becomes $4\sum e_t^2$. In that case equation B.14 becomes

$$\frac{4\sum e_t^2}{\sum e_t^2} = 4$$

If there is no serial correlation at all, the d statistic is equal to 2. Hence, if the d statistic is close to either 0 or 4, you should suspect serial correlation.

Unfortunately, the correction for serial correlation is beyond the scope of this introductory textbook. If you are interested in knowing more about these problems, you may consult one of many excellent texts on econometrics.[8]

Heteroskedasticity: The Problem of Scaling Variables

One of the important conditions for the least squares method is that the variability (standard deviation) of the error term of the observations does not vary with the size of the dependent variable. This is the condition of homoskedasticity. Figure B.11 demonstrates the implication of this assumption.

As you can see, the variance of the error term corresponding to the three observations of the dependent variable X falls within the same band. However, this happy situation may not hold true if the independent variables vary a great deal with the size of the dependent variable. In that case, as the scale of the dependent variable increases, so does the variability of the error term. This situation of increasing variability of the error term is called heteroskedasticity and is shown in Figure B.12.

Heteroskedasticity, therefore, is caused essentially by mixing apples with oranges in the data set and is typically encountered in cross-section models. Suppose we are trying to account for urban crime in America. If our data set contains the number of high crimes committed in large cities, along with those perpetrated in small towns in primarily agricultural states, we are likely to encounter heteroskedasticity. If the model is not properly specified, differences in the variance of the error terms may result. This is called impure heteroskedasticity. If, on the other hand, despite the best specification of the model, the error terms show signs of heteroskedasticity, this is known as pure heteroskedasticity.

FIGURE B.11   **Homoskedastic Distribution of Errors**

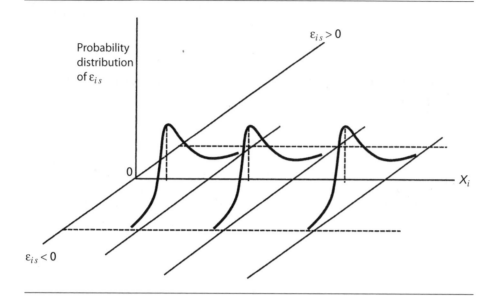

FIGURE B.12   **Heteroskedastic Distribution of Errors**

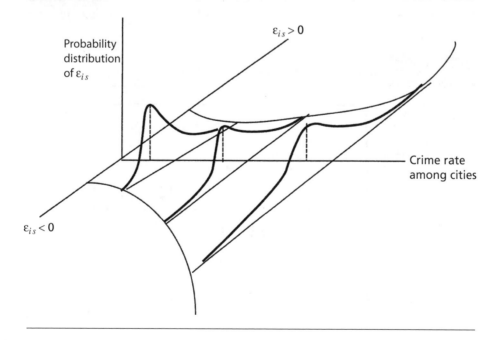

Detecting Heteroskedasticity

Heteroskedasticity can be visually inspected by plotting the error terms. If we do not have heteroskedasticity, the errors will be distributed randomly around zero. However, if it is present, the errors will show a flaring-out pattern, as in Figure B.13.

FIGURE B.13 **Hypothetical Errors Showing Presence and Absence of Heteroskedasticity**

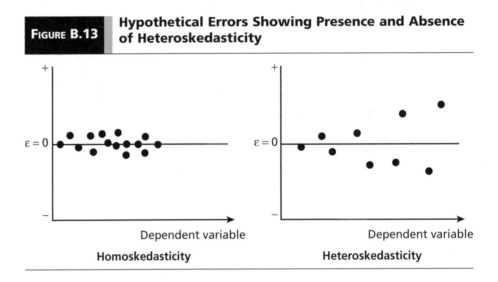

To explain the point, let us return to our example of estimating housing prices. Using the results of equation B.3, we have obtained the predicted value for each of the homes in the sample. The difference between the actual and the predicted value is the error term. The error terms of the housing price data have been plotted in Figure B.14.

FIGURE B.14 **Error Terms of Housing Price Data**

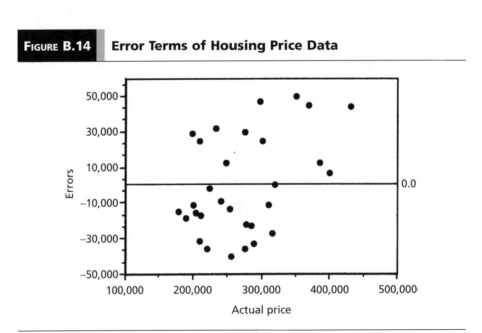

TABLE B.6	Housing Prices with Data for a Dissimilar Neighborhood		
Observation	Price ($)	Predicted price ($)	Error (residuals)
1	310,000	320,733	–10,733
2	233,000	168,067	64,933
3	400,000	422,349	–22,349
4	430,000	436,803	–6,803
5	210,000	168,067	41,933
6	240,000	262,698	–22,698
7	300,000	263,770	36,230
8	350,000	309,126	40,874
9	385,000	367,161	17,839
10	368,000	307,351	60,649
11	200,000	191,281	8,719
12	298,000	268,501	29,498
13	275,000	228,949	46,051
14	198,000	168,067	29,933
15	253,000	271,458	–18,458
16	278,000	309,126	–31,126
17	320,000	317,251	2,749
18	178,000	204,663	–26,663
19	225,000	191,281	33,719
20	212,000	228,949	–16,949
21	288,000	333,412	–45,412
22	315,000	332,340	–17,340
23	255,000	310,198	–55,198
24	284,000	329,493	45,493
25	189,000	206,458	–17,459
26	220,000	260,923	–40,923
27	248,000	236,637	11,363
28	276,000	297,519	–21,519
29	210,000	226,102	–16,102
30	205,000	214,495	–9,495
31	535,000	548,433	–13,433
32	648,000	640,217	7,783
33	656,000	606,468	49,532
34	802,000	814,322	–12,322
35	735,000	724,313	10,687
36	546,000	658,699	–112,699
37	762,900	944,846	–181,946
38	485,000	546,637	–61,637
39	942,000	979,667	–37,667
40	1,250,000	898,418	351,582

The plot in Figure B.14 does not indicate overwhelming heteroskedasticity, since the housing prices are fairly close to one another. Now suppose we included in the sample data an adjoining but dissimilar neighborhood. Whereas the original sample contains data from an upper-middle-class area, the next sample is from a decidedly more affluent one.

The expanded data set, with ten new entries of extremely high-priced homes, is presented in Table B.6. In this table, we have included a column of predicted values of house prices by using the specification of equation B.15 and adding a dummy variable for the two communities. The value of this newly created dummy variable is 0 for the moderately priced community (Comm) is 0 and 1 for the wealthy community. The estimated equation is as follows:

$$\text{Price} = -40,859.71 + 116.07 \text{ Area} + 56,963.41 \text{ View} + 49,275 \text{ Cul-de-sac}$$
$$+ 275,903.98 \text{ Comm}$$

$$t = \quad (0.94) \quad (6.20)^* \quad\quad (2.11)^* \quad\quad\quad (1.88)^* \quad (6.73)^*$$

$$R^2 = 0.905$$
$$\text{Adjusted } R^2 = 0.894$$
$$F(4, 35) = 83.57^*$$
$$n = 40$$

(B.15)

*Significant at the .05 level

The column "Predicted price" was created using this formula. The error terms were calculated by subtracting the predicted price from the actual price (the price variable).

The terms shown in the "Error" column of Table B.6 are plotted against price in Figure B.15. By comparing this figure with the previous one (Figure B.14), you can clearly see that the introduction to the sample of high-priced homes has created heteroskedasticity.

FIGURE B.15 **Error Terms Showing Heteroskedasticity**

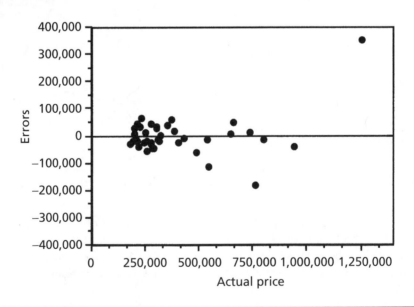

Effects of Heteroskedasticity

Pure heteroskedasticity can increase the variance of the estimated coefficients in a way that will cause the t and F values to come out stronger than what is warranted by the data. Therefore, though the estimates will remain unbiased, all the measures of hypothesis testing will be suspect. On the other hand, if there is impure heteroskedasticity resulting from a poor specification of the equation, its impact on the estimators will be similar to the effect of serial correlation discussed earlier.

Correcting Heteroskedasticity

The error of heteroskedasticity is primarily caused by a variable that is too diverse. For that reason, heteroskedasticity should be suspected in cross-section data with samples varying greatly in size. Time-series data stretching over a long period of time are also suspect, as are data series in which the magnitude of the dependent variable increases with time at a very high rate. If we are trying to predict the number of homicides in our city on the basis of the number of homicides committed this year in a large number of diverse cities and towns, we are likely to encounter heteroskedasticity. Also, it is likely to exist in time-series data showing the number of individuals with AIDS, since the actual number of individuals with the disease keeps increasing every year.

Heteroskedasticity can be detected with the help of some of the more sophisticated tests, which are beyond the scope of this introductory book. However, we may say a few words about correcting heteroskedasticity at this point. First, if heteroskedasticity is impure, it can be corrected simply by better specifying the model. To repeat our discussion of proper specification, developing a better model requires a great deal of hard work in thinking through the proper theoretical structure.

If, on the other hand, heteroskedasticity is pure, the very nature of the data causes the variance of the error terms to change, and we need to think about the dependent variable. For example, if we encounter strong heteroskedasticity in trying to work with data on the number of homicides in cities and towns across the nation, we may separate the sample into two groups: large cities and small towns. Or we may express the absolute numbers in ratios, such as homicide rate per 1,000 inhabitants. Sometimes this kind of data transformation can reduce the variance to such an extent that heteroskedasticity can be significantly reduced.

When the Data Are Imperfect

Finally, in forecasting with regression models, serious errors occur when the data are spurious. In statistics this situation is known as the error in variable, or the measurement problem. The problem can creep in because of various factors. Many sociological data, when available, often contain severe measurement errors. Thus, information on child and spousal abuse, rape, and incest are significantly underrepresented. Even economic data, such as unemployment or inflation figures, are often criticized for containing biases of all sorts. Unemployment data are typically collected by adding the numbers of all those who registered at unemployment offices. This list, then, does not include those whose unemployment benefits have run out, students or homemakers seeking employment for the first time, or the underemployed (those who are working at levels far below their capabilities, such as an engineer working as a waiter in a restaurant). The data on inflation are computed by comparing the prices of items in a basket of goods a "typical" consumer would buy. Because of wide differences in consumption habits, the inflation figures published by the Bureau of Labor Statistics are likely to affect individuals differently.

Therefore, when data containing biases are used in a regression model, the accuracy of statistical explanation and prediction is affected. Errors can occur if the dependent variable is biased or if there is measurement error in the independent variable as well. If the dependent variable contains measurement error but the independent variable is generally free of it, and the bias is random, then the measurement error will increase the errors of prediction, while the estimated coefficients remain unbiased. Thus, the predicted results will have more variation, although the estimated coefficients will be unbiased. In other words, if we were to repeat the experiment a sufficient number of times with different samples, the average of all the estimated coefficients would approach the actual coefficient. Theoretically at least, this is a lesser problem than the one caused by an error in the independent variable.

If the independent variables contain measurement biases, bias spreads through the error term (ε) in the estimated equation, and this problem cannot be corrected easily. In effect, this bias in the independent variable will cause the independent variable to be correlated with the error term (ε).[9]

Beta Coefficient: Measuring the Relative Strength of the Independent Variables

The regression coefficients measure the slope of the independent variable in explaining the dependent variable. However, the size of the coefficient depends on the relative size of the independent variable. If you use actual years as independent variables (for example, 2001, 2002, 2003, and so on), the estimated coefficient will be much smaller than if you use time (1, 2, 3, and so forth). This change does not affect the R^2 value or the t and F values. It simply adjusts the absolute size of the coefficient to fit the relationship. Thus, when we estimate a quadratic relationship ($Y = a + bX + cX^2$), the estimated coefficient c turns out to be a lot smaller than b.

This dependence of the coefficients on the size of the independent variables may pose a problem for someone interested in finding out the relative strength of the independent variables in explaining the dependent variable. One way to determine this relative strength is to standardize the variables. You can standardize a variable by calculating

$$SD(X_i) = \frac{X_i - \overline{X}}{s} \tag{B.16}$$

where $SD(X_i)$ is the standardized value of the variable X, $\overline{X}$ is the mean of X_i, and s is the standard deviation of X_i.

Most statistical software packages provide you with the β coefficient along with the estimated coefficients of the nonstandardized variables.

SUMMARY: STEP-BY-STEP SUGGESTIONS FOR BUILDING A MODEL OF CAUSAL PREDICTION

1. **Develop a theory.** The first step in building a causal model is to have an excellent understanding of causality. Do a thorough job of reading the existing literature on the issues. Then, on the basis of your theoretical understanding of the relation between the dependent and independent variables, develop your hypothesis in terms of an implicit model.
2. **Operationalize variables.** Having developed your hypothesis, think of how you can measure the relevant variables. You have to make sure that you are measuring what you intend to measure and nothing else.
3. **Collect clean data.** If there are built-in biases, make sure you are aware of them and can make the necessary adjustments to your model.
4. **Plot the dependent variable against each independent variable.** To formulate the explicit functional form, plot the dependent variable against the independent variables. Determine which form is most appropriate.
5. **Estimate the regression equation** and make necessary adjustments to omit unnecessary variables and include necessary ones.
6. **Check for multicollinearity.** Calculate the correlation matrix. If the problem of multicollinearity is not acute, leave it alone. Otherwise, see if you can pick one variable from the collinear ones to represent the set. Also, see if adding the variables or taking the first difference makes theoretical sense.
7. If there is reason, **check for heteroskedasticity.**
8. **Check for serial correlation.** Use Durbin-Watson statistics, if available.
9. **Present estimation results clearly** and draw conclusions.
10. **Explain all the assumptions** and point out the possible sources of biases in your conclusions.

Tips: Go for parsimony. If two models explain approximately the same amount, choose the one with fewer variables. Moreover, **keep it simple**. Unless a more complicated functional form is truly necessary, choose the simpler one. When forecasting the future, remember that the error of estimation will flare out as you move away from the sample mean. Therefore, the difficulty of making accurate predictions increases exponentially as you go farther into the future.

EXERCISES

1. What is causal prediction? What are its advantages over trend projection? What are its relative shortcomings?
2. Refer to our estimated model of housing price in equation B.3, then comment on the following four units presently on the market:

	Area (square feet)	View	Cul-de-sac	Asking price ($)
a.	2,500	Yes	No	295,000
b.	3,200	Yes	Yes	325,000
c.	1,500	No	No	162,000
d.	1,950	No	Yes	182,000

To explain housing prices more thoroughly, what are some other variables you would include in the model?

3. Suppose you have been asked to forecast the crime rate of your city. You have decided to use a cross-sectional model of fifty-five cities across the nation.
   a. What measure of the dependent variable would you use?
   b. Which variables would you include as the independent variables, and what signs for their coefficients would you postulate?
   c. What would be the source(s) of your information?
   d. Explain the various statistical problems that you would face when estimating this model.
   e. What actions would you take to correct these problems?

4. Suppose your state legislature is considering legalizing a state-run lottery. One aspect of the lottery that is under scrutiny is the demographic profile of the prospective players. A survey of total yearly purchases of lottery tickets by 500 participants in a neighboring state shows the following relation:

$$\text{Total purchases} = 10.51 - 0.086 \text{ PI} + 1.23 \text{ Age} - 0.162 \text{ Ed} + 2.59 \text{ Min} + 3.05 \text{ Male}$$
$$t = (6.78) \quad (3.67) \quad (2.46) \quad (2.01) \quad (2.01) \quad (1.14)$$
$$R^2 = 0.68$$
$$\text{Adjusted } R^2 = 0.59$$
$$F(5,494) = 189.95$$
$$n = 500$$

where PI is personal income ($\times$ \$1,000), age is the age of the lottery player, ed is years of education, min is a dummy variable (minority = 1, nonminority = 0), and male is a dummy variable (male = 1, female = 0).
   a. Write a detailed report explaining the results.
   b. What are the important policy implications the legislators should be aware of?
   c. What are some of the other independent variables that could have been included?
   d. On the basis of this estimated model, how much are you expected to spend on the lottery per month?

5. The water utility department of your town has estimated the following model of water use per capita:

$$\text{PWU} = 15.64 + 1.86 \text{ Y} + 3.29 \text{ CH} + 2.87 \text{ AD} + 0.029 \text{ SQ} + 0.009 \text{ LS}$$
$$t = (2.39) \quad (7.85) \quad (3.99) \quad (1.99) \quad (2.53) \quad (2.01)$$
$$R^2 = 0.76$$
$$\text{Adjusted } R^2 = 0.74$$
$$F(5.344) = 189.95$$
$$n = 350$$

where PWU is per capita water use (in gallons), Y is income per household ($\times$ \$1,000), CH is the number of children in the house, AD is the number of adults in the house, SQ is the square footage of covered area, and LS is the lot size (land area).

Interpret this equation and write a report explaining the significance of these findings.

6. What are the possible sources of bias in the estimation of a classical least squares method? Explain the terms *multicollinearity*, *heteroskedasticity*, and *serial correlation*. Discuss how you would detect them in an estimated relationship. What are some of the ways of eliminating multicollinearity and heteroskedasticity?

7. Suppose there are fifteen counties in your state. You are given the current year's sales tax revenue and a number of independent variables. Estimate the equation and, on the basis of the projected growth of the independent variables, forecast the state's total sales tax revenue five years from now. Also, comment on the relative size of the β coefficients. (Hint: Estimate the equation, examine it for various errors, and, on the basis of the correct specification, reestimate the equation. Using the revised equation, forecast each county's tax revenue and then add the county revenue figures to forecast the state's tax revenue.)

	Current year's data			Forecasted data		
County	Tax revenue (× $1 million)	Population (×1,000)	Per capita income (× $1,000)	Land area devoted to agriculture (percent)	Population (×1,000)	Per capita income (× $1,000)
A	38.7	50.0	23.2	60.0	52.0	24.0
B	156.0	75.0	32.8	20.0	86.5	36.2
C	115.9	151.1	22.1	75.0	153.0	22.8
D	98.7	45.6	36.9	15.0	54.0	39.7
E	68.3	98.0	24.1	62.0	101.0	24.9
F	220.8	94.0	36.0	18.0	99.0	38.6
G	75.2	102.9	23.0	62.0	105.0	23.2
H	268.8	91.7	41.0	3.0	110.0	46.2
I	32.1	65.0	21.9	82.0	61.0	22.1
J	69.2	47.1	34.6	59.7	49.5	33.6
K	199.9	98.0	35.6	21.0	106.0	37.8
L	86.0	110.0	23.8	58.0	111.8	24.3
M	112.8	202.0	25.0	66.0	198.0	25.0
N	209.0	85.3	40.1	5.0	96.7	46.5
O	116.0	66.0	39.0	22.0	121.0	41.2

Notes

1. For an excellent discussion of computer-assisted mass appraisal of property value, see Glenn W. Fisher, *The Worst Tax? A History of the Property Tax in America* (Lawrence: University of Kansas Press, 1996), 176–186. See also J. Richard Aronson and Eli Schwartz, eds., *Management Policies in Local Government Finance*, 4th ed. (Washington, D.C.: International City/County Management Association, 1996), 211.

2. In most states, property tax is 1 percent of the assessed value.

3. I did not write the formula for deriving multiple regression coefficients. The formula is complex, and calculating it is extremely time consuming. For estimating multiple correlation,

you should familiarize yourself with available statistical packages. There are a number of excellent and user-friendly software programs, of which SPSS and Minitab are perhaps the most widely used.

4. Our problem has been compounded by the fact that we have a percentage measure as a dependent variable and are therefore restricted between 0 and 1. However, even without this restriction, higher order polynomials can quickly ascend or descend to absurd levels of prediction, particularly for the values of the independent variable outside the sample range.

5. You may test this statement by creating a linearly dependent variable and then including both independent variables in a regression model. Most software will give you an error message stating that the coefficients cannot be computed. A few software programs will give you highly imprecise estimates due to rounding errors.

6. The presence of multicollinearity is best determined by the test of variance inflation factor. However, this test is a bit too complicated for this book. See O. E. Farrat and R. R. Glauber, "Multicollinearity in Regression Analysis: The Problem Revisited," *Review of Economics and Statistics* (1967): 92–107; and David A. Belsley, Edwin Kuh, and Roy E. Welsch, *Regression Diagnostics: Identifying Influential Data and Sources of Collinearity* (New York: John Wiley, 1980). For an excellent overall discussion, see A. H. Studenmund, *Using Econometrics: A Practical Guide*, 2nd ed. (New York: HarperCollins, 1992).

7. This test is based on J. Durbin and G. S. Watson, "Testing for Serial Correlation in Least-Square Regression," *Biometrica* (1951): 159–177.

8. See, for example, Harry H. Kelejian and Wallace E. Oates, *Introduction to Econometrics: Principles and Applications* (New York: Harper & Row, 1981); and Studenmund, *Using Econometrics*.

9. This situation will be close to the simultaneous bias. However, the bias of simultaneity has been deliberately left out of this introductory book. Without explanation, I will simply state that this bias can be corrected by using the instrumental variable approach. If you are interested in learning more about this problem, see Peter Kennedy, *A Guide to Econometrics*, 4th ed. (Cambridge, Mass.: MIT Press, 1998). Also see Studenmund, *Using Econometrics*, or Robert S. Pindyck and Daniel L. Rubinfeld, *Econometric Models and Econometric Forecasts*, 2nd ed. (New York: McGraw-Hill, 1981).

Appendix C

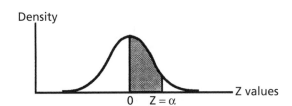

Density

0   Z = α

Z values

Areas of the Standard Normal Distribution (the Z table)

Z	0.00	0.01	0.02	0.03	0.04	0.05	0.06	0.07	0.08	0.09
0.0	.0000	.0040	.0080	.0120	.0160	.0199	.0239	.0279	.0319	.0359
0.1	.0398	.0438	.0478	.0517	.0557	.0596	.0636	.0675	.0714	.0753
0.2	.0793	.0832	.0871	.0910	.0948	.0987	.1026	.1064	.1103	.1141
0.3	.1179	.1217	.1255	.1293	.1331	.1368	.1406	.1443	.1480	.1517
0.4	.1554	.1591	.1628	.1664	.1700	.1736	.1772	.1808	.1844	.1879
0.5	.1915	.1950	.1985	.2019	.2054	.2088	.2123	.2157	.2190	.2224
0.6	.2257	.2291	.2324	.2357	.2389	.2422	.2454	.2486	.2517	.2549
0.7	.2580	.2611	.2642	.2673	.2703	.2734	.2764	.2793	.2823	.2852
0.8	.2881	.2910	.2939	.2967	.2995	.3023	.3051	.3078	.3106	.3133
0.9	.3159	.3186	.3212	.3238	.3264	.3289	.3315	.3340	.3365	.3389
1.0	.3413	.3438	.3461	.3485	.3508	.3531	.3554	.3577	.3599	.3621
1.1	.3643	.3665	.3686	.3708	.3729	.3749	.3770	.3790	.3810	.3830
1.2	.3849	.3869	.3888	.3907	.3925	.3944	.3962	.3980	.3997	.4015
1.3	.4032	.4049	.4066	.4082	.4099	.4115	.4131	.4147	.4162	.4177
1.4	.4192	.4207	.4222	.4236	.4251	.4265	.4279	.4292	.4306	.4319
1.5	.4332	.4345	.4357	.4370	.4382	.4394	.4406	.4418	.4429	.4441
1.6	.4452	.4463	.4474	.4484	.4495	.4505	.4515	.4525	.4535	.4545
1.7	.4554	.4564	.4573	.4582	.4591	.4599	.4608	.4616	.4625	.4633
1.8	.4641	.4649	.4656	.4664	.4671	.4678	.4686	.4693	.4699	.4706
1.9	.4713	.4719	.4726	.4732	.4738	.4744	.4750	.4756	.4761	.4767
2.0	.4772	.4778	.4783	.4788	.4793	.4798	.4803	.4808	.4812	.4817
2.1	.4821	.4826	.4830	.4834	.4838	.4842	.4846	.4850	.4854	.4857
2.2	.4861	.4864	.4868	.4871	.4875	.4878	.4881	.4884	.4887	.4890
2.3	.4893	.4896	.4898	.4901	.4904	.4906	.4909	.4911	.4913	.4916
2.4	.4918	.4920	.4922	.4925	.4927	.4929	.4931	.4932	.4934	.4936
2.5	.4938	.4940	.4941	.4943	.4945	.4946	.4848	.4949	.4951	.4952
2.6	.4953	.4955	.4956	.4957	.4959	.4960	.4961	.4962	.4963	.4964
2.7	.4965	.4966	.4967	.4968	.4969	.4970	.4971	.4972	.4973	.4974
2.8	.4974	.4975	.4976	.4977	.4977	.4978	.4979	.4979	.4980	.4981
2.9	.4981	.4982	.4982	.4983	.4984	.4984	.4985	.4985	.4986	.4986
3.0	.4987	.4987	.4987	.4988	.4988	.4989	.4989	.4989	.4990	.4990
3.5	.4998	.4998	.4998	.4998	.4998	.4998	.4998	.4998	.4998	.4998

Note: Suppose you want to find the area under the standard normal curve between the values $Z = 0$ and $Z_a = 1.77$. In that case, read down the first column of Z values and locate the row for $Z = 1.7$. Then read along this row and find the number corresponding to the column 0.07 (in effect, you have added 1.70 to 0.07 to obtain the value for 1.77). This value is .4616.

Appendix D

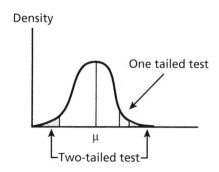

Density

One tailed test

μ

└─Two-tailed test─┘

Critical Values of the *t* Distribution

	Level of significance				
	One-tailed test				
	10%	*5%*	*2.5%*	*1%*	*0.5%*
Degrees of	*Two-tailed test*				
freedom	*20%*	*10%*	*5%*	*2%*	*1%*
1	3.078	6.314	12.706	31.821	63.657
2	1.886	2.920	4.303	6.965	9.925
3	1.638	2.353	3.182	4.541	5.841
4	1.533	2.132	2.776	3.747	4.604
5	1.476	2.015	2.571	3.365	4.032
6	1.440	1.943	2.447	3.143	3.707
7	1.415	1.895	2.365	2.998	3.499
8	1.397	1.860	2.306	2.898	3.355
9	1.383	1.833	2.262	2.821	3.250
10	1.372	1.812	2.228	2.764	3.169
11	1.363	1.796	2.201	2.718	3.106
12	1.356	1.782	2.179	2.681	3.055
13	1.350	1.771	2.160	2.650	3.012
14	1.345	1.761	2.145	2.624	2.977
15	1.341	1.753	2.131	2.602	2.947
16	1.337	1.746	2.120	2.583	2.921
17	1.333	1.740	2.110	2.567	2.898
18	1.330	1.734	2.101	2.552	2.878
20	1.325	1.725	2.086	2.528	2.845
21	1.323	1.721	2.080	2.518	2.831
22	1.321	1.717	2.074	2.508	2.819
23	1.319	1.714	2.069	2.500	2.807
24	1.318	1.711	2.064	2.492	2.797
25	1.316	1.708	2.060	2.485	2.787
26	1.315	1.706	2.056	2.479	2.779
28	1.313	1.701	2.048	2.467	2.763
30	1.310	1.697	2.042	2.457	2.750
60	1.296	1.671	2.000	2.390	2.660
120	1.289	1.658	1.980	2.358	2.617
Infinity (normal distribution)	1.282	1.645	1.960	2.326	2.576

Appendix E

Critical Values of the F Statistic: 5 Percent Level of Significance

		v_1 = degrees of freedom for numerator								
	1	**2**	**3**	**4**	**5**	**6**	**7**	**8**	**10**	**20**
1	161	200	216	225	230	234	237	239	242	248
2	18.5	19.0	19.2	19.2	19.2	19.3	19.4	19.4	19.4	19.4
3	10.1	9.55	9.28	9.12	9.01	8.94	8.89	8.85	8.79	8.66
4	7.71	6.94	6.59	6.39	6.26	6.16	6.09	6.04	5.96	5.80
5	6.61	5.79	5.41	5.19	5.05	4.95	4.88	4.82	4.74	4.56
6	5.99	5.14	4.76	4.53	4.39	4.28	4.21	4.15	4.06	3.87
7	5.59	4.74	4.35	4.12	3.97	3.87	3.79	3.73	3.64	3.44
8	5.32	4.46	4.07	3.84	3.69	3.58	3.50	3.44	3.35	3.15
9	5.12	4.26	3.86	3.63	3.48	3.37	3.29	3.23	3.14	2.94
10	4.96	4.10	3.71	3.48	3.33	3.22	3.14	3.07	2.98	2.77
11	4.84	3.98	3.59	3.36	3.20	3.09	3.01	2.95	2.85	2.65
12	4.75	3.89	3.49	3.26	3.11	3.00	2.91	2.85	2.75	2.54
13	4.67	3.81	3.41	3.18	3.03	2.92	2.83	2.77	2.67	2.46
14	4.60	3.74	3.34	3.11	2.96	2.85	2.76	2.70	2.60	2.39
15	4.54	3.68	3.29	3.06	2.90	2.79	2.71	2.64	2.54	2.33
16	4.49	3.63	3.24	3.01	2.85	2.74	2.66	2.59	2.49	2.28
17	4.45	3.59	3.20	2.96	2.81	2.70	2.61	2.55	2.45	2.23
18	4.41	3.55	3.16	2.93	2.77	2.66	2.58	2.51	2.41	2.19
19	4.38	3.52	3.13	2.90	2.74	2.63	2.54	2.48	2.38	2.16
20	4.35	3.49	3.10	2.87	2.71	2.60	2.51	2.45	2.35	2.12
21	4.32	3.47	3.07	2.84	2.68	2.57	2.49	2.42	2.32	2.10
22	4.30	3.44	3.05	2.82	2.66	2.55	2.46	2.40	2.30	2.07
23	4.28	3.42	3.03	2.80	2.64	2.53	2.44	2.37	2.27	2.05
24	4.26	3.40	3.01	2.78	2.62	2.51	2.42	2.36	2.25	2.03
25	4.24	3.39	2.99	2.76	2.60	2.49	2.40	2.34	2.24	2.10
30	4.17	3.32	2.92	2.69	2.53	2.42	2.33	2.27	2.16	1.93
60	4.00	3.23	2.84	2.61	2.45	2.34	2.25	2.18	2.08	1.84
120	3.92	3.07	2.68	2.45	2.29	2.18	2.09	2.02	1.91	1.66
Infinity	3.84	3.00	2.60	2.37	2.21	2.10	2.01	1.94	1.83	1.57

v_2 = degrees of freedom for denominator

Note: The F statistic is a joint probability distribution that measures statistical significance on the basis of two-sided hypotheses about more than one regression coefficient at a time. Unlike the t statistic, the F statistic is measured by two sets of degrees of freedom. The degrees of freedom for the numerator (the column values), v_1, is calculated by K, the number of restrictions (coefficients for the independent variables plus the intercept term), and the denominator (the row values), $v_2 = n - K - 1$, where n is the number of observations. Thus, if in an estimated equation there are fifty observations and five independent variables, the numerator value (v_2) for the F statistic is 5 + 1 = 6, and the denominator value (v_2) is 50 − 5 − 1 = 44. Since we do not have the exact value corresponding to these degrees of freedom, approximate it with the closest number, which is $F(6, 30) = 2.42$.

Appendix F

Critical Values of the F Statistic: 1 Percent Level of Significance

		v_1 = degrees of freedom for numerator								
	1	**2**	**3**	**4**	**5**	**6**	**7**	**8**	**10**	**20**
1	4,052	5,000	5,403	5,625	5,764	5,859	5,928	5,982	6,056	6,209
2	98.5	99.0	99.2	99.2	99.3	99.3	99.4	99.4	99.4	99.4
3	34.1	30.8	29.5	28.7	28.2	27.9	27.7	27.5	27.2	26.7
4	21.2	18.0	16.7	16.0	15.5	15.2	15.0	14.8	14.5	14.0
5	16.3	13.3	12.1	11.4	11.0	10.7	10.5	10.3	10.1	9.55
6	13.7	10.9	9.78	9.15	8.75	8.47	8.26	8.10	7.87	7.40
7	12.2	9.55	8.45	7.85	7.46	7.19	6.99	6.84	6.62	6.16
8	11.3	8.65	7.59	7.01	6.63	6.37	6.28	6.03	5.81	5.36
9	10.6	8.02	6.99	6.42	6.06	5.80	5.61	5.47	5.26	4.81
10	10.0	7.56	6.55	5.99	5.64	5.39	5.20	5.06	4.85	4.41
11	9.65	7.21	6.22	5.67	5.32	5.07	4.89	4.74	4.30	4.10
12	9.33	6.93	5.95	5.41	5.06	4.82	4.64	4.50	4.10	3.86
13	9.07	6.70	5.74	5.21	4.86	4.62	4.44	4.30	3.94	3.66
14	8.86	6.51	5.56	5.04	4.70	4.46	4.28	4.14	3.80	3.51
15	8.68	6.36	5.42	4.89	4.56	4.32	4.14	4.00	3.69	3.37
16	8.53	6.23	5.29	4.77	4.44	4.20	4.03	3.89	3.59	3.26
17	8.40	6.11	5.19	4.67	4.34	4.10	3.93	3.79	3.51	3.16
18	8.29	6.01	5.09	4.58	4.25	4.01	3.84	3.71	3.43	3.08
19	8.19	5.93	5.01	4.50	4.17	3.94	3.77	3.63	3.37	3.00
20	8.10	5.85	4.94	4.43	4.10	3.87	3.70	3.56	3.31	2.94
21	8.02	5.78	4.87	4.37	4.04	3.81	3.64	3.25	3.51	2.88
22	7.95	5.72	4.82	4.31	3.99	3.76	3.59	3.45	3.26	2.83
23	7.88	5.66	4.76	4.26	3.94	3.71	3.54	3.41	3.21	2.78
24	7.82	5.61	4.72	4.22	3.90	3.67	3.50	3.36	3.17	2.74
25	7.77	5.57	4.68	4.18	3.86	3.63	3.46	3.32	3.13	2.70
30	7.56	5.39	4.51	4.02	3.70	3.47	3.30	3.17	2.98	2.55
40	7.31	5.18	4.31	3.83	3.51	3.29	3.12	2.99	2.80	2.37
60	7.08	4.98	4.13	3.65	3.34	3.12	2.95	2.82	2.63	2.20
120	6.85	4.79	3.95	3.48	3.17	2.96	2.79	2.66	2.47	2.03
Infinity	6.63	4.61	3.78	3.32	3.02	2.80	2.64	2.51	2.32	1.88

v_2 = degrees of freedom for denominator

Appendix G

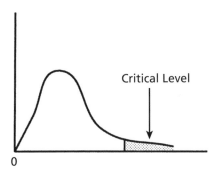

Critical Level

0

The Chi-square Distribution

Degrees of freedom	Level of significance (probability of a value of at least as large as the table entry)			
	10%	*5%*	*2.5%*	*1%*
1	2.71	3.84	5.20	6.63
2	4.61	5.99	7.38	9.21
3	6.25	7.81	9.35	11.34
4	7.78	9.49	11.14	13.28
5	9.24	11.07	12.83	15.09
6	10.64	12.59	14.45	16.81
7	12.02	14.07	16.01	18.48
8	13.36	15.51	17.53	20.1
9	14.68	16.92	19.02	21.7
10	15.99	18.31	20.5	23.2
11	17.28	19.68	21.9	24.7
12	18.55	21.0	23.3	26.2
13	19.81	22.4	24.7	27.7
14	21.1	23.7	26.1	29.1
15	22.3	25.0	27.5	30.6
16	23.5	26.3	28.8	32.0
17	24.8	27.6	30.2	33.4
18	26.0	28.9	31.5	34.8
19	27.2	30.1	32.9	36.2
20	28.4	31.4	34.2	37.6

Index

Figures and tables are indicated by f and t following page numbers.

Abandoned Mine Reclamation Fund, 91
Absolute measure of efficiency, 16
Abu Ghraib prison abuses, 37
Academic performance, ranking of nations, 4, 4t
Academics as analysts, 28
Accuracy
  of measuring scales, 178–179, 179f
  of simple regression analysis, 278–280
ACLU (American Civil Liberties Union), 84
Actions, 323
  alternate courses of, 103–105
Adjusted R^2, 303–304
Adjustment and anchoring as biases, 127
Adoption lag and delay in policy implementation, 67
Advanced searches, 194
Advocacy, 233–234
  analysts and, 28–34
Affirmative action plans, 120
African Americans
  life insurance of, 223
  tyranny of the majority and, 21
Agenda setting models, 76–87
  cost-benefit analysis, 86–87
  neglect or deliberate inaction and, 89–91, 90f
  pluralist vs. elitist models, 83, 83t

school safety as example of pluralist model, 84
types of, 76–77
AIDS, information about, 197, 227–228, 230, 234
Aitkens, Alexander, 317
Akerlof, George, 67, 68, 73, 74, 343
Alchain, Armen, 25
Alexander, Matthew, 44
Allais, Maurice, 125, 130
Allais paradox, 124–125, 331
Allocation, 53
Alonso, William, 197, 202
Alternate courses of action, 103–105
  consistency with goals, 103
  evaluation of, 104
  feasibility of, 103
  forecasting, 103
  identification of, 103
  policy goal achievement and, 4–5
American Civil Liberties Union (ACLU), 84
American Economic Association, 39
American Enterprise Institute, 28
Ames, E., 280, 317
Analysis of historical data, 249–269, 311–313. *See also* Projection techniques
Analysts, role and tools of, 27–45
  client groups of, 28

domain of, 29
limitations of, 38–39
models of analysis, 30–32, 31f
quantitative techniques, use of, 35–40
statistical techniques used by, 42–43
types of analysts, 28–34
Analytical constraints on role of government, 66–67
Anchoring as bias, 122, 127
Anderson, Benedict, 13, 25
Anderson, James E., 98, 99
Animal spirit, 67
Annual Statistical Abstract of the United States, 196
Anonymity, 233
Antilog, 301
Aronson, J. Richard, 344
Ascher, William, 45
Assumption of continuity, 225
Assumptions regarding human behavior, 38–39
Asymmetric distributions, 143–144, 143–144t, 143f. *See also* Symmetric distribution
Asymptotic convergence, 133
Asymptotic probability, 151
Audience, knowledge of, 383
Autoregressive model, 311
Availability of information, 122, 125–126
Average price vs. marginal costs, 51

Axelrod, Robert, 340, 344
Ayton, Peter, 176

Baade, Robert A., 129
Bachrach, Peter, 99
Bagley, Charles E., 371
Bailout money, 8, 16
Baim, Dean V., 129
Baker, James, 36
Baldassare, Mark, 344
Ball, George, 387
Banking crisis of 2008, 10–11
Bank insurance, 68
Banks, Arthur, 202
Baratz, Morton S., 99
Bar charts, 144, 210
Bardach, Eugene, 379, 387
Bardes, Barbara A., 100
Bargaining, 341
Bar graphs, 144, 210
Barrett, Louise, 25
Barrett, William P., 202
Baseball and probability, 152–153
Base figure, 209
Battle of the Bismarck
    Sea (game theory case), 335, 335–336f
Baumol, William J., 25, 74
Beck, Douglas, 248
Becker, Gary S., 370
Behavioral models, 88
Behn, Robert, 377, 387
Behrens, William W., III, 269
Bell curve, 141–142
Benefits analysis. *See* Cost-benefit analysis
Bentham, Jeremy, 106
Bernanke, Ben, 14
Bernstein, Carl, 36
Beta coefficient, 276
Biases
    awareness of, 375–376
    in data/observations, 39
    ideological, 41, 42
    of imaginability, 126
    of reasoning, 122–127, 321

in statistical interpretation, 214
    systematic, 42
Biddie, Andrea K., 371
bin Laden, Osama, 13, 33
Birkland, Thomas, 83, 85, 99
Birody, Dan, 130
"Blackmail" potential, 103–104
Black Panthers, 9
Blaug, Mark, 73
Blimes, Linda, 99
Boolean searches, 194
Borger, Mya M., 129
Bradford, David F., 370
Brandt, Allan, 44
Brewer, Gary D., 96, 100
Brinkley, Joel, 73
Broad, William, 388
Brookings Institution, 28, 41
Brooks, David, 10–11
Bruce, Neil, 75
Budget, federal
    deficit as percentage of GDP, 297–299, 297t, 298f, 298t, 299f
    systems vs. incremental approach, 35–36
    2000 presidential election debate over surplus, 266
Bueno de Mesquita, Bruce, 242, 248, 344
Buford, Bill, 25
Bulow, Jeremy, 344
Burchell, Robert W., 247
Bureaucracy
    elitist model of agenda setting and, 81, 81f
    pluralist model of agenda setting and, 77, 77f
Bureau of Labor Statistics, 199, 205
Bush, George H. W., 36, 243, 245
Bush, George W.
    Abu Ghraib prison abuses, 37
    antiterrorism actions of, 32

Enron investigation and, 36–37
Halliburton and, 118–119
ideological slant of efficiency and, 17–18
neocon counterterrorism policy of, 33
9/11 terrorist attacks, 22
presidential debates (2000), 266
presidential election (2004), 12
Butts, R. E., 344

Cagan, Joanna, 129
California. *See also* San Diego, California
    defense expenditures, 120
    DNA testing of criminal defendants, 91
    electricity deregulation, 68
    gold rush, 292
    immigration controversy, 51
    Mammoth, and predictions of volcano eruption, 265
    milk producers, 56
    Orange County bankruptcy, 332–333
    Proposition 13 (tax revolt), 70, 332–333
Campaign contributions, 282–283
Capital punishment. *See* Death penalty
Carter, Douglas, 98
Carter, Jimmy, 12, 91, 121
Case study method, 230
Casti, John, 38, 45, 99, 176, 344
Catastrophic trend, 255–256, 256f
Categorical precedence and pluralist model of agenda setting, 80
Cato Institute, 28
Causal connections/links, identification of, 109, 110f, 114, 225

Causal regression model, 353–354

CDC (Centers for Disease Control), 78, 197

Census Bureau, 40

Census Bureau Catalog and Guide, 196

Census of Governments, 196

Center on Budget and Policy Priorities, 267

Centers for Disease Control (CDC), 78, 197

Central Intelligence Agency (CIA), 21, 197, 245

Central limit theorem, 155–156

Central tendency, 131, 132–137, 144

Chances, failure to self-correct and dilution, 123–124

Chandler, Ralph C., 130

Changes in slope, 292–296, 292t, 293f, 295f, 296t

Changes in trend, 288–292, 288t, 289–290f

Chatterjee, Pratap, 129

Cheney, Dick, 18, 33, 37, 118–119

Cheung, Richard, 344

Chi-squared test, 165–169

Choi, Young Back, 321, 343

CIA. *See* Central Intelligence Agency

Cialdini, Robert, 26

Citizen activist groups
elitist model of agenda setting and, 81, 81f
pluralist model of agenda setting and, 77, 77f

Citron, Robert, 332–333

Clark, Christie, 75

Clarke, Richard, 33

Class divisions in presidential voting, 132f

Classification of goods, 6–7, 6t

Clayton Act of 1914, 54

Clean Air Act of 1990, 37, 71

Clines, Francis X., 99

Clinton, Bill
banking regulations and, 11
navy ships, 64
oil industry and, 55
terrorist attacks and, 33

Club goods (common pooled resources), 6t, 7

Cluster samples, 186

Coalitions formed around institutional agendas, 92, 93f

Coase, Ronald, 71

Cobb, Roger, 77, 80, 98

COE (U.S. Army Corps of Engineers), 325, 343

Coefficient for trend (slope), 275

Coefficient of determination. *See* R^2

Coefficient of variation, 141

Coefficients
beta coefficient, 276
relevance of estimated coefficients, 280–283
significance of individual coefficients, 283–286, 286t
significance when taken together, 304–305

Coequal (nonhierarchical) model, 31, 31f

Cohen, David K., 21, 36–37, 45

Cohen, Richard, 99

Collapse (Diamond), 9

Collection bias, 182

Collection costs, outweighing benefit of charging fees, 72

Collection of data. *See* Sources of data; Surveys

Collective action problem, 8

Collectively exhaustive inclusion of alternatives in decision tree, 324

Columbine High School incident, 84

Column marginal, 166

Common good, 39

Common log, 301

Common pooled resources (club goods), 6t, 7

Community security, 23

Comparable city method, 230

Comparison of different series of numbers, 162–164

Compound interest, 355

Conditional forecasting, 306–307

Confidence interval, 159–161

Conflict, 89–91

Conflict in values, responses to, 32–34, 34f, 36–37

Conflict of interest, 42

Congress
agenda setting by, 77
policy adoption considerations, 91–92
self-interest and ideology as influencing, 92

Congressional Budget Office, 198, 266, 362, 375

Consequences, forecasting, 116–117

Consistency with goals, 103

Consolidated policy change, 95

Constant, 133

Constant vs. current dollars, 204–208, 204t, 205f, 207f, 208t

Constitution, U.S., 5
Fourth Amendment, 37

Consumer price index, 206–207, 206t, 214

Consumer surplus, 50, 50f, 346, 350, 350f

Consumption efficiency, 70

Contingency table, 165, 166t

Control variables, 89, 109, 110f

Convincing decision makers, 385–386

Core values of policy coalitions, 92

Correlation analyses, 114, 114t

Correlation coefficient (Pearson's r), 145–147, 146f, 147t, 167

Corrigan, Tim, 224

Cost-benefit analysis, 345–371
  agenda setting using, 86–87
  case study using, 367–368
  choice of best alternative,
    364–368, 365*t*
  choice of discount rate,
    360–362
  classifications of, 348, 348*f*
  defining goals, 346
  estimation of costs and
    benefits, 349*t*, 350–355
  examples of, 120
  forecasting using, 88–89
  identifying alternatives,
    346–347
  intangible costs and benefits,
    348, 351–353, 354
  internal rate of return,
    362–363, 363*f*
  listing alternatives' costs and
    benefits, 347–348
  measurement of future loss
    or gain, 353–355
  policy cycle and, 5
  present value analysis,
    355–363. *See also*
    Present value
  public goods allocation
    and, 7
  ratio, 364–365
  redistribution of income,
    366
  social vs. private, 346–347
  steps in process of, 346
  valuation of costs and
    benefits, 349*t*, 350–355
Cost-effectiveness analysis,
  366–368
County and City Data Book,
  196
County Yearbook, 196
Court agenda setting, 77
Credible commitment
  problem, 8
Crime rates, 114
  autoregressive model to
    forecast, 311–312, 312*t*

Critical thinking and research
  design, 101–130
  challenges to critical
    thinking, 122–127
  choosing method of analysis,
    109–115
  designing policy research,
    117–122
  goal setting, 104–109
  objective analysis, 102–104
Critical value, 158
Cross-section analyses, 114
Cullen, Dave, 99
Cultural constraints on role of
  government, 65
Cumulative probability
  distribution, 151, 153*t*
Current vs. constant dollars,
  204–208, 204*t*, 205*f*,
  207*f*, 208*t*
Curve fitting, forecasting by,
  312–313
Cyclical trend, 252

Damasio, Antonio, 11–12, 25
D.A.R.E. (Drug Abuse
  Resistance Education), 88
Databases, 195
Data sources, 177–202. *See also*
  Sources of data
Davis, Robert K., 130
Death penalty, 90–91, 95
Deceptive use of statistics,
  213–222
Decision making
  choice of best alternative,
    364–368, 365*t*
  criteria for choosing among
    alternatives, 104
  expected payoff as factor,
    321–322, 330–332, 331*f*,
    334*t*
  game theory, 332–339. *See*
    also Game theory
  graphical methods in,
    211–212
  rules to apply under
    uncertainty, 338–339

Decision tree analysis,
  322–332
  actions, 323
  chance nodes, 323, 325
  collectively exhaustive
    inclusion of
    alternatives, 324
  decision nodes, 323, 325
  do-nothing option, 322–323,
    325, 327
  folding backwards, 330
  mutually exclusive
    alternatives, 324
  outcomes, 322–323
  payoffs, 323, 327, 330–332,
    331*f*, 334*t*
  probabilities, 323, 327
  structuring of tree, 324–325
Declaration of Independence
  (U.S.), 18, 63
Dede, Martha J., 248
de Graaf, Janny, 84, 99
Degrees of freedom, 140, 161
DeLeon, Peter, 37, 44, 45,
  96, 100
Delphi technique, 232–237
deMause, Neil, 129
Democracy, limits of, 63–64
Demsetz, Harold, 25
Dependent variables, 109, 110*f*,
  225, 275
  lag dependent variables,
    311–313
Deregulation, 68–69
Descartes, René, 3
Designing policy research,
  117–122
Diamond, Jared, 9
Dickey, Christopher, 26
Difference of proportions test,
  164–165
Diffuse costs and benefits,
  86–87, 86*t*
Direct costs and benefits, 348
Direct infusion of money, 69
Direct observation to collect
  primary data, 179
  errors due to, 182–184

Disasters' effect on agenda setting, 83–84

Disclosure of information, 57

Discounted future earnings method, 352

Discount rate, 356–359
  choice of, 360–362
  plot of present values as function of, 359*f*
  time preference and, 357*f*

Discrimination, 120, 223

Dispersion
  of distributions, 141–142, 141*t*
  ex post data, analysis of, 131
  measures of, 137–144, 152
  normal distributions with various levels of, 155*f*

Disraeli, Benjamin, 213

Dissertation Abstracts/Digital Dissertations, 200

Distribution
  bell-shaped distribution, 141–142
  dispersion of distributions, 141–142, 141*t*
  as government role, 53
  joint probability distribution, 167
  probability distribution, 151–157, 153*t*, 154*f*
  skewed distributions, 141–144
  of statistical summary, 233
  stem-leaf method, 144–145, 145*f*, 145*t*
  Z distribution, 158

Dixit, Avinash, 340–341, 343

DNA testing to determine guilt, 90–91, 96

Dominant strategy, 337, 338–339

Do-nothing option, 322–323, 325, 327

Douglas, Susan, 26

Downs, Anthony, 89, 90, 99

Druckman, James, 25

Drug Abuse Resistance Education (D.A.R.E.), 88

Drugs, illegal
  education about, 88, 115–116, 211–212, 212*f*
  forecasting use of, 1 15–116
  long-term programs for dealing with, 359
  regulation, 87
  trafficking, 56, 58, 87, 359

Drunk driving, 87

Dubnick, Melvin J., 100

Dummy variable, 288–292, 290*t*

Dunbar, Robin, 25

Dunn, William, 234, 248

Dye, Richard F., 129

Dye, Thomas R., 81, 98

e (equal to 2.71828), 301

Easton, David, 45

Ebbert, Stephanie, 73

EBSCOhost Academic Search Elite, 196

Economic analyses, fundamentals of, 49–52

Economic cycles, 252, 252*f*

Economic rationality, 50–51

Economic security, 23

Education. *See* Schools

Effectiveness of presentation, 382–386

Effectiveness of search, 126

Efficiency as policy goal, 15, 15*f*, 16–18

Efficiency-equity trade-off, 17, 19

Elder, Charles D., 98

Elections
  limits of democracy, 63–64
  polls, 182
  predictions, 243
  2000 presidential election, 216–217, 266
  2004 presidential election, 12

Electricity deregulation, 68

Elitist model of agenda setting, 77, 81–83, 81*f*

Elkind, Peter, 44

Ellerman, A. Denny, 75

Ellison, Brian, 93, 100

Eminent domain, 120

Emissions trading, 71

Endangered Species Act, 120, 121

Enron investigation, 36–37

Entrepreneurs, political, 13

Environment
  Animas-La Plata River project, 93
  Clean Air Act of 1990, 37, 71
  endangered species, 120, 121, 353
  energy and dam construction, 121
  Exxon *Valdez* settlement, 353
  knowledge constraints on role of government, 66
  PCBs, 352–353

Environmental security, 23

Equilibrium, 48–49, 48*f*

Equity as policy goal, 15, 15*f*, 17, 18–19

Equity-efficiency trade-off, 17, 19

Equity in distribution of income, 19

Erickson, Carrolly, 44

Errors. *See* Biases; Estimation errors; Random errors; Systematic errors in sampling

Error term, 277

Estimation errors, 274, 274*f*, 276

Estimation of costs and benefits, 349*t*, 350–355

Ethics
  public policy analysis and, 9–14, 40–42
  value conflict and, 32–34, 34*f*, 36–37

Evaluation
  of policy, 93–94
  of possible outcomes, 104

Evidence chosen to prove event, 124
Ex ante facto, 131
Ex ante forecasting, 306
Excludability as classification of goods, 6, 6t
Exhaustibility (rivalrous quality) of a good, 6, 6t
Expected payoff and decision making, 321–322, 330–332, 331f, 334t
Expected utility model, 242–244, 243–244f
Experience goods, 59
Experimental research designs, 110–112. See also Quasi-experimental research designs
Exponential trend, 254–255, 255f
Exports and imports
  institutional constraints on, 65–66
  mercantilism and, 47
Ex post facto, 131
Ex post forecasting, 306
Externalities
  awareness of, 376–377
  negative externalities, 59–61, 71, 104, 347
  positive externalities, 59–61, 103, 347, 362
  social costs and, 59–61
External threats to security, 21
Exxon Valdez settlement, 353

Face-to-face interviews, 189
Face value of life insurance method, 352
Factor mobility, 55
Factual information, 88
Fairness, 121–122
Falsifiability, 5
Family Support Act of 1988, 37
FAT. See Feasibility assessment technique
FDA (Food and Drug Administration), 76, 168

FDIC (Federal Deposit Insurance Corp.), 10, 68
Fear, 339–340
Feasibility assessment technique (FAT), 238–241
  calculated influence, 241t
  numbers, origin of, 244
  potential for influence, 240t
  relative issue positions, 238t, 239f
  resource availability, 239t
  resource rankings, 240t
Feasibility of alternatives, 103
Federal budget. See Budget, federal
Federal debt, 29
Federal Deposit Insurance Corp. (FDIC), 10, 68
Federal Emergency Management Agency (FEMA), 325
Federal Reserve, 14, 37
Feedback, 94
Feingold, Stephen, 197, 202
Feldman, Martha, 388
Felt, Mark ("Deep Throat"), 36
FEMA (Federal Emergency Management Agency), 325
FIA (fiscal impact analysis), 229–230, 229t
Financing of sports stadiums, 101, 103–106
Fineberg, Harvey V., 343
Fiscal impact analysis (FIA), 229–230, 229t
Fischer, Frank, 45
Fisher, Anthony C., 130
Fisher, Roger, 341, 344
Fisher, Ronald A., 317
Fixed weight, 205
Flood damage, 325–330
  decision tree for flood control, 326f, 328f
  decision tree with total expected costs, 329f
  estimation of, 325t, 327t
  probability of, 326f
  total estimated cost, 330t

Florida
  Palm Beach County's growth management policies, 191
  2000 presidential election results, 216–217
Focus events, 85
Focus groups, 190–192
Food and Drug Administration (FDA), 76, 168
Food security, 23
Forbes magazine, 29
Ford, Gerald, 91, 319–320, 322–324
Forecasting, 88–89. See also Probability; Projection techniques
  alternate courses of action, 103
  by curve fitting, 312–313
  history, inadequacy of, 225–226
  interval forecasts, 307–311, 310f
  least squares, 271–318. See also Least squares method
  multiple regression, 272, 287–296. See also Multiple regression
  point forecasts, 306–307
  politics of, 265–267
  problems of, 305–311
  random errors in, 273–274, 274f
  without relevant information, 124
Foucault, Michel, 24
Fourth Amendment, 37
Fowler, James, 26
Framers of Constitution, 30
Framing, 13
Frantz, Roger S., 73, 176, 387
Freed, Stanley, 129
Freeman, J.L., 98
Free market
  correction by government, 53

government and, 47–74
market failure, 52–62
perfectly competitive
    market, 53
Free riders, 8, 9, 87
F test, 305
Functional termination of
    policy, 96
Fundamental issue,
    identification of, 103

Galton, Francis, 124
Game theory, 332–339
    defection and its
        consequences, 339–340
    dominant strategy, 337,
        338–339
    local government decision
        making using, 337–338
    minimax strategy, 334, 337
    Nash equilibrium, 335, 337
    prisoner's dilemma,
        337–338, 338*t*
    tit-for-tat strategy, 340
    zero-sum games, 338–339
Gandhi, 13
GAO (Government
    Accountability Office),
    196, 362
Garbage can model of agenda
    setting, 82–83
Gart, Alan, 75
Gauss, Carl Friedrich, 317
GDP
    deflator, 206
    federal budget deficit as
        percentage of, 297–299,
        297*t*, 298*f*, 298*t*, 299*f*
    per capita, 271–273, 272*f*,
        288, 304
Geanakopolos, John, 344
*The General Theory of
    Employment, Interest and
    Money* (Keynes), 43
General will, 105
Geneva Convention, 22, 37
Gillespie, Kate, 73
Glaberson, William, 100

Glaeser, Bernhard, 129
Glass-Steagall Act of 1933, 11
Gleick, James, 179, 202
Glezer, Vadim D., 248
Goals
    consistency with, 103
    for cost-benefit analysis, 347
    of government intervention,
        15–23, 15*f*
    setting, 104–109
Goldhamer, Herbert, 44
Goleman, Daniel, 25
Gonzales, Elian, 78–79, 80
Gore, Al, 266
Gossett, W. S. *(Student),* 161
Gould, Stephen Jay, 224
Government Accountability
    Office (GAO),
    40, 196, 362
Governmental agendas, 76–77
Government decision making
    and game theory, 337–338
Government-funded
    institutes, 28
Government publications, 197
Government rate of return, 362
Government role
    failure of government, 62–67
    in free market, 47–74
    goals desired in policies of,
        15–23, 15*f*
    market correction, 53
    pervasiveness in daily life,
        1–2
Government staff
    analysts, 28
Gramlich, Edward, 370, 371
Graphical methods, 203–212
    choosing type of, 210–211,
        210*t*, 211*f*
    current vs. constant dollars,
        204–208, 204*t*, 205*f*,
        207*f*, 208*t*
    decision making and,
        211–212
    index, 209–210, 210*f*
    percentage change, 208–209,
        208*t*

pictorial presentation
    of data, 218–219*f,*
    218–220, 220*t*
tabular presentation of data,
    221–222, 222*t*
Gray, Scott, 176
Great Depression, 3, 10, 32,
    38, 52
Great Leap Forward plan, 17
Great Society program, 62, 292
Greed, 339–340
Greek characters for statistical
    terminology, 140, 277
Grossbard-Shechtman,
    Shoshana, 370
Gross domestic product.
    See GDP
Group consensus, 233
Grouped data, 136–137, 137*t*
Group identity, 12–14, 183
Groupthink, 232
Growth, 53
Guantanamo Bay detention
    center, 22, 32
Gun control. *See* Violence
Gupta, Dipak K., 25, 26, 99,
    202, 343, 387
Gurr, Ted, 202

Hagen, Ole, 130
Haidt, Jonathan, 14, 26
Halliburton, 118–119
Hamm, Mark, 26
*Handbook of Labor
    Statistics,* 196
Hanrahan, Jennifer, 98, 100
Haq, Mahbub ul, 23
Hardin, Garrett, 25
Harsanyi, John C., 344
Haskins, Ron, 41
Haveman, Robert H., 370
Hawthorne experiment, 183
Health care costs, 120, 225–226,
    226*f*
Health security, 23
Heath, Chip, 388
Heath, Dan, 388
Heclo, H., 98

Heineman, Robert A., 44

Heisenberg, Werner, 182, 382

Held, Virginia, 45

Helms, Jesse, 197

Henry, Clement M., 73

Henry, Patrick, 20

Heritage Foundation, 40

Heuristics, 122

Hicks, John, 107

Higher-order polynomials, 299–301, 300*f*

Highway construction, 366

Hinges, in statistics, 137, 139*f*

Hintikka, J., 344

Hirschman, Albert, 32, 34*f*, 44

Histograms, 144

Historical data analysis, 249–269, 311–313. *See also* Projection techniques

Hoffman, Bruce, 202

Hoffman, Frederick L., 223, 224

Holmstrom, Bengt, 25

Holtz, Robert Lee, 269

Homo economicus (self-utility-maximizing economic being), 8, 9, 13, 23, 39, 67

Honest graft situations, 42

Hoover Institution, 28

Horizontal trend, 251, 251*f*

Housing prices, 133*t*, 134

Hudson, Michael, 202

Huff, Darrell, 215, 218, 221, 224

Human behavior
    behavioral models, 88
    economic rationality to predict, 50

Human security, factors of, 23

Hurricane Katrina, 21, 83

Hussein, Saddam, 33, 245

Hypothesis testing, 157–165
    confidence interval and, 159–161
    critical value, 158
    level of significance, 157
    one-tailed test, 158, 159*f*

quantitative techniques of analysis and, 38
    risks in, 167–169, 168*t*
    steps in, 168–169
    t test, 161–162
    two-tailed test, 160–161, 161*f*, 162

ICMA (International City/County Management Association), 182

Ideological bias, 41, 42

Ideologies, 28–29

Illegal immigration, 182, 231

Illusory correlation, 126

Imaginability, 126

Implementation of policy, 5, 67, 92–93

Inadequacy of knowledge and uncertainty, 321

Income
    nominal income, 206
    real income, 206
    as welfare proxy, 118–119

Independent probability, 150

Independent variables
    intercept dummy variable, 288–292, 290*t*, 292
    irrelevant, 303–304
    method of analysis, 109, 110*f*
    prediction, 225
    regression model and, 275

Index, 209–210, 210*f*

Index to Current Urban Documents, 200

Indifference map, 357

Indirect costs and benefits, 348

Indivisibility, 56

Inefficiency, 18

Inflation, 206–207

Information disclosure restrictions, 57–59

In-house political analysts (staff analysts), 30–32

Input-output ratio (efficiency), 16

Institute for Social Research at University of Michigan, 198

Institutional agendas, 76–77
    conflict's effect on, 89–91
    nondecision's effect on, 89–91, 90*f*
    pluralist model and, 77–80, 77*f*

Institutional constraints on role of government, 65–66

Insurance
    African Americans and life insurance, 223
    bank insurance, 68
    face value of life insurance method, 352

Intangible costs and benefits, 348, 354

Integrity, 41–42

Intercept dummy variable, 288–292, 290*t*

Intercept term, 275, 285

Interdependence of human actions and uncertainty, 321

Internal rate of return, 362–363, 363*f*

Internal security, 22

International City/County Management Association (ICMA), 182

International Labour Organization, 28

International Monetary Fund, 28

Internet searches, 193–200, 194*f*

Interval forecasts, 307–311, 310*f*

Intervals, 136–137

Interval scales, 178

Intervening variables and research design, 112

Interviews. *See* Opinion polls

Inverse forms, 302–303, 303*f*

Invisible hand of market forces, 3, 21, 48–49

Iron triangle, 82

Irrelevant information, 123

Iteration, 233

Jacobson, Louis, 100

Janis, Irving, 248, 376, 387

Jenkins-Smith, Hank, 92, 98, 99, 100

Jensen, Ronald, 26

Jim Crow legislation, 21

Jodice, David, 202

Jodice, Michael, 182

Johnson, Arthur, 129

Johnson, Kirk, 370

Johnson, Lyndon B., 35, 62

Joint probability distribution, 167

JSTOR, 195, 196

Judgmental methods
problems of, 245
of projection, 227, 232–245
of sampling, 185

Judicial impartiality, 282–283

Kahneman, Daniel, 14, 26, 122, 124, 125, 130

Kaldor, Nicholas, 107, 129

Kaldor-Hicks compensation principle, 107–108, 119

Kaletsky, Anatole, 39

Kalt, Joseph, 91, 99

Kant, Immanuel, 3

Kantrow, Buster, 75

Kau, J. B., 99

Keefer, Philip, 26

Kelly, Raymond, 21

Kemperer, Paul, 344

Kennedy, Peter, 317

Kenney, George C., 335–337

Kernell, Samuel, 26

Kerry, John, 12

Keynes, John Maynard
animal spirit, 67
government role in market correction, 3, 52, 69
ideas, power of, 43, 45
policy termination, 96
political constraints, 65

Keynesian economics, 32

Keyword search, 194

Khemani, Stuti, 26

King, A., 98

King, Martin Luther, Jr., 9, 13

Kingdon, John, 82–83, 98

Kinsey, Alfred, 387

Klahr, David, 248

Klein, Joe, 20

Knight, Frank, 320, 343

Knowledge
of audience, 383
constraints on role of government, 66
inadequacy of, and uncertainty, 321
ordinary knowledge as approach to setting policy, 374–375, 383–384

Kotovsky, Kenneth, 248

Kranton, Rachel E., 343

Kreps, David M., 344

Krutilla, John V., 130

Kuran, Timur, 248, 343

Labor unions and game theory, 334–335, 337

Lad, Frank, 169, 176

Lag dependent variables, 311–313

Lagging, 261, 263

Lakoff, George, 5, 24

Lane, Robert, 122

Laplace, Pierre-Simon de, 317

Lasswell, Harold, 35, 44

LaVelle, Phillip J., 129

Law enforcement, 92. *See also* Violence

Law of large numbers, 155, 184, 281, 282, 284, 286

Lay, Kenneth, 36

Least squares method, 271–318
logic of, 272–275
multiple regression analysis, 272, 287–296. *See also* Multiple regression
nonlinear trends, 296–305
simple regression analysis, 271, 275–287, 277–278t. *See also* Simple regression model

Legal constraints on role of government, 66

Legalization, 68

Legalization of marijuana, 20

Legendre, Adrien-Marie, 317

Leibenstein, Harvey, 54, 73

Lerner, Daniel, 44

Lester, James P., 98, 100

Level of significance, 157

Lewis, Michael, 176

Lexis/Nexis Academic Universe, 196

Liberty as policy goal, 15, 15f, 17, 20–21

Liberty-security trade-off, 17, 22–23

Lichbach, Mark I., 45

Liebenstein, Harvey, 343

Lieberman, Trudy, 98

Life insurance
African Americans and, 223
face value of life insurance method, 352

Likert scales, 190

Lilla, Mark T., 43, 45

Lincoln, Abraham, 13

Lindblom, Charles, 36–37, 45

Linear functional form
choice of, 305
simple regression model of, 275–287, 277–278t

Linear policy change, 95

Linear trend, 250, 251f

Liquidity, 332

Listokin, David, 247

Literature review. *See* Sources of data

Liu, Zinan, 75

ln (natural log), 301

Lobbyists, 82, 82f

Local government decision making and game theory, 337–338

Logarithms and logs, 301–302, 302f

Logging moratorium, 353

Logistic trend, 254–255, 255f

Log-log functions, 301

Log-transformed forms, 301–302
Lotteries, 121
Lower hinge, 137
Lycett, John, 25
Lying in response to survey questions, 182
Lynd, Robert, 35, 44
Lynk, E. L., 75

Mabey, Nick, 98
MacArthur, Douglas, 335
Mafia, 340
Mailed questionnaires, 189
Mainzer, Lewis C., 44
Majone, Giandomenico, 130
Makridakis, Spyros, 269
March, James G., 81, 98
Marcos, Ferdinand, 243–244
Mares, David, 73
Marginal, 166
Marginal analysis, 49–51, 50f
Marginal costs and benefits of public goods, 64–65
Marginal revenue, 50–51
  vs. average price, 51
Margolis, Howard, 99, 343
Margolis, Julius, 370
Mariani, Mack, 148
Marijuana legalization and commercialization, 20
Market. See Free market
Market cost, 60
Market failure, 52–62
  barriers to entry and exit, 55–57
  externalities and social costs, 59–61
  lack of competition, 53–55
  restricted flow of information, 57–59
  rising service costs and, 61–62
Markov, Andrey, 317
Martin, Clyde, 387
Massachusetts, housing crisis in Boston, 47, 52

Master's theses as sources of data, 200
Mayer, Jane, 26, 44
Mayo, Elton, 183
Mazmanian, D., 99
McCafferty, Stephen, 45
McCall, Madhavi, 282–283, 318
McCollum, Kelly, 75
McDermott, Rose, 26
McGee, Victor, 269
McLean, Bethany, 44
McNamara, Robert, 388
Meadows, Dennis L., 269
Meadows, Donella, 269
Mean, 133–134. See also Central tendency
  comparison, 164, 164t
  population mean, 281
  of probability distribution, 152, 154f
  projecting by the mean, 263
  skewed distributions and, 144, 144t
Mean absolute deviation, 139, 139t
Median, 134. See also Central tendency
  skewed distributions and, 144, 144t
  stem-leaf method and, 144
Medicaid, 17
Meltsner, Arnold, 44
Mercantilism, 47
Michaels, Meredith, 26
Microeconomics, 51
Microsoft antitrust case, 53–54
Midspread, in statistics, 137, 139f
Mikesell, John, 371
Milgram, Stanley, 183, 202
Military
  expenditures, global, 21, 22f
  external factors in valuing loss of life, 352–353
  use of game theory, 335–337

Milk producers in California, 56
Mill, John Stuart, 20–21, 42
Miller, Gary, 25
Minimax strategy, 334, 337
Minimum wage, 56
Mitchell, E. J., 99
Mixture-in-administration model, 31–32, 31f
Mixture-in-policy model, 31f, 32
Mode, 134. See also Central tendency
Models of analysis for public policy
  choice of right model, 115–116
  coequal (nonhierarchical) model, 31, 31f
  definitions of, 115
  examples of, 31f
  limitations of, 38–39
  mixture-in-administration model, 31–32, 31f
  mixture-in-policy model, 31f, 32
  policy-administration dichotomy model, 30, 31f
  scientific analysis, steps in, 5
  types, 30–32
Monopolies, 53–55
Monroe, Kristen Renwick, 25
Moral hazard, 8, 10–11
Moral Majority, 241
Morgenstern, Oscar, 321
MOSAIC-2000, 84
Moving average, 260, 263–264, 264f
Mueller, John, 99
Multimodal response, 234
Multinational agencies, analysts and, 28
Multiple regression, 287–296. See also Estimation errors
  beta coefficient, 276
  changes in slope, 292–296, 292t, 293f, 295f, 296t

changes in trend, 288–292, 288*t*, 289–290*f*
defined, 272
Municipal Yearbook, 196
Mutually exclusive options in decision tree, 324
Mutually exclusive probability, 150
Myths, 126

Nachmias, Chava, 129
Nachmias, David, 129
Naive projection, 261–263, 262*t*
Nalebuff, Barry, 340–341, 343, 344
Nash, John, 335
Nash equilibrium, 335, 337
National Center for Public Policy and Higher Education, 60, 61
National Institutes of Health (NIH), 28
National Public Radio (NPR), 8, 14
National Science Foundation, 28
Natural log, 301
Needs assessments, 180
Negative correlation, 145–147
Negative externalities, 59–61, 71, 104, 347
Negative incentives, 88
Negatively skewed distribution, 142, 144
Negative trend, 249
Nelson, Barbara, 98
Net social benefit, 351
Neustadt, Richard E., 343
Newman, David, 248
"New public administration" of 1960s, 30–31
New York City and labor unions, 337
New York Police Department (NYPD), 21
New York Times, 10–11
NIMBY (Not In My Backyard) factor, 14, 353

9/11 terrorist attacks, 21, 22, 33
Nixon, Richard
  illegalities by, 36
  job performance of, 12
  Watergate crisis, 126
No-bid contracts, 18
Nominal income, 206
Nominal scales, 177
Nondecision, 89–91, 90*f*
Nongovernmental organizations, 28
Noninstitutional agendas, 76–77
Nonlinear policy change, 95
Nonlinear trends, 296–305
  inverse forms, 302–303, 303*f*
  irrelevant independent variables, 303–304
  log-transformed forms, 301–302, 302*f*
  polynomial forms, 296–299
Non-parametric tests, 167
Nonrepresentative samples, 181
Normal distribution, 152, 155*f*, 281, 281*f*
Null hypothesis
  coefficients and, 284, 305
  defined, 156–157
  rejection of, 159, 162, 285, 305

Obama, Barack
  antitrust policy, 55
  banking crisis and, 10–11
  economic stimulus, 3, 69
  equity-efficiency trade-off and, 19
  group identity and, 13
  job performance of, 12
  stimulus money and, 29
Objective analysis, 42–43
Objective probability, 149–169
Objective professionalism, 102
Objective sampling, 185–186
Observation, number needed for simple regression, 286–287, 287*f*
Observed frequency, 149–150

Office of Management and Budget (OMB), 39, 221, 362
Ohio school violence and safety, 84
Oil industry, 55
Oligopoly, 55, 56
Olsen, Johan P., 81, 98
Olson, Mancur, 8, 9–10, 25, 87, 99
One-shot case studies, 114
One-tailed test, 158, 159*f*
"On Liberty" (Mill), 20
Online searches, 193–200, 194*f*
Open society and problems of formulating policy for, 113, 114
Opinion polls, 180. *See also* Sources of data
  methods, 189
  survey instruments, 187–189
Opportunity costs, 16, 49, 52, 360
Ordinal scales, 178
Organizational termination of policy, 96
Ostrom, Elinor, 24, 39, 45
Ostrowski, John W., 248
Outcomes
  decision tree analysis, 322–323
  evaluation of possible outcomes, 104
  forecasting, 116–117
  policy outcomes, 94
  target outcome, 150
Outsourcing, 68, 69

Pabushka, Alvin, 248
PAIS. *See* Public Affairs Information Service
Pandemics, 78–79
Pareto, Vilfredo, 106
Pareto inferior, 107
Pareto principle, 106–107, 107*f*, 119
Pareto superior, 107

Passage of time, effect on research design, 114–115

Patton, Carl V., 129

PCBs, 352–353

Pearson, Clifford A., 202

Pearson's r, 145–147, 167

Pecuniary effect, 351

Pendleton Act of 1883, 30

Per capita multiplier method, 230

Percentage change, 208–209, 208t

Perfectly competitive market, 53

Performance evaluation, 94

Personal security, 23

Persuasion
of decision makers, 385–386
by statistics, 384–385

Pew Research Center, 12, 22

Ph.D. dissertations as sources of data, 200

Pictorial presentation of statistics, 218–219f, 218–220, 220t

Pie charts, 210

Pill, Juri, 248

Pindyck, Robert S., 176

Planning-Programming Budgeting System (PPBS), 35, 62

Plano, Jack, 130

Plato, 3

Pluralist model of agenda setting, 77–80, 77f, 85

Point forecasts, 306–307

Policy-administration dichotomy model, 30, 31f

Policy adoption, 67, 91–92

Policy analyst's role, 373–374, 374t

Policy change, 94–95

Policy cycle, 3–5, 75, 76, 76f

Policy Delphi technique, 233–234

Policy evaluation, 93–94

Policy formation, 75, 76, 76f, 87–91, 377–382

Policy objectives, 109, 110f

Policy outcomes, 94

Policy output, 94

Policy termination, 96–97

Political constraints on role of government, 65

Political entrepreneurs, 13

Political Science and Government, 200

Political security, 23

Politics
defined, 2
rationality and, 2–5

Polling methods, 189

Pollution. *See* Environment

Polynomial forms, 296–299

Pomeroy, Wardell, 387

Pontell, Henry N., 344

Popper, Karl R., 5, 40–41, 45, 129

Population, 133, 180

Population mean, 281

Population standard deviation, 281

"Pork barrel spending," 16

Positive correlation, 145–147

Positive externalities, 59–61, 103, 347, 362

Positive incentives, 88

Positively skewed distribution, 142, 144

Positive trend, 249

Post-test-only control group experimental design, 111–112, 112f, 113

Powell, Colin, 37

PPBS (Planning-Programming Budgeting System), 35, 62

Predictions. *See* Forecasting; Projection techniques

Prescription lag and delay in policy implementation, 67

Presentation, effectiveness of, 382–386

Present value, 355–363
choice of discount rate, 360–362
definition of, 356

internal rate of return, 362–363, 363f

long-term vs. short-term solutions, 359–360

President, U.S
agenda setting by, 77
policy adoption considerations, 91–92
Report of the President, 196

Price deflator, 204

Price increases in services, 61–62

Price indexes, 206

Price makers, 53

Price takers, 50, 53

Primary data, 88, 177, 179–189. *See also* Sources of data

Prisoner's dilemma, 337–338, 338t
strategies to overcome, 339–341

Private cost, 60

Private goods, 6–7, 6t

Privatization, 68, 69

Probability, 149–176
asymptotic, 151
baseball, 152–153
central limit theorem, 155–156
chi-squared test, 165–169
comparison of different series of numbers, 162–164
confidence interval, 159–161
decision tree analysis and, 323
distribution, 151–157, 153t, 154f
hypothesis testing, 157–165
independent events and, 150
joint probability distribution, 167
mutually exclusive events and, 150
null hypothesis, 156–157
number of tries and, 150–151, 151f, 322

objective probability, 149–169
Pearson's *r* (correlation coefficient), 167
risk vs. uncertainty, 320
subjective probability, 169–170, 170*t*
t distribution, 161–162, 284–285
Probability-based sampling, 185–186
Procedural justice, 121
Production efficiency, 70
Program termination, 96
Project acceptance or rejection, 119–121
Projection techniques, 225–318
adjustment methods, 256–260, 257*f*
analysis, elaborateness of, 378–382
analysis of historical data, 249–269
calculating the mean, 263
causal prediction vs., 225–226, 226*f*
choice of, 265
components of trend, 249–253, 250*f*, 253*f*, 256
Delphi technique, 232–237
expected utility model, 242–244, 243–244*f*
explaining the present with the past, 249–269, 311–313
feasibility assessment technique (FAT), 238–241. *See also* Feasibility assessment technique
fiscal impact analysis (FIA), 229–230, 229*t*
higher-order polynomials, 299–301, 300*f*
inadequate history available, 227–231
interval forecasts, 307–311, 310*f*
inverse forms, 302–303, 303*f*

irrelevant independent variables, 303–304
judgmental method of projection, 227, 232–245
least squares, 271–318
log-transformed forms, 301–302, 302*f*
moving average, 263–264, 264*f*
multiple regression, 272, 287–296
naive projection of immediate past, 261–263, 262*t*
nonlinear trends, 296–305
patterns of time trend, 253–256
point forecasts, 306–307
polynomial forms, 296–299
seasonal adjustment, 256–259, 258*t*, 259*f*
simple regression, 271, 275–287, 277–278*t*. *See also* Simple regression model
single-factor projection, 227–229, 230–231, 231*f*
smoothing out fluctuations, 260–265
trend adjustment, 259–260, 260*t*, 261*f*
Property values, 353–354
Proportions test, 164–165
ProQuest database, 195, 196
Prospect theory, 14
Public Affairs Information Service (PAIS)
PAIS International (online), 196
Public Affairs Information Service Bulletin, 200
Public goods
allocation of, 7–8, 53
care of, 9
costs of, 64–65
definition and classification, 6, 6*t*

ideological positions and, 18
Pareto principle applied to, 107
Public policy curriculum, 236–237
Public policy process, 75–100
agenda setting models, 76–87
behavioral models, 88
conflict, 89–91
costs and benefits analysis, 86–87
ethics and, 9–14, 40–42
forecasting, 88–89
goals of governmental interventions, 15–23, 15*f*
individualistic vs. collective societies and, 2
policy adoption, 91–92
policy change, 94–95
policy evaluation, 93–94
policy formulation, 87–91
policy implementation, 92–93
policy termination, 96–97
sensational events' impact on, 83–85
Public services, charging for, 70–72
Pure public goods, 6*t*, 7

al-Qaida, 33
Quade, E. S., 130
Quadratic score, 169, 170*t*
Quadratic trends, 253, 297, 298*t*, 299*f*
Qualitative change, 288
Quantification of survey data, 189–190
Quantitative techniques, use of, 35–40
Quasi-experimental research designs, 110, 112–115
Questionnaires. *See* Survey instruments
Quick decision making, 67–68, 144, 377–378

R^2 (coefficient of
determination)
adjusted R^2, 303–304
calculation of, 280*t*
defined, 279
problems when high, 280
$\bar{R}^2$, 303–304
*Race Traits and Tendencies
of the American Negro*
(Hoffman), 223
Racial profiling, 212–213
Rafool, Mandy, 128
Raiffa, Howard, 344
Randa, Laura E., 100
Randers, Jorgen, 269
Random errors
in forecasting, 273–274, 274*f*
in sampling, 184–185, 185*f*
in trends, 249–250
Random sampling, 185–186
Range, 137–138, 139*f*, 159
Ranking of resources, 240, 240*t*
Raphael, David D., 73
Rappaport, Anatol, 340
"Rational Fools" (Sen), 5
Rational fools, world of, 5–14
Rationality, 1–26
illogic of "rational beings,"
6–9
and politics, 2–5
un-rationality in political
behavior, 9–14
Rational model of decision
making, 35
Ratio scales, 178
Rawls, John, 42, 108, 129
Rawlsian criterion, 108, 119
Reagan, Ronald
defense budget and, 221
federal assistance to state and
local governments, 292
federal regulations and, 11
job performance of, 12
navy ships, 64
privatization and, 69
rational decision making
and, 35

on social welfare
inefficiency, 17
Real income, 206
Real terms, 207
Reason, rationality, and public
policy, 1–26
Recognition gap and delay
in policy
implementation, 67
Rector, Robert, 40, 41
Reggio, Michael H., 100
Regression analysis, 301
autoregressive model, 311
causal regression model,
353–354
multiple regression, 272,
287–296. *See also*
Multiple regression
simple regression, 271,
275–287, 277–278*t*. *See
also* Simple regression
model
Regression equation, 275
Regression toward the
mean, 124
Regulatory action for public
good, 9
Reiter, S., 280, 317
Relative frequency, 133, 149
Relative measure of efficiency
(opportunity cost), 16
Rent seeking, 18, 56–57, 57*f*,
118–119
Report of the President, 196
Representativeness, 122–125,
181
Required compensation
method, 352
Research design. *See* Critical
thinking and research
design
Research institutes (think
tanks), 28
Retrievability, 125–126
Revealed preference, 184
Reverse U-shaped pattern,
253–254, 254*f*

Ridley, Jasper, 44, 100
Risk
required compensation
method in risky jobs,
352–353
tolerance, 330–332, 331*f*
uncertainty vs., 320
Risk averters, 104, 331
Risk neutral, 331
Risk takers, 104, 331
Rivalrous quality
(exhaustibility) of a good,
6, 6*t*
Rivlin, Alice, 39, 45
Roe v. Wade (1973), 68–69
Roelithsberger, F. J., 183
Roosevelt, Franklin D., 10, 38,
65, 68, 181
Ross, Jennie-Keith, 98
Ross, Marc H., 98
Rousseau, Jean-Jacques, 105
Row marginal, 166
Rubin, P. H., 99
Rubinfeld, Daniel L., 176
Rumsfeld, Donald, 33, 37

Sabatier, Paul, 92, 98, 99, 100
Sabine, George, 105, 129
Sackman, Harold, 248
Sageman, Marc, 116, 129
St. Claire, G. K., 99
Saint-Germain,
Michelle A., 248
Samet, Jonathan N., 371
Sample error, 187
Sample population, 180,
185–186
Samples, 133
Sample size, 123
Sample standard
deviation, 140
Sampling theory, 180, 185–186
San Diego, California
garbage collection fees, 72
illegal immigration, 231
racial profiling in police
stops, 212

sports stadium, public
    financing of, 104
San Diego Union Tribune, 212
Sapolsky, Harvey, 130
Satisficing behavior in agenda
    setting, 83
Sawhill, Isabel, 41
Sawicki, David S., 129
Scatter plots, 210
Schattschneider, E. E., 99
Schick, Allen, 130
Schmid, Alex P., 84, 99
Schools
    benefits of free public
        education, 70
    California immigration
        controversy in, 51
    Drug Abuse Resistance
        Education
        (D.A.R.E.), 88
    higher education costs,
        52, 60–61
    safety and violence, 84
    testing, programs to improve
        performance, 93–94
    vouchers, 113
Schumpeter, Joseph, 25
Schwartz, Eli, 344
Scientifically based public
    policy, 373
Search engines, 194
Search goods, 57, 59
Searching for information, 126,
    193–200, 194f
Seasonal adjustment, 256–259,
    258t, 259f
Seasonal trend, 251, 252f
Seat belt use on Texas school
    buses, 367–368
Secondary data, 192–200
    defined, 177
    hypothesis testing, use
        in, 88
    online searches, 193–200,
        194f
    searching for information,
        193

Securities and Exchange
    Commission (SEC), 11, 11f
Security as policy goal, 15, 15f,
    21–22
Security-liberty trade-off, 22–23
Self-interest
    Congress, when voting on
        legislation, 87
    as determinant in agenda
        setting, 87
    as human motivation, 5–14
Self-selection bias within the
    sample, 181–182
Self-utility-maximizing
    economic being *(homo
    economicus),* 8, 9, 67
Self-utility-maximizing human
    being, 6
Sen, Amartya K., 5, 23, 24, 26,
    99, 343
Sensational events' impact on
    agenda setting, 83–85
Sensitivity analysis, 364
Service costs, 61–62
Service delivery systems, 180
Shadow price, 360
Sherman Act of 1890, 54
Shiller, Robert, 67, 68, 75
Significance tests
    hypothesis testing and level
        of significance, 157
    for individual coefficients,
        283–286, 286t
Silverstein, Arthur M., 343
Simon, Dorothea, 248
Simon, Herbert, 98, 248, 376
Simple regression model,
    275–287
    accuracy of results, 278–280
    estimation results, 286
    high R^2, 280
    linear trends, use in, 271
    number of observations
        needed for, 286–287, 287f
    population over time, 277t
    relevance of estimated
        coefficients, 280–283

significance of individual
    coefficients, 283–286,
    286t
straight-line regression
    equation calculations,
    278t
Simplicity and pluralist model
    of agenda setting, 80
Simulation of the market, 68,
    69–72
Singer, David, 198
Singh, Harinder, 176, 387
Single-factor projection,
    227–229, 230–231, 231f
Size of sample, 186–187
Skewed distribution, 142
Skewness and symmetry of
    distribution, 141–144
Slope dummy, 294, 294t
Small, Melvin, 198
SMCRA (Surface Mining
    Control and Reclamation
    Act), 91
Smirnov, Oleg, 26
Smith, Adam
    invisible hand, 21
    mercantilism, 47–48
    rationality, 3, 5, 24
    self-correcting market, 52
Smoking
    social costs of, 60
    teen smoking, 79–80
Snail darter, 121
Social costs and benefits,
    59–61, 346–347, 350,
    350f, 351
Social objectives, 106
Social Security, 17, 267
Social significance and
    pluralist model of agenda
    setting, 80
Social time preference, 361
Social tyranny, 21
Social welfare
    designing research for, 118
    problem of defining, 39, 63,
        107–108, 117

Solomon four-group
experimental design,
110–111, 111*f*
Sources of data, 177–202
accuracy of measuring scales,
178–179, 179*f*
choosing the sample
population, 185–186
focus groups, 190–192
online searches, 193–200,
194*f*
polling methods, 189
primary data, 88, 177,
179–189
print publications, 200
quantification of survey
data, 189–190
random errors in sampling,
184–185, 185*f*
reporting of survey results,
190
secondary data, 88, 177,
192–200
size of sample, 186–187
survey instruments, 187–189
systematic errors in
sampling, 180–184, 181*f*
terrorism research, 198–199
types of measurement,
177–178
unavailable data, 200
Soviet Union, 245
Space program, 292, 361
Specific costs and benefits,
86–87, 86*t*
Specificity and pluralist model
of agenda setting, 79–80
Split policy change, 95
Sports stadiums, financing
of, 101, 103–106, 105*t*,
117–118
Spotted owl, 353
Squared deviation, 275
S-shaped trend, 254–255, 255*f*
Stabilization, 53
Standard deviation, 140
population standard
deviation, 187, 281

of probability distribution,
152
sample standard deviation,
140, 187
Standard normal distribution,
152, 154, 155*f*
Starr, Paul, 197, 202
Stationary series, 251
*Statistical Abstract of the United
States,* 199
Statistically significant
coefficients, 284–285
Statistics, 131–148
behavioral model validated
by, 88
central limit theorem,
155–156
central tendency,
131, 132–137, 144
deceptive use of, 213–222
dispersion, 131, 137–144,
138*f,* 138*t*
government publications
of, 197
grouped data, 136–137, 137*t*
interpretation of, 214–221
lagging, 261, 263
methods of descriptive
statistics, 131–147
persuasion by, 384–385
pictorial presentation of,
218–219*f,* 218–220, 220*t*
presentation of, 203–224
printed publication of
government data, 200
skewness and symmetry of
distribution, 141–144
stem-leaf method, 144–145,
145*f,* 145*t*
tabular presentation of,
221–222, 222*t*
techniques used for analysis,
42–43
weighted estimates, 135–136,
136*t*
STAT-USA, 199
Stem-leaf method, 144–145,
145*f,* 145*t*

Stewart, Joseph, 98, 100
Stiglitz, Joseph, 99
Stimulation of the market,
68–69
Stockholm International Peace
Research Institute, 21
Stokey, Edith, 117, 130,
363, 371
Stone, Deborah A., 26, 99
Stonecash, Jeffrey, 148
Stratified sampling, 186
Strikes, 334–335, 337
Structured conflict, 234
Student's *T* distribution,
161–162, 284–285
Subgovernmental model of
agenda setting, 82, 82*f*
Subjective judgment, 39–40
Subjective probability, 169–170,
170*t*
Summing the errors, 275, 275*f,*
279
Surface Mining Control
and Reclamation Act
(SMCRA), 91
Survey instruments, 184,
187–189
Surveys, 180
errors in. *See* Random errors;
Systematic errors in
sampling
quantification of data,
189–190
reporting of results, 190
Svara, James H., 44
Swine flu, 319–320, 322,
323–324*f*
Symbionese Liberation
Army, 9
Symmetric distribution
asymmetric distributions
compared, 143*t*
asymmetric series compared,
143*f*
data showing, 142*t*
distribution with extreme
value, 135*f*
example of, 142*f*

mean, median, and
  mode, 144*t*
shapes of, 152
skewness and, 141–144
statistics, 134, 134*f*
Systematic errors in sampling,
    180–184
  bias in survey instrument, 184
  collection bias, 182
  example of, 181*f*
  lying by survey
    respondents, 182
  nonrepresentative
    sample, 181
  observation errors, 182–184
  self-selection bias, 181–182
Systemic (noninstitutional)
    agendas, 76–77

Tajfel, Henri, 12–13
Target outcome, 150
Taxation
  California Proposition
    13 (tax revolt), 70,
    332–333
  increased revenues as benefit
    from subsidized sports
    stadium, 103
Taylor, Charles, 182, 202
T distribution, 161–162,
    284–285
Teen smoking, 79–80
Telephone interviews, 189
Temporal relevance and
    pluralist model of agenda
    setting, 80
Tennessee Valley Authority
    (TVA), 121
Termination of policy, 96–97
Terrorist attacks
  9/11 terrorist attacks,
    21, 22, 33
  on U.S. embassies in East
    Africa, 33
  on *U.S.S. Cole,* 33
Texas school buses and seat belt
    use, 367–368
Thayer, Frederick, 44

Thornton, Robert J., 344
Time
  effect on research design,
    114–115, 273, 273*f*
  governmental policy, timing
    of, 15–16, 67
  patterns of time trend,
    253–256
  present value analysis,
    355–363
Time, 20
Time horizon, 359–360, 360*f*
Time preference, 356, 357*f*
Time-series data
  graphical presentation of,
    211
  method of least squares
    for trend projection,
    271–272
Tit-for-tat strategy, 340
Tobacco Institute, 28
Toll goods, 6*t,* 7
Torgerson, Douglas, 45
Trade. *See* Exports and imports
Trade-offs in public policy,
    15–16, 15*f,* 19, 22–23
Trade secrets, 57
Traffic, 75, 94, 119–120, 212,
    353–354
Tragedy of the commons, 9
Transportation and highway
    construction, 366
Trend adjustment, 259–260,
    260*t,* 261*f*
Trend coefficient, 276
Trends, 225
  abrupt changes in, 288–292,
    288*t,* 289*f,* 290*f*
  analysis, 115, 249–253, 250*f,*
    253*f,* 256
  multiple regression analysis,
    272
  simple regression analysis,
    271, 275–287, 277–
    278*t. See also* Simple
    regression model
Truman, David B., 98
Trust, 338–339, 341

TVA (Tennessee Valley
    Authority), 121
Tversky, Amos, 14, 26, 122, 124,
    125, 130
Two-tailed test, 160–161, 161*f,*
    162
Type I error, 167
Type II error, 167
Tyranny of the majority, 21

Uncertainty, 38, 320–321,
    338–339
Unconditional forecasting,
    306–307
Undocumented aliens. *See*
    Illegal immigration
Unemployment, 55–56
Unintended consequences,
    109, 110*f*
United Nations
  Children's Fund, 28
  Commission on Human
    Security report of
    2003, 23
  Development Programme
    report on human
    security of 1994, 23
  statistical publications, 197
United States Institute of
    Peace, 28
Universal Declaration of
    Human Rights, 37
"Un-rational being" and
    political behavior,
    9–14
Upper hinge, 137
Ury, William, 341, 344
U.S. Army Corps of Engineers
    (COE), 325, 343
USA PATRIOT Act of 2001, 32
U-shaped pattern, 253–254,
    254*f*
Utilitarians, 106

Valuation of costs and benefits,
    349*t,* 350–355
Value conflict, responses to,
    32–34, 34*f,* 36–37

Variables, 133–134, 294, 294*t*. *See also* Dependent variables; Independent variables
Variable weight, 205
Variance, 139–140, 140*t*
Vaupel, James, 377, 387
Vertical shifts, 288
Vining, Aidan, 32, 34*f*, 43, 44, 45
Violence
   cost-benefit analysis for gun control, 86
   political division over gun control, 89
   school violence as example of pluralist model of agenda setting, 84
Voting and limits of democracy, 63–64, 64*t*, 65*t*

Wall Street Journal, 221
Walmsley, Julian, 344
War on terror, 33
War Powers Resolution of 1973, 66
Washington Post, 36
Watkins, Sherron, 36–37

The Wealth of Nations [An Inquiry into the Nature and Causes of the Wealth of Nations] (Smith), 3, 47, 49
Wealth transfer, 104
Weather Underground Organization, 9
Web searches, 193–200, 194*f*
Weighted estimates, 135–136, 136*t*
Weimer, David, 32, 34*f*, 43, 44, 45
Weinberger, Caspar, 221
"Welfare queen," 17
Westen, Drew, 12, 14, 25
Wheelwright, Steven, 269
Whistleblowers, 34, 36–37
Wildavsky, Aaron, 35–36, 45
Will, Susan, 344
Williamson, Joel, 224
Wilson, Woodrow, 30, 44
Woods, B., 99
Woodward, Bob, 36
World Bank statistical publications, 28, 197
World Factbook, 197, 309
World Handbook of Political and Social Indicators, 182

World Health Organization, 78
World Meterological Organization, 28
World War II battle and use of game theory, 335–337, 336*t*
Wright, George, 176

X-inefficiency, 54

Y^1 ("Y hat one"), 274
Yates, J. Frank, 176
Yearbook of International Trade Statistics, 197
Yergin, Daniel, 73
Yoo, John, 37

Zagare, Frank C., 344
Z distribution, 158
Zeckhauser, Richard, 117, 130, 363, 371
Zero-sum games, 338–339
Ziegler, Harmon, 81, 98
Zone of ignorance, 107
Z score, 158, 159, 162, 164, 186
Z test, 158–159
Zupan, Mark, 91, 99